ROLL, JORDAN, ROLL

ROLL, JORDAN, ROLL

THE WORLD THE SLAVES MADE

EUGENE D. GENOVESE

*The earth is the Lord's, and
the fulness thereof; the world,
and they that dwell therein.*
—Psalms 24:1

VINTAGE BOOKS

A DIVISION OF RANDOM HOUSE,
NEW YORK

FIRST VINTAGE BOOKS EDITION, February 1976

Copyright © 1972, 1974 by Eugene D. Genovese

All rights reserved under International and Pan-American Copyright Conventions. Published in the United States by Random House, Inc., New York, and simultaneously in Canada by Random House of Canada Limited, Toronto. Originally published by Pantheon Books, a division of Random House, Inc., in 1974.

Library of Congress Cataloging in Publication Data

Genovese, Eugene D   1930–
  Roll, Jordan, roll.

  Includes bibliographical references.
  1. Slavery in the United States—Condition of Slaves.
I. Title.
E443.G46 1975   975'.004'96073   75–26906
ISBN 0–394–71652–3

Manufactured in the United States of America

Since this copyright page cannot accommodate all acknowledgments, they can be found on the following two pages.

Grateful acknowledgment is made to the following for permission to reprint previously published material:

AMS Press, Inc.: For excerpts from *The Papers of Thomas Ruffin*, edited by J. G. Hamilton. Reprinted by AMS Press, Inc., 1973.

Arno Press Inc.: For excerpts from *The Negro in Virginia* by the Virginia Public Works Administration. Reprinted by Arno Press Inc., 1969.

John Anthony Caruso: For an excerpt of 10 lines of song from Dorothy Scarborough, *On the Trail of Negro Folk-Songs*, pp. 66–67, quoted in *The Southern Frontier* by John Anthony Caruso (New York, 1963).

Columbia University Press: For an excerpt of 6 lines of song from *Negro Folk Music, U.S.A.* by Harold Courlander, p. 156 (New York, 1963). Reprinted by permission of the publisher.

The Dial Press: For excerpts from *To Be a Slave* by Julius Lester. Copyright © 1968 by Julius Lester. Used with permission of The Dial Press.

Duke University Press: For an excerpt of six lines of song from "Wild Nigger Bill," quoted in H. C. Brearly, "Ba-ad Nigger," pp. 116–117 in *The South Atlantic Quarterly*, vol. 38, January 1939. Reprinted by permission of Duke University Press.

Fisk University: For excerpts from *The Unwritten History of Slavery* by Fisk University Social Science Institute. Reprinted by permission of the Fisk University Library.

Greenwood Press: For excerpts from *The American Slave* by George P. Rawick. Reprinted by kind permission of George P. Rawick and Greenwood Press.

Harcourt Brace Jovanovich, Inc.: For an excerpt of 3 lines of poetry from "The Love Song of J. Alfred Prufrock" by T. S. Eliot from his *Collected Poems 1909–1962*, and for "The Naming of Cats" from *Old Possum's Book of Practical Cats* by T. S. Eliot. Copyright, 1939, by T. S. Eliot, renewed 1967, by Esmé Valerie Eliot. Reprinted by permission of Harcourt Brace Jovanich, Inc.

Harper & Row, Publishers, Inc.: For an excerpt of 2 lines of verse from Howard Thurman, *The Negro Spiritual Speaks of Life and Death*. p. 46, Copyright 1947 by Harper & Row, Publishers, Inc. By permission of the publishers.

Holt, Rinehart & Winston, Inc.: For excerpts from *Life Under the "Peculiar Institution": Selections from the Slave Narrative Collection* by Norman R. Yetman. Copyright © 1970 by Holt, Rinehart & Winston, Inc.

Houghton Miffllin Company: For excerpts of 6 lines of song from p. 430 and 4 lines of song from p. 447 of *Gumbo Ya-Ya* by Lyle Saxon *et al.* Copyright © renewed 1973 by the Louisiana State Library; excerpts from *North Toward Home* by Willie Morris; excerpts from *A Diary from Dixie* by Mary Boykin Chestnut, edited by Ben Ames Williams. All excerpts reprinted by permission of Houghton Miffllin Company.

Macmillan Publishing Co., Inc.: For excerpts from *A History of the Old South* by Clement Eaton. Copyright 1949 by The Macmillan Company.

ROLL, JORDAN, ROLL

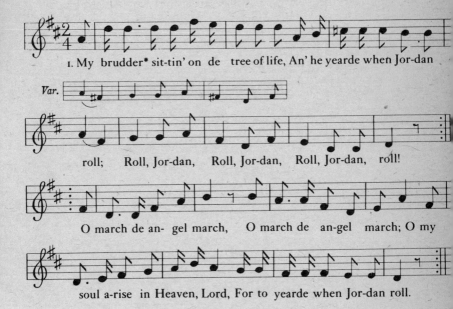

1. My brudder* sit-tin' on de tree of life, An' he yearde when Jor-dan

Var.

roll; Roll, Jor-dan, Roll, Jor-dan, Roll, Jor-dan, roll!

O march de an- gel march, O march de an-gel march; O my

soul a-rise in Heaven, Lord, For to yearde when Jor-dan roll.

2. Little chil'en, learn to fear de Lord,
   And let your days be long;
   Roll, Jordan, &c.

3. O, let no false nor spiteful word
   Be found upon your tongue;
   Roll, Jordan, &c.

From W. F. Allen, *et al., Slave Songs of the United States* (New York, 1871).

*[sister, etc.]

For MISS BETSEY

My own personal Bright and Morning Star

CONTENTS

PREFACE

The question of nationality—of "identity"—has stalked Afro-American history from its colonial beginnings, when the expression "a nation within a nation" was already being heard. In recent decades it has re-emerged fiercely in political debates, and it is destined to remain with us, however triumphant "integrationist" or "separatist" tendencies appear at a given moment. Some historians, black and white, interpret the Afro-American experience as a separate national experience; others, black and white, interpret it as a more or less ethnically distinct component of a single regional or national experience. The closer one looks at the quarrel, the clearer it becomes that no such formula can account for so rich and contradictory an experience.

In this book I refer to the "black nation" and argue that the slaves, as an objective social class, laid the foundations for a separate black national culture while enormously enriching American culture as a whole. But that separate black national culture has always been American, however much it has drawn on African origins or reflected the distinct development of black people in America. White and black southerners, however different they may claim to be and in some ways are, have come to form one people in vital respects. As C. Vann Woodward observes, in *American Counterpoint:*

> The ironic thing about these two great hyphenate minorities, Southern-Americans and Afro-Americans, confronting each other on their native soil for three and a half centuries, is the degree to which they have shaped each other's destiny, determined each other's isolation, shared and molded a common culture. It is, in fact, impossible to imagine the one without the other and quite futile to try.

Originally, I had planned to explore the theme of nationality throughout the book and to examine its political implications in an epilogue. I have decided, however, to leave the matter for a later date and a more appropriate format. My reading of the evidence as constituting a national thrust—in its objective significance more than as a conscious effort by the slaves—may therefore appear as an *obiter dictum*. Yet I trust that every reader is capable of recasting certain formulations in useful alternative terms. I hope I have shown that the slaves made an indispensable contribution to the development of black culture and black national consciousness as well as to American nationality as a whole. But, knowing that the ambiguity of the black experience as a national question lends the evidence to different readings, I have chosen to stay close to my primary responsibility: to tell the story of slave life as carefully and accurately as possible. Many years of studying the astonishing effort of black people to live decently as human beings even in slavery has convinced me that no theoretical advance suggested in their experience could ever deserve as much attention as that demanded by their demonstration of the beauty and power of the human spirit under conditions of extreme oppression.

The reception accorded by white America to the black people brought here in chains and raised in slavery and under racist oppression has, first and foremost, provided a record of one of history's greatest crimes. I have tried to tell the story not so much of the crime itself, although I hope I have not slighted it, as of the black struggle to survive spiritually as well as physically—to make a livable world for themselves and their children within the narrowest living space and harshest adversity. And if I have tried to present the slaveholders not as monsters but as human beings with solid virtues of their own, my intention has hardly been to spare them condemnation for their crimes. They commanded and profited from an evil social system; whatever the extenuating circumstances, qualifications, and complexities, they remained in the end responsible for what they wrought. But I have also tried to show that, for a complex of reasons of self-interest, common humanity, and Christian sensibility, they could not help contributing to their slaves' creative survival; that many slaveholders even took some pride and pleasure in their slaves' accomplishment; and that they imbibed much of their slaves' culture and sensibility while imparting to their slaves much of their own.

Slavery, especially in its plantation setting and in its paternalistic aspect, made white and black southerners one people while making them two. As in a lasting although not necessarily happy marriage, two discrete individuals shared, for better or worse, one life. I must therefore ask readers to be patient with Book One, Part 1, and with some other sections of this volume that treat the masters and other white people much more fully than the slaves and that move abruptly from one general aspect of life to another (for example, from descriptions of social relations to analyses of law and ideology). An understanding of the slaves requires some understanding of the masters and of others who helped shape a complex slave society. Masters and slaves shaped each other and cannot be discussed or analyzed in isolation.

Some of the language in this book may disturb readers; it disturbs me. Whenever "nigger" appears in the sources, it has been retained; moreover, I have used it myself when it seemed the best way to capture the spirit of a contemporary situation. The word is offensive, but I believe that its omission would only anesthetize subject matter infinitely more offensive. In Book Three, Part 1—in the section entitled "The Language of Class and Nation"—I have discussed the use of the word by black people themselves.

As for the dialect used in quotations, I have transcribed it from the sources. In many cases whites took down black comments and rendered them as they thought proper. I have not tampered with these sources and assume that every reader can judge for himself or herself the probable accuracy of the rendering.

I have used "black" and "Afro-American" in preference to "Negro" out of respect for what I perceive to be the present preference of the majority of the black community. I have, however, used "free Negro" because it was the most common contemporary term and also because it more accurately captures the color duality of that group as black and mulatto. When discussing the Caribbean, I have followed regional procedure and used "colored" to refer to those who were part white.

So many errors of spelling and grammar appear in the contemporary sources that I have omitted [sic] except in a few cases when it seemed necessary. All words in italics have been transcribed from the texts and indicate the original author's emphasis.

E.D.G.

Palo Alto, California
August, 1973

ACKNOWLEDGMENTS

I wish to thank *Louisiana Studies: An Interdisciplinary Journal of the South* for permission to use material from "The Black Preachers," a version of which originally appeared in Volume XI (Fall, 1972), 188–214; and Johns Hopkins University Press for permission to reprint material from my essay on "Free Negroes" that originally appeared in David W. Cohen and Jack P. Greene, eds., *Neither Slave Nor Free: The Freedmen of African Descent in the Slave Societies of the New World* (Baltimore, 1972), pp. 258–277.

Many friends and colleagues devoted time and effort to criticizing manuscript versions of this book. I am deeply indebted to them for correcting errors and helping me to improve the style and content. It is not their fault if I did not always follow their advice or heed their warnings.

I could not have arranged to send the manuscript to so many people—and indeed, I might not have been able to write it at all —had it not been for the generosity of the Center for Advanced Study in the Behavioral Sciences at Stanford, California, which provided the fellowship that enabled me to devote a year's full attention to writing and which made available its remarkable facilities. I must especially thank Susan Custer, who skillfully and promptly duplicated a long manuscript, section by section, so that it could be sent to critics in time to have them comment. The typing of Dee Decker and Val Faulkenburg was excellent, and the kindness of the others on the center's staff cannot be repaid.

I have been singularly fortunate in having Jeannette Hopkins to edit the manuscript and Jeanne Morton to copy edit it. I would also like to thank John Higham for the encouragement he gave an assistant professor a decade ago when this book was a two-page outline.

During the decade this book has been in progress, a number of institutions have made it possible for me to devote shorter periods of time to it and to travel to southern libraries: the Social Science Research Council, the American Council of Learned Societies, the Canada Council, and the Rabinowitz Foundation. In addition, I received generous assistance from the universities at which I was teaching—Rutgers, Sir George Williams, and the University of Rochester. The staffs of the libraries in the southern universities noted in the list of manuscript collections were helpful and gracious as only southern librarians can be; in particular, I must thank John Price, then director of the Department of Archives and History at Louisiana State University and now editor of *Louisiana Studies*, for much help well beyond the call of duty and even beyond the canons of southern courtesy.

Early sketches of the material on religion were criticized by Henry H. Mitchell, John S. Walker, Winthrop Hudson, and Jacques Marchand. A later version was presented as the Commonwealth Lecture at the University of London and was then criticized by Duncan McLeod, H. C. Allen, George Shepperson, and others in a splendid seminar. I have also benefitted from the dissenting comments and constructive criticism of Timothy Smith.

While in residence at the Center for Advanced Study, I had the opportunity to discuss various problems and to show written material to Steven Channing, Natalie Davis, Carl Degler, John Whitney Hall, Donald Harris, Steven Marcus, Kenneth M. Stampp, Daniel Thompson, and Stephen Tonsor, among others to whom I am indebted for criticism and encouragement,

The section on law benefitted from the expert criticism of Terence Sandalow, Douglas Ayer, George Dennison, and Irving Leonard Feder.

I am indebted to many friends and scholars for reading long sections of the manuscript, or indeed all of it, and for the help they provided: Roger D. Abrahams, Olli Alho, Marvin Becker, Ira Berlin, Clement Eaton, Sanford Elwitt, Eric Foner, Ella Laffey, John Laffey, Sidney W. Mintz, Brenda Meehan-Waters, Jesse T. Moore, Willie Lee Rose, John F. Szwed, Bennett H. Wall, Michael Wallace, John Waters, Jonathan Weiner, Peter H. Wood, and Harold D. Woodman. In addition to help with the manuscript, George P. Rawick taught me a great deal in stimulating discussions of the subject matter and in his own fine book *Sundown to Sunup: The Making of the Black Community*.

I have a special debt to Frank Otto Gatell and William K. Scarborough, who made meticulous comments on a manuscript with which they often disagreed. The hard criticism of friends who think you are wrong does not make pleasant reading, but friends who withhold their considered judgment are no friends at all. If Professors Gatell and Scarborough did not change my mind on the essentials, they did, in radically different ways, force me to make significant adjustments and to correct flagrant errors.

Lawrence Levine and Leon Litwack shared ideas and materials with me while working on their own books, which overlap with this one. The academic world boasts of being a community of scholars, free of petty proprietorship in ideas and sources, but, alas, the reality is usually something else. Professor Levine's and Professor Litwack's support for a "competitor" was an act of friendship and generosity not often encountered. It is such people who make work in the academic world a joy.

Stanley Engerman read the entire manuscript and offered exhaustive and splendid criticisms. Moreover, he and Robert W. Fogel discussed the materials with me at length and placed their own statistical and analytical work on the slave economy at my disposal.

The warm encouragement, advice, and criticism of C. Vann Woodward were indispensable, as on so many other occasions. And I must pay tribute to David Brion Davis who—to my great good fortune—was in residence at Stanford while I was. He read the manuscript section by section, took time from writing his own book to share ideas, and helped me over numerous rough spots.

With a book like this one the use of research assistants would, to say the least, be a mistake. But I did cheat a little and call on the services of James and Janice McGowan for some peripheral work. My real debt to them, however, lies elsewhere. They, and my other graduate students, offered criticism of ideas tried out in seminar and added ideas of their own. It is impossible to know how much one learns from one's students, but there can be no doubt that the debt is large. I also wish to thank Paolo Ceccarelli for checking the quotations and sources.

My wife, Elizabeth Fox-Genovese, to whom this book is dedicated, did not type the manuscript, do my research, darn my socks, or do those other wonderful things one reads about in acknowledgments to someone "without whom this book could not have been written." Nor did she work so hard on this book that she deserves to be listed as co-author; if she had, she would be listed as co-author. She did, however, take time from writing her doctoral dissertation to criticize each draft, review painstakingly the materials, help me rewrite awkward sections and rethink awkward formulations, and offer countless suggestions, corrections, and revisions. And while under the pressure that anyone who has written a dissertation will readily appreciate, she made an immeasurable if intangible contribution to the writing of this book by living it with me.

BOOK ONE

GOD IS NOT MOCKED

Be not deceived; God is not mocked: for whatsoever a man soweth, that shall he also reap.
—Galatians 6:7

PART 1

OF THE WILLING AND THE OBEDIENT

If ye be willing and obedient, ye shall eat the good of the land:

But if ye refuse and rebel, ye shall be devoured with the sword: for the mouth of the Lord hath spoken it.
—Isaiah 1:19–20

ON PATERNALISM

Cruel, unjust, exploitative, oppressive, slavery bound two peoples together in bitter antagonism while creating an organic relationship so complex and ambivalent that neither could express the simplest human feelings without reference to the other. Slavery rested on the principle of property in man—of one man's appropriation of another's person as well as of the fruits of his labor. By definition and in essence it was a system of class rule, in which some people lived off the labor of others. American slavery subordinated one race to another and thereby rendered its fundamental class relationships more complex and ambiguous; but they remained class relationships. The racism that developed from racial subordination influenced every aspect of American life and remains powerful. But slavery as a system of class rule predated racism and racial subordination in world history and once existed without them. Racial subordination, as postbellum American developments and the history of modern colonialism demonstrate, need not rest on slavery. Wherever racial subordination exists, racism exists; therefore, southern slave society and its racist ideology had much in common with other systems and societies. But southern slave society was not merely one more manifestation of some abstraction called racist society. Its history was essentially determined by particular relationships of class power in racial form.

The Old South, black and white, created a historically unique kind of paternalist society. To insist upon the centrality of class relations as manifested in paternalism is not to slight the inherent racism or to deny the intolerable contradictions at the heart of paternalism itself. Imamu Amiri Baraka captures the tragic irony of paternalist social relations when he writes that slavery "was, most of all, a paternal institution" and yet refers to "the filthy paternalism and cruelty of slavery."[1] Southern paternalism, like every other paternalism, had little to do with Ole Massa's ostensible benevolence, kindness, and good cheer. It grew out of the necessity to discipline and morally justify a system of exploitation. It did encourage kindness and affection, but it simultaneously encouraged cruelty and hatred. The racial distinction between master and slave heightened the tension inherent in an unjust social order.

Southern slave society grew out of the same general historical conditions that produced the other slave regimes of the modern world. The rise of a world market—the development of new tastes and of manufactures dependent upon non-European sources of raw materials—encouraged the rationalization of colonial agriculture under the ferocious domination of a few Europeans. African labor provided the human power to fuel the new system of production in all the New World slave societies, which, however, had roots in different European experiences and emerged in different geographical, economic, and cultural conditions. They had much in common, but each was unique.[2]

Theoretically, modern slavery rested, as had ancient slavery, on the idea of a slave as *instrumentum vocale*—a chattel, a possession, a thing, a mere extension of his master's will. But the vacuousness of such pretensions had been exposed long before the growth of New World slave societies.[3] The closing of the ancient slave trade, the political crisis of ancient civilization, and the subtle moral pressure of an ascendant Christianity had converged in the early centuries of the new era to shape a seigneurial world in which lords and serfs (not slaves) faced each other with reciprocal demands and expectations. This land-oriented world of medieval Europe slowly forged the traditional paternalist ideology to which the southern slaveholders fell heir.

The slaveholders of the South, unlike those of the Caribbean, increasingly resided on their plantations and by the end of the eighteenth century had become an entrenched regional ruling class. The paternalism encouraged by the close living of masters and slaves was enormously reinforced by the closing of the African slave trade, which compelled masters to pay greater attention to the reproduction of their labor force. Of all the slave societies in the New World, that of the Old South alone maintained a slave force that reproduced itself. Less than 400,000 imported Africans had, by 1860, become an American black population of more than 4,000,000.[4]

A paternalism accepted by both masters and slaves—but with radically different interpretations—afforded a fragile bridge across the intolerable contradictions inherent in a society based on racism, slavery, and class exploitation that had to depend on the willing reproduction and productivity of its victims. For the slaveholders paternalism represented an attempt to overcome the fundamental contradiction in slavery: the impossibility of the slaves' ever becoming the things they were supposed to be. Paternalism defined the involuntary labor of the slaves as a legitimate return to their masters for protection and direction. But, the masters' need to see their slaves as acquiescent human beings constituted a moral victory for the slaves themselves. Paternalism's insistence upon mutual obligations—duties, responsibilities, and ultimately even rights—implicitly recognized the slaves' humanity.

Wherever paternalism exists, it undermines solidarity among the oppressed by linking them as individuals to their oppressors.[5] A lord (master, *padrone, patron, padrón, patrão*) functions as a direct provider and protector to each individual or family, as well as to the community as a whole. The slaves of the Old South displayed impressive solidarity and collective resistance to their masters, but in a web of paternalistic relationships their action tended to become defensive and to aim at protecting the individuals against aggression and abuse; it could not readily pass into an effective weapon for liberation. Black leaders, especially the preachers, won loyalty and respect and fought heroically to defend their people. But despite their will and considerable ability, they could not lead their people over to the attack against the paternalist ideology itself.

In the Old South the tendencies inherent in all paternalistic class systems intersected with and acquired enormous reinforcement from the tendencies inherent in an analytically distinct system of racial subordination. The two appeared to be a single system. Paternalism created a tendency for the slaves to identify with a particular community through identification with its master; it reduced the possibilities for their identification with each other as a class. Racism undermined the slaves' sense of worth as black people and reinforced their dependence on white masters. But these were tendencies, not absolute laws, and the slaves forged weapons of defense, the most important of which was a religion that taught them to love and value each other, to take a critical view of their masters, and to reject the ideological rationales for their own enslavement.

The slaveholders had to establish a stable regime with which their slaves could live. Slaves remained slaves. They could be bought and sold like any other property and were subject to despotic personal power. And blacks remained rigidly subordinated to whites. But masters and slaves, whites and blacks, lived as well as worked together. The existence of the community required that all find some measure of self-interest and self-respect. Southern paternalism developed as a way of mediating irreconcilable class and racial conflicts; it was an anomaly even at the moment of its greatest apparent strength. But, for about a century, it protected both masters and slaves from the worst tendencies inherent in their respective conditions. It mediated, however unfairly and even cruelly, between masters and slaves, and it disguised, however imperfectly, the appropriation of one man's labor power by another. Paternalism in any historical setting defines relations of superordination and subordination. Its strength as a prevailing ethos increases as the members of the community accept—or feel compelled to accept—these relations as legitimate. Brutality lies inherent in this acceptance of patronage and dependence, no matter how organic the paternalistic order. But southern paternalism necessarily recognized the slaves' humanity—not only their free will but the very talent and ability without which their acceptance of a doctrine of reciprocal obligations would have made no sense. Thus, the slaves found an opportunity to translate paternalism itself into a doctrine different from that understood by their masters and to forge it into a weapon of resistance to assertions that slavery was a natural condition for blacks, that blacks were racially inferior, and that black slaves had no rights or legitimate claims of their own.

Thus, the slaves, by accepting a paternalistic ethos and legitimizing class rule, developed their most powerful defense against the dehumanization implicit in slavery. Southern paternalism may have reinforced racism as well as class exploitation, but it also unwittingly invited its victims to fashion their own interpretation of the social order it was intended to justify. And the slaves, drawing on a religion that was supposed to assure their compliance and docility, rejected the essence of slavery by projecting their own rights and value as human beings.

FARMERS, PLANTERS, AND OVERSEERS

Half the slaves in the South lived on farms, not on plantations as defined by contemporaries—that is, units of twenty slaves or more. Typically, a twenty-slave unit would embrace only four families. If a big plantation is to be defined as a unit of fifty slaves, then only one-quarter of the southern slaves lived on big plantations.[1] The slaveholders of the Caribbean or Brazil would have been amused by this definition, for their own plantations usually had more than one hundred slaves. For the slaves in those areas dominated by farms, some degree of contact among slaves of different masters compensated for the absence of the big plantation community. But slaves on small farms within the areas dominated by large plantations risked greater isolation unless neighboring planters and slaves welcomed them as guests.

By reputation farmers treated their slaves better than planters did, but this reputation depended on a questionable belief in a major difference between practices in the predominantly small-farm Upper South and those in the plantation Lower South. Good treatment of slaves, as defined by the masters, did not necessarily constitute good treatment from the slaves' point of view. Travelers usually reported that most small farmers showed their slaves greater consideration and worked them more humanely. At the beginning of the nineteenth century Isaac Weld, Jr., and La Rochefoucauld-Liancourt made opposing judgments, with the latter's positive estimate being the more widely held.[2] E. S. Abdy, during the early thirties, expressed considerable admiration for the way in which the farmers and small planters of Kentucky worked with and treated their slaves, and Frederick Law Olmsted and James Stirling, among other travelers in the fifties, concurred for the South as a whole.[3] Fredrika Bremer of Sweden thought that the farmers of the Shenandoah Valley deserved their reputation but that the struggling small farmers of the Deep South too often could not feed and quarter their slaves adequately.[4] J. P. Flournoy, Sr., an old patriarchal planter in Caddo Parish, Louisiana, considered the small farmers harsher and more cruel to their slaves than big planters like himself, but other planters decried the evils of excessive size and the attendant necessity of using overseers.[5]

No clear verdict emerges from the slaves' reports. Farmers, small planters, and big planters seem to have been more or less alike in this respect. To Anna Hawkins, an ex-slave from Georgia, her alcoholic small-farm master was "the meanest man that ever lived,"[6] and the evidence of a number of ex-slaves lent credence to the charge that some small farmers bought slaves before they could profitably use them or decently feed and care for them.[7] Others reported that they received kind treatment and said they felt like part of the family. Hannah Scott, who had been one of nine slaves on a farm in Alabama, said of her master, "I guess he what you calls 'poor folks,' but he mighty good to he black folks." Such slaves recalled the intimacy and the easy style of life of the farmstead.[8] If white and black accounts are weighed, the pace of work and the material conditions seem to have differed on the small farms, but the range of treatment seems about the same as that prevailing on the big plantations.

Farms of ten slaves or less did not develop an extensive division of labor. The white farmer and his wife divided chores, but the extent of specialization among the slaves rarely went beyond the assignment of one or two women to house work; and even they had to work in the fields when needed. A common effort by master and slave at work together produced an easy familiarity, reinforced by living arrangements. The mistress or perhaps a female slave cooked for all at the same time and in the same way. Only segregation at table drew a caste line. The slaves either slept in one small house with the master's family or in a cabin that faced on the same yard. Slave and free, black and white, lived close to one another, and their relationship led to a widespread reputation for "better treatment." Thus C. C. Baldwin of Virginia, who owned only eight slaves, could boast that his people had "no domestic restraints" and returned his indulgence with faithful service, while D. R. Hundley, the planter-ideologue, could rail against the small-holders for extending too many privileges to the slaves and thereby spoiling them.[9] This familiarity did not prevent the subjection of the slaves to the punitive measures of slaveholders whose closeness encouraged the indulgence of daily passions. It did not prevent the breaking up of family units by masters whose precarious financial position often left them without much choice. And among small white farmers of modest means the hiring out of slaves, with its attendant uncertainties, became all the more common.[10]

The argument for the greater humanity of the small slaveholders turned, to a great extent, on the fact of greater intimacy, of rough camaraderie, and of mutual sympathy born in common quarters. But, as Kenneth Stampp observes, there is no reason to believe that the slaves always welcomed this intimacy, for it meant constant scrutiny by whites and drastically reduced contact with fellow blacks.[11] Olmsted and Sir Charles Lyell felt certain that the greater contact with whites helped to "civilize" the blacks, but Ulrich Bonnell Phillips, who agreed with their view, sharply pointed out that these particular whites did not usually have the highest claims to "civilization" themselves.[12]

Plantation slaves did not clamor to be sold to small farmers even when they had a choice. After noting that slaves on small farms had more freedom of movement than those on the plantations, Olmsted added that they rarely wanted to be sold to the up country. When he asked a slaveholder for an explanation, he was told that blacks feared the mountains. He regarded the answer as irrational and suggested that the slaves did not want to find themselves among an overwhelming white majority.[13] The slaveholder might have had a point, for among some West Africans highlands and mountains are regarded as the dwelling place of the gods and are indeed to be feared.[14] But above all, slaves wanted to avoid sale to masters of scanty means, not primarily for reasons of the status attached to a rich master—an attitude much exaggerated by contemporary and subsequent commentators—but because they understood that their own family and community security depended upon their owner's solvency.

Historians have long insisted that the planters hardly knew their field hands and that even middle-sized planters restricted their contacts to the house slaves, a few skilled mechanics, and special hands.[15] Actually, very few planters held so many slaves on so many different plantations that such distance was required. Even most absentee owners knew the names of their field hands and something of their personal qualities, and even some of those slaveholders who had too many slaves to keep track of were regarded by their own field hands as kind masters.[16]

Slaveholders corresponded regularly with their overseers and members of their own family. In their journals and diaries their slaves regularly appear by name, with strong indications of their owners' consciousness of their individuality. George Washington, who had a reputation for keeping his distance from "my people," knew most of his large slave force by name. He was no exception among Virginia planters.[17] During the last few decades of the antebellum period, masters and mistresses regularly visited the quarters in order to establish personal contact with individual slaves, to encourage them to take their problems to the Big House, and to observe their work personally. The whites particularly enjoyed participating in the slaves' "plantation balls" and other social events. The death of a well-liked field hand might inspire a written tribute, and the slackers, the inept, and the troublemakers got much more personal attention than they wanted. Between these extremes, slaveholders made simple inquiries and reports about the health, morals, or activities of the ordinary hands.[18]

Corroboration comes from the narratives of former slaves who had worked in the fields. Charlotte Foster recalled getting sick headaches in the hot sun and having her master insist that she rest in the shade when necessary. She also recalled that many masters and especially mistresses taught Sunday school for the children and enjoyed playing with them until they grew up enough to be sent to the fields. Mary Kincheon Edwards—to cite another example—borrowed some of her mistress's jewelry for plantation parties.[19]

The slaves of the Old South, unlike the slaves of the Caribbean,[20] lived on plantations with resident masters. Absenteeism was limited. During the eighteenth century the planters of Virginia spent most of the year on their estates, whereas those of coastal South Carolina, which echoed the experience of the Caribbean, often did not. By the time of the rise of the Cotton Kingdom and the consolidation of the slave regime in the South as a whole, even coastal South Carolina had changed appreciably, although as late as 1845, J. H. Hammond, in the midst of a determined defense of slavery, referred to absenteeism as an "evil greatly [felt] even here."[21] The evil, however narrow its limits, drew heavy and effective criticism from abolitionists.[22]

North Carolina, lying between the two great slave states, ranged closer to Virginia in this respect and probably had an even greater preponderance of resident planters. In this basically farming state, even the eastern lowlands, where the great plantations could be found, had little absenteeism. Planters might own more than one place within walking or easy riding distance in a single county or neighboring counties.[23]

On the Rice Coast of Georgia, resident planters were less common, but even there most slaveholders stayed on their plantations for much of the year. They might live in Savannah or elsewhere, but they would visit their plantations twice a week or so in summer and spend at least half the year on them during the cooler and less unhealthful months. The Sea Island planters would escape during the worst months or even live in Beaufort or Charleston, but they tried to stay close and visit the plantations often.[24] Unfortunately, the growing season fell precisely during those months in which the overseers had the least supervision.

Farther west, on some plantations owned by easterners who could not visit often, a son or other relative might be in residence. Or, a friend or agent might live close by and look in from time to time. Absentees owned enough plantations in Alabama to evoke a serious protest movement and demands for restrictive legislation, but they did not dominate the plantation regions. Elisha F. King, who owned 186 slaves and three plantations in Perry County and another in nearby Bibb County, ran two himself, trusted the third to his son, and the fourth to an overseer whom he or his son visited once a week. Clement C. Clay had two plantations, and for a while three. Members of his immediate family visited the second and third regularly and stayed for long enough periods to guarantee proper order.[25]

This "local absenteeism" marked the Mississippi Valley, where a number of slaveholders who owned several plantations within riding distance of each other preferred to live in Natchez, Vicksburg, or New Orleans. About half the plantations on the Mississippi side of the river had absentee owners, although most owners lived close enough to visit regularly and spend part of the year.[26] On the Louisiana side and in the sugar region, planters more frequently lived on the place or close enough to spend much time there. Away from the river in either direction, even local absenteeism faded.[27]

A large majority of plantation slaves lived with resident owners, and a large additional minority with part-time resident owners. If the approximate half of all rural slaves who lived on units smaller than plantations are included, then the overwhelming majority of the slaves of the South lived with their masters and worked under their supervision. The correlation between cruelty and absenteeism proposed by some abolitionists and by planters with uneasy consciences has some truth, but it breaks down. The blame for too many evils falls directly upon the shoulders of resident planters, who caused them themselves or whose overseers did while working under their daily review, whereas too many other masters, with hundreds of slaves on scattered plantations, strove to guarantee humane treatment, to keep families together, and to keep their overseers on as tight a leash as circumstances permitted. If the absence of these masters exposed the slaves to their overseers' harsher side, the solidity of the masters' fortunes also minimized the risk of sale and community disruption.[28]

The blame for much of the cruelty to slaves, as well as for much of the inefficiency in southern agriculture, nevertheless fell on the overseers. Hardly a planter could be found, except on the South Carolina and Georgia coast where a particularly respected class of overseers operated, who did not claim that they were at best a necessary evil. Planters must attend to their own business if they expect humanity and efficiency, warned leading reformers from John Taylor of Caroline to Edmund Ruffin. But Gideon Bridgers, editor of the *American Farmer*, put these complaints into perspective when he bluntly told the planters to accept responsibility and stop blaming others for a situation of their own making.[29] Maunsel White wrote in exasperation in 1860: "From what I can see no man nowadays should own a plantation without living on it all the time."[30] The planters took it for granted that the overseers preferred the absence of their employers and craved a free hand.

A. H. Arrington of North Carolina wrote his wife from their Alabama place that he had hired a new overseer "who is so well pleased at getting on my plantation that I think he will do his best to try to please me—overseers in Ala. prefer hiring with me to any one else in that vicinity for two reasons, one is that my negroes are obedient and work well and the other is that I am away and can't find fault till the end of the year."[31]

As Arrington must have understood, overseers on plantations with a planter in residence often found themselves no more than glorified drivers.[32] As one of many such sermons in *De Bow's Review* put it: "Nothing more reconciles the negro to his work than the overseer's sharing with him. If they shuck corn at night, let him be present till the last moment; if the sun shines hot, let him stand it as much as they do; if it rains, let him take his share of it; if it is cold, let him not go to the fire oftener than they do. . . ."[33]

Contrary to legend, no more than one-third and possibly only one-fourth of the rural slaves worked under overseers, and many of these either worked under an overseer and a resident planter simultaneously or under an overseer who was a relative of the planter. Kenneth Stampp has suggested that the total number of overseers roughly equaled the number of units with thirty or more slaves, but most of these units probably had resident owners.[34] The twin evils of absenteeism and overseer control may well have been growing in the 1850s, for the number of overseers doubled during those prosperous years, as the expansion and consolidation of the plantation system pressed forward.[35] The dip in the reproduction rate for slaves during the fifties, considered in this light, lends some credence to W. E. B. Du Bois's charge that the rate of exploitation was rising. But if so, the overseers can hardly be taxed with full or even primary responsibility.

Overseers were either the sons or close kin of the planters, who were learning to be planters in their own right; or floaters who usually lived up to the reputation of their class, the "po' white trash," and created for all overseers a particularly bad reputation; or, the largest group, a semiprofessional class of men who expected to spend their lives overseeing or wanted to earn enough money to buy a farm. However much the professionals, who constituted the majority, may have striven to meet their responsibilities to masters and even slaves, their chances for success rarely ran high. Outside the aristocratic low country of the eastern seaboard and the Mississippi Delta, overseers came and went every two or three years. When they did not fall short in performance, they often fell victim to the slaveholders' notion that a change of overseers was good in itself. Whatever the reasons and whoever among the whites deserves the blame, those slaves who worked under these rough and exploited men often suffered much harshness.

Slaveholders fired overseers for a variety of reasons. They fired those who treated their slaves too leniently, and much more often, those who treated them too harshly. "It is an indisputable fact," reported Solon Robinson, "that an overseer who urged the slaves beyond their strength, or that inflicted cruel or unnecessary punishment, or failed to see them well-fed, or kindly taken care of when sick, would be as sure to lose his place, as though he permitted them to be idle and waste their time."[36] With some exceptions during the nineteenth century, the slaveholders gave up the self-defeating system of paying overseers with a share of the crop and thus had good reason to try, as best they could, to live up to Robinson's glowing account. Yet even under the salary system, no overseer who failed to make a good crop would be retained, or would easily get another job if fired. So, the pressure to be crop-happy at the expense of the slaves, however much curtailed, remained.[37]

The slaveholders, however, regularly fired their overseers for cruelty. David Gavin of South Carolina exploded with rage when his overseer's wife beat slaves without cause; his diary shows that he was more concerned with the injustice to his people than with the damage to plantation efficiency. John C. Burruss of Louisiana wasted no time in firing an overseer who had had his throat cut, almost fatally, by slaves whom he victimized while drunk. When Haller Nutt of Louisiana visited his plantation to find "a horrid account of negligence and ill-treatment," he fired the overseer. Henry Palfrey of Louisiana fired an overseer for mistreating his slaves and explained, "He is a man of violent and ungovernable temper and of a jealous, suspicious, and vindictive disposition." Jerry Boykins, an ex-slave from Georgia, recalled that his master did all the whipping on the plantation because his slaves had killed two overseers for whipping cruelly. The courts upheld masters in civil suits when they summarily discharged overseers for cruelty, and occasionally an overseer went to jail for it.[38]

These irate and perhaps self-righteous masters may be given as much credit as one wishes for defending their slaves, but little could or would have happened if the slaves had not been willing to brave a cruel overseer's wrath to complain or take direct action. The slaves spoke up, and the masters had to listen. There were limits, which the slaves understood because they helped to set them, beyond which an overseer normally dared not go. As A. H. Arrington wrote after visiting his Alabama plantation: "I have this day discharged my overseer, Mr. Brewer. I found so much dissatisfaction amongst the negroes that I placed under his charge that I could not feel satisfied to continue him in my employment."[39]

Those overseers who lost their jobs for excessive leniency included some who simply shirked their duty, so that the charge of leniency tells us nothing about their attitudes toward the slaves.[40] Some slaveholders accused their overseers of being too familiar, but the accusation could mean anything from sleeping with the women to being too solicitous of the slaves' comfort. The extreme case occurred on the Manigault rice plantation in South Carolina. "Elated by a strong and very false religious feeling," Manigault wrote of his twenty-four-year-old overseer, "he began to injure the plantation a vast deal by placing himself on a par with the negroes. . . ."[41] But for most planters the big problem lay elsewhere. Francis Terry Leak of Mississippi provides a hint:

> Rec'd a letter from Wm. Hall making enquiry about Mr. Robinson's qualifications as an overseer. In reply I gave Mr. R. credit for honesty, sobriety, and agreeableness; for great industry & close attention to business, but objected to his want of authority among the negroes, & the reckless manner in which he permitted them to do their work—alledging that, owing to these causes, he had never succeeded in retaining a good stand of Cotton or in gathering the crop in good order. I expressed the opinion that he would probably succeed very well with a set of well-trained hands, accustomed to stand in fear of their overseer & execute their work well, but thought with my hands, *who knew him*, he never could. His wife I represented as a quiet, discreet lady, who would never occasion the employee of her husband the least trouble.[42]

The overseers who fell under the charge of indulgence did not necessarily have a more humane or less racist attitude toward the slaves. Rather, they knew that they would not keep their jobs without some degree of support in the quarters, and accordingly, they tried to curry favor. No sensible slaveholder wanted a man who could not maintain a certain level of morale among the slaves. Thus, the slaves had an opening. They knew it, and they seized it.

The overseers' problems included the effect that the class distance between them and their employers had on the slaves. Confronted with employers who, even when respectful and friendly, held them at arm's length, the overseers could hardly have expected the slaves to offer them more respect than that which fear induced. As William Kauffman Scarborough aptly concludes, the overseers, ostracized by those above and forbidden by edict and convention from associating with those below, lived in a social vacuum.[43] When they deferred to their employers, they courted disdain; when they showed some spirit, they courted dismissal. In either case they were branded as lacking "dignity"—no small charge in this quasi-traditional society.[44] Since the overseer lacked status and dignity, he had for the most part to rely on force; but since, in the diabolical workings of the world in which he found himself, he ultimately needed the approval of the victims of his force, he also had to win friends.

Whatever the racist pretensions, whatever the cries for white unity across class lines, whatever the "obvious fact" that a sane master should take the word of his overseer against that of his slaves, the masters, who were indeed sane, did no such stupid thing. An overseer had to control the people: that was what he got paid for. To control the people meant maintaining a certain level of morale. How he did it was his business. If he did not do it, the reason and the fault were of academic interest. He had to go. But beneath this ruthless indifference lay a simple truth. The masters understood that their slaves had brains, ability, self-discipline, and an interest, however psychologically antagonistic, in the smooth running of the plantation which fed black and white alike. Therefore, it was the overseer's business to manage them, not vice versa.

A slave boy, aged twelve, arrived at a wheat farm in Virginia to which he had been hired. The overseer, with customary delicacy, greeted him: "Whose nigger is you?" The boy, who had come from the city, was a bit too well dressed and provided a perfect target for bullying. The overseer yelled to the field hands, "Stop that threshing, here is a new nigger, a city nigger." Eyeing the boy's dress, he asked if he had planned to go to a ball; without waiting for an answer, he decided that he had acquired a spoiled nigger. All according to script. And yet, as that slave recalled much later in life, "The overseer, however, tried after showing me around to impress me with the belief that I had done well in reaching that plantation, as none others within many miles of the place afforded such simple and comfortable accommodations."[45] Neither for the first nor the last time, a tough, caustic overseer had found it necessary to try to win favor with a wretched young slave.

"The master and the overseer," wrote a slaveholding sage, "should always pull the same end of the rope. Negroes soon discover any little jarring between the master and overseer, and are sure to take advantage of it."[46] Overseers deserved their reputation for brutality toward slaves, and yet, as if to prove that impish paradox rules the world, they were, for all their bravado, pathetically aware of their dependence upon the good will of those whom they whipped with impunity. William M. Otey visited his family's plantation in Mississippi in 1851 and reported reassuringly that the overseer and his wife were doing just fine: the slaves were "very much pleased with them."[47] Seven years later, Otey found that they "all like him very well [and] I hear know [sic] complaint from them."[48] Further east, in South Carolina, a planter who owned several plantations got a report from his manager about one of the overseers, who had been much too severe. The overseer got the message. All was well: "The negroes said that they got along very well yesterday."[49] But no master wanted his overseer to get too close to the slaves, and so, they argued that overseers should treat all slaves alike and show no favoritism.[50] No wonder the weaker overseers took to drink and the stronger did as they pleased on the principle that the devil might take the hindmost.

Any sensible master, notwithstanding all pretensions and professions, trusted his slaves against his overseer. Overseers came and went; the slaves remained. A shrewd and successful Alabama planter, who said that "an overseer is only wanted because the negroes can't be trusted," demanded that his overseers hide their faults from the slaves: "But if not possible then never in any event whatever request or require the negroes to conceal his faults from the employer—In such case the overseer is unmanned—better to retire at once from a place he can but disgrace, when afraid his hands may tell on him."[51]

From colonial times to secession the masters consulted their slaves about the performance of the overseers. In eighteenth-century Virginia Robert Carter, in the words of his biographer, "never hesitated to censure an overseer or a white artisan when a Negro had a legitimate grievance."[52] By the eve of secession, attitudes had not much changed. "My negroes," wrote J. W. Fowler of Mississippi to his overseer in 1858, "are permitted to come to me with their complaints and grievances and in no instance shall they be punished for so doing."[53]

Frederick Douglass had a cousin who had been abused outrageously. She ran to her master, who rebuked her and insisted that the overseer had his full support. But Douglass reflected that such courage as his cousin had shown usually found a reward in greater leniency thereafter: "When a slave had nerve enough to go straight to his master with a well-founded complaint against the overseer, though he might be repelled . . . and though he might be beaten by his master, as well as by the overseer, for his temerity, the policy of complaining was, in the end, generally vindicated by the relaxed rigor of the overseer's treatment."[54]

John Berkley Grimball of the South Carolina low country, who lived in Charleston but kept a sharp eye on his plantations, received an unwelcome visit from Bachus, a trusted slave. Not liking what he heard, Grimball wrote to William McKendree, his overseer:

> SIR:
> Bachus has just come down with your letter, which I am sorry to say contains *nothing whatever*—and his verbal account—which I have got after close examination, is altogether displeasing to me—
>
> From him I learn what *you did not mention*, that your brother from Georgia has been staying at my plantation for several weeks and feeding his horse on my blades and my corn, which he had about as much right to do, as to put his hand into my pocket and take my money—
>
> And for which I shall certainly *expect you to pay* at our settlement.

About six weeks later Grimball noted in his diary that "Negro property is certainly the most troublesome in the world." He continued:

> This morning—Richard, the Driver at Slann's Island made his appearance—
>
> It seems from his story that McKendree was exceedingly angry at the receipt of my last letter and accusing Richard of sending me all the news of the Plantation broke him and made Robin Driver—and gave him reason to believe that he would punish him further.—
>
> He tells me, what I can scarcely credit, but which if true is a most impudently dishonest thing on the part of McKendree, to wit: That McK's Negroes to the number of five, have during the whole summer taken out allowance out of my corn House and regularly every week—and he brought me a stick with the number of bushels notched upon it.—The quantity they have used is 25 bushels up to this day.—

I shall send him back tomorrow and have written the following to McK to go by him.—

SIR:

Richard came to me this morning with a complaint—When I go into the country his conduct will be examined and if he requires it he shall be punished. He tells me you have broken him and made Robin *driver*. Now although Richard is far from giving me satisfaction as Driver, yet the right of making and displacing drivers is one which no one has a liberty to exercise without my permission—and as that permission has not been given to you, I am surprised at your doing so in the present instance. I'll thank you to put him back into his office as soon as you receive this.—

As Richard will be examined when I go up he is not to be punished for *this offence*.

The overseer, sensing the impending disaster, went to Charleston to plead his case and satisfied Grimball that the driver had been lying about the raiding of the corncrib. Grimball noted that the overseer's health was wretched to the point of collapse and that he intended to leave the coast for a more healthful climate as soon as practicable. No doubt the overseer knew he would need a strong letter of recommendation from Grimball in the near future. Because the issue reduced to one of man to man—or rather, overseer to slave—because the overseer had given three years of good service and was himself a slaveholder and man of property, because the driver was not among Grimball's favorites, and because the overseer's physical condition evoked sympathy, Grimball felt compelled to believe him.[55] Still, it was a close call, and therein lies the story. Grimball's negative evidence begins to explain D. R. Hundley's outburst against the "cotton snobs" who indulged their slaves by encouraging them to look down on the poor whites and to rebel against their overseers by carrying tales to their masters.[56]

In keeping overseers they neither trusted nor fully respected under surveillance, masters necessarily relied on their slaves for information. After Charles M. Manigault received a letter attributing an unexpectedly short rice crop to weather and tides, he wrote back: "You must make use of your usual prudence to ferret out *this mystery* by enquiring of the driver, trunkminder & without shewing that you believe in the Overseer's incapacity. Then make up your mind whether he is an *imbécille* [sic]—or whether he be not in fault & all other qualities are tolerable."[57] A. T. Goodloe, with plantations in Tennessee and Arkansas, publicly denounced the practice of listening to slaves' tales about their overseers after almost becoming a victim of his slaves' ability to take advantage of such division between master and overseer. His slaves had been caught holding a meeting to discuss the best way to frame the overseer and get him fired.[58] Other planters appeared to reject the practice of consulting slaves against their overseers, only to give it new support. T. E. Blont of Sussex County, Virginia, wrote:

> The overseer will be expected not to degrade himself by charging any slave with carrying news to the employer. There must be no news to carry. The employer will not encourage tale-bearing, but will question every slave, indiscriminately, whenever he thinks proper about all matters connected with the plantation, and require him to tell the truth.[59]

The overseers, smarting under these rebukes and this implicit denigration, struck back when they could. William Capers, one of Manigault's strong overseers, who had been taught his job by an uncle, asserted, as his uncle had before him, that a man who would place any confidence in a Negro was a damned fool. A writer in the *American Cotton Planter* defended overseers by appealing to race pride: "Generally speaking, employers have more confidence in their negroes than in their overseers. If they wish to know how business progresses, they seldom, if ever, inquire of the white man, but call up some negro, and ask him questions that ought to make any gentleman blush to think of asking a negro about a white man."[60] J. L. Eubanks, an overseer who assumed responsibility for the Arrington estate in Alabama, reported that the slaves had been negligent and unruly under his predecessor. He intended to restore order; the slaves' opinion of him would not be allowed to influence his policy. He charged that the dreadful situation he was inheriting "has been concealed from you to keep the good will of the negroes." As for himself, he hoped they would like him, but he would not try to curry favor with them.[61]

The slaves took advantage of these conflicts to make life easier for themselves, and even tough taskmasters among the slaveholders intervened occasionally in their behalf. In some cases the overseers adjusted well and actually won the affection of the slaves, who would praise their fairness. But usually tension prevailed. And with it, the slaves ran great risks, for whenever they succeeded in curbing an overseer's power and wringing some additional living space, they incurred his wrath and, one way or another, had to take blows.[62]

The slaves' success in playing master and overseer against each other emerged in stark form in an article written by a slaveholder for a widely read agricultural journal. He quoted "a very shrewd old negro man" as saying, "Dese nic' yune oberseers ain't wut nuthin; one man like mas' Dick is wut more'n all uv em put together." Naturally, the writer approved the old slave's stated preference for Ole Massa, which "struck me as sensible."[63] The old slave was much shrewder than the writer knew. He had calmly set himself up to judge the relative merits of white men and demonstrated that all he had to do to get away with it was to indulge in a little flattery.

The game had unpleasant consequences. Most obviously, it reinforced the slaves' dependence on the master. Negatively, it provided, in the overseer, a conducting rod for their dissatisfactions; the master often dropped from sight as the man responsible for their condition. Positively, the periodic intervention of the master in their defense against excesses reinforced his self-image and his image in the quarters as a protector. As Bobby Frank Jones observes, both masters and slaves in effect used the overseers to detach themselves from the harsher side of the regime, so that each new overseer represented a new beginning and a hoped-for return to normality. "The master and slaves," he concludes, "regrouped, wiped the slate clean, and prepared to make the same mistakes another year."[64]

In other ways the three-way relationship affected class and race relations in the South over the long run. A white person put to manage black plantation workers, Frances Butler Leigh wrote from postwar Georgia, must be a gentleman to get results. The blacks know the real thing, she added, and have contempt for anything less.[65] Isaac DuBose Seabrook, a descendant of South Carolina's low-country aristocracy, recalled in 1895 how the slaves could appeal to their masters against cruel overseers: "The slave thus came to look down on the working white man, overseer or other, and up to his owner who grew to be in his eyes a superior being immensely removed above the common fate of mankind."[66] Seabrook exaggerated, or rather, he described only the tendency; but his point was well taken. The overseer as a reference point and the slaves' very ability to place some limits on his power did widen the gulf between black and white labor and strengthen the blacks' ties to the white upper classes. George Young, an ex-slave from Alabama who had suffered from cruel overseers on an absentee plantation, concluded, "De Lawd wouldn' trusted Peter wid no keys to Heaven."[67]

The hostility between slaves and overseers reflected a more general hostility between slaves and lower-class whites. Several famous runaways left biting accounts of those they perceived as "poor whites." Frederick Douglass opened his famous *Life and Times* with a reference to having been born among "a white population of the lowest order, indolent and drunken to a proverb."[68] He provided a portrait of Edward Covey, a poor white man working his way up as a professional "nigger breaker," who obtained needed labor for his farm by renting slaves at a nominal sum from planters who wanted them cured of "impudence." Douglass added a moving account of being beaten and abused by white shipyard workers, yet he also testified to some sympathy from Irish workers on the Baltimore wharf.[69] Another celebrated runaway, H. C. Bruce, wrote acidly in *The New Man* of poor whites who did odd jobs for planters and spied on the slaves, who sold their votes to the leading planters, and whose degeneracy was proven by their unwillingness to move to the free states where they could have earned a decent living.[70]

Ex-slaves later recalled poor white neighbors as "one of our biggest troubles." Those poor whites would encourage slaves to steal and then cheat them in trade; would steal themselves and blame slaves; would seduce impressionable young slave girls; and above all, provided the backbone of the hated slave patrols, which whipped and terrorized slaves caught without passes after curfew.[71] And besides, the slaves regarded the poor whites as the laziest and most dissolute people on earth; it was probably the slaves who dubbed the poor whites "trash."[72]

The slaveholders heartily concurred in their slaves' attitude toward the poor whites and tried to strengthen it. But actual relations between slaves and local poor whites were complex and included much more than mutual distaste and hatred. Many of the slaves who stole their masters' goods sold them to poor whites at drinking and gambling parties, which could promote genuine friendships and encourage a dangerous ambivalence on both sides. The same poor white who proved a brute on patrol might help a particular slave to run away or to outwit his master. Sometimes, the poor whites befriended slaves in order to spite a slaveholder they hated or envied, or conversely, out of a sudden burst of *noblesse oblige* modeled on the planters; sometimes, because of a particular friendship with a slave that had developed despite racist attitudes. The slaveholders felt that no white man other than the most degraded would enter into such illicit and even leveling associations with blacks, and that nothing except trouble for the plantation community would come from these contacts.[73]

But, the slaveholders could go only so far in encouraging their slaves' contempt for the poor whites, for it quickly became a safe vehicle for expressing contempt for all whites. When the slaves sang, "I'd rather be a nigger than a poor white man," they were attacking prevalent racist doctrine, at least in its most extreme form.[74] Gustavus A. Ingraham of Maine, trying to build up a small business in Augusta, Georgia, wrote in 1840 that the Negroes "are however too sycophantic as a race but there are some exceptions and these are too proud to speak to a common white man like myself."[75]

The slaveholders had other worries. Many suspected that non-slaveholders would encourage slave disobedience and even rebellion, not so much out of sympathy for the blacks as out of hatred for the rich planters and resentment of their own poverty. White men sometimes were linked to slave insurrectionary plots, and each such incident rekindled fears.[76] By deciding that lower-class whites who associated with blacks were "degraded," the slaveholders explained away the existence of such racial contacts and avoided reflecting on the possibility that genuine sympathy might exist across racial lines. They also upheld stern police measures against whites who illicitly fraternized with blacks, and justified a widespread attempt to keep white and black laborers apart. The circumstances of lower-class white-black contact therefore encouraged racist hostilities and inhibited the maturation of relationships of mutual sympathy if not equality.

Such relationships of mutual sympathy between slaves and poor whites did exist. They remained few in number, but their existence was ominous in a society in which no sane member of the ruling class wanted to take chances. Lewis Clarke, a successful runaway, recalled a slave woman who suffered fifty lashes for slipping food to a sick old poor white neighbor. Olmsted reported a slave's stout defense of poor Cajuns as good, hard-working people.[77] Recollections by former slaves during the twentieth century are especially compelling since their postemancipation relationships with poor whites could rarely have been such as to inspire a romantic reading of the long past. Most spoke harshly of the poor whites and especially recalled their vicious behavior as members of the patrols. But some added other information and judgments. They recalled poor whites and immigrant laborers who appealed to the slaves, often successfully, for food and help in desperate circumstances. They spoke compassionately of the terrible struggle the poor whites had and of how their suffering often rivaled or exceeded that of the slaves. They spoke of kindnesses shown by poor whites to slaves of hard masters and of hired white laborers who worked side by side with the slaves ("helped us") and who shared the good times as well as the backbreaking labor.[78]

Fanny Kemble, in an account of the hiring of Irishmen and blacks to dig a canal, captured the quality of race relations among the poor as well as the potential. The planters, she wrote, insisted on segregating the laborers ostensibly to prevent violence, for the Irish were believed anxious to take every opportunity to abuse the blacks. Mrs. Kemble reflected:

> They [the Irish] have been oppressed enough themselves to be oppressive whenever they have a chance; and the despised and degraded condition of the blacks, presenting to them a very ugly resemblance of their own home circumstances, naturally excites in them the exercise of the disgust and contempt of which they themselves are very habitually the objects; and that such circular distribution of wrongs may not only be pleasant, but have something like the air of retributive right to very ignorant folks, is not much to be wondered at. . . . But the Irish are not only quarrelers, and rioters, and fighters, and drinkers, and despisers of niggers—they are a passionate, impulsive, warm-hearted, generous people, much given to powerful indignations, which break out suddenly when not compelled to smoulder sullenly—pestilent sympathizers too, and with a sufficient dose of American atmospheric air in their lungs, properly mixed with a right proportion of ardent spirits, there is no saying but what they might actually take to sympathy with the slaves, and I leave you to judge of the possible consequences. You perceive, I am sure, that they can by no means be allowed to work together on the Brunswick Canal.[79]

The scattered incidents recalled by ex-slaves merely hint at the potential perceived by Mrs. Kemble and feared by the slaveholders. Whether in time changing conditions would have created a new political situation remains a matter of speculation; under the political and social conditions of the Old South, interracial solidarity could not develop into a serious threat to the regime. The hostility of the poor whites toward the blacks reinforced the regime and forced the slaves into increased reliance on the protection of their masters and other "good" and "quality" whites. The overseers thus came to symbolize not so much the class oppression of slavery as the racist hostility of all lower-class whites. The attitudes of the blacks and poor whites were not to pass away easily, and their consequences during Reconstruction and the Populist period were devastating.

THE HEGEMONIC FUNCTION OF THE LAW

When Mao Tse-tung told his revolutionary army, "Political power grows out of the barrel of a gun," he stated the obvious, for as Max Weber long before had observed as a matter of scientific detachment, "The decisive means for politics is violence."[1] This viewpoint does not deny an ethical dimension to state power; it asserts that state power, the conquest of which constitutes the object of all serious political struggle, represents an attempt to monopolize and therefore both discipline and legitimize the weapons of violence.

One of the primary functions of the law concerns the means by which command of the gun becomes ethically sanctioned. But if we left it at that, we could never account for the dignity and élan of a legal profession in, say, England, that has itself become a social force; much less could we account for the undeniable influence of the law in shaping the class relations of which it is an instrument of domination. Thus, the fashionable relegation of law to the rank of a superstructural and derivative phenomenon obscures the degree of autonomy it creates for itself. In modern societies, at least, the theoretical and moral foundations of the legal order and the actual, specific history of its ideas and institutions influence, step by step, the wider social order and system of class rule, for no class in the modern Western world could rule for long without some ability to present itself as the guardian of the interests and sentiments of those being ruled.

The idea of "hegemony," which since Gramsci has become central to Western Marxism, implies class antagonisms; but it also implies, for a given historical epoch, the ability of a particular class to contain those antagonisms on a terrain in which its legitimacy is not dangerously questioned. As regards the law specifically, note should be taken of the unhappy fate of natural-law doctrines and assorted other excursions into "revolutionary" legal theory. The revolutionary bourgeoisie, during its rise to power in Europe, counterposed natural-law doctrines to feudal theory but once in power rushed to embrace a positive theory of law, even while assimilating natural-law doctrines to a new defense of property. Nor did the experience of the Communist movement in Russia differ after its conquest of power. However much sentimentalists and utopians may rail at the monotonous recurrence of a positive theory of law whenever revolutionaries settle down to rebuild the world they have shattered, any other course would be doomed to failure. Ruling classes differ, and each must rule differently. But all modern ruling classes have much in common in their attitude toward the law, for each must confront the problem of coercion in such a way as to minimize the necessity for its use, and each must disguise the extent to which state power does not so much rest on force as represent its actuality. Even Marxian theory, therefore, must end with the assertion of a positive theory of law and judge natural-law and "higher-law" doctrines to be tactical devices in the extralegal struggle.[2]

In southern slave society, as in other societies, the law, even narrowly defined as a system of institutionalized jurisprudence, constituted a principal vehicle for the hegemony of the ruling class. Since the slaveholders, like other ruling classes, arose and grew in dialectical response to the other classes of society—since they were molded by white yeomen and black slaves as much as they molded them—the law cannot be viewed as something passive and reflective, but must be viewed as an active, partially autonomous force, which mediated among the several classes and compelled the rulers to bend to the demands of the ruled. The slaveholders faced an unusually complex problem since their regional power was embedded in a national system in which they had to share power with an antagonistic northern bourgeoisie. A full evaluation of the significance of the law of slavery will have to await an adequate history of the southern legal system in relation to the national; until then a preliminary analysis that risks too much abstraction must serve.[3]

The slaveholders as a socio-economic class shaped the legal system to their interests. But within that socio-economic class—the class as a whole—there were elements competing for power. Within it, a political center arose, consolidated itself, and assumed a commanding position during the 1850s. The most advanced fraction of the slaveholders—those who most clearly perceived the interests and needs of the class as a whole—steadily worked to make their class more conscious of its nature, spirit, and destiny. In the process it created a world-view appropriate to a slaveholders' regime.

For any such political center, the class as a whole must be brought to a higher understanding of itself—transformed from a class-in-itself, reacting to pressures on its objective position, into a class-for-itself, consciously striving to shape the world in its own image. Only possession of public power can discipline a class as a whole, and through it, the other classes of society. The juridical system may become, then, not merely an expression of class interest, nor even merely an expression of the willingness of the rulers to mediate with the ruled; it may become an instrument by which the advanced section of the ruling class imposes its viewpoint upon the class as a whole and the wider society. The law must discipline the ruling class and guide and educate the masses. To accomplish these tasks it must manifest a degree of evenhandedness sufficient to compel social conformity; it must, that is, validate itself ethically in the eyes of the several classes, not just the ruling class. Both criminal and civil law set standards of behavior and sanction norms that extend well beyond strictly legal matters. The death penalty for murder, for example, need not arise from a pragmatic concern with deterrence, and its defenders could justifiably resist psychological arguments. It may arise from the demand for implementation of a certain idea of justice and from the educational requirement to set a firm standard of right and wrong. "The Law," as Gramsci says, "is the repressive and negative aspect of the entire positive civilising activity undertaken by the State."[4]

The law acts hegemonically to assure people that their particular consciences can be subordinated—indeed, morally must be subordinated—to the collective judgment of society. It may compel conformity by granting each individual his right of private judgment, but it must deny him the right to take action based on that judgment when in conflict with the general will. Those who would act on their own judgment as against the collective judgment embodied in the law find themselves pressed from the moral question implicit in any particular law to the moral question of obedience to constituted authority. It appears mere egotism and antisocial behavior to attempt to go outside the law unless one is prepared to attack the entire legal system and therefore the consensual framework of the body politic.[5]

The white South shaped its attitude toward its slaves in this context.[6] With high, malicious humor, William Styron has his fictional T. R. Gray explain to Nat Turner how he, a mere chattel, can be tried for the very human acts of murder and insurrection:

> ". . . The point is that *you* are *animate* chattel and animate chattel is capable of craft and connivery and wily stealth. You ain't a wagon, Reverend, but chattel that possesses moral choice and spiritual volition. Remember that well. Because that's how come the law provides that animate chattel like you can be tried for a felony, and that's how come you're goin' to be tried next Sattidy."
>
> He paused, then said softly without emotion: "And hung by the neck until dead."[7]

Styron may well have meant to satirize Judge Green of the Tennessee Supreme Court, who declared in 1846, "A slave is not in the condition of a horse." The slave, Judge Green continued, is made in the image of the Creator: "He has mental capacities, and an immortal principle in his nature that constitute him equal to his owner, but for the accidental position in which fortune has placed him. . . . The laws . . . cannot extinguish his high born nature, nor deprive him of many rights which are inherent in man."[8] The idea that chattels, as the states usually defined slaves, could have a highborn nature, complete with rights inherent in man, went down hard with those who thought that even the law should obey the rules of logic.

Four years before Judge Green's humane observations, Judge Turley of the same court unwittingly presented the dilemma. "The right to obedience . . ." he declared in *Jacob (a Slave) v. State*, "in all lawful things . . . is perfect in the master; and the power to inflict any punishment, not affecting life or limb . . . is secured to him by law."[9] The slave, being neither a wagon nor a horse, had to be dealt with as a man, but the law dared not address itself direct to the point. Had the law declared the slave a person in a specific class relationship to another person, two unpleasant consequences would have followed. First, the demand that such elementary rights as those of the family be respected would have become irresistible in a commercialized society that required the opposite in order to guarantee an adequate mobility of capital and labor. Second, the slaveholders would have had to surrender in principle, much as they often had to do in practice, their insistence that a slave was morally obligated to function as an extension of his master's will. However much the law generally seeks to adjust conflicting principles in society, in this case it risked undermining the one principle the slaveholders viewed as a *sine qua non*.

Yet, as Styron correctly emphasizes in the words he gives to T. R. Gray, the courts had to recognize the humanity—and therefore the free will—of the slave or be unable to hold him accountable for antisocial acts. Judge Bunning of Georgia plainly said, "It is not true that slaves are only chattels . . . and therefore, it is not true that it is not possible for them to be prisoners. . . ."[10] He did not tell us how a chattel (a thing) could also be nonchattel in any sense other than an agreed-upon fiction, nor did he wish to explore the question why a fiction should have become necessary. Since much of the law concerns agreed-upon fictions, the judges, as judges, did not have to become nervous about their diverse legal opinions, but as slaveholders, they could not avoid the prospect of disarray being introduced into their social philosophy. Repeatedly, the courts struggled with and tripped over the slave's humanity. Judge Hall of North Carolina, contrary to reason, nature, and the opinion of his fellow judges, could blurt out, *en passant*, "Being slaves, they had no will of their own. . . ."[11] If so, then what of the opinion expressed by the State Supreme Court of Missouri: "The power of the master being limited, his responsibility is proportioned accordingly"?[12]

The high court of South Carolina wrestled with the conflicting principles of slave society and came up with an assortment of mutually exclusive answers. Judge Waites, in *State v. Cynthia Simmons and Lawrence Kitchen* (1794): "Negroes are under the protection of the laws, and have personal rights, and cannot be considered on a footing only with domestic animals. They have wills of their own —capacities to commit crimes; and are responsible for offences against society." The court in *Fairchild v. Bell* (1807): "The slave lives for his master's service. His time, his labor, his comforts, are all at the master's disposal." Judge John Belton O'Neall in *Tennent v. Dendy* (1837): "Slaves are our most valuable property. . . . Too many guards cannot be interposed between it and violent unprincipled men. . . . The slave ought to be fully aware that his master is to him . . . a perfect security from injury. When this is the case, the relation of master and servant becomes little short of that of parent and child."[13] But in Kentucky, the high court had pronounced in 1828: "However deeply it may be regretted, and whether it be politic or impolitic, a slave by our code is not treated as a person, but *(negotium)* a thing, as he stood in the civil code of the Roman Empire." But one year later we hear: "A slave has volition, and has feelings which cannot be entirely disregarded." And again in 1836: "But, although the law of this state considers slaves as property, yet it recognizes their personal existence, and, to a qualified extent, their natural rights."[14]

The South had discovered, as had every previous slave society, that it could not deny the slave's humanity, however many preposterous legal fictions it invented.[15] That discovery ought to have told the slaveholders much more. Had they reflected on the implications of a wagon's inability to raise an insurrection, they might have understood that the slaves as well as the masters were creating the law. The slaves' action proceeded within narrow limits, but it realized one vital objective: it exposed the deception on which the slave society rested—the notion that in fact, not merely in one's fantasy life, some human beings could become mere extensions of the will of another. The slaves grasped the significance of their victory with deeper insight than they have usually been given credit for. They saw that they had few rights at law and that those could easily be violated by the whites. But even one right, imperfectly defended, was enough to tell them that the pretensions of the master class could be resisted. Before long, law or no law, they were adding a great many "customary rights" of their own and learning how to get them respected.

The slaves understood that the law offered them little or no protection, and in self-defense they turned to two alternatives: to their master, if he was decent, or his neighbors, if he was not; and to their own resources. Their commitment to a paternalistic system deepened accordingly, but in such a way as to allow them to define rights for themselves. For reasons of their own the slaveholders relied heavily on local custom and tradition; so did the slaves, who turned this reliance into a weapon. If the law said they had no right to property, for example, but local custom accorded them private garden plots, then woe to the master or overseer who summarily withdrew the "privilege." To those slaves the privilege had become a right, and the withdrawal an act of aggression not to be borne. The slaveholders, understanding this attitude, rationalized their willingness to compromise. The slaves forced themselves upon the law, for the courts repeatedly sustained such ostensibly extralegal arrangements as having the force of law because sanctioned by time-honored practice. It was a small victory so far as everyday protection was concerned, but not so small psychologically; it gave the slaves some sense of having rights of their own and also made them more aware of those rights withheld.[16] W. W. Hazard of Georgia ran the risk of telling his slaves about their legal rights and of stressing the legal limits of his own power over them. He made it clear that he had an obligation to take care of them in their old age, whereas free white workers had no such protection, and argued deftly that their being whipped for insubordination represented a humane alternative to the practice of shooting soldiers and sailors for insubordination. His was an unusual act, but perhaps not so risky after all. He may have scored a few points while not revealing much they did not already know.[17]

The legal status of the slave during the seventeenth century, particularly in Virginia, still occasions dispute. We cannot be sure that the position of the earliest Africans differed markedly from that of the white indentured servants. The debate has considerable significance for the interpretation of race relations in American history. It remains possible that for a brief period a less oppressive pattern of race relations had had a chance to develop in the Upper South; it is doubtful that any such alternative ever existed in South Carolina, which as a slave society virtually derived from Barbados. In any case, before the turn of the century the issue had been resolved and blacks condemned to the status of slaves for life.[18]

The laws of Virginia and Maryland, as well as those of the colonies to the south, increasingly gave masters the widest possible power over the slaves and also, through prohibition of interracial marriage and the general restriction of slave status to nonwhites, codified and simultaneously preached white supremacy. Kenneth Stampp writes: "Thus the master class, for its own purposes, wrote chattel slavery, the caste system, and color prejudice into American custom and law."[19] These earliest, Draconian slave codes served as a model for those adopted by new slave states during the nineteenth century. Over time they became harsher with respect to manumission, education, and the status of the free Negro and milder with respect to protection for slave life; but most of the amelioration that occurred came through the courts and the force of public opinion rather than from the codes themselves. At the end of the antebellum period the laws remained Draconian and the enormous power of the masters had received only modest qualification. The best that might be said is that the list of capital crimes had shrunk considerably, in accordance with the movement toward general sensibility, and that the ruthless enforcement of the eighteenth century had given way to greater flexibility during the nineteenth.[20] The laws, at least as amended during the early nineteenth century, tried to protect the lives of the slaves and provided for murder indictments against masters and other whites. They also demanded that masters, under penalty of fine or imprisonment, give adequate food, clothing, shelter, and support to the elderly. But these qualifications added confirmation to the power of the master over the slaves' bodies as well as labor-time. Nowhere did slave marriages win legal sanction, and therefore families could be separated with impunity. Only Louisiana effectively limited this outrage by forbidding the sale away from their mothers of children under the age of ten. Most significantly, blacks could not testify against whites in court, so that enforcement of the laws against cruel or even murderous masters became extremely difficult.

If harsh laws did not mean equally harsh practice, neither did mild laws mean equally mild practice. Kentucky had one of the mildest of slave codes, including the notable absence of an antiliteracy provision, but it probably suffered more personal violence and lynching than most other states, although much more often directed against allegedly negrophile whites than against blacks. The South had become the region of lynching *par excellence* during antebellum times, but of the three hundred or so victims recorded between 1840 and 1860, probably less than 10 percent were blacks. Occasionally, the lynch fever struck hard, as in the wake of an insurrection scare. In these cases the most respectable planters might find themselves side by side with the poor whites in meting out fearful summary punishments; but for the blacks the danger of lynching remained minimal until after emancipation.[21] The direct power of the masters over their slaves and in society as a whole, where they had little need for extralegal measures against blacks, provided the slaves with extensive protection against mob violence. So strong a hold did this sense of justice take on the master class that even during the war prominent voices could be heard in opposition to panicky summary actions against defecting slaves. Charles C. Jones, Jr., then a lieutenant in the Confederate army, wrote his father: "A trial by jury is accorded to everyone, whether white or black, where life is at stake. . . . Any other procedure, although possibly to a certain extent justified by the aggravated character of the offense and upon the grounds of public good, would in a strictly legal sense certainly be *coram non judice*, and would savor of mob law."[22] As Lieutenant Jones undoubtedly understood, an easy attitude toward indiscriminate mob violence against blacks would do more than threaten slave property; it would also threaten the position of the master class in society and open the way to initiatives by the white lower classes that might not remain within racial bounds. The masters felt that their own direct action, buttressed by a legal system of their own construction, needed little or no support from poor white trash. Order meant order.

The extent to which the law, rather than mobs, dealt with slave criminals appeared nowhere so starkly as in the response to rape cases. Rape meant, by definition, rape of white women, for no such crime as rape of a black woman existed at law. Even when a black man sexually attacked a black woman he could only be punished by his master; no way existed to bring him to trial or to convict him if so brought.[23] In one case an appellate court reversed the conviction of a black man for attempted rape, probably of a white woman, because the indictment had failed to specify the race of the victim.[24]

Rape and attempted rape of white women by black men did not occur frequently. Ulrich Bonnell Phillips found 105 cases in Virginia for 1780 to 1864, with a few years unaccounted for.[25] Other states kept poor records on slave crime, although enough cases reached the appellate courts to make it clear that every slaveholding area had to face the issue once in a while.[26] But even these infrequent cases provide a body of evidence of contemporary white southern attitudes.

On the whole, the racist fantasy so familiar after emancipation did not grip the South in slavery times. Slaves accused of rape occasionally suffered lynching, but the overwhelming majority, so far as existing evidence may be trusted, received trials as fair and careful as the fundamental injustice of the legal system made possible. Sometimes slaves did run into injustices even at law. A slave accused of raping a widow in Louisiana in 1859 went to the gallows on evidence that a local planter thought woefully insufficient. No positive identification had been made, he charged, and the evidence as a whole was slender. "I consider him," he wrote in his diary, "to be a victim of what is deemed a necessary example."[27]

The astonishing facts—astonishing in view of postemancipation outrages—are that public opinion usually remained calm enough to leave the matter in the hands of the courts and that the courts usually performed their duty scrupulously. The appellate courts in every southern state threw out convictions for rape and attempted rape on every possible ground, including the purely technical. They overturned convictions because the indictments had not been drawn up properly; because the lower courts had based their convictions on possibly coerced confessions; or because the reputation of the white victim had not been admitted as evidence. The calmness of the public and the judicial system, relative to that of postbellum years, appeared most pointedly in reversals based on the failure to prove that black men who approached white women actually intended to use force. The Supreme Court of Alabama declared in one such instance: "An indecent advance, or importunity, however revolting, would not constitute the offense. . . ."[28] The punishment for rape remained death; punishment by castration receded, although in Missouri it survived into the late antebellum period.[29]

The scrupulousness of the high courts extended to cases of slaves' murdering or attempting to murder whites. In Mississippi during 1834–1861, five of thirteen convictions were reversed or remanded; in Alabama during 1825–1864, nine of fourteen; in Louisiana during 1844–1859, two of five. The same pattern appeared in other states.[30]

A slave could kill a white man in self-defense and escape conviction, provided that his own life stood in clear and imminent danger. In a celebrated case in Virginia in 1791, Moses, a slave, killed his overseer and escaped conviction despite much controversy in the white community. The court accepted testimony that Moses had served honestly and faithfully and that he had killed only when the overseer tried to kill him.[31] During the nineteenth century the southern courts said plainly that a slave had the right to resist an assault that threatened his life, even to the point of killing his attacker. In practice, these rulings meant that a white man who attacked a slave with a deadly weapon risked the consequences; they did not mean that a slave had the right to make a judgment on the potential effects of, say, a prolonged whipping.[32]

A brace of famous cases in North Carolina brought the theoretical questions to the surface and exposed the ultimate absurdity of defining a slave as chattel. In 1829, Judge Thomas Ruffin, one of the South's most respected jurists, handed down a decision he freely admitted to have ghastly implications.[33] A lower court had held that, as a matter of law, a master could be charged with committing battery upon a slave, much as a parent could be charged with unduly harsh physical punishment of a child. Judge Ruffin explained the Supreme Court's reversal in words that reveal as much about new attitudes toward the rights of children and the limits of parental authority as about anything else:

> There is no likeness between the cases. They are in opposition to each other and there is an impassable gulf between them—the difference is that which exists between freedom and slavery—and a greater cannot be imagined. In the one the end in view is the happiness of the youth born to equal rights with that governor on whom the duty devolves of training the young to usefulness in a status which he is afterwards to assume among free men.
>
> With slavery it is far otherwise. The end is the profit of the master, his security and public safety; the subject, one doomed in his own person, and his posterity, to live without knowledge, and without the capacity to make anything his own, and to toil that another may reap the fruits. What moral considerations, such as a father might give to a son, shall be addressed to such a being, to convince him what, it is impossible but that the most stupid must feel and know can never be true—that he is thus to labour upon a principle of natural duty, or for the sake of his own personal happiness, such services can only be expected from one who has no will of his own; who surrenders his will in implicit obedience to that of another. Such obedience is the consequence only of uncontrolled authority over the body. There is nothing else which can operate to produce the effect. The power of the master must be absolute to render the submission of the slave perfect. I must freely confess my sense of the harshness of this proposition, I feel it as deeply as any man can. And as a principle of moral right, every person in his retirement must repudiate it. But in the actual condition of things, it must be so. There is no remedy. This discipline belongs to the state of slavery.[34]

Never has the logic of slavery been followed so faithfully by a humane and responsible man. As Ruffin knew, no civilized community could live with such a view. Perhaps he had hoped that the legislature would find a way to remove the high court's dilemma. It did not. The court had to reconsider its attitude.

In 1834, in *State v. Will*, the liberal Judge Gaston, speaking for the same court, handed down a radically different doctrine at once infinitely more humane and considerably less logical. Judge Gaston considered some things more important than logical consistency. Will, a slave, had tried to run away from an overseer who was attempting to whip him. The overseer thereupon got a gun and tried to shoot him. Will killed the overseer; accordingly, he entered a plea of innocent by reason of self-defense. The Supreme Court, under Judge Gaston's leadership, overturned Will's conviction and sustained the plea. Judge Ruffin must have been relieved; he remained silent and did not dissent from a ruling that so clearly contradicted the philosophy inherent in his own previous judgment.[35] The aftermath of the case also reveals something about the southern legal system. On the assumption that Will's life would be unsafe from extralegal white retaliation, his master sold him and his wife to Mississippi. A few years later she arranged to be sold back to her old place. Her fellow slaves greeted her with surprise, for they had not expected her to leave her husband. She had not. Will had killed another slave in Mississippi and had been convicted of murder and executed. As the poor woman recalled, "Will sho'ly had hard luck. He killed a white man in North Carolina and got off, and then was hung for killing a nigger in Mississippi."[36]

The courts could never have sustained the right of a slave to self-defense if public opinion had been hostile. For the most part, it was not. Especially in cases in which the victim was an overseer or a poor man, the white attitude was that he got what he deserved. Armstead Barrett, an ex-slave of Texas, recalled that when a brutal overseer finally went too far, two slaves picked up their hoes one day and hacked his head off. The master calmly sold them.[37] In so doing, he protected his investment, for compensation never equaled market value; but we can hardly believe that in such cases of violence against whites monetary considerations easily overpowered the others. In South Carolina a master abused his slaves and was believed responsible for the death of one or more. A committee of local citizens waited on the master to suggest, no doubt with grave courtesy and respect, that he leave the area immediately. He did.[38] In Georgia slaves killed a cruel master without evoking the ire of local whites, who considered that he had deserved his fate.[39] In Missouri, an ex-slave recalled that at the age of ten she had blinded her old mistress by hitting her with a rock in retaliation for the wanton and unpunished murder of her baby sister, who had made a nuisance of herself by excessive crying. The slave girl was owned by the mistress's daughter, who refused to have her punished and said, "Well, I guess mamma has larnt her lesson at last."[40]

In seventeenth-century Virginia a master could not murder a slave. He might cause his death, but he could not, legally, murder him. Would a man willingly destroy his own property? Certainly not. Therefore, no such crime as the murder of one's own slave could present itself to a court of reasonable men.[41] In time, Virginia and the other slave states thought better of the matter. In 1821, South Carolina became the last of the slave states to declare itself clearly in protection of slave life. During the nineteenth century, despite state-by-state variations, slaveholders theoretically faced murder charges for wantonly killing a slave or for causing his death by excessive punishment. The Virginia Supreme Court in 1851 upheld the conviction of a master for causing the death of a slave by "cruel and excessive whipping and torture": "But in so inflicting punishment for the sake of punishment, the owner of the slave acts at his peril; and if death ensues in consequence of such punishment, the relation of master and slave affords no ground or excuse or palliation." The court unanimously ruled that a murder had been committed.[42]

South Carolina responded more slowly to the demands for liberalization than did other states, although Chancellor Harper may have been right in declaring: "It is a somewhat singular fact that when there existed in our State no law for punishing the murder of a slave other than a pecuniary fine, there were, I will venture to say, at least ten murders of freemen for one murder of a slave."[43] White folks in South Carolina, gentlemen all, always had played rough with each other and everyone else. When whites were convicted of killing slaves, they usually got off lightly, although less so as time went on. By 1791 the prosecution insisted that a white man deserved the death penalty in a clear case of murder, especially since such crimes against slaves were increasing and had to be deterred. The murderer received a fine of £700, which he was unable to pay; accordingly, he went to prison for seven years at hard labor. The same year a white man convicted of manslaughter of a slave paid £50. After a tougher law was passed in 1821 in South Carolina a man killed a slave, not with premeditation but "in heat of passion," and received a fine of $350.

The law of 1821 established three categories: murder, killing in heat of passion, and killing by undue correction—generally, excessive whipping. The change aimed at increasing the penalty for murder. Judge O'Neall commented: "The act of 1821 changed the murder of a slave from a mere misdemeanor, which it was under the act of 1740, to a felony. . . . It, in a criminal point of view, elevated slaves from chattels personal to human beings in the place of the State." The authorities enforced the law as best they could, but its strength may be measured by the sentence meted out to a woman convicted of killing a slave by undue correction in 1840— a fine of $214.28.[44]

The courts moved to eliminate the excuses for killing blacks. In Louisiana, for example, a white man was found guilty of killing a free man of color who had insulted him. The court observed that whites did not have to suffer insults from Negroes, slave or free, and had adequate recourse at law; therefore, the provocation could not excuse the defendant's extralegal action.[45] In Texas a white man killed another man's slave, who had raised a hand to him. He was found guilty of manslaughter and appealed, but the high court sustained the verdict, citing precedent in Tennessee, and added, "The only matter of surprise is that it should ever have been doubted."[46]

When whites did find themselves before the bar of justice, especially during the late antebellum period, they could expect greater severity than might be imagined. The penalties seldom reached the extreme or the level they would have if the victim had been white; but neither did they usually qualify as a slap on the wrist. If one murderer in North Carolina got off with only eleven months in prison in 1825, most fared a good deal worse. Ten-year sentences were common, and occasionally the death penalty was invoked.[47]

The greatest difficulty in securing enforcement of the laws against murdering or mistreating slaves did not stem from the laxness of the authorities or from the unwillingness of juries to convict, or from any softness in the appellate courts. Public opinion might remain silent in the face of harsh treatment by masters; it did not readily suffer known sadists and killers.[48] But neither did it suffer blacks to testify against whites, and therein lay the fatal weakness of the law. Moreover, the authorities and public opinion

THE HEGEMONIC FUNCTION OF THE LAW

more readily came down hard upon overseers or small slaveholders than upon gentlemen of standing.

Despite the efforts of the authorities and the courts, masters and overseers undoubtedly murdered more slaves than we shall ever know. If the number did not reach heights worthy of classification as "statistically significant," it probably did loom large enough to strike terror into the quarters. It could happen. It sometimes did. And the arrests, convictions, and punishment never remotely kept pace with the number of victims.

Despite so weak a legal structure, the slaves in the United States probably suffered the ultimate crime of violence less frequently than did those in other American slave socieites, and white killers probably faced justice more often in the Old South than elsewhere. The murder of a slave in Barbados drew little attention or likelihood of punishment. Effective protection was out of the question in Saint-Domingue. The Catholic slaveholding countries of Spanish and Portuguese America abounded in unenforceable and unenforced protective codes. Wherever the blacks heavily outnumbered the whites, as they did in so much of the Caribbean, fear of insurrection and insubordination strangled pleas for humanity. The bleak record of the southern slave states actually glows in comparison. These observations reveal something about the sociology of law and power. But they would not likely have provided much comfort to the slaves of South Carolina or Mississippi.[49]

Frederick Law Olmsted pointed out the consequences of the South's position, especially for those regions in which white testimony could not be expected:

> The precariousness of the much-vaunted happiness of the slaves can need but one further reflection to be appreciated. No white man can be condemned for any cruelty or neglect, no matter how fiendish, on slave testimony. The rice plantations are in a region very sparcely occupied by whites: the plantations are nearly all very large —often miles across: many a one of them occupying the whole of an island—and rarely is there more than one white man upon a plantation at a time, during the summer. Upon this one man each slave is dependent, even for the necessities of life.[50]

South Carolina tried to protect its slaves in cases of wanton cruelty or murder by providing that the master had responsibility for their condition, so that physical evidence on a body or the condition of a corpse could constitute circumstantial evidence adequate for conviction. What the law gave, the law took away, for it also provided that a master's oath of innocence had to be respected. Apart from the general absurdity of such a provision, the State Supreme Court's outstanding jurist, John Belton O'Neall, fumed, "This is the greatest temptation ever presented to perjury, and the Legislature ought speedily to remove it."[51]

The tenacious opposition to black testimony against whites proved a disadvantage to the planters themselves. If, for example, a white man robbed a plantation, the testimony of the owner's slaves had to be ignored. If a white man killed another's slave and thereby also robbed him of hundreds or thousands of dollars, the slaveholder had to settle accounts by personal violence or not at all unless some other white man had witnessed the crime. In Louisiana in 1840 the ultimate irony occurred, when a white man who had incited slaves to insurrection had to be acquitted because their confessions could not be used against him.[52] In this as in so many other ways, the racism of the whites worked against them; but they regarded these expensive inconveniences as necessary evils and bore them doggedly.

"It is remarkable at first view," wrote George Fitzhugh, the proslavery ideologue of Virginia, "that in Cuba, where the law attempts to secure mild treatment to the slave, he is inhumanely treated; and in Virginia, where there is scarce any law to protect him, he is very humanely governed and provided for."[53] This self-serving sermon, with its exaggeration and its kernel of truth, became standard fare for the apologists for slavery and has won some support from subsequent historians. The slaveholders did not intend to enforce their severe legislation strictly and considered it a device to be reserved for periods of disquiet and especially for periods of rumored insurrectionary plots. In practice this easy attitude confirmed the direct power of the master. For example, although state or local laws might forbid large meetings of slaves from several plantations, the planters normally permitted religious services or balls and barbecues unless they had some reason to fear trouble. The local authorities, generally subservient to the planters, usually looked the other way. Thus in Ascension Parish, Louisiana, the local ordinance declared: "Every person is prohibited from permitting in his negro quarters any other assemblies but those of his slaves and from allowing his slaves to dance during the night."[54] Enforcement of such an edict would have required that masters constantly punish their slaves, who were not to be denied, and thereby ruin the morale of their labor force. Planters who agreed to such an edict had either let themselves be swept away by some momentary passion or intended it for emergency enforcement. The laws of most states also forbade teaching slaves to read and write. Most slaveholders obeyed these laws because they thought them wise, not because they expected punishment of violators. In many of the great planter families various individuals, especially the white children, taught slaves to read. Some slaveholders violated the laws against giving slaves guns to hunt with, although they no doubt screened the beneficiaries with care. The law existed as a resource to provide means for meeting any emergency and to curb permissive masters. But the heart of the slave law lay with the master's prerogatives and depended upon his discretion. In this sense alone did practice generally veer from statute.

A slaveholding community did not intervene against a brutal master because of moral outrage alone; it intervened to protect its interests. Or rather, its strong sense of interest informed its moral sensibilities. "Harmony among neighbors is very important in the successful management of slaves," wrote a planter in an article directed to his own class. A good manager among bad ones, he explained, faces a hopeless task, for the slaves easily perceive differences and become dissatisfied.[55] It does no good, wrote another, to enforce discipline on your plantation if the next planter does not.[56] These arguments cut in both directions. They called for strict discipline from those who tended to be lax and for restraint from those who tended to be harsh.

What the law could not accomplish, public opinion might. A brutal overseer threatened by arrest could be made to understand that, however his trial might turn out, the community would welcome his departure. J. H. Bills reported from one of his plantations in Mississippi: "A jury of inquest was held yesterday over the body of a negro fellow, the property of the John Fowler estate, whose verdict was, I understand, that he came to his death by a blow given him on the head by Mahlon Hix a few days before. Hix left the country this morning."[57]

A more difficult question concerned atrocities by respected masters. When in Richmond, Virginia, Fredrika Bremer heard some slaveholders talking about a rich neighbor who treated his slaves savagely. They condemned him, but had nevertheless accepted an invitation to his party. When questioned, they explained that they did not wish to offend his wife and daughters. Miss Bremer thought that his money and power had played a part in their decision. She noted a five-year sentence handed down on a master for barbarously killing a favorite house slave. When the entire community expressed outrage at the crime and approved the prison term, she concluded that that was about what it took to provoke a meaningful reaction.[58]

Ex-slaves from various parts of the South recalled community interventions and moral pressure on cruel masters. Hagar Lewis of Texas said that her master filed charges against some neighbors for underfeeding and excessive whipping. A. M. Moore, an educated preacher from Harrison County, Texas, added, "I've known courts in this county to fine slaveowners for not feeding and clothing their slaves right." George Teamoh of Virginia recalled that his mistress gave runaways from cruelty refuge on her place. Lou Smith of South Carolina recalled a slave's slipping off to tell white neighbors that his master had savagely whipped a slave and left him bleeding. The neighbors forced the master to have the slave attended by a doctor. And others testified that brutal masters had constant trouble from irate fellow slaveholders, none of whom, however, seemed willing to take direct action unless something atrocious had occurred.[59]

Cruel and negligent masters did not often face trial. Some did, primarily because of the efforts of other slaveholders. A slaveholder in certain states could be convicted on circumstancial evidence alone, if the decision in *State of Louisiana v. Morris* (1849) may be taken as a guide. Even then, no conviction was likely without an aroused public opinion. These convictions, inadequate as they were, reminded the community of what was expected of individual behavior.[60]

Fortunately for the slaves, in many communities one or two souls among the slaveholders ran the risks of personal retaliation to keep an eye on everyone else's plantations. Captain J. G. Richardson of New Iberia, Louisiana, made no few enemies by compelling prosecution of delinquent fellow slaveholders, and others like him cropped up here and there.[61] The private papers of the slaveholders, as well as their public efforts, suggest that they could become enraged at local sadists and would take action in the extreme cases.[62]

Moral suasion and active intervention had limits. Much cruelty occurred because average masters lost their tempers—something any other master had to excuse unless he saw himself as a saint who could never be riled—and little could be done about someone who stopped short of atrocities as defined by other slaveholders and who did not much care about his neighbors' criticism. Yet moral pressure, if it could not prevent savages from acting savagely, did set a standard of behavior to which men who cared about their reputations tried to adhere.

Although we do not have a thorough study of the place of the slave law in the southern legal system and of the relationship of the southern legal system as a whole to that of the United States and Western Europe, tentative appraisals must be risked if much sense is to be made out of the broader aspects of the master-slave relationship. Two questions in particular present themselves: the general character of the southern legal system; and the relationship between the legal status of the slave and his position in what appears to many to have been extralegal practice.

The two questions merge. The dichotomy, made current by Ulrich Bonnell Phillips, of a decisive distinction between law and practice or custom, requires critical examination. W. E. B. Du Bois's comment on the proslavery apologetics to which such a distinction has sometimes been applied says enough on the level on which he chose to leave the matter:

> It may be said with truth that the law was often harsher than the practice. Nevertheless, these laws and decisions represent the legally permissible possibilities, and the only curb upon the power of the master was his sense of humanity and decency, on the one hand, and the conserving of his investment on the other. Of the humanity of large numbers of Southern masters there can be no doubt.[63]

The frontier quality of much of the Old South inhibited the growth of strong law-enforcement agencies, but this quality itself cannot be separated from the geographic advance of slave society.[64] The plantation system produced an extensive pattern of settlement, relative to that of the Northwest, and resulted in the establishment of a multitude of separate centers of power in the plantations themselves. At the same time, the nonplantation areas found themselves developing as enclaves more or less detached from the mainstream of southern society. Thus, whereas the frontier steadily passed in the free states and even the formative stages of civilization rested on a certain civic consciousness, it not only passed less rapidly in the slave states but actually entrenched itself within the civilization being built. This process imparted a higher degree of apparent lawlessness—of the extralegal settlement of personal disputes—to southern life. Its spirit might be illustrated by the advice given to Andrew Jackson by his mother: "Never tell a lie, nor take what is not your own, nor sue anybody for slander or assault and battery. *Always settle them cases yourself!*"[65]

This "violent tenor of life," to use an expression Johan Huizinga applied to late medieval Europe,[66] provided one side of the story; the intrinsic difficulty of developing a modern legal system in a slave society provided another. Southerners considered themselves law-abiding and considered northerners lawless. After all, southerners did not assert higher-law doctrines and broad interpretations of the Constitution. Rather, as Charles S. Sydnor has argued, they understood the law in a much different way and professed to see no contradiction between their code of honor, with its appeal to extralegal personal force, and a respect for the law itself.[67] Notwithstanding some hypocrisy, their view represented a clumsy but authentic adjustment to the necessity for a dualistic, even self-contradictory, concept of law prefigured in the rise of a rational system of law in European civilization.

At first glance, the legal history of Western Europe represents an anomaly. The law arose in early modern times on rational rather than traditional, patrimonial, or charismatic foundations, however many elements of these remained.[68] As such, it assumed an equality of persons before the law that could only have arisen from the social relationships introduced by the expansion of capitalism and the spread of bourgeois, marketplace values, although to a considerable extent it derived from Roman tradition. Max Weber's distinction between "capitalism in general" and "modern capitalism," however suggestive, cannot resolve the apparent contradiction.[69]

As Weber clearly understood, the ruling class of Roman society, and therefore the society itself, rested on slave-labor foundations.[70] We do not have to follow Rostovtzeff, Salvioli, and others in projecting an ancient capitalism or a cycle of capitalisms in order to establish a firm link between ancient and modern civilization in Western Europe, as manifested in the continuity of legal tradition. Slavery as a mode of production creates a market for labor, much as capitalism creates a market for labor-power. Both encourage commercial development, which is by no means to be equated with capitalist development (understood as a system of social relations within which labor-power has become a commodity).[71] Ancient slave society could not, however, remove the limits to commercial expansion—could not raise the marketplace to the center of the society as well as the economy—for its very capitalization of labor established the firmest of those limits. The modern bourgeoisie, on the other hand, arose and throve on its ability to transform labor-power into a commodity and thereby revolutionize every feature of thought and feeling in accordance with the fundamental change in social relations.[72] It thereby created the appearance of human equality, for the laborer faced the capitalist in a relation of seller and buyer of labor-power—an ostensibly disembodied commodity. The relationship of each to the other took on the fetishistic aspect of a relationship of both to a commodity—a thing—and cloaked the reality of the domination of one man by another. Although ancient slavery did not create a market for labor-power, it did, by creating a market for human beings and their economic products, induce a high level of commercialization that, together with the successful consolidation of a centralized state, combined to bequeath a system of law upon which modern bourgeois society could build. The rise of capitalism out of a seigneurial society in the West owed much to cultural roots that that particular kind of seigneurialism had in a long slaveholding past.

The slave South inherited English common law as well as elements and influences from continental Roman and Germanic communal and feudal law. But by the time the slave regime underwent consolidation, the legal system of the Western world had succumbed to a bourgeois idea of private property. The southern slaveholders had been nurtured on that idea but also had to draw upon earlier traditions in order to justify their assimilation of human beings to property. In so doing, they contradicted, however discreetly, that idea of property which had provided the foundation for their class claims.[73]

The slaveholders could not simply tack the idea of property in man onto their inherited ideas of property in general, for those inherited ideas, as manifested in the bourgeois transformation of Roman law and common law, rested precisely upon a doctrine of marketplace equality within which—however various the actual practice for a protracted period of time—slavery contradicted first principles.[74] The southern legal system increasingly came to accept an implicit duality: a recognition of the rights of the state over individuals, slave or free, and a recognition of the rights of the slaveholders over their slaves. Since the slaveholders' property in man had to be respected, the state's rights over the slaveholders as well as the slaves had to be circumscribed. At first glance, this arrangement appears simple enough: considered abstractly, a system in which the state, representing above all the collective will of the slaveholding class, could lay down rules for the individual slaveholders, who would, however, have full power over their chattels. But the slaves, simply by asserting their humanity, quickly demolished this nice arrangement. The moral, not to mention political, needs of the ruling class as a whole required that it interpose itself, by the instrument of state power, between individual masters and their slaves. It is less important that it did so within narrow bounds than that it did so at all. The resultant ambiguity, however functional in quiet times, ill prepared the South to meet the test of modern war.

Even in peacetime the slaveholders had to pay dearly for their compromises. Among other things, as Charles S. Sydnor saw and as Robert Fogel and Stanley Engerman have reflected on further, the reintroduction of precapitalist elements into the legal system weakened the economic organization and business capacity of the planters.[75] These questions await a full exploration at other hands.

The immediate concern is with the effect of the imposed duality created by the reintroduction as well as the continuation of precapitalist ideas of power and property into an inherited system of bourgeois-shaped rational jurisprudence. This momentous reintroduction was effected with some ease because the idea of the state's having a monopoly of the legal means of coercion by violence had had only a brief history—roughly, from the conquest of state power by the bourgeoisies of England and Holland during the seventeenth century and of France at the end of the eighteenth.[76] Nor had traditional ideas simply disappeared. Not only from the Left, but more powerfully from the Right, they continued to do battle within even the most advanced capitalist countries.

The slaveholders fell back on a kind of dual power: that which they collectively exercised as a class, even against their own individual impulses, through their effective control of state power; and that which they reserved to themselves as individuals who commanded other human beings in bondage. In general, this duality appears in all systems of class rule, for the collective judgment of the ruling class, coherently organized in the common interest, cannot be expected to coincide with the sum total of the individual interests and judgments of its members; first, because the law tends to reflect the will of the most politically coherent and determined fraction, and second, because the sum total of the individual interests and judgments of the members of the ruling class generally, rather than occasionally, pulls against the collective needs of a class that must appeal to other classes for support at critical junctures. But the slaveholders' problem ran much deeper, for the idea of slavery cannot easily be divorced from the idea of total power— of the reduction of one human being to the status of an extension of another's will—which is phenomenologically impossible, and more to the point, as Judge Ruffin had to face, politically impossible as well. Repeatedly, the slaveholders' own legal apparatus had to intervene, not primarily to protect the slaves from their masters, but to mediate certain questions among contending manifestations of human action. In so doing, it discredited the essential philosophical idea on which slavery rested and, simultaneously, bore witness to the slaves' ability to register the claims of their humanity.

Confronted with these painful and contradictory necessities, the slaveholders chose to keep their options open. They erected a legal system the implications of which should have embarrassed them, and sometimes did; and then they tried to hold it as a reserve. They repeatedly had to violate their own laws without feeling themselves lawbreakers. The slave laws existed as a moral guide and an instrument for emergency use, although the legal profession and especially the judges struggled to enforce them as a matter of positive law; wherever possible, the authority of the master class, considered as a perfectly proper system of complementary plantation law, remained in effect. But since no reasonable formula could be devised to mediate between counterclaims arising from the two sides of this dual system, much had to be left outside the law altogether.

Several of the many ramifications of this interpretation bear on the position and condition of the slaves. We have already found reason to qualify the oft-repeated charge that the legal system of the South did not offer the slaves the protection offered by the slave codes of the Catholic countries. Further observations are now in order. The ethos informing the Catholic slave codes did play a significant role in shaping the slave societies of Portuguese and

Spanish America, but the role of the law itself cannot readily be deduced either from that ethos or from the codes themselves.[77] The system of enforcement in the United States, conditioned by Anglo-American standards of efficiency and civic discipline, generally exceeded that in, say, Brazil, where effective power lay with the *senhores de engenho*—the great sugar planters. And the Spanish slogan, *¡Obedezco pero no cumplo!* (I obey, but I do not comply) says enough.[78] More to the point, the slave codes of Brazil, the various Caribbean colonies, and Spanish South America had been drafted by nonslaveholders in the several metropolitan capitals and had had to be imposed upon resistant planters with enormous power of their own. The British, for their part, showed great reluctance to impose a slave code on the Caribbean planters. The slave codes of the southern United States came from the slaveholders themselves and represented their collective estimate of right and wrong and of the limits that should hedge in their own individual power. Their positive value lay not in the probability of scrupulous enforcement but in the standards of decency they laid down in a world inhabited, like most worlds, by men who strove to be considered decent. These standards could be violated with impunity and often were, but their educational and moral effect remained to offer the slaves the little protection they had.

For the slaves, two major consequences flowed from the ambiguities of the system. First, they constantly had before them evidence of what they could only see as white hypocrisy. An ex-slave commented on the antimiscegenation laws and their fate at the hands of the white man: "He made that law himself and he is the first to violation."[79] No respect for the law could easily rise on such a foundation. Since the slaves knew that the law protected them little and could not readily be enforced even in that little, the second consequence followed. For protection against every possible assault on their being they had to turn to a human protector —in effect, a lord. They had to look to their masters for protection against patrollers, against lynching, against the strict enforcement of the law itself, as well as against hunger and physical deprivation. And they had to look to some other white man to shield them against a harsh or sadistic master. Thus, the implicit hegemonic function of the dual system of law conquered the quarters. But not wholly and not without encouraging a dangerous misunderstanding.

As the masters saw, the working out of the legal system drove the slaves deeper into an acceptance of paternalism. As the masters did not see, it did not drive them into an acceptance of slavery as such. On the contrary, the contradictions in the dual system and in the slave law per se, which had developed in the first place because of the slaves' assertion of their humanity, constantly reminded the slaves of the fundamental injustice to which they were being subjected. Paternalism and slavery merged into a single idea to the masters. But the slaves proved much more astute in separating the two; they acted consciously and unconsciously to transform paternalism into a doctrine of protection of their own rights —a doctrine that represented the negation of the idea of slavery itself.

IN THE NAME OF HUMANITY AND THE CAUSE OF REFORM

Since the great object of social reform is to prevent a fundamental change in class relations, sensible reformers must fight on two fronts within the ruling class. They must fight against those reactionaries who cannot understand the need for secondary, although not necessarily trivial, change in order to prevent deeper change; and they must fight against cheerful fools who think that change is intrinsically wonderful and who therefore cannot distinguish between the safe and the dangerous. Since reactionaries will insist that any change, no matter how slight, will set in motion forces of dissolution and since nothing will convince them other than the experience they fear to obtain, reformers face a formidable task; it becomes the more so as the enthusiasts for change demonstrate blindness toward the reality of the danger. The reactionary argument has a truth of its own, which curiously betrays respect for the personalities of those whom reckless reformers too easily view as mere objects of their schemes—a respect which flows from an awareness that lower-class beneficiaries of change may choose to seize a good deal more than they have been offered, once they have been offered anything at all. And it is no answer that force alone cannot keep people in subjugation, for as G. G. Coulton has re-marked, "The gospel of the uselessness of persecution is true only if we look forward to a far longer time than the vast majority of men take into their calculations."[1]

The history of the South from the Revolution to secession con-stitutes a glorious story of wise self-reformation at once conserva-tive in its preservation of the social order and liberal in its flexible response to altered conditions—glorious, that is, from the point of view of the master class. Step by step, those changes which would strengthen the regime took effect and those which might have opened the floodgates did not. Those who deserve credit for the achievement met the one great challenge they faced: they had to convince a skeptical slaveholding class that the humanization of slave life would strengthen rather than weaken the regime. They controlled the press, stocked the state legislatures with safe men, and compromised the churches.[2] Only occasionally did trou-blemakers have to be killed. Since the usefulness of violent mea-sures stems primarily from their threat, which calls forth a reaction when carried out too often and too far, the slaveholders preferred restraint.[3] But the slaveholders did use a combination of measures to crush the antislavery movement in the South; they thereby freed themselves to civilize their society according to their own lights. They removed the dangers reform so often entails. The death of southern liberalism, as Ulrich Bonnell Phillips called it, marked the birth of a new effort to ameliorate the conditions of slave life.[4] Phillips shared with most of those who have criticized him the doubtful assumption that southern reform should be iden-tified with moves toward emancipation. Even his leading critics have thought so, the great difference being that he blamed the demise of reform on the northern abolitionists and thought that their defeat would have resurrected it, whereas they have blamed the demise on southern intransigence and have doubted that it could ever have been resurrected while the old regime lasted. But the kind of structural reform that pointed toward emancipation represented only one tendency within the reform movement as a whole, and its defeat increasingly became the *sine qua non* for the ultimately successful opposite tendency, which sought to make reform serve the slavery interest.

Hence the paradox. Historians have correctly viewed the period from 1831 to 1861 as one of reaction. Yet they have also correctly viewed it as one in which the treatment of slaves became progressively better. Both views have been correct in that they refer to different aspects of a single process. The condition of the slaves worsened with respect to access to freedom and the promise of eventual emancipation; it got better with respect to material conditions of life. The same men who fought for the one more often than not fought for the other. Their position made perfect sense: Make the South safe for slaveholders by confirming the blacks in perpetual slavery and by making it possible for them to accept their fate.

The constitutions of the slave states left room for manumissions, but the laws made them increasingly difficult. Virginia's attitude hardened after a flurry of liberalism during the Revolutionary era. By the end of 1793 the legislature had banned free-Negro immigration, and by 1806 it had declared that a freedman must leave the state within a year or suffer re-enslavement. South Carolina maintained a passive attitude until 1800, when it raised bars; in 1841 it moved to seal the escape route altogether. Even states like Tennessee followed the same path. By the late antebellum period every slave state had tightened its procedures so as to confirm blacks in slavery and to dash hopes for personal and collective emancipation.[5]

Thus, the steady progress of anti-emancipation sentiment went hand in hand with demands for amelioration and greater humanity. A petition from citizens of Hanover County to the General Assembly of Virginia, dated January 30, 1831, stated the position plainly:

> Slaves while kept in subjection are submissive and easily controlled, but let any number of them be indulged with the hope of freedom, one must have but little knowledge of their nature, who is to be informed that they reject restraint and become almost wholly unmanageable. It is by the expectation of liberty, and by that alone, that they can be rendered a dangerous population. So long as we are true to ourselves there can be nothing to fear.[6]

In 1854, the *Richmond Examiner* explained: "True philanthropy to the Negro begins, like charity, at home; and if Southern men would act as if the canopy of heaven were inscribed with a covenant, in letters of fire, that *the Negro is here, and here forever; is our property, and ours forever* . . . they would accomplish more good for the race in five years than they boast the institution itself to have accomplished in two centuries. . . ."[7]

Dissenters continued to speak out in favor of a more liberal policy, but they usually argued that slavery needed a safety valve, not that emancipation ought to be encouraged widely. Some, like Judge O'Neall of South Carolina, may have held broader views than they generally expressed, but even they generally stayed within the white consensus. Others, like William Gilmore Simms, took unambiguous proslavery ground and yet favored reform as being wise and safe. These voices, however distinguished, grew fainter over time, for they could not easily argue with those who, like Edward Pollard of Virginia, pointed out that if emancipation were a suitable reward for meritorious service, then the idea that slavery benefitted the blacks had to be wrong.[8]

The great reaction of 1831–1861 cannot be made the responsibility of abolitionist criticism, as it has been by apologists for the old regime; nor can it be laid to Nat Turner, although this contention has much more force. Abolitionism itself had taken on a shriller tone because the dream of slow and peaceful emancipation had been evaporating. If Mr. Jefferson and his brilliant entourage in Virginia had not succeeded even in getting the matter discussed seriously, what hopes were left? South Carolina and Georgia had always been intransigent, and the derived demand for Virginia's slaves effected by the westward cotton movement sealed the fate of the forces in the Upper South that continued to hope for emancipation. The Virginia debates, which opened the period of reaction, represented the last attempt of forces that had long been in retreat.[9] Once the devil of emancipation had been exorcised, the South could reform itself. The nature and limits of that reform reveal much about the society that was coming to maturity.

No feature of the slave law stirred so many misgivings as the lack of protection for family life. Even that pillar of the slaveholders' regime, Robert Toombs, squirmed badly and joined his fellow Georgian, Alexander Stephens, in calling for reform. But the timidity of the call from the usually firm, blunt planter-politician spoke as loud as his criticism. "We are reproached," he said, "that the marriage relation is neither recognized nor protected by law. This reproach is not wholly unjust, this is an evil not yet remedied by law, but marriage is not inconsistent with the institution of slavery as it exists among us, and the objection therefore lies rather to an incident than to the essence of the system."[10]

Leading proslavery intellectuals like George Frederick Holmes, Henry Hughes, and George Fitzhugh and leading jurists like John Belton O'Neall joined in advocating laws to recognize slave marriages. As late as 1855 a group of North Carolinians made a major effort to humanize the slave code especially with respect to marriage and literacy, but got nowhere. Their proposals concerning protection of family life evoked more praise than censure across the South, but most of all they evoked silence. The slaveholders understood that such reforms threatened the economic viability of the capital and labor markets. No other issue so clearly exposed the hybrid nature of the regime; so clearly pitted economic interest against paternalism and defined the limits beyond which the one could not reinforce the other.

The long-run prospects for this reform did not look bright, although increasing discussion of compromise proposals suggested some possibilities. Some reformers, as well as thoughtful planters like Samuel Walker of Louisiana, were beginning to work out ideas for legislation to entail the estates of the bankrupt or deceased so as to keep family units together.[11] The fate of such ideas, had the Confederacy won, must remain a matter of conjecture, but the discernible uneasiness of the slaveholders did have the effect of making the separation of families more odious. Such moral pressure alone could not have reduced the evil to the level of Toombs's "incident," for had such ever become the case, that same public opinion, noticeably writhing over the issue, would surely have become ready for a direct attack. The problem and the contradiction it called forth therefore remained—and so did the agony.

What of the material conditions of slave life? Slaveholders claimed, and some slaves acknowledged, that conditions were improving as the nineteenth century progressed and the frontier receded. The most skeptical travelers agreed.[12] During the 1830s and 1840s Louisiana and Texas suffered from a reputation, probably deserved, for hard driving. Adeline Cunningham, who had been a slave in Texas, recalled, "Dey was rough people and dey treat ev'ry body rough."[13] But even in Texas conditions improved markedly during the 1850s as communities became more stable and as rising slave prices compelled greater attention to reproduction. The sugar plantations of Louisiana, for all their reputation as hellholes, usually provided better care than the small farms, for they were solvent and did not have to skimp on food and clothing. By the 1850s word had traveled back to slaves in Virginia that the more favorable economic conditions of the Southwest meant more comfort.[14]

The idea that slaveholders in the Upper South treated their

slaves much better than did those in the Lower South arose during
the eighteenth century. The slaveholders of eighteenth-century
Virginia acquired a good reputation for humanity toward their
slaves, at least relative to the slaveholders of South Carolina, about
whom Forrest McDonald has written: "The South Carolina planters' callous disregard for human life and suffering was probably
unmatched anywhere west of the Dnieper."[15] South Carolina's
black population reproduced itself adequately during the early
decades of the eighteenth century but suffered a negative rate of
natural increase after the big importations from Africa that followed 1720. The treatment of slaves grew increasingly harsh between 1720 and the Stono rising of 1739, which compelled the
slaveholders to reflect on their policies. Thereafter, fear of insurrection accomplished what appeals to humanity had not, and conditions gradually improved.[16]

The living conditions of slaves in South Carolina were considerably better at the end of the eighteenth century than they had been
at the beginning, nor did the temporary reopening of the African
slave trade reverse the gradual amelioration. The regime had settled by then, and the rich coastal areas had developed stable communities in which the expectations of the highly productive slaves
in the rice and Sea Island cotton districts could not easily be
tampered with. Besides, the planters, knowing that the slave trade
would close definitively in 1808, had to look to the future.[17] During
the nineteenth century the difference in treatment between the
Upper and Lower South became steadily less noteworthy.[18]

During the late antebellum period J. H. Hammond of South
Carolina accused the abolitionists of compelling a reversal in the
trend toward amelioration. Their agitation, he argued, was result-
ing in a withdrawal of privileges, which "is painful to us."[19] But
his remarks, dubious in any case, applied to matters other than
such material conditions as food, clothing, shelter, or even punishment. Harriet Martineau asserted that the abolitionist attacks had,
on the contrary, resulted in a decided improvement in the treatment of slaves. Ezekiel Birdseye, an abolitionist in East Tennessee,
concurred in her judgment, as did John Flournoy, the rabidly
negrophobic antislavery eccentric, who fumed that the slaves in
Georgia were receiving more consideration than the poor
whites.[20] A. T. Goodloe in effect conceded the point in a harsh
attack on his fellow slaveholders, who, he said, were ruining the
blacks in an ill-considered attempt to ward off abolitionist criticism. N. D. Guerry of Alabama denounced Goodloe's inhumane

tone and insisted that the discernible improvement in treatment had long been overdue. "The days of fogyism in the management of Negroes," he snapped, "have gone, the time for brute force is past. . . ."[21]

The campaign to improve the lot of the slaves predated the abolitionist agitation, as did the campaign to confirm the blacks in perpetual slavery. Abolitionism and the southern reaction to it accelerated forces already in motion. As early as the 1820s agricultural journals like Legaré's *Southern Agriculturalist,* published in Charleston, were running a steady stream of articles to encourage better treatment, although other journals—the *Southern Planter,* for example—did not pick up the theme until much later. Some writers frankly placed the discussion in political perspective, but even they demonstrated a wider effort to sharpen their fellow slaveholders' class consciousness by appealing to a sense of moral responsibility. Chancellor Harper set the tone in the 1830s in his militant contribution to the proslavery argument:

> It is wise, too, in relation to the civilized world around us, to avoid giving occasion to the odium which is so industriously excited against ourselves and our institutions. For this reason, public opinion should, if possible, bear even more strongly and indignantly than it does at present, on masters who practice any wanton cruelty on their slaves. The miscreant who is guilty of this not only violates the law of God and of humanity, but as far as in him lies, by bringing odium upon, endangers the institutions of his country, and the safety of his countrymen.[22]

Writing about the same time, an anonymous contributor to the *Southern Agriculturalist* bluntly related the confirmation of the slaves' status to progress in their material comfort: "Is then the condition of the slaves as a caste never to be mitigated? We answer that such mitigation is to be looked for only in the improvement of their masters. That it has already derived much amelioration from this source is a sure harbinger of its future improvement."[23] In 1851, Garnett Andrews warned the Southern Central Agricultural Society of Georgia not to allow unscrupulous masters to use the abolitionist agitation to excuse undue severity toward their slaves.[24] In 1860, Dr. John Stainback Wilson condemned those slaveholders who failed to meet their responsibilities toward their slaves. Apparently fearful of being charged with giving aid and comfort to the abolitionists, he added:

Duty requires that errors and abuses should be pointed out, with the hope of correction and reformation. This is a duty to the dependent creatures whom God has committed to our charge; it is due to ourselves individually as slaveholders; and it is due to us collectively as a community of slaveholders, deeply, vitally interested in the vindication of our institution before a misguided and gainsaying world. Yes, it is the duty of all slaveowners, of all who are interested either directly, or indirectly, in the perpetuation of the institution, to disclose its abuses . . . with a design of correcting those abuses and thus disarming our enemies.[25]

Dr. Wilson quoted the Reverend C. F. Sturgis's "Prize Essay on the Duties of Masters to Their Servants" as saying: "As a farmer and a Southerner, I boldly declare that as long as such bad economy is practiced, even in a few cases, it will be impossible to gag the abolitionists. . . ."[26]

The mounting abolitionist critique forced the slaveholders to take a long look at themselves and at others, especially other slaveholders. Proslavery ideologues had difficulty in evaluating Caribbean and South American slavery. They felt the need to defend slavery as a social system in all parts of the world, but wanted to dissociate themselves from the special evils of other regimes and to claim special virtues for their own. As the slaveholders' ideological struggle with the abolitionists sharpened during the 1840s and 1850s, their criticism of the Cuban regime mounted, and they increasingly praised themselves for the excellence of their treatment of their own slaves. In part they coveted Cuba and were trying to create humanitarian grounds for annexation, but they also genuinely recoiled at what they saw and heard there. Cuban slavery, a mild system during the eighteenth century, became a horror story during the nineteenth, when the sugar boom swept the island.[27] The southern slaveholders derived particular satisfaction from the favorable comparisons of their own regime with that of Cuba which were appearing in books by critical European travelers.[28]

Much of the controversy over "treatment" of slaves turns on a confusion of meanings. The slaveholders could proclaim their slaves the best treated in the world and even compare their condition favorably with that of European workers and peasants, but their evidence rested entirely on data about the material conditions of life. They did not talk much about the protection of family life or other features of cultural autonomy. Nor did they care to discuss access to freedom and citizenship. Ulrich Bonnell Phillips was probably right in arguing that American slaves were better treated than Caribbean or Brazilian, for he too was thinking of material conditions. Stanley M. Elkins was probably right in saying that American slaves were much worse treated, for he clearly was thinking of other matters.[29]

The slave regime of the Old South became progressively more repressive with respect to manumission as it became progressively more humane with respect to the material conditions of life. In the specific conditions of southern slavery the one required the other, or rather, each formed part of a single process of social cohesion. The slaveholders did not defend their regime by distinguishing among the several meanings of "treatment," for they would have exposed the negative side of their practice; nor did the abolitionists usually make such distinctions in their assaults, for they did not wish to concede any ground to an enemy perceived as purely evil.[30] Did the white racism of the slaveholders lead them to value black life so little as to treat their slaves like animals? The rhetoric of paternalism aside, the slaveholders knew and said what the abolitionists knew and tried not to say: The South had the only slave system in the New World in which the slaves reproduced themselves. The less than 400,000 Africans imported into the North American British colonies and the United States had become a black population ten times greater by 1860, whereas despite much larger importations by Jamaica, Saint-Domingue, Brazil, and Cuba, these and other slave countries struggled to balance imports against mortality in order to hold their own in population.[31]

The slaveholders sometimes asked: What does racism have to do with the waste of human life? What has race to do with business? Do you not know that the poor whites who worked on the slave ships suffered a significantly higher death rate than did the enslaved Africans themselves?[32] In the South and in the Caribbean the treatment meted out to white indentured servants had rivaled and often exceeded in brutality that meted out to black slaves; brutality to white servants preceded brutality to black slaves. The slaveholders did not treat their slaves with contempt because of racist feeling; they had learned long before to hold the lives of the lower classes cheap.[33] Rich Europeans had always been willing to use up their own lower classes as readily as they would Africans; it was not their fault that their own lower classes had learned how to protect themselves.

The slaveholders did not tell the other side of the story. As the workers and peasants of Europe and America forged weapons of self-defense, the ruling classes increasingly turned to the exploitation of nonwhite labor, and a virulent racism became the indispensable rationalization for their policies. But during the nineteenth century the "treatment" of black labor relative to white in the capitalist world remained a legitimate matter of dispute.

Southern intellectuals kept the slaveholders informed about living conditions among the world's laboring classes. Journals like *De Bow's Review* abounded in such material, as did the speeches and books of Hammond, Hughes, Fitzhugh, Holmes, Grayson, and many others. D. R. Hundley scored heavily in 1860 when he contrasted the conditions of slave life with those of the Mexican peons, who were bought and sold like cattle and then turned loose in old age.[34] European travelers with no sympathy for slavery gloomily admitted that the slaveholders had entirely too much truth for comfort on their side of this argument.[35] After all, Richard Pilling, an English workingman sentenced as a strike leader in 1842, described to the court as grim a picture as a slave might have:

> I have seen in the factory in which I worked wives and mothers working from morning to night with only one meal; and a child brought to suck at them thrice a day. I have seen fathers of families coming in the morning and working till night and having only one meal, or two at the farthest extent.[36]

Slaveholders generally believed that their slaves lived better than the great mass of peasants and industrial workers of the world. Virtually every southerner who raised his voice at all on this subject insisted on the point, not only those who wrote articles and made speeches for propaganda but those who commented privately in family letters and wills.[37] Surrounded by the extreme wretchedness of their own déclassé poor whites, whom the slaves contemptuously called "trash," and informed of general conditions abroad by an effective proslavery press, the slaveholders saw no reason to apologize for the treatment of their slaves. Fanny Kemble, who understood the value of freedom even for the starving, could not deny that the slaves, whose oppressive conditions she so ruthlessly exposed, lived better than a substantial portion of the Irish.[38] Johann Koepff, a German who settled in Texas, wrote in a German newspaper: "Slavery belongs to the curses of the land and fills one with sorrow. Yet the position of the poor negro is not as unhappy as one often pictures. I know for certain that one third of the population in a German village is not any better off than the Texas negro."[39]

Reviewing the conditions of the workers and peasants of Europe, Raimondo Luraghi, the learned Italian historian who has written a detailed study of the United States during this period, concludes that the slaves fared as well, in material terms, as a substantial portion of the workers and peasants of Western Europe and "certainly better" than the mass of the Russian, Hungarian, Polish, and even Italian peasants.[40] To which Jürgen Kuczynski, the noted statistician and historian of the working class, adds after a glance at the more brutal side of proletarian life in the mid-nineteenth century: "It is precisely these bad conditions which justify the arguments of the slaveowners of the South, that the slaves are materially better off than the workers in the north. This would in many cases have been true. . . ."[41] Those who fear that Luraghi and Kuczynski or such other Marxists as Eric Hobsbawm, George Rudé, and E. P. Thompson take too hard a view of European conditions are at liberty to contrast the material conditions of slave life with those of the European peasants and workers described—to cite a few recent historians untainted by Marxism —by Clough or Mandrou on France or G. T. Robinson on Russia or Hamerow on Germany or anyone at all with the stomach to have written on the million casualties suffered by the Irish during the great famine.[42] And if the slaveholders could have been convinced that the English working class, despite everything, was improving its lot during the nineteenth century, they still might have a final word. Were anyone perverse enough to bother, he might easily find that the living conditions of a large minority or even a majority of the world's population during the twentieth century might not compare in comfort with those of the slaves of Mississippi a century earlier.

Consider the length of the working day. The actual length varied according to the amount of daylight as well as according to the attitude of the master and the seasonal pressures of planting and the harvest. In colonial times a fourteen-hour day received legal sanction in South Carolina after the Stono rebellion had made the slaveholders thoughtful, whereas in Georgia the law, which Phillips excoriated as "positively barbarous," fixed the limit at sixteen hours until 1765.[43] During the nineteenth century the slaveholders learned that excessive driving came at the expense of their slaves' health and a consequent capital loss. They even enlisted racist arguments to advocate a more humane course, explaining that blacks constitutionally could not work as long as whites.[44]

The range of waking time in all parts of the South extended from about 3:30 A.M. to 5 A.M. The reports of ex-slaves suggest 4 A.M. as the mode; if anything, the white sources tend slightly to an earlier rather than a later average.[45] Few slaveholders risked the health of their slaves by keeping them in the fields after sunset except during the harvest season, which required crash methods. On the sugar plantations the crop had to be brought in quickly or spoil, and a sixteen- to eighteen-hour day could be expected. But masters, overseers, hired whites and blacks, house slaves, mechanics, and craftsmen all worked together under conditions made as festive as possible. During most of the year the slaves had the nights off, although too often they had additional small chores in the Big House or the quarters which reduced their leisure time. The slave women, in particular, had to cook for their families, sew, wash, and even fulfill assigned quotas for making clothes. The men had to gather firewood, feed the stock, and attend to tasks that might have seemed trivial if they had not come at the end of a long day in the fields. Sunup to sundown in the Gulf states meant about fourteen daylight hours in summer and somewhat more than ten in winter, but the actual day stretched in both directions since the slaves had to be ready to start work at daybreak and had those extra chores after dark. To risk a generalization for the South as a whole: The slaves' workday, as perceived by their masters, averaged about twelve hours, and as perceived by the slaves, who calculated the extras and shared a portal-to-portal mentality with laborers elsewhere, averaged about fifteen hours. That is, the slaves worked about twelve hours in the fields and a few hours more in getting to and from work and doing odd jobs.[46]

Although the sunup-to-sundown rule might have led to a longer working day during the summer, masters generally compensated their slaves with a midday break of two hours or more. "I heard," Mrs. E. C. Hamilton wrote her son in 1860, " . . . that Mr. Jackson was losing his negroes with pneumonia. Be careful to lett [sic] the negroes rest in the heat of the day."[47] As a rule, provision of a long midday break came during June, July, and August but might also come at other times, even during the picking season when the temperatures rose to summer levels. The slaves worked much better during the hot weather if they had rest periods. James Thomas of Hancock County, Georgia, made a careful test of performance and found that a five-minute break every half hour increased the output of his slaves by 15 percent.[48]

The normal working day in the rice fields of the low country of Georgia and South Carolina did not exceed ten hours and sometimes did not exceed five or six. Masters assigned the slaves individual tasks instead of driving them in gangs, so that an especially strong and efficient man or woman could finish early. Solon Robinson thought the day so short as to encourage idleness, but the masters found the system best for getting a high output from those who had to do particularly hard work under unhealthful conditions.[49]

However the hours in the sugar, rice, cotton, and tobacco fields are calculated, the slaves thought them long and hard, and the slaveholders did not gain much by telling them that their workday compared favorably with that of other laboring classes. Overseers had their own reasons for stressing the comparison, for their workday was, if anything, longer than that of the slaves. Many of the more efficient planters were themselves up before daybreak and attending to their responsibilities until well after dark, although they did little or no physical labor. Farmers, northern and southern, worked as long as or longer than most slaves. "The day begins at sunrise and ends at dark," Sidney Andrews wrote of the small farmers of North Carolina. But, he added, they punctuate their long day by pausing to lean on the fence and chatting with neighbors, and they proceed according to their own notions.[50] A good master might give his slaves breaks to rest or go swimming, but he could not give them that sense of controlling their own time and labor which might have made even the longest hours and most arduous work seem reasonable and pleasant. For the slaves the workday remained an absolute, if for no other reason than that it left them no opportunity to take a few minutes to play with their children or fuss over a new baby or enjoy a glass of whiskey or do anything else to break the monotony and enjoy each other.

The slaveholders alone took comfort in the comparative perspective. They believed that their slaves worked a shorter day than the slaves of Brazil or the Caribbean, who could often expect an eighteen-hour day during the long sugar-grinding season and who worked as long as or longer than American slaves during the rest of the year.[51] The slaveholders knew that even during the 1850s when conditions were improving, proletarians and handicraft workers in the North and in Europe worked twelve to fourteen hours, if not longer, exclusive of traveling time to work.[52] The slaveholders knew the approximate length of the working day of Chinese, Indian, Arab, and even European peasants. They could not know, but would have enjoyed knowing, that during the first decade of the twentieth century the miners and other workers of Sardinia—to take one example—worked a fifteen-hour day for seven days a week and had to wage a bitter and protracted struggle to get that one day off a week which American slaves had enjoyed.[53] Even if the slaves had worked a sixteen-hour day and a full six-day week, their hours of labor would have fallen short of those of the Sardinian workers by 10 percent; calculated more realistically but still conservatively, the differential was 20 percent.

From their self-congratulatory comparative perspective, the slaveholders asserted in good faith during the late antebellum period that both interest and sentiment led them to do everything possible to protect the health of the slaves. Most slaveholders provided physicians' services for their slaves at an average cost of three dollars per slave per year, and many spent large sums—ten dollars to more than a hundred—to provide medical care for slaves, often under circumstances in which the economic motive does not appear to have been dominant.[54] The actual health of the slaves nevertheless remains a matter of sharp disagreement among scholars. The wide range in practice among slaveholders meant that even if most slaves received good care, a large number of others did not. And the poor quality of the medical profession may well have resulted in worse conditions for slaves with concerned masters who provided physicians than for those who had to rely on folk medicine and trust to nature. But the slaveholders could not see matters in this light. They knew that most of their number were doing their best and that most laborers in the world did not receive such care and attention. From the slaveholders' point of view, the treatment of the slaves had already reached heights unprecedented for common laborers and was steadily improving.

The slaveholders also insisted that their slaves ate well and that, in particular, they ate more meat than laborers elsewhere could dream of. During the nineteenth century the amount of meat available to the slaves did in fact increase. Standard rations during most of the eighteenth century called for meat only on special occasions, although the slaves took the initiative to raise chickens and to hunt and fish. Meat as a daily staple came during the post-Revolutionary era and especially during the first decade of the nineteenth century. Thereafter, masters usually provided a half pound of pork per day for each adult. Only a few masters withheld this ration as a means of punishment.[55]

The slaveholders believed, with reason, that their slaves ate more and better food than the slaves of the Caribbean and Brazil. Closer to home, the slaveholders thought that their slaves ate as well as the smaller white farmers and considerably better than the largely landless poor whites. The diet of the lower-class rural whites, including the less favored yeomen, was in fact often not much different from that of the slaves.[56]

Abolitionists railed at the insufficiency of the slaves' meat ration, only to incur the slaveholders' wrath and incredulity. Theodore Weld's *American Slavery as It Is* told unwary readers that the inhabitants of English prisons ate better than southern slaves. It did not mention the widespread English complaint that those prisoners and paupers on relief were eating better than a large part of the working class and that honest workmen were being tempted into petty crimes with the aim of getting a decent meal in jail.[57]

How much meat did European workers and peasants eat? In Holland at its zenith during the seventeenth century even the moderately well-to-do seldom ate meat once a week, whereas peasants and workers did well to get meat once a month. Weld told his readers how much better European seamen ate than American slaves; he did not mention how well the European laboring classes were eating relative to those seamen.[58] That Russian peasants got little meat will surprise no one. But the English rural laborers, as well as the French workers and peasants, with a better general diet, rarely tasted meat more than once a week in the mid-nineteenth century, and the Irish have not done better in the twentieth. As late as 1910, Mrs. Pember Reeves could report that if the poor workingmen of London were eating meat regularly, their women and children were not.[59] The slaves' basic ration of a half pound of low-grade pork was certainly miserable, but the slaveholders knew very well that it was as good as or better than workers and peasants were getting elsewhere. They also knew that the slaves, unlike urban workers, could hunt, fish, and raise chickens to supplement their food supply.

The slaveholders told those who cried out against the inhumane punishment of whipping to preach reform to their own navies and merchant marines. England had counted two hundred capital offenses at the end of the eighteenth century and retained whipping as a humane substitute in many crimes for which capital punishment was abolished during the 1830s. Civilized countries like Germany permitted young mine workers—mere boys—to be whipped. Atrocities were a daily affair in Russia. And the slaveholders also knew, even if they exaggerated, that West Africans dealt out horrible punishments to their own slaves.[60]

Nor did the slaveholders think that they were committing a crime by whipping their slaves. Throughout the South whites submitted to public whippings for minor crimes; pupils, especially of the lower classes, suffered more corporal punishment than even its advocates might have approved of; white men whipped their wives and parents their children. Frederick Douglass observed that in the South everyone seemed to want the privilege of whipping someone else.[61] Yet, the rabidly proslavery *Planters' Banner* in Louisiana saluted, without a trace of sarcasm, the wonderful and humane reform that abolished flogging in the United States Navy.[62]

Colonel Charles J. Faulkner, a large slaveholder who insisted that he had spent his whole life among slaveholders, assured Fitzgerald Ross—who apparently believed him!—that he had never heard of, much less seen, an adult slave being whipped. Susan Dabney Smedes more cautiously suggested that "many" slaves never suffered a whipping and many others no more than once in a lifetime. She was right—just so long as we do not look too closely at the word "many."[63] Ex-slaves told of masters who refused to whip their slaves or who whipped them only rarely.[64] There were such masters, and not so few that they qualified as curiosities; but they were still atypical by a good deal. The typical master went to his whip often—much more often than he himself would usually have preferred.

Masters who were not slaves to their passions tried to hold corporal punishment to a minimum. The harsh Bennet H. Barrow of Louisiana used his whip more than most: his slaves averaged one whipping a month and many only once a year.[65] When possible, masters and overseers tried to control their slaves by withdrawing visiting privileges, forbidding a Saturday night dance, scheduling extra work, or putting an offender in the stocks or in solitary confinement. But too many high-spirited slaves scorned such measures. Sooner or later the masters fell back on the whip. If a master lacked the will to use it, he would have to sell his "incorrigibles," in which case someone else had to use it. "Were *fidelity* the only security we enjoyed," wrote a planter in the *Southern Patriot*, "deplorable indeed would be our situation. The fear of punishment is the principle to which we must and do appeal, to keep them in awe and order."[66] On a well-run plantation the whip did not crack often or excessively; the threat of its use, in combination with other incentives and threats, preserved order.[67] The whip, *Affleck's Cotton Plantation Record and Account Book* instructed overseers, ought to be used sparingly but cannot be dispensed with. From colonial times to the end of the regime intelligent masters tried to reduce their dependency on the whip but admitted that they could not do without it.[68] The slaveholders believed that corporal punishment did much more good than harm—that if it hardened some who would be intractable anyway, it successfully restrained many more. A planter mused over the changed situation of 1866:

> Eaton [the overseer] must find it very hard to lay aside the old strap —As for myself, I would give a good deal to amuse myself with it, a little while. I have come to the conclusion that the great secret of our success was the great motive power contained in that little instrument.[69]

The accounts of ex-slaves suggest that many slaves grudgingly acknowledged the power of the whip. Some were not so grudging: "Dem whippin's done me good. Dey break me up from thievin' and make de man of me."[70]

Planters instructed their overseers to give twenty lashes for ordinary offenses and thirty-nine for the more serious ones, but many slaves suffered many more.[71] More important than the number was the vigor with which the lashes were laid on. On some Sea Island plantations every slave's back had scars, and the narratives of ex-slaves reveal many stories of slaves whipped to death.[72] Running away ranked as the number one offense requiring "correction," but stealing and poor work did not lag far behind.[73] Poor work might have ranked higher except that the whip went to the fields with the slaves, forcing better performance and obviating "correction."

Badly scarred slaves dropped in value, so that slave traders and some planters devised methods for inflicting severe punishment without breaking the skin. A cowhide paddle served admirably, for it left no scars while inflicting terrible pain.[74] Solomon Northup's first beating came at the hands of a slave trader who used a paddle with holes in it and then a rope-whip.

I struggled with all my power, but it was in vain. I prayed for mercy, but my prayer was only answered with imprecations and with stripes. I thought I must die beneath the lashes of the accursed brute. Even now the flesh crawls upon my bones, as I recall the scene. I was all on fire. My sufferings I can compare to nothing else than the burning agonies of hell![75]

Andy Marion of Texas vividly remembered a whipping inflicted by a new master: "I's jus' 'bout half died. I lays in de bunk two days, gittin' over dat whippin,' gittin' over it in de body but not de heart. No, suh, I has dat in de heart till dis day."[76]

The psychological damage to the slaves inflicted by the whip did not escape white notice. Apply the whip calmly and as a last resort, cautioned Nathan Bass of Georgia, "for the slave knows when he intentionally violates orders, and when he deserves correction; and if inflicted capriciously or cruelly, it has a tendency to make him reckless and harden him in crime."[77] Susan Cornwall of Georgia understood the question in her own way. She scoffed at northern threats of coercion in January, 1861, and defiantly asked, "Do they think that we are as degenerate as our slaves, to be whipped into obedience at the command of our self-styled masters?"[78] And Thomas Wentworth Higginson marveled at the contradictions in the make-up of his black troops. "Severe penalties," he remarked, "would be wasted on these people, accustomed as they have been to the most violent passions on the part of white men. . . ." He noted that they behaved much better than white troops when taking a town and gave vent to much less hatred and thirst for vengeance, but that they also appeared insensitive to the pain they could inflict and would unfeelingly raze a town if ordered to.[79]

Hegel observes in his wry, satirical, but deadly serious defense of stern punishments, including capital punishment:

If you adopt that superficial attitude to punishment, you brush aside the objective treatment of the righting of wrong, which is the primary and fundamental attitude in considering crime; and the natural consequence is that you take as essential the moral attitude, i.e., the subjective aspect of crime, intermingled with trivial psychological ideas of stimuli, impulses too strong for reason, and psychological factors coercing and working on our ideas (as if freedom were not equally capable of thrusting an idea aside and reducing it to something fortuitous!). . . . In discussing this matter the only important things are, first, that crime is to be annulled, not because it is the producing of an evil, but because it is an infringement of the right as right, and secondly, the question of what that positive existence is which crime possesses and which must be annulled; it is this existence which is the real evil to be removed, and the essential point is the question of where it lies. . . . He [the criminal] does not receive this due of honor unless the concept and measure of his punishment are derived from his own act. Still less does he receive it if he is to be treated either as a harmful animal who has to be made harmless, or with a view to deterring and reforming him.[80]

The slaves proved themselves good Hegelians. The frequent references in the accounts of former slaves to the efficacy of the discipline and exemplary punishments imposed by their masters must be read in this light. But so must the frequent condemnations of cruelty and oppression. The slaves objected not so much to punishment for disobeying the rules, even when they thought the rules unfair, as to the arbitrariness, the caprice, the inhumanity that allowed one man to vent his passions on another. Mary Boykin Chesnut understood their disgust. "I wonder if it be a sin," she wrote, "to think slavery a curse to any land. Men and women are punished when their masters and mistresses are brutes, not when they do wrong."[81]

The slaveholders insisted nevertheless that the frequent use of the whip testified to their own improvement and reformation. During the nineteenth century branding, ear cropping, and assorted mutilations gradually disappeared from the list of punishments prescribed at law and shrank to a minimum in plantation practice. The burning alive of alleged rapists and murderers also declined, although this and other atrocities never disappeared. Iron collars and "nigger boxes"—cells with a few air holes and just enough room to allow a slight shift in position—continued in effect on some plantations. Still, however great the atrocities during the late antebellum period—and they were fearful—they did not rival the widespread fiendishness committed, say, in Saint-Domingue on the eve of the great revolution.[82]

Castration, a popular remedy for high spirits during the eighteenth century, decreased considerably during the nineteenth, much as it did earlier in Spanish America.[83] Most southern colonies had curbed the practice during the eighteenth century by restricting it to punishment at law for attempted rape. This reform ended castration as punishment for chronic running away, plotting insurrection, and other offenses.[84] Privately inflicted castration did not disappear; scattered evidence suggests that some masters continued to apply it especially to slaves who had become their rivals for coveted black women.[85] Public opinion had turned, however, and sadistic slaveholders could no longer exercise their will with impunity. In Tennessee in 1850, for example, a slave-holder with a reputation for outstanding humanity toward his slaves castrated a "turbulent, insolent, and ungovernable slave" only to find himself sent to jail for two years for "mayhem." Judge Totten of the State Supreme Court upheld the conviction with the sardonic observation: "We utterly repudiate the idea of any such power . . . of the master over the slave, as would authorize him thus to maim his slave for the purpose of his moral reform."[86]

The decline, although not disappearance, of castration, the low incidence of slave lynchings, and the rising opposition to cruelties —or what the slaveholders could recognize as cruelties—were cited as evidence by the slaveholders that they treated their slaves no worse than other ruling classes treated their lower classes. As they compared their behavior with that of other ruling classes, they could not understand the charge that their system was cruel, much less that they were sadists. Everyone knew that the rabble responded only to force. The unpleasant necessities attendant upon slave ownership seemed unexceptionable to them. Notwithstanding twinges of conscience, which generally concerned the excesses and not the exigencies of the system, the slaveholders increasingly saw themselves as good men who were doing what had to be done—men who acted in the best interests of their dependent beings and for the prosperity and happiness of the world.

The slaves saw matters differently. Their miserable standard of living may have been just high enough to give them a sense of having something to lose, but they could hardly have been im-pressed by arguments justifying or minimizing the physical cruel-ties and deprivations. And beyond these matters lay others, discussed by W.E.B. Du Bois, who freely admitted that the living conditions of the slaves compared reasonably well with those of the mass of laborers elsewhere:

> What did it mean to be a slave? It is hard to imagine it today. We think of oppression beyond all conception: cruelty, degradation, whipping and starvation, the absolute negation of human rights; or on the contrary, we may think of the ordinary worker the world over today [1935], slaving ten, twelve, or fourteen hours a day, with not

enough to eat, compelled by his physical necessities to do this and not to do that, curtailed in his movements and his possibilities; and we say, here, too, is a slave called a "free worker," and slavery is merely a matter of name.

But there was in 1863 a real meaning to slavery different from that we may apply to the laborer today. It was in part psychological, the enforced personal feeling of inferiority, the calling of another Master; the standing with hat in hand. It was the helplessness. It was the defenselessness of family life. It was the submergence below the arbitrary will of any sort of individual. It was without doubt worse in these vital respects than that which exists today in Europe or America.[87]

The movement for humanitarian reform reappeared in the Confederacy and soared to new heights. Led by such distinguished figures as the Right Reverend Stephen Elliott of Georgia, Calvin Henderson Wiley of North Carolina, the Reverend James A. Lyon of Mississippi, the Reverend W. B. W. Howe of South Carolina, and Edward A. Pollard of Virginia, demands grew to validate slave marriages, to prevent the separation of families, to permit the education of slaves, to protect slaves against cruelty and inhumanity, and even to admit black testimony against whites in court. In 1863, Georgia repealed its law against the licensing of black preachers, and Alabama improved its protection of slave rights in court. Beyond these modest accomplishments, the reformers had little of a tangible nature to show for their efforts, although they expressed considerable satisfaction with the building sentiment for change.

These proposed reforms did not strike at slavery itself, and the question remains whether their eventual enactment would have strengthened or slowly undermined the regime. The reformers themselves genuinely believed that the proposed changes would not threaten the master-slave relation, but the most careful historian of the question believes that they were deceiving themselves.[88] The continued opposition to black testimony after the war suggests that that reform never had much chance, and it is doubtful that the others did either. At best, some protection for family life that would not cripple the market mechanism might have been devised in the form of a partial entail. The reformers' greatest accomplishment probably lay with the intangible effect that their agitation had on the moral consciousness of the slaveholders. Increasing public hostility toward brutal masters could have been consolidated and rendered more effective. Certainly, the Confederate setbacks during the war and the fact of the war itself on southern soil made many cry out that God was punishing them, not for slavery, but for its worst evils.[89] All that may be said with assurance is that the long-developing tendency to try to humanize slavery without striking at its essence was gaining strength toward the end of the regime and that the improvement in the physical conditions of slave life continued, even if slowly. The slaveholders were closing ranks.

OUR BLACK FAMILY

"Before I go," Robert Lowell has Captain Amasa Delano say to Benito Cereno, "I want to propose a last toast to you! *A good master deserves good servants!*"[1] Here, as elsewhere in his magnificent play, Lowell has gone to the heart of the slaveholding regime as perceived by its participants. From the masters' side, the right of property in man had to be taken for granted but had to be made responsible. The master must be a "good" master; he had to understand and execute his duties.[2] "His intercourse with the people," the Reverend C. C. Jones explained, "will be made pleasant by kindness and condescension, without too great familiarity or sacrifice of becoming dignity and self-respect."[3] According to the plantation manual prepared for the estate of Philip St. George Cocke, " 'Tis but just and humane, when they [slaves] have done their duty, to treat them with kindness, and even sometimes with indulgence." It emphasized: "No man can enforce a system of rules and discipline, unless he himself conform strictly to the system. There never was a truer maxim than the old one, 'Like master, like man.' . . ."[4]

These ideal statements tell us much more about the actual practice than might be imagined, for although a good master should be "kind," circumstances must first allow him to be kind. He must fulfill his duties to his slaves; they will, of course, do their duty to him and respond positively to his demands, so that his kindness and even indulgence may become natural gestures. Kindness does not define this social ideal; kindness crowns it. A particular notion of reciprocal duties defines it. Thus, no hypocrisy necessarily marked the outrage of the white preacher who berated some plantation slaves in Louisiana for doing the devil while their master was killing himself to look after them. And something much more complex than "Tomism" marked the reaction of the ex-slave who described the sermon: "I 'spect dat was jest about de truth."[5]

The white South, almost with one voice in the late antebellum period, denounced cruelty to slaves and denied that much of it occurred. Here and there, yes, one could find it; to a significant or noteworthy extent, no. Northerners who knew the South well often agreed. Thomas P. Jones, a supporter of the movement to bring industry to the South, wrote: "Examples of cruelty are very rare, and indelible disgrace affixes itself to him who has the character of being a bad master." Mrs. Eleanor J. W. Baker of Massachusetts insisted that cruel masters were few and far between and were held in great distaste in aristocratic Charleston society.[6] Abolitionists and other critics quickly and unanswerably pointed out that any social system that left room for such cruelty deserved to be condemned, even if most masters did in fact behave decently. From everywhere within the South itself came damning admissions. Most obviously, the prospects for cruel and sadistic treatment rose appreciably when masters displayed severe psychological instability. Slaveholders apparently did not go insane more often than others, but when they did, the slaves could expect no protection until so much damage had been done to them that the law or the community felt compelled to intervene.[7]

Short of this extreme, questions steadily arose. If the character of the masters could be depended upon to prevent cruelty, why did Dr. Josiah Nott, an ardent proslavery polemicist, discreetly warn: "Life insurance on negroes offers strong temptations to be feared, many of which I have not time to enumerate"? Why did Kate Stone have to single out a neighbor in these terms: "We admire Dr. Carson greatly. He is such a humane master and good Christian"? Humane masters and good Christians supposedly inhabited virtually every plantation. William Henry Holcombe of Natchez said much too much when he described three captured runaways, chained together by an overseer who was returning them: "Mr. Davis remarked that if those creatures were his, he would sell them, rather than subject them to the torture necessary to 'break them in'.—They belonged to his brother."[8] He might have noted that, sold or not, someone had to "break them in." A young woman from Maryland, who had grown up among masters and slaves, married her old beau and moved to his sugar plantation in Louisiana. She wrote in her diary in 1861:

> Oh, how my ears have been stunned today by the cry of the distressed. How bestial it is to whip the negro so; surely God will not wink at such cruelty. . . .
>
> *Tuesday, Aug. 27.* I feel sad—more whipping going on. One poor old man the sufferer of man's passion. Thank God my husband is not so heartless. It is indeed hard to bear, to be compelled to stay where such is carried on daily. All are not like him here. He is the father of my husband, but I can never love him as such. I have no respect for him. He is too mean for anything. I wish he was not Howard's father.[9]

These and much worse items could be multiplied indefinitely. In North Carolina a slaveholder was sentenced to death for the murder of his female slave. The indictment charged:

> Through a period of four months, including the latter stages of pregnancy, delivery, and recent recovery therefrom . . . he beat her with clubs, iron chains, and other deadly weapons, time after time; burnt her; inflicted stripes over and often, with scourges, which literally excoriated her whole body; forced her to work in inclement seasons, without being duly clad; provided for her insufficient food; exacted labor beyond her strength, and wantonly beat her because she could not comply with his requisitions. These enormities, besides others too disgusting to be particularly designated, the prisoner, without his heart once relenting, practiced . . . even up to the last hours of his victim's existence.[10]

The State Supreme Court, presided over by a wildly indignant Judge Thomas Ruffin, sustained the conviction and the judgment of death. Yet this same Judge Ruffin, a man of exceptional intellectual acuteness and moral credibility—a first-rate jurist in every respect—was the author of that famous decision which affirmed that slavery, by definition, made the slave into an extension of the master's will. Thus, cruelty had to be and generally was condemned as barbarous, unchristian, and unacceptable to civilized society but could only be recognized in its more extreme manifestations; cruelty, that is, could not easily be defined in a master-slave relationship. Outraged conscience aside, perceived cruelty seems to have been intolerable to society as a whole primarily because it threatened a delicate fabric of implicit reciprocal duties, the acceptance of which by both masters and slaves alone could keep the regime intact.

In 1865, the Confederate Congress passed tax legislation with exemptions for "goods manufactured by any person for the use and consumption of his family, including slaves."[11] Despite the formality of the legal language, which dictated the word "slaves," the Congress was following the general antebellum practice of alluding to the centrality of the "family, white and black," in southern society. Duncan McCall of Jefferson County, Mississippi, made a typical entry in his diary. He had, he recorded, killed a hog for his guests—"Mr. Watson's family, black and white." And Eliza Frances Andrews, while years later introducing her diary entries for 1865, found it necessary to qualify her account: "My sister's white family at the time of arrival consisted of . . ."[12] Every planter boasted of the physical or intellectual prowess of one or more of his blacks, much as the strictest father might boast of the prowess of a favored child.[13] And therein lay dangerous implications.

After describing how the Eastern slaves of Renaissance Tuscany lived as part of a household but took merciless beatings and suffered considerable cruelty, Iris Origo notes that in these respects they did not always fare much worse than the master's wife and children.[14] From ancient to modern times we hear this theme. According to Roman legend, Manlius Torquatus, beheaded his son, who had just returned victorious from combat, for breaking ranks; and Gilberto Freyre describes similar actions by patriarchal Brazilian masters.[15]

In the Old South the lines blurred. Heir to a softening Anglo-Saxon tradition and constantly reacting to it, the slaveholders could not treat their women and children so, and their women especially did not so readily stand for abuse. But the same tendency appeared in weaker manifestations. "Neither his affection for his immediate family," writes Jack P. Greene of Landon Carter, "nor the fatherly affection he felt toward some of his overseers ever prevented him from trying to hold them in a strict adherence to the same rigid code by which he lived."[16] "Flog my godson," wrote Isaac L. Baker of Louisiana in 1823, "whenever occasion requires. Nothing you know is so wholesome as discipline. It may pester the youngster a little for the time being but will greatly benefit him hereafter."[17] Mary Boykin Chesnut put the women's case bluntly:

How men can go blustering around, making everybody uncomfortable, simply to show that they are masters and we are only women and children at their mercy! My husband's father is kind, and amiable when not crossed, given to hospitality on a grand scale, jovial, genial, friendly, courtly in his politeness. But he is as absolute a tyrant as the Czar of Russia, the Khan of Tartary, or the Sultan of Turkey.[18]

The blacks did not fail to see the connection between their masters' patriarchal stance toward their wives and children and that toward their slaves. Andrew Goodman, an ex-slave, remembered a neighboring slaveholder who terrorized his slaves but also savagely beat his own children. Harriett Robinson of Texas remembered her Mis' Julia's treating the slaves badly and hitting her own children hard for such crimes as misspelling and lagging in their lessons. Gus Smith of Missouri told of a master who beat his own son to death. And George Rogers of North Carolina praised his master as a man who never whipped his slaves harder than he did his own children.[19]

The slaveholders' vision of themselves as authoritarian fathers who presided over an extended and subservient family, white and black, grew up naturally in the process of founding plantations.[20] Hence Seargent S. Prentiss could introduce a resolution in his state legislature in 1836 that declared: "We hold discussions upon the subject [slavery] as equally impertinent with discussion upon our relations, wives, and children. . . ."[21]

This special sense of family shaped southern culture. In its positive aspect, it brought white and black together and welded them into one people with genuine elements of affection and intimacy that may yet, as a black historian has prayerfully suggested, blossom into a wholesome new relationship.[22] But in its overwhelming negative aspect—its arrogant doctrine of domination and its inherent cruelty toward disobedient "children"—it pitted blacks against whites in bitter antagonism and simultaneously poisoned the life of the dominant white community itself. Anne Firor Scott points out, in her admirable book *The Southern Lady*, that women, children, and slaves were expected to accept subordination and obey the head of the white family. She adds: "Any tendency on the part of any of the members of the system to assert themselves against the master threatened the whole, and therefore slavery itself."[23] Thus, the slaveholders' insistence on having a "black family" must be taken with deadly seriousness. Its contradictory quality and dangerous consequences, however, were much different than anything they could have understood.

A DUTY AND A BURDEN

John S. Wise of Virginia, looking back on the fall of the Confederacy from the vantage point of the turn of the century, condemned slavery as a curse and expressed relief that it had passed. But he also observed: "There is not a graveyard in Old Virginia but has some tombstone marking the restingplace of somebody who accepted slavery as he or she found it, who bore it as a duty and a burden, and who wore himself or herself out in the conscientious effort to perform that duty well."[1] Those words "duty" and "burden" recurred time and again. They must be appreciated as being central to the self-image and self-respect of the master class if either the slaveholders or the slaves are to be understood.

The twin themes sounded in eighteenth-century Virginia. William Byrd wrote to an English earl in 1726:

> Besides the advantage of a pure Air, we abound in all kinds of Provisions without expence (I mean we who have Plantations). I have a large Family of my own, and my Doors are open to Every Body, yet I have no Bills to pay, and half-a-Crown will rest undisturbed in my Pocket for many Moons together. Like one of the Patriarchs, I have my Flocks and my Herds, my Bond-men and Bond-women, and every Soart of Trade amongst my own Servants, so that I live in a kind of Independence on everyone but Providence. However this Soart of Life is without expence, yet it is attended with a great deal of trouble. I must take care to keep all my people to their Duty, to set all the Springs in motion and make every one draw his equal Share to carry the Machine forward. But then 'tis an amusement in this silent Country and a continual exercise of our Patience and Economy.

Later in the century the tart Landon Carter denounced blacks as "devils" and concluded that emancipation would be madness since it would unleash them. Yet, his diary for 1757 shows him following an ill field hand through an assortment of miseries and cures with the utmost care and concern. His diary reveals constant attention to the needs of his slaves.[2]

For the nineteenth century, these themes are reflected in the policy statements of the regime's intellectual leaders, which might be considered with skepticism, in the remarks of travelers, and above all, in the private expressions of planters within their own family circles. Sanctimoniously, the Reverend Dr. Thornwell, professor of theology in the Presbyterian Seminary of Charleston, South Carolina, declared: "Our slaves are our solemn trust and while we have a right to use and direct their labors, we are bound to feed, clothe, and protect them. . . . They are moral beings, and it will be found that in the culture of their moral nature we reap the largest reward from their service. *The relation itself is moral. . . .*"[3] The major contributors to the "proslavery argument" spoke up in a similar vein. E. N. Elliott, president of Planters' College in Mississippi, defined slavery:

> Slavery is the duty and obligation of the slave to labor for the mutual benefit of both master and slave, under a warrant to the slave of protection, and a comfortable subsistence, under all circumstances. . . . The master, as the head of the system, has a right to the obedience and labor of the slave, but the slave has also his mutual rights in the master; the right of protection, the right of counsel and guidance, the right of subsistence, the right of care and attention in sickness and old age. He has also a right in his master as the sole arbiter in all his wrongs and difficulties, and as a merciful judge and dispenser of law to award the penalty of his misdeeds.[4]

The manifestation of the slaves' humanity drove the slaveholders into this attempt to distinguish property in man from property in man's labor, but they could not sustain the distinction at law nor transform it into a consistent philosophy. No matter how subtle the dialectical gyrations, either slavery meant property in man or it meant nothing at all; and property in man was precisely what defined the essentials of the system. Southern ideologues repeatedly retreated into the view, to which their racism lent plausibility, that the slaves could not take care of themselves and that their masters had a Christian duty to do it for them. They thereby turned aside the abolitionists' religious attack and mounted a powerful counterattack by interpreting the demand for abolition as a call for unchristian irresponsibility toward the fate of one's fellow man. They convinced themselves that the religious doctrine of the abolitionists, not their own, constituted heresy. But the deeper they plunged into this line of defense, whether justified by an appeal to race or class or both, the more enmeshed they became in the contradictions inherent in that idea of property in man with which they remained so uncomfortable.

Thus, William Gilmore Simms, one of the Old South's most prestigious literary figures, proclaimed that slaveholders had no moral right to free their slaves unless absolutely sure they could take care of themselves. He took high ground:

> The question with us is, simply as to the manner in which we have fulfilled our trust. How have we employed the talents which were given us—how have we discharged the duties of our guardianships? What is the condition of the dependant? Have we been careful to graduate his labors to his capacities? Have we bestowed upon him a fair proportion of the fruits of his industry? Have we sought to improve his mind in correspondence with his condition? Have we raised his condition to the level of his improved mind? Have we duly taught him his moral duties—his duties to God and man? And have we, in obedience to a scrutinizing conscience, been careful to punish only in compliance with his deserts, and never in brutality or wantonness? These are the only questions, and they apply equally to all his other relations in society. Let him carefully put them to himself, and shape his conduct, as a just man, in compliance with what he should consider a sacred duty, undertaken to God and man alike.[5]

Facets of this point of view appeared in the writings of other prominent figures. Edward A. Pollard, Virginia's controversial journalist and propagandist, spelled out the ideological mood of the late antebellum period in his book, *Black Diamonds:*

> In the midst of my own boyish enjoyments . . . I have suddenly thought of my poor little slave companions, how they had to work in the fields, how they were made to tote burdens under the summer's sun, what poor food they had, and with what raptures they would devour "the cake" with which I was pampering myself. Then would I become gloomy, embittered, and strangely anxious to inflict pain and privation on myself; and with vague enthusiasm would accuse the law that had made the lots of men so different. . . .
>
> But the bitter experiences of life have cured these feelings. In its sad and painful struggles has expired my juvenile and false philosophy, and I have awakened to the calm, serious, profound conviction that every human lot has its sorrow and its agony. . . . I am profoundly concerned that the negro-slave has naturally as much happiness as I. . . . when will the world learn the plain lesson, wipe away

all tears of sentimental sympathy, and adopt, as the great rule of life, that every man should bear his own burdens; that the object of sympathy is individual; and that it is equally senseless and sinful to sorrow over lots inferior to our own, as to repine for and envy those which are superior. . . .

I just felt that every man has his own burden to bear in this life; that, while (I hope to God) I would always be found ready to sympathize with and assist any individual tangible case of suffering, I would never be such a fool thereafter as to make the abstract lots of men in this world an object of sympathy. I venture to say that I have suffered more of unhappiness in a short worldly career then ever did my "Uncle Jim" or any other well conditioned negro slave in a whole lifetime.[6]

James C. Coggesball, a successful planter of West Tennessee, writing in the state comptroller's report for 1855–1856, put the case defiantly: "For myself, my relation to slavery is one that I allow no man, even my neighbor, who is a nonslave holder, to counsel me respecting. . . ." He insisted that slaveownership was a "duty" and that "God and my country recognize it, and I care not what others think of me respecting it." And he expressed confidence "that slavery is a blessing to the slave in the largest extent, produced by the wisdom of God, and retained as such by his overruling providence, and that the Christian slaveholder is the true friend of the black man."[7]

The twin themes of duty and burden, which grew stronger over time, appeared throughout the master class, not merely in the more propagandistic writings of public figures. "It must be remembered," wrote Harriet Martineau in the 1830s, "that the greater number of slaveholders have no other idea than of holding slaves." She pointed out that they could cultivate mercy, kindness, and indulgence toward their slaves because they took their inferiority for granted. Hence, she concluded, they could be astonishingly patient with slaves and inferiors generally but were hardly so with those they regarded as equals. What did the slaveholders understand by "human rights"? "Sufficient subsistence in return for labor," she explained.[8]

Almost a quarter of a century later, Frederick Law Olmsted and William Howard Russell, two of the most acute travelers, neither of whom approved of slavery, testified to the strong sense of duty among the slaveholders and to their constant attention to the slaves. From a plantation in Virginia, Olmsted wrote: "During three hours, or more, in which I was with the proprietor, I do not think there were ten consecutive minutes uninterrupted by some of the slaves requiring his personal direction or assistance." The planter told Olmsted that he wished slavery could be abolished and slaveholders released from their burden. But, the planter added, "The trouble and the responsibility of properly taking care of our negroes, you may judge from what you see yourself here, is anything but enviable. . . . I am satisfied, too, that our slaves are better off, as they are, than the majority of your free laboring class at the North."[9] From South Carolina, Russell described a plantation mistress who spent the whole night attending a slave birth. Antislavery though he was, he commented that such acts of kindness were much more common than generally supposed and that they could not fairly be attributed solely to material interest. He quoted the mistress: "It is the slaves who own me. Morning, noon, and night, I'm obliged to look after them, to doctor them, and attend to them in every way."[10]

Some nonslaveholders denounced the slaveholders for taking care of the blacks instead of sending them back to Africa to take care of themselves.[11] Garland D. Harmon, one of the South's most successful and respected overseers and an outspoken defender of his class, complained that the slaves plagued him every night with requests and problems of one or another kind. "I can't even read at night," he protested, ". . . without being bedeviled with forty niggers—here after everything you can mention."[12]

The slaveholders spoke up in their diaries and family letters. Rachel Weeks O'Connor wrote her brother in 1824 that a planter and his wife among her neighbors had had to remain on their plantation in New Iberia, Louisiana, because their slaves had taken sick and required personal attention and because the overseer had been cruel.[13] Jefferson T. Craig of Georgetown, Kentucky, commented on the impending death of a slave:

> Jim has declined rapidly today, and now is past all hope. He has long been idle and intemperate, and I thought dishonest, and I have often thought of selling him, but have still put it off as a disagreeable business. I felt as if we should be better off without him, though death in our household is a solemn thing.[14]

Mary Burruss McGehee wrote to her brother to assail him for his contempt for money and preference for a literary life:

> In relieving father and securing your own interest you will have motive enough for cheerful and pleasant exertion, even without the additional motive of making your poor dependents happy, exalting

them in the scale of being and making their labors light by kindness. Think of them as the laboring class in every community (there is always such a class) and see if their burthen is not lighter and their lot less hard in many respects. Anxiety for the future never disturbs their spirits. In richness and health, in youth or old age they are alike easy and provided for by the watchful care of another. Of course this exists only under a humane master, but you will be such a master.[15]

"It seems to me," wrote R. L. Dabney of Virginia, "there could be no greater curse inflicted on us than to be compelled to manage a parcel of Negroes."[16] Moses Liddell of Louisiana, ill and concerned with the proper instruction of his son and heir, wrote him in 1841:

But there is a kind of responsibility placed on your shoulders that you have to fulfill—that is the relation in which you stand as to Master and Slave of which you understand as well as I can tell you —Never require of your slaves too much. Treat them with kindness. Chastise them well for disobedience and refractory conduct. Keep a clear conscience in these matters. . . .[17]

Another Louisiana planter, deep in financial difficulty, wrote an associate from New Orleans a few years later: "I shall get through my business as quickly as I can, and return to the miserable occupation of seeing to negroes, and attending to their wants and sickness and to making them do their duty—and after all have no prospect of being paid for my trouble."[18]

In the 1850s, with the proslavery argument triumphant and the secessionist thrust mounting, the slaveholders became steadily more self-conscious and reflective. "If the master contend that he cannot make the situation one of advantage to the servant," wrote Calvin Henderson Wiley of North Carolina, "then he argues against slavery as an absolute moral evil, a sin not to be tolerated by the Christian." A slaveholder, he continued, must not only try to repay a slave for his labor; he must make the slave comfortable in recognition of the sacred trust that has fallen to him.[19] As if to say "Amen," a planter in Washington County, Mississippi, made the following entry in his diary on Christmas Day, 1858: "Killed a sheep and a hog for my negroes. Clay [overseer] gave them two bbls. of flour. Spent the day waiting on the negroes, and making them as comfortable as possible."[20] And Samuel Walker, sugar planter of Louisiana, insisted that the planters of Louisiana worked harder than their slaves, taking care of blacks as well as whites.[21]

The war years brought with them a severe test of the slaveholders' commitment to "duty," much as it threatened their "interest" and increased their "burden." Charles C. Jones, Jr., former mayor of Savannah and son of the Reverend C. C. Jones, asked his parents' advice about taking a proffered captaincy of a military unit in Virginia. His father being absent, his mother replied and then wrote to her husband: "In your absence, I could only say what I thought and felt, and told him I did not think it his duty to leave his present post, where he was defending his native soil, his home and servants, his infant daughter, his father and mother."[22] While Lieutenant Jones was receiving advice to stay in Georgia to defend his own family, black and white, Mary Boykin Chesnut was recording her planter-politician husband's insistence that his slaves owed him $50,000 for the food and clothing he had given them. "Why the lazy rascals," she quoted him as saying, "steal all of my hogs, and I have to buy meat for them, and they will not make cotton." Asked if he had had any runaways, he roared, "Never. It's pretty hard work to keep me from running away from them!" Furious with his slaves, he loudly proclaimed that they should all go to the Yankees and stop living off him. "But," wrote Mrs. Chesnut, "when he went over to the plantation, he came back charmed with their loyalty and affection for him."[23] With the desertion of the blacks during the war, Chesnut would find them other than charming and would return to his previous view, much as he would have an opportunity to calculate his economic relationship to them more realistically.

The relationship of the plantation mistress to the slaves requires special comment, and life among the white and black women of the Big House presents a problem in itself. It has been a familiar claim that the white ladies provided a mediatory force and appreciably softened the master-slave relationship, and here too the question of duty emerges as paramount.

The mistresses, however much they conformed to the image of the "southern lady" in important respects, worked too hard under too many limitations to live up to their reputation as ethereal beings who wallowed in leisure. That, as a class, they earned their reputation for graciousness and ladylike accomplishments while having to perform the grubbiest of chores speaks well for their character, but then, only prigs think that graciousness and dirty hands are incompatible.[24] Joel B. Fort, son of a large slaveholder in Robertson County, Tennessee, remembered his mother and grandmother as "the busiest women I ever saw, they did all the sewing and cutting out for all the negroes."[25] Eliza Magruder, while living with her aunt on a large plantation near Natchez, went back and forth to the quarters several times a day on one chore or another.[26] John Brown, an ex-slave from Talladega, Alabama, recalled his mistress: "She was with all the slave women every time a baby was born. Or, when a plague of misery hit the folks she knew what to do and what kind of medicine to chase off the aches and pains. God bless her! She sure loved us Negroes."[27] James Lucas, who had been a slave in Mississippi, said, "Wives made a big difference. Dey was kind and went about amongst de slaves a-lookin' after 'em. . . ." George Teamoh of Virginia added, "I do not believe that the high of God's sun ever looked upon a more generous, virtuous and fair minded Christian lady than Mistress Jane Thomas. . . ." And Phillip Rice of South Carolina spoke for a great many others in recalling how his mistress had checked the overseers' tendency to be rough on the people.[28]

Such testimony from the black side makes more comprehensible the attitude expressed by one mistress, Catherine Carson, to her father:

> They are much attached to me and protest against my return to Kentucky. So far from being afraid of them I feel they would be a protection; often after their day's labor is finished they will all come to see me and inquire after young Mistress's health, then I have the gratification of giving them apples or some other little rarity which they consider a great *"treat."* On every Saturday I have flour and molasses given out to them all; this little kindness they have not known for a long time and I assure you they appreciate it.[29]

Harriet Martineau, who had no inclination to romanticize the master class, paid a critical tribute to its women: "Women who have to rule over a barbarous society (small though it may be), to make and enforce laws, provide for all kinds of physical wants, and regulate the entire habits of a number of persons who can in no respect take care of themselves, must be strong and strongly disciplined, if they in any degree discharge this duty." But she added, "Those who shrink from it become perhaps the weakest women I have anywhere seen. . . ."[30]

The ladies had their critics. A significant minority of former slaves complained bitterly about cruel mistresses even on plantations with good masters.[31] Many black troops, themselves ex-slaves, who occupied the South Carolina coast during the war ridiculed those who thought that the professions of loyalty by white residents could be credited, and especially reviled the women. Thomas Wentworth Higginson of Massachusetts, who led the black troops, may have exaggerated, but he was too honest and acute an observer to be ignored: "The [black] men never showed disrespect to these women by word or deed, but they hated them from the bottom of their hearts." Joel R. Poinsett of South Carolina had told Fredrika Bremer a decade earlier that slavery had worked more prejudicially upon white women than upon the men and that the difference expressed itself in a harsher attitude toward the slaves. Yet, the arrival of "white ladies"—northerners, to be sure—reassured the Sea Island blacks, who had initially distrusted the occupying white forces. And the regularity with which plantation slaves appealed to mistresses for protection against masters and overseers cannot be ignored.[32]

These diverse reactions reflect the expected range of human behavior from kind to cruel but also something deeper. A hint comes in the remark of Silas Green, an ex-slave from South Carolina, who spoke for many others in recalling that his mistress had treated her slaves well but had been harsh to those owned by her husband.[33] A sense of stereotyped "stepmother" behavior bristles from the pages of the slave narratives. Through the range of human behavior, including the ambivalence, ramifications of sexual frustration, and outright brutality that have drawn so much comment, the mistresses apparently did live up to their reputation as a humanizing force in the master-slave relationship. But Higginson may not have been wrong. The black troops under his command had learned much during the war and would have been the first to understand that, kind or cruel, the white women were fiercely devoted to the southern cause. These women, as Miss Martineau saw, were tough. Even more than their men, they understood their duty, including both their duty to minister to the slaves and to maintain a social order based on strict superordination and subordination. For them, in a manner splendidly representative of those ideals of their class which they often adhered to more fully than their men, duty meant, above all, family—direct response to one's own. Hence, the repeated references by ex-slaves to a duality in the behavior of some of these women toward their own and their husbands' slaves suggest much more about the attitude of those particular women toward their husbands than about their attitude toward slaves. The kindness and delicate affection toward slaves were there, but so were their human antitheses. Holding their contradictions in behavior together was the strong sense of duty to family, however broadly or narrowly each individual chose to define her particular family.

The whites' view of slaveholding as a duty and a burden was clearly self-serving and should hardly be taken at face value. When Eliza Frances Andrews' mother proclaimed in 1865 that she expected to enjoy her emancipation from the blacks more than they would enjoy their emancipation from her, she was making the best of a situation that she had not invited but could no longer avoid.[34] The themes of duty and burden nevertheless were reflected even in the prevalent idea of economic interest; they constituted its moral justification. The notion that most slaveholders felt guilt-stricken over owning slaves has no basis in fact. No doubt some did, but most accepted the world into which they had been born and took for granted both its advantages and its hardships. Even when we confront a transplanted New Englander, full of that sense of guilt for which the people he had left behind became famous, we hear a different if nonetheless ambiguous voice. "If it is sinful," wrote Hiram B. Tibbetts, a planter of Louisiana, to his brother in Massachusetts, "to own Negroes treated as I treat mine, I am willing to live and die under that sin. I feel no misgivings about it at all."[35] Everard Green Baker of Mississippi, who supported John Bell, the Unionist, for the presidency in 1860, wrote on behalf of innumerable others that year: "I fear there are terrible times ahead of us, the bloodiest civil war that has ever darkened the pages of history—There is this consolation—that we will be fighting for our homes, our families & our property,—"[36]

Chancellor Harper had presented the essential argument almost a quarter century earlier. The abolitionists, he declared, alarm us because they encourage us to fear our slaves and seek to instill in us a sense of guilt. But, he struck back, "It is natural that the oppressed should hate the oppressor. It is still more natural that the oppressor should hate the victim. Convince the master that he is doing an injustice to his slave, and he at once begins to regard him with distrust and malignity."[37]

Kate Stone, reflecting in 1900 on her antebellum diary, sounded a long-familiar note, which historians have too often confused with guilt: "The great load of accountability was lifted, and we could save our souls alive. God would not require the souls of the Negroes at our hands. Everyone would give account of himself to

God. . . ."[38] That a Christian God could ever have demanded that one person assume responsibility for another's soul would appear, to say the least, theologically doubtful. But emerging from this assertion of a widely held view are those two themes of duty and burden, which, however self-serving and self-deceiving, constituted the rock on which the slaveholders' ideology, morality, and self-image had had to be built. This point of view toward the world and toward themselves served them well so long as they held power, but it betrayed them when war and emancipation allowed the blacks—the objects of this paternalism—to speak openly for themselves.

The white South's sense of carrying a burden and a trust crystallized in the claim that, without slavery, the blacks would be exterminated. Such outstanding ideologues as George Fitzhugh, Henry Hughes, C. C. Jones, George Frederick Holmes, J. H. Hammond, T. R. Dew, and Edmund Ruffin sounded the theme often. They vigorously insisted that blacks could never survive in the cutthroat world of the capitalist marketplace; that they would drop to the bottom of the social scale as unwanted and improvident unskilled workers and would starve to death. Slavery represented white protection against this horror; it gave the masters an interest in the preservation of the blacks and created a bond of human sympathy that led to an interest in their happiness as well. Judge Lumpkin of the State Supreme Court of Georgia asked: "What friend of the African or of humanity would desire to see these children of the sun, who . . . perish with cold in higher latitudes, brought into close contact and competition with the hardy and industrious population . . . northwest of the Ohio, and who loathe negroes as they would so many lepers?"[39] As if to prove him right, Julian M. Sturtevant, president of Illinois College and a Republican, called for the abolition of slavery on the grounds that it alone pampered and protected the blacks, who, he believed, would disappear without it.[40]

The slaveholders' pretensions accompanied their counterattack on free labor as wage slavery, their increasing rejection of egalitarian doctrines, and their defense of the subordination of class to class in all societies. George Fitzhugh and Henry Hughes led the way with a defense of slavery in the abstract as the natural condition of all labor. Others settled for more moderate claims but exhibited the same tendency. Edmund Ruffin wrote of that "slavery of class to class which in one or another form either now prevails, or will soon occur in every civilized country where domestic slavery is not found." "All men are born dependant," wrote a slaveholder. "More than one half the human race in fact, and at least one-fifth slaves in name." Southern slavery, Andrew Garnett told the Southern Central Agricultural Society of Georgia, "has solved the difficulties of communism, so long and so fruitlessly dreamed of by French philosophers; because associated labor, when controlled by the governing power of a master, encourages in consumption, and augments in production." Mrs. Henry Rowe Schoolcraft ridiculed Harriet Beecher Stowe's "millennial world" and quoted Hegel without having understood a word of him: "South Carolinians, you know, are 'old fogies,' and consequently *they* do not believe with the Abolitionists that *God* is a progressive being; but that throughout eternity *He* has been the same; perfect in wisdom, perfect in justice, and perfect in love to all his creatures. . . ." Mrs. Schoolcraft concluded: "There scarcely ever was a time in the history of the world, when one man did not enslave his fellow-man, and, probably, this will continue until the glorious season of the millennium. . . ."[41]

This ideology, whether viewed as an extravagance or not, developed in tandem with that self-serving designation of the slaves as a duty and a burden which formed the core of the slaveholders' self-image. Step by step, they reinforced each other as parts of an unfolding proslavery argument that helped mold a special psychology for master as well as for slave. The slaveholders' ideology constituted an authentic world-view in the sense that it developed in accordance with the reality of social relations. If it was nonetheless self-serving and radically false in its fundamental philosophical content, so is every other ruling-class ideology. The slaveholders understood as much and could therefore embrace it without hypocrisy—or rather, without a larger dose of hypocrisy than must attend every attempt to justify the exploitation and oppression of others. The kind of men and women the slaveholders became, their vision of the slave, and their ultimate traumatic confrontation with the reality of their slaves' consciousness cannot be grasped unless this ideology is treated as an authentic, if disagreeable, manifestation of an increasingly coherent world outlook.

OF CONCUBINES AND HORSES

Edward L. Keenan has recently had the bad taste to expose as a forgery the extraordinary correspondence between Tsar Ivan IV and Prince Alexander Kurbskii, thereby casting a pall over those who have been able to enjoy reading some astonishing documents. Notwithstanding Keenan's exposure, the "correspondence," whoever actually wrote it, strikes at the heart of the problem of absolute authority. Prince Kurbskii, former friend and supporter of the Tsar, fled to Lithuania and allegedly wrote back bitter letters of rebuke, to which the Tsar Ivan IV, who was not called "The Terrible" for nothing, allegedly replied:

> How can you not understand that the ruler must neither act like a beast nor submit silently? . . . Even during the times of the most pious tsars one can find many cases of the most cruel punishments. Are you really capable, in your unreason, to suppose that the tsar must always act the same way, irrespective of time and circumstances? . . . Tsars must always be circumspect, sometimes gentle, sometimes cruel, merciful, and gentle to the good, while the evil ones get cruel punishments. If this is not the case [there is] no tsar.[1]

Charles Pettigrew, a large planter in North Carolina, made the point in his will in 1806 when he declared: "It is a pity that agreeably to the nature of things, Slavery & tyranny must go together —and that there is no such thing as having an obedient & useful slave without painful exercise of undue & tyrannical authority."[2] William Elliott of South Carolina spoke with much truth when he said that masters were generally kind but added, "Against *insubordination alone*, we are severe."[3] Elliott probably did not know the Akan proverb and would not have quoted it if he had: "One does not acquire a slave in order to be affronted by him."[4]

"Absolute obedience and subordination to the lawful authority of the master," the Supreme Court of Alabama announced in 1861, "are the duty of the slave."[5] The centrality of this demand to the lives and thought of the slaveholders appeared in the will of Ste-

phen Henderson of Louisiana. He wished to free his slaves but
inveighed against abolitionist fanatics and troublemakers. While
still slaves, his people were to receive kind treatment, details of
which he carefully spelled out; but, "There must be strict discipline."[6] Andrew Jackson, whose 150 to 200 slaves made him one of
the biggest slaveholders in Tennessee, cried out, "I could not bear
the idea of inhumanity to my poor negroes." He saw no more
incompatibility in the juxtaposition of that sentiment and his frequent and severe use of the whip to punish impertinence and
violations of discipline than in that which characterized his relationship to the troops under his firm command.[7]

The problems inherent in the contradiction in the slave's legal
existence as man and thing constantly emerged. Those who demanded absolute obedience were trying to reduce the slave to an
extension of the master's will, which the best of the slaveholders
took for granted as humane and just. But the effort could not be
sustained even when supported by terror and the greatest violence.
At law and in the community, limitations everywhere arose, in no
small part because the slaves fought to impose them. Solomon
Northup recalled a decent master's remonstrating with a brutal
one: "This is no way of dealing with them, when first brought into
the country. It will have a pernicious influence and set them all
running away. The swamps will be full of them."[8]

The humanity of the slave implied his action, and his action
implied his will. Hegel was therefore right in arguing that slavery
constituted an outrage, for, in effect, it has always rested on the
falsehood that one man could become an extension of another's
will. If one man could so transform himself, he could do it only
by an act of that very will supposedly being surrendered, and he
would remain so only while he himself chose to. The clumsy
attempt of the slaveholders to invoke a religious sanction did not
extricate them from this contradiction. The Christian tradition,
from the early debates over the implications of original sin
through the attempts of Hobbes and others to secularize the problem, could not rationally defend the idea of permanent and total
submission rooted in a temporally precise surrender of will. The
idea of man's surrender to God cannot be equated with the idea
of man's surrender to man, but even if it could, the problem would
remain. The Catholic and Arminian struggle for constant rededication to God as an act of free will avoided the difficulty, and only
the extreme forms of antinomianism took the plunge into a doc-

trine of continuous and permanent submission. By so doing—the politically radical ramifications notwithstanding—antinomianism passed into a hysterical abnegation of humanity. But apart from the ultras among the South's predestinarian Regular Baptists, and by no means always among them, the southern versions of Protestantism did not take that road. Moreover, the slaveholders perceived the revolutionary political dangers in such a doctrine, as their mounting attacks on northern "religious fanaticism" reveal. Hence, their attempt to justify slavery philosophically contradicted their increasing need for a moderate theology, no matter how fundamentalist its dress. They ended, therefore, with no reply at all to the liberal challenge, epitomized in Hegel's critique, and had to fall back on the assertion of naked power. And at that, they ruined themselves, for their recognition of the slaves' right to life, explicitly endorsed in the laws against the murdering of slaves, both exposed the absurdity of the assertion of a doctrine of total surrender of will and registered their own inability to justify even to themselves the unlimited use of force.

Why, then, did the slaveholders so often reiterate their demand for absolute obedience while repudiating its theoretical foundation explicitly in their courts and implicitly in their daily behavior? Because in no other way could they justify themselves to themselves. Because in no other way could they see themselves as morally responsible beings who were doing their duty. We must therefore accept the naiveté of Mrs. Schoolcraft as an ideological position essential to the self-esteem, self-confidence, and moral strength of her class. Commenting on Trollope's observation that slaves love their masters in the same way that dogs do, she agreed, but with a difference. "The slave," she told herself, "can never be treated with the hardness of heart that poor white operators are, because the fact of his being dependent makes his master love to patronize him." And more sharply, "How thankful I am to God that the slave, who seems given up to the will of his master, should have the very strongest passion of that master's heart enlisted to protect him and provide for his every want."[9]

The slaveholders found themselves trapped by the exigencies of their untenable view of their relationship to their slaves. Their position suffered the more from an awareness of dependency upon their slaves' labor, which necessarily transformed a doctrine of absolute property and absolute will into a doctrine of reciprocity.

Everard Green Baker of Panola, Mississippi, a thoughtful young man and perhaps a model master, wrestled with the problem in his diary and vowed to avoid waste. "A man," he explained, "should not squander what another accumulates with the exposure of health & the wearing out of the physical powers, & is not that the case with the man who needlessly parts with that which the negro by the hardest labor & often undergoing what he in like situation would call the greatest deprivation?" The slave's body, he added later, "has been worn out in hard service for us [so] that the decrepitude of age [must] receive our tenderest notice, since the vigor of life—the buoyancy of spirit, & strength of arm has worn itself away with many a hard year's labor—through suns & tempests, to enable us to indulge in the comforts & niceties of this world. . . ." A few years later, he wrote on Christmas Day: "I have endeavored too to make my Negroes joyous and happy—& am glad to see them enjoying themselves with such a contented hearty good will. . . . Thus I commenced another year under favorable auspices as far as my domestic affairs are concerned—I did all I could to make their hollidays pleasant to them & they seem to appreciate my endeavors."[10]

Insisting that a master had a duty to provide a slave with legal counsel, Judge Starnes of the State Supreme Court of Georgia explained that this duty must be understood as being "in return for the profit of the bondman's labor." Yet he ruled in the case at issue that unless the master's punishment aimed to kill, the slave must submit and had no right to make a judgment on its severity.[11] The slaves saw this attitude in their masters' behavior. Robert McKinley, an ex-slave of North Carolina, remembered a local slaveholder who explained his kindness toward his slaves as a necessary return to people whose hard work made his own easier life possible. Louise Jones, an ex-slave of Virginia, described how her master had enjoyed himself at his slaves' Christmas balls, which his wife hated:

> Den ole Missus say to Marsa, "I b'lieve you lak dem niggers better'n you do me." Den Marsa say, "Sho, I lak my niggers. Dey works hard an' makes money fo' me, an' I'm goin' to see dat dey have a good time. You go back to de house ef you don' wanna stay here. I'se gwine stay an' see dat my niggers have a good time."[12]

The slaves understood these impulses in their masters and seized the significant concession they implied. Unable to challenge the system as such—unable to resist it frontally except on desperate occasions and then with little hope of success—they accepted what could not be avoided. In its positive aspect this accommodation represented a commitment, shared by most peoples, however oppressed, to the belief that a harsh and unjust social order is preferable to the insecurities of no order at all. It also represented an awareness that the masters required their affection, or at least the appearance of it, in order to curb their own tendencies toward cruelty and even greater injustice. Slaveholders had the great advantage over colonizers of being an intrinsic part of their society rather than marginal men who were imposing themselves on a conquered country. Thus, they could reverse the assumption that those who conquer and dominate others must hate them if they are to justify themselves as Christians and human beings. The slaveholders struggled to reverse the pattern and to "love" those whom they made suffer. They could deny to themselves that in fact they did cause suffering and could assert that their domination liberated the slaves from a more deprived existence. Such a view demanded the doctrine of reciprocal duties implicit and sometimes explicit in their defense of their regime and their own lives. Inherent in this doctrine were dangerously deceptive ideas of "gratitude," "loyalty," and "family." Inherent also was an intimacy that turned every act of impudence and insubordination—every act of unsanctioned self-assertion—into an act of treason and disloyalty, for by repudiating the principle of submission it struck at the heart of the master's moral self-justification and therefore at his self-esteem. Nothing else, apart from personal idiosyncrasy, can explain the ferocity and cruelty of masters who normally appeared kind and even indulgent.[13] The slaves accepted the doctrine of reciprocity, but with a profound difference. To the idea of reciprocal duties they added their own doctrine of reciprocal rights. To the tendency to make them creatures of another's will they counterposed a tendency to assert themselves as autonomous human beings. And they thereby contributed, as they had to, to the generation of conflict and great violence.

This paternalism of the masters toward their slaves influenced and was in turn reinforced by the relationship of the planters to middle-class and lower-class whites. Those nonslaveholders who lived as farmers and herdsmen in the up country and well back of the plantation districts had only minimal contact with the great planters and created a world of their own, presenting to the slaveholders' regime a complex of problems beyond the scope of this discussion. Those nonslaveholders who lived in the interstices of the plantation districts further divided into strata: solid yeomen; respectable sub-subsistence farmers who supplemented their incomes by working as day laborers; skilled and semiskilled mechanics; and dissolute, déclassé "poor white trash." The relationship between the planters and these several strata varied in time and place and requires discrete analysis, but a few generalizations of special importance may be risked here. Each of these strata had its own stake in slavery, however much the slaveholders' regime, considered as social system, may have oppressed them. The yeomen who raised a little cotton often relied on the planters to gin and market it for them. Those who raised primarily corn and pork found their market in the nearby plantations and planter-dominated towns. The day laborers and mechanics worked for these same planters, and the poor whites depended to some extent on their charity as well as on their patronage for such odd jobs as hunting runaway slaves. The economic relationship of the upper and lower classes, in short, bound them together without economic exploitation. If anything, the planters proved generous in dealings with surrounding whites. Slavery as a system did oppress the nonslaveholders but in a disguised and impersonal way, while creating personal bonds across class lines. A full analysis of these bonds would have to go well beyond economics and take account of kinship patterns and social intercourse. A single family, defined in this quasi-traditional society as extending to fourth or fifth cousins, often had members among the richest and poorest strata of a given county. And any planter with social pretensions or a modest spirit of neighborliness, not to mention political ambitions, would periodically throw a big barbecue for the whole community, white and black.

Thus, the paternalist spirit readily extended beyond the black-white relationship and impinged upon the relationship of rich to poorer whites. As such, it reinforced the paternalism of the master-slave relationship itself. The slaves saw proud, free white men willingly defer to the great and powerful planters. This wider paternalism—or rather, pseudopaternalist element in a complex system of class relations—ran into strong countertendencies. The meanest whites could participate in the political process, claim equality with the rich, and thumb their noses at the high and mighty. The social relationships of poorer to richer whites involved much more than a pattern of deference. Rather, that pattern provided one element in a contradictory and potentially explosive whole.[14] For present purposes, however, it is enough that that element existed, fortified plantation paternalism, and strengthened the impulse of both masters and slaves to see paternalism as the normal and proper form of class relations.[15]

The German saying that whoever would command must first learn to obey, Hannah Arendt reminds us, rests on the psychological truth that the will to power and the will to submission rise and fall together; that a strong inclination to disobey normally accompanies an equally strong reluctance to dominate and command.[16] But this truth rests on a contradiction of its own, for those raised to command do not happily recognize that superiority in others which alone requires their submission. In practice, therefore, men raised to command will learn to submit, but neither easily nor often. The slaveholders paid heavily for this tension in their make-up; it cost them dearly when they had to wage a desperate war for survival with a great residue of courage and ferocity to draw upon but with an undeveloped sense of civic discipline. Perhaps in no more ironical way did that habituated submission of the slaves which the masters chose to interpret as docility and lack of will strike back to claim a final revenge.

Although the slaveholders displayed all the qualities of ordinary humanity and shared a common national experience with their northern neighbors, in essential respects they grew to be a particular type of men and women. In the middle of the twentieth century a gifted white writer tells of growing up in the Delta:

> My mother's people . . . captured my imagination when I was growing up, were of the Deep South—emotional, changeable, touched with charisma and given to histrionic flourishes. They were courageous under tension and unexpectedly tough beneath their wild eccentricities, for they had a close working agreement with God. They also had an unusually high quota in bullshit.[17]

The slaveholders normally spoke about themselves with greater delicacy but to the same effect. William Henry Holcombe of Natchez, in a diary entry dated August 5, 1855, but undoubtedly written at the beginning of the war, contrasted northerners and southerners:

> Northerners.—Individually cautious and timid—collectively bold and courageous. Individually cool and calm—collectively excitable.

Individually resorting to law or suasion—collectively to force. Individually insensible to points of honor—collectively very much so.

Southerners.—Individually brave to rashness—collectively cautious and wise. Individually excitable—collectively possessed and dignified. Individually resorting to violence—collectively to suasion. Individually sensitive to the point of honor—collectively less so, singularly calm and forebearing and forgiving.[18]

A gentleman in Charleston, whom G. W. Featherstonhaugh admired for "intelligence and liberality of sentiments on other subjects," insisted that slavery elevated the character of the master by making him jealous of that which was his own, a friend of public liberty, a man of surpassing dignity.[19] Sir Charles Lyell, the noted scientist, no friend to slavery and not a man to be taken in by cant, observed on his visit to Hopeton Plantation that to manage a plantation properly required a just-so combination of "firmness, forbearance, and kindness."[20] He reflected further: "The relation of the slaves to their owners resembles nothing in the northern states. There is a hereditary regard and often attachment on both sides, more like that formerly existing between lords and their retainers in the old feudal times of Europe, than to any thing now to be found in America."[21] And Hugh Davis, a cultured big planter of Alabama, loved Pope's *Essay on Man*, especially the lines:

> Order is Heavens first law and this confessed
> Some are, and must be greater than the rest,
> More rich than wise; but who infers from hence
> That such are happier shocks all common sense.[22]

These and many similar comments by slaveholders cannot be dismissed as so much self-congratulatory rubbish, for few perceptive critics of the regime disputed the essentials of the description, however much they inverted the value judgments. Dr. Francis Lieber, who had known the South well, wrote from the safety of the North that slavery, "while degrading human beings—persons —to things, engendered in the owner that reckless and cruel pride which made even angels fall."[23] The son of an aristocratic South Carolina planter, writing in 1895 in criticism of racial segregation, recalled sadly:

> An unconquerable pride grew up in the hearts of this class—the pride of unchallenged domination, of irresponsible control of others, of unquestioned power, of uncriticized conduct. Each man became a lord within his own domain. He was the source of law among his

slaves; and his self interest and good or ill will was the rule of his actions: the laws of the state did not readily reach him and public opinion among his own class naturally coincided with his views. There thus resulted an absolute indifference to the opinions of others: an entire independence of the objects, needs or aims of the other classes of the population.[24]

And W. E. B. Du Bois, the greatest of black scholars, years later penned a biting passage about the planters, which represented a judgment of agreed-upon qualities:

> The psychological effect of slavery upon him was fatal. The mere fact that a man could be, under the law, the actual master of the mind and body of human beings had to have disastrous effects. . . . Their "honor" became a vast and awful thing, requiring wide and insistent deference. Such of them as were inherently weak and inefficient were all the more easily angered, jealous and resentful; while the few who were superior, physically or mentally, conceived no bounds to their power and personal prestige.[25]

Among the harshest of contemporary indictments was Fanny Kemble's. High-spirited, intelligent, sharp-tongued and sharp-penned, although certainly not always fair or accurate, she had lived as a planter's wife and was at her considerable best in studying the character of the men of the master class. She began: "If the accounts given by these ladies of the character of the planters in this part of the South may be believed, they must be as idle, arrogant, ignorant, dissolute, and ferocious as that medieval chivalry to which they are fond of comparing themselves. . . ." The southern women, she continued, staunchly defended slavery and justified it as an indulgent system. "It is not surprising that women should regard the question from this point of view; they are very seldom *just*, and are generally treated with more indulgence than justice by men." She asked a planter if he was not proud of his son for having heroically risked his life and displayed firmness and self-control when others had panicked. She took full note of his brief reply: "I am glad, madam, my son was not selfish." She reflected:

> Now, E——, I have often spoken with you and written to you of the disastrous effect of slavery upon the character of the white man implicated in it; . . . but the devil must have his due, and men brought up in habits of peremptory command over their fellow men, and under the constant apprehension of danger, and awful necessity of

immediate readiness to meet it, acquire qualities precious to themselves and others in hours of supreme peril such as this man passed through, saving by their exercise himself and all committed to his charge.

Mrs. Kemble, as she called herself after her divorce from Pierce Butler, saw the slaveholders as "a very different race of men from either Manchester manufacturers or Massachusetts merchants; they are a remnant of barbarism and feudalism, maintaining itself with infinite difficulty and danger by the side of the latest and most powerful development of commercial civilization." They were, she admitted, well-bred men, in the English sense, with good manners. But, "Their temperament is impulsive and enthusiastic, and their manners have the grace and spirit which seldom belong to the deportment of a Northern people." She continued:

> The South Carolina gentry have been fond of styling themselves the chivalry of the South, and perhaps not badly represent in their relations with their dependents, the nobility of France before the purifying hurricane of the Revolution swept the rights of the suzerain and the wrongs of the serf together into one bloody abyss. The planters of the interior of the Southern and Southwestern states, with their furious feuds and slaughterous combats, their stabbings and pistolings, their gross sensuality, brutal ignorance, and despotic cruelty, resemble the chivalry of France before the horrors of the Jacquerie admonished them that there was a limit even to the endurance of slaves.

She concluded with a reference to "overbearing irritability, effeminate indolence, reckless extravagance, and a union of profligacy and cruelty, which is the immediate result of their irresponsible power over their dependents."[26]

The most flattering self-portraits of the slaveholders and the harshest and most exaggerated indictments of their critics have much in common despite conflicts of emphasis, balance, and above all, value judgment. The men who emerge from the one can be recognized with little difficulty as those who emerge from the other. They were tough, proud, and arrogant; liberal-spirited in all that did not touch their honor; gracious and courteous; generous and kind; quick to anger and extraordinarily cruel; attentive to duty and careless of any time and effort that did not control their direct interests. They had been molded by their slaves as much as their slaves had been molded by them. They were not men to be taken lightly, not men frivolously to be made enemies of. And they wallowed in those deformities which their slaves had thrust upon them in the revenge of historical silence—deformities which would eventually lead them to destruction as a class. The Chinese have a proverb: "A hero may risk his whole world but will never surrender his concubine or his horse." The slaveholders were heroes.

THE MOMENT OF TRUTH

The slaveholders' understanding of themselves and their world suffered a severe shock during and immediately after the war, when "their black family" appeared in a new light. How new the blacks had become—how much they had actually changed—remains a question, especially since perhaps 80 percent remained on the plantations instead of deserting during the war. But their behavior suggests that to a significant extent they had not so much changed as come into the open. Their behavior presented their masters with a terrible moment of truth. Could it be that they had never known "their people" at all? that they had been deceiving themselves? Yes, it could be, and it was. Willie Lee Rose has aptly called this historical moment "traumatic" for the slaveholders.[1]

The masters had expected more than obedience from their slaves; they had expected faithfulness—obedience internalized as duty, respect, and love. They had had little choice, for anything less would have meant a self-image as exploitative brutes. This insistence on the slaves' constituting part of the family and these expressions of belief in their loyalty lay at the heart of the masters' world-view and, abolitionist criticism notwithstanding, embraced little insincerity. Thus the leading southern ideologues, who wrote the proslavery polemics of the late antebellum period, were deceiving none so much as themselves. In 1837, Chancellor Harper blithely wrote of docile and faithful slaves' adding greatly to southern military strength. J. H. Hammond, erratic and flamboyant but anything except an ass, added that the slaves would "delight" in helping disarm and enslave an invading black army.[2] In 1850, a young aristocratic South Carolinian gloomily told Fredrika Bremer, "The world is against us, and we shall be overpowered by voices and condemned without justice, for what we are, and for what we are doing on behalf of our servants." And as late as 1864, with the cause lost, a lawyer in Memphis lamented, "I believe too that a very large number of the negroes will not accept their freedom and that, by one name or another, pretty much of the old relations will be re-established."[3] These sentiments help explain the temper of those whites who angrily shot down deserting blacks even before they could have been sure that they would be unable to recover their slave property.[4]

The wartime and immediate postwar trauma derived less from the sudden confrontation with the true attitudes of their slaves than from the enforced confrontation with themselves. The experience proved all the more bitter since that organic relationship of master and slave which the slaveholders always celebrated had so clearly rebounded against them: any change in their perception of the slaves intrinsically meant a change in their perception of themselves. The freedmen often had a better sense of this relationship and of the nature of the slaveholders' reaction than did the slaveholders. They spoke of masters and mistresses who died of broken hearts both for the loss of their property and for their sense of having been betrayed. Some blacks were saddened by what they saw, others delighted; few seem to have been surprised. One old man, who had been a body servant, told a story that may stand for many others. He had been literate but had hid his talent from his master. After the war, he signed his name and watched his old master "faint" and then expel him from the place. As he remembered the white man's words: "You done stayed in war wid me four years and I ain't know that was in you. Now I ain't got no confidence in you."[5]

The great shock to the planters came with the defection of their most trusted and pampered slaves—the drivers and especially the more intimate of the house servants. That many of these remained loyal did not offset the shock at the behavior of those who did not. The slaveholders might reconcile themselves to the defection of their field hands, for it struck at their pocketbooks but not necessarily at their self-esteem. They could explain the exodus from the fields by reasoning that these were inexperienced, simple people whom the Yankees could mislead. No such reasoning would serve to explain the behavior of the house slaves or the drivers. Their desertion, in the minds of the slaveholders, constituted the essence of ingratitude, of unfaithfulness, of disloyalty, of treason.

The cries of anguish reverberated across the South. To begin with Virginia: "I am beginning to lose confidence *in the whole race,*" Catherine Barbara Broun concluded from the desertion of those very house slaves whom the whites had expected to protect them from the Yankees. Judith Brockenbrough McGuire described the slaves as "servants deserting their homes." John H. Phillips wrote to B. O. Tayloe that he had talked to the slaves "as a father" but that they had laughed. A white man told Lucy Chase, "I should not have cared, if they'd only given notice that they were going." Frank Fikes, who had been well treated as a slave, left his version:

> Ol' miss and massa was not mean to us at all until after surrender and we were freed. We did not have a hard time until after we were freed. They got mad at us because we was free and they let us go without a crumb of anything and without a penny and nothing but what we had on our backs. . . . We had a hard time then and I've been having a hard time ever since.[6]

In North Carolina, Catherine Devereaux Edmondston wrote of a neighbor's male house servant who drew a knife to defend his mistress against Yankee troops and of "Aunt Susan" who wanted to have General Lee tarred and feathered for surrendering the Confederate cause. But she also told us the story of Fanny, whose behavior had equivalents throughout the South: "During the whole of my sickness I was nursed in a most devoted and affectionate manner by my maid Fanny. At times she actually wept over me. . . . And yet—when I was scarce able to walk without assistance—she left me without provocation or reason—left me in the night, and that too without the slightest notice."[7]

South Carolina provided some of the most articulate cries of pain. Duncan Clinch Heyward, the son of one of the biggest of rice planters and slaveowners, wrote years later, in calmer and (for him) better times:

> Late one afternoon in early January, 1867 . . . my father arrived at Combalee. . . . What seemed to surprise and hurt him most of all was the changed attitude toward himself of the Negroes, who had so feelingly bade him goodbye when, only a year before, they had left his plantation on the Wateree.
>
> In a letter to my mother . . . he comments on the rundown condition of everything, and says: "But as to the human part of it! Oh!

what a change. It would have killed my father and worries me more than I expected, or rather the condition of the Negroes on the place is worse than I expected. It is so very evident that they are disappointed at my coming here; they were in hopes of getting off again this year and having the place to themselves. They received me very coldly; in fact it it was some time before they came out of their houses to speak to me. . . . They are as familiar as possible and surprise me in their newly acquired 'Beaufort manner.' They are constantly in Beaufort, quite too much for their good."[8]

"Today," wrote the brilliant Mary Boykin Chesnut in 1865, "I was telling Mrs. Johnston the first time I ever heard the word 'nigger' used by people *comme il faut*. Now it is in everybody's mouth, but I have never become accustomed to it." But that was in 1865. In 1861 she had written in high spirits of the loyalty of the slaves in the face of Yankee invasion: "Now if slavery is as disagreeable as we think it, why don't they all march over the border where they would be received with open arms." She expressed amazement, adding, "I am always studying these creatures. They are to me inscrutable in their ways, and past finding out." Two years later she began to "scent" a desire for freedom in an extremely bright, grave, dignified butler whom she had taught to read and befriended. "He is the first Negro that I have felt a change in. They go about in their black masks, not a ripple or an emotion showing; and yet on all other subjects except the War they are the most excitable of races." In 1864, in Richmond, she expressed sympathy for President and Mrs. Davis over the defection of their closest servants. She understood that the Davises had loved and trusted them in the grand southern manner and that the shock had to be great. No matter, then, the momentary pretenses. Mrs. Chesnut knew better than most how painfully deceived her class had been—how painfully they had deceived themselves.[9]

It may be objected that Mrs. Chesnut cannot serve as a model. She had an extraordinary intelligence, as well as a sensitivity to everyone and everything around her. But corroboration appeared everywhere. Louis Manigault, great patriarchal planter of the South Carolina and Georgia low country, wrote in May, 1862:

> With us upon Savannah River, my favorite Board Hand, a Man who had rowed me to and from Savannah from my earliest recollections of Gowrie Plantation (1839), one who had been kindly treated by my Father and family upon numerous occasions, a man bought with Gowrie (1833), my constant companion when previous to my

marriage I would be quite alone upon the plantation, and a Negro We all of us esteemed highly. Singular to say, this man "Hector" was the very first to murmur, and would have hastened to the embrace of his Northern Brethren, could he have forseen the least prospect of a successful escape. He was the first Negro I took with me from the plantation on to Charleston and is now (May, 1862) safe. Such is only one of the numerous instances of ingratitude evinced in the African character.

A month or so later, on June 12, 1862, he expanded his exposition and protest:

This war has taught us the perfect impossibility of placing the least confidence in the negro. In too numerous instances those we esteemed the most have been the first to desert us. House Servants, from their constant contact with the family become more conversant with passing events are often the first to have their minds polluted with evil thoughts. For my own part I am more than ever convinced that the only suitable occupation for the Negro is to be a Labourer of the Earth, and to work as a field hand upon a well disciplined plantation. It has now been proven that those Planters who were the most indulgent to their Negroes when we were at peace, have since the commencement of the war encountered the greatest trouble in the management of this species of property.

When the war ended, Manigault began to grasp the paradox of the "bad nigger" and the "loyal black family" in their infinite and surprising complexity. He wrote in 1867: "So deceitful is the Negro that as far as my own experience extends I could never in a single instance decipher his character. . . . In former days also fear in a great measure guided the action of the Negro and we Planters could never get at the truth." Manigault contrasted, with astonishment, the postwar experience with Jack Savage, local "bad nigger," with those whom he looked to affectionately. On March 22, 1867, he recalled antebellum days when Jack Savage was "the greatest Villain on the plantation, most notoriously bad character & worst Negro on the place." He described Savage, who had been bought in 1839, as "an exceedingly lazy man, although quite smart and our best plantation carpenter." Jack Savage had been "the only Negro ever in our possession who I considered capable of murdering me, or burning my dwelling at night." Despite his "perfect" work in building trunks and floodgates, Savage had been sold in 1863 for causing trouble. Manigault returned to the plantation in 1867. Savage had also returned and was there to greet him: "As we met I gave him my hand and made a few friendly remarks. I always gave him many presents such as bacon, & tobacco & rice." To his surprise, Savage's response was warm, whereas the women who had also been recipients of his presents and who had always gushed upon his appearance sat glumly and did not even say hello. The paradox drove him wild. All he knew was that everything was upside down.[10]

Aunt Charlotte Foster, who had lived as a slave near Spartanburg, South Carolina, was also puzzled by her experience, but not quite in the same way. After the war her mother had taken her to live with her father on another plantation. Her master had wanted to help them, but his sons refused and preferred to let them risk starvation. She may not have understood their motives, but there is no reason that she should have tried.[11]

In Georgia after the war, a former servant of Mary A. H. Gay asked her to take care of her children. She had to go to work in a laundry and expected Ole Missus to care for her "little niggers" same as before. No. Never again would Mrs. Gay assume such heavy responsibility for those who "have shown very little gratitude for what has been done for them."[12] An omen of that which would come appeared in 1865 in the journal of Ella Gertrude Clanton Thomas:

> Susan, Kate's nurse, most trusty servant, her advice, right hand woman and best liked house servant has left here. I am under too many obligations to Susan to have hard feelings toward her. During six confinements Susan has been with me, the best of servants, rendering the most efficient help. To Ma she has always been invaluable and in case of sickness there was no one like Susan. Her husband Anthony was one of the first to leave the Cumming Plantation and incited others to do the same. I expect he influenced Susan, altho I have often heard Pa say that in case of a revolt among Negroes he thought that Susan would serve as ringleader. She was the first servant to leave Ma's yard and left without one word of warning.[13]

Eliza Frances Andrews noted in her diary for January 16, 1865, that the most well-behaved and docile blacks became increasingly unruly as Yankee troops got close. On May 27, she celebrated the loyalty of her own servants, whom she called "treasures": "I really love them for the way they have stood by us." A month later she told of the adventures of a neighbor's favorite pampered, loyal, religiously devout, superannuated slave. One day, as usual without the slightest provocation so far as the slaveholders were concerned, he slandered his white family, which had sheltered and befriended him, and—of all things—had the temerity to claim the plantation as his own. Years later, when Miss Andrews had grown into a woman of considerable intellectual sophistication, she reflected on these pages of her diary and recalled how her aunt, who had had no children of her own, had compensated by spoiling a "pet" servant. The boy had been orphaned by the death of his mother, the aunt's favorite maid. As soon as the war ended he "deserted." "The kind-hearted old lady never ceased to mourn over his ingratitude." Miss Andrews recalled this story along with another. Arch, her father's favorite dining-room servant, was the first black to leave the plantation. Yet he had not sneaked off. He had asked his old master's permission, which could hardly have been refused, and had expressed all possible respect. But the time had come. For many years afterwards he visited the white family, which continued to employ his sister.[14]

This ambivalence in the Big House often broke into its antagonistic components, with some white families experiencing only the slaves' "loyalty" and others only their "desertion." And for many whites the fact of freedom itself constituted a desertion. One planter in Georgia burned his slave cabins to the ground and expelled his people. He had no use for them any longer, he said, nor they for him.[15] In 1871 a hysterical old white man "denounced, with bitter curses, his negroes, saying that they had abandoned him when set free and left him to starve in his old age, knowing as they did what he had intended to do for them [that is, to care for them] if he could have had his own way."[16]

Also in Georgia, the family of the Reverend C. C. Jones had always concerned itself, according to its own understanding, with the material and spiritual welfare of the slaves. During the worst days of the war, faced with the greatest privations and shaken by defections among their own people as well as those of their neighbors, this devoutly religious, high-minded, duty-conscious family fought desperately to preserve its sense of Christian love and obligation. Amidst the despair of war, destruction, and imminent invasion, time was always made to inquire about sick slaves, to express condolences, to attend to those details of life which affected the standard of comfort. "Your brother," wrote the Reverend Mr. Jones to his son, Charles Jr., in April, 1862, "stayed to take care of the people." But in the same letter he described a scene while missing its biting irony. A boat was approaching. "When the Negroes ran to the brick shed, someone called to the old patriarch Tony to go along. Said he: 'Where is Massa?' 'Gone!' 'Where is Mistress?' 'Gone!' 'Well, I am too old to run. I will stay and throw myself into the hands of the Lord.' "

A few months later the Reverend Mr. Jones again wrote Charles Jr.:

> A public meeting of the citizens was called on the 8th at Hinesville to adopt some measures for suppressing if possible the escape of our Negroes to the enemy on the coast. Fifty-one have already gone from this county. . . . One of these was *Joefinny!* Such is the report. The temptation of *cheap goods, freedom,* and *paid labor* cannot be withstood. None may absolutely be depended on. The only preservation is *to remove them beyond the temptation,* or *seal* by the most rigid police all ingress and egress; and this is most difficult. . . . They are traitors who may pilot an enemy into your *bedchamber!* They know every road and swamp and creek and plantation in the country, and are the worst of spies.

Charles C. Jones, Jr., formerly mayor of Savannah and then a lieutenant in the Confederate army, wrote back: "I deeply regret to learn that the Negroes still continue to desert to the enemy. Joefinny's conduct surprises me." He urged that all deserting whites be shot but only the worst of the blacks: "Ignorance, credulity, pliability, desire for change, the absence of political ties of allegiance, the peculiar status of the race—all are to be considered and must exert their influence in behalf of the slave." His benevolent father remained beside himself and reiterated: "They are traitors of the worst kind, and spies also who may pilot the enemy into your bedchamber. It is those caught *going* that we wish to know what to do with. Those who are caught *coming back* may no doubt be treated summarily as spies."

Through all this bitterness the family tried to maintain its old stance. Mrs. Mary S. Mallard, in the spring of 1865, was still ending her letters to her mother with the customary "Howdy to the servants." Trying to pick his way through the confusion and mixed emotions of the family, the Reverend John Jones wrote to his sister:

> I am truly tired of my daily cares; they are without number. To clothe and shoe and properly feed our Negroes and pay our taxes requires more than we make by planting, especially when debts have

to be paid. I believe the most pressed people in our Confederacy are the owners of slaves who have no way to support them. Sometimes I think that Providence by this cruel war is intruding to make us willing to relinquish slavery by feeling its burdens and cares.

Mrs. Mary Jones wrote to her daughter, Mrs. Mary Mallard, in the old vein as late as February, 1864: "Howdies from all the *servants here* and at *Montevideo.* Old Andrew and Sue were very much hurt at not seeing you before you left home. The old man says you know he was always a "sponsible man in the family.' " By the end of the year even the most stalwart members of the Big House had lost heart.

Several entries in the journal of Mrs. Mary Jones during January, 1865, taken together, reveal the deepening despair and sense of abandonment and betrayal:

[Jan. 6, 1865.] The people are all idle on the plantations, most of them seeking their own pleasure. Many servants have proven faithful, others false and rebellious against all authority and restraint. Susan, a Virginia Negro and nurse to my little Mary Ruth, went off with Mac, her husband, to Arcadia the night after the first day the Yankees appeared, with whom she took every opportunity of conversing, informing them that the baby's father was Colonel Jones. She has acted a faithless part as soon as she could. Porter left three weeks since. . . . Gilbert, Flora, Lucy, Tenah, Sue, Rosetta, Fanny, Little Gilbert, Charles, Milton, and Elsie and Kate have been faithful to us. Milton has been a model of fidelity. He will not even converse with the Yankees. . . . His brother, Little Pulaski . . . took himself off a week since.

[Jan. 21, 1865.] Kate, daughter's servant who has been cooking for us, took herself off today, influenced, as we believe, by her father. Sent for cook Kate to Arcadia. She refuses to come.

Their condition is one of perfect anarchy and rebellion. They have placed themselves in perfect antagonism to their owners and to all government and control.

[Jan. 24, 1865.] Nearly all the house servants have left their homes; and from most of the plantations they have gone in a body.

In June, 1865, Mrs. Jones received a letter from her daughter-in-law, Mrs. Eva B. Jones, who lamented: "Adeline, Grace, and Polly have all departed in search of freedom, without bidding any of us an affectionate adieu." A month later she again wrote of the desertion of some slaves and of the increased thievery of others. After much exchanging of letters on the deplorable state of black life,

Mrs. Mary Jones wrote to her daughter-in-law: "I truly regret to know that your mother's servants have given her so much trouble. We cannot but feel such ingratitude." The Reverend John Jones wrote to his sister-in-law, Mrs. Mary Jones: "Some great change, have come over us since you left. The dark, dissolving, disquieting wave of emancipation has broken over this sequestered region. . . . It has been like the iceberg, withering and deadening the best sensibilities of master and servant, and fast sundering the domestic ties of years." After receiving more reports of the awful behavior of trusted servants, Mrs. Mary Jones pronounced herself "thoroughly disgusted with the whole race." By November, 1865, despite continued affectionate references to some of the old servants, she burst out:

> My life long (I mean since I had a home) I have been laboring and caring for them, and since the war have labored with all my might to supply their wants, and expended everything I had upon their support, directly or indirectly; and this is their return.
>
> You can have no conception of the condition of things. I understand Dr. Harris and Mr. Varnedoe will rent their lands to the Negroes! The conduct of some of the citizens has been very injurious to the best interests of the community. . . .
>
> I have just called Charles and asked if he had any messages. "He sends love to Lucy and Tenah, and begs to be remembered to you, and says he will make an opportunity to come and see them before long." This is the sum and substance of his message. It is impossible to get at any of their intentions, and it is useless to ask them. I see only a dark future for the whole race.

A month later, with cotton stolen, Mrs. Mary Jones's "heart is pained and sickened with their vileness and falsehood in every way. I long to be delivered from the race." Still, on May 18, 1866, she could write to her small granddaughter: "Your dear papa has no doubt told you that your nurse Peggy was dead. She took care of and nursed you for the first year of your life, and loved you very dearly. She wanted to go to New York to wait on you, but it is the will of our Heavenly Father that she should not live even to take care of her own child. I hope poor Peggy was a Christian and has gone to heaven."

The struggle of the members of the Jones family to keep faith with their past in the face of what they regarded as the most severe provocations emerges from two letters with which we may close our account of them. Charles C. Jones wrote to his mother from New York in May, 1866:

I regret deeply to hear that you have been subjected to "severe trials" at Montevideo, and heartily unite with you in the hope that they are now overpassed. The transition in the status of the Negro has been such a marked and violent one that we cannot wonder that he does not at once adapt himself rationally and intelligently to the change. He has always been a child in intellect—improvident, incapable of appreciating the obligations of a contract, ignorant of the operation of any law other than the will of his master, careless of the future, and without the most distant conception of the duties of life and labor now devolved upon him. Time alone can impart the necessary intelligence; and the fear of the law, as well as kindness and instruction, must unite in compelling an appreciation and discharge of the novel duties and responsibilities resting upon him.

But his mother had remained on the plantation and could not manage to be quite so philosophical. On May 28, she replied with news about a strike over contract terms that had been put down by Federal troops:

I have told the people that in doubting my word they have offered me the greatest insult I ever received in my life; that I had considered them friends and treated them as such, giving them gallons of clabber every day and syrup once a week, with rice and extra dinners; but that now they were only laborers under contract, and only the law would rule between us, and I would require every one of them to come up to the mark in their duty on the plantation. The effect has been decided, and I am not sorry for the position we hold mutually. They have relieved me of the constant desire and effort to do something to promote their comfort. . . . Gilbert has maintained his fidelity on all occasions, and Kate and Lucy are great comforts to me.

Everything lies bare in these letters and in numerous others like them.[17] The "ingratitude" of the blacks. But then, we must try to understand that their condition opens them to temptation and error. Still, how could they do this to us? What about Cato—a favorite, wonderful at ingratiating himself? Why was he the one to stir up trouble among the slaves so much earlier than the bad characters among them? They are hateful. But we cannot hate them, for we are good Christians. And, they really still do love us. Of course they do—some of them. They must. They are confused. They will come to their senses. Some of the old affection remains. How are we supposed to live without it? They do love us, in their own irritating, childish, perverse way. The ungrateful wretches. What can they be thinking of? What is in their enigmatic heads? They should talk to us. We would understand. We have always understood them. Why not just talk to us? Just talk. Just say something.

The desolation fell over the whole South and not merely the patriarchal coastal lowlands. At "Brokenburn" in northeast Louisiana, Kate Stone railed against Webster, the dining-room attendant and family coachman, "our most trusted servant," who "claims the plantation as his own and is renowned as the greatest villain in the country." Faithful old Uncle Bob doggedly stayed loyal to the end, but even he was leaving to farm for himself. His demeanor at least helped to soften the impact of the defection of Webster and the field hands. But, "What a treacherous race they are!"[18]

Elsewhere in Louisiana the desertion of the favorites, particularly the house servants, provoked gasps of outrage and wails of sorrow. On many plantations the departure of the house servants preceded rather than followed that of the field hands or was simultaneous with it; in these cases the masters' agony was the greater. "They left," cried Emily Caroline Douglas, "without even a good-bye."[19] Catherine S. Minor, from a family of Unionist big planters in Alabama and Mississippi, told her slaves that the Yankees would kill or exploit them and that they needed her protection. She confessed to a friend that she had tried to frighten them into staying and explained, "You know how hard it is for persons who raised up negroes in this way to have them leave." She felt certain, "If they will only stay with me a while until after the excitement gets over, they will not leave then if they know I will treat them well." A few years later she told the federal commissioners who were hearing her case for compensation for depredations: "We had nothing in the world: we lived within our resources. We wove our own clothes for the Negroes, our people."[20]

The message was the same everywhere. In the happy days of 1853, Elise Young had written her cousin, W. N. Mercer, a big planter in Adams County, Mississippi: "The Negroes seem to have a merry Christmas. They all ask after you, many with tears in their eyes." A decade later, with the war lost, Mercer received a letter from his manager telling him bluntly that the slaves would soon desert; they were, he was certain, only waiting for warmer weather. Many, including house slaves, did leave; others stayed for adequate wages.[21] Apparently, those who left did so without fanfare or bitterness; they simply wanted to pursue their own lives.

The Reverend Samuel A. Agnew discussed the situation in Mississippi:

Oct. 29, 1862. On my arrival was surprised to hear that our negroes stampeded to the Yankees last night or rather a portion of them. . . . The children who have been taken away by their misguided parents, are to be pitied. I don't commisserate the men and women if they do suffer. . . . Have reason to believe that our [other] negroes are in communication with the enemy. Some of them are not willing to go untill they get their clothing and their shoes. I think every one, but with one or two exceptions will go to the Yankees. Eliza and her family are certain to go. She does not conceal her thoughts but plainly manifests her opinions by her conduct—insolent and insulting.

Oct. 31, 1862. Some of our negroes will not go to the Yankees, I think —but they may all prove faithless. Hear that Big George has no use for me, do not believe it.—If they go they will just have to go and risk the consequences.

Nov. 1, 1862. The negroes still "carry a high head." Eliza is ranting because I have no confidence in her veracity. Big George admits to me that he said "he had no use for me." Verily I repose very little confidence in any of them.[22]

In Texas, Mrs. W. H. Neblett wrote her husband during the difficult spring of 1864 that "the black wretches" were "aggravating" her in every way. "The negroes," she observed with uncommon delicacy, "care no more for me than if I was an old free darkey."[23] Apparently, they cared a good deal less. Three ex-slaves from Texas said their own piece, in terms essentially the same as those used everywhere else. Anderson Edwards had been a slave on a small unit of three black families. His master had treated them with kindness and as part of his own family but could not cope with their emancipation. "Gawd," he exploded, "never did 'tend to free niggers." Isaac Martin described how his master grieved himself to death, although his own slaves had remained loyal and had cried when freedom came. And Anne Miller watched her master go mad when emancipation came. He left the area, screaming that he would not live in a country in which blacks were free. A year later he committed suicide.[24]

The blacks knew what they saw. They saw the trauma and often felt compassion despite their determination to assert themselves. Jane Simpson of Kentucky was stern: "I never heard of white folks giving niggers nothing. . . . Dey was so mad 'cause dey had to set 'em free, dey just stayed mean as dey would allow 'em to be anyhow, and is yet, most of 'em." Willis of Georgia, who had been foreman of a plow gang, recalled that he had wanted to stay with his former master but that his wife had insisted on leaving. Naturally, he chose his wife. But his master had trouble understanding the decision. He burst out crying: "I didn't thought I could raise up a darkey dat would talk dat-a-way." Robert Falls of Tennessee told of his good master's announcement that his slaves had been freed:

> "Sit down there all of you and listen to what I got to tell you. I hates to do it but I must. You-all ain't my niggers no more. You is free. Just as free as I am. Here I have raised you all to work for me, and now you are going to leave me. I am an old man, and I can't get along without you. I don't know what I am going to do." Well, sir, it killed him. He was dead in less than ten months.[25]

The Memphis *Argus,* a conservative southern newspaper, summed up part of the story in 1865:

> The events of the last five years have produced an entire revolution in the social system of the entire Southern country. The old arrangement of things is broken up. The relation of master and servant is severed. Doubt and uncertainty pervade the mind of both. . . . The transition state of the African from the condition of slaves to that of freeman has placed him in a condition where he cannot avoid being suspicious of his newly acquired privilege of freedom. He looks with a jealous eye upon anything like an encroachment on what he esteems his rights. . . . We fear that too many of the former masters of the negro, forced by the events of a mighty revolution to relinquish their rights in the persons of slaves as property, do it with a bitter reluctance, amounting to absolute hatred.[26]

Not all planters reacted with consternation. Some surprises came from the opposite direction. Betty Simmons had been a slave in Texas for a master who had been "pretty hard on us." Yet, when freedom came at lay-by time, "He give us a gen'rous part of dat crop." Mariah Snyder's master had apparently been decent but not especially indulgent. When freedom came he lay dying from an accident. He called in the black children to see them before he died and then shook hands with the field hands and bade them take care of themselves.[27] Throughout the South many old masters or their descendants helped their former slaves to survive the difficulties of a poverty-stricken old age, as both black and white sources reveal.[28]

For many, the old paternalism died hard. The old families struggled to understand, adjust, and, in their own terms, forgive. John

Berkley Grimball, for example, could cry out at the desertion of seventy-four slaves during the war, "This is a terrible blow and has probably ruined me. . . ." To cover the loss he had to sell forty-eight more. In that moment of despair and disillusion, he took financial losses in order to keep families together and to sell them to someone he thought would be kind.[29] This residue of a sense of duty faced an unbearable test in the years ahead. Even many of the great low-country families slowly succumbed, for financial stress compelled that hardness which even the emotional shock of the transition had failed to achieve. For many, life had already changed utterly. One had to survive. And for the more cynical spirits, tomorrow was another day.[30]

But for many, especially those whose spirit had shaped the old ruling class, the defection of so many blacks had spelled the end. No matter that 80 percent or more had stood fast. More would have gone if they had had the chance or the courage. Many others wisely waited for the end of the war to go their own way. They were faithless. The "loyalty" of the many could never, in any case, have compensated for the "betrayal" of so many trusted others. Betrayal! For that was the point. The slaveholders had been deserted in their time of need. Abandoned. Octave Mannoni was right about a dependency complex in traditional, patriarchal societies, but he failed to notice that that dependency worked in both directions.

The old paternalistic sensibility, in its best and basest manifestations, withered. In some cases it died quickly, with screams of most foul and bloody murder; in others, it declined slowly, with brave attempts to forget and forgive or with pathetic groans. To a decreasing extent it lingered on well into the twentieth century, but for the most part after emancipation the John T. Morgans and Hoke Smiths would surrender to the harsher racists, while the Wade Hamptons, enfeebled and torn, would be dragged by the vicissitudes of political realities down the same road.[31]

The temper of the times may be discerned in a deposition filed by a Louisiana planter with the Union army: "When I owned niggers, I used to pay medical bills. I do not think I shall trouble myself."[32] It may be discerned in the caustic but soul-searching recollection of John S. Wise:

Were not the negroes perfectly content and happy? Had I not often talked to them on the subject? Had not every one of them told me repeatedly that they loved "old Marster" better than anybody in the world, and would not have freedom if he offered it to them? Of course they did—many and many a time. And that settled it.[33]

And above all, it may be discerned in a letter to the *New York Tribune*, written in 1865 by Augustin L. Taveau of Charleston, South Carolina, whom Manigault described as "a gentleman known to our family & a planter." For Manigault, Taveau's analysis was "correct."

Apart from religious considerations, by the loss of the cause and the institution I have suffered like the rest, yet am I content, for the conduct of the Negro in the late crisis of our affairs has convinced me that we were all laboring under a delusion. Good masters and bad masters all alike, shared the same fate—the sea of the Revolution confounded good and evil; and, in the chaotic turbulence, all suffer in degree. Born and raised amid the institution, like a great many others, I believed it was necessary, to our welfare, if not to our very existence. I believed that these people were content, happy, and attached to their masters. But events and reflection have caused me to change these opinions; for if they were necessary to our welfare, why were four-fifths of the plantations of the Southern States dilapidated caricatures of that elegance and neatness which adorn the Country-seats of other people? If as a matter of profit they were so valuable, why was it that nine-tenths of our planters were always in debt and at the mercy of their factors? If they were content, happy and attached to their masters, why did they desert him in the moment of his need and flock to an enemy, whom they did not know; and thus left their, perhaps really good masters whom they did know from infancy?[34]

PART 2

████████

...AND THE CHILDREN BROUGHT UP

> Hear, O heavens, and give ear, O earth: for the Lord hath spoken, I have nourished and brought up children, and they have rebelled against me.
> —Isaiah 1:2

TO THE MANOR BORN

"In no hands," wrote Susan Dabney Smedes, the nostalgic and romantic daughter of a great planter, "was the dignity of the family so safe as with the negro slaves. . . . They greatly magnified the importance of their owners, and were readily affronted if aspersion of any sort were cast on their master's family." The blacks, she added, "are all aristocrats by nature." Without understanding all the implications, Mrs. Smedes told of a family servant who had carried a letter from her father to an illiterate neighbor. Embarrassed, the neighbor pretended that he could not read the planter's handwriting. The indignant servant insisted that his master was too well educated to write poorly: "You cannot read, Sir!"[1] The master had provided a vantage point from which to flaunt contempt for a white man for whom respect and deference had been demanded by law and custom.

A genuinely aristocratic ethos characterized by something other than a supine quest for identification with the strong emerged among the slaves. White southerners forever spoke of the slaves' pride in belonging to a great planter family, and the slave narratives bear them out; but the whites saw only envy and pretension and missed the deeper attitude.[2] So many blacks did assure interviewers of having lived on plantations with hundreds of slaves that great exaggeration or distorted memory appears obvious. "It was," said Charles Davenport of Mississippi in a typical flurry, "only one o' de marster's places 'cause he was one o' de richest and highest quality gentlemen in de whole country. I'se tellin' you de truth, us didn't belong to no white trash." In another vein, slaves from the Upper South who had been sent to the sugar region would boast of having come from "Old Ferginny."[3] Solomon Northup recalled a popular slave song, which had parallels among the white rural lower classes:

> Harper's creek and roarin' ribber,
> Thar, my dear, we'll live forebber;
> Den we'll go to the Ingin nation,
> All I want in dis creation,
> Is pretty little wife and big plantation.[4]

A black soldier in Colonel Higginson's regiment roared, "I ain't got colored-man's principles. I'se got white geneman principles. I'se do my best."[5] Charles S. Sydnor, the gifted southern historian, saw this complex of attitudes much more clearly than most. He quoted an old family retainer in Mississippi as having condemned a recently employed tutor: "Lord, what sort of a man is this master is got to teach his children! He don't even know how to get on a horse!" Sydnor commented that for black as well as white southerners, riding a horse "was an outward symbol of a way of life."[6]

Implicit in this demand for doing things properly lay an insistence upon order. The freedmen, wrote Harriet Ware, a northern abolitionist, from the Sea Islands in 1863, "hate all change and confusion."[7] Years before, Aunt Lethe Jackson, the gardener on a Virginia plantation, wrote to her young mistress, Virginia Campbell:

> Tell My Master I think all the world of him and long once more to see his dignified steps up our hill. . . . Tell Mistress I hope I shall soon hear of her recovery and that we long for the time when she will be again here to give her directions and have everything as it ought to be and as she wants it—We have all done the best we could since she

went away but still there is nothing like having a person of sense to dictate—and then if we are obedient every thing goes on smoothly and happy. . . .[8]

Only those who romanticize—and therefore do not respect—the laboring classes would fail to understand their deep commitment to "law and order." Life is difficult enough without added uncertainty and "confusion." Even an oppressive and unjust order is better than none. People with such rich experience as that of the meanest slaves quickly learn to distrust utopian nostrums. As Machiavelli so brilliantly revealed, most people refuse to believe in anything they have not experienced. Such negativity must be understood as a challenge to demonstrate that a better, firmer, more just social order can replace the one to be torn down. But this innate conservatism, which rests on a wisdom rooted in much experience of the disasters that accompany the efforts of well-meaning fools, can be transformed into a powerful positive force as a demand for a responsible and constructive alternative to a tenaciously held security.[9] And at the least, it implies a series of expectations, which when not met can produce stunning outbreaks of apparently irrational violence.

The slaves' notion of order assumed a special aspect: it personalized everything. "Mr. Lincum," remarked Isaac Stier, an ex-slave from Natchez, "was a good man, but dey tells me he was poor an' never cut much figger in his clothes. Dat's why he never did un'erstan' how us felt 'bout us white folks. It takes de quality to un'erstan' such things."[10] The slaves' much celebrated—and denigrated—identification with their own white folks, especially the rich, undoubtedly had its elements of servility, envy, and idolatry, but it remained a respect for "de quality." They by no means deceived themselves about the brutal and seamy side of their masters' lives. But when they expressed admiration for the aristocratic features of southern life, they set a high standard for themselves. They noted that the more patriarchal masters could display grace, dignity, courtesy, and coolness under fire. Why should the slaves not have admired these qualities? The pity was that they seem no longer to have recognized how many such virtues their own forefathers had brought from Africa and contributed to the southern way of life—that they could not appreciate how great a contribution blacks had made to whites as well as vice versa. And the pity for the white South was that, as William Faulkner and Ralph

Ellison have stressed, the slaves probably took these qualities much more seriously than did those they ostensibly imitated.[11]

The slaves' commitment to the aristocratic ethos and to a sense of order emerged in their contribution to that pattern of behavior known as southern courtesy. Both blacks and whites contributed to the South's deserved reputation for that formal courtesy and graciousness which helped define its aristocratic ethos. Necessarily, they did so in different ways. Whites dealt with whites with a grave formality that won the admiration of visitors and also protected them from getting killed in a hot-tempered environment which encouraged an inflated sense of personal honor. Blacks dealt with blacks in a parallel way under less compulsion. Fanny Kemble referred to the slaves' "courtesy and affable condescension" and to their remarkably good manners, which she thought more a product of their African heritage than of slavery. Her daughter, whose own social views were plainly racist, made a similar point three decades later. Referring to a boorish country schoolteacher, she said, "I hope he might learn in time from the negroes in return for some book learning, as they are singularly gentle and courteous in their manners."[12]

Mrs. Kemble's observation on the African past had insight, for the complex social conditions in Africa did produce high standards of formal courtesy and good manners.[13] White southerners had their own traditions, which undoubtedly flourished in a society that kept every man on his guard and that also introduced those supporting tendencies which normally accompany lordship and its attendant condescension. Southern courtesy grew out of the interchange of these black and white attitudes.

If formal courtesy became a weapon of defense for whites, much more so did it become one for blacks. Bertram Wilbur Doyle writes in his study of "the etiquette of race relations" that a certain standard of deference, imposed by the whites as their due, led the slaves to devise a well-ordered pattern of protective behavior.[14] I received an intimation of this kind of courtesy on my first visit to the Deep South during the 1950s. Many southern blacks still seemed obsequious in the presence of whites. A stranger with an undisguisable Brooklyn accent, I often had to ask directions and assistance from people who might not be expected to be friendly. Both whites and blacks responded with unfailing graciousness. The blacks even seemed to fawn. Yet, after a few days I had to reflect on the curious difference in outcome. Whites would, if necessary, drop what they were doing to lead me by the hand to make certain I did not get lost. In one instance this same courtesy was bestowed by characters around a poolroom who displayed all the outward characteristics of the kind of hooligans I knew too well in New York, whose normal reception for strangers would not command the Lord's approval. On the other hand, what of those obsequious, fawning blacks? Never, not once, did I get proper directions. Either I found myself being sent in the wrong direction to the accompaniment of rousing yassuhs, or I found that a chap who had clearly lived in town all his life and whose manners were impeccable somehow did not know where Main Street was. I recalled these incidents when subsequently I read in Lyell's *Second Visit:* "The negroes here have certainly not the manners of an oppressed race." He added that they displayed admirable courtesy but knew how to stand their ground when they chose to.[15]

Another incident, illustrating the unpleasant side of southern courtesy, occurred in New Orleans at a time when segregation prevailed in public transportation. People were lining up to enter a bus in ninety-degree heat, a young black woman, heavy with child, among them. I stopped to watch perhaps a dozen well-attired white men board that bus while she waited under an unbearable sun. New Orleans not being New York, I am certain that any of those men would have cut off his right arm before doing such a thing to a white woman, and I suspect that any number of them were mortified at having to do it to a black woman—at not having the courage to behave like civilized human beings, not to mention like southern gentlemen. But of course, a southern gentleman was never expected to show the same courtesy to a black woman or indeed even to notice her. It was for good reason that black women were referred to, in the old days, not merely as "girls" (or even "women," in sharp contradistinction to "ladies"), but less ambiguously as "wenches."

W. E. B. Du Bois, who came closer to the ideal of an aristocrat than any man it has been my honor to meet, once wrote:

> There are two situations where it is hard to be courteous: when courtesy involves public condemnation; and when courtesy is demanded by the discourteous. . . . For a Negro to offer courtesies to white people usually means that the courtesy will be snatched as a right, or angrily refused; even if it is graciously accepted there re-

mains in the Negro's breast the knowledge that he is giving what he, his wife, or his child would never receive under reversed circumstances, and he half despises himself for being a gentleman.[16]

The slaves' standard of formal courtesy toward the whites arose not only from their servile condition but from a sense of justice inherited from Africa and confirmed by the better standards of the whites around them. Above all, courtesy became an instrument in their determined effort to take care of each other in a painful common struggle to live decently. As virtually every possible white and black source attests, blacks treated each other as they treated whites but without the element of protective dissembling. An oppressive system forced them to extend their high standard to those outside their own group, although it denied them proper reciprocity. But to say as much is to say, without in any way slighting the excellent features of antebellum southern white life, that the finest, if rudest, examples of the southern lady and gentlemen were to be found in the quarters even more readily than in the Big House.

The slaves' version of the southern ethos had a special quality. "When Bernsdorf, the great statesman of Denmark, emancipated the peasant serfs on his estate," Fredrika Bremer recalled, "these assembled to a man, and besought him with tears, that he would not give them up but still continue to be their paternal lord and master. . . ." According to Miss Bremer, he refused and said that their children and grandchildren eventually would understand.[17] In the Black Belt during the first half of the twentieth century, Charles S. Johnson, the sociologist, found: "For those [blacks] still living in the country there is, it would appear, one unfailing rule of life. If they would get along with least difficulty, they should get for themselves a protecting white family." Johnson adds that this attitude reflected more than fear. "There is," he notes, "a solid and sympathetic paternalism among some of the white planters toward their Negro dependents which is felt by them."[18]

Beyond racial dependency, a special sense of relationship to a particular person or persons emerges here. The abolitionists who went to the Sea Islands confronted this attitude immediately. When they told the freedmen that the government must be obeyed, they were met with blank stares. Persons, particular human beings, had to be obeyed. What was a government? The assassination of Lincoln stunned the freedmen not only because they had come to love him as a deliverer but because they had great difficulty in imagining that the government, which was protecting them, could survive or indeed had ever existed apart from his person.

The slaveholders for once grasped the slaves' attitude. Edmund Ruffin, in the introduction to his diary, noted that he had transferred his property to his children, who had appointed a manager. He tried to explain the change to his slaves. "But," he added, "I was sure the negroes would continue to regard me as still their master, & their judge of appeals—& the new owners would not assume their full authority & will, but would continue to refer, & to defer, to me, as their father & head of the household."[19] An important feature of this relationship appeared in relief in an unsigned article published in a leading agricultural journal:

> You must provide for him yourself, and by that means create in him a habit of perfect dependence on you. Allow it once to be understood by a negro that he is to provide for himself, and you that moment give him an undeniable claim on you for a portion of his time to make this provision; and should you from necessity, or any other cause, encroach upon his time, disappointment and discontent are seriously felt.[20]

Morris Shepherd, an ex-slave from Oklahoma, gave this white testimony a different twist. His children had told him that Lincoln had set him free, but he did not believe it. He believed his master had, for no northerner had ever given him anything.[21]

The tendency to identify the protective side of paternalism with a particular master and to elevate that master to great heights may be discerned in a comment made by a black boatman to Colonel Miles of the Confederate army. Notwithstanding the clearly "put-on" aspect of the reply, it remains revealing. Asked by Colonel Miles, "Are you not afraid of Colonel Anderson's cannon?" he proclaimed, "No, sar, Marse Anderson ain't darsn't to hit me. He know Marster wouldn't 'low it."[22] Miemy Johnson, an ex-slave from South Carolina, spoke of her master in the context of an event long after the war: "It's a pow'ful comfort to have a brave white man 'round at sich a time 'mongst a passle of terrified niggers, I tells you!" Aunt Nicey Pugh, an ex-slave from Alabama, cut a wider swath:

> But all and all, white folks, den was de really happy days for us niggers. Course we didn't hab de 'vantages dat we has now, but dere

> wus somp'n back dere dat we ain't got now, an' dat secu'aty. Yassuh,
> we had somebody to go to when we was in trouble. We had a Massa
> dat would fight fo' us an' help us an' laugh wid us an' cry wid us.
> We had a Mistus dat would nuss us when we was sick, an' comfort
> us when we hadda be punished.

And George Young of Alabama cut wider still: "All de nations
couldn't rule, jes lak hit is now. De stronges' people mus' rule."[23]

These ideas long outlived the war. The black work songs of the
New South constantly speak of the white "captain," who generally
appears as a mean man but also as one worthy of admiration for
his toughness, strength, and power.[24] In a broader setting, as Ambrosio Donini points out, all slave and seigneurial societies throw
up the figure of the *padrone*, who simultaneously protects and
abuses, nourishes and punishes. So, even when the people seek a
savior, whether in this world or the next, they tend to cast him in
the same mold and thereby to circumscribe the act of rebellion
itself.[25] Perhaps in no greater way did the slaves' acceptance of the
aristocratic ethos, for all its positive contributions, trap them in a
dependency relationship.

However dangerous that trap, other impressive sides of the
slaves' peculiar contribution to the aristocratic ethos also manifested themselves, including a strong sense of shame among the
slaves. To understand it, we shall have to consider the opposing
tendency among the masters. The slaveholders of the nineteenth-
century South did not wallow in guilt over their ownership of
slaves. They took their world for granted. Yet, many perceptive
and knowledgeable historians have interpreted their behavior as
guilt-ridden. In a sense, they have not been mistaken. The whites
of the South inherited an Anglo-Saxon civilization based on religions that profoundly deepened whatever sense of guilt may be
inherent in human experience. But for precisely that reason the
notion that the slaveholders' relationship to their slaves can be
understood as a function of guilt must be scouted. They felt guilt
about everything. But everything in this respect equals nothing.
Their guilt feelings ended, as they began, as a personal matter.
And in no sense can their response to slavery be interpreted as a
function of a pervasive and yet ultimately self-indulgent expression of this general sensibility. Still, for general purposes, it would
not be amiss to regard, however roughly, the white South as a guilt
culture, if only to sharpen our awareness of the black South as the
alternative—a shame culture. "A society that inculcates absolute

standards of morality and relies on men's developing a conscience is a guilt culture by definition," writes Ruth Benedict, "but a man in such a society may, as in the United States, suffer in addition from shame when he accuses himself of gaucheries that are in no way sins." She adds: "Shame is a reaction to other people's criticism. A man is ashamed by being openly ridiculed and rejected. . . ."[26] However the debate over the significance of guilt in the white culture of the white South proceeds, in these anthropological terms it was a guilt culture, and the culture of the black South, like that of Africa, was a shame culture.

Shame, Helen Merrell Lynd tells us in her stimulating book, *On Shame and the Search for Identity*, does not imply acceptance of standards measured against which one has failed. That criticism, characteristic of guilt cultures, does not apply, except inasmuch as all experience both guilt and shame to some extent. Rather, shame implies a sense of inadequacy. The blacks' equivalent of the whites' sense of betrayal upon exposure to the true face of the other grew out of the sense of shame so profoundly manifested in their experience. Mrs. Lynd writes:

> In an experience of shame trust is seriously jeopardized or destroyed. Emphasis may fall on one side or the other: on the questioning of one's adequacy or on the questioning of the values in the world of reality which so contradict what one has been led to expect. Or both may be doubted. In any case, suddenly exposed discrepancy threatens trust. Part of the difficulty in admitting shame to oneself arises from reluctance to recognize that one has built on false assumptions about what the world one lives in is and about the ways others will respond to oneself.[27]

The slaveholders well understood the meaning of shame in the quarters. When Bennet H. Barrow of Louisiana wanted to punish a runaway, he hit upon the idea of exhibiting him on a scaffold in the middle of the quarter on Christmas Day with a red flannel cap on.[28] A slaveholder in Virginia returned a recently purchased seamstress to the slave traders because, although she tried to please, she was too anemic and unskilled to do the job properly. The slave trader wrote back that the poor woman had broken into tears over the "rejection."[29] In Rowan County, North Carolina, in 1865, John Richard Dennett came across a black man whose mistress had not yet told him he had been freed, although he knew as much; still, he planned to work until Christmas and then leave if not paid. But why? "Ye see, master," he explained, "I am ashamed to say anything to her."[30] He may have been ashamed for himself or for her; but if for her, then the evidence of paternalistic identification is even stronger. This strong sense of shame among the slaves helps explain that pride in belonging to "de quality" masters which so many contemporaries and so many later historians have interpreted as servility. In an organic relationship based on reciprocal obligations, pride in belonging to a rich and powerful gentleman constituted the reverse side of shame at belonging to poor white trash, for the slaves could not escape identification with their white folks and had to share the shame they thought their cruel or indifferent or improvident masters ought to feel.

A strong sense of shame—of injured pride—strengthened resistance to insult. James Knox Polk's overseer defended his treatment of a runaway slave by insisting that the slave had not been "insulted in any way."[31] And in 1865, a slave in Georgia, captured by the Yankees, made his way back to his master. The Yankees had laughed at his strong dialect. They had been "impolite" and had failed to respect his "feelin's."[32]

The sense of shame could become a formidable defensive weapon and even lead to grim consequences. A slave who had never suffered the whip one day did, after having been unjustly accused of negligence in an injury to the master's child. He took an axe and chopped off his right hand, exclaiming, "You have mortified me, so I have made myself useless. Now you must maintain me as long as I live."[33] Shame and manly pride went hand in hand. Without a strong sense of shame, however much masters may have been able to turn it to advantage, the slaves could not have developed that pride in themselves and their efforts which provided a means to defend and develop their personalities. They could not easily have produced men like Prince Lambkin, an astonishing if unsung figure in Colonel Higginson's regiment, who could describe a German shopkeeper by saying, "He hab true colored-man heart."[34] Nor could they have produced that splendid temper displayed by Sue, a faithful, efficient, pleasant house servant in the C. C. Jones family. Despite her record of fidelity to the Joneses, she was primarily responsible for convincing the freedmen not to return to the household in 1866. Why? Her husband had elected to leave and she had naturally chosen to go with him. Mrs. Jones tried unsuccessfully to dissuade her and then sharply told her to go immediately. But, she added, as her feelings softened, do not hesitate to return if you are not well treated. The reply: "No, ma'am, I'll never come back, for you told me to go."[35] Sue had been insulted.

The two-sidedness of the shame complex appears in the testimony of Josiah Henson:

> I was as lively as a young buck, and running over with animal spirits. I could run faster, wrestle better, and jump higher than anybody about me. . . . All this caused my master and my fellow slaves to look upon me as a wonderfully smart fellow, and prophesy the great things I should do when I became a man. My vanity became vastly inflamed. . . . Julius Caesar never aspired and plotted for the imperial crown more ambitiously than did I to out-hoe, out-reap, out-husk, out-dance, out-everything every competitor; and from all I can learn he never enjoyed his triumph half as much. One word of commendation from the petty despot who ruled over us would set me up for a month.[36]

So proud a man might be shamed but would not easily take insults from any quarter. Such accounts simultaneously underscore the slaves' dependence upon their masters, their accommodation, and their pride, which together laid the basis for the destruction of the paternalistic relationship. The idea of reciprocity, which in contradictory ways underlay the masters' and the slaves' understanding of paternalism, illuminates this dialectic.

DE GOOD MASSA

If the slave narratives were to be taken at face value, the moonlight-and-magnolias interpretation of slavery might appear to stand up reasonably well. However many reports we find of "de mean massa," we are flooded with those of "de good massa" and of "de bestes' massa in de worl'." Less ebullient ex-slaves also denied mistreatment and insisted that their masters, if not especially generous or lovable, behaved decently.[1] Occasionally, a balanced estimate emerges, laconically delivered: "Some of us had good owners and some of us had bad. . . ."[2] Martin Jackson of Texas, who had had life fairly easy as the son of a cook with the

Confederate army, clear-headed and articulate at the age of ninety, warns us of one of the pitfalls in the narratives:

> Lot of old slaves closes the door before they tell the truth about their days of slavery. When the door is open, they tell how kind their masters was and how rosy it all was. You can't blame them for this, because they had plenty of early discipline, making them cautious about saying anything uncomplimentary about their masters. I, myself, was in a little different position than most slaves and, as a consequence, have no grudges or resentment. However, I can tell you the life of the average slave was not rosy. They were dealt out plenty of cruel suffering.[3]

Conditions and experiences varied enormously, but the important question concerns the standards the slaves applied: What did they expect? or, What did they feel they had to settle for? The compilers of the valuable book based on the narratives, *The Negro in Virginia*, make a helpful observation: "Of great significance, however, is the common statement that worse conditions prevailed 'on the next plantation.'" This observation cuts two ways. Those on plantations with cruel masters saw others who lived much better; hence, an association of their unfortunate condition with slavery per se was tempered, whereas those who lived under more favorable conditions were prevented from taking too sanguine a view of the master-slave relationship. Virtually all slaves experienced "de good massa" and "de mean massa." Either they had belonged to different masters, or their master and mistress differed in virtue, or their overseer differed from their master, or neighboring slaveholders behaved differently from their master.[4]

The slaves disagreed about what constituted a good master but did agree on a minimum. A good master fed, housed, and clothed them at the prevailing standard of decency, as understood by masters and slaves alike. In times of great economic hardship the slaves could see a master's effort to do his best and could excuse some failure; but for the most part excuses did not mean much. They expected the minimum due. The good master allowed the slaves their holidays and good times and, above all, stayed out of their religious life. Beyond this minimum the slaves applied different criteria. With notable exceptions they did not rail against whipping as such, long enforced as a common method of punishment; they did rail against cruel, excessive, and especially arbitrary whipping. A master who used his whip too often or with too much vigor risked their hatred. Masters who failed to respect family sensibilities or who separated husbands from wives could be sure of it. The slaves grieved over the sale of their children but accepted it as a fact of life; however much they suffered, they did not necessarily hate their individual masters for it. But a husband and wife who cared for each other could never accept being parted.

The slaves set their individual priorities. Some would accept much deprivation on one level and little on another; others would reverse the choice. Few expected their masters to be saints and to get top marks on all counts. "De bestes' massa in de worl' " came reasonably close to the highest accolade; "de mean massa" did badly across the board. Between the two, the slaves applied their judgments according to their private rating. Their willingness to make the best of what had to be endured broke through the testimony of an ex-slave, whose hindsight and postemancipation perspective probably only helped make articulate, if in exaggerated form, a widespread feeling among many slaves: "Well, she was good as most any old white woman. She was the best white woman that ever broke bread, but you know, honey, that wasn't much, 'cause they all hated the po' nigger."[5]

The shifting priorities in the slaves' consciousness explain many apparent anomalies. Some slaves described as "kind" not only masters who used the whip often but also those who broke up families with impunity and even those who traded in slaves. An ex-slave from Georgia recalled a slave-trading master by saying, "He wuz a good man an lot uh his slaves stay wid him on duh fahm attuh freedom."[6] To others, such a master ranked as a criminal no matter how well he provided for his slaves or how much leisure he accorded them.

These varied responses reveal both an act of judgment, which in itself carries significance, and an acceptance of the state of things, not as a preference but as a realistic adjustment to a given world. From this very act of qualified acquiescence, the slaves moved to create as much living space as possible. Their acceptance of paternalism allowed them, even in so unjust a relationship, to perceive that they had rights, which the whites could trample on only by committing a specific act of injustice. The practical question facing the slaves was not whether slavery itself was a proper relation but how to survive it with the greatest degree of self-determination.

Did many slaves prefer slavery, as so many whites alleged while taking measures to crush abolitionist activities and to prevent insurrections? "Sometimes," said Annie Flowers, an ex-slave of Louisiana, "I think them days was happier, sometimes dese. But so much trouble done gone over this old haid I ain't sure of nothin' no more. I just don't know." And Jane Booker added, "Sometimes I think I wanted to be free, but I got more to eat than I do now."[7] Andrew Goodman, at the age of ninety-seven, said:

> I was born in slavery and I think them days was better for the niggers than the days we see now. One thing was, I never was cold and hungry when my old master lived, and I has been plenty hungry and cold a lot of times since he is gone. But sometimes I think Marse Goodman was the bestest man God made in a long time. . . . [The slaves cried when told they were free] 'cause they don't know where to go, and they's always 'pend on old Marse to look after them.[8]

Abram Harris, from a small farm with a kind master in South Carolina, thought, "After us was free, de white folks have to teach us just like you teach a child."[9] Another ex-slave recalled his master's announcement of emancipation with the comment, "Nigger was wondering what he was going to do, for he still had to look to the white man, for he didn't know what to do with hisself."[10] Henri Necaise of Mississippi summed up these attitudes:

> To tell de truth, de fact of de business is, my marster took care of me better'n I can take care of myself now.
> When us was slaves Marster tell us what to do. He say, "Henri, do dis, do dat." And us done it. Den us didn't have to think where de next meal comin' from, or de next pair of shoes or pants. De grub and clothes give us was better'n I ever gets now.

After blaming the Yankee carpetbaggers for ruining the country, he continued:

> Dey went and turned us loose, just like a passel of cattle, and didn't show us nothin' or give us nothin'. . . . Dey should-a give each one of us a little farm and let us get out timber and build houses. Dey ought to put a white marster over us, to show us and make us work, only let us be free 'stead of slaves.[11]

Some slaves steadfastly refused to accept freedom on condition that they go to Liberia. They preferred to remain where they were.[12] About ten thousand did go to Liberia, where they compiled an uneven record. They accomplished much under difficult conditions, but allegedly displayed much of the tyrannical temper they had fled. Some oppressed, whipped, and abused the native Africans and too readily fell back into old patterns by relying on public agencies for those kinds of support to which they had grown accustomed during slavery.[13] Afro-American settlers kept up a respectful correspondence with their former masters in the South. Since they had received their freedom from these whites the continued contact was to be expected. But that correspondence included requests for money, supplies, and other forms of assistance, asked for with an air that almost assumed an unyielding obligation.[14] During the antebellum period a few free Negroes, here and there, enslaved themselves in an effort to obtain protection. The proslavery press made much of each occasion, but the very paucity refuted the propagandistic pretensions.[15]

The nostalgia for the good old days that breaks through the slave narratives with disturbing frequency must be set in temporal perspective. Most of the respondents had been children under the slave regime and had not yet suffered its worst miseries. Thus William Henry Towns, who as a child in Alabama had fared well, could say, "Life was kiner happy durin' slavery 'cause we never knowed nothing about any yuther sort of life or freedom."[16] Most ex-slaves had grown old in desperate poverty and many, including those whose rejection of slavery had remained strong or grown stronger, could not help wondering if they would not have been better off as superannuated slaves on the old master's plantation.

Other testimony edges closer to the more typical attitude. Victoria Adams of South Carolina refused to admit to the Yankees that she wanted to be free. She loved her master and mistress and would not hurt them. Yet, she told her interviewer that she preferred freedom: "Any niggers what like slavery time better is lazy people dat don't want to do nothing."[17] "I felt like it be Heaven here on earth to git freedom," exulted Green Cumby of Texas, " 'spite de fac' I allus had de good marster. He sho' was good to us, but you knows dat ain't de same as bein' free."[18] These old people, having long tasted freedom, did not necessarily speak for the slaves of antebellum times. But if they did not come close enough, how shall we account for the hysterical reaction of the whites every time they heard a hint about freedom whispered in the quarters? Henry Palfrey, a planter of St. Mary's Parish, Louisiana, wrote his brother, William, a distressed letter about their other brother, John Gorham Palfrey, who had petitioned to free all the slaves he had inherited from their father's estate. The authorities unanimously rejected the petition, but the newspapers published the story. "I wrote Gorham last evening," fretted Henry Palfrey, "& informed him of the result of his application—& regretted that he should have sent it—owing to the disaffection which it will create among *all* the negroes."[19]

A southern lady, Fredrika Bremer reported, freed her slaves, among whom one went on to considerable economic success. But his son spent him into bankruptcy, and in his old age he had to work hard to pay off the debts. Knowing that he was dying, he went to his old mistress to ask if she would assume the remaining portion of the debt—a mere fifteen dollars—so that he might die with a clear conscience. Of course she would. But, she asked, had you been happier under slavery? No, he replied. Freedom had brought much suffering, but he had been free to choose the responsibilities that brought it.[20] A newly emancipated black, who spoke with unabashed affection for his master, said more simply, "Liberty is as good for us as for the birds of the air. Slavery is not so bad, but liberty is so good."[21]

Despite the hesitations, timidity, and caution, the vibrant freedom themes of the spirituals and the sermons of the black plantation preachers echoed throughout the quarters. The slaves wanted a freedom that gave them more, not less, than they had had in slavery. Hence, the touch of bitterness as well as of nostalgia among the freedmen in their old age, for it was not slavery but a healthier version of its doctrine of reciprocal obligations that remained attractive to them. On the central question of slavery itself most were clear enough. "In slavery," said Margrett Nullin of Texas, "I owns nothin' and never owns nothing.' In freedom I's own de home and raise de family. All dat cause me worryment and in slavery I has no worryment. But I takes de freedom."[22] An unidentified slave spoke with James Stirling in the late 1850s. I am told, Stirling said, that the blacks prefer slavery. "His only answer was a short contemptuous laugh."[23]

The slaves' alleged contentment in slavery and loyalty to the Confederacy, so elaborately celebrated on the political stump during the years after the overthrow of Reconstruction, had not quite convinced their masters during the war. Judah P. Benjamin, the ablest man in the Confederate government, who later changed his mind when faced with the probability of military defeat, argued against arming the slaves on three grounds: the government could not raise the money to compensate masters; the blacks had more important work to do as plantation laborers and construction workers; and the desertion rate would be unacceptably high. General Beauregard, who remained intransigent, invoked Napoleon's horror of popular insurrection and had no doubt about the risks entailed by an armed black population. Confederate officers in the Army of Tennessee, led by General Patrick R. Cleburne, pleaded for black troops in 1864 on the obvious ground, to be accepted by President Davis, that the Confederacy was losing the war and that desperate measures had to be taken. They understood, however, that those enlisted would have to be offered freedom if the Confederacy's weakness were to be turned into a source of strength. "The approach of the enemy," they pointed out, "would no longer find every household surrounded by spies." As if this admission were not sufficiently damning, they added: "The negro slaves of Santo Domingo, fighting for freedom, defeated their white masters and the French troops sent against them . . . and the experience of this war has been so far that half-trained negroes have fought as bravely as many other half-trained Yankees."[24]

Under prodding from General Lee, President Davis and his government finally decided to face up to a hopeless situation and to reach for the dreaded expedient. But the decision came too late for implementation and for the historic test it would have created. The howls of rage from Davis's opponents, even faced with the annihilation of their dreams, remain revealing both for their implicit fears and for the tenacity of the dying order's central myth. Roared Howell Cobb:

> I think that the proposition to make soldiers of our slaves is the most pernicious idea that has been suggested since the war began. . . . You cannot make soldiers of slaves or slaves of soldiers. . . . The day you make soldiers of them is the beginning of the end of the revolution. If slaves make good soldiers, our whole theory of slavery is wrong.[25]

The *Richmond Examiner* joined the assault:

> We have been accustomed to think in this Southern country that the best friends of the Negroes were their own masters. . . . But now the President of the Confederate States opens quite another view of the matter. According to his message it is a rich reward for faithful services to turn a Negro wild. Slavery, then, in the eyes of Mr. Davis, keeps the Negro out of something which he has the capacity to enjoy. . . . If the case be so, then slavery is originally, radically, incurably wrong and sinful, and the sum of barbarism.[26]

Catherine Devereaux Edmondston of North Carolina got a taste of what to expect when some of her neighbors discussed the proposal to draft slaves into the army. The house slaves were listening.

The next day the plantation was deserted. Two earlier entries in her diary indicate that she had prepared herself for the worst:

Nov. 17, 1864: President Davis in his late message suggests the propriety of taking forty thousand slaves and making pioneer laborers and engineers of them—hinting at the promise of ultimate freedom —and pointing plainly to the fact that should we find it necessary to arm our slaves—this forty thousand trained and disciplined body would be the nucleus of the organization. Can one credit it? . . . But that silly Congress should consume their time and our money in a grave discussion over the best means to destroy the country is a depth of folly too deep for me to fathom!

Dec. 30, 1864: We give up a principle when we offer emancipation as a reward or boon, for we have hitherto contended that slavery was Cuffee's normal condition, the very best position he could occupy. . . .[27]

"Mr. Chesnut's Negroes," noted Mary Boykin Chesnut in 1862, "offered to fight for him if he would arm them. He pretended to believe them. He says one man cannot do it." During 1863, she discussed with Mr. Venable the question of arming the slaves. As she summarized their discussion: "Would they fight on our side, or desert to the enemy? They don't go to the enemy now, because they are comfortable where they are, and expect to be free anyway." By November, 1864, she was noting how her husband had told his drivers, who previously had expressed a great desire to fight for the Confederacy in return for freedom, that they might have their chance. "Now," she mused, "they say coolly that they don't want freedom if they have to fight for it. That means they are pretty sure of having it anyway."[28]

White nostalgia for the good old-time darkies who hid the family silver from the hated Yankees has drawn justifiable ridicule in recent years, but it rested on widespread if exaggerated incidents. Slaves and freedmen often rallied to their white folks in times of danger. Since they had always expected protection as well as sustenance in return for labor and loyalty, some readily seized the opportunity to reverse roles and to protect those from whom they had demanded protection. In such terms, and not as Uncle Tomism, the terse comment of Al Roseboro, an ex-slave from South Carolina, must be understood. He had been told to take care of the young massa to whom he had been assigned: "I always did. . . ."[29]

Susan Dabney Smedes gives the more romantic white version,

which nonetheless hints at the complex truth. "They seemed to do better," she thought, "when there was trouble in the white family, and they knew that there was trouble enough when all the young men in the family were off at the wars. . . . They were our greatest comfort during the war."[30] A biographer of Booker T. Washington comes even closer when he recounts, from Washington's autobiographical writings, the events on a small farm in Virginia. When the master's sons came home wounded, the slaves vied with each other for the privilege of caring for them; when one got killed, they mourned sincerely. They did in fact bury the family silver and did stand ready to defend the white family against assault. When emancipation came, they asked their master's advice. For all that, "They rejoiced at the news of every success of the Union armies."[31] John Petty, an ex-slave of South Carolina, spoke with unambiguous joy of freedom, but—

> Us never sassed our white folks like it appears to be the knowledge up North. I've done been there and they thinks us turned our backs on our white folks, but I never seed nothing but scalawag niggers and poor white trash a-doing that, that I ain't.[32]

Elizabeth Keckley, who had worked as a maid for the Jefferson Davises and later for the Lincolns and who exhibited great pride in being a black woman, did not hesitate to cry out in 1865: "Even I, who was once a slave, who have been punished with the cruel lash, who have experienced the heart and soul torture of a slave's life, can say to Mr. Jefferson Davis, 'Peace! you have suffered! Go in peace!' " And Elizabeth Hyde Botume summed up the attitude of the freedmen: "They literally said of their old owners, 'Father, forgive them, for they know not what they do.' "[33]

A drunken soldier on the streets of Columbia, South Carolina, began to abuse a white southern lady. The soldier was armed and ugly. Two blacks, unarmed, immediately intervened to defend her.[34] Charley Williams, an ex-slave, described how Yankee troops ordered his master either to dance for them or to make his blacks dance. He refused on both counts. The blacks moved in and danced, in Williams's account, "trying to please Marster and Old Mistress more than anything." Pleasing or no pleasing, they probably quite knowingly saved a man's life. Another ex-slave recalled wresting a gun from his master and locking him in the smokehouse to keep him from a suicidal confrontation with Union troops.[35] Old Charlie, sole male protector of the mistress of the Henry Tabb plantation in Virginia, stood in the doorway to block the entrance of Union troops. He shook his fist at them: "Don't you know dis is de Tabb place? Ain't you never heard of States' rights? Git on off wid you."[36] Those who wish to read the many such accounts as Uncle Tomism are at liberty to do so, just so long as they do not tax us with misguided judgments about unmanliness. People who risk their lives to defend those perceived to be in their charge, whatever else may be said about them, are acting like nothing if not like men.

The ambiguity of the slaves' and freedmen's talk about freedom comes through two testimonies, which ought to show how even embittered blacks tried to grant the whites the benefit of the gravest doubts and how the organic aspect of paternalism separated itself, to some extent, from slavery as such. People who say that slavery days were better, said Katie Rose of Arkansas, "didn't have no white master and overseer lak we all had on our place. . . . I hear my chillun read about General Lee, and I know he was a good man, but I didn't know nothing about him den, but I know he wasn't fighting for dat kind of white folks."[37] And Charley Moses of Mississippi added: "Slavery days was bitter an' I can't forgit the sufferin'. Oh, God! I hates 'em, hates 'em. . . . If all marsters had been good like some, the slaves would all a-been happy. But marsters like mine ought never been allowed to own Niggers."[38]

The attitudes of the slaves grew out of the adjustment they had made to a paternalistic relationship, within which they had defined their role in their own way. When Uncle Osborne, a carpenter in Georgia, remained to work for wages so that, in a variety of ways, he could take care of the distressed white family, he did not thereby display servility or reject freedom. We know as much because as soon as the worst had passed for the whites, he courteously took himself off to work for himself.[39] "Shorty" Wadley Clemons of Alabama could not stand by and watch his old mistress starve after her husband had died and she had lost her land. He had worked himself into a comfortable station and had become well off; so, he supported her until her death and would have paid for her funeral, had the local whites not decided that he had done more than enough and that they ought to assume responsibility.[40] Charles Davenport of Mississippi stayed with his master after the war. "When I looked at my marster," he explained, "and knowed he needed me, I pleased to stay." Liza Jones of Texas, among many others, told a similar story.[41] The freedmen in the Sea Islands, disappointed and disgruntled as they were by the dashing of their hopes for land, did not enjoy seeing their old masters suffer, whether because they were old masters or because they were human beings in trouble. They offered help and even, when they could, gave them money.[42] When the Union troops entered Richmond a servant told Jennie D. Harrold's mother, who like others had only Confederate money, which is to say no money at all: "Miss Thomasia, I expect to have more money than you have now, in silver and gold, so we wish to give you each a 25 cents to start life with." A nasty thrust? Yes, but more to the point, a comment on how the mighty have fallen.[43]

Three strands run through these incidents: a compassion for others born of their own suffering; the recurring idea of mutual obligations in an organic relationship; and a new sense of having the strength to reverse traditional roles within that organic relationship. Mrs. Chesnut told of an old black man who comforted his destitute master at the end of the war: "When you 'all had de power you was good to me, and I'll protect you now. No nigger, nor Yankee, shall touch you. If you want anything, call for Sambo. I mean, call for Mr. Samuel—that's my name now."[44] As W. E. B. Du Bois expressed it, the blacks "felt pity and responsibility and also a certain new undercurrent of independence."[45] This new sense of responsibility and power, even with its undeniable element of satisfaction in the agony of old tyrants who had caused others agony, fitted within long-established paternalistic patterns. Those patterns retained great strength, but the world had changed nonetheless, for "de bottom rail was on de top." It was no fault of the blacks that their choice of generosity and compassion over retribution and vengeance did not prove adequate "t' keep hit dar."

OUR WHITE FOLKS

The whites came to grief over the self-deception inherent in the idea of a "family, white and black," but they could plead some excuse in encouragement from the blacks themselves. The frequent references to "our white folks" in the slave narratives and in sociological and anthropological reports from the Deep South during the twentieth century warn that the black attitude embraced much more than dissembling. The racial catastrophe that accompanied the whites' moment of truth had its roots in a genuine intimacy, not merely in black pretense. But the blacks' understanding of that intimacy rested on different ground from that of the whites. The implicitly antagonistic definitions of an organic relationship seemingly agreed upon wrought much more havoc than the dissembling and protective deception that also marked the black response to white paternalism.

A variety of comments from black sources expose a much more complex relationship. Elizabeth Keckley had had unpleasant masters and had hardly been a cringing slave in spirit. Yet, when she wrote her mother in 1838, she did not forget the customary gracious message, "Give my love to all the family, both white and black." After the war she spoke with kindness about those whites without hiding their cruelty. Despite everything, she insisted, the master-slave relationship had always been "warm." She explained that, for better or worse, the joys of childhood and of black life, as well as the pain, had become inextricably bound up with those of the whites.[1] Alice Houston, an ex-slave of Texas who stayed with her good masters after the war, said pathetically, "We stayed with Miss Watkins, and here I is an ole nigga, still adoin' good in dis world, atellin' de white folks how to take care of de chillun." The implicit notion of reciprocal service formed part of the attitude and recurred constantly in the reports of ex-slaves. "Long as nigger do right," said John McCoy of Texas, "old Marse pertect him. Old Marse feed he niggers good, too, and we has plenty clothes." Mandy Morrow, who had worked as a cook for Governor Stephen Hogg of Texas and might be expected to have been close to her white folks, nevertheless expressed herself in an illuminating way: "Yes, suh, de Gov'nor am de good man. You knows, when he old nigger mammy die in Temple, him drap all he work and goes to de fun'ral and dat show him don't forgit de kindness."[2]

One theme runs through such testimony: that of reciprocal obligations ("de kindness"). To this extent the slaves' attitude seems to have complemented that of the masters. But a slight, portentous shift of emphasis lay inherent within it, for "de kindness," in the slaves' view, deserved to be repaid with equivalent service and respect. The white doctrine of reciprocal duties, defined from above to equate demands upon the slaves with privileges bestowed by the masters, was edging toward an equation of demands and, therefore, toward an assertion of "rights." That old Mammy of Governor Hogg's had not simply obeyed commands; she had offered "kindness," which cannot be commanded. And the good governor was expected to know it. When these expectations were met, the behavior of an ex-slave like Bill Simms of Missouri becomes comprehensible. An intelligent, articulate man, he took his stand with the Union and condemned pro-Confederate slaves as "ignorant." Yet, he loved his old master and willingly returned to work for him after the war.[3] No less comprehensible becomes the action of those five thousand or so freedmen who boldly struck out to work the southwestern cattle drives and yet fitted easily into an almost feudal pattern of personal loyalty to an accepted chieftain who offered protection and sustenance in return.[4]

Protection had always loomed large. An ex-slave from Tennessee spoke for countless others in praising a stern master who had not spared the whip and who had enforced strict order and discipline. Yet local whites considered the master too soft on his slaves and called them his "free niggers." He had kept a slave mistress and defined his relationship with his people in his own way. As one result, he had prevented the patrols from entering his plantation and bothering his slaves; he had thereby protected them against a dreaded foe.[5] To take another example, Phyllis Jenkins, who had accompanied her husband to Guadeloupe when he was sold for intractability, wrote back in 1803:

My Dear Mother
I imbrace this opportunity to inquire after your health which I hope you happily enjoys with all my family and friends particularly my Mistress—and Children, and Master James and Miss Nancy Blunt—all whom I hope enjoys good health—better than I do at present—pray do not forget Mrs Beasley and family—but I am truly sorry to hear of the Death of my Master, but as I happy enough to find an opportunity of writing you where I am. I hope you will be good enough to write me by all opportunity Directing me as above mentioned, nothing can afford me more pleasure than a letter from you. I have nothing at present to send you but hopes you will be kind enough to write me by all opportunity—but really [?] I am ever to be your affectionate daughter—and always ready to find all Service—but do not forget Mass' Jacke—whom I nurse—tell him I hope he has not

forgot me—since I left you I never sent you any thing but two juggs—by Pollidore, Betsy Whites husband—my love to my brother forchin [Fortune, the driver], & Aron, and Children and believe me ever to be your dutiful Daughter.

PHYLLIS JENNINGS[6]

And Solomon Northup described his father as a man who had always understood slavery to have been a great wrong but who "at all times cherish[ed] the warmest emotions of kindness, and even of affection towards the family, in whose house he had been a bondsman."[7]

The white trauma over the defection of favorite slaves and freedmen needs reconsideration in the light of these expressions, for the self-deception had arisen less from fantasy than from an erroneous perception of something real. William Henry Holcombe of Natchez chatted with a group of slaves who were moving from Alabama to Texas; they had belonged to his cousin. "Some of the older Negroes," he beamed, "remembered my father and mother and their six little boys and crowded up to shake hands with me." Frank E. Steel wrote his family in Ohio from Mississippi: "I have never seen a family show more pleasure at the return of a long-absent parent than Major Redd's servants did at his. Indeed he was obliged to keep 'open house' for two days after his arrival to allow the negroes an opportunity of 'paying their devoirs' to the family."[8]

Kindness as a free act worthy of reciprocation worked both ways. The slaves' view of reciprocity required that acts of kindness by their masters and especially by their mistresses be repaid. Thus, a body servant in Georgia, left behind when his young master went off to war, sent him some valuable cloth, obtained in a trade for the products of his own labor.[9] Thus, common field hands felt an obligation to present Missus with a few eggs or a chicken or some other small gift when she visited the quarters. These gifts would be freely given, but if they did not repay some previous kindness, the slaves could expect to be and normally would be recompensed in some way.[10]

The blacks' sense of having white folks—of being part of a family, white and black—differed from that of the whites in emphasis, but the emphasis meant everything. Sir Charles Lyell asked a black woman in Georgia if she belonged to a white family of his acquaintance, and she replied "merrily," "Yes, I belong to them, and they belong to me." J. W. DuBose recalled after the war the attitude of the typical slave on his Alabama plantation: "He was proud of the beautiful cotton growing under his toil, proud of the majestic corn he cultivated, proud of the colts he broke to the bridle, of the fat hogs he slaughtered for 'our' people. . . . It was to him, all 'ours.' " During and after the war the children in the Sea Islands vied with each other for the privilege of calling the Yankee schoolteachers "my missus." Willie Lee Rose, the distinguished historian, has put their attitude in perspective for us: "Seemingly the possessive pronoun worked both ways."[11] Thus, the freedmen sometimes genuinely welcomed their old masters back and offered every courtesy, but when they did, they expected strict respect for their newly acquired rights, especially to the land. All that had changed were the specifics of a system of reciprocal rights. But that was quite enough.[12] And lest we conclude that their vision of an organic society precluded an appeal to violence, we might reflect on the "joke" going around Salisbury, Rhodesia, in 1960, which might easily have been going around Salisbury, North Carolina, a century earlier. Black riots had erupted in South Africa, and white Rhodesians had begun to shake. Mary Cable, wife of a prominent white man, reported:

> There was a joke going around the Salisbury tea tables about a houseboy and the white lady he worked for. Madam said to the houseboy, "Joseph, I suppose that if there were to be a Kaffir revolution here, you'd kill me." "Oh, no, Madam," said Joseph. "I'd go next door and kill Gilbert's Madam. Then Gilbert would come over here and kill you."[13]

One does not kill a member of one's own family. Still, what has to be done has to be done.

Not many slaves defined what had to be done as the murder of their white folks. On the eve of the war a portion of public opinion in the North expected the slaves to rise once hostilities began, and that which marked hope in the North marked fear in the South. When the time came, the hope and the fear proved groundless. The slaves' response to the war ranged widely and cannot be subsumed under a simple formula. In a variety of ways they helped to bury the Confederate cause, but those ways were of their own choosing and did not follow the scenarios of either their friends or their enemies. The war provided their finest and their worst hour. They displayed superb qualities of self-discipline, decency, restraint, and toughness; they also proved unwilling or unable to take certain measures that, however dangerous, might have helped to avoid the catastrophe of the postwar years. The charge of "cowardice" may be dismissed; too many slaves behaved too well for us to waste time on such nonexplanations. Nor are references to "civilized restraint," however valid up to a point, especially helpful.[14] The specific roots of the slaves' response and the political consequences of their actions require attention.

Here and there insurrectionary plots and even modest risings did occur. In Lafayette County, Mississippi, slaves responded to the Emancipation Proclamation by driving off their overseers and dividing the land and implements among themselves. In 1864, they burned the courthouse and more than a dozen homes in Yazoo City. In a few places they killed their masters or overseers in concerted local actions.[15] No large-scale or general rising took place.

Yet, as Willie Lee Rose says of the Sea Islands, "The revolution began with considerable destruction of property." As their masters scurried for cover and the Federals approached, the slaves smashed cotton gins, looted the Big House, and burned buildings symbolic of the old regime. They looted the fashionable town houses of Beaufort. When necessary, they stood bravely against their old masters. Rarely, however, did they show any disposition to hurt them.[16] On the coast of South Carolina in 1863 and inland by 1865, the whites suffered substantial attacks on their property but few on their persons. In Georgia, Mississippi, Louisiana, everywhere, the story was repeated.[17] Even the presence of militant black soldiers did not much alter the balance between blows at property and restraint toward people. And when possible, even the old courtesy remained, if with a difference. The blacks, reported Kate Stone, were sacking plantations in northern Louisiana in the wake of Federal invasion. Her own people remained as polite as ever, "But you could see it was only because they knew we would soon be gone. We were only on suffrance."[18]

The blacks' distaste for violence against anyone, including and perhaps especially their old masters, did not preclude their defending themselves when they had to and when they could. Rather, it suggested an attitude caught by the sensitive northern free Negro, Charlotte Forten, years before she went south to teach the freedmen. August 11, 1854: "Hatred of oppression seems to me so blended with hatred of the oppressor I cannot separate them." But September 12, 1855: "Oh! it is hard to go through life meeting contempt with contempt, hatred with hatred, fearing, with too good reason, to love and trust hardly any one whose skin is white—however lovable, attractive, and congenial in seeming." Almost a decade later, on January 24, 1863, Miss Forten told of a slave who ran off to the Yankees. His master pursued him and shot him through the arm. He turned, fought, and beat the white man senseless. Miss Forten did not find it necessary to comment upon a feature of the story that some might find most striking. In the face of this extreme provocation, to which he had responded with such manly courage, the slave did not kill his master when he had the opportunity.[19]

Kelly Miller finds the best evidence for the blacks' qualities as a people in their folksongs. "This race," he writes, "uttered the burden of its soul in these songs of sorrow without the slightest tinge of bitterness, animosity, or revenge."[20] One might sense some exaggeration and argue for at least an occasional "tinge," but the point remains well taken. "No Man Can Hinder Me" expresses the positive emphasis of the spirituals. The closest the spirituals come to an appeal for retribution—"And drownded old Pharaoh's army. Hallelu!"—speaks more of justice for the escaping and of a deserved fate for God's transgressors than of vengeance.

Many plantations did have those who dreamed other dreams. Solomon Northup recalled Lethe: "She had sharp and spiteful eyes, and continually gave utterance to the language of hatred and revenge. . . . Pointing to the scars upon her face, the desperate creature wished that she might see the day when she could wipe them off in some man's blood!" She provided the exception to the rule that Northup had laid down.[21] The Lethes had to be restrained partly because their sensibilities were not those of the others but also because, even if they had been, the relationship of forces demanded cooler heads. W. L. Bost, an ex-slave of North Carolina, said, "Then after the War was over we was afraid to move. Just like tarpins or turtles after 'mancipation. Just stick our heads out to see how the land lay."[22] Kate Stone saw more than timidity in the slaves' response to the war: "We would be practically helpless should the Negroes rise, since there are so few men left at home. It is only because the Negroes do not want to kill us that we are still alive." The blacks, she added, were not "revengeful." In 1865, Jane Pringle wrote to Adele Petigru Allston, widow of the great planter and former governor of South Carolina: "You do not run the slightest risk . . . from the negroes unless you try to dispossess them of the property they have seized. . . . No outrage has been committed against the whites except in the matter of property." This attitude of the slaves did not arise overnight. During the Nat Turner rebellion, for example, Mrs. Nathaniel Francis hid in a closet while she listened to the cries of whites who were being murdered in her house. Her fears of being betrayed by her house servants proved groundless. They knew she was there but protected her by their silence. While doing so, however, they quarreled bitterly over the division of her clothes.[23] Ordinary humanity, shrewd restraint, and plantation-nurtured timidity proceeded in concert, or rather, merged into a single stance.[24]

Felix Haywood, an ex-slave of Texas, reflected:

> Did you ever stop to think that thinking don't do any good when you do it too late? Well, that's how it was with us. If every mother's son of a black had thrown 'way his hoe and took up a gun to fight for his own freedom along with the Yankees, the war'd be over before it began. But we didn't do it. We couldn't help stick to our masters. We couldn't no more shoot them than we could fly. My father and me used to talk 'bout it. We decided we was too soft and freedom wasn't goin' to be much to our good even if we had a education.[25]

As if to offer one possible answer, Benjamin Russell, an ex-slave from South Carolina, described how the slaves on his plantation received the news of their emancipation. "Some were sorry," he said, "some hurt, but a few were silent and glad."[26] That a few were silent and glad requires no comment, nor even that some, timid and confused, were sorry. That some were "hurt" does. Freedom brought a newly felt strength along with new fears, and it provided the slaves with the means to contain their own sense of having been betrayed. Yet the sense of betrayal did appear. Not merely some but many felt "hurt," for they felt in danger of being abandoned by those, kind or harsh, on whom they had always relied. The whites' trauma had its parallel among the blacks, for they too had accepted a doctrine of reciprocity. Silas Smith, also of South Carolina, caught the positive and negative sides of the moment: "It was the awfulest feeling dat everything in dem quarters laid down wid dat night, de feeling dat dey was free and never had no marster to tell dem what to do."[27]

The slaves displayed more pride and self-esteem than they are usually credited with, despite the marks of servility and domination they bore. Fanny Kemble provides a clue to this curious ambiguity. "I next proceeded to make up the fire," she wrote, "but, there was universal outcry of horror, and old Rose, attempting to snatch it from me, exclaimed, 'Let alone, missus—let be, what for you lift wood? You have nigger enough, missus, to do it!' " Decades later, during the war, Lucy Chase, a northern teacher to the freedmen, wrote her family from Craney Island, Virginia, that the blacks were "too respectful to fawn and cringe, but ready and expectant to save the whites from all meaningful labor. A broom in my hand brings them to their feet."[28] These blacks accepted a certain division of labor in which they had the short end. For them, it had become a duty, no matter what they thought of individual masters. But so far as possible, they also shaped that duty to suit themselves.

The freedmen, E. S. Philbrick, a northerner, wrote from South Carolina, would work much better if the government would provide the regular allotments of tobacco and molasses they had expected and received from their old masters.[29] Such allotments had never been the slaves' right, according to the theory of the master class; they had merely been privileges bestowed by kind masters who looked after their happiness. To the slaves, however, they had quickly become small parts of their return for services rendered. Anthony Dawson, an ex-slave from North Carolina, explained to his interviewer:

> The nigger during slavery was like the sheep. He couldn't take care of hisself, but his master looked out for him, and he didn't have to use his brains. The master's protection was like the woolly coat. But the 'mancipation come and take off the woolly coat and leave the nigger with no protection and he can't take care of hisself either.

Allen V. Manning, who had lived in Mississippi, Louisiana, and Texas, said of his master, a minister and a kind man: "He treated the Negroes just like they treated him. He been taught that they was just like his work hosses, and if they act like they his work hosses they got along all right. But if they don't—oh, oh!" Charley Williams of Louisiana recalled how his old master said to him, "Charley, you ain't got no sense but you is a good boy." Harriet McFarlin Payne of Arkansas thought, "If all slaves had belonged to white folks like ours, there wouldn't been no freedom wanted." One slave, upon being told by his master that he was free, protested. You, he insisted, brought our people from Africa to America and from North Carolina to Arkansas. Now take care of us.[30]

These attitudes reverberated through the plantation districts of the South well into the twentieth century. David Blont, an ex-slave of North Carolina, remembered how at Cape Fear on hot summer days the master would signal for a swimming break. "After we come out'n de water we would work harder dan ever and de marster was good to us, 'cause we did work and we done what he asked us."[31] Repaying kindness with loyal service was one element in the system of expectations and duties. Lyell hinted at another. A superannuated black woman in Alabama asked her master to free her, for she thought she could do better as a free beggar. But, her master asked, what will you do in winter? The reply: "I will come back to you then, and you will take care of me in the cold weather."[32]

The demand for protection and succor in a strange and hostile white world sounded again and again and could become self-deprecating, as some selections from the South Carolina slave narratives will show. "I knows I'se a nigger," said Samuel Boulware, "and I tries to know my place. If white folks had drapped us long time ago, us would now be next to de rovin' beasts of de woods." The theme of reciprocity in dependence recurs even among the more abject. "Freedom come too soon," thought Moses Lyles. "De nigger was de right arm of de buckra class. De buckra was de horn of plenty for de nigger. Both suffer in consequence of freedom." Granny Cain expressed certainty that she would not be suffering if her old mistress were still alive, for she would have "somebody to take care of you and help you. If my mistress was living I would rather be back in slavery." Louisa Davis might have agreed, for like many others she was being supported in her old age by her "white folks." Charlie Davis revealed how far the tendency in paternalism to destroy the self-reliance of those protected could go. "Boss," he said, "I is kinda glad I is a black man, 'cause you knows dere ain't much expected of them nohow and dat, by itself, takes a big and heavy burden off deir shoulders."[33] And the slaves in Florida put the message into song:

> Don't mind workin' from Sun to Sun
> Iffen you give me my dinner
> When dinner time come.[34]

Ezra Adams summed up the viewpoint:

De slaves on our plantation didn't stop workin' for old marster, even when dey was told dat dey was free. Us didn't want no more freedom than us was gittin' on our plantation already. Us knowed too well dat us was well took care of, wid plenty of vittles to eat and tight log and board houses to live in. De slaves, where I lived, knowed after de war dat they had abundance of dat somethin' called freedom, what they could not eat, wear, and sleep in. Yes, sir, they soon found out dat freedom ain't nothin' 'less you is got somethin' to live on and a place to call home. Dis livin' on liberty is lak young folks livin' on love after they gits married. It just don't work.

Yet, even this black man could add that to enjoy freedom a poor man had to work for himself: "It is sho' worth somethin' to be boss. . . ."[35]

Other blacks displayed much greater self-confidence, although they too sounded the same themes of protection and reciprocity. Stephen McCray of Alabama did not stand alone in taking high ground.

> Every time I think of slavery and if it done the race any good, I think of the story of the coon and the dog who met. The coon said to the dog, "Why is it you're so fat and I am so poor, and we is both animals?" The dog said: "I lay round Master's house and let him kick me and he gives me a piece of bread right on." Said the coon to the dog: "Better then that I stay poor." Them's my sentiment. I'm lak the coon; I don't believe in 'buse.[36]

Closer to the center we have the remarks of Anne Broom of South Carolina, who spoke for many of those whose narratives we have in stressing the expectation of at least a minimal return for work well done.

> You through wid me now, boss? I sho' is glad of dat. Help all you kin to git me dat pension [New Deal social security] befo'-I die and de Lord will bless you, honey. De Lord not gwine to hold His hand any longer 'ginst us. Us cleared de forests, built de railroads, cleaned up de swamps, and nursed de white folks. Now in our old ages, I hope, they lets de old slaves like me see de shine of some of dat money I hears so much talk 'bout. . . .[37]

The range from abject acceptance of slavery through insistence on a decent return to outright defiance should not obscure the underlying thread. Some accepted slavery in fear of freedom; others in awareness of superior force; others only because they were held down by the manifestation of that force. Almost all, however, with lesser or greater intensity, fell into a paternalistic pattern of thought, and almost all redefined that pattern into a doctrine of self-protection. For the masters, paternalism meant reciprocal duties within which the master had a duty to provide for his people and to treat them with humanity, and the slaves had a duty to work properly and to do as they were told. Necessarily, the slaves also had, from the white point of view, incurred an obligation to be grateful. The white point of view, however, rested on a catastrophic misunderstanding.

The slaveholders' rage over the desertion of their pet slaves and, less frequently, over that of their field hands usually included references to "ingratitude." Before the war, the slaveholders were of two minds about the existence of a sense of gratitude among the blacks. Lyell received assurances in Virginia during the 1840s that the slaves were kind, obedient, loving, and grateful.[38] But throughout the antebellum period uneasiness appeared everywhere. As early as 1770, the suspicious and contentious Colonel Landon Carter expressed a view that would recur during the next century: "I think I have the clearest evidence in the world that kindness to a Negroe by way of reward for having done well is the surest way to spoil him. . . . This species of gratitude is seldom experienced in a slave."[39] In the 1830s, Harriet Martineau told of a frost-bitten young runaway who had had to have both legs amputated. He did not attribute his flight to ill-treatment and freely acknowledged that his master and mistress had always shown him kindness. His mistress responded to his flight and subsequent misfortune with rage at his ingratitude. Miss Martineau found complaints about the ingratitude of slaves everywhere. Too shrewd not to see beneath this surface and yet incapable of explaining anything to her hosts, she became "heartsick."[40]

War and defeat brought white and black attitudes to the fore. Fitzgerald Ross, strongly pro-Confederate on his tour of army camps, met a soldier from Louisiana: "He told me that if he met a negro in a fight, he should give him no quarter—that they had always treated the negroes well, and if they fought against them now, they deserved no quarter, and he, for one, should give them none."[41] A northern woman who had settled in North Carolina upon marrying a planter wrote two letters to her parents, which, taken together, tell a story. The first, written in 1856: "I wish as sincerely as you possibly can that we lived near you. . . . And, yet, to gain that end I should be very unwilling to sell our servants. I know that they are kindly cared for now, and they might easily fall into worse hands." The second, written in 1867: "As for the hired help, I get along fast. Change almost every month. Three have run away during the last few months that we had clothed up to be decent. They came to us all but naked. They are an ungrateful race."[42]

Northerners, including the sympathetic missionaries who went to the Sea Islands, could not understand the apparent lack of gratitude in the freedmen.[43] Sidney Andrews, a northern reporter, told of a planter whom an ostensibly well-treated black man had beaten up. "It never don't do no good," the planter said to Andrews, "to show favor to a nigger, for they's the most ongratefullest creeturs in the world." The yeomen farmers, according to Andrews, also argued that ingratitude marked the blacks as a race. A former Confederate soldier told him that the kindest and most benevolent masters had suffered the worst manifestations of their ingratitude.[44] In a calmer tone a planter at Lynchburg, Virginia, sadly suggested to John Richard Dennett: "I begin to believe that they are without gratitude. Mine appear to have forgotten all the kindness and lenity with which they have been treated by me and my family."[45]

Matthew Gregory Lewis, best known as the author of *The Monk*, who spent some time on his Jamaican plantation in 1816 and left us a notable record of his experience and impressions, defended his slaves against the charge of ingratitude, as familiar in the Caribbean as in the United States. No, he insisted, not ungrateful, "only selfish." He explained, "They love me very well, but they love themselves a great deal better." He ended his book with a tribute to their "gratitude, affection, and good-will." Earlier in his book he had made an observation that might have helped him to understand the slaves' attitude, had he reflected on it. Jamaican blacks, he wrote, always called ingratitude "bad manners."[46]

But just what is gratitude? Why did the slaveholders dwell on it so? And why did the slaves, who showed so little spirit of vengeance and so much kindness toward distressed whites who had hurt them in the past, earn such a reputation? Mrs. Mary Jones revealed much in a letter to Charles C. Jones, Jr.: "If it be dreadful to have the cry of the poor and the oppressed rising up to God against us, how sweet like incense poured forth their tributes of gratitude and affection, their prayers and benedictions."[47] In society much turns on the giving and receiving of equivalences, but where equivalence is out of the question, gratitude enters as a substitute. People are expected to be grateful not so much for the object received as for the experience of the giver himself. Between equals gratitude becomes a mediating force, which binds men into an organic relationship.[48] But paternalism rested precisely on inequality. The masters desperately needed the gratitude of their slaves in order to define themselves as moral human beings. The slaves, by withholding it, drove a dagger into their masters' self-image. But their purpose had less to do with their masters, one way or the other, than with something entirely their own—something entirely, to use Lewis's word, "selfish."

The slaves impaled their masters on the central point of slave-holding hegemonic ideology—the dependency relationship. The Malagasy, like other colonial peoples, suffered accusations of ingratitude from their French masters. Like the slaveholders of the Old South and like colonialists everywhere, the French first did everything to instill—or reinforce—a dependency complex in their subjects and then howled with rage when they met ingratitude. But what else should they have expected? As Octave Mannoni writes: "Dependence excludes gratitude. That this is so is shown by the fact that we have to *teach* European children to be grateful, and even then there is an element of hypocrisy in it, for the child cannot really learn gratitude until he has attained a certain independence."[49]

Gratitude implies equality. The slaveholders had committed the grotesque blunder of assuming that it could be forthcoming from a people who had had an acceptance of inequality literally whipped into them. The slaves' ingratitude was not incompatible with a measure of good will toward particular masters, and it was entirely compatible with an acceptance of—indeed, a demand for —protection and support. The slaves had turned the dependency relationship to their own limited advantage. Their version of paternalistic dependency stressed reciprocity. What, then, were they supposed to be grateful for? From their point of view, the genuine acts of kindness and material support, to which they were by no means insensible, were in fact their due—payment, as it were, for services loyally rendered. And the crowning irony was that their own services rendered were precisely those offered within the dependency relationship itself.

To the slaves, the white point of view looked a bit bizarre, and the very meaning of paternalism shifted to one of interdependence. If the master had a duty to provide for his people and to behave like a decent human being, then his duty had to become the slave's right. Where the masters preferred to translate their own self-defined duties into privileges for their people—an utter absurdity the illogic of which the most servile slave could see through—the slaves understood duties to be duties. Because they knew that their masters depended upon their labor, which they sometimes even preferred to think freely given despite the obvious coercion—hence their strictures to Fanny Kemble and Lucy Chase upon manual work—they felt that they had earned their masters' protection and care.

Out of necessity they had made an uneven agreement, but it was nonetheless an agreement. In this context the apparent anomalies begin to clear. Any given slave on any given day might decide he had had enough and kill his overseer or even his master. But in too many instances, "good Negroes" suddenly turned into murderous avengers. These instances foreshadowed the white trauma of the war and postwar years, for they stemmed from the same root. The slaves had made their agreement, and most did their best to keep it, whether from necessity or honor or both. Hence, they would usually submit calmly to whipping for some wrongdoing, as conventionally defined, but would become enraged at being punished arbitrarily or for something they did not feel they had done. And they resented insults. Their explosions or, less dramatically, their sullen withdrawals displayed a feeling the slaveholders themselves would come to know—a feeling of having been betrayed. The slaves' acceptance of paternalism, therefore, signaled acceptance of an imposed white domination within which they drew their own lines, asserted rights, and preserved their self-respect.

The slaves thereby provide an excellent illustration of Antonio Gramsci's incisive thesis on popular consciousness. The active man of the masses, he writes,

> has two theoretical consciousnesses (or one contradictory consciousness), one implicit in his actions, which unites him with all his colleagues in the practical transformation of reality, and one superficially explicit or verbal which he has inherited from the past and which he accepts without criticism. . . . Nevertheless, this (superficial) "verbal" conception is not without consequence; it binds him to a certain social group, influences his moral behavior and the direction of his will in a more or less powerful way, and it can reach the point where the contradiction of his conscience will not permit any action, any decision, any choice, and produces a state of moral and political passivity. Critical understanding of oneself, therefore,

comes through the struggle of political "hegemonies," of opposing directions, first in the field of ethics, then of politics, culminating in a higher elaboration of one's own conception of reality.[50]

The masters and the slaves ended in the same place. Consider the question once more from the masters' point of view. For the sake of their own self-image they had to force themselves to believe that they sought happiness for their slaves. But the "happiness" of the slaves could never have arisen from an acceptance of slavery. At best, it had to arise as a function of the living space created by the paternalistic compromise forced on them. That living space meant the possibility of the creation of an autonomous spiritual life—a religion of their own with which they could be "happy"—that is, they could live in reasonable peace with themselves. The masters, seeing their apparent contentment, took credit and congratulated themselves for the slaves' acceptance of slavery, whereas in fact the slaves had only accepted the limited protection that even slavery had to offer, while acknowledging the reality of the power over them. The masters then had to hold the slaves' religion in contempt, for in truth they feared it. And properly so, for it meant that the slaves had achieved a degree of psychological and cultural autonomy and therefore had successfully resisted becoming extensions of their masters' wills—the one thing they were supposed to become. It made all the difference that the masters' claims to be bestowing privileges were greeted by the slaves as a recognition of their own rights. "Men," writes Gramsci, "when they feel their strength and are conscious of their responsibility and their value, do not want another man to impose his will on theirs and undertake to control their thoughts and actions."[51] The everyday instances in which "docile" slaves suddenly rebelled and "kind" masters suddenly behaved like wild beasts had their origins, apart from frequent instabilities in the participating personalities, in this dialectic. Master and slave had both "agreed" on the paternalistic basis of their relationship, the one from reasons of self-aggrandizement and the other from lack of an alternative. But they understood very different things by their apparently common assent. And every manifestation of that contradiction threatened the utmost violence.

The slaves defended themselves effectively against the worst of their masters' aggression, but they paid a high price. They fought for their right to think and act as autonomous human beings, but it was a desperate fight in which they could easily slip backward. We still hear the words of such black leaders as the late Malcolm X and Dr. Martin Luther King, admonishing their people to get off their knees and act like men. Indeed, such authorities as Imamu Amiri Baraka and Stanley Elkins have insisted that the slaves had been emasculated and could not become men at all. This judgment cannot be sustained by the evidence. Most found ways to develop and assert their manhood and womanhood despite the dangerous compromises forced upon them. They had manifested strength. But the legacy of paternalism, no matter how brilliantly manipulated to protect their own interests, kept the slaves and generations of later blacks from a full appreciation of that individual strength. And the intersection of paternalism with racism worked a catastrophe, for it transformed elements of personal dependency into a sense of collective weakness. Thus, Colonel Higginson confronted black troops who wanted the whites out of their lives and yet placed "childlike confidence" in one or two white officers— who could not wholly sever their deep commitment to a paternalistic dependency, within which they asserted themselves as strong men, from the effects of a white racism they were bravely ready to challenge.[52] In Gramsci's terms, they had had to wage a prolonged, embittered struggle with themselves as well as with their oppressors to "feel their strength" and to become "conscious of their responsibility and their value." It was not that the slaves did not act like men. Rather, it was that they could not grasp their collective strength as a people and act like political men. The black struggle on that front, which has not yet been won, has paralleled that of every other oppressed people. It is the most difficult because it is the final struggle a people must wage to forge themselves into a nation.

SOME VALIANT SOLDIER HERE

The slaves' record during and after the war lends itself to opposite readings. The vast majority neither struck out for freedom nor cheerfully served the Confederate cause. Those who see in their responses evidence of docility and servility misread behavior that, at most, exhibited a political paralysis which requires close examination; those who see evidence of militant opposition to the regime and of a "general strike" (the term is W.E.B. Du Bois's) come much closer to the truth but claim too much. Sidney Andrews guessed in 1865 that only 10 percent of the blacks of North Carolina had left their plantations; the rest had stayed and were trying to work in familiar surroundings in order to accumulate a little property. He scoffed at white fears of a general rising at Christmas aimed at seizing the land. The blacks, he wrongly thought, were passive and, he rightly thought, knew too well that they lacked the power to command events in that way.[1] North Carolina's strategic position between the battle zones in Virginia and the South Carolina coast gave its food-growing capacity a special role. Without steady black labor to build fortifications and produce the crops, Confederate North Carolina would have collapsed early in the war.[2]

In Virginia, closer to the Yankee lines, the slaves responded in about the same way. James H. Brewer's careful study shows a desertion rate of about 10 percent and concludes that compulsory black labor effectively sustained the Confederate war effort in all phases of military and economic performance. In the particular case of the essential Tredegar ironworks, as Charles B. Dew reveals, black defections to the Yankees did not swell until June, 1864. Before that, when slaves deserted the dangerous underground pits, they usually ran home to their plantations, not to the Yankees.[3] But the slaves faced the Confederacy's greatest army, the failure of the Union army to launch large-scale raiding parties, and the general uncertainties of the war. Flight to the Union lines usually required daring, courage, physical strength, and a greater degree of confidence in the intentions of the invading troops than the slaves had reason to have. The danger of capture by the Confederates, to be followed by summary execution, made many pause. The slaves rarely had shoes to wear on long journeys over rugged terrain. The swamps and woods inspired fear in people who were not accustomed to being far from home. Securing food under wartime conditions posed a big problem. The slaves hesitated to leave homes, families, friends, and to strike out on so uncharted and doubtful a course. Their determination to stay in place itself propelled them into flight, for many did not desert the plantations until their masters tried to "refugee" them to areas well behind the battle lines. The combination of hesitation and initiative manifested itself in Mississippi, where at first the slaves performed their plantation tasks adequately and produced ample supplies of food for the war effort—although the Confederate government bungled the distribution—but in 1863 and subsequently, when the Yankees drew close and the Confederate army no longer effectively commanded its own terrain, the desertions began. Where the slaves could not or would not desert, they slowed down the pace of work appreciably.[4]

The slaves were staying calm. Occasionally, some would run great risks to get food or supplies for their white families or to render exemplary service in some other way.[5] These incidents demonstrated a sense of personal responsibility and loyalty to particular whites. Only rarely did slaves defiantly take pro-Confederate ground as a matter of political choice.[6] Even those who accepted a certain passivity during the war had their own vision of what they had done. Black delegates to a freedmen's convention in North Carolina in 1865 drew up a conciliatory petition to the Constitutional Convention which asserted that cordial relations had existed between the races and which pretended to believe that slaves had deserted only bad masters. With dignified restraint, however, they made their point:

> Though it was impossible for us to be indifferent spectators of such a struggle, you will do us the justice to admit that we have remained throughout obedient and passive, acting such part only as has been assigned us, and calmly waiting upon Providence. Our brethren have fought on the side of the Union, while we have been obliged to serve in the camp, to build fortifications, and raise subsistence for the Confederate army. Do you blame us that we have, meantime, prayed for the freedom of our race?[7]

Thus, the heroic efforts of black troops, Union spies, and runaways represented the exception—a judgment that will surprise only those who expect heroic efforts from majorities without the resources to impose a stern collective discipline on themselves. Frederick Douglass understood that the slaves could not be expected to move as a mass in opposition to the regime and that a struggle to convince them to assert themselves would have to be waged inside and outside the South. "The very stomach of this rebellion," he wrote, "is the negro in the condition of a slave. Arrest that hoe in the hands of the negro and you smite rebellion in the very seat of its life."[8] Lee and Davis, as well as Grant and

Lincoln, understood the slaves' importance, but political pressures in the North resulted in measures that hardly reassured the slaves as to Federal intentions. It was one thing for the slaves to hope that a Union victory would free them; it would have been quite another for them to make the foolhardy error of transforming that hope into a certainty in the face of the North's manifest racism or even to assume that freedom under such auspices would prove a blessing. The bold spirits gambled; the majority waited for a sign.[9] Too often, the behavior of their northern "friends" must have made them recall the chilling words that Jesus poured over the Pharisees: "And there shall no sign be given unto [ye], but the sign of the prophet Jonas" (Matthew 16:4).

The more dramatic efforts of the slaves in their own cause achieved their peak moment when Robert Smalls and a band of fellow blacks took over the steam-powered ship, *The Planter*, with stolen guns aboard, and deftly sailed it past Confederate batteries to deliver it into Union hands. "I thought," the future congressman from South Carolina remarked, "that 'The Planter' might be of some use to Uncle Abe."[10] As for the dangerous matter of spying, Allan Pinkerton, chief of the United States Secret Service, who later went on to less admirable work, remarked when on a spying expedition to Memphis in 1861, "Here, as in many other places, I found that my best source of information was the colored man." Particularly valuable, he added, were those who were working for the Confederate army.[11]

The caution displayed by so many other slaves reflected their experience with the Yankees. "In the Civil War," writes the South's greatest historian, "the Negroes who crowded into Union lines were made to order for the role of scapegoat. The treatment they received at the hands of their liberators makes one of the darkest pages of war history." Another "shameful chapter," he adds, concerned the treatment of the almost 180,000 blacks who served in the Union army. In the background lurked a fierce white racism, which, although courageously fought by some northern whites, exploded in antiblack violence, euphemistically called "race riots," in Cleveland, Cincinnati, Chicago, Detroit, Buffalo, Albany, Brooklyn, and New York City; in campaigns to restrict the civil rights of blacks in the northern states; and, most absurdly, in efforts to exclude blacks from fighting in a war that would determine the fate of their own people.[12]

Invading armies rarely behave well, as the performance of the

German, Soviet, American, Indian, Nigerian, and Israeli armies among others in recent decades grimly reminds us. But, as the American performance in Korea and Vietnam especially suggests, they may be expected to behave in a particularly disgusting manner when they consist of troops from a racist culture who are turned loose on defenseless civilians of an ostensibly inferior race. Union troops raped black women with an impunity that would have outraged the white South, had it not had so uneasy a conscience on this matter. Even more shocking—if only because assaults on women are, however sickeningly, to be expected from occupying soldiers—was the looting of the slave cabins. That did shock the white South. The spectacle of a liberating army's stealing the meager possessions of poor blacks made a deep impression on all who witnessed it. But one soldier put it all in perspective. Rebuked by a slave woman for stealing her quilts when he was supposed to be fighting for the freedom of black people, this gallant shouted, "You're a goddam liar. I'm fighting for $14 a month and the Union."[13] Those who choose to disregard the testimony of the slaveholders on these outrages, including the wanton murder of blacks who refused to leave their homes or who resisted abuse, can hardly doubt the corroborative testimony in the slave narratives or the pained reports of abolitionists like Lucy Chase. Henry D. Jenkins, an ex-slave from South Carolina, remembered the Yankees as "a army dat seemed more concerned 'bout stealin' than they was 'bout de Holy War for de liberation of de poor African slave people."[14] Fortunately, many officers and common soldiers intervened to prevent abuses, and many more at least abstained from perpetrating them. The record was by no means wholly bad, and a large part was splendid. But enough damage had been done to shake the confidence of the blacks, to add plausibility to Confederate propaganda about Yankee intentions, and to caution the boldest slaves against taking anything for granted.

Slowly, after the Emancipation Proclamation and especially after the appearance of Union troops, the slaves began to edge toward support of the Union cause—that is, toward a willingness to accept the abuses and disillusionments as part of the price to be paid for a freedom they could see coming. A white woman in Louisiana noted on March 12, 1862, that with the Yankees approaching, the slaves were becoming even more frightened than their masters. But by November 15, with the Yankees arriving and apparently behaving well, she wrote: "Oh yes, the Negroes are very,

very sweet! They [the Yankees] seem to gain all their information from the *unbleached gentlemen and ladies*. They asked a Negro man if any rebbles [*sic*] in town. 'Oh yes, plenty in every house!' "[15]

The slaves' disgust at the Yankees had another root. They did not only react to the abuses heaped upon themselves; they also reacted against the destruction of the plantations, which, however necessary as a war measure, often seemed to them wanton cruelty and evil. One ex-slave after another recalled with disgust the devastation wrought by Union troops, especially the burning of homes and the seizing of food supplies.[16] Those plantations that the Union troops were burning happened to be their homes and those crops their food supply. The harsh measures applied by Sherman's troops on their way to the sea and then north toward Virginia may be defended as necessary war measures, but the slaves found it difficult to perceive any connection between this destruction, no matter how necessary to the Union cause, and their own hopes for freedom and for land. They increasingly saw the plantations as their own property, and they took their razing personally. "Our Darkies," said George Briggs, an ex-slave from South Carolina, "tried hard to be obedient to our master so dat we might obtain [keep] our pleasant home."[17]

White and black troops did not behave in the same way. When James Montgomery, a white Kansas jayhawker, ordered the black troops under his command to burn the town of Darien in Georgia, they obeyed orders but without enthusiasm. Except under such orders they had done their best to behave scrupulously and to bring down no censure upon their people.[18]

The freedmen's land hunger marked the extent to which they had prepared themselves to break the old dependencies and assert themselves as free men. Demands for the division of the land reverberated during Reconstruction and demonstrated how closely the slaves had come to associate freedom with economic independence. They could not take up the gun for it in a country occupied by white troops. That they did not organize themselves more effectively in politics, if only to protect themselves against the subsequent terror and defrauding of established claims, shows how frail their new position was—how far they had to go to transform their newly proclaimed aspirations, which were not necessarily new aspirations, into an effective collective movement. An understanding of their weakness requires a closer look at the old plantation dependency, at the world-view it nurtured, and at the details of their lives as slaves. But the emergence of the aspiration demonstrates the limits beyond which their acceptance of plantation paternalism did not drive them.[19]

Had Draconian war measures been linked with the blacks' own aspirations and even had the torch been applied much more widely than in fact it was, the slaves' sentiment for "de ole plantation" and "our pleasant home" might well have given way to the exhilaration of participating in a destruction perceived as constructive. As it was, they found themselves in the infuriating position of knowing themselves to have been the chief victims of a regime they wanted destroyed without recourse to vengeance and unnecessary personal suffering and yet having to watch others, who had not so suffered, take vengeance for reasons that were at best puzzling and at worst contemptible.

The slaves sometimes gave way to self-denigrating cynicism. One asked another if the Emancipation Proclamation meant the general arming of the slaves. "Yo' talkin' fool talk, nigger!" was the reply. "Ain't yo' nebber seen two dogs fightin' ober bone 'fo' now? Well, den, yo' ain't nebber seen de bone fight none, is yo'?"[20] But in the end they did fight, some with gun in hand or by brave desertions and many more quietly and even timidly by slowing down production and forcing themselves upon a sometimes unwilling army of liberation. Julius Lester, discussing the resistance of the Federals to the first wave of slave deserters, comments appropriately: "As far as the slaves were concerned, the 'bluecoats,' as they called the northern army, had come to liberate them, and they weren't going to take no for an answer."[21] As the war dragged on, the slaves' resolve, even in silence, stiffened. Perhaps nothing helped so much to stiffen it as the electrifying arrival of black Union troops.

The greatest significance of the black troops' worthy effort did not lie in the demonstration of black manhood to white America. They did receive acclaim and did score important points there. But black soldiers had fought bravely for their country during the Revolution and especially during the War of 1812, when they won a ringing proclamation from Andrew Jackson for their bravery at the battle of New Orleans. White memories proved short. They were to prove short again after the Spanish-American War and especially after World War I, when black servicemen returned from Europe to face the worst orgy of lynching ever to disgrace our country.[22] The greatest significance lay, rather, in their contribution to the historical development of their own people.

The history of how the North had to be dragged against its will into turning the war into a war against slavery and into recruiting black troops needs no review here. Nor does the history of the discrimination against those blacks who finally had to be recruited to help save a flagging war effort.[23] The recruitment, when it came, virtually destroyed slavery in the border states of the Union. The promise of freedom for those enlisting helped; the promise of freedom for the families of those entering helped much more.[24] Notwithstanding evidence of considerable coercion in some areas, blacks throughout the Union signed up in impressive numbers to free their brethren. They never doubted that, whatever others might say or do, they were fighting for a great deal more than fourteen dollars a month—which they did not get anyway—and the Union.

The record of these troops in battle became a political and ideological plaything, with a deluge of lies about their alleged cowardice under fire and general ineffectiveness and of accolades for supposedly unprecedented heroism. The truth is that they overcame unspeakable insults and discrimination, not to mention inexperience and insufficient training, to acquit themselves well. Like most armies, they had bad moments as well as heroic ones. On balance, they performed with honor—which was enough.

But when some of President Andrew Johnson's Reconstruction governors and military officers addressed the freedmen right after the war, they blithely informed even the veterans of the black regiments that blacks had had no part in the struggle for their own freedom, that the war had been a white man's affair, that equality remained something to be earned by future effort, and that blacks had to prove their worth by staying on the land and calling their old master, master, and their old mistress, mistress. The freedmen everywhere heard this splendid oration in one form or another from Yankee officers. To the satisfaction of Laura E. Buttolph of the slaveholding Jones family in Georgia, "The Nigs were quite disgusted."[25] Nor was this message delivered only to those whom insensitive officials perceived to have been passive during the days of hard fighting. Listen to the words of James Montgomery as he tried to intimidate his black troops into accepting a lower rate of pay than the whites with whom they were fighting side by side. "I was the first person in the country," he crowed, "to employ niggers and a lot of mules; and you know a nigger and a mule go well together."[26] In such accents did this worthy representative of a conquering bourgeoisie address the indignant heroes of the battle of Fort Wagner, whom he had had the honor to command.

The black troops did something as important as their fighting. They transformed the black countryside, or as much of it as they were permitted to reach. Imagine the impact on the more timid slaves when they saw black men, many of them newly freed from slavery, in the uniform of their country, occupying the plantation districts, singing:

> Don't you see the lightning?
> Don't you hear the thunder?
> It isn't the lightning,
> It isn't the thunder,
> It's the buttons on
> The Negro uniforms!

and their own version of "The Battle Hymn of the Republic":

> We are done with hoeing cotton,
> We are done with hoeing corn.
> We are colored Yankee soldiers,
> As sure as you are born.
> When Massa hears us shouting,
> He will think 'tis Gabriel's horn,
> As we go marching on.[27]

The slaves marveled at the soldiers' pride in dealing with whites, including their own officers, at their self-control and self-confidence, at their determination to make the occupying officials keep their promises. The slaveholders marveled too, but in quite another way. The Beast of the Apocalypse had arrived. The black troops encouraged slave desertions, dealt firmly with abusive whites, and frightened everyone. These slaveholders rarely commented, however, on what their own testimony makes clear—that the black soldiers eschewed vengeance and personal vindictiveness and attended to the business of strengthening the morale and position of their own people. The slaveholders had long feared precisely that result, much more than they ever feared for their lives.

Writing in 1866, John Richard Dennett claimed that the slaveholders of Alabama regarded their blacks as much less militant and troublesome than those of Georgia.[28] Perhaps they were right. The slaves in Georgia had felt the presence of the Union army, had seen their vaunted masters thoroughly humbled, and had had greater contact with black troops, including many recruited from their own quarters. The caution and timidity of so many slaves do not require elaborate explanation; the new spirit of so many others does. They had begun to feel their strength and to calculate their responsibilities. They had begun, however hesitantly, to learn the meaning of the words that John M. Langston had used in Ohio in 1862 in urging fellow blacks to resist provocations and to join the army despite humiliating discrimination: "Pay or no pay, let us volunteer. The good results of such a course are manifold. But this one alone is all that needs to be mentioned in this connection. I refer to thorough organization. This is the great need of the colored Americans."[29]

Those black troops represented the first great encounter of the free Negroes of the North, as well as the South, with the slaves of the countryside. For the first time on a mass scale they could all see how slavery and freedom shaped men and women differently and yet how much they had in common as black men and women. They could see, that is, a black nation at its genesis.

BOOK TWO

THE ROCK AND THE CHURCH

Upon this rock I will build my church; and the gates of hell shall not prevail against it.

—Matthew 16:18

PART 1

OF THE GOD OF THE LIVING

But as touching the resurrection of the dead, have ye not read that which was spoken unto you by God, saying,

I am the God of Abraham, and the God of Isaac, and the God of Jacob? God is not the God of the dead, but of the living.

—Matthew 22:31–32

THE CHRISTIAN TRADITION

In this secular, not to say cynical, age few tasks present greater difficulty than that of compelling the well educated to take religious matters seriously. Yet, for all except the most recent phase of the history of a minority of the world's peoples, religion has been embedded in the core of human life, material as well as spiritual. Bishop Berkeley spoke a simple truth: "Whatever the world thinks, he who hath not much meditated upon God, the human mind, and the *summum bonum* may possibly make a thriving earthworm, but will most indubitably make a sorry patriot and a sorry statesman."[1]

The philosophical problem of religion, its truth and falsehood, represents a domain only partially separate from that of politics.[2] Since religion expresses the antagonisms between the life of the individual and that of society and between the life of civil society and that of political society, it cannot escape being profoundly political.[3] The truth of religion comes from its symbolic rendering of man's moral experience; it proceeds intuitively and imaginatively. Its falsehood comes from its attempt to substitute itself for science and to pretend that its poetic statements are information about reality. In either case, religion makes statements about man in his world—about his moral and social relationships—even when it makes statements about his relationship to God. Even when a man's adherence to a religion is purely formal or ritualistic, essential elements of his politics are thereby exposed, for participation in rites normally means participation in social acts that precede, rather than follow, individual emotional response. He enters, usually as a child, into a pattern of socially directed behavior that conditions his subsequent emotional development and that, from the beginning, presupposes a community and a sense of common interest.[4] For good reason the whites of the Old South tried to shape the religious life of their slaves, and the slaves overtly, covertly, and even intuitively fought to shape it themselves.

The religion of Afro-American slaves, like all religion, grew as a way of ordering the world and of providing a vantage point from which to judge it. Like all religion it laid down a basis for moral conduct and an explanation for the existence of evil and injustice. The religion of the slaves manifested many African "traits" and exhibited greater continuity with African ideas than has generally been appreciated. But it reflected a different reality in a vastly different land and in the end emerged as something new. If black religion in America today still echoes Africa and expresses something of the common fate of black people on four continents, it has remained nonetheless a distinct product of the American slave experience. It could not have been other. But the religion of the slaves became Christian and unfolded as a special chapter in the general history of the Christian religions.

The notion of Christianity as pre-eminently a religion of slaves arose long before Nietzsche's polemics, which nonetheless must be credited with imparting to it special force and clarity. "The Christian faith, from the beginning," Nietzsche insists, "is sacrifice: the sacrifice of all freedom, all pride, all self-confidence of spirit; it is at the same time subjection, self-derision, and self-mutilation."[5] This cruel religion of painful subjection, he continues, softened the slaves by drawing the hatred from their souls, and without hatred there could be no revolt.[6] Africans eventually provided their own version of this interpretation of Christianity's political role. According to their widespread saying: "At first we had the land and you had the Bible. Now we have the Bible and you have the land."

The Nietzschean view of Christianity contains an element of truth, but remains a one-sided and therefore superficial judgment upon a religion that carried the ideas of spiritual equality and of the freedom of the will and soul across Europe and the world. Christianity has been a powerful conservative force, but it has been other things as well, even for slaves. Certainly, as Ernst Troeltsch suggests, its political conservatism—its willingness to render unto Caesar the things which are Caesar's—appeared as a powerful tendency from its beginnings in a patriarchal family based on strict submission of women to men, and worked its way out in slave and seigneurial society.[7] Certainly, Karl Kautsky has a point when he argues that ancient slaves obeyed their masters out of fear, whereas Christianity raised the spineless obedience of the slaves to a moral duty incumbent even upon free men.[8] However true, these strictures constitute only one side of that process we know as the history of the Christian religion. To see only that side is to surrender all chance to understand the contribution of Afro-American Christianity to the survival and mobilization of black America.

Early Christianity and the historical Jesus need not be interpreted as politically revolutionary, in either a social or a national-liberation sense, as some radical critics have tried to do.[9] The living history of the Church has been primarily a history of submission to class stratification and the powers that be, but there has remained, despite all attempts at extirpation, a legacy of resistance that could appeal to certain parts of the New Testament and especially to the prophetic parts of the Old. The gods must surely enjoy their joke. Christianity's greatest bequest to Western civilization lies in its doctrines of spiritual freedom and equality before God —those flaming ideas that Nietzsche and so many others have worked so hard to drown in contempt—but this bequest, these doctrines, negated and continue to negate the brilliant accomplishment of the Church in establishing and consolidating the principle of social order. Social order has always rested on a delicate reconciliation of the claims of society and those of the individual, but Christianity's courageous recognition that the antagonism must remain irreconcilable in this world has always tempted the wrath of those with apocalyptic visions and murderous commitment to the Kingdom of God on Earth.

Christianity did not spread as a cry from the hearts of slaves but, as Ambrosio Donini so suggestively argues, from the totality of slave society at the beginning of its disintegration.[10] Individual suffering by itself could not point away from the world toward a spiritual reconciliation beyond; only a widespread sense of being trapped in a world of general insecurity and disorder could do so. For this reason alone, in that day as in this, an ideology, to triumph, must appeal across class lines even while it justifies the hegemony of that particular class which has the wherewithal to rule.

From its beginnings Christianity has precariously balanced submission to authority against the courage of the individual will. In a special way, fraught with consequences for the oppressed of that time and after, it has not been able to maintain this balance without great violence, for it has never been able to impose permanent restraint on the socially subversive impulses of the will. But, for an impressively long epoch, it did influence the channels through which those impulses worked themselves out.

Even Troeltsch, who vigorously defends the ethical-religious against the social interpretation of the Jesus legend, admits that Jesus addressed himself primarily to the poor and oppressed and that the rich were not won to the Christian banner until the second century—that is, after the impact of Paul's crusade.[11] Whatever the historical Jesus may have preached, the fact remains that Mark, in his account of Barabbas, refers not to *an* insurrection but to *the* insurrection; that Jesus on the eve of his arrest tells his disciples to sell their cloaks and buy swords; that all the Gospels agree on his having entered Jerusalem to the politically seditious popular cry of *Hosannah;* that the Anabaptists had good reason to love and Luther good reason to hate the Book of James—"this revolutionary pamphlet," as Archibald Robertson calls it.[12] Whatever interpretation one chooses to put on the words that burn the pages of the Book of Matthew, it is easy to see how they could spur some men and women to radical action: "And ye shall be hated of all men for my name's sake: but he that endureth to the end shall be saved"

(10:22). "Think not that I am come to send peace on earth: I came not to send peace, but a sword" (10:34). "And from the days of John the Baptist until now the kingdom of heaven suffereth violence, and the violent take it by force" (11:12). And with or without the specific sanction of the Gospels, Christianity offered to the oppressed and the despised the image of God crucified by power, greed, and malice and yet in the end resurrected, triumphant, and redeeming the faithful. However much Christianity taught submission to slavery, it also carried a message of foreboding to the master class and of resistance to the enslaved.

Christianity, even as expressed in the ostensibly conservative formulations of Paul, preached the dignity and worth of the individual and therefore threatened to stimulate defiance to authority, even as it preached submission. For no class was this message more vital than for slaves. The doctrine, "Render therefore unto Caesar the things which are Caesar's; and unto God the things that are God's," is deceptively two-edged. If it calls for political submission to the powers that be, it also calls for militant defense of the freedom of the spirit and the autonomy of the personality. But the master-slave relationship rests, psychologically as well as ideologically, on the transformation of the will of the slave into an extension of the will of the master. Thus, no matter how obedient—how Uncle Tomish—Christianity made a slave, it also drove deep into his soul an awareness of the moral limits of submission, for it placed a master above his own master and thereby dissolved the moral and ideological ground on which the very principle of absolute human lordship must rest. It was much more than malice that drove so many Southern masters to whip slaves for praying to God for this or that and to demand that they address all grievances and wishes to their earthly masters.[13]

Troeltsch finds it "most remarkable" that radical individualism should appear, in however conservative a form, in Paul himself. Pondering the sociopolitical conservatism of Paul in relation to the Christian doctrine of individual freedom, Troeltsch comments that the doctrine of submission contained within it much less love than resignation and contempt for existing institutions. The Christian utopia always carried radical political implications even in its more conservative, accommodationist, and otherworldly forms. It was, however, as Gramsci says, a gigantic attempt in mythological form to reconcile the actual contradictions of life in this world. When it proclaimed a single nature, endowed by God, for every man, it also proclaimed all men brothers. But in so doing, despite every attempt to separate the Kingdom of God from the kingdoms of man, it illuminated the chasm that separated the equality of men before God from the grim inequality of man before man.[14]

Christianity, like other religions, grew out of and based its strength upon the collective. In early tribal religions, African as well as European, God is at once a supreme member of the family —a veritable *paterfamilias*—and an independent force above the family who embodies its ideal life and symbolizes its unity.[15] The essentially tribal idea of God, however modified, never wholly departs from the sophisticated religions of civilized society. Afro-American slaves, drawing on both Euro-Christianity and their own African past, combined the two and in the process created a religion of their own while contributing to the shape of Christianity as a whole.

The genius of Christianity has appeared nowhere so impressively as in its struggle to reconcile freedom with order, the individual personality with the demands of society. From the consolidation of the Roman Catholic Church, with its central idea from Saint Cyprian—far less arrogant and far more humane than it might appear to Americans—"Outside the Church there is no salvation," to the heroic effort of the Puritans to build their City on a Hill, the Christian churches have fought to embody an acceptance of the dignity and sanctity of the human personality in submission to a collective discipline that alone can guarantee the freedom of the individual in a world haunted by the evil inherent in the nature of man. Those who are purified are so for His sake and through their unity in Him. Thus Troeltsch: "Absolute individualism and universalism . . . require each other. For individualism only becomes absolute through the ethical surrender of the individual to God, and being filled with God; and, on the other hand, in possession of the Absolute, individual differences merge into an unlimited love. . . ."[16]

The religious tradition to which the Afro-American slaves fell heir and to which they contributed more than has yet been generally recognized by no means unambiguously inspired docility and blind submission. Many of the white preachers to the slaves sought to sterilize the message, but they were condemned to eventual defeat. Too many carriers of the Word were themselves black men who interpreted in their own way. The Word transmitted itself, for some slaves and free Negroes in touch with slaves could read the Bible and counter the special pleading of the white preachers. And the black community in slavery, oppressed and degraded as it was, summoned up too much spirit and inner resourcefulness to be denied. In their own way the slaves demonstrated that, whatever the full truth or falsity of Christianity, it spoke for all humanity when it proclaimed the freedom and inviolability of the human soul.

Christianity as a religion of salvation that had arisen from and that had internalized a particular form of class relations, including and especially relations of lordship and bondage, impressed itself even upon its dissidents and transmitted to them the idealization of those very social relations which dissent had meant to challenge. As Ambrosio Donini writes: "In all the mystery religions, from that of Dionysus to that of Christ, the relationship between the faithful and the savior is seen as a relationship between a 'slave' . . . and his lord [*padrone*]."[17] In all precapitalist class societies man has had a lord and has sought a savior, who quite naturally has been cast in the image of the lord himself. The egalitarian doctrines associated with the Cargo Cults of Melanesia strikingly identified the expected "cargo" with the achievements of the European masters who were to be displaced. By making the cargo (the products of European technical and material superiority) an object of worship, the natives declared for their own freedom and for equality with the whites, but they sometimes came close to expecting the cargo as a gift from those same whites. Donini's words receive striking support from the slaves of the Old South as well, for some could think of no better way to refer to God than as "de Big Massa."[18]

The revolutionary danger point to the ruling classes came from the millennialist movements when the authority and legitimacy of lordship had been badly shaken—when submission to an earthly lord receded in society and could therefore recede in spiritual consciousness. Christianity could offer Roman slaves solace, a sense of personal worth, and even some hope of personal deliverance in this world through emancipation or amelioration of treatment, but it could offer no sense of the possibilities of liberation as a class.[19] That sense could only emerge among Christian slaves whose very enslavement was imbedded in a world of bourgeois social relations and bourgeois consciousness. But by then Christianity, in its several post-Reformation forms, had undergone profound transformations.

The general significance of the rise of Christianity among black slaves in the United States must be assessed as part of the centuries-long development of Christianity as a whole and therefore of the development of the civilization within which Christianity became the dominant religion. However much the rise of Christianity in the ancient world had been prepared, in Troeltsch's words, "by the destruction of national religions, which was the natural result of the loss of national independence,"[20] the fateful splits occasioned by the Reformation closed the circle and reconstructed Christianity as a series of discrete national religions even within the Roman Catholic sphere—one need only reflect on the French Church since the time of Philip the Fair and especially since the time of Napoleon. The Afro-American slaves of the United States, in contradistinction to those in Brazil, Cuba, or Saint-Domingue, inherited Protestant Christianity. Even this diluted and perverted Protestantism lent itself, in various subtle but discernible ways, to the creation of a protonational black consciousness.

SLAVE RELIGION IN HEMISPHERIC PERSPECTIVE

To put the religious experience of the southern slaves into perspective and to evaluate the relationship between religion and resistance (or accommodation), it is necessary to survey, however briefly and inadequately, the evidence from the British Caribbean, the French Caribbean, and Catholic Brazil and Spanish America.

At the beginning of the nineteenth century the slave population of Jamaica adhered to traditional African, or rather Afro-Jamaican, religions and remained largely ignorant of Christianity.[1] During the first half of the nineteenth century the dissenting sects spread rapidly among blacks and coloreds but probably never reached the great majority of the slaves in any direct and hegemonic way. Not until the second half of the century, after emancipation, did the Christian sects become a prime fact of life for the Jamaican population as a whole, in part perhaps because of their work in support of the social and economic initiatives of the freedmen.

The Anglicans bore chief responsibility for the religious life of the colony. At the beginning of the eighteenth century the moral condition of the clergy was deplorable. No doubt it improved with time, but never did it effectively undertake the conversion, much less protection, of the slaves. Jamaica and the other British sugar islands would not have had a clergy large enough to work properly, even if the will had been present and if political relationships had become favorable—neither of which in fact obtained. In the Leeward Islands the small clergy attended to the whites and concerned itself with the slaves primarily as an excuse for collecting fees for meaningless mass baptisms. Its concern for the slaves remained carefully circumscribed by its virtually total submission to the local ruling class.

The experience of the Society for the Propagation of the Gospel in Foreign Parts proved instructive and disheartening. The society's purpose, as set by its founders in 1701, was to spread the word of the Established Church among the heathen of the world. It failed, although here and there, notably in colonial South Carolina, it did some worthy educational work among the blacks. Its great test came in Barbados, where it bravely intervened in the master-slave relationship in the most direct way.

Christopher Codrington, preparing to die in Christ, left his huge slave estate to the society and bade it show the world what true and wise Christians could bring to enslaved blacks. Naturally, the society, as a pillar of the Church that stood at the very center of social order, had to be careful not to offend the secular men of property on Barbados. Naturally, it cared for the souls of men, not for the bagatelle of their class condition. And so, it made clear that it would prove Christian blacks to be the most useful and industrious of servants. To make a long story short, the "conversions" effected by its missionaries, the noble ones as well as the drunken whoremasters, proved superficial and in time virtually ceased. The feeble attempts to teach the slaves to read ended under secular pressure. Nothing changed—not even the regularity of the whip.

In the final decade or two of British West Indian slavery, the Baptists and Methodists came under increasing fire from the planters for allegedly encouraging slave revolt. A wave of revival meetings about 1830 received credit for exciting the expectations and hostility of the blacks. Planters charged that the Baptists, in particular, were paid by Negro congregations and were politically hostile to the existing regime. Long after emancipation Baptist ministers and congregations were considered to be at the center of lower-class and racially egalitarian resistance movements. The resident planters of the British islands could not move against these sects with impunity, for they received some measure of protection from the mother country, from which they had imbibed their attitudes.

The reputation of the Baptists had not always been so low among slaveholders. In the 1780s the Baptists, largely through the perseverance of a dedicated Negro preacher from Georgia, George Liele, had made converts even on Jamaica. The reliance of the Baptists on black preachers undoubtedly helps account for their success among the slaves. In time the strains caused by the exigencies of courting white approval and by the constant pressure of the African religious impulse from the slave quarters resulted in deep rifts among the black Baptists.

By the time of the suspected Baptist complicity in the nineteenth-century slave revolts, we find unmistakable evidence of heavy infusions of Afro-Jamaican Myalism in the Christianity of the younger preachers. To take root as a religion of the slaves, in contradistinction to the free Negroes, Baptist Christianity had to Africanize itself. In so doing, it made its own long-range accommodations with white rule, but it also forged new possibilities for the sharpening of revolutionary ideologies and, less explosively, for the creative blending of traditional African impulses with the doctrines of the dominant culture.

As for the Methodists, they have been done too much honor. John Wesley's *Thoughts upon Slavery* (1774), subsequently taken up by the abolitionists, struck hard at the foundations of Caribbean slavery and earned him and his followers a reputation for antislavery radicalism. By the end of the century, however, the Methodists, under the leadership of Thomas Coke, had trimmed their sails and eased toward accommodation. Methodist preachers, like the Moravian, went among the slaves and in time built up an impressive following.

The Methodists, and even more the Moravians, undermined the unity and the subversive potential of the slaves in ways more effective than by inculcating submissiveness. The Danes, who also housed Moravian missionaries on their Caribbean slave plantations, boasted that their Christian Negroes provided greater security against insurrection than their forts. In time they would question their boast, but everywhere Christianization did create new divisions and new hostilities among the slaves. In particular, it greatly exacerbated the dangerous cultural division between the creoles and the African-born. As Christian profession became a symbol of being civilized, it narrowed the apparent gulf between master and slave, white and black; in precisely the same way, it weakened the unity of the quarters.

The Methodists relentlessly warred on African "superstition" and preached the Protestant virtues of thrift, industry, and social peace. Dr. Coke even claimed credit for keeping the British islands calm during the explosion in Saint-Domingue. Whatever the truth of his claim, Methodist efforts do appear to have improved the living conditions of the slaves. Although the success of Methodism among the slaves accompanied the progress of accommodationism, the planters never wholly reconciled themselves to these outsiders. Somehow, the turbulence among the slaves more and more took on a Christian tone; and if the Methodist preachers indignantly proclaimed their innocence, the questions remained. The slaves and free coloreds were taking the message as they saw fit, not necessarily as the white missionaries intended. If Methodism did reduce the revolutionary thrust inherent in the African cults, the accommodation it provided was based on the principle of human brotherhood in Christ, which could be transformed into a rather bloody reformism by those with imagination. There are accommodations and accommodations, and this one had its particular price, which the ruling whites had little wish to pay. Methodism's compromise appealed especially to free blacks and coloreds, who filled its ranks. By the second quarter of the nineteenth century, with its conjuncture of metropolitan abolitionism, slave revolt and disobedience, and internal political crisis, this religion of pacification and social reconciliation looked dangerous to the ruling class, for the growing demands for an end to racism, as much as the demand for abolition, sounded the death knell of the old regime.

With the Established Church ineffective, with the Methodists and Moravians oriented primarily toward the free colored and the house-slave elite, and with the Baptists alone a serious challenge, the Afro-Caribbean religions swept the quarters. During the eighteenth century the transatlantic African trade had remained open; despite a moderate domestic slave trade, most slaves remained in one place, where they could develop strong community ties, and, until after the turn of the century, they received infusions from Africa from living carriers of the traditional ways of life and thought.

Afro-Caribbean religion manifested itself in two forms, Obeah and Myalism, although the distinction became less clear with time. The Obeah men worked in secret and concerned themselves largely with private matters. In societies marked by acute sexual imbalance, not to mention the grave everyday problem of dealing with harsh taskmasters, slaves needed personal help. The magic of the Obeah men, including their ability to poison and to heal with herbs and folk medicine, comforted the tormented and tormented the comfortable, according to circumstances and the right price. The reputation of the Obeah men spread to Europe and North America, although whites at home and abroad rarely distinguished between Obeah and Myalism. The missionaries of the Society for the Propagation of the Gospel in Foreign Parts were scandalized in Barbados; the planters of the southern United States were solemnly warned about the power of Obeah long after Caribbean emancipation. Eric Williams, the prime minister of Trinidad, himself a historian of note, speaks of the continued strength of the African cults among the Caribbean masses in the middle of the twentieth century.

African practices did not reappear in the New World in their traditional forms. Many of them, including the cult of the dead, the worship of certain gods, and the use of particular charms and potions, fused somewhat incoherently into new and much less structured patterns of belief and ritual. Obeah aimed specifically at harming individuals at the behest of others and relied on the skill of professional sorcerers to manipulate fetishes in order to detect and punish the crimes of slave against slave. The Obeah men were generally African-born, as was their following. Accordingly, their influence waned as creolization advanced during the nineteenth century.

Myalism became a more politically dangerous tendency. The Ashanti are supposed to have predominated in Myalism and the Popos in Obeah. These ascriptions of ethnic origins cannot wholly be credited, but the alleged role of the Ashanti in Myalism is noteworthy in view of the frequent identification of the Ashanti and Myalism in Caribbean slave revolts. The Myal men concerned themselves with group worship and welfare rather than with personal vendettas, and, if anything, arose as anti-Obeah men, much as African witch doctors had arisen as antiwitches. Since, like the Obeah men, they represented an avowedly anti-Christian religious movement, they too were suppressed. As a result, these ethnic and religious leaders emerged in enforced hostility to the regime and curbed the accommodationist attitudes that might have developed in a more relaxed atmosphere.

Myalism spread among the slaves and became deeply implicated in such major risings as that of 1760 in Jamaica. Although rivalry divided the Obeah and Myal men, the two seem to have cooperated effectively during a number of revolts and disturbances. The Myal men compelled fear and respect among the slaves, noticeably in a manner especially attuned to political resistance: they administered mixtures of gunpowder, rum, human blood, and grave-dirt to rebels, who swore loyalty and silence. The draught, with its accompanying oaths and ritual dance, ostensibly protected the rebels so that the white man's bullets would bounce off or facilitate reincarnation in Africa.

With the spread of Methodism in the nineteenth century a decided Afro-Christian syncretism arose. The persecuted Myal men often became Methodist preachers. Not until the 1840s, after abolition, does the Christian element in Jamaica appear to have begun to gain the upper hand at the expense of the Myalist. During slavery the Myalist Methodists posed a grave problem for the planters and the government; they probably were responsible for much of the widespread criticism of the Methodists.

British imperial policy had generally tended toward toleration of native customs, but in religion the British worked harder to influence the Negroes than in any other area of culture. Yet, as Philip Curtin suggests, the strongest African survivals in Jamaican culture are to be found precisely in religion. Afro-Christian sects did not take form there until the end of the eighteenth century, when the traditional features of African religion had already struck firm colonial roots. When the time came for compromise and syncretism, such traditionalism proved a formidable rival to Christianity. The political consequences in Jamaica as elsewhere in the hemisphere depended on the totality of political and cultural conditions, but clearly the high level of religious autonomy among the slaves and the decidedly African cast of that autonomy created unusual insurrectionary possibilities.

In the Dutch colonies the Dutch East and West India Companies cooperated with the Calvinist ministry to send out hundreds of ministers and religious teachers every year, but only in New Amsterdam, among the New World colonies, did they accomplish much.[2] In the plantation colonies Christian instruction of the slaves received little attention; in the extreme case, Demerara forbade it altogether until the colony passed into English hands. In Surinam religious neglect and a standard of cruelty extreme even for the Caribbean contributed to strengthen African religious life and with it a state of constant agitation and rebellion. With the opportunity for slaves to flee to the bush, organize themselves, and wage guerrilla warfare, the weakness, not to say absence, of white-dominated religious controls provided ideal conditions for a protracted struggle to rebuild African society in a New World setting.

The religion that the French brought to the sugar islands, particularly to Saint-Domingue, did not represent the best the Roman Catholic Church had to offer.[3] The Church had long had to wage a rear-guard action against the encroachments of the French state, and however one may assign responsibility, it found itself in no position to play a vigorous proselytizing and humanizing role in the French Caribbean. The French priests in the islands generally behaved badly, and those in Saint-Domingue reputedly behaved worst of all. The Abbé Raynal charged in 1770: "A succession of bad and ignorant priests has destroyed both respect for the cloth and the practice of religion in almost every parish of the colony. An atrocious greed has become the habitual vice of most of the parish priests." Five years later the Baron de Wimpffen spoke even more severely. As time went on the Church struggled to send more dedicated priests, but the cynicism of the government officials, the indifference of the planters, the miserable conditions of life, and the temptations offered by slave women, an impossible climate, and a hopeless cause combined to drag down all except the most resolute.

The wonder, as elsewhere, was that Catholicism took hold at all. Most of the slaves had been born in Africa, received little or no religious instruction from the whites, and had every reason to associate Christianity with sadism. Yet, even as they preserved their own religions in the form of Vodûn, it is of no small significance that they did so syncretically and insisted on being good Catholics. The Catholic Church remained the church of Europe and of the master class; only fools would refuse to identify with its power and its magic. On another plane, how significant that Toussaint L'Ouverture, upon consolidating his power, moved to suppress the Vodûn priests: "We are no [African] coast Negroes!" Dessalines, that specialist in revolutionary butchery, almost ruined himself by the ruthlessness with which he carried out Toussaint's orders to purge the infidels. Toussaint knew what he wanted, and even his ultimate failure marked his greatness. An independent Haiti had to be a modern state with a modern economy and a modern social order. It therefore had to have a religion in touch with and reflecting the modern world.

Haitian Vodûn and the Afro-Catholicism with which it came to be intimately identified have exemplified the political adaptability of popular religion in general. When the great revolution exploded, the Vodûn priests called on the slaves, so many of whom had recently come from Africa, to rise in holy war against their white Catholic masters. The exigencies of that extended revolutionary war called for new and more worldly-wise leadership. When it came forward in the person of Toussaint, a figure of unquestionable political genius, it offered a brilliant compromise of Christian adherence and the secular political ideology of Jacobinism. Yet, the victory of the revolution spelled the defeat of Toussaint's vision. Not even the savage repressions of a Dessalines or the political agility of a Christophe—not even the genius of Toussaint, had he been spared to preside over the transition to freedom—could save a Haiti confronted by hostile white imperialists without and an ex-slave population hungry for land and "freedom" within. The country slipped inexorably into a subsistence peasant economy. The religious syncretism that arose from the confusion and hope of the revolutionary period splendidly affirmed the traditions and cultural autonomy of the newly created, or re-created, peasantry. And it reinforced its backwardness, its isolation, and its poverty.

Still, it had not always been so. Before and even during the great revolution Vodûn meant resistance and war. Probably, an Afro-Catholic Vodûn spread ever more widely among the Haitian masses after the revolution. Before, it was the religious cry of the revolutionary elements among the slaves and the maroons, and in its early emphasis on the gods of Dahomey it helped open a fissure between the slaveholders and their slaves that would widen into a chasm. The essential ingredient in the revolutionary role assumed by Vodûn during the revolution, then, came not from the special character of the African elements in its theology but from the sense of social distance and hostility that it imparted to the slaves and the spiritual power this sense gave to an oppressed people who finally found themselves in a position to strike. With the removal of these conditions in the later period, Vodûn emerged as decidedly less African and more clearly syncretic. As such it proved itself quite as able as other religions, European and African alike, to bind oppressed and poverty-stricken masses to ruling elites.

The Portuguese Church took pride in its attention to the conversion of the heathens of Angola and elsewhere on the African coast.[4] The secular authorities, accompanied by Catholic priests, herded enslaved Africans at overseas departure points and baptized them *en masse*. Interpreters were supposed to translate the Portuguese renditions of the mysteries of the Faith into one or another African language and somehow have the spiritual message understood. No doubt this performance contained a positive meaning. If nothing else, it declared that Catholic Portugal regarded these black men as human beings and potential brothers in Christ; it at least represented a promise of decent treatment and provided a theoretical check to the white racism inherent in a master-slave relationship based on the principle of white over black.

The Jesuits, Dominicans, and others nonetheless supported and participated in the horrors of the Atlantic slave trade. The slave traders and missionaries in Angola worked closely together with little difficulty. The holiest of Catholic institutions in Luanda—the Holy House of Mercy—took its share from the slave trade. The bishop, like the colonial governor, the civil and ecclesiastical officials, the army, and the municipal council, received his income from precisely this source.

By the middle of the seventeenth century Portuguese proselytism in the Congo and Angola had spent its force. The priests died under the rigors of a strange climate and difficult circumstances, and the recruitment of high-level personnel, never easy, grew ever more difficult. Laymen, despite the noblest of protestations, went to Africa to get rich and easily corrupted a frail and undermanned clergy. Governors such as Fernão de Mello of São Tomé hardly hid their primary interest in the trade and their indifference to conversion. Notwithstanding subsequent Roman denunciations of the trade, those charged with Church policy in slaveholding countries themselves almost invariably entered the practical workings of the system. As late as the second quarter of the nineteenth century the Catholic bishops of Brazil split over the question of whether to support the anti-slave-trade conventions that the British were attempting to impose upon a disgruntled Brazilian government. Not until the middle of the eighteenth century had slavery been dramatically condemned by a man of the Church—Father Manoel Ribeiro Rocha in his great tract, *Ethiope resgatado*—and a hundred years later the ambiguity still persisted. Lacking the religious pluralism and attendant room for organized dissent of the Protestant United States, the Catholic Church of Brazil could never live up to its early promise as a force against the slave regime. When the abolitionist movement burst upon Brazil during the nineteenth century, the message of the Faith was almost nowhere in evidence.

The experience of the Jesuits reveals much about the relationship of Church and state in Brazil and about the problems facing those within the Church who might have had the desire to intervene on behalf of the cause of freedom. The Jesuits grew stronger in Brazil than in Spanish America, where other orders predominated, and they took up the cause of the Indians with the utmost dedication. They inspired laws to defend the Indians against enslavement, built missions to civilize and protect them, and when necessary led them in defensive warfare. The difficulties appeared in 1639 with startling force. The pope issued a bull of excommunication against anyone who enslaved Indians, but the reading of the bull in Rio de Janeiro provoked a riot in which the Jesuit college was attacked and priests almost murdered. The vicar general of Santos was trampled when he tried to publish the bull. When the Catholic residents of São Paulo drove the Jesuits out altogether, they demonstrated that their material interests and emotions had coalesced into a demand for the most extreme measures. The Jesuits had themselves unwittingly fired those emotions, for the "domestication" of the Indians and their reduction to disciplined labor had contributed immensely to their potential value as slaves.

In refusing to condemn African slavery as they had condemned Indian slavery and in strengthening the principle of race and class subordination, the Jesuits added their weight to black oppression. Their failure to establish hegemony over colonial Brazilian society may have contributed as much or more to the abandonment of the blacks. The Jesuits had a great tradition of mass guidance and had always demonstrated exceptional flexibility in adjusting to social change. By the eighteenth century, when Portugal's strong man, the Marquis of Pombal, launched his attack, they had already succumbed to the corrupting influence of Brazilian frontier-slave society; they too had come to look like just one more vehicle for the commercial exploitation of subject peoples. Thus, the one great force within the Church that had staked out implacable opposition to the pretensions of the planters, the one order capable of building a clericalism to rival the secular power of the slaveholders, went down to defeat and left the field to a clergy all too willing to accommodate to the regime.

The Catholic Church internationally and within Brazil had an easier time with the problem of slavery than did the Protestant churches of Anglo-Dutch America. With firm roots in ancient and medieval systems of class stratification, and having internalized those systems within its own theology as well as organization, it was able to accept slavery as one more unfortunate consequence of the Fall of Man and yet insist upon the spiritual equality of master and slave before God. Not as yet infected with bourgeois ideas of property and freedom, it saw no contradiction between the idea of property in man and the idea of man's property in his own soul.

As a result, the Church could demand attention to the spiritual life of the slaves, not merely in the *pro forma* Protestant manner of the churches of the Old South, but in a manner designed to sanctify marriage and family life. The Hispanic powers took their Catholicism seriously and responded with such memorable pronouncements as the *Siete Partidas* of Alfonso the Wise during the thirteenth century and the socially advanced Spanish slave code of 1789, which were models of humane law by the standards of slaveholding societies. In the colonies, however, the planters, not the metropolitan officials and intellectuals, had the last word, and everywhere tension arose between the spirit of the Church-influenced laws and the exigencies, as well as the pretensions and abuses, of direct lordship.

Protection of the slaves rested with Church and state, but those great institutions remained mere abstractions apart from their living representatives. The *senhores de engenho* and *fazendeiros* controlled their little worlds, standing as giant patriarchs astride their slaves, their numerous sharecroppers and tenants, their retainers, and their own wives and children. The Portuguese authorities came and went and sometimes did intervene to prevent or punish atrocities, but for the most part the *senhores* dealt with local authorities, who, happily for them, were generally their own fathers, sons, uncles, cousins, retainers, and friends, when they were not themselves.

Never was the number of priests adequate to the task of shepherding the flock; never did the moral quality of the priests rise to the level required by circumstances or expected by Rome. Gilberto Freyre writes that each Big House had its own church or chapel and its own chaplain. That most plantations had a clergyman in residence is more than doubtful, but in any case, as Freyre himself adds, the chaplain was almost invariably more dependent upon the *senhor* than upon the bishop; indeed, he was often a member of the *senhor*'s family. Whether kin or not, he ranked as a member of the family, in the wider sense; no doubt he had special influence with the *patrão*; but he remained subservient.

Yet, Frank Tannenbaum was right to assert that Catholicism made a profound difference in the lives of the slaves. Catholicism imparted to Brazilian and Spanish American slave societies an ethos—or, for those who prefer, a hegemonic ideology and psychology—that profoundly reflected premodern, seigneurial rather than bourgeois ideas of property, class, status, and spiritual brotherhood. Accordingly, the white racism and cruel discrimination that inevitably accompanied the enslavement of black to white emerged against countervailing forces of genuine spiritual power. All the evidence now being accumulated to prove the existence and severity of white racism in Brazil cannot explain away the chasm that separates Brazil from the United States in rate of intermarriage, access of blacks to positions of respect and power, and the integration of people of color into a single nationality. Catholicism does not by itself account for the difference, but from the beginning it played its part by the force of its impact on society as a whole.

This accomplishment did not necessarily include special favors to the slaves, apart from its help in facilitating individual manumissions. The Catholicism of Rome (or of Portugal or of Luso-Brazil) may not even have prevailed in the slave quarters, for the very flexibility of Luso-Brazilian Catholicism left much room for Afro-Brazilian religious syncretism and for a wide measure of Afro-Brazilian cultural autonomy within the process of national consolidation. Brazil today features large and strong Afro-Brazilian religious cults in which specifically African elements have acquired a depth and visibility virtually unknown in the United States. Some of these cults exist outside the Catholic Church, but most within, and it has plausibly been argued that the very definition of a "Negro" in racially mixed Brazil must include reference to the way in which a person practices his Catholicism. The cults correspond roughly to the Vodûn of Haiti and enjoy considerable support along the coast, especially in the patriarchal Northeast, which cradled Brazilian slave civilization. Candomble in Bahia, Xangô in Pernambuco, and Macumba in Rio de Janeiro emerged as highly organized, ritually complex movements of distinctly West African origin and no less distinctly Catholic influence. Religions both from the Guinea Coast, especially from among the Yoruba and the peoples of Dahomey, and from the Bantu-speaking Angola-Congo region have their particular geographic settings and ethnic clientele.

Freyre may be right in arguing that the African cults greatly expanded with the waning of the plantation system and especially with the abolition of slavery, when the blacks drifted into the urban slums and occupied shanties that no longer were organically linked to the culture of the Big House. But the roots of this religious diversity, as Freyre's own books demonstrate, lay in the slave plantations themselves. The power of African religions in Catholic Brazil and in Brazilian Catholicism itself arose from various interlocking sources. The Luso-Brazilian Church offered its own strength and weakness: its strength as manifested in a capacity to tolerate, absorb, and eventually discipline the beliefs and rites of those heathen whose conversion to the True Faith would take time and patience; its weakness as manifested in the corruption, indiscipline, and lack of resources of the priests and planters who had responsibility for the souls of those in their charge. And in Brazil there were just not enough whites relative to Indians, Negroes, and mixed peoples to prevent the maintenance of traditional beliefs and practices. Much of the police apparatus on the countryside and on the plantations was in the hands of men of color—one color or another—who were themselves susceptible to other than orthodox ideas and practices. Many of the whites, including the proudest and most Catholic of the *senhores*, could not wholly resist the mysteries of those African spirit religions which had acquired plausible Christian coloration. Many slaves lived on huge sugar and coffee plantations with few whites to survey their every movement. The wonder is that so much Christianity entered the life of the country, rather than that so much traditional African belief entered Brazilian Christianity.

The Saint George cult, which grew particularly strong in Rio de Janeiro, provides a useful illustration of Afro-Brazilian syncretism. The cult achieved considerable popularity among both masters and slaves, but with a different content. The slaves identified Saint George with Ogun, the African god who represented, among other things, war and vengeance. The Ogun cult gained notable popularity among urban ruffians and hoodlums, who sometimes translated their hero into Saint Anthony rather than Saint George and who sparked a number of big riots in Recife and elsewhere. This "fighting aristocracy of the slave population," as Freyre calls them, became notorious for proficiency in a type of street brawling known as *capoeiragem,* the repertoire of which included head-batting, tripping, and kicking the feet out from under one's opponent.

Such cults provided the psychological and ideological ground on which slaves and desperately poor Negroes, oppressed by class and race in a conjuncture that defies separation, could stand and strike back at their tormentors. Religion did not simply color the social revolt, as an early social interpretation suggested; rather, as Roger Bastide insists, it was "the very heart of the revolt." The actual political context of such rebelliousness is another matter, for it can and usually does quickly pass into reactionary channels, much in the manner of the lower-class royalism of Naples or the anti-Jacobinism of the Vendée or the church-and-crown mobs of England. Freyre undoubtedly presses his case too far when he denies all politically radical significance to the cults and even, astonishingly, to Bahian Islam. But his remarks are worthy of attention: "It was these Negroes, these slaves, these ruffians, these idlers, held down and repressed in their youthful virile manifestations as though their games, their dance steps, their songs of praise of Ogun, their whistles, were a crime or indignity against the colony or the Empire, who put down the uprising of Irish and German mercenaries, the favorite troops of Pedro I, when they revolted in 1828." Social readings other than Freyre's are possible, especially when we recall that 1828 fell during that great period of slave violence and insurrection which culminated in the massive rising in Bahia in 1835. But he is right to suggest that the rebellious spirit of oppressed peoples can be directed into safe channels by rulers. Religious ideology invariably is politically ambiguous.

The Brazilian blacks, unlike the North American, clustered around their traditional African gods to an impressive extent, but very much like the North American, they translated their religious particularism into a strategy for the survival of their individuality and some measure of group autonomy. They did not, as a rule, translate it into a revolutionary weapon. There have been few revolutionary-prophetic religious movements among black Brazilians, but adherence to religious cults that separated them from the ruling class retained its revolutionary potential. From time to time, that potential became realized under the leadership of charismatic militants and rebellion became holy war. Here as everywhere, religion proved a two-edged sword for the enslaved. It enabled them to accommodate with some measure of cultural autonomy and personal dignity, and, more rarely but ominously, it provided the war cry for determined insurgents.

The Catholic Church in Cuba, and in much of Spanish America, scored some success during the early centuries of colonization in its work of conversion.[5] In much of Spanish America, African slaves worked in a diversified economy and received closer attention from the Church than was possible in the profit-hungry plantation islands and enclaves. In Cuba, which became Spain's greatest sugar colony, the efforts of the Church to humanize slavery and to convert the slaves received their severest test.

Cuba did not experience its sugar boom until after the collapse of Saint-Domingue. During the eighteenth century, when Cuban society was moving forward as a relatively benign slaveholding colony, the Church exerted considerable influence over both masters and slaves and set certain standards that could not wholly be disregarded. When the sugar craze began and a new and more vicious plantation system arose during the nineteenth century, the impact of the Church receded. It remained strong in the cities and on the small tobacco *vegas* but never conquered the great slave-driven sugar estates with their steady infusions of newly imported Africans. It is enough to note that by 1860 there were slightly more priests in Havana than in all the rest of the country. An ex-slave tells us that on the big estates Catholicism became the religion of the house slaves, but that the African religions dominated the quarters. He adds that at least two types of African religions vied with each other, one of Guinean origin and one of Congolese. As in Brazil, the slaves worshipped Ogun, the god of war, but in this case he appeared as Saint John rather than as Saint George or Saint Anthony.

In Cuba, as elsewhere, the Church struck vigorously at African religious beliefs and rites even as it bent to absorb as much as seemed necessary and safe. Everywhere in Spanish America the

Negro confraternities served as mechanisms of political and ideological control and at the same time eased the path of acceptance of blacks into white-dominated societies. This success, measured against Catholic performance in Saint-Domingue or even Brazil, weakened the political separatist thrust of slave rebelliousness, which in Cuba tended to express itself within the wider movement for insular freedom or at least in closer association with nonslave and nonblack sectors of the population. Afro-Catholic syncretism went forward and infected whites as well as blacks. It proved a powerful mechanism for psychological and cultural survival, but its stimulus to slave insurrection is by no means clear.

Even so brief a sketch warns of two major pitfalls in the evaluation of the religion of the southern slave quarters: the facile tendency to assume that the southern slaves passively absorbed a religion handed down from above and completely relinquished their African heritage without replacing it with anything new; and the mechanistic error of assuming that religion either sparked the slaves to rebellion or rendered them docile. The religion fashioned by the slaves of the Old South did not replicate that fashioned by the slaves of Brazil or Saint-Domingue or Jamaica, but it did display the same creative impulse to blend ideas from diverse sources into the formulation of a world-view sufficiently complex to link acceptance of what had to be endured with a determined resistance to the pressures for despair and dehumanization.

BLACK CONVERSION AND WHITE SENSIBILITY

The processes by which and the rate at which black slaves converted to Christianity remain unclear. Edmund Ruffin thought that Africans had rarely become Christians in Virginia and that conversion came with the first generation born into slavery.[1] Since those early slaves, African-born and American-born alike, began to see some element of safety in conversion, if only because it gave them stronger claims to the sympathy of their masters, the spiritual significance of their conversion cannot readily be assessed. Even in cases of conversions of convenience, however, religious sincerity played a role, for the protection it sought rested on a spiritual doctrine of equality before God and the recognition of every man's "human claims upon other men."[2]

A pioneer historian of the conversion problem has argued that during the colonial period most of the slaves retained much of their African religious beliefs and lived and died strangers to Christianity.[3] In its own terms, this judgment may be correct, but it can nonetheless prove misleading. From the moment the Africans lost the social basis of their religious community life, their religion itself had to disintegrate as a coherent system of belief. From the moment they arrived in America and began to toil as slaves, they could not help absorbing the religion of the master class. But, the conditions of their new social life forced them to combine their African inheritance with the dominant power they confronted and to shape a religion of their own. In time they would produce a religion—or perhaps it would be better to say a sensibility on which a religious system could be built—that would help shape the mainstream of American Christianity and yet retain its special aspect as a black cultural expression.

In terms recognizable to the white America in which the black development was lodged, the mass of the slaves apparently became Christians during the late eighteenth and early nineteenth centuries. By the last antebellum decade blacks constituted a large proportion of those attending Christian services. Northern abolitionists, for self-serving reasons but also because they rarely took pains to acquaint themselves with the actual life of the slaves, made themselves ridiculous by pointing to low figures for black church membership. The figures, unreliable as they are, in fact suggested large enough totals to lead W. E. B. Du Bois and other scholars to estimate that about one of every six adult slaves considered himself or herself attached to a Christian sect. Most southern whites did not hold formal church membership either, nor even attend services regularly. More often than not, those who did consider themselves staunch Christians did not join a church until late in life. In the rural, quasi-frontier slave states good Christians went to the services that were available and had little opportunity to join the church that most suited their theological preference. Black professions and actual church membership must be evaluated in this wider social context and cannot provide a suitable measure of concern and commitment.

Little is known about the religious beliefs of the slaves during the seventeenth or most of the eighteenth century. Whites paid scant attention to them and did little to convert the slaves to Christianity. The white attitude grew initially out of fear as well as out of a cultural distance that bred indifference. Although during the seventeenth century the law clearly stated that baptism would not imply emancipation, slaveholders throughout the British and even French colonies continued to fear that Christian slaves would be declared free.[4] Under the circumstances whites believed, and some historians have continued to believe, either that the slaves wallowed in "superstition"—a word that Sidney Mintz has properly defined as "the other man's religion"—or, even more absurdly, that they had no spiritual life at all. Probably, the slaves retained their traditional African beliefs, but the coherence of traditional African religion must have steadily disintegrated under the several pressures of life in a new environment and under a new regimentation.

Thus, it is necessary to follow Luther P. Jackson's suggestion and to begin the story with 1760, when black conversion to Christianity started to assume noticeable proportions. Jackson divided the history of black Christianity in Virginia into three periods: 1750–1790, 1790–1830, and 1830–1860.[5] During the first period, 1750–1790, colonial religion took a popular turn, exhibiting an awakened consciousness and mass enthusiasm. Blacks responded to the roughhewn frontier preaching and were, for the most part, welcomed as participants. No few blacks appeared as preachers and acquired followings among both blacks and whites. The Baptists and Methodists who carried much of the new religious drive often expressed hostility toward slavery and a hope that it would vanish. Throughout the Upper South the spirit of the revivals manifested itself in a demand, often backed by administrative measures within the churches, for humane treatment of slaves and for recognition that they were brothers in Christ.[6] The inclusion of blacks and indeed the religious Awakening itself did not, however, extend much below Virginia; South Carolina, even then, stood as a bulwark of conservatism in religion as in most else.[7]

During the second period, 1790–1830, antislavery feelings in the churches began to dissolve under pressure from the slaveholders, who naturally dominated institutions based on participatory democracy within a slaveholding society. Simultaneously, enthusiasm for enlisting black brethren also waned, although something of a struggle went on.[8]

A great burst of proselytizing among the slaves followed the Nat Turner revolt. Whereas previously many slaveholders had feared slaves with religion—and the example of Turner himself confirmed their fears—now they feared slaves without religion even more. They came to see Christianity primarily as a means of social control. Hence the apparent contradictions of the period: a decline of antislavery sentiment in the southern churches; laws against black preachers; laws against teaching slaves to read and write; encouragement of oral instruction of slaves in the Christian faith; and campaigns to encourage more humane treatment of slaves. The religious history of the period formed part of the great thrust to reform slavery as a way of life and to make it bearable for the slaves.

They ordered things differently in South Carolina—as always. Unencumbered by a colonial past mired in religious enthusiasm and secure under the steady guidance of a cohesive low-country aristocracy, South Carolina proceeded slowly in the religious instruction of its slaves, much as it proceeded slowly in everything except proslavery extremism. Before the insurrectionary plot of 1822 the planters generally opposed religious instruction of the slaves. In part this hostility derived from a suspicion that many ministers and preachers held antislavery views.[9] William W. Freehling, our best authority, has even suggested that the ministry did not become safely proslavery until about 1840.[10] After the Denmark Vesey plot, however, despite the momentary hysteria over the alleged role of the churches in encouraging slave insubordination, South Carolina's great planter aristocracy began going to church, or rather began making sure that the slaves were going. As was to happen in Virginia a decade later, once faced with an insurrection of slaves who displayed religious inclinations, the slaveholders sobered up. If the slaves were going to get religion, then religion had to be made safe for slaveholders.

This progress of slaveholder sensitivity to the spiritual needs of the slaves called forth its echo within the churches. The clergy faced a choice. Should it follow the example of the Quakers or of other small groups and take high ground against slavery?[11] If so, it would be rendered, perhaps with no small amount of violence, irrelevant to the lives of the slaves. Or should it place the souls of the slaves above all material considerations and render unto Caesar the things which are Caesar's? The troublemakers were dealt with, and the deed was done. Step by step, the several churches embraced the proslavery argument. They won the trust of the masters and freed themselves to preach the gospel to the slaves. The Reverend Edward Thomas's view may stand for that of many others:

> I have some hope, too, of being able to effect some spiritual good among the Blacks, who abound in this Parish [St. John's Berkeley, South Carolina], and many of whose owners are quite willing that they should receive religious instruction from their Parish minister. If our Northern brethren would let our domestic institutions alone, the poor negroes would fare much better as to their souls; but the abolition measures have excited such a spirit of jealousy and suspicion that some Planters will not listen to the introduction of religion on their places.[12]

With a few notable exceptions, each denomination made its own accommodation in due time, and the schism of northern and southern branches merely strengthened a *fait accompli*. Thus, the General Assembly of the Presbyterian Church declared in 1861 that the slave system had generally proven "kindly and benevolent" and had provided "real effective discipline" to a people who could not be elevated in any other way. Slavery, it concluded, was the black man's "normal condition."[13]

The soul-searching struggles in the eastern and border states did not recapitulate themselves in the western cotton states despite occasional mutterings. The turbulent slaveholders who conquered the Old Southwest in the 1820s and 1830s came to religion slowly and could hardly have been expected to try to bring their slaves on any faster. But they also had fewer fears. Indifference, not hostility, created the greatest obstacle to those who would convert the slaves. The slaveholders of Alabama never mounted a notable campaign against religious instruction. Those of Mississippi gave support early to the principle. And those of Arkansas and Louisiana, despite carping from the *Planters' Banner*, slowly overcame their own indifference and undertook the task. By 1850, Fredrika Bremer could report that although religious instruction in the western states moved slowly, a general advance was occurring.[14]

The rhythm of advance differed in the older and newer slave states but manifested the same tendency, although at different historical moments. After 1831, however, the southern slaveholders began to move in tandem. The unfolding unity on this special question reflected a growing sectional unity on the larger question of slavery itself, and it received considerable support from within the churches. As the churches overcame their qualms about slavery and either grudgingly accepted the facts of life or warmly embraced the proslavery argument, they put themselves in a position to proselytize among the slaves with the blessings and active support of the masters. In 1845, the flower of the South Carolina planter aristocracy assumed the lead in sponsoring the efforts of proslavery clergymen to bring their version of the gospel to the slaves.[15] The conscientious work of a Presbyterian minister, C. C. Jones of Georgia, provided the most famous instance. His book, *Religious Instruction of the Negroes*, and his pamphlet, *Suggestions for the Religious Instruction of the Negroes*, gained wide circulation, as did other such writings. Ministers like the Reverend William Capers in North Carolina prepared their ground carefully and sought, by patient effort, to convince the planters that "the novel experiment was a safe and judicious one."[16] Generally, they succeeded.

A few small scruples did have to be overcome along the way, even apart from the big one of slavery itself. Had the clergy been Roman Catholic, life might have been easier. But it was hard for Protestants, who had a clear idea of the role of mass literacy and use of the vernacular in their movement's great Reformation, to swallow the laws against teaching slaves to read and write. Still, how could they argue with South Carolina's Whitemarsh B. Seabrook, who sensibly pointed out that anyone who wanted slaves to read the entire Bible belonged in a lunatic asylum?[17] The answer conformed to necessity. It would be purely oral instruction. Nothing was lost save their own historic tradition—a small matter, despite pretensions, for any conservative movement.

As the slaveholders themselves became more self-consciously religious during the late antebellum period, they increasingly paid white preachers to conduct services for their slaves. If preachers could not come, or even if they could, the slaveholders would preach to the slaves themselves, and their wives would conduct Sunday school for the children or Bible readings for the adults. Governor Hammond of South Carolina insisted that those slaves who wished could attend plantation or town services at least once a month and that in the sparsely settled South whites fared no better. Plantation records throughout the South bear him out, and the testimony of ex-slaves contains little to raise suspicions.[18]

In the South Carolina low country many—some insist the great majority—of the slaveholders built chapels or "praise-houses" on their plantations, and the practice spread to the western cotton belt, at least among the larger planters. These efforts, along with the insistence on taking some of the house slaves to the white family's church, did not always evoke enthusiasm among the slaves.[19] The slave narratives contain numerous complaints of having been forced to attend service against their will. To make matters worse, when a master got religion he might do as William Wells Brown's master did: end all that Sunday frolic and foolishness and see to it that his slaves kept their minds on the Good Lord.[20]

Masters did not normally force their slaves to adopt their own denomination. The slaves preferred to become Baptists or Methodists, and even Roman Catholic planters were known to let them have their way. In South Carolina, for example, a large portion of the low-country planters remained Episcopalian throughout the antebellum period, but many of their slaves became Baptists. In some cases coercion did occur, as the postwar exodus of so many blacks from other denominations into the ranks of the Baptists and Methodists suggests.[21] But in most cases, a plantation had to take whatever preacher came through the area regardless of his sect.

The slaveholders' motives combined self-interest with a genuine concern for the spiritual welfare of their slaves and indeed of themselves. Many slaveholders came to believe that religion served them well as a means of control; others, who remained skeptical or held a contrary opinion, nevertheless would not deprive the slaves of preaching. Some had the good sense to know that if the slaves were listening to a reliable white preacher, they could not —not that moment, at any rate—be off in the woods listening to some suspect black exhorter. R. F. W. Allston, South Carolina's great planter, built a prayer house for his slaves and reported them "attentive to religious instruction, and greatly improved in intelligence and morals, in domestic relations, etc. . . . Indeed, the degree of intelligence which as a class they are acquiring is worthy of deep consideration."[22] The Alabama Baptist Association at its annual meeting in 1850 called for greater efforts to instruct the slaves: "Intelligent masters with the light of experience before them will regard the communication of sound religious instruction as the truest economy and the most efficient police and as tending to the greatest utility, with regard to every interest involved."[23] And Thomas Affleck included the following instructions to overseers in his *Cotton Plantation Record and Account Book*, which sold widely in the cotton states:

You will find that an hour devoted every Sabbath morning to their
moral and religious instruction would prove a great aid to you in
bringing about a better state of things amongst the Negroes. It has
been thoroughly tried, and with the most satisfactory results, in
many parts of the South. As a matter of mere interest it has proved
to be advisable, to say nothing of it as a point of duty. The effect upon
their general good behavior, their cleanliness and good conduct on
the Sabbath is such as alone to recommend it to the Planter and
Overseer.[24]

These remarks, which echoed across the South with increasing
force after 1831, revealed the place of religious instruction in the
development of the proslavery argument. They formed part of the
swelling demand to make slavery safer for the masters by making
it more tolerable for the slaves—a demand that implicitly deepened the South's commitment to slavery as a permanent social
order.[25]

The strategy of using religion as a method of social control could
never have served its purpose had it been only that. The success
of the political strategy for attention to the slaves' religious life
paradoxically required a considerable degree of genuine Christian
concern by the masters, for it depended upon the slaves' perception of a degree of sincere white interest in their welfare. The
slaves did not often accept professions of white sincerity at face
value; on the contrary, they seized the opportunity to turn even
white preaching into a weapon of their own. White preaching
could have a degree of conservative political effectiveness only
when the slaves could accept the sincerity of the gesture.

Fortunately for the regime, the religious feelings of the masters
were deepening during the nineteenth century, and their efforts
for the slaves were taking on a stronger moral tone. There is no
other way of reading the slaveholders' private diaries, journals,
and letters. George De Berniere Hooper of Alabama referred to
the death of a slave as the loss not only of a "friend" but of a
"Brother in Christ." "I verily believe," he wrote to his wife, "that
God has a high place prepared for them." John Rogers of Charleston, South Carolina, believing himself near the end, addressed his
children: "I wish you also to give all the indulgence you possibly
can to the negroes in going to Church, and making them repeat
their questions, for this reason that if neglected we will have to
answer for the loss of their souls. . . ." Everard Green Baker
penned a prayer in his diary: "Oh my God enable me to live as a
Christian should live to be a faithful husband, a kind father and

master and an exemplary Christian, that I may set my family such
an example as will be agreeable in the eyes of my Maker, and that
I may be spared to rear my children in the fear and nurture of the
Lord." Baker went to considerable trouble to swap land strips with
his neighbors so that his slaves would have an easier time getting
to church. Ebenezer Jones of Tennessee wrote to his children:

> Dear son and daughter may you ever mind
> And to your slaves be always very kind
> You soon with them on a level must meet
> When Christ doth call you to his judgment seat
> Christ will not ask if folks are black or white
> But judge the deeds and pass a sentence right
> The earth is not a place for our abode
> Prepare, prepare to meet a righteous God.[26]

The slaves could not remain insensible to such attitudes. Rather,
as in so many other ways, they turned them to advantage. They
used them as a yardstick with which to measure their masters and
to strengthen their sense of themselves. John Brown, an ex-slave
from Talladega, Alabama, whose master had taught his slaves to
read and write, recalled:

> Sunday was a great day around the plantation. The fields was
> forgotten, the light chores was hurried through, and everybody
> got ready for the church meeting. It was out of the doors, in the
> yard fronting the big lot where the Browns all lived. Master
> John's wife would start the meeting with a prayer and then
> would come the singing—the old timey songs. But white folks on
> the next plantation would lick their slaves for trying to do like
> we did. No praying there, and no singing.[27]

The complexity of the masters' attitudes appears in such reports as that of Elige Davison, an ex-slave from Virginia. His
master's religious sincerity expressed itself in his willingness to
ignore the law and to teach his slaves to read the Bible. It did
not, however, prevent his regularly breaking up slave families
by sale.[28]

No matter how often such anomalies occurred, the masters'
religious conversion more often than not benefitted the slaves,
even if only slightly. In rare and extreme cases, such as those of
John Rogers of Kentucky and James Hervey Greenlee of North
Carolina, it led them to conclude that proper religious instruction
would prepare the slaves for freedom. There can be no question
of the depth of feeling expressed by Greenlee in his diary:

Explained them there nature, the great importance of studying and practicing the truths they contain, that they should try to understand, for they gave information of things that belong to there future happiness, & point them to Jesus, as the great attoning sacrifice for man accepted of the Father as our surity and answered the demands of the Holy Law of God which we had violated—opened up the way by which God can be reconsiled to man, admitted through his righteousness to his favor, and adopted as his children. Lord grant that they may be made wise unto salvation, receive Christ as their Lord & portion and serve him with their whole heart. May we who have charge of them feel it is our indispensable duty to instruct them tho they are in a degraded and dependent condition . . . ever bearing in mind that their souls are as precious in the sight of him with whom we have to do, as tho they were as free as we are, or as white as the fairest son of Adam.[29]

Continued indifference, rather than hostility, explained the lack of religious instruction on most plantations where it was absent, but outright hostility never completely disappeared. Instructions such as those of a Louisiana sugar planter to his overseers in 1861 grew less frequent as time went on, but still appeared: "He must not allow preaching of any sort on the place nor allow the Negroes to go off the place to hear any kind of exhortation."[30] This hostility had several sources: in a few cases, a fanatical racist rejection of the idea that blacks could have souls or profit from any religious message; in most cases, a grave suspicion that religion, even in the anesthetized form of customary white preaching, undermined the social order of slavery. The critics may not have been wrong; the gains to the whites always accompanied risks. The Christian message, no matter how censored, took its toll on whites and blacks alike. The passionately pro-Confederate Eliza Frances Andrews wrote in 1865: "I don't think there ought to be any distinction of classes or races in religion. We all have too little 'gentility' in the sight of God for that."[31]

Throughout the nineteenth century, quite apart from the implications of the religious message of a Nat Turner, slaves drew their own conclusions from the most apparently innocuous preaching. In 1807 a Baptist church in Kentucky had to exclude a black woman because, on becoming a Christian, she denounced slavery. She had acquired the crazy idea that no Christian should hold slaves.[32] In the 1830s a slave girl who had repeatedly rebuked her mistress for running off to parties on Saturday night when she ought to have been preparing for the Sabbath, finally lost patience and tried to kill several whites.[33] In 1856, an old slave in Georgia sent his young master a touching acknowledgment for a gift of some tobacco: "Do, Missis, write and give him tousand tanks. Tell him *I can do nothing for him, but the Lord can do everything for him;* and I pray the Lord to bless him and make him a good Christian."[34] Missus and Young Massa took the message, as it was probably intended, as evidence of warm affection. They do not appear to have noticed the simple assumption of spiritual equality—indeed of the old slave's superiority—that it contained.

These recurring themes kept some slaveholders nervous to the end. They had company. Ruling classes have usually had to worry about the other side of the control mechanism inherent in the Christian religion. In 1811, an overseer in Virginia who had visited the British Isles wrote to his employer and put the debate in a larger perspective that deserves notice, whatever we think of his evaluations:

> As to the instructing and enlightening of Negroes whether it would be an advantage or a disadvantage to them I really can form no opinion, numerous indeed are the arguments used against it. I am clearly of opinion that it would be of great advantage to them while young by employing their minds in that manner & keeping them in proper subjection, and it certainly would be a means of keeping them from vicious habits which they imbibe while young, but what effect it would have upon them afterwards, I am unable to judge. In some counties in England where I visited where the Servants are totally ignorant the farmers there use the same arguments against instructing & enlightening them as are used here against the negroes. I have heard some of them assert that they never knew one of them that was educated turn out well. But in Scotland where almost all of them are educated more or less and numbers of them pretty well informed I presume that there are not more obedient, industrious & faithful servants any where.[35]

LET THE DEAD BURY THE DEAD

As part of the white attempt to control black religion, the slave-holders' regime tried to supervise slave funerals and feared their providing the occasion for insurrectionary plots. In 1687 authorities in the Northern Neck of Virginia banned public funerals for slaves because they had become convinced of their role in hatching a dangerous conspiracy.[1] In 1772 the corporation of New York City required that slave funerals be held during daylight hours and that maximum attendance be held to twelve. Both justifications for the edict are illuminating, especially in combination: unrestricted slave funerals tended toward sedition and toward the encouragement of "heathenish services."[2] These fears betrayed caution, not paranoia. The famous insurrectionary plot associated with Gabriel Prosser in Virginia in 1800 had, as its organizational occasion, the gathering of slaves for a child's funeral,[3] and the circumstances surrounding the Nat Turner revolt of 1831 chilled the white South. "A Farmer of Lower Virginia," as he signed himself, wrote in 1836 of the decision to bar black preachers and to forbid public funerals without a white man present to officiate:

> Their funerals formerly gave them great satisfaction, and it was customary here to furnish the relations of the deceased with bacon, spirit, flour, sugar and butter, with which a grand entertainment, in their way, was got up. We were once amused by a hearty fellow requesting his mistress to let him have his funeral during his lifetime, when it would do him some good. The waggish request was granted; and I venture to say there was never a funeral, the subject of which enjoyed it so much.[4]

After 1831, as our farmer suggested, the slaveholders found it a good deal harder to enjoy the carefree antics of their "happy niggers." But never did the white reaction succeed in suppressing big slave funerals. Too many planters considered the repressive regulations inhuman, and others noted that they either could not be enforced or would so embitter the slaves as to increase, rather than decrease, the threat of violent resistance. In one way or another, however, the whites missed the point. The significance of proper funerals for the slaves lay, not in the peripheral if real danger of conspiracy, but in the extent to which they allowed the participants to feel themselves a human community unto themselves. To that extent the slaves decisively negated the mythical foundation of the slaveholders' world.

The majority of ex-slaves whose testimony we have did recall that masters permitted their slaves to have funeral ceremonies. Most acknowledged that whites made no attempt to deprive the slave dead of proper respect, although enough recalled white callousness to form an indictment.[5] "When a slave die," Elige Davison of Virginia bitterly charged, "he just another dead nigger. Massa, he builded a wooden box and put the nigger in and carry him to the hole in the ground. Us march around the grave three times and that all."[6] Even when masters provided the opportunity for decent funerals, the coffins were of the simplest and roughest construction. Small slaveholders, many of whom did their own carpentering, sometimes made them themselves. Planters assigned the task to a slave carpenter or hired a free white or black, or the slaves simply stepped in and did it themselves. Occasionally, planters bought coffins. Robert H. Stewart, a big mortician, furniture dealer, gravedigger, and planter of the Natchez region, did a thriving business in coffins for urban slaves and some rural ones as well.[7]

The death of beloved Mammies, respected "old family servants," drivers of long service, and even favorites among the field hands brought out strong sentimental efforts by the more patriarchal masters. When Susan Dabney Smedes's Mammy died, her father would allow no sermon: "I do not know anybody good enough to preach a sermon over her." The master led the funeral procession, and all his children followed the coffin as mourners. "He ordered out the whole plantation, every one who could walk, and every man, woman, and child carried a torch." So painful did Miss Susan find the prospect of the funeral that she sought to be excused: "But the master seemed unapproachable in his grief, and I was afraid of incurring his displeasure if he should discover that I was unwilling to pay what he considered fitting respect to the memory of this trusted friend."[8]

Plantation family records reveal any number of such occasions, marked by the same sense of grief and the same respect. One other, a letter from Judith Page Rives of Albemarle County, Virginia, may suffice:

> It was also the day of poor Mammy's interment. She was attacked monday the 1st. I am thankful to say that she apparently suffered little or no pain, and that in the brief intervals of lethargic but tranquil sleep that marked the progress of the fatal malady she was sufficiently conscious to join in the prayers of High at her bed side, and to express to me her firm faith in a savior's love and pardon. Every mark of respect was shown to this good and faithful servant, who I trust, has entered into joy of her Lord. Mr. Boyden performed the service, and we attended with the people of the neighboring farms and our own.[9]

What Mrs. Smedes and Mrs. Rives seem to have missed in their touching recollections is the manner in which the masters appropriated these Mammies to the white family and thereby simply assumed their severance from the black; they also took for granted the way in which the masters defined the terms of respect itself. Possibly, the slaves might have seen those Mammies that way; possibly, the Mammies might have seen themselves that way. But no one ever thought to inquire. These funerals, moving as they were, were for the whites. The blacks never had the chance to show their own grief and their own respect in their own black way.

"Foby," in one of those essays on the "Management of Servants" that so frequently appeared in antebellum agricultural and political journals, included a section on burials (1853): "The dead are decently shrouded, decently confined, and decently buried. This is due to the wounded feelings of the afflicted and should not be neglected."[10] Too many masters ignored the advice, and many slaves suffered terribly from their masters' indifference. Most planters understood, however, that the advice addressed considerations of interest and policy quite as much as considerations of humanity, and they responded accordingly. The extent to which the whites understood that they had to accommodate to their slaves may be measured by the action of an overseer who refused to send his slaves to help a neighbor raise a ginhouse—something every good neighbor simply just did—because they had to go to a funeral. His one concession consisted of polling the slaves to see if there might not be a few who might prefer to pass up the funeral.[11] The importance attached by the slaves to their funerals appeared in their willingness to give up Sundays as a day of leisure in order to participate in a proper ceremony for a fellow who had died during the week and been buried hastily.[12]

How many masters allowed their slaves to quit work in order to attend a funeral and how many did not? Enough ex-slaves answered the question affirmatively to lend credence to the whites' own claims of benevolence.[13] But neither benevolence nor a self-interested concern with slave morale tells the main story. A great many, perhaps a large majority, of slave funerals occurred at night. In the South Carolina and Georgia low country, among other areas of heavy black concentration, they may, as Mrs. Schoolcraft claimed, "invariably" have been held at night.[14] Often, as several ex-slaves insisted, the slaves held their funerals at night because masters refused to allow time during the day.[15] But there is no doubt that the slaves frequently preferred night funerals, if only because it provided an opportunity for friends from neighboring farms and plantations to attend.[16] This preference existed throughout the South but especially in areas of high black density and cultural continuity with Africa, and it strongly suggests African patterns. That the slaves did not simply yield to pressure from their masters is attested to by the persistence of the practice among the freedmen long after the war.[17]

A slave funeral became a pageant, a major event, a community effort at once solemn and spirited. The slaves preferred to have a service, but they would not readily do without a display.[18] In this way they carried on West African tradition, according to which a proper funeral would put the departed spirit to rest and would guarantee against the return of a stirring ghost—a view held by some rural southern blacks during the twentieth century. Funerals thus served as a conduit for the departed's entrance into the spirit world.[19] At the same time the slaves could draw on traditional and frontier white experiences that pointed in the same direction. In seventeenth-century Virginia, funerals among the planters necessarily took on a festive aspect, for mourners had to congregate from long distances. Funerals required considerable expenditure for feeding and quartering; and the occasion, no matter how grim, brought together friends and relatives who normally did not see each other.[20]

The slaves' African inheritance, albeit adapted, modified, and transformed, showed through. Thomas Wentworth Higginson helped arrange a collective black funeral during the war and recalled: "Just before the coffins were lowered, an old man whispered to me that I must have their positions altered—the heads must be towards the west."[21] For the slaves of the eastern seaboard, and for many of the interior as well, graves had to be dug east-west, with the deceased's head to the west, for a man should neither sleep nor be buried "crossways uv de world." The dead should not have to turn around when Gabriel blows his trumpet in the eastern sunrise.[22] African burial customs lingered on in the Old South and in fact into the twentieth century, although by the end of the first decade of the nineteenth century the slaves had merged them with white and Indian customs to form new ones. Throughout the slave period, the West African practice of burying food with the dead reappeared in direct form in the Georgia and South Carolina low country and in one or another variation in Virginia and elsewhere.[23]

As among some West African peoples for whom a "second burial"—that is, a memorial at which all are gathered—is *de rigueur*, so it became among the slaves and freedmen, especially in the extreme Southeast. They would wait for days or weeks after the actual burial to hold a proper funeral. Much of the original African religious rationale fell away, and the practice appeared to be a necessary response to the exigencies of time and distance. As such, the black response did not sharply differ from the white in regions in which similar conditions prevailed,[24] but the practice sank deeper roots and carried on long after it had become rare among the whites.

Physical conditions required speedy burials, whatever might follow. When they could, the slaves held wakes, which struck white observers as rivaling those famous Irish wakes in their raucousness.[25] Here too we find an echo of Africa in the implicit idea of death, but it must also be considered a comment on the relationship of life to death under conditions of sorrow and oppression. Whether raucously or not, the slaves insisted on maintaining a death watch whenever they could get permission. An African insistence? Yes, but also one general among preindustrial peoples. And more to the point, there was a less spiritual explanation. Slave cabins had no glass windows, and the shutters usually had to be left open in the warm southern climate. Dead bodies rotted quickly in the heat, and cats and other animals had little trouble getting in to eat the decaying flesh. The slaves had to protect their dead.

To the horror of many whites, especially the Regular Baptists, who were simply scandalized, the slaves organized processions to and from the cemetery, complete with chanting and singing and "shouts" at the grave. The white Baptists were certain that the proceedings had pagan origins, and by their own definition they were right.[26] The processions moved slowly, led by six or more pallbearers, their way through the dark woods lit by pine torches. The slaves sang their mournful dirges going to, at, and returning from a grave that had earlier been prepared for the body. The sermon would usually be brief.

During the entire period of the slave regime, from eighteenth-century Virginia and South Carolina to nineteenth-century Mississippi and Louisiana, whites frequently preached at slave funerals or at least attended them.[27] More frequently, the slaves by preference conducted their own services. Black preachers, despite restrictive laws, appeared everywhere, and where they were unavailable, drivers, craftsmen, exhorters, or other prestigious slaves filled in. The most common slave funeral had a black man, trained or untrained, literate or illiterate, to add the necessary solemnity, dignity, and religious sanctification to the ceremony.[28]

The slaves' favorite funeral hymn, which could be heard across the South in one of several versions, was "Hark from the Tomb."

> Hark from de tomb a doleful soun'
> My ears hear a tender cry.
> A livin' man come through the groun'
> Whar we may shortly lie.
> Heah in dis clay may be you bed
> In spite ob all you toil
> Let all de wise bow rev'rent head
> Mus' lie as low as ours.

They sang other hymns as well.

> I
>
> We're a marching to the grave,
> We're a marching to the grave, my Lord,
> We're a marching to the grave,
> To lay this body down.

> II
>
> My sister says she's happy,
> By de grace of God we'll meet her,
> In de last long solemn day,
> When we stand around de throne.[29]

From beginning to end, unless well-meaning whites appropriated to themselves the right to make the funeral arrangements, the slaves moved in their own time.

The solemnity dissolved afterwards in a convivial dinner at which tensions broke. It was the combination of more vigorous moments in the procession, especially the use of those drums which were so reminiscent of Africa and so threatening to white ears, and the sometimes boisterous dinners held subsequently that provided the occasion for many whites to consider these funerals "pagan festivals" and to interpret them in one or another self-serving racist way.

The practice of throwing dirt into the grave has not been restricted to Africa and Afro-America and does not in itself prove cultural continuity; but there is no reason to doubt that the blacks of the eastern tidewater and low country brought it from Africa and made it largely their own in the New World. It was not unknown at white funerals, and an ex-slave, Willis Winn of Texas, caustically recalled that although slaves on his plantation were denied their own funerals, they had to attend funerals of whites to throw dirt in their graves.[30] The custom among blacks extended across the South and took especially deep root in the Southeast.[31] However much European practice influenced American practice, white southerners—Edward A. Pollard for one—referred to it as "the negro custom."[32] The significance of the custom remains obscure, at least in its American manifestation, but it loomed large in slave belief. Black conjurers made much of graveyard dirt, mixing it with whiskey or the shavings of the graveboard from the head of the tomb and sometimes including it in the preparation of poisons.[33]

The funeral over, the graves remained. "Broken earthenware," writes Robert Farris Thompson, "adorns the surface of the graves of some Afro-Americans in remote areas of Mississippi, Georgia, and South Carolina, and carved wooden grave-markers have been found in association with these remarkable deposits at Pine Harbor and Sunburg in Georgia."[34] Thompson links these especially to the practice of the Bakongo of northern Angola—a view that has gained in credibility since he put it forward, for new evidence indicates a greater movement of Angolans to the port of Charleston than had previously been thought.[35] The apparent symbolism, he argues, invokes the destruction of the body by death. The broken earthenware, which appears in both West African and

Afro-American practice,[36] has no widespread counterpart among southern Euro-Americans. Afro-American slaves and, long after, freedmen offer hesitant and differing explanations, which lack the coherence of West African traditional belief, but sooner or later they too return to a sense of death as a broken body and to the need to compensate the spirit.

"No Negro in Cottonville," wrote Hortense Powdermaker of the Yazoo Delta in the 1930s, "can live content unless he is assured of a fine funeral when he dies."[37] The funeral has figured prominently as a religious ritual, a social event, and an expression of community. However much the concern with the celebration of death may have arisen from immediate circumstances, it drew upon a long history. The slaves cared passionately about their funerals and demanded that they be elaborate.[38] White southerners, for the most part, yielded to this black demand, as well they might have. Burial of the dead has had a special meaning in the South; white southerners could not, unless their racism totally blinded them, have found the black attitude strange.[39]

Bourgeois opinion in the Western world generally has manifested outrage at the apparently irrational compulsion of the lower classes to insist on funerals beyond their means. For the slaves, means did not present an important problem, but their attitude toward the scale and shape of the event ran true to lower-class form, whatever its special ethnic characteristics. The deluded creatures of the lower classes are generally absurd enough to take religious and family responsibilities seriously and quaint enough to think that their lives, too, ought to be marked by respect. For such people funerals either are proper or they are not. Eric Hobsbawm remarks on the English migrants from country to city during the early part of the nineteenth century: "The irrationally expensive funerals and wakes on which labourers insisted as a traditional tribute to the dead and communal reaffirmation of the living were incomprehensible to a middle class. . . . The first benefit paid by a trade union and friendly society was almost invariably funeral benefit."[40] The familiar charge that the laboring poor could bury their dead at half the price has almost always been naive. Even during the twentieth century an English worker who, say, gave his child a pauper's funeral would thereby pauperize himself—that is, would diminish his credibility as a "respectable" working man—in the eyes of prospective employers.[41] The laborers found themselves propelled by vicious economic pressures into spending much more than their strong sense of the right and the proper required. Thus, they suffered a degree of exploitation well beyond that suffered even by slaves, and they were enmeshed in a tragic complicity in a contemptible and thoroughly bourgeois reduction of respect to the level of dollars and cents. But in the world they knew they dared not, if they could possibly avoid it, refuse to pay whatever it took to provide that decent respect for the dead which helps define respect for the living.

The Nazis knew what they were doing when they refused to bury concentration-camp victims. Considerations of cost and convenience were not paramount. Joost A. M. Meerlo comments: "There is in this mass murder and defiance of the dead the defiance of life itself, the defiance of the vital and moral forces guiding men. It is the denial of any aim in this world."[42] Conversely, respect for the dead signifies respect for the living—respect for the continuity of the human community and recognition of each man's place within it. The slaves understood their responsibilities.[43]

THE WHITE PREACHERS

The slaveholders' effort to control black religion depended ultimately on the work of the white preachers. Throughout the nineteenth century a substantial number of the white preachers themselves owned slaves. In South Carolina during 1780–1800, for example, of the one hundred preachers or licentiates, 40 percent owned some slaves and one ranked as a big planter.[1] What kind of slaveholders were they? The fragmentary accounts in the slave narratives leave the impression that most qualified, by the slaves' standard of judgment, as humane, although some had no difficulty in reconciling their Christianity with cruelty.[2]

The white ministry had accumulated some spiritual capital with the slaves during the eighteenth and early nineteenth centuries by its hostility, or at least coolness, toward the institution of slavery; but by the time of the Nat Turner revolt it had squandered most of it. Some antislavery ministers continued to work in the Upper South throughout the antebellum period, but fewer and fewer, especially as community opposition grew harsher and more threatening.[3] William Henry Holcombe of Natchez, Mississippi, himself moderately proslavery, penned a recollection of his father, William James Holcombe of Virginia, who later freed his slaves and resettled them in Ohio and Liberia:

> [My father] devoted himself without reward or self-seeking of any kind, to the spiritual welfare of the poor and the outcasts, especially of the slave population, became the trusted friend and even idol of the impressible, affectionate negroes, preaching for them on Sunday afternoons, superintending their prayer-meeting and revivals, baptizing, marrying, burying, bearing their burdens, entering with his whole Soul into the joys, the sufferings, the sorrows of these feeblest and humblest children of Christ.[4]

But by the 1830s such men had become rare in the Upper South and virtually nonexistent in the Lower. When ministers did have doubts about slavery, they usually took the ground of the Reverend John H. Witherspoon, who wrote to his wife:

> I have been from my youth up, opposed to slavery as it exists in the South, *on the score of expediency.* Nothing has so prostrated our Southern country in point of domestic improvement as slavery.
> And yet I believe African Slavery, lawful & not unchristian, and that it is better for them, on the whole, *than liberty* without a due *preparation* for the reception of the blessing.
> Some may attribute this view to selfish motives but I have nothing to gain from it. I never willingly and heartily *bought* or *sold* a human being. I have done so, for the accommodation of the slave & my own domestic peace & comfort but *never* for *gain*, from the "love of filthy lucre."[5]

The slaves, therefore, made their judgments on other grounds. The whites took the political orthodoxy of their ministers increasingly for granted and came to regard them as supporters of the plantation social order.

White ministers who preached to the slaves congratulated themselves on the excellence of their performance. Joseph B. Stratton, a Presbyterian minister, reported contentedly that his services in the Natchez region were "interesting and solemn." Willis P. Hill, an itinerant Baptist preacher in South Carolina, found the slaves "remarkably attentive" to his sermons. John H. Witherspoon, a Presbyterian minister of Greensboro, Alabama, fully expected that the slaves on the plantation to which he was going would flock to hear him. To Francis Hanson, an Episcopal minister of Marengo County, Alabama, the blacks "seemed to be interested in the services." N. L. Garfield saw the distinguished Bishop Leonidas Polk of Louisiana preach at the confirmation of slaves: "I noticed one of those confirmed that when the Bishop laid his hands on his head, the tears ran down his cheeks!" The Reverend John Hamilton Cornish visited the plantation of Colonel Joseph E. Jenkins in South Carolina and expressed delight when several dozen field hands called his name, jumped the fence, and ran to express their pleasure at seeing him. Other whites expressed satisfaction with those who preached to their slaves. Leonidas Pendleton Spyker of Louisiana noted that Mr. Trippett "is an excellent preacher either for white or black." And after the war, Martha Schofield told of a white preacher in South Carolina whose prestige allowed him to intercede to save some ex-Rebel troops from the wrath of the freedmen.[6]

Notwithstanding these rosy recollections, which may have been fair enough so far as they went, the slaves frequently gave the white preachers a rough time. Not that they often displayed hostility—although they did walk out on the Reverend John B. Pinney when he recounted his impressions of the degradation he had witnessed in Africa and told them how lucky they were[7]—they just responded, in the words of one editor, with "a loud, comfortable, snoring nap."[8] Eliza Frances Andrews' diary for January 15, 1865, noted the black response to the Reverend Dr. Hillyer's service: "They kept awake and looked very much edified while the singing was going on, but most of them slept through the sermon."[9]

The first, although not the most serious, problem facing the white preachers concerned language and style. What, after all, can be said about the young white minister who began his sermon to the slaves with, "Primarily, we must postulate the existence of a deity"? Bertram Wilbur Doyle, who tells this story in his *Etiquette of Race Relations in the South*, adds that after a short pause an old black man responded, "Yes, Lord, dat's so. Bless de Lord."[10] Everyone may interpret the old man's response for himself. I can only find in it further evidence that black slaves were compassionate people, always ready to rescue a conscientious ass from the consequences of his own acts. Another white preacher had a similar problem but an earthier capacity to deal with it. An ex-slave recalled that when the preacher grew frustrated at seeing the slaves unable or unwilling to comprehend his sermon, he would curse them. That they understood.[11]

There is no record of the sermons of Samuel A. Agnew, a Presbyterian minister in Mississippi, but none is needed to know what he was about. The good minister thought, "There is not much faith to be reposed in a negroe" (sic). He noticed in particular that the slaves did not keep their word.[12] One night he wandered into a black prayer meeting by mistake and left us his Christian reaction as a timeless memorial to the sensitivity of his class:

> Went in and heard the negroes conduct a prayer meeting and remained untill an old negro commenced preaching. This was the first time I ever saw "Afric s ebon sons" conduct the public services of the sanctuary. I tried to keep my mind in the proper frame for such services but the "King's English" was so mercilessly cut up that often I could scarce restrain a smile. "Dis" "dat" "Warship" "source" "retentions" are given as specimens. I became tired of the moans etc and mounted my mule and sped on my way home.[13]

John Hamilton Cornish, a much better human being, gave an instructive account of a different kind: "Evening—Negroes came to chant—have learned this winter *Benedic, Anima, mei* and sing it well—under Martha's instruction. Last winter I taught them *Vente, exulternos Domino.*"[14] The Reverend Mr. Cornish at least had the good sense to stress singing, which the slaves loved so much they would even do it in Latin. Fredrika Bremer saw the point in her own way. She had heard a white preacher deliver an "unusually wooden" sermon to the slaves on a rice plantation in South Carolina. "But," she remarked, "I was astonished at the people's quick and glad reception of every single expression of beauty or of feeling."[15]

The problem of communication did not lend itself to solution nearly so readily as might be assumed. If all at issue had been the stiffness of the white preachers, it would have easily been overcome, especially since the fiery Baptists and Methodists, who made up the great majority of the white preachers, did not suffer from the inhibitions of the Presbyterians or Episcopalians. A glimpse of how much a sympathetic white Methodist preacher might accomplish comes from a report by a North Carolinian who stumbled on a service for slaves. William D. Valentine described the Reverend Sam Wright Hayse as a feeling although not profound preacher. The Reverend Mr. Hayse began gravely to establish decorum but soon warmed up. The blacks "vibrated." Valentine described the congregation as being "charged as with electric influence that quickened, not deadened." He expressed wonder at "such fierce, rough struggle of gesticulation and shouting" and added, "It seemed the preacher had said as they wanted him say it."[16] The Reverend C. C. Jones thus had to worry about another problem—that of preaching in the blacks' own style and ostensibly sacrificing the dignity of the service and the purity of the message. He acknowledged that slaves were "good judges of a good sermon," but he saw only the issues of theological content and proper English. Appropriately, John Edwin Fripp of St. Helena, South Carolina, used the word "lectures" to describe the preaching done by a Reverend Mr. Welch to the slaves.[17] In Louisiana, the editor of the *Planters' Banner* fumed that the blacks understood nothing and merely responded to intonations, gestures, and emotional cues.[18] Like most whites, he could not understand that the black response to tone and gesture implied its own content.

The white ministers had a credibility problem as well. John Hamilton Cornish, for example, worked with the slaves well enough to earn their contributions of pennies and nickels to his collection plate, and he displayed genuine concern for their welfare. But what were they to think when, albeit with grave misgivings, he dutifully served his turn on the hated and feared slave patrols?[19] How were they to interpret the restraint of a man like the Reverend Sidney D. Bumpus of North Carolina, who could write: "Performed the disagreeable task of praying for two criminals at the gallows who were hung today. George had accidentally killed a white man, in self defense who attempted to beat him with a hoe . . ."?[20]

There is hardly a word in Bumpus's private journal, or in Cornish's diary, or in the private papers even of the most dedicated ministers, about the wordly hopes, fears, sorrows, aspirations, and travail of those slaves whom they felt it a duty to attend. They dared not concern themselves. The Reverend C. C. Jones himself had warned them to "have nothing to do with the civil condition of the negroes, or with their plantation affairs." Listen to no complaints, he insisted, and take no part in their quarrels. These charges laid bare the terms on which the slaveholders would allow the preachers to set foot on their plantations at all.[21]

Yet the slaves knew that many of these white preachers, in their own brittle way, genuinely cared about them. The Reverend C. C.

Jones wore himself out in pursuit of the religious instruction of the blacks, as he called it. His son fearfully begged him to give up night rides to plantation services, which were undermining his health. When he died, his family had reason to believe that this overwork had hastened the end.[22] Many other ministers—the Reverend Mr. Cornish among them—did their best and meant well, and the slaves often responded with kind appreciation. Mandy Hadnot of Texas, for example, remembered a white preacher fondly as a "big jolly man." But the positive attitude toward some white ministers generally had a practical edge. For sixteen years Andy Marion waited on a Presbyterian pastor, who finally died and left him a house and forty acres. "Dat's what I calls religion," Marion exulted.[23] For the most part, however, the slaves did not so much like or dislike the white preachers as manifest indifference to them. With notable exceptions, the preachers did not figure much in their lives.

At their best the white preachers had much to say to the slaves and made an indispensable contribution to the spiritual life of the quarters. A few regularly struck a responsive chord, and many others might suddenly make the slaves come alive at any given moment. It did matter, and the slaves did remember, when a preacher had the courage to dwell on the theme that God made no distinction between the souls of white masters and black slaves. The tough-minded Solomon Northup thought William Ford, a cotton planter in Avoyelles Parish, Louisiana, to be the best of masters and particularly remembered his preaching to the slaves on Sunday. "He sought," Northup wrote, "to inculcate in our minds feelings of kindness toward each other, of dependence upon God—setting forth the rewards promised unto those who lead an upright and prayerful life."[24] Let the record show that good white men in good faith did good deeds. Let it also show that much of the time the slaves, ungrateful as usual, fell asleep.

Sometimes they stayed awake and smothered their anger. Hannah Scott of Arkansas: "But all he say is 'bedience to de white folks, and we hears 'nough of dat without him tellin' us." Lizzie Hughes of Texas: "The whites preached to the niggers and the niggers preached to theyselves." Jenny Proctor of Alabama especially remembered a white preacher who coldly told the slaves that they had no souls and could expect no afterlife. Maria, Mary Boykin Chesnut's slave, forcefully explained that she preferred the Reverend Manning Brown to a circuit rider, the Reverend Mr. Shuford:

"He [Brown] is ole Marster's nephew, a gentleman born, and he preaches to black and to white just the same. . . . Mr. Shuford he goes for low life things, hurting people's feeling. 'Don't you tell lies. Don't you steal!' Worse things, real indecent. Before God, we are white as he is, and in the pulpit he no need to make us feel we are servants." Nancy Williams of Virginia summed up: "Dat ole white preachin' wasn't nothin.' Ole white preachers used to talk wid dey tongues widdout sayin' nothin' but Jesus told us slaves to talk wid our hearts."[25]

The slaves understood the assigned political task of the white preachers and naturally resented it. The favorite text of the white preachers, as the Reverend C. C. Jones proudly acknowledged, was Paul's "Servants, obey in all things your masters according to the flesh; not with eyeservice, as menpleasers; but in singleness of heart, fearing God: And whatsoever ye do, do it heartily, as to the Lord, and not unto men. . . ." To which the Reverend Mr. Jones pointedly added the even more direct words of the Apostle Peter: "Servants, be subject to your masters with all fear; not only to the good and gentle, but also to the froward."[26]

The prize for sermons from such texts must, however, go to the Right Reverend William Meade, Episcopal bishop of Virginia, by no means a bad soul as these things go. Indeed, his reputation as a man with genuine feeling for the slaves underscores the significance of his performance. His subject was "correction"—that is, whipping.

> Now, when *correction* is given you, you either deserve it, or you do not deserve it. But whether you deserve it or not it is your duty, and Almighty God requires, that you bear it patiently. You may, perhaps, think that this is a hard doctrine; but if you consider it rightly, you must needs think otherwise of it. . . . Suppose you do not, or at least you do not deserve so much or so severe a correction for the fault you have committed; you perhaps have escaped a great many more, and are at last paid for all. Or suppose you are quite innocent of what is laid to your charge, and suffer wrongfully in that particular thing; is it not possible that you may have done some other bad which was never discovered, and that Almighty God, who saw you doing it, would not let you escape without punishment some time or another? And ought you not in such a case to give glory to Him, and be thankful that He would rather punish you in this life for your wickedness, than destroy your souls for it in the next life? But suppose that even this was not the case—a case hardly to be imagined

—and that you have by no means, known or unknown, deserved the correction you suffered; there is great comfort in it, that if you bear it patiently, and leave your cause in the hands of God, He will reward you for it in heaven, and the punishment you suffer unjustly here shall turn to your exceeding great glory hereafter.[27]

The bishop's theology ranks in soundness with that of the celebrated Roman theologian, Spina, who, according to Michelet, never worried whether the Inquisition's victims were guilty. Father Spina explained to his squeamish associates that even if those executed were innocent, they deserved death anyway by reason of original sin.[28]

However much such sermons as that of Bishop Meade may have reeked of racist arrogance and insensitivity, they expressed, *par excellence*, traditional European class attitudes. All Bishop Meade had done was to adapt the classic formula of, for example, the eighteenth-century priests who went among the poor of Paris. Honor God for your poverty, they implored, for He has, in His infinite mercy, spared you the temptations attendant upon wealth and thereby rendered your souls so much the safer.[29] And little if anything in the sermons of the white preachers could overmatch the wonderful tidings announced by a Kentish parson in 1543. He taught that God had constructed not one but three heavens—one for the poor, one for the men of mean estate, and one for society's great.[30] Even the Reverend Samuel A. Agnew, if his sermons could be consulted, could not have improved upon the theme. The racism permeating the white sermons left its own deep scar, but the sermons themselves had been built on class pretensions that had proceeded fearlessly through the ages without regard to race, color, creed, or previous condition of servitude.

ORIGINS OF THE FOLK RELIGION

Afro-American religion arose from a conjuncture of many streams —African, European, classic Judeo-Christian, and Amerindian— but pre-eminently it emerged as a Christian faith both black and American. The argument over African "survivals" and "influence," which once engaged the formidable talent of Melville J. Herskovits, who argued for continuity, and of E. Franklin Frazier, who argued for a sharp break, will no doubt go on.[1] Neither position in stark form is tenable, but each has made valuable contributions to the discussion.

In ways indirect, distorted, ambiguous, and even confused, the spiritual experience of the slaves took shape as part of a tradition emanating from Africa. To seek, as so many have done, for European antecedents for every feature of black culture is to collapse into absurdity. Of course, the blacks took much from the whites; of course, the whites took much from the blacks. Blacks and whites in America may be viewed as one nation or two or as a nation within a nation, but their common history guarantees that, one way or another, they are both American. The fact remains that a significant thrust in black culture emanated from the African tradition. If that thrust had European counterparts, so be it. If those counterparts reinforced or encouraged certain features of black religion, well and good. Black America's tie with an African tradition nonetheless remained and helped shape a culture entirely its own. And, no—*pace* all "scientific" historians—it cannot be measured.

Traditional West African religion provided an integrated world-view. G. J. A. Ojo writes: "African life in general is thoroughly permeated by religion. It is no overstatement to say that religion is not just one complex of African culture but the catalyst of the other complexes."[2] For West Africans, as for earlier Euro-Christians, religion was an aspect, not a feature, of society—the vital way in which the entire human body collectively expressed its essence. Among other ramifications, no clear distinction could develop in Akan religion, for example, between wrong and sin.[3] Thus, the insistence of slaves on a Christian message that was this-worldly at the very moment of its most apparently other-worldly pronouncements had deep roots.

The West African belief in a pantheon of gods passed to drastically different political settings in the New World. Without doubt it syncretized much better with Catholic than with Protestant Christianity. West Africans generally believed in a Supreme God who presided in some ultimate sense over human morality, but they also believed in a large body of specific gods. One normally reached the Supreme God through an appeal for the intercession of a lesser god, much as Catholics reach God by an appeal for the intercession of the saints or the Virgin Mary.

> Holy Mary, Mother of God,
> Pray for us sinners,
> Now and at the hour of our death.

Protestantism, especially in its Baptist and Methodist forms, offered a poor refuge. Where was one to find room for an Ogun cult translated into homage to Saint George or Saint Anthony? Yet, as the experience of the British Caribbean reveals, the austerity and exclusiveness of the Protestant denominations left room for the retention of a much purer African religious tradition than did the universalism of the Church of Rome, which so much more easily absorbed the cults once they became diluted. In the southern United States the combination of hostile white power, small plantation and farm units, and the early closing of the slave trade crushed much of the specific African religious memory. But since the denominations could not easily absorb the African impulse, they found themselves defeated by it in two sometimes complementary and sometimes antagonistic ways: large residues of "superstition" remained in the interstices of the black community; and Afro-Christianity arose as something within the Euro-Christian community and yet remained very much without.

African belief in a pantheon of gods facilitated conversion to both Catholic and Protestant Christianity, for it carried with it the perfectly sensible principle that no one could afford total reliance on a god who allows his people to get beaten, whereas everyone could use identification with a god who leads his people to victory. This tribal principle existed among the peoples of the ancient Near East, including the early Jews. Adherence to local or tribal deities strengthened the political particularism that had given rise to it. The movement from a tribal god, which implied spiritual allegiance to a single nation, to a universal community of men grew out of a primitive Jewish form into a Catholic form in the Christian Church. With the development of the Jewish view came the shift from blaming a weak god for tribal defeat to blaming one's own people for the infidelity that had provoked His wrath. When Africans took over the Christian God they simultaneously extended, rather than transcended, their own particularist practice.

Traditional West African religions did not espouse a doctrine of original sin, and the acceptance of Christianity by African peoples never did result in a full surrender to this most profound and fateful of Christian ideas. The idea of original sin lies at the heart of the Western formulation of the problem of freedom and order. In time it tipped the ideological scales decisively toward the side of individual freedom in its perpetual struggle with the demands for social order. For the West Africans the scales remained tipped toward social order so long as their world-view and the social basis on which it rested remained traditional.

This spiritual collectivism retreated before the advance of Christianity, but it preserved something of its older quality. Afro-Americans accepted Christianity's celebration of the individual soul and turned it into a weapon of personal and community survival. But their apparent indifference to sin, not to be confused with an indifference to injustice or wrongdoing, guaranteed retention of the collective, life-affirming quality of the African tradition and thus also became a weapon for personal and community survival. The slaves reshaped the Christianity they had embraced; they conquered the religion of those who had conquered them. In their formulation, Christianity lacked that terrible inner tension between the sense of guilt and the sense of mission which once provided the ideological dynamism for Western civilization's march to world power. But in return for this loss of revolutionary dynamism, the slaves developed an Afro-American and Christian humanism that affirmed joy in life in the face of every trial.

The African principle of acquiring stronger gods did not require or even encourage the surrender of one's own gods. The diversity of gods resembles that of the Greeks and Hindus, among other great peoples, and hardly implies intellectual backwardness, as so many whites have charged. On the combination of monotheism and polytheism among the Greeks, which in this respect resembles that of the Africans, Santayana writes that it "is no contradiction, but merely an intelligent variation of phrase to indicate various aspects or functions in physical and moral things."[4]

Two other interrelated features of West African religion especially bear on the black experience in America. First, West Africans practiced what has often dubiously been called "ancestor worship"; second, they believed in a kind of reincarnation and strongly adhered to an idea of the world as a good, warm, light place. West African religion affirmed life and linked concern for the deceased and belief in rebirth not with suffering but with the celebration of existence. The traditional attitude toward ancestors, and therefore toward the aged, perpetuated a profoundly "Eastern" rather than "Western" view of the world. Whereas Western civilization bequeathed to Euro-Americans, especially to Anglo-Saxons, a vision of being heirs of the ages, African civilization bequeathed to Afro-Americans a vision of being debtors to the ages and, accordingly, a sense of responsibility to those who came before.[5] African tradition imparted to the religion of the slaves an irrepressible affirmation of life—an ability to see the world as a "vale of tears" and yet experience a joy in life that has sometimes evoked admiration from whites, sometimes contempt, but almost always astonishment.

White contemporaries, resident and nonresident, agreed that the religious life of the slaves embraced much more than anything they were capable of recognizing as Christianity. Most also agreed that the slaves' religious feeling, whatever its elements, ran deep. During the war Thomas Wentworth Higginson recounted with wonder and admiration the spirit of the black troops, most of whom had only recently been slaves. Not since Cromwell's time, he exulted, have we seen so religious an army. The blacks called it a "Gospel Army." Among the more significant features of his account are these: the blacks spoke and sang incessantly of Moses and associated him with all the great events of history, including the most recent; their services displayed drumming, clapping, and bodily movement in the African manner; and the praise-house they built reminded him of nothing so much as a "regular African hut." He observed wisely that the deep religious faith of the slaves had saved them from the dehumanization the abolitionists had feared inevitable under slavery.[6]

The stubborn insistence of the slaves on their right to touch God received poignant expression from an ex-slave who acidly commented on white attempts to exclude them from Christian communion: "Dey law us out of church, but dey couldn't law 'way Christ."[7] The religious fervor of the slaves became a matter of general comment among the whites and a matter of widespread recollection among ex-slaves, some of whom—in this respect, anyway—wished for a return of the old times.[8] Plantation records, travelers' accounts, and other contemporary sources reflect the considerable and somewhat surprised interest with which whites viewed the tenacity as well as the spirit of religious expression among the slaves.

The slaves, however, did not always admire white religious expressions and markedly preferred their own. Henrietta Perry, an ex-slave from Virginia, said, "White folks can't pray right to de black man's God. Can't nobody do it for you. You got to call on God yourself when de spirit tell you and let God know dat you bin washed free from sin."[9] "Many of the blacks," noted a pained white clergyman in 1832, "look upon white people as merely taught by the Book; they consider themselves instructed by the inspiration of the Spirit."[10] Whites fear religion, charged Anderson Jackson, an ex-slave of South Carolina: "I stays independent of what white folks tells me when I shouts. De Spirit moves me every day, dat's how I stays in. White folks don't feel sech as I does; so dey stays out."[11]

Some northern abolitionists and southern slaveholders alike doubted the depth of the slaves' Christian commitment. For some southerners, not necessarily the most flagrantly racist, the quality of religious expression among the blacks belied a Christian sensibility; for some northern critics, the slave system was so vicious that no one could possibly expect the slaves to be capable of understanding the Christian message. Thus James Redpath, whose youth may excuse his insufferable self-righteousness:

> I have investigated the character of too many of the "pious negroes" to feel any respect either for their religion or their teachers. Church membership does not prevent fornication, bigamy, adultery, lying, theft, or hypocrisy. It is a cloak, in nine cases out of ten, which the slaves find convenient to wear, and in the exceptional cases, it is a union of meaningless cant and wildest fanaticism. A single spark of true Christianity among the slave population would set the plantations in a blaze. Christianity and slavery cannot live together; but churchianity and slavery are twins.[12]

It is painful to have to report that even the Reverend R. Q. Mallard, son-in-law of the Reverend C. C. Jones and a stalwart supporter of the slave regime, showed greater sensitivity, not to mention decency, when he discussed the same question. He was "shocked" by a black revival meeting and wrote to his wife: "I could but ask: What religion is there in this? And yet I could scarcely doubt the sincerity and even piety of some who offered prayer. Some allowance, of course, must be made for the *excitability* of the Negro temperament. What better, indeed, could we expect of those who only imitate (somewhat exaggerating it, of course) the conduct of some of their masters, who should know better?"[13] Throughout the South many slaveholders showed far less condescension than the Reverend Mr. Mallard in paying tribute to the slaves' deep religious conviction.[14] Even the State Supreme Court of Mississippi took note of it. A lower court had refused to admit the dying words of a pious slave as testimony against the slave who had attacked him. The Supreme Court reversed the ruling with the observation: "The simple, elementary truths of Christianity, the immortality of the soul, and a future accountability are generally . . . believed by this portion of our population."[15]

With the war and emancipation the strength of the slaves' religion became clear. The religious intensity of the ex-slave Union troops, the freedmen's translation of their political position into religious terms, and the extraordinary mushrooming of black churches told their own story. Redpath and most other whites, northern and southern, had been misled because the Christian expression of the slaves burst forth as something so different from anything they knew. For such critics the slaves had to become, in effect, either white Christians or no Christians at all. The slaves saw it differently. For them, the more honest efforts of the whites to bring them Christianity served primarily to provide a spiritual basis compatible with the Euro-American world into which they had been forced and from which they would never wholly separate themselves. But as such, it gave them the wherewithal to fashion a religion of their own—one no less Christian than that of the whites and one that would gradually insinuate itself into the "white" American Christianity so anxious to disown it.

But what kind of Christianity? Did Africa intrude itself into the slaves' religious life, and if so, did it present a direct challenge to Christianity? How can we speak of a genuine Christianity among slaves if we also insist that their most solemn beliefs and practices could not be isolated from what so many contemporaries called "superstition"—from conjuring, magic, and witchcraft?

Few would doubt the strength of "Africanisms" or indeed of African religion per se among the blacks during the eighteenth century, but many have doubted their persistence into the late antebellum period outside New Orleans and the coast of Georgia and South Carolina. Yet, white as well as black sources attest to persistence all across the South even after slavery had passed. The real problem concerns the meaning of the beliefs. Along the coast, even in the Virginia tidewater, African-born conjurers, quasi-African practices and beliefs, and strange "superstitions" abounded.[16] The Reverend C. C. Jones wrote in the early 1840s that African "paganism" had been dying out since the closing of the slave trade but that the Negroes of Georgia still typically believed in "second-sight, in apparitions, charms, witchcraft, and in a kind of irresist-ible Satanic influence."[17]

A writer who identified himself as a "minister of the gospel" gave his own report to the *Southern Cultivator*, which should com-mand special attention because of the nature of that publication. Southern agricultural periodicals went to planters and overseers who were quick to reply to humbug when they saw it. This report drew no fire.

> Another fact, equally notorious, is that on almost every large planta-tion of Negroes there is one among them who holds a kind of magical sway over the minds and opinions of the rest; to him they look as their oracle—and this same oracle, though most generally a *preacher*, is, in ninety-nine cases out of a hundred, the most consummate villain and hypocrite on the premises. It is more likely that he has seen sundry miraculous visions, equal to those of John on the Isle of Patmos; angels have talked with him, etc. etc. The influence of such a negro on the quarter is incalculable. He *steals* his master's pigs, and is still an object commanding the peculiar regard of Heaven, and why may not his disciples? It may be, and in most cases this influence is, such an obstacle in the way of the missionary, that he can accom-plish but little unless his preaching is in unison with the theology of this sage old *Doctor of Divinity*.[18]

The slaves, wrote Olmsted from the interior as well as the coast, generally use religious figures of speech, refer to visions, and give signs of deep fervor. "The result," he added, "in the majority of cases has been merely to furnish a delusive clothing of Christian forms and phrases, to the original vague superstition of the African savage."[19] Few slaves, wrote the astute slaveholding intellectual, D. R. Hundley, any longer believe in the African religions as such, but most continue to believe in witchcraft, sorcery, conjuring, and other forms of "paganism."[20] Similar observations appear in pri-vate plantation letters and memoirs. The planters never doubted that their slaves' Christianity contained a good dose of African belief.[21]

Leading Southern physicians especially concerned themselves with black religious beliefs and practices. Dr. Samuel Cartwright, a racist ideologue with some standing in the medical profession, warned that every large plantation had one or more conjurers who ruled the other slaves by terror. He expressed dismay that even the intelligent Negroes, despite their shamefaced denials, believed in witchcraft and sorcery and yielded to the leadership of conjurers.[22] Belief in witchcraft and conjuring, according to Dr. John Stainback Wilson, prevailed among plantation Negroes. He charged that it induced depressions which predisposed the slaves to disease and ruled the course of their ensuing illnesses.[23] Dr. W. M. Carpenter expressed particular concern for the fatalistic resignation that gripped many slaves addicted to dirt eating. He believed that Obeah or some equivalent lay at the root of the trouble.[24]

Negro beliefs of distinctly African origin, prevalent in slavery times, continued well into the twentieth century and have not disappeared in the rural South or in the innermost parts of the great cities. The dead can return to the living in spiritual visitations that are not necessarily ill-intentioned or dangerous. Children born with teeth or as twins come under an ominous sign. Conjuring is the cause of insanity. Many maladies must be attributed to the insertion of a snake into the human body by a conjurer in the service of some enemy. Frizzled chickens should be kept to dig up any conjure bag an enemy may place near your house.[25]

Belief in conjuring, voodoo, Obeah, and witchcraft among rural and urban southern blacks has not proven incompatible with a fervid commitment to Christianity. In some areas ministers themselves have openly shared the attitudes of their congregations, much as the poor parish priests in traditional Catholic countries have often shared their congregations' belief in magic.[26] Southern black "superstition," on closer inspection, takes on the attributes of a folk religion, which has not in its manifold forms been limited to New Orleans or the Sea Islands. If in those areas of strongest continuing African presence they appear in more disciplined and structured form, elsewhere they have persisted under various guises.[27]

Southern conjurers have almost always been black, but their clientele has often been interracial.[28] And white participants have not always come from the rural lower classes. Julia E. Harn writes in her account of black life in Georgia: "So firm a hold upon the youthful mind have the things we learned in childhood, few of those brought up with Negro nurses are really free of every vestige of superstition."[29] Among the mountain whites and the poor whites of the plantation districts, belief in witches and in magic initially derived from Europe; but it merged with black and Indian lore and sometimes produced respect for black conjurers.[30] Weyman Williams, an ex-slave from Texas, had no trouble understanding his mistress's willingness to let her slaves openly express a belief in conjuring: "She partly believe it too."[31] William Wells Brown remembered a black fortune teller whose clients included young white ladies in search of true love. Court records identify black conjurers whose white clientele had more serious interests: here, a case in which a master fell under the power of a conjurer on his plantation; there, a small slaveholder who sought a conjurer's help in business matters. And then, too, one chap enlisted a black conjurer to help murder his wife.[32]

Slaves and ex-slaves, including Frederick Douglass, described the conjurers' power over the quarters.[33] Ex-slaves often identified the conjurers as having been African-born, but possibly those African-born slaves who still remained in late antebellum times came to be thought of as natural conjurers. The blacks believed that only blacks, especially those born with a caul, had the secret power and that it was somehow a gift of their African heritage.[34]

The strength of the African element in the religion of the slaves emerges even from antivoodoo pronouncements. Martha Colquitt, who had been a house slave in Georgia, recalled: "Us all de time heard folkses talkin' about voodoo, but my grandma was powerful religious, and her and Ma tell us chillen voodoo was a no 'count doin' of de devil, and Christians was never to pay it no attention."[35] An ex-slave from Alabama spoke up: "But I'm a believer, and this here voodoo and hoodoo and spirits ain't nothing but a lot of folks outen Christ. Haunts ain't nothin' but somebody died outen Christ and his spirit ain't at rest, just in a wandering condition in the world."[36] In these expressions the blacks inadvertently affirmed strong African ideas. The devil appears alive and specific. Disturbed spirits wander in and out of the world of the living.

On closer inspection, the devil of the black stories, songs, and accounts is usually a trickster and often a demon in the form of a man. He is both terrifying and a source of mirth. In the spiritual, "You Must Be Pure and Holy," we hear:

> De debbil am a liah an' a conjurer too.
> Ef you doan look out, he'll conjure you.

The fiddle and the banjo were the devil's tools. You communicated with him by playing, and simultaneously you had a good time yourself.[37] Devil's tools or no, plantation preachers did not hesitate to double as fiddlers at parties in the quarters.[38] Ingraham tells of a complaint by a planter who for years had tried to teach his slaves Christianity. It was, he said, hopeless. One day he questioned a slave whom he had long been drilling: "In whose image were you made?" The reply exasperated him: "In de image ob de debil, master." Edward A. Pollard described an illuminating incident without seeing anything in it besides the comic quality of black religion:

> A minister was telling Uncle Junk, to work him to repentance, how the devil tormented those who went to hell. Junk hoped that "good Mass'r Debble" wouldn't be so cruel. The minister reproved him from speaking of Satan in such polite terms. "Well, you see, Mass'r," replied the old negro, "no tellin' but de enemy might cotch me, and den I trust he remember as how I spoke of him perlitely, and jes de same as if he was a white man."

Or, as the old Gullah saying had it: "De buckruh hab scheme, en de nigger hab trick, en ebry time de buckruh scheme once, de nigger trick twice."[39] The slaves' idea of the devil appeared strange to the whites for the same reason that the idea of so many West Africans would have. Good and evil could not easily be separated in the projection of discrete personalities. However terrifying to the slaves in some of his aspects, the devil could also be a friend in need and a laughing matter.[40]

William E. Barton, a white minister, observed an element of insincerity in black demonology: "Satan is a decided convenience. It is always possible to load on him what else might be a weight upon the conscience."[41] Barton missed the African trickster in this demonology, but he did have a point. In Africa the social setting kept the devil under ethical restraints and made men responsible for their own spirit. In the religiously disorganized social setting of the plantations the devil-as-trickster sometimes led to an evasion of personal responsibility and presented a formidable challenge to the effort of the black preachers to shape an appropriate moral consciousness among the slaves.

Black belief in ghosts was not distinguished from that of southern whites, but one feature of their belief was. Many of the slaves believed not only in ghosts to be feared but in ghosts to be befriended—in benign spirits of old friends who returned to visit and to see if everything was all right.[42] This African belief does not seem to have been widespread among the poor whites, and if it existed at all, it was probably learned from the blacks. In white belief, as well as in much black, ghosts were purely evil spirits or the souls of the restless dead; they might not be dangerous, but they were always to be dreaded.

Southern voodoo, much confused with other manifestations of what the whites called superstition, separated blacks from those whites commonly thought to have been wallowing in witchcraft and magic. However fascinated whites have always been by voodoo, it has been a black religion.[43] As a system of belief, Southern voodoo never reached the internal coherence of Haitian Vodûn, but, relative to the "Africanisms" dissolved in black folk religion, it has maintained a distinct character. In its classic form it has been primarily associated with New Orleans, although well after emancipation it demonstrated surprising strength in Atlanta and other cities.

According to Robert Tallant, voodoo arose during the eighteenth century with the arrival of slaves from Africa and the West Indies, who adapted their "snake cults" to new surroundings; but it did not spread.[44] The slaveholders associated it with rebellion as well as heathenism and suppressed it ruthlessly.[45] The influx of West Indian slaves after the American annexation broke the dikes. Thereafter the authorities in New Orleans tried various measures to defeat it, including sponsorship of black dances in Congo Square. They remained convinced that the voodoo priests were stirring up hatred for whites, although this fear may have arisen more from the secretiveness of the ceremonies than from overt acts. Moreover, free Negroes and women notably predominated in the leadership of the cult. This set it off from the various manifestations of black Christianity that swept through the South. Voodoo itself, however, fused with Christian beliefs and probably reached its height in the 1850s.

At no time during the slave period did voodoo become a major force outside New Orleans, although scattered manifestations appeared on the Louisiana plantations and spread in all directions. The many references to voodoo, or hoodoo as the plantation slaves usually called it, commonly refer to unorganized conjuring, witchcraft, and magic. Voodoo remained peripheral to the slave experience, but as its reputation and fragments of its practice spread, they strengthened the slaves' commitment to the folk aspect of their religion and their sense of being in the hands of powers other than those of the whites.

Newbell Niles Puckett, among others, suggests that the masters deliberately instilled fear of the supernatural into their slaves or at least encouraged it as a means of control.[46] No doubt some did, but most feared the effects of strange beliefs on their slaves and tried to suppress them. Plantation papers usually mention voodoo, conjure, and superstition as something to be abhorred and punished, and the blacks similarly reported their masters' hostility. "Old Miss wouldn't stand for no such thing as voodoo and haunts," said Prince Johnson of Yazoo, Mississippi. "When she inspected us once a week, you better not have no charm around your neck, neither."[47] When blacks spoke of conjure as a means of social control they usually referred to the power of some slaves over others. For example, an ex-slave recalled an old conjure man who looked after the children and used their fear of his magic to keep them obedient.[48]

The social significance of voodoo and conjure among the slaves lay less in some direct threat to the whites, much less in their alleged use by whites to control blacks, than in the degree of autonomy they provided the quarters. The slaves saw other slaves with great power, and by that belief alone they offered resistance to that doctrine of black impotence which the slaveholders worked incessantly to fasten on them.

The slaves had few illusions about the power of the conjurers over whites, and the conjurers usually had enough sense to limit their claims. Sylvia King, an ex-slave from Texas, remembered that the local conjurer would predict whippings, not prevent them.[49] Occasionally a bold soul would try his luck and get away with it. Mrs. Sarah Carpenter Colbert, an ex-slave from Kentucky, told of a slave who, having received a whipping, went to a "witch doctor." The conjurer made him walk backwards, drive nails into the side of a barn, and "do such." His master never whipped him again.[50] Since the master appears to have been a kind man who rarely whipped his slaves, some doubts about the conjurer's power may be permitted. But his reputation undoubtedly soared. Most conjurers exercised greater caution. At the hanging of a cook for attempted murder by poison, the assembled slaves asked their conjure woman to intervene. She demurred; it was too late now. Some slaves played safe. Hoodoo, Lucy Davis of Kentucky explained, did not prevent Master's beating us, but "mebby dey'd a beat um up worser or mebby killed 'em."[51]

Sometimes the conjurers committed the sin of pride. One put a spell on the master to keep him from noticing that the slaves were stealing hogs for weekly barbecues. It worked, until one day the master started to count his hogs. Another gave a woman a charm that would keep her master from whipping her. Her faith in her protector was so great that she tempted fate and sassed the master. He whipped her brutally. "Dat," reflected the old ex-slave who told the story, "ruint de conjure man business."[52]

According to an ex-slave who assured the interviewer that he did not believe in conjuring, "The niggers could conjure each other but they couldn't do nothing to the white folks." Another ex-slave said more forcefully, "They had in those days a hoodoo nigger who could hoodoo niggers, but couldn't hoodoo masters. He couldn't make ole master stop whipping him, with the hoodooism, but they could make Negroes crawl to them."[53] The slaves interpreted this limitation on the conjurers' power in a way that was both sensible and fraught with implications. We believe in these things, they would say, whereas the whites do not; hence it works for us and not for them. But such an interpretation would carry with it the advice to stop believing, if all that it meant was a recognition of the psychological basis of the conjurer's power over those who made a choice to believe. All except the most stupid slaves could surely have seen that much. The deeper implication, which made the dualism inherent in their explanation rational if not necessarily convincing, was that whites and blacks believed in different things because the one had originated in Europe and the other in Africa, and because this difference in origin somehow meant that they were subject to different natural forces.[54]

The political power of the Obeah men, the Myal men, and the Vodûn priests of the West Indies and their occasional emergence as revolutionary leaders[55] could not be reproduced in the United States, except on a trivial scale, because the necessary revolutionary conjuncture did not exist. Hence the conjurers of the Old South were accommodationists in the same sense as were the black preachers. Indeed, the two may sometimes even have been the same men. Their accommodationism, however, like that of the preachers, must not be confused with Uncle Tomism, docility, or servility, although it might have elements of each; rather, it must be understood as a double-edged adjustment to political reality. It represented a tactical withdrawal into a black world that offered joys, fears, and a sense of existence as a people apart; but it presented no direct threat to the regime, for its formula for survival rested precisely on acceptance of the existing relationship of forces. When that hoodoo conjurer could make the blacks crawl to him and yet could not keep himself from being whipped by his master, he simultaneously helped build an inner and autonomous black world for his brothers and sisters and reinforced the image of the master as a great power. After all, if the slaves so feared and respected the conjurer that they would crawl to him and if in their own eyes the master was yet more powerful, then . . . ? The impact of the conjurer was, therefore, profoundly conservative at the same time and in the same way that it was ultimately subversive.

The conjurers primarily related in a direct and personal way to other slaves. Lorenzo Ezell, an ex-slave from a small farm near Orangeburg, South Carolina, talked about them: "In slavery times dey's men like dat regarded as bein' dangerous. Dey make charms and put bad mouth on you. De old folks wears de rabbit foot or coon foot and sometimes a silver dime on a fishin' string to keep off de witches. Some dem old conjure people make lots of money for charm against ruin or cripplin' or dry up de blood. But I don't take up no truck with things like dat."[56] Slaves like Richard Carruthers of Texas spoke of conjurers who "would take hair and brass nails and thimbles and needles and mix them up in a conjure bag. But I knows one thing. They was a old gin between Wilbarger and Colorado and it was haunted with spirits of kilt niggers."[57]

If the black preachers throve on love, the conjurers throve on fear. "Dem conjure men sho' bad," complained Willis Easter, an ex-slave from Texas, who attributed to their evil magic everything from pneumonia to boils. Rosanna Frazer, who had been a slave in Mississippi, blamed a conjurer for her blindness. And Nicey Kinney of Georgia thought "some old witch man conjured me into marrying Jordan Jackson."[58] A white plantation mistress left a description of Uncle Guinea George, whose sharpened teeth lent credence to his claim that he had been a cannibal in Africa. He terrified the blacks, who respected and feared his power.[59] Conjurers might be evildoers; they might be people who, like the witches of the European persecutions, had been wronged themselves and sought revenge on mankind.[60] In either case, fear had to be their weapon, for even a good deed for one person normally had to come at the expense of someone else. Down to our own time, hoodoo doctors, not being fools, have studied their people and learned how to provide them with advice designed to produce results an expensive psychoanalyst might envy.[61] They have put this talent to particular use in their work as "root doctors" and have thereby performed the closest thing to an unambiguously positive service. But, however positive their role in the struggle of the slave quarters for psychological survival, they never could have matched the preachers as a force for cohesion, moral guidance, and cultural growth.

What of the charms themselves? In the African tradition, as in the medieval European, the old gods disappeared, but the magical charms associated with them long survived. Africans, in their traditional religious practices, did not worship those material objects we call fetishes. Their belief, rather, rested on an idea of God as intruding Himself everywhere. Those "fetishes" supposedly held a particular spirit temporarily; the material and spiritual elements of life penetrated each other, with the former becoming a vehicle for the latter. The Afro-American South held to that belief. Hardly a source, black or white, fails to mention their ubiquity. Puckett, in his valuable *Folk Beliefs of the Southern Negro*, documents for the twentieth century, as do the slave narratives for the nineteenth, the widespread use of charms and their attendant magical spells. The most important positive application of charms came in slave medical practice, which illustrated the way in which black folk religion permeated every part of the slaves' lives and served their daily interests.[62]

Black doctors treated whites as well as blacks in eighteenth-century Virginia. Not until the legislation of 1748 did white tolerance give way to repression. At that, whites had not so much lost confidence in the ability of black doctors as they had developed an understandable aversion to being murdered by adeptly prepared poisons. Ulrich Bonnell Phillips describes the two relevant convictions in Virginia after 1748 as being for "the fantastic offense of administering medicines to white persons." Cases of poisoning occurred in greater numbers, but the law notwithstanding, planters continued to accept the presence of black doctors among their own slaves and to recognize the strong preference of the slaves for them. Robert Carter's coachman, Tom, performed so well that he was hired out to treat white neighbors.[63]

The fear of poison may to some extent have been an excuse to underscore the racist view that black doctors necessarily had to be either quacks or murderers, but outside a self-serving medical profession the disdain never reached the heights we might have expected in so racist a society. The fear itself did not betray paranoia; it reflected a healthy awareness that, propaganda aside, not all slaves were happy, sweet-tempered, and fun-loving. Even the religious argument for suppression, which focused on the connection between black medical practice and African "heathenism," came down to the same fear, for white Virginians appreciated the support given by persistent African beliefs and practices to the spirit of resistance.[64]

During the nineteenth century, states and localities periodically tried to eliminate the practice of medicine by blacks.[65] The extreme attempt to destroy it among the blacks themselves never had a chance for success. The more practicable attempt to end black treatment of whites scored better results but never fully succeeded either. From time to time, surreptitiously or not, whites went to black herb doctors either when white doctors failed them or by preference.[66]

However many jeremiads against black quackery appeared in the medical journals, rural whites, including some big planters, acquired respect for local black practitioners. Since the medical profession did not enjoy a reputation for infallibility—since it remains an open question whether attendance by a licensed doctor prolonged or shortened the life of a patient—sensible whites learned what they could from anyone, white or black, who produced results. *Gunn's Domestic Medicine*, the medical bible of the eighteenth century, extolled the use of herbs, and although whites, blacks, and Indians all practiced herb medicine, the reputation of the blacks in the plantation districts exceeded that of the others. Plantation prescription books, in which many planters took pride, abounded in black herbal lore.[67] Many planters were themselves doctors, whether professionally trained or self-taught. Weymouth T. Jordan's remarks on one of them, Martin Marshall of Alabama, may serve for many others: "Many of his cures were his own; others came to him from neighbors and friends; some were picked up from Indian lore; some were brought to Alabama from Africa by Negro slaves. He practiced empiricism at its best, or worst."[68] All that might be added is that the slaves made a contribution beyond that of applying their African inheritance, for they developed their own skill at experimentation and freely admitted learning much from the Indians.[69]

The slaves' distrust of white doctors evoked some sympathy from the planters. John Hamilton of Williamsport, Louisiana, wrote to his brother: "I am sorry to learn that you have been unfortunate with the Negroes. Your Doctors are rather a rough set —they give too much medicine. It is seldom that I call in a physician. We Doctor upon the old woman slave and have first-rate luck."[70] Fanny Kemble wrote of a slave's performance: "I was sorry not to ascertain what leaves she had applied to her ear. These simple remedies resorted to by savages, and people as ignorant, are generally approved by experience, and sometimes condescendingly adopted by science." She cited a planter's comment that the only relief for his rheumatism came from a treatment his doctor had learned from blacks in Virginia.[71]

Much of the case for black practitioners rested upon a negative judgment on white. Southern physicians made a good living from plantation practice, and reliance on them constituted a measure of the planters' concern for the welfare of their slaves. The deficiencies of the medical profession, however, led planters to rely either on their own resources or on the efforts of their slaves or both. The slaves took a more sanguine view of the efforts of their masters, and especially their mistresses, than they did of the efforts of hired doctors, but they did tend to fall back on their own folk remedies. Their hostility toward white physicians had roots not only in an awareness of widespread ignorance and incompetence in the medical profession, but in their awareness that too many physicians used slaves as guinea pigs for their pet theories and remedies.[72]

Other whites turned the guns around and assailed the slaves' "superstitions." Mrs. Schoolcraft wrote that black plantation nurses always supported the patients' efforts to frustrate treatment by white doctors; like so many others, she noted that slaves would accept medicine only from whites who were their mistresses or masters, if they could help it. Ingraham reported that slaves would go without medication or "take some concoction in repute among the old African beldames in the 'quarters,' by which they are sickened if well, and made worse if ill."[73] Kate Stone returned to her old plantation in Louisiana after the war to find the freedmen with cholera. They refused medicine and ate green figs and salt instead, with predictable results.[74]

Frederick Douglass, who dismissed the slaves' medical initiatives as evidence of the slaveholders' failure to provide adequate professional attention, recalled Uncle Isaac Cooper, a preacher and a doctor: "His remedial prescriptions embraced four articles. For diseases of the body epsom salts and castor oil; for those of the soul, the 'Lord's Prayer,' and a few stout hickory switches."[75] Notwithstanding Douglass's understandable ire, black plantation medicine and its practitioners should not so easily be dismissed. At the very least, they constituted part of a complex tendency on the part of the slaves to take care of themselves and each other. White southerners sometimes noted these efforts with admiration.[76]

The methods used by black herb doctors and conjurers ranged from the maddest quackery and outright charlatanry to pragmatically effective folk medicine. Not a few of the remedies found their way into the planters' own repertory for the good reason that they produced better results than available alternatives.[77] Even some planters who were themselves doctors did not hesitate to turn to black herb doctors for help.[78] "There's allus some old time nigger what knowed all dif'rent kinds of yarbs and roots," recalled Abram Sells of Texas, who insisted that his grandfather could stop bleeding and conjure away fevers and warts. "On nearly all plantations there were 'traiteurs,' " according to an ex-slave from creole Louisiana. Josephine Bacchus, an ex-slave from South Carolina, told her interviewer: "Oh, de people never didn' put much faith to de doctors in dem days. Mostly, dey would use de herbs in de fields for dey medicine." She thought that the slaves had been "wiser" than latter-day blacks because they had had "signs" to guide their behavior.[79] Josephine Bacchus's linking of the slaves' medical practice with their religious beliefs went to the heart of the matter. "Root doctors," often trained from boyhood, have done a thriving business among southern blacks down to the present day, and their popularity, as might be expected, has been greatest in those areas in which the old rural folk religion has retained its force.[80]

The decision of the freedmen on Kate Stone's plantation to eat green figs and salt to cure cholera did not commend itself to posterity, and neither did cat soup, boiled cockroaches, or any number of other pleasantries to which slave practitioners subscribed.[81] Human beings are tough creatures, however, and nature is often kind enough to heal us in spite of our doctors' most determined efforts. Not only did the slaves often survive the bleeding and purging so frequently resorted to by white doctors, they also survived black efforts to prove that whites have no monopoly of cures that kill. When slaves recovered after having had some dreadful potion poured into their already weakened system, they did as most people still do: they declared the doctor a genius and his remedy the cause of recovery. The probabilities being what they were, the reputation of the quacks and fraudulent doctors rose along with that of genuinely talented herb practitioners, quite apart from considerations of scientific judgment. Any given black practitioner might well have qualified as a quack in some respects and as an excellent experimental physician in others. The white medical profession was therefore both right and wrong in charging that the slaves were being victimized by ignorance and "superstition," much as the slaves were both right and wrong in thinking that most white doctors were primarily useful as business agents for morticians.

The deeper meaning of the widespread use of folk medicine by the slaves lay not in its contribution to medical science, although some valuable contribution may well have been made, but in its function as an agency for the transmission of black religious sensibility into a defense against the psychological assaults of slavery and racial oppression. Much of whatever success "untrained" slave medical practitioners could claim rested on their ability as psychologists and on the faith of their patients. The best of the practitioners were untrained only in the formal, professional sense, for they studied their subject during many years and drew on a lively oral tradition and on training by older slaves. W. E. B. Du Bois describes the loss of African traditional religion among the slaves as a "terrific revolution." But some traces did remain. He continues: "The chief remaining institution was the Priest or Medicine-Man. He early appeared on the plantation and found his function as the healer of the sick, the interpreter of the Unknown, the comforter of the sorrowing, the supernatural avenger of wrong, and the one who rudely but picturesquely expressed the longing, disappointment and resentment of a stolen and oppressed people."[82]

Black practitioners paid as much attention to the mode of treatment as to its content. Much of the treatment centered on such devices as the use of charms, and even the most pragmatically efficacious use of herbs took ritualistic form. Africans traditionally regarded disease as the product of an indwelling evil spirit and did not separate the spiritual (or psychological) from the material realms of being. This belief faded among the slaves as an intellectually coherent system, but it lingered on as a tendency.[83]

The cultural continuity with Africa was reinforced and reshaped by the impact of European and Euro-American culture, into which it itself fed. These African ideas have constituted a variant or variants of ideas prevalent among many preindustrial peoples. As late as the seventeenth century in England and much later in, say, Eastern Europe, many among the poor relied on a folk medicine that sometimes brought good results and sometimes killed. For those patients medicine ultimately presented itself as occult, as indeed it does among the most sophisticated of patients today. What theory of causation exists to explain anything? And without one, why should not common sense reach for nonmedical, nonmaterial explanations? Medieval and early modern Western Europeans, as well as Africans, could see that specific ailments had specific remedies and that treatment should proceed accordingly. But disease in general eluded explanation, and rational men, however "primitive," preferred a supernatural explanation to none at all or, worse, to an explanation based on chance, which would seem to condemn them to a purposeless world.

When the most intellectually progressive currents in countries such as China or India today take folk medicine seriously, they do so only partly to learn what they can from an empirically rich tradition; they also seek to understand the psychological dimension of the medical problem. No romantic veil need be cast over slave practice, much of which was destructive or medically useless, to recognize that it offered the slaves a necessary degree of psychological support and produced positive physical results.[84]

The readiness of the slaveholders to denounce black folk beliefs as so much superstition to be exorcised by proper Christian instruction betrayed a studied unwillingness to consider the history of their own religion. For them the folk cults and the Christian adherence of the slaves were implacably hostile to each other or blended only in the minds of the more depressed and ignorant field hands. Yet, early Christianity itself absorbed much from the so-called pagan cults. The determined effort of the Church to drive out the vestiges of paganism had much more to do with the need to purge politically and theologically unassimilable elements than with a determination to purge beliefs of prior origin simply for being so.

Christianity never ceased assimilating pagan beliefs to itself, and had it ceased, it probably could not have maintained its hold on the masses. G. G. Coulton writes of the Middle Ages: "It is absolutely necessary to realize that nobody whatever doubted the actual existence of these old pagan gods. They existed as truly as the great God; but whereas the pagans had taken them for gods, the Christians knew them to be devils."[85] The churches have sought to tolerate, or at worst only slowly undermine, harmless residues of older beliefs and to crush those that threatened their power or the social order generally. The Catholic Church could therefore grudgingly tolerate peasant celebrations of saints' days in which blatantly pagan dances were featured, but had to smash, violently when necessary, the apparently deep Catholic absorption in miracles, which for a variety of reasons too often led the people into insubordination.[86] However much the Catholic Church might explain the true meaning of its use of holy water and resolutely deny that it is a magical potion to exorcise devils, the peasants of medieval Europe, and many of the workers of our own cities, have more often than not believed what they have wanted to believe. Despite the demystification introduced by the Reformation, the witch mania of the seventeenth century and the waffling on such matters as the existence of ghosts demonstrated that the new churches could not so easily fend off the pressures from the folk tradition.[87] As has often been said by both friends and foes of the Christian churches, religion even in recent times has generally meant rationalism for the few and magic for the many.

An appreciation of the wisdom of the churches in struggling to accommodate to beliefs considered pagan and the wisdom of those whose tenacity has forced the issue requires an appreciation of the claims of magic itself. In folk religions supernatural beings and their power usually have both good and bad elements. As they have passed into Christianity, this duality has reappeared, for example, in the juxtaposition of saints and devils. Historically, the struggle, in whatever form, has reflected and reacted upon the social struggle of the oppressed and helped them to make sense out of an unjust and disorderly world. Ivar Paulson is describing "the old Estonian folk religion," but his words have much wider application: "The heavy taxes, serfdom, slavery, and corvée which developed from the feudal order promoted the spread of a corresponding religious and magic ideology accompanied by the religious images, customs and activities of witchcraft which arose from this ideology." Or as Julia Brown, an ex-slave of Georgia, said more simply, God in those days had to work through miracles, for the people were illiterate and had to be shown His presence.[88]

Magic, in the widest sense of the word, as Frazer, Tylor, and other pioneer anthropologists taught, is a false science with an erroneous idea of cause and effect, but it is akin to science nonetheless in its appeal to human devices for control of the world. If religion arose on the failure of magic as science, it has, in its many varieties, suffered a similar fate. All prayer that aims at material benefit, as most does, rather than contenting itself with being a poetic statement of the ideal, betrays precisely this deficiency of magic and corrupts its own spirit. The slaves' efforts, therefore, aimed at ordering this world, at rendering it rational, and at explaining those things which their oppressors could not or would not explain to them. The specific elements of "superstition" that they carried into their Christianity provided the means for easing the transition to a higher realm of thought and were themselves not essential. The mediatory role these elements played in the slaves' lives and the particular ways of thought they introduced into their more systematic religion—as yet an inadequately studied subject—constituted their deepest significance.

The slaves had to pay a price for the strength brought by the folk elements in their religion. For peasantries magic, however petty many of its applications, has served the vital social function of providing some defense, no matter how futile in the end, against natural disasters and forces beyond their control. Peasants have relied on their own skills to work their land and do their chores; they have invoked magic to deal with soil conditions, weather, the health of their animals, and other matters they have not yet learned to control. Hence magic, or the magical element in religion, has been rooted in the process of production and has strengthened the community in its collective as well as individual aspects. For the slaves, who found themselves severed from the means of production, this strengthening of the collective occurred only in one important sense—it helped identify them with each other in contradistinction to their masters. But within the community it functioned primarily as a device for settling personal affairs and thereby undermined the very sense of solidarity it had helped to create. The psychological use of magic as an outlet for socially acceptable hostility only deepened the contradiction on which this process was based. This negative feature of the political legacy of the slaves' folk beliefs provides the element of truth in Frantz Fanon's bitter, one-sided critique of the colonials' world-view:

> The native will strengthen the inhibitions which contain his aggressiveness by drawing on the terrifying myths which are so frequently found in underdeveloped communities. There are maleficent spirits which intervene every time a step is taken in the wrong direction,

leopard-men, serpent-men, six-legged dogs, zombies—a whole series of tiny animals or giants which create around the native a world of prohibitions, of barriers and of inhibitions far more terrifying than the world of the settler.[89]

THE GOSPEL IN THE QUARTERS

Folk beliefs might not so easily have passed into the heart of black Christianity had the slaves and free Negroes of the cities not wrested some degree of control of the churches from the whites. Without that degree of autonomy within the structure of formal religion folk belief might have remained an antithesis, and the slaves might have had to make the hard choice between Christianity and an anti-Christianity. Institutional developments and the ability of preachers and the slaves themselves to take advantage of them opened the way toward the absorption of much of the folk culture into the Christian faith.

Whatever the religion of the masters, the slaves, when given a choice, overwhelmingly preferred the Baptists and secondarily the Methodists. By the 1850s the recruitment of blacks to the Episcopal Church in Virginia had virtually ceased.[1] In the South as a whole the Presbyterians had a small following, especially in the up country, and the Catholics scored some success in Louisiana. Melville J. Herskovits has advanced the provocative thesis that the slaves' preference for the Baptists reflected the continued strength of traditional West African religion. Noting the practice of total immersion, he has suggested a connection in the slaves' mind with the powerful river spirits in the West African religions; in particular, he thinks that enslaved priests from Dahomey must have provided leadership and continuity from Africa to Afro-America.[2] E. Franklin Frazier, who has led the attack on Herskovits's thesis, dismisses the argument on the grounds that enslavement and the slave trade had effectively destroyed the social basis of African religion among the blacks and that Herskovits's speculations hardly constitute evidence. He suggests, instead, that the slaves responded to the fiery style and uninhibited emotionalism of the frontier Baptist and Methodist preachers and that the Baptists had the additional advantage of a loose church structure to accommodate slaves more easily.[3] Although Frazier's views have come under withering fire for their extreme formulation of a break with the African past, he clearly has had the better of this particular argument. Herskovits's insistence on links between West African and Afro-American folk religion has merit, but it simply cannot be stretched to account for the slaves' preference for the Baptists. Arthur Huff Fauset has pointed out that the same blacks who chose the Baptists might have chosen the Methodists, the Baptists' hottest rivals in the plantation districts—and the Methodists' greatest fun in life was ridiculing total immersion and adult baptism.[4]

Methodism, on the face of it, hardly seems a likely candidate for the affections of a high-spirited, life-loving people. Grim, humorless, breathing the fires of damnation—notwithstanding love feasts and some joyful hymns—it was more calculated to associate Jesus with discipline and order than with love. The slaves adjusted Methodism, as they adjusted every other creed, to their own way of life, and they transformed each in the process, as the ring shout may demonstrate. Once converted, the slaves had to stop dancing, for it was sinful. Dutifully, they stopped going to dances and went to the praise-house instead. What they did there looked like dancing to the white uninitiated and still looks like dancing to those who recognize the origin of the Charleston and several other popular dances. But no: it could not have been dancing. Dancing was sinful, and these slaves had been converted. They were not dancing; they were "shouting." Henry George Spaulding, a white Unitarian minister who visited Port Royal, South Carolina, with the United States Sanitary Commission during the war, left us a description of the ring shout, which he insisted was the "religious dance of the Negroes":

> Three or four, standing still, clapping their hands and beating time with their feet, commence singing in unison one of the peculiar shout melodies, while the others walk around in a ring, in single file, joining also in the song. Soon those in the ring leave off their singing, the others keeping it up the while with increased vigor, and strike into the shout step, observing most accurate time with the music. . . . They will often dance to the same song for twenty or thirty minutes. . . .[5]

Whatever Spaulding thought, the blacks convinced themselves that they did not dance the shout, for as everyone knows, you cross your feet when you dance; and since they did not tolerate crossing of feet, they clearly were not dancing.

The slaves' insistence on shouting harked back to Africa in both form and content. The style, which subsequently came to dominate American popular dancing in a variety of versions, could not have been more clearly African. The same might also be said about the insistence that the community worship God in a way that integrated the various forms of human expression—song, dance, and prayer, all with call-and-response, as parts of a single offering the beauty of which pays homage to God. This idea of beauty as deriving from the whole of human expression rather than from its separate manifestations, or even its artifacts, was not entirely new to the Christian tradition. It had originally been as much a part of Euro-Christian tradition as of African but had been lost during the Middle Ages and especially after the Reformation. Thomas Merton ends his study of the reform of the Roman Catholic liturgy: "One thing that is certain to come out of Africa is the revival of the ancient liturgical art of *the dance*, traditionally a problem to Western Christianity."[6]

The Methodists had in common with the Baptists certain features, beyond those mentioned by Frazier, that did appeal to the slaves. They had retained some interest in ameliorating plantation conditions; their congregations had long been racially mixed and never wholly accepted the white pressures to segregate; and above all, their preachers spoke plainly. Richard Allen, founder of the Bethel African Methodist Episcopal Church of Philadelphia and himself an ex-slave, explained: "I was confident that no religious sect or denomination would suit the capacity of the colored people so well as the Methodists, for the plain simple gospel suits best for any people, for the unlearned can understand, and the learned are sure to understand."[7] But the greatest advantage held by both Baptists and Methodists, with their particular strength in the countryside and in the cities respectively, was that they worked hard to reach the blacks and understood the need to enlist black preachers and "assistants" to work with them. Emotional appeal and organizational flexibility gave the Baptists the edge, but they might have thrown it away had they not undertaken the task of conversion with the vigor they did. The organizational flexibility of the Baptists provided a particularly good opportunity for the retention of magic and folk belief despite the theological strictures against them. Excommunications for backsliding into paganism occurred, but the loose methods of organization made surveillance difficult; and the black preachers found it easy to look the other way without incurring the wrath of a watchful hierarchy.

The Baptists' efforts to proselytize among slaves and their willingness to rely on, or at least not exclude, black preachers did not prove them less racist or more deeply concerned with the secular fate of the blacks than were others. Whatever advantage they may have derived from their early hostility to slavery and later concern with amelioration faded as the several southern churches closed ranks behind the single reform formula of confirming slavery as a normal condition for blacks and urging more humane treatment. During the last three decades of the antebellum period Baptists, Methodists, Presbyterians, and others accelerated, both by design and simply by taking the path of least resistance, the long-developing trend toward racial separation within the churches.[8]

Even during the eighteenth century a double push for separation had been taking place. Hostile whites steadily tried to push the blacks into separate congregations, especially where the black population was substantial, and blacks often moved to facilitate the split, partly because they felt uncomfortable and wished to practice their religion in their own way, and partly because they resented the inferior position into which they were being thrust within the white churches. For the blacks the move to separate was thus both a positive desire for independent cultural expression and a defense against racism.[9]

The rise of the independent black churches in Philadelphia and other cities of both North and South, often under the leadership of strong personalities, did make the task of the white segregationists all the easier.[10] At the same time the trend toward separation affected the plantation belt itself in less dramatic and less formal ways. By the end of the antebellum period most southern blacks who professed Christianity called themselves Baptists, and so they were. But they had become black Baptists—a category increasingly of their own making. The division had fateful consequences. Ulrich Bonnell Phillips clearly saw the negative implications for both black and white, but especially white: "In general, the less the cleavage of creed between master and man, the better for both, since every factor conducing to solidarity of sentiment was of advantage in promoting harmony and progress. When the planter went to sit under his rector while the slave stayed at home to hear an exhorter, just so much was lost in the sense of fellowship."[11] What Phillips did not wish to see was that the consequences for the slaves were not entirely negative, for separation helped them to widen the degree of autonomy they were steadily carving out of their oppressors' regime.[12]

On the plantations and farms the slaves met for services apart from the whites whenever they could. Weekly services on Sunday evenings were common. Where masters were indulgent, additional meetings might take place during the week, and where they were not, they might take place anyway. Masters and overseers often accepted the Sunday meetings but not the others, for the slaves would stay up much of the night praying, singing, and dancing. The next day being a workday, the meetings were bad for business.[13]

The slaves' religious meetings would be held in secret when their masters forbade all such; or when their masters forbade all except Sunday meetings; or when rumors of rebellion or disaffection led even indulgent masters to forbid them so as to protect the people from trigger-happy patrollers; or when the slaves wanted to make sure that no white would hear them. Only during insurrection scares or tense moments occasioned by political turmoil could the laws against such meetings be enforced. Too many planters did not want them enforced. They regarded their slaves as peaceful, respected their religious sensibilities, and considered such interference dangerous to plantation morale and productivity. Others agreed that the slaves presented no threat of rising and did not care about their meetings. Had the slaves been less determined, the regime probably would have been far more stringent; but so long as they avoided conspiracies and accepted harsh punishment as the price for getting caught by patrols, they raised the price of suppression much too high to make it seem worthwhile to planters with steady nerves.[14]

When the meetings had to be held in secret, the slaves confronted a security problem. They would announce the event by such devices as that of singing "Steal Away to Jesus" at work.[15] To protect the meeting itself, they had an infallible method. They would turn over a pot "to catch the sound" and keep it in the cabin or immediate area of the woods. Almost infallible: "Of course, sometimes they might happen to slip up on them on suspicion."[16] George P. Rawick suggests that the practice of turning over a pot probably had African origins, and John F. Szwed links it to rituals designed to sanctify the ground. The slaves' belief in its efficacy gave them additional confidence to brave the risks, and their success in avoiding detection led some whites to think that there might just be something to the pot technique.[17]

The desire of the slaves for religious privacy took a limited as well as a general form. Eliza Frances Andrews went down to the plantation praise-house after dinner one night to hear the slaves sing. "At their 'praise meetings,'" she commented, "they go through all sorts of motions in connection with their songs, but they won't give way to their wildest gesticulations or engage in their sacred dances before white people for fear of being laughed at."[18] But the slaves had no objection to pleasing curious whites when they expected an appreciative response. They took enormous pride in their singing and in the depth of their religious expression. They resisted being laughed at, but they responded to expressions of respect. Gus Feaster, an ex-slave from Union County, South Carolina, proudly told of such instances:

> At night when the meeting done busted till next day was when the darkies really did have they freedom of spirit. As the wagon be creeping along in the late hours of moonlight, the darkies would raise a tune. Then the air soon be filled with the sweetest tune as us rid on home and sung all the old hymns that us loved. It was always some big black nigger with a deep bass voice like a frog that'd start up the tune. Then the other mens jine in, followed up by the fine little voices of the gals and the cracked voices of the old womens and the grannies. When us reach near the big house us soften down to a deep hum that the missus like! Sometimes she hist up the window and tell us sing "Swing Low, Sweet Chariot" for her and the visiting guests. That all us want to hear. Us open up, and the niggers near the big house that hadn't been to church would wake up and come out to the cabin door and jine in the refrain. From that we'd swing on into all the old spirituals that us love so well and that us knowed how to sing. Missus often 'low that her darkies could sing with heaven's inspiration.[19]

This pride, this self-respect, this astonishing confidence in their own spiritual quality, explain the slaves' willingness to spend so much of their day of leisure at prayer meetings. Often they would hear the white preacher or the master himself on Sunday morning, but the "real meetin'" and the "real preachin'" came later, among themselves.[20] Richard Carruthers, an ex-slave from Texas, explained another feature of the concern with prayer. "Us niggers," he said, "used to have a prayin' ground down in the hollow and some time we come out of the field, between eleven and twelve at night, scorchin' and burnin' up with nothin' to eat, and we wants to ask the good Lord to have mercy."[21]

The meetings gave the slaves strength derived from direct communion with God and each other. When not monitored, they allowed the message of promised deliverance to be heard. If the slaves had received false information or had been misled by the whites, they provided an opportunity for correction, as when the white preachers led them in prayers for the Confederacy, and their black preachers, in secret session, led them in prayers for the Union.[22] But above all, the meetings provided a sense of autonomy —of constituting not merely a community unto themselves but a community with leaders of their own choice.

The slaves' religious frenzy startled white onlookers, although few ever saw it fully unleashed. The more austere masters tried to curb it but usually had little success. Emoline Glasgow of South Carolina had a Methodist master who took one of his slaves to church and determined to keep him in line by bribery if necessary. He offered to give the slave a new pair of boots if he behaved himself. All went well until about the middle of the service, when the slave let go: "Boots or no boots, I gwine to shout today."[23] The slaves took their letting-go seriously and condemned those who simulated emotion. When the Catholic priests forbade shouting in Louisiana, Catherine Cornelius spoke for the slaves in insisting that "the angels shout in heaven" and in doggedly proclaiming, "The Lawd said you gotta shout if you want to be saved. That's in the Bible." Sincerity meant everything. Emma Fraser, an ex-slave from South Carolina, talked about her singing in church in the way that others talked about shouting. "But ef I sing an' it doan move me any, den dat a sin on de Holy Ghost; I be tell a lie on de Lord."[24] The frenzy, as W. E. B. Du Bois called it, brought the slaves together in a special kind of communion, which brought out the most individual expressions and yet disciplined the collective. The people protected each other against the excesses of their release and encouraged each other to shed inhibitions. Everyone responded according to his own spirit but ended in a spiritual union with everyone else.[25]

Possession appeared much less often among the slaves of the Old South than among those of Saint-Domingue or Brazil, where the practice of Vodûn and the rites of the African cults ran high. Yet ecstatic seizures, however defined, appeared frequently and submit to differing interpretations. Critics have recognized in them a form of hysteria, and Frantz Fanon even speaks of a kind of madness. Roger Bastide has suggested that they are vehicles by which repressed personalities surface in symbolic form. Many anthropologists, however, have remained skeptical of psychoanalytic explanations and have pointed out that no genuine schizophrenic could possibly adjust to the firm system of control that the rituals demand. No matter how wild and disorderly they look to the uninitiated, they are in fact tightly controlled; certain things must be done and others not done. They thus require, according to Alfred Métraux, social, not psychological, explanation. Yet, schizophrenia aside, a psychoanalytic explanation is compatible with a social one. The question may be left for experts, if any. Two things are clear. First, the slaves' wildest emotionalism, even when it passed into actual possession, formed part of a system of collective behavior, which the slaves themselves controlled. The slaves may have been driven wild with ecstasy when dancing during their services, but never so wild that their feet would cross without evoking sharp rebuke. And second, the slaves' behavior brought out a determination to assert their power and the freedom of their spirit, for, as Max Weber says, ecstasy may become an instrument of salvation or self-deification.[26]

If emotional fervor alone had distinguished black religion, the usual interpretations would take on greater credibility—that no great difference existed between the religion of the slaves and that of the lower-class whites who followed the frontier Baptist and Methodist preachers. The frequently heard assertion that the blacks merely copied the whites may be left aside as unworthy of discussion. If one must choose between the two separate tendencies, the view of Dr. Du Bois, according to which the style of the poor whites has been a "plain copy" of the style of the blacks, easily holds the field.[27] White and black responses reinforced each other, as they had to in an interracial setting. Their blending reflected a common frontier Christian character and no doubt contributed something toward bringing together two antagonistic peoples. But there were differences that illuminate the special quality of the black experience.

Neither a common body of belief—to the extent that it was in fact common—nor even common rites could guarantee a common spiritual experience. Rites reflect, and in turn reshape, the communities that practice them. Slaves and poorer rural whites (that is, small farmers and actual "poor whites") brought fundamentally different community settings to their common rites, and they therefore brought fundamentally different spiritual needs, responses, and values.[28] When slaves from small farms shared religious meetings and churchgoing with their white yeomen and poor white neighbors, they no doubt drew closer to their inner experience, but even then some distance was inevitable. For plantation blacks, the distance had to be much greater.

The blacks did not hide their disdain for white shouters, whom they regarded, as Dr. Du Bois did later, as a plain copy of themselves. Even in the early camp meetings the blacks notoriously outshouted the whites and stayed up singing and praying long after the whites had retired. They made up their own hymns, which drew protests from orthodox whites because they were their own and because they came too close to sounding like plantation jubilee melodies.[29] Viewing a meeting in Georgia, which attracted even more blacks than whites, Olmsted observed: "The Negroes kept their place during all the tumult; there may have been a sympathetic groan or exclamation uttered by one or two of them, but generally they expressed only the interest of curiosity. . . . There was generally a self-satisfied smile upon their faces; and I have no doubt they felt they could do it with a great deal more energy and abandon, if they were called upon."[30] Beneath the similarities and differences of style lay a divergence of meanings, including some divergence in the very meaning of God.

The slaves drew their call-and-response pattern from their African heritage, however important the reinforcing elements from the Europeans. Europeans had also used something like a song-style of preaching and responding, which had somewhat different qualities. Blacks and whites in the South performed in distinct ways. The content of the white responses to a preacher—undoubtedly with many exceptions—consisted of "Amens" and the like. The whites cheered their preacher on or let him know they were moved. The preacher needed that response, craved it, even demanded it. But the black preacher had to evoke it, not for his own satisfaction, subjectively important as that may have been, but because without it the service had no relationship to God.[31] This difference in style betrayed a difference in theological tendency. The whites were fundamentalists to the core, the blacks only apparently so. Both preached the Bible in fiery style, but as the Reverend Henry H. Mitchell suggests, the whites were fiery mad, while the blacks were fiery glad.[32] Or as Martin Ruffin, an ex-slave from Texas, said of a black preacher, Sam Jones, he "preached Hell-fire and judgment like the white preachers."[33]

While the religion of the slaves, as everyone saw, exhibited joy much as the religion of their African forebears had, who in his right mind would say the same thing of the religion of the whites? W. J. Cash writes of white southern religion:

> What our Southerner required . . . was a faith as simple and emotional as himself. A faith to draw men together in hordes, to terrify them with Apocalyptic rhetoric, to cast them into the pit, rescue them, and at last bring them shouting back into the fold of Grace. . . . The God demanded was an anthropomorphic God—the Jehovah of the Old Testament: a God who might be seen, a God who *had* been seen. A passionate, whimsical tyrant to be trembled before, but whose favor was the sweeter for that. A personal God, a God for the individualist, a God whose representatives were not silken priests but preachers risen from the people themselves.
>
> What was demanded here, in other words, was the God and the faith of the Methodists and the Baptists and the Presbyterians.[34]

Cash fails to note that the blacks identified with the same churches and turned them into something rather different.

Olmsted's description of that white hellfire preacher in action before a congregation of lower-class whites says a great deal:

> The preliminary devotional exercises—a Scripture reading, singing, and painfully irreverential and meaningless harangues nominally addressed to the Deity, but really to the audience—being concluded, the sermon was commenced by reading a text, with which, however, it had, so far as I could discover, no further association. Without often being violent in his manner, the speaker nearly all the time cried aloud at the utmost stretch of his voice, as if calling to some one a long distance off; . . . and as he was gifted with a strong imagination, and possessed of a good deal of dramatic power, he kept the attention of the people very well. There was no argument upon any point that the congregation were likely to have much difference of opinion upon, nor any special connection between one sentence and another; yet there was a constant, sly, sectarian skirmishing, and a frequently recurring cannonade upon French infidelity and socialism, and several crushing charges upon Fourier, the Pope of Rome, Tom Paine, Voltaire, "Roosu," and Jo Smith. . . . He had the habit

of frequently repeating a phrase, or of bringing forward the same idea in a slightly different form, a great many times. The following passage, of which I took notes, presents an example of this, followed by one of the best instances of his dramatic talent that occurred. He was leaning far over the desk, with his arm stretched forward, gesticulating violently, yelling at the highest key, and catching breath with an effort:

"A—ah! why don't you come to Christ? ah! what's the reason? ah! Is it because he was of *lowly birth?* ah! Is that it? *Is it* because he was born in a manger? ah! Is it because he was of a humble origin? ah! Is it because he was lowly born? a-ha! . . . Perhaps you don't like the messenger—is that the reason? I'm the Ambassador of the great and glorious King; it's his invitation, 'taint mine. You musn't mind me. I ain't no account. Suppose a ragged, insignificant little boy should come running in here and tell you, 'Mister, your house's a-fire!' would you mind the ragged, insignificant little boy, and refuse to listen to him, because he didn't look respectable?"[35]

It is not easy to imagine a black preacher's wanting to know if his slave congregation despised Jesus for being poor and not looking respectable. Time and again, the message of the black preachers turned precisely on the low earthly station of the Son of God.

Dr. Mitchell draws for us a sharp distinction between southern black and white uses of the Bible. "A Black preacher," he notes, "is more likely to say, 'Didn't He say it!' than to be officious about what 'the Word of God declares!' " For the blacks the Bible provides an inexhaustible store of good advice for a proper life; it does not usually provide an unchanging body of doctrine, as with the white fundamentalists. Hence, biblical figures must come alive, must be present, must somehow provide a historical example for modern application. Black religion eschews bibliolatry and does not have a strong anti-intellectual bias.[36] Those who might suspect that Dr. Mitchell is being carried into romantic exaggeration might note that social scientists who have closely studied black religious behavior in the South have unearthed materials that lend firm support to his analysis.[37] At issue, therefore, are the slaves' notions of heaven, hell, sin, and soul.

White Methodist and Baptist preachers ripped each other up in theological debates all over the South and did not let up when singly preaching to the slaves. The slaves turned out to cheer them on. Olmsted, after remarking that Baptist and Methodist preachers spent much of their time denouncing each other's doctrines, added, "The negroes are represented to have a great taste for theological controversy."[38] Eliza Frances Andrews described a Methodist slave in Georgia who had a staunch Baptist master: "They used to have some high old religious discussions together."[39]

The slaves' penchant for theological disputation ought neither to be dismissed as a ridiculous spectacle nor accepted at face value. There is nothing ridiculous in the idea of illiterate field hands' trying to follow an argument about God, for He was ever-present in their lives, even if they did respond more readily to evidence of spiritual motivation in the preacher than they did to his argument. Then too, the white Baptist and Methodist preachers had learned to translate the most difficult points of theology into unadorned English for their frontier congregations. If they could not make themselves understood to the slaves, it was usually for reasons other than their inability to speak plain English. But neither should the slaves' reaction be taken straight, first, because the theological questions that most interested them were of a different order, and second, because they had too high a sense of humor not to respond to a good show when they saw one.

The Baptist churches in the South ran the gamut from Calvinism to Arminianism, but the powerful tendency, especially in the rougher terrain of the Mississippi Valley, took extreme predestinarian ground. Now, Regular Baptists who talk like John Calvin on the fate of man present something of a puzzle. The accepted and plausible, if somewhat impish, explanation is that the free-will polemics of the rough-and-tumble Methodists drove their Baptist adversaries further and further into extreme formulations of their standpoint. So far did one wing go that its famous two-seed doctrine, according to which Eve produced two seeds only one of which originated with God, has quite sensibly been classified by some scholars as thinly disguised Manichaeanism.[40] Yet, predestinarian doctrine did not appear in black religion. In part, the explanation may lie in a greater attention to preaching among the slaves by the free-will Baptists and those who glided over the issue. But the deeper reason must be sought in the slaves' own inclinations. Only rarely did orthodox Calvinism come from the mouths of black preachers, and even in those cases its uses remain in doubt. In 1793, a black preacher upset Harry Toulmin by preaching Calvinist doctrine, but the point he was making in his excellent sermon was the equality of man before God.[41] The slave quarters provided poor ground for predestinarianism. When slaves and ex-slaves insisted that God had foreordained everything, they usually meant that even slavery had an appropriate place in His eternal design. And at that, their reaction could turn bitter. In Wilkinson County, Mississippi, an old slave gravedigger, accompanied by a young helper, asked a white stranger a question:

> "Massa, may I ask you something?"
> "Ask what you please."
> "Can you 'splain how it happened in the fust place, that the white folks got the start of the black folks, so as to make dem slaves and do all de work?"
> The younger helper, fearing the white man's wrath, broke in: "Uncle Pete, it's no use talking.' It's fo'ordained. The Bible tells you that. The Lord fo'ordained the Nigger to work, and the white man to boss."
> "Dat's so. Dat's so. But if dat's so, then God's no fair man!"[42]

Since predestination leaves no room for magic, its attraction for people whose religious sensibility retained the features of folk origin was almost nonexistent. No socially deprived lower class has found it easy to warm to Calvinist theology. As Keith Thomas writes:

> The doctrine of providence was always less likely to appeal to those at the bottom end of the social scale than the rival doctrine of luck. For the believer in luck can account for his misfortune without jeopardizing his self-esteem. The concept of luck explains any apparent discrepancy between merit and reward and thus helps to reconcile men to the environment in which they live.[43]

The slaves stayed close to their conjurers, and the preachers who could reach them knew enough not to force the issue.

For the slaves, salvation came through an uneasy combination of free will and faith—faith in God and faith in each other—because faith meant love. An old preacher, who had been a slave in South Carolina, remarked, "Brother, you has to have faith in your fellow man befo' you has faith in de lawd."[44] The spirituals vibrated with the message: God will deliver us if we have faith in Him. And they emphasized the idea of collective deliverance of the slaves as a people by their choice of such heroes as Moses, Jonah, and Daniel.[45] The slaves' attachment to the doctrine of salvation by faith, their ability to turn the most serious matters to good-humored advantage, and their inexhaustible penchant for puttin' on Ole Massa all appeared in an incident described by Olmsted. A formally pious slave was plaguing his master by his persistence in undefined immorality. The master asked a minister to intercede and try to appeal to the slave's religious nature. As Olmsted told it:

> The clergyman did so, and endeavored to bring the terrors of the law to bear upon his conscience. "Look yeah, massa," said the backslider, "don't de Scriptur say, 'Dem who believes an' is baptize shall be save'?" "Certainly," the clergyman answered; and went on to explain and expound the passage: but directly the slave interrupted him again.
>
> "Jus you tell me now, massa, don't de good book say dese word: 'Dem as believes and is baptize, shall be save'; want to know dat."
> "Yes, but . . ."
> "Das all I want to know, sar; wat's de use o' talkin' to me. You ain't a going to make me bleve wat de blessed Lord says, ain't so, not ef you tries forever."
> The clergyman again attempted to explain. . . . "De Scriptur say, if a man believe and be baptize he *shall* be save. Now, massa minister, I *done* believe and I *done* baptize, an I *shall be save suah*—Dere's no use talkin', sar."[46]

According to the scriptural defense of slavery, which commanded enormous attention throughout the white South during the forties and fifties, the enslavement of the blacks by the whites fulfilled the biblical curse on Ham, much as for the Russian landlords the curse had fallen on their serfs. Japheth's predicted dwelling in the tents of Shem accounted for the expropriation of the Indians' lands, and the enforced service of blacks to whites took care of the sons of Ham. The suggestion that in time Ethiopia would stretch out her hand to God caused some misgivings, but not many. "Panola," as a planter from Mississippi signed himself in the agricultural journals, nicely took care of any qualms. Was Ethiopia ready to stretch out her hand to God? No. How did he know? "Niggers are too *high* for that."[47] The imagery extended even to militant black sources and appears, for example, although with a quite different meaning, in David Walker's famous *Appeal to the Colored Citizens of the World*.

Despite a few hints to the contrary, the slaves did not view their predicament as punishment for the collective sin of black people. No amount of white propaganda could bring them to accept such an idea. Occasionally, blacks spoke of slavery as a punishment for sin, but even then the precise meaning remained vague. The stark assertion of the white preachers that blacks suffered from the sin of Ham had few if any echoes in the quarters. When Eli Coleman, an ex-slave from Kentucky, spoke of blacks' being under God's curse and therefore in a living hell, he insisted that their great problem was lack of higher vocational and educational skills.[48] Rarely if ever has the transition from John Calvin to Adam Smith been so tightly telescoped. Charity Moore remembered her father's interpretation of the Bible and original sin. The story is charming enough, but its finale demands attention. Adam, it seems, had been so frightened by his sin that he turned white. The rest of the story she "disremembered."[49] Another version, by Ezra Adams, who had been a plowhand on a South Carolina slave plantation, took a plainly secular turn: Adam sinned by taking what did not belong to him. "If what Adam done back yonder," he explained, "would happen now, he would be guilty of crime. Dat's how 'ciety names sin." Thus black preachers invoked parables to demonstrate that God could make good come from evil; that there was good in the most errant brother and sister; and, by implication, that He was bringing good to His enslaved people whose conditions rather than themselves were evil.[50]

For the slaves, sin meant wrongdoing—injustice to others and violation of accepted moral codes. Their otherworldly idea of Heaven shared its place with a this-worldly idea that stressed freedom and a community of love for one's brothers and sisters; little room remained for a theology based on original sin. Hence, black theology largely ignored the one doctrine that might have reconciled the slaves to their bondage on a spiritual plane.

Original sin does not appear in African religions, and the problem of freedom and order therefore assumes radically different forms. Without such a doctrine the delicate balance between the two tips toward the claims of the collective against those of the individual. Much as the doctrine of original sin reflects the class divisions in Western society, whatever its deeper insight into human nature, it also creates greater possibilities for individual freedom, particularly since the cause of individual freedom has historically been inseparable from the use of private property. When the Christian faith took its stand on the doctrine of original sin, it constructed a defense of the individual personality on which the most secularized ideologies of liberalism came to be built. But Christianity's world-shaking achievement also rested on guilt and self-contempt, without which its doctrine of freedom could not have been theologically and socially disciplined. This particular tension between freedom and order provided the driving force of Western culture, as well as the basis for its pessimism.

The African legacy to Afro-America—that celebrated joy in life which is so often denigrated or explained away—represented a life-affirming faith that stressed shame and minimized guilt. Enslavement might be shameful and an expression of weakness, but it could not easily produce a sense of guilt—of getting what you deserved and of being punished for having offended God. Christianity might have transformed the slaves into the slavish robots of Nietzsche's polemic or the Sambos of Stanley Elkins's model, if they had not virtually reshaped it to fit their own psychic needs and their own sensibility.

The ambiguity of the slaves' Heaven and of the limitations on their idea of sin had roots in African ideas of the Soul. Again, it is not possible to know to what extent they stubbornly clung to African ideas and to what extent plantation slave conditions recreated certain patterns of thought. But, clearly, no sharp break occurred. Their life as slaves in the New World, even after conversion to Christianity, did not destroy the traditional sensibility. Newbell Niles Puckett, in his study of folk beliefs among southern blacks during the twentieth century, pointedly insists that their idea of the Soul comes close to traditional African ideas. In some cases he finds "a definite belief in a *kra* or dream-soul," according to which a dream becomes the actual experience of the dreamer's Soul wandering into another world.[51]

A more significant question concerns the relationship of the Soul to the natural order. In the classical Christian tradition man is unique; he alone has a Soul, which establishes his claims to freedom as a matter of responsibility before God. Even in Calvinist theology, in which man's Soul is predestined to salvation or damnation, man himself chose not to obey God in the first place. African ideas place man himself and therefore his Soul within nature. Reincarnation and the return of spirits to the world of the living may occur. Man's Soul is one spirit among many, for all things are infused with spirits. Man himself is one of many material hosts. For traditional Africans, like many non-Christian peoples elsewhere, the Soul came to mean the inner life—the quintessential experience of which matter was merely the form. Thus the Soul, crystallized in a man's shadow, could be detached from his person. Hence, spirits wandered in this world.[52]

The theology of the black preachers made peace with folk ideas of the Soul when it slid over the meaning of Heaven. In so doing, it strengthened the slaves' sense of belonging to the world and of being promised deliverance through faith in Jesus Christ. The compromise was effected on Christian ground, but it necessarily had to reduce that very otherworldliness on which classical Christian individualism in general and antinomianism in particular had arisen. This adjustment entailed sacrifice of considerable revolutionary power.

The idea that the slaves' repeated references to Heaven prove their religious orientation to have been primarily otherworldly rests on a narrow reading of their complex thought. The most obvious function of a concern with Heaven among preachers to the slaves would appear to have been a determination to reconcile them to their lot and turn their attention to an ideal realm. The sermons of black preachers, not to mention white, often centered on this theme. E. S. Abdy heard a slave preacher in Kentucky in 1834 and described him and his performance: "He was about sixty years of age—shrewd and sensible, and, as far as I could judge from some of his observations, a very religious man. What he said upon the duty of submission to his lot here, and his reliance on Divine justice hereafter would have done no discredit to the best educated white."[53] Yet, such messages contain much ambiguity, and so did the very language and delivery of those who spoke them.

Miles Mark Fisher, in a provocative, controversial, but often strained study of the slave songs, vigorously denies that the slaves had any understanding of or interest in the immortality of the Soul. The part of his interpretation that evokes most querulousness is his insistence that Africa played the central role in slave consciousness and that references to Heaven in the spirituals should be understood as meaning Africa or other earthly places of refuge. He does not prove this part of his case, but he does suggest a deep ambiguity in the slaves' apparently otherworldly references.[54]

The slaves' concern with Heaven cannot be interpreted as escapism, especially since, as Howard Thurman and Lawrence Levine point out, a rigid separation of the sacred and the secular had no place in the slaves' view of the world.[55] The several meanings of Heaven in the spirituals must therefore be seen as one—as a necessary and intrinsic ambiguity that reflects a view of the world in which the spiritual and the material merge. No choice need be made between this-worldly and otherworldly interpretations of the song sung by slaves in Mississippi:

> But some ob dese days my time will come,
> I'll year dat bugle, I'll year dat drum,
> I'll see dem armies, marchin' along,
> I'll lif' my head an' jine der song.[56]

Or of "Didn't My Lord Deliver Daniel," or of "Joshua Fit de Battle ob Jericho," or of "Oh, Mary, Don't You Weep," or of "Go Down, Moses." They do not necessarily refer to deliverance in this world or in the other, for they might easily mean either or both. But either way or both ways, they did imply the immanence of God's justice here or hereafter, as He sees fit to bestow it. In this sense, the spirituals were, as Dr. Du Bois himself suggested, "Sorrow Songs" that transcended their sorrow and became hymns of joy.

> Through all the sorrow of the Sorrow Songs there breathes a hope —a faith in the ultimate justice of things. The minor cadences of despair change often to triumph and calm confidence. Sometimes it is faith in life, sometimes a faith in death, sometimes assurances of boundless justice in some fair world beyond. But whichever it is, the meaning is always clear: that sometime, somewhere, men will judge men by their souls and not by their skins.[57]

The slaves' talent for improvisation, as well as their deep religious conviction, drew expressions of wonder and admiration from almost everyone who heard them sing. The boatmen of Georgia and South Carolina and of the Mississippi River received the most attention and drew the most comment, but the common field hands of the Cotton Belt did not lag far behind in performance. The words "wild" and "weird" recurred among white observers, from the abolitionists to the slaveholders to the merely curious. Harriet Beecher Stowe heard Sojourner Truth sing "There Is a Holy City" and remarked, "Sojourner, singing this hymn seemed to impersonate the fervor of Ethiopia, wild, savage, hunted of all nations, but burning after God in her tropic heart and stretching her scarred hands towards the glory to be revealed."[58] Eliza Frances Andrews, listening to the slaves on her plantation singing at a praise-meeting, called their songs "mostly a sort of weird chant that makes me feel all out of myself when I hear it way in the night, too far off to catch the words."[59]
Asked how the songs originated, a black man replied:

I'll tell you; it's dis way. My master call me up and order me a short peck of corn and a hundred lash. My friends see it and is sorry for me. When dey come to de praise meeting dat night dey sing about it. Some's very good singers and know how; and dey work it in, work it in, you know; till dey get it right; and dat's de way.[60]

In 1845, J. Kennard wrote in *Knickerbocker Magazine:*

Who are the true rulers? The Negro poets to be sure. Do they not set the fashion, and give laws to the public taste? Let one of them, in the swamps of Carolina, compose a new song, and it no sooner reaches the ear of a white amateur, than it is written down, amended (that is, almost spoilt), printed and then put upon a course of rapid dissemination, to cease only with the utmost bounds of Anglo-Saxon-dom, perhaps with the world. Meanwhile, the the poor author digs away with his hoe, utterly ignorant of his greatness.[61]

T. S. Eliot observed:

When a poet's mind is perfectly equipped for its work, it is constantly amalgamating disparate experience; the ordinary man's experience is chaotic, irregular, fragmentary. The latter falls in love, or reads Spinoza, and these two experiences have nothing to do with each other, or with the noise of the typewriter or the smell of cooking; in the mind of the poet these experiences are always forming new wholes.[62]

It is doubtful that, by this standard, the world has ever seen so many poets whose minds were "perfectly equipped" simultaneously at work to produce so powerful a synthesis of sacred and secular themes.

Alexander K. Farrar, a planter in Adams County, Mississippi, provided an illuminating illustration of the slaves' understanding of Heaven and its worldly uses. Some slaves had committed murder and had been sentenced to hang. A public display was in order, he thought, for too many slaves believed that the punishment for murder would be transportation, and they had to be disabused. Farrar urged that the bodies be exhibited to the slaves but strongly opposed a public hanging. "If the Negroes are brought out in public to be hung," he explained, "and they get up and talk out that they have got religion and are ready to go home to heaven, etc. etc. —it will have a bad effect upon the other Negroes."[63]

In its blandest and most accommodationist forms, the orientation of oppressed classes toward an afterlife contains important elements of political judgment that help to counteract the pressures for dehumanization and despair and contribute toward the formation of class consciousness. If the lower classes cannot claim to be much, the idea of Heaven, with its equality before God, gives them a strong sense of what they are destined to become. It thereby introduces a sense of worth and reduces the stature of the powerful men of the world. The emphasis on Heaven metamorphoses from the otherworldly into the inner-worldly and creates its own ground for dissent in this world.[64] The other side of this lower-class concern with Heaven is its vision of Hell–the afterlife appropriate to the oppressor. Of the Methodists' influence on the British working class, E. P. Thompson writes: "Faith in a life to come served not only as a consolation to the poor but also as some emotional compensation for present sufferings and grievances: it was possible not only to imagine the 'reward' of the humble but also to enjoy some revenge upon their oppressors, by imagining their torments to come."[65] This sense of a revenge to come always carried with it the thrust of a political quiescence accompanied by vicarious thrills. Its positive political significance remained only a tendency. By sharpening a sense of class justice it prepared the way for explosive hostility, should circumstances present an opportunity for aggressive action.

In less dramatic ways, the slaves manipulated the idea of Heaven both defensively and offensively. It could become a vehicle for a sarcastic judgment of the masters, as it did for Andrew Moss of Georgia: "De white folks what owned slaves thought that when dey go to Heaven de colored folks would be dere to wait on 'em."[66] One theme that recurs is love for each other. The slaves viewed Heaven as a place of reconciliation with each other; only sometimes did they view it as a place of reconciliation with whites. Annie Laurie Broiderick, a white woman from a slaveholding family in Vicksburg, Mississippi, recalled the activities of the Methodist slaves. "During their protracted meetings," she wrote, "after becoming pious, they would work themselves into a frenzy, and begin their shouting by walking up to each other, taking and shaking the hand with words, 'I hope to meet you in heaven. . . .' "[67] Anne Bell, an ex-slave from South Carolina, made the same point in her own way: "Does I believe in 'ligion? What else good for colored folks? I ask you if dere ain't a heaven, what's colored folks got to look forward to? They can't git anywhere down here. De only joy they can have here is servin' and lovin'; us can git dat in 'ligion but dere is a limit to de nigger in everything else."[68]

Fanny Kemble's three-year-old daughter confronted the maid: "Mary, some persons are free and some are not." No reply. "I am a free person. I say, I am a free person, Mary—do you know that?" Acknowledgment: "Yes, missus." Relentless child: "Some persons are free and some are not—do you know that, Mary?" Reply: "Yes, missus, *here;* I know it is so here, in this world."[69]

Did the slaves sing of God's Heaven and a life beyond this life? Or of a return to Africa? Or of a Heaven that was anywhere they would be free? Or of an undefined state in which they could love each other without fear? On any given occasion they did any one of these; probably, in most instances they did all at once. Men and women who dare to dream of deliverance from suffering rarely fit their dreams into neat packages.

Black eschatology emerges more clearly from the slaves' treatment of Moses and Jesus. The slaves did not draw a sharp line between them but merged them into the image of a single deliverer, at once this-worldly and otherworldly. Colonel Higginson said that their heads held a jumble of Jewish biblical history and that they associated Moses with all great historical events, including the most recent. After the war black preachers took the political stump to tell the freedmen in South Carolina that the Republican gubernatorial candidate, Franklin J. Moses, was none other than the man himself, who had come to lead them to the Promised Land. All across the South blacks insisted that they had seen Mr. Linkum visit their locality as part of his work of deliverance.

The image of Moses, the this-worldly leader of his people out of bondage, and Jesus, the otherworldly Redeemer, blended into a pervasive theme of deliverance. A former house slave, who considered himself superior to the field hands, admitted praying with them. "Well, yes'm," he explained, "we would pray the Lord to deliver us." Eliza Frances Andrews waxed indignant over the freedmen's adulation for the abolitionist who had come to teach them during the Union occupation. They think he is Jesus Christ, she protested. "Anyhow," she paraphrased them, "he has done more for them than Jesus Christ ever did." The Reverend C. C. Jones observed that the few remaining Muslim slaves on the Georgia coast identified Muhammed with Jesus, and he might have added, therefore with Moses too.[70]

The variety of uses to which the slaves put Moses may be glimpsed in two comments by ex-slaves. Savilla Burrell of South Carolina said:

Young Marse Sam Still got killed in de Civil War. Old Marse live on. I went to see him in his last days and I set by him and kept de flies off while dere. I see the lines of sorrow had plowed on dat old face and I 'membered he'd been a captain on hoss back in dat war. It come into my 'membrance de song of Moses; "de Lord had triumphed glorily and de hoss and his rider have been throwed into de sea."[71]

And George Briggs, also from South Carolina, himself an old preacher, commented: "Man learns right smart from Exodus 'bout how to lead. . . . Moses still de strongest impression dat we has as rulers. God gits His-self into de heads of men dat He wants to rule and He don't tell nobody else nothing 'bout it neither."[72] The great heroes of the spirituals, even when Jesus' name appears, often turn out to be the deliverers of the people as a whole in this world.[73]

The slaves had a special and central place for Jesus, but a place that whites had difficulty recognizing. Julius Lester has given us, with a few short strokes, a convincing reading. The slaves, he writes, "fashioned their own kind of Christianity, which they turned to for strength in the constant times of need. In the Old Testament story of the enslavement of the Hebrews by the Egyptians, they found their own story. In the figure of Jesus Christ, they found someone who had suffered as they suffered, someone who understood, someone who offered them rest from their suffering."[74] Moses had become Jesus, and Jesus, Moses; and with their union the two aspects of the slaves' religious quest—collective deliverance as a people and redemption from their terrible personal sufferings—had become one through the mediation of that imaginative power so beautifully manifested in the spirituals.

If Jesus had suffered as they had suffered, if He had in fact died to relieve their suffering, He necessarily took on an aspect apart from the Moses figure. "The death of the savior," writes Max Weber, "may be viewed as a means of mollifying the wrath of god, before whom the savior appears as an intercessor for men. . . ."[75] He therefore assumed a double aspect for the slaves, much as Moses did in a somewhat different way. In this sense the slaves were no more "confused" than are those who would accept the Trinity as a single manifestation of a monotheist's God and yet insist on preserving the identities and discrete meanings of the Father, the Son, and the Holy Ghost.

Jesus was closer to them than Moses, as He has so often been to the poor, by virtue of the low earthly station the Son of God chose as His own. In the words of G. G. Coulton:

Gibbon sneers at Tertullian's boast that a Christian mechanic could give an answer to problems which had puzzled the wisest heads of antiquity. But is not Gibbon's criticism a dangerous half-truth? From a wider point of view, must we not count it a real step forward in civilization that the artisan should seriously attempt to answer these questions at all? Christianity certainly brought in a new spirit; and the spirit is all-important. The belief in a crucified carpenter— the conviction that the highest triumph may be gotten of the completest earthly failure—did, as a matter of fact, take more men out of themselves, and took them further out of themselves than anything else since the dawn of history.[76]

Appropriately, Christianity spread across the Mediterranean basin, not as a religion of slaves, but primarily as a religion of artisans. In time, the Roman ruling class did everything in its power to impose it on the slaves in order to reconcile them to their lot and point them toward otherworldly concerns. When the black slaves of the New World made it their own, they transformed it into a religion of resistance—not often of revolutionary defiance, but of a spiritual resistance that accepted the limits of the politically possible. Paul Radin observes that whereas the whites asked Jesus for forgiveness, the blacks primarily asked for recognition.[77] The slaves' assimilation of Moses to Jesus represented a vital mechanism for that transformation.

However politically radical the historical Jesus may have been and however subversive some may wish to understand the New Testament as being, Christian revolutionaries have always had a hard time explaining away the Epistles of Paul and too much else. Sooner or later, usually sooner, they have summoned the God of Wrath of the Old Testament. For black slaves who were determined to resist the powers that be and yet powerless to defy them openly, who looked longingly toward delivery from bondage and yet had little thirst or opportunity for vengeance, who sought spiritual redemption in Heaven and yet could not ignore their need for bodily redemption in this world, the assimilation of Moses to Jesus provided the way to reconcile all contradictions. Moses, once become Jesus, had his dangerous message muted, and the gloomy implications of the forty years in the wilderness could be forgotten. Jesus, once become Moses, underwent a transubstantiation that carried with it the promise of this-worldly salvation without suicidal adventures. The assimilation solved the problem of how to achieve spiritual freedom, retain faith in earthly deliverance, instill a spirit of pride and love in each other, and make peace with a political reality within which revolutionary solutions no longer had much prospect.

It bridged another painful gap as well. At the risk of oversimplification, the God of the Old Testament may be taken as a national deity—Lord of the Chosen People and God of Wrath—and the God of the New Testament may be taken as the first projected Lord of the entire human community and a God of Love. Then the slaves' "confusion" appears as a necessary, if not firmly consistent, response to their objective position in white America. It allowed them to preserve, in muted form, a sense of being God's special children and yet allowed them to accept, or at least not deny, the whites, whose lives were so intimately bound up with their own as brothers in Christ. An ex-slave said, "The love of God is beyond understanding. It makes you love everybody."[78] For people who, even as slaves, were creating an incipient nation within a nation, it would be difficult to imagine a more satisfactory solution.

THE BLACK PREACHERS

In the cities, slaves and free Negroes heard black denominational ministers who were at least as well trained as their white counterparts and innumerable class leaders or assistants or prayer leaders, who ostensibly assisted a white minister but who, more often than not, did most of the effective preaching to the blacks. In the countryside, especially, exhorters got the spirit and preached the Word with or without any training or guidance at all.[1]

Every plantation had its exhorter. The great pity is that so little is known about his relationship to the black preachers who passed through and so little about the relationship between both and the plantation conjurers. It would not be surprising if some black preachers were all three at once. On the Georgia coast as late as the 1930s black Baptist and Methodist preachers openly shared their congregations' retention of African beliefs in ghosts and witches. In antebellum days some outstanding black leaders, like Bishop Daniel Alexander Payne of the African Methodist Episcopal Church, waged a stubborn fight against the "heathenish" and "outlandish" beliefs and practices of their country brethren. Despite every effort, a white pastor wrote the Richmond, Virginia, *Religious Herald*, the blacks were clinging to old beliefs, and none bore so much responsibility as the preachers.

The plantation preachers, like the itinerants, often commanded the respect of their masters as well as of the slaves, but no less often they faced the whip or worse for their efforts. If they sought and often gained respect, prestige, influence, and special favors for themselves, they also exposed themselves to dangers. William Wells Brown recalled a preacher who belonged to the same church as his master but was nonetheless sold away from wife and children. Other preachers, like Salomon Oliver, were repeatedly beaten for defying orders not to preach to the slaves. If there were rewards to tempt the vain and the ambitious, the risks guaranteed considerable dedication.

When white travelers said that Negro preachers were mulattoes, as they often did, they were merely reflecting circumstances as they existed in the tourist-attracting cities of Charleston, New Orleans, and Richmond. Black and mulatto preachers worked side by side, and there is little indication of special rivalry and caste consciousness outside the ranks of the small urban brown elite. Sir Charles Lyell, Fredrika Bremer, and other astute travelers found black preachers everywhere, and both plantation records and the accounts of former slaves concur.

Those clearly identified by both whites and blacks as regular preachers, in contradistinction to those identified as plantation hands who preached in lieu of a regular preacher, often could read and often knew the Bible. No doubt many were illiterate or poorly educated, but the proportion may not have been much higher than among the poor white preachers. The reputation of the black preachers for illiteracy and extreme ignorance stemmed primarily from white and black reports on those slaves who took up preaching on their own plantations in the absence of a regular preacher. Even these efforts often reflected tremendous dedication. For example, two such slaves who performed plantation weddings pretended to read the appropriate wedding service, probably less to impress their fellow slaves, who surely knew they could not read, than to establish the dignity of the occasion. They knew the service, as written, by heart, having learned it from the master's grandson.

During the eighteenth century free Negro preachers had enjoyed a considerable reputation in the South. When confronted with white hostility, they organized clandestine plantation meetings and took the beatings that rewarded their efforts. Forbidden by law from functioning as preachers during the nineteenth century, they insinuated themselves into the confidence of local whites as "assistants" to white clergymen and went about their own business. Law or no law, repression or no repression, the slaves heard their own black preachers, if not regularly, then at least frequently enough to make a difference in their lives.

Although blacks preached with some ease during the eighteenth century, they were severely curbed during the nineteenth. Each insurrectionary scare from Gabriel's to Vesey's to Nat Turner's led to a wave of repression. Especially after 1831, laws forbade free Negroes to preach to slaves or sought to register and control them or required whites to be present when any black man preached. But the preachers, free and slave, carried on. In Virginia between 1770 and 1780, at least half a dozen regularly ministered to whites. John Chavis, a free Negro Presbyterian minister who had won over large numbers of initially hostile whites, had to stop preaching in the wake of the repression that followed the Nat Turner revolt. Undaunted, he opened a private school—for whites—which he conducted until his death in 1838. According to the Reverend R. C. Medaris, a white Baptist minister of Arkansas, Uncle Tom Clements, a black slave preacher freed late in life, officiated at perhaps as many as one hundred white Baptist funerals. Even in the deepest South—Alabama, Mississippi, Louisiana—black preachers had large numbers of whites among their communicants right down until the war; in fact, they seem to have worked more easily and in greater numbers in Texas and the western Cotton Belt than they did further east. Respected black ministers, like Jacob Walker of Augusta, Georgia, or Joseph Wills of Opelousas, Louisiana, met their responsibility to reach the slaves, even as they ministered to the free men of both races. But the repression of the post–Nat Turner era took its toll. Some of the finest black ministers had to leave the South or fall silent.

Ex-slaves recalled with pride particularly accomplished preachers. Elizabeth Ross Hite remembered a local preacher in Louisiana who spoke five languages—not so surprising in a state in which slaves not infrequently knew French and Spanish as well as English. Andrew Goodman, an ex-slave from Virginia, recalled a preacher named Kenneth Lyons as a "man of good learnin' and the best preacher I ever heard." Feribe Rogers, an ex-slave of Georgia, spoke of a literate preacher who presided at weddings and taught others to read. W. L. Bost, an ex-slave of North Carolina, recalled a "terrible smart" young preacher who paid special attention to the plantation children. Throughout the South so many whites as well as blacks commented on the literacy and sophistication of black preachers that we are left to wonder if these did not constitute a majority. The Reverend C. C. Jones, for example, could write that some consideration should be given to the circumstance that not all black ministers could read; he apparently took it for granted, and expected his readers to, that most could.

Majority or no, they existed in sufficient numbers to guarantee that most slaves heard reasonably well-trained and well-educated black preachers once in a while. And once in a while would have been quite enough to let them know that, notwithstanding their alleged inferiority, black men could rival and surpass the white preachers, not only in the spirit but by the Book.

W. E. B. Du Bois writes, in *Souls of Black Folk*, that the black slave religion displayed three particular characteristics: "The Preacher, the Music, and the Frenzy." He continues:

> The Preacher is the most unique personality developed by the Negro on American soil. A leader, a politician, an orator, a "boss," an intriguer, an idealist—all these he is, and ever too, the center of a group of men, now twenty, now a thousand in number. The combination of a certain adroitness with deep-seated earnestness, of tact with consummate ability, gave him his preeminence, and helps him maintain it.

Given the specific character of their religion—its African soul and utter, slave-conditioned necessity for a plain message to the heart—the slaves naturally looked to those who could understand and address themselves to their hopes and their misery. Drivers, artisans, and ordinary field slaves of special force of personality turned to preaching. Precisely those slaves and free Negroes who had the strength to lead their fellows took up the Word. The experience of slavery, and of Reconstruction too, suggests that rather than preachers somehow usurping community leadership, the natural leaders of the community, as defined by the slaves themselves, felt the call to preach and knew that preaching was their road to prestige, power, and deepest service within the black community.

White attitudes toward black preachers varied widely according to time and place. Whenever trouble occurred, the preachers took the blame. The aftermath of the Nat Turner revolt provided only the most dramatic illustration of a reaction that had come in the wake of every major disturbance after the Revolutionary War. Governor Floyd of Virginia believed that the evil doings of the black preachers lay at the heart of the insurrection. According to his information, the rebels sought to establish a black government under the dictatorship of their preachers. In view of the low incidence of revolts in the South and of the unblemished record as nonrevolutionaries accumulated by the vast majority of the preachers, Governor Floyd's response, so characteristic of white reaction, might seem excessive. Yet, the evidence accumulated by Herbert Aptheker, James Hugo Johnston, and other historians adds up to a defense of Governor Floyd's sanity.[2]

The preachers did not typically call for revolt and violence, for conditions overwhelmingly discouraged insurrectionary ideas among sober black men. But many could turn into revolutionaries if conditions changed. Neither their temperament nor the quality of their religious faith prohibited a call to arms. Under the best of circumstances many had to be judged by the slaveholders as dangerous men of unpredictable political tendency. That more of them did not call their people to arms may say more about the relationship of forces than about their inclinations.

The white South could ill afford to take chances. A favorable balance of power might convince sober heads that insurrectionary appeals were not likely, but "not likely" is rarely good enough for men with wives, children, and property to worry about. Besides, preachers could cause a great deal of mischief short of appeals to bloodshed. To cite a common case, in 1854 a grand jury in Madison County, Alabama, recommended that only whites be allowed to preach to slaves because too many black preachers were troublemakers.[3] A grand jury normally consisted of people who knew their county and the people in it, black and white. Not above being panicked, it nonetheless could usually be counted on to act with restraint and a strong sense of self-interest in matters affecting master-slave relations. Many apparently felt as did the Royalist duke of Newcastle during England's time of troubles in the seventeenth century: "There should be more praying and less preaching, for preaching breeds faction, but much praying causes devotion."[4]

From the earliest period advertisements tell of runaway slaves who insisted they were preachers and who had proven themselves faithless scoundrels in the eyes of the master class.[5] Olmsted tells us that southern whites merely took for granted the bad character of the preachers.[6] Time and time again the plantation preacher would be described as the "worst Negro on the place." A liar. A thief. A troublemaker. A braggart. A faker. A consummate opportunist. Show a slaveowner a slave preacher and he would show you a very bad nigger. In some cases slaveowners reacted with contempt and cynicism. A slaveowner in Mobile, Alabama, offered to sell a black preacher: "I will warrant him sound enough in wind, if not in doctrine." The prospective buyer's reply was instructive: "I wouldn't care for his doctrine, if I bought him; I don't care how black he is, feed him right, and in a month, he will be as orthodox as the archbishop."[7]

Hostility, suspicion, contempt, and cynicism do not tell the whole story of white attitudes. Too many whites became infected with the genuine spiritual appeal of the black preachers, including their own slaves, not to take measures to protect them. When the preachers expressed socially orthodox views, whether honestly or for white consumption, they were the more valued. A great southern planter could write in his diary with evident interest about a free Negro preacher who disliked abolitionists and refused to do missionary work in Africa ostensibly because no whites lived there.[8] The wife of a planter, himself a minister, could write movingly of "faithful old Uncle Nat," the plantation's slave preacher. According to her description, he was literate and "trusted and respected by every one." Her ambiguous remark that he reported to the master on the Negroes' "condition" and "acts" suggests that, although he may have played the informer, he may also have represented the slaves' interests, or most likely, done both at once.[9]

Many slaveholders, especially those in the clergy themselves, understood that whatever the law might say or the whites might demand, the blacks would find a way to hear their own preachers. Accordingly, they urged a reversal of policy and an acceptance of the inevitable. Let the white churches encourage black preaching, they argued, and thereby put themselves in a position to supervise it. The Reverend C. C. Jones, indefatigable in his efforts at converting the slaves, vigorously championed the formal use of unlicensed, untrained Negro "exhorters" as supplementary preachers. He pointed out that "numerous" black preachers and exhorters serviced the plantations with or without official sanction and that many of them did a good job from the white point of view. With unusual insight but his usual courage, he argued that God always preaches to His people in part through their own. Blacks deserved to hear black preachers.[10]

The Reverend Mr. Jones was merely facing facts. The only question concerned the degree of white influence and supervision. Even those white ministers energetically servicing the plantations had to appoint black assistants, who did most of the actual preaching. From Charleston to Jackson, in town and in country, the report was the same: the laws against black preachers could not be enforced.[11]

White toleration of the preachers, which always existed in an uneasy balance with repression and abuse, became part of the growing tendency to promote religious segregation. As such it represented at once a steady strengthening of the more virulent forms of white racism and a major concession to black sensibilities and the slaves' covert power over their own lives. By the time of the war Fitzgerald Ross could say plainly that the blacks attached to the Confederate army openly preferred their own religious meetings, presided over by their own preachers, and that the whites were happy to leave them alone.[12] Black tributes as well as white claims reveal that many masters appreciated a slave's talent and encouraged him to preach. Robert Toombs, the distinguished planter and politician from Georgia, taught his coachman to read and write and allowed him to preach widely on the countryside. In South Carolina a slave got the call but was ridiculed by his master, who reminded him that he was both illiterate and ignorant. He persisted, and the master let him try. In the words of the ex-slave who had witnessed the scene, "Bird preached the hair-raisingest sermon you ever heard." His master freed him, gave him a horse, and sent him on the circuit. Other ex-slaves, including some who later became ministers, recorded evidences of white support and generosity.[13]

The slaves preferred their own black preachers. Anthony Dawson, himself the nephew of a literate driver-preacher, said, "Mostly we had white preachers, but when we had a black preacher, that was heaven."[14] Former slaves from Virginia recall that long after the repressive laws of the early 1830s had gone into effect the slaves demanded and got black preachers for their funerals.[15] Charlie Meadow of South Carolina: "My favorite preacher was a big black African named Williams who came to preach in de darky church for us every now and den." Pet Franks of Mississippi: "Old Daddy Young was 'bout de bes' preacher us ever had." Walter Calloway of Alabama added simply that the people preferred Joe, their slave preacher, to the occasional white preachers.[16] The slaves collected a little money for the preachers when they could and at least quartered them and took care of their mules and horses.[17]

The reputation of the preachers among the slaves was never entirely unblemished, as some satirical songs show:[18]

> Some folks say preachers won't steal,
>   Ha, ha, Rosie!
> But I caught two in my cornfield,
>   Ha, ha, Rosie!

or:

> Say, I wouldn't trust a preacher out o' my sight,
> 'Cause dey believes in doin' too many things far in de night.

or the one supposedly sung by a preacher:

> Brother, if you want mo' preachin'
> Save a little [money] for me.

The preachers in antebellum as well as postbellum times often faced accusations from blacks of promiscuity, extortion, and infidelity, but no more often than white frontier preachers faced such accusations from their own people.[19] Never did the blacks' criticism of their preachers run so deep or extend so wide as to discredit them as a group. The frailty of the man was not essential. Faith in the preacher gave a personal expression to faith in God, and for slaves especially, faith in God meant faith in oneself—in one's own soul and worth. The relationship of the slave community to their preachers provides a wonderful example of the wisdom of Georg Simmel's remarks on the sociology of religion:

> Faith in a human being, even though it be objectively unjustified, has the immense advantage of kindling many things in our soul and uniting passing events which otherwise would have remained unconscious or ineffective. . . . He supports us in our suffering with inadequate and improper palliatives, but trusting his help we take new courage and strength. He tries to prove something to us by way of a poor argument, and in accepting it as true we discover for ourselves the correct answer. Very often we do confer on someone in whom we trust those treasures which are our very own; yet he has inspired us to dig into ourselves for these treasures. What it all comes to is the belief of man in himself.[20]

The slaves sometimes had reasons other than personal ones for criticizing their preachers. Charley Williams, an ex-slave who had lived in Mississippi, Louisiana, and Texas, reported: "We had meetings sometimes, but the nigger preacher just talk about being a good nigger, and doin' to please the master."[21] Other ex-slaves told of black preachers brought in by the whites to do their bidding. During the war many of them could be heard to pray for the Confederate cause, although what they said to their brethren privately was often another matter.[22]

The preachers walked a tightrope. They knew that they had to rely on the protection of their masters. As men of God who cared about the spiritual life of the slaves, their unwillingness to separate theology from sociopolitical questions did not arise from an indifference to theology but from a holistic vision of life. Thus, they had to make many compromises in order to be able to do the very first thing incumbent upon them—to preach the Word. When Old Alfred Williams, a slave preacher of Tennessee, had to contend with the hostility of patrollers to his prayer meetings, he had a ready response: he sent for his master on whose protection he knew he could depend.[23]

In the absence of white observers the preachers became bolder, but even so they always had to be careful of informers and showed little inclination to turn inflammatory. Hiram R. Revels, a preacher who later served as a United States senator from the reconstructed state of Mississippi, wrote: "I sedulously refrained from doing anything that would incite the slaves to run away from their masters. It being understood that my object was to preach the gospel to them, and improve their moral and spiritual condition, even slave holders were tolerant toward me."[24] The Reverend Henry H. Mitchell has pointed out that even the conservative John Jasper, who was a great favorite among the whites and entirely safe on political questions, did important work for his people by instilling in them a strong sense of moral values, without which no future movement for liberation would have been possible.[25]

Some preachers struck out more boldly than others when the opportunity arose. "When I starts preachin'," recalled the Reverend Anderson Edwards, who had been a slave in Texas, "I couldn't read or write and had to preach what massa told me. And he say tell them niggers iffen they obeys the massa they goes to heaven, but I knowed there's something better for them, but daren't tell them 'cept on the sly. That I done lots. I tells 'em iffen they keeps prayin' the Lord will set 'em free."[26] And James Childress, an ex-slave from Tennessee, remembered nothing about the preachers so much as that they promised deliverance from slavery through faith in God.[27] Litt Young, a former slave from Mississippi, reported that her mistress had built the slaves a fine and well-appointed church and had provided a mulatto preacher. Under orders from his mistress and in her presence, he would stay close to the "Obey your master" theme. When she was not present, "He come out with straight preachin' from the Bible."[28]

"Straight preachin' from the Bible" does not suggest political fireworks, but neither does it suggest ideological neutrality. The slaves appreciated the artificial construction and political purpose of the white man's words and opposed to them a biblical view of the world, which implied a sense of a higher organic order in the universe and therefore a Truth far above the claims of temporal relations. Consider a few "nonpolitical" sermons. Lyell visited a black Methodist church in Louisville and heard a well-spoken, fully black preacher address his congregation as "Sirs and Madams" and insist that all humanity descends from Adam and Eve. It would be difficult to imagine anything so tame and yet so quietly subversive of the hegemony of a white-supremacist master class.[29] In Savannah, Lyell heard a black man preach to a congregation of about six hundred mostly dark Negroes. He spoke so well that Lyell thought his occasional ungrammatical lapses and "Negro idiom" to have been deliberate. His thesis: Lead a moral life so that you can get to Heaven. And, oh yes, he defined Heaven as a future state in which God would deal impartially with "the poor and the rich, the black man and the white."[30] To remind black slaves that God made no distinction of class or race was not revolutionary, but neither was it without dissident ideological content. It had been a favorite theme since the earliest days, and its invocation could be enough to get a black preacher sent to the cotton fields by an irate master.[31] When freedom came and the favorite text of the white preachers—"Obey your masters"—disappeared, there stood in its place Malachi 2:10: "Have we not all one father? hath not one God created us?"[32] A white southerner witnessed the baptism of slaves by a slave preacher in Augusta, Georgia, and heard the preacher call to his people, "All who hear me, black and white, bond and free." They called back, "Black and white, bond and free."[33]

Fredrika Bremer tells of slaves on a South Carolina rice plantation who listened to a dull white Methodist preacher during the day and then assembled to hear a black preacher at night. She paraphrased the black preacher's message as "Let us do as Christ has commanded us; let us do as he wishes, let us love one another."[34] Not a message of physical resistance, it was a message of reaffirmation of slave personality and worth. A people who can be fired with love for each other have set strict limits to the degradation that the most evil of social systems can impose upon them. Miss Bremer was right to call the preacher's message one of "spiritual freedom." She had heard an old theme among the slaves. Edmund Botsford, a white minister, on the revival circuit in 1790, commented on the results. The blacks, he said, "in general far exceed the whites in love to each other and in most other duties."[35]

The Reverend J. G. Williams, a white man who lived among the Gullah slaves, left us some instructive illustrations of the subtle techniques of the plantation preachers. He reconstructed from memory and perhaps from notes the sermons of Brudder Paul Coteny, who never so much as hinted that his fellow slaves ought to protest against their enslavement. "Good Negro" that he ostensibly was, he dutifully preached the standard sermon against stealing from dear Old Maussah, whose Christian devotion to the slaves he warmly praised. Yet step by step, right under the nose of the Reverend Mr. Williams, Brudder Coteny drove home his attack on the whites:

> Mind you, nigger! de debil ent shine you eye wid dem buckra watermillion. Watermillion is berry shine eye ting to nigger eye. Buckra chicken and buckra hog—dems a shine eye ting. . . . And dem shinin silver and gold dollar is a shine eye ting to buckra, an dat's de reason some dem buckra want to get to hebin—case so much gold da, till de berry street pave wid gold. And nigger is a shine eye ting to buckra. Ef he look pun a nigger he say: "A thousand dollar in dat nigger." O, I tell you, nigger gwine send heap of dem buckra to struckshun.

In other sermons Brudder Coteny innocently railed against sin by comparing sinners to goats and Christians to sheep. He made no overtly antiwhite remarks and insisted, "Buckra an nigger skin different, but dem haht is same color." He ended on the familiar biblical note that on Judgment Day the Lord would separate the sheep from the goats. What the Reverend Mr. Williams apparently missed was that black folklore assigns a special meaning to goats: they are white people. He ought not to have missed the special meaning assigned by antebellum whites to sheep: they were akin

to blacks since both had "wool," not hair. The slaves did not miss
the reference, for they roared back at Brudder Coteny, "Bless de
Lawd, we nigger know who hab de wool!"[36]

Scholars may be right in insisting that black religion in the
postbellum South oriented itself toward the status quo when it
taught that roles would be reversed in Heaven.[37] But such teaching
cannot be dismissed as being oriented toward the status quo when
directed to slaves. The religious leaders first had to combat that
sense of unworthiness and inferiority which the slaveholders constantly tried to infuse in the slaves. The doctrine of spiritual equality and a future without white supremacy therefore had great
positive value despite its restricted and conservative political content.

Fredrika Bremer could find only one black preacher—a Methodist in Cincinnati—who invoked blunt black nationalism: "Is God
with us? I speak of our nation, my brethren. . . ." He told the story
of the Israelites as the story of the oppressed black nation and cast
the Negroes in the role of the Chosen People for whom slavery and
oppression constituted God's test.[38] Such a message might have
been preached at secret slave meetings in the South, but there is
no evidence that it was much heard. Yet, in holding their people
together spiritually, in teaching them to value themselves, to love
one another, to trust in ultimate deliverance, the preachers contributed more to the formation of a black national sensibility than
perhaps they ever knew.

The black preachers faced a problem analogous to that of the
early Christian preachers: they had to speak a language defiant
enough to hold the high-spirited among their flock but neither so
inflammatory as to rouse them to battles they could not win nor
so ominous as to rouse the ire of ruling powers.[39] Like Justin, they
often had to preach peace and loyalty to their general public and
to reserve more radical messages for those congregations prepared
to receive them. Unlike Justin, they performed with sufficient skill
to avoid execution. The preachers benefitted in their deception by
the low cultural level of the whites usually assigned to observe
them; white overseers normally lacked the intellectual sophistication to detect a subversive sermon unless flagrantly delivered.[40]

The preachers, among other accomplishments, made a significant contribution to general southern culture as well as to specifically black culture. Their preaching style was their own, although
it owed much to the African call-and-response song-style and
something to the florid oratorical style of the white politicians and

preachers all around them. Every successful preacher knew the power of a rhythmic progression of words and knew how, at first slowly and softly and then with deceptive quickness, to move his audience to a crescendo of frenzied response. It is impossible to believe that, apart from the uniquely Afro-American style they were creating, they did not profoundly, if subtly and inadvertently, add much to that great tradition of southern oratory ordinarily attributed solely to white men of power and standing.

The words used by the preachers often could not be understood by whites fortunate enough to hear them. The enthusiastic black audiences did not always understand their words either; at least, white observers often thought not. Many plantation preachers were illiterate and not entirely comfortable in standard English, and sometimes the whites could not understand because they were straining to hear standard English from men speaking a black dialect. Yet, sensitive whites like Mary Boykin Chesnut found themselves deeply moved. She described a plantation congregation which had just heard a fiery white Methodist minister, after which the blacks took over:

> Jim Nelson, the driver, the stateliest darky I ever saw, tall and straight as a pine tree, with a fine face, and not so very black but a full-blooded African, was asked to lead a prayer. . . . The words had no meaning at all. It was the devotional passion of voice and manner which was so magnetic. The Negroes sobbed and shouted and swayed backward and forward, some with aprons to their eyes, most of them clapping their hands and responding in shrill tones: "Yes, God!" "Jesus!" "Savior!" "Bless de Lord, amen," etc. It was a little too exciting for me. I would very much have liked to shout too. . . .[41]

No doubt the style of the black preachers in slavery times differed from the style of rural black preachers today; no doubt it would be an error to read the one back into the other. Yet the evidence suggests far greater continuity than discontinuity, and much can be learned about the antebellum preachers by following the accounts of today's black "folk preachers" in the studies by Bruce A. Rosenberg and the Reverend Henry H. Mitchell. Their preaching has a strong element of chanting—virtually, of singing. For some reason, Rosenberg, whose valuable book is marred by an astonishing inattention to African culture, attributes this style to European rather than to African influences or to a conjuncture of both.

Typically, the preacher begins in a carefully measured way and steadily works toward a more rhythmical and intense delivery. As the rhythm, rising and falling, builds toward a climax, punctuated by groans, grunts, and cries, the preacher virtually breaks into a chant and then a song. In effect, he guides his congregation toward a musical response that may provide an important clue to the origin of those wonderful and spontaneous songs created by the slaves. No two sermons can be alike, and each shows the marked influence of the spirituals and vice versa. Each sermon becomes a new poetic construction and a new combination of artistic elements.[42]

Many black preachers swung easily between congregations of rough, dialect-speaking field hands and congregations of house slaves, urban slaves, free Negroes, and even whites. Most impressively, many were able to preach effectively to all at once. In such cases the procedure called for delivering sermons in standard English, with enough intrusions of vocabulary and expression from the dialect of the field hands to make them comfortable, and then for relying on para-language—tone, gesture, rhythm—to complete the message to those unable or unwilling to follow a sophisticated sermon. The results often astonished white observers. Henry E. Simmons, a Union soldier from Rhode Island who normally took a condescending attitude toward the blacks, attended a meeting at a contraband camp in Virginia in 1863 and reported to his wife: "The old [black] minister began to preach and in fifteen minutes he gave us a better sermon than the chaplain this morning did in an hour."[43]

The most literate slave preachers used black English, much as some of the most sophisticated black ministers do now, not as an affected talking down to congregations of the uneducated, but as a natural resort to the accepted and preferred language. The reliance on repetition, for example, established its own context by emphasizing, in the words of Dr. Mitchell, "intensity of response" rather than "extensity of material covered." Educated ministers today—see the printed excerpts from the sermons of Dr. Mitchell, who is a scholar and university professor as well as a minister, or recall the powerful sermons and speeches of the late Dr. Martin Luther King—will freely slip into double negatives and other forms of "bad English," which in fact represent, in the context of southern-born audiences, a perfectly straightforward and clear use of dialect. As Dr. Mitchell suggests, the preachers must resort to the language of the people, not simply to get a hearing, but to deliver an important thought through the medium itself. The people must hear God's Word spoken in their own language. With this one stroke the preachers have brought God to black people as their own, not as some remote white father-image.

Ruder antebellum preachers, especially the illiterates, sometimes strove to impress the whites in their audience or to awe their own people by fancifying their speech with phrases like "agnominious sinners" or "His glorifious presence," which were no more ludicrous than those used by a multitude of poor-white Baptist preachers on the frontier.[44] Many whites laughed and congratulated themselves on their own superiority. Almost invariably the blacks, whether or not taken in by the charlatanry and the pathetic lapses, responded with enthusiasm. The whites took the joyous black responses as further evidence of inferiority. Even the most culturally backward of the slaves, however, were responding to something more than to the formal features of the sermons.

The slaves did not mindlessly cheer every black preacher, any more than they automatically refused to respond to every white preacher. The preachers had to communicate with more than words, if only because too often whites were listening. Even when whites were not listening, the tradition of indirection, necessary for survival under conditions of white domination, manifested itself as a way of life, not merely as a mask to be put on and dropped at will. Thus, the preachers relied heavily on tone, gesture, and rhythm and combined an adequate verbal message with a deep emotional appeal that transcended the words themselves. In a sense every preacher has to do so, but the problem facing the black preachers was specific and especially difficult.

The success of black preachers like John Jasper of Virginia is instructive. Slaves would defer funeral ceremonies for as long as necessary in order to bring him to the plantation for the service. During the war he won a warm response from the Confederate wounded to whom he preached and offered solace. Consider his most famous sermon, which he reputedly gave on several hundred occasions to whites and blacks alike. Jasper had heard that some heretics were misleading his people into believing that the earth moved around a stationary sun. Richmond's most fashionable whites and the countryside's poorest slaves flocked to hear his reply, which came to be known as his "De Sun Do Move an' de Earth Am Square" sermon.

> Joshuar tell de sun ter stand' still till he could finish whippin' de enemy an' de sun was travellin' long dar thew de sky when it stopt for Joshuar. It stopt fer business an' it went on when it got thew.

Before we assume that the whites, many of whom had undoubtedly come for laughs, left the service laughing, we should hear the report of Dr. William E. Hatcher, pastor of the Grace Street Baptist Church (white). To illustrate Jasper's power to spellbind, Hatcher told of a newspaper reporter who had listened, stunned, until the end of the sermon, when Jasper, as usual, had asked all those who agreed that "de Sun do move" to hold up their hands. Hatcher was not at all surprised to see the reporter suddenly stretch his hand up just as high as he could get it, for he himself had done the same.[45]

The sermons displayed those special characteristics of language that have become part of the quality of life in black America. In their technical aspect they relied on copiousness and verbal adaptability. Fredrika Bremer referred to "that talent of improvisation, and of strikingly applying theoretical truths to the occurrences of daily life, which I have often admired among the negroes."[46] With each reference to sin, the black Methodist preacher of whom she wrote supplied descriptions "as graphic as his gestures." Olmsted reported on a sermon by a black preacher in New Orleans: "Much of his language was highly metaphorical; the figures long, strange, and complicated, yet some times, however, beautiful. Words were frequently misplaced, and their meaning evidently misapprehended, while the grammar and pronounciation were sometimes such as to make the idea intended to be conveyed by the speaker incomprehensible to me." The congregation reacted with excitement and enthusiasm, which Olmsted took to be primarily a response to the preacher's action—to his total performance rather than to the words of the formal sermon. A white minister who spent much of his youth among the Gullah slaves of the South Carolina low country commented on the difference between the style and content of their preachers and that of the poor white preachers:

> The [Gullah] preaching, if we may so call it, in these meetings, was very different from the preaching generally heard in churches of white people in that day, however illiterate the preacher and the people might be. The plantation "brudder" . . . couldn't read the Bible but his imagination, with which faculty the negro is largely

endowed in common with most people of Eastern origin, gave him eyes to see "sermons" in the familiar objects that were around him. . . . Illiterate white preachers are generally too apt to spiritualize the Bible and too often to make nonsense out of it, but the old-time plantation negro preacher spiritualized the familiar objects and common things of life, and used them as object lessons, picturing to the eye and to the heart great spiritual truths.

Long before, Lyell had written of a group of blacks who struck up a Methodist hymn, "in which the most sacred subjects were handled with strange familiarity, and which, though nothing irreverent was meant, sounded oddly to our ears, and, when following a love ditty, almost profane."[47]

The response of the black congregations to a strong preacher played an absolutely essential part in the proceedings. The praise-houses and churches rang with "Dat's de truth!" "Praise Jesus!" "That's right!" "Uh-huh!" "So true!" "Preach de Word, brudder!" The preacher had to evoke mass response, not only as a much-sought encouragement and sign of approval, but as the other half of a living process of communion over which he had been called to preside. As in the African tradition from which it arose and as in the Afro-American song and dance forms into which it fed, the call-and-response pattern represented community solidarity and yet demanded the fullest expression of the individual. The preacher's congregation had to talk back, for he was not there to give opinions but to deliver God's Word to a people who insisted on receiving it actively. Black congregations distinguished between a preacher with the Spirit and an aspiring crowd pleaser. They expected their own responses to be genuine and would greet with stares of contempt those who tried to turn the occasion into a forum for puttin'-on-dog. "Question to Little Jr. Parker: 'What does your audience expect from you?' Answer: 'They expect what you are.' "[48]

An understanding of what the black preachers did for their people requires an understanding of what they did not do. The preachers preached; they did not prophesy, except in the narrowest meaning of the word. The somber political implications of the black folk religion—to recall Fanon's hostility—and the long shadow they have cast over the black liberation movement were reflected in the rarity of prophets and the virtual absence of a prophetic tradition among the slaves.[49] To be sure, the generalization is shorthand. Nat Turner was rightly called "Ole Prophet

Nat," and other such revolutionary prophets appeared from time to time.[50] Every time a preacher assured his flock of their deliverance by Almighty God, he did make a prophecy of sorts. The slaves hailed their emancipation as the Day of Jubilo and waited again for the Year of Jubilo, in which they would receive those forty acres and a mule. A case, then, could be made for some kind of prophetic and millennialist tradition.

But although Nat Turner had predecessors and successors, the revolts themselves never created a tradition and a powerful myth that could grip the slave quarters in story and song. When Jesus entered Jerusalem to cries of *Hosannah*, he represented the latest of a long line of deliverers whose pretensions and possibilities had fired the imagination of Israel. And it was not for nothing that Muhammed spoke of himself as Jesus' heir—as the end of a great prophetic tradition. But, the black preachers had too strong a grip on reality to identify their promise of freedom with some promise of the Kingdom of God on Earth. Deliverance had a limited and immediate meaning. The slaves' idea of freedom did not include an implication of perfection and the Kingdom of God on Earth. The joyous cries of Jubilee-Jubilo came down with overwhelming frequency to refer to distinct and realistic goals, not to a transition to the Christian Paradise.

Millennial movements have, throughout history, appeared in quietist garb, but usually only after the defeat of the militant millennialist thrust. However militant the slaves may have been and however revolutionary on occasion, they never mounted a sustained militant millennialism. Their quietist version of millennialism, therefore, looks like a very different matter.

Nor was the slaves' religion essentially messianic in the political sense. The quarters did not throw up a succession of would-be deliverers to whom substantial numbers tensed themselves to rally. The sermons of the black preachers did not call on the people to be ready to follow a black messiah who would arise to lead them out of bondage. The deliverer of the people was to be God Himself, expressed in the image of Moses (or Moses-Jesus), and he was to be called forth by faith. The preachers could have done no more. Their power did not rest on a charisma that made them direct political leaders; if anything, it rested on a willingness to forgo that role for a more practicable one. They could not possibly create such a role in the dangerous and fragmented condition of slave life. Their great accomplishment was to bend to the actual conditions of slave life and to transform themselves into teachers and moral guides with a responsibility to keep the people together with faith in themselves. The negative side of their accomplishment was the necessary surrender of the principle of political leadership and authority. Nat Turner's appeal to a handful of slaves does not alter this general picture.

The slender messianic thread among the slaves did, nonetheless, have an ominous feature. The slave narratives do throw up something of a messiah figure, but he is Massa Linkum, not Nat Turner, who hardly appears at all. And when a Union army officer dropped into Elizabeth Hyde Botume's school for freedmen and asked, "Children, who is Jesus Christ?" he heard, "General Saxby, sar," and then, "Not so, boy! Him's Massa Linkum." The preacher at the memorial meeting for Lincoln aroused no objection from the freedmen when he referred to "Massa Linkum! our 'dored Redeemer an' Saviour an' Frien'! Amen!"[51] In no other way did slavery and white racism do such deadly work in the quarters. The slaves relied on their black preachers for solace and moral guidance, but the preachers could not transform that support into political action. After the war the preachers began to develop themselves into a political leadership, and the freedmen did respect them. But politicization, other than that defensive strategy which was the preachers' old role, had to be a long and painful process, which did not run its course until the emergence of Dr. Martin Luther King in the 1950s.

How bitter the irony. The slaves, guided by their preachers, resisted slavery's psychological assault manfully; they learned to love each other and have faith in their deliverance. These things they did for themselves. But they could not carry their struggle onto political terrain. Once deliverance became a political question the slaves looked to white leadership; they had no confidence in each other in this realm. It would take a long time before black people could win this struggle with themselves and understand that they had in fact made themselves into a people—that having done without black messiahs, they could trust black leaders and do without white messiahs as well.

The lack of a politically militant millennial and prophetic tradition helps explain the limits of the revolutionary impulse among the slaves, for there have been few more dreaded and deadly messages preached to the wretched of the earth than those which have begun, "It is written . . . but I say unto you . . ." Revolutionary millennialism originally had a precise meaning drawn from the belief of some Christians, on the authority of Revelation 20:4–6, that after His second coming Christ would establish a kingdom on earth that would last for a thousand years until the Day of Judgment.[52] "It is," Norman Cohn writes, "utterly to transform life on earth, so that the new dispensation will be no mere improvement on the present but perfection itself."[53] The oldest form of millennialism of which much is known accompanied the messianism of the Jews, and Cohn describes Chapter 7 of the Book of Daniel as virtually a millennialist manifesto. Not accidentally, the Book of Daniel dates from about 165 B.C. at the height of the Maccabean revolt. After tracing the political and doctrinal history of Jewish messianism, he concludes that the expectation of deliverance became tense and urgent whenever a massacre or some other disaster threatened.

Here are two clues to the lack of a revolutionary or politically militant millennialism and messianism among the slaves of the South. First, the regime was too pervasive, too strong, too stable. The oppressiveness of slavery always threatened personal disaster for the enslaved, but the entrenched regime of the slaveholders and the collective nature of slave life shielded the slaves from the broader social disasters that have so often befallen subject nationalities and atomized peasantries. As Eric Wolf points out, the emergence of those large and powerful millennial movements which have so often laid the groundwork for peasant revolts even in the twentieth century—for example, in Vietnam—have appealed particularly to people who were isolated in their social relationships and yet collectively confronted with devastating cultural and social changes.[54] Second, we find a clash of two peoples but not of two civilizations each of which has reached a peak of development. Such civilizational clash has provided fertile ground for militant millennial movements. Those movements do indeed appear in colonial Africa, but among southern slaves African civilization had been reduced to a much-muted, if still living, presence. The slave quarters, denied a direct apprehension of their African political past, proved infertile soil for prophets, for whom the call to return to pure and sanctified origins has constituted a God-inspired mission. And since the quarters retained an African-like rejection of original and collective sin, the task of would-be prophets became the more difficult, for how do you demand that such a people renounce their collective guilt and return to the covenant with God? They demonstrated no such sense of guilt or of having broken faith. The slaves had to build their own culture and community within a wider American civilization.

Revolutionary, politically militant millennial movements, born in social catastrophe or in the fear of impending catastrophe, have normally fed on the conviction that those responsible for mediating between man and God have betrayed their trust. Such movements consequently have arisen with some leaders as well as followers drawn from the ruling classes themselves, for they have reflected a crisis in the society as a whole.[55] The spiritual malaise that feeds them has produced the defection of members of the ruling class, who contribute to the political power of the revolutionary movement but more often than not also blunt its revolutionary edge.

Black slaves could and did have their own religious leaders, but these were necessarily thrown up and cast down locally and in accordance with particular conditions; they represented no institutional authority the moral collapse of which would provoke that anti-authoritarian rebellion among the true believers which has been one of the hallmarks of revolutionary millennialism. The racist nature of the white churches and their congregations effectively removed, with only occasional exceptions, the threat of defection from above that played so important a role in the formation of millennial movements elsewhere.

Even if the African impulse had remained stronger than it did in Afro-American Christianity, it would have offered little support to revolutionary millennialism. Traditional African religions were decidedly life-affirming rather than otherworldly and provided poor ground for that subtle transformation of the Kingdom of God into the Kingdom of God on Earth which propelled millennial ideologies. On the contrary, traditional African religions preached reincarnation and attention to life in this world. In the West African tradition, in contradistinction to the Judeo-Christian, time is cyclical and eternal; the religious tradition cannot therefore readily provide for an apocalypse.[56] When Afro-American slaves embraced Christianity, they infused their African sensibility into the acquired doctrine. In so doing, they could look to deliverance from their bondage but could also resist or ignore that millennialist perfectionism which, in the specific conditions of their political world, could only have collapsed into otherworldly passivity.

The emergence of a revolutionary millennial thrust requires a mass psychological predisposition toward withdrawal from the world in combination with a practical inability to withdraw.[57] That is, it requires a psychological receptivity to an ideology of sectarian election that life-affirming religions, however attractive in themselves, have been ill-equipped to provide. From the peasant revolts of medieval Europe, to revolutionary Puritanism, to the early working-class organizations, to the great revolutionary movements of our day, asceticism has provided a decisive ingredient in the mobilization of popular risings. Engels observes:

> Asceticism . . . is to be found in all medieval uprisings that were tinged with religion, and also in modern times at the beginning of every proletarian movement. This austerity of behavior, this insistence on relinquishing all enjoyment of life . . . is a necessary transitional stage without which the lowest strata of society could never start a movement. In order to develop revolutionary energy, in order to become conscious of their own hostile position towards all other elements of society . . . [they] must begin with stripping themselves of everything that could reconcile them to the existing system of society. They must renounce all pleasures which would make their subdued position in the least tolerable. . . .[58]

The lack of revolutionary millennialism does not in itself explain the lack of sustained revolts, especially when we recall that most medieval peasant revolts had no discernible millennial ideologies. Had revolutionary millennialism developed among the slaves, Afro-American Christianity could no doubt have been credited with just enough of an ideal foundation to account for it. After all, Afro-American Christianity, like all Christianity, would be unthinkable without messianic and millennialist impulses, however politically quietist; and these always retain some potential political danger. But the ideal foundation was extremely weak, and its strengthening would have required exceptionally favorable political conditions. The political stability of the regime—its ability to crush rebellion and especially to render most rebellions abortive —had an opposite effect.

Even in Melanesia and other areas of rampant militant millennialism, the prophets of the Kingdom must sooner or later deliver on their promises. When they cannot, the movements disappear or become accommodationist and politically quietist.[59] Vittorio Lanternari's study of "the religions of the oppressed" demonstrates that the usual path of millennial movements has been from

revolutionary violence to defeat to some form of nonrevolutionary, accommodationist, reformist prophetic cult. The African
cults generally manifested this tendency; the American Indians
moved from ghost dance to peyote; the extreme Protestant radicals
rallied to Thomas Münzer and then, after his defeat, adopted a
quietist compromise. But as Lanternari also shows, the retreat
from revolutionary violence to politically quietist accommodationism often protected the cultural autonomy of the dissidents and
provided a means by which they could resist the domination of
their subduers.

The slaves had their own version of "postmillennial" accommodation, understood as a strategy for survival and not as a lapse into
passivity, but they had been forced by tradition and circumstance
to take a route dictated by their own experiences and reflecting
their own unique, emergent view of the world. The preachers, in
rejecting the role of prophets except in a strictly limited sense,
showed how well they grasped the implications of their political
position.[60] The prophet is so by vocational calling; he arrives with
personal revelation and rests his authority on appeal to a new law.
Unlike the priest, who guards the sacred tradition, the prophet
proclaims the new. Unlike the sorcerer, who deals in magic, the
prophet announces a doctrine of obligation. If he arrives as a
lawgiver, he is usually driven toward the usurpation of political
power; if he contents himself with being a teacher, he usually
avoids direct political action but cannot avoid speaking in accents
others see as politically charged. In either case, he is, from the
point of view of any established regime, a dangerous man.

The prophet is a man in grace, both in the theological sense of
inner assurance and in the political sense of having a magnetic
appeal for others. Black preachers displayed charisma in both
senses, but in a way definitely outside the prophetic tradition. That
tradition has had two streams, each of which southern slave society
effectively dammed up. In the stream of exemplary prophecy the
preacher has appealed to his followers to imitate his own conduct.
But what could such an appeal come to in plantation society except
at rare moments of desperation? If anything, it could only come to
a supine call for accommodation to secular power and a retreat into
the world of the spirit. In the stream of ethical prophecy, with its
implied separation of man from God, the preacher has appealed
for a worldly asceticism the revolutionary implications of which
would have guaranteed his early demise in the South and, in any

case, have fallen on deaf ears among a people who confronted overwhelming force.

The black preachers had to face the realities of class power and the realities of a coherent slave community with little disposition toward apocalyptic visions and suicidal adventures. The great prophets—from the ancient Jews to the ghost-dance Paiute leaders and Melanesian millenarians of more recent times–were outsiders who often, like Muhammed, had to leave home to gain a following among strangers. Normally, they preached to hostile audiences. Even in the Christian Era, with its organized communities of the faithful, the prophet appears as an individual agent of challenge to the religious and secular order. In proclaiming a new law, even in the guise of a return to an older interpretation of existing law— "It is written . . . but I say unto you . . ."—the prophet assumes the role of revolutionary leader.

The rise of a revolutionary leader, in contradistinction to a suicidal psychotic or foolhardy, desperate rebel, presupposes a revolutionary conjuncture in a community the experience of which has been leading it toward confrontation with its rulers. Prophets have appeared among peoples who can no longer tolerate their political reality and are already in motion. Thomas Münzer, Savonarola, and closer to our own day, in Brazil, Antonio Conselheiro, in effect intervened in rather than incited political turmoil. But among such peoples it is often the prophet who can transform mass disaffection into a movement by meeting the need for spiritual justification and by raising the act of resistance to the level of moral imperative.

Black preachers faced these conditions and possibilities with steady realism. If, as Lanternari suggests, the revolutionary prophet is one in whom past and future converge, then they had little to work with. The African tradition was dim enough in the slave quarters and, in any case, led away from millennialism and apocalyptic desperation. If the theological effect was nonrevolutionary, it was by no means without positive political meaning. One of the most dramatic messages of the ancient Jewish prophets assigned the cause of Israel's misfortunes not to the weakness of Jehovah, as would have been the typical response in tribal religion, but to His wrath. The Israelites by their infidelity and immorality had brought a terrible judgment down upon themselves. Their own slavery and misfortune came as punishment for their sins. Western civilization had begun its guilt-ridden march to salvation, led by one people after another who craved the role of the Chosen and the Elect. Pity the poor Africans. So backward did they remain in their theology, which absurdly concerned itself with making life more reasonable and pleasurable for the men and women living it, that they never did quite get the classical Judeo-Christian point even after their conversion. Few came to regard their enslavement as punishment for their collective sin.

But without a sense of being God's Chosen People—chosen, that is, to bring His Kingdom, not merely to be delivered by Him—the slaves could not easily develop that sense of national mission which has been so efficacious in the formation of revolutionary ideology—which has so marvelously sparked the liberation of nations and classes and simultaneously brought so much imperialist gangsterism into the world. The black preachers saw Africa in America as it was, not as they may have wished it. Their realism reflected that of the masses they sought to sway. The African religious tradition helped shape an Afro-American religion that had long since forgotten its origins. The slave communities, embedded as they were among numerically preponderant and militarily powerful whites, counseled a strategy of patience, of acceptance of what could not be helped, of a dogged effort to keep the black community alive and healthy—a strategy of survival that, like its African prototype, above all said yes to life in this world. Two recent comments by black ministers go to the heart of the matter. The Reverend Henry H. Mitchell: "Indeed, even that outstanding spiritual of accommodation, 'Humble Yourself,' was a message designed to keep more people from being slaughtered like Nat Turner and his followers." The Reverend Albert Cleage: "The Black Church has not always been revolutionary, but it has always been relevant to the everyday needs of black people. The old down-home black preacher who 'shouted' his congregation on Sunday morning was realistically ministering to the needs of a black people who could not yet conceive of changing the conditions which oppressed them."[61] The slave preachers understood their people and their world, and if they turned away from the prophetic vision, they did so because of an understanding in harmony with that of the people they had to lead.

RELIGIOUS FOUNDATIONS OF THE BLACK NATION

The slaves' Christianity cannot be understood as a façade behind which the countryside practiced pagan rites or wallowed in something called superstition. Nor, alternatively, can the beliefs and practices of the folk be understood as having corrupted the slaves' Christianity. Folk belief, including the belief in magic, constituted a vital element in the making of the slaves' own version of Christianity, and does not appear to have introduced any greater distortion into a supposedly pure Christianity than did those folk beliefs of ancient, medieval, or even modern Europe which steadily helped shape the formation of the high religion.

Even when the churches resolutely fought popular "superstition," they had to absorb much of it either by direct appropriation or by bending formal doctrine to provide the spiritual elements that made folk belief attractive. Thus, however harshly the sophisticated urban black ministers waged war on what they considered the pagan residues of their flock, they could not easily convince the conjurers or their supporters of any unchristian doing, nor could they avoid shaping their own doctrine in such a way as to answer the questions that the resort to magic posed.

The folk dynamic in the historical development of Afro-American Christianity saved the slaves from the disaster that some historians erroneously think they suffered—that of being suspended between a lost African culture and a forbidden European one. It enabled them to retain enough of Africa to help them create an appropriate form for the new content they were forging and to contribute to the mainstream of American national culture while shaping an autonomous identity. Their religion simultaneously helped build an "American" Christianity both directly and as a counterpoint and laid the foundation for a "black" Christianity of their own. That is, it made possible a universal statement because it made possible a national statement. But, for blacks, the national statement expressed a duality as something both black and American, not in the mechanical sense of being an ethnic component in a pluralistic society, but in the dialectical sense of simultaneously being itself and the other, both separately and together, and of developing as a religion within a religion in a nation within a nation.

Black religion had to be more than slave religion, not only or even mainly because many of its most articulate and sophisticated spokesmen were southern free Negroes and northerners who lived outside slave society, but because the racial basis of slavery laid the foundations for a black identity that crossed class lines and demanded protonational identification. The horror of American racism, as if to prove Hegel right about "the cunning of Reason," forced the slaves out of themselves—forced them to glimpse the possibilities of nationality rather than class. Had it not been so, they would have been condemned to the fate of the slaves of the ancient world; they would have remained a pathetic and disorganized mass at the bottom of a single social scale, with no possibility of building an autonomous culture or rising above the role of historical witness to the crime of ultimate class oppression. The Moorish black nationalists of the 1930s knew what they were talking about when they said, "Before you have a God you must have a nationality."[1] What they could not see was just how far the slaves had gone toward establishing both.

The origins of black Christian religion in the slave quarters—the roots of an embryonic national religion in the consciousness of the slave class—embodied two contradictions, the transcendence of which has yet to be effected. First, Christianity bound master and slave together in universal communion while it contributed to their separation into antagonistic peoples. Second, it imparted to the slaves, and through them to black America, a collective strength that rested on a politically dangerous kind of individualism.

In entering into Christian fellowship with each other the slaves set themselves apart from the whites by creating a distinctive style, sensibility, and theology. In the hands of militants and revolutionaries, the sense of being a people apart could lead to a belief that whites were the antichrist, but the universality of the Christian religion, embedded in an intimate, paternalistic plantation world, militated against such an interpretation and rendered it an idiosyncratic footnote. For the slaves, whites lived under God and were brothers in Christ. In its positive aspects, this sense of racial brotherhood gave the slaves a measuring rod with which to hold slaveowners to a standard of behavior appropriate to their own professions of Christian faith. By its very nature it forbade slaves to accept the idea that they had no right to judge their masters; it made judgment a duty. In thus being compelled to see some masters as "good" and some as "bad," the slaves had to take conservative ground and admit that a man did not necessarily stop being a Christian by holding slaves, although they did not take this concession to mean that slavery itself could be a proper order for a Christian society. This compromise strengthened their resistance to dehumanization, for it curbed the self-destructive tendency toward hatred. It left them free to hate slavery but not necessarily their individual masters. It left them free to love their masters as fellow sinners before God and yet to judge their relative merits as Christians and human beings. W. E. B. Du Bois could therefore express admiration for their profoundly Christian ability to love their enemies and yet defend them against the notion that in so doing they surrendered their manhood or accepted their masters' world view.[2]

Thus, slave parents could teach their children to pray before going to bed:

> Now I lay me down to sleep,
> I pray de Lord my soul to keep,
> If I should die befo' I wake,
> I pray de Lord my soul to take.
>   Bless pappy, bless mammy,
>   Bless marster, bless missie,
>   And bless me, Amen![3]

Thus, a body servant could write a member of his master's family about the death of his young master in battle: "Dear Master Richard, You sent me word some time ago to write this morning. I will now try to give you an account of my feelings toward my young master who is now dead." He expressed sorrow that he was not there at the end to comfort him and drew from his young master's death a meaning for himself. "Master Richard, I say to you it is good to be religious. . . . I believe it as much as I ever believed anything in my life, that he is at rest. My heart believes it. I desire to be a better Christian. I want to go to Heaven. . . . My earnest desire is to be at rest after this life."[4] Thus, masters and slaves turned to each other for solace in times of grief with no sense of doing anything odd. When Pierce Butler, Fanny Kemble's ex-husband, died, their distraught daughter took comfort from an old woman who had been a slave on their Georgia plantation: "Missus, don't cry; it vex de Lord. I had t'irteen children, and I ain't got one left to put even a coal in my pipe, and if I did not trust de Lord Jesus what would become of me?"[5] It would be hard to hammer a revolutionary commitment out of such a spirit and even harder to raise a cry for holy war, but the generous legacy it bequeathed would provide enormous compensation for a people who had to survive and who never lost faith in a future built on human brotherhood.

If the contradictory nature of the slaves' religion as part of American Christianity and yet as a faith apart lessened revolutionary inclinations, the contradiction between its individual and its collective aspects proved even more fateful. The religion practiced in the quarters gave the slaves the one thing they absolutely had to have if they were to resist being transformed into the Sambos they had been programmed to become. It fired them with a sense of their own worth before God and man. It enabled them to prove to themselves, and to a world that never ceased to need reminding, that no man's will can become that of another unless he himself wills it—that the ideal of slavery cannot be realized, no matter how badly the body is broken and the spirit tormented.

The spiritual emancipation of the individual therefore constituted the decisive task of religion and the necessary foundation for black collectivity. But communion as a people, under so pressing a demand, reinforced that tendency toward atomization of the quarters which it was combatting. At the very moment that it was helping to create a sense of solidarity through mutual respect and love for each other, it was strengthening an extreme doctrine of the equality of individuals. The slaves desperately needed that doctrine to confront their masters, but they were whole men and women, not a jumble of abstractions; they could not easily assert their claims against the authority of their masters without asserting them against the claims of each other. The Reverend Henry H. Mitchell tells us: "The black preacher is not an army officer ordering men to their death. Rather he is a crucial witness declaring how men ought to *live*."[6] But, he adds, the tendency inherent in this role is to strengthen the individual at the expense of collective political assertion.

These contradictions propelled black religion forward to the creation of collective identity and pride. The black variant of Christianity laid the foundations of protonational consciousness and at the same time stretched a universalist offer of forgiveness and ultimate reconciliation to white America; and it gave the individual slave the wherewithal to hold himself intact and to love his brothers and sisters in the quarters, even as it blocked the emergence of political consciousness and a willingness to create a legitimate black authority. The synthesis that became black Christianity offered profound spiritual strength to a people at bay; but it also imparted a political weakness, which dictated, however necessarily and realistically, acceptance of the hegemony of the oppressor. It enabled the slaves to do battle against the slaveholders' ideology, but defensively within the system it opposed; offensively, it proved a poor instrument. The accomplishment soared heroically to great heights, but so did the price, which even now has not been fully paid.

PART 2

...AND EVERY MAN ACCORDING AS HIS WORK SHALL BE

> And, behold, I come quickly; and my reward is with me, to give every man according as his work shall be.
> —Revelation 22:12

TIME AND WORK RHYTHMS

It goes without saying that "niggers are lazy": the planters always said so, as did the "poor white trash," whose own famous commitment to hard and steady work doubtless assured their entrance into John Calvin's Kingdom of Heaven. Some of the refrain may be dismissed as obvious ideological rationalization and self-serving cant or a distorted interpretation of the effects of a lack of adequate incentives. Yet much more needs to be said, for the slaves themselves sang at their work:

> Nigger mighty happy when he layin' by the corn,
> Nigger mighty happy when he hear dat dinner horn;
> But he more happy when de night come on,
> Dat sun's a slantin', as sho's you born!

Dat old cow's a shakin' dat great big bell,
And de frogs tunin' up, 'cause de dew's done fell.[1]

"The white men," Johann David Schoepf observed on his travels during the 1780s, "are all the time complaining that the blacks will not work, and they themselves do nothing." Virginia's great humorist, George W. Bagby, once reflected on the complacency and self-satisfaction of antebellum life: "Time was abundant in those days. It was made for slaves, and we had the slaves."[2]

The slaveholders presided over a plantation system that constituted a halfway house between peasant and factory cultures. The tobacco and cotton plantations, which dominated the slave economy in the United States, ranged closer to the peasant than the factory model, in contradistinction to the great sugar plantations of the Caribbean, which in some respects resembled factories in the field; but even the small holders pushed their laborers toward modern work discipline. The planters' problem came to this: How could they themselves preserve as much as possible of that older way of life to which they aspired and yet convince their slaves to repudiate it? How could they instill factorylike discipline into a working population engaged in a rural system that, for all its tendencies toward modern discipline, remained bound to the rhythms of nature and to traditional ideas of work, time, and leisure?

They succeeded in overcoming this contradiction only to the extent that they got enough work out of their slaves to make the system pay at a level necessary to their survival as a slaveholding class in a capitalist world market. But they failed in deeper ways that cast a shadow over the long-range prospects for that very survival and over the future of both blacks and whites in American society. Too often they fell back on the whip and thereby taught and learned little. When they went to other incentives, as fortunately most tried to do, they did get satisfactory economic results, but at the same time they reinforced traditional attitudes and values instead of replacing them with more advanced ones.

The black work ethic grew up within a wider Protestant Euro-American community with a work ethic of its own. The black ethic represented at once a defense against an enforced system of economic exploitation and an autonomous assertion of values generally associated with preindustrial peoples. As such, it formed part of a more general southern work ethic, which developed in antagonism to that of the wider American society. A Euro-Ameri-

can, basically Anglo-Saxon work ethic helped shape that of southerners in general and slaves in particular and yet, simultaneously,
generated a profound antithesis.

In the medieval Catholic formulation the necessity to work both
derived from the Fall of Man and served as an expression of
humility and submission. In the words of Ernst Troeltsch, "Labor
is thus both a penalty and a means of salvation."[3] The Lutheran
doctrine of the calling emphasized the means to salvation rather
than the penalty, and thereby strengthened the Christian insistence on being satisfied with one's station in life. Calvinism, which
so profoundly altered Anglo-American culture, raised the idea of
the calling to a religious duty in itself. Whereas in the Lutheran
formulation work, with its rigor and anxiety, continued to contra-
dict fundamental features of man's nature, in the Calvinist formulation it became an expression of Grace and therefore an end in
itself as a worthy and agreeable means to salvation. Troeltsch
writes:

> To people who have been educated on Calvinistic principles the
> lazy habit of living on an inherited income seems a downright sin;
> to follow a calling which has no definite end and which yields no
> material profit seems a foolish waste of time and energy, and failure
> to make full use of chances of gaining material profit seems like
> indifference towards God. From the Calvinistic point of view lazi-
> ness is the most dangerous vice. . . .
>
> The principles and ideals of Ascetic Protestantism may therefore
> be summarized thus: the inner severance of feeling and enjoyment
> from all the objects of labour; the unceasing harnessing of labour to
> an aim which lies in the other world, and therefore must occupy us
> till death; the depreciation of possessions, of all things earthly, to the
> level of expediency; the habit of industry in order to suppress all
> distracting and idle impulses; and the willing use of profit for the
> religious community and for public welfare. . . .[4]

To this stern doctrine of work as duty the slave opposed a religion
of joy in life that echoed traditional Africa and, surprising as it
may seem, even more firmly echoed the spirit of the plantation
community itself. To speak of a "calling" or vocation for slaves
would be absurd; but more to the point, worldly asceticism neither
corresponded to the sensibilities shaped by the historic development from Africa to the New World nor could take root among
a people who had no material stake in its flowering.

For bourgeois society in sixteenth- and seventeenth-century England a regular rhythm of labor had to be established. From a

steady work week punctuated by one day of Sabbath rest to such household details as regular mealtimes, the middle classes vigorously campaigned for a philosophy of saving time and doing things on schedule. Work increasingly passed from being one part of an organically integrated life into being a discrete central fact of existence. This ideological process, accompanying the transformation of labor-power into a commodity, required and conditioned new personalities for whom rest and leisure had lower value; for whom life had to be economically rationalized; and for whom the rising concern with individualism prepared the way, however ironically, for the subordination of man to the means of production.[5]

"World-rejecting asceticism," as Weber called it, led not to a flight from the world but to a continuous battle against it—to the demand to rationalize everything and to subject all spheres of life to systematic conduct. Such a world-view, to be transformed into a social power, had to rest on the assent of free men; it became inseparable from the right of private judgment and its attendant concern for individual liberty.[6] A great deal more than the fervor of white Baptist and Methodist preachers would be required to make the message meaningful to enslaved Afro-Americans. The Baptist Christianity of the slaves had neither the capacity nor the aim to do to the slaves what Methodism did to the English working class.

The heart of black slave culture rested in a religion that, however intimate its connections with white religion, emerged as a product of the black experience. For the slaves and for black people generally, religion did not constitute one feature of life or merely one element in an ideological complex; rather, it constituted the fundamental spiritual expression of their entire world-view, as manifested in attitudes toward time and work. An ex-slave described his conversion experience: "He spoke to me once after I had prayed and prayed trying to hurry him and get religion. He said, 'I am a time-God. Behold, I work after the counsel of my own will and in due time I will visit whomsoever I will.' "[7] The Reverend Henry H. Mitchell has addressed himself to current criticisms that black church services are too long and undisciplined:

> Yet Black tradition holds that the Holy Spirit does not follow white clocks. The Spirit must have its way, and whatever God does is right on time. It is believed that the true Presence is intellectually as well as emotionally enlightening, and that it takes *time* for the Spirit to

involve a congregation which must first be emptied of private concern for mundane interests.

Dr. Mitchell also hints at a special sense of historical time when
he notes that blacks see the Bible, not as white fundamentalists do,
as the repository of unchanging truths, but as a source of historical
experience and a moral context for discussion of their own world.[8]

The slaves' attitude toward time and work arose primarily from
their own experience on the plantations of the South. Comparisons with Africa suggest some important cultural continuities.
Traditional African time-reckoning focuses on present and past,
not future. Time, being two-dimensional, moves, as it were, backward into a long past; the future, not having been experienced,
appears senseless. This idea of time, which inhibited the appearance of an indigenous millennialism prior to Islamic and Christian
penetration, encouraged economic attitudes not readily assimila-
ble to early bourgeois demands for saving, thrift, and accumulation.[9] But, however strong the specifically African influence, even
more important are those tendencies which characterize preindustrial agricultural peoples in general, for whom the Africans provided a variant or, rather, a series of variants.

G. J. O. Ojo, in *Yoruba Culture*, offers a reference point when he
notes that "within the tropics and particularly close to the equator,
within about 10°, the almost uniform length of day and night lends
itself as the standard reference of time."[10] The Yoruba gave no
thought to scientific explanations of the day; they began the day
at sunrise and measured the month by the phases of the moon.
They had the great advantage of a climate in which the sun rarely
disappeared behind clouds, but when it did, they estimated time
by the amount of work completed and by the behavior of birds and
animals. Measurement of a year was not precise, nor need it have
been, for the important marks lay in the intersection of work and
season.

The Yoruba experience provided one variant of the West African, and the West African provided one complex of variants of a
more general traditional, rural preindustrial experience. Traditional society measured its time by calendars based on agricultural
and seasonal patterns, which themselves formed part of an integrated religious world-view. The year proceeded according to a
certain rhythm, not according to equal units of time; appropriate
festivals and rites broke its continuity and marked the points at
which the human spirit celebrated the rhythm of the natural or-

der. Not pure quantities of time obtained, but such flexible units as the beginning of planting and of the harvest. Time became subordinated to the natural order of work and leisure, as their servant rather than their master.[11]

Whereas in peasant farming the work tasks and such natural conditions as the amount of daylight determine the length of the workday, the acceptable number and duration of breaks, and the amount and type of leisure, in factory work "the arbitrarily fixed time schedule determines the beginning and the end of work periods."[12] In peasant societies work tasks such as planting and harvesting, which appear to conform to the demands of nature, have oriented the notation of time. E. P. Thompson argues convincingly that this "task orientation" has rendered work more humanly comprehensible: "The peasant or labourer appears to attend upon what is an observed necessity."[13] For the preindustrial English community as a whole the distinction between "work" and "life" was much less clear than it was to become; the working day itself lengthened and contracted according to necessary tasks, and no great conflict appeared between the demands of work and those of leisure. One need not idealize the undoubtedly harsh physical conditions of preindustrial rural life to appreciate the force of Thompson's argument, especially since those who passed under industrial work discipline probably were themselves the ones who came most to idealize their previous existence and thereby to heighten either their resistance or their despair. Eric Hobsbawm writes:

> Industrial labour—and especially mechanized factory labour—imposes a regularity, routine and monotony quite unlike pre-industrial rhythms of work, which depend on the variation of the seasons or the weather, the multiplicity of tasks in occupations unaffected by the rational division of labour, the vagaries of other human beings or animals, or even a man's own desire to play instead of working. This was so even in skilled pre-industrial wage-work, such as that of journeymen craftsmen, whose ineradicable taste for not starting the week's work until the Tuesday ("Saint Monday") was the despair of their masters. Industry brings the tyranny of the clock, the pace-setting machine, and the complex and carefully-timed interaction of processes: the measurement of life, not in seasons ("Michaelmas term" or "Lent term") or even in weeks and days, but in minutes, and above all a mechanized *regularity* of work which conflicts not only with tradition, but with all the inclinations of a humanity as yet unconditioned into it.[14]

The advent of clock time represented more than a marking of regular work units—of minutes and hours—and of arbitrary schedules, for it supported the increasing division of labor and transformed that division of labor into a division of time itself. Capitalist production had to be measured in units of labor-time, and those units themselves took on the mysterious and apparently self-determining properties of commodities. When Benjamin Franklin said that time is money, he said much more than is generally understood. E. P. Thompson comments: "In a mature capitalist society all time must be consumed, marketed, put to *use;* it is offensive for the labour force merely to pass the time."[15] Natural rhythms of work and leisure gave place to arbitrary schedules, which were, however, arbitrary only from the point of view of the laborers. The capitalists and those ideologues who were developing a new idea of rationality based on the demands of a rapidly developing economy saw the matter differently. The process of cultural transformation had to rest on economic and extra-economic compulsion and ultimately on violence. It served as the industrial equivalent of that which the West Indian slaveholders, with fewer inhibitions, called "seasoning."

The transformation in the labor force was complete. Thompson writes: "The first generation of factory workers were taught by their masters the importance of time; the second generation formed their short-time committees in the ten-hour movement; the third generation struck for overtime or time-and-a-half. They had accepted the categories of their employers and learned their lesson, that time is money, only too well."[16]

The slaves could not reckon time either according to preindustrial peasant models or according to industrial factory models. The plantations, especially the sugar plantations that dominated most of the slaveholding regions of the New World, although not of the United States, did resemble factories in the field, but even if we take them as our norm we cannot escape the implications of their preindustrial side. However much their economic organization required and tried to compel quasi-industrial discipline, they also threw up countervailing pressures and embodied inescapable internal contradictions.

The setting remained rural, and the rhythm of work followed seasonal fluctuations. Nature remained the temporal reference point for the slaves. However much the slaveholders might have wished to transform their slaves into clock-punchers, they could not, for in a variety of senses both literal and metaphoric, there were no clocks to punch.[17] The planters, especially the resident planters of the United States and Brazil but even the typical West Indian agents of absentee owners, hardly lived in a factory world themselves and at best could only preach what the most docile or stupid slave knew very well they did not and could not practice. Since the plantation economy required extraordinary exertion at critical points of the year, notably the harvest, it required measures to capitalize on the slaves' willingness to work in spurts rather than steadily. The slaveholders turned the inclinations of the slaves to their own advantage, but simultaneously they made far greater concessions to the value system and collective sensibility of the quarters than they intended.

The slaveholders, as usual, had their way but paid a price. The slaves, as usual, fell victim to the demands of their exploiters but had some success in pressing their own advantage. Thus, the plantation system served as a halfway house for Africans between their agricultural past and their imposed industrial future. But, it froze them into a position that allowed for their exploitation on the margins of industrial society. The advantage of this compromise, from the black point of view, lay in the protection it provided for their rich community life and its cultural consolidation. The disadvantage lay in its encouragement of a way of life that, however admirable intrinsically, ill prepared black people to compete in the economic world into which they would be catapulted by emancipation.

John Horton observes, in a stimulating essay entitled "Time and Cool People": "Time in industrial society is clock time. It seems to be an external, objective regulator of human activities. But for the sociologist . . . time is diverse; it is always social and subjective. A man's sense of time derives from his place in the social structure and his lived experience." Horton concludes that "street people," as he calls them, plan their time quite deliberately and rationally but in accordance with their own priorities. The same dude who can never be counted on to show up for work on time will arrive at his girlfriend's schoolyard precisely at noon to pick her up on her lunch hour. Leithman Spinks, an ex-slave from Louisiana, recalled that his master fed the slaves communally. "Dat de one time," he chuckled, "massa could allus 'pend on de niggers. When de bell say, 'Come and git it,' all us am there."[18] And no one ever accused the slaves of lacking a sense of "time" in their singing. The attitude Horton discusses developed out of the plantation experience, rather than out of the preindustrial agricultural experience in general. It combined the ostensibly natural sense of time found among traditional agriculturalists with an attitude of disguised disobedience—of apparent shiftlessness—which marks a slave class as at once sullen, "stupid," and uncooperative and yet enormously resourceful at doing what it wants to do.

The contradiction between the slave's nature as a human being and his status as a thing with irritating human complications repeatedly drove the slaveholders into responses that, if economically and even socially rational in a direct sense, invariably proved self-defeating with respect to larger ends. Consider Frederick Douglass's bitter indictment:

> I never met with a slave in that part of the country [eastern Maryland] who could tell me with any certainty how old he was. Few at the time knew anything of the months of the year or the days of the month. They measured the ages of their children by spring-time, winter-time, harvest-time, planting-time, and the like. Masters allowed no questions concerning their ages to be put to them by slaves. Such questions were regarded by the masters as evidence of an impudent curiosity.[19]

Douglass may have exaggerated the determination of the slaveholders as a class to suppress information and may have underestimated their carelessness and indifference, but most slaves in the South probably did not know their exact age.[20] On some plantations masters and overseers took care to record birth dates, whether or not they imparted the information to the slaves themselves; the more paternalistic masters would even record the data in the family Bible. Many plantation journals, however, contain entries such as these: "List of Negroes of the Estate of William Robertson, with their supposed ages"; "bought a boy . . . about fourteen years old;" or simply a list of slaves with their ages recorded as "about . . ."[21]

The slaveholders' objections to having slaves know their age, or their sheer indifference to this feature of the slaves' humanity, proved most obviously self-defeating in the element of irrationality it introduced into slave sales. Without adequate records unscrupulous slave dealers could disguise the age of their human commodities with impunity. Even experienced planters could never be certain of what they were buying. George S. Barnsley of Georgia wrote in 1860: "Took Dick to Maj. Wooley's to see how old he was. The maj. considers him 40 years old and his present value to be $1100. I don't think that he is much over 33 years old."[22]

The planters had to sacrifice more than commercial inconvenience. As Douglass saw, the slave children's imprecise notions about their age reinforced a much more general education in the meaning of time. Carelessness about ages and indifference to or ignorance of exact temporal information reinforced the already strong tendency toward preindustrial and natural patterns of thought. Since children acquire a sense of time from their particular environment, since from an early age they "sense the cycles of change in their environment,"[23] and since slave children did not normally break into field work until the age of twelve, their masters had an uphill battle to make them time-conscious in the industrial sense of the word. The young slaves began with half-time labor and were eased toward full-time labor over a period of years. Masters and overseers tried to bring them on slowly and safely, but the battle to make them into workers with good Calvinist attitudes had been unwittingly surrendered before it began.

The black view of time, conditioned by the plantation slave experience, has provided a great source of strength for a people at bay, as one of Bishop A. G. Dunston's sermons makes clear:

> You know, that's the way God does it. Same as you can't hurry God— so why don't you wait, just wait. Everybody's ripping and racing and rushing. And God is taking his time. Because he knows that it isn't hurtin' nearly so bad as you and I think it's hurtin'—and that is the way he wants us to go. But by and by he brings relief....[24]

Black people, in short, learned to take the blow and to parry it as best they could. They found themselves shut out by white racism from part of the dominant culture's value system, and they simultaneously resisted that system both by historically developed sensibility and by necessity. Accordingly, they developed their own values as a force for community cohesion and survival, but in so doing they widened the cultural gap and exposed themselves to even harder blows from a white nation that could neither understand their behavior nor respect its moral foundations.

A "LAZY" PEOPLE

The divergence in values occurred within a wider effort to accultu-
rate Africans to a single southern ethos. Landon Carter, an aristocratic planter of eighteenth-century Virginia, never could
reconcile himself to the way his slaves worked, but his experience
and comments shed even more light on white than on black work
attitudes and habits. He complained that the introduction of new
and better equipment merely made both white overseers and black
laborers lazy. He insisted that his overseers should set an example
for the slaves by hard work, and he himself tried to set an example
for the overseers. Success eluded him. He found that the slaves had
an inexhaustible storehouse of devices for shamming and dissembling. Nothing but frustration would follow an attempt to send a
slave for supplies, for he would invariably bring back less than the
amount needed so that he would be sent again.[1] Carter was a
grumpy man, rarely satisfied with anything, but his complaints,
such as the one that follows, echoed among planters during the
nineteenth century and are especially valuable for their awareness
of the organic relationship between the white and the black work
ethic in the South.

> *Sept. 11, 1771.* This [poor work] confirmed me in my past experience
> that neither overseer nor negroes, when they have but one short crop
> to tend, ever do that to more advantage than when they have a large
> crop to manage. The only evident reason seems to be, they think they
> shall presently get over their crops; and become quite indifferent
> both as to the time they go about it, and indeed the care they ought
> to use. I have seen it so all my life; and can say that I never saw a
> short crop made so even by accident, ever managed either in time or
> really well.[2]

If Carter and many others spoke of overseers, still others spoke
of hired white labor in general. Olmsted, more than three-quarters
of a century later, wrote: "Wherever there are slaves, I have found
that farmers universally testify that white laborers adopt their

careless habits, and that they are even more indifferent than negroes to the interests of their employers." Olmsted reported that slaveholders denied the allegation that slavery degraded labor, but he suggested that it might be more correct to say that "slavery breeds unfaithful, meretricious, inexact, and non-persistent habits of working." He added, significantly, that the mountain whites showed much greater industry than the nonslaveholding whites of the plantation districts, although they too felt the effects of the slaveholding culture.[3]

The nonplantation regions of the up country and back country were embedded in a greater slave society and felt its effects, but the primary effect was a degree of economic isolation and self-sufficiency on which considerable cultural autonomy could be based. The yeomen of the plantation regions, however, constituted an integral part of the mainstream slaveholding culture. The yeomen, the white agricultural laborers, and the poor whites in different ways had their world-view shaped by the presence of a powerful planter class above them and a degraded, racially despised slave class below.[4] Southern yeomen worked hard, but a substantial number seem to have been less attracted by the lure of upward mobility within the slave system than by a way of life reminiscent of self-sufficient peasantries. The greater problem for the slave regime as a whole came with the agricultural laborers and the poor whites who functioned as occasional day laborers. The recruitment of white labor for factories or for the plantation harvest and odd jobs presented serious difficulties. White laborers, with some exceptions in the industrial villages, proved no more productive than black and often much less so. They were deeply infected by attitudes passed down from the leisured group at the top of the slaveholding class, and so resented being in competition or parallel status with the slaves that, as if by God's special vengeance, they increasingly came to resemble those whom they most despised.[5]

The question, in the end, came down to the attitudes of the planters, for if the nonslaveholders and the slaves did not merely imitate those attitudes—if they brought their own sensibilities and experiences with them—they did imbibe much and did shape their lives under this influence from above. With some exceptions the slaveholders, even the great planters, did not spend their lives in leisure, sipping mint juleps and courting the lovely young belles. However much leisure they permitted themselves, they worked hard enough in their fashion and carried heavy responsibilities.

But they could hardly be accused of Puritanical steadiness, of bourgeois respect for time and attention to duty, of single-minded devotion to the calling of business. Like the great landed classes of medieval and early modern Europe, the slaveholders exhibited a strong acquisitive spirit and seized the chance to make their fortune; but also like them, they saw money as a means to a particular kind of good life, not as an end in itself; and more important, they showed little respect for steadiness, regularity, and sustained effort. Hardly a southern intellectual could be found, no matter how passionately proslavery, who did not point to this trait as being fundamental to the southern ethic and as representing the dividing line between southern and northern sensibilities. Some wrote with sorrow and fear of the military and political consequences; others wrote with joy and expressions of superior virtue. But almost all agreed on the fact.

Whether the planters' aristocratic ethos—some would call it a pose—should be admired for its repudiation of bourgeois insistence on work and profit for their own sake is a matter of taste or, as our sociologists would say, of value judgment. Whatever one's judgment, dangerous consequences attended it. The slaveholders operated in a capitalist world market, they presided over the production of commodities, and they had to pay attention to profit-and-loss statements. Consequently, they developed a strong commitment to the Puritan work ethic—but only so far as their slaves were concerned. Slaves ought to be steady, regular, continent, disciplined clock-punchers. God Himself required it. Now, it is not the easiest of tasks to live by one code and to preach another to people who live close enough to see the difference. The doctrine, "Do as I tell you, not as I do," has never been received with enthusiasm by the lower classes, which, however degraded in condition, are rarely as stupid as their lords would like to believe.

The slaveholders taught by example the opposite of what they hoped to teach by exhortation. During Reconstruction, David Macrae observed: "It was part of the teachings of slavery that a gentleman was one who lived without working. Is it wonderful that some of the negroes, who want now to be gentlemen, should have thought of trying this as the easiest way?" Faced with the destruction of their fortunes by war and emancipation, many of these planter gentlemen, in the phrase used by Emma LeConte about her father, "worked like a negro." Their strong sense of patriarchal pride and duty served them well in adversity, but the adversity itself provided the framework necessary for them to take the step.[6] The class and race bias of the slaveholders, in this as in so many other ways, struck back at them. If the blacks absorbed much of the aristocratic world-view of the planters and perhaps took it more seriously than the whites themselves, the other side of this absorption proved to be a reaction among the slaves that checked the demands of the white regime. The extent to which the slaveholders exercised hegemony over their slaves measured the extent to which the slaves forged weapons of resistance.

The blacks saw the slaveholders as northern white bourgeois saw them: as people who lived on other people's labor, which they were, and as people who did not work themselves, which for the most part they were not. As an ex-slave, Josephine Bacchus put it: "Lord, pray Jesus, de white people sho' been mightly proud to see dey niggers spreadin' out in dem days, so dey tell me. Yes, ma'am . . . 'cause white folks couldn' work den no more den dey can work dese days like de colored people can."[7]

The notion that black slaves, being intrinsically lazy, would work only under compulsion did not arise from some timeless racist bias; rather, it reinforced a developing Euro-American racism, the roots of which lay in centuries of ruling-class European attitudes toward their own laboring poor. When slaveholders insisted that blacks would work only long enough to provide for elementary needs and occasional debauchery, they were associating themselves with a theory generally held by English manufacturers, not to mention the clergy, about the laboring poor.[8]

Northern and English travelers to the South repeatedly compared the slaves to the Irish, often to the detriment of the latter, and hardly a racial stereotype of the blacks poured forth without its being a modest modification of familiar descriptions of the Irish. J. H. Ingraham, in *The South-West*, chose the Italians and the Latin Americans to the same effect. In complaining about the blacks in Mississippi in the 1830s, he likened their work habits to those of the *lazzaroni* and the rural poor he had seen crowded into Buenos Aires. He told of once approaching a poor man in Buenos Aires to get a job done and having him reply, *"Tengo dos reales, señor"* (I have a little money, sir). He pursued his comparison: "Individuals of them I have known to work with great industry for a day or two, and earn a few dollars, when they would cease from their usual labor, and until their last penny was expended, no remuneration would prevail on them to carry a trunk across the square. . . ." Ingraham concluded: "Slaves in their present moral condition, if emancipated, would be lazzaroni in everything but colour."[9] Fanny Kemble expressed amazement when she heard blacks spoken of as incapable, lazy, or stupid. "In my own country," she protested, referring to England, "the very same order of language is perpetually applied to these very Irish, here spoken of as a sort of race of demigods by negro comparison. And it is most true that in Ireland nothing can be more savage, brutish, filthy, idle, and incorrigibly and hopelessly helpless and incapable than the Irish appear. . . ."[10]

After the war the complaints of planters against the irregular work habits of the freedmen paralleled those of the railroad and lumber bosses against their white workers, who allegedly worked a few days and then took time off to enjoy the fruits of their toil.[11] The similarity had less to do with race and ethnicity than with the chasm between the representatives of a bourgeois and increasingly industrial civilization and those who were emerging from preindustrial cultures and had to be disciplined, against their every effort, to a new pattern of work and a diminished idea of the value of extended leisure. "It takes two white men," a southerner told Harriet Martineau, "to make a black man work."[12] He expressed the common view. "With negro slaves," wrote Susan Dabney Smedes of Mississippi, "it seemed impossible for one of them to do a thing, it mattered not how insignificant, without the assistance of one or two others. It was often said with a laugh by their owners that it took two to help one to do nothing."[13]

From colonial times to the end of the slave regime and beyond, the planters described the work habits of the blacks as simply impossible. "There is nothing so absurd," wrote a Virginia planter in 1772, "as the generality of negroes are. If in the beginning of cutting tobacco without watching they will cut all before them, and now, when there is danger of the tobacco by the frost, should it happen, they will not cut the plants really ripe because they may be thicker just as if there was time to let it stand longer. . . . I find it almost impossible to make a negro do his work well. No orders can engage it, no encouragement persuade it, nor no Punishment oblige it."[14] C. W. Gooch, also of Virginia, wrote many years later that blacks made little effort to work well and that their maxim remained "Come day, go day, God send Sunday."[15] In 1849, Daniel Dennett of Louisiana, editor of the *Planters' Banner*, wrote in exasperation:

On a plantation they can neither hoe, nor ditch, chop wood, nor perform any kind of labor with a white man's skill. They break and destroy more farming utensils, ruin more carts, break more gates, spoil more cattle and horses, and commit more waste than five times the number of white laborers do. They are under instruction relative to labor from their childhood, and still when they are grey headed they are the same heedless botches; the negro traits predominate over all artificial training.[16]

A mechanic in Savannah exclaimed, "I happened to be swearing at a negro who was helping me or rather hindering me,"[17] and the refrain echoes through the diaries and journals of the planters, the reports of travelers, and the outcries of editors and reformers.[18] When the war ended slavery, the white evaluation of black attitudes toward work took on new importance. An editor in Athens, Georgia, wrote in 1865 of the transition to free labor:

Those [Negroes] who are able to work will now find it necessary to establish good characters for industry, sobriety, honesty, and fidelity. When detected in his frequent delinquencies, Sambo will have no "maussa" to step in between him and danger. . . . Under the new system the planter will hire only such as are willing and able to work—and when we say work, we mean work in earnest, and not the half play and half work to which many of the slaves have been accustomed. That has "played out"—they will now have to work like white men.[19]

Perhaps the most impressive example of white perceptions came from Frances Butler Leigh, the high-spirited daughter of Fanny Kemble and Pierce Butler, who returned to her father's plantation in Georgia after the war and spent a decade trying to recoup its fortunes. "The negroes," she began, "talked a great deal about their desire and intention to work for us, but their idea of work, unaided by the stern law of necessity, is very vague, some of them working only half a day and some even less."[20] She proceeded to file a complaint reminiscent of those which representatives of the industrial economic order have periodically filed against preindustrial laborers. The Negroes, she fumed, only wish to earn subsistence and prefer to work half a day and then to relax. She criticized northerners, as many had done in antebellum times, for not recognizing that Negroes would not automatically respond to wage incentives and would assert their own preferences in matters of work and leisure.[21] Finally, in exasperation, she burst forth: "I generally found that if I wanted a thing done I first had to tell the negroes to do it, then show them how, and finally do it myself. Their way of managing not to do it was very ingenious, for they always were perfectly good-tempered, and received my orders with, 'Dat's so, missus; just as missus says,' and then somehow or other left the thing undone."[22] Mrs. Leigh's traditional white southern attitude toward blacks, so different from that of her mother and so reminiscent of that of her father, did not blind her to certain realities. She observed that the blacks wanted land of their own; that they preferred to eke out existence on their own inadequate plots of land rather than work for whites; that they hated regular work, not hard work; and that they performed no worse and often better than English laborers who had been imported to work under similar conditions.[23]

Mrs. Leigh's remarks on the difference between regular work and hard work went to the core of the issue. The usually perceptive Thomas Wentworth Higginson missed this distinction when he wrote of his recently liberated black troops: "How absurd is the impression bequeathed by Slavery in regard to these Southern blacks that they are sluggish and inefficient in labor." On the contrary, he insisted, his troops worked hard day and night with good humor.[24] Old planters, too, could recall the other side of the slaves' work habits and marvel, as did D. E. Huger Smith, at the extraordinary proficiency of plow hands, as well as carpenters.[25] The slaves' reputation for being lazy and inattentive long plagued black workers, no matter what their actual performance. Thus, in the postwar Far West, Negroes established themselves as among the best horse trainers and riders, and yet the term "nigger brand" was used to describe those sores on a horse's back caused by careless saddling or riding.[26]

The slaveholders responded in a characteristically self-defeating way, although it is difficult to imagine anything else they could have done. They decided that the slaves worked as they did because that was the only way blacks could be expected to work. Even Mary Boykin Chesnut came close to adhering to the usual rationalization: "The Northern men and women who came here were always hardest [on their slaves], for they expected an African to work and behave as a white man. We do not."[27] Yet the use of the word "African" requires comment. Most white southerners believed the slaves to be anything except white men in black skins, but they disagreed on whether the difference was rooted in biology and heredity or in previous conditioning in a primitive society. In either case they transformed their awareness of difference into a double-edged racist argument. Since blacks were inferior, they had to be enslaved and taught to work; but, being inferior, they could hardly be expected to work up to Anglo-Saxon expectations. Therefore, the racist argument in defense of slavery reinforced the slaveholders' tendency to tolerate, with an infinite patience that amazed others, a level of performance that appalled northern and foreign visitors.

According to one corollary of this ideology, it was not possible to overwork the slaves. "All experience in the South," wrote Mrs. Henry Rowe Schoolcraft, "proves that you cannot overwork a negro. He will do his task, and no human power can make him do any more. . . ."[28] The ideologues of the medical profession rallied to support this interpretation. Such leading physicians as Josiah Nott and Samuel A. Cartwright contributed to the development of the proslavery argument and insisted that blacks constitutionally could not work like whites and required patient handling and some tolerance of their slow rhythm and irregular habits.[29] An unsigned article in the *American Cotton Planter* in 1854 suggestively explored this line of thought:

> [We must resolutely keep the black] in the place where he was placed by God, and at the same time take care that contact *do not assimilate us too much to him.* To use him, we must unavoidably be a *little* like him; we must be more given to self indulgence—we *must* be content to advance less rapidly than the energetic North; but we need not be altogether Sybarites, we should not fall into an intellectual paralysis. We must take the good with the accompanying evil. For the docility which makes him obey, we must take the laziness which makes him hate forethought; for the strength which he wields in the world's service, we must be content to take the conservative stubbornness which makes it impossible to work him to death. We must touch him in the play-ground, set before him at the table, hear him in the council, see him in the church, for in all he has his place, which he claims as the wages of his birth-right service.[30]

The process of accommodation of master to slave naturally looked different to outsiders. Harriet Martineau, from her deeply felt attachment to the Anglo-Saxon work ethic, saw another facet of the relationship. The slave, she agreed, rarely suffered from overwork.

> He knows the evil of toil, the reluctance, the lassitude, but with it he knows also the evil of idleness; the vacuity, the hopelessness. He

has neither the privilege of the brute, to exercise himself vigorously upon instinct, for an immediate object, to be gained and forgotten; nor the privilege of the man, to toil, by moral necessity, with some pain, for results which yield an ever glowing pleasure. It is not work which is the curse of the slave: he is rarely so blessed as to know what it is.[31]

The actual work rhythm of the slaves, then, had to be hammered out as a compromise between themselves and their masters. The masters held the upper hand, but the slaves set limits as best they could.[32] When war and the Confederate impressment of slaves came, the planters balked not only because they resented losing part of their labor force to the war effort, but because they feared that the army officers would not understand or respect those patterns of work and life which had been established on their particular plantations.[33]

Occasionally, masters interpreted the facts realistically. Charles Pettigrew of North Carolina instructed his sons in his last will and testament:

> To manage *negroes* without the exercise of too much passion, is next to an impossibility, after our strongest endeavors to the contrary; I have found it so. . . . Let this consideration plead in their favor, and at all time mitigate your resentments. They are slaves for life. They are not stimulated to care and industry as white people are, who labor for themselves. They do not feel themselves *interested* in what they do, for arbitrary masters and mistresses, and their education is not such as can be expected to inspire them with sentiments of honor and gratitude. . . .[34]

The other side of this thinking came from an old ex-slave, Doc Daniel Dowdy of Georgia. "The white folks," he explained, "was ignorant. You know the better you prepare yourself the better you act. Iffen they had put some sense in our heads 'stead of sticks on our heads, we'ud been better off and more benefit to 'em."[35]

Africans and Afro-Americans presented whites with an alternative work ethic, as W. E. B. Du Bois suggested, but that alternative was a variation of what the whites themselves had once embraced. Hence, the reaction of working-class whites represented a strong assault on what they themselves had only recently been. The social history of the United States has been pre-eminently a history of waves of European immigrants each of whom in turn had to be subjected to industrial discipline. With each wave a painful shift in values and style of life had to occur. With each shift and its consolidation of a new viewpoint the converts became, as usual, more Catholic than the pope. What the blacks confronted them with, as Winthrop Jordan and George Rawick have so suggestively argued, was a constant reminder of a way of life they themselves had had to repudiate. The familiar refrain "We made it, why can't they?" expresses far more than ignorance of the special effects of white racism's socio-economic discrimination.[36]

The slaves' estimates of the charge that they would work only under compulsion ranged widely from an apparent acceptance of the white man's indictment to a sophisticated dissent. Within this range certain common features illuminated underlying attitudes toward work and leisure. Even those blacks who viewed their people as being naturally lazy agreed that, whether from fear of punishment or internal compulsion, the slaves worked hard. Jim Henry, an aged ex-slave from South Carolina, commented on his being part white, part Indian, and part black: "Derefore, us been thrifty like de white man, crafty like de Indians, and hard workin' like de negroes."[37]

Chancellor Harper, in his contribution to *The Pro-slavery Argument*, declared that the blacks "are undergoing the very best education which it is possible to give. They are in the course of being taught habits of regular and patient industry, and this is the first lesson which is required." Harper at least phrased the argument more plausibly than most of the slaveholders when he stressed regular rather than hard work. Normally, both southern and northern whites simply assumed that Africans had been food gatherers who had learned the rudiments of agricultural labor only when enslaved in the New World.[38]

The slaves, whose own view of their African past blended black folklore with considerable acceptance of white propaganda, imbibed a good deal of their masters' viewpoint. The testimony of ex-slaves reveals some harsh judgments. According to Charlie Davis of South Carolina, "Dere ain't no doubt dat many a slave learnt good lessons dat showed them how to work and stay out of de jail or poorhouse, dat's worth a little." Similarly, Sam Rawls, from the vantage point of old age during the 1930s, complained: "De present generation of niggers ain't got much sense. Dey work when dey want to and have dere own way about it. De old niggers was learned to work when dey was little." James Johnson put the case more philosophically: "De black man is natchally lazy, you knows dat. De reason he talks lak he does, is 'cause he don't want

to go to de trouble to 'nounce his words lak dey ought to be."
Another ex-slave gave the same point of view a different twist:
"When he come here, de white man made him work, and he didn't
like dat. He is natchally lazy. . . . Ever since the first time de nigger
found out he had to work, he has silently despised the white man."
Added Mary Johnson: "Slavery did good to nigger, made him
careful and know how to work." Sam Polite went further: "W'at
I t'ink 'bout slabery? I t'ink it been good t'ing. It larn nigger to
wuk. If it ain't mek nigger wuk, he wouldn't do nutting but tief."
And Fanny Smith Hodges spoke for a surprising number of old
ex-slaves when she said, "Slaves was whipped when dey wouldn't
work right. Sometimes dey was lazy."[39]
Such sentiments notwithstanding, the slaves had some sense of
being an exploited class, not merely an oppressed race. The evidence bears out the generalization made by W. Arthur Lewis:

> Slaves are notoriously inefficient and unwilling. A horse, if it is well
> treated and well cared for, will gladly give all the effort which a well
> loved master demands. Some slaves are like horses in this respect, but
> most are not. The difference arises in their humanity; their sense of
> justice revolts against a system which uses their labour to enrich
> others; and their sense of freedom chafes against restraint. Even if
> the majority of the slaves would rest content, there is always a
> minority who feel their humanity strongly, and who communicate
> their feelings to the others.[40]

Fanny Kemble reported a conversation on the Butler plantation in
which the slave complained that his master would not plow the
ground and continued to depend on the hoe " 'cause horses more
costly to keep than colored folks."[41] A postwar song brought a
traditional black criticism up to date; it was entitled "Ain't It Hard
to Be a Nigger."

> Well, it make no difference
>   How yo' make out yo' time;
> White man sho bring a
>   Nigger out behin'.
>
> If you work all the week,
>   An' work all the time,
> White man sho to bring
>   Nigger out behin'.[42]

If the extent to which black slaves saw themselves as an exploited class remains somewhat cloudy, no doubt should remain

about their awareness of making a fundamental economic contribution to southern society. Writing in 1891, F. D. Srygley commented: "They seemed to forget all the toils and sufferings of their slavery, in their admiration of the plantation built up by their labor."[43] The most poignant expressions came from the blacks themselves during the war, when they expressed disgust and horror at the Yankees' destruction of the plantations. Charles Davenport, an ex-slave from the Natchez region, recalled: "It make my innards hurt to see fire attached to somethin' dat had cost us niggers so much labor and honest sweat."[44]

The slaves' sense of being productive members of society emerges from two incidents. Harriet Martineau tells us of a conversation between slave and master in Kentucky: "One of the slaves of a neighboring gentleman came and asked his master what he would give him for two bee-holes. 'You are a pretty fellow,' said his master, 'to ask me to pay for my own trees.' The negro urged that his master would never have found the bee-holes for himself; which was very true."[45] In the second case a contraband slave defended himself when a Union man accused him of "stealing" his owner's horse in order to escape and then for good measure accused him of "stealing" himself at a cost of about $1,000 to his owner. The slave replied, "*I don't look at it jis dat way, massa. I wo'ked ha'd for missus mor'n thirty yea's, an' I reckon in dat time I 'bout pay fo' meself.*"[46]

The slaves had their own labor theory of value, but, as might be expected, they interpreted it to suit themselves. And why not? Whatever the claims to genius that may be made for ruling classes, the poor, dull-witted, no-'count members of the degraded classes are at least entitled to match the elite's talent for self-serving theories. Accordingly, the slaves never did understand that their food, clothing, and shelter represented payment for work done and constituted the equivalent of a minimum wage. Their apparent dull-wittedness expressed the underside of the paternalist ideology, for in effect, it declared acceptance of a traditional society's notion of reciprocal obligations. When the slaves took their keep for granted, they simultaneously bowed to the hegemony of ruling-class ideology and announced the price to be exacted for their submission. The evidence from the antebellum period and from early Reconstruction demonstrates that the most ignorant slaves knew very well who raised the crops, generated the profits, and formed the indispensable element in the productive system.[47]

Ex-slaves generally insisted that they had worked much better for kind masters than for harsh ones. Solomon Northup, a talented northern free black who, having been kidnapped and sold into slavery, worked for both types, asserted forcibly that the kinder the master the better the work.[48] Adeline Johnson of South Carolina remarked, "In slavery, us have all de clothes us need, all de food us want, and work all de harder 'cause us love de white folks dat cared for us." Another recalled a song sung by the field hands:

> Go way, Ole Man
> Go way, Ole Man
> W'ere you bin all day?
> If you treat me good
> I'll stay 'till de Judgment Day,
> But if you treat me bad,
> I'll sho' to run away.[49]

Support for Northup's contention also came from the Texas ranch country, where slaves reputedly received friendly treatment and responded with loyalty and good work. Significantly, similar reports came from the slave-run ranches of Brazil's Rio Grande do Sul.[50]

Ex-slaves expressed the same idea negatively. Andy Anderson of Texas, who had never been whipped by his old master but who was immediately whipped by his new one, said, "After dat whippin' I doesn't have de heart to work for de massa. If I seed de cattle in de cornfield, I turns de back, 'stead of chasin' 'em out."[51] For most slaves matters were not so simple. Most did fear and respond to the whip. Austin Grant, also of Texas, told of his early education in the quarters: "My grandfather, he would tell us things, to keep the whip off our backs. He would say, 'Chillen, work, work and work hard. You know you hate to be whipped, so work hard.' And of course we chillen tried, but of course we would git careless sometimes."[52]

The slaveholders' views corresponded roughly to those of the blacks: Spare the whip and spoil the slave. Yet, kindness and patience often produced better results than harshness. A maddening ambiguity defined this feature of the master-slave relationship, much as it defined every other. Thomas Dabney of Mississippi explained how he got his slaves to work so well by saying that a man would do more and better work in five and a half days than in six. Harrod C. Anderson, a particularly tough planter from West Tennessee who used his whip often, understood that he had to do more than apply force. A simple entry in his plantation diary may speak for others: "Having given the servants a Dinner on Saturday in commemoration of their faithful working & expectation of a good crop of cotton . . ."[53]

According to George Washington in an earlier day, "When an overlooker's back is turned, the most of them will slight their work, or be idle altogether; in which case correction cannot retrieve either but often produces evils which are worse than the disease."[54] In the 1850s Samuel A. Cartwright, one of the South's leading racist ideologues in the medical profession, insisted that blacks yielded naturally to white command; he tried, with some charming dance steps, to use this extreme racist theory to encourage more humane treatment:

> The empire of the white man's will over the prognathous race is not absolute, however. It cannot force exercise beyond a certain speed; neither the will nor physical force can drive negroes for a number of days in succession, beyond a very moderate daily labor—about one-third less than what the white man voluntarily imposes upon himself. If force be used to make them do more, they invariably do less and less, until they fall into a state of impassivity, in which they are more plague than profit—worthless as laborers, insensible and indifferent to punishment, or even to life; or in other words, they fall into the disease which I have named Dysesthaesia Ethiopica, characterized by hebetude of mind and insensitivity of body, caused by overworking and bad treatment.[55]

The slaveholders could never quite resolve the contradictions in their attitude. They had to rely on force to drive unwilling laborers. They knew that they could get results from incentives and acts of kindness, which, however, would backfire if the blacks set their own work pace or applied their own ideas of what good work should be. They decided that blacks could not work steadily and so concluded that they ought not to expect them to. The work had to be done, and the general level of economic performance for the plantation South as a whole indicates that it was done. But it indicates only that it was done under the special conditions of plantation life and organization and says nothing about the extent to which a labor force was being disciplined to the growing demands of a more modern and diversified society. In this context we must reflect on the fame justly achieved by the planters for their patience and good humor with sloppiness, incompetence, and dissembling and on the inability of northern and European visitors to understand how they could stand living that way. It is also clear that the planters had few illusions about the damage being done.

The slaves could and did work hard, as their African ancestors had before them. The charge of laziness has missed the mark. But they resisted that regularity and routine which became the *sine qua non* for industrial society and which the planters, despite their own rejection of so much of the bourgeois work ethic, tried to impose upon them. The slaves developed their own notion of work and its relationship to leisure, which did suggest some continuing African cultural influence but which was much less specifically African than generally rural, prebourgeois, and especially preindustrial. Despite the wide differences between the world of the Africans and that of the Afro-American slaves, they did have certain features in common, which allowed for some continuity in collective sensibility. The slaves' attitude toward work, time, and leisure undoubtedly arose primarily from plantation life itself, which provided a harsh variant of traditional agricultural community life, just as African agricultural life provided another and much less harsh variant. To the extent that Africa continued to exert an influence in the slave quarters, it reinforced the exigencies of the slave condition itself.

THE BLACK WORK ETHIC

The slaves' world outlook, as manifested in their attitude toward work, has usually been treated as a mechanism of resistance to labor or to the demoralization occasioned by an especially oppressive labor system. Older and openly racist writers like Ulrich Bonnell Phillips or A. H. Stone accounted for it primarily by reference to "Negro traits." Ironically, W. E. B. Du Bois, the one scholar who attacked the question without bias and with sympathetic care, came out closer to the white racists than to the liberals, for he too proclaimed profound cultural differences; but he simultaneously stripped away the racists' distortions and, as it were, turned their arguments back on them. Any consideration of this question—indeed, any consideration of any question concerning slave life—must begin with a careful reconsideration of Dr. Du Bois's great work.

Perhaps Dr. Du Bois's best discussion of the black work ethic is the one in *The Gift of Black Folk:*

> The black slave brought into common labor certain new spiritual values not yet fully realized. As a tropical product with a sensuous receptivity to the beauty of the world, he was not as easily reduced to be the mechanical draft-horse which the northern European laborer became. He was not easily brought to recognize any ethical sanctions in work as such but tended to work as the results pleased him and refused to work or sought to refuse when he did not find the spiritual returns adequate; thus he was easily accused of laziness and driven as a slave when in truth he brought to modern manual labor a renewed valuation of life.

And again:

> Many a northern manager has seen the contradiction when, facing the apparent laziness of Negro hands, he has attempted to drive them and found out that he could not and at the same time has afterward seen someone used to Negro labor get a tremendous amount of work out of the same gangs. The explanation of all this is clear and simple: the Negro laborer has not been trained in modern organized industry but rather in a quite different school.[1]

Dr. Du Bois located the difference in the attitudes of Euro-American and Afro-American workers in the difference between the bourgeois social system of the one and the ostensibly "communistic" social system of the other. The white worker worked hard not only to avoid starvation but to avoid disgracing himself and his family, whereas the black worker "looked upon work as a necessary evil and maintained his right to balance the relative allurements of leisure and satisfaction at any particular day, hour, or season."[2] Ever alert to complexities, Dr. Du Bois suggested that the white worker brought to America the habit of regular toil as a great moral duty and used it to make America rich, whereas the black worker brought the idea of work as a necessary evil and could, if allowed, use it to make America happy.

There is much that is wise as well as humane in Dr. Du Bois's point of view, and it seems incomprehensible that it should so long have been ignored, if only because it raises so many questions of a kind that now threaten to tear the country apart generationally as well as racially. Santayana, with whom Dr. Du Bois studied at Harvard, once wrote: "Certain moralists, without meaning to be satirical, often say that the sovereign cure for unhappiness is work. Unhappily, the work they recommend is better fitted to dull pain than to remove its cause. It occupies the faculties without rationalising the life."[3] Notwithstanding the great merit of Dr. Du Bois's interpretation, its historical specifics cannot go unchallenged. The blacks may indeed be seen as "a tropical product with a sensuous receptivity to the beauty of the world." Despite appearances, there is nothing mystical here—merely a proper concern for the impact of physical environment on the historically developed, collective sensibilities of peoples. But, Dr. Du Bois made a costly error in assuming that white European workers came to the United States after having internalized the Puritan work ethic, and he thereby drew attention away from the central character of the slave experience and moved it to the African experience, which was only a special case in the general immigrant experience.

The immigrants who filled the ranks of the unskilled labor force during the nineteenth century came, to a great extent, from peasant societies with a rural work ethic reinforced by Roman Catholicism. The Sicilians and East Europeans who followed did not bring the maxims of Benjamin Franklin with them. Each wave of immigrants had to undergo a process of acculturation that meant a harsh struggle to break down an established set of values and the slow inculcation of those values we associate with specifically industrial discipline. Moreover, as E. P. Thompson has so well demonstrated, the English working class itself had arisen from the countryside amidst the bitter contention of rival value systems in general and work ethics in particular. Thus, the contribution of Africa came not from some supposed communistic tradition but from its particular participation in a much broader tradition that we associate with most agrarian peoples. But whereas the Europeans found themselves drawn into an industrial system that slowly transformed them into suitable industrial workers, the Africans found themselves drawn into a plantation system that, despite certain similarities to an industrial setting, immensely reinforced traditional values and also added elements of corruption and degradation.

The African tradition, like the European peasant tradition, stressed hard work and condemned and derided laziness in any form.⁴ Not hard work but steady, routinized work as moral duty was discounted. In this attitude African agriculturalists resembled preindustrial peoples in general, including urban peoples. The familiar assertion that certain people would work only long enough to earn the money they needed to live was leveled not only against day laborers but against the finest and most prestigious artisans in early modern Europe.⁵

Olmsted reported that the slaves could be and often were driven into hard, unremitting toil but that they responded with a dull, stupid, plodding effort which severely reduced their productive contribution.⁶ The slaves, he added, "are far less adapted for steady, uninterrupted labor than we are, but excel us in feats demanding agility and tempestuous energy." Olmsted's argument became standard among postbellum employers who were trying to rebuild with a labor force of freedmen. As one farmer in North Carolina told John Richard Dennett in 1865, "You know how it is with them—for about three days it's work as if they'd break everything to pieces; but after that it's go out late and come in soon."⁷ Ironically, this distinction parallels precisely the one made by proslavery ideologues who wished to describe the cultural differences between themselves and the Yankees. It is also the distinction made by scholars in describing the position of southern blacks who went north to cities like Chicago during the twentieth century.⁸

What did the blacks themselves say? Isaac Adams, who had been a slave on a big plantation in Louisiana, recalled that most of the blacks remained there when the Yankees emancipated them. "But," he added, "they didn't do very much work. Just enough to take care of themselves and their white folks."⁹ Frank Smith, an ex-slave who went north from Alabama to Illinois, complained: "I didn't lak de Yankees. Dey wanted you to wuk *all de time*, and dat's sump'n I hadn't been brung up to do."¹⁰ Colin Clark and Margaret Haswell may have a point when they argue, in *The Economics of Subsistence Agriculture*, that subsistence laborers will overcome their attachment to leisure and work steadily once they have been brought into contact with communities and values strong enough to stimulate their wants.¹¹ But powerful cultural resistance to any such tendency must be overcome, and the projected outcome of such a confrontation is not inevitable. In part the outcome must depend on the extent to which the more traditional group has organized itself into a community rather than continuing as a

conglomerate of individuals and on the extent to which assimilation to the more economically advanced community is blocked by
discrimination.

The slaves' willingness to work extraordinarily hard and yet to
resist the discipline of regularity accompanied certain desires and
expectations. During Reconstruction the blacks sought their own
land; worked it conscientiously when they could get it; resisted
being forced back into anything resembling gang labor for the
white man; and had to be terrorized, swindled, and murdered to
prevent their working for themselves.[12] This story was prefigured
in antebellum times when slaves were often allowed garden plots
for their families and willingly worked them late at night or on
Sundays in order to provide extra food or clothing. The men did
not generally let their families subsist on the usual allotments of
pork and corn. In addition to working with their wives in the
gardens, they fished and hunted and trapped animals. In these and
other ways they demonstrated considerable concern for the welfare of their families and a strong desire to take care of them. But
in such instances they were working for themselves and at their
own pace. Less frequently, slaves received permission to hire out
their own time after having completed the week's assigned tasks.
They were lured, not by some internal pressure to work steadily,
but by the opportunity to work for themselves and their families
in their own way.[13]

Many slaves voluntarily worked for their masters on Sundays or
holidays in return for money or goods. This arrangement demonstrated how far the notion of the slaves' "right" to a certain amount
of time had been accepted by the masters; how readily the slaves
would work for themselves; and how far the notion of reciprocity
had entered the thinking of both masters and slaves.

The slaves responded to moral as well as economic incentives.
They often took pride in their work, but not necessarily in the
ways most important to their masters. Solomon Northup designed
a better way to transport lumber only to find himself ridiculed by
the overseer. In this case it was in the master's interest to intervene, and he did. He praised Northup and adopted the plan.
Northup comments: "I was not insensible to the praise bestowed
upon me, and enjoyed especially, my triumph over Taydem [the
overseer], whose half-malicious ridicule had stung my pride."[14]

From colonial days onward plantation slaves, as well as those in
industry, mining, and town services, received payments in money

and goods as part of a wider system of social control.[15] These payments served either as incentive bonuses designed to stimulate productivity, or more frequently, as a return for work done during the time recognized as the slaves' own. Many planters, including those who most clearly got the best results, used such incentives. Bennet H. Barrow of Louisiana provides a noteworthy illustration, for he was a not a man to spare the whip. Yet his system of rewards included frequent holidays and dinners, as well as cash bonuses and presents for outstanding work. In Hinds County, Mississippi, Thomas Dabney gave small cash prizes—a few cents, really—to his best pickers and then smaller prizes to others who worked diligently even if they could not match the output of the leaders. In Perry County, Alabama, Hugh Davis divided his workers into rival teams and had them compete for prizes. He supplemented this collective competition with individual contests. In North Carolina at the end of the eighteenth century Charles Pettigrew, like many others before and after him, paid slaves for superior or extra work.[16]

The amounts sometimes reached substantial proportions. Captain Frederick Marryat complained that in Lexington, Kentucky, during the late 1830s a gentleman could not rent a carriage on Sundays because slaves with ready money invariably rented them first for their own pleasure. Occasionally, plantation records reported surprising figures. One slave in Georgia earned fifty to sixty dollars per year by attending to pine trees in his off hours. Others earned money by applying particular skills or by doing jobs that had to be done individually and carefully without supervision. Amounts in the tens and even hundreds of dollars, although not common, caused no astonishment.[17]

The more significant feature of these practices, for the society as a whole if not for the economy in particular, was the regularity —almost the institutionalization—of payments for work on Sundays or holidays. Apart from occasional assignments of Sunday or holiday work as punishment and apart from self-defeating greed, not to say stupidity, which led a few masters to violate the social norm, Sunday was the slaves' day by custom as well as law.[18] The collective agreement of the slaveholders on these measures had its origin in a concern for social peace and reflected a sensible attitude toward economic efficiency. But once the practice took root, with or without legal sanction, the slaves transformed it into a "right." So successfully did they do so that the Supreme Court of Louisiana ruled in 1836: "According to . . . law, slaves are entitled to the produce of their labor on Sunday; even the master is bound to remunerate them, if he employs them." Here again the slaves turned the paternalist doctrine of reciprocity to advantage while demonstrating the extent to which that doctrine dominated the lives of both masters and slaves.[19]

Ralph Ellison writes of his experience as a boy: "Those trips to the cotton patch seemed to me an enviable experience because the kids came back with such wonderful stories. And it wasn't the hard work which they stressed, but the communion, the playing, the eating, the dancing and the singing."[20] A leading theme in the blues tradition of black "soul" music is "Do your best." The emphasis in both performance and lyrics rests not on the degree of success but on the extent and especially the sincerity of effort.[21] Underlying black resistance to prevailing white values, then, has been a set of particular ideas concerning individual and community responsibility. It is often asserted that blacks spend rather than save as someone else thinks they should. But the considerable evidence for this assertion must be qualified by the no less considerable evidence of the heartbreaking scraping together of nickels and dimes to pay for such things as the education of children, which will generally draw Anglo-Saxon applause, and the provision of elaborate funerals, which generally will not but which for many peoples besides blacks constitutes a necessary measure of respect for the living as well as the dead.

The slaves could, when they chose, astonish the whites by their worktime élan and expenditure of energy. The demands of corn shucking, hog killing, logrolling, cotton picking, and especially sugar grinding confronted the slaves with particularly heavy burdens and yet drew from them particularly positive responses.

With the exception of the Christmas holiday—and not always that—former slaves recalled having looked forward to corn shucking most of all.[22] Sam Colquitt of Alabama explained:

> Next to our dances, de most fun was corn-shucking. Marsa would have de corn hauled up to de crib, and piled as a house. Den he would invite de hands 'round to come and hope shuck it. Us had two leaders or generals and choose up two sides. Den us see which side would win first and holler and sing. . . . Marsa would pass de jug around too. Den dey sho' could work and dat pile'd just vanish.[23]

Some ex-slaves remembered corn shuckings as their only good time, but many more said simply that they were the best. Occasionally a sour note appeared, as when Jenny Proctor of Alabama said, "We had some co'n shuckin's sometimes but de white folks gits de fun and de nigger gits de work."[24] For the vast majority, however, they were "de big times."

The descriptions that have been preserved provide essential clues for an understanding of plantation life and its work rhythms. According to Robert Shepherd of Kentucky:

> Dem corn shuckin's was sure 'nough big times. When us got all de corn gathered up and put in great long piles, den de gettin' ready started. Why, dem womans cooked for days, and de mens would get de shoats ready to barbecue. Master would send us out to get de slaves from de farms round about dere. De place was all lit up with light-wood knot torches and bonfires, and dere was 'citement a-plenty when all niggers get to singin' and shoutin' as dey made de shucks fly.[25]

An ex-slave from Georgia recalled:

> In corn shucking time no padderollers would ever bother you. We would have a big time at corn shuckings. They would call up the crowd and line the men up and give them a drink. I was a corn general—would stand out high above everybody, giving out corn songs and throwing down corn to them. There would be two sides of them, one side trying to outshuck the other. Such times we have.[26]

White contemporaries provided comments that complement those of former slaves. Fredrika Bremer, one of the more astute and thoughtful travelers to the South, wrote that corn shuckings "are to the negroes what the harvest-home is to our [Swedish] peasants."[27]

Certainly, the slaves had some material incentives. The best shuckers would get a dollar or a suit of clothes, as might those who found a red ear. But these incentives do not look impressive and do not loom large in the testimony. Those plantations on which the prize for finding a red ear consisted of a dollar do not seem to have done any better than those on which the prize consisted of an extra swig of whiskey or a chance to kiss the prettiest girl. The shucking was generally night work—overtime, as it were—and one might have expected the slaves to resent it and to consider the modest material incentives, which came to a special dinner and dance and a lot of whiskey, to be inadequate.

The most important feature of these occasions and the most

important incentive to these long hours of extra work was the community life they called forth. They were gala affairs. The jug passed freely, although drunkenness was discouraged; the work went on amidst singing and dancing; friends and acquaintances congregated from several plantations and farms; the house slaves joined the field slaves in common labor; and the work was followed by an all-night dinner and ball at which inhibitions, especially those of class and race, were lowered as far as anyone dared.

Slavery, a particularly savage system of oppression and exploitation, made its slaves victims. But the human beings it made victims did not consent to be just that; they struggled to make life bearable and to find as much joy in it as they could. Up to a point even the harshest of masters had to help them do so. The logic of slavery pushed the masters to try to break their slaves' spirit and to reconstruct it as an unthinking and unfeeling extension of their own will, but the slaves' own resistance to dehumanization compelled the masters to compromise in order to get an adequate level of work out of them.

The combination of festive spirit and joint effort appears to have engaged the attention of the slaves more than anything else. Gus Brown, an ex-slave from Alabama, said simply, "On those occasions we all got together and had a regular good time." The heightened sense of fellowship with their masters also drew much comment. Even big slaveholders would join in the work, as well as in the festivities and the drinking, albeit not without the customary patriarchal qualifications. They would demand that the slaves sing, and the slaves would respond boisterously. Visitors expressed wonder at the spontaneity and improvisation the slaves displayed. The songs, often made up on the spot, bristled with sharp wit, both malicious and gentle. The slaves sang of their courtships and their lovers' quarrels; sometimes the songs got bawdy, and the children had to be hustled off to bed. They sang of their setbacks in love:

> When I'se here you calls me honey.
> When I'se gone you honies everybody.

They sang of their defeats in competition:

> You jumped and I jumped;
> Swear by God you outjumped me,
> Huh, huh, round de corn, Sally.

and of their victories:

> Pull de husk, break de ear
> Whoa, I'se got de red ear here.

But the songs also turned to satire. White participation in these festivals was always condescending and self-serving, and the slaves' acceptance of it displayed something other than childlike gratitude for small favors. They turned their wit and incredible talent for improvisation into social criticism. Occasionally they risked a direct, if muted, thrust in their "corn songs," as they came to be called.

> Massa in the great house, counting out his money,
> Oh, shuck that corn and throw it in the barn.
> Mistis in the parlor, eating bread and honey,
> Oh, shuck that corn and throw it in the barn.

More often, they used a simpler and safer technique. Ole Massa was always God's gift to humanity, the salt of the earth, de bestest massa in de whole wide worl'. But somehow, one or more of his neighbors was mighty bad buckra.

> I
> Massa's niggers am slick and fat,
>   Oh! Oh! Oh!
> Shine jes like a new beaver hat,
>   Oh! Oh! Oh!
>
> *Refrain:* Tùrn out here and shuck dis corn.
>   Oh! Oh! Oh!
> Biggest pile o' corn since I was born,
>   Oh! Oh! Oh!
>
> II
> Jones' niggers am lean an po',
>   Oh! Oh! Oh!
> Don't know whether they git 'nough ter eat or no,
>   Oh! Oh! Oh![28]

Blacks—any blacks—were not supposed to sass whites—any whites; slaves—any slaves—were not supposed to sit in judgment on masters—any masters. By the device of a little flattery and by taking advantage of the looseness of the occasion, they asserted their personalities and made their judgments.

A curious sexual division of labor marked the corn shuckings. Only occasionally did women participate in the shucking. The reason for the exclusion is by no means clear. Field women matched the men in hard work, not only in picking cotton but in rolling logs, chopping wood, and plowing. Yet at corn shuckings they divided their time between preparing an elaborate spread for the dinner and taking part in quilting bees and the like. As a result, the corn shuckings took on a peculiarly male tone, replete with raucous songs and jokes not normally told in front of women, as well as with those manifestations of boyish prancing associated with what is called—as if by some delightful Freudian slip—a "man's man."

The vigor with which the men worked and the insistence on a rigid sexual separation raise the central question of the slaves' attitude toward work in its relationship to their sense of family and community. The sense of community established by bringing together house and field slaves and especially slaves from several plantations undoubtedly underlay much of the slaves' positive response, and recalled the festivities, ceremonials, and rituals of traditional societies in a way no office Christmas party in an industrial firm has ever done. And corn shucking, like hog killing, had a special meaning, for at these times the slaves were literally working for themselves. The corn and pork fed them and their families; completion of these tasks carried a special satisfaction.

From this point of view the sexual division of labor, whatever its origins, takes on new meaning. In a limited way it strengthened that role of direct provider to which the men laid claim by hunting and fishing to supplement the family diet. Even the less attractive features of the evening in effect reinforced this male self-image. Nor did the women show signs of resentment. On the contrary, they seem to have grasped the opportunity to underscore a division of labor and authority in the family and to support the pretensions of their men. Slavery represented a terrible onslaught on the personalities and spirit of the slaves, and whatever unfairness manifested itself in this sexual bias, the efforts of male and female slaves to create and support their separate roles provided a weapon for joint resistance to dehumanization.

Hog-killing time rivaled corn shucking as a grand occasion. Consider two accounts from Virginia—one from J. S. Wise's well-known memoir, *The End of an Era*, and the other from Joseph Holmes's account of his life as a slave.[29] First, Wise:

> Then there was hog-killing time, when long before day, the whole plantation force was up with knives for killing, and seething caul-

drons for scalding, and great doors for scraping, and long racks for cooling the slaughtered swine. Out to the farmyard rallied all the farm hands. Into the pens dashed the boldest and most active. Harrowing was the squealing of the victims; quick was the stroke that slew them, and quicker the sousing of the dead hog into the scalding water; busy the scraping of his hair away; strong the arms that bore him to the beams, and hung him there head downward to cool; clumsy the old woman who brought tubs to place under him; deft the strong hands that disemboweled him.

And now, Joseph Holmes:

Dat was de time of times. For weeks de mens would haul wood an' big rocks, an' pile 'em together as high as dis house, an' den have several piles, lak dat 'roun' a big hole in de groun' what has been filled wid water. Den jus' a little atter midnight, de boss would blow de ole hawn, an' all de mens would git up an' git in dem big pens. Den dey would sot dat pile of wood on fire an' den start knockin' dem hogs in de haid. Us neber shot a hog lak us does now; us always used an axe to kill 'em wid. Atter knockin' de hog in de haid, dey would tie a rope on his leg an' atter de water got to de right heat, fum dose red-hot rocks de hog would be throwed in an' drug aroun' a while, den taken out an' cleaned. Atter he was cleaned he was cut up into sections an' hung up in de smoke house. Lawsie, lady, dey don't cure meat dese days; dey jus' uses some kind of liquid to bresh over it. We useta have sho' nuff meat.

The slaves enjoyed a special and delightful inducement here, for they could eat as they worked and could display pride in their individual skills within the totality of a community effort. As in corn shucking, they did this work for themselves and poured enthusiasm into it.

Logrollings called forth some of the same festive spirit but came less frequently. They had some direct reference to the slaves' own life when they contributed to building the quarters. Women worked along with the men, and teams competed against each other. In other respects the event had the same style as the corn shuckings. As Frank Gill, an ex-slave from Alabama, recalled:

Talkin' 'bout log rollin', dem was great times, 'ca'se if some ob dem neighborin' plantations wanted to get up a house, dey would invite all de slaves, men and women, to come wid dere masters. De women would help wid de cookin' an' you may be shore dey had something to cook. Dey would kill a cow, or three or four hogs, and den hab peas, cabbage, an' everything lack grows on de farm.[30]

The evidence from the sugar plantations is especially instructive. Louisiana's sugar planters reputedly drove their slaves harder than any others in the slave states. Such reputations are by no means to be accepted at face value, but they certainly drove them hard during the grinding season. Yet, slaves took to the woods as limited and local runaways more often during the spring and summer months than during the autumn grinding season, when the work reached a peak of intensity and when the time for rest and sleep contracted sharply.[31] Once again, the small material incentives cannot account for the slaves' behavior.[32]

The slaves brought to their labor a gaiety and élan that perplexed observers, who saw them work at night with hardly a moment to catch their breath. Many, perhaps most, found themselves with special tasks to perform and special demands upon them; by all accounts they strained to rise to the occasion. The planters, knowing that the season lasted too long to sustain a fever pitch of effort, tried to break it up with parties and barbecues and at the very least promised and delivered a gala dinner and ball at the end. Ellen Betts, an ex-slave from Texas, recalled: "Massa sho' good to dem gals and bucks what cuttin' de cane. When dey git done makin' sugar, he give a drink called 'Peach 'n' Honey' to de women folk and whiskey and brandy to de men." Another ex-slave, William Stone of Alabama, said that the slaves were "happy" to work during the sugar harvest " 'cause we knowed it mean us have plenty 'lasses in winter."[33]

Still, the demands of the sugar crop meant the sacrifice of some Sundays and even the Christmas holiday. The slaves showed no resentment at the postponement of the holiday. It would come in due time, usually in mid-January, and the greater their sacrifices, the longer and fuller the holiday would likely be. For the slaves on the sugar plantations Christmas did not mean December 25; it meant the great holiday that honored the Lord's birth, brought joy to His children, and properly fell at the end of the productive season.

Cotton picking was another matter. One ex-slave recalled cotton-picking parties along with corn-shucking parties but added, "Dere wasn't so much foolishness at cotton pickin' time." The slaves missed, in particular, the fellowship of slaves from other plantations. An exchange of labor forces on a crash basis sometimes occurred, and ex-slaves remembered precisely those times warmly. The planters had to have their cotton picked at about the same time and could not easily exchange labor forces. But the neighborly tradition was too strong to be denied entirely, and when a planter fell dangerously behind, others would come to his aid. Unable to take time away from their own work unless well ahead of schedule, friendly planters had to send their slaves after hours to pick by moonlight. The slaves, instead of becoming indignant over the imposition, responded with enthusiasm and extra effort. Many of them later recalled this grueling all-night work as "big times," for they were helping their own friends and combining the work with festivity. Bonuses, parties, and relaxed discipline rewarded their cooperation. Scattered evidence suggests less whipping and harsh driving during the cotton-picking season on some plantations but the opposite on others.[34]

Some planters congratulated themselves on their success in getting a good response during the critical cotton harvest. Virginia Clay visited Governor Hammond's noteworthy plantation in South Carolina and enthusiastically reported on the magnificent singing and general spirit of the slaves, and Kate Stone was sure that "the Negroes really seemed to like the cotton picking best of all." Henry William Ravenel, in his private journal, made an interesting observation that provides a better clue to the slaves' attitude. Writing in 1865, immediately after their emancipation, he declared that the slaves had always disliked planting and cultivating cotton and would now prefer almost any alternative labor.[35] The picking season must have struck the slaves as a mixed affair. It meant hard and distasteful work and sometimes punishment for failure to meet quotas, but also the end of a tough season, prizes for good performances, and the prelude to relaxation and a big celebration. Yet, the special spirit of the season was not strong enough to carry the slaves through the rigors of labor; the whip remained the indispensable spur.

Some anthropologists and cultural historians, noting the tradition of collective work among West Africans, have suggested its continuing influence among Afro-Americans. The Yoruba, for example, ingeniously combine community spirit and individual initiative by organizing hoeing in a line, so that everyone works alongside someone else and yet has his own task. But evidence of direct influence remains elusive, and, as William R. Bascom points out, collective patterns of work abounded in medieval Europe too.[36] Whatever the origins of the slaves' strong preference for collective work, it drew the attention of their masters, who knew that they would have to come to terms with it. Edmund Ruffin, the

South's great soil chemist and authority on plantation agriculture, complained that the pinewoods of North Carolina were set afire every spring by inconsiderate poor whites who cared nothing for the damage they did in order to provide grazing land for their few cows. He added that the slaves also set many fires because they intensely disliked collecting turpentine from the trees. This work was light and easy in Ruffin's estimation, but the slaves resisted it anyway because it had to be performed in isolation. "A negro," Ruffin explained from long experience, "cannot abide being alone and will prefer work of much exposure and severe toil, in company, to any lighter work, without any company."[37]

This preference for work in company manifested itself in a readiness to help each other in field labor. Richard Mack, among others, recalled that he could finish a given task quickly and would then help others so that they would avoid punishment. This attitude, by no means rare, led another ex-slave, Sylvia Durant of South Carolina, to protest in the 1930s, "Peoples used to help one another out more en didn't somebody be tryin' to pull you down all de time."[38]

Mrs. Durant's lament, common in the testimony of ex-slaves, hints at an anomaly reminiscent of the attitude of the Russian peasants who left the *mir*. The powerful community spirit and preference for collective patterns of working and living had their antithesis in an equally powerful individualism, manifested most attractively during and after Reconstruction in an attempt to transform themselves into peasant proprietors. This particular kind of individualism has also had less attractive manifestations, from the creation of the ghetto hustler and the devil-take-the-hindmost predator to the creation of a set of attitudes that many blacks hold responsible for a chronic lack of political unity. Certainly, the old collective spirit remains powerful, as the very notion of a black "brotherhood" demonstrates, but it does rest on a contradictory historical base. The work ethic of the slaves provided a firm defense against the excesses of an oppressive labor system, but like the religious tradition on which it rested, it did not easily lend itself to counterattack. Once the worst features of the old regime fell away, the ethic itself began to dissolve into its component parts. Even today we witness the depressing effects of this dissolution in a futile and pathetic caricature of bourgeois individualism, manifested both in the frustrated aspirations so angrily depicted in E. Franklin Frazier's *Black Bourgeoisie* and in violent, antisocial nihilism. But we also witness the continued power of a collective sensibility regarded by some as "race pride" and by others as a developing black national consciousness.

The slaves expressed their attitude in song. The masters encouraged quick-time singing among their field slaves, but the slaves proved themselves masters of slowing down the songs and the work. They willingly sang at work, as well as going to work, coming from work, and at almost any time. While assembling for field work they might sing individually.

> Saturday night and Sunday too
> Young gals on my mind.
> Monday morning 'way 'fore day,
> Old master's got me gwine.
> Peggy, does you love me now?

But whenever possible they sang collectively, in ways derived from Africa but rooted in their own experience. When they had to work alone or when they felt alone even in a group, they "hollered." Imamu Amiri Baraka's extraordinary analysis of the historical development of black music, however controversial, speculative, and tentative it may be judged, remains the indispensable introduction to the subject. He remarks on the roots of the blues: "The shouts and hollers were strident laments, more than anything. They were also chronicles but of such a mean kind of existence that they could not assume the universality any lasting musical form must have."[39] Imamu Baraka traces the spread of hollers during and after Reconstruction when work patterns fragmented; but even during slavery a large portion of the slaves worked in isolation on small farms. Their hollers provided a counterpart to plantation work songs, but ranged beyond a direct concern with labor to a concern with the most personal expressions of life's travail. As such, they created a piercing history of the impact of hardship and sorrow on solitary black men. Their power notwithstanding, they represented a burning negative statement of the blacks' desire for community in labor as well as in life generally. As positive expression, both in themselves and in the legacy they left for blues singers to come, they contributed to the collective in a strikingly dialectical way, for they provided a form for a highly individualistic self-expression among a people whose very collectivity desperately required methods of individual self-assertion in order to combat the debilitating thrust of slavery's paternalistic aggression.

BOOK THREE

THE VALLEY OF THE SHADOW

Yea, though I walk through the valley of the shadow of death, I will fear no evil: for thou art with me; thy rod and thy staff they comfort me.

Thou preparest a table before me in the presence of mine enemies: thou anointest my head with oil; my cup runneth over.

Surely goodness and mercy shall follow me all the days of my life: and I will dwell in the house of the Lord for ever.

—Psalms 23:4–6

PART 1

OF THE SONS OF JACOB

> And Jacob called unto his sons, and said, Gather yourselves together, that I may tell you that which shall befall you in the last days.
>
> —Genesis 49:1

LIFE IN THE BIG HOUSE

"The slaves," recalled Annie Laurie Broidrick of Vicksburg, Mississippi, in accordance with the plantation legend, "were of two classes; the bright [colored] darky who was trained for house service, and the 'corn-field nigger'; the latter being usually the black, shiny darky who could sleep all day.... The dining-room servants or butlers were usually mulattoes, who were great dandies, having all the graces and mannerisms of their masters...."[1] However much the quadroon and mulatto servants, stiffly parading in full dress, dominated the Big House of the legend, they did not dominate the Big House of reality. A preference for light-skinned slaves to work in the house existed in Charleston, New Orleans, and some other cities, but even there it was far from general. As often as not, southern slaveholders, in sharp contradistinction to the slaveholders of the British Caribbean, enjoyed being served by blacks—the blacker the better—as well as by light-skinned

Negroes. Even during the colonial period, whites did not show any great partiality to mulattoes, except when they were blood relatives.[2] Mulattoes came to be preferred for house work roughly to the extent that they had acquired certain cultural advantages that made them more presentable to upper-class white society. Typically, the great plantations and town houses employed servants of every shade, and no caste lines grew up except in a few places like New Orleans and Charleston, where the Caribbean three-caste tradition had never wholly disappeared.[3]

According to guesswork honored by time and repetition, about a quarter of the southern slaves worked in or around the house rather than in the fields. So high a percentage appears plausible only when qualified by a consideration of its component parts. The figure includes slaves owned by yeomen, who frequently bought a single slave or a family to help in the house while the farmer worked his own land; a small army of domestics held in groups of one to five or so by townspeople; and plantation slaves who did menial work in the house and more or less specialized outside work like gardening and coach driving.[4] Thus, those who might have formed an elite status group on the plantations constituted only a small minority of the total number of house slaves. Five percent of the total number of adult slaves or 20 percent of the total number of house slaves would seem the highest reasonable estimate, although the figure would have to be much higher for the South Carolina and Georgia low country, the Natchez district, and a few pockets here and there.[5] Even many large plantations, and not only those under absentee owners, had small household staffs of, say, a half dozen out of a slave force of fifty to one hundred.[6]

The legend of the house-slave elite grew up primarily in the cities, where town-house slaves and the more economically secure free Negroes combined in a special way. Nehemiah Adams, a New Englander, recorded his impression of the urban scene:

> To see slaves with broadcloth suits, well-fitted and nicely ironed fine shirts, polished boots, gloves, umbrellas for sunshade, the best of hats, their young men with their blue coats and bright buttons, in the latest style, white Marseilles vests, white pantaloons, brooches in their shirt-bosoms, gold chains, elegant sticks and some old men leaning on their ivory and silver headed staves, as respectable in their attire as any who that day went to the House of God, was more than I was prepared to see.[7]

Olmsted added:

> In what I suppose to be the fashionable streets [of Washington], there
> were many more well-dressed and highly-dressed colored people
> than white, and among this dark gentry the finest French cloths,
> embroidered waistcoats, patent-leather shoes, resplendent brooches,
> silk hats, kid gloves, and *eau de mille fleurs*, were quite as common as
> among the New York "dry-goods clerks," in their Sunday prome-
> nades in Broadway. . . . Many of the colored ladies were dressed not
> only expensively, but with good taste and effect, after the latest
> Parisian mode. Many of them were quite attractive in appearance,
> and some would have produced a decided sensation in any Europe
> drawing room. Their walk and carriage was more often stylish and
> graceful than that of the white ladies who were out.[8]

On the great plantations even the more favored house slaves had
few such frills, but they did live with greater security than others,
not so much because they came to be respected as a hereditary caste
—something that happened only in the most aristocratic districts[9]
—as because servants trained and polished for elegant performance as butlers, cooks, and dining-room attendants were hard to
obtain and not easily spared. "Will you please keep George, if
convenient, with you on the Island, about the house," Charles C.
Jones, Jr., wrote to his father, "as I do not wish that he should
forget his training. I want him to acquire a *house look*, which you
know is not the acquisition of a day."[10] Masters and mistresses
therefore had to bear with their servants' peccadillos and imperti-
nences as best they could. Not often did they reduce them to field
labor except temporarily as a punishment for a specific action.[11]

The masters of the more aristocratic plantations, especially in
the Sea Island cotton, rice, and sugar districts, encouraged pride
of caste in their house servants. Undoubtedly they sometimes succeeded, and when they did, a sharp social line arose between the
slaves of the Big House and those of the quarters. Mary Colquitt
of Georgia recalled that her mother, a cook, forbade her to play
with the children of the field slaves. According to a member of the
mighty Heyward family, the house slaves on their huge estates
lived apart from the field slaves and associated with them little. Sir
Charles Lyell wrote of a superb black house woman who managed
everything for her master and mistress but who could never find
anyone worthy of becoming her husband among country people
so much ruder than herself. A male ex-slave reflected: "We house
slaves thought we was better'n the others what worked in the field.

We really was raised a little different, you know. . . ."[12]

These elite house servants stood on their dignity. The classic story comes from Natchez, as told by Ingraham:

> "You know dat nigger, they gwine to sell, George?"
> "No, he field nigger; I nebber has no 'quaintance wid dat class."
> "Well, nor no oder gentlemens would."[13]

By expressing contempt for the field hands—by putting on more airs than the white folks, as a former field hand expressed it[14]— they tried to raise their own image in society at the expense of other slaves, but simultaneously they were narrowing the distance between white and black. They felt superior to the poor whites and even to some solid yeomen; their identification with their masters, far from representing an acceptance of inferiority, gave them a device for asserting superiority over many whites. As such, it constituted acceptance of class paternalism and its pecking order but a determined rejection of the extreme formulations of racial subordination. The field hands did not readily accept the pretensions of the elite house servants except in the most caste-ridden regions of the eastern low country, but they did observe that some blacks carried themselves haughtily toward most whites—and got away with it.[15]

If some field hands envied those who worked in the Big House and hoped to change their own status, others did not. Many preferred field work and chose it when given the chance. No doubt some of this preference resulted from a sense of caste inferiority, for field hands who were pressed into service in the Big House sometimes found themselves humiliated by the patronizing and contemptuous attitudes of the more sophisticated house servants on the great plantations. Edward A. Pollard left an account of Pompey, an old slave who had to fill in for the butler from time to time. Pompey ordinarily did odd jobs and did not have the polish of a well-trained servant in an aristocratic Big House. When he made mistakes and fell into gaucheries, his mistress not merely scolded but ridiculed him, and the housemaids promptly joined in the fun and added to his humiliation. "Pompey," wrote Pollard, "is greatly cut up by such scoldings; and to be made a jest of before the genteeler and more precise servants, is his especial punishment and pain in this world."[16] Such cases illustrate Helen Merrell Lynd's formulation on the genesis of shame:

> It is peculiarly characteristic of these situations of suddenly experienced incongruity or discrepancy that evoke shame that they are

often occasioned by what seems a "ridiculously" slight incident. An ostensibly trivial incident has precipitated intense emotion. What has occurred is harmless in itself and has no evil pragmatic outcome. It is the very triviality of the cause—an awkward gesture, a gaucherie in dress or table manners, "an untimely joke" always "a source of bitter regret," a gift or a witticism that falls flat, an expressed naïveté in taste, a mispronounced word, ignorance of some important detail that everyone else surprisingly knows—that helps to give shame its unbearable character.[17]

Even on the more typical plantations, on which field hands had easy and pleasant intercourse with house servants, they often preferred the fields, and some house servants shared that preference and grumbled at having to stay in their ostensibly privileged position. A few simply liked the rough outdoor work better than the physically less demanding house chores. Others wanted to work alongside a husband or wife or wanted to avoid proximity to ever-demanding whites whom one had to wait on hand and foot. These slaves spoke of the camaraderie of field work and the constricting atmosphere of the Big House. In particular, field hands often enjoyed more leisure time and freedom of movement at the end of a day's work and on weekends. A well-treated cook who had to help out in the fields when needed explained her positive attitude toward cotton picking: "We could talk and do anything we wanted to, just so we picked the cotton; we used to sing and have lots of fun."[18] These attitudes did not appear often enough to warrant a conclusion that most field hands wanted to remain in their station, much less that most house slaves would have preferred field work; but they cast doubt on the common assumption that great status and prestige accrued to work in the Big House on other than the largest plantations.

Reputedly, house servants fared much better than field hands: they had more and better food and clothing, more comfortable quarters, and more personal consideration from the whites. Those who, like Fredrika Bremer, visited the plantations of the great planters thought the house servants better treated than the hired servants who worked in the homes of Europe's wealthy.[19] That which was reputed existed in fact—up to a point. Materially, the house servants often did live better, partly because of the closer sympathy and attention they received from one or more members of the white family and partly because they were in a position to take what they wanted anyway. Poorly fed house servants could and would steal everything in sight.[20] Perhaps their greatest advantage lay in a familiarity with the whites that gave some protection against the breakup of families when conditions necessitated sales. Here too, their own initiative helped, for house servants could ruin a sale by petulance or an unpleasant demeanor. Slaveholders wanted those who worked in their homes to be cheerful and content; house servants distraught on the auction block commanded lower prices when they moved at all.[21] House servants appeared frequently in the trade in slaves, perhaps in proportion to their numbers, but they retained two advantages over the field hands. First, they were not sold promiscuously and could feel more secure when working for an economically solvent master. Second, and perhaps more important, when they were sold they had a much better chance of being sold as a family.[22]

Those who lived and worked intimately with their white folks in the Big House became members of the family in a more literal sense than the others. The whites cared for them in ways that transcended anything the kindest master felt for his other slaves. Eliza Eve Carmichael of Georgia showed neither irritation nor surprise when her friends canceled a visit in order to take care of a sick servant. Eliza L. Magruder of Mississippi, like so many others, enjoyed reading to her allegedly exasperating and perverse women servants during the afternoon.[23] Masters and mistresses would give their house servants, or at least the favorites among them, privileges they would never think of bestowing on field hands.

The Big House had its gloomy side. Fanny Kemble pointed out that although the servants had access to good and plentiful food, they ate, "if possible, with even less comfort . . . inasmuch as no time whatever is set apart for their meals, which they snatch at any hour, and in any way they can." Their quarters, she said, did not exceed those of the field hands in comfort, and they had to feel the relative deprivation all the more since the example of the Big House was in front of them every day. "In the North," she concluded, "we could not hope to keep the worst and poorest servant for a single day in the wretched discomfit in which our negro servants are forced habitually to live."[24]

Mrs. Kemble had little respect for the plantation regime, but, as in so many cases, she scored her points. If many slaveholders pampered their house servants, or at least some of them, others dealt with them harshly. A position in the Big House did not guarantee an easier life, and it remains problematical that it provided one more often than not. Brutal and sadistic masters and mistresses did not represent the norm, but they did exist. At their hands the house servants sometimes fared much worse than the field hands and lived in torment, for they had little chance to avoid the constant observation and wrath of their superiors. But even more average and basically humane slaveholders had their share of bad moments and acute irritability. Typically, they always wanted something; typically, the servants failed to measure up to the constant demand for steady, cheerful, reliable, total service; typically, blows fell.[25]

Ill-treatment of house servants arose from a variety of sources besides the obvious ones. More than a few mistresses hated pretty young maids who had attracted, or were feared to have attracted, the attentions of the white men of the house or who had caught the eye of Young Missus' suitor. In such cases the punitive violence could reach terrible proportions. Sometimes, master and mistress did not enjoy their life together and took out their frustrations on each other's favorite servants or on anyone close at hand. In other cases, the master might protect the servants against an unwarranted outburst by the mistress—or vice versa—only to have the restrained and sullen party wait for a legitimate excuse to give the intended victims a double dose. The white women became aggressors much more often than their husbands, in part because of sexual jealousies and frustrations, but also because the men had field hands to vent their spleen upon. In the close conditions of life in the Big House anything and everything could trigger violence, including violence against a favorite later regretted by its perpetrator.[26]

When masters and mistresses controlled the urge to violence, they often settled for insults and deprecations, which plagued, angered, and even enraged servants, whose pride and sensitivity to being shamed far exceeded anything their masters usually appreciated. In many cases, ill-tempered masters and mistresses combined physical and verbal assaults. Austin Steward, who worked in a Big House in Virginia at the beginning of the nineteenth century, remarked:

> Mrs. Helm was a very industrious woman, and generally busy in her household affairs—sewing, knitting, and looking after the servants; but she was a great scold—continually finding fault with some

of the servants, and frequently punishing the young slaves herself, by striking them over the head with a heavy iron key, until the blood ran; or else whipping them with a cowhide, which she always kept by her side when sitting in her room. . . . No slave could possibly escape being punished.[27]

Among the more galling features of life in the Big House about which the slaves complained bitterly was having to stand constantly in the presence of whites. The line in the spiritual that says "I want to be in heaven sittin' down" particularly expresses the resentment of the house servants. Such small indignities and inconveniences could make life seem intolerable—but then, they only seem small to those who do not have to suffer them.[28]

According to the slaveholders, especially the ladies, the house servants were insufferably lazy, incompetent, dishonest, and impudent; even the best servants would periodically lapse into the impossible habits of the race. Olmsted quoted a southern lady as saying to a friend whom she had been visiting in New York:

> I can not tell you how much . . . I dread to go home and have to take care of our servants again. We have a much smaller family of whites than you, but we have twelve servants, and your two accomplish a great deal more, and do their work a great deal better than our twelve. You think your girls are very stupid, and that they give you much trouble: but it is as nothing. There is hardly one of our servants that can be trusted to do the simplest work without being stood over. If I order a room to be cleaned, or a fire to be made in a distant chamber, I never can be sure I am obeyed unless I go there and see for myself. If I send a girl out to get anything I want for preparing the dinner, she is as likely as not to forget what is wanted, and not to come back till after the time at which dinner should be ready. . . . And, when I reprimand them, they only say they don't mean to do anything wrong, or they won't do it again, all the time laughing as though it was all a joke.[29]

A writer in the *Southern Planter* charged in 1843 that Virginia mistresses did not manage their homes well because they depended on their servants.

> Most servants are incapable of understanding the explanation of anything which they cannot *see* with their *eyes*; therefore it is useless to tell them to do anything which requires a long explanation, or which they are not daily accustomed to. . . . One can do more work with two or three if they are employed closely together; probably some will not believe this, but let them try it. . . . Be always concise

in giving orders; for servants cannot retain many things in their heads at one time. Never scold when a servant neglects his duty, but *always punish* him, no matter how mildly, for mild treatment is the best; severity hardens them. Be firm in this, that no neglect go unpunished. Never let a servant say to you, "*I forgot it.*" That sentence, so often used, is no excuse at all.[30]

A usually even-tempered woman from New York who married into a family of big slaveholders in North Carolina wrote her parents that one house girl in New York would do as much as two on a southern plantation. The editor of the *Planters' Banner* of St. Mary's Parish, Louisiana, complained: "House servants have to be taught over and over almost every day of their lives things that white people almost learn by instinct, and when they have served twenty years in a house under good domestic instruction they are still heedless and unskillful." In the asperity of old age and postwar disillusionment, Charles Manigault asked himself how his former slaves were faring and answered: "I *know nor care not;* badly enough with some of them no doubt. But *this I do know,* that we with *less than half their number* of Servants are getting much more satisfactorily in service as, in all our domestic affairs *now* than when we had double their number of drones formerly." Mary Boykin Chesnut was gentler. "The Chesnut Negroes," she wrote in 1861, "are spoiled to a degree; but then they have such good manners, they are so polite you forget everything else. And they make you so comfortable, if you can afford ten to do the work of one servant." Some years later she added, "Ellen is a poor servant, but if I do a little work, it is quite enough to show me how dreadful it would be if I should have to do it all!"[31]

Mingo White, an ex-slave from Alabama, spoke of his mother: "Her task was too hard for any one person. She had to serve as maid to Mr. White's daughter, cook for all de hands, spin and card four cuts of thread a day, and den wash. Dere was one hundred and forty-four threads to de cut. If she didn't get all dis done she got fifty lashes dat night." And Jacob Branch of Texas added: "My pore mama! Every washday old Missy give her de beating." Old Missy, it seems, never thought the washing good enough. Many years after the war Kate Stone reflected, as she had not bothered to do while she was the young mistress of a Louisiana plantation, that the washerwomen had had to work long and exhausting hours.[32]

The antagonism gripped not only those masters and mistresses who made unreasonable demands and perhaps enjoyed indulging their passions when the demands could not be met, and not only those servants who could not or would not do a minimum amount of work. The very intimacy of life in the Big House meant that every fault and every passion appeared in full view. Only model masters and mistresses could constantly swallow their expectations and hold their tempers. Only model slaves could cheerfully and efficiently do everything demanded of them. For average masters, mistresses, and servants, the relationship proceeded fraught with frustration, outburst, and violence.

Young house servants, as well as some older ones, ran special risks attendant upon the intimacy of the Big House, for they often slept in the same room as their masters and mistresses. The more aristocratic families sometimes had separate bedrooms for husbands and wives, in which case a slave boy or girl or even an adult would attend to each. Where master and mistress slept together, as most did, either a boy or a girl would sleep in the room with them. Sometimes these youngsters were in their teens, well on their way to becoming men and women; sometimes they were much older. Normally, they slept on the floor; sometimes, in a bed of their own; occasionally, in the same bed as the master or mistress.[33] When a house servant did not sleep in the same room as master or mistress, one or more had free access and, at the least, had to enter quietly and unannounced to make the fire in the morning. Sarah Hicks Williams, who left New York for plantation life in North Carolina, assured her parents that house servants were treated with kindness and a degree of familiarity rarely seen in the North.

> They are in the parlor & in your rooms & all over. The first night we spent in the slaveholding states, we slept in a room without a lock —twice before we were up a waiting girl came into the room & while I was dressing in she came to look at me—she seemed perfectly at home, took up the locket with your miniatures in it & wanted to know if it was a watch. I showed it to her. "Well," said she, "I should think your Father and Mother were mighty old folks."[34]

One danger in this familiarity may be dismissed: I know of no cases of sexual violation of white women by their male servants. Rather, it was the black girls and young women who ran the risk of being forced or tempted into intimacies by their masters, and especially by their masters' sons, when the mistress was not at home. The servants, male and female, calmly attended their mistresses and walked in and out of their bedrooms; the mistresses felt no danger at all. On occasion, however, a servant decided he or she had had enough and murdered the white family.[35]

Field hands had one big advantage over house servants: firmer control of assigned periods of leisure time. The field hands had Sundays, certain prescribed holidays, and the late evening of each day to relax as best they could. House servants had to remain on call, for these were precisely the times at which visitors would descend on the plantation and have to be served. Even laws requiring Sunday as a day of rest for the slaves provided an exception for house servants.[36] When the extra work consisted in staying up all night to prepare a holiday barbecue for fellow slaves, the cooks and their helpers showed no resentment and usually welcomed the chance. The same chore for the whites called forth less enthusiasm.[37]

The house servants took these demands on their time in stride as the price to be paid for the advantages of their position, but for just that reason they had to feel those advantages in the first place. The more responsible and sensitive slaveholders appreciated the difficult position of their house servants and tried to make life easier for them. Mrs. Isaac Hilliard of Arkansas described nothing unusual in a diary entry for 1850: "Attend Church—unwilling to deprive [carriage] driver, every Sunday of his holy day, we walk." The Dabneys rotated slaves in and out of the Big House in order to give their regular house servants most Sundays off.[38] Edmund Ruffin took pleasure in the inconvenience attendant upon the absence of servants when he visited Governor Letcher of Virginia in 1860, for he thoroughly approved the decision to give them the day off despite the expected arrival of guests.[39] Marriah Hines, who had been a slave in Virginia, recalled that her white folks had allowed their servants to prepare dinner on Saturday, to be eaten cold on Sunday. Sometimes, she added, especially when a preacher would be visiting, the slaves showed their appreciation by voluntarily preparing hot meals on Sunday at the cost of their leisure time.[40]

House servants were treated with consideration on the plantations of the more thoughtful planters, but as a rule even there they had to be constantly on call. In 1900, Kate Stone wrote about her old cook, Lucy: "Her office was no sinecure, as there were always from thirteen to maybe twenty white people and all the house servants to cook three abundant warm meals for every day. . . ." Miss Stone admitted that her view had changed: "I know our cook was a hard-worked creature. Then, we never thought about it."[41]

House slaves and field slaves did not generally constitute separate and mutually hostile groups; on the contrary, a variety of circumstances, including the exposure of the house servants to much abuse, bound them closely together. According to one of the main tenets of the legend of status division, house servants disdained to marry field hands. Blacks as well as whites so testify. Rosa Starke, formerly a slave for a haughty, aristocratic, highly class-conscious family, insisted:

> A house nigger man might swoop down and mate wid a field hand's good lookin' daughter, now and then, for pure love of her, but you never see a house gal lower herself by marryin' and matin' wid a common field-hand nigger. Dat offend de white folks, 'specially de young misses, who liked de business of match makin' and matin' of de young slaves.[42]

Yet, apart from the status-bound great plantations—apart, that is, from a small elite—house servants regularly married field hands with no suggestion of loss of caste. The three-quarters of all slaves who lived on units of fifty or less slaves could hardly afford such pretensions, for the staff of house servants did not reach a size appropriate for inbreeding; and even on the largest plantations the status lines appeared only in some cases, probably not nearly a majority. Since women house servants usually outnumbered men, nature took its course. Marriages between house slaves and field slaves occurred without notice on all except a few plantations. Mildred Graves of Virginia explained: "I was a house gal, an' stayed in de house, an' he work in de field, so we didn't git chance to git together often." But love had its way, and he proposed. "I say all right 'cause I was tired livin' in de house where dey wasn't no fun."[43] Some whites tried to impose caste distinctions upon resistant house women, who often wished to accept the attentions of field hands and whose carryings-on around the house looked scandalous to their self-appointed white guardians.[44] Frequently, house women married such prestigious hands as drivers and skilled workers, but many married common field hands, however much their masters and mistresses disapproved.[45]

House servants and field hands often came from a single family. Commonly, the children of house slaves went to the fields or vice versa; brothers and sisters and uncles and nephews regularly fell into separate categories. Jake Green of Alabama recalled that his father worked in the house, one uncle drove the carriage, and two others served as foremen of the plow and hoe hands respectively. When needed, all worked in the fields: "An dem fo' niggers could chop much cotton in a day as de mule could plow."[46] Caroline Wright of Virginia and her sister worked in the house while their parents and brothers worked in the fields. Members of a single slave family could run the gamut of occupations and yet live closely as a family.[47]

Some house slaves lived in the quarters, many more in cabins that stood closer to the Big House; but almost all who did not work in the aristocratic Big Houses of the plantation legend sought a close social relationship with the field slaves. Life would have been dreary and lonely without it. Some masters tried to reduce these contacts. Hugh Davis, with a large plantation in Alabama, declared: "All communication between house servants and those at the cabins strictly forbidden after [9 P.M.]."[48] But, Austin Steward pointed out, the social intercourse of house and field slaves did not necessarily destroy caste lines and might even reinforce them.

> House servants were, of course, "the stars" of the party; all eyes were turned to them to see how they conducted [themselves]. . . . The field hands . . . look to the house servant as a pattern of politeness and gentility. And indeed, it is often the only method of obtaining any knowledge of the manners of what is called "genteel society"; hence they are even regarded as a privileged class; and are sometimes greatly envied, while others are bitterly hated.[49]

Steward's remarks applied, however, to the small elite group, not to the generality, and even they, airs or no, showed up at the plantation balls.

On farms and small plantations most house servants had to do double duty as field hands. Only on the largest plantations did a clear-cut division between house and field become possible; and not even there did house servants always escape entirely from field labor, for the harvest season in particular demanded the services of everyone who could be spared from other tasks. Other activities such as corn shucking drew the house servants into a more pleasant and often welcome camaraderie with the field hands. All except a small minority of house servants experienced the hardest field work now and then and often developed some sympathy for their brothers and sisters in the quarters.[50]

Some slaves worked in the Big House only because they lacked the physical strength for field work. Such work as spinning and making clothes fell to women who were or pretended to be unfit for outside work. Catherine Devereaux Edmondston cried out in 1860: "I wish I could for once see a hearty negro woman . . . who was not 'poorly, thank God!' To be 'poorly' is their aim and object, as it ends in the house and spinning."[51]

Masters sometimes punished disobedient or unruly house servants by sending them to the fields, where their pretensions, if any, would be undermined. House servants normally resented such punitive action. Hugh Davis of Alabama took a $750 loss when a demoted coachman burned down a barn in revenge.[52] Yet, house servants who were sold often ended by being reassigned to field work, or to a combination of house and field work if they had been sold to a smaller place. Such transfers appear to have been resented more for the inconvenience than for loss of caste.[53]

The social distance between house servants and field hands even on the larger plantations was reduced in childhood. Many children destined for field work began by helping around the house from, say, age nine to twelve. As a result of this early training they could more easily be impressed into house service in their adult years when emergencies arose. Enduring friendships grew between field hands and the house servants with whom they had played as children, as well as the older ones who had come to fancy them as pets.[54]

When well-treated house servants witnessed overseers' cruelty to field slaves they reacted, so far as the evidence speaks at all, sympathetically and compassionately. When they too suffered indignities and cruelties, their sense of solidarity with the field hands became all the stronger.[55] A male house servant insisted that a real difference in quality separated those who, like himself, worked in the Big House from ordinary field hands, but he added: "They would steal the pigs. I would help them out, too. I never would steal, but if they tell me to say some certain thing, I would always do it."[56]

House slaves and field slaves often helped each other to run away.[57] The attitude of the house servants no doubt sometimes smacked of *noblesse oblige* and showed some caste feeling, but it also reflected a strong sense of racial identification and responsibility. The elite mulatto house servants of Washington, D.C., for example, responded with extraordinary kindness and generosity to the influx of black field hands during the war despite the danger posed by the whites' increasing tendency to lump them all together as "niggers."[58]

These manifold bonds between house servants and field hands had far-reaching consequences, including a growing sense of common oppression and national solidarity. Had the elitist patterns of Charleston, New Orleans, Natchez, and the great low-country districts set the norm, an enormous schism might have torn the slaves' ranks apart and possibly condemned the field hands to that degradation so often attributed to them.[59] The conditions of plantation and farm life in the Old South created powerful impediments to any such tendency among the slaves and encouraged considerable sympathy across the lines of color and pseudoclass in the slave community.

The house servants' inclination to identify with their masters constantly ran into limits, which reminded even the most caste-conscious that they too were slaves. Their masters resembled other employers of household labor in at least one important respect: they acted as if their house servants had neither eyes nor ears—as if they hardly existed at all. Just as many parents will speak between themselves and with their guests about the qualities and deportment of their children as if the children were not present, so the slaveholders, in the words of Frances Trollope, talked of their slaves, "of their condition, of their faculties, of their conduct, exactly as if they were incapable of hearing."[60] Olmsted reported from a plantation in Virginia that the master "frequently addressed the servant familiarly, and drew him into our conversation as if he were a family friend, better informed, on some local and domestic points, than himself,"[61] but generally the slaves heard themselves discussed in a manner that could only generate shame and resentment.

Some house servants who felt their inferior social position acutely interpreted their masters' attitude as a sign of confidence that required special loyalty and protection, but many others drew closer to their brothers and sisters in the quarters. The political danger to the whites became apparent. "The negroes are in every family," said David Bard of Pennsylvania in 1804 while leading a fight to tax slave imports in order to restrict the size of the slave population. "They are waiting on every table; they are present on numerous occasions when the conversation turns on political subjects, and cannot fail to catch ideas that will excite discontentment with their condition."[62]

The slaveholders experienced nothing unique. Tsar Nicholas addressed the representatives of the St. Petersburg nobility in 1848:

> These people [house serfs] generally are demoralized and are threats to society and their own masters. I ask you to be extremely cautious with respect to them. Frequently, at table or in an evening conversation, you discuss political or governmental or similar matters, forgetting that these people listen to you, and from their ignorance and stupidity construe your conversation in their own way, that is, incorrectly. Moreover, these conversations, harmless among educated people, often suggest to your servants ideas that they never would have thought of themselves. That is very dangerous![63]

The secession crisis and the war years revealed the extent of the links between house and field slaves. The desertions to the Union lines could never have proceeded so far had the field slaves not been well informed by the house servants about the course of the war and the shifting battle lines.[64] The Chesnuts, more alert than most, began speaking French at their dinner parties. "We are," wrote Mrs. Chesnut, "using French against Africa."[65]

Some house servants openly identified with their masters against the field hands, but many others did not. Uncle Jackson of Virginia, who had virtual immunity from whipping because of his long service to the white family, made the perfect sentry to warn illegally assembled slaves of the approach of white men. Others relayed information when patrols were expected. Discussions in the Big House of the pending sale or whipping of some field hand would quickly be passed on to the intended victim so that he might make his escape.[66] Andy Marion of South Carolina recalled: "In slavery I was de carriage driver . . . I used to hear lots of things from behind me, while drivin' de folks and sayin' nothin'."[67] Some slaves, like Red Ann, never admitted their literacy, read the newspapers in the Big House, and carried essential information to the quarters.[68] A great deal more than the mindlessness and carelessness attributed to them accounts for the house servants' never closing a door in the house unless specifically ordered to.[69]

Many outsiders found the apparently advantageous condition of the house servants of the big planters, especially the Mammies, nurses, body servants, and personal maids, distasteful. Eleanor J. W. Baker of Massachusetts, on a visit to Charleston in 1848, wrote in her journal:

They are mostly well fed and well dressed & well cared for, & the house servants of the rich are often-times a lazy, pampered set. I look with perfect wonder at the indulgence & patience of Southern housewives. The ladies take as much care of their slaves as if they were children & I am quite shocked to see the familiar way in which many are treated. Then again you see the reverse treatment.[70]

The disapproval fell less upon the personal deportment and work habits of the servants than upon the intimacy across racial and class lines that they exposed. Frederick Law Olmsted sat on a train in Virginia and watched a white woman, her daughter, a stout black woman, and a pretty mulatto girl board and sit together.

They all talked and laughed together, and the girls munched confectionery out of the same paper, with a familiarity and closeness of intimacy that would have been noticed with astonishment, if not with manifest displeasure, in almost any chance company at the North. When the negro is definitely a slave, it would seem that the alleged natural antipathy of the white race to associate with him is lost.[71]

The black and white women of the Big House needed each other. They lived as part of a single family, although by no means always a happy, peaceful, or loving one. If black Mammies and nurses usually delivered the white babies, white mistresses sometimes delivered the black and more often helped look after both mother and infant. If Mammies and nurses raised the white children, mistresses helped raise the black, so that the children, white and black, were constantly underfoot and a joy and a trial to all. Mistresses with drunken, dissolute, spendthrift, or brutal husbands poured out their troubles to their maids, who poured out their own troubles to their mistresses and to each other. If a woman, white or black, woke up at night terrified by a dream of impending death, she would run to her maid or her mistress for comfort.[72]

The great planters and especially their sons found their body servants indispensable. Those with access to Charleston, Louisville, Natchez, and of course New Orleans, not to mention less notorious high spots, gambled, whored, and brawled in a manner worthy of the greatest of those medieval and early modern aristocracies they so much admired. Josiah Henson described a master's debauchery and a body servant's role. Although primarily a driver, he served as his master's personal servant as well.

> My master's habits were such as were common enough among the dissipated planters of the neighborhood; and one of their frequent practices was to assemble on Saturday or Sunday . . . and gamble, run horses, or fight game-cocks, discuss politics, and drink whisky and brandy and water all day long. Perfectly aware that they would not be able to find their own way home at night, each one ordered his body-servant to come after him and help him home. . . . Quarrels and brawls of the most violent description were frequent consequences of these meetings; and whenever they became especially dangerous, and glasses were thrown, dirks drawn, and pistols fired, it was the duty of the slaves to rush in, and each one drag his master from the fight, and carry him home. To tell the truth, this was a part of my business for which I felt no reluctance. . . . I knew I was doing for him what he could not do for himself, and showing my superiority to others, and acquiring their respect in some degree, at the same time.[73]

The mistresses and maids back home had a few things to talk about among themselves.

Mistress and servants found themselves bound together in mutual dependency in spite of themselves. The house servants required the protection and support of their white folks, much as the field hands did, and in addition, they needed to maintain their special advantages. The whites required that the house servants, like the field hands, work to provide for them, but in addition, they required their love and emotional support far beyond anything the servants needed in return. In the reciprocal dependency of slavery, especially in the Big House, the slaves needed masters and mistresses they could depend on; they did not need masters and mistresses to love them. But the whites needed their servants' love and trust. The slaves had the upper hand, and many of them learned how to use it.

The black and white women of the Big House reached the peak of intimacy in their involvement in each other's love lives. The young white ladies occupied much of their time in exchanging love letters with beaux and arranging rendezvous, the safe execution of which—not to mention half the fun—required secrecy and cunning in a society that demanded female chastity and feared sexual scandal. Loyal and discreet allies among the house servants became the *sine qua non* of romance. As Annie Laurie Broidrick of Mississippi insisted, "Many a romantic tale was confided by mistress and maid to each other during the hours the hair was being brushed and the soft wrapper donned."[74]

The servants often had access to information not easily obtained by their mistresses. If the beau lived on a nearby plantation, the servants of the two households probably knew each other or could arrange to know each other. The young lady's servants then became privy to the beau's private life and could report on his character, morals, and other love interests. They could learn much about his true feelings for their mistress. When he lived a bit farther away, this access to private information might even be enhanced, for an excuse could be found to send a servant to his home, and she would be likely to receive an invitation to spend the night among his house servants. Sometimes, the servants decided against a gentleman whose attentions their mistress fancied and were not bashful about saying so. The servants appropriated to themselves some of the duties and rights of Big Sister, not to say Mother.[75]

The presumption cut both ways. Young Missus normally expected to have something to say about whom her favorite servants cavorted with and did not hesitate to intervene in their marital affairs. Yet, the black women seem to have protected their independence better than the white. In any case, the bonds between mistress and servant grew stronger with each shared secret. And so did the boldness and pretensions of the servants, who readily felt the strength that shared secrets carry with them. Machado de Assis shrewdly suggests in one of his novels: "The lie was one of those [told by] servants who are quick to reply to visitors that 'madam has gone out,' when madam does not wish to talk to anyone. This complicity has a certain relish. The sin shared in common makes the condition of the persons involved, for the time being, equal...."[76] And the dangers inherent in the servant's carrying the feeling of equality too far appear in a dramatic passage from Lorca's *House of Bernarda Alba*, in which the servant, La Poncia, rebukes the *senõra* for the way in which she has raised her daughters:

> *Bernarda:* Hold your tormenting tongue!
> *Poncia:* One can't even talk to you. Do we not share secrets?
> *Bernarda:* We do not. You're a servant, and I pay you. Nothing more.[77]

The intimacy of shared secret lives brought the black and white women of the Big House together in a relationship of mutual dependence, but it thereby threatened the mistress-servant relation itself. At its best, the women's feelings for each other would deepen, but the inevitable resentments easily generated moments of hatred and fierce violence.

When the house servants could, they risked pressing their masters and mistresses into a reversal of roles. They throve on the manifest dependency of their superiors. When the mistress of the Dabney plantation died and her daughters had to step in, the servants made their bid for supremacy. Susan Dabney Smedes recalled: "These were days of trial and perplexity for the young mistresses. The old house-servants, though having at heart an affection for them, considered or pretended to consider them too young to know what they wanted." Mrs. Smedes paraphrased the servants' attitude: "Besides, had they not known these young ladies ever since they were born? And did they not call them mammy or aunt in consideration of superior age?" The young white ladies had no easy time establishing their authority and might have failed if Mammy had not rallied to them and helped put the others in their place.[78]

Usually, the dependency stayed within limits and allowed the ladies to maintain a condescending view. Mrs. Chesnut allowed her servants to order her to rest after working too hard: "I am very docile now, and I obeyed orders."[79] And Virginia Tunstall Clay, wife of the Confederate senator from Alabama, found charming her altercation with a maid as they were preparing to leave for Richmond. The maid started to pack an evening dress.

> "We are going to war, Emily. We shall have no need for velvet or jewels. We are going to nurse the sick; not to dress and dance."
>
> Emily rebelled: "There's bound to be somethin' goin' on, Miss 'Ginnia, an' I ain't goin' to let my Mistis be outshined by Mis'——
> —an' dem other ladies."
>
> There were many occasions afterwards when I blessed the thoughtfulness of my little maid; for there were heroes to dine and to cheer in Richmond, both civil and military, and somber garments are a sorry garb in which to greet or brighten the thoughts of men tired with the strain of fighting for a government.[80]

Wherever slavery existed, the mistresses yielded to increased dependency. In the French islands an eighteenth-century print has a planter's wife order her slave, "Mimbo, tell Quasheba to tell Dido to tell Sue to come and pick up my needle." The slave replies that Quasheba has gone to market and will not be back for three hours and that Sue will be scratching master's legs for two. "Oh, dear me, one must have the patience of Job to live in this world with any comfort. Here I must wait two hours for my needle."[81] In the Old South the ladies, according to one of their number, had their own refrain:

> Oh, that I had a million slaves or more,
> To catch the rain drops as they pour.[82]

The reality ranged far from such wishes. The ladies kept busy in a thousand ways and worked hard enough themselves, but the ideal of leisure took hold. Many succumbed to the temptation to let strong servants have their way and run their lives; most fell into some compromise for the sake of their sanity as well as their comfort. When they did, they undermined their image as all-powerful beings and emboldened their slaves in proportion.

Nor did the men escape. An old body servant reported that his master could not brush his teeth in the morning unless he had his toothbrush handed to him.[83] And a slaveholding Confederate soldier who had to send his body servant home insisted upon his early return. "He is a great darky—worth his weight in gold even in these hard times," he glowed, explaining, "He can tell you what things I principally need & more fully than I can write—he knows more about it anyway than I do, knows more about what I have and what I need—he attends to it all."[84]

Not all these incidents were so innocent. Many mistresses and some masters became imprisoned by their dependency, and the slaves knew as much. A former slave from Texas said that she had hardly known herself to be a slave, " 'cause I was really only ole Mis' housekeeper; kept house, took care of her money and everything; she was one o' these kinds women that couldn't keep up with nothing, and I just handled her money like it was mine almost." A coachman in the Sea Islands spoke more sharply about the farm girl his master had married. She was, he said, "as much a lady as anybody—couldn't get a glass of water for herself nor nothin'."[85] The whites' reliance upon their slaves created much of that family feeling they were so fond of talking about, but it also often reduced the whites' prestige and gave the slaves a vantage point from which to assess their own capabilities.

In view of the close bonds forged in the Big House, the death of a favorite slave fell heavily on the whites as the loss of a friend rather than of an investment. Close relationships developed more readily among the women than among the men, but the men too had deep and intimate friendships, if such a word may be applied to so unequal a relationship. Frequently, a body servant would be buried close to his master, sometimes according to the most careful instructions in the master's will.[86] The many eulogies by slaveholders upon departed body servants reveal both the depths of genuine affection and the contribution that such servants made to their masters' self-esteem. In 1846, Hugh Lawson Clay of Alabama wrote to Susanna Clay:

> Jim died. . . . You know how devotedly attached and faithful he was to me, and know what must be my feelings in writing, the melancholy intelligence of his death. . . . No other servant in the place would have been attended in sickness with as much care and constancy as he was. The young gentlemen of the place, when I became prostrated by anxiety and fatigue from watching, sat by his bedside, *day and night*, administering to his wants rather with the solicitude of friends, than with a thought of his being a slave and their inferior. . . . I feel desolate—my most devoted friend is gone and *his place* can never be supplied by another placed in his situation.[87]

In 1854, Everard Green Baker of Mississippi penned a long obituary to his favorite servant—longer, in fact, than the touching one to the wife he apparently loved deeply.

OBITUARY—

Died the 30th of June, 1854 (yesterday Friday about breakfast time) at the residence of Dr. Wm. I. Menn in Panola, my faithful & dearly beloved servant Jack, aged about 65 years—He has been in my mothers family since he was quite small, served my mother faithfully during his life time, & stood high in her regard. Since I have owned him he has been true to me in all respects.—He was an obedient trusty servant to his master & mistress, an affectionate husband & father to his family—I never knew him to steal nor lie & he ever set a moral & industrious example to those around him.—I was in to see him on last Wednesday & he seemed quite weak but well otherwise —He was attacked last winter with diarrhoea which was followed by the dropsy—The water all left him in two days which prostrated him. But the doctor seemed to think that tonics would enable him to regain his strength & Jack when I saw him on Wednesday seemed hopeful as to his situation & I left him cheered up with the belief that he would soon mend—He seemed mending up to the very moment that he became insensible—no one was with him at the time but it seems he attempted to get up to a chair & fainted & fell against the chair—& was discovered soon after it must have occurred in that situation. He never spoke & died about one o'clock P. M. same day. —I regret that he did not see his family before death. I would have sent some of them onto him on Sunday—the Doctor & myself had no idea his end was so near—and I do not think Jack either. He fainted in consequence of trying to get up & his system was unable to circulate the blood in an upright position—Altho' he died suddenly yet his long indisposition together with his age must have caused him to know that he could not live much longer—& altho' he was not a professing Christian—yet no man white or black I have ever known was more exemplary in his conduct. He was kind— moral—sober—industrious, obedient—& honest—I never knew one who kept closer to the path of rectitude—He was unwilling to die & who is there not who has a good home & a loving family?—I shall ever cherish his memory, & now vow most solemnly to repay to those he has left behind & who were dear to him, the kindness & gratitude which his services on earth has merited. He deserves a better reward than can be given in this world.—

"Requiescat in pace."[88]

Ruffin Thomson of Mississippi wrote home from the war to praise his servant, Preston, and to report on his health and activity. They had grown up together and had remained close. Preston suddenly died, apparently from pneumonia, and his distraught young master filled eight pages of a letter in describing the circumstances, the soldier's burial he had arranged, and his sorrow. Such instances typified the relationship between a planter and his man as seen through white eyes.[89]

On the slaves' side, the ambivalence inherent in close-quarter living with the whites rarely showed itself so forcefully as when a master or mistress came to grief. "Massa Garlic," said Delia Garlic, who had been a field hand on his Louisiana plantation, "had two boys in de War. When dey went off de massa and missus cried, but it made us glad to see dem cry. Dey made us cry so much." Annie Hawkins, an ex-slave from a small farm in Georgia, commented on the death of her dissolute and vicious master: "He finally killed himself drinking, and I remember Old Mistress called us in to look at him in his coffin. We all marched by him slow like, and I jest happened to look up and caught my sister's eye and we both just natchally laughed—Why shouldn't we? We was glad he was dead." When William Wells Brown heard that his master had become ill, "Nothing brought more joy to my heart than that intelligence. I prayed fervently for him—not for his recovery, but for his death."[90] But these extreme reactions occurred even less frequently than their opposite, and neither alone says more than the obvious.

The narratives of former slaves describe much genuine grief at the death of masters and mistresses, apart from the testimony of those who told their interviewers what they thought they should and of those who might have been embarrassed to admit having enjoyed another's death. Abram Harris, who had labored on a small farm in South Carolina, remembered the master's son, who died in battle during the war: "It sure did hurt me when Marse Hampton got kilt, 'cause I loved dat white man. He sure was good to me."[91] Ezra Adams, who had been a field hand while still a boy near Columbia, South Carolina, said, "When marster died, dat was my first real sorrow. Three years later, missus passed 'way, dat was de time of my second sorrow." Ellen Botts, from a big sugar plantation in Louisiana, had had a kind master. "Us niggers," she recalled, "went to de graveyard and us sho' cry over old Marse."[92] When the master had been a particularly kind man, the slaves' grief came naturally, but the many expressions of grief at the death of masters of average temperament and behavior demand closer attention.

Austin Steward suggested the range of response in describing how the slaves saw a tough mistress die in great agony: "The slaves were all deeply affected by the scene; some doubtless truly lamented the death of their mistress; others rejoiced that she was no more, and all were more or less frightened." Mrs. Kemble heard the slaves of an absentee master express distress at his illness: "Massa die, what become of all him people?"[93] If the master had not been a brute, the slaves had reason to lament and to be frightened. The death of a master threatened a property division and sale of a plantation that, whatever else it was, was the only home they knew; it threatened a scattering of Ole Massa's people—of the family, white and black—even if nuclear family units were respected. It threatened, if not disaster, at least disorder and difficult adjustment. Ole Massa may not have been ideal, but the slaves had learned, through many painful experiments, how to handle him. Now they would have to begin all over again with a new and often unknown quantity.

The grief had another and deeper meaning. To turn it around: when a mistress in Tennessee broke down in tears at the death of a slave whom she had beaten repeatedly over the years, a black woman remarked caustically, "Huh, crying because she didn't have nobody to whip no more."[94] However much truth may be found in this reaction, the death of any human being brings home to us our own fate. Masters and slaves alike, when they had not totally surrendered their humanity, had to be moved by the death of someone they knew so well. Many of the slaves' expressions of mourning may have been no more than simple decency plus a renewed awareness of their own mortality. For masters and slaves, whites and blacks, these elementary human reactions had a special significance, for they brought out clearly the extent to which plantation slavery in general and life in the Big House in particular had tied them together, however antagonistically. Neither could easily make any statement about the human condition and their own place within it without some reference to the life of the other.

The intimacy of the Big House and its resultant ambivalence come into sharper focus with those most privileged of slaves—the body servants and Mammies. Slaveholders responded with disbelief when the Confederate government, faced with imminent collapse, issued a new ration law in 1864 that would have made it difficult for gentlemen officers to maintain personal servants in the army.[95] However much the gentlemen would have missed the amenities guaranteed by a constant attendant, much more was at issue for them. They, after all, were enduring every hardship in the field and can hardly be thought unwilling to sacrifice some creature comforts. The presence of their body servants provided a needed confidant in times of great emotional stress, as well as the most intimate contact with their normal lives at home.

The resultant intimacy allowed the servants to take liberties. They knew too much of their masters' character and weaknesses to idolize them, although they often genuinely admired and liked them. A great deal of affectionate teasing followed, as did a certain amount of malicious criticism in witty garb. A servant, making up his master's bed in a Confederate army camp, received sharp instructions to be sure it was long enough. The servant grinned, looked up, and chided, "S'pose, Master William, you'se now grown taller since you was major."[96]

The perfect body servant comes to us through white testimony, or rather, testimonial. When Charles C. Jones, Jr., moved to Savannah, his parents decided that it was time for him to have his own personal servant. They picked a man carefully and made sure he learned how to cook and wash, among other things, so that he might perform any duty and assist in any emergency.[97] Henry Clay's valet, Charles, accompanied him to Washington and elsewhere. As reported by a traveler in 1845, Charles, the perfect servant, functioned as

> a kind of second master of household to Mr. Clay, and enjoys the greatest trust and confidence. To him can the keys of the wine-cellar be given without fear and on all occasions where help was needed, Mr. C. called for Charles. Charles brought us wine, Charles was at the door, at the carriage, at the gate, every where in fact, and as polite and civil as a man asking for office. He is a fine looking middle-sized negro, about thirty years old and I do not believe he could be drawn from Mr. Clay except by absolute animal force, so great is his devotion to him.[98]

Amelia Thompson Watts, when in St. Landry Parish, Louisiana, described a typical specimen of the small group of highly trained body servants to the great planters:

> There were several servants who waited on the table, and my grandfather's body servant, Uncle Lea always stood back of his chair and poured the wine. Claret was always drunk with an equal quantity of water. Uncle Lea had special care of his master [Judge Seth Lewis], and always accompanied him when he held Court in the other parishes. They always went on horseback, and Uncle Lea packed the saddle bags, took care of the horses, shaved his master, took care of his clothes, and assisted him in dressing. Naturally he fell heir to all of Grandpa's discarded clothing, and it was hard to say which had the more personal dignity.[99]

The body servant who shared his young master's danger at the front during the war and even forfeited his own life to protect him assumed a central place in the postbellum plantation legend. There is no reason to doubt that most served as faithfully as claimed; neither is there reason to doubt that a significant number did not —significant in that enough desertions occurred to underscore the fundamental ambivalence that entered into all such relationships. Desertions and duplicity among trusted body servants did not appear for the first time during the war. Such cases have reached us from eighteenth-century sources as well as nineteenth. On the aristocratic Eastern Shore, William Paca's "complete body servant" took off for the North one day with no prior indication of trouble. The grumpy Landon Carter rebuked his faithful Moses ever so slightly only to have him leave the plantation at the head of a party of runaways. Others took advantage of their ability to forge passes and left when they could.[100] Some servants deserted their masters to join the Union cause or simply to get away. That trusted servants of patriarchal planters like R. F. W. Allston were among them tells us that none could be taken for granted.[101]

Others stayed with their masters but not exactly faithfully. Taking advantage of their knowledge and position, some ran private black-market operations and looted their masters' resources. Others, while not necessarily disloyal to their particular masters, returned home from the front to brief their fellow slaves on the course of the war and to encourage their desertion.[102]

The complex character of these body servants emerged in full view during and after the war. The formidable Prince Rivers—a heroic and commanding figure in Colonel Higginson's black army unit—had been a personal servant and first-class coachman before joining the Union cause and rising to postwar prominence. Others also went on to political careers, including such men as State Assemblyman Ambrose Henderson and United States Senator Blanche K. Bruce of Mississippi. Their old ties to the whites appeared in their political moderation during Reconstruction, but so did their sense of responsibility toward their fellow blacks.[103]

The Daughters of the Confederacy suggested in 1923 that Congress set aside a site in Washington for a suitable memorial to the antebellum plantation Mammy. The good ladies had picked their symbol carefully, for no figure stands out so prominently in the moonlight-and-magnolias legend of the Old South. The hostile reaction of so many blacks confirmed the judgment. As the Phillips tradition in southern historiography has waned and as the old regime has come under increasingly critical scrutiny, Mammy has had a steadily worsening press. She remains the most elusive and important black presence in the Big House. To understand her is to move toward understanding the tragedy of plantation paternalism.

First, the white legend. Lewis H. Blair, attacking racial segregation in 1889, wrote:

> Most of us above thirty years of age had our mammy, and generally she was the first to receive us from the doctor's hands, and was the first to proclaim, with heart bursting with pride, the arrival of a fine baby. Up to the age of ten we saw as much of the mammy as of the

mother, perhaps more, and we loved her quite as well. The mammy first taught us to lisp and to walk, played with us and told us wonderful stories, taught us who made us and who redeemed us, dried our tears and soothed our bursting hearts, and saved us many a well-deserved whipping. . . .[104]

A few years later, Annie Laurie Broidrick of Mississippi provided her own sketch:

Consequential, important, and next in authority to the owners were the old "black mammies," who raised and superintended the care of the children. As they grew old they were exempt from hard work, and ruled white and black with impartial severity. Our old "mammy Harriet" raised two or three generations of children. We had the greatest love for her, but it was tempered with fear, for she never overlooked a fault and was ready to tell "old miss" how "de chillun was carrying on." She never allowed us to go into the kitchen. That was considered extremely low taste; and she would say with an emphatic shake of her old, turbaned head, "Nobody but niggers go in thar. Sit in de parlor wid'er book in y'or hand like little white ladies." Once mammy was in disgrace, when she slapped my mother, after her marriage. My father said he used some pretty strong language to the old lady, and she never repeated the offense.

But if Mammy punished, Mammy forgave and consoled. She would wipe away the white child's tears while defending her mistress's action: "But, honey, why does yer make y'r ma so mad, acting like sich po'r white trash?" The report concluded:

Numbers of little "darkies" were always around and the children often begged the privilege of having them in the house to show off an accomplishment, such as a dance, or a tune on the jewsharp or banjo. I have seen dusky feet flying over the velvet carpet in the large drawing-room, and heard the hearty applause given by master and mistress. . . . Then mammy would come in, "hustle" them all out, grumbling that she "would like to know what white folks meant having all these niggers bout starting things."[105]

Without contradicting Mrs. Broidrick's implicit reading, a skeptic might at least wonder if Mammy was not as shamed by the spectacle being made of the black children as she was concerned with the maintenance of class and racial mores in the Big House.

This picture did not stem simply from postwar nostalgia; it had already appeared in antebellum days in the expressions of those who sought to paint slavery in the brightest possible colors. Edward A. Pollard wrote during the 1850s in his well-known defense of the regime, *Black Diamonds:* "Aunt Debby is an aged colored female of the very highest respectability, and with her white apron, and her head mysteriously enveloped in the brightest of bandannas, she looks (to use one of her own rather obscure similes) 'like a new pin.' " Aunt Debby slept in the Big House and referred to slaves of lesser social position as "de niggers." She was, in Pollard's word, "spoiled" and used to having her own way. "If at times her mistress is roused to dispute her authority, Aunt Debby is sure to resume the reins when quiet ensues." She particularly upset her mistress by using stern methods on the house servants, including rather free use of the whip. She professed the deepest religious sentiment, which Pollard thought was "not to be taken at its word" in view of her irrepressible *joie de vivre.* Her death, the first he had witnessed, brought unfeigned sorrow and grief to the household.[106]

Mammy comes through the black sources in much the same way, but only so far. Lindey Faucette of North Carolina remembered her grandmother, Mammie Beckie, who "toted de keys," whose word had the force of law with Marse John and Mis' Annie, and who slept in the bed with her mistress when the master's law practice kept him in town all night. Alice Sewell of Alabama especially recalled the plantation Mammy's comforting the relatives of deceased slaves, arranging for the burial, and leading the funeral services. Ellen Botts of Louisiana noted: "All de niggers have to stoop to Aunt Rachel like they curtsy to Missy."[107] And Adeline Johnson, who had served as a Mammy in South Carolina, spoke in her old age in accents that would have warmed the hearts of those Daughters of the Confederacy:

> I hope and prays to git to hebben. Whether I's white or black when I git dere, I'll be satisfied to see my Savior dat my old marster worshipped and my husband preached 'bout. I wants to be in hebben wid all my white folks, just to wait on them and love them and serve them, sorta lak I did in slavery time. Dat will be 'nough hebben for Adeline.[108]

Who were these Mammies? What did they actually do?[109] Primarily, the Mammy raised the white children and ran the Big House either as the mistress's executive officer or her *de facto* superior. Her power extended over black and white so long as she exercised restraint, and she was not to be crossed. She carried herself like a surrogate mistress—neatly attired, barking orders, conscious of her dignity, full of self-respect. She played the diplomat and settled the interminable disputes that arose among the house servants; when diplomacy failed, she resorted to her whip and restored order. She served as confidante to the children, the mistress, and even the master. She expected to be consulted on the love affairs and marriages of the white children and might even be consulted on the business affairs of the plantation. She presided over the dignity of the whole plantation and taught the courtesies to the white children as well as to those black children destined to work in the Big House. On the small and medium-sized plantations she had to carry much of the house work herself, and her relationship to the field slaves drew closer. In general, she gave the whites the perfect slave—a loyal, faithful, contented, efficient, conscientious member of the family who always knew her place; and she gave the slaves a white-approved standard of black behavior. She also had to be a tough, worldly-wise, enormously resourceful woman; that is, she had to develop all the strength of character not usually attributed to an Aunt Jane.

Mammy supposedly paid more attention to the white children than to her own. Even W. E. B. Du Bois, who was rarely taken in by appearances and legends, thought so. He described the Mammy as "one of the most pitiful of the world's Christs. . . . She was an embodied Sorrow, an anomaly crucified on the cross of her own neglected children for the sake of the children of masters who bought and sold her as they bought and sold cattle."[110] The Mammy typically took her responsibilities to the white family as a matter of high personal honor and in so doing undoubtedly could not give her own children as much love and attention as they deserved. House nannies, white and black, free and slave, have often fallen into this trap, as Olmsted, for one, observed.[111] But willful neglect of or indifference to their own children cannot be deduced from their behavior. In particular, the idea that the Mammies actually loved the white children more than their own rests on nothing more than wishful white perceptions. That they loved the white children they themselves raised—hardly astonishing for warm, sensitive, generous women—in no way proves that they loved their own children the less. Rather, their position in the Big House, including their close attention to the white children sometimes at the expense of their own, constituted the firmest protection they could have acquired for themselves and their immediate families. Mammies did not often have to worry about being sold or about having their husbands or children sold. The sacrifices they made for the whites earned them genuine affection in return, which provided a guarantee of protection, safety, and privilege for their own children. The relationship between the Mammies and their white folks exhibited that reciprocity so characteristic of paternalism. "Of course," a planter in Virginia told a northern reporter in 1865, "if a servant has the charge of one of my little ones, and I see the child grow fond of her, and that she loves the child, I cannot but feel kindly towards her." Of course, Mom Genia Woodbury, who had been a slave in South Carolina, acknowledged that when white folks treat you kindly, you develop kind feelings toward their children.[112]

The devotion of the white children, who regularly sought her as their protector, confidante, and substitute mother, established a considerable barrier against the abuse of Mammy or her family. "We would not hesitate about coming to see you," Laura S. Tibbetts of Louisiana wrote her sister-in-law, "if I could bring my servants, but I could not bring my baby without assistance. She is a great deal fonder of her *Mammy* than she is of me. She nurses her and it would be a great trial to go without her."[113] The implicit intimacy of Mammy and the white children grew over time. A young white woman who had grievously offended her sister received a sharp rebuke from her mother: "I should not offer my services to walk out with you to Mrs. A's any more, and indeed I do not expect *your old nurse* will be anxious to go with you again. She said she was very sorry you behaved as you did." The rebuke concluded: "If you do not treat your brothers and sisters well you will never be respected by any one, either old or young, black or white."[114]

The immunity that Mammy secured for herself did not fully cover husband and children, but it went far enough to shield them from the worst. Mammy distraught, hurt, or angry was not to be borne. More than one overseer learned to his cost to walk gingerly around her and hers. Ma Eppes of Alabama said that an overseer had whipped the plantation Mammy when the mistress was away.

> When Miss Sarah comed back and found it out she was the maddest white lady I ever seed. She sent for the overseer and she say, "Allen, what you mean by whipping Mammy? You know I don't allow you to touch my house servants. . . . I'd rather see them marks on my old

shoulders than to see 'em on Mammy's. They wouldn't hurt me no worse." Then she say, "Allen, take your family and git offen my place. Don't you let sundown catch you here." So he left. He wasn't nothing but white trash nohow.[115]

Another overseer made the incredible mistake of asking his employer for permission to punish Mammy. The reply: "What! What! Why I would as soon think of punishing my own mother! Why man you'd have four of the biggest men in Mississippi down on you if you even dare suggest such a thing, and she knows it! All you can do is to knuckle down to Mammy."[116]

Violence against Mammies and old nurses did sometimes occur. Francis Henderson, who fled a plantation near Washington, D.C., and settled in Canada, said that his master's son treated all the slaves cruelly: "I have known him to kick my aunt, an old woman who had raised and nursed him. . . ." And Ellen Cragin of Mississippi said that her mother fell asleep at a loom one day to be wakened by blows from her master's young son. She grabbed a stick and beat him badly, crying out, "I'm going to kill you. These black titties sucked you, and then you come here to beat me."[117]

The Mammies, strictly speaking, inhabited only the large plantation households. A much larger group, the nurses, took on many of their attributes. Even where a powerful Mammy presided, one or more nurses would be on hand, and plantations and good-sized farms usually had a black nurse for the white children, as well as a midwife, when the two were not the same person. Frequently, one black woman nursed and raised black and white children alike. White opinion of the nurses' qualities as midwives and medical practitioners varied, but the sources reveal much more praise than censure.[118] Beyond their medical services, to these nurses fell most of the duties associated with the more formally designated and prestigious Mammies. It was they who imparted the speech of the quarters to the children of the Big House, who introduced them to black folklore, who taught them to love black music, and who helped bend their Christianity in the folkish direction the black preachers were taking it.

The uses to which Mammy put her power and influence included protection of her own family. If her loyalty to her white folks took priority over her loyalty to the blacks in the quarters—and it did not always—she cannot be convicted of slighting her own flesh and blood. At the end of the war some Mammies did choose to stay with their white folks in preference to following a husband or children. But the departing children were usually full-grown and ready to make their own lives, and there is no evidence that the Mammy left her husband in cases other than those in which the marriage had deteriorated anyway. Normally, the husband held a position of importance in his own right—butler, coachman, blacksmith—and the couple would have been foolish to leave white people with whom they had developed kind and warm relationships for the vicissitudes of life in an uncertain world. The decision to stay demonstrated genuine affection and loyalty to the whites; it did not demonstrate servility or disloyalty to their own color, much less to their own family.

The same testimony from the Big House that created the legend of the faithful Mammy as contented slave *par excellence* also provided some warnings. Mrs. Chesnut wrote in 1865: "My ideas of those last days in Columbia are confused. The Martins left the Friday before I did, and their Mammy refused to go with them. That daunted me."[119] Elizabeth Allston Pringle, of a great low-country slaveholding family, told of her mother's attempt to return to the plantation during the war and of Mammy's message to desist or take another road:

> I never understood that message from Maum Milly, whether it was genuine anxiety on her part, or whether it was to keep mamma from coming and asserting her rights, by intimidating her. Maum Milly had always been greatly considered and trusted. She held herself and her family as vastly superior to the ordinary run of negroes, the aristocracy of the race.[120]

And Eliza Frances Andrews told how "dear old mammy—Sophia by name—while so superior, and as genuine a 'lady' as I ever knew," fell under suspicion of being a Yankee spy.[121]

Having begun our discussion with the comments of nostalgic whites, let us end with one more, which brings Mammy's complex significance into full view. According to Susan Dabney Smedes, her father consulted Mammy on all important plantation affairs and usually took her advice. Upon returning home from a tour of the fields in the middle of each day, he sat, laughed, and talked with the old woman in what appears to have been among the more pleasurable moments in both their lives. As for Mrs. Smedes herself, "Our childish associations with Grannie Harriet were delightful. She petted and spoiled us to our heart's content, and could not bear to have any fault found with us." Grannie Harriet was virtually Mammy Emeritus by that time. The younger and more vigorous Mammy Maria, who was old enough to have raised Mrs. Smedes's mother "and had come to love the white family better than her own blood and race," had assumed the actual duties. Having to call on white support to discipline unruly and quarrelsome house servants, Mammy Maria came to be regarded by the slaves as "a white folks' servant." But if she usually agreed with the whites' notions of order and discipline, she also carried great weight whenever she championed the cause of some abused slave.

> The place that she made for herself was one that would, in a character less true and strong, have brought on herself the hatred and distrust of her race. But they knew her to be just, one who never assailed the innocent, and with so warm and compassionate a heart in real trouble that none were afraid to come to her. From being a confidential servant she grew into being a kind of prime minister, and it was well known that if she espoused a cause and took it to the master it was sure to be attended to at once, and according to her advice.

And in her own way Mammy defended black dignity. A fellow slave who qualified as a good church member received her special respect, even to her calling him or her Mr. or Mrs.—something that would have gotten any other slave's head cracked. Mrs. Smedes recalled having once asked her, "Mammy, what makes you call Henry Mr. Ferguson?" "Do you think," she replied with undisguised indignation, " 'cause we are black that we cyarnt have no names?"

After the war Mammy Maria got whatever she wanted from the Dabneys, in return for which she gave them much they could not readily do without. When Mr. Dabney died, one of his daughters asked Mammy if he should be afraid to meet any of his former slaves at the bar of God's justice. Mrs. Smedes ended her book by recalling that Mammy gave the family assurances that her old master had nothing to fear.[122]

In her own romantic way Mrs. Smedes laid bare the tragedy of the plantation Mammy. She was not, as is so easily assumed, some "white man's nigger," some pathetic appendage to the powerful whites of the Big House. Her strength of character, iron will, and impressive self-discipline belie any glib generalizations. More than any other slave, she had absorbed the paternalist ethos and accepted her place in a system of reciprocal obligations defined from above. In so doing, she developed pride, resourcefulness, and a high sense of responsibility to white and black people alike, as conditioned by the prevalent system of values and notions of duty. She did not reject her people in order to identify with stronger whites, but she did place herself in a relationship to her own people that reinforced the paternalist social order. Thus, she carried herself with courage, compassion, dignity, and self-respect and might have provided a black model for these qualities among people who needed one, had not the constricting circumstances of her own development cut her off, in essential respects, from playing that role. Her tragedy lay, not in her abandonment of her own people, but in her inability to offer her individual power and beauty to black people on terms they could accept without themselves sliding further into a system of paternalistic dependency.

The high spirit of the house slaves, including some body servants and Mammies, during and after the war surprised and offended their masters, but it had long been foreshadowed in daily behavior. Famous runaways like Austin Steward, William Wells Brown, and Frederick Douglass had worked in the Big House as well as outside it, and newspaper advertisements for uncelebrated runaways had always included a healthy portion of those described as house servants. The Big House itself often resembled a battlefield. If closeness bred affection and warmth, it also bred hatred and violence; often it bred all at once, according to circumstances, moods, and momentary passions.

As a group, the house servants appear to have been more rather than less troublesome to the whites than the field hands, even if in less dramatic ways.[123] They quarreled among themselves and with the whites, sulked, shouted, and in a variety of ways did not, or could not, conceal their hostility to harsh, unsteady, or even unexceptionable mistresses. Life had to be lived at such close quarters that antagonism broke out everywhere. High-strung white mistresses and sensitive servants clashed over words, deeds, and mere looks. Field slaves normally got whipped for poor work, house servants for "impudence" and "impertinence." "Really well-trained, accomplished, and docile houseservants," wrote Olmsted, "are seldom to be purchased or hired at the South. . . ."[124]

Impertinence could pass into such unpleasantries as murder. When the beautiful young Miss Virginia Frost of Richmond, Virginia, reproached her servant for insolent language, the servant shot her dead.[125] House servants did not often kill their masters or mistresses. But when they did, well-bred house servants preferred the more genteel device of poison, which had the great advantage, apart from its propriety, of sometimes escaping detection. Cases of poisoning and suspected poisoning, however infrequent, kept the slaveholders nervous, especially since any undiagnosed or strange death could raise suspicion of foul play.[126]

The soberest and most secure whites had bad moments. Eliza L. Magruder, who did not fear for her life among her servants and who took the racial serenity of her plantation for granted, might not have become upset when a slave tried to poison her neighbor, Olivia Donoho, if it had not been the second such case in a short period and if a major incident of arson had not also disturbed the countryside.[127] This less idyllic side of life in the Big House emerged from an account by the cool and sophisticated Mrs. Chesnut, whose steadiness under adversity and general good sense made her an exemplary witness.

> [*Sept. 21, 1861.*] I began to read one of [the letters] aloud. It was from Mary Witherspoon, and I broke down; horror and amazement was [*sic*] too much for me. Poor cousin Betsy Witherspoon was murdered! . . . [She] was murdered by her own people, her Negroes. . . . Her household Negroes were so insolent, so pampered, and insubordinate. She lived alone. She knew, she said, that none of her children would have the patience she had with these people who had been indulged and spoiled by her until they were like spoiled children, simply intolerable. . . .
>
> [*Sept. 24.*] William and Cousin Betsy's old maid, Rhody, are in jail; strong suspicion but as yet no proof of their guilt. . . .
>
> [*Sept. 24.*] Hitherto I have never thought of being afraid of Negroes. I had never injured any of them; why should they want to hurt me? Two thirds of my religion consists in trying to be good to Negroes, because they are so in our power, and it would be so easy to be the other thing. Somehow today I feel that the ground is cut away from under my feet. Why should they treat me any better than they have done Cousin Betsy Witherspoon?

The story came out by October 7. It seems that Mrs. Witherspoon's son, John, had heard of certain misdeeds by William and Rhody and threatened to whip them when he visited the plantation the next day. Mrs. Witherspoon, however, had told her young grandson, "I do not intend John to punish these Negroes. It is too late to begin discipline now. I have indulged them past bearing. They all say I ought to have tried to control them, that it is all my fault." The slaves nevertheless expected to be punished and apparently decided to give John something else to think about. Mrs. Chesnut recalled the other such case she knew of; it too involved indulged, pampered house servants and a mistress who had spoiled them.

[*Oct. 7*] If they want to kill us, they can do it when they please, they are noiseless as panthers. . . . We ought to be grateful that anyone of us is alive, but nobody is afraid of their own Negroes. I find everyone, like myself, ready to trust their own yard. I would go down on the plantation tomorrow and stay there even if there were no white person in twenty miles. My Molly and all the rest I believe would keep me as safe as I should be in the Tower of London.

On October 18, Mrs. Chesnut's mother-in-law cried out at table not to eat the soup: it was bitter and she feared poison. Mrs. Chesnut: "Mrs. Witherspoon's death has clearly driven us all wild." She then recalled the case of Dr. Keith, who recognized that he was slowly being poisoned—a little dose each day—by his house slaves, who promptly responded to his discovery by cutting his throat.[128]

If this great southern lady, possessed of a brilliant mind and a character of steel, was having these nightmares, what should be surmised about her more limited and frail sisters—and brothers— among the planter class? Perhaps that lower level of sensitivity which leads people not to know what they do know saved them. But the hysteria accompanying each insurrection scare, no matter how unsubstantiated the rumors, suggests that even those who preferred to sleep in the illusion of safety had bad moments from time to time.

Life in the Big House, with its affection and hatreds, its interracial attachments and intolerance, its extraordinary kindnesses and uncontrollable violence, represented in all of these contradictions paternalism in its most heightened form. The house servants' psychological and physical dependence upon their masters and mistresses proceeded hand in hand with their acute awareness of the whites' weaknesses, foibles, and insecurities. The masters' and mistresses' psychological and physical dependence upon their slaves proceeded hand in hand with gnawing intimations of the blacks' hostility, resentment, and suppressed anger. With steady nerves and a reasonable amount of good will on both sides, life could be lived decently. Too often, even with good will, the contradictions exploded in sudden violence. A field hand could lower his eyes, shuffle, and keep control of himself in the face of provocations, but a house servant had to live with a master and mistress who knew him or her well enough to read insubordination into a glance, a shift in tone, or a quick motion of the shoulders.

The deeper commitment of the house servants to a dependency relationship—that closer identification with their white folks which has always drawn so much comment—did not imply a commitment to slavery. The house servants knew their white folks too well to see them as ten feet tall. No evidence exists that the house servants more readily accepted slavery than did the field hands, and much evidence exists to suggest the reverse. The impudence and impertinence of which they were always quite rightly (by white standards) accused laid bare a good dose of contempt for their superiors, who learned to fear much more than having their throats cut in bed one night. More than one master and mistress learned the lesson that T. S. Eliot put in the mouth of J. Alfred Prufrock:

> I have seen the moment of my greatness flicker,
> And I have seen the eternal Footman hold my coat, and snicker,
> And in short, I was afraid.[129]

The heightened paternalism of the Big House placed the servants in a special position vis-à-vis both whites and other blacks. They, above all others, carried Afro-American culture into the cooking, the folklore, the religion, and the sensibility of whites who have not yet ceased pretending that southern culture comes straight from Europe and the white experience in America. Simultaneously, the house servants transmitted the culture of the Big House to the quarters and themselves came to embody the best and worst of both. The white children they raised rarely lost completely the peculiar speech patterns most directly associated with the quarters; the field slaves who looked to the servants for the graces learned from them whatever standard English they came to speak. Of all the slaves the house servants most clearly approximated what the whites considered proper Christianity. Their religion manifested a greater degree of biblical and church orthodoxy than did that of the field hands. Accordingly, they imparted a large measure of Euro-American Christianity to the quarters. But most of them remained people of both worlds and hence carried the folk religion of the quarters into the Big House. The sources continue to hold many secrets, but the house servants appear to have been the primary agents for that cultural fusion of Africa and Europe and of diverse white and black experiences in the plantation community, which resulted, among other things, in an Afro-American Christianity and guaranteed it some influence on the religion of the whites. The house servants, then, no more stood between two cultures than did the slaves as a whole. On the threshold of both, they became the principal carriers of a third culture, neither African nor Euro-American.

The house servants did not so much stand between two cultures as they remained suspended between two politics. Their intimacy with the whites more readily represented an exaggerated form of the master-slave relationship in general than a counterpoint to a separation of masters and field hands. As such, it drew the teeth of politically relevant class hatreds even while it nurtured no few personal hatreds. The contradictory conditions generated by so close a life with the whites provided a critical standpoint that eventually led to a desire for freedom and equality, but the very intimacy of those conditions made it difficult for most—notwithstanding the many exceptions noted—to make a complete break. The house servants emerged as the great "integrationists" in the black community, culturally as well as politically—the one demanded the other—but without them, the seeds of a separate nationality in the quarters could not have sprouted in the first place.

THE MEN BETWEEN

Most planters of the Lower South and some of the Upper appointed drivers whether or not they hired white overseers. The drivers, slaves themselves, acted as foremen of the labor gangs and supervisors of the decorum of the quarters. Capable drivers—and there were many such—readily became the most important slaves on the place and often knew more about management than did the whites. The term "driver" itself expresses the primary function of keeping the field hands moving. Yet, formally designated drivers did not constitute the whole of the foreman category, for the farms and small plantations that had no such designated personages normally did have, with or without some title, slave leaders on whom the masters relied. No formula governed the number of drivers per slaveholding unit, but one driver would usually suffice for a plantation of fifty slaves or less, with others added on the larger units. Where there was more than one driver, usually but with many exceptions one would be designated head driver and given supervision of the others.[1]

The slave codes discouraged the use of black overseers, in contradistinction to drivers, by demanding the presence of white men among the slaves. Some planters simply defied the law.[2] Others who lived on their own plantations all year long did without a white overseer, so that their drivers became *de facto* overseers, albeit under the direct supervision of the master. During the war especially, with many slaveholders in the army and good white overseers scarce, many a mistress ran her plantation by relying on an experienced and trusted driver. From the seventeenth century onward, many Virginia planters preferred black overseers, and many more low-country South Carolina and Georgia planters relied on them than cared to admit as much. Everywhere in the South black overseers ran large plantations for absentee owners and, more often, for residents who left their plantations for months at a time. The percentage of southern slaves who worked under formally designated black overseers could not have been large, but the percentage who worked under *de facto* black overseers undoubtedly was. The small slaveholders who dominated the Upper South, and many of those who lived within the great plantation belts of the Lower South, could not afford and did not need white overseers. Their drivers or simply their ablest men assumed many of the responsibilities normally associated with white overseers. In addition to the southern rural slaves who lived on units too small to support an overseer, others lived on units that relied on a black overseer or a driver with extensive powers. Probably, at least two-thirds of the slaves in the South worked under a black man who had direct access to the master with no white overseer between them—probably at least two-thirds, that is, experienced responsible and direct black leadership in their everyday work life.[3]

Even planters who did not appoint drivers often provided for a lower order of black leadership in the fields and shops. Plow or hoe gangs, blacksmith shops, a room full of spinners, and other such groups would, if large enough, have a foreman or captain or leader who assumed responsibility for the pace and quality of work. Of special importance, trained slaves supervised cotton-ginning, sugar-boiling, and tobacco-curing crews in exacting work that demanded some skill and care. Personnel changed frequently because different slaves were tried and found wanting, or because masters and drivers preferred to rotate group leaders, or because generally good leaders would fall off from time to time. As a result, many ordinary slaves got a taste of giving orders once in a while and of assuming responsibility for some small phase of management. In this way, they came out of slavery with much wider experience than their masters usually realized or had intended.[4]

Those drivers who won a firm position and held it for many years enjoyed an excellent reputation. The qualities for which they received the greatest praise were intelligence, managerial skill, and practical knowledge of the intricacies of farming. Drivers of top quality made up a considerable portion of the whole and typically had the experience to run a plantation without white direction in all respects except marketing and finance. When masters fled the plantations of the South Carolina low country during the war, many drivers took over and managed well without them.[5]

The drivers knew their worth. Lyell described one on an up-country Georgia plantation who knew everything possible about soil and crop conditions. Not only overseers but several owners had come and gone while he held office. "This personage," commented Lyell, "conscious of his importance, would begin by enlarging, with much self-complacency, on the ignorance of his master. . . ."[6]

Masters valued good drivers and often paid tribute to their intellect and ability. Duncan Clinch Heyward wrote: "March was then in his prime, being in his forty-third year, tall and straight and of powerful build. Intelligence and understanding showed in his face, and force in his every movement. He looked indeed like one born to command. . . ."[7] In a similar vein the manager of the R. R. Barrow estates in Louisiana penned an obituary on April 21, 1858:

Andrew the Driver Died

The Residence has met with a great loss in the death of this valuable man, in the loss of Andrew I suppose the Plantation will materially suffer as his services as a driver cannot be replaced. He was about 60 years old. He was well liked by all who knew him. He was a negro of uncommon good mind and I have regarded him as one who possess good Judgment about Plantation work. He was Buried this evening and all the negroes on the Residence & Mertle Grove [another Barrow plantation, here misspelled] attended his funeral. He was aware of his approaching death and expressed an entire willingness to die. He conversed freely an hour before his death with many of his fellow-servants and expressed a hope that he would meet them all in heaven—He was certain that he would go to heaven. Before his death he bid all an affectionate farewell and died about 7 o'clock in the morning triumphantly and thanked his god that he should soon be in heaven. His loss was generally and universally regretted and deep sorrow was depicted on the countenance of every one who knew him both white & black. He was buried tonight.[8]

The drivers had to be extraordinary men to discharge effectively the heavy responsibilities that fell to them. The "Duties of the First Driver," as recorded in the papers of William J. Minor's sugar plantation in Louisiana, provide a fair statement of what was expected:

He must obey all the orders of the Overseer. He must see that all the hands under him in the field do their duty and punish them in a proper manner unless they do. He must not allow any loud talking or quarreling in the fields or in the Quarters on the place.

He must give the whole of his time and attention to the interest of the place. He must [report] everything he sees going wrong or that he believes to be wrong w[h]ether the person guilty of the crime is under his particular orders at the time or not.

He must take care that the people do not leave the Quarters without permission, that they are all at their houses at the proper time after the wringing of the bell.

He must wring the bell morning and evening at such hours as he may be ordered to by the Overseer. Immediately after wringing the bell in the morning he must call the Overseer. He must not allow the negroes to use or keep or drink spirituous liquors of any kind, and above all he must not do it himself.

He must never in punishment cut the skin or bruise in any way the persons punished. If he is resisted he must call others by name to help him, if they refuse he [must] report the case to the Overseer.

He must never strike with any thing else but the lash of his whip.

He must treat all the negroes alike, showing neither love nor hatred to any one, but be just in all things to all.

He must so conduct himself that there shall be no complaint of his being too intimate with the wives and daughters of the other men. He must by no means attempt to become the Ondidonk over the people for if he does burnt brandy should not save him from the most severe punishment.[9]

A few masters raised particular slaves to become drivers and kept the post within a single family. A driver who held his job for decades obviously had his master's confidence, and if he had a bright, strong, ambitious son, he could train him to inherit the job.[10] These cases were, however, highly exceptional, for masters had to look for physically strong, intelligent, businesslike men who could command respect in the quarters, and could not afford to play favorites.

A master or overseer might appoint as driver a slave in his twenties, if he showed unusual qualities and there were no other likely candidates; normally, they preferred more mature men. Since drivers often remained in their jobs for long periods, even for life, the average age probably fell in the forties, and many were, by the standards of the day, old men.[11] A letter from William S. Pettigrew of North Carolina to his sister reveals some of the problems, as well as something of the qualities sought. Moses, the old driver, had died, and Pettigrew had appointed Glasgow, a cousin of Moses and the son of a deceased driver named Uncle Bill.

> Glasgow possesses many qualities that will, I think if cultivated, adapt him to his present position. He is honest, industrious, not too *talkative* (which is a necessary qualification) a man of good sense, a good hand himself, and has been hitherto faithful in the discharge of whatever may have been committed to his care. He is but thirty-two years of age. This comparative youth may militate against him for a short while, if he prove to be in possession of the abilities requisite for his station. The man of 32 will, in ten year's time, find in any company of persons a far greater number behind him than are in advance of him. It will be many years before those disqualifications for command that usually characterize old persons will overtake the man of 30. While he who has attained 50 must soon expect the inexorable hand of time to soften that vigour which is all important in a ruler and without which he soon permits some stronger spirit than his own to assume the mastery over him. Withal, the young man grows up with the business of the plantation, and it becomes incorporated in his very mind.[12]

Thus, typically, at the time of his appointment the driver, even if relatively young for the post, had acquired much knowledge of plantation affairs, much experience in relating to both whites and blacks, and considerable personal maturity.

The great majority of drivers could not read or write. Only a few masters thought that literacy would make them better managers. Some drivers learned anyway in the same variety of ways and with the same risks as ordinary slaves.[13] A few, with or without the master's permission, taught some of the others to read.[14] Their greatest contributions to the education of the slaves fell elsewhere. They taught them the rudiments of farm work, as well as special skills, and during the early period of the regime they taught the incoming Africans to speak English.

The privileges accruing to drivers varied a great deal but usually included some extra food and clothing, as well as allotments of tobacco and whiskey. Sometimes they lived in more comfortable quarters than the others. The most valued could expect cash bonuses of five or ten dollars at Christmas time. Although these perquisites did not come to much in absolute material terms, they did contribute to a more comfortable life for the driver's family.[15]

The most entrenched and responsible drivers did not do much field work themselves, but the more typical drivers often did work alongside the others and set the pace. Even so, their varied responsibilities allowed them to move around a good deal and attend to different matters; hence, they escaped the most boring, brutal, and demoralizing features of the gang-labor system. Of considerable importance to them, they could generally protect their wives and children from the worst rigors of field work and at least keep the whip off their backs. If they had garden plots, they might arrange to have the work done by other slaves as a kind of *corvée.*[16]

To be able to carry a whip, as well as a watch, and to bark commands no doubt meant much to some. An ex-slave revealed a good deal when he said of his father, who had been a driver, that he was "de only slave dat was give de honor to wear boots."[17] And Andrew Dirt of Alabama commented:

> I was a driver during slavery and I reckons I was about twenty sompin'. I don't remember nothin' in particular that caused me to get dat drivin' job, 'ceptin' hard work, but I knows I was proud of it 'cause I didn't have to work so hard no mo'. And den it sorta made de other niggers look up to me, an' you knows us niggers, boss. Nothin' makes us happier dan to strut in front of other niggers.[18]

One perquisite had special attraction for some. Occasionally, a driver obtained his master's permission to have more than one wife. More often, his prestige and actual power guaranteed him the favors of the less scrupulous young women or, more honorably, the pick of the prettiest girl for a wife. Some drivers forced the slave women in much the same way as did some masters and overseers. It remains an open question which of these powerful white and black males forced the female slaves more often. Under the task system the driver set the day's work for each slave and had no trouble making a woman's life miserable if she refused him. Under the more prevalent gang system, drivers could lay the whip on with impunity—if they had the power to whip at all, as many did—or they could find any number of other ways to reward and punish. One illustration may suffice. Fanny Kemble rebuked Sophy, an unmarried slave, for having had a child by a driver who had forced her. Mrs. Kemble thought she might have done a better job of defending her honor. Sophy replied, "Oh, yes, missis, we know—we know all about dat well enough; but we do anything to get our poor flesh some rest from de whip; when he made me follow him into de bush, what use me tell him no? He have strength to make me." Mrs. Kemble commented: "I have written down the woman's words; I wish I could write down the abject misery with which they were spoken."[19]

The drivers did not enjoy an enviable reputation in their day and have not enjoyed one since. Usually they have been portrayed as brutal men who won a few privileges for themselves by beating and betraying their fellow slaves. This reputation has rested on surprisingly slim evidence; or rather, it has rested on evidence for which we find a steady counterpoint of reverse testimony.

The legend of the cruel driver grew up in the Caribbean islands and, like so much else about slavery, was simply transferred to the South. In much of the Caribbean, most notably Jamaica, the drivers apparently earned their reputation and earned the hatred of the slaves. But the position of the driver, like so much else, had to differ markedly between a slave society of absentee owners, an overwhelmingly black population, and a three-caste system, and a slave society of resident planters, a large white and free majority, and a two-caste system. Also, however much the drivers of the Caribbean lived up to their reputation as traitors and brutes, a number of them joined slave insurrections.

The drivers of the Old South ran the gamut from sadistic monsters to compassionate leaders of their people. It is not possible to judge, even roughly, the proportions at the extremes, especially since so much depends on the very definition of driver. Should, for example, the many less formally designated foremen or captains on farms with only two or three slave families be included, or merely the leaders of the gangs on the large plantations? Moreover, a succession of cruel men contributed much to the image of the drivers as a group, but their cruelty resulted in short terms of office. These and other problems must remain insoluble in view of the state of the evidence. The position of the drivers on the medium-sized and large plantations—the ones most criticized in contemporary and later historical accounts—was in fact fraught with ambiguity. By taking note of the extremes while concentrating on the men who had to wrestle with that ambiguity, we can make a judgment, however tentative, about these most fascinating and important of slaves.

To begin with those drivers who measured up to notice for cruelty to blacks and subservience to whites, the slave narratives contain many horror stories, which by themselves would fully justify the indictment so often leveled. "De meanest man, white or black, I ever see," Jane Johnson of South Carolina called her former driver. Gus Feaster spoke with more restraint, but in context the message was the same: "He was a sorry nigger dat never had no quality in him a-tall, no sir-ee." More forcefully, Henry Cheatam of Mississippi said of his black overseer: "Dat was de meanest devil dat ever lived on de Lord's green earth. I promised myself when I growed up dat I was a-goin' to kill dat nigger if it was de last thing I ever done."[20] Not only did ex-slaves say that their drivers behaved as badly as their masters or overseers; many proclaimed that they behaved worse.[21] And worst of all were the drivers for the slave traders, who ranked, along with their masters, as the fiends of the regime. Their brutality provided a conjuncture for two of the three meanings of the word "driver" in the Old South; it could also mean a slave trader or a carriage driver.[22]

The slaves dealt with particularly harsh drivers much as they dealt with particularly harsh overseers. Occasionally, they beat or killed them. "A few days ago," wrote A. M. Lobdell of West Feliciana Parish, Louisiana, to her brother, "a favorite Negro [of the neighboring Mulford family], their driver, was murdered by one of the other Negroes. He is said to have been horribly cut to pieces. The one that killed him has run away."[23] More often, the slaves conspired to have the driver broken. They appealed to the overseer or the master and asked for a change. Risking additional punishment, they slowed down or sabotaged the work until they got a new man. But in so doing, they found their dependence on the whites reinforced and the solidarity of their own ranks undermined. They paid this price when they had to, and the whites were quick to assert themselves as the protectors of the blacks against the tyranny of other blacks. Black as well as white sources suggest that the slaves sometimes felt that their masters and even overseers were protecting them against the excesses of drivers.[24]

Thus, the manager of the huge Butler estate of many hundreds of slaves had the external support he needed for his one-sided and self-serving characterization of his own role. His father, who had managed before him, had inherited disorder.

> The grand point was to suppress the brutality and licentiousness practiced by the principal men on it; (say the drivers and tradesmen). More punishment is inflicted on every plantation by the men in power, from private pique, than from a neglect of duty. . . . The owner or overseer knows, that with a given number of hands, such a portion of work is to be done. The driver, to screen favorites, or apply their time to his own purposes, imposes a heavy task on some. Should they murmur, an opportunity is taken, months after, to punish those unfortunate fellows for not doing their own and others' tasks. Should they not come at the immediate offenders, it will descend on the nearest kindred. As an evidence of the various opportunities that a brutal driver has to gratify his revenge (the predominant principle of the human race), let any planter go into his field, and in any Negro's task, he can find apparently just grounds for punishment. To prevent this abuse, no driver in the field is allowed to inflict punishment, until after a regular trial. . . . An order from a driver is to be as implicitly obeyed as if it came from myself, nor do I counteract the execution (unless it is injurious) but direct his immediate attention to it. It would be endless for me to superintend the drivers and field hands too, and would of course make them useless. . . . It is a great point in having the principal drivers men that can support their dignity; a condescension to familiarity should be prohibited.[25]

So many whites and blacks put the drivers in this light that contemporaries and historians may be forgiven for taking the version for granted. What they failed to notice was that many other whites and blacks saw the drivers differently and made a good case of their own. After reporting that the slaves "shore hated that old black man," Allen V. Manning of Texas said of his driver that, after all, he had never been allowed to think for himself, had had to work at least as hard as any of the others, and never knew any better. Sarah Ford described her black overseer as mean, quick with the whip, and hated by the other slaves. Yet her father, a tough and recalcitrant slave who had suffered from the lash, took him in after the war when he was alone and near death. Campbell Davis of Texas remarked that his uncle, the driver, had no choice except to use the whip as directed. And a variety of sources reveal that masters and overseers made it clear to all that the driver would himself feel the lash if he used it too sparingly on others.[26] A forceful illustration of the hardening of attitudes under extreme pressure comes from the statement of a Jamaican driver who was whipped for not getting enough work out of the hands. He turned on them and whipped them all savagely, saying, "Never mind, I don't blame Busha [overseer] for this; but I will know what to do —I'm not going to take a lick for all the gang in this way, and I don't care what I do—I will cut and chop away right and left."[27] Only the bluntness of speech distinguished this driver from many in the Old South. Such comments compel a closer look at the anomalous position in which the drivers found themselves.

W. W. Hazard of Georgia revealed some of the ways in which whites sought to manipulate their drivers. He explained that he rarely whipped slaves himself and preferred to let the driver do it. Thus, "I may remove from the mind of the servant who commits a fault, the unfavorable impression, too apt to be indulged in, that it is for the pleasure of punishing, rather than for the purpose of enforcing obedience and establishing good order that punishments are inflicted." Hazard added that if the driver does something wrong, "I reprimand him in private, then publicly." He tried to appeal, he said, to the driver's religious sense of obedience and only then to his fear of punishment: "This being one of the rare instances, where the master or manager should inflict the punishment, and not degrade the driver by allowing a private to punish; which will humble a driver and prostrate his authority that should be absolute."[28]

Skillful masters used methods other than bribery and threats to get the most out of their drivers. They flattered them and appealed to their pride; more revealingly, they stressed that the slaves as well as their master benefited from a proper level of production and from good order in the quarters. That is, they exhorted the drivers to impose strict discipline for the good of the slaves themselves. The Pettigrew family papers contain a remarkable set of letters that illustrate the complexities of the relationship. William S. Pettigrew, an Episcopal priest who had to be away from his North Carolina plantation for months at a time, despised white overseers and relied on two drivers, each of whom had charge of one of two adjoining plantations. To stay within the law and to facilitate his correspondence with the illiterate drivers, he employed Malachi White, a neighboring farmer, to look in periodically and also to read his letters to the drivers and to write back as they dictated. They, however, not he, were in charge.

> *William S. Pettigrew to Moses, June 24, 1856.* I have placed much reliance in your management, industry & honesty by thus leaving the plantation & all on it in your charge, nor have I any fear that you will fall short of the confidence I have placed in you. . . . You & Henry must endeavor to manage to the best advantage & occasionally you should talk together on the subject of what should be done. You must not be unfriendly to each other, as it would injure both places & yourselves, as well as myself. You may give them much time on Saturdays as you think proper. . . .
>
> YOUR FRIEND,
> /s/
>
> I hope your Uncle Charles feet are improving.

> *Moses to W.S.P., July 5, 1856.* I was happy to hear from master and am thankful to receive the lines which master sent to me. . . . Dear Master . . . the people has been faithful and all have agreed together since master left home.
>
> YOUR SERVANT,
> [dictated but signed by
> Mr. White for Moses]

> *W.S.P. To Moses, July 12, 1856.* [A certain Mr. Johnston] hopes he may continue to receive good news from Belgrade; but he says, if he should hear bad reports he would have to write you himself. You see from this, Moses, how much interest Mr. Johnston takes in you and your people, and that should things take an unfavorable turn, in consequence of my long absence, not only would I be distressed, but he would also; and you & all your people would not only be disgraced in my estimation, but also in his.

> *Henry to W.S.P., July 5, 1856.* Dear Master, I return my respects to you. I was glad to hear from Master. I have done all day in my power towards your benefit. . . . The hands has bin faithful to their duty an all has agreed well together. I wish to indulge all in my power. All is well at present, master. . . .

Henry to W.S.P., Aug. 2, 1856. [After expressions of love and regards from all the people, Henry asks if Mr. Johnston is privy to all his letters. If so, please let him know because certain things must be for his master's eyes only: "You will excuse this, master."]

W.S.P. to Moses, Aug. 30, 1856. [Expresses sorrow to hear of a death and a miscarriage on the place.] Remember me very kindly to the people, particularly the older ones; & say to them that I frequently think of them & am glad to hear they are well, also that Jack is no worse than when I left home.

The letters continue along the same lines, except for lengthy discussions of crop conditions and plantation affairs that amply demonstrate the extent of the drivers' knowledge and sense of responsibility. Increasingly, they are signed "Your Servant Henry [or Moses] and friend." Long silences about misbehavior are striking; no doubt Moses and Henry played down any trouble, both to protect the slaves from further punishment and to put their own regime in the most favorable light. But in November, 1857, a carpenter ran away and Pettigrew began to smell trouble.

W.S.P. to Moses & Henry, Dec. 18, 1857. The misconduct of some of the people, whilst I was with you, has much impaired my confidence & renders me apprehensive of a renewal of misconduct in some shape or other. Should there be any outbreak requiring my attention, be assured I will be with you within a few days after you have informed me of the fact, in order to adopt such course as circumstances may require. No molasses is to be given to any one who is confined in the penitentiary; that is, to Frank or Jack or Patience—Nor is Venus to have molasses given her unless she requires it in consequence of sickness. . . . Do not allow Patience's children to be neglected while she is in the penitentiary. Does Frank make any further confessions as to the money stolen? I have no idea Patience has much of it. During my absence, it is my wish that the people go from home as little as possible. If I were they, I would be ashamed to be seen away from home after the plantation has been so disgraced by these criminals, Jack, Venus, Frank, Patience & Bill. It is painful to me, even now & at this distance from home, to think of such wicked creatures & such crimes. I do not give a positive order, but I think the people had better stay at home during the Christmas holidays. . . .

W.S.P. to Moses & Henry, Dec. 25, 1857. Of course, you are not expected to carry out any order unless you see it can be done to advantage, and that I would have it done myself, if at home.

The drivers continued to remain silent about misbehavior and to concentrate their attention on matters of work routine and expressions of fidelity and affection for their master. On February 6, 1858, however, Moses wrote about an old neighbor, Mr. Davenport, who was shot by "his own negro man . . . an awful case." Pettigrew's reliance on the discretion of his drivers was again highlighted in a letter on September 11, 1858, in which he withdrew an order to begin planting wheat and decided that they ought to use their own judgment. Exhorting the people to greater efforts, Pettigrew wrote: "Their good conduct will be very gratifying to me and will add greatly to their credit & to the good name of their home."

> *Moses to W.S.P., Sept. 25, 1858.* The fracus that I sent the word to master was between me and Cousin Jerry. I rang the Bell an Jerry was whip[p]ing of the Boy an I told him to stop an he did not an gave words an I hit him an it all was between me an him. As to the work tha have been faithful.

On October 20, 1860, Mr. White wrote Pettigrew that an insurrection scare had hit the area and that patrols had seized all the arms and gunpowder on his plantations. The slaves with whom those arms had confidently been left by Pettigrew had grown frightened and petitioned for his return home.

These letters are open to various interpretations, but certain things are clear. The drivers knew their business and enjoyed Pettigrew's trust not only because of their loyalty but because of their demonstrated ability. Their silence about disorders was obviously self-serving, but nothing in these voluminous papers indicates that they were hard on their people or unpopular with them. On the contrary, they appear to have done their best to contain quarrels and outbreaks and to maintain discipline without Draconian methods. The slaves could easily have gotten word to Pettigrew that the drivers were abusing them. Malachi White looked in regularly, and Pettigrew himself, no man to stand for petty tyranny from his drivers, returned home periodically. It is hard, therefore, to avoid the conclusion that however genuine the drivers' expressions of loyalty to and affection for him, they were also looking after the interests of the quarters.

In 1860, Pettigrew wrote his sister:

> Please accept my thanks for your very kind and affectionate letter of the 21st ult., in which you make especial allusion to the death of my faithful Servant, Moses. He is entitled to all that any one can say in his praise; and as to my own feelings, I shall ever regard it as a duty

and a pleasure to cherish for his memory the highest respect, as long as I retain any recollection of the merits of those who have aided me in acting my part amid the toils of life. I humbly trust he has exchanged the duties of this world for the result & enjoyment of a better. If so, the loss is only ours, the gain is his.[29]

Throughout the South masters had to deal with drivers who ran away from beatings, from insults, and from orders they had no stomach to carry out, or from a wish to gain freedom.[30] In a few cases drivers led plots to murder masters or raise insurrections. Were these rebels men who had especially suffered or who had personal resentments? Only some. One driver, who admitted planning to raise a bloody insurrection, insisted that he dearly loved his master and mistress but would nonetheless have slain them first. He thought enough of his white folks to rely on them to protect his allegedly innocent wife after he was hanged and to announce, "Master, I shall die in peace, and I give you a dying man's blessing."[31]

Or take an opposite case. Dan Josiah Lockhart, a driver or black overseer who later fled to Canada, explained that his master had whipped him for being too hard on the people. Lockhart had strict ideas of proper order and discipline and refused to pursue his master's more passive course. A proud family man who eventually fled after a second owner had whipped his wife, he could be called a harsh driver but hardly a "white man's nigger."[32] Confronted by impossible demands and conflicting loyalties, it is no wonder that some drivers became drunken and dissolute.[33]

Most drivers did not murder their masters, raise insurrections, or run away; neither did they become drunkards, Toms, or sadists. They struggled to assert their own manhood vis-à-vis both their masters and the other slaves. To keep their position and their privileges, they had to do the masters' bidding. They had to demand a certain level of discipline and performance from the hands. When they did not get it, they used their whip. They asserted their authority and resolutely crushed, when they could, all challenges from below. But they too were black slaves and knew that no accomplishment would change their station—the constraints of being black inexorably prevailed. They lived among the others in the quarters and did not participate, as did many drivers in the Caribbean, in a separate privileged group. Consequently, they strove to mediate between the Big House and the quarters, to lower the level of violence, to maintain order in the most humane way available—which, to be sure, was not always all that humane. They were men between.

The labor demands of the plantation brought the ambiguity of the drivers' position into sharp focus. For whatever reasons—from conscious resistance to indifference born of lack of incentives to ordinary shiftlessness—some slaves did anything possible to get out of hard work. On such slaves the driver used his lash. But in so doing, he did not necessarily ruin himself with the other slaves, for they often resented the shirkers, whose nonperformance threw a heavier burden on the rest. Thus, a tough driver who kept the work moving represented the interests of both the master and the slaves. But only up to a point. The difference between a good driver and a mean one, from the slaves' point of view, centered not on whether or not he commanded hard work—he had to—but on whether or not he proceeded according to reason. For the slaves reason meant evenhandedness, a decent respect for individual weakness and unfeigned illness, and an ability to adjust, so far as he could, to their preferred work rhythms.

The driver's job ultimately became impossible, for the masters pressed toward clock-time work patterns, whereas the slaves resisted and tried to substitute their own ideas of productive work. A good driver had to mediate: to keep the slaves working as steadily as possible, especially during the harvest season, and to remonstrate with master and overseer not to demand what they could not get without brutality if indeed at all. To the extent that the driver succeeded in this mediation he played a decisive role in instilling a more modern work discipline in his people, and, at the same time, he offered some protection—for better or worse—against factorylike regimentation.

Some drivers whipped hard; others whipped lightly or not at all. Particularly kind masters who prohibited whipping altogether or allowed it only sparingly relied on their drivers to keep the work going without physical punishment. In some cases white overseers had specific instructions to let the drivers do the whipping in order to guarantee against excesses.[34]

Some drivers, perhaps many, behaved like beasts, but those who did not often had to go through the motions of enforcing harsh discipline. Solomon Northup's account of his work as a driver might be suspect as self-exculpating, if similar accounts were not available from disinterested sources. "I learned," wrote Northup, "to handle the whip with marvellous dexterity and precision, throwing the lash within a hair's breadth of the back, the ear, the nose, without, however, touching either of them." The slaves would dutifully howl with simulated pain and complain to the master about Northup's severity.[35] West Turner of Virginia told of Old Gabe who did the whipping for his master:

> Ole Gabe didn't like dat whippin' bus'ness, but he couldn't he'p hisself. When Marsa was dere, he would lay it on 'cause he had to. But when ole Marsa wasn't lookin,' he never would beat dem slaves. Would tie de slave up to one post an' lash another one. 'Cose de slave would scream an' yell to satisfy Marsa. . . .[36]

Similarly, Miss Bongy Jackson of Louisiana recalled a driver whose skill with the whip rivaled Northup's:

> That nigger would holler jest like he was being beat bad. I recollect one time a Massa come out the house and told the driver to stop. He thought that coon was gittin' whipped to death, and that nigger ain't never been touched.[37]

Fanny Kemble, among others, let herself be deceived by appearances. She described with disgust the rough manner in which the drivers urged the slaves on:

> The command of one slave to another is altogether the most uncompromising utterance of insolent, truculent despotism that it ever befell my lot to witness or listen to. "You nigger—I say you black nigger—you no hear me call you—what for you no run quick?" . . . "Hi! you boy!" and "Hi, you girl!" shouted in an imperious scream, is the civilest mode of apostrophizing those at a distance from them; more frequently it is "You, nigger, you hear? hi, you nigger." And I assure you no contemptuous white intonation ever equaled the *prepotenza* of the despotic insolence of this address of these poor wretches to each other.[38]

John James Audubon, with greater discernment, described a driver in 1821: "He spoke roughly to his underservants but had a good indulgent Eye, and no doubt does what he Can to Accomodate [sic] Master and all."[39] Some drivers punctuated rude commands and apparent insults by cracking a whip over the slaves' heads or on the ground beside them. The language and threatening gestures did two jobs at once: convinced the whites that their driver was a tough taskmaster who was taking no nonsense, and urged the slaves to maintain the pace necessary to allow him to keep the whip off their backs. Masters as well as slaves praised some drivers for their humanity and restraint—for their ability to get the hands to work without resorting to more force than was absolutely necessary. It is especially noteworthy that many blacks became virtual overseers because masters had dismissed white overseers for cruelty and sought a more humane leadership.[40]

If many slaves complained that the driver enforced strict discipline, many others observed that he set a reasonable work pace, which did not always enchant his white overlords.[41] Some drivers took advantage of their authority by setting tasks and controlling work breaks in a petty or spiteful way; many others dealt in an evenhanded way with their charges and made their lives more comfortable. In innumerable ways, they did the best they could for their own people.

The power the slaves manifested in making and breaking overseers turned largely on the prestige and influence of the driver and on his ability to get the master's ear. When Isaac Stephens, a driver for William Elliott, wrote his master about crop conditions, he did not hesitate to include a word of praise for the overseer and to express the wish that his master might find so good a man for his other plantation.[42] If masters expected their overseers to keep the slaves from stealing too much, they also expected their drivers to keep an eye on the overseers, who were known to do a little stealing themselves. Some masters gave their drivers the keys to the storerooms in preference to giving them to the overseers.[43] Josiah Henson explained how he rose to become a driver:

> And by the detection of the knavery of the overseer, who plundered his employer . . . and through my watchfulness was caught in the act and dismissed, I was promoted to be the superintendant of the farm work, and managed to raise more than double the crops, with more cheerful and willing labor than was ever seen on the estate before.

Another ex-slave told of "an old go-ahead Negro" whose "word went further with the master than the overseer's." And Henrietta Perry of Virginia described how her father won the job as well as his master's admiration. He beat up the overseer one day for cursing him. The master decided to fire the overseer and put him in charge.[44]

The driver's latitude and direct access to his master received sanction in a contemporary plantation manual:

> The head driver is the most important negro on the plantation. He is to be treated with more respect than any other negro by both

master and overseer. He is on no occasion to be treated with any indignation calculated to lose the respect of the other negroes without breaking him. He is required to maintain proper discipline at all times. To see that no negro idles or does bad work in the field, and to punish it with discretion on the spot. The driver is not to be flogged except by the master but in emergencies that will not admit of delay. He is permitted to visit the master at any time without being required to get a card though in general he must inform the overseer when he leaves the place and present himself on returning. He is expected to communicate freely whatever attracts his attention or he thinks information to the owner.[45]

Overseers had to tread carefully with any driver who had won his master's confidence, especially since normally a good driver would remain in his job while one overseer followed another. Besides, overseers needed the support of good drivers for reasons of their own. Contrary to rules, they liked to leave the plantation on Sundays and at other times for a little recreation or to attend to personal business. The drivers' ability to maintain order without them—and to keep quiet about their absence—made such lapses possible. In the daily running of the plantation cooperation between overseers and drivers usually meant that the job would get done without embarrassing incidents. An overseer who did not get along with his driver assured himself of endless headaches even if he could count on the owner's support, for he would have to supervise everything himself, could not efficiently delegate authority, and risked constant sabotage. Occasionally, overseers established excellent relations with their drivers for dishonorable reasons: more than one overseer and driver happily collaborated to loot the property of an absentee owner.[46]

Drivers tried to protect their people and to represent their interests in the Big House in countless little ways. They might, for example, ignore the rules and look the other way when a strong and quick slave took up the slack for a weak and slow one. Although the overseers had responsibility for determining whether a slave was sick or shamming, the task often fell to the drivers, some of whom risked getting a beating themselves by deciding in favor of the claimant.[47] Sometimes the drivers cut up the meat rations for the slaves. When they did, they could not easily give anyone too little, for such an action would draw immediate protest and the intervention, probably by violence, of the master. They could, however, sometimes err on the side of generosity.

The intermediary position of the driver between the whites and fellow blacks created ambiguities for everyone. The whites required a regime of peace, quiet, law, and order in the quarters and had to rely on their drivers to maintain it. But the paternalistic white ideal required that masters or overseers, not black drivers, should have the last word on the slaves' lives. Indeed, proslavery propaganda insisted that the blacks could not govern themselves, that the drivers were naturally despotic and cruel, and that white supervision alone protected the slaves from abuse.[48] A good driver, however, usurped the roles of prosecutor, judge, jury, and arbiter in the quarters. When possible, he settled quarrels that threatened to erupt into violence or disrupt the lives of others, and he intervened to deal with bullies.[49] Since the masters demanded order in the quarters, a tough driver who insisted on discipline appeared to be carrying out instructions. But he was also often keeping the slaves from severe punishment, from allowing their frustrations to pit them against each other in fratricidal struggles, and from having white folks intervene in their lives even more than they so readily presumed to do.

The regularity with which the slaves left their cabins to attend unauthorized religious meetings says something about how the drivers met their responsibility to enforce curfew. Undoubtedly, the willingness of the drivers to wink at the violations of curfew —to protect young lovers as well as those going to prayer meetings[50]—sometimes meant no more than that they wanted a good night's sleep and did not want to be bothered. Even so, some degree of sympathy was implicit, and their indulgence earned for them a certain amount of appreciation and confidence. Many drivers also attended, presided over, and preached to unauthorized prayer meetings.

Some drivers openly conspired with their fellow slaves to break rules or raise hell. Thomas Goodwater, an ex-slave of South Carolina, told of a driver who would shoot cows from other plantations and then skin and prepare them for his own people. He would go from cabin to cabin with the cryptic message that those who wanted fish had better go fishing before the supply ran out. The slaves translated fish as beef and repaired to an appointed spot for a barbecue.[51]

More typically, the drivers simply did the day-to-day things expected of community leaders, including or especially authoritarian ones. Here, a driver saved the life of a woman who had been bitten by a rattlesnake by quickly and efficiently amputating her finger. There, drivers spotted the approach of a storm or hurricane and led their people—in one case a driver literally had to lash them —to places of refuge. Here and there, drivers enlisted the intervention of their masters against the ravages of the patrols or the abuse of local whites. Even harsh drivers, like so many harsh masters, stood up for their people when they thought they deserved protection.[52]

The frequency with which drivers assumed the role of preachers raises a difficult and ultimately insoluble question: Did they do so because the master directed them to in an effort to keep trained preachers away,[53] or because the people naturally looked to them for leadership? The two possibilities were not mutually exclusive but were distinct. Most drivers probably had the support and trust of their masters and therefore acquired prestige in the quarters so long as they also tried to represent the people. Enough drivers performed well as preachers and won the respect of their congregations to compel the tentative conclusion that they combined the ambiguous role of foreman with that of spiritual leader and thereby assumed a commanding place in the lives of the slaves.[54] In this way they could combine the threat of punishment not only with exhortation but with the threat of scandal and shame at the slaves' own meetings. If they used this power to get more and better work for the master, they also used it to raise the standard of civility, cleanliness, and morality among the people. To the extent to which they succeeded as religious leaders they could spare themselves having to do the uglier side of their job as foremen. This juggling did not imply Tomming for the Man, although it did imply a strategy of accommodation designed to make life in the quarters as safe and rich as possible.

The hostility of the slaves toward many of their drivers, so frequently expressed in their songs as well as in the narratives of ex-slaves and other sources,[55] was matched by a strong preference for them over white overseers and by heavy reliance on their leadership. When Edmund Ruffin wanted to get his version of the John Brown affair across to his slaves, he did not speak to them directly; he spoke at length to his driver with the expectation that he could transmit a message to the slaves and have it accepted.[56] Josiah Henson deeply regretted leading the slaves in his charge back to their owner when he might have effected their freedom upon crossing into Ohio. But Henson could not have led his people back across the Ohio River unless they had trusted him. He explained: "These people had long been under my direction, and were devotedly attached to me in return for the many alleviations I had afforded to their miserable condition, the comforts I had procured them, and the consideration I had always manifested for them."[57] These and similar incidents demonstrate that many drivers earned and kept the trust of their fellow slaves by dealing with them fairly, if often sternly, and by representing their interests as best they could. As a result, after the war many continued to enjoy the support of their people and to provide leadership during the period of transition.[58]

The defection of many drivers to the Union side had a profound effect on the whites, who had long confused black accommodation with servility. The stepfather of Henry F. Pyles, an ex-slave of Tennessee, had deserted his post as driver to join a black Union regiment. After the war he returned "a changed nigger," joined the Republican Party, was elected a delegate to the state convention, and campaigned for William Gannaway Brownlow. The most unusual part of the story concerns the attitude of his master, who, virtually alone among the whites, bore him no grudge and saved him from a lynching during the subsequent period of political reaction.[59] In some cases the drivers did not simply desert; they led mass defections. "The drivers everywhere have proved the worst negroes," wrote John H. Ransdell, a planter, to Governor T. O. Moore of Louisiana in 1863.[60] In many other cases drivers remained loyal but seized the opportunity to negotiate favorable working conditions for their people, who often accepted their advice to stay on the old place after emancipation.[61]

The leadership that the drivers gave to the quarters reflected the contradictory nature of their loyalties, experience, and social position. In certain essential respects they provided a valuable symbol and rallying point for the slaves, but their ultimate reliance upon white sanction destroyed much of the potential long-term advantage. To serve their people at all, as well as to look after their personal interests, the drivers had to win the confidence of the masters. They had to become agents of order and discipline in the fields and the quarters. Necessarily, they had to crack the whip and to enforce not only those rules which the community as a whole required for good order but also those which the masters required for their own narrower purposes. The drivers' submission to their masters' authority, in fact, legitimized their demands for the hands' submission to themselves. To this extent, every driver assumed the role of accommodationist and became the master's man.

Many no doubt went much further and identified as completely as circumstances permitted with the Man. Many no doubt fell into the classic foreman pattern so aptly caught by the proletarian ditty:

> The working class
> Can kiss my ass.
> I've got the foreman's job
> At last!

The masters encouraged this attitude, as rulers have always done in comparable situations; but they could do so only up to a point, for in the end they needed the driver's moral authority in the quarters as much as his ability to intimidate.[62]

More than pride in such symbols of power and authority as the whip and the boots or such perquisites as extra food and whiskey and access to women encouraged the drivers to identify with the whites. They accompanied masters and overseers on hunting trips, drank whiskey with them while discussing plantation management on close to equal terms, ran errands that would only be assigned to trusted and respected men, and in a variety of ways received the respect that men normally demand for themselves.[63] The other side of this tendency was contempt for their fellow slaves. "For years after the war," wrote Duncan Clinch Heyward, "the foremen, and the other old Negroes, liked to pretend, especially in my presence, that they did not know the surnames, or the 'titles' as they termed them, of the younger and more trifling of the hands they worked."[64] As a result of this attitude, many blacks came to prefer to work for whites rather than suffer the pretensions of those blacks whose station was not, after all, so far above their own.[65]

The acceptance of the prevailing social attitudes by some drivers did not, however, stamp them as Toms. It sometimes became the vehicle for asserting personal power within the old mold, but even so, the substitution of a black for a white usurper had posititive significance for a people who had to resist racial subordination as well as class paternalism. A single illustration from Charles Manigault's postwar diatribe will demonstrate the possibilities. The blacks whom he had kept on a profitless forty-slave plantation out of sentimental attachment to them—kept, that is, apart from his other quite profitable and more demanding plantations—looted the premises in 1865.

> But *Frederick* (the Driver) was ringleader, & at the head of all the iniquity committed *there*. He encouraged all the Negroes *to believe* that the Farm, and everything on it, *now since Emancipation*, belonged *solely to him*, & *that their former owners* had now no rights, or control there whatever. And he accordingly encouraged them to lay by *seed potatoes* & other things & several of them were preparing little patches of land for planting on their own account. *Frederick* went daily upon the Publick Road, to converse with & compare notes with the numerous Negroes who in Enjoyment of freedom were leaving the plantations (above us) for the City. *He* then selected from them a gang of about fourteen of these Negroes, whom he conducted into the Farm & placed them all to reside permanently in *Our Fine Dwelling House*, where *they all remained*, during two months—*then leaving it like a Pig Sty*. *He* immediately apportioned to *these 14 Negroes*, a section of my farm to work *there on shares* with him—but without assisting them in their work. *He* being *lord & master* of *everything there*. He was to receive half their years crop when ripe and harvested in the autumn.[66]

Many drivers resisted falling prey to this extreme tendency and tried to defend their people, but even some of the harshest provided the slaves with everyday proof that black men could manage production, compel labor and social discipline, and, in a word, rule. Only when their authority rested wholly on white patronage did they fail to do this much, which was no small contribution to a people who had to fight continuously against succumbing to the whites' image of them as inept, incompetent, stupid, and unable to take care of themselves.

Basically, the drivers promoted accommodation and accepted the ambiguity of their role. Rarely did they use their moral authority in the quarters to promote direct resistance and insurrection. The brutal and hated drivers of the Caribbean led or at least participated in insurrections much more readily,[67] for, in essence, they had developed qualities of leadership and strength that could be turned in any direction as circumstances dictated. In the Old South the drivers, like the preachers, avoided suicidal gestures and bargained for what they could get. As Northup recalled:

> Such an idea as insurrection, however, is not new among the enslaved population of Bayou Boeuf. More than once I have joined in

serious consultation, when the subject has been discussed, and there have been times when a word from me would have placed hundreds of my fellow-bondsmen in an attitude of defiance. Without arms or ammunition, or even with them, I saw such a step would result in certain defeat, disaster and death, and always raised my voice against it.[68]

After the war an old driver carried on this tradition in a confrontation with carpetbaggers who were trying to encourage the freedmen to turn against their old masters. "Listen, white folks," his son quoted him as saying, "you is gwine to start a graveyard if you come round here teachin' niggers to sass white folks."[69] It was rather late by then for such black men to transform themselves into revolutionaries.

The drivers had acquitted themselves reasonably well under slavery. Enough of them had become first-rate economic managers and skilled defenders of their people through the art of compromise and the juggling of contradictory demands from above and below to have laid the groundwork for a substantial postwar leadership. They and the preachers might have provided the leaders that an emancipated black community badly needed. But the postwar reaction hurled the blacks back under white domination and thereby once more reduced the drivers—or foremen and captains, as they came to be called—to their old accommodationist role. Slavery had prepared them for something better but at the same time had hemmed them in. Emancipation did not provide them the chance to become wholly black leaders. An incipient autonomous black leadership had died a-borning.[70]

MEN OF SKILL

During the colonial period the plantations of Maryland, Virginia, and South Carolina hummed with the sounds of the blacksmith and the carpenter, the cooper and the stonemason, the miller and the shoemaker. The wealthier plantations resembled industrial villages, and substantial numbers of slaves acquired a high level of skill in a wide variety of trades. "Indeed," writes Marcus W. Jernegan, "it is hard to see how the eighteenth-century plantation could have survived if the negro slave had not made his important contributions as an artisan. . . ."[1]

During the nineteenth century the slaveholders boasted that they had civilized savage Africans and taught them skills and even how to do any work at all. In truth, however, the West African peoples who filled the slave ships brought magnificent skills with them. Reports of mining and metal work had originally prompted the Portuguese and other Europeans to probe the African coast. West African craftsmanship in the production of hoes and farm tools, as well as in handicrafts, won the praise of Europeans.[2] Throughout the Americas the Africans displayed a high level of mechanical skill, and where they had the chance, as in Cuba, they often came to dominate particular trades. If, during the nineteenth century, southern slaveholders had to enlist white artisans to teach their slaves trades, they had only themselves to blame.

The alleged (and I think actual) decline of skills during the nineteenth century resulted from the South's growing dependence on northern manufactures and from increasingly exclusionist policies enforced by hostile white labor in the towns. Although white mechanics did not succeed in driving the slaves and free Negroes out of the urban trades, their hostility did brake and reverse black industrial progress.[3] On the plantations the decline in extent and quality of craftsmanship had other roots. As transportation improved and the reliance on staple production increased, more and more slaveholders found it cheaper to buy implements or shoes from New England or even from southern industry than to divert labor to the trades. As a result, the percentage of full-time mechanics and craftsmen on the plantations declined steadily, although the data for precise measurement are lacking. Even in 1860 every plantation had mechanics and craftsmen, some of whom displayed considerable skill, but greater reliance was being placed on semi-skilled slaves who alternated between particular jobs and common field work.

The records even of the great plantations during the late antebellum period show surprisingly large payments to skilled white workers for jobs that slaves normally had done on the colonial plantations. An owner of more than fifty slaves in Holmes County, Mississippi, spent $73.56 for blacksmith work during an eight-month period in 1839; an owner of seventy-five in Alabama spent $142 in 1847; and other such cases could be multiplied at random from all parts of the South.[4] Plantation records reveal heavy expenditures for carpentry, masonry, and almost every kind of work slaves might have done.[5] An average plantation would list at least a carpenter, a blacksmith, and one or two other skilled slaves, but the number of full-time mechanics and craftsmen appears to have contracted. If jacks-of-all-trades are excluded, probably no more than 5 percent of the country slaves achieved a notable level of skill.

Numbers do not tell the whole story. On the eastern seaboard and the Mississippi River slaves continued to excel in making, manning, and piloting boats and ships, and the rice and sugar plantations could not have remained in business without the effort of some skilled trunk minders and machine operators.[6] The general level of carpentry among the slaves probably remained low or even declined, but many individual slaves established formidable reputations. Genuinely first-rate carpenters brought two to three times as much as prime field hands on the auction block, and others did well for themselves and their masters when hired out on the countryside. Many of the slaves hired out in the plantation districts were skilled. As the economic pressure mounted to keep slaves in the fields, it created room for some specialists whom masters rented to neighboring planters. The contribution of slave and free Negro mechanics to the technological development of the South has not yet been properly assessed. One slave, Barclay, working from a traveler's account and a rude drawing of Whitney's cotton gin, built the first gin in Mississippi. A free man of color, Norbert Rillieux, revolutionized sugar production in Louisiana by his work on sugar machinery.[7]

The general decline in the number of mechanics and in the quality of work may have been undergoing reversal in the older states by the 1850s. In Georgia, the relative decline in cotton production, attendant upon competitive pressure from the states to the west in the 1840s and 1850s, led to a renewed emphasis on plantation self-sufficiency and increased encouragement of slave skills.[8] In Virginia, which had undergone a similar readjustment much earlier, slave skills remained high enough to allow the Confederate government to sustain a war effort that might have collapsed without them.[9]

Between 5 and 10 percent of the slaves of the South could expect to be hired out during any given year in the late antebellum period.

Slave hiring was nothing new; it had appeared throughout the colonies during the colonial period.[10] Those hired out were primarily common field hands and secondarily domestics, but the practice had special significance for the mechanics and craftsmen. Planters had surplus hands after lay-by and would hire some of them out, if they could, for short periods. Ordinarily, however, they had to hire slaves out by the year—actually, for a period of fifty-one weeks with a stipulated return for Christmas vacation. These slaves came from relatives of deceased slaveowners, who were settling the estate; from authorities who were sorting out a bankruptcy; from mobile planters who were setting up new plantations and needed time to get ready for a full work force; and from settled planters who had bought a large group of slaves and could not absorb it immediately.[11] Small farmers and even overseers added to the supply as they hired out the slaves they were accumulating one by one until they could profitably employ them on a home place.[12]

The cities, towns, and industrial villages hired thousands of country slaves every year. Throughout the South the railroads both hired and bought slaves, many of whom had special skills or soon acquired them. In the Upper South the tobacco and hemp factories hired large numbers; in the tobacco factories of Virginia, for example, hired slaves constituted more than half the hands. They constituted half of the slaves in all occupations in Lynchburg, a quarter of those in Nashville, and 16 percent of those in Louisville. In all towns and cities, hired craftsmen and mechanics, as well as common laborers and domestics, swelled the slave population.[13]

Masters seized the opportunity to hire out their slaves and to hire those of others as a matter of good business and convenience, but they often disliked doing either. Sometimes they punished unruly slaves by sending them away from family and friends, but they also often complained about the deportment and work habits of those they hired themselves.[14] In some cases the slaves came to prefer living with those who had hired them, and difficulties ensued for all parties; but slaveholders worried about the kind of treatment their slaves would receive from temporary masters and about their condition on return.[15] With so many skilled slaves among the hired, the evidence of inferior treatment suggests that the relatively privileged life of the mechanics and craftsmen had its negative side.[16]

The mechanics and craftsmen among those hired out did have an enormous advantage over the laborers and domestics. Often, they could "hire their own time"—that is, choose their own masters and make their own arrangements. In effect, they could live approximately as did the free Negroes, except that they had to surrender a large part of their income to their owners. When they were particularly efficient or when the demand for their trade ran high, they could drive good bargains and pocket substantial earnings. Although one state after another outlawed this practice as subversive of social order, screams of protest from those opposing the practice grew louder as time went on.[17] In every part of the South, whether in town or country, the laws could not be enforced, for too many able slaves could relieve too many masters of concern by shifting for themselves and paying a rent for the use of their own time and effort.[18]

Hundreds of slaves took the opportunity to accumulate and save money. Some bought their freedom despite antimanumission laws. Many more used their earnings to establish a better standard of living for their families and to build churches for their people. When emancipation came, many had accumulated the money and skill to do well as free workers.[19] Although slave hiring has often been interpreted as "a step toward freedom," at least in the Upper South,[20] the number of self-purchases appears much too small to justify such a conclusion. Richard B. Morris has demonstrated, moreover, that these gains must be evaluated in the context of a general deterioration in the freedom of the labor force, white as well as black.[21] The great contribution that the practice of allowing slaves to hire themselves out made to the black community must be sought in the strong reinforcement it gave to the thirst for freedom and economic advance among those mechanics and craftsmen who were its primary beneficiaries.

The mechanics and craftsmen enjoyed a reputation for being the proudest and most independent of all slaves. The slaveholders had mixed feelings about their pride in self and in their work. Landon Carter became enraged with carpenters who disregarded his orders to erect two rough buildings to store corn and instead put up strong, tight buildings of the kind used to store tobacco. "I find," he fumed, "there is no making my carpenters understand me. . . . Thus it is each rascal will be a director. I must now add to it that we may also hang tobacco in; therefore it will be still of a greater service than I intended it should be."[22] The carpenters may well have understood him perfectly. The spirit of the mechanics and craftsmen arose not only from the nature of their work and its opportunities for pride in performance, but also from their ability to control their work pace, to move about the countryside and towns, and to relate to a wide variety of consumers as well as employers and masters.

This independence of spirit and greater knowledge of the world expressed themselves in the prominent place occupied by skilled slaves in the advertisements for runaways, as well as in the frequency of their appearance at the center of insurrectionary plots. Contrary to legend, no evidence exists of widespread contempt for the field hands among the more privileged skilled slaves, who lived among and mingled with their less advantaged brothers and sisters and joined them periodically in harvests and corn shuckings. The field hands brought up their children to respect the mechanics and craftsmen as men of accomplishment, especially since so many of them could read and write. Blacksmiths and carpenters appeared in the slave quarters as highly valued preachers.[23] The bonds between the skilled slaves and the common field hands extended into family life. Prized mechanics often found themselves able to woo the prettiest and most sophisticated house servants; many others married field hands whose treatment by the whites did not necessarily improve because of their husbands' status.[24] So far as the whites were concerned, these bonds reinforced the potential danger of unrest among the mechanics and craftsmen.

"Whenever a slave is made a mechanic," J. H. Hammond told the South Carolina Institute in 1849, "he is more than half freed, and soon becomes, as we too well know, and all history attests, with rare exceptions, the most corrupt and turbulent of his class."[25] Hammond had his eye primarily on the urban and industrial slaves, but plantation mechanics and craftsmen also came under fire as dangerous to plantation discipline. They had greater control of their own labor-time and could more easily get into mischief. They received cash gratuities—many whites called them bribes—for good or fast work and could gamble and drink. Most developed considerable pride in themselves, their families, and their work and too often became known as "uppity niggers." In short, all the measures encouraging their economic performance had the disadvantage of making them considerably less servile than slaves were supposed to be. The slaveholders took the risks, bestowed the privileges, and winked at the manifestations of independence, for their business operations benefitted thereby. But had the number of mechanics and craftsmen risen well above that estimated level of 5 percent, the slaveholders might have reconsidered.[26]

The mechanics' and craftsmen's sturdy qualities of independence, pride, and defiance of the high and mighty paralleled those of the artisans of eighteenth-century America, England, and France on whose shoulders political and social democracy was hoisted into the modern world in volatile and radical forms.[27] More than linguistic confusion may be detected in the common description of black mechanics and craftsmen as "slave artisans" —an expression that is a contradiction in terms. These men provided the firmest social basis for a radical political leadership, as their repeated appearance in insurrectionary plots shows, but the general impediments to violent mass action by the slaves muted the danger. Their leadership normally expressed itself in three other ways: as preachers and moral guides and examples; as frequent runaways and individual defiers of coercive authority; and, more subtly, as specific contributors to Afro-American culture. The first two roles—the more obvious—made them manly examples to the youth of the quarters. The last requires special comment.

Slave craftsmen made a special contribution, as yet virtually unstudied, to Afro-American culture. Fragmentary evidence suggests a noteworthy artistic accomplishment in blending certain African and Western elements into an aesthetically impressive performance, the long-term significance of which demands careful analysis.

West African culture did not separate art, much less religion, from practical life. Music and the dance formed part of the religious outlook that brought unity and coherence to material and spiritual life, and this holistic view remained strong as a tendency among Afro-American slaves even after they had forgotten its African origins. West Africans developed a formidable reputation for other kinds of artistic achievement within the context of their religious world-view. Pottery, weaving, sculpture, masks of bronze, ivory, and wood, as well as extraordinary metal forging in gold and iron, rose to technical and aesthetic heights now much admired by the Euro-American art world, which had so long assumed Africa to be a cultural desert. The work of these first-rate craftsmen represented an organic combination of practical needs with the aesthetic they had brought to America from Africa.

Neither the talent nor the cultural heritage disappeared in America. The slaveholders of colonial Virginia and South Carolina hired white artisans to teach slaves the crafts and even sent slaves to England for training, but they also assigned skilled slaves to teach white children.[28] The work of the slaves in building the great plantation homes extended well beyond manual labor and included the fashioning of many of the highly praised hand-wrought grilles and balconies, beautifully carved cabinets, and other decorative furnishings. Even during the late antebellum period when the slaves' level of craftsmanship had declined in the wake of growing occupational exclusion, they furnished much of the artistic beauty found in the Big Houses.[29]

During the eighteenth century every plantation had skilled craftsmen, many of whom did remarkable work in wood carving in the African manner. In the low country of South Carolina and Georgia strong African influence continued in the production of wood carvings, masks, wooden chains and figures, spoons, walking sticks, and banjos.[30] As the South as a whole experienced a forced decline of slave craftsmanship and especially of distinctly African styles and concerns, the slaves continued, however weakly, to embody one tradition and to lay the foundation for another. A resurgent Afro-American art, owing much to that history, may well lie ahead of us.

Robert Farris Thompson, the art historian of Africa who has turned his talent to Afro-America and sketched the course that creative new work is likely to follow, concludes his preliminary investigation:

> Contrary to general opinion, important Afro-American and African-influenced art exists in the United States. The tradition lacks the richness of the Afro-Caribbean and Afro-Brazilian aesthetic, but there are a number of sculptures of comparable merit. The fact that wood sculpture is the predominant medium suggests the depth of the tradition, for while painting is the classic art of the West, sculpture in wood plays a comparably central role south of the Sahara.[31]

Thompson's conclusions follow an analysis of scattered evidence drawn primarily but not exclusively from South Carolina and Georgia, where African influence has remained strongest. He draws attention to the African influence in the "amazing stoneware vessels shaped in the form of anguished human faces made by Afro-Americans in South Carolina during the last century, multiple wood carving modes in tidewater Georgia basketry . . . [and] the deliberate decoration of graves in the African manner." He traces the spread of artwork in walking sticks as far west as Missouri and focuses especially on the pottery of the eastern low country.

On the larger questions, Thompson finds certain common traits in this Afro-American art suggestive of African influence: monochromy or bichromy; smooth, luminous surfaces; frozen faces; beaded shell or metal eyes; synoptic vision, especially reminiscent of the famous art of Benin; and a particular repertory of motifs, most notably the recurrence of reptiles. He asks, "What is the meaning of the stylized anguish which contorts the face of the vessels, and for whom were the vessels made?" To the first question he replies:

> The artists of imperial Benin worked images of long-nosed Portuguese soldiers into the coiffure of an ivory representation of the ruler as a suggestion of the power of their state to incorporate the power of the foreigner. So the potters of South Carolina may have alluded to their oppressor the better to absorb his power.[32]

This suggestion appears the more plausible when we consider it as a specific manifestation of the general tendency in African and Afro-American religion to assimilate the gods of the conqueror. As for the second question, Thompson remarks that the whites must have thought the satirical and grotesque elements of slave artwork to have been amusing curiosities.

> A patronizing patronage does not make much sense as a sustaining force for the autonomous wit and invention and care which went into the making of the finest of these vessels. Their excellence goes against the grain of what we know about the low productivity of slaves in the ante-bellum South. . . . In the presence of the ferocity and energy expressed by the best of these Afro-Carolinian vessels, one senses a shift in attitude, a craft based on the self-generated incentive of a vital culture, standing apart from the nature of most pre–Civil War Southern Afro-American industry. The distinction, the writer would guess, stems from the fact that the Afro-American craftsmen made these vessels for themselves and their people for traditional reasons of their own. Under the noses of their masters they succeeded in carving out a world of aesthetic autonomy.[33]

Afro-American tradition extended into the late antebellum period and beyond. Since the craftsmen tended to be among the most acculturated of the slaves and since the African tendencies in their work grew noticeably weaker over time, a high degree of African consciousness cannot be assumed. The craftsmen, in fact, often took the lead in manifesting that denigration of things African so common among the slaves. Moreover, the persistence of certain "Africanisms" in their work suggests much less the strength of a tradition of technique and subject matter than that tradition of sensibility observed in their religion—that is, a recurrent tendency toward a holistic world-view.

African motifs and techniques faded in the products of slave craftsmanship of the nineteenth century, although in view of the experience of music and the dance, future archaeological work may turn up some surprises. This fading African expression in the crafts cannot be explained by the decline of the crafts themselves. Craftsmen generally perpetuate the collective sensibility of the community as well as their individual sensibility by passing their skills on from father to son in a social structure that permits forms even more than themes to express a traditional sensibility the specific roots of which may no longer be understood by the artists themselves. With a few exceptions the slaves could not follow this traditional course of a well-established artisanate, although the free Negroes could. But the free Negroes' circumscribed social position and dependence upon a white clientele led them away from a sustained effort to preserve African cultural elements and toward the adoption of Euro-American norms. Thus, the black craftsmen most likely to maintain high standards and to seek the fullest cultural expression in their work were increasingly those furthest removed from the folk roots of Afro-America. Still, without much more archaeological and historical investigation, the extent to which the free Negroes contributed to an Afro-American art cannot be assessed; much significant work may subsequently have disappeared or passed into forms not yet fully understood. Those Afro-American walking sticks in Missouri, which Thompson so suggestively analyzes, may have been much more than an echo of the South Carolina and Georgia lowlands. Until extensive archaeological excavations are undertaken throughout the South, as well as expert analyses of cemetery decorations, those who insist on the disappearance of an African impulse in black craftsmanship or who deny any strong artistic impulse are running well ahead of the evidence. The black craftsmen of the South, both slave and free, did, however modestly, metamorphose African impulses into ingredients of a discernible Afro-American spirit as well as style. The cultural and political direction in which Afro-America will carry their achievement remains an open question.

More research into the lives of the mechanics and craftsmen is needed, but certain conclusions already emerge. Many slaves seized every opportunity to acquire skills when they had adequate incentives, and they expressed their aesthetic sensibilities through their work to a degree greater than generally appreciated. If the numbers and skills of the mechanics and craftsmen did decline during the nineteenth century, the explanation must be sought primarily in the decreasing opportunities which accompanied increased reliance by the plantations on the products of northern industry, and secondarily, in the discriminatory pressures arising in the southern towns and cities.

The quality of these men, as men, nonetheless left a deep impression on the quarters and contributed much to the spiritual survival of Afro-America. They lacked the numbers and the opportunity to emerge as a coherent political leadership until after emancipation, when they gave a good account of themselves. Their achievement remained circumscribed and was forced into other than political channels. But they allowed those with eyes among whites and blacks alike to glimpse the potential strength of an Afro-America free to rely on its own resources and to follow its own course.

FREE NEGROES

Despite protestations of loyalty and a low incidence of seditious and rebellious behavior, free Negroes inspired fear and apprehension among the whites of the Old South. In the words of Ulrich Bonnell Phillips, "Many men of the South thought of themselves and their neighbors as living above a loaded mine, in which the negro slaves were the powder, the abolitionists the spark, and the free negroes the fuse."[1] Therefore, says Phillips, the official policy of the southern states was to reduce access to freedom and to narrow the mobility of those Negroes already free. At the same time, he adds, "The private attitude of a great number of persons toward free Negroes differed radically from the official attitude." And he continues: "Men whose main concern was with industry and commerce and not with police were disposed to judge other men more upon their industrial ability and worth than upon their color or their legal status."[2] Communities everywhere ignored a variety of restrictions placed upon manumission and the rights of free Negroes. In general the free Negro appears to have been, in the words of Caleb Perry Patterson, "a sort of inmate on parole";[3] nonetheless, even after 1830 he had just enough support from the white community to find the wherewithal to survive.

Yet, the fears and hostility of the white community as a whole constantly threatened the security and disturbed the peace of mind of the free Negroes. During the late antebellum period and early war years, pressure mounted to induce free Negroes to re-enslave themselves and to restrict their rights further. The actual change in the circumstances of free Negro life probably was not great, but the insecurity and fear induced even by public discussion of proposed changes must have been intense.[4]

A number of southern states, especially in the late antebellum period, defeated bills to expel all free Negroes or passed them in such modified form as to negate their original purpose. In the debates, arguments took one of two directions, the first alleging that most free Negroes, contrary to reputation, were industrious, loyal, and valuable members of society, and the other, that humanity forbade any such wholesale condemnation and uprooting. Whichever argument is judged the stronger, and however much the first conditioned the second, the fact remains that the extreme negrophobes never got their way, although they did win concessions. Between 1830 and 1860 one state after another closed off manumissions altogether or insisted on the removal of freedmen from the state.[5] In the 1850s the position of the free Negro in New Orleans and some other cities rapidly deteriorated through increasingly harsh attacks in the press, police harassment, and restrictions against keeping coffeehouses or entering special fields of employment.[6] The state courts, even those that acted to soften the force of the slave codes, did little or nothing to ease the plight of the free Negroes.[7] As a particularly vicious counterpart of these legal and social developments, free Negroes faced the persistent danger of being kidnapped and sold into slavery, especially during the 1850s, when slave prices rose steeply, and especially in the newly settled regions of the South.[8] Despite these difficulties, free-Negro protest and petition for redress of grievances increased during the 1850s, and so did white concern about free-Negro "impudence."[9]

In 1860 there were close to half a million free Negroes in the United States, roughly half of them in the slave states. In 1790 there had been fewer than 60,000, but the next decade saw an 82 percent increase; ten years later, thanks primarily to the annexation of Louisiana, the total free Negro population rose by about 72 percent. Thereafter, the rate of increase fell off sharply to 25 percent between 1810 and 1820, 37 percent during the twenties, 21 percent during the thirties, 12.5 percent during the forties, and 12.25 percent during the fifties. In the slave states the period 1830–1860 was one of increasing restrictions on manumission, expulsion of freedmen, and a general deterioration in the free Negroes' conditions of life. By the end of the antebellum period four states (Mississippi, Florida, Texas, and Arkansas) had fewer than 1,000 free Negro residents; and Mississippi's population declined more than 40 percent in twenty years. Five other states (Missouri, Tennessee, Alabama, Georgia, and South Carolina) had fewer than 10,000, and Kentucky had only a few hundred more than that. Louisiana had 18,600; North Carolina, 30,400; Virginia, 58,000; and Maryland, 83,900. Delaware, which had virtually ceased being a slave state, had just below 20,000. In other words, the mass of southern free Negroes were in the Southeast, from Maryland to North Carolina, with a large supplement in Louisiana.[10]

A large minority of the free Negroes—about one-third—lived in the cities and towns. Of the 83,900 in Maryland, almost 25,600 lived in Baltimore; of the 18,600 in Louisiana, 10,700 lived in New Orleans. Elsewhere, free Negroes tended to cluster in cities like Memphis, Natchez, Vicksburg, and Mobile, although a large if undetermined number lived in the countryside, especially in the Virginia-Maryland tidewater and in Arkansas and North Carolina. How many free Negroes in villages, towns, and even cities earned part of their income by occasional labor on nearby farms and plantations remains an open question, and herein lies a major clue to the ambivalence of southern whites. In the cities local white residents and nearby farmers and planters needed the skilled and unskilled labor of the free Negroes, especially before the influx of white immigrants during the 1840s and 1850s. The secular agricultural depression in the Virginia-Maryland tidewater created a curious shortage of labor at the very time when so many slaves were being sold south. The same economic factors that drove the planters to reduce the size of their slave force for reasons of efficiency and in order to raise funds to supplement low agricultural profits also drove them to hire short-term skilled labor and to seek supplementary hands during critical periods of the crop year.[11] Under these circumstances free Negroes could find work as craftsmen and ordinary laborers in town and country. Contrary to the trend in Charleston and New Orleans, economic opportunities in eastern Virginia and Maryland improved for free Negroes during the late antebellum period, although they never became secure. In Louisiana, sugar plantations needing extra labor during peak months found it among free Negroes as well as among whites. Free Negroes worked at both skilled and unskilled jobs, and many of the coopers were reputedly free Negroes. To some extent those demographic and economic forces which Marvin Harris credits with easing the path to freedom for the colored in Brazil and elsewhere and with inhibiting the development of a two-caste system played some role even within the two-caste system of the Old South.[12]

Outside Delaware, whites presumed all Negroes—that is, black and colored—to be slaves and required those who claimed to be free to produce papers to prove it. As time went on, this presumption passed into a program of restriction, culminating in the 1850s in a series of state laws that invited free Negroes to enslave themselves.[13] Only a few did so, but that some did suggests that often their legal and economic position was so precarious as to throw them on the mercy of a trusted white man.[14] In Georgia and Florida all free Negroes had to have white guardians, and elsewhere increasing pressures for guardianship led to one or another *de facto* or *de jure* response.[15]

In view of the racial basis of the slave regime and the attendant two-caste system, it is not surprising that free Negroes were generally excluded from the franchise. What is surprising is that they had the right to vote in North Carolina and Tennessee until 1835 and that they voted illegally in Rapides Parish, Louisiana, until the 1850s. In several counties of North Carolina and Tennessee and in Rapides Parish they were alleged to have the balance of power.[16]

More to the point, the free Negro had been deliberately enfranchised by the Tennessee Constitutional Convention of 1796: Negro suffrage had been the conscious will of the leading men of the state.[17] This early liberalism was all the more remarkable since Negroes had generally been denied the franchise in North America from colonial days. Both Carolinas had forbidden Negro voting by about 1715, but North Carolina reversed itself fifteen years later. Virginia excluded Negroes in 1723, Georgia in 1761.[18]

Only Delaware and Louisiana allowed free Negroes to testify against whites, although some exceptions seem to have been allowed elsewhere. In an act passed in 1732, Virginia had prohibited such testimony on the grounds that "they are people of such base and corrupt natures."[19] During the eighteenth century in Maryland, Negroes seem to have enjoyed the right, but it did not survive into the nineteenth century.[20] In Louisiana, the right of Negroes to testify against whites was reaffirmed as late as 1852, when the state legislature voted down a bill to bar such testimony in criminal cases, but the courts accepted Negro testimony with the clear understanding that the social status of the witness diminished his credibility.[21]

The laws against mixed marriage clearly reflected the racist attitude of the white community. Virginia forbade such marriages in 1705, Maryland in 1717, North Carolina not until 1838.[22] Despite such laws in most southern states and despite the stern condemnation of white public opinion, mixed marriages did occur and were sometimes even flaunted. Free Negroes married whites, especially immigrants, or rather entered into common-law arrangements with them. A number of these people felt secure enough to tell the census takers about their domestic arrangements, and many more no doubt kept them to themselves. Even in the countryside, interracial common-law marriages occasionally existed in peace. In Jefferson and Orange counties, in the extreme southeastern corner of Texas, five free Negroes, three of them men, lived openly with whites.[23] The more frontierlike the community was, the more relaxed the local whites' attitude toward miscegenation appears to have been, especially when white women were in short supply. Free Negroes were among the pioneer settlers of Texas. They and the manumitted offspring of whites and slaves combined to produce a small but stable free Negro community in Texas as early as the days of the Republic.[24]

The extent of education among the free Negroes of the South

is by no means clear, but Carter Woodson has suggested that, despite restrictive legislation, most could at least read and write. Certainly, in cities like Baltimore, New Orleans, and Mobile, where restrictions were fewer, they managed through their own efforts to get some education.[25] Negro money and talent accounted for the greater part of their modest achievement; white philanthropy helped but does not appear to have played the overwhelming role generally assumed.[26] In Maryland, Negroes somehow managed to support their own educational programs while being taxed to help pay for white schools.[27] In Virginia and Georgia, Negro educational efforts were prohibited, but travelers and other contemporaries made it clear that many Negroes managed to learn to read and write. Free Negroes in the large cities erected churches and schools, more often than not clandestine, and organized various kinds of improvement associations. Southern whites might have feared free Negroes who could read, but they also needed them in many jobs that required some skill and education. In the end the laws remained only halfheartedly enforced.

If whites hindered the free Negro in his quest for an education, they raised no objection to his paying taxes. Georgia and South Carolina enacted discriminatory taxes shortly after the Revolutionary War, and other states followed suit. "Taxes and road duty," wrote John Spencer Bassett, "alone of all their functions of citizenship were at last preserved."[28] Added to this indignity was a growing tendency to prosecute and punish free Negroes in a manner befitting slaves rather than free whites. The rest of the catalogue is familiar. Free Negroes were pariahs who nonetheless proved too valuable to expel.

Economic competition between free Negroes and whites did not reach dangerous proportions during the colonial period outside Charleston, Savannah, and perhaps a few other places. Winthrop D. Jordan accounts for the low level of white resentment toward Negro labor by saying that it "reflected the prevailing shortage of all kinds of labor in America."[29] He notes outbursts of white resentment, especially among the skilled craftsmen of the towns, but stresses their occasional character:

> In Williamsburg, for instance, white and Negro craftsmen seem to have felt no sense of racial competition. Only in Charleston was there evidence of widespread and continuing resentment and there distaste for the Negro as a job competitor was closely linked to fear

that South Carolina was running dangerously short of white men. No important movement for restricting Negroes to chores of servile drudgery developed, and of course no one tried to claim that Negroes were incapable of engaging in skilled crafts—a notion concocted after the abolition of slavery.[30]

As a matter of fact, the notion that Negroes were incapable as craftsmen grew up during the late antebellum period—in the face of overwhelming evidence to the contrary—although it does not appear to have swept the South until after the war. It grew, along with a broader sentiment for racial exclusiveness, as two major trends unfolded in the Old South: the first, the perfection of the proslavery argument, which somewhat paradoxically included a stronger racist component than ever before; and the second a marked influx of Irish and other immigrants who sought to capture the labor market of the larger towns and cities.[31]

In the light of the colonial acceptance of free Negro labor, the nineteenth-century legend of a free Negro population wallowing in poverty, crime, drunkenness, and depravity must be discarded. Many contemporary slaveholders praised the free Negro's industry, sobriety, and loyalty and asked that he be left alone. Later generations of specialized historians, from Phillips on, have generally expressed doubt that the free Negro deserved the negative reputation. An abundance of evidence demonstrates that the free Negro community, although poor and struggling, held an honorable and useful place in the southern economy.[32]

A high percentage of free Negroes lived in towns, cities, and industrial villages, but the majority lived in the countryside. Black labor in the countryside included a small, but in some places important, class of yeomen; a somewhat larger class of tenant farmers and sub-subsistence landowners who supplemented their income by working part-time for others; and a large group with little or no land, who lived as occasional laborers and had a reputation for trading illicitly with slaves, especially in stolen goods.

In some states, notably Arkansas and North Carolina, the free Negro population was overwhelmingly rural and self-supporting.[33] In North Carolina, only about 10 percent of the free Negroes lived in towns and cities, and almost 60 percent were farmhands in the big plantation counties of the eastern part of the state. Some Negroes owned their own farms, but most worked, at least part-time, on the plantations and small farms of the whites. Here as elsewhere, a substantial if minor portion lived with white families.[34]

Most of the large free Negro population of Maryland and Virginia lived and worked at or near the tidewater. White Maryland farmers needed their labor and were quick to say so whenever racist fanatics demanded their expulsion. Despite the large number of free Negroes, whites complained about the high wages that resulted from a shortage of labor. Some Negroes did well enough as farmers to hire others, including slaves.[35] In Virginia, free Negroes constituted a large proportion of the rural labor force in many counties. Data from Lunenburg County in 1814 suggest that more than 60 percent of the free Negroes there owned some land and that many more were in ancillary occupations.[36] Luther Porter Jackson's excellent study of the period 1830–1860 demonstrates that the major component of Virginia's free Negro population, with 12 percent of the total black and colored population in 1860, worked on the land and supplemented slave labor. Mechanics and artisans were found everywhere and in significant numbers, but the mass of the free Negro population consisted primarily of farmhands and unskilled laborers. Considerable tenancy and the presence of the crop lien help fill out the rural picture. Among the small class of black yeomen there were a few commercial farmers and a much larger number of subsistence farmers.[37] In Tennessee, free Negroes tended to concentrate in Memphis and other cities and towns, but even so, between 20 and 25 percent were farmers or farm laborers, and another 50 percent worked in trades that suggest possible links to the countryside.[38]

In the cities, including the big ones like New Orleans, Charleston, Mobile, and Richmond, a general decline occurred in the economic strength of the free Negroes during the nineteenth century. Although long entrenched as barbers, carpenters, bricklayers, draymen, and of course house servants, they found themselves pressed hard, if unevenly, by the Irish, Germans, and other immigrants during the nineteenth century. The most striking and yet widely ignored feature of the southern cities was the growing ethnic competition and antagonism of the last few antebellum decades. In Mobile, for example, Negroes were only 4 percent of the free male labor force in 1860 and southern-born whites only 18 percent—the rest, 15 percent from the North and 62 percent from other countries. Data from Charleston in 1848 and 1860 demonstrate a headlong decline in the absolute as well as relative position of the free Negro workers, even in such traditionally Negro occupations as barbers, blacksmiths, and tailors.[39] Free Negro artisans and laborers, and slave craftsmen and hired laborers too, doggedly held on in the cities, but by the 1850s they were losing ground, while their brothers in the countryside, although perhaps more restricted, appear to have been more secure. Indeed, one of the reasons given for the peaceful relations between free Negro and white laborers in St. Louis during the 1850s was the employment of a majority of the Negroes in the surrounding countryside. Whites and blacks worked together without much antagonism on jobs in St. Louis, but it is doubtful that the peace could have been maintained had their relative proportions been altered by a closing of the rural safety valve.[40] Neither in town nor country, with the possible exceptions of New Orleans and Charleston, was there a Negro middle class of significant proportions.

Some groups of free Negroes even owned slaves, usually as a way of circumventing laws against manumission. In the late antebellum period one state after another passed laws that required manumitted slaves to leave the state and made manumission as difficult as possible. As a result, a free Negro who wished to purchase the freedom of a wife, husband, child, parent, or friend normally had to acquire and maintain property rights in his or her person; if this was not done, the emancipated Negro faced expulsion from the state. The great majority of Negro slaveholders—the total number of which was never large, although it has yet to be tabulated properly—owned relatives or friends as a mere formality. The frequency with which Negro slaveholders appeared as owners of their own children and grandchildren resulted from the particular difficulties attached to manumitting slaves under thirty years of age, even when manumission was still a legal possibility.[41] Negro slaveholders faced their slaves in a relationship such as that Judge Manly of North Carolina described as existing between free Negroes and particular whites—that of *"patron* and *client."*[42]

The efforts, successful and unsuccessful, of slaves and free Negroes to free themselves and their loved ones often reached heroic proportions. Most slaves who bought their own freedom had been skilled workers whose masters had permitted them to "hire their own time," but the economic position of a larger portion of the free Negro community made small savings possible. Some free Negroes, themselves sometimes only recently freed, devoted their efforts to buying freedom for others and accomplished what can only be judged as extraordinary feats of industry and selflessness.[43] To cite only one of many cases, Samuel Martin, who was called "the oldest resident of Port Gibson, Mississippi," bought his freedom in 1829 with the greatest effort and difficulty and then worked to buy six others, all of whom he freed and took to Cincinnati in 1844.[44]

Not all Negroes who owned only a few slaves were so selfless. Even among these cases some were interested solely or largely in profit making. Thomas Bonneau of South Carolina, founder of a school for free Negroes, left two slave girls to his heir. His will stipulated that if the girls did not behave, they were to be sold— "in that case," he added, "the money will be sure."[45] Litigation arising from disputes over the condition of the merchandise indicates that even free Negro slaveholders sometimes were merely engaged in business.[46]

Even when relatives were bought, their fate necessarily remained precarious while they were legally slaves. Carter Woodson found cases of husbands who bought their wives and deliberately kept them as slaves to ensure their fidelity and good behavior. One Negro shoemaker in Charleston, South Carolina, bought his wife for $700, found her impossible to please, and sold her some months later for $750.[47]

The white community accepted the necessity of a few exceptions to the manumission laws and was prepared to look the other way, especially since the forces of custom and local usage so often modified southern legal arrangements. The right of Negroes to own slaves had been firmly upheld by the courts in Virginia as early as 1654. Not until 1832 was this right effectively challenged, and then only to the extent of limiting further purchases by Negroes to their spouses or children.[48] In North Carolina, the right of free Negroes to accumulate property was never seriously challenged except when that property consisted of slaves. Even so, the Supreme Court reaffirmed Negro slaveownership in 1833. Not until the secessionist legislature of 1860–1861 was this right withdrawn, and then not retroactively.[49] Curiously, the decision of 1860–1861 came when it was hardly needed. John Hope Franklin points out that the decline in the economic condition of the free Negroes in North Carolina had reduced their efforts to buy slaves to a mere trickle during the closing decades of the antebellum period. Only Arkansas and the virtually free state of Delaware specifically prohibited Negro slaveownership, although other states increasingly created obstacles.[50]

Still, the presence of affluent Negro slaveholders caused apprehension among the whites. Those Negroes who were genuine

slaveholders presented several knotty problems for white southerners. Since the basis of southern slavery was racial, there was
something strange and disquieting about the existence of black and
brown slaveholders. In Jamaica, Saint-Domingue, Cuba, Brazil,
and elsewhere a three-caste system or something more fluid existed; consequently, the existence of a colored, as distinct from a
black, class of slaveholders created fewer ideological difficulties,
although much trouble ensued anyway. There was no such bridge
in the Old South.

Two states of the Old South stand out as having had highly
visible if small groups of large slaveholders within the free Negro
population: Louisiana easily ranked first, with South Carolina second.[51] The existence of a small class of colored slaveholders and
their reputation for cruelty, whether deserved or not, present two
questions: the first concerns the circumscribed three-caste system
of New Orleans and Charleston, which had at least feeble echoes
elsewhere; the second concerns the more general problem of free
Negro relationships with slaves. A circumscribed three-caste system appeared precisely in the areas of French and Spanish influence: Louisiana, of course; Charleston and lowland South
Carolina, with their early Huguenot settlers and later émigrés
from Saint-Domingue; and the Gulf coast of Alabama, which came
to the United States as part of the Florida cession.[52]

Economic circumstances strengthened the hand of the free
Negroes but were far from strong enough to account for their
relatively favored position. Culture and tradition more than economic advantage protected the free Negroes in their caste pretensions, especially the well-to-do mulattoes. These pretensions,
especially in Louisiana where they were strongest, were reinforced by the cumulative effect of political divisions among the
whites. When the Spanish took Louisiana from the French, they
so feared the pro-French feeling among the whites that they deliberately set out to placate the free Negroes. By this time, in any case,
the free Negroes were firmly entrenched in the economy and
could, with reasonable legal protection, hold their own against
white immigration. Subsequently, even under the Americans,
military conditions during Indian wars, slave risings, and the War
of 1812 allowed the free Negroes to maintain their traditional rights
by loyalty to the slaveholders' regime.[53]

The actual relationship that existed between free Negroes and
slaves remains to be discovered. It would be surprising if major

differences between town and country were not uncovered. In the towns and especially in the larger cities, many slaves "hired their own time" and lived away from their masters. Although these practices were generally illegal, they were sanctioned almost everywhere, by custom and in accordance with white business interests. Consequently, free Negroes, whose freedom was always precarious, interacted every day, socially and at work, with slaves who were close to being half-free. A certain amount of intermarriage occurred, and little in the social setting generated antipathy. Exclude for the moment the haughty but tiny mulatto bourgeoisie of New Orleans and Charleston and the small class of slaves attached as house servants to the town houses of the great white planters and who took on airs from the attachment: the numerous free Negroes and urban slaves who worked at similar skilled and unskilled jobs apparently displayed little of the caste feeling that allegedly divided the Negro population of the cities. On the contrary, as Richard B. Morris has shown, the improvement in the condition of some slaves, effected through the hiring system, was largely offset by the deterioration in the economic and social position of the free Negro working class.[54]

Fragmentary evidence suggests that with the possible exception of New Orleans, Charleston, and a few other cities, free Negroes and upward-mobile slaves saw each other as brothers in a different legal condition rather than as competitors from rival status groups, although in those larger cities the process of stratification and caste distinction within the free Negro community appears to have gone far by 1860. This identification was strongest when many in both groups had relatives in the other, even a wife or husband. In North Carolina, for example, John Hope Franklin finds: "It was not unusual for free Negroes to live on slave plantations and to participate in the life there. Some of them had slave wives or husbands, and the benevolent master frequently permitted them to live there together, hiring the services of the free person."[55] Some free Negroes worked as overseers, some earned a living by tracking runaways, and others lived on mutually hostile terms with the slaves.[56] Many more lived on such close and sympathetic terms with them that some masters tried to prevent any contact.[57] Free Negroes and slaves faced the hostility and harsh competition of increasing numbers of European immigrants, who were quick to seize upon white racism as a way of securing a position in the job market.

The churches and, where circumstances permitted, the schools and social activities sponsored by free Negroes in the large cities were usually open to slaves. Certainly the white community, even in cities like Charleston, believed that relations between the slaves and free Negroes were close.[58] Ira Berlin observes:

> Some freedmen organized churches, schools, and benevolent societies. On the surface, these institutions were but a weak image of those of white society. They reflected middle class values and aped the structure of their white counterparts. But slowly their own special style began to emerge, so that African churches, schools, and benevolent societies not only gave their members a measure of security and a richer life, but provided a base from which to attack white racism.
>
> From the beginning, free Negroes expressed their desire for independence by creating and controlling their own institutions.[59]

Both whites and slaves told contradictory stories about free Negroes. Some runaways remembered the free Negroes with loathing; John Little, who fled North Carolina for Canada, recalled how a free Negro had once betrayed him for ten dollars.[60] James Redpath, the abolitionist editor, recalled a revealing conversation with a Negro, presumably a slave, in North Carolina: "He advised me not to trust the free colored population, because many of them were mean enough to go straight to the white people and tell them that a stranger had been talking to them about freedom." In other words, treachery lurked everywhere; but recognition of the presence of many informers would hardly justify a conclusion that it defined the primary relationship of slaves to free Negroes. Consider the next sentence of Redpath's report: "He advised me also to be cautious with many of the slaves."[61]

White slaveholders and black abolitionists both saw the free Negro, at least potentially, as an ally of slave insurgents. Whites throughout the South charged that free Negroes corrupted the slaves, encouraged them to steal and defect, and generally led them astray. David Walker, in his famous *Appeal*, attacked colonization as designed to separate resourceful and intelligent free Negroes from the slaves whom they could teach and lead. He added that the whites recognized how disturbing the mere presence of free black men was to the slave system.[62] The sight of free black caulkers in Baltimore exhibiting both class and racial militancy by celebrating John Brown's raid was inevitably disquieting.[63] Frederick Douglass added a special dimension to Walker's older argument. As a boy he had been taught that God made all whites masters and all blacks slaves, but he saw clearly that in fact all whites were not masters and all blacks were not slaves.[64] Douglass also paid tribute to the active contribution of some free Negroes to the freedom of their brothers. He described in particular how some free Negroes lent manumission papers to runaways to facilitate their escape. The runaway would then mail the papers back from the free states. Douglass insists that many free Negroes gambled on their own freedom in this way. The odds were dangerous, for return of the papers depended on the runaway's making good his escape to free territory and having the presence of mind and integrity to send the papers back quickly and safely.[65]

Free Negro participation in slave revolts had a cloudy history. White fears and the fierce legal retaliation after almost every insurrection scare suggest that free Negroes were at the center of the black revolutionary impulse from Virginia to Texas, but few free Negroes have ever been found to have taken part in the actual revolts or in the many incipient revolts or scares. Denmark Vesey stands out as a great exception, and it is possible that one or two free Negroes joined Gabriel Prosser's movement and one or two other early risings, notably that of 1795.[66] Other free Negroes were known to have betrayed slave plots, as in the projected rising in Frederick, Maryland, in 1814.[67] During the rising in Louisiana in 1811—probably the greatest in the history of the slave South—free colored men offered their services to the governor and played an important role in the suppression of the rebellious slaves.[68] The ambivalence of the free Negro community appeared most sharply during the so-called Seminole War in Florida, which was really a Negro war more than an Indian one. Many free Negroes supported the Indian and black forces during the long struggle, and some fought in their ranks; others were to be found on the side of the whites.[69] During the War for Southern Independence, free colored militia units, most notably at New Orleans, offered their services to the Confederacy and then changed sides at the appropriate moment—a record each of us may interpret for himself. Elsewhere, free Negroes worked for the Confederacy when they had to, but identified with the cause of freedom when Union generals sought to organize quasi-forced-labor battalions.[70]

In view of the slender support given by free Negroes to slave revolts, and in view of the willingness of some—in fact, of many in Louisiana—to side with the whites against the slaves, how should the wrath that followed every slave revolt be interpreted? A review of the restrictive legislation on manumission and the status of free Negroes shows that the worst blows fell after slave insurrections or scares. Almost invariably, free Negroes were thought to be responsible, despite a monotonously consistent lack of evidence. Yet, the slaveholder had every reason to worry about the free Negroes, even when he knew very well that few of them were likely to meddle in seditious or insurrectionary plots. As a "Memorial of the Citizens of Charleston to the Senate and House of Representatives of the State of South Carolina" observed in 1822, the mere presence of free Negroes reminded the slaves of what they would like to be but could not become and rendered their own labor the more irksome. The memorial pointed out that, among other evils, the free colored population served as a transmitter of information and seditious ideas to the slaves. Since almost all ideas were seditious when not those of the master, the claim was not so far-fetched. From elsewhere in the South came reports that the presence of free Negroes disturbed the slaves; that free Negroes traded illegally with slaves, usually in stolen goods; and that free Negroes more often than not aided and abetted runaways and in general acted like Negroes first and free men second.[71] Rarely did white southerners consider that the increasing tendency to treat slaves and free Negroes alike under the law and the successful circumscription of the incipient three-caste system of New Orleans and Charleston made the result inevitable.

Slaveholders agreed almost unanimously that the free Negroes of the towns corrupted their slaves, although their complaints fell just as heavily on the town slaves and therefore on the general conditions of town life rather than on the free Negroes per se. If the freedom of the free Negroes existed within narrow limits, the slavery of the town slaves was so loose as to make them look almost free. The complaints fell on the blacks' gambling, whoring, and drinking, but principally on their ease of movement and control of time in both work and leisure.[72] In New Orleans, conditions hit bottom from the white point of view. Joseph G. Tregle, Jr., observes:

> The whole behavior of the Negro toward the whites, as a matter of fact, was singularly free of that deference and circumspection which might have been expected in a slave community. It was not

unusual for slaves to gather on street corners at night, for example, where they challenged whites to attempt to pass, hurled taunts at white women, and kept whole neighborhoods disturbed by shouts and curses. Nor was it safe to accost them, as many went armed with knives and pistols in flagrant defiance of all precautions of the Black Code.[73]

The black population of the towns and cities, both slave and free, did not live in racially segregated areas. The slaves typically lived in quarters behind their masters' houses, and the free Negroes lived in almost every part of town, often near a white patron. Thus, despite forming a single black community centered in the churches—but also in the gambling houses and brothels and on street corners—the blacks constituted an intimate part of the general community.

Notwithstanding the boldness, the most extreme manifestation of which Tregle so strikingly describes, the urban blacks had to make widespread accommodation to white hegemony. The cultural influence, particularly that of the free Negroes among them, on the southern black community as a whole tended toward assimilation of white values and away from those of rural black folk. If, under the circumstances, the free Negroes never rose against the regime in a suicidal gesture, neither did they ever give clear evidence of their loyalty and reliability to the master class. They kept their own counsel and held on to what they had as best they could. Their course may have lacked the theatrics that nowadays pass for revolutionary heroics in middle-class circles, but it had dignity, purpose, and wisdom.

MISCEGENATION

W. E. B. Du Bois, discussing antebellum miscegenation, referred to it as "stark, ugly, painful, beautiful," and added, "The colored slave woman became the medium through which two great races were united."[1] The intimacy of the Big House and of the paternalistic master-slave relationship in general manifested itself as acts of love in the best cases, sadistic violence in the worst, and ostensible seduction and imposed lust in the typical. "You're not worried about me marrying *your* daughter," James Baldwin told a white southerner during a television debate. "You're worried about me marrying your *wife's* daughter. I've been marrying your daughter ever since the days of slavery."[2]

Because three-quarters or so of today's Afro-American population in the United States reputedly has some white ancestry, we seek its origins primarily in the easy access to slave women provided by plantation slavery. Yet, only about 13 percent of the Afro-American population of 1860 had white ancestry, according to the census reports, although some scholars have estimated 20 percent or more.[3] According to the official statistics, the percentage of "mulattoes" (as all with some white ancestry came to be called) in the slave population was about twice as high in the states of the Upper South as in the Lower. The figure was close to 20 percent in Missouri and Kentucky and about 15 percent in Virginia but only between 5 and 9 percent in South Carolina, Alabama, Mississippi, and Georgia. These figures do not support the hypothesis about slave breeding, although mulattoes show up most frequently in the slave-exporting states and in such new slave-importing states as Arkansas and Texas.[4] The size of the slaveholding units in the slave-exporting states ranged well below that of the slave-importing states; slaveholding farms and small plantations dominated the Upper South, and interracial intimacy prevailed, in sexual and other matters. And with the exception of New Orleans and Charleston, the cities were in the Upper South, as were the great majority of large towns.

In 1850 an estimated 37 percent of the free Negro population of the United States was part white, although the figure was much higher for the half of the free Negro population living in the South. Probably, little more than 10 percent of the slave population had white ancestry.[5] Those who distrust the low census figures— and it is easy to distrust them—point out that mulattoes were so designated by the crudest observation and that a tendency to underreport was manifest. The crude observations also produced counterdistortions. All Africans are not "black"; they vary considerably in skin color. Whether the lighter-skinned African peoples have white ancestry remains in doubt, but for our purposes it is beside the point. Many apparent mulattoes must have fallen into the category provided by an advertisement for a runaway in North Carolina: "His color is tolerably bright, but he has no white blood in him."[6]

The plantations hardly emerge from the statistics looking like the harems of abolitionist fantasy. Many of the free Negroes did originate in plantation unions, but their very freedom suggests that many of the original sexual unions had been other than rape and debauchery. To risk some generalizations: (1) Enough violations of black women occurred on the plantations to constitute a scandal and make life hell for a discernible minority of black women and their men. (2) Much of the plantation miscegenation occurred with single girls under circumstances that varied from seduction to rape and typically fell between the two. (3) Married black women and their men did not take white sexual aggression lightly and resisted effectively enough to hold it to a minimum. (4) Most of the miscegenation in the South occurred in the towns and cities, not on the plantations or even farms. With all these qualifications, miscegenation had a profound and in some respects devastating effect on southern life.

The towns and cities provided the favored setting and housed the larger numbers of the mulattoes, some of whom had doubtless stemmed from rural unions. Sexual ratios in the towns and cities propelled interracial concubinage, for white males usually outnumbered white females, whereas black females usually outnumbered black males.[7] Urban life generally moved at a faster pace and in a looser manner. Miscegenation primarily occurred outside the plantation heartland, although when it occurred inside, it tended to be the more violent and cruel.

Many white men who began by taking a slave girl in an act of sexual exploitation ended by loving her and the children she bore. They were not supposed to, but they did—and in larger numbers than they or subsequent generations of white and black southerners have ever wanted to admit. The Supreme Court of Kentucky refused to judge insane a white man who wanted to marry the slave he had just emancipated. However repugnant, the court declared, such concubinage occurred too often to permit denial of the attraction.[8] The courts handled many divorce cases and squabbles over wills in which a genuinely affectionate and lasting relationship between a master and a slave led to litigation.[9] With increasingly strict manumission laws in effect, the efforts of the masters to free concubines and children ran into great obstacles, but the court records contain many such attempts. In the twentieth century no small number of southern white families have retained close links with the colored descendants of these relationships.[10]

The freeing of mulatto children does not necessarily reveal

much about the quality of the sexual union, for it may have come about solely from guilt, a sense of parental responsibility, or pride of race; but it does weigh on the side of the meaningful rather than the promiscuous. Throughout the history of the slave regime there were planters who openly or surreptitiously accepted responsibility for the paternity of mulattoes, educated them, freed them, and, when manumission became difficult, made special provisions for their care. Much of the free Negro population came from this source.[11] William Gilmore Simms spoke openly of the force of these interracial ties when he rebuked Harriet Martineau for suggesting that slaveholders deliberately got their slave girls pregnant in order to increase their capital assets.

> The rule that the child shall follow the condition of the mother is not a stimulant to licentiousness among the whites. . . . [Miss Martineau] certainly knows but little of human passion, if she supposes that, in matters of this nature, the mercenary desire of gain will prompt the white man to such excesses, other provocatives being wanting. So far from this being the motive, it may be stated here with perfect safety that the greater number of Southern mulattoes have been made free in consequence of their relationship to their owners.[12]

But if most of those emancipated originated in miscegenation, most issue from miscegenation did not gain their freedom. Olmsted's reports from Virginia applied to the whole South: a large majority of mulatto children born to slaveholders lived their lives as slaves, often with no special consideration or privileges.[13]

Some light on the quality of the more tangled relations comes from an unlikely source. For the pleasure of the wealthiest planters, or more likely their unmarried sons, New Orleans, Louisville, and a few other cities maintained "fancy-girl" markets, which aroused the special ire of the northern abolitionists. These girls, young, shapely, and usually light in color, went as house servants with special services required. First-class blacksmiths were being sold for $2,500 and prime field hands for about $1,800, but a particularly beautiful girl or young woman might bring $5,000. Wherever slavery has existed such markets have existed also. "With this, as with any other merchandise," writes Iris Origo about the market for Eastern European fancy girls in Renaissance Tuscany, "peculiarly attractive wares could command what the Italian phrase aptly calls a *prezzo d'affezione.*"[14]

These sales, private and public, went on in full view, drew

attention but not much censure from the southern press, and were considered by the slaveholder's society more of a curiosity of up-per-class life than a moral problem. Northern antislavery writers expressed outrage on two counts: concern for the young women forced into degrading relationships with debauched white men; and special concern about the young women's so often being virtu-ally white. A touch of racism may have paid political dividends, for northern opinion responded so much more readily to the exploita-tion of quadroons and octoroons than it ever would have if the preference of the southern gentlemen had been for blacks. The fate of these young women varied greatly. Some of their purchasers undoubtedly were the most dissolute members of the planter class, although their having been so did not necessarily mean that they treated their concubines worse than did the less tainted souls. The women left no record of their attitudes. Some may have resembled Maria, whom Solomon Northup described:

> Maria was a rather genteel looking colored girl, with a faultless form, but ignorant and extremely vain. The idea of going to New-Orleans was pleasing to her. She entertained an extravagantly high opinion of her own attractions. Assuming a haughty mien, she declared to her companions, that immediately on our arrival in New-Orleans, she had no doubt some wealthy single gentleman of good taste would purchase her at once![15]

For many other young women, raised by slave mothers with strong moral values or unlucky enough to fall into the hands of a sadistic master, life could become grim. But most men, even most free-wheeling, gambling, whoring young aristocrats, do not readily indulge their sadistic impulses. It would be hard to live with a beautiful and submissive young woman for long and to continue to consider her mere property or a mere object of sexual gratification, especially since the free gift of her beauty has so much more to offer than her yielding to force. The *prezzo d'affezione* was usually just that: it would not be astonishing if many of these fancy girls, like their famous free quadroon sisters in New Orleans who entered into an institutionally structured concubinage with wealthy whites, often ended by falling in love with their men, and vice versa.[16]

Some prominent planters flaunted their slave mistresses and mulatto children. David Dickson of Georgia, one of the most cele-brated leaders in the movement to reform southern agriculture,

lost his wife early in life, took a mistress, and accepted a measure
of social disapproval to live openly with her and their children.[17]
Bennet H. Barrow of Louisiana exploded with rage over similar
conduct on the part of his neighbors. His fellow planters of West
Feliciana Parish were, he said, of course all opponents of the abolitionists: "Yet the people submit to amalgamation in its worse form
in this Parish, Josias Grey takes his mulatto children with him to
public places etc. and receives similar company from New Orleans. . . ."[18] The first mayor of Memphis, Marcus Winchester, had
a beautiful free quadroon mistress whom he married and took to
Louisiana. His successor, Ike Rawlins, lived with a slave woman.
He did not marry her but did provide handsomely for their son.
And the haughty nabobs of Natchez had their own scandals. Other
white observers report such relationships, displayed publicly and
accepted by society with nothing worse than muttering and minor
social ostracism.[19] Several daughters of wealthy free Negroes married respectable white men.[20]

Ex-slaves talked both about the forcing of black women by white
men and about strong and affectionate interracial relationships.
James Dallas Burruss, Fisk University's first professor of math-
ematics, who had been one of three children born in Tennessee to
a white father and a slave mother, said that his parents "lived
together in affectionate and respectful companionship." And an
ex-slave in Arkansas described his white father as having been "a
fool" about his mother.[21] The slave narratives reveal such relationships and hint at still more in reports of planters and overseers
who kept one woman as a mistress for many years and in descriptions of violent jealousy shown by the white men.[22] Evidence from
the slaveholders themselves confirms the existence of the stable
interracial unions suggested in the narratives.[23]

White southerners admitted their sexual exploitation of black
women but tried to deny that anything like love ever could enter
into white men's feelings about them. Henry Hughes of Mississippi, oblivious to the sport that later generations might make with
his words, burst forth: "Hybridism is heinous. Impurity of races
is against the law of nature. Mulattoes are monsters. The law of
nature is the law of God. The same law which forbids consanguin-
ous amalgamation forbids ethnical amalgamation. Both are incestuous. Amalgamation is incest."[24] Heinously incestuous or not,
white men slept with black women and less often black men slept
with white women; and, much more often than they were sup-

posed to, those who began by seeking casual pleasure ended by caring.[25] Still, "caring," "affection," and "love" could not be simple matters in these tortured circumstances. "A central tragedy of the slave-white relationship," writes Earl E. Thorpe, "was that neither side could love or hate in anything like fullness of dimension."[26] Individual exceptions aside, blacks and whites were not free to love each other without considerable emotional confusion, marked in part by a self-contempt projected onto the other. The tragedy of miscegenation lay, not in its collapse into lust and sexual exploitation, but in the terrible pressure to deny the delight, affection, and love that so often grew from tawdry beginnings. Whites as well as blacks found themselves tortured as well as degraded, but not always for the reasons they thought.

Despite pretenses that miscegenation occurred primarily between lower-class whites and slaves, many slaveholders and their growing sons took slave mistresses or forced reluctant women and fathered mulatto children. Some of the black people interviewed in the 1930s traced their ancestry to a former master or related incidents from their own plantations with a ring of authenticity.[27] Some reports from ex-slaves refer to the reaction of the slaveholder and his wife to the presence of her husband's mulatto children. No pattern emerges. Many masters disposed of their own children in the slave trade, but others sold them to a friend who offered protection and kindness or looked after them on their own plantation. Many wives forced the sale of their husband's children or treated them cruelly, but a surprising number showed them tenderness and played the kind stepmother. Southern court records containing divorce suits in which slaves are mentioned, in effect, as corespondents suggest that meaningful affairs, if not common, were not rare.[28]

The slaveholders refuted their own claims that the white lower classes, not themselves, forced or seduced the slave women. No modern historian who has examined the evidence from the slaveholders' papers and records accepts those claims.[29] The great slave traders knew better. Gardner, Smith & Co. of New Orleans kept a boarding house for prospective buyers who wanted accommodations with their women slaves.[30] A slaveholder, writing in a journal read largely by other slaveholders, admonished:

> Every effort should be used to prevent that sexual intercourse, which degrades the master and is the cause of discontent to the slave. As far

as is practical, it would be advisable to have elderly servants only in families, and the young should be employed wholly in agrestic and other manual labours. The custom of bringing up negro children in towns or about the dwellings of their owners is fraught with evil and should be avoided.[31]

But listen to Chancellor Harper:

> And can it be doubted that this purity [of the white women] is caused by, and is a compensation for, the evils resulting from the existence of an enslaved class of more relaxed morals? . . . It is mostly the warm passions of youth, which give rise to licentious intercourse. But I do not hesitate to say that the intercourse which takes place with enslaved females is less depraving in its effects than when it is carried on with females of their own caste. In the first place, as like attracts like, that which is unlike repels; and though the strength of passion be sufficient to overcome the revulsion, still the attraction is less. He feels that he is connecting himself with one of an inferior and servile caste, and there is something of degradation in the act. The intercourse is generally casual; he does not make her habitually an associate, and is less likely to receive any taint from her habits and manners.[32]

State laws carefully defined those with up to seven-eighths white ancestry as "Negroes." To have pushed the definition any further would have embarrassed too many prominent "white" families.[33] In 1854 a vigorous debate engulfed the Louisiana legislature over a proposal to refuse all petitions for emancipation. Peter Tanner, representative of Rapides Parish, rose to speak in opposition:

> Do you wish to retain a negress with whom he had lived in concubinage under the roof or in the neighborhood of the legitimate white wife? Will you by your action inflict upon a white lady such a monstrous wrong as this? . . . Sir, the woman and her bastard brood should be sent away. Her presence can only engender quarrels and turn the domestic hearth into a mortal hell.
>
> Sir, if an examination be made, it will be found that such cases as this have led to numberless applications for divorces. We cannot by our act stifle or destroy the feelings of human nature.[34]

Mr. Tanner took for granted the quality of the interracial relationships; he did not, for example, worry about those masters who, once they married, callously sold their former mistresses to slave traders.

Some white southerners frankly admitted that personal maids

and body servants in the homes of some of the best families were in fact children of the Big House. "In numbers of cases," wrote M. T. Judge of Mobile, Alabama, "the girl picked out for the young lady was her half-sister. This was also applied to the young man, but in those cases I have never heard of any great devotion. In the case of the pure slaves, the devotion was at times sublime."[35]

Apologists for the slave regime have charged overseers and other lower-class white men with responsibility for most of the abuse of slave women on the plantations. Most planters discouraged such liaisons if for no other reason than that they caused great trouble in the quarters. When the slave men did not resort to violence, they ran away, sulked, or shirked work. Haller Nutt, one of the biggest planters of the Natchez region, wrote in his "General Rules to Govern Time of an Overseer":

> Above all things avoid all intercourse with negro women. It breeds more trouble, more neglect, more idleness, more rascality, more stealing, & more lieing [sic] up in the quarters & more everything that is wrong on a plantation than all else put together. Instead of studying or thinking about women in bed or out of bed, a man should think about what he has to do tomorrow—or for a week ahead, or for a month or year.... In fact such intercourse is out of the question —it must not be tolerated.[36]

No few overseers found themselves summarily dismissed when their employers found out that they were keeping black mistresses or behaving promiscuously with the slave women.[37] But many overseers took black women anyway, sometimes with the knowledge of their employers.[38] Slaveholders decided not to notice when both the overseers and the black women were single, when no special resentment arose among the black men, and when the relationship was stable. Few slaveholders tolerated overseers who promiscuously trifled in the quarters or whose actions infuriated the men or caused a commotion. Married overseers had the better chance to secure employment, for single men could be expected to take a mistress and might be tempted into disorderly living. Yet, as William Kauffman Scarborough shows, some areas of the South had large numbers of unmarried overseers.[39] Many more overseers may have taken unmarried mistresses more or less with their consent than forced women, particularly married women. Either way, a discernible crop of "yellow" babies were born. White laborers and local poor whites also fathered an undetermined number of mulatto children, but in most such cases the women had the option of refusal.

According to legend, antebellum miscegenation coupled white men and black women, and occasionally black men and poor white women, but rarely if ever black men and white women of the planter class. The upper-class young ladies enjoyed much less freedom of movement than the young men. Still, white women with black lovers or even husbands—Missouri did not forbid mixed marriages until 1835 nor did South Carolina until the postbellum period—appear in the records of the state appellate courts. It is not possible to estimate the number of such unions; most never came into public view.[40]

Despite the legend, white women of all classes had black lovers and sometimes husbands in all parts of the South, especially in the towns and cities. Ex-slaves recalled a number of instances on the plantations.[41] One wife of a brutal slaveholder defiantly took the carriage driver for a lover and bore his child. A planter's daughter ran off with a slave, bore his child, and refused to leave him. When measured by postbellum probabilities, the interesting feature of these and similar cases is that the black men did not suffer lynching; the whites apparently took these matters much more in stride than they were able to do later.[42] The eccentric and explosive J. J. Flournoy of Georgia did not qualify as a sober witness on most questions, but sometimes only such a man dares to speak the truth. "Do not many of our pretty white girls," he thundered in a letter to Governor R. F. W. Allston of South Carolina, "even now permit illicit negro embrace at the South?"[43] The governor did not reply.

The frequent charge that slaveholders and overseers seduced or forced most of the young, sexually attractive slave girls appears to be a great exaggeration and an injustice to blacks as well as whites. The big plantations of the South Carolina and Georgia low country, for example, had few mulatto children, much to the surprise of the northerners who accompanied the Union occupation.[44] Many ex-slaves told stories about the seduction and rape of black women; others insisted that their masters permitted no such nonsense and that the black women lived without dread of white sexual violence.[45] This white disapproval of the exploitation of black women—or rather, of sexual irregularities in general—requires a close look, but by itself it cannot explain the large number of plantations on which little or no miscegenation occurred. Many black women fiercely resisted such aggression, and many black men proved willing to die in defense of their women.[46] Planters and overseers who confronted resistant women and dangerous men usually had the good sense to content themselves with trying to seduce attractive single girls by using a combination of flattery, bribes, and the ever-present threat of force. The atrocious aggression of some masters and overseers against married women (and their husbands) or against unwilling single women must not be minimized, especially since rape did not have to occur everywhere or every day to add up to an overpowering indictment against the regime as a whole. On this evidence alone, slavery stands convicted of inexpiable crimes against black people. But black women and their men were able to set limits by their own actions.

The sexual exploitation of black women, however outrageous, will startle no one. The problem is to explain why it did not go much further. The resistance of the women and their men, important as it was, does not provide a full explanation, for the restraint shown by so many whites must also be accounted for. Brazil offers an illuminating contrast. The Portuguese settlers and their descendants availed themselves freely and openly of Indian and then African women. The shortage of white women explains little. Wherever white women were in short supply, as in the Caribbean, masters and overseers took black or mulatto concubines, but Luso-Brazilian men won a reputation for widespread philandering and for openly flaunting colored mistresses long after their marriages to upper-class ladies. A slaveholder's son who reached his teens without having sampled the slave girls cast grave doubts on his masculinity. Something had to be wrong with him. Perhaps his earlier indulgence in *leva-pancadas* with the slave boys, instead of whetting his appetite for richer treasures, had caught his fancy as a way of life. Had he become a "sissy"?[47]

No mystifications about Latin versus Anglo-Saxon sexuality need be invoked to explain a profound cultural difference. Latin and Anglo-Saxon Europe, both Protestant and Catholic, had their share of virtuous and lascivious men, however defined, but mores diverged with the Reformation and its Puritan development. The permissible and the taken-for-granted changed radically even if the impulses to violation did not. This shift in values itself reflected a shift in social conditions that helps explain the growing restraints in areas of Anglo-Saxon ascendancy. The decline of seigneurialism in England and Holland, in contradistinction to its continued strength in Portugal, meant a decline in the easy attitude that "that's what servant girls are for." This attitude never wholly died among the English upper classes, and Fielding among other novelists entertained his own and future generations with the theme; but it became increasingly gauche to flaunt it. Until the nineteenth century, upper-class marriage had little to do with initial love. Its purpose was to secure the family fortune, to legitimize issue, and to sustain the public order. Mistresses and lovers, naturally, had their place in any civilized relationship. With the coming of the nineteenth century these eminently sensible views gave way to the idea that marriage ought to follow love instead of vice versa, and that nice people did not engage in extracurricular activity. Although the upper classes violated their own precepts, which like most precepts were intended to guide the masses rather than their betters, the new sentiments made steady progress. One might even measure the progress by measuring the decline in the number of retainers attached to the great families, were not such a procedure to betray a cynicism not to be countenanced. With whatever qualifications, playing around in the pantry no longer amused society in the old way; husbands and wives were expected to observe their marriage vows, or rather, to exercise discretion and respect each other's sensibilities.

Typically, the slaveholders could not take their black "wenches" without suffering psychic agony and social opprobrium.[48] The men could not sow their wild oats with the happy abandon of the Brazilians. Could any sane Brazilian have agonized in the manner of David Gavin of the South Carolina low country?

Sept. 29, 1855. I am not in good health, and am now convinced it is not healthy to live singly or without intercourse between the sexes. I have always been opposed to intercourse between the sexes before marriage or unlawful intercourse, but I believe now that if a man lives until he is forty years old, he should have intercourse, even unlawfully, or his health will be impaired. In 1853 I first began to feel the bad effects of it, was more confirmed in the summer of 1854 and now 1855 am fully convinced. I was born 15th Nov. 1811 and will be forty-four years old in Nov. next. I feel dull and heavy, little desire for exertion and little desire for women. I have no doubt haveing [sic] no sexual intercourse with them is the cause. I have no doubt it affects the health of women as well as men, perhaps not as much as men, and some men sooner than others. I think therefore that illicit intercourse in both male and female is better than injury to health, although the world may condemn it because it is ignorant of the bad effect of non intercourse on health. I never had the least idea of its bad effect on the health of men until as above stated and therefore sternly condemned all sexual intercourse or libertinism. I wish I had only known it sooner, God grant I may be able to restore my health. I still condemn what may be termed *libertinism* but not the moderate or occasional sexual intercourse which is necessary to health.

Poor Gavin's resolution to end his self-imposed oppression wavered. In 1856 he kept dreaming of large rattlesnakes and of losing his hat, and in 1859 he returned to the theme of nonintercourse by again complaining about the injury to his health, the need for sexual activity, and the hope that he could bring himself to do something about it.[49]

Gavin's large plantation housed its share of young black women, to whom he never refers; his speculations concerned the white whores in town. And if he was lying to himself, so much the more significant. That Gavin was not typical is beside the point. Even in the Victorian South forty-four-year-old male virgins did not abound. Yet, he can hardly be thought unique when the *New Orleans Medical and Surgical Journal* could publish a grave warning about the dangers of abstinence among men, who suffer in consequence from "irritable state of the testes, headaches, malaise, etc. and from nocturnal emissions." The anonymous author challenged a moral code that so clearly contradicted nature.[50] Men with such problems did not exist in Brazil outside the ranks of the demented. Nor would an irate slaveholder disown his son for sleeping with a slave girl[51]—unless, of course, she was his own mistress, in which case he might kill his son. Nor would a planter tear his church apart over his demand for the censure of a respectable young man who had fathered a mulatto while visiting his plantation.[52] Southern slaveholders, like respectable Anglo-Saxons everywhere, had come a long way since the days when William Byrd of Virginia could confide to his diary that he had "rogered my wife with vigor"; had "good sport" with an Indian girl; "asked a negro girl to kiss me"; and indulged himself royally with pliable servant girls and miscellaneous wenches, white, red, and black.[53]

By the early nineteenth century many slaveholders had become prudes, with enough exceptions to torment the quarters. Even the prudes took their share, but with an uneasy conscience. Their own women had not been brought up to share their husbands with a mistress and a procession of one-night stands in the quarters. C. Vann Woodward points out:

It is plain enough that the ladies in crinoline had a lot to put up with. And they did put up with it, many of them, but only in their own fashion. . . . The ladies were reticent, evasive, often willfully blind about what sometimes went on in their own backyards. But what was shameful was regarded as shameful. It was not condoned as the legitimate prerogative of patriarchs, the proper initiation to manhood for one's sons, or an acceptable means of increasing one's labor supply. Nor was it brought into the parlor and flaunted in the streets.[54]

As for the havoc done the white family, the protests remained muffled in the South: few listened to the cries of the unwilling black women and their men; and few listened to the cries of the white women either, for they rarely dared utter them aloud. No doubt they had their own ways of paying their men back—the oppressed and wronged always do—but those ways hardly contributed much to their own happiness. Those strong enough to admit the truth even to themselves poured out their anguish in the privacy of their diaries.[55] The most telling indictment comes, as expected, from Mary Boykin Chesnut. Indeed, her indictment has attracted so much attention that readers of her diary often miss its many other excellent features, which add up to overwhelming evidence that she had much greater intellectual power and political acumen than her prestigious husband and the other famous worthies she suffered to entertain.

[*March 14, 1861.*] Under slavery, we live surrounded by prostitutes, yet an abandoned woman is sent out of any decent house. Who thinks any worse of a Negro or mulatto woman for being a thing we can't name? God forgive us, but ours is a monstrous system, a wrong and an iniquity! Like the patriarchs of old, our men live all in one house with their wives and their concubines; and the mulattoes one sees in every family partly resemble the white children. Any lady is ready to tell you who is the father of all the mulatto children in everybody's household but her own. Those, she seems to think, drop from the clouds. My disgust sometimes is boiling over. Thank God for my country women, but alas for the men! They are probably no worse than men everywhere, but the lower the mistress, the more degraded they must be.

[*April 20, 1861.*] Bad books are not allowed house room except in the library and under lock and key, the key in the Master's pocket; but bad women, if they are not white and serve in a menial capacity, may swarm the house unmolested. The ostrich game is thought a Chris-

tian act. These women are no more regarded as a dangerous contin-
gent than canary birds would be. . . .

There are certain subjects pure-minded ladies never touch upon,
even in their thoughts.

[*Aug. 22, 1861.*] I hate slavery. You say there are no more fallen women
on a plantation than in London, in proportion to numbers; but what
do you say to this? A magnate who runs a hideous black harem with
its consequences under the same roof with his lovely white wife and
his beautiful and accomplished daughters? . . . Fancy such a man
finding his daughter reading "Don Juan." "You with that immoral
book!" And he orders her out of his sight. You see, Mrs. Stowe did
not hit the sorest spot. She makes Legree a bachelor.[56]

This extraordinary southern lady, who proclaimed her hatred for
slavery, remained a fierce partisan of the Confederate cause until
the end.

Mrs. Chesnut lived in Charleston, which had arisen as an off-
shoot of Caribbean plantation society and which boasted a cosmo-
politan population that aspired to the stance of the English
aristocracy. Only New Orleans and Mobile, and Natchez on a
smaller scale, rivaled its sophistication in these matters. Some of
its women, much more freely than other southern women, could
pour the goose's sauce over the gander and revenge themselves
with love affairs of their own. But even they could not have been
wholly immune to the devastation wrought by their men. Husbands who cheated on their wives were nothing new. But, as
Chancellor Harper admitted, slavery provided for a special kind of
cheating, which converted white woman into ethereal beings even
as it degraded black women into alleged whores. Winthrop D.
Jordan writes: "The dissipation of the white gentlemen was as
much a tragedy for his white lady as for him. A biracial environment warped her affective life in two directions at once, for she
was made to feel that sensual involvement with the opposite sex
burned bright and hot with unquenchable passion and at the same
time that any such involvement was utterly repulsive."[57]

The resultant sexual and racial myths did not disappear with
slavery. In our own day Willie Morris can write of growing up
white in the Mississippi Delta:

I knew all about the sexual act, but not until I was twelve years old
did I know that it was performed with white women for pleasure;
I had thought that only Negro women engaged in the act of love with
white men just for fun, because they were the only ones with the

animal desire to submit that way. So that Negro girls and women were a source of constant excitement and sexual feeling for me, and filled my day-dreams with delights and wonders.[58]

The white South's sexual fantasies increased enormously after slavery ended—that is, after whites no longer exercised a seemingly total power over blacks—but they had appeared with the earliest racial contacts, circumscribed as they were by a rigid system of class and racial subordination. The Old South's relatively restrained response to rapes by black men of white women suggests that conditions deteriorated drastically after the war. But even before, the beginnings of those pathologies which slavery made inevitable could be discerned. Winthrop D. Jordan has found seventeenth-century evidence of white concern about that allegedly enormous black penis and with it the myth of superior potency. Even in Brazil these superstitions have poisoned the relations of men and women, black and white. The white man, some Brazilians insist, lacks a black man's prowess *(não e tão persistente)* —everyone knows that![59] All of which might entertain us, especially since blacks have the same fantasies about white sexuality,[60] did it not come drenched in so much innocent blood.

Slave women, like their men, brought a healthy attitude to sex and did not deserve the reputation for lewdness that white propaganda hung upon them. For some that attitude may have helped them to take in stride what could not be avoided. But the incidents of force or seduction under implicit threat of force must have taken a fearful toll. These women paid a higher price than the white women or the men, white and black, for it was they who suffered the violence and the attendant degradation of being held responsible for their own victimization, while their white mistresses—in this case I am tempted to write in all seriousness, their white sisters —became, with or without their own consent, symbols of asexual purity.

With little or nothing in their society to justify sexual aggression, the white men too often succumbed to that impetus toward sadism which accompanies self-contempt and self-hatred. Miscegenation poisoned southern race relations much less through those acts of violence which lower-class women—and their men— have always had to suffer in hierarchical social systems, than through the psychological devastation it wrought upon white society and black. What the white men might have viewed, even if perversely, as joyous and lusty, they generally had to view as a self-degradation easily projected into hatred and violence toward its victims.[61] The rape and quasi-rape of slave women in a society that condemned sexual irregularity generally and viewed sexual intimacy with blacks as especially degrading represented an acting-out of those essentially childish fantasies to which Willie Morris refers and associated sexual pleasure inextricably with violence. The men may have displayed a raucous male bravado when they got together to drink or, more flamboyantly, when they defended the honor of the South and its ladies by challenging hostile northern congressmen to duels, but they could not escape their slaves' revenge. The planters had good reason to flaunt their prized manhood so ludicrously while worrying about the size of the black man's penis, for their abuse of black women undermined them as men. And if the shrill tone with which they were forever proclaiming their own masculinity to the world reveals anything, they knew it.

And what of the fruits? Mulattoes did not constitute a separate caste in the Old South except among the well-to-do free Negroes of a few cities. Blacks and mulattoes worked side by side in the plantation Big House and in the fields. Those mulattoes who received special treatment usually were kin to their white folks, and the special treatment was not always favorable. The South Carolina low country provided some exception to this generalization, as did a few other areas in which the slave system reflected Caribbean origins. The mulatto elite that existed in the South was overwhelmingly concentrated in a few cities and rural pockets. Typically, the mulatto, especially the mulatto slave, was "just another nigger" to the whites.

Little is known about the attitude of the black and mulatto slaves toward each other, but that little suggests more fraternity than hostility. The widespread idea that the blacks envied the mulattoes and that the mulattoes looked down on the blacks came largely from postbellum sources. The slave narratives are especially suspect here, for caste lines had hardened during the post-Reconstruction years, and twentieth-century attitudes should not be read back into the antebellum period without adequate contemporary support. Even so, attitudes varied sharply. "I got both blood," said Susan Hamlin of South Carolina, "so how I going to quarrel wid either side?" But, added Ed Barber, also of South Carolina, "them was scary times! Me being' jus' half nigger and half white man, I knowed which side de butter was on de bread."[62]

The plantation slaves did react with hostility toward those mu-lattoes who claimed and received privileges based on their color and relationship to the white family and who put on airs in the quarters. The slave songs and stories sometimes describe "yaller gals" as dangerous temptresses while making clear their sexual desirability; but when not more in fun than in hostility, these songs and stories suggest criticism of the sexual irregularity that marked the girls' origins. On the other hand, the slaves responded to black and mulatto preachers according to talent; we find no evidence that color made a difference either way.

So far as impressions go, the slaves did value white as the color of those with power and accomplishment but did not despise their own blackness. Evidence of a thirst for whiteness comes largely from the war years and long after, when new forces came into play within and without the black community. The fateful division between lighter- and darker-skinned Negroes, so often correlated with distinctions of class, income, and education, had remained weak during slavery. The mulatto elites of New Orleans and Charleston had to discover their own blackness when they made their bid for political power during Reconstruction, for the coun-try blacks did not flock to them unless they demonstrated the value of their education and experience in combination with a fraternal attitude toward the ex-slaves. The leadership that emerged after the war had a disproportionate share of mulattoes because the better-educated northern and southern free Negroes and privi-leged town slaves were in the best position to step out front. They did so, however, by strengthening their ties to their black brothers and sisters—a task made easier by previous associations. In short, the divisions and attitudes that manifested themselves later had their roots in the slave period, but those roots were fragile and might have been cut. Nothing in the slave experience made the future shape of the black community inevitable.

The mulattoes of Jamaica and Saint-Domingue stood in a differ-ent relationship to the blacks. In both colonies they constituted a separate caste in a three-caste system. Generally, they were free; often they occupied positions in the skilled trades or as overseers or, especially in Saint-Domingue, as wealthy slaveholding plant-ers. Their class interests bound them to the whites, and their political efforts were devoted to attempts to win white acceptance as partners in the business of exploiting the slaves. But white racism set limits to the conservatism of the mulattoes. In both colonies they waged a stubborn battle for equality with the whites and ended by contributing to the liberation of the blacks. The racist myopia of the French drove the mulattoes of southern Saint-Domingue into insurrection at a time when the black slaves of the northern plain were also rising. The unity of the nonwhite rebels, while always frail, proved strong enough to guarantee the success of the Haitian Revolution.

The two-caste system in the Old South drove the mulattoes into the arms of the blacks, no matter how hard some tried to build a make-believe third world for themselves. Although in Charleston, New Orleans, and Mobile some semblance of a three-caste system appeared and played an important role within the local Negro community, for the South as a whole whites made little distinction between blacks and mulattoes. In the Caribbean whites constituted a small minority of the population and had to build up an intermediary colored class of managers, tradesmen, and small proprietors. In the South, whites constituted the majority and had no such problem. Those mulattoes who came out of paternalistic or guilt-stricken white families secured advantages and often freedom. They had greater access to education and skills and provided a natural leadership among the blacks during and after the war. But they could play that role—to the still undetermined extent they did—because the social and cultural distance between blacks and mulattoes had not become the chasm that it had in the Caribbean.

THE LANGUAGE OF CLASS AND NATION

The duality of the black experience both within and without the American national experience, and the contribution of different classes and strata of the black community to that duality, appeared in the kind of English spoken on the farms and plantations and in the towns and cities. The slave, Kelly Miller remarks, had to be ear-minded, whereas the master could be eye-minded.[1] Up to a point the ear-mindedness of Afro-American slaves did not differ essentially from that of, say, Eastern European slaves in the cities of Renaissance Italy.[2] Even today in the black urban ghettos verbal ability contributes at least as much as physical strength to individual prestige. Thomas Kochman writes: "The prestige norms which influence black speech behavior are those which have been successful in manipulating and controlling people and situations."[3] But the slaves did more than set the pace for a certain verbal style; they created, or at least elaborated, their own version of the English language.[4]

Although the slave traders wanted to reduce communication within their human cargoes, they never wholly succeeded. The two great West African language families, the Bantu and the Sudanese, did not exclude passage from one variant to another within each nor even between them.[5] More important, the slaves often had to be held for reshipment at various points on the coast, where pidgin English (or pidgin French or especially pidgin Portuguese) served as a lingua franca. Based on English vocabulary but perhaps with some West African grammatical influence and tonal characteristics, it provided these Africans with the first English they were to learn, and by its very nature it could be learned quickly. When on the New World plantations these slaves taught those who came after them. Gerald W. Mullin has estimated that slaves in Virginia were speaking an adequate amount of English within six months and that they were speaking well in about two and a half years.[6] From those days forward, blacks, not whites, took primary responsibility for teaching other blacks on the plantation.[7] The English they taught was based on the pidgin that had arisen in the slave trade. The principal need of the slaves was communication with the other slaves, not with whites. The terms "pidgin" and "creole" (the development of pidgin into a first language for a new generation) evoke peculiar reactions, for they are for some reason regarded as pejorative. They are, however, technical linguistic terms that imply no value judgment. Pidgin English, which became common in the New World, probably arose, in the manifestation relevant to Afro-Americans, on the slave-trading coast of West Africa. It appeared wherever British slave traders appeared.[8]

Linguists have variously interpreted the special qualities of southern speech, in its wide variety of forms, and until recently have denied much of an African contribution, much less the existence of a separate black dialect. Clement Eaton has admirably summed up and applied the views of such linguists as Cleanth Brooks and G. P. Krapp:

> Modern students believe that the most important cause for the peculiarities of Southern speech was the survival in the South of the English language as spoken in the seventeenth and eighteenth centuries, which was brought over by the colonists. The pronunciations of *get* as "git," *ask* as "ax," *boil* as "bile," *oblige* as "obleege," and *master* as "marster" or "marse," were common usages in the southern part of England during the seventeenth century. Even the dropping of the final *g* as in "darlin" for *darling*, or elision of *r*—supposedly common Southern failings—were practices of old English speech during the period of emigration. . . . Furthermore, the Southern colonists brought over with them pronunciations peculiar to the numerous dialects of the mother country, especially those of southern and southwestern England. Expressions such as "gwine" for *going* and "ain't" for *isn't* antedate the coming of the Negroes to the South. Many of the pronunciations and even the drawl which are regarded today as peculiarly "Southern" were also current in New England in the seventeenth and eighteenth centuries.

And further:

> The places where old English speech survived most tenaciously were the eastern sand banks and the mountains. Here the inhabitants were insulated from progressive currents and also only to a slight degree were affected by the controls of the printed page. They seldom saw a Negro, and consequently could not have been influenced by Negro corruptions of speech. Yet many of their pronunciations and expressions were similar to those used by the Negroes, such as "hit" for *it* and "tote" for *carry* and "pore" for *poor*. Old pronunciations and archaic words were also preserved by the continuance of folksongs and ballads brought from the British Isles by the colonists.[9]

The force of these arguments, however strong within certain limits, fades abruptly when some specific questions are considered, quite apart from such obvious objections as that "tote" is clearly of African origin. White and black speech converged and always influenced each other, as evidenced by the strong black influence, including its African element, on the plantation whites and even on the more remotely placed small farmers.[10]

However much the speech of whites and blacks merged to become, on one level, a single regional dialect or group of dialects, a certain structural distinctiveness remained primarily, almost exclusively, black, and black uses of para-language had no important white equivalents.[11] As George W. Cable pointed out for French-speaking Louisiana, planters often learned their slaves' dialect but sought to maintain the difference of speech as a mark of caste. From time to time, throughout the South, masters punished slaves for trying to speak "good English" rather than black dialect.[12] Beyond the occasional use of such African words as goober, tote, juba, jigger, okra, yam, or banjo,[13] and beyond the more frequent use of African words in the Gullah dialect, so well studied by Lorenzo Dow Turner, a consideration of language must include discussion of the structural features of slave-quarter speech and of the para-language with which it developed.

The principal features of black English have been elaborated in the work of William A. Stewart, J. L. Dillard, and others and are attested to in a wide variety of antebellum sources.

First, the slaves normally relied on a zero copula; that is, they dropped the verb "to be"—and other verbs as well—and left it understood. "Which is that one?" became "Which dat one?" and "Mary is our daughter" was reduced to "Mary we daughter."

Second, the slaves appeared to disregard gender. Nothing drove northern whites like Elizabeth Hyde Botume quite so wild as the blacks' blurring of male and female. The slaves had no difficulty understanding each other in this or any other regard, for they relied on context and familiarity to identify the sexes; they found the pronoun unnecessary. An ex-slave told her interviewer about a grandchild: "I raise him from baby." The interviewer then asked if her grandson helped her. Amused, she replied, "Wat dat? Him ain't no man, him my granddaughter, Ellen Jenkins. . . ."[14]

Third, the personal pronoun usually accompanied the noun, as well as substituting for it. Thus, to say "Mary is in the cabin," a slave normally would say "Mary, he in cabin."

Fourth, pronoun forms were invariant. "His wife" became "he wife"; "our" and "us" usually became "we." When house slaves, or later, the freedmen as a group, learned "us," the old pattern often continued. But instead of saying "We like he," they might say "Us like he."

Fifth, possession was marked by juxtaposition, not by the addition of "'s" or by the form of the pronoun. Thus, "Mary's hat" became "Mary hat" or "he hat."[15]

Sixth, the slaves negated with "no." The word "not" appeared in the speech of the house slaves and others, who copied the whites closely, but "no" was standard in both verbal and adjectival formulations. Thus: "He no mind we" and "He no wicked."

Seventh, the slaves normally dropped suffix markers and reduced consonant clusters. "The girls are dressed" would certainly become "The girls is dress." And "stop" would become "'top" or "divorce," "'vorce." Gradually, words like "revorce" appeared, but these marked an attempt to speak standard English. The effort of uneducated blacks to speak as the whites did passed through an awkward stage of fancification. Thus, instead of the simple "'vorce," some would reach for "revorce," and eventually, "divorcement." By the time of emancipation the speech of the more assimilated slaves was riddled with "scatterment," "dividement," "separament," "worryment," and the like. The original speech of the field slaves had the virtue of a crisp directness that had stripped nouns of apparently superfluous prefixes and suffixes.[16]

Eighth, the expression "There go [or, Here go] we-all stockings," does not mean "There go our stockings" but "There are our stockings." The use of "there go" and "here go" corresponds to the French use of *voilà* and *voici*, or the Spanish use of *hay*, or similar phrases in other Romance languages, and may reflect the influence of the European slave traders on the formation of pidgin English.

Ninth, among other features of slave speech which carried over into modern black English were the dropping of words like "if," so that "See if he can go" would become "See can he go," and "What did you say?" would become the ubiquitous "Say what?" Also, multiple negation became the rule and greater emphasis accompanied the extended use of the negative: "He ain't never give none of we nothin'."

Tenth, slaves did not form plurals in the manner of standard English. Their own formulation was nonredundant. Thus, "Gib massa tousand tank" for "Give master a thousand thanks"; or "some valiant soldier here" rather than "soldiers"; or "How much wife?" for "How many wives?"

Travelers and others thought that field hands had no sense of grammar and talked gibberish. They might have reflected on the need of the field hands to understand each other and their obvious ability to do so, even if they were delinquent—perhaps deliberately so—in making themselves understood to outsiders. Accordingly, in their own way they made distinctions of tense and of all else they needed. Here, we may quote William A. Stewart on black

English in general, with the observation that the field slaves probably spoke the closest thing to the "Negro dialect" he describes:

> In Negro dialect, *be* is used with adjectives and the *in'* (-ing) form of
> verbs to indicate an extended or repeated state or action, e.g., *He be
> busy, He be workin'*. On the other hand, the absence of this *be* usually
> indicates that the state or action is immediate or momentary, e.g.,
> *He busy, He workin'*. The auxiliary or tag for *be* in Negro dialect is
> *do*, e.g., *Do he be busy?* as a question form of *He be busy*, while the
> explicit form use in the non-be construction is usually *is*, e.g., *Is he
> busy?* as a question form of *He busy*. This means, of course, that *be* and
> *is* are entirely different morphemes in Negro dialect. But in standard
> English, there is no grammatical distinction, and *be* and *is* are merely
> inflectional variants of one and the same verb. Thus, for the two
> grammatical constructions of Negro dialect, standard English has
> but one grammatical equivalent, e.g., *He is busy, He is working*, in
> which the immediacy or duration of the state or action is left entirely
> unspecified.[17]

The slaves' language displayed much more than an African and
plantation vocabulary, much of which passed into and also reflected rural and lower-class white dialect; and it displayed much
more than that grammatical variation which set it off decisively
from white speech patterns. It throve on ambiguity and *double-
entendre* and passed into para-language. Africa contributed to this
development, for everyday speaking in parables frequently appears in Africa and influenced black English.[18]

Roger D. Abrahams has drawn attention to the tendency to
collapse words in such a way as to impart, often deliberately, a
desired ambiguity. Thus, in the Caribbean the name of the African
spider-trickster, Anansi, appears as "Nansi," and, by extension in
the folktales, "Nansi 'tory" may be pronounced in a way to suggest
"nonsense story." In the United States "right on," which has now
become standard in white as well as black slang, expresses a deliberate ambiguity when pronounced in the southern black manner,
for it collapses "right" and "ride" and therefore not only expresses
approbation but encourages further action. Moreover, words
themselves often have directly opposite meanings, in accordance
with the way in which they are pronounced, the gestures that
accompany them, and the context in which they appear. Thus, the
"ba-ad nigger" who appears frequently in the plantation literature
was a very special sort of person to the slaves, who might say "Yo'
a mighty *ba-ad* nigger" with unquestionable delight whereas they

would say "Yo' a mighty bad *nigger*" with extreme distaste.

The slaves fell back on ambiguity at every point. What, for example, is to be made of the natural, perfectly unaffected, and seemingly unconscious way in which the freedmen and later blacks referred to slavery times? To say "during slavery" they more often than not would say "endurin' slavery." James Redpath was right for once in noting that the slaves referred not so much to slavery as to "bondage," as if to identify themselves with the ancient Jews, who after all were delivered in God's good time.[19]

Whatever parable and ambiguity have meant in traditional African cultures, their importance to Afro-American slaves needs no elaboration. The slaves, in effect, learned to communicate with each other in the presence of whites with some measure of safety, and the studied ambiguity of their speech, reinforced by reliance upon tone and gesture, helped immeasurably to prevent informers from having too much to convey to the masters beyond impressions and suspicions. If a slave informer heard a black preacher praise a runaway by calling him a "*ba-ad* nigger," what could he tell his master beyond saying that he thought the preacher meant the opposite of what he had said? Even slaveholders usually required better evidence.

Yet, the slaves could not escape some negative consequences from their use of ambiguity, as consideration of their use of the word "nigger" will show. Well-bred planters rarely used the word "nigger" before the war, and their increasing use of it after the war provides one measure of their manner of experiencing the shock of emancipation. The yeomen used it more frequently and the poor whites almost invariably. But its greatest devotees were the slaves themselves, who provided a case study in black uses of black English. They called themselves and each other "nigger" as a matter of course and referred to "nigger quarters," "nigger meetings," "nigger preachers," and even "nigger dogs." Julius Lester says of this word among the slaves:

> It was a brutal, violent word that stung the soul of the slave more than the whip did his back. But the slaves took this ugly word and like the white man's religion, made it their own. In their mouths it became an affectionate, endearing word. As much as was possible they robbed it of its ability to spiritually maim them.[20]

Lester's point is well taken, as even the occasional quotations from black sources in this book ought to show. But the linguistic ambiguity in which the slaves specialized obtained here too. Colonel Higginson thought, for example, that they used it for field hands much more readily than for elite house servants, as if to mark their acceptance of the white man's pecking order.[21] Or more to the point, an insulting black man called to some white ruffians in the streets of Washington, D.C., "You come back here, and I'll make you laugh; you is jus' three white nigger cowards, dat what *you* are."[22] From slavery days to the present blacks have varied the meaning of the word, from tenderness toward a loved one to a replica of the white man's usage, by shifting their tone. "Dese niggers here in Carlisles," began an ex-slave, "—and niggers is all dey is too. . . ."[23]

By accepting the word and varying its meaning, the slaves went far toward denigrating themselves and accepting the white man's version of them, although, as Lester says, in the end they at least destroyed its most poisonous effects and turned it to whatever advantage they could. Harriet Tubman, that great "Moses of her people" of Underground Railroad fame, provided a lesson in how to accept the implicit denigration and yet transform it into its opposite. She told an audience in 1861 that she retained her optimism about the Union cause, for "God's ahead of Massa Linkum."

> God won't let Massa Linkum beat de South till he do right ting. Massa Linkum he great man, and I'se poor nigger; but dis nigger can tell Massa Linkum how to save de money and de young men. He do it by setting de niggers free. S'pose dar was awfu' big snake down dar, on de floor. He bite you. Folks all skeered, cause you die. You send for doctor to cut de bite; but snake he rolled up dar, and while doctor dwine it, he bite you agin. De doctor cut out dat bite; but while he dwine it, de snake he spring up and bite you agin, and so he keep dwine, till you kill him. Dat's what Massa Linkum orta know.[24]

The more pronounced forms of black English during the slave period were heard primarily among the plantation field slaves. Yet even among house slaves, small-farm slaves, and southern and northern urban free Negroes strong elements of black English appeared and created a special bond among all blacks, slave and free, southern and northern. The main obstacle to the development of this variation of English as a protonational black language lay not in its absence among other than field slaves, but in its association with the lowest status group of American blacks. Too

often, the others found it shameful and tried to dissociate themselves from it.[25]

Frederick Douglass, often asked why he exhibited so little "slave
speech," answered that his language had been formed in association with the white children from the Big House. "The law of
compensation holds here as well as elsewhere," he explained.
"While this lad could not associate with ignorance without sharing
its shade, he could not give his black playmates his company without giving them his superior intelligence as well."[26] Mary Anderson, who had been a slave in Wake County, North Carolina, said
in a similar vein, "Marster's children and the slave children played
together. I went around with the baby girl Carrie to the other
plantations visiting. She taught me how to talk low and how to act
in company. My association with white folks and my training
while I was a slave is why I talk like white folks."[27] Ellen Thomas,
formerly a house slave on Judge F. G. Kemball's place in Alabama,
said simply that the judge insisted on "good English" in the Big
House.[28]

In the Gullah-Geechee regions of the South Carolina and
Georgia coast, where black language ranged furthest from white,
the house slaves rarely spoke other than standard English in the
Big House, although they had no trouble speaking Gullah (called
Geechee in Georgia) with the field hands.[29] These house slaves
brought "good" English to the field hands, for the two groups lived
close together. To the extent that they accepted the idea of white
cultural superiority, they also transmitted to the field hands some
sense of linguistic deprivation, although how much remains unclear. The influence of the house slaves worked toward racial integration in the form of the decreolization of black English and its
development toward standard English. The process of decreolization, therefore, worked itself out almost from the beginning, however tenaciously the language of the quarters held on and spread
back to the house slaves and, through them, to the whites.

A role similar to that of the house slaves appeared among urban
blacks, slave and free, and among the slaves on small farms, especially in regions not dominated by the plantations. Hence, travelers like James Stirling could assert that the slaves of the Border
States were decidedly "more intelligent" than those of the Deep
South. He also insisted that the free Negroes of the North did not
use "nigger gibberish."[30] Still, the plantation dialect cannot be
dismissed as a minor matter, or as a language of poverty and

deprivation that was overcome with time and freedom. The survival of so much of the dialect into the twentieth century, even among the educated, suggests that it has served as an important element of black cultural unity. Decreolization and the use of standard English have progressed steadily, but the retention of something of the original language, not as evidence of a "culture of poverty" but as a conscious cultural mechanism for community solidarity and defense, ought to alert us to its power and significance in the slave quarters.[31]

Conversely, the process of decreolization strengthened the unity of the blacks before and especially after emancipation by overcoming linguistic differences. The emergence of skilled mechanics, preachers, and urban free Negroes as postwar leaders undoubtedly rested in part on their greater command of standard English. They were more intellectually developed than the field hands to begin with, but their greater familiarity with standard English provided the vehicle for their more rapid assimilation of the most advanced ideas of world culture as a whole.

The cultural relativists among the linguists have contributed a great deal toward an understanding of black English. They have properly insisted that it deserves to be treated with respect and that it could be expanded to do the work of any national language. But, as Gramsci has pointed out, dialects always must suffer in relation to developed national languages in their reduced ability to absorb the universalistic elements in world culture. This reduced ability arises from the realities of political life without regard for the intrinsic merits of the dialects themselves. Thus, Gramsci argued for the progressive role of the Italian language in Sicily, not because he thought the Sicilian dialect intrinsically inferior to Italian, which itself began as just one dialect in Florence, but because he was committed to the principle of Italian national unity.[32] John S. Mbiti made this point forcefully in *African Religions and Philosophy* when he noted the spread of the English and French languages in Africa: "They are the greatest legacy we have inherited from the colonial powers, and this inheritance nobody can take away from us."[33]

The decreolization of black English therefore represented a great victory for the integrationist tendency of the free Negroes and house slaves over the protonationalist tendency of the field slaves. But even from a black nationalist point of view, the result served essential purposes for the long run. Without it, the struggle for unity of the black community would have been severely retarded. Mammy's "code-switching" ability to talk one way in the Big House and another in the quarters contributed more than she could have known, or probably would have approved of, to the development of the black nation within the American nation.

A Conclusion and a Preface

These house servants, drivers, mechanics, and free Negroes, black and mulatto, contributed much to the plantation community but did not constitute its mass. These more privileged blacks did not wallow in sinecures, pampered and made haughty by baubles and flattery. Their lives were generally hard, and the force of white racism, as well as their own inclinations, drew them close to the field hands in kinship, religion, interest, and sympathy. Their greater access to the printed word and their wider knowledge of the world made them natural leaders but also introduced caste pretensions and possibilities for making private accommodations at the expense of their own people. These divisive tendencies might have gone much further if the whites had felt the need to make major concessions to a free mulatto class in order to maintain social order. The security and power of the regime in a region with a white majority reduced the need for such concessions and repeatedly forced the blacks and mulattoes, the slaves and free Negroes, to consider themselves a single people.

The house slaves, mechanics, free Negroes, even to a lesser extent the drivers, paced the black community's absorption of Euro-American culture, for they lived intimately with the whites at the same time as they remained attached to their own people. They led the transformation of Africans into Americans. But the Americans they became were Afro-Americans, not merely in the sense of being another ethnic component in a variegated American nationality but in the deeper sense of contributing to and absorbing American national culture and yet remaining apart from it on some important levels. In language, the integrationist impulse of the privileged slaves and the separatist impulse of the mass of field hands combined to create a culture very much American and yet significantly special.

PART 2

...AND THE COAT OF MANY COLORS

Now Israel loved Joseph more than all his children, because he was the son of his old age: and he made him a coat of many colors. . . .

And it came to pass when Joseph was come unto his brethren, that they stript Joseph out of his coat, his coat of many colors that was on him.
—Genesis 37:3, 23

THE NAMING OF CATS

The Naming of Cats is a difficult matter,
   It isn't just one of your holiday games;
You may think at first I'm as mad as a hatter
   When I tell you, a cat must have THREE DIFFERENT
   NAMES.
First of all, there's the name that the family use daily,
   Such as Peter, Augustus, Alonzo or James
Such as Victor or Jonathan, George or Bill Bailey—
   All of them sensible everyday names.

There are fancier names if you think they sound sweeter,
  Some for the gentlemen, some for the dames:
Such as Plato, Admetus, Electra, Demeter—
  But all of them sensible everyday names.
But I tell you, a cat needs a name that's particular,
  A name that's peculiar, and more dignified,
Else how can he keep up his tail perpendicular,
  Or spread out his whiskers, or cherish his pride?
Of names of this kind, I can give you a quorum,
  Such as Munkustrap, Quaxo, or Coricopat,
Such as Bombalurina, or else Jellylorum—
  Names that never belong to more than one cat.
But above and beyond there's still one name left over,
  And that is the name that you never will guess;
The name that no human research can discover—
  But THE CAT HIMSELF KNOWS, and will never confess.
When you notice a cat in profound meditation,
  The reason, I tell you, is always the same:
His mind is engaged in a rapt contemplation
  Of the thought, of the thought, of the thought of his
name:
      His ineffable effable
      Effanineffable
Deep and inscrutable singular Name.

                                        —T. S. Eliot[1]

"Slaves being men," the Supreme Court of Louisiana declared sternly—if not without some ambiguity—in 1827, "are to be identified by their proper names."[2] If any class in the United States understood the importance of names, the slaveholders did. In the early days of settlement in Virginia planters tried to assimilate the name of their locality, or more modestly of their residence, to their own surname in accordance with the custom prevalent in Scotland and the more seigneurial areas of northern England.[3] The practice, in restricted form, spread across the Lower South during the nineteenth century. The planters, while curbing its more pretentious features, aspired to that aristocratic style associated with great landowning classes. From a practical point of view, the association of family name with residence made sense in a rural society spread over great distances in which kinship played so great a role; but significantly, yeomen farmers solved their problem of identity in other ways.

Masters and slaves considered slave names in the same context, although from opposite points of view. Both understood that names identified class and status and marked an appropriate degree of respect. No greater sign of respect could be assigned a village headman in feudal Japan than to allow him to wear a sword and take a surname, for these normally were forbidden to peasants and reserved for the higher classes.[4] Years after the war white southerners sighed with relief when Booker T. Washington received a doctorate. They had too much respect for him to call him "Booker" and could not call any black man "Mr."; but "Dr. Washington" presented no problem. The slaves cared about their names and about the attitude of the whites to them. When married in formal ceremonies they often wanted to see their names written down in the master's family Bible, although they themselves usually could not read them. When they wanted to put a mistress in perspective, they called her by her first name behind her back. William Wells Brown recalled that he had "lost" his name, William, when his master's nephew of that name arrived to live with them. Ordered to change his name in deference to the white boy, he balked. "This at the time, I thought to be one of the most cruel acts that could be committed upon my rights; and I received several severe whippings for telling people that my name was William, after orders were given to change it."[5] Later, when free, he hated the idea of keeping the surname of his white father and took instead the name of the Quaker abolitionist who had helped him to escape. But to his benefactor's name, Wells Brown, he prefixed the William, for it had been given to him by his mother and remained his own.

Masters sometimes gave their slaves surnames; more often, with or without their masters' consent or even knowledge, the slaves took surnames for themselves. The percentage of slaves with surnames is unknown, but they did appear in all parts of the South. In Louisiana, for example, surnames appeared frequently among the slaves of Anglo-Saxon planters, although some influence from early French and Spanish practice may have been at work.[6]

The strongest evidence for the appropriation of surnames by the slaves or of their pressure to compel slaveholders to grant them the "privilege" comes from the Mississippi Valley and the South Carolina and Georgia coast, for these were the regions with the biggest plantations and the greatest degree of stability. Elsewhere surnames appeared less frequently, but there was a tendency toward their use, which may well have paralleled the growth in community stability. Duncan Clinch Heyward wrote that the slaves of the Rice Coast all used surnames among themselves, and "scarcely ever did the Negro choose the name of his or her owner, but often took that of some other slaveholding family of which he knew."[7]

After the war slaves throughout the South took surnames or openly announced those they already had. Appropriately, they called them "entitles." As Heyward suggests, they did not usually take their master's name, but neither did they always repudiate it. When all the slaves from a large plantation took their master's name the subsequent confusion in the community may be imagined. Their sense of specific family could not then easily be protected; but, on the other hand, the old sense of the whole plantation as a family would be strengthened.[8] They had another and more significant reason for going back in time to take the name of the first master they had ever had, or perhaps of the first whom they could remember as having been a decent man: by so doing, they recaptured, as best they could, their own history. That the name had its origin with whites, sometimes even cruel whites, mattered little: for better or worse, it had become their own property. Thus, Susan Hamilton's father took his master's name although he had considered him "very mean." The important thing was to establish a real history, preferably well back in time but in any event in a family experience. Many freedmen went to lengths to find out the name of the whites who had owned their parents or grandparents; others took a master's name and altered it. One way or another, the name had to be "real"; it had to embody a living history without which genuine identity could not have become possible.[9]

To establish a link with the master's family, or with some master's family, often meant to establish a link with one's own father. The idea that black people's names today are "slave names" is true but distressingly twisted, for it overlooks the formidable black initiative in their creation. Whatever later ideologues might say, the slaves and freedmen knew that their lives had grown intertwined with those of the whites; that in some ways and to some extent no divorce would ever be possible because it would rob them of the only history they had and, more specifically, rob them of contact with the black fathers who had so often been ripped from them.[10] Jacob Branch of Texas had been a little boy when his father was sold, but he took the name Branch after the war because he knew it to have been his father's.[11] Henry D. Jenkins, an ex-slave from South Carolina, had a special story. His father had been named Dinkins but had deserted the family after the war for another woman. Henry and his brother took the name Jenkins for unstated reasons, but they both used the middle initial *D*, "so if anything come up, de 'D' could 'cite 'membrance of who us really is."[12]

With freedom, many blacks took particular surnames for reasons other than to establish a historical link with their own family, especially since it was often difficult or impossible to do so. At the very least, they wanted the privilege of selecting a name and thereby establishing their right to make a choice.[13] In some cases they were resorting to a ruse. "When us black folks got set free," explained Alice Wilkins, "us'n change our names, so effen the white folks get together and change their minds and don't let us be free any more, then they have a hard time finding us."[14] Others were seeking protection. By reaching for the name of a big and respected planter they hoped to enlist his sympathy should trouble come, or to fool the rougher element among the whites into thinking that they had a protector.[15] Tom Roseboro, an ex-slave from South Carolina, took his name because it had been his father's, because it was prettier than his own master's name, and because the Roseboros were "big buckra in dat time."[16] Well into the twentieth century, blacks in the plantation districts of the South were naming their children after local whites to whom they looked for friendship and protection in a dangerous world.[17] Others took names to celebrate their new status or attitude: Freedman, Freeland, Justice, Lincoln, Grant. Still others, like earlier Europeans, took the name of a skill of which they were proud: Taylor, Mason, Wheeler, Carpenter.

Generally, slave parents named their own children, although in numerous instances slaveholders presumed to do it for them. On the great patriarchal plantations the planters had the inconvenience of numbers to encourage them to mind their own business. The slaves' choices varied from concern with family continuity to whim, but rarely did they choose those pompous, classical, or comical names which masters sometimes inflicted on them.[18] Very few Caesars, Catos, and Pompeys survived the war; the freedmen divested themselves of these names so quickly that one wonders if they had ever used them among themselves in the quarters. Slaves often accepted a master's choice passively, especially if the name was unexceptionable, but sometimes they resisted. Sarah Wilson of Oklahoma had been named Annie by her mistress, who was herself named Annie and no doubt thought that she was bestowing an honor. Sarah Wilson's mother did not feel honored and, as soon as the mistress died, she renamed her daughter to suit herself.[19] Nathaniel Heyward, the South's greatest rice planter, must have learned something of the slaves' tenacity in naming processes from his experience in trying to name his own plantations. He loved Holland so much that he named his plantations Rotterdam, Amsterdam, and the like. "But," wrote Duncan Clinch Heyward, "it was one thing for 'Ole Maussuh' . . . to give his plantations such names, and quite another to get his Negroes to call them by these names." The slaves, he explained, changed the names to "De Swamp" and "De Lower Swamp," and "these names stuck in spite of 'Ole Maussuh.' "[20]

If so many first names chosen by masters and mistresses stuck, it was in part because of their plausibility and the probability that the slave parents had been consulted in the first place. Contrary to legend, most slaveholders did not give their slaves ridiculous or fanciful names. When Landon Carter named a slave girl "Sukey," the parents, whatever else they felt, could not have thought that he was making fun of them, for his own daughter, Susannah, was another plantation "Sukey."[21] Slaves rarely if ever used diminutives. A slave Sukey was in fact Sukey, not Susannah, and a John would not become Johnnie. Perhaps by avoiding diminutives the slaves tried to resist succumbing to the white designations "boy" and "girl," for they did not so refer to themselves; they were men and women, or rather, "mens" and "womens." Classical or whimsical names appeared on the slave lists much less frequently than generally believed. Most large plantations sported a few, but the great majority of names were straightforward.[22]

Slave names that seemed strange or ridiculous to white outsiders often had African origins. Africans commonly would name a child after the day or month of birth (day-name), or they might name him or her after a particular personality trait discerned immediately. The slaves of the South Carolina and Georgia low country never gave up this practice, which echoed across the South. A slave named Quack would be taken by white travelers to be the victim of some master's bad taste, but probably his own parents had simply adapted the African Quaco, meaning a male born on Wednesday. A woman named Squash probably got her name from Quashee—a female born on Sunday. The common name Cuffee suggests both a male born on Friday and the Ashanti name Kofi. Some variation of Phoebe might look like a master's fancy, but Phiba or Phibbi means a female born on Friday. These names and others with clear African origins, such as Cudjo and Juba, existed all over the South, although nowhere so prominently as on the southeastern coast. In time, the slaves anglicized these African names in their own way. Thus, Cudjo might become Monday in one generation and Joe in the next; Quaco might become Wednesday but sooner or later would end up as Jacco, Jacky, or Jack. If a master wanted to name a slave Hercules, the slave parents might think it a fine idea, for *heke* means "large wild animal" in Mende. Cato suggests several perfectly good West African names, whatever the master may have intended. Thus, names that were assumed to have been absurdities imposed by whites often reflected black initiatives or interpretations, and suggest a line of continuity in the life of the quarters even when the origins of that line had been forgotten.[23]

African names steadily receded after the turn of the nineteenth century, as a review of the slave names that appear in court records will immediately show, but they never wholly disappeared. And for what it may be worth, there is the case of Martin Jackson of Texas:

> The master's name was usually adopted by a slave after he was set free. This was done more because it was the logical thing to do and the easiest way to be identified than it was through affection for the master. Also, the government seemed to be in a almighty hurry to have us get names. We had to register as someone, so we could be citizens. Well, I got to thinking about all us slaves that was going to take the name Fitzpatrick. I made up my mind I'd find me a different one. One of my grandfathers in Africa was called Jeaceo, and so I decided to be Jackson.[24]

The slaves blended their African origins into the New World and turned their "twoness" as blacks and as Americans to advantage in all directions. Slaves repatriated to West Africa would flash their Christian names as a badge of superiority in a world becoming colonized by Europeans. "Superstitious" slaves in the South would refuse to name their children until the ninth day after birth, for, however puzzled their masters might be, it was common knowledge among West Africans that infants might fall prey to tetanism ("ninth-day fits").[25] The importance of the shift from, say, Cudjo to Joe lies less in the African origin or in the "Americanization" than in the extent to which the slaves were trying to live their own lives in their own way.

Slave practice in its many variations represented a striving toward personal identity and self-respect, which the names marked. The spirituals tell us that the slaves knew they had a "real" name, known to God, and that a man's identity would emerge on Judgment Day.

> O nobody knows who I am, who I am
> Till the Judgment morning.

Or:

> My name is written in the book of life
> Turn, sinner, turn O.[26]

In Darien, Georgia, a kindly, patriarchal planter and renowned Presbyterian minister spoke to a little black boy: "Howdy, John" —he was too sensitive to call him "Sambo." "My name is Norman, sir." "Ah, yes, Norman." As the patriarch and his son-in-law, who later told the story, passed on, they heard someone ask Norman who the old man was. "I don't know who he is," he replied, *but he know me.*"[27]

THE MYTH OF THE ABSENT FAMILY

The recent controversy over the ill-fated Moynihan Report has brought the question of the black family in general and the slave family in particular into full review. Largely following the pioneering work of E. Franklin Frazier, the report summarized the conventional wisdom according to which slavery had emasculated black men, created a matriarchy, and prevented the emergence of a strong sense of family.[1] Historians and sociologists, black and white, have been led astray in two ways. First, they have read the story of the twentieth-century black ghettos backward in time and have assumed a historical continuity with slavery days. Second, they have looked too closely at slave law and at the externals of family life and not closely enough at the actual temper of the quarters.

During the twentieth century blacks went north in great waves and faced enormous hardship. The women often could find work as domestics; the men found themselves shut out of employment not so much by their lack of skills as by fierce racial discrimination. Some disorientation of the black family apparently followed; evaluation of its extent and social content must be left to others who can get beyond simple statistical reports to an examination of the quality of life.[2] But those inclined to read the presumed present record back into the past have always had a special problem, for by any standard of judgment the southern rural black family, which remained closer to the antebellum experience, always appeared to be much stronger than the northern urban family.[3]

The evidence from the war years and Reconstruction, now emerging in more systematic studies than were previously available, long ago should have given us pause.[4] Every student of the Union occupation and early Reconstruction has known of the rush of the freedmen to legalize their marriages; of the widespread desertion of the plantations by whole families; of the demands by men and women for a division of labor that would send the women out of the fields and into the homes; of the militancy of parents seeking to keep their children from apprenticeship to whites even when it would have been to their economic advantage; and especially of the heart-rending effort of thousands of freedmen to find long-lost loved ones all over the South. These events were prefigured in antebellum times. Almost every study of runaway slaves uncovers the importance of the family motive: thousands of slaves ran away to find children, parents, wives, or husbands from whom they had been separated by sale. Next to resentment over punishment, the attempt to find relatives was the most prevalent cause of flight.[5]

These data demand a reassessment of slave family life as having had much greater power than generally believed. But a word of warning: the pressures on the family, as E. Franklin Frazier, W. E. B. Du Bois, Kenneth M. Stampp, Stanley M. Elkins, and other scholars have pointed out, were extraordinary and took a terrible toll. My claims must be read within limits—as a record of the countervailing forces even within the slavocracy but especially within the slave community. I suggest only that the slaves created impressive norms of family life, including as much of a nuclear family norm as conditions permitted, and that they entered the postwar social system with a remarkably stable base. Many families became indifferent or demoralized, but those with a strong desire for family stability were able to set norms for life in freedom that could serve their own interests and function reasonably well within the wider social system of white-dominated America.

The masters understood the strength of the marital and family ties among their slaves well enough to see in them a powerful means of social control. As a Dutch slaveholder wrote from Louisiana in the 1750s: "It is necessary that the Negroes have wives, and you ought to know that nothing attaches them so much to a plantation as children."[6] No threat carried such force as a threat to sell the children, except the threat to separate husband and wife. The consequences for the children loomed large in the actions of their parents. When—to take an extreme example—a group of slaves planned a mass suicide, concern for their children provided the ground for sober second thoughts.[7]

Evidence of the slaveholders' awareness of the importance of family to the slaves may be found in almost any well-kept set of plantation records. Masters and overseers normally listed their slaves by households and shaped disciplinary procedures to take full account of family relationships. The sale of a recalcitrant slave might be delayed or avoided because it would cause resentment among his family of normally good workers. Conversely, a slave might be sold as the only way to break his influence over valuable relatives.[8] Could whites possibly have missed the content of their slaves' marital relationships when faced with such incidents as the one reported by James W. Melvin, an overseer, to his employer, Audley Clark Britton?

> [Old Bill] breathed his last on Saturday the 31st, Jan. about 8-1/2 o'clock in the morning. He appeared prepared for Death and said he was going to heaven and wanted his wife to meet him there. When he took sick he told all it would be his last sickness—I was very sorry to lose him.[9]

The pretensions of racist propagandists that slaves did not value the marriage relation fell apart in the courts, which in a variety of ways wrestled with the problems caused by the lack of legal sanction for slave marriages. However much they insisted on treating the slaves' marriages as mere concubinage, they rarely if ever denied the moral content of the relationship or the common devotion of the parties to each other. Thus, Georgia and Texas illogically and humanely would not permit slave wives to testify against their husbands while continuing to insist that their relationship had no standing at law. The high courts of South Carolina and other states took a more consistent stand on the question of testimony but repeatedly acknowledged the painful problems caused by the lack of legal sanction for relationships everyone knew to be meaningful and worthy of respect.[10]

Many slaveholders went to impressive lengths to keep families together even at the price of considerable pecuniary loss, although, as Kenneth Stampp forcefully insists, the great majority of slaveholders chose business over sentiment and broke up families when under financial pressure. But the choice did not rest easy on their conscience. The kernel of truth in the notion that the slaveholders felt guilty about owning human beings resides largely in this issue. They did feel guilty about their inability to live up to their own paternalistic justification for slavery in the face of market pressure.[11]

The more paternalistic masters betrayed evidence of considerable emotional strain. In 1858, William Massie of Virginia, forced to decrease his debts, chose to sell a beloved and newly improved homestead rather than his slaves. "To know," he explained, "that my little family, white and *black*, [is] to be fixed permanently together would be as near that thing happiness as I ever expect to get. . . . Elizabeth has raised and taught most of them, and having no children, like every other woman under like circumstances, has tender feelings toward them."[12] An impressive number of slaveholders took losses they could ill afford in an effort to keep families together.[13] For the great families, from colonial times to the fall of the regime, the maintenance of family units was a matter of honor.[14] Foreign travelers not easily taken in by appearances testified to the lengths to which slaveholders went at auctions to compel the callous among them to keep family units together.[15] Finally, many ex-slaves testified about masters who steadfastly refused to separate families; who, if they could not avoid separations, sold the children within visiting distance of their parents; and who took losses to buy wives or husbands in order to prevent permanent separations.[16] Stampp's insistence that such evidence revealed the exception rather than the rule is probably true, al-

though I think that exceptions occurred more frequently than he
seems to allow for. But it does demonstrate how well the whites
understood the strength of the slaves' family ties and the devastating consequences of their own brutal disregard of the sensibilities
of those they were selling.

Masters could not afford to be wholly indifferent to slave sensibilities. "Who buys me must buy my son too," a slave defiantly
shouted from an auction block. Better to buy in Virginia than
Louisiana, wrote J. W. Metcalfe to St. John R. Liddell, for we stand
a better chance of buying whole families, whose attachments will
make them better and less troublesome workers. Enough slaves
risked severe punishment in demanding that their families be kept
intact to make masters thoughtful of their own self-interest.[17] So
far as circumstances permitted, the slaves tried to stay close to
brothers and sisters, aunts and uncles.[18] A woman with a husband
who struck her too freely might turn to her brother for protection.
A widowed or abandoned aunt could expect to live in a cabin with
an affectionate niece and her husband. An old slave without spouse
or children could expect attention and comfort from nieces,
nephews, and cousins when facing illness and death.[19] Brothers
looked after their sisters or at least tried to. An overseer killed a
slave girl in Kentucky and paid with his own life at the hands of
her brother, who then made a successful escape. In Virginia terrible whippings could not prevent a young man from sneaking off
to visit a cherished sister on another plantation.[20]

The more humane masters took full account of their slaves'
affection for and sense of responsibility toward relatives. Charles
West wrote to the Reverend John Jones of Georgia to ask if a
certain Clarissa was alive and about, for her sister, Hannah, in
Alabama wanted to visit her during the summer. Dr. Bradford, a
slaveholder in Florida, hired out three sisters at a lower price than
he could have gotten because he would not separate them even for
a year.[21] Few slaveholders took such pains to respect the strong ties
of brothers and sisters, but fewer still could claim as excuse that
they did not have evidence of the slaves' feelings. Three-quarters
of a century after slavery, Anne Harris of Virginia, at age ninety-
two, told her interviewer that no white person had ever set foot
in her house.

> Don't 'low it. Dey sole my sister Kate. I saw it wid dese here eyes.
> Sole her in 1860, and I ain't seed nor heard of her since. Folks say

white folks is all right dese days. Maybe dey is, maybe dey isn't. But I can't stand to see 'em. Not on my place.[22]

In the late antebellum period several states moved to forbid the sale of children away from their mother, but only Louisiana's law appears to have been effective. At that, Governor Hammond of South Carolina had the audacity to argue that the slaveholders deserved credit for efforts to hold slave families together and that the slaves themselves cared little.[23]

Masters not only saw the bonds between husbands and wives, parents and children, they saw the bonds between nieces and nephews and aunts and uncles and especially between brothers and sisters. Nowhere did the slaveholders' willful blindness, not to say hypocrisy, concerning the strength of their slaves' family ties appear so baldly as in their reaction to separations attendant upon sales. They told themselves and anyone who would listen that husbands and wives, despite momentary distress, did not mind separations and would quickly adjust to new mates. Not content with this fabrication, some slaveholders went so far as to assert that separation of mothers from children caused only minimal hardship. Most slaveholders knew this claim to be nonsense, but they nevertheless argued that the separation of fathers from their children was of little consequence.

From time to time a slave did prefer to stay with a good master or mistress rather than follow a spouse who was being sold away. In these cases and in many others in which slaves displayed indifference, the marriage had probably already been weakened, and sale provided the most convenient and painless form of divorce. Such incidents reveal nothing about the depth of grief aroused by the sale of cherished wives and husbands. The slaveholders knew that many slave marriages rested on solid foundations of affection. Slaves on all except the most entrenched and stable plantations lived in constant fear of such separations and steeled themselves against them. When the blow came, the slaves often took it with outward calm. A discernible decline in a master's fortune or growing trouble with the overseer or master might have given warning of what was coming. If the slaves suffered quietly and cried alone, their masters had an excuse to declare them indifferent.

No such excuses, frail as they were, could explain the slaveholders' frequent assertions that mothers and children adjusted easily to separations. The slaveholders saw the depth of the anguish constantly, and only the most crass tried to deny it. John A. Quitman said that he had witnessed the separation of a family only once. It was enough: "I never saw such profound grief as the poor creatures manifested." Mary Boykin Chesnut remarked to a visiting Englishwoman as they passed a slave auction, "If you can stand that, no other Southern thing need choke you."[24]

John S. Wise's testimony may stand for many others. An apologist who put the best face he could on the old regime, he described an auction in which a crippled man of limited use was in danger of being separated from his wife and children. Israel, the man, spoke up in his own behalf:

> "Yes, sir, I kin do as much ez ennybody; and marsters, ef you'll only buy me and de chillum with Martha Ann, Gord knows I'll wuk myself to deth for you." The poor little darkeys, Cephas and Melinda, sat there frightened and silent, their white eyes dancing like monkey-eyes, and gleaming in the shadows. As her husband's voice broke on her ear, Martha Ann, who had been looking sadly out of the window in a pose of quiet dignity, turned her face with an expression of exquisite love and gratitude towards Israel. She gazed for a moment at her husband and at her children, and then looked away once more, her eyes brimming with tears.[25]

Wise's story—of course—ended happily when a slaveholder accepted a loss he could not easily afford in order to buy the family as a unit. But Wise, a man of the world, had to know, as Brecht later reminded us, "In real life, the ending is not so fine / Victoria's Messenger does not come riding often."

John Randolph of Roanoke, a slaveholder himself, who had known Patrick Henry, Henry Clay, and all the great political orators of the day and who himself ranked at the top, was asked whom he thought to have pride of place. "The greatest orator I ever heard," he replied, "was a woman. She was a slave and a mother and her rostrum was an auction block."[26]

All except the most dehumanized slaveholders knew of the attachments that the slaves had to their more extended families, to their friends, and to most of those who made up their little communities and called each other "brother" and "sister." Kate Stone wrote in 1862: "Separating the old family Negroes who have lived and worked together for so many years is a great grief to them and a distress to us."[27] Those who pretended that the separations came easy never explained why so many ruses had to be used to keep men and women occupied while one or another of their children was being whisked off. Robert Applegarth, an Englishman, described a common scene in which slaves suffered threats and punishments at auctions in response to their wailing and pleading to be kept together.[28] So well did the slaveholders understand the strength of these family ties that the more humane among them found it useful to argue against separations on the grounds of economic expediency by pointing out that the slaves worked much better when kept together.[29]

The extent of separation of wives from husbands and children from parents will probably remain in dispute. The impressive econometric work by Robert Fogel and Stanley Engerman suggests that separations occurred less frequently than has generally been believed, but the data do not permit precise measurement.[30] The nostalgic son of an antebellum planter did not fear contradiction when he recalled long after emancipation: "Were families separated by sale, etc.? Yes, quite often."[31] The potential for forced separation—whatever the ultimate measure of its realization—struck fear into the quarters, especially in the slave-exporting states of the Upper South. If the rich and powerful Pierce Butler of the Sea Islands had to sell hundreds of slaves to cover debts in the 1850s, was anyone safe? Even planters willing to take financial losses to keep families intact could not always control events. Once slaves passed out of the hands of their old masters, their fate depended upon the willingness of professional traders to honor commitments to keep families together or upon the attitude of new masters. And many masters did not respect their slaves' family feelings and did not hesitate to sell them as individuals.

Frederick Douglass referred to "that painful uncertainty which in one form or another was ever obtruding itself in the pathway of the slave."[32] Perhaps no single hardship or danger, not even the ever-present whip, struck such terror into the slaves and accounted for so much of that "fatalism" often attributed to them. If the spirit of many did crack and if many did become numb, nothing weighs so heavily among the reasons as the constant fear of losing loved ones. In the weakest slaves it instilled reckless irresponsibility and a fear of risking attachments—of feeling anything—and in the strongest, a heroic stoicism in the face of unbearable pain. A majority of the slaves probably suffered from some effects of these fears, but their vibrant love of life and of each other checked the slide into despair.

But the pain remained, and the slaveholders knew as much. Is it possible that no slaveholder noticed the grief of the woman who told Fredrika Bremer that she had had six children, three of whom had died and three of whom had been sold: "When they took from me the last little girl, oh, I believed I never should have got over it! It almost broke my heart!"[33] Could any white southerner pretend not to know from direct observation the meaning of Sojourner Truth's statement: "I have borne thirteen chillun and seen 'em mos' all sold off into slavery, and when I cried out with a mother's grief, none but Jesus heard. . . ."[34] Whatever the whites admitted to others or even themselves, they knew what they wrought. And the slaves knew that they knew. A black woman, speaking to Lucy Chase, recalled her first husband's being sold away from her: "White folks got a heap to answer for the way they've done to colored folks! So much they won't never pray it away!"[35]

ROMANCES OF THE FIELD

During the seventeenth and eighteenth centuries West African sexual mores had shocked Europeans. The extent of nakedness; the free use of sexual jokes, allusions, and symbols; the apparent ease with which sexual partners could sometimes be exchanged—in a word, the different standards of behavior—convinced Europeans that Africans had no standards, no morals, no restraints. Before long, Europe and America were hearing lurid tales of giant penises, intercourse with apes, and assorted unspeakable (but much spoken of) transgressions against God and nature. Occasionally, some European might notice that in fact West Africans demanded chastity in their youngsters and severely punished adultery; but since these same Africans had the audacity to define chastity, adultery, and other relevant terms to suit themselves, and since their views of sexual freedom largely applied to women as well as men, they continued to be regarded as amoral by Europeans. Some African peoples, for example, held the view that hospitality should include the offering of one's daughter or wife for the night, but only under strictly defined circumstances and to certain parties. Thus, whereas adultery constituted a deadly offense, its definition varied considerably from the one accepted in Europe.[1] The Africans who came to America brought with them strict sets of family and sexual mores, which proved impossible to maintain under slavery in a foreign land, and they had to fashion new and more appropriate ones. Even if the legend of black sexual promiscuity had had the substance attributed to it, slavery in a white man's country, not the African heritage, would have to be held accountable.[2]

In one positive respect the African heritage retained great force. The life-affirming spirit of the traditional religion and the sense of sin as primarily a moral offense to the community rather than to God had both passed into Afro-American Christianity and created formidable obstacles to the denigration of sex as sinful, dirty, or anything other than delightfully human and pleasurable. Although Victorianism made surprising progress in the quarters, especially among slave mothers who worried about their daughters' happiness, it never destroyed that earthy attitude toward sex which a life-affirming world-view imparted. The brutal side of slavery—the precariousness of the family, the exploitation of black women by white men, the attempts of some masters to mate their slaves like cattle—could not wholly demoralize the quarters, which adhered to definite if flexible standards of sexual morality. The source of the slaves' rejection of guilt-stricken white sexual attitudes lay deep in a religious world-view that had originated in Africa and had embodied itself in the sensibility of the slave quarters of the New World.

If the slaves had been half as loose sexually as whites have usually blithely assumed, the plantations ought to have been filled with cases of venereal disease, as they were in Brazil or as they appear to have been in some sections of the Deep South during the twentieth century.[3] For the Old South such evidence is lacking. Rumors and reports occurred more frequently during the eighteenth century than during the nineteenth, but since doctors confused yaws with venereal disease, such evidence cannot wholly be trusted.[4] Gonorrhea and syphilis engaged the attention of the medical profession in the South, as it did the fantasy life of the novel-reading white ladies of the upper class, but it did not become a matter of major concern.[5] These diseases may well have struck southern whites more often than blacks; in any case, they appeared among both much more frequently in the towns than on the plantations.[6] Although the evidence is scanty and even treacherous, it would also appear that plantations situated close to towns and cities had a much higher incidence than those more remote.[7] Planters in eighteenth-century Virginia showed some concern about the diseases and discussed remedies. During the late antebellum period, Louisiana and Arkansas appear to have had a higher incidence than the states to the east, but the difference may have reflected nothing more than greater frankness.[8] Cases appeared everywhere, but only rarely did they involve more than one or two slaves. Nothing like the epidemic proportions attained in Europe at certain times or in the United States in the 1970s ever occurred.[9]

Despite white pretense that venereal disease was a black problem in the Old South, everything suggests, on the contrary, that it struck with particular force among the poor whites and the townspeople. The incidence of venereal disease among the plantation blacks of the Sea Islands did upset the abolitionists who went down to teach and work during the war, but the suspicion grew that much of it had been introduced by Union troops in the best tradition of occupying armies.[10] Southern slaves identified venereal disease as a white man's malady, much as the English called it the French disease and vice versa. One old black man commented on another, whose deformities strongly suggested the effects of syphilis: "Dat dere fellow am as ill as if he were one of de white pop'lation."[11]

"History tells us also," Representative Keitt of South Carolina told the Congress of the United States in 1857, "that when the working classes stepped out of the condition of bondage, by the process of emancipation, they branched into four recurring subordinations—the hireling, the beggar, the thief, and the prostitute—which have no general existence in slave countries."[12] Representative Keitt did not explain the apparent disappearance of the white laborers of the Old South, whose condition and prospects caused so much debate in the southern press; of the white and black beggars who outraged respectable opinion in New Orleans and other cities; or of the slaves and free Negroes, who, as white southerners never tired of insisting, were all thieves by nature. The abolitionists argued that slavery as a system turned black women into prostitutes against their will, but Representative Keitt was referring to prostitutes strictly defined. Brothels abounded in southern cities, and most of their ladies-in-waiting were not black.

In the capital of Georgia, for example, the poor black whores had a difficult time competing with their white sisters. The white politicians who provided the clientele preferred white to black women, contrary to customary speculation. Evidence from other cities suggests that the preference for white whores was general. Some slave women in New Orleans, the South's capital of debauchery, hired their own time on the streets, and some free Negro women did good business in various cities; but most southern prostitutes appear to have been poor white girls, some of whom serviced both races and concerned themselves only with the color of their clients' money.[13]

Sidney W. Mintz, the distinguished anthropologist, has drolly defined "superstition" as some other man's religion and "promiscuity" as some other man's sex life. The sex life of the slaves might have created an uproar among the whites if their racism had not led to the smug judgment that it hardly mattered. The slaves, not being subject to the same ideological ravages, remained free to judge the sex life of the whites. Not surprisingly, they found it morally deficient. The unquestionably chaste and even Victorian among the slaves did not condemn their brothers and sisters in the terms used by the whites, however much they expressed disgust with particular indiscretions. The idea that the slaves hopped in and out of bed with each other as well as with the whites originated among self-serving slaveholders concerned to prove that the separation of families and the sexual exploitation of black women by white men aroused little or no resentment or moral revulsion in the quarters.

On what evidence does this legend of slave promiscuity rest? The sexual code of the slaves did in fact differ from that of the whites, even if less in practice than in theory. The whites perceived the difference as proof of the immorality of the slaves, especially the slave women; the slaves reversed the judgment. All the white critics ever demonstrated was that the slaves did not demand premarital chastity; that they freely experimented before marriage; that they would drop one husband for another if he proved unsatisfactory; and that, relative to their white mistresses at least, they enjoyed a relaxed attitude toward their own sexuality. The white critics never proved—and in truth did not even often allege—that slave women easily entered into adultery or that they often had more than one man at a time.

Whites did not focus on the sexuality of black men. The titillating and violence-provoking theory of the superpotency of that black superpenis, while whispered about for several centuries, did not become an obsession in the South until after emancipation, when it served the purposes of racial segregationists.[14] The double standard among the whites, which had a much weaker parallel among the blacks, shielded the black men from censure; but more important, the whites needed to denigrate black women in order to excuse their own impudent trifling with them. Yet, rarely did anyone accuse black women of polyandry, whereas polygyny, although not frequent, periodically surfaced. Some men preferred to have " 'broad wives" (wives who lived "abroad" on another place; I have seen no reference to " 'broad husbands") because it enabled them to have more than one household, and drivers and other privileged male slaves sometimes obtained their master's permission to have more than one wife. Occasionally, slaveholders deliberately assigned slave men to live and work as studs.[15] The black women bore the transgressions of black men with much less equanimity than did the white men, whose indifference no doubt reflected a certain male camaraderie across class and racial lines. White men preferred to base their charge of black promiscuity on the alleged behavior of the women. But they never had much of a case.

Slave children, recalled Mary Ellen Johnson, an ex-slave from Texas, were not supposed to ask questions about delicate subjects. Maggie Black, an ex-slave from South Carolina, agreed: "De little chillum was jes uz foolish den cause de peoples ne'er tell dem 'bout nuthin tall in dat time." Anne Broome from South Carolina told of being ridiculed by whites as "a big girl" because she had accepted her mother's story of having been delivered by a railroad train. Mom Ryer Emmanuel asked her mother where she had come from and received the same reply as many other slave children: "I got you out de hollow log." When Andy Marion was about ten years old, his mother told him that she had found him in the bushes. Katie Sutton of Kentucky was told by her mistress that she had been hatched, and long believed it. The lullabies her mother had sung to her had reinforced this idea.[16]

One woman from Texas recalled having been forced to marry a man she disliked and then trying to fight him off when he went to her bed; although sixteen years old, she had not known what was expected of her.[17] Another, from Tennessee, insisted that girls in their late teens often knew nothing and would look for babies in parsley beds and hollow logs. "I was twenty years old when my first baby came," she continued. "I didn't know nothing then. I didn't know how long I had to carry my baby. We never saw nothing when we were children."[18] A mother told her daughter that doctors brought babies and then, questioned further about the screams of a woman in childbirth, told her to get out or she would kill her. Other ex-slaves, usually but not always the women, told similar stories. As one said, "We never seed nothing. People was very particular in them days. They wouldn't let children know anything like they do now."[19]

For a rural society in which the example of barnyard animals appeared everywhere and in which adults and children of both sexes usually slept in the same room, these claims cannot easily be accepted, especially since many years, conditioned by a new morality, had passed by the time of the interviews. Yet they cannot be dismissed either, for surprisingly little evidence exists on the other side, despite the conventional white wisdom about black promiscuity. Many slaves struggled to establish some degree of privacy in sleeping arrangements and in family life generally. George Conred, Jr., remembered the beds being curtained off. Many slave children slept in trundle beds, which would usually be spread over the floor at night but might be locked under their parents' bed; others slept on bunks above those of their parents. These measures reinforced the element of privacy, but the children could hardly help hearing if not seeing their parents' love-making.[20] They might hear, as one did, a mother playfully singing to her husband:

> Sleepy creature, sleepy creature,
> There's something to do 'sides sleeping.

The adults did not find it necessary to disguise their affection. "Daddy used to play wid mammy just lak she was a child," recalled John Collins of South Carolina. "He'd ketch her under de armpits and jump her up mighty nigh to the rafters in de little house us lived in."[21]

These scattered recollections take on additional meaning in view of the ages at which the slaves courted and married. The widely believed notion that masters compelled their slaves to marry at tender ages is not true. Enough masters did interfere to create an evil of noticeable proportions, but the overwhelming majority did not. Slaves do not seem to have married at young ages relative to the standards of most rural societies. Some masters would not permit their slaves to marry earlier than twenty or so, apparently in the hope of encouraging more stable unions, for they appreciated that stable unions yielded children and contributed to a level of plantation morale which would be reflected in higher economic productivity.[22]

Many slaves, if not most, married in their mid-teens or later, possibly earlier than most well-to-do whites. Kate Stone's sister was not a rarity in marrying at sixteen after rejecting ten proposals.[23] This pattern continued among blacks after emancipation.[24] The pressure to marry young, in most cases, came not from the Big House but from Mamma. Normally, slave parents, not masters, supervised marriages; the master's permission followed the consent of the parents. Many, perhaps most, slave mothers wanted their children, especially their daughters, to "grow up right." Early marriages cut down the chances of their "going wrong." As one woman who married with her mother's consent at fourteen pointed out, Mamma knew that, marriage or no marriage, she was about ready to have a good time. But these early marriages also set the stage for a high rate of divorce.[25]

Most masters let the slaves pick their own partners at their own pace and relied on natural desires to accomplish reasonably early mating. But enough masters did compel unwelcome unions to call forth considerable protest from the blacks, and some of the separations accompanying emancipation had their origins in this initial compulsion.[26] Forced marriages affected perhaps one out of ten and became all the more galling in view of the contrary dominant practice. Kate Darling, who had had a harsh master in Texas, said, "Niggers didn't court then, like they do now. Massa pick out a portly man and a portly gal and just put 'em together. What he want am the stock."[27] But Clara C. Young, an ex-slave of Mississippi, came closer to the norm when she reflected on the efforts of masters to prevent their slaves from getting to know those of other plantations. The masters, she thought, feared romances that would create 'broad wives, in which case "dey would either have to buy or sell a nigger before you could get any work out of him."[28] William Wells Brown recalled how his mistress tried to convince him to marry so as to guarantee his ties to family and home; and in many other cases, masters bought mates for single slaves more or less to please them and with their consent.[29]

Although most white southerners allowed their daughters to pick out their own husbands, many of the richest and most powerful made arrangements commensurate with the interests of family power. J. S. Buckingham attributed the noticeable number of unhappy marriages to this source, and a Gullah slave preacher could think of no better way to urge his people to live right than to make a biting reference to the behavior of the big buckra who married for money and property instead of for love.[30] Prearranged marriages have appeared as a fact of life in many traditional societies, including the African, and have remained the custom in countries from Ireland to Indonesia during the twentieth century. However jarring to modern American sensibilities, they had their virtues; Hegel made out an attractive case for their moral superiority to marriages based on initial love and self-selection.[31] But in slavery masters, not parents, arranged matters, and the moral sanction suffered accordingly. Not acts directed by the family in its own collective interest, but efforts by a force outside the family circle to increase the level of expropriated wealth, these marriages constituted an alien imposition on the slaves.

Teen-age slave girls did often slip into sexual adventures despite their mothers' efforts. The young house servants in particular had ample opportunity and rarely lacked suitors. The field hands lived on a tighter leash but had opportunity enough. The Victorianism of Mamma and the admonitions of Missus did not always prevail against a thirst for life in a slave community that simply could not bring itself to decry love-making as a crime, even when it dutifully pronounced it to be wrong. Given the attitude of the slaves toward sin, they found it difficult to see some offense against God in behavior they willingly described as not nice or not respectable.[32] Some of the young men, therefore, happily went a-courting. John White, who had been a cook on a plantation in Texas, chuckled: "Sometimes I'd slip some things from out of the kitchen. The single womenfolks was bad that way. I favors them with something extra from the kitchen. Then they favors me—at night."[33]

Even the more conservative parents who married their daughters off young did not get hysterical if their unmarried daughters got pregnant. It was not a nice thing to do, but it was not a moral disaster either. The object became to live respectably and happily with one man, or at least with one man at a time. A slave girl's chances to get the man she wanted did not slip much because she had had an "illegitimate" child. A male ex-slave replied with astonishment when asked if an unwed mother would be ostracized: "No, they wouldn't do that."[34] Virginity at marriage carried only small prestige; cooperation within the larger family reduced the burden of having children early; and the children themselves were often welcomed as a pleasure, especially since they did not constitute a direct economic burden. A "good girl," therefore, was one who could be expected to be a loving and faithful wife, not one who could claim to have been untouched by human hands. That particular pretension, staunchly adhered to by the whites, although much less in their guilt-producing practice than in their hotly maintained theory, the slaves found slightly ridiculous. Even so, the extent of illegitimacy among the slaves may well have been exaggerated by hostile whites. Prominent contemporaries like Toombs of Georgia and DuBose of Alabama thought so, as have Dr. Du Bois and other subsequent investigators.[35] A planter in Tennessee recorded in his diary in 1854: "The girl, Martha, wife of Willis, is delivered of a daughter this morning—she has been married only two months. Her mother says 'she makes quick Work of it' and seems distressed. I comfort her by telling her such things often happen with the first born, but never afterwards."[36]

"As to their habits of amalgamation and intercourse," wrote a Mississippi planter, "I know of no means whereby to regulate them: I attempted to for many years by preaching virtue and decency, encouraging marriages, and by punishing, with some severity, departures from marital obligations, but it was all in vain."[37] Not one black woman in six, a North Carolina sage told a northern reporter in 1865, remained faithful to her husband.[38] He did not, unfortunately, explain his sampling method. Several decades earlier, the urbane Charles Cotesworth Pinckney had put the white South's judgment in perspective. Why, he observed, the black wenches take their marital vows even more lightly than do the fashionable ladies of the European capitals.[39] Had he been less solicitous of local sensibilities, he might easily have added, "or of Charleston," for the most responsible studies of recent years demonstrate that the ladies of the planter class filled their own quota of premarital and extramarital adventures. The slaves did not fail to notice.[40] Church records and other sources reveal fornication, illegitimacy, and adultery in the life of the white lower classes in the countryside and in the towns. Their extent remains problematical, but there is no reason to believe that it was one whit less than among the slaves.[41]

Intermittent outbursts of *crimes passionnels* did disturb the quarters, but these hardly testified to an easy attitude toward adultery.

Existing evidence cannot sustain the charge of widespread marital infidelity, which may in fact largely reflect perceptions of postbellum conditions of social disorganization.[42] Circumstances varied widely, but the slaves accepted marital fidelity as a personal and social responsibility. However generously they treated lapses by their women from a white-inspired standard of premarital sexual morality, they took a stern view of postmarital philandering. In some cases masters and especially mistresses enforced discipline with an iron hand,[43] but the insistence on regularity generally arose from within the quarters. Susan Snow, an ex-slave of Alabama, described a common although by no means universal attitude when she said, "De women had to walk a chalk line. I never heard tell o' wives runnin' round with other men in dem days."[44] During the war the women in the contraband camps who had husbands in the Union army made it a point of honor to reassure them of their fidelity and showed considerable steadfastness under trying conditions.[45] Adultery among the slaves did occur, but it ranked as a serious offense against their own standard of decency.

Many sober heads among the slaveholders had long scoffed at the conventional charges. Governor R. F. W. Allston of South Carolina, one of the largest slaveholders in the South, calmly stated that adultery and sexual scandals rarely occurred among the slaves. The Supreme Court of North Carolina noted in passing that the slaves generally respected each other's marital rights. The wife of a white pastor in Montgomery, Alabama, who said that the slaves took sexual matters lightly, reported that most proved loyal when married. Other prominent slaveholders like R. Q. Mallard and D. E. Huger Smith concurred. And Mrs. Chesnut, a determined enemy of cant, replied to charges by William Howard Russell about the moral laxity of female slaves, ridiculing him for going "on in indignation because there were women in the Negro plantations who were not vestal virgins! Negro women are married, and after marriage behave as well as other people." And Governor Collier of Alabama, advocating compliance with the weak law of 1851 against separation of families, declared as a matter of common knowledge that husbands and wives generally held each other in affection.[46] Frances Butler Leigh, who rarely lost a chance to impugn the character of the blacks, wrote shortly after the war: "The negroes had their own ideas of morality, and they held to them very strictly; they did not consider it wrong for a girl to have a child before she married, but afterwards were extremely severe upon anything like infidelity on her part." Mrs. Leigh wryly added: "Indeed, the good old law of female submission to the husband's will on all points held good."[47]

However much some whites followed the logic of chattel slavery and sought to degrade the sexual relations of their slaves to an animal level while fuming about innate black amorality, the slaves shaped a world of their own. They did not always have an easy time doing so, and many succumbed to demoralization. "Dat courtin' stuff," said Jane Johnson, an ex-slave of South Carolina, "is what white folks does, no nigger knows what dat fancy thing is. Us just natchally lives together; men and women mates lak de animals out dere. Colored people don't pay no 'tention to what white folks call love, they just 'sires de woman they wants, dat's all."[48] Others disagreed sharply but pointed to frustrations. "I been married four times since de war," said Andy Marion, also of South Carolina, "and I'm here to tell you dat a nigger had a hell of a time gettin' a wife durin' slavery. If you didn't see one on de place to suit you, and chances was you didn't suit them, why what could you do?" He added that to get a wife from another place meant getting regular passes and then the permission of both of the girl's parents plus that of two sets of masters.[49]

The "romances of the field," as the Reverend Elijah P. Marrs, an ex-slave turned Union soldier, preacher, and author, called them, nevertheless proved irrepressible.[50] When his interviewer asked Frank Adamson of South Carolina if he had courted under slavery, he replied forcefully, with an appropriate touch of contempt:

> Now what make you ask dat? Did me ever do any courtin'? You knows I did. Every he thing from a he king down to a bunty rooster gits 'cited 'bout she things. . . . It's de nature of a he, to take after de she. They do say dat a he angel ain't got dis to worry 'bout.[51]

The men spoke plainly about wanting to marry for love. Asked by a skeptical mistress how he knew he really loved his intended, Francis Frederick replied, "because since me lub Fanny me lub everything on de plantation, de hosses and all de tings." A black soldier went to Colonel Higginson for advice, which he then refused, about marrying a woman another officer had already cautioned him not to. "Cap'n Scroby [Trowbridge] he advise me not for marry dis lady, 'cause she had seben chil'en. What for use? Cap'n Scroby can't lub for me. I mus' lub for myself, and I lub he."[52] Lucy Ann Dunn of North Carolina recalled that her man never kissed her until he proposed marriage shortly after emancipation.

> It was in de little Baptist church at Neuse where I first seed big black Jim Dunn and I fell in love with him den I reckons. He said dat he loved me den too, but it was three Sundays before he asked to see me home.
>
> We walked dat mile home in front of my Mammy, and I was so happy dat I ain't thought it half a mile home. We et corn bread and turnips for dinner and it was night before he went home. Mammy wouldn't let me walk with him to de gate, I knowed, so I just set dere on de porch and says goodnight.
>
> He come every Sunday for a year and finally he proposed. I had told Mammy dat I thought dat I ought to be allowed to walk to the gate with Jim and she said all right, iffen she was settin' dere on de porch lookin'.[53]

The wonder is not that many slaves slipped into the insensitive and even brutal patterns of life they were being pushed toward by a demoralizing social system, but that so many others, possibly a commanding majority, fought for human ground on which to live even as slaves. From black and white sources we learn of the tenderness, gentleness, charm, and modesty that often marked the love lives of ordinary field hands as well as of more privileged house slaves. Consider some random recollections from the Fisk University narratives:

> Niggers didn't have time to do much courting in them days. White folks would let them have suppers 'round Christmas time, then after that it was all over and no more gatherings till the next summer; then they would let them set out under the shade trees on Sunday evening, and all like that.
>
> They courted then just like they do now. Only they wasn't fast like they are now. I never in all my born days went out at night by myself and stayed out like these young folks do now. When I went out I always had company.
>
> They courted nicer than they do now. They would come to the girl they liked, and talk to them at night after the work was done.
>
> Would not have no courting. They just laughed and talked. Didn't let the boys get around the gals like they do now. He sat over there and you sat here and do your courting.

> I wasn't big enough to court; I had to slip. I knowed the road she'd come, and I could slip off and meet her sometimes, but we had to dodge the old folks 'cause they would whip me sho'.

> We would just sit and talk with each other. I told him once I didn't love him; I hated him, and then I told him again that I loved him so much I just loved to see him walk. You had to court right there on the place, 'cause they had padderollers. . . .[54]

Many of the slaveholders and travelers noted the widespread affection and delicacy among the courting slaves and tried to show them respect, however little they could resist condescension. Joel B. Fort of Tennessee remembered Shed, "a traveling man" in more than one sense of the word, who convinced the elder Fort to buy him from the traders so that, ostensibly, he could end his "wanderings." "The truth of the matter," wrote Fort, "he met Aunt Chaney who was a plump girl of eighteen, and it was love at first sight." Their marriage lasted until death, almost fifty years later.[55] A friend of Harriet Martineau described having walked behind two black men who were courting a young woman. "He told me," she wrote, "that nothing could be more admirable than the coyness of the lady, and the compliments of the gallant and his friend."[56] Olmsted reported on the teasing behavior of a big South Carolina rice planter toward one of his field women:

> While watching the negroes in the field, Mr. X addressed a girl, who was vigorously plying a hoe near us.
> "Is that Lucy?—Ah, Lucy, what's this I hear about you?"
> The girl simpered; but did not answer nor discontinue her work.
> "What is that I hear about you and Sam, eh?"
> The girl grinned; and still hoeing away with all her might, whispered, "Yes, sir."
> "Sam came to see me this morning."
> "If master pleases."
> "Very well; you may come up to the house Saturday night, and your mistress will have something for you."[57]

Devices to win the affections of one's beloved ran the usual gamut, but with two notable additions. The signs, charms, and love potions, so much a part of the folk religion, came into full sway and received much credit for winning over ostensibly reluctant young women. And the slaves' talent for improvising songs of wit and beauty had a special outlet among the suitors. In competition for a young woman the ability to out-sweet-sing one's rival could easily prove decisive. When disappointed or merely sowing wild oats, they sang too and carried on their flirtations with all who would respond.

> Ol' Mars'r had a pretty yaller gal,
> He brought her fum de Souf;
> Her hair it curled so berry tight
> She couldn't shut her mouf.

> Way down in Mississippi,
> Where de gals dey are so pretty,
> W'at a happy time way down in old Car'line!
> Dis darky fell in love
> Wid a han'some yaller Dinah.
> Higho—higho—higho.[58]

Gallantry and modesty existed alongside crudeness, coarseness, and demoralization. In a world in which black women regularly had to strip to the waist to be whipped and sometimes had to strip naked to be displayed at auction, it was no small matter that they could mingle shame with their bitter resentment. The shame marked their determination to carry themselves as women with sensibilities as delicate as those of the finest white ladies. Many of the young men protected this attitude and simultaneously claimed their own manhood by showing elementary courtesies and trying to shield their young women from indignities. A well-brought-up field hand would stop chewing or smoking tobacco when he approached a young woman. If caught by patrols at night he would offer to take her whipping as well as his own. In one instance a youngster begged the patrollers not to make him remove his jacket in the presence of his girlfriend, for he had no shirt under it and did not want to be embarrassed. With such trifles have the efforts of ostensibly degraded field hands to bring their children up "respectable" been recorded.[59]

Two general conclusions flow from this complex story. First, the slaves fashioned their own standards of morality and sexual propriety, which deviated from prevailing white standards but not necessarily in ways our own age would judge negatively. The standards brought a measure of order and dignity to life in the quarters. Their hostility toward adultery, no matter how many lapses occurred among the frail, demonstrated a rejection of the indifference the whites had often tried to guide them into while preaching the opposite. The legal and social system devised by the whites from the earliest days often tended to undermine the self-respect of the slaves. Virginia's Act of 1705 provided punishment for "adultery or fornication." By omitting slaves from the terms of the act, the Virginia Assembly eliminated the legal responsibility of slaves for actions defined as immoral and illegal for whites.[60] The evidence of slave violation of the quarters' own code against adultery and of the personal violence provoked by jealousy must be weighed as part of the evidence for a wider standard of behavior that sanctioned divorce. Much of the transgression occurred as marriages were disintegrating and as one or both parties sought new alliances.

Thus, the second conclusion: The slaves did not separate marriage or sex itself from love. Indeed, they held the theory that good Christians did not sin by sleeping together out of wedlock, for they were pure and therefore could not defile each other.[61] They never fully recognized conjugal responsibilities attendant upon involuntary marriages, and they saw no reason to live forever with their mistakes. Their easy attitude toward divorce was strongly reinforced by the knowledge that the blow to the children would be greatly softened in a community in which all looked after all and the master had to feed all. The whites had good reason to envy their slaves, not because the legendary "happy niggers" could throw social responsibility to the winds and indulge their animal passions, as Stephen Pearl Andrews, among others, claimed,[62] but because the slaves had transformed the ghastly conditions under which they labored into living space within which they could love each other.[63]

Masters wanted their slaves to marry someone from the same farm or plantation, but as in so many other cases, the wishes of these all-powerful lords did not prevail. So many slaves had 'broad wives that they may well have constituted a majority in some sections of the South. Even on the great plantations pressure from the slaves for freedom of movement overcame the hostility of all except the most determined masters to allow interplantation marriages. 'Broad wives could be found everywhere.[64] In the Upper South and in those districts of the Lower South in which small units prevailed, slaveholders had little choice except to authorize marriages off the place.[65] In such cases the men generally got passes to visit their wives on weekends; many for Wednesday night also; some, whose wives lived on a neighboring farm, nightly.

Marriages off the place meant considerable inconvenience to masters as well as to slaves. The masters of the slave men had to forgo any claim to their children. Since slave marriages had no status at law and children followed the condition of the mother, the economic advantage fell to the masters of the slave women. But the masters of the men did not necessarily sacrifice their economic interests. They knew that a man who fell in love with a woman off the place would be a poor and sullen worker, and probably soon a runaway, if deprived of his choice. Positively, the man had to work especially hard and to avoid trouble, for if he incurred his master's displeasure, he might lose his visiting privileges. The slaves took advantage of their masters' economic interests and forced them to weigh the cost of forfeiting the capital gains inherent in slave children against the potential losses inherent in having demoralized or vengeful workers.

The ease with which so many masters capitulated speaks well for their humanity as well as their practicality; it also demonstrates that, notwithstanding their propaganda about slave promiscuity, they understood the depth of the feelings which went into many slave marriages. The slaveholders' courts registered this knowledge. In *Woodhouse v. McRae* (1857) the Supreme Court of North Carolina threw out a slaveholder's suit against someone who rented a slave and who inadvertently abetted his escape by giving him a pass to visit his wife. The court held that common practice sanctioned such visits and that the renter had behaved properly.[66]

The slaveholders permitted these interplantation marriages, but they did not like them. Many warned of the dangers. The opposition combined a variety of arguments, some of which concerned dangers to the slaveholders' interests; some of which concerned dangers to the slaves themselves; and all of which concerned dangers to good order. The greatest threat to the slaveholders' interests—the loss of capital gains by the owners of the men—was too obvious to require discussion. The greatest complaint was that the slaves derived too much independence from their increased freedom of movement. The slaves begin to think, wrote a hostile planter, that they have "an uncontrollable right to be frequently absent." They become indifferent to their master's interests and consider their wife's plantation their own home. Their presence disrupts the quarters, for they bring news, habits, and attitudes from the outside. They expose themselves to a much greater risk of separation from loved ones since the risk of sale from insolvency now arises from the condition of having two masters instead of one. But especially, interplantation marriage "creates a feeling of independence, from being of right, out of the control of their master for a time."[67]

The slaves preferred to marry off the plantation for the very reasons their masters preferred them not to, although they too feared the higher risk of sale and permanent separation. That risk took a particularly dreaded form, for a slave on his usual Wednesday or Saturday visit might discover that his wife had disappeared. A wife whose husband did not appear at the appointed time had much more to worry about than the possibility of his being sick, punished, or unfaithful.[68] Still, as Ella Thomas, a slaveholder of Georgia, said with some exaggeration, the slaves "all preferred having husbands off the plantation [and] thought it was exceedingly hard if they could not marry away from home." The slaves themselves stressed the much greater variety of choice of mates that interplantation marriages afforded and the pleasures of getting away, visiting, and changing pace.[69]

Many whites suspected that the women and especially the men enjoyed the sexual freedom distance made possible and were restoring African polygamy. These suspicions were wildly exaggerated, but some black men with freedom of movement did help create the image of the "travelin' man" who was to emerge so picturesquely in postwar black folklore. No doubt some of the wives had lovers in between their husbands' visits.[70] There is no reason to assume greater irregularity than such circumstances made inevitable. Living apart during the week generated tensions and fed jealousies. The men, as an ex-slave remarked, would be "'stracted" by jealousy all week long, the more so the more they loved their wives.[71]

Polygamy, travelin' men, and young women with a taste for adventure spiced but by no means typified interplantation marriages, many of which gave every indication of being held together by devotion and a high sense of responsibility. A man who could only visit his wife once or twice a week had to cook for himself or eat at a communal kitchen most of the time, but he could expect special treatment when he saw his wife. The women took pains to prepare a "big dinner" and to make the visits as festive as possible. They cleaned and repaired their husbands' clothes and made a fuss over them. When the men could, they brought an opossum or chicken or some vegetables or a little gift. Husbands and wives turned to each other for care and comfort, as when Mary Bell's mother would patiently bathe her husband and attend to the effects of frequent whippings. The whip had always played a big part in the slaves' preference for marrying off the plantation. By living apart the men and women did not have to witness the beatings and humiliations their loved ones took.[72]

The masters, despite pretenses, knew that these interplantation marriages rested on affection and commitment. They often made efforts to unite the couple through purchase when the slaves found the physical distance too difficult. Those masters who took their slaves' feelings lightly paid for their mistake during the war. Forbidden to visit 'broad wives because their masters feared desertion, the slaves responded by deserting in larger numbers.[73] Masters could not afford to believe their own propaganda about slave infidelity and marital indifference. The determination of the slaves to have their own way could not so easily be turned aside.

BROOMSTICKS AND ORANGE BLOSSOMS

As masters became convinced of the social and economic utility of stable unions among their slaves, they reflected on the importance of ceremonies to celebrate the seriousness of the marital tie. Weddings, simultaneously dignified and gay, received sanction from the masters, who saw them as necessary for the preservation of social control.[1] Planters themselves often performed wedding services, and many took impressive pains with the festivities. They paid special attention to the weddings of the house servants, but did not ignore those of the field hands. Many planters married their house servants in the Big House, and some married their field hands there. Curiously, the Big House occasionally hosted broomstick weddings—the customary slave wedding in which the ceremony consisted of having the couple jump over a broomstick— each planter having his own idea of what was proper to celebrate the occasion.[2]

To avoid loss of work time and also to provide maximum festivity, masters preferred weddings to be held during the Christmas holidays. During the year the masters tried to schedule the weddings for the weekends; but their motives were not entirely mercenary, for they often made arrangements for Saturday night, rather than Sunday, and allowed the hands to quit work early to dress up for the party. Christmas weddings had the additional advantage of permitting the white children who had returned from boarding school to attend and the white family as a whole to gather, the attendance of the whites at slave weddings being considered no small matter.[3]

White ministers often officiated at the weddings of slaves who worked in the Big Houses of the elite plantations and sometimes officiated at the weddings of ordinary field hands as well. Particularly in the aristocratic low country of Georgia and South Carolina, many ministers performed this service on the plantations, although some resisted by insisting on performing all weddings in their churches, thereby encouraging masters to take care of their slaves' weddings themselves.[4] In North Carolina and Tennessee white ministers reputedly regularly married the slaves on the farms and plantations.[5] Quite possibly, the practice would have become more general if the slaves had wanted it, for in many cases they had a choice and opted for a black preacher or even their own master.[6] Black preachers performed many weddings in all parts of the South, and many slaves clearly preferred them.[7]

The whites, especially the ladies, often went to considerable lengths to prepare big wedding parties for their house servants and sometimes put themselves out almost as much for the field hands. Many of the white ladies enjoyed the fuss and filled days with writing invitations to their own relatives and friends, as well as to neighboring planters, who were invited to bring their slaves. They wanted their people, especially the bridal party, to enjoy a memorable occasion, and they expected to enjoy it themselves.[8]

Two descriptions of slave weddings in Mississippi provide an idea of the event. Ingraham wrote during the 1830s:

> The negroes are usually married by the planter, who reads the service from the gallery [of the Big House]—the couple with their attendants standing upon the steps or on the green in front. These marriages, in the eye of the slave, are binding. Clergymen are sometimes invited to officiate by those planters who feel that respect for the marriage covenant, which leads them to desire its strict observance, where human legislation has not provided for it.

The ladies, he added, would bring delicacies and presents for the couple.[9]

In October, 1856, Francis Terry Leak of Mississippi recorded preparations for the wedding of some of his slaves:

> *Oct. 2, 1856.* Wrote to Margaret [his daughter who was away at school] informing her that her Mother would send for her on the 18th to help prepare for the Negro wedding on the 25th.
>
> *Oct. 17, 1856.* Wrote to Jane telling her that we would send for her next Friday to attend the Negro wedding, etc.
>
> *Oct. 27, 1856.* Mr. Mayo came down to the Negro wedding on Saturday night. Several white persons besides the owners of the Bridegrooms attended the wedding.
>
> There were seven couples married at the Negro wedding on Saturday night. The ceremony employed here is copied for future use. It was as follows, viz:
>
>> We are assembled together tonight on an occasion of much interest. It is a marriage occasion, but it is of a novel and peculiar character. It is not the ordinary occasion of the marriage of one couple of persons, but the very unusual one—perhaps unprecedented one, of the marriage at the same time, and with the same ceremony, of seven separate couples. The parties, who are to be married now stand in a circle before us, each couple hand in hand. The couples are Alfred & Ermine, Isaac & Rosa, Bennett & Catherine, Allen & Harriet, Ben & Emma, Lewis & Peggy, & Horace & Betty.
>>
>> With this brief statement of the nature & unusual character of the occasion that has brought us together tonight, we will now proceed to solemnize the rites of matrimony between the several couples, by asking the usual question & exacting the usual vow, of the parties individually.
>>
>> Alfred—Do you agree, before me & these witnesses to take Ermine as your wife, & to solemnly pledge yourself to discharge towards her the duties of an affectionate & faithful husband?
>>
>> Ermine—Do you agree, before me & these witnesses, to take Alfred as your husband, & Do you solemnly pledge yourself to discharge towards him the duties of an affectionate & faithful wife? . . . [Questions repeated to each couple]
>>
>> We have now gone through with every form necessary to authorize me to pronounce each of these several couples as man & wife. We have heard each party, of each couple, agree to enter into the married relation with the other party; and we have heard, from each to the other, a solemn vow of fidelity to the obligations of the

married state. It only remains, therefore, that I should pronounce, and accordingly, in the presence of these witnesses, I do pronounce Alfred & Ermine, as man and wife, Isaac & Rosa . . . [etc.]

And in conclusion I enjoin, according to the good old custom of our fathers and mothers, that each Bridegroom now salute the bride.[10]

Tempie Herndon remembered her own wedding to a slave from another plantation:

When I growed up I married Exter Durham. He belonged to Marse Snipes Durham who had de plantation 'cross de county line in Orange County. We had a big weddin'. We was married on de front porch of de Big House. Marse George killed a shoat and Mis' Betsy had Georgianna, de cook, to bake a big weddin' cake all iced up white as snow with a bride and groom stand' in de middle holdin' hands. De table was set out in de yard under de trees, and you ain't never seed de like of eats. All de niggers come to de feast and Marse George had a dram for everybody. Dat was some weddin'. I had on a white dress, white shoes, and long white gloves dat come to my elbow, and Mis' Betsy done made me a weddin' veil out of a white net window curtain. When she played de weddin' march on de piano, me and Exter marched down de walk and up on de porch to de altar Mis' Betsy done fixed. Dat de prettiest altar I ever seed. Back 'against de rose vine dat was full of red roses, Mis' Betsy done put tables filled with flowers and white candles. She done spread down a bed sheet, a sure 'nough linen sheet, for us to stand on, and dey was a white pillow to kneel down on. Exter done made me a weddin' ring. He made it out of a big red button with his pocket knife. He done cut it so round and polished it so smooth dat it looked like a red satin ribbon tied round my finger. Dat sure was a pretty ring. I wore it about fifty years. Den it got so thin dat I lost it one day in de wash tub when I was washin' clothes.

Uncle Edmond Kirby married us. He was de nigger preacher dat preached at de plantation church. After Uncle Edmond said de last words over me and Exter, Marse George got to have his little fun. He say, "Come on, Exter, you and Tempie got to jump over de broom stick backwards. You got to do dat to see which one gwine be boss of your household." Everybody come stand round to watch. Marse George hold de broom about a foot high off de floor. De one dat jump over it backwards, and never touch handle, gwine boss de house. If both of dem jump over without touchin' it, dey won't gwine be no bossin', dey just gwine be congenial. I jumped first, and you ought to seed me. I sailed right over dat broom stick same as a cricket. But when Exter jump he done had a big dram and his feets was so big and clumsy dat dey got all tangled up in day broom and he fell headlong. Marse George he laugh and laugh, and told Exter he gwine be bossed 'twell he scared to speak lessen I told him to speak. After de weddin' we went down to de cabin Mis' Betsy done all dressed up, but Exter couldn't stay no longer den dat night 'cause he belonged to Marse Snipes Durham and he had to go back home. He left de next day for his plantation, but he come back every Saturday night and stay 'twell Sunday night.[11]

The paternalistic effort of the whites had its less attractive side, as Kenneth Stampp has well said:

> The weddings, balls, and other social functions which a generous master arranged for his slaves were equally "irresistible." The white family found it a pure delight to watch a bride and groom move awkwardly through the wedding ceremony, to hear a solemn preacher mispronounce and misuse polysyllabic words, or to witness the incredible maneuvers and gyrations of a "shakedown." . . . In the sentimental recollections of the whites, these gay times in the quarters gave plantation life much of its charm. But these affairs were as much performances for the whites as celebrations for the slaves.[12]

But for the slaves the occasions had their own meaning, which they valued and converted into a mark of their own humanity. More than one white had to acknowledge the dignity and seriousness that the slaves brought to the ceremonies. The Reverend John Hamilton Cornish of South Carolina wrote in his diary an account of a wedding at which he had officiated:

> Paul & I took tea with Mr. Andrew Johnston. Between 8 & 9 in the evening the room was cleared, & a company of servants came in. Six Bride grooms & six Brides ranged themselves in order about the room, all decently, & some of them quite tastefully dressed—& I joined them together in a holy state of matrimony. There was no trifling or levity on the occasion—but a decent reverence & solemnity was preserved through the whole ceremony [sic].
> We then went to another building where a supper table was spread for the newly married & their near relatives—covered with Venison, wild Ducks, ham & rice—Nice pound cakes, custards & coffee. We saw them seated, which was done very decently—then went to another part of the yard where was a large pot of rice & Venison for a general feast. Mrs. J. staid [sic] by table till she saw them seated, & everything in order. The wild Ducks were, I suppose, mostly shot by the master—Mr. Wm. caught the Venison for them. I looked in upon them before we returned to the house. They were conducting

themselves with order, & as ceremoniously as any company of Gentlemen & Ladies.

This is the first wedding I have attended in Caroline except my own. I do not know that I ever attended one in any place that left with better feelings. Mr. J. & Mrs. J. are doubtless well ripaid [*sic*] for their trouble & kindness they have ministered to so bountifully this evening.[13]

To the Reverend Mr. Cornish's report we may add that of Judith Page Rives of Albemarle County, Virginia:

Pauline took it into her wise young head to be married, and though the arrangement is anything but convenient to me I could not object on the score of her youth as she is a year older than I was when I took that important step. We expected to have a little fun in this exhibition of "high life below stairs," but the imitation of a fashionable bridal was really so perfect that it ceased to be ridiculous. The kitchen and wash house were decorated with evergreens, and lighted up for the reception of the company which was numerous—the gentlemen in white gloves and cravats, the ladies in white muslins and pink ribbons—even the wreath of orange blossoms was conspicuous on the head of the bride, while the bridal veil, modestly drawn down, concealed the blushes of the bashful wearer. To our surprise the ebony minister drew from his pocket an episcopal prayer book, and with the exception of the interpolation of one word which would have puzzled a lexicographer, as it did me, and making the lady promise to obey the gentlemen, at which there was a supressed titter among the brides-maids and grooms-men, the services were as impressive as they often are on such occasions.[14]

Not many slaves could expect such lavish weddings; the great majority were undoubtedly married in broomstick ceremonies. But these cannot be dismissed as without ritual value and significance. The slaves may well have resented the implicit slight; at the least, they came to resent it after they had tasted emancipation. Resentment or no, they often did what they could to make a ceremony out of it. To some extent the whites helped. If many whites demanded broomstick weddings as the form appropriate to slaves, others did so to avoid the embarrassment of having to perform a Christian ceremony that had no status in law and could not include the usual words "Till death do you part." Where possible, the slaves seized the chance to make the occasion as dignified as this central indignity allowed. Where masters made even that much difficult, the slaves often arranged a prayer meeting of their own and provided what formality they could. Most slaves. largely through their own efforts with or without their masters' sanction and support, got married "right"—or as right as circumstances made possible.[15]

No matter how simple, some ceremony was necessary if the slaves were to feel properly married at all. For Africans, white southerners, and black slaves too, the wedding ceremony served the vital function of lifting the couple out of their private relationship and reminding them that the bond between them also bound them to their community and entailed wider responsibilities. Masters and slaves both sought this effect as a means of social control, but not quite the same kind of control.[16]

The great trouble with the slave wedding ceremonies, even the most solemn, elaborate, and dignified, lay in the inevitable collapse of the essential Christian message during the exchange of vows. The slaves knew very well that weddings were supposed to reach a climax with "Till death do you part," and they were bound to react grimly to the absence of such words in their own ceremonies. Not many blacks could have thought it clever when a white minister offered "Until death or distance do you part."[17] Matthew Jarrett, an ex-slave from Virginia, remarked on the usual practice:

> We slaves knowed that them words wasn't bindin'. Don't mean nothin' lessen you say, "What God has jined, caint no man pull asunder." But dey never would say dat. Jus' say, "Now you married."[18]

Whites apparently found it amusing when a popular black preacher in Alabama, whose miseries with the King's English and alleged clownishness provided them with great sport, offered his own version: "Now before God and the witness, I pronounce you man and woman. And whomsoever God hap solated to be jined together, let no man part a thunder. Cursed is he that part man and wife—Amen."[19] But if the whites had trouble getting that message, which one would think clear enough, perhaps they did better with that of an old Gullah preacher who had a particular penchant for crispness: "Till death or buckra part you."[20]

HUSBANDS AND FATHERS

According to the slaveholders, slave men had little sense of responsibility toward their families and abused them so mercilessly that
Ole Massa constantly had to intervene to protect the women and
children. Skeptics might wonder how these allegedly emasculated
men so easily dominated the strong-willed and physically powerful women of the matriarchal legend, but the slaveholders never
troubled themselves about such inconsistencies. "Negroes are by
nature tyrannical in their dispositions," Robert Collins of Macon,
Georgia, announced, "and, if allowed, the stronger will abuse the
weaker; husbands will often abuse their wives and mothers their
children." Thus, he concluded, masters and overseers must protect
the peace of the quarters and punish aggressors.[1] "Foby," writing
on the proper way to manage servants, proudly announced: "The
husbands are taught by sad experience to know that they shall not
abuse their better halves." Planters frequently instructed their
overseers to protect the poor black women against their unfeeling
husbands.[2] The great white fathers spoke without a touch of irony.
Listen to W. W. Hazard of Georgia:

> I never permit a husband to abuse, strike or whip his wife, and tell
> them it is disgraceful for a man to raise his hand in violence against
> a feeble woman, and that woman too, the wife of his bosom, the
> mother of his children, and the companion of his leisure, his mid-
> night hours. If the wife teases and provokes him by her nightly
> chatter, or crabbed deportment, and he complains and establishes
> the fact, she is punished, but it sometimes happens that the husband
> petitions for his freedom, which I make it a rule not to refuse, as it
> imposes a strong obligation on the wife to use her tongue with less
> bitterness, and be more conciliating in her behavior.[3]

This outrage at the thought of a man's beating a woman—unless,
of course, the man was white and the woman black, in which case,
one supposes, she metamorphosed from a woman into a "wench"
—reached imposing theoretical heights in the pronouncements of
leading proslavery ideologues. Chancellor Harper, deeply con-

cerned over the world-wide tendency of lower-class men to abuse their women, sighed with relief at the protection offered by slavery.

> The [slaves] are placed under the control of others, who are interested to restrain their excesses of cruelty or rage. Wives are protected from their husbands, and children from their parents. And this is no inconsiderable compensation of the evils of our system and would so appear, if we could form any conception of the immense amount of misery which is elsewhere inflicted.[4]

Life in the quarters, like lower-class life generally, sometimes exploded in violence. Court records, plantation papers, and ex-slave accounts reveal evidence of wife-beating but do not remotely sustain the pretension that without white interference the quarters would have rung with the groans of abused womanhood. Too many black men did not believe in beating their wives, and too many black women, made physically strong by hard field work, were not about to be beaten. So, why should slaveholders, who thought nothing of stripping a woman naked and whipping her till she bled, express so much concern? The pontificating of the ideologues might be dismissed as politically serviceable rubbish, but the concern of the slaveholders who wrote in agricultural journals primarily for each other's eyes and who penned private instructions for overseers demands explanation.

The slaveholders needed order and feared that domestic abuse would undermine the morale of the labor force. But, then, why not require the drivers to enforce peace and quiet? Why not refrain from intervening unless plantation morale actually sagged? After all, the intervention and whipping might easily provoke a worse reaction than the incident itself. But, by asserting himself as the protector of black women and domestic peace, the slaveholder asserted himself as *paterfamilias* and reinforced his claims to being sole father of a "family, black and white." In this light, the efforts of the drivers or plantation preachers or other prestigious slaves to restrain abusive husbands represented an attempt by the quarters to rule themselves. When a driver intervened and usurped the role of *paterfamilias*, he may have thereby underscored the paternalist ideology of the plantation; but, by keeping the white man out of the picture, he set limits to the slaves' internalization of racist norms.

The slaveholders intuitively grasped something else. A black man whose authority in the house rested on his use of force may have picked the worst way to assert himself, but in a world in which so much conspired to reduce men to "guests in the house" and to emasculate them, even this kind of assertion, however unmanly by external standards, held some positive meaning.

The slave women did not often welcome Ole Massa's protection. They preferred to take care of themselves or, when they needed help, to turn to their fathers, brothers, or friends. As any policeman in a lower-class neighborhood, white or black, knows, a woman who is getting the worst of a street fight with her man and who is screaming for help usually wants relief from the blows; she does not want her man subjected to an outsider's righteous indignation and may well join him in repelling an attack. When Ellen Botts's mother—the much-respected Mammy of a sugar plantation —showed up with a lump on her head inflicted by her hot-tempered husband, she told her master that she had had an accident. She would deal with her husband herself and certainly did not want to see him whipped. When James Redpath asked a slave woman in South Carolina if slave women expected to leave their husbands when they fell out, he got the contemptuous answer meddlers in other people's love lives ought to expect: "Oh, no, not allus; we sometimes quarrel in de daytime and make all up at night."[5]

The slaveholders did not want their slaves to abuse each other. Rather, they could not abide their slaves' living together without outside interference. They therefore read the signs as they wished. The slaves, for their part, did not live like saints but did take care of each other quite as well as any other people raised in a less than genteel world.

The slaveholders, in their tender concern for black women who suffered abuse from their husbands, remained curiously silent about those who fell back on their husbands' protection. Laura Bell's father won her mother's hand by volunteering to take a whipping in her place. Most slaveholders had the sense to prohibit such gallantry, but no few black men braved their wrath by interposing themselves between their wives or daughters and the white man who sought to harm them.[6] Not only husbands but male friends killed, beat, or drove off overseers for whipping their women.[7]

Black women fell victims to white lust, but many escaped because the whites knew they had black men who would rather die than stand idly by. In some cases black men protected their women and got off with a whipping or no punishment at all; in other cases they sacrificed their lives. Knowledge of their inevitable response prevented many outrages from happening.[8] Eliza Frances Andrews need not have expressed surprise when one of the first acts of the freedmen in Georgia was to organize a "Sons of Benevolence" to protect "female virtue." And Kate Stone should have known better than to say of the battle of Milliken's Bend, "It is said the Negro regiments fought like demons but we cannot believe that. We know from long experience they are cowards."[9]

In view of the risks, the wonder is not that more black men did not defend their women but that so many did, especially since the women had to caution restraint or risk their men's lives. With children and each other to consider, the slaves had to strengthen each other in a course of acceptance of what could be prevented only at too high a price. If submission to outrage sometimes revealed cowardice, so did it often reveal a far greater strength than most men and women are ever asked—or ever should be asked—to display.[10]

Even short of death, the pride of assertive manliness could reach fearful proportions. An overseer tried to rape Josiah Henson's mother but was overpowered by his father. Yielding to his wife's pleas and the overseer's promise of no reprisal, the enraged slave desisted from killing him. The overseer broke his promise. Henson's father suffered one hundred lashes and had an ear nailed to the whipping post and then severed.

> Previous to this affair my father, from all I can learn, had been a good-humored and light-hearted man, the ringleader in all fun at corn-huskings and Christmas buffoonery. His banjo was the life of the farm, and all night long at a merry-making would he play on it while the other Negroes danced. But from this hour he became utterly changed. Sullen, morose, and dogged, nothing could be done with him.

Threats of being sold south had no effect on him. The thoughts running through his mind as he came to prefer separation from the wife he loved to enduring life there must remain a matter of speculation. His master sold him to Alabama, and he was never heard from again.[11]

What kind of evidence and how much of it is needed to convince skeptics that the essential story of black men in slavery lay with the many who overcame every possible hardship and humiliation to stand fast to their families? Elizabeth Keckley's father, sold away a long distance from her mother, returned to visit his family every Christmas and Easter. Later sent to the Caribbean, he regularly exchanged letters with the wife he was never to see again. A slave in Georgia prevailed on his master to sell him to Jamaica so that he could find his wife, despite warnings that his chances of finding her on so large an island were remote. Renty, a slave on the George Noble Jones plantation in Florida, divorced his wife and married again only when his new favorite promised to take care of his children. George Payne of Virginia wept when his child was sold away from him, and another slave in Virginia chopped his left hand off with a hatchet to prevent being sold away from his son. Stepfathers everywhere reportedly treated their newly acquired children as if they had been their own. Freedmen in Louisiana stubbornly resisted impressment by the Union army because, as their old master explained, their families were suffering. John Blassingame has convincingly demonstrated how the slave men of the Union border states flocked into the army once their families were guaranteed freedom in return for their enlistment.[12]

Slave men provided for their families to a greater extent than has been appreciated. The overwhelming majority of the masters gave their slaves enough to eat but did not err on the side of generosity; and the fare was coarse and monotonous. The slaves would have suffered much more than many in fact did from malnutrition and the hidden hungers of nutritional deficiencies if the men had not taken the initiative to hunt and trap animals. "My old daddy," recalled Louisa Adams of North Carolina, "partly raised his chilluns on game. He caught rabbits, coons an' possums. He would work all day and hunt at night."[13] Mothers sang to their babies:

> Bye baby buntin'
> Daddy's gone a-huntin'
> Ter fetch a little rabbit skin
> Ter wrap de baby buntin' in.[14]

The men took pride in their effort. Edgar Bendy of Texas boasted, "I used to be plumb give up to be de best hunter in Tyler and in de whole country. I kilt more deer dan any other man in de country. . . ." And the boys took pride in their fathers, grandfathers, and uncles. A half century later John Glover of South Carolina remembered his grandfather as "a great 'possum hunter."[15] The men had some justification for their boasting. Trapping wild turkeys, for example, required considerable skill; not everyone could construct a "rabbit gum" equal to the guile of the rabbits; and running down the quick, battling raccoon took pluck.[16] For a boy growing up, the moment when his father thought him ready to join in the hunting and to learn to trap was a much-sought recognition of his own manhood.

For the slaves fishing was much more than the lazy pastime of white plantation romance. They varied monotonous and inadequate diets by catching fish, crabs, and gathering oysters, clams, conchs, turtles, terrapins, shrimp, and prawns, and anything else available. The coastal lowlands of Maryland, Virginia, South Carolina, and Georgia as well as the bayou country of Louisiana offered special opportunities, but most regions had some kind of stream with something worth catching. According to Mrs. Schoolcraft, every black man on the South Carolina coast made his own canoe "by burning the inside, and then scraping out a great oaken log, some ten or twelve feet long."[17]

The archaeological excavation of a slave cabin in Georgia by Robert Ascher and Charles H. Fairbanks turned up evidence of a wide assortment of animals, birds, and fish. "The animals," they write, "were young, old, and in-between, suggesting that their pursuer took whatever he could find." Their study supports the insistence of ex-slaves and antebellum travelers that the men put much effort into supplementing their families' diet. As they conclude: "In sum, through excavation, we have learned that the people in one cabin managed to add considerable protein to their diet, apparently through their own efforts."[18]

Many slaves had Saturday afternoons free for hunting and trapping, but many more had to find time after a long day's work during the week. A free afternoon did not always avail anyway since opossum and raccoon, the slaves' great favorites, run at night. When the masters allowed the slaves to roam about at night, they turned the hunt into a great collective sport and shared the spoils. When the masters frowned on this activity, they had to go singly or in pairs and risk punishment. Although few masters wanted their slaves to run about at night instead of resting for the next day's work, most saw the advantage in allowing the slaves to get some of their own food, and the masters also needed these efforts to help control the ravages of raccoons, squirrels, and crows in their fields.[19]

The slaves' great allies in hunting opossum and raccoon were their dogs. The dogs treed the prey and fought them when the slaves had shaken them down. The slaves took particular pride in their dogs and insisted that a first-class 'possum dog should not be confused with a first-class 'coon dog. To each dog his own work.[20] The slaves' dogs created many problems for the slaveholders and for the neighborhood generally. They sometimes killed domestic animals; they barked too much; they ran around filthy and constituted a nuisance. In 1752, Virginia's House of Burgesses gravely debated a proposal for destroying the slaves' dogs. During the nineteenth century Alabama outlawed them but could not enforce the law. The slaves everywhere had their way. "Our greatest trial," wrote Elizabeth Hyde Botume, "was the dogs. No colored man considered himself safe, or even respectable, without one or more miserable-looking curs."[21]

Many plantations had at least one slave who used a gun for hunting on a larger scale. Some masters simply allowed one or two reliable men to carry a gun in order to bring in large game for the quarters; others designated one or two slaves as plantation specialists who worked for the Big House table as well or even exclusively. In some cases the hunting guns had been given to slaves assigned to guard the plantation.[22] The states generally outlawed the practice of giving slaves guns, although localities often made room for exceptions. With or without legal sanction, masters did as they pleased, and the sight of slaves hunting with guns rarely raised eyebrows.[23]

The big all-plantation hunts came during the winter, which by happy coincidence combined an easier work pace with a great abundance of opossum and raccoon. White and black men turned the opportunity into a holiday.

> Possum up de gum stump,
> Raccoon in de hollow—
> Git him down and twist him out,
> And I'll give you a dollar.[24]

As in corn shuckings, the accompanying camaraderie strengthened paternalist ties, especially since the masters so clearly played the leading organizational role while the slaves did most of the work and provided the marvelous stories and gaiety that made the subsequent bonfires so memorable. At the same time, the slave men accumulated a supply of their favorite foods for their families and gave their women the wherewithal and the occasion to demonstrate their culinary skills.

Sensible masters actually encouraged a limited sexual division of labor among their slaves and saw some advantage in strengthening the power of the male in the household. Many planters identified slave women by their husbands' names: Tom's Sue or Joe's Mary. A strong man who kept his wife and children in line contributed to social peace and good order. William Ervin of Lowndes County, Mississippi, laid down the following as the second point in his Rules for the Plantation:

> 2nd. Each family to live in their own house. The husband to provide fire wood and see that they are all provided for and wait on his wife. The wife to cook & wash for the husband and her children and attend to the mending of clothes. Failure on either part when proven shall and must be corrected by words first but if not reformed to be corrected by the Whip.[25]

Hugh Davis, whose scrupulous biographer considers him typical of the bigger planters of the Alabama Black Belt, included among his rules:

> Men alone are required to feed and perform all lot work [animal care] at the close of every day. The women are required, when work is done in the field, to sweep their houses and yards and receive their supper [communally prepared] at the call of the cook, after which they may sew or knit but not leave their houses otherwise.[26]

On the large plantations, which displayed a greater division of labor than the small plantations and farms, men did heavy work on rainy days or in slack periods while the women sewed, cleaned up the grounds, and did assorted lighter tasks. Even then, the foreman of the women's crew was often a man.[27]

This division of labor and the strengthened male role within it, which so many planters encouraged, helped shape the kind of men who might prove more independent than slaves were supposed to be. The slaveholders, therefore, here as elsewhere, had to live with a contradiction: dispirited slave men could not keep the good order necessary for efficiency and, besides, might become troublesome in their very irresponsibility; spirited slaves with a sense of being men would help keep good order and render the plantation more efficient, but they too, in different ways, might become troublesome in their very responsibility. Slaves remained a troublesome property.

Meanwhile, in ways wholesome and not so wholesome, the men asserted themselves. If Nancy Williams's mother spent extra hours in making quilts for the family, her father built the shelves and closets to house them. If Mary Ann Lipscomb's mother had to weave when tired from a day's labor, her father did his best to help. Other men asserted themselves at the expense of their wives by contemptuously refusing to do "women's work."[28]

The struggle to become and to remain men, not the "boys" their masters called them, included some unattractive manifestations of male aggression. The freedmen, Miss Botume noted, spoke affectionately of their wives but in such a way as to suggest that they were property, virtually slaves, helpless children who had to be taught everything.[29] Almost everywhere in the South the freedmen demanded wages high enough to allow them to support their families. They wanted their women home with the children, and the women supported the demand vigorously. Many women may have preferred housekeeping to the rigors of farm work and thought they were choosing an easier life, but most seem to have felt a great need to give their children a full-time mother. In any case, these tough women, who so often proved militant during the political struggles of Reconstruction, displayed not merely a willingness but a desire to defer to their husbands both at home and in the new political world they were entering together. For all the deformations introduced by slavery, they knew that many of their men were strong and dependable and wanted the others to become so.

The slaveholders deprived black men of the role of provider; refused to dignify their marriages or legitimize their issue; compelled them to submit to physical abuse in the presence of their women and children; made them choose between remaining silent while their wives and daughters were raped or seduced and risking death; and threatened them with separation from their family at any moment. Many men caved in under the onslaught and became irresponsible husbands and indifferent fathers. The women who had to contend with such men sometimes showed stubborn cheerfulness and sometimes raging bitterness; they raised the children, maintained order at home, and rotated men in and out of bed.

Enough men and women fell into this pattern to give rise to the legends of the matriarchy, the emasculated but brutal male, and the fatherless children. These legends did not merely arise from contemporary proslavery propagandistic fantasies or from the ethnocentricity of later historians and social scientists; they rest on unquestionable evidence, which, being partial, has misled its interpreters.

The inability of the slave men to protect their women against the insults and abuse of masters and overseers hardly put them in a unique or unusual position. For centuries, the mass of European serfs and dependent peasants suffered such indignities at the hands of lords and warlords, yet no one questions their masculinity. Men cannot define the tests of masculinity in a manner abstracted from the web of class power in which they find themselves; women do not normally expect their men to get themselves killed in a fruitless attempt to prevent what cannot be prevented. In a paternalistic system men defer to their lords in a variety of ways without losing a sense of themselves as men in relation to their women. Although slave men suffered deeply, there is no evidence that most felt themselves less than men. But white racism did undermine them in other ways. It created among them and their women a tendency to doubt that black men could play all the roles that whites could, but these generally concerned matters of political, economic, and intellectual leadership rather than male-female relations.

Many men and women resisted the "infantilization," "emasculation," and "dehumanization" inherent in the system's aggression against the slave family. How many? No one will ever know. At issue is the quality of human relationships, which cannot be measured. But there exists as much evidence of resistance and of a struggle for a decent family life as of demoralization. A brutal social system broke the spirit of many and rendered others less responsible than human beings ought to be. But enough men came out of this test of fire whole, if necessarily scarred, to demonstrate that the slaves had powerful inner resources. A terrible system of human oppression took a heavy toll of its victims, but their collective accomplishment in resisting the system constitutes a heroic story. That resistance provided black people with solid norms for family life and role differentiation, even if circumstances caused a dangerously high lapse from those norms. The slaves from their own experience had come to value a two-parent, male-centered household, no matter how much difficulty they had in realizing the ideal.

The role of the male slave as husband and father therefore requires a fresh look. If many men lived up to their assigned irresponsibility, others, probably a majority, overcame all obstacles and provided a positive male image for their wives and children. An ex-slave recalled his boyhood:

> I loved my father. He was such a good man. He was a good carpenter and could do anything. My mother just rejoiced in him. Whenever he sat down to talk she just sat and looked and listened. She would never cross him for anything. If they went to church together she always waited for him to interpret what the preacher had said or what he thought was the will of God. I was small but I noticed all of these things. I sometimes think I learned more in my early childhood about how to live than I have learned since.[30]

Protective fathers appeared in the lullabies slave mothers sang to their children.

> Kink head, wherefore you skeered?
> Old snake crawled off, 'cause he's a-feared.
> Pappy will smite him on de back
> With a great big club—Ker whack! Ker whack![31]

Many ex-slaves recalled their fathers as stern disciplinarians, and the slaveholders' complaints about fathers' abusing their children may be read as supporting evidence. Other slave men left their children a memory of kindness and affection that remained through life. Will Adams's father, a foreman on a Texas plantation, came in exhausted after a long day's work but never failed to take his son out of bed and to play with him for hours.[32] The spirituals and other slave songs reflected the importance of the father in the lives of the children; many of them sang of the reunification of the family in heaven and of the father's return.[33]

Men knew that they might have to part from their wives and children, but that knowledge did not engender indifference so much as a certain stoical submission to that which had to be endured. Under painful conditions, many did their best even while others succumbed. Mingo White's father, upon being sold, did nothing unusual when he charged a male friend with responsibility for looking after his son.[34] A principle of stewardship had arisen in the quarters. Even in the absence of a father, some male would likely step in to help raise a boy to manhood. When the war ended, men crisscrossed the South to reclaim their families and to assert authority over their children.[35]

Slave children usually did have an image of a strong black man before them. Critical scholars have made the mistake of measuring the slave family by middle-class norms; naturally, they have found it wanting. Even when a slave boy was growing up without a father in the house, he had as a model a tough, resourceful driver, a skilled mechanic or two, and older field hands with some time for the children of the quarters. Some of those men devoted themselves to playing surrogate father to all the children. They told them stories, taught them to fish and trap animals, and instructed them in the ways of survival in a hostile white world. The norm in the quarters called for adults to look after children, whether blood relatives or not. Every plantation had some men who played this role. Under the worst of circumstances, one or two would have been enough; usually, however, there were a number. And there were the preachers. To the extent that the slaves heard their preachers, the children saw before them influential black men whose eloquence and moral force commanded the respect of the adults.

A positive male image existed even in those cabins without resident fathers. In the urban ghettos of the twentieth century, where the one-parent household has taken on greater prominence, the children have not suffered from a lack of a masculine presence. Ulf Hannerz observes: "More or less steady boyfriends (sometimes including the separated father) go in and out. Even if these men do not assume a central household role, the boys can obviously use them as source material for the identification of male behavior."[36] And more sharply, Charles Keil:

> Clearly, lower-class Negro culture includes a concept of manhood that differs in kind from the white middle-class definition of a man as a head of household, who holds down a steady job and sends his kids to college. . . . But as far as he and his women are concerned, he spends his money freely, dresses well, and is great in bed. That's just the way he is—*a man*—and they like him that way, despite the fact that he's obviously "no good."[37]

However outsiders may judge the kind of masculinity projected by these circumstances, claims of emasculation and infantilization do not ring true. The slave children, like the ghetto children of later decades, saw a pattern of behavior that implied clear sexual differentiation and a notion of masculinity with its own strengths and weaknesses.

What happened to a slave boy who witnessed, as many did, his father's being whipped by a white man, or worse, his father's standing by helplessly while his mother was being whipped? Clearly, the moment had to be traumatic and the boy's confidence in his father had to be shaken. Children apparently did not often witness such scenes: most masters preferred to discipline their slaves at times and in places unavailable to the children, and the slave parents conspired to keep their children ignorant. As for those children who saw and suffered, many possibly never got over the shock. But there is no evidence that many despised their fathers, especially since their mothers tried to explain the acquiescence and instruct their children in the ways of survival. Nor do we know how many children reacted like that Mexican peasant boy who saw his father collapse helplessly in tears when a treacherous landowner expropriated his land. Emiliano Zapata did not despise his father. He swore vengeance.[38]

Peter Poyas, Denmark Vesey's lieutenant in the abortive rising of 1822, is remembered as the man who showed his troops how to face execution: "Do not open your lips; die silent, as you shall see me do." He might also be remembered for his restrained comment to the judge who sentenced him to death: "I suppose you'll let me see my wife and family before I die?"[39]

WIVES AND MOTHERS

Elizabeth Hyde Botume in her wonderful book, *First Days Amongst the Contrabands*, tells of the black women recently emancipated by the Yankee invasion:

> When the women found me so unsuspicious, they exhibited their handicraft with no small degree of pride. It was not an unusual thing to meet a woman coming from the fields, where she had been hoeing cotton, with a small bucket or cup on her head, and a hoe over her shoulder, contentedly smoking a pipe and briskly knitting as she strode along. I have seen, added to all these, a baby strapped to her

back. The patient devotion of these negro women was most admirable.[1]

The women field hands generally had a longer day than their men.
Even the critical Fanny Kemble thought that the middle-aged men
did not appear overworked but that the women did. She particularly drew attention to the effects of hard field work in combination with childbearing.[2] Ex-slaves said much more. In addition to
the usual work load, the women had to cook for their families, put
the children to bed, and often spin, weave, and sew well into the
night. On many plantations masters and overseers released them
from field work early to attend to their household chores, but on
many others they did not, except perhaps on Saturday to get the
week's washing done. Many of the women rose early to feed their
men, although most masters sensibly preferred to arrange for communal preparation of the morning's meal. Harrison Beckett of
Texas grimly recalled his mother's coming in exhausted from the
fields and having to cook for her husband and children: "Lots of
times she's so tired she go to bed without eatin' nothin' herself."[3]

Usually men, not women, plowed on the large plantations, but
when the minority of plantation women who did plow are added
to those on smaller units who had to work alongside their men or
even alone, it would appear that the rigors of plowing engaged the
efforts of a substantial minority of southern slave women.[4] On
many plantations the women proved superior to the men in picking cotton; in general, men and women did about equally well. Not
unusually a woman would rate as the most valuable field hand on
the place or as the single most physically powerful individual.
Some excelled in such exacting roles as logrollers and even lumber-
jacks.[5] And if the men often helped their wives to keep up with
their tasks, the roles could be reversed. "My daddy was a field
hand," recalled Pierce Harper, who had been a slave in North
Carolina, "and my mother worked in the field, too, right 'longside
my daddy, so she could keep him lined up." Her mother had a
reputation as the best field hand on the place and her father as the
worst. "My mother," she explained, "used to say he was chile-
some."[6]

White southerners, who usually knew better, sometimes pretended that black mothers cared little about children. The whites
might have been referring to that stoicism toward the death of an
infant which appears in all societies with high infant mortality,

especially among the poor; yet even upper-class southern whites suffered too often from the death of their own infants not to understand the necessity for a certain amount of fatalism and self-control. They did not confuse their own self-discipline with lack of grief. The white women and even the men frequently commented on the grief felt by particular slave parents when they lost a child.[7] The sadistic mistress who whipped a slave girl to death fully appreciated the maternal affection of her slaves: she sent for the girl's mother to watch her die.[8]

The calmness of many slave mothers and fathers in the face of the death of their infants and young children recalls that of many other peoples who simply had to live with the probability of losing some of their children. Keith Thomas writes: "In Tudor and Stuart England men were fully accustomed to disease and a low expectation of life. Parents were slower to recognize the individuality of their children, for they well knew that they might lose them in their infancy."[9] Philippe Ariès adds that such conditions existed in France well into the nineteenth century: "Nobody thought, as we ordinarily think today, that every child already contained a man's personality. Too many of them died."[10]

Mrs. Kemble, commenting on the apparent indifference of parents to the death of a boy, recounted a telling incident: "The mother merely repeated over and over again, 'I've lost a many; they all goes so'; and the father, without a word or comment, went out to his enforced labor."[11] This self-protective hardening of parents' attitudes toward their children, reinforced under slavery by fear of sale, did not appear in the quarters any more noticeably than elsewhere under conditions of high infant mortality; it may even have appeared less often. Most black women welcomed their babies as a joy, loved them, and braced themselves for inevitable losses and heartaches.

Some slave women took little interest in their children either because they succumbed to the terrific pressures of overwork, insufficient time for child care, and general demoralization or because they did not want to raise them as slaves.[12] But much of what has been called indifference was no more than the effects of exhaustion on women who loved the children they could not always find patience for. Women who had been forced into cohabitation might especially have resented the children of these unions; yet there is no evidence that even they usually did so.

Women who did not want children knew how to abort or to

arrange to have a child die soon after birth. With childbirth deaths so common from natural causes, the deed could not easily be detected. But birth and reproduction rates remained high. Slave abortions, much less infanticide, did not become a major problem for the slave holders or an ordinary form of "resistance" for the slaves. Infanticide occurred, but so far as the detected cases reveal anything, only in some special circumstance. The white citizens of Virginia petitioned in 1822 to spare a slave condemned to death for killing her infant. The child's father was a respectable, married white man, and the woman insisted she would not have killed a child of her own color. Lou Smith, an ex-slave from South Carolina, recalled a woman who had had one child after another sold away from her. Finally, she poisoned her next child and swore to have no more. The other slaves knew what she had done but protected her.[13] For the most part, however, the slaves recognized infanticide as murder. They loved their children too much to do away with them; courageously, they resolved to raise them as best they could, and entrusted their fate to God. Nothing like the widespread infanticide of, say, nineteenth-century Japan, with its economic rationale, ever swept the quarters.[14]

Particularly humane or closely calculating masters released their slave women from field work for a full month before and after childbirth, but many fell short of this model. Normally, the women would have their tasks lightened or cut in half during the last month of pregnancy and then would not be expected back at work until a month after delivery.[15]

Plantation midwives usually attended the deliveries, although mistresses sometimes helped. Slaveholders turned to physicians rarely, but the substantial fees recorded in physicians' account books suggest that they regularly attended the difficult cases.[16] The women often complained bitterly that they needed more time before and after delivery, but they may have been more concerned about the care of their infants than about their own health. The slaveholders thought a month's rest after delivery ample and pointed out, accurately, that the peasant and working-class women of Europe had no such good fortune.[17]

Black women supposedly needed less consideration than the weaker white women anyway, but the statistics on death in childbed as well as on disease and deformity following childbirth provide no support for this rationalization.[18] Nor did lectures on the superiority of their treatment relative to that of, say, English peasant and working-class women who had to endure the physical and psychological hardships attendant upon pregnancy, delivery, and nursing. Kenneth Stampp, admittedly working from shaky data, plausibly estimates many more spontaneous abortions and stillbirths in black women than in white. Whatever the precise differential, the slave women's particular vulnerability to this group of maladies largely resulted from overwork, inadequate prenatal care, and enforced performance of tasks beyond their strength.[19]

The women complained especially about the inadequate conditions for nursing. Landon Carter permitted his slaves to leave the fields three times a day to attend to their babies; the women thought five times would be proper and caused themselves no little trouble by lying or trying to maneuver the overseer into giving them more time. During the nineteenth century three or four times became standard. On M. W. Philips's plantation in Hinds County, Mississippi, the women went into the cookhouse to nurse at breakfast, at 9:30 A.M., at noon, and once during the afternoon. On some plantations mothers could remain with their infants for two hours at midday.[20] Often, the nurses brought the children to their mothers in the field. Overseers and nurses had instructions to keep mothers from nursing their children for fifteen minutes or so after they had stopped working in hot weather or had walked the long distance from the fields. Such instructions could not readily be enforced; too often, hot and tired mothers picked their children up eagerly and nursed them under conditions that might easily have done psychological and physical damage.[21]

If slave mothers viewed their infants with indifference as many slaveholders claimed, they had some strange ways of showing it. Notwithstanding the objective difficulties in nursing, they showed, by more recent standards, a marked unwillingness to wean them early. "We sucked till we was a fair size," said Mary Reynolds of Louisiana in expressing a common view. The Gullah slaves, like the West Africans to whom they remained culturally closer than did other slaves, nursed their children two or three years and even longer. The slaves' practice did not vary greatly from southern practice in general, especially that of the lower classes. Mrs. Kemble, Olmsted, and others were taken aback at the prolonged nursing among the whites. The little evidence we have indicates that the blacks followed the same course and nursed their babies as long as they reasonably could.[22]

Many women saw their children only for a few minutes at night and then on weekends. That some became indifferent ought to cause no surprise; and yet, clearly, most did not.

> My mammy [recalled Fannie Moore of South Carolina] she work in de field all day and piece and quilt all night. . . . I never see how my mammy stand such hard work. She stand up for her chillen though. De old overseer he hate my mammy, 'cause she fought him for beatin' her chillen. Why she get more whippin' for dat dan anythin' else.[23]

Fannie Moore's mother had plenty of company in slave mothers who forcibly defended their children against white abuse.[24]

Although often accused of indifference to their children, slave mothers could hardly have made a deeper impression on the children themselves. The lifelong love of the children, male and female, for their mothers shines through the narratives, as it does through the earlier writings of successful runaways and the occasional observations of whites. Martha Schofield recorded in her diary the dying words of her male cook: "Lord forgive them. I am coming mother, I am coming. Oh! This is pleasant, my mother's grave."[25] William Wells Brown reflected on his mother's having been sold south and on the probability of her early death: "As I thought of my mother, I could not but feel that I had lost, 'The glory of my life/ My blessing and my pride!/ I half forgot the name of slave/ When she was by my side.'"[26] Josiah Henson wrote of the mother from whom he was separated by sale only to be reunited by repurchase after he had fallen ill:

> We had been in the main very happy. She was a good mother to us, a woman of deep piety, anxious above all things to touch our hearts with a sense of religion. . . . Now, I was once more with my best friend on earth, and under her care. . . .[27]

George Teamoh of Virginia recalled his mother in a letter to Carter G. Woodson that might have spoken for numerous others:

> My mother—whom I well remember—bore the common name "Winnie." She died when I was quite small. My father, who was not her husband by the usages of custom died some time after. She was the mother of three or four children, whether all by the same man I am not prepared to say, but what I do know is, she was a kind and

affectionate mother and true to her offspring. She was raised with my old mistress, to whom we both belonged.[28]

These were not occasional pronouncements. When added to the powerful image of the mother that comes through the spirituals, as well as to the overwhelming evidence of maternal devotion in the plantation records and the slave narratives, they compel the conclusion that the children felt loved and experienced their mothers' tenderness and warmth. In view of how much conspired to thwart the maternal instincts of these black women, their achievement reached heroic proportions.

The story of the slave women as wives requires indirect examination. To deduce from it an assumption that the man was a guest in the house will not do. A review of the actual position of the men as husbands and fathers suggests that the position of the women was much more complex than usually credited. The women's attitude toward house work, especially cooking, and toward their own femininity by itself belies the conventional wisdom according to which the women unwittingly helped ruin their men by asserting themselves in the home, protecting their children, and assuming other normally masculine responsibilities.[29]

A remarkable number of women did everything possible to strengthen their men's self-esteem and to defer to their leadership. What has usually been viewed as a debilitating female supremacy was in fact a closer approximation to a healthy sexual equality than was possible for whites and perhaps even for many postbellum blacks. The men did not play the provider for their families in a full and direct sense, but they did everything they could to approximate it. They could have scored few successes without the sympathetic cooperation of their women, many—by no means all—of whom yielded their own prerogatives. This female deference represented an effort by the women to support their men—an effort that could only have flowed from a judgment on what men ought to be and an awareness of the terrible ravages being wrought by slavery. On whatever level of consciousness, many women— perhaps a substantial majority—understood that the degradation of their men represented their own degradation as black women and that of their children. They wanted their boys to grow up to be men and knew perfectly well that, to do so, they needed the example of a strong black man in front of them.

The struggle of the women to define a feminine role for themselves and to strengthen their men's sense of their own masculinity came to fruition after the war when the women so readily deferred to their men without surrendering their own opinions and activities, which were often militant. Black people found themselves in a brutal battle for genuine freedom in a postwar world in which certain norms reigned. They knew that in order to win, they would have to accommodate to those norms—specifically, the norms according to which men, not women, controlled the political process and supported the family. The ease with which black men and women made that transition, when not prevented by forces beyond their control, demonstrates how well prepared they already were.

The slave family had, however, rested on a much greater equality between men and women than had the white family. It had bred strong women. The strength of the women did not necessarily undermine the men; often, it supported them. It took enormous strength for a woman to keep her man from avenging an insult or a beating she had suffered and to convince him that the test of his masculinity was self-restraint, not some action that would deprive her of a husband and her children of a father. He needed that assurance to survive, and only she could give it to him. But with freedom the women had to strengthen their men in ways that separated themselves from some of the major sources of their own strength, especially their place in the economy. Their withdrawal from field work undoubtedly would have gone much further if new systems of exploitation had not forced many of them to help their tenant-farmer and sharecropper husbands. The subsequent history of the black family is another matter. New conditions of oppression made it difficult for black men and women to build on their past and create the new and more sexually equitable family inherent in it.

The postbellum record should not be projected backward. A substantial number of black women came out of slavery just as strong as some historians insist. But, in a sense, they had always been even stronger: strong enough to know that their own dignity required having strong men who could meet their responsibilities; strong enough to support their men in those very aspirations.

THE CHILDREN

In 1857 the Supreme Court of Georgia upheld the conviction of a planter for manslaughter in the whipping of a thirteen-year-old girl. The Supreme Court agreed with the lower court's opinion that a girl of that age ought not to be hit with anything more than a switch and indignantly suggested that the only error in the case lay in the failure to convict for murder.[1] The courts and public opinion considered slaves children until about twelve and tender adolescents until their late teens. Boys of twelve might already be plowing, but they remained boys at the beginning of a slow breaking-in process.[2] On the recommendation of the Caroline County Court, Governor James Monroe of Virginia pardoned Scipio for his part in Gabriel's rebellion because he was a mere lad, no older than eighteen or nineteen.[3] Not until the age of ten— usually twelve—did humane masters consider selling a child away from the mother, although a great many less humane masters sold children at any age.[4] From a strictly economic point of view, slaveholders thought that children under ten did not pay their way and that they did not earn a profit for their masters until their late teens.[5]

Plantation records and slave narratives give qualified support to J. H. Hammond's boast that no slave did any work before the age of ten; that most did not work until the age of twelve; and that they did light field work for the first few years thereafter.[6] Hammond came as close to the truth as a propagandist could be expected to, for a majority of the slaves went to the fields at twelve.[7] A noticeable minority began field work before twelve, mostly at ten and sometimes even earlier,[8] but another minority did not begin until thirteen, fourteen, or fifteen.[9]

Before the age of about eight most children did little or no work apart from looking after ("nursing") those younger than themselves, although in every part of the South some masters worked the little ones unmercifully from the time they could toddle. Between eight and twelve the children graduated to such responsibilities as cleaning up the yards, digging up potatoes, many of which they appropriated for their own illicit roasting parties, shelling peas for the kitchen, or more laboriously, toting water to the field hands. Their hardest work came during the cotton-picking season, when they were sometimes called upon to help. In the fields, with little expected of them and with normal childish pride in doing the work of adults, they often enjoyed themselves.[10] Mrs. Schoolcraft wrote truthfully about the children who had such tasks as chasing birds out of the fields: "The little rascals are, however, such 'cute eye-servants that they make traps and pick blackberries, and roast potatoes and groundnuts in the rice and corn patches, leaving the birds full swing. . . ."[11] Despite a quota of abuse and danger, the slave children had a childhood, however much misery awaited them.

The children's release from field labor gave them time to help their parents in ways other than looking after the babies. Their work in the garden plots, for example, reduced the burden on their overworked parents. The older boys learned to trap squirrels and other small animals to augment and vary the family's diet. Slave parents did not ruthlessly exploit their children in these ways; the children willingly contributed to the household.[12]

To appreciate the significance of these protected years, consider the lot of the peasants and workers of other mid-nineteenth-century societies. "I was glad," wrote William Howard Russell, the English correspondent, from Louisiana, "to see the boys and girls of nine, ten, and eleven years of age were at this season, at all events, exempted from the cruel fate which befalls poor children of their age in the mining and manufacturing districts of England."[13] In the British Isles in 1835, about 13 percent of the more than 220,000 workers in the cotton industry were twelve years of age or less. Their working conditions, exposed in parliamentary investigations, not to mention the searing indictments in Engels's *Condition of the Working Class in England in 1844* and Marx's *Capital,* produced a measure of drunkenness, debauchery, and moral degradation among the children that no amount of bourgeois apologetics on the glories of the industrial revolution will ever erase. By 1853, children of eight were still lawfully employed in English and French industry, and children of nine to eleven in much of Germany. Not until 1853 did Prussia take the lead by abolishing child labor under the age of twelve and by restricting the length of the working day to six hours for children under sixteen.[14]

A doctor described the children who worked in the Manchester cotton mills as "almost universally ill-looking, small, sickly, barefoot, and ill-clad. Many appeared to be no older than seven."[15] They had not started out well. As tots, many had had to be shifted into incompetent hands, while their young mothers worked all day; many had been fed laudanum and other opiates to keep them quiet and numb their hunger. At work in pits and factories at seven years of age, they worked twelve, sixteen, eighteen hours. Did they fall asleep? Not likely. The whip kept them awake. The rest of the story—the desperation of their exhausted mothers and fathers, the inattention to their most elementary needs, the utter brutalization of their formative years—we need only note in passing. "The exploitation of little children, on this scale and with this intensity," writes E. P. Thompson with all the restraint he can muster, "was one of the most shameful events in our history."[16]

Most abolitionists pretended not to know the relative conditions of English working-class and southern slave children, or worse, actually did not know; but the slaveholders knew precisely and commended themselves on their own humanity, which had something to be said for it, especially since the slaveholders of the British Caribbean used their slave children in a manner more reminiscent of the factory owners of Manchester than of the planters of Mississippi.[17] The southern slaveholders knew, too, that their slave children fared closer to the style of their own pampered children than to that of the children of nonslaveholders, who had to help their parents by doing rough work at early ages.[18] The better impulses of the master class combined with a good deal of solid economic rationality to bring the slave children to maturity slowly and in a manner designed to guarantee their eventual maximum productivity. Southern ideologues extolled slavery precisely for this blending of self-interest and humane consideration. George Fitzhugh, among many others, regarded such self-interest as the indispensable foundation of all viable humanitarianism.

The slaveholders in this case and in their more general treatment of slaves looked at the condition of the European working class, at the abolitionists' indifference and even hypocrisy concerning that condition, and at the condition of their own slaves and drew their own conclusion: they saw themselves as misunderstood, misrepresented, wronged. Those leisurely and playful black children were inadvertently strengthening the intransigence of their masters' commitment to slavery. More important for immediate purposes, the prolonged childhood of the slaves provided a foundation of physical health for their potential development as independent, spirited adults, even if many broke along the way. Once they went to the fields they experienced the full misery of their condition, and the abrupt shift must have been traumatic despite the painstaking efforts of so many masters to break them in to hard labor slowly over a period of years. Not that the slaves suffered initially from being sent to the fields. Many youngsters could hardly wait, for the work assignment itself marked their arrival as young men. Often they were, in the word of an ex-slave, "crazy" to get behind a plow and show their stuff.[19]

The lives of the children changed dramatically at about the age of twelve. The eagerness of many to get behind a plow carried with it other recognitions of manhood. The sexual prudery of the whites always went along with a failure to notice blacks, so that naked slave children, not always small, romped everywhere.[20] Boys, like girls, wore dresses until the age of about twelve or when they went to the fields. Usually, the boys' dresses could not be distinguished from the girls'; by the time the boys reached ten or so and were growing rapidly, the dresses did not always comfortably cover private parts. Under the embarrassment of such exposure, the boys' desire to put on men's clothing requires no explanation.

For some, the shocking awareness of slave conditions came during childhood, and for others later, when they went to the fields and felt the whip. For most, their early and formative years had offered a semblance of childhood, at least relative to the children of other laboring classes. They had had time to grow physically and to parry the most brutal features of their bondage through games. Within limits they had been able to feel and enjoy life. Within these limits they absorbed the rules and values of the dominant culture, but their early freedom from mind- and body-breaking toil contributed to the strength of the many adult slaves who emerged as high-spirited men and women.

The children devised games to fill their spare time. With woods and streams to explore and to provide a setting for mischievous adventures, they did not have to rely as much as children in crowded urban environments on formal games to amuse themselves. But they had some games, most commonly marbles, which slave children and even some adults played everywhere in the South. Other games included hide-and-seek and hide-the-switch,

pitching horseshoes, and variations on handball and stickball. The
girls liked to jump rope. Boys and girls played ring games, to
which the older children added some sportive kissing.[21] The
bolder spirits among the boys sometimes took to shooting craps
and playing cards, but to do so they had to avoid the eyes of their
parents as well as those of the master; and they rarely had much
to gamble with.

Some of the games reflected the children's slave condition. Julia
Blanks of Texas remembered the children's favorite game as whipping each other with switches. "You know," she added, "after you
was hit several times it didn't hurt much."[22] And then, there was
the game of playing auction. One child would play the auctioneer
and pretend to sell others to prospective buyers. They learned
early in life that they had a price tag, and as children are wont to
do, took pride in their prospective value. They could in fact turn
it to some advantage with their white playmates. Two boys were
boasting to each other about how much they were worth, when a
white boy asked about himself. The scornful reply: "Lord, Marse
Frank, you'se white. You ain't worth nothing!"[23] When the children played their ring games they sometimes castigated the whites
in song.

> My old mistress promised me,
> Before she dies she would set me free.
> Now she's dead and gone to hell,
> I hope the devil will burn her well.[24]

The adult slaves wrestled and fought each other, primarily at the
behest of and for the enjoyment of the whites, but do not seem to
have encouraged their children to follow suit. Slave children took
part in some combative and team sports, but apparently not on a
large scale. Somewhere, sometime, some slave children played any
and every game, but mostly they romped in the woods, played
marbles or skipped rope, and looked after each other with surprisingly good spirit. But that good spirit should not obscure the inner
reality of games like those mock auctions and whippings. Children
use games to neutralize the things they most fear. The slave children were exorcising devils and demonstrating how much insecurity and panic were built into a seemingly carefree existence.

The slaveholders always insisted, without meaning to misrepre-
sent the facts, that an old nurse cared for the slave children under

the watchful eye of Ole Missus while the parents worked in the fields. Every plantation had one or more old women to look after the children, to cook for them, and to keep them out of mischief. The arrangement described by an anonymous planter in Mississippi may be taken as representative:

> A large house is provided as a nursery for the children, where all are taken at daylight, and placed under the charge of a careful and experienced woman, whose sole occupation is to attend to them, and see that they are properly fed and attended to, and above all things to keep them as dry and cleanly as possible, under the circumstances. . . . The suckling women come in to nurse their children four times during the day; and it is the duty of the nurse to see that they do not perform this duty until they have become properly cool, after walking from the field.[25]

One of the most important tasks of the old nurse in relation to the growing children—the one most keenly and resentfully commented on in the slave narratives—concerned feeding. Although the old nurse fed them conscientiously, according to instructions, the children later recalled the procedure with distaste. Robert Shepherd of Kentucky said:

> Dere was a great long trough what went plum across de yard, and dat was where us et. For dinner us had peas or some other sort of vegetables, and corn bread. Aunt Viney crumbled up dat bread in de trough and poured de vegetables and pot likker over it. Den she blowed de horn and chillen come-a-runnin' from every which way. If us et it all up, she had to put more victuals in de trough. At nights, she crumbled de corn bread in de trough and poured buttermilk over it. Us never had nothin' but corn bread and buttermilk at night. Sometimes dat trough would be a sight, 'cause us never stopped to wash our hands, and before us had been eatin' more dan a minute or two what was in de trough would look like real mud what had come off our hands. Sometimes Aunt Viney would fuss at us and make us clean it out.[26]

Many ex-slaves described such scenes but added that the quantity of food was inflexible, so that the children scrambled to slop up as much as they could as fast as they could. Time and time again they referred to having to eat "like pigs." If nothing else had told them, at a tender age, that they were of inferior caste, the trough must have; no white child ate that way. The children's diet, however, had much to commend it. Contrary to the usual assertion that the slaves drank little milk, the narratives strongly suggest that the children, at least, got large quantities, usually in soured form. The plantations had great difficulty in producing milk, but they did well enough to provide for the children.

The old nurses came under fire from antislavery travelers and even from many slaveholders for incompetence and indifference, but other slaveholders and ex-slaves reported kind and conscientious nurses as well as tyrannical or lazy ones. The slaves themselves often turned to these old nurses to give their children religious and moral instruction.[27] The ambiguity so characteristic of plantation life was reflected in the words of an ex-slave: "Yes, ma'am, he name Rachel, and he lick we. We haffa love um or she lick we."[28]

Without denigrating the role of these old women, most of whom probably did their best, it is necessary to correct the false impression that they, or more preposterously the plantation mistresses, had the major role in raising the children whose parents worked in the fields all day. By and large, the children raised each other. The nurses did not so much attend to the younger children as supervise the older children who attended to them. Olmsted described a well-ordered rice plantation in South Carolina, which in this respect appears typical of larger plantations in all regions of the South:

> On the verandah and the steps of the nursery, there were twenty-seven children, most of them infants, that had been left there by their mothers, while they were working their tasks in the fields. They probably make a visit to them once or twice during the day to nurse them. . . . A number of girls, eight or ten years old, were occupied in holding and tending the youngest infants. . . .[29]

The narratives reveal that, late in life, ex-slaves remembered raising children and being raised by older children.[30] The slave children, male as well as female, called the task of looking after younger children "nursing" them. That strong sense of discipline which parents, if necessary, whipped into their children paid off early: if the children grew up showing respect to their elders, they also grew up knowing they had a duty to look after those weaker than themselves.

The "nursing" of little children by bigger ones did not always end well. "Amy's child died this morning," noted M. W. Philips of Mississippi, "choked by a child's feeding it."[31] "My experience," protested a planter from Marengo County, Alabama, "is that small nurses have been the cause of death and many cripples among infants, which would not have occurred if the old and invalid grown negroes on the plantation had been put to nursing. . . ."[32] Fanny Kemble looked askance at every feature of the practice. She grew particularly irate because the older children, often already in their teens, played roughly with the little ones and rolled around with them indecently. And she disapproved of the effects on the "nurses": "Stout, hale, hearty girls and boys, of eight to twelve and older, are allowed to lounge about, filthy and idle, with no pretense of occupation but what they call 'tend baby.' . . ."[33]

These caveats notwithstanding, the narratives and other admittedly fragmentary sources suggest that the children looked after each other with considerable kindness and a healthy sense of responsibility. They did not always keep the little ones clean or teach them the amenities, but they did offer them attention and affection.[34] The success of these eight-to-twelve-year-olds received its warmest tribute from their masters and mistresses, who thought nothing of leaving their own children in the care of black children only a few years older.[35]

Concerned slaveholders insisted that the slaves hit their children too hard and too often, and some of the slave children thought so too. "What the Lord Almighty make trees for," asked an old black woman, "if they ain't for lick boy chillen?"[36] Black mothers expected the northern teachers who came south with the Union army to apply the rule, Spare the rod and spoil the child. Yet, as Lucy Chase recalled, these mothers could treat the very same children they whipped, and wanted her to whip, with loving kindness.[37] Much later in life the children generally recalled that their parents had been "strict" and quick with their hands. Fathers as well as mothers "whipped"—that is, applied a switch to—girls and boys alike.[38]

In retrospect the children showed little resentment and insisted that they needed the discipline. Some remembered their parents as mean but excused them, as one did her sadistic mother: "She had been treated so bad during slavery, she just thought she ought to treat everybody the same way. . . ."[39] These assurances and excuses cannot be accepted at face value. Children usually love their parents, no matter how many beatings they get, and grow up trying to excuse, minimize, and explain away actions they do not want to remember as evidence of a lack of parental affection. But these black reflections cannot be taken as simple equivalents of those familiar from white experience. No doubt a good dose of sadism and brutality went into the harsh discipline. Some slaves must have succumbed to the dehumanizing force of the regime, and many others must have been too weary to put up with their children's mischief and exuberance. But the majority displayed much tenderness and kindliness toward each other as well as toward their children.

Slave parents knowingly carried a heavy responsibility. They had to teach their children how to survive in an extraordinarily dangerous world. They had little margin for error and could not permit their children to learn from their own mistakes. A slave who grew to manhood without the special kind of self-control required in a system of strict racial and class subordination would get himself killed. The "etiquette of race relations" had to be beaten into him if necessary. Many slave parents laid on the switch with a heart as heavy as their hand. Ralph Ellison has written about the twentieth-century southern black family words that apply with even greater force to the slave family:

> One of the Southern Negro family's methods of protecting the child is the severe beating—a homeopathic dose of the violence generated by black and white relationships. Such beatings . . . were administered for the child's own good; a good which the child resisted, thus giving family relationships an undercurrent of fear and hostility, which differs qualitatively from that found in patriarchal middle-class families, because here the severe beating is administered by the mother, leaving the child no parental sanctuary. He must ever embrace violence along with maternal tenderness, or else reject; in his helpless way, the mother. . . .
>
> Even parental love is given a qualitative balance akin to "sadism." And the extent of beatings and psychological maimings meted out by Southern Negro parents rivals those described by the nineteenth century Russian writers as characteristic of peasant life under the Czars. The horrible thing is that cruelty is also an expression of concern, of love.[40]

Fathers as well as mothers imposed a strict discipline and enforced it vigorously. The Reverend Elijah P. Marrs, who had grown up as a slave in Kentucky and later fought with the Union army, recalled his mother's severity but defended her and other slave mothers in terms suggestive of Ellison's. Slave children, like other children, he pointed out, could easily talk too much. Parents had to shield their children from knowing too much and had to instill reticence in them at the earliest possible age. If the children repeated conversations heard in the quarters to the whites or to those who would run to the whites, the people would have to take blows or worse.[41] Lizzie Davis of South Carolina added, "No mam, de older people was mighty careful of de words dey let slip dey lips."[42] When the adults' conversation turned to serious matters the children had to leave the cabin.[43] Late at night parents took care that the children fell asleep, a favorite method being to tell them frightening stories of how "Rawhead-and-Bloody-Bones" or some other demon was on the prowl for children still awake.[44] Much of this effort to keep the adult world from falling too quickly on the children went into protecting them against sexual precocity. What the Reverend Mr. Marrs and other ex-slaves might not have recalled is that the parents' harshness had an especially poignant aspect: since they struggled so hard to give their children as carefree a childhood as possible—since they shielded them as much as possible from an early knowledge of their fate as slaves—they had to be all the more tyrannical and severe in discouraging behavior that, however innocent in other environments, would be dangerous in the quarters.

Parents used their hands and switches on the children for a variety of educational purposes. Ellen Renwick of South Carolina recalled her mother's whipping her for doing poor work.[45] Masters and overseers usually showed young slaves some indulgence, but the parents knew that soon enough the indulgence would give way to the whip. Better that they instill elementary habits and discipline in their children early and according to their own measure. More broadly, slave parents taught their children manners. Obviously, the children had to learn racial etiquette as early as possible if they were to grow up at all, but parents taught etiquette for other than strategic reasons. For the slaves good manners meant respect for and deference to parents and all adults, black and white. In the family cabin children literally were expected to be seen and not heard. Children were expected to know they were children, and they risked a thrashing for prematurely using tobacco or drinking or in any way disobeying their parents.[46]

Slave parents barked orders and applied the switch, but they also manifestly loved and delighted in their children. Even without the constant necessity to train their children to survive in a white-dominated world, their own traditions and temperament would have produced a strong emphasis on courtesy and deference to adults.."My grandma say to me," recalled Gus Bradshaw, " 'Gus, don't run you mouth too much and allus have manners to whites and blacks.' "[47] No small part of the parents' effort went into teaching the children to do the things that might brighten life: to cook and to sew, to weave and to quilt, to fish and to trap, and above all, to trust God and respect the preacher.

If the severity of the household regime poisoned the relationship of some children and adults and produced distorted personalities, primary responsibility must rest with the masters, who commanded a social system that introduced extreme provocations and tensions into a family life that would have remained difficult in the best of worlds. If a large number of parents found ways to express love and protection through a necessary severity, and to guide their children to a stronger manhood and womanhood, the credit belongs to themselves.

Occasionally masters and mistresses mistreated the slave children, but generally they doted on them as if they were playthings or pets. Even harsh masters often took great delight in their "pickaninnies" and treated them with a kindness and affection that provided no warning of the privations and cruelty to come. Masters, harsh and kind, loved nothing so much as to "spoil the little niggers." Masters and mistresses played with the children of field hands and house servants alike; brought them presents, not only at Christmas but whenever they returned from trips; and tolerated no end of mischief. "All us little chillun," recalled Ida Akins of North Carolina, "called [Marse Frank] Big Pappy. He went to Raleigh erbout twice a year. Every time he came back he brings us niggers some candy." Josephine Barrow of South Carolina explained:

> Old Massa, he used to come to de plantation drivin' his rockaway en my Lord a mercy, we chillun did love to run en meet him. . . . "Massa comin'!" "Massa comin'!" En he would come ridin' through de big gate and say, "Yonder my little niggers! How my little niggers? Come here and tell me how you all!"[48]

The masters' affection appeared with deepest poignancy in their private communications of the death of the little ones. Both pecuniary interest and human response appear in such statements as that of M. W. Philips of Mississippi: "Mary's son Richard died tonight. Oh! my losses almost make me crazy." But his earlier comment on Scott cannot be misunderstood:

> Died this morning, Monday, 23rd Sept., Scott, Emily's next to oldest boy—a remarkable child of his age and a pet of us all. I feel as if I had lost some dear relative. We know he is better by the change. May God make us all resigned and able to say, "Thy will, O God, be done."[49]

Rachel Weeks O'Connor said enough in a letter to her sister: "My little Negro babe is dead," as did W. C. Harrison in a letter to William H. Taylor: "She dies after suffering more than any little thing I ever saw."[50]

Masters as well as mistresses made Sunday morning a big time for the children. The scene described by Mary Anderson, who had been a slave in Wake County, North Carolina, recurred in all parts of the South, although not on every plantation:

> Every Sunday morning all the children had to be bathed, dressed, and their hair combed, and carried down to marster's for breakfast. It was a rule that all the little colored children eat at the great house every Sunday morning in order that marster and missus could watch them eat so they could know which ones were sickly and have them doctored.[51]

Mrs. Anderson went on to suggest some of the consequences of this paternalism:

> Some of the slave children wanted to stay with them at the great house all the time. They knew no better of course and seemed to love marster and missus as much as they did their own mother and father. Marster and missus always used gentle means to get the children out of their way when they bothered them an' the way the children loved and trusted them wus a beautiful sight to see.[52]

The slaves' adjustment to paternalism, in contradistinction to some implicit acceptance of slavery, arose in part from these childhood experiences. The children grew up with loving mothers and often fathers too; with the attention of older slave children; with the affection if also the rough discipline of the older slaves. Their masters and mistresses not only pampered them but presided over the plantation family in a way that enabled them to get some of the credit for what slave parents and friends were doing for the children. The more credit the master could claim, the greater the danger to the child. Consider the scenario: The master takes great pleasure in the black children, plays with them, pets them, spoils them. Meanwhile, the parents, with the encouragement of the same master but primarily for their own reasons, are enforcing a strict discipline and freely using the switch. The master, patient and pleasant, delights in the occasional company of the children; the parents, worn out by long hours in the fields, are often cross or short-tempered or simply distracted. The same benevolent, kind, indulgent master—this Big Pappy—also whips and disciplines the parents. If the tendency to worship the master and scorn the parents did not take a greater toll than it apparently did, the credit belongs to the slave parents, whose love for their children went a long way toward offsetting the ravages inherent in this scenario. And credit belongs to the children themselves, for by taking care of each other all day they built up a sense of black community and minimized the necessity for contact with the parents. Not having seen their children all day meant that parents did not constantly feel annoyed and pressed by them. When they got back to their cabins, tired as they were, they often wanted some time with the children, and their display of affection helped undo the damage.

In due time the children went to the fields, and the attentions of the whites waned or even became inverted. But the impressions of those formative years lingered on; not easily did the image of playful Ole Massa and kindly Ole Missus give way to their opposites, even when the whipping began. How much easier to blame the overseer or the driver and to cry out, like the Russian serfs, "If only the Tsar knew!" Underlying the difficulties of the transition lay the sense of shame. To have grown up believing a master to be a kind, fatherly figure and then to have to admit to his being a harsh and unfeeling taskmaster, or even simply a man whose concern had narrow limits and his "love" narrower, required the courage to admit having been taken. The admission of self-deception, for slaves as for the rest of us, did not come easy: it had to be particularly painful because so shameful. Many children did not grow up in such idyllic circumstances and did not suffer this trauma. But many in the majority who did resisted the full recognition of what they were seeing happen. The masters understood the consequences of their own behavior. As R. R. Gibbes of Columbia, South Carolina, wrote in 1858: "The kindness in sickness in seeing after the comforts of these dependent beings causes a strong attachment from early childhood towards their masters and mistresses; and this grows with their growth and strengthens with their strength."[53]

Some masters, afraid of the "corrupting influence" of the slave children on their own, forbade contact or tried to restrict it to the children of the house servants. But such rules usually proved unenforceable, for the white children eagerly sought the companionship of the black children their own age and loved nothing better than to romp in the quarters.[54] The children, black and white, generally had their way.[55]

White boys usually played with black boys and white girls played with black girls as a matter of preference. When boys and girls sought each other out for games, few adult eyebrows flickered. There is little evidence of those postbellum sexual fears which might have made masters and mistresses aghast at seeing their lily-white daughters playing with black boys. Amelia Thompson Watts, recalling a summer on a Louisiana cotton plantation in 1832, described an unexceptional occurrence:

> One of the negro boys had found a dead chicken and we arranged for a great funeral. The boys made a wagon of fig branches, and four of them as horses. We tied a bow of black ribbon around the chicken's neck, and covered him with a white rag, and then marched in a procession singing one of the quaint negro hymns, all the white children next to the hearses, marching two by two, and the colored children following in the same order. . . . After marching all the way up the avenue and down again, we stopped at the grave, under the big magnolia tree by the gate, and my sister Maria preached a sermon from the text, "We must all die," and the chicken was buried with great solemnity.[56]

Had the children been a little younger, the caste distinction between white and black, which shows through the account, probably would have been much weaker.

Often, white and black children conspired not only to commit mischief but to help each other. Together they did no small amount of stealing and of mutually advantageous trading. Marbles for buttered biscuits, for example, offered an attractive deal to whites and blacks. Some ex-slaves tell of white children who, in a variety of ways, protected their black friends from punishment by white adults or slipped food to hungry playmates.[57] Most important, white children frequently defied their parents to teach the black children to read and write.

Sometimes, lifelong friendships grew out of these early years. "When I's a chile we'uns played togedder," Betty Farrow said of her childhood with her master's three girls and four boys, "and we'uns 'tached to each other all our lives."[58] Usually, those friendships only persisted between the white children and one or two blacks who became body servants or occupied some special station. For most slaves the moment came when the awareness of class and race, of superordination and subordination, surfaced; for many, that moment of explicit recognition came as a shock.

Some slave children learned early and others late that they were slaves and that their white playmates stood in a superior position to them. The moment might come, as Kenneth Stampp suggests, when their parents had to explain matters so as to protect them from dangerous breaches of etiquette; or when the attitude of a growing white child began to change; or when the master or overseer superseded parental authority in some dramatic way.[59] On many plantations it came at the beginning, for the black children might be commanded to call even a newly born white baby "Young Massa" or "Young Missus."[60] Some black youngsters learned the difference when they found themselves being punished for the whites' mischief and had no way to protest.[61]

The moment could come in a sudden exchange. A white boy called Francis Black of Texas out to play: "Come on, nigger." When answered, "I'm no nigger," he responded, "Yes, you is, my pa paid $200 for you. He bought you for to play with me."[62] Or it could come much more gently. Dr. George Washington Buckner, who had been a slave on a small farm in Kentucky, remembered his young master so fondly that he could still recall grieving so much at his deathbed that he could not even bear to look at his toys. He also recalled that, besides playing happily with him, he used to have to polish his boots, put away his toys, and do his bidding.[63] The kindest white children learned at a tender age to sport their authority, however gently. The white children on the Tooke plantation in Georgia, for example, loved to fill Christmas stockings for the blacks and, like so many other children of the more benevolent Big Houses, to accompany their mothers on friendly but patronizing Sunday visits to the quarters.[64] The black children must always have felt a difference. The white boys did not eat at a trough or wear dresses until almost full grown. The etiquette of race relations began early.

For those children, white and black, who grew up amicably and warmly the break usually came when the white children began to go to school. At that point the difference in condition became manifest, for the black children often wanted to go too, and the white children often demanded that they be allowed to. As if this distinction were not painful enough, the blacks at that moment often began to function as body servants. The remarks of Henry Johnson, who had been a slave boy in Georgia, described a common occurrence: "When my young master went three miles to school, he rode on a horse. I had to walk alongside de horse to carry his books, den go home and fetch him a hot dinner for noon and go back at night to carry dem books."[65] Life for both had begun in earnest, but in radically different ways.

The behavior of many white children protected the black children against any subsequent shock of awareness of their respective conditions by making the difference clear from the beginning. Harriet Martineau and Frances Trollope, as well as a disgusted southern gentleman, left a record of the ease with which too many of the white children learned, virtually in their cradles, to torment black children and even adults and to play lord of the manor with all the cruelty that undisciplined children can muster.[66] Solomon Northup especially recalled the intelligent ten- or twelve-year-old son of a brutal parvenu slaveholder who picked up all his father's habits with the greatest ease. "Mounted on his pony," wrote Northup, "he often rides into the field with his whip, playing the overseer, greatly to his father's delight."[67] White cruelty to black among children did not always end well for the aggressors. Slave children who had not yet come to understand their condition were quick to return blows. And they might even get away with winning, for some masters did not enjoy seeing their children play the despot and thought the rebukes salutary.[68] The fondness of many masters for the slave children, as well as their pecuniary interest in them, might work to the slaves' advantage even as it aggravated the sibling rivalries inherent in the confrontation of black and white children with the plantation family. Edmund, a bright slave boy who had taught himself to read on a South Carolina plantation, tasted both sides of his master's admiration and affection. The master's two young boys tormented him and one day beat him badly. The master "wore them out" for doing so.[69]

The slave children received some measure of protection against the aggression of the white children from the concern of more sensible white adults who saw the long-range dangers to their own children. A slaveholder, writing in a prominent agricultural journal, warned:

> Children in this section of the Union should be educated with a reference to the relation of masters and slaves. No terms of familiarity should ever be permitted between them, while at the same time, they should be taught that it is their duty to regard them with benevolence, to administer to their wants, and to protect them from injury.[70]

Many tried to bring their children up with an attitude of *noblesse oblige* toward their slaves and took the attitude of Leonidas L. Polk, who believed that it took twenty-one years to make a man and who let his son know that he would tolerate no fourteen-year-old gentlemen on his premises. To drive the point home many planters freely let adult slaves inflict light physical punishment on misbehaving white children.[71]

Well they might have, for white southerners, like Americans generally, were increasingly loath to apply old-fashioned methods of discipline to their own children. Foreign visitors thought that southern whites dealt entirely too permissively with their children, although by twentieth-century bourgeois standards they were clearly rough enough. Sir Charles Lyell suggested that the planters fell into the worst possible practice of combining tyrannical scoldings and threats with an absence of force.[72] Southern women worried about the effects of slavery on their children, particularly their sons. A "noble lady of New Orleans" told Fredrika Bremer that everything conspired to make the white children stubborn and intractable. In Miss Bremer's paraphrase: "The child, surrounded by slaves from the cradle, accustoms himself to command them, to have all his caprices gratified, or to see the refusal punished, often with cruelty."[73] Fanny Kemble added her own judgment:

> I do not think that a residence on a slave plantation is likely to be particularly advantageous to a child like my eldest. I was observing her today among her swarthy worshipers, for they follow her as such, and saw, with dismay, the universal eagerness with which they sprang to obey her little gestures of command. She said something about a swing, and in less than five minutes head man Frank had erected it for her, and a dozen young slaves were ready to swing little "missis."—Think of learning to rule despotically your fellow-creatures before the first lesson of self-government has been well-spelt over![74]

And Amos Kendall, the tutor of Henry Clay's children, penned some notes in his journal:

> *May 29, 1814* Yesterday, Mrs. Clay being absent, Thomas [aged twelve] got into a mighty rage with some of the negroes, and threatened and exerted all his little power to kill them.
>
> *Aug. 23, 1814* Hearing a great noise in the kitchen, I went in and found Theodore swearing in a great rage with a knife drawn in attitude to stab one of the big negroes.[75]

That so many white youngsters behaved with so much kindness and friendship toward their black playmates speaks well for the generous impulses of human beings not yet hardened to the possibilities for oppressing others. But sooner or later, although often without entirely losing that decent spirit, the white children grew into the perquisites and responsibilities of their lordly station. For the slaveholders, as for the rest of humanity, the child was father to the man.

THE OLD FOLKS

The slaveholders congratulated themselves on their solicitude for the aged slaves and loudly claimed that no free laboring class could look forward so securely to decent retirement. Eliza Frances Andrews thought the old slaves privileged to the point of being pampered. Mrs. Schoolcraft insisted that a planter who shirked his duty toward the aged would meet with scorn and expulsion from society. Mrs. Schoolcraft may have been a romantic apologist for the regime, but she was neither stupid nor dishonest. She added that, the hostility of white neighbors aside, a slaveholder who mistreated his old slaves would arouse dangerous discontent among the younger ones.[1]

Many slaveholders lived up to their self-created reputation and left an impressive record of concern. A Virginian, traveling in France, wrote home in 1860 and asked about the condition of the old slaves. "They must be very helpless," he wrote, "and will soon, if not now, require the personal attention of a young negro. Suggest some mode of making them comfortable the balance of their lives, and at the present or a less expense."[2] William S. Pettigrew wrote his driver, Moses, in 1856 to acknowledge the news of the death of Uncle Charles. He regretted not being able to return for the funeral and added, "You inform me that he had every attention, which I am satisfied of, & would be much pained if there were reason to think otherwise."[3] Solon Robinson described Joseph Dunbar's plantation in Mississippi as containing a large number of superannuated slaves. According to Robinson, Dunbar brought the old slaves together from his several plantations so that he could personally attend to their needs.[4] Such cases could be multiplied; they did not occur rarely and may have matched in numbers those of indifference and cruelty.[5] Between the two, the great majority of slaveholders at least provided minimal material comfort.

But the slaveholders' proud boast of tender care cannot be taken at face value; there is too much evidence of cruel neglect and worse. The whites of Maryland, for example, expressed outrage at the extent to which slaveholders were manumitting their old slaves in order to escape responsibility for them. In Baltimore, as in other southern cities, incensed residents protested against the influx of manumitted country blacks who could only become a public charge, and fought for tough laws to curb the practice.[6] No less staunch a proslavery writer than Dr. Josiah Nott of Mobile revealed the fragility of paternalistic concerns in his attack on the practice of insuring slaves. "As long as a negro is sound," he wrote, "and worth more than the amount insured, self-interest will prompt the owner to preserve the life of the slave; but, if the slave becomes unsound and there is little prospect of perfect recovery, the underwriters cannot expect fair play—the insurance money is worth more than the slave, and the latter is regarded rather in the light of a super-annuated horse."[7]

With blacks as well as whites considered "old" at fifty, slaves of that age commanded no higher a purchase price than eight-year-old children on the open market during the 1850s, and the temptation to cut them loose remained strong among less scrupulous masters.[8] Ironically, the stiffening laws against manumission may have provided the slaves with firm protection at this point. Some urban slaveholders solved the problem by sending their old slaves out to peddle or beg and thereby bring in some income as well as support themselves.[9]

The behavior of the slaveholders toward the superannuated ranged widely from full and kind concern through minimum attention to paternalistic responsibilities to indifference and sheer barbarism. Thus, both James R. Sparkman and Fredrika Bremer doubtless told the truth in their contradictory accounts of the South Carolina low country. Sparkman, a prominent plantation physician, assured R. F. W. Allston that the planters he attended did not skimp on medical care for their old slaves, whereas Miss Bremer recorded instances of deplorable abuse.[10] The war brought no change in the spectrum. If many slaveholders went to great lengths to take care of the old and infirm, many others brutally abandoned them when they herded their productive slaves to places safe from Yankee advance.[11] Notwithstanding the admirable sense of responsibility exhibited by many slaveholders, there is enough evidence to justify Kenneth Stampp's harsh reading:

> The combination of lower living standards, greater exposure, heavier labor, and poorer medical care gave slaves a higher mortality rate than whites. The census of 1850 reported average ages of 21.4 for Negroes and 25.5 for whites at the time of death. In 1860, 3.5 per cent of the slaves and 4.4 per cent of the whites were over sixty; the death rate was 1.8 per cent for the slaves and 1.2 per cent for the whites. . . .
>
> These statistics discredit one of the traditions about slavery: that a substantial number of aged "aunties" and "uncles" spent their declining years as pensioners living leisurely and comfortably off their masters' bounty. A few did, of course, but not enough reached retirement age to be more than a negligible expense to the average owner.[12]

As the slaves grew old—if they grew old—they asserted the right to that comfortable old age which a paternalistic system ostensibly guaranteed. "Just come to tell you, Massa," an old man announced, "that I've labored for you for forty years now. And I done earned my keep. You can sell me, lash me, or kill me. I ain't caring which but you can't make me work no more." The response of the shocked master is no less instructive: "All right, Jake. I'm retiring you, but for God's sake, don't say anything to the other niggers."[13] The sense of reciprocal obligations usually emerged in less dramatic but no less telling ways. On the Rice Coast of Georgia, for example, planters relied on superannuated slaves to curb the ravages of the rats. Significantly, the slaveholders knew enough to pay a bounty of tobacco at the rate of a pound per hundred rats killed.[14] Many old slaves throughout the South slipped into "retirement" well before their laboring powers had given out. Many slaveholders always knew as much, and those who did not learned after the war. No sooner had old, crippled, helpless, useless blacks become freedmen and gotten a chance to work their own land than they astonished everyone by their physical vigor and output.[15]

Those slaveholders who pointed to the pleasant condition of the old slaves did not lie; they deceived themselves. Their description, as a balanced judgment on a wide range of circumstances, conformed closely enough to reality. Their self-deception concerned the credit they took for themselves. They could never recognize that the credit belonged much less to themselves than to the young and middle-aged slaves. Lyell glimpsed the truth when he wrote of the comfortable superannuated slaves on the great Hopeton plantation in Georgia, "who would be supported in a poor-house in England [but who] enjoy here, to the end of their days, the society of their neighbors and kinfolk, and live at large in separate houses assigned to them."[16]

The slaves, including the children, looked to the needs of their old people and treated them with a respect and deference that offset the humiliations heaped on them by condescending, not to mention unkind, whites. Seventy-year-old slaves, for example, were called on to race fifty yards under the orders of ten-year-old Massa Robert and to receive prizes from young Massa Will and Missus Annie.[17] An old man in the Sea Islands, rejoicing over freedom, spoke for many others in telling Charlotte Forten: "Don't hab me feelins hurt now. Used to hab me feelins hurt all de time. But don't hab em hurt now, no more."[18]

The slaves themselves did everything possible to allow their old people to end their lives with dignity. If some responded to their parents or grandparents with indifference or hostility, others in the community would step in to assume responsibility. When freedom came, the old slaves faced the withdrawal of their masters serenely, confident that they would be taken care of by family, friends, and the black community at large, as they always had been.[19]

Careful attention to and respect for the aged carried on a classic African attitude. In West African traditional religions the spirits of ancestors continue to relate to the living, and old people are viewed as approaching the time of that power. More broadly, Africans, like many other non-Western peoples, venerate wisdom and experience. As the Akan say, there was an old man before a lord was born.[20]

The dignity of the old people rested on much more than attentions received, for they felt not only wanted but needed. With parents in the field all day, the old folks had the responsibility of disciplining unruly children and keeping an eye on the tiny "nurses" to the tinier tots. They taught the little ones how to pray and how to fish; how to show courtesy and how to feed the chickens.[21] Solomon Northup recalled Old Abram: "a kind hearted being—a sort of patriarch among us, fond of entertaining his younger brethren with grave and serious discourse. He was deeply versed in such philosophy as is taught in the cabin of the slave. . . ."[22] With vegetable gardens requiring attention beyond that which tired field hands could provide after hours, the old folks helped out and contributed something to the comfort of their neighbors and kin.[23]

The reliance of the quarters on folk medicine gave the old folks a special role—one that made them feel especially useful and respected and that brought them a consideration born of religious sanction as well as physical service. Typically, it was the old folks who "studied"—and here this ambiguous word of the blacks must be taken literally—herb medicine and "doctoring." They attended the sick, comforted those in pain, and taught the younger slaves the mysteries of medical magic. The line between these efforts and protective conjuring was a fine one, and they attracted to themselves all the more respect for their sanctity as well as their wisdom.[24]

No one, therefore, need be surprised that suicide appeared so rarely among old slaves, although its incidence in modern American society has been especially high among old people.[25] The aged slaves had a high degree of security, emotional as well as physical. Their masters' error lay in the supposition that the modest protection of the Big House accounted for their widespread cheerfulness and contentment, for the old folks' ability to live decently and with self-respect depended primarily on the support of their younger fellow slaves.

HEARTH AND HOME

From the late 1830s to the war southern agricultural journals mounted a determined campaign to improve the quality of slave housing. Primarily, they rested their case on the planters' interest in protecting the health and reproductive powers of their chattels, although they also included the usual arguments from humanity and some concern for morale and good order. "In no case," wrote a planter, "should two families be allowed to occupy the same house. The crowding [of] a number into one house is unhealthy. It breeds contention; is destructive of delicacy of feeling, and it promotes immorality between the sexes."[1]

The standards called for by these reformers and concerned citizens included log cabins of sixteen by eighteen (or twenty) feet, located as many as seventy-five yards apart, raised two or three feet off the ground, and equipped with large fireplaces and chimneys, plank floors, and large if unglazed windows.[2] By the 1850s the great majority of the slave cabins in all parts of the South met the specifications as to size and the restriction to one family unit. The census reports from 1850 and 1860, as well as plantation records, show that, on the average, five to six slaves—one family unit—occupied a cabin.[3] Where crowding occurred the masters were not always at fault, for the slaves often took orphans, old people, or single friends in to live with them rather than leave them to a barrackslike existence.[4]

Many plantations had cabins of two rooms separated by a "dog trot," or open hall. The Reverend C. C. Jones complained that these cabins deprived families of privacy and increased the dangers of quarreling and trouble. They may, however, have been to the slaves' taste, for they enabled them to live closely as an extended family and to take better care of their children and old folks.[5]

In other respects, only the more patriarchal planters carried out these ideal specifications. Some cabins had no windows at all. Spaces between the logs were daubed with mud or clay, which could be knocked out to provide ventilation in the hot weather. As a result, the slaves had inadequate ventilation in summer and too often suffered from drafts in winter.[6] Most cabins had windows with shutters but no panes. Thus, in winter the slaves had to choose between getting fresh air and being cold or smothering and keeping warm, whereas in summer they could not prevent massive invasions of insects.[7] Margaret Nillin of Texas commented on the use of shutters, which "lets flies in durin' de summer an' col' in durin' de winter. But if you shuts dat window dat shuts out de light."[8] Savilla Burrell of South Carolina added: "Dere was plenty to eat sich as it was, but in the summer time before us git dere to eat de flies would be all over de food and some was swimmin' in de gravy and milk pots. Marse laugh 'bout dat, and say, it made us fat."[9] Nor did the slaveholders usually provide plank floors or raised houses during the 1850s, although more and more were doing so.[10]

Although some slave cabins had chimneys made of brick or tabby (a mixture of oyster shells, lime, and sand),[11] the overwhelming majority had chimneys made of mud, clay, and sticks, which had the great disadvantage of catching fire. Fatalities occurred rarely, but minor injuries must have been frequent.[12] The archaeological excavation conducted by Ascher and Fairbanks in Georgia reveals a considerable spilling of ashes across the cabin, and children as well as adults often huddled close to the fireplaces.[13] Cabins burned down often, for the slaves loved to have them well lit and heated and would build roaring fires even in warm weather.[14] Richard Carruthers of Texas recalled cabins catching fire from the chimneys. "Many the time," he added, "we have to get up at midnight and push the chimney away from the house to keep the house from burning up."[15]

The men collected firewood, usually plentiful; the women tended the fires and provided other forms of illumination. With matches scarce, the slaves often had to rub flint rocks together and apply the sparks to cotton lint. This work could be tedious and difficult, so it was easier to keep a fire going as long as possible.[16] Slaves made their own candles, as a rule, although some masters provided candles and even brass holders. The women took tallow from cow innards, boiled out the fat, and inserted string, which being in short supply, they carefully saved on every occasion. Some raised bees for the wax.[17]

The cabins improved in size and construction as the nineteenth century progressed. At least, the practice of quartering slaves in barn lofts and barrackslike makeshifts, all too common during the eighteenth century, gave way to individual family units. Under pressure from physicians and reformers, planters increasingly appreciated the importance of better housing, even from a strictly economic point of view, so that conditions improved steadily although not dramatically.[18]

The slaveholders expressed satisfaction with their slave quarters while admitting deplorable conditions and prodding each other for improvements. Their satisfaction rested on the thought that most of the world's peasants and workers lived in dirty, dark, overcrowded dwellings and that, by comparison, their slaves lived decently. In 1798 Julian Ursyn Niemcewicz, the Polish poet, described the slave quarters at George Washington's Mount Vernon as "far more miserable than the poorest of the cottages of our peasants," but he was not the most reliable of witnesses.[19] During the nineteenth century such perceptive travelers as Basil Hall, Harriet Martineau, James Stirling, and Sir Charles Lyell thought the slaves at least as well housed as the English and Scottish poor, and Olmsted thought the slaves on the large plantations as well situated as the workmen of New England. Hinton R. Helper, the abolitionist firebrand, visited Chile and admitted thinking the housing of the peasants near Valparaiso worse than that of southern slaves. Even Fanny Kemble thought conditions no worse than among the European poor.[20]

As late as 1914 a substantial portion of the London working class was crowded into wretchedly small rooms without hope of privacy, comfort, or elementary convenience—rooms the size and furnishing of which readily remind us of the slave quarters of the Old South.[21] The laboring poor of France, England, and even the urban Northeast of the United States, not to mention Sicily or Russia, lived in crowded hovels little better and often worse than the slave quarters.[22] No matter how the "optimist" historians of the industrial revolution try to minimize the misery by recording improvement and progress, the fact remains that the rural and urban poor even of the advanced countries lived in squalor. The slaveholders may have been self-serving in their comparisons; they may even have been hypocritical. But they were not fools. They knew that their slaves had housing comparable to that of the free workers and peasants of the bourgeois world, and this knowledge strengthened their commitment to their own way of life.

By the late 1850s great housing problems nonetheless remained.

"More disease and loss of time on plantations," thundered the *Practical Farmer and Mechanic* of Somerville, Tennessee, in 1857, "are engendered from crowded negro cabins than from almost any other cause."[23] Slaveholders, travelers, and especially physicians heartily agreed, describing the cabins and the immediate grounds as intolerably filthy and breeding places of disease.[24] During the 1840s and especially the 1850s, with improved dissemination of medical information, planters required regular cleaning and weekly inspections.[25] Some planters tore down their quarters every few years and rebuilt them on a fresh spot.[26]

As time went on, more and more slaveholders arranged springtime whitewashing parties in the quarters.[27] The slave women sometimes did this work while the men cut firewood.[28] Most slave cabins may never have received a coat of whitewash—the record is unclear—but an increasing number did, at least on the outside, during the last decade of the regime.

Some slaves tried to improve the appearance of their cabins. A woman would take great pride in keeping her cabin "clean and neat as a pin" or would collect flowers and ornaments to add a pretty touch.[29] Solon Robinson did not describe a typical slave cabin, but he may well have described more than an occasional one when he wrote about the plantation of Joseph Dunbar of Jefferson County, Mississippi:

> His negro quarters look more like a neat, pleasant, New England village than they do like what we have often been taught to believe was the residence of the poor, oppressed and wretched slaves. I did not give them a mere passing view, but examined the interior, and in some of them saw what might be seen in some white people's houses—a great want of neatness and care—but, so far as the master was concerned, all were comfortable, roomy and provided with beds and bedding in abundance. In others there was a show of enviable neatness and luxury; high-post bedsteads, handsomely curtained . . . with musketo netting, cupboards of blue Liverpool ware, coffee mills, looking glasses, tables, chairs, trunks and chests of as good clothes as I clothe myself or family with.[30]

A slave who prided himself on his prowess in hunting opossum and raccoon decorated his walls with their skins, and others occasionally built decorative furniture in an effort "to make it look nice."[31] Most slaves took no such pains with their cabins, but they did develop a reputation for such particular practices as fastidiously scrubbing their cooking pots.[32] And their sense of beauty led them to press their masters to build the quarters amidst trees and flowers, even if the cabins themselves were slighted. John H. Ingraham described the China trees of the Natchez region, which the slaves so admired:

> This . . . is the universal shade tree for cabin and villa in this state. It is in leaf about seven months in the year, and bears early in the spring a delicate and beautiful flower, of a pale pink ground slightly tinged with purple. In appearance and fragrance it resembles the lilac, though the cluster of flowers is larger and more irregularly formed. . . . The chief beauty of this tree consists in the richness and arrangement of its foliage.[33]

By and large, however, the slaves fussed no more over the appearance of their cabins than did, say, French or Balkan peasants. With the cabins cramped, with the physical demands of daily labor so pressing, with insects impossible to control, and with poultry and small animals virtually part of the household, clean, neat, well-ordered cabins required herculean effort and an improbable degree of concern. Community life centered in the praise-houses and brush-arbors. The slaves, like so many traditional agriculturalists, did not draw a sharp line between house and yard and did not highly value household regularity and order.[34]

Yet, the cabins provided more than a place to eat and sleep. In important if limited ways they strengthened the sense of family. The slaves might have done more with them if they had had a chance to shape their building in the first place. Generally the slaves built their own cabins, but with little room for innovation. The masters provided the specifications and organized the construction by gangs of laborers and by housing units rather than by individuals or families and single dwellings.[35] Occasionally, the slaves tried to assert themselves, but with little success. An African-born slave on St. Simon's Island, Georgia, built a traditional African hut only to have his master tear it down.[36] Many slaveholders hired carpenters and laborers, white and free Negro, to build the slave cabins, and others used specially assigned slave carpenters.[37] The slaves had little opportunity to build their houses as they might have wished or to adjust specifications to the needs of their families. They did often have the opportunity to build hogpens and fowl houses for their stock, and more important, additions to their cabins. A fourteen-by-eighteen-foot cabin did not lend itself to privacy. The slaves perpetually felt the need to preserve as much delicacy as possible in their love-making and to protect their children from seeing more than they should. Accordingly, they built lean-to extensions to their cabins or lofts or simple partitions in order to put the children to sleep as privately as possible.[38]

In contrast, the slaves of the Caribbean, who built their own cabins with materials provided by their masters and with fewer restrictions, had a more onerous task but a greater cultural opportunity. Their cabins may not have provided more room and a greater degree of comfort than those of the American slaves, but the persistence of African styles and patterns wherever the slaves had wide choice suggests a measure of self-expression.[39]

Particularly cruel or irresponsible masters withheld adequate beds and bedding from their slaves. Josiah Henson, writing about a slaveholding in Maryland at the end of the eighteenth century, described log huts without floors:

> In a single room were huddled, like cattle, ten or a dozen persons, men, women and children. . . . There were neither bedsteads, nor furniture of any description. Our beds were collections of straw and old rags, thrown down in the corner and boxed in with boards; a single blanket the only covering. Our favorite way of sleeping, however, was on a plank, our heads raised on an old jacket and our feet toasting before the smouldering fire.[40]

Solomon Northup, whose testimony ranks as one of the most authoritative of the slave narratives, told of a cotton plantation in Louisiana in the 1840s on which beds consisted of twelve-inch planks with sticks of wood for pillows.[41] The slaveholders of the late antebellum South usually insisted that they provided good beds, but even they admitted that too many of their number skimped on bedding and blankets. As late as 1860, John Stainback Wilson warned slaveholders to pay more attention to these matters or continue to accept heavy losses from sickness and death, and that rock-ribbed journal of proslavery extremism, the *Planters' Banner*, joined the chorus calling for improvement.[42]

Throughout the nineteenth century slaves received light cotton blankets every third year and had to make do through southern winters, which, however mild in general, could turn dangerously raw for short periods.[43] In cold weather the slaves would sleep on the floor huddled around the fire, but the "floor" was usually the ground, damp and cold, and thus the slaves took considerable risks. By the 1850s conditions had improved. Blankets still had to do for three years, but were of somewhat better quality, and the beds were more comfortable. Hostile travelers described slaves sleeping on the bare ground but did not inquire whether the slaves did so by choice. In the hot weather the children often preferred the cool ground and so did many adults.[44]

Some of the slow improvement in sleeping arrangements occurred because of the initiative of the slaves. Sensible masters provided the necessary lumber, and male slaves built solid bedsteads, usually on two or three legs with one side attached to the wall. Many masters provided cotton for mattresses; more provided straw. If the slaves got neither, they collected moss and scalded it in an often futile attempt to keep out insects. The women did their best to make comfortable mattresses and keep them repaired.[45] More important to the family's health, the women supplemented the light blankets by making warm, heavy, and often attractive quilts. Plantation mistresses organized quilting parties; so did slave women. They got together at night to help each other and to chat, laugh, and gossip. Largely because of these efforts, the abolitionists' grim picture of freezing slaves huddled around the fire, while no invention and often accurate, prove to be much exaggerated.[46] The slaves took their sleeping arrangements seriously. They slept in accordance with prescribed folk customs: the blankets were pulled over their heads, even if their feet froze; and they built their bedsteads east to west in the African manner, so as not to sleep "crossways of the world."[47]

From the seventeenth century to the end of the regime little change took place in the furnishing of slave cabins. An inventory from Henrico County, Virginia, in 1697 could easily have come from Mississippi in 1861: several chairs and a bed, an iron kettle and a brass kettle, an iron pot, a pair of potracks, a pothook, a frying pan, and a beer barrel.[48] In the 1860s, William Howard Russell reported from Louisiana:

> There is a partition dividing the hut into two departments, one of which is used as the sleeping-room, and contains a truckle bedstead and a mattress stuffed with cotton wool, or the hair-like fibres of dried Spanish moss. The wardrobes of the inmates hang from nails or pegs driven into the wall. The other room is furnished with a dresser, on which are arranged a few articles of crockery and kitchen utensils. Sometimes there is a table in addition to the plain wooden chairs, more or less dilapidated, constituting the furniture. . . .[49]

In the 1850s M. W. Philips of Mississippi, the well-known planter and agricultural writer, said, "Negroes have no need of furniture; they have bedsteads, bedding and seats, with chests or trunks for clothes—almost as much as laborers anywhere."[50] The slaves may not have entirely agreed with Philips, for they collected jars, bottles, and stoneware, converted the skins of cattle into rawhide for chairs, obtained pots and pans suitable for proper cooking, and built odd pieces of furniture to suit their taste. When freed during and after the war, they spent part of their first wages for better cooking and eating utensils, for cooking had always been important to them.[51]

The slaves generally made their own furniture or bought it out of their small earnings from their gardens or odd jobs. The men made simple chests or tables as well as benches for the family's use around the fire.[52] They sometimes built a table or chair to give each other as wedding presents.[53] Rarely did masters buy furniture for the quarters. When the men did not provide for their own families, one or two slave carpenters built furniture for all.[54]

Slaves who wished to cook and eat decently, as most clearly did, had to improvise. Only a few masters provided tin dishes, although considerably more provided knives and wooden spoons.[55] If the slaves were not to eat with their hands—and contrary to outraged reports in such abolitionist tracts as Weld's *American Slavery as It Is*, few adults sank into that degradation—they had to provide utensils for themselves. Where possible, they collected mussel or oyster shells to serve as spoons and knives. They raised gourds, which they dried, processed, and converted into bowls, dishes, ladles, jugs, and anything else their ingenuity and skill could shape.[56]

In St. Francisville, Louisiana, about halfway between Baton Rouge and Natchez, Rosedown still stands. Built by Daniel Turnbull and his wife, Martha Hilliard Barrow, in 1835, it represented the plantation ideal in the architecture of the Lower South as well as any Big House could. With two stories, wooden Doric columns, and a gabled roof, built of cedar and cypress but with one-story brick wings added some years after the initial construction, it recaptured the spirit of the great houses of colonial Virginia. Rosedown had beautiful furnishings and a noteworthy library and sat among a formidable collection of secondary buildings: a detached kitchen, a milking shed, and a doctor's office, as well as barns and woodsheds. Most impressively, it looked down a breathtaking avenue of oaks, behind which stood marble statues of Greek and Roman goddesses. The gardens, designed by a Parisian landscape artist, long remained among the loveliest in the South.[57] Frederick Douglass described growing up in the shadow of a less formidable "great house" and seeing it for the first time as a child: "It was a treat to my young and gradually opening mind to behold this elaborate exhibition of wealth, power, and beauty."[58]

Rosedown represents the pinnacle, the ideal, and by no means the common reality of plantation homes. The overwhelming majority of the big planters, as well as the moderate to small planters, lived in simple two-story log houses, tolerably spacious and comfortable but hardly the mansions of *Gone with the Wind* and the plantation legend.[59] Yet, mansions like Rosedown dotted the landscape and fired the imagination of white and black alike, imparting that sense of power and permanence so necessary to sustain the claims of a landed ruling class.

For poorer white farmers as well as for slaves, who lived at best in adequate, tight cabins and at worst in hovels, even a modest rustic Big House commanded awe and respect. Will Baily, an ex-slave from Missouri, could recall that his master built the Big House out of the same logs he provided for the quarters, but Octavia George of Louisiana more typically commented on the relative smallness of the cabin she had lived in.[60]

However the Big House may have looked to a critical and sophisticated eye, it loomed as a "mansion" to the slaves. Isaac Martin of Texas burst out:

> My ol' marster he live in a big house. Oh, it was a palace. It had eight or nine rooms. It was buil' outer logs, and moss and clay was stuff' twixt de logs. Dere was boards on de outside and it was all ceil' nice on de inside. He lived in a mansion.[61]

After a long life in freedom in which to reflect on the reality, James Southall of Tennessee concluded: "It really wasn't such a big house as it had only four or five rooms in it. It was a common boxed house, painted white and wid a long gallery across de front. Maybe it was de gallery dat made it look so big to us."[62] When Benjamin Johnson of Georgia went up to the Big House one day, the other field hands waited for his return and fired questions. Like others who had glimpsed the inside, he was impressed: "It's pretty!" Susan Merritt of Texas remarked, "Massa Watt lived in a big log house what set on a hill so you could see it round for miles, and us lived over in the field in little log huts, all huddled along together."[63] However those Big Houses are now judged, the slaves could not see them as in fact most of them were. Some spirituals, for example, refer to God ("de Big Massa," as some slaves called him) as living in a "mansion in de sky." The Big House might have provided a dangerous reference point for the slaves by underlining the wretchedness of their own cabins. The record suggests, however, that it provided a positive reference point by reaffirming the slaves' image of their master as a powerful and dominating figure, appropriate to a system of paternalistic hegemony.

The contrast between the planters' large and imposing homes, no matter how rude, and the hovels of the poor and even not-so-poor whites similarly strengthened the paternalist vision, even as it checked racist pretensions. Sarah Debro of North Carolina derided the cabins of the poor whites as "little shacks made of sticks and mud with stick and mud chimneys" and contrasted them sharply with the "planked up and warm" cabins that Marse Cain provided for his slaves.[64] The slaves saw how the marginal white farmers and especially the déclassé poor whites lived. Even their overseers rarely if ever had more than three rooms and sometimes not that many.[65] "The many descriptions left by the antebellum travelers," writes Avery O. Craven, "indicate that the home of the poor white and the cabin of the Negro slave varied little in size or comfort. Both were apt to be of but a single room whose plain walls of log were broken only by doorways and an open fireplace. . . ."[66] Eliza Frances Andrews described her nearest poor white neighbor as living in "a cabin that Brother Troup wouldn't put one of his negroes into."[67] Nor did the solid yeomen always do better; many did just as badly. Large families often crowded into one room in a manner that would have made most slaveholders blush were their slaves in such condition.[68] Sidney Andrews described as typical a yeoman cabin in North Carolina in 1865:

> His house has two rooms and a loft, and is meanly furnished,—one, and possibly two, beds, three or four chairs, half a dozen stools, a cheap pine table, an old spinning wheel, a water-bucket and drinking gourd, two tin washbasins, half a dozen tin platters, a few cooking utensils, and a dozen old pieces of crockery. Paint and whitewash and wallpaper and window-curtains are to him needless luxuries.[69]

The variety of reports by the observant and scrupulous Frederick Law Olmsted confirmed the strictures of such southerners as D.

R. Hundley and the disgust of northern and English travelers. Whether in the Upper South or the Lower, the older cotton states or the newer, the up country or the low, he reported the yeomen's living either in hovels as bad as or worse than the slave cabins or in homes only one notch better.[70]

The slaves looked up to Rosedown and to the pseudo-Rosedown big log cabins of the typical masters; and they looked down on the homes of the poor and middling whites, as well as on their own cabins. From any angle the apparently unshakable power of the master class received daily confirmation.

But within the cabin the power of the master could be shut out temporarily. The fireplace centered the family. "We worked hard in de field all day," said Clara C. Young of Mississippi, "but when dark come we would all go to de quarters and after supper we would set around and sing and talk."[71] The cheerful singing and dancing, reported John Mason Brown, the Kentucky Unionist, contrasted with the sad, plaintive songs that the slaves sang going and coming from work and with their slow, rhythmic work songs.[72] Olmsted reported from a modest plantation in Mississippi:

> During the evening all the cabins were illuminated by great fires, and looking into one of them, I saw a very picturesque family group; a man sat on the ground making a basket, a woman lounged on a chest in the chimney corner smoking a pipe, and a boy and two girls sat in a bed which had been drawn up opposite to her, completing the fireside circle. They were talking and laughing cheerfully.[73]

Many masters took measures to get their slaves to bed early and some even forbade nocturnal singing and audible recreation. When the slaves lacked permission to unwind before their own fires, they often did it anyway at the risk of punishment. They valued their privacy, especially from whites. "When left to themselves," Julia E. Harn writes of the Georgia Rice Coast, "they wanted their cabins in some secluded place, down in the hollow, or amid the trees, with only a path to their abode."[74] The slave women puzzled their masters by insisting on delivering their babies at home among family and friends, instead of in the more comfortable plantation hospitals.[75] Alexander Humboldt pointedly contrasted the family-centered cabins in the United States, for all their wretchedness, with the grim slave barracks in Cuba.[76] He might have called Charles Davis of South Carolina as a witness:

"De 'possum in his hollow, de squirrel in his nest, and de rabbit in his bed, is at home. So, de nigger, in a tight house wid a big hot fire, in winter, is at home, too."[77]

GARDENS

To a greater or lesser extent most slaveholders permitted their slaves to keep chickens and sometimes hogs and to raise vegetables. Most slaves in northwest Louisiana, Kate Stone thought, had their own gardens. "It was," she wrote, "a very lazy 'cullud pusson' who did not raise chickens and have eggs." These gardens allowed the slaves to improve and vary their diet and reduced the cost to the masters of maintaining a healthy labor force. From the eighteenth century onward many slaves had a better diet than rural whites simply because they made an effort to raise vegetables.[1]

Having gardens meant working at night after having finished a long day in the fields. The slaves did this work by moonlight or provided illumination by lighting grease in a frying pan strategically placed on a stump.[2] The women have generally been credited with working the gardens.[3] But some men assumed responsibility, no doubt in appreciation of such late-night work as weaving and sewing as their women had to do. The evidence is too fragmentary for an appraisal, but it does show that at least a substantial minority and quite possibly even a majority of the men worked the gardens.[4] Men and women often helped each other and their neighbors to harvest the crops during their allotted leisure time on Saturday night.[5]

Most slaves used their gardens to grow cabbages, collards, turnips, and extra corn for themselves, but many others raised these vegetables and even a little cotton or tobacco for sale. In some cases they earned substantial amounts of money.[6] Wise slaveholders feared the temptation to illicit trade with unscrupulous poor whites presented by the slave gardens, and responded by buying the produce themselves. To do so, they had to make the price attractive to the slaves, and as a result, the slaves found themselves in a position to strike good bargains.[7] The slaves used their money or credits to buy fishhooks or kitchen utensils or to buy marbles for their children or to keep their women in ribbons, bandannas, and assorted finery.[8]

The deeper significance of these slave gardens emerges from a contrast of their scope and marketing apparatus with those of the British Caribbean.[9] In Jamaica and such smaller islands as Grenada and St. Vincent the slaves had provision grounds (palinkas) in nearby hills and mountains in addition to their plantation gardens (yards). On islands such as Barbados and St. Kitts the yards had to do double duty, and the slaves' independent production was naturally much smaller. By assigning palinkas to the Jamaican slaves, the planters saved themselves a good deal of money for food supplies. The slaves had to produce for themselves, for they could not scrape by on the limited rations provided by their masters. Since the slaves needed time to get to and from the distant palinkas, their masters had to release them from plantation duties for most of the weekend. Since the slaves needed and emphatically wanted to use their palinkas to raise crops for sale, their masters had to allow them virtually a free hand to buy and sell in town and village markets on Sundays. In his *History of Jamaica* Edward Long estimated that the slaves controlled 20 percent of the cash circulating on the island.

The palinkas and related Market Sundays transformed the slaves into part-time peasants and petty traders. When emancipated, they had already acquired the habits, experience, and talents of an independent peasantry and petty bourgeoisie. Their masters had underestimated this side of the system and had seen only its integrative functions—especially its tendency to curb rebelliousness by giving the slaves a stake in the system. The slaves' performance reached such impressive proportions that William Pitt, demanding abolition of the slave trade in Parliament, could taunt the slaveholders with references to the Jamaican experience, not merely to liberal economic theory: "Why, Sir, a negro, if he works for himself, and not for a master, will do double work."[10]

The Jamaican planters particularly miscalculated in thinking that, after abolition, the slaves would remain as plantation laborers because of their special attachment to their yards. When the time came, the strong sense of personal independence rooted in landowning, which their experience on the palinkas had given them, prevailed over that attachment, and they retreated to the mountains. But the choice was hard, for their yards did hold a special place in their lives.

Every Jamaican slave family had its house and shared a yard, which together provided the center for family life. The yard served more than one family and became the place for gossip, interfamilial decision making, and normal social exchange. It also served for raising chickens and small domestic animals, as well as a few fruit and coconut trees and plots of such favored vegetables as plantains and yams. But it was much more than a social center and a source of additional food. The slaves buried their dead there; the yard took on a religious significance and contributed to the slaves' sense of familial roots. One did not walk into another's yard without permission. Thus the yards and palinkas, considered together, shaped the cultural life of the slaves in ways economic, social, and religious and blended these elements into a strong tendency toward independence and pride in self and in family.

The slaves of the Old South did not have an equivalent. The other side of the slaveholders' boast that their slaves were well fed was that they did not, anywhere near to the extent of the Jamaican slaves, learn to take care of themselves in a world of production for market. The gardens, like the palinkas and yards of the Jamaicans, gradually became recognized by common consent as the slaves' private property, however unsanctioned by law. But for the southern slaves they were not an essential source of food. Many slaves lacked the energy or desire to work them when given the chance; many others never got the chance.

Southern slaves did not have Market Sundays and could not create an incipient petty bourgeoisie within their ranks. Officials and citizens of Natchez and many other southern cities complained bitterly about country blacks who crowded in on Sundays to drink, gamble, and trade in goods, including stolen goods.[11] But the extent of the trading and of the organized production it represented paled in comparison with Jamaican practice.

Southern slaves valued their gardens, worked hard in them, and enjoyed the opportunities for trading in town. Richard Soule, a northerner, was struck by the "manorial attitude" of the slaves toward their garden plots. Olmsted and Russell noted that the slaves expressed a proprietary interest in their chickens by cutting claws, wattles, tails, or wings in order to identify them.[12] The difference between these slaves and those of Jamaica did not arise from a variant initial attitude toward the prospects for making a partially independent livelihood; it arose from the much narrower scope of the gardens and from the economically and institutionally weaker market setting. The gardens nonetheless played an important role in the slaves' lives. Even on a small scale they gave the slaves a chance to learn to get along without a master. They provided a focus for a family effort in which parents could assume the role of provider normally usurped by the master and in which the children themselves could contribute some labor to their own home. Some slaves did learn the arts of sharp dealing in town, although without adequate legal markets too many fell victim to unscrupulous whites.

Black performance in the contraband camps and during early Reconstruction shows clearly that a substantial majority of the freedmen, even though suffering from the demoralization of war, quickly became self-supporting when given any opportunity. John Eaton, superintendent of the Freedmen's Bureau, reported from Tennessee and Arkansas in 1864 that of the 113,650 freedmen for whom he was responsible, more than 40,000 were in the military service, 62,000 were completely self-supporting, and slightly more than 10,000 were getting aid. Thirty percent of those getting aid were from working families and expected to repay. Those remaining were the aged, the children, the hospitalized, and the crippled.[13] The full story of the freedmen's efforts to educate themselves and their children, to build churches, and to support themselves out of meager earnings is slowly coming to be told. W. E. B. Du Bois plausibly suggested that the slaves' experience with their gardens had generated that land hunger which became an important if unattained demand during Reconstruction.[14]

The slaveholders recognized the tenacity with which the slaves held on to their garden privileges and transformed them into "rights." Noah Cloud, a prominent agricultural editor in Alabama, warned that garden privileges only encouraged the slaves to become thieves and complained that some masters were forcing others to give in to the slaves' demands. He pointed out that once a single planter allotted gardens, all the others in the neighborhood would have to follow suit or risk a deterioration in the morale of the labor force.[15] Where the practice took firm hold the property accumulated by the deceased slaves passed to their next of kin as surely as if slave rights had had legal sanction.[16] Sometimes even an element of legal sanction appeared. In *Waddill v. Martin* (1845) the Supreme Court of North Carolina faced the question whether the estate of a deceased planter should include the value of the little crops of cotton he had allowed his slaves to raise for themselves. The executor dutifully paid the slaves $143.97 for the cotton, but made a cross entry to debit the estate. Judge Ruffin overruled him and called the claim "ungracious." He noted the extent of such slave privileges, calling them wholesome, and insisted that although slaves could not legally own property, their right to the product had received the sanction of custom and public sentiment.[17]

The gardens provided a strong basis for the development of an independent spirit, but were not extensive enough to generate an incipient petty bourgeoisie. The slaves learned to value their own land and to work for themselves but not how to defend and expand their interests in vigorous marketplace competition. The enhanced sense of independence they acquired from the control of a little property and their role as providers for their own families received both positive and negative recognition from the slaveholders. "Rusticus," writing in 1857, argued for more extensive garden privileges: "These little gardens contribute much of the comfort during the year and give a cheerful, home-like appearance to that quarter. Besides, they attach the negro to his home and makes [sic] him feel that he has more than a passing interest in the things about him."[18] A tough overseer argued the case for garden privileges as a means of social control even more bluntly:

> Every means are used to encourage them, and impress on their minds the advantage of holding property, and the disgrace attached to idleness. Surely, if industrious for themselves, they will be so for their masters, and no Negro, with a well stocked poultry house, a small crop advancing, a canoe partly finished, or a few tubs unsold, all of which he calculates soon to enjoy, will ever run away. In ten years I have lost by absconding, forty-seven days, out of nearly six hundred Negroes.[19]

Not every slaveholder agreed. Many complained about the encouragement to theft and others about the slaves' habit of conserving their energy while working for their masters so that they could work for themselves at night and on weekends.[20] The more reflective saw deeper problems and cautioned against reducing the slaves' dependence on their masters. In his "Plantation Rules," Bennet H. Barrow of Louisiana unwittingly revealed the slaves' resourcefulness at transforming every privilege into a claim: "Allow it once to be understood by a negro that he is to provide for himself, and you that moment give him an undeniable claim on you for a portion of his time to make this provision, and should you from necessity, or another cause, encroach upon his time—disappointment and discontent are seriously felt. . . ."[21]

KITCHENS, HIGH AND LOW

The food in Washington, protested Benjamin F. Wade, the rough-hewn abolitionist from Ohio, upon taking his seat in the Senate in 1851, "is all cooked by niggers until I can smell and taste the nigger."[1] He was, of course, commenting on southern cooking. Southerners themselves have tended to discuss the subject with greater respect, not to mention delicacy. Willie Morris, from the Mississippi Delta, writes in *North Toward Home* of a dinner party in New York with southern black friends and fellow writers:

> At Al Murray's apartment in Harlem, on New Year's Day, 1967, the Murrays, the Ellisons, and the Morrises congregated for an unusual feast: bourbon, collard greens, black-eyed peas, ham-hocks, and corn-bread—a kind of ritual for all of us. Where else in the east but in Harlem could a Southern white boy greet the New Year with the good-luck food he had as a child, and feel at home as he seldom had thought he could in the Cave [New York City]?[2]

That antebellum southern kitchen of which Senator Wade complained in his customarily bluff manner moved John S. Wise to write with some nostalgia: "The Virginia cook and the Virginia cooking of that time were the full realization of the dreams of epicures for centuries."[3] Whether or not Wise knew it—he probably did—he was paying his compliments to the slaves' culinary skill. The high praise of southern cooking, which has undeniably been our most impressive regional cuisine, has usually been lavished on Ole Missus. Even today, almost any southern cookbook recounts the glories of her performance in the kitchen. The truth is that Ole Mammy, or merely "the cook," usually ran the kitchen with an iron hand and had learned what she knew from generations of black predecessors. What Missus knew, she usually learned from her cook, not vice versa.[4]

Discerning slaveholders knew and said as much. R. Q. Mallard of Georgia referred to "the kitchen, where French cooks are completely outdistanced in the production of wholesome, dainty and appetizing food; for if there is any one thing for which the African female intellect has natural genius, it is for cooking."[5] Mallard need not have limited himself to the women, although they did dominate the Big House kitchens, in contradistinction to those of the inns, hotels, coastal ships, and, later, the cattle drives.[6] A few black men in Louisiana went to Paris for special training, and some Big Houses across the South sported male cooks.[7] Male or female, black cooks took great pride in their work. When more than one worked on a plantation, which was often the case, the chief cook ruled the others despotically.[8]

On the great plantations and on many of the more modest ones, everything did have to be just so. Breakfast, dinner, and supper in the Big House became major productions, especially on the innumerable occasions when guests had arrived. William Howard Russell visited a Louisiana plantation and had trouble believing his eyes when breakfast was served: "There is on the table a profusion of dishes—grilled fowl, prawns, eggs and ham, fish from New Orleans, potted salmon from England, preserved meats from France, claret, iced water, coffee and tea, varieties of hominy, mush, and African vegetable preparations."[9]

Dinner, which would be served about two o'clock in the afternoon, constituted "the great business of the day." As synthesized in Sam Hilliard's study of antebellum southern food habits, the great low-country South Carolina planters might find themselves confronted at a single sitting with turtle soup, boiled mutton, turtle steaks and fins, macaroni pie, oysters, boiled ham, venison, roast turkey, bread pudding, ice cream, pie, and fruit. Madeira, sherry, and champagne normally stood in for dinner wines, and cordials would follow dessert.[10]

The overwhelming majority of slaveholders, even the more affluent, lived a good deal more modestly, but the standard set by the great planters of the low country, the Delta, and the sugar parishes made its impact. Dinner was an important matter for which pains had to be taken, however much the effort might be scaled down, finer dishes replaced by rougher ones, and whiskey substituted for Madeira and sherry during the meal. Large staffs worked in the kitchens of the big plantations, and the cook needed some help even on the smaller ones. The kitchens threw up much noise and bustle, quarrels, confusion, and the sometime crack of Mammy's whip across the back of a stupid, slovenly, or incompetent helper. The odors, noise, and activity did not so easily filter into the Big House proper, for the kitchen stood as a building well apart. On some of the more comfortable plantations even the dining room was separated from the rest of the Big House by a porch.

To know what came out of most of those kitchens, look at the items advertised in any of Harlem's "soul food" restaurants. Bob Jeffries, a black chef from Alabama who established a formidable reputation for himself in New York, writes:

> When people ask me about soul food, I tell them that I have been cooking "soul" for over forty years—only we did not call it that back home. We just called it real good cooking, southern style. However, if you want to be real technical on the subject, while all soul food is southern food, not all southern food is "soul." . . . Soul food cooking is an example of how really good southern Negro cooks cooked with what they had available to them, such as chickens from their own back yard and collard greens they grew themselves, as well as home-cured ham, and bakin' powder biscuits, chit'lins, and dubie [berry cobbler].[11]

The secret of soul food, Mr. Jeffries adds, lies in its spices and herbs.

The slave cooks established their reputation, to no small degree, by their imaginative spicing. The subtle flavors of the gumbos and jambalayas—"two distinct dishes foreign to European cookery"— arose primarily from black skill in combining herbs.[12] Sesame seeds and oil, as well as red pepper, came from Africa with the slaves and became central to southern cooking. "Red pepper," wrote Sarah Hicks Williams to her parents in New York in 1853, "is much used to flavor meat with the famous 'barbecue' of the South & which I believe they esteem above all dishes is roasted pig dressed with red pepper and vinegar."[13] Malaguetta (melegueta) pepper from the West African coast had been freely used to season food in the slave trade, as it was thought to prevent dysentery.[14] In the Caribbean as well as in the southern slave states, the slaves used heavy doses of pepper and other sharp spices, whether out of African conditioning or a need to enliven the taste of their plain fare or both. They developed a taste for highly spiced cooking, mastered its art, and transmitted their preference to the whites via their command of the Big House kitchen.[15] As for sesame seeds, the effects of which drew compliments from Thomas Jefferson among many others, the slaves regarded them as bearers of good luck and planted them everywhere they could for use in candies, cookies, and desserts,—most of which, however, were enjoyed by their masters.[16]

The identification of pork, especially chitterlings and the like, collard greens, black-eyed peas, cornbread, and hominy with slave life has been general, but these dishes were by no means restricted to blacks. Nor were the poor whites, who also needed cheap, substantial nourishment, alone among the white population in developing a strong taste for them. They made their way into the Big House and became a much larger part of upper-class preference than some among later generations of white southerners have wanted to admit. However much soul food may be despised by today's Black Muslims as an ugly cuisine imposed from above, it represented the culinary despotism of the quarters over the Big House in antebellum times.[17] The slaves in Brazil and the Caribbean helped shape the cuisine of those regions by introducing African foods and methods and by transmitting their plantation preferences, born of necessity, to the whites, and the slaves of the southern states decisively shaped that which came to be known and prized as "southern cooking."[18] The spread of southern cooking to the North in our own day, like the spread of so much else in southern culture, has represented, above all, the triumph of its black component.

The accomplishment of the slave cooks could never have been so complete if only a few highly trained elite cooks had been at work. They were able to bend the taste of the Big House toward that of the quarters because the slaves as a class, including the rudest field hands, had quietly been making a life for themselves that included a healthy concern with cooking. "The negroes," exulted Mrs. Schoolcraft, "are born cooks." And she added with only slight exaggeration that when a cook fell ill, it was only necessary to send the driver to the quarters for any one of a number of male or female field slaves. The Big House kitchen would be in safe hands.[19]

Some years ago a woman, recalling her experience in a Nazi concentration camp, said that the inmates always knew when one of their number had lost her will to live and would soon die. When someone no longer bothered with the wretched fare of potato peels for dinner or lined up to wash with the dirty water in the basin, the end was in sight. These were elementary matters of self-respect quite as much as of physical survival: with them, hope remained; without them, none. The slaves had a good deal more than potato peels to eat, but the conditions of their life might easily have led to a demoralization that expressed itself in indifference. That for many, even most, it manifestly did not provide a measure of their will to survive; more impressively, it provides a measure of their spiritual power and ability to make a harsh world as pleasurable as possible.

Most masters would have preferred to distribute food to their slaves on Monday or Tuesday rather than on weekends and would have preferred to establish a communal kitchen rather than to allot portions of uncooked food to slave families. Yet, the great majority distributed food on weekends in response to strong pressure from the slaves, for whom the weekend, especially Sunday, called for a special culinary effort.[20] The masters welcomed their slaves' spirit, but feared that too much of the week's ration would disappear in a few days and that either hunger or stealing would follow during the rest of the week.

The unwillingness of most slaveholders to establish a common kitchen implicitly demolished the claim that slaves had no strong sense of family. A common kitchen guaranteed the master control of the quantity and quality of his slaves' food and removed the danger that the slaves, weary from a long day in the fields, would undercook the pork or not bother with the corn and vegetables or gulp their food down in a manner injurious to their health.[21] Yet, most slaveholders nonetheless yielded to their slaves' insistence on eating as families with some measure of privacy. "Southron" wrote in the *American Cotton Planter and Soil of the South* that although some planters insisted upon a common kitchen for their slaves as the most economical and healthful practice, "We prefer to give each one his separate weekly allowance of meal and bacon, allowing sufficient time at mid-day for cooking and rest. They are better satisfied to have it themselves, to cook according to their fancy."[22] "Rusticus" added a few months later that he would prefer a common kitchen for his slaves but that "those among them who have families prefer to serve up their food for themselves in their own peculiar way."[23]

The slaveholders understood their slaves' concern for food as being more than a matter of sustenance. The more patriarchal made a small ceremony out of the distribution of the week's rations and used the occasion to greet the male field hands with hand-shakes and inquiries about the health of their families. As Gus Feaster, who had been a slave in South Carolina, recalled, "It was a special day on each plantation when de Master and de o'seer give out de week's rations."[24]

Returning from the fields after an exhausting day, some slave women would toss their cornmeal and fat pork on the fire and serve it indifferently. Dinner had already been eaten anyway haphazardly, for dinner meant the midday meal. At night they had supper, a less important matter. Yet to a surprising extent, many took pains with supper despite their fatigue. When their husbands lived on another farm or plantation and visited once or twice a week, those evenings became a special occasion. And it was a poor wife and mother who did not put herself out for her family on weekends. On plantations on which religious services or relaxation occupied most of Sunday but some extra time was available on Saturday afternoon, they did part of their cooking in advance. Mom Hester Hunter, an ex-slave from South Carolina, fondly recalled, "De people sho cook dey dinner fer Sunday on Saturday."[25]

The slaves cooked in large fireplaces that extended four feet or so across and served many purposes at once. Benny Dillard of Georgia described a typical fireplace:

> De fireplaces was a heap bigger dan dey has now, for all de cookin' was done in open fireplaces den. 'Taters and cornpone was roasted in de ashes and most of de other victuals was biled in de big old pots what swing on cranes over de coals. Dey had long-handled fryin' pans and heavy iron skillets wid big, thick, tight-fittin' lids, and ovens of all sizes to bake in. All of dem things was used right dar in de fireplace. Dere never was no better tastin' somepin t' eat dan dat cooked in dem old cook-things in open fireplaces.[26]

The Yankee troops who occupied the Sea Islands during the war expressed surprise at the resourcefulness displayed by the freed-women in cooking for special occasions.[27] Those who came out of slavery spoke with impressive pride of their parents' ability. To Alonza Fantroy Tombs of Georgia, his mother was surely "one of de bes' cooks in de lan'." To Wills Easter of Texas, "Mammy de bes' cook in de country." In more general terms, Lizzie Davis of South Carolina proclaimed, "Yes, child, de slavery people sho had de hand to cook."[28] Children, both male and female, learned to cook before they grew large enough for field work. Their mothers taught them when they could, and when they could not or would not, some old slave usually stepped in.[29]

The slave recipe that has come down to us most prominently is for opossum—significantly, a food they obtained for themselves. "The flesh of the coon," wrote Solomon Northup, who had lived as a free man in the North before being kidnapped into slavery and who did not suffer from nostalgia for the old plantation in Louisiana, "is palatable, but verily there is nothing in all butcherdom so delicious as a roasted 'possum."[30] Raccoon, ground hog, and other self-procured foods had their supporters. Anthony Dawson, an ex-slave from South Carolina, declared, "I love 'possum and sweet 'taters, but de coon meat more delicate, and de hair don't stink up de meat."[31] But opossum remained the favorite of the great majority.

From one end of the South to the other, the slaves prepared opossum in roughly the same way: parboiled and then roasted with lard or fatback. They used locust or persimmon beer to wash the meat down, and roasted it with sweet potatoes.[32] For variety, the slaves might dry and smoke opossum as they would hams. If the animal was young, they had the option of frying it, but frying was, for the most part, reserved for young rabbits, which were considered especially tender.[33] Prepared one way or the other, opossum inspired the slaves to sing:

I

Well, 'possum meat's so nice an' sweet,
  Carve 'im to de heart;
You'll always find hit good ter eat.
  Carve 'im to de heart.

Refrain: Carve dat 'possum,
Carve dat 'possum, chillun.
Carve dat 'possum,
Oh, carve 'im to de heart.

II

De way ter cook de 'possum nice,
  Carve 'im to de heart,
First parbile 'im, stir 'im twice,
  Carve 'im to de heart.

III

Den lay sweet taters in de pan,
  Carve 'im to de heart;
Nuthin' beats dat in de lan'.
  Carve 'im to de heart.[34]

Cooking opossum was a serious matter, which one had to learn to do right. "Ma was sick in de bed," recalled Emma Virgil of Georgia, "and de mens had done been 'possum huntin'. Ma said I would jus' have to cook dem 'possums. She told me to fix 'em and she said to fix 'em wid potatoes and plenty of butter and red pepper. Den she looked at me right hard and said dat dey had better be jus' right."[35]

Squirrel meat was tough, so the women had to use violent measures even while following the same basic system. The boiling had to be more vigorous, but it had the advantage of offering a treasured broth. Squirrel pie, served with dumplings, qualified as a delicacy. The slaves' experience with squirrels served them well during the war, when they made an easy adjustment to cooking rats, while the squeamish upper-class whites went hungry.[36] The slaves usually raised chickens themselves, and J. S. Buckingham expressed astonishment at their ability to pluck, dissect, and fry them in less than half an hour.[37] Mrs. Harriet Chester, an ex-slave from Tennessee, described the basic method of preparation:

> When we roasted a chicken, we got it all nice and clean, stuffed him with dressing, greased him all over good, put a cabbage leaf on the floor of the fireplace, put the chicken on the cabbage leaf, then covered him good with another cabbage leaf, and put hot coals all over and around him, and left him to roast. That is the best way to cook chicken.[38]

The slaves in French-speaking Louisiana combined African, French, Anglo-Saxon, and other cooking procedures to develop a style of their own. Ex-slaves especially spoke highly of coosh-coosh (or *couche-couche*), the name of which suggests a Muslim West African influence. To make coosh-coosh, the slaves boiled meal in salted water, stirred in milk, clabber, or syrup, preferably molasses, added beef parts when available, and produced a dish that, when done with care, evoked great compliments. Variations on coosh-coosh, often meatless, appeared as far east as North Carolina.[39]

White southerners dreadfully overcooked their vegetables and threw away the liquid, which contained most of the nutritional value. They thought that vegetables had to be cooked "thoroughly," and thus made a great contribution to one of the worst features of our national cuisine.⁴⁰ The slaves followed suit but with a difference: they highly valued the liquid and drank it. As a result of their penchant for this "pot-likker" (or pot-liquor or pot-licker), they probably gained much more value from their method of preparation than did the whites, except for those poorer whites who copied them. During the twentieth century and perhaps earlier, lower-class southern whites have disdained pot-likker—or pretended to—as something fit for the pigs and, of course, the blacks.⁴¹

The slaves did not prepare their vegetables haphazardly. As reported by Lizzie Farmer, an ex-slave of Texas, their method required care and patience. They began by putting a piece of hog jowl in a pot and then added beans. When the beans were half done, they added "a mess of cabbage," and when the cabbage was half done, put in squash. When the squash was half done, they added okra. The vegetables, when cooked through, would be removed a layer at a time. With less time to fuss, they would cook field peas, for which they had considerable enthusiasm, heavily seasoned with red pepper.⁴² Another vegetable dish, also popular among the whites, to which meat would normally be added, was "Hopping John." Cowpeas would be boiled with or without rice and then pork or bacon would be stirred in. Vegetables and herbs also served as emetics and purgatives. "Poke salad," explained Gus Feaster, an ex-slave from South Carolina, "was et in dem days to clean a feller out. Hit come up tender every spring and when it cut deep down in sand it looked white. It's an herb." After being cut and parboiled, it would be fried in hot grease, seasoned with pepper and salt, and eaten with new spring onions.⁴³

Poke salad went well with ashcake or hoecake, as well as with clabber, buttermilk, and especially sweet milk. Ashcake and hoecake, which probably derived from West African practice, were great favorites with anything or by themselves. An ex-slave recalled: "They would cook in ashes. We could get old cabbage leaves and wrap up corn pones in it, and rake the ashes and put them in hot ashes to cook. We would wrap potatoes up in cabbage leaves, too, and cook them in ashes."⁴⁴ When the opportunity permitted, they might make 'simmon bread by adding persimmon juice to flour.⁴⁵ And they sang:

I
If you wants to bake a hoecake,
To bake it good and done,
Slap it on a nigger's heel,
And hold it to de sun.

II
My mammy baked a hoecake,
As big as Alabama.
She throwed it 'gainst a nigger's head,
It rang just like a hammer.

III
De way you bake a hoecake,
De old Virginny way,
Wrap it round a nigger's stomach,
And hold it dere all day.[46]

Coffee was another matter. Until recently a good cup of coffee could not be obtained in the South outside private homes and in Louisiana, where the addition of chicory saved it. Olmsted spoke for most travelers when he referred to "the abominable preparation which passes for coffee."[47] Once the war came, whatever standards may have previously obtained gave way to necessity. Well-parched cottonseed, among other things, had to do. "It should be soaked over night," noted a South Carolina planter, "and thoroughly parched while still damp." The slaves never had much choice even before the war; they made their coffee by roasting okra, corn, or other grain. No wonder, then, that they earned a reputation for having a sweet tooth—to make it palatable, they poured in huge quantities of sugar or molasses. Those who preferred tea made it from sassafras or various wild weeds.[48]

The slaves let their masters know that they had standards. The hominy did not taste right if the corn was too yellowish, and the master was expected to provide the proper kind. The steam mill at Beaufort relieved the blacks of Port Royal of the arduous task of grinding the corn by hand, but they preferred to do the hard work and enjoy the sweeter meal and grits it produced.[49] They made an effort to mold whatever was available into something a little better. The great complaint of the slaves was the monotony of their assigned diet. They responded by varying it themselves. The poorer whites often did the same, and the two styles had much in common. But what the slaves did, they taught themselves to do, and they contributed more to the diet of the poorer whites than the poorer whites ever had the chance to contribute to theirs.

CLOTHES MAKE THE MAN AND THE WOMAN

Slaveholders took the normally mild southern winters too much for granted. Their clothing allotments kept the slaves warm most of the time but provided little or no insurance against the brief but bitter cold snaps that struck periodically. During the seventeenth century and much of the eighteenth, reports from the slaveholders themselves suggested that the slaves often suffered terribly, but conditions seem to have improved after the Revolution.[1]

During the nineteenth century the demands for improvement sounded on all sides. The Reverend C. F. Sturgis of South Carolina, in his "Prize Essay on the Duties of Masters to Servants," thundered against "the miserable policy of allowing servants to go to their labor in rags, for want of comfortable clothing, and to employ the hours of Saturday night, almost to Sabbath morning, in washing those miserable garments, then to lie down about half naked on Sunday, until these garments are dry, or put them on half dry, and thereby bring on rheumatic and other acute inflammatory diseases."[2] *The Planters' Banner* denounced the prevalent indifference to the quality of slave clothing while admitting that masters generally paid attention to quantity, and other journals joined the chorus.[3]

These efforts bore some fruit. The slave narratives, for example, more often than not report at least adequate clothing. Yet, reports of dangerous shortages cropped up periodically even during the late antebellum period. T. T. Bouldin, a congressman from Virginia, charged in 1835: "Many negroes had died from exposure as a consequence of flimsy fabric that will turn neither wind nor weather." From time to time cries of alarm reverberated through the slaveholders' correspondence and publications.[4] The clothing allowance, although normally adequate, had no margin for safety, so that the slaves could expect to suffer occasional hardship.

During the last few antebellum decades slaveholders spent between seven and ten dollars per year to clothe an adult slave; some spent fifteen dollars or even more.[5] Those who considered the bill too high made efforts to have the clothes made on the plantation. In 1854 Robert Collins of Macon, Georgia, wrote from the vantage point of thirty years as a planter: "The proper and usual quantity of clothes for plantation hands is two suits of cotton for spring and summer, and two suits of woolen for winter; four pair of shoes and three hats, which with such articles of dress the negro merits, and the owner chooses to give, make up the year's allowance."[6] The usual distribution probably included only two or three pairs of shoes, but Collins's report was basically accurate. Many planters provided socks and underclothes. Even the most generous allotments, however, left the slaves little opportunity to wash and change their clothes more than once a week.[7]

Many slaveholders bought their slaves' clothing, but others, especially the biggest, bought cloth and other materials for plantation manufacture. Even many of those who bought the basic items expected their slaves to make their own socks and accessories. Plantation mistresses often supervised the production of clothing and some worked hard themselves in the actual production.[8] On some of the larger plantations a few slave women specialized in making clothes for all. But with or without the direction and assistance of the mistress and the slave seamstresses, the field women had to do extra work to provide some of their family's clothing, as well as to wash it and keep it in good repair.[9]

The slaves complained about the texture of the fabrics at least as readily as about the quantity of the clothing. Their cotton garments—"osnaburgs"—had the advantage of durability and sturdiness but the disadvantage of roughness. "Dat ole nigger-cloth," protested a slave from Virginia, "was jus' like needles when it was new. Never did have to scratch our back. Jus' wriggle yo' shoulders an' yo' back was scratched."[10] Booker T. Washington probably had a great deal of company in being grateful to his older brother for taking pity on him and breaking in his boyish shirttails for him.[11]

No article of slave clothing called forth so much complaint as the shoes. Large numbers of slaves worked barefoot in all but the worst weather, partly from habit and preference but mostly from dissatisfaction with their shoes, which were too stiff and did not fit. Masters made an effort to provide comfortable shoes: they measured their slaves' feet and ordered by size.[12] But crude measurements and rough materials and production added up to discomfort. Masters too easily assumed that the slaves would have scorned the most comfortable shoes. Ex-slaves said something else. "A nigger man with white beard," said Mary Reynolds of Louisiana, "told us a day am coming when niggers only be slaves of God. We prays for the end of tribulation and the end of beatings and for shoes that fit our feet."[13]

The slaves could not do much about the size of the shoes, but they could reduce the discomfort caused by the stiffness. Irella Battle Walker's father patiently rubbed grease into her shoes to make them comfortable for her, and he repeated the operation whenever they hardened again in the hot sun. Kate Stone, looking back on the privations of her slaves, exclaimed, "After many, many greasings, the poor darkies could at least bend their feet in them."[14]

During the late antebellum period, when the division of labor on the plantation had declined and the number of good shoe-makers with it, slaveholders had to spend $1.00 to $1.25 per pair for slave shoes, which wore out in a year, if they lasted that long.[15] Disgust with shoddy New England manufacture of "Negro shoes," and especially with the mixture of sheepskin and cardboard that sometimes passed for leather, probably accounts for the widespread use of wooden shoes.[16] The slaves turned this uncomfortable feature of their shoes to some advantage. Many wore, if not wooden shoes, then shoes with wooden soles, and many others wore shoes with brass tips. As Nellie Lloyd of South Carolina explained: "Dey danced de 'flat-foot.' Dat was when a nigger would slam his foot flat down on de floor. De wooden bottom shoes sho would make a loud noise."[17]

Alert masters took measures to enforce minimum standards of cleanliness among their slaves. They insisted that the slaves sweep their quarters and yards during the weekend and that they report for work in clean clothes on Monday morning. The whip enforced the rules.[18] But the slaves took their own measures on weekends, when the black preachers exhorted their people to cleanliness.[19] The slaves cleaned themselves up and put on fresh clothes for their Saturday night parties and especially for church on Sunday.[20] The women assumed responsibility for picking the lice out of the hair of their husbands, their children, and each other. Eliza Frances Andrews bristled at having to watch some of this activity at church services, but in this respect the slaves did not behave differently from the poor whites.[21] In dressing up for the weekend the women took particular care with their hair. They rolled it up indifferently during the week but combed it out on Sunday to look as pretty as possible.[22]

Cleaning up meant extra work for the slave women, for often they had to make their own soap. They poured hickory ashes and water over straw in a large barrel and later added fat and grease. They then drew out the lye and boiled it with more grease. "Dis," said Gracie Gibson of Florida, "was lye-soap, good to wash wid."[23]

It would be easy enough to conclude, in the best manner of a bourgeois social worker, that the poor, overworked, inadequately housed slaves just gave up on themselves. Poor peasants and agriculturalists the world over have lived in crowded cabins with pigs and chickens in and out and have been unable to keep their cabins, clothes, and persons clean even when they have wanted to. (Ex-GIs may recall from basic training, not to mention combat, what their fatigues looked and smelled like after a few summer days in the fields, notwithstanding access to showers and other modern facilities.) But the slaves, like other poor rural folk who appear so disgusting to outsiders, had their own standards and made their own distinctions. They cleaned up for certain occasions, drawing laughter from the whites for wasting time, effort, and the little money they had in order to dress up "fine." Their attitude toward their clothes became inseparable from their attitude toward personal cleanliness.

Nineteenth-century propagandists notwithstanding, West Africans enjoyed a great reputation for personal cleanliness, whereas Europeans, including if not especially the English, suffered from an equally emphatic and well-deserved reputation for avoiding soap and water at all costs. Africans bathed daily and could hardly believe the filthiness of their European captors. The Europeans—Portuguese, Spanish, Dutch, and English—paid high tribute to the Africans' fastidiousness, although they often found it a bit eccentric.[24] K. Onwuka Dike, a distinguished African historian, permits himself some sport in discussing the Niger Delta's shift from slave exporting to palm-oil exporting during the nineteenth century: "With the increasing population at the time of the industrial revolution in Britain came changes in social customs and industrial requirements. As British people began to take washing seriously, the demand for soap rose considerably, and palm oil was the chief constituent in its manufacture."[25]

White southerners, despite their references to the filthiness of their slaves, won no medals for cleanliness. The English and Yankees, having become converted to bathing, assumed, as was their wont, that everyone else ought to convert also. In the 1840s, Featherstonhaugh expressed indignation at the condition of the South's highly touted watering places:

> Language cannot do justice to the scenes we have witnessed, and through which we had to pass at the White Sulpher Springs. It must appear incredible to those who have heard so much of the celebrity of this watering place, but who have never been here, to be told that this, the most filthy, disorderly place in the United States, with less method and cleanliness about it than belongs to the common jails of the country, and where it is quite as impossible to be comfortable, should from year to year be flocked to by great numbers of polite and well-bred people who have comfortable homes of their own. . . .[26]

Fanny Kemble, J. S. Buckingham, Sidney Andrews, and many others poured down their scorn on the lack of cleanliness among the whites, rich and poor alike.[27] But for the most part, the opprobrium fell on the slaves.

The slaveholders expressed concern about the slaves' inattention to cleanliness; in particular, socially conscious physicians repeatedly warned that unsanitary conditions and habits were causing much sickness and death.[28] The complaints about the slaves' being "disgustingly dirty"[29] and unresponsive to exhortations measured the distance that they had traveled from their African origins and the extent to which they had blended into their rural American surroundings.

The slaves had their own complaints. Asked by James Redpath how many shirts he had, a slave in Virginia replied that he had one. He explained that it had to be washed at night in the hope that it would be dry in the morning.[30] During the summer the slaves had access to streams and made some effort to bathe, but during the cold months many made no attempt during the week. Peter Clifton of South Carolina spoke about the slave children: "Us was fed up to de neck all de time, though us never had a change of clothes. Us smell pretty rancid maybe, in de winter time."[31]

Not surprisingly, many slaves did become demoralized and indifferent to filth. "When I asked Mary-Jane, this evening, to hand me a tumbler of water," reported Lucy Chase, "I called her attention to the unclean tumbler, which she speedily made clean with the towel to which I was indebted for clean feet." The abolitionists who went south with the Union occupation moaned that they would have to teach the reluctant freedmen the simplest features of personal hygiene.[32]

Meticulous masters treated the semiannual distribution of slave clothing as a paternalistic ritual. Although John Berkley Grimball had superior overseers and disliked leaving Charleston for his country plantations, he made the trip regularly in order to hand out clothing personally. Charles Manigault, also of the eastern low country, listed as one of the reasons for residing on his plantations at least half the year the necessity personally "to give them punctually their clothes, blankets, etc., *calling each by name* and handing it to them." And Moses Liddell of Louisiana wrote to his brother: "I have purchased more [calico] for the other negroes than I intended but I trust that they will feel a disposition to appreciate what we give them & behave accordingly."[33] Throughout the South, masters and especially mistresses distributed clothing in a manner designed to underscore their own benevolence and to evoke gratitude for a supposed gift[34]—a sensitivity to the social significance of clothing that suggests an awareness of the slaves' own positive attitude toward their appearance and comfort.

"On the way to our friends' plantation," wrote Harriet Martineau from the outskirts of Montgomery, Alabama, "we passed a party of negroes, enjoying their Sunday drive. They never appear better than on such occasions, as they all ride and drive well, and are very gallant to their ladies."[35] Plantation, small-farm, and urban slaves scrubbed themselves for Sunday. "You cannot conceive anything more grotesque," wrote Fanny Kemble with mixed feelings, "than the Sunday trim of the poor people."[36] Gabe Emmanuel, an ex-slave from Mississippi, with a less jaundiced eye, suggested that the slaves loved to "dike out in spick an' span clean clothes come Sund'ys."[37]

The slaves surprised contemporaries by a combination of indifference toward their appearance during the week and concern with their appearance on Sundays and holidays. "With a passion for dress," complained the Reverend C. C. Jones, "they frequently spend all they make in fine clothes; their appearance on the Sabbath and on public days is anything but an index of their fortunes and comfort at home."[38] Gus Feaster of South Carolina recalled: "Sunday clothes was dyed red for de gals; boys wore de same. We made de gals' hoops out'n grapevines. Dey give us a dime, if dey had one, fer a set of hoops."[39]

Sunday was church day; one had to dress appropriately. Thus, slaves who would not wear shoes during the week, if for no other reason than that they rarely fit properly, would commonly wear them to church. The more fastidious improvised a shoebrush or borrowed one from the Big House and shined their shoes with grease or a mixture of soot and syrup. When, as often happened, they had to walk long distances to church, they would carry their shoes and put them on before going in. Church was a place where you showed respect for God, for your brothers and sisters, for yourself. Often the slaves dressed better for church than did the yeomen whites.[40] Carrying the shoes rather than wearing them had a special significance for some. A black man carrying his shoes down a road on the Rice Coast of South Carolina was stopped by a curious white man, who asked why he did not put them on. "Well," he answered, "oonuh see dese duh me shoosh; me feet dem blonx tuh Maussah." (Well, you see, these shoes are mine; my feet belong to Master.)[41]

The dichotomy in the slaves' attitude toward their clothes puzzled Harriet Martineau: "The slave women cannot be taught, it is said, to cut out even their scanty and unshapely garments economically. Nothing can be more hideous than their working costume."[42] Yet, these same slave women took the trouble to learn to make starch so as to look pretty on Sunday, which belonged to the Lord—and therefore to His people, to themselves.[43] And not only did they dress up on Sundays; they dressed up for their Saturday night and holiday parties. To these they went, as one put it, "dressed to death."[44] These parties, like their religious meetings, belonged to them, not to their masters. They represented their own time, which meant a time to be together. An old Gullah preacher understood the dichotomy in the slaves' attitude and appealed to their pride:

> An dem man, dat is man, lub fur be clean, an look nice demself wen Sunday come, an dat show dat yunner ooman is to keep yunner husban clode patch an wash. Das heaper lub in dat. Man lub to brag bout dem smaht wife.[45]

Masters and especially mistresses took great pleasure in passing their used clothing on to the slaves and understood this gift relationship as maintaining if not widening social distance. An ex-slave from Virginia recalled that every spring "Aunt Emma" would tote a big bundle of discarded clothes from the Big House to the quarters and watch the field women scurry to claim and trade off the various articles.[46] House slaves would get the choicest items, which might include lace, silks, petticoats, velvet waistcoats for the men, and almost anything that the master or mistress might wear; but the field slaves also sometimes got a share of these.[47]

Often the masters would buy "Sunday clothes" for their slaves, to be distributed at Christmas and sometimes again at lay-by or some other midyear holiday. Martha Bradley, who had been a field hand in Alabama, said of these dresses and shoes, "We'd sho' be proud of 'em."[48] Before long, the slaves began to translate these "gifts" into "rights" and to let their masters understand as much. Ingraham reported a conversation between slave and mistress:

> "Missus, you promise me a Chrismus gif'."
> "Well, Jane, there is a new calico frock for you."
> "It werry pretty, missus, but me prefer muslin, if you please; muslin de fashion dis Chrismus."
> "Very well, Jane, call to-morrow and you shall have a muslin."[49]

But much of the slaves' special clothing came through their own effort. They spent much of their earnings from garden plots or bonus work in this manner. They also made their own "fine" clothes when they could and made or bought buttons to decorate their clothing. Nancy Williams, who had been a field slave in Virginia, boasted: "Clothes, chile, I done had plenty clothes in slavery days. Christmas time used to wear sometimes three or four different dresses de same day. How I git money to buy clothes? Used to quilt de prettiest quilts you ever see. . . . Used to sell 'em to de white folks; de best ones Missus hers'f would buy."[50] Whites always complained loudly that the slaves "threw away" the money they earned from their garden plots on finery and baubles, and a field hand in Alabama complained that he would never marry because the women demanded too much effort to keep them well dressed.[51]

The Lord's people wore red:

> Who is that yonder all dressed in red?
> I heard the angels singin'.
> It looks like the children Moses led,
> I heard the angels singin'.[52]

Both males and females greatly preferred red articles of clothing to those of any other color. Cureton Milling, an ex-slave from

South Carolina, remarked, rather perversely: "Then came Hampton and de Red Shirts. Had they a black shirt I don't believe niggers would ever have took to it. 'Dog for bread, nigger for red,' they likes dat color."[53]

The origins of the preference remain obscure but may have been African. So strongly did the West Africans enjoy red that among southern as well Caribbean slaves the legend grew that it had betrayed them into slavery by laying them open to white deception.[54] Red served as the royal color at Ardra, one of the great African centers of those religious rites which became voodoo in the New World, and it continued to serve similar purposes in the United States as well as Haiti. Theories vary, but the African attitude has plausibly been interpreted as an identification of red with life and fertility. As the color of blood it is made to represent the birth process for women and the roles of warrior and hunter for men.[55]

Masters and mistresses would buy or make red articles for the slaves from time to time, but the field hands could not depend on occasional handouts. They learned to make and use dyes. When, for example, the slaves received white jeans and shirts, they would dye them tan, gray, or red, according to whether they intended them for work or for Sunday dress. They used walnut, elm, cherry, and red oak in various combinations to make red dye, cedar moss to make yellow dye, and walnut alone to make brown. They usually had to do this work on their own time. They did it willingly as a matter of pride, "to look nice" on special occasions.[56]

A curious historical irony surrounds the use of headkerchiefs or bandannas. Carried into the twentieth century in the rural South, it became a mark of servility, of Aunt Jemimaism, of everything to be exorcised, so far as militant blacks were concerned. The headkerchief became the mark of that "old-time Negro," whose gradual passing has always brought tears of nostalgia and regret to the eyes of racist whites. Yet originally, nothing so clearly signified African origins and personal pride. That whites transformed it into a badge of servility merely provides one more indication of how people with physical power over others can, to their own satisfaction, transform anything into a badge of servility. The willingness of whites to view the slaves' headkerchiefs with pleasure and of later blacks to view them with distaste stemmed, in large measure, from their association with house slaves and especially with plantation Mammies. The Mammies of the South Carolina low country marked their status by wearing white turbans, and the house slaves more generally by wearing brightly colored, tastefully wound headkerchiefs. But throughout the South even the field women would wear them when they could. In some areas, headkerchiefs became the sign of a married woman.[57] The custom of wearing those headkerchiefs originated in Africa and appeared most strongly in those areas of the New World in which African values retained their greatest strength—the same areas, in some cases, in which revolutionary resistance to slavery had been most pronounced and successful.[58]

As in many other class-bound and caste-bound societies, the ruling class understood the importance of dress as an index of social position.[59] South Carolina's slave code of 1740 strictly regulated dress. Except for livery, which rated as properly servile, slaves were to wear only coarse clothing. The authorities never enforced the law; the planters ignored it; and in the 1840s Judge John Belton O'Neall pronounced it unenforceable and worthy only of repeal.[60] So determined were the slaves to assert themselves and so indulgent were many masters that only reformers and other self-appointed guardians of the public morals could be naive enough to try to set things right. Their biggest attempt had fallen flat in 1822, when the famous "Memorial of the Citizens of Charleston," sent to the legislature in the wake of the Denmark Vesey plot, had declared:

> Your memorialists also recommend to the Legislature to prescribe the mode in which our persons of color shall dress. [These leading citizens apparently did not know that such a law had been on the books for eighty-two years.] Their apparel has become so expensive as to tempt the slaves to dishonesty; to give them ideas not consistent with their condition; to render them insolent to whites, and so fond of parade and show as to cause it extremely difficult to keep them at home.[61]

Cooler heads continued to prevail, no doubt in large part because the slaveholders thought the slaves' fancy dress rather comical and decided that it marked inferiority as well as anything else.[62] Historians have been too quick to agree. "The exaggerated importance given to fine clothing was a natural reaction of the slaves to the general deprivations inherent in bondage," writes Edgar J.

McManus. "Slaves obtained in expensive attire an illusion of importance that their real condition denied them." He adds that finery contributed to the slaves' "mean and frivolous" view of themselves.[63] This view contains too much truth to be disregarded, but it is a partial and ultimately misleading truth. When slaves came off the auction block and settled in a new plantation, they discarded their clothes and expected to receive others which had no association with their sale.[64] In so doing, they taught something. Those who see only servility and self-degradation in the slaves' concern for clothes and their quest for fancy clothing might reflect on those ridiculous Russian workers whom Gorky describes in his novel *Mother*. Regardless of the weather, they would wear rubbers and carry umbrellas on their Sunday promenades. Those who view this behavior as a sign of self-deception and self-degradation might remember that these poor deluded, degraded, and benumbed creatures shortly thereafter executed the Tsar of All the Russias and turned the world upside down.

Sidney Andrews, visiting North Carolina in 1865 and reporting that the black women rushed to fancify their dress, quoted a white lady in Salisbury as saying in disgust, "The chief ambition of a wench seems to be to wear a veil and carry a parasol." To which another furious matron added, "The nasty niggers must have a parasol when they ha'nt got no shoes." Andrews himself commented: "Does this matter of veils and parasols and handkerchiefs seem a small one? Yet it is one of serious import to the bitter, spiteful women whose passionate hearts nursed the Rebellion."[65] The white ladies may have been bitter—they may even have been spiteful—but they understood a bid for equality when they saw one. The poor whites who made up the hated patrols understood too. Why else would they have spit tobacco juice on the Sunday clothes of an inoffensive slave?[66]

The bid by the freedwomen could never have occurred had it not had roots in a long, if often pathetically manifested, struggle for dignity. The Charleston Memorialists of 1822 had been right: there was something impudent, and therefore subversive, about the slaves' finery. But that something would have had only limited significance if it had been confined to an urge to imitate or rival white dress. Its more important meaning emerges from the slaves' insistence on dressing up for church and for plantation parties. In those instances they demonstrated respect for their brothers and sisters and therefore that self-respect without which respect for others is impossible. During the week they belonged to Ole Massa;

what they looked like was of little importance. On Saturday night and Sunday, among themselves, they asserted themselves as proud men and women.

READING, WRITING, AND PROSPECTS

"From any point of the exegetical compass," exclaimed a Jesuit father who opposed making the Bible available to Chinese peasants, "a Chinaman can find his way up to the great rice problem."[1] When, during the seventeenth century, the Puritans asserted that learning meant power and pushed forward one of the most fateful of cultural revolutions, English conservatives reacted with horror. An appeal to Scripture, the men of order pointed out, could not be separated from an appeal to conscience, for men can always find an appropriate text to justify their wishes.[2] A president of the Royal Society spoke out against education for the working class in plain terms:

> However specious in theory the project might be, of giving education to the labouring classes of the poor, it would in effect be found to be prejudicial to their morals and happiness; it would teach them to despise their lot in life, instead of making them good servants in agriculture, and other laborious employments to which their rank in society had destined them; instead of teaching them subordination, it would render them fractious and refractory. . . .It would enable them to read seditious pamphlets, and. . .would render them insolent to their superiors. . . .[3]

The slaveholders understood the issue. The laws against teaching slaves to read and write grew out of a variety of fears, the simplest of which concerned the forging of passes by potential runaways. The argument expressed with greatest agitation concerned the dangers of incendiary literature. Proslavery ideologues like Chancellor Harper and J. H. Hammond of South Carolina thought that only madmen would risk having their slaves read abolitionist pamphlets. But each carried the argument further. Hammond pointed out that even the Catholic Church had long denied the Scriptures to the ignorant and impressionable—quite an argument from a Protestant—and Harper, with greater restraint, added, "The slave receives such instruction as qualifies him for his particular station." In a similar vein Judge Lumpkin of the Supreme Court of Georgia spoke out in favor of the repressive laws: "These severe restrictions. . .have my hearty and cordial approval. Everything must be interdicted which is calculated to render the slave discontented."[4] Perhaps these gentlemen had a point. Michele Caruso, the popular Italian shepherd-bandit, at Benevento in 1863, cried out to his captors in accents of the dispossessed of the earth: "Ah, gentlemen, if I had been able to read and write, I'd have destroyed the human race."[5]

Even in colonial times powerful opposition to slave literacy arose among slaveholders in an attempt to prevent the forging of passes but also to head off insurrection or at least to weaken any prospective insurrectionary leadership. South Carolina and Georgia pioneered in repressive legislation during the middle of the eighteenth century. Despite periods of modest liberalization, the restrictions grew worse over time. Local ordinances supplemented state laws; in some places it became a crime merely to sell writing materials to slaves.[6] The Nat Turner revolt completed the reactionary course in the Lower South and influenced the Upper South as well. Alabama's harsh legislation grew directly out of the postinsurrectionary panic of 1831–1832. In Arkansas and Tennessee the legislatures resisted the exponents of legal repression, but public opinion had so hardened that the actual opportunities for slaves to learn had probably decreased as much as elsewhere. Kentucky also held out, and, possibly, public opinion remained calmer and opportunities more available. Missouri caught up with the Lower South in the late 1840s, when ideological lines were being drawn across the nation.[7] The specific reasons for the reaction notwithstanding, Josiah Henson expressed the more general reason in his reflections on having eventually learned to read:

> It was, and has been ever since, a great comfort to me to have made this acquisition; though it has made me comprehend better the terrible abyss of ignorance in which I had been plunged all my previous life. It made me also feel more deeply and bitterly the oppression under which I had toiled and groaned; but the crushing and cruel nature of which I had not appreciated, till I found out, in some slight degree, from what I had been debarred. At the same time it made me more anxious than before to do something for the rescue and the

elevation of those who were suffering the same evils I had endured, and who did not know how degraded and ignorant they really were.[8]

The estimate by W.E.B. Du Bois that, despite prohibitions and negative public opinion, about 5 percent of the slaves had learned to read by 1860 is entirely plausible and may even be too low.[9] Undoubtedly, most of the literate slaves lived in the towns and cities or had worked in them for some time. Towns and cities provided a friendlier climate, not so much because of a more liberal white public opinion as because of the favorable opportunities that local condtions opened up to black initiatives. Free Negroes and literate slaves had some space to teach others, even at the risk of punishment. Black efforts appear to have been more important than white in this respect, although some whites, either out of a sense of duty or for pecuniary gain, conducted illegal schools.[10]

The least advance in literacy in the countryside undoubtedly occurred on the large plantations of the Black Belt, for both law and a hostile public opinion operated there with the greatest force and effectiveness. Yet, literate slaves appeared everywhere, no matter how unfavorable the atmosphere. Slaveholders, travelers, and ex-slaves agreed that many plantations had one or more literate slaves and that any given locality had some. Thus, the most restricted and isolated plantation slaves normally had contact with some who could transmit information about the wider world, and who were probably responsible for the rapid spread of political news among the slaves, especially just before and during the war. Each of these disparate historical sources contains the observation that the blacks had a much greater desire to learn than the poor whites or even the solid yeomen.[11]

How did the country slaves learn? Who taught them? The most obvious part of the answer came from the slaveholders, who, as usual, took full credit. Throughout the South some masters, more mistresses, and even more white children scoffed at the law, which was unenforceable on the plantations anyway, and instructed a favorite or two or some other slave who persisted in the demand.[12] Ex-slaves tell of masters who would teach mulatto children but not black, or house slaves but not field hands, but these distinctions did not prevail. House slaves received more attention because of their greater intimacy with the whites, but most of the masters' efforts went to the children, who rarely were segregated according to the status of their parents. A master or mistress who felt it a duty to teach the slaves generally taught those for whom he or she had time or whose determination had become apparent. The greatest effort seems to have come from the white children, who often disobeyed their parents' orders and taught their black playmates. These efforts proceeded within narrow limits, but without them the slaves' lot would have been infinitely harder. The slaves' own attempts to teach each other had to begin with an opportunity created by some friendly white person.[13] The impulses among the whites varied from those of interest, such as that of a young master who said the law could go to hell since he simply had to have someone literate among the slaves, to those of conscience, such as that suggested in 1860 by a mistress who had failed in her perceived duty. "This teaching of Negroes," she wrote, "is a sore problem to me! It ought to be done and I ought to do it. . . .My difficulties I am convinced beset many a well-intentioned mistress who, like me, does nothing because she cannot do what she feels she *ought*."[14]

This occasional white support would have come to naught had the slaves not responded to the opportunity and had they not used their acquired skill to teach others. Elijah P. Marrs recalled an old plantation slave who had taught others after ten o'clock at night. Sometimes a literate slave taught others with his master's permission, more often without it. An old black preacher in Georgia moaned on his dying bed that he had caused the death of many slaves by teaching them to read and write. More commonly, slave children who had to carry the books of the white children to school would sit outside, listen, and try to keep up with the lessons. Here and there a slave such as George Teamoh of Virginia, or the one met by Dennett after the war, or the one Edmund Carlisle, himself an ex-slave from South Carolina, recalled as "the smartest nigger I is ever seed," taught themselves to read by sheer act of will.[15]

Dr. Du Bois observed: "There is no doubt but that the thirst of the black man for knowledge—a thirst which has been too persistent and durable to be mere curiosity or whim—gave birth to the public free-school system of the South. It was the question upon which black voters and legislators insisted more than anything else. . . ."[16] Sidney Andrews made the point in 1865 when he visited a freedmen's convention in North Carolina and expressed surprise at the seriousness of the delegates. Freedom of labor remained uppermost in their minds, but no more so than the education of their people. He contrasted sharply the indifference of the yeomen whites to the education of their children with the passion of the blacks. Writing later from Georgia, he continued:

However poor or ignorant or unclean, or improvident he may be, I never yet found a negro who had not at least a vague desire for a better condition, an undefined longing for something called freedom, a shrewd instinct of self-preservation. These three ideas—or, let me say, shadows of ideas—do not make the creature a man, but they lift him out of the bounds of brutedom. The Georgia "cracker" . . . seems to me to lack not only all that the negro does, but also even the desire for a better condition and the vague longing for an enlargement of his liberties and his rights.[17]

The freedmen's efforts to educate themselves and their children provide one of the most moving chapters in American social history, and historians are finally giving it the attention it deserves. Northern white support played an important role, but the extent to which blacks with few resources and little experience scraped to pay for schools and teachers stands out like a miracle.[18] Escaped slaves like Susie King and free Negroes like Charlotte Forten did everything they could to teach the freedmen, and others, newly freed themselves, taught what little they knew to those who knew less. The desire for education everywhere exploded. For the freedmen, as for the slaves before them, it represented the Keys of the Kingdom.

The roots of black enthusiasm for education lay deep in the slave past. As early as the 1750s, Samuel Davies found the slaves eager pupils when he sought to teach them to read as part of his campaign to win converts.[19] The poignancy of the slaves' struggle for learning appeared everywhere. Fredrika Bremer found a young woman desperately trying to read the Bible. "Oh, this book," she cried out to Miss Bremer. "I turn and turn over its leaves, and I wish I understood what is on them. I try and try; I should be so happy if I could read, but I can not."[20] An ex-slave woman from Tennessee recalled: "I remember once I was hired out and I was trying to say my alphabets backward and forward by memory. I just cried because I couldn't say them backward from memory . . .but I could say them forward."[21] Among the bitterest recollections of ex-slaves were those of whippings for trying to learn to read. Few things so outraged their sense of justice. Dr. LeConte told Sir Charles Lyell that his black carpenter once came to him in great delight. He had determined that each side of a hexagon equaled the radius of a circle drawn around it. When LeConte told him that the "discovery" was common knowledge, he replied that, had he been taught it, he could have made great use of it in his work.[22] This attitude, less dramatically manifested, inspired many slaves and guaranteed that, in George Brown Tindall's words, "Even behind the façade of slavery, a Negro leadership was developing."[23]

These herculean, if exceptional, efforts by people with little leisure and less encouragement provide the context for Susan Dabney Smedes's smug but typical assertion: "Some of the sons taught those of the plantation negroes who cared to learn, but very few were willing to take the trouble to study." Even so, she recalled some successful scholars, five of whom went on to become preachers.[24] Fanny Kemble saw things differently: "If they are incapable of profiting by instruction, I do not see the necessity for laws inflicting heavy penalties on those who offer it to them. . . .We have no laws forbidding us to teach our dogs and horses as much as they can comprehend." The slaves, she added, would seize the chance to learn, and their masters knew it.[25] During the war Elizabeth Hyde Botume taunted some southern white women in the same manner when they insisted that the blacks were unteachable. Oh, they replied, we meant the country niggers. The house slaves, it seems, "were smart enough for anything."[26]

That more slaves did not perform heroically and kill themselves trying to grasp the mysteries of the book means little, for the conditions were appallingly difficult. The story lies with those who managed to do it. The obstacles did not all concern fatigue, limited cultural horizons, a lack of books and paper or of an available tutor. Beyond all these lurked another. Mrs. Kemble suggested to the son of a literate plantation slave that he ask his father to teach him to read. He answered "with a look and manner that went to my very heart. 'Missus, what for me learn to read? me have no prospect.' "[27]

DE BIG TIMES

Claims by the spokesmen of the regime that a majority of slaveholders worked their slaves only a half day on Saturday receive considerable support from plantation records and from the slave narratives. The fragmentary evidence suggests that a substantial number of slaves quit work sometime between late morning and 3 P.M. on Saturdays.[1] Even masters who worked their male slaves all day on Saturday usually let the women off early to do household chores. The women's domestic responsibilities, which included the week's washing and mending, were inescapable and entailed hard work. The men's comparable chores, hunting, fishing, working the garden, or earning extra money at odd jobs, could be more easily shirked. Many of the men, however, willingly shouldered these responsibilities.[2]

Law, custom, explosive white opinion, and slave resistance combined to prevent masters from working their slaves on Sunday. When planters needed work done on Sunday, they called for volunteers and paid them. During the sugar harvest the slaves sometimes had to work on Sunday or the crop would spoil, but they usually received compensation in the form of time off, extra holidays, or bonuses. Many masters and mistresses tried to make Sunday a pleasant day by teaching Sunday school, arranging for a preacher to visit, and visiting the quarters themselves. Others did the slaves an even bigger favor: they left them alone. Among the special touches provided by masters and mistresses to brighten the slaves' Sundays, the ex-slaves especially remembered the distribution of biscuits baked in the Big House or, alternatively, the distribution of flour so that the slaves could bake their own. Perhaps no single gesture by the masters went so far with the slaves, however trivial it might now seem.[3]

In addition to Sundays, part of Saturdays, and holidays, the slaves enjoyed free time and semifree time on rainy days. Unlike the slaves of the Caribbean and Brazil, who regularly worked in inclement weather, those of the Old South normally quit the fields when the rains came. "All hands idle," runs a typical notation in a plantation diary. "Rained in torrents last night and all day, with every prospect of it continuing all night. The whole plantation is submerged."[4] Although the average period of wet weather in the Cotton Belt rarely extended beyond five days, spring often brought thunderstorms and rains heavy enough to compel masters to pull their slaves out of the fields.[5] Ingraham noted that in the Natchez region rainy and snowy days averaged 78.6 per year.[6] With prevalent practices, a great many of these must have resulted in idle and semi-idle hands. The time was not wholly lost, and "idle" usually meant something less than the ordinary meaning of the word. Masters would direct the men to clean out their houses, shuck corn, repair tools, and cut firewood, and the women to make baskets and mats and to catch up on their sewing.[7] But with masters and overseers snugly indoors themselves and the assigned tasks not pressing, the slaves converted these frequent hours and days into occasions to gossip, sing, nap, and lounge around. Some masters preferred to avoid the pretense and inevitable frustration and simply sent the hands back to their cabins.[8] Occasionally, slaves had to work in the rain or acute cold. Olmsted made a surprising observation while in the lower Mississippi Valley: "Only once did I see a gang which had been allowed to discontinue its work on account of the rain." And Rosa Washington, an ex-slave from Louisiana, told of a particularly mean overseer who made the hands keep working in the rain.[9] Some masters tried, with doubtful success, to get some night work out of the slaves to compensate for time lost on rainy days, and others tried to get some work done on rainy days by building sheds in the fields.[10]

For the most part, masters resigned themselves to giving their slaves time off, or at best, to getting a little indoor work done. They accepted the judgment of their physicians that exposure would result in much more loss of time and money through sickness and death than could be compensated for by extra field work; and the susceptibility of the slaves to pneumonia served as a constant reminder. "The Negroes must be kept as much as possible out of the rain," Andrew Flinn of Mississippi sternly ordered his overseer. "It is much better to lose some time than to run the risk of sickness and death."[11] M. W. Philips explained: "Negroes cannot bear the same exposure to wet and cold that whites can. . . . They require warmer clothing than whites, and better protection from the inclementness of winter."[12] The Reverend J. N. Pendleton of Tennessee claimed: "When I went North, nothing surprised me more than to see laborers at work in the rain and snow. In such weather, slaves in Kentucky and Tennessee would have been under shelter."[13]

The narratives of ex-slaves support these claims. Charley Williams of Louisiana recalled his master's deathbed cry: "I don't want my niggers working in the rain. Go down to the quarters and see they all dried off good. They ain't got no sense, but they all good niggers."[14] Andrew Goodman insisted that his master "didn't never put the niggers out in bad weather. He give us somethin' to do, in out of the weather, like shellin' corn and the women could spin and knit."[15] Ex-slaves, with the partial exception of those who had worked in the sugar and rice fields, reported either being idle in rainy weather or working indoors on light tasks.[16] Not all the credit goes to the humanity and wise self-interest of the slaveholders, for the slaves had something to say about their working conditions. An overseer complained in 1857 that the only way he could have gotten his hands to work in the rain would have been to stand out there himself and watch them every minute.[17] The slaves had assimilated one more "privilege" to their notion of "rights."

All except the most unfeeling masters threw Saturday night parties for their slaves once in a while. Even those who normally worked their slaves a full day on Saturday would release them early to get cleaned up. On some plantations these parties came every Saturday night, although in such cases the master's material contribution may have been slight.[18] Most masters contributed some whiskey and a hog or chickens for a barbecue and left the slaves alone to enjoy themselves; but others meddled. Whites who attended these black social events expected gratitude in return for their generous offer to play chaperone. The presence of older whites provided only a minor irritant in most cases and occasionally even some pleasure despite its condescension.[19] Here and there white presumption extended to organizing and directing these events and even to using them for self-amusement by arranging to have the blacks fight each other in gladiator style.[20]

The mature whites usually looked on and enjoyed themselves vicariously, but the younger ones sometimes made trouble. Those "white sports," as one ex-slave called them, crashed the slave parties and danced with the prettiest black girls, with predictable if well-controlled reactions from the slaves themselves. Frank Adamson of South Carolina recalled having had a good master but complained that his sons would "mix in wid de 'fairs of slave 'musements." Sometimes slaves welcomed the arrival of whites who wanted to join in the singing and dancing, but more often they resented it.[21]

On a number of plantations the slaves abruptly quit having dances when they got religion. The proscription drove some of the younger men into such alternative amusements as gambling and carousing, but most of the slaves spent more time in the praise-houses, where they replaced their secular dancing with the ring shout. By the 1850s any large plantation would have at least a few slaves whose conversion had led them to give up dancing as sinful.[22] The slaves created the occasion for Saturday night parties when they wanted to. Some planter in the neighborhood likely had given permission for one, and slaves from the area flocked in with or without passes.

The slaves enjoyed the illicit parties most of all. Lack of permission meant lack of supervision and interference, except from a patrol that might appear to break up the evening's fun. Masters generally imposed a nine o'clock curfew; some even tried to enforce an eight o'clock curfew during the winter months. But the overseers rarely bothered to check more than once, so the slaves simply had to bide their time and slip out later in the evening. When, as often happened, the drivers had responsibility for checking and when they too wanted to join the party or prayer meeting, only the unexpected intervention of a patrol was likely to spoil the night.

Masters allowed Saturday night parties in the particular hope of keeping the slaves home during the week, and some of the bigger slaveholders built recreation halls to accommodate the festivities.[23] Only the most unfeeling resented their slaves' having fun on the night before their day off. The real problem lay elsewhere: in the penchant of the slaves for impromptu partying during the week. Josiah Henson was not stargazing when he observed: "Ours is a light-hearted race. The sternest and most covetous master cannot frighten or whip the fun out of us."[24] However many of the older slaves settled in with their families around a fire at night or fell asleep after a day in the fields, the younger ones flew out to have a good time. A master who allowed a weekend party could keep the week-night excursions down to manageable proportions, but he had a constant struggle.

The slaveholders brooded over the unreasonableness of their slaves, who preferred to party and court when they ought to have been resting up for the next day's labor. W. W. Gilmer of Virginia suggested that the slaves had to be made to work hard or "they become restive, run about at night for want of exercise in the day, to pilfer, and visit, hear the news, etc. etc." He sputtered, "Adams & Co.'s Express can't beat them in the transmission of all sorts of reports; they travel from ten to thirty miles in a night, and many it seems do with less sleep than almost any other animal."[25] Slaves who worked listlessly through the day and complained of impossible demands on their strength miraculously came to life and walked eight or ten miles to dance all night on a neighboring plantation. Some planters caustically suggested that their slaves did not need to sleep at night since they had mastered the art of sleeping at work during the day.[26] (Ex-GIs who mastered the art of executing close-order drill while being more asleep than awake will testify that it can be done.) One way or another, the slaves found the energy to have a good time whenever the opportunity arose.

If a master did not magnanimously offer a hog or some chickens for the preparty supper, the slaves would help themselves anyway. When discovered by their master or overseer, the slaves took their punishment without much rancor; they considered a good party cheap at the price. As Charles Grandy of Virginia explained:

> Might whip us de nex' day, but we done had our dance. Stay as late as we want—don't care ef we is got to be in de field at sunrise. When de dance break up we go out, slam de do' ef we wants, an' shout back at de man what had de party:
>
> > "Eat yo' meat an' chaw yo bone,
> > Goodbye, Charlie, I'se gwine home."[27]

Masters could not hope to prevent interplantation visiting unless they owned, say, more than fifty slaves on a single place, and even then they had their hands full. However much they might rail against the ostensibly demoralizing effects that contact with other slaves had on their own, all except a few found it impossible to prevent intercourse. David Gavin might complain that his people became "very impudent" when away from his plantation. B. McBride might thunder, "All intercourse with negroes of other plantations is strictly forbidden." And the agricultural journals could pontificate on the joys of splendid isolation and the evils of interplantation partying. In the end the slaves, especially those of courting age, slipped off to see their friends and join a barbecue or dance, authorized or not, on some neighboring plantation. Judge Bay of South Carolina remarked from the bench, "The strictest watching could not at times prevent them from visiting their acquaintances. . . ."[28] From the seventeenth century onward, masters especially exploded at the incredible impertinence of slaves who would appropriate plantation horses for transportation to unauthorized meetings.[29]

Singing and dancing marked the parties, but the musical instruments were not easily come by. The slaves had to make their own or find ways of doing without. Sometimes they got a fiddle or banjo from a solicitous master or bought one with the earnings from their gardens or extra work. More often, they had to improvise. With little or no opportunity to secure professional training, they needed technically simple instruments that could be handled and carried easily. The slaves made an assortment of instruments, including many of the fiddles and banjos so often in evidence at their parties.[30] They made stringed instruments out of horsehair, animal skin or bladders, and gourds, and percussion instruments out of tin pans, logs, and other available items. As Wash Wilson recalled:

> There wasn't no musical instruments. Us take pieces of sheep's rib or cow's jaw or a piece of iron, with an old kettle or a hollow gourd and some horsehair to make the drum. Sometimes they'd git a piece of tree trunk and hollow it out and stretch a goat's or sheep's skin over it for the drum. . . . They'd take the buffalo horn and scrape it out to make the flute.[31]

With instruments scarce and good players tired out during a long night, the slaves would use their feet to work up a tune. Their coordinated foot tapping did what instruments would normally be expected to. Much of their dancing consisted of "patting juba," in which they sang as they danced:

> Juba this and Juba that.
> Juba killed a yaller cat.
> Juba this and Juba that.
> Hold your partner where you at.[32]

The favorite dances included "Cuttin' the Pigeon Wings," in which the dancers flapped their arms while holding their necks stiff; "Going to the East and Going to the West," in which the less inhibited kissed without wrapping arms; and "Set de Flo'," which couples did in turn by facing each other and bowing while "patting" the floor in place. Individual contests featured those who could dance with a glass of water on their head. Betty Jones told of "Settin' de Flo' with Jenny"—"Jenny" being code for the dance, the dancer, the unauthorized party, the spirit of the occasion, or all four.

> Every gal with her beau and such music! Had two fiddles, two tangerines, two banjos, and two sets of bones. Was a boy named Joe who used to whistle, too. Them devilish boys would get out in the

middle of the flo' and me, Jenny and the devil right with 'em. Set a glass of water on my head and the boys would bet on it. I had a great wreath roun' my head an' a big ribbon bow on each side, and didn't waste a drop of water on none of 'em.[33]

A white woman who spent eight years in the South with her daughter and son-in-law, an Episcopal minister, finally managed to attend one of these occasions. She described a substantial supper and dance that ran well into the night: "There were so many huddled together in a small room that it was impossible for more than two couples to dance at once. . . . After dancing a short time they began a play so that more could participate, and all joined in singing."[34] Fanny Berry of Virginia gave a description of "Set de Flo'" after making a spirited case for the high moral standards of the slaves' dancing:

> Wasn't none of this sinful dancin' where yo' partner off wid man an' woman squeezed up close to one another. Danced 'spectable, de slaves did, shiftin' round from one partner to 'nother an' holdin' one 'nother out at arm's length. . . . De couples would do dat in turn. Dey come up an' bend over toward each other at de waist, an' de woman put her hands on her hips an' de man roll his eyes all roun' an' grin an' dey pat de flo' wid dey feet jus' like dey was puttin' it in place. Used to do dat bes' on de dirt flo' so de feet could slap down hard against it. Sometimes dey would set de flo' alone—either a man or a woman. Den dey would set a glass of water on dey haid an' see how many kinds of steps dey could make widout spillin' de water.[35]

These parties and dances, or "balls" as the slaves called the more elaborate ones, provided a series of warm-ups for "de big times" —the holidays.

The slaves made the Christmas holidays a time of joy. Even harsh masters usually provided a three-day holiday at Christmas. A few especially brutal ones gave only one or two days, but they were outnumbered by those who gave a longer holiday than the average—five days, a week, or even more. In some cases the length of the holiday depended on the burning of a log, with the slaves scurrying about to find the largest and slowest-burning candidate. If the weather was bad anyway or the work well under control, masters took the opportunity to display their benevolence by extending the holiday.[36] The weather favored the slaves. Although late December in the Deep South can be mild, it is often raw, rainy, cold, and a poor time for work on crops. Slaveholders saw a chance to enlist the aid of their slaves in cleaning up the plantations, for the coming of Christmas provided incentive enough to get things in proper order.[37]

Few masters punished slaves by depriving them of their Christmas holiday, but the threat of deprivation went a long way toward maintaining good plantation order during the previous month or two. On the few occasions when a slave did lose his holiday—general cancellation rarely occurred—he regarded it as cruel and unusual punishment.[38]

However long the holiday, it featured constant partying, with the plantation Christmas tree, studded with candles and gifts, serving as the center of the festivities. "It sho' was a picture of beautifulness," Junius Quattelbaum, who had been a slave in South Carolina, said of the tree, and others retained similar fond memories throughout their lives.[39] With three days or more available, the more considerate masters staggered the parties so that the slaves on a given plantation could entertain slaves from neighboring plantations and then be entertained in turn. The parties featured lavish barbecues, much whiskey, and all-night singing and dancing. The slaves of less considerate masters generally moved about freely and would be welcome guests at one party or another.[40]

The slaves made up for their customary sobriety during the Christmas holiday, when large numbers got roaring drunk, especially those who could go to nearby towns.[41] In addition to hard liquor the masters dispensed generous quantities of eggnog, which the white family prepared both for itself and the slaves, each of whom expected his or her "customary bowl" to mark the holiday.[42]

Masters generally gave all their slaves Christmas presents. Most preferred to give tobacco, ribbons, and other articles, but many distributed a little cash. Random observation of plantation accounts suggests that adult slaves got two and a half to three dollars each, with a dollar or so the floor and five dollars the ceiling.[43] In addition to cash presents many slaves acquired a little money at Christmas time by doing extra jobs or selling their chickens.[44] These sums, together with the produce of their gardens, allowed the slaves to give each other presents. In this setting, the master and mistress scored extra points by doling out extra food and clothing and playing Lord and Lady Bountiful.

In time the slaves took up the privileges of an extended holiday with barbecues and presents and claimed them as rights. Thomas C. Clemson of South Carolina wrote to John C. Calhoun that he simply could not afford to give his slaves a four-day holiday, but that his overseer had warned him that a four-day holiday was the custom and that his slaves had better get it. Throughout the South, and more widely throughout the hemisphere, the slaves claimed those arrangements sanctioned by local custom and generally got their way.[45]

The slaveholders tried to use these occasions to impose their own version of paternalism and to tighten their control. John Stainback Wilson wrote in 1860:

> Fourth of July, or laying-by-crop jubilee, should be observed on every Southern plantation; for apart from their health-promoting tendencies of cheerfulness . . . this festival may be made a powerful controlling power in the management of negroes, by having it understood that the dinner is a mere gratuity to be given or withheld according to merit or demerit. With the prospect of the "big dinner" ahead, they will be greatly animated and encouraged in their labors; and the fear of losing it will often be more more effective in keeping such childish and sensual creatures "straight" than the terrors of the rod itself.[46]

Marvelous thinking. But evidence that slaveholders in fact withheld these "privileges" cannot easily be found. To have withheld them in any except the most extreme instances of general insubordination would have invited the deepest resentment, sulking, disorder, and breakdown of morale and productivity. The slaves here as elsewhere had seized "rights."

For the slaves, as for the whites, Christmas Day belonged especially to the children. Masters and mistresses collected the black children with their own, played Santa Claus, told stories, and distributed presents. The memories of kindly Ole Massa that some slave children carried all their lives had strong roots in these moments, when he dressed as Santa Claus and handed out the goodies to the happy cries of "Christmas gif'!" Prince Johnson of Yazoo, Mississippi, recalled:

> Christmas was de time o' all times on dat old plantation. Dey don' have no such as dat now. Every child brought a stockin' up to de Big House to be filled. Dey all wanted one o' de mistis' stockin's, 'cause now she weighed nigh on to three hundred pounds. Candy and

presents was put in piles for everyone. When de names was called dey walked up and got it.

And Junius Quattelbaum of South Carolina added more extravagantly:

> Christmas mornin', marster would call all de slaves to come to de Christmas tree. He made all de chillun set down close to de tree and de grown slaves jined hands and make a circle 'round all. Then marster and missus would give de chillun deir gifts, fust, then they would take presents from de tree and call one slave at a time to step out and git deirs. After all de presents was give out, missus would stand in de middle of de ring and raise her hand and bow her head in silent thanks to God. All de slaves done lak her done. After all dis, everybody was happy, singin' and laughin' all over de place. Go 'way from here, white man! Don't tell me dat wasn't de next step to heaven to de slaves on our plantation. I sees and dreams 'bout them good old times, back yonder, to dis day.[47]

The children capped the day by exploding firecrackers, which they made by blowing up hog bladders, tying them tight, and popping them in the flames.[48]

The slaves enjoyed a New Year's Day as a special holiday within the Christmas holiday, although they sometimes had to celebrate it on December 27 or 28. "The hands as usual came to greet the New Year with their good wishes," wrote a planter in Louisiana, "[and] the scene is well calculated to excite sympathies: notwithstanding bondage, affections find roots in the heart of the slave for the master."[49] For many slaves, however, January 1 brought the holiday season to a grim close, for those hired out had to bid friends and families farewell as they left to take up their duties for the coming year. The slaves often called New Year's Day "heart-break day."[50]

The slaves also enjoyed other holidays. Those masters who celebrated Thanksgiving—a substantial but undetermined number—gave their slaves a holiday too, and many others gave their slaves Easter Monday if the work schedule permitted.[51] When the slaves laid by the crops they usually got a day off and a big barbecue, and most masters would declare an impromptu holiday once in a while during the slack season. Masters and slaves looked forward to these occasions as a kind of one-day, midyear opportunity to relax and have a good time separately and together.[52] "De han's," recalled William Henry Towns, an ex-slave from Alabama, "celebrated ever' holiday dat deir white folks celebrated."[53] On occasion even a slave's birthday called forth a celebration.[54]

The blacks benefitted from the whites' fondness for parties and holidays. As Johann David Schoepf grumpily remarked when in Virginia, "No people can be so greedy after holidays as the whites and blacks here, and none with less reason, for at no time do they work so much as to need a long rest."[55] The slaves merrily played upon their masters' whims. Did Ole Massa or Ole Missus or Li'l Missy have a birthday? Their own black family could not let the day pass without a barbecue to mark it. Did Ole Massa return from a trip? His own black folks could not fail to honor him by taking a half day off to shake hands, toast his health, and sing and dance for his very own pleasure. Was a member of the white family getting married or having a baby? Certainly not without a big time from their loving darkies who, after all, lived only for the white folks' pleasure.[56]

The Fourth of July provided another occasion for a big barbecue and the gathering of slaves from various plantations. When the Fourth coincided with lay-by the slaves usually got the day itself. When it did not and they had to work, masters might throw a big party on the nearest weekend.[57] The slaves looked forward to it with special excitement as "de biggest day to blacks and whites."[58] The Fourth, however, had unusual characteristics, for it often gave the slaves access to political speeches not suited to their condition. Words and phrases like "freedom," "independence," "revolution," and "death to tyrants" did not escape their ears.

These holidays, especially the extended Christmas holiday, have lent themselves to different interpretations. The harshest judgment came from Frederick Douglass. He began by describing the almost total cessation of work and the gathering of families and friends, including those who had been hired away all year. Some slaves, he noted, hunted game or worked their gardens, but most simply frolicked. The masters, he thought, encouraged drunkenness and uninhibited displays. "I believe," he wrote, "those holidays were among the most effective means in the hands of the slaveholders of keeping down the spirit of insurrection among the slaves." They kept the slaves' minds on such immediate pleasures as eating, drinking, courting, singing, dancing, and playing. "But for these," he concluded, "the rigors of bondage would have become too severe for endurance, and the slave would have been forced to a dangerous desperation."[59]

Supporting evidence for Douglass's view comes from a variety of sources. John Pierpont of Boston, who spent a brief period of his youth as a tutor on the William Allston plantation in South Carolina, left a description of a Christmas celebration that illustrates, in its own way, Douglass's argument. Pierpont's account takes on special significance because he had no fondness for slavery and soon declared himself a firm abolitionist.

> *Dec. 25th, Christmas*—Throughout the state of South Carolina, Christmas is a holiday, together with 2 of the succeeding days . . . especially for the negroes. On these days the chains of slavery with which the blacks are loaded and in which they toil unceasingly for their masters, are loosed. A smile is seen on every countenance, and the miseries of the year seem amply recompensed by this season of hilarity and festivity. No restraint is imposed upon their inclinations, no lash calls their attention from the enjoyment of all those delights which the most unconstrained freedom profers [*sic*]. Children visit their parents; husbands, their wives; brothers & sisters each other, who live at a distance. . . . On The morning of Christmas, Col. Alston gave orders that as many beeves might be butchered as to supply all with meat, which as a general thing is not allow'd them. No less than 21 bullocks fell sacrifices to the festivity. On my first waking, the sound of the serenading violin and drum saluted my ears, and for some time continued to prove that no mind is below feeling the powerful effects of music. *Merry Christmas* met me at every corner, and sounded in my ears even in retirement. During almost the whole of the second and 3 afternoons, the portico was crowded with these dancers. . . . Some of them who were native Africans did not join the dance with the others but, by themselves gave us a specimen of the sports and amusements with which the benighted & uncivilized children of nature, divest themselves, before they become acquainted with the more refined & civilized amusements of life. Clapping their hands was their music and distorting their frames into the most unnatural figures and emiting the most hideous noises is their dancing. Jumping, running, and climbing trees was last recourse in the interval and the whole exhibited a scene which might more than compare with the bachannal feasts and amusements of antiquity. Their drink (Rum, sugar, & water) was prepared in large tubs of 2 or 3 pailfulls, and carried about them so that each one might drink his fill of the intoxicating and Lethean draught. Nor was this opportunity suffered to pass unimproved; many for a while forgot both their sorrows and their joys, their hopes and their fears, and proved "That Negroes like their masters will get drunk."[60]

An overseer stressed the whites' interest in the Christmas holiday as a means of social control when he reported to his employer: "I killed twenty-eight head of beef for the people's Christmas dinner. I can do more with them in this way that if all the hides of the cattle were made into lashes."[61] Writing of the slaves' leisure time in general, Francis de Castelnau complained in 1837:

> Nothing proves better the moral degradation of the negro than the joy and content he shows in the state of slavery. Draw near a plantation and the noisy outbursts of laughter that you hear there will make you forget the overseer who goes about with his huge whip. Then come the rest days and all the miseries of the week are forgotten in the wildest dances and the most ridiculous capers.[62]

Christmas in particular and the slaves' leisure time in general meant much more than social control to the masters, who found in them confirmation of their paternalistic claims to stewardship. John Nevitt of Adams County, Mississippi, noted his slaves' Christmas frolic and added, "[I] sat up untill 2 o'clock in the morning to keep order with them."[63] Many masters and mistresses took pleasure in giving up much of their own holiday to provide for their people in a manner that heightened their own self-esteem and sense of performing selfless service.[64] They then needed to take only one short step to express the typical wish, "If only the abolitionists could see how happy our people are . . ." Hiram B. Tibbetts of Louisiana wrote his brother, John, in 1848: "The idea of unhappiness would never enter the mind of any one witnessing their enjoyments. The truth is that negroes well situated on Plantations with kind masters & mistresses are the happiest beings on the face of the earth."[65] And "Foby" added: "During this *jubilee* it is difficult to say who is master. The servants are allowed the largest liberty."[66] Perhaps the clearest expression of where this line of thought could lead came from John N. Evans of West Feliciana Parish, Louisiana, who wrote to a fellow slaveholder:

> We have had a "right merrie" Christmas; and I do not know where I have seen such expression of content and happiness, as my negroes exhibited during the festival. Some of them seem to have their countenances perfectly set to an expression of good humor, and all of them meet me today with a smile and a "happy new year to you, master." I am much more reconciled to my condition as slave owner, when I see how cheerful and happy my fellow creatures can be in a state of servitude, how much I have it in my power to minister to

their happiness, and when I reflect that most of the evils of slavery neither result inevitably from it, nor as a consequence, nor are invited by the interest of the master, which is always in accordance with the welfare of his subjects.[67]

But Evans said more than he intended when he added that the abolitionists could not understand attitudes like his, "for they do not consider how much the sources of human pleasure are varied by education and habit."

Evans had glimpsed another side of the story, one which Douglass, the revolutionary, probably also glimpsed but on principle had to slight. The slaveholders were taking solace, not from the slaves' self-degradation, but from their irrepressible ability to find joy in life—even in slave life. That black achievement the slaveholders perverted for their own ends. Douglass was right in thinking that the holidays and good times undermined the revolutionary impulse of the slaves, but he was wrong, I believe, in thinking that the cause lay in the slaves' being trapped into triviality and self-degradation. Rather, it lay in the double sense of community inherent in these occasions, which the slaveholders more fully appreciated, however much they twisted the meaning into self-justification. The slaves developed a sense of community among themselves and, to a much lesser but still vital extent, a sense of community with their white folks. Thus, the holidays weakened the slaves' impulse to challenge the regime frontally while they contributed to an ability to create a healthy black community and to guarantee its survival.[68]

The slaves themselves saw these implications in their own way. Northup described in detail the huge barbecues, the reunion of families, the courting, and the fun, but he also noted the way the slaves cleaned up and took pride in themselves. "They are," he wrote, "different beings from what they are in the field; the temporary relaxation, the brief deliverance from fear, and from the lash, producing an entire metamorphosis in their appearance and demeanor."[69] Charley Hunt of Georgia added, "Anyway, dat one day on massa's place all am happy and forgits dey am slaves."[70] And Fannie Berry of Virginia recalled:

Slaves lived jus' fo' Christmas to come round. Start gittin' ready de fus snow fall. Commence to savin' nuts and apples, fixin' up party clothes, snitchin' lace and beads fum de big house. General celebratin' time, you see, 'cause husbands is comin' home an' families is gittin' 'nunited agin. Husbands hurry on home to see dey new babies. Ev'ybody happy.[71]

The slaves' ability to let themselves go expressed itself not only in their courting, dancing, drinking, and cavorting but in their satirical thrusts at the whites. Douglass himself recorded a memorable example:

The fiddling, dancing, and "jubilee beating" was carried on in all directions. The latter performance was strictly southern. It supplied the place of the violin or other musical instruments and was played so easily that almost every farm had its juba beater. The performer improvised as he beat the instrument, marking the words as he sang so as to have them fall pat with the movement of his hands. Once in a while among a mass of nonsense and wild frolic, a sharp hit was given to the meanness of the slaveholders. Take the following example:

> We raise de wheat,
> Dey gib us de corn;
> We bake de bread,
> Dey gib us de crust;
> We sif' de meal,
> Dey gib us de huss;
> We peel de meat,
> Dey gib us de skin;
> And dat's de way
> Dey take us in;
> We skim de pot,
> Dey gib us de liquor;
> And say dat's good enough for nigger.
> Walk over! Walk over!
> Your butter and de fat;
> Poor nigger, you can't git over dat!
> Walk over—[72]

A few other such songs have survived, along with hints of many others lost. Since the slaves did not sing them in front of whites the written record remained slim. Millie Williams, an ex-slave from Texas, recalled:

> Massa sleep in de feather bed,
> Nigger sleeps on de floor;
> When we'uns gits to Heaven,
> Dey'll be no slaves no mo'e.[73]

To which John Moore of Louisiana added:

> My old missus promise me
>   Shoo a la a day.
> When she die she set me free,
> Shoo a la a day.
> She live so long her head git bald,
>   Shoo a la a day.
> She give up de idea of dyin' a-tall,
>   Shoo a la a day.[74]

The slaves also turned their satire against themselves. They resorted to public ridicule and scandal in order to make lazy fellow slaves carry their share of the work, or to straighten out an errant husband or wife, or to curb the tongue of a scold or gossip. Their songs and jokes, designed to shame wrongdoers, provided their own means of social control for life in the quarters. Those means were neither pleasant nor harmless; they could in fact be cruel. But they were decidedly preferable to Ole Massa's whip.

The holidays, like the Saturday night parties, provided the occasion for the unleashing of satirical black storytelling and singing. In the South as in the Caribbean, Brazil, and elsewhere in the Americas, the slaves spun out folktales of weak creatures who outwitted oppressors and bullies by guile and trickery. In the Brer Rabbit stories, as in the Jamaican Anansi stories, the trickster, so reminiscent of African folklore, appeared everywhere.[75] The devices for lampooning the whites took extraordinarily clever forms. Here, a body servant who had accompanied his master to France vilified the French as a barbarous and ridiculous people; there, the slaves poured out scorn on the Irish in jokes that sent masters into fits of appreciative laughter. However the prejudices of the masters conspired to make these jokes acceptable, the slaves surely knew that Frenchmen and Irishmen are white and that blacks were not supposed to ridicule any whites.[76]

The forms appear to have had African origins, but they also no doubt arose from other sources. Ralph Ellison has pointed to the figure of the trickster in Elizabethan literature and throughout Western civilization, and the idea of "wearing a mask" before the oppressor loomed large, say, in Renaissance Italy.[77] Ellison says of the man behind the mask: "Nor is he so much a 'smart-man-playing-dumb' as a weak man who knows the nature of his oppressor's weakness. . . . Thus, the mask of meekness conceals the wisdom of one who has learned the secret of saying the 'yes' which accomplishes the expressive 'no.' "[78] Taking something from their African tradition and something from the traditions of the whites around them, the slaves created symbolic expressions that not only defended them against those who would denigrate them but also delivered no few direct blows of their own.

The masters saw as much. Along with their self-congratulations over the slaves' happiness and contentment, they uneasily reflected on the ambiguity and deception. In their own way they echoed Nietzsche's remark on what he called the superficiality of men: "It is their preservative instinct which teaches them to be flighty, lightsome, and false."[79] Hear the Reverend C. C. Jones:

> The Negroes are a distinct class in community and keep themselves very much *to themselves*. They are one thing before the whites, and another before their own color. Deception toward the former is characteristic of them, whether bond or free, throughout the whole United States. It is habit—a long established custom which descends from generation to generation.[80]

Hear J. S. Brisbane, president of the St. Andrews, Ashby, and Stone River Agricultural Association:

> Slaves are an impelling power; and if not properly directed will lead to failure. . . . Nothing but an early knowledge of their powers of evasion will allow us to detect their duplicity, and prevent us from becoming the dupes of their superior cunning, or sagacity in roguery, if you please, in our relative situations. It is their business to deceive us, and ours to detect the deceit.[81]

Hear an anonymous planter, writing in Ruffin's *Farmers' Register:*

> They soon ascertain the character of those in authority over them, their peculiarities of temperament and disposition, and frequently under the cloak of great stupidity, make dupes of the master and overseer. The most general defect in the character of the negro is hypocrisy; and this hypocrisy frequently makes him pretend to more ignorance than he possesses; and if his master treats him as a fool, he will be sure to act the fool's part. This is a very convenient trait, as it frequently serves as an apology for awkwardness and neglect of duty.[82]

The slaves' will to live with as much joy as possible guaranteed their spiritual as well as physical survival—their survival as a people as well as their survival as individuals—and it allowed them to establish a degree of dignity not always found in servile classes. The slaves' spirit transformed their lives into tragicomedy. They bore their adversity so well because they never ceased to laugh at themselves. And by laughing at themselves, they freed themselves to laugh at their masters. Through their satire and behind their masks, they asserted their rights as men and women to the fullness of the Lord's earth.

Oppressed peoples who can laugh at their oppressors contain within themselves a politically dangerous potential, but the weapons of popular culture also betray a conservative political bias. They direct criticism, as Douglass feared, into channels acceptable to the regime—acceptable because in themselves they pose no direct political threat and may even function as a safety valve for pent-up discontent. Their more dangerous content remains latent so long as the general conditions of life do not generate a crisis that heightens their critical thrust and points it to political terrain—a crisis that upsets the balance within the bitter-sweet laughter and liberates the anger behind the laughter. At those moments the oppressor's legitimacy, which the laughter ironically helps to authenticate by its very playfulness, suddenly faces challenge. The slaves' weapons of cultural defense, however, did not often contribute to a frontal assault on the regime, for the ingredients of insurrectionary confrontation rarely appeared. Their resistance to slavery remained indirect and defensive. But, the slaveholders' placid acceptance of the self-assertion implicit in the slaves' cultural life—their awareness of its political limits and its function as safety valve—never extended so far as to disguise completely a deep uneasiness.

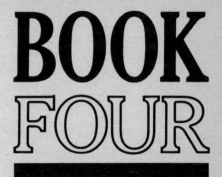

BOOK FOUR

WHOM GOD HATH HEDGED IN

Why is light given to a man whose way is hid, and whom God hath hedged in?

—Job 3:23

THE SLAVE REVOLTS

The slaves of the Old South, unlike those of the Caribbean and Brazil, did not take up arms often enough or in large enough numbers to forge a revolutionary tradition.[1] The southern slaves' role in shaping an organic master-slave relationship unfolded under objectively unfavorable military and political circumstances that compelled a different course. But those slaves who rejected the dialectic of accommodation and resistance at its root bore witness, by their rebellion, not only to their own personal courage but to the limits of their masters' hegemony.

More than any other scholar Herbert Aptheker, in his *American Negro Slave Revolts* and pioneering essays, has argued for a revolutionary tradition among the slaves. He demolished the legend of the contented slave, which Ulrich Bonnell Phillips especially promoted despite his own excellent work showing the opposite. Whatever Aptheker's exaggerations and doubtful evaluations, his careful analysis, sharpened by that passionate commitment to the struggle for black liberation which has informed his life's work, unearthed much evidence of insurrection, maroon activity, and other forms of physical resistance and compelled a new departure in the historiography. Kenneth M. Stampp's *Peculiar Institution*, which in 1956 delivered the *coup de grâce* to Phillips's more tendentious interpretations, could not so easily have swept the field had not Aptheker and a few others already cleared away so much rubbish. But in arguing for a revolutionary tradition from a slim evidential base, Aptheker drew attention away from the slaves' deeper cultural and social resistance and from the organic relationships inherent in the slaveholders' hegemony; he focused instead on forms of overt resistance that, while important in their own right, did not lay bare the essence of the slave experience. By no means unaware of those dimensions, he was among the first to follow W. E. B. Du Bois in pointing out their strength; but his choice of emphasis flowed from an empirical error and led to an incorrect theoretical assessment. Satisfied that he had discovered a revolutionary tradition, he missed the chance to apply his considerable professional talent and critical Marxist perspective to the problem of the weakness and limited extent of the revolts and to move the discussion toward a reconsideration of those preconditions for hemispheric slave revolt which can tell us so much about the general conditions of slave life. That problem remains.

The significance of the slave revolts in the United States lies neither in their frequency nor in their extent, but in their very existence as the ultimate manifestation of class war under the most unfavorable conditions. The resort to insurrection in the United States, especially when more than merely a violent outburst against vicious local conditions, provides a yardstick with which to measure the smoldering resentment of an enslaved people who normally had to find radically different forms of struggle. A Gabriel Prosser or a Nat Turner presents the opposite limiting case to the slavish personality delineated in Stanley Elkins's celebrated model. The slaves as a class cannot be understood apart from the combination of these two images, for every slave, being flesh and blood, necessarily had within him elements of both. The preponderance of the one over the other in their peculiar and innumerable combinations ultimately depended on the totality of social conditions.

Notwithstanding the occurrence of insurrections in the Old South that command attention, they did not compare in size, frequency, intensity, or general historical significance with those of the Caribbean or South America. The largest slave revolt in the United States took place in Louisiana in 1811 and involved between 300 and 500 slaves; it alone was comparable in size to those of the Caribbean—that is, comparable to the modest ones. Nat Turner had about 70 slaves with him. Gabriel Prosser and Denmark Vesey apparently expected to raise many more but never had the chance. Risings such as those of 25 or so in New York City in 1712 or of 50 to 100 at Stono, South Carolina, in 1739, although impressive in themselves, qualify as minor events in the general history of slave revolts in the Americas.

Consider the magnitude of a few lesser-known eighteenth-century revolts. In the almost successful insurrection of 1733 on the small island of St. John in the Danish West Indies, 150 slaves were directly implicated and so many others simultaneously slaughtered and punished as to suggest the participation of many more. Thirty years later an estimated 2,000 slaves rose in Berbice and claimed the lives of about 200 of the colony's 350 whites. A few years later 100 or so slaves rose once more. During the eighteenth century a series of slave revolts erupted in Venezuela, culminating in one of about 300 at Coro in 1795, and shook Spanish power. In the first half of the nineteenth century slave risings in Cuba, the heir to the ill-fated sugar boom on Saint-Domingue, featured many hundreds of slaves at a time.

Saint-Domingue aside, Jamaica and the Guianas stand out in the history of slave revolts during the eighteenth and nineteenth centuries. The reports and correspondence in the British Colonial Office demonstrate that the authorities frequently found themselves confronting not merely rebellion but large-scale war. Jamaican revolts varied greatly in size but averaged, according to Orlando Patterson, about 400 slave participants. The first serious revolt broke out in 1669 on a plantation in St. Dorothy's Parish. Several took place in the 1690s and marked virtually every year of the decade 1730–1740. Tacky's rebellion in 1760 numbered about 1,000 slaves. During the eighteenth century more than a dozen slave revolts matured in a contradictory relationship to the great maroon wars that threatened the foundations of white power. By the nineteenth century, when the Jamaican slaves moved into revolutionary action, which profoundly influenced the politics of abolition in England, they had a powerful tradition and body of experience to draw upon. Their movement peaked in the great Christmas rising of 1831.

Or consider the Guianas. The first slave revolt on record broke out on a plantation in Essequibo in 1731, when under the Dutch. As usually happened later, slave revolts in the Guianas centered on a single plantation and could be contained, if with difficulty. Between 1731 and the abolition of slavery at least eighteen revolts occurred in Essequibo, Berbice, and Demerara—present-day Guyana—exclusive of abortive risings and protracted and extensive maroon wars. That is, these colonies averaged one significant slave revolt per decade. In 1823 between 10,000 and 20,000 slaves on some fifty plantations rose in Demerara and almost tore it apart.

The British finally put a hard core of 700 slaves to flight, but only after 100 were dead, whether more or less than the number subsequently executed remains unclear. In sheer numbers and power the whole record of the slave revolts in the Old South did not equal this drama, much less that of Palmares or Saint-Domingue. Even little Barbados had one turn. On Easter Sunday in 1816 some sixty plantations felt the impact of a general rising that, in the words of one historian, "brought fire and pillage to a great part of the colony."

Brazilian slaves raised a number of major insurrections as well as sustaining guerrilla warfare from runaway or maroon colonies known as *quilombos*. For more than half a century a great *quilombo*, Palmares, waged war against the Dutch and Portuguese and at its peak housed an estimated 20,000 blacks. Some 3,000 blacks subsequently participated in the movement known as the Balaiada. Major risings took place during every century of the Brazilian slave regime.

The period 1807–1835 in Bahia opened with an abortive plot among Hausa and Mandinka blacks and closed with a primarily Yoruba rising. In the interim the Yoruba rose in 1809, the Hausa in 1814, blacks of undetermined origin in 1816, and the Yoruba and Fon in 1826 and 1830. The Bahian revolt of several hundred slaves and free Negroes in 1835 suggests the general conditions that encouraged the revolts of the whole period. Despite British pressure and treaty obligations, Brazil continued to import Africans, whose numbers in Bahia increased steadily. Although these new slaves came from various areas, certain groups, notably the Hausa and Yoruba, clung together in large numbers. Many went to the city of Bahia as skilled workers and craftsmen, where they established ties with free Negroes of similar background and together formed a coherent community with literate and sophisticated leaders. The surrounding plantations, once filled with Angolan-Congolese slaves who had only a tenuous relationship with the urban Guineans, increasingly received Hausa and Yoruba imports.

A comparative analysis of the slave revolts of the New World will have to await an extended analysis at a more appropriate place. But even a brief review of the general conditions which favored the massive risings and maroon activities elsewhere in the Americas will illuminate the nonrevolutionary self-assertion of the slaves of the Old South. Slave revolt flourished particularly where the master-slave relationship had developed more as a matter of business than paternalistically; where economic distress and unusual hardship prevailed with greater frequency and intensity than in the Old South; and where slaveholding units were large— the great plantations of the Caribbean and Brazil averaged 100 to 200 slaves, not the 20 or so that marked the plantations of the South. Revolts occurred in both town and country; on the whole, urban centers, like the great plantation districts, offered especially favorable conditions. Revolts also germinated in areas in which a high ratio of slave to free and black to white prevailed and in which the slaves had had a chance to acquire military experience. The constant warfare that marked the Caribbean and South America forced the regimes to arm black volunteers periodically in return for promises of freedom. The slaves of the Old South lived under an enormously powerful regime with a white majority and did not face the divisions in the ruling class that marked Saint-Domingue, Brazil, and other countries. Southern slaves developed their own religion and turned it to good effect, but they were not able to retain such African religions as Islam or develop heavily African syncretisms capable of calling them to holy war.

The revolts in Jamaica, Surinam, Saint-Domingue, Brazil, and elsewhere accompanied and followed large-scale maroon wars. In a number of cases the maroons prevailed and forced the regimes to sign peace treaties and recognize their autonomy. The relationship between maroons and slaves was complex and by no means always friendly. The peace treaties between maroons and white regimes usually provided for black autonomy in return for military support against slave revolts and for the return of new runaways. But the existence of militarily respected maroon colonies destroyed in a single stroke the more extravagant racist pretensions of the whites and provided a beacon to spirited slaves.

In the South slaves also ran away in groups, tried to organize colonies, and struggled for autonomy. During the colonial period they even scored some local successes, and in the 1830s some blacks merged with the Seminoles to make a heroic stand against white power in Florida. But the rapid development of the southern back country confronted slaves with a formidable white power and reduced possibilities for sustained guerrilla warfare to a minimum. Thus, the slave might know of small groups of desperate holdouts here and there, but he had no example of an autonomous black movement to guide him.

* * *

The two big eighteenth-century revolts in New York City and Stono, South Carolina—not really so big since they respectively involved 30 and 100 slaves, at the very most—shared certain of the features noticeable in risings elsewhere in the hemisphere. In both instances the slaves took advantage of white divisions. The whites in New York had remained politically rent and in constant agitation since Leisler's rebellion in 1689. The whites in South Carolina had had constant trouble with the Indians and with black maroons operating in Florida; worse, everyone, black and white, knew that Spain and England hovered on the brink of war and that the Spanish were providing sanctuary for slaves from the British colonies. In both revolts African-born slaves predominated and raised the religious question. In New York the rebels flew an openly anti-Christian banner; in South Carolina Angolan slaves espoused an Afro-Catholicism that drew them to the Spanish while providing autonomous ground of their own. In New York the rebels drew their leadership and perhaps their following from skilled mechanics, craftsmen, and other privileged slaves; in South Carolina the rebels probably did also, although the record is unclear.

Little is known about the revolt in St. John the Baptist Parish, Louisiana, in 1811, although it has pride of place as the biggest in our history. Between 300 and 500 slaves, armed with pikes, hoes, and axes but few firearms, marched on New Orleans with flags flying and drums beating. Haiti still loomed large among these slaves, some of whom had originated there. Free Negroes generally supported the regime and helped crush the revolt, but at least one rebel leader from Saint-Domingue, Charles Deslondes, was a free mulatto. The rebels organized well, dividing themselves into companies commanded by officers, but they quickly collapsed in combat against the well-armed militia and regular troops under the command of Wade Hampton.

Three nineteenth-century revolts, two of them abortive, received the notoriety that that of 1811, despite its scope, did not. Since the United States had only recently annexed Louisiana, events there seemed peripheral and no more than what might be expected from an untamed frontier region. The other revolts, which occurred in the oldest and most stable slaveholding regions, stunned the whole South. Nat Turner raised only about seventy slaves but won fame by killing an unprecedented number of whites. Since the previous plots and risings in Virginia had failed to draw white blood, Turner's accomplishment stood out all the more. The Gabriel Prosser and Denmark Vesey plots never had their moment but in some ways emerged as more impressive than Turner's.

These three revolts shared certain features. Each had literate leaders drawn from the ranks of privileged slaves: Gabriel Prosser, a blacksmith; Nat Turner, a foreman and exhorter; Denmark Vesey, a free Negro who had bought his own freedom after having worked as a seaman and visited Haiti among other places. The Vesey plot had such leaders as Peter Poyas, a ship's carpenter, as well as a black overseer, house servants, and skilled mechanics. Each revolt had an urban dimension: Gabriel Prosser planned to seize Richmond; Vesey, Charleston; and Nat Turner, the town of Jerusalem. Each matured in the wake of divisions or apparent divisions in the ruling classes. Gabriel Prosser organized his plot when many slaves believed that the United States had gone to war with France, and they counted on French help. The bitter struggle between Federalists and Republicans also created an impression of deeper divisions than in fact existed. Vesey and his literate fellow conspirators had followed the congressional debate over the Missouri Compromise and knew that slavery evoked no enthusiasm in a large part of the country. The Turner revolt erupted after Virginia's tense Constitutional Convention of 1829–1830, from which the representatives of the antislavery western part of the state had gone home bitter at the slaveholding east's continuing strangle hold over state politics.

In some respects, notably religious ideology, the movements diverged. Gabriel Prosser relied on Christian preaching but stressed secular themes and, possibly to his cost, ignored appeals to the folk religion of the "outlandish people"—the African-born slaves and those country slaves of the first generation who remained close to the African origins of their parents. Nat Turner, of all the North American slave-revolt leaders we know much about, came closest to assuming a messianic and apocalyptic stance. Whereas Prosser and Vesey died more or less in silence, Turner talked about himself, his hopes, and his plans. An exhorter, he told us a great deal about himself and his world when T. R. Gray asked, "Do you not find yourself mistaken now?" His terrifying and self-revealing answer: "Was not Christ crucified?" Denmark Vesey offered the most complex response. He appealed to the Bible and invoked Christian sanction for his revolt. He also drew upon the services of Jack Purcell ("Gullah Jack"), an Angolan who appealed to traditional African beliefs and relied heavily on magic. Contemporaries and historians have suggested that Vesey behaved cynically and used opposite appeals in order to unite creole and African-born slaves. But there is no evidence that such a dichotomy existed. Vesey seems to have come closest to formulating a flexible religious appeal based on the folk religion and both African and classical Christian ideas and appeals. Gabriel Prosser slighted the folk religion; Nat Turner assumed a messianic stance among a people not prone to following messiahs; Denmark Vesey most creatively captured the complex tradition of the people he sought to lead.

The slaves of the United States had always faced hopeless odds. A slave revolt anywhere in the Americas, at any time, had poor prospects and required organizers with extraordinary daring and resourcefulness. In the United States those prospects, minimal during the eighteenth century, declined toward zero during the nineteenth. The slaves of the Old South should not have to answer for their failure to mount more frequent and effective revolts; they should be honored for having tried at all under the most discouraging circumstances.

As time went on those conditions became steadily more discouraging: the hinterland filled up with armed whites; the population ratios swung against the blacks; creoles replaced Africans; and the regime grew in power and cohesion. Each new defeat, each abortive conspiracy, confirmed the slaves in the thought that rebellion meant suicide. Meeting necessity with their own creativity, the slaves built an Afro-American community life in the interstices of the system and laid the foundations for their future as a people. But their very strategy for survival enmeshed them in a web of paternalistic relationships which sustained the slaveholders' regime despite the deep antagonisms it engendered.

The slaves' success in forging a world of their own within a wider world shaped primarily by their oppressors sapped their will to revolt, not so much because they succumbed to the baubles of amelioration as because they themselves were creating conditions worth living in as slaves while simultaneously facing overwhelming power that discouraged frontal attack. The slaves of the Old South could not readily throw up a Toussaint—a revolutionary of measured temperament, scorning fanaticism, coolly studying his terrain, alternating compromise with intransigence. They came close enough with Denmark Vesey, Peter Poyas, and perhaps Gabriel Prosser. Nat Turner, on the other hand, foreshadowed his white counterpart, John Brown—fanatic, millenarian, and possibly mad. If so, the question presents itself: What judgment should be rendered on a society the evils of which reach such proportions that only madmen are sane enough to challenge them? It was no accident that a Nat Turner arose after the despair occasioned by the defeats of 1800, 1811, and 1822.

Should the slave revolts, then, be viewed as increasingly futile, pathetic, or even insane efforts doomed to defeat and historically productive of no better result than the inevitable ensuing repression? Should we say of the slave revolts, as Marc Bloch did of the peasant revolts of medieval France, that they qualified as disorganized outbursts which counted for little or nothing when weighed against the achievements of the peasants in building their village communities? The question, however compelling, must be turned around: What could the slaves have accomplished if they had totally lacked an insurrectionary spirit and if their masters had had no fear of getting their throats cut?

The panic of the slaveholders at the slightest hint of slave insurrection revealed what lay beneath their endless self-congratulations over the supposed docility, contentment, and loyalty of their slaves. Almost every slaveholder claimed to trust his own slaves but to fear his neighbor's. As Ulrich Bonnell Phillips—of all people—wrote:

> A great number of southerners at all times held the firm belief that the negro population was so docile, so little cohesive, and in the main so friendly toward the whites and so contented that a disastrous insurrection by them would be impossible. But on the whole there was much greater anxiety abroad in the land than historians have told of, and its influence in shaping southern policy was much greater than they have appreciated.[2]

The slaveholders simply did not know what to think. Mary Boykin Chesnut read a book on the Sepoy mutiny and then saw a play.

> What a thrill of terror ran through me as those yellow and black brutes came jumping over the parapets! Their faces were like so many of the same sort at home. To be sure, John Brown had failed to fire their hearts here, and they saw no cause to rise and burn and murder us all. . . . But how long would they resist the seductive and irresistible call: "Rise, kill, and be free!"[3]

In 1856, William Proctor Gould of Greene County, Alabama, reacted to news of an insurrection scare and to the execution of alleged conspirators by warning his own slaves against getting involved. They denied knowledge of any plot and assured him of their loyalty.

> This may or may not be so—but from nothing I have noticed in their conduct can I bring myself to believe that any of them were looking forward to a change in their situation. What they might have done if there had been an actual outbreak must forever remain unknown to us.[4]

The slaveholders sometimes stimulated fears of slave revolt for political purposes. An occasional scare went a long way toward justifying measures to suppress political opposition to the regime. Sam Houston of Texas did not stand alone in accusing the Fire-Eaters of manufacturing slave plots in order to silence their white opponents. As Clement Eaton argues, fear of slave revolt enhanced the pressures for conformity, white unity, and "a profoundly conservative attitude toward social reforms."[5] Politically moderate slaveholders often denounced, at least privately, "sham" insurrections and vigilante hysteria.[6] But no amount of drumbeating by slaveholding extremists would have succeeded in whipping up so much panic so often if the whites had not believed that their slaves had cause to rise and might find the resources and opportunity.[7]

For the slaves, the revolts, however rare, served a purpose. Revolt and white fear of revolt encouraged not only repression—all action calls forth reaction, which hardly constitutes an excuse for inaction—but also amelioration of material conditions. Much more important, they combatted, in the most decisive way among both whites and blacks, the racist myth of black docility. T. R. Dew, J. H. Hammond, and other proslavery writers ironically expressed certainty that their slaves, being creoles, were too "civilized" to rise. Others scoffed that all blacks were "arrant cowards." And Garnett Andrews of Georgia rubbed it in: "If unfitted for the relation, the African would—instead of affection, have the greatest hostility to those under whose immediate rule he serves."[8] Every slave revolt or even aborted plot set limits to these white self-deceptions and to the tendency for the slaves to accept them themselves.

There is little evidence of a revolutionary folk tradition among the southern slaves of the kind that Palmares inspired among the slaves of the Brazilian Northeast or that Rákóczy and Stenka Razin inspired among the peasants of Hungary and Russia. Songs and stories about Gabriel Prosser and Nat Turner did exist, and some tradition has passed down to the present in localities like Southampton County, Virginia. But as the slave narratives suggest, southern slaves as a whole knew little about the great slave rebels. No powerful tradition emerged, perhaps simply because the revolts never achieved an appropriate size or duration. But the rebels did their best, and weak as their effort was, it was a great deal better than nothing.

ON RESISTANCE

Those slaves whose disaffection turned into violence and hatred— those who resisted the regime physically—included slaves who made stealing almost a way of life, killed their overseers and masters, fought back against patrollers, burned down plantation buildings, and ran away either to freedom or to the woods for a short while in order to effect some specific end, as well as those who took the ultimate measures and rose in revolt. Class oppression, whether or not reinforced and modified by racism, induces servility and feelings of inferiority in the oppressed. Force alone usually has not sufficed to keep the lower classes in subjugation. Slavishness constitutes the extreme form of the psychology of the oppressed, although we may doubt that it ever appears in pure form. It longs for acceptance by the other, perceived as the epitome of such superior qualities as beauty, goodness, virtue, and above all, power. But the inevitable inability of the lower classes, especially but not uniquely slave classes, to attain that acceptance generates disaffection, hatred, and violence.

The slaves' response to paternalism and their imaginative creation of a partially autonomous religion provided a record of simultaneous accommodation and resistance to slavery. Accommodation itself breathed a critical spirit and disguised subversive actions and often embraced its apparent opposite—resistance. In fact, accommodation might best be understood as a way of accepting what could not be helped without falling prey to the pressures for dehumanization, emasculation, and self-hatred. In particular, the slaves' accommodation to paternalism enabled them to assert rights, which by their very nature not only set limits to their surrender of self but actually constituted an implicit rejection of slavery.

Stark physical resistance did not represent a sharp break with the process of accommodation except in its most extreme forms—running away to freedom and insurrection. Strictly speaking, only insurrection represented political action, which some choose to define as the only genuine resistance since it alone directly challenged the power of the regime. From that point of view, those activities which others call "day-to-day resistance to slavery"—stealing, lying, dissembling, shirking, murder, infanticide, suicide, arson—qualify at best as prepolitical and at worst as apolitical.

These distinctions have only a limited usefulness and quickly lose their force. Such apparently innocuous and apolitical measures as a preacher's sermon on love and dignity or the mutual support offered by husbands and wives played—under the specific conditions of slave life—an indispensable part in providing the groundwork for the most obviously political action, for they contributed to the cohesion and strength of a social class threatened by disintegration and demoralization. But "day-to-day resistance to slavery" generally implied accommodation and made no sense except on the assumption of an accepted status quo the norms of which, as perceived or defined by the slaves, had been violated.

The definition of resistance as political response nonetheless draws attention to a break—a qualitative leap—in the continuum of resistance in accommodation and accommodation in resistance. The slaves who unambiguously chose to fight for or fly to freedom represented a new quality. They remained a small portion of the total, but their significance far transcended their numbers. The maturation of that new quality, so vital to the health and future of the black community, depended upon those less dramatic efforts in the quarters which produced a collective spiritual life.

"ROAST PIG IS A WONDERFUL DELICACY, ESPECIALLY WHEN STOLEN"

To the slaveholders and whites generally, all blacks stole by nature. They defined "a thieving Negro" simply as one who stole much more than the average. In colonial days Robert Carter even complained that universal stealing by slaves rendered Virginia's plantations unprofitable. Hog stealing reached such proportions that in 1748 Virginia decreed the death penalty for a third offense. George Washington solemnly declared some years later that for every two bottles of his fine wine he drank, thievish slaves enjoyed five. In South Carolina on the eve of the Revolution a plantation manager reported a wave of cattle thefts to his employer and added, "This kind of work prevails so much in your neighborhood that I fear few of your Creatures will be left by the year's end."[1]

Not much changed during the nineteenth century. Charles C. Pinckney asserted, however implausibly, that 25 percent of the rice crop was entering the market through the hands of pilfering slaves. Southern churches more often disciplined their slave communicants for stealing than for any other offense.[2] Even on the best-managed plantations, which boasted well-fed slaves, the plundering of the hogpen, the smokehouse, the chicken coop, and the corncrib constituted a normal feature of plantation life.[3] In its more extreme manifestations widespread stealing forced masters to curtail or abandon hog raising, or to build their own mills in order to forestall thefts during deliveries to a neighborhood mill, or to take other expensive measures.[4]

The slaveholders responded to their slaves' stealing variously but, most noticeably and ominously, with increasing equanimity. They slowly convinced themselves that blacks would steal and that they, as good fathers and mothers, had to take the peccadillos in stride. Joe Gray Taylor observes: "Thieving habits on the part of the slave were not unforgivable. . . . The slaveholder might look with a relatively tolerant eye on thefts from the smokehouse or his larder so long as the black thief consumed his loot, but he was less tolerant when goods were purloined for trading purposes."[5] The slaveholders excused these thefts not only on grounds of congenital black character but on grounds of general experience with slaves throughout history and with all lower classes—most notably, of course, the Irish.[6]

With whatever excuse, the slaveholders, as their private papers as well as public pronouncements show, increasingly took the slaves' stealing for granted. Olmsted reported from a well-managed plantation in the lower Mississippi Valley that generously fed slaves were regularly looting the corncrib to feed their own hogs and fowls. "This," he noted with raised eyebrows, "was mentioned to me by the overseer as if it were a matter of course."[7] In North Carolina, Mary Branch wrote William Branch that the hands had slaughtered enough hogs to feed the plantation, "unless too much is consumed by the negroes before they are divided."[8]

This equanimity sometimes passed into levity. "It so happened," wrote a contributor to the *Southern Agriculturalist*, "that if I took a special fancy for any pig, some rogue took an equal fancy for the same; and somehow or other, he continued to strengthen his fancy by 'nine points of the law.' His fancy thus became stronger than mine, and I was obliged to yield."[9] Thomas Affleck, the vigorous agricultural reformer and promoter, wrote to the United States commissioner of patents in 1849: "Many planters raise an ample supply of hogs for their families, black and white. Many more find it a thing impossible, from the destruction of their young stock by the negroes, who have all a particular penchant for roast pig, and especially when stolen; and many never make the effort to raise pork."[10] Judge O'Neall of South Carolina spoke more seriously but to the same effect: "Occasional thefts among the tolerably good slaves may be expected."[11]

Not all slaveholders took the thefts so lightly, especially not those whose losses reached serious proportions. From time to time the themes of ingratitude and betrayal sounded. In 1834 a planter in Georgia lamented:

> 1830—1831—1832—1833—I have every year experienced from some unknown scoundrel the robbery of my garden—I have every year planted a few watermelons for the eating of my little family—my wife, two young daughters, son and myself. . . . Certainly it cannot

be a servant of my own. I cannot bear the thought that I have among my servants a wretch so depraved of every sense of gratitude to his mistress and myself as to break open the garden fence in order to rob my small patch of ten or fifteen small watermelons for to eat or sell in Town, when the price it would bring could not be more than perhaps a dollar or a dollar and a half.

He added that he would rather pay the slaves, whom he had just ostensibly absolved on principle, the value of the watermelons if only he could guarantee their availability to his little daughter.[12] In North Carolina in 1851, William D. Valentine reported:

A most disagreeable but necessary duty devolved on the heads of this family yesterday. It was to redress most gross conduct of our slaves (some of them). . . .

Slaves we have raised and have ever been well treated, as well as we Know How, according to the nature of master and slave as the relation exists among us, had been stealing—had killed and cleaned a hog, the property of a neighbor and carried it to a poor white man to sell to him but he refused to buy and disclosed the fact. . . . He [the accused slave] was obstinate and would not tell—but told many evident falsehoods. So his punishment was greater than it would have been and rightly. . . . Some others are behind the curtain. Of such is family police in a slave country. There is one fact incident to negro slaves—they *will steal*—So will lazy, mean unprincipled white men steal and the non-Slaveholding States have their share of this class. They steal to satisfy necessity. Not so our slaves, who are fed and clothed well.

Stealing is common to all negro slaves in this country. It is distressing to contemplate. Unless we have good evidence against them, they will suffer more punishment than we are willing to inflict rather than confess the truth. And it is bad policy, often cruel, to whip on mere suspicion to make them tell what may be supposed to be their guilt. . . .

Some white people in all slaveholding communities are worse than slaves. . . . In this case the hog was carried to a white man. A great audacious piece of presumption indeed, if the negro had not cause or reason to believe the white man would buy of him. . . .

There having not been an affair of the kind in this family for some seventeen years, and these being young negroes we have raised, it is really rending. But firm duty must be met.[13]

Probably, less fuss would have followed if the stolen hog had not been a neighbor's, for the sense of family disgrace and the disillusionment would not have been so strong.

The ambivalence of the slaveholders toward their slaves' stealing burst forth in various forms. "Pray my son be careful," Charles Pettigrew wrote to his son, Ebenezer, in 1804, "and put no dependence in their honesty, for be assured their condition scarce admits of honesty, and they will improve opportunities of getting for themselves."[14] A quarter century later a low-country planter wrote for public consumption: "To keep a diary of their conduct would be a record nothing short of a series of violations of the laws of God and man. To moralize and induce the slave to assimilate with the master and his interest has been and is the great desideration aimed at; but I am sorry to say I have long since desponded in the completion of this task." But, he insisted, slaveholders are nonetheless "bound under many sacred obligations, to treat them with humanity at all times, and under all circumstances."[15] And in the closing days of the old regime, Adele Petigru Allston confided to her son: "The conduct of the negroes in robbing our house, store room, meat house, etc. and refusing to restore anything shows you they *think it right* to steal from us, to spoil us, as the Israelites did the Egyptians."[16]

Mrs. Allston had glimpsed, as many slaveholders had long before, that the slaves had their own notion of morality. In 1855 a slaveholder in Alabama reported that a slave, Tom, had stolen his master's turkey and, when caught, confessed without remorse. "When I tuk the turkey and eat it," Tom insisted, "it got to be part of me."[17] The slaves made a distinction: they stole from each other but merely took from their masters. Their logic was impeccable. If they belonged to their masters—if they were in fact his chattels —how could they steal from him? Suppose they ate one of his chickens or hogs or some of his corn? They had only transformed his property from one form into another, much as they did when they fed the master's corn to the master's chickens. Olmsted explained from Virginia:

> It is told me as a singular fact, that everywhere on the plantations, the agrarian notion has become a fixed point of the negro system of ethics: that the result of labor belongs of right to the laborer, and on this ground, even the religious feel justified in using "Massa's property" for their own temporal benefit. This they term "taking," and it is never admitted to be a reproach to a man among them that he is charged with it, though "stealing," or taking from another man than their master, and particularly from one another, is so. They almost universally pilfer from the household stores when they have a safe opportunity.[18]

The slaves in the Old South did not invent the distinction be-tween stealing and taking or the idea that slaves, being property, logically could not steal from their own masters. Brazilian slaves scoffed at the charge of stealing from their masters by arguing that a son could not steal from his own father. The distinction between stealing and taking rebounded throughout the Caribbean as well. "What I take from my master being for my own use, who am his slave or property," they reasoned, "he loses nothing by its trans-fer." Throughout history, wherever slaves have existed, this theme has recurred.[19] And not only among slaves. During the nineteenth century young criminals in the slums of English cities developed their own variation by distinguishing between petty theft, which they defined as taking, and grand larceny, which they acknowl-edged to be stealing.[20]

The slaves' main excuse for stealing rested on the countercharge of underfeeding. Some, in fact, did not get enough to eat. Two slaves, sentenced to hang for stealing food in eighteenth-century Virginia, pleaded hunger and threw themselves on the mercy of the governor.[21] Long after slavery had passed, Richard Carruthers of Texas reflected:

> If they didn't provision you 'nough, you just had to slip round and get a chicken. That easy 'nough, but grabbin' a pig sure 'nough problem. You have to catch him by the snoot so he won't squeal, and clomp him tight while you knife him. That ain't stealin', is it? You has to keep right on workin' in the field, if you ain't allowanced 'nough, and no nigger like to work with his belly groanin'.[22]

The slaveholders admitted that much stealing was caused by un-derfeeding. "The very best remedy for hog stealing," wrote a planter in Virginia, "is to give the rougues a plenty of pork to eat." And Mrs. Schoolcraft, among many other self-satisfied slavehold-ers, remarked: "Having every necessity of life and being con-stantly employed, the plantation negro rarely steals from his master."[23] The law in Tennessee made its own admission when it held masters who underfed their slaves responsible for any steal-ing they might do from others.[24]

Plantation plunder occurred too often to be attributed mostly to underfeeding, not only because the evidence refutes the charge of widespread underfeeding but also because the blacks so often rested their case elsewhere. Betty Powers of Texas, for example, suggested that her plantation suffered from short—that is, too closely calculated—rations but certainly not from hunger. But why should hard-working people settle for so marginal a sustenance? They preferred to help themselves to something extra.[25] Others said that even when they had no complaint about the quantity of food dispensed, they resented the lack of variety and the assumption that they did not care about anything other than a full dinner pail of pork and cornmeal. "We has some good eats," remarked Walter Rimm of Texas, "but has to steal de best things from de white folks." Sara Colquitt of Virginia offered: "All us niggers was fed from de big kitchen and wasn't hongry, but sometimes us would steal more food dan was give us anyhow." Mrs. M. E. Adams of South Carolina added that the slaves stole hogs to supply their Saturday night barbecues and that "nigger has de mos'es fun at a barbecue dat dere is to be had."[26]

The diet itself invited trouble and complicates the question of underfeeding, for many plantations did not provide enough vegetables and other foods to offer the slaves an adequate nutrition. Hidden hungers associated with nutritional deficiencies may have impelled some of the attempt to supplement the diet, but even without these the slaves loved good food too much to settle for bare rations. In particular, they enjoyed fresh meat and would not tolerate a steady diet of mess pork. When the slaves felt hungry or in any way inadequately fed according to their own standards, they defended their stealing with particular indignation on the principle that their work had earned them a proper dinner.[27]

The slaves had good reason to doubt the honesty of some masters who were forever bringing in white preachers to help lecture on honesty. Those poor whites whom Sidney Andrews described in North Carolina—"They are lazy and thriftless, mostly choose to live by begging or pilfering"[28]—hardly set the best white example in the plantation districts. Nor did slaveholders who disdained to hide their cynicism. Miss Botume quoted one: "I never whip a nigger for stealing, but I'll lick him half to death for being found out. They *will* steal; all the nigs will; but if they ain't smart enough to hide it, they deserve to be thrashed, and I tell my niggers so."[29] Far short of this extreme, the slaves had other grounds on which to consider some stealing much worse than others. In Louisiana they sang:

> Negro cannot walk without corn in his pocket,
>   It is to steal chickens.
> Mulatto cannot walk without rope in his pocket,
>   It is to steal horses.

White man cannot walk without money in his pocket,
It is to steal girls.[30]

Or, in the words of a saying that might have come from the Caribbean: "When buckra tief, he tief plantation; when nigger tief, he
tief piece of cane."

The slaves also asked a few embarrassing questions about a particular kind of stealing. "Dey allus done tell us it am wrong to lie
and steal," exploded Josephine Howard of Texas, "but why did de
white folks steal my mammy and her mammy? Dey lives clost to
some water, somewhere over in Africy. . . . Dat de sinfulles' stealin'
dey is." The whites did the first stealing, sneered another ex-slave,
when they stole our people from Africa.[31] Or as Brudder Coteny,
that old Gullah preacher, asked his flock: "Ef buckra neber tief,
how come nigger yer? . . . How about de tief dat steal nigger not
from e mossa [in which case the white man would hang], but fum
e fadder an mudder?"[32]

The whites' exhortations against stealing fell on deaf ears especially when the slaves had masters—or knew of other masters—
who actually encouraged their slaves to steal from neighboring
farms and plantations. Henry Johnson of Georgia insisted that his
master would bring in a preacher to demand honesty and then
would himself order his slaves to steal from neighbors. Ex-slaves
from various parts of the South told similar stories. And in Louisiana, Bennet H. Barrow concluded that slaves from another plantation were stealing his cotton at the behest of their master.[33] Even
if only a small minority of masters used their slaves as thieves, the
slaves needed only to know of one or two to question the sincerity
of their masters' admonitions, so many of which addressed the
ostensibly special penchant of black people for stealing.

Masters who encouraged their slaves to steal from neighbors
accomplished something for themselves they probably did not
often recognize. To the extent that the slaves took the demand in
stride, they strengthened the sense among both whites and blacks
of their plantation as a discrete community which stood alone
against all outsiders. In this subtle way masters bound their slaves
to their own white folks and drove a wedge between them and
their neighbors, black and white. By the same process the slaves
on those plantations which were being robbed of foodstuffs and
supplies felt a loss that tied them to their own white folks in
opposition to outsiders, black and white.

For many slaves, stealing from their own or other masters became a science and an art, employed as much for the satisfaction of outwitting Ole Massa as anything else. "We stole so many chickens," chuckled an ex-slave, "that if a chicken would see a darkey he'd run right straight to the house."[34] An ex-slave from Tennessee remarked that his master provided gardens and plenty of food for the slaves, "but we would steal anyhow." He explained:

> It is just natural for Negroes to steal. Our folks would do it, and they had plenty. They would kill a hog and put it under the bed and cook it at night, and they would eat what they wanted and then put a top over the skillet and set it back under the table and nobody would never know nothing about it.[35]

To steal a hog or chicken successfully required skill, for they had to be prevented from squealing. The slaves learned how to strike a single blow and silence their prey, but their problems did not end there. "You had to be careful and bury all de [chicken] feathers in de ground," said Benjamin Johnson of Georgia, " 'cause if you burned 'em de white folks would smell 'em."[36] The slaves stored cooked surplus meat in holes under their cabin floors, but often chose to eat their loot immediately and called on their fellow slaves to share the spoils.[37] If they could slip into the woods all would probably end well, but often they had to cook and eat a stolen pig or chicken in their cabin. Lewis Clarke told of a particularly adept woman whose overseer once almost caught her boiling a pig. Upon hearing his approach, she placed the pot on the floor, covered it with a board, and sat her young daughter upon it. It seemed the poor child had a terrible cold that just had to be sweated out of her. Quick thinking, but not so quick. Like many other slaves this woman had done her thinking in advance and tried to have a contingency plan for every emergency.[38] The slaves enjoyed the sporting element in their stealing, and they sang:

> Sorry dat if I leave my home,
> I gwine to my shack
> Wid de chicken on my back
> Nobody business but mine.[39]

If the slaves themselves defined stealing as thefts from each other and if they enjoyed a sporting element in taking from their masters, the question remains: How frequently did they in fact steal from each other? The evidence does not permit a firm answer, but such stealing did constitute a problem on some plantations. Lyell,

Olmsted, and Russell all reported that slaves on particular plantations they visited either locked their cabins during the day or
locked closets or sleeping rooms inside their cabins in order to
keep out thieves.[40] On Thomas Dabney's plantation in Mississippi
the slaves successfully petitioned their master to sell a woman
whom they could not keep from stealing from them. In Georgia
a blacksmith killed a fellow slave for stealing the keys to his shop.
In Alabama a number of slaveholders declared in favor of communal kitchens as a device to keep slaves from stealing each other's
food. And here and there slaveholders publicized measures for
reducing thefts within the quarters.[41] The black preachers' exhortations not to steal from one another demonstrated that a problem
existed in more than the imagination of the masters.[42] Not many
slaves seem to have stolen from each other, but one or two thieves
would keep an entire plantation agitated and foster mutual suspicion.

Evidence of blacks' stealing from blacks after the war suggests
that for too many it had become a way of life, although we cannot
measure the effect of the new conditions of deprivation and community instability.[43] Reports from Liberia also suggest that the
habit of stealing did not so readily vanish with new conditions.[44]
And in Haiti Henri-Christophe resorted to Draconian measures to
stamp out the widespread thieving his people had carried from
slavery days into their lives as free men.[45]

The slaves' distinction between stealing and taking and their
rejection of white standards of morality, which so often seemed
flagrantly hypocritical, have commanded the sympathetic attention of historians, most notably and eloquently Herbert Aptheker
and Kenneth M. Stampp, who have stressed the implicit elements
of resistance and initiative.[46] These historians certainly do not
intend to make a virtue of theft, lying, and deception but rather
—if I read them correctly—to argue that the oppressed have a right
to use available weapons to protect themselves, their families, and
their people against continuous aggression from above. The valid-
ity of this viewpoint is apparent, but the slaves' practice also had
negative implications; like so much else in the slaves' arsenal of
weapons, thieving from Ole Massa cost the slaves more than meets
the eye.

The doctrine of the legitimacy of taking from Ole Massa could
not arise simply as an alternative morality, securely rooted in the
slaves' autonomous world-view. However distinct the slaves'

Christianity, it remained Christianity. When the black preachers joined the white in denouncing slaves' thefts from their masters, they were not simply appeasing their white patrons and eavesdroppers; they were also fighting to instill a more coherent morality in their people and to prevent their slipping into degradation, division, and self-contempt. They undoubtedly understood the provocations to theft and sympathized with some of the response, especially that which followed upon short rations. But they also knew that excuses accuse—that the response, however understandable, took a toll in the quarters.

At the least, the slaves' actions strengthened the slaveholders' self-esteem and sense of commanding a moral social system. Long after slavery ended, this ideological consequence persisted. Hortense Powdermaker writes of the justifications put forward by black servants for pilfering from whites in the twentieth-century Black Belt: "It fits very comfortably into the traditional pattern, which made the master responsible for feeding his dependents, and which prescribed a certain indulgence for the 'childlike, irresponsible' Negro."[47] The white press had an easy justification for their sneers that the black delegates to Reconstruction legislatures and conventions were "henroost and pigsty thieves."

The slaves could not take so easy a view of their own behavior as folklore suggests, for their religiously informed sensibility could not offer adequate justification. The morality of the Ten Commandments or the Sermon on the Mount, like that implied by so much of the legal system even in grossly unjust class societies, has a double aspect. To a great extent it offers standards of behavior, sanctioned by experience, that appear to be and in fact often are necessary to the conduct of civilized life. A ruling class consolidates its hegemony precisely by presenting itself as the guardian, even the embodiment, of a moral code much of which represents the interests and sentiments of all classes and by disguising the purely exploitative and manipulative features of the prevailing code. The slaves could challenge the moral code, but could not readily counterpose a coherent alternative. At best, they could challenge the workings of a specific item, as they did in their distinction between taking and stealing, but for the most part they —or rather, the most sensitive, decent, and responsible among them—had to have mixed feelings and to experience some degradation. Notwithstanding Dostoevski's reactionary politics and his harsh judgment on the lower classes, the words he gave to Father

Zossima contain an element of truth: "The common man is vile, he cannot stop himself from committing the foulest of sins, but he still knows that it is a foul sin. . . . Always our people believes in truth, recognizes God, weeps in joyous repentance."[48] This element of self-contempt in those slaves who easily resorted to stealing need not be exaggerated, especially since their religion did not dwell on guilt; but neither can it be ignored. The tragedy was for the very best of the slaves—those who most keenly felt the shame —for they were precisely the ones who understood that there were better ways to live.[49] The slaves did protect themselves by stealing freely, and Aptheker and Stampp wisely defend them against superficial moralizing. But the slaves' resistance inevitably weakened their self-respect and their ability to forge a collective discipline appropriate to the long-term demands of their national liberation.

From colonial days to the end of the regime the slaveholders wrung their hands over the slaves' apparently congenital inability to tell the truth. "Their veracity," roared the Reverend C. C. Jones, self-appointed guardian of black morals, "is nominal. Duplicity is one of the most prominent traits in their character, practiced between themselves, but more especially towards their masters and managers. . . . The number, the veracity, and the ingenuity of falsehoods that can be told by them in a few brief moments is astonishing."[50] The good minister's remark might have been made by a Roman slaveholder about his white slaves or a West Indian slaveholder about his black slaves, or by any slaveholder anywhere, any time, about his slaves of any nationality or color. Throughout history slaveholders have assumed that slave testimony could be accepted, if at all, only when procured by torture.[51]

Concern about the slaves' lying was expressed also by those who were more sympathetic. Fredrika Bremer caught slaves in flagrant lying about being underfed and overworked when surrounded by evidence to the contrary. She quoted Joel Poinsett as saying to her: "[Slave] children learn from their parents to regard white people with fear, and to deceive them. They are always suspicious, and endeavor by their complainings to get some advantage."[52] William Wells Brown, himself a famous runaway, remarked: "Slavery makes its victims lying and mean; for which vices it afterwards reproaches them, and uses them as arguments to prove that they deserve no better fate."[53]

Most southern slaveholders who commented on the slaves'

prevarication attributed it to their being black rather than to their being slaves. Notwithstanding the large element of self-serving cant in their position, it may have contained an undigested and misunderstood kernel of truth. Africans considered lying—or what Europeans and white Americans understood as lying—an ingredient of courtesy. European travelers as well as anthropologists reported that Africans repeatedly "lied" to each other in matters of no importance when they had nothing to gain. In time these Europeans learned that Africans regarded as discourtesy the telling of something the other party did not want to hear. Much as sin constituted an offense against the community more readily than against God, truth and falsehood constituted devices for human comfort rather than moral imperatives. The appropriate became more important than the strictly-speaking true. Thus, the freedmen who infuriated Union troops by giving them false information about local conditions usually had no desire to mislead or endanger them; they were being gracious and perhaps were also ashamed to admit ignorance.[54] This traditional African view, which has appeared in other societies, presents no threat, moral or other, to community order unless that order rests on close calculation and economic credibility—in a word, on credit.[55]

Traditional African attitudes passed to the New World as part of the "etiquette of race relations" within which courtesy and self-protective dissembling became inseparable. Even before the rise of the slave trade the Africans' view of courtesy and truthfulness had its element of protection against a dangerous world, as perhaps does every other people's view. The West African admonition never to tell anyone more than half of that which you know, makes sense for more than West Africans or any other special people in time and place.[56] With the rise of the slave trade and the enforced transfer to slave plantations in a strange land, lying, which came to be known more delicately as "puttin' Ole Massa on," became a way of life. James Pope-Hennessy writes in his history of the slave trade:

> The first line of defense for any vanquished or occupied nation, as for any camp of war-prisoners, is calculated cunning and deceit. It was thus that the Negro slaves in the European colonies made lying their second nature. An analogy can be found in the history of Ireland. More than seven centuries of brutal English oppression produced a race of the most persuasive, adept, and incorrigible liars in the world. . . . These piccaninnies were patiently taught by their

mothers and fathers with all the earnest diligence white parents would employ to ensure that their own offspring were instructed in Latin, or riding, or arithmetic. The water-tight lie became a vital piece of the slave-baby's equipment at the outset of his sad career.[57]

Colonel Higginson, in *Army Life in a Black Regiment*, reports having overheard a black soldier telling the others how he escaped to the Yankees and specifically how he got a white man to tell him where the Federals were:

"Den I go up to de white man, berry humble, and say, would he please git ole man a mouthful for eat?"

"He say he must hab de valeration ob half a dollar."

"Den I look berry sorry, and turn for go away."

"Den he say I might gib him dat hatchet I had."

"Den I say," (this in a tragic vein) "dat I must hab dat hatchet for defend myself *from de dogs!*"

[Immense applause and one appreciating auditor says, chuckling, "Dat was your *arms*, ole man," which brings the house down again.]

"Den he say de Yankee pickets was near by, and I must be very keerful."

"Den I say, 'Good Lord, Mas'r, am dey?' "

Words cannot express the complete dissimulation with which these accents of terror were uttered—this being precisely the piece of information he wished to obtain.[58]

These put-ons, this wit and ingenuity, displayed by the slaves in defense of their interests came at a cost. The slaves were not merely applying an alternative standard of morality or mindlessly reaching for anything available to ward off a blow. Their own version of Christianity did not encourage lying any more than stealing. The slaves had to struggle with a contradictory code, and many made admirable efforts to live truthful, honest lives even as slaves. To the extent that they made the effort they suffered from every lie they had to tell. Elijah Green of South Carolina, honored by an invitation to a white wedding in the Big House, had to pretend that he liked the new member of the family. "I didn't like that 'cause I had to lie on myself by sayin' nice things about the person and hated the person at the same time."[59] A lie "on myself." Most slaves probably did not worry so, but some did.[60] The crime against the black community implicit in the trap in which it found itself lay in the quality, not the numbers, of those who were torn, for they were precisely those who were struggling toward a morality necessary to function in a modern economy and society. To the extent that the exigencies of survival suffocated their impulses, they dealt crippling blows to the long-run prospects for the black community, while protecting it against its oppressors. The question cannot be posed as a choice of moralities. The slaves did what they had to do to survive but at the same time had to sacrifice much that the black community would need for the long haul. That maddening dialectic constituted, as Elijah Green so incisively suggested, "a lie on myself."

The slaves' necessary resort to put-ons and lies had other ramifications, which might even fall under the rubric of ruling-class control. The masters often knew they were being deceived. Sometimes they fretted; sometimes they chuckled, as if delighted by the cleverness of their mischievous children. In either case, they took their slaves' behavior as confirmation of their own superiority. J. D. B. De Bow announced in 1861 that the South's vaunted and unquestioned chivalry and high sense of honor—certainly no one in his right mind would have dared question them in the South of 1861—grew out of the white man's awareness of the slaves' moral defects and of his determination to place maximum distance between his own behavior and that of his despised underlings.[61] Southern whites may not have behaved as honestly and truthfully as they so modestly claimed, but they had to think they did. The ex-slave brother of Blanche K. Bruce, Mississippi's Reconstruction senator, told of having been brought up to believe that whites never lied. H. C. Bruce insisted that many of the slaves actually believed that only blacks lied. Reflecting on his boyhood naiveté, he thought that in fact perhaps whites rarely had lied to their slaves. They normally scorned to lie to them, he thought, for they could simply refuse to answer embarrassing questions and did not have to fear harsh reactions to unpleasant truths. Thus, the whites could make a point of honor out of telling the slaves either the truth or nothing at all.[62] In fact, the whites often lied to their slaves, who were not fooled. But Bruce had seen how the whites, as a matter of ideological control, welcomed—although with some fear—their slaves' prevarication and dissembling, and how they tried to strengthen their own claims to being men of honor.

STANDING UP TO THE MAN

For the slaves, as for lower classes in other times and places, arson had much to recommend it as a way of settling scores, for as a historian of seventeenth-century England remarks, "Arson required no great physical strength or financial resources and could easily be concealed."[1] As late as the great "Captain Swing" disorders of the nineteenth century, the rural English laborers readily used the torch as social protest.[2] Kenneth Stampp reasonably asserts: "Next to theft, arson was the most common slave 'crime,' one which slaveholders dreaded almost constantly. . . . More than one planter thus saw the better part of a year's harvest go up in flames."[3]

The evidence of arson calls for caution and some qualification. Since the authorities and aggrieved parties could not easily detect arson, they often simply assumed it and further assumed its perpetration by slaves. When a wave of destructive fires ravaged Texas during the politically charged, not to say hysterical, days of 1860, the cry of Republican-inspired slave arson went up everywhere. Yet, the summer of 1860 had been unusually dry; despite evidence of arson in Dallas, the origin of most of the fires remains in doubt.[4] Urban conditions especially lent themselves to fires caused by carelessness or of spontaneous origin, but when the public became upset over an insurrectionary plot or the national political struggle, it looked to slave and abolitionist arsonists. In some cases, arsonists, white or black, had in fact been busy at the behest of local businessmen interested in collecting insurance or leveling a competitor. Many factories were firetraps, and when those using slave labor burned down, suspicion quickly fell on the slaves. Some slave arson undoubtedly occurred; but how much will remain in doubt. But a large portion of southern white opinion, especially in the cities, had so little confidence in the loyalty, contentment, and docility of the slaves that it regularly assumed the worst.[5]

The plantations probably suffered less from slave arson than the towns and cities, but they had their share. Since ginhouses, barns, and stockpiles presented far fewer fire hazards than urban dwellings, suspicions of arson had much more to recommend them. Sometimes, planters could only report that a ginhouse had burned down and that they had reason to suspect their slaves. Sometimes, they knew or thought they knew that slaves had done the deed for their own reasons or at the urging of another slaveholder with a grudge. Occasionally, they caught the culprits.[6]

The reaction of the slaveholders reveals much about their contradictory attitude toward their slaves. The sister-in-law of Bishop Leonidas Polk, herself with qualifications as a "kind slaveholder," wrote in her diary in 1850:

> Deplorable state of things here. Negroes are nothing but a tax & an annoyance to their owners—from fear, or mistaken indulgence, any degree of impertinence & idleness is tolerated. Within the last few months, Mr. Marshall's, Throckmorton's, Grey's, and several other persons' dwellings have been set on fire and burned to the ground. Idleness is the devil's workshop, and they have abundant time to hatch plenty mischief. I believe it to be my duty, so long as I own slaves, to keep them in proper subjection and well employed. So come what may, I intend to make mine do "service."[7]

A few years later Eliza L. Magruder wrote from the Natchez region: "Oh! what wickedness is in the world. I heard yesterday that one of William's negroes (from hatred of S. Haggart) had set fire to the carriage house and burned it down with three carriages."[8] Miss Magruder did not qualify as tough-minded about slaves or anything else and often expressed shock at occurrences others might have taken in stride. But what of the hardened, experienced Edmund Ruffin, who refused to credit others' suspicions that his own slaves had set the fires plaguing his plantation? Not until the fifth serious fire during the late 1850s did he finally face the truth. William Kauffman Scarborough, who has so ably edited Ruffin's diary for publication, remarks: "Like most of his peers, however, the venerable Virginian badly misjudged the aspirations and loyalties of southern Negroes."[9] Ruffin simply did not want to believe that the culprits came from within his own black family; he did not want to believe that plantations with good masters housed slaves ready to burn them down. And indeed, during the war his slaves did not defect until the arrival, replete with assurances and exhortations, of the Union troops.[10]

The arsonists' courageous display of militancy did not always win support and encouragement in the quarters. Arsonists usually worked alone or at most in groups of two or three; their action usually represented retaliation for some private offense or injustice. During the "Captain Swing" rebellion on the English countryside, for example, arson consisted of "individual acts and, even if related to the general labourers' movement, were rarely part of any organized plan." The laborers resorted to the torch primarily after the defeat of their collective resistance.[11] For the slaves, arson took on even greater individual and restricted character. If an insulted, injured, irate slave burned down the Big House, which few ever did, or the carriage house, or some other building of little direct economic significance, the slaves might easily sympathize with and protect them. But when, as so often happened, one or two slaves burned down the corncrib, the smokehouse, or the ginhouse, what were the others to think and do? Destruction of food stores meant their own deprivation. Destruction of the cotton meant severe losses to their master, but this furious vengeance also threatened the sale of one or more members of the slave community or, worse, bankruptcy and the breakup of the community altogether. The slaves who failed to sympathize with their arsonists, or who took a harsh attitude toward them, or who handed them over for punishment, were not necessarily playing the Tom. They had to weigh the impulses behind the brave deeds against their effect on the community, and often they found them wanting.

Masters and mistresses overwhelmingly insisted that they did not fear their slaves and in fact relied on them for protection against hostile outsiders, black and white. Since they rarely locked the doors of the Big House and seldom locked the slaves in at night, their claims must be taken seriously. Even during insurrection scares, when the whites so often panicked, they usually believed that their own slaves would protect them against other masters' rebels. Yet, in every decade slaveholders in every part of the South got an occasional jolt from news that normally obedient slaves had killed a master, mistress, or overseer. Thad Tate writes of eighteenth-century Virginia: "There were just enough instances of masters who had been killed by a slave in this way to lend a certain amount of justification to the whites' perpetual sense of insecurity."[12] That perpetual sense of insecurity existed at the same time, in the same place, and often in the same persons as the professed reliance on loyal slaves. As one result the slaveholders developed into fearless people, or rather, people who swallowed their fears and determined to live their lives as if nothing could frighten them. Their slaves could not help noticing, and to the extent they did, the hegemonic position of the master class became the more secure despite the periodic challenge posed by murder and lesser forms of individual physical resistance.

Poison held a special place in the arsenal of slave weapons throughout the Americas. The planters of the British and French Caribbean in particular lived in terror of being poisoned by their slaves.[13] Long before Africans fell prey to the slave trade they had mastered the art of poisoning as a means of dealing with enemies. From the moment they embarked for the New World, they resorted to poison against the whites, and they continued to practice the art throughout the eighteenth century.[14] Poisoning, at least as reported in an era of growing self-censorship by the press, declined during the nineteenth century but recurred often enough to suggest a pervasive nervousness.[15]

Historians differ about whether slaves killed masters more frequently than they did overseers. No one has yet studied local sources in depth and, as Ulrich Bonnell Phillips's analysis of Virginia's uniquely assembled crime records warns, those sources could prove misleading. The newspapers sometimes advertised the murder of a master widely in order to warn others, but at all other times they preferred restraint in reporting so as not to put ideas in the heads of imitative slaves. The murder of a master would usually provoke a serious investigation, and word would get out. Normally, so would the murder of an overseer, but often not, for many masters supported their slaves in the murder of a cruel overseer and effectively blocked inquiry. Much more often, masters ran off overseers whom the slaves had physically assaulted but not killed. In 1849 an overseer replied to charges against his class by insisting, "He [an overseer] has to punish and keep in order the negroes, at the risk of his life," and Olmsted reported from the Mississippi Valley that overseers carried arms in constant fear of their lives.[16]

From colonial times to the end of the regime murders of whites by slaves, whatever the proportion of overseers to masters, made everyone thoughtful. Murder did not have to occur often: one nearby, perhaps no closer than a neighboring county and perhaps only once in a decade, made a deep impression on masters as well as slaves. From time to time matters grew graver, and the killing of masters and overseers became, as one Texan said, "painfully frequent."[17] Slaves especially challenged overseers and, less readily, masters who were trying to whip or abuse them. These cases occurred much more often than generally believed, and sometimes they ended in death, by no means always the slave's. The frequency and numbers remain elusive, but the ubiquity of the reports from so many different sources suggests that life in the fields as well as in the Big House was often lived on the edge of violence.[18]

Sometimes the slaves on a plantation, or a substantial portion of them, conspired to murder a master or overseer; sometimes, that is, a murder reflected the collective judgment of the quarters. Presumably, these actions struck at particularly brutal whites, but in some cases they claimed the lives of reputedly kind masters and thereby suggested intense hostility toward slavery itself.[19]

The significance of slaves' murdering their masters or overseers cannot be reduced simply to "resistance to slavery," although all such action marked the limits beyond which slaves resisted becoming creatures of their master's will. Many of the slaves who committed these murders had had records as "good Negroes"—as men and women who seemed to accept their condition, do their work, and follow orders.[20] Such outbursts puzzled and distressed the whites who knew them. These slaves represented most clearly the internalization of paternalistic norms, according to which masters and slaves—or more properly from the slaves' point of view, lords and dependents—had specific rights and duties toward each other. In other words, the plantations contained many slaves who gave little or no indication of rebelliousness and dutifully accepted their subservient roles but who nonetheless did not surrender their will or their honor—who stayed in place so long as their expectations did not suffer a severe jolt and so long as they did not feel betrayed. These slaves made a contradictory impact on the quarters. Their day-to-day behavior taught manly self-discipline to others, but it also taught acquiescence in the status quo. And their sudden explosion taught the same lesson at a higher level, for their protest, as an individual reaction to individual abuses, set a model that reinforced the regime.

To curb runaways, hold down interplantation theft, and prevent the formation of insurrectionary plots, the slaveholders developed an elaborate system of patrols. Some states required them, whereas others merely authorized local communities to organize them. Usually a captain and three others, appointed for a period of a few months, worked the roads and checked the plantation quarters every few weeks or as often as the current temper dictated. Slaves caught without passes could expect summary punishment of about twenty lashes.

In normal times the patrols slacked off as conscripted citizens found the task irksome. In South Carolina and Alabama they functioned better than elsewhere, but in most states they periodically lapsed into passivity. A Georgia planter complained: "Our patrol laws are seldom enforced, and even where there is a mock observance of them, it is by a parcel of boys or idle men, the height of whose ambition is to 'ketch a nigger.' "[21]

Complaints against the patrols came from both masters and slaves. The masters, in ordinary times, bought their way out of patrol duty and then fumed because the poor whites who replaced them abused the slaves and unsettled the quarters. The brutality of the patrols drew widespread protest from the slaves who suffered from arbitrary or excessive beating. As a result, the slaves often regarded their masters as protectors against the patrols, and sometimes the masters in fact were. However irregular and lax, the patrols accomplished their main purpose: they struck terror in the slaves, who sang:

> Run, nigger, run,
> De Patteroll git you.

"Dat one of the songs de slaves all knowed," said Anthony Dawson of North Carolina. "Sometimes I wonder iffen de white folks didn't make dat song up so us niggers would keep in line."[22] If we may judge from the blacks' own alarmed accounts and expressions of fear and loathing, they generally did "keep in line."

Yet, terrified as the slaves were by the patrols, they often did resist them. Mostly, they resorted to such preventive mechanisms as learning when to expect a patrol, setting up a warning system, and playing stupid and innocent when caught.[23] They also built trapdoors in their cabins, especially those raised above ground, and slipped slaves without passes to safety when the patrols came through.[24] More aggressively, they tied ropes or vines across the roads leading to their meeting places and tripped the horses of those approaching. The injuries to the riders could be serious, and those slaves careless enough to get caught paid dearly. Sometimes, they fought their way out of their meeting places or threw hot coals in the faces of the intruders. Patrollers often beat and even killed slaves in these encounters, but the slaves sometimes beat and even killed patrollers. In some districts slave resistance to patrols reached high levels and produced alarm and emergency measures among the whites.[25]

One of the most impressive forms of slave self-assertion has remained largely unsung, for it rarely reached public notice. A surprising number of slaves would not submit to the whip. As Frederick Douglass asserted, overseers "prefer to whip those who are most easily whipped."[26] In some cases masters and overseers took the cowardly way out, avoided use of the whip, and slyly gave tough slaves passes ostensibly for safe conduct to visit a friend but actually directing patrollers to whip the bearer hard.[27]

To refuse to submit to a whipping meant to risk death or sale away from family and friends or an especially vicious beating after being subdued. The stakes being high, many slaves struck back or struck first and beat or killed their tormentors. Whatever their numbers, slaves who would not submit to whippings existed in every part of the South. All available sources refer to them, and every district, if not every large plantation, had one or two.[28] An overseer told Olmsted that he would kill a slave as readily as a dog, for "some negroes are determined never to let a white man whip them and will resist you, when you attempt it; of course you must kill them in that case."[29]

In some cases overseers took severe beatings from slave women whom they had tried to whip, or whose children they had abused, and then had to suffer additional humiliation from masters who refused to discipline the women and rebuked them instead. As one master told his overseer, "Well, if that is the best you could do with her, damned if you won't just have to take it."[30]

Occasionally, a group of slaves stood together to protect a brother who would not submit. Dr. G. M. Wharton of Alabama wrote to a planter in 1850:

> The men talk politics. They all go for dissolution. They say it is time —that the North has "spoilt" the "niggers" already. Yesterday, ten miles off, an overseer stabbed one to the heart for "sarseeing" him. Last week below Pikeville, another driver [i.e., overseer] attempted

to flog a boy. Four of the ploughmen stopped their mules, and taking out their singletrees, advanced upon him in battle array. [The plowmen were shot to death.][31]

Some planters examined their conscience in the wake of a slave's resistance. David Gavin of South Carolina reflected in 1861:

> I yesterday undertook to correct Big Jim and he resisted me, bit the fore finger of my hand and ran off. I am very sorry the circumstance occurred for Big Jim was a lively, brisk hand to work, generally did his work cheerfully and well, and I believe I was wrong for going to correct him, for I believe he overloaded the wagon honestly to do good work and stalled it, he erred in judgment and not by design, I think, but he has done very wrong in resisting me, he has always been a good boy, this is his first offense, except fighting some years ago another boy, Mike. O! How I regret it, Lord forgive me and enable me to do better hereafter, Give me strength and courage to act and think right and proper, & Knowledge, wisdom, and virtue to be honest, generous and upright, humble and thankful.[32]

These isolated but not necessarily infrequent incidents of resistance represent the high point of slave assertion within the system, for although they concerned individuals and only occasionally a group, they did not threaten the interests of the collective and reminded all that the Man's power could effectively be challenged.

Since the slaves understood their economic value they sometimes struck at their master's pocketbook. Feigning illness, a favorite tactic, especially recommended itself to the slaves, and masters and overseers complained loudly about its frequency.[33] Those slaves who used the tactic had chosen a reasonably safe one, for masters did not readily endanger the longevity of their capital investment and normally gave a slave who claimed illness the benefit of the doubt. The other slaves, however, did not necessarily cheer their clever brother on, for the work had to get done. Those slaves who successfully begged off placed a heavier burden on the others; the overseer cracked his whip the more readily to meet quotas and protect his job. Up to a point, feigning did represent a form of resistance, but only so far as all could take their share of time in the sickhouse and collectively slow down the general pace. When, as usually happened, a few played the game well while others did not or could not, the advantage of a few became the disadvantage of the rest. The slaves consequently often rode their shirkers hard, ridiculing them in the quarters and especially at their parties and denouncing them at their religious meetings. The slaves did everything possible to shame shirkers into doing their share, not only because they resented being put upon, but because they might all get punished for poor or insufficient work.[34]

Other methods of resisting work schedules proved more advantageous. In a few instances the slaves combined in actions that qualified as strikes in order to get better working conditions.[35] At other times they took action that hurt the interests of their masters without seriously jeopardizing the interests of their fellow slaves. For example, they killed and maimed livestock frequently, whether from indifference, carelessness, or a wish to sabotage.[36]

The slaves tried in a variety of ways to slow down the pace of work and to set norms they considered reasonable. By moving only so fast and by being willing to take some blows, they compelled even an overseer who used his whip with minimum provocation to adjust his sights. Those overseers who tried to bully the hands into picking a certain quota of cotton each day had to spend much time checking every detail, for the slaves falsified the weight by wetting the cotton or slipping rocks into the bags. The slaves learned that even some of the harshest overseers might wink at these tactics, for they too thought to gain by deceiving the master. More experienced overseers or those certain of contract renewals would not readily take the chance, but others would.[37]

Thus, the slaves struggled to influence their own working conditions. Their actions did not challenge slavery *per se*, nor were they often meant to, any more than striking workers often mean to challenge the capitalist system. Yet, in an important sense the slowdowns and resistance to overwork contributed more to the slaves' struggle for survival than did many bolder individual acts that may have reflected a willingness to attack slavery itself. The slaves did make gains in their everyday living conditions, which some latter-day ideologues, in the comfort of their studies, dismiss as mere sops to keep people quiet but which often meant the difference between agony and a chance to live with at least a minimum of decency. But more important, the collective form of this kind of resistance imparted a sense of community strength and taught the rudiments of organization in a way that individual acts of resistance, no matter how courageous or admirable, rarely could.

BROTHERS, SISTERS, AND
NO-'COUNTS

While in slavery, blacks protected each other much more readily than they undermined or betrayed each other. "People in my day," said Susan Davis, an ex-slave from Missouri, "didn't know book learning but dey studied how to protect each other, and save 'em from such misery as dey could."[1] Leading slaveholders agreed. Judge Green of the Tennessee State Supreme Court declared from the bench in 1844 that a slave who supported his white folks by exposing or betraying a fellow black would become "an object of general aversion among Negroes."[2] The Reverend C. C. Jones added more explicitly:

> The Negroes are scrupulous on one point, they make common cause, as servants, in *concealing* their faults from their owners. Inquiry elicits no information; no one feels at liberty to disclose the transgressor; all are profoundly ignorant; the matter assumes the sacredness of a "professional secret." . . . [3]

C. W. Gooch, in his "Prize Essay on Agriculture in Virginia," added that no greater crime existed for the slaves than that of betraying one another to the whites. In a similar vein, Whitemarsh B. Seabrook wrote: "Between slaves on the same plantation there is a deep sympathy of feeling which binds them so closely together that a crime committed by one of their number is seldom discovered through their instrumentality."[4] Charles P. Ware, who went to Port Royal to work with the freedmen during the Union occupation, contributed an exasperated corroboration:

> Their skill in lying, their great reticence, their habit of shielding one another (generally by silence), their invariable habit of taking a rod when you, after much persuasion, have been induced to grant an inch, their assumed innocence and ignorance of the slightest rules of *meum* and *teum*, joined with an amazing impudence in making claims. . . .[5]

An ex-slave who went on to achieve some distinction made the point differently several decades later: "Slaves were much truer to one another in those days than they have been since made free, and I am unable to assign any reason for it. . . ."[6]

Some former slaves complained bitterly that their people had not stuck together enough. "They taught us to be against one another," said an ex-slave from Tennessee, "and no matter where you would go you would always find one that would be tattling and would have the white folks pecking on you." Others insisted that some of the house slaves had acted as spies and gotten field hands into trouble.[7] But significantly, these stories center on a few slaves, often only on one or two, who broke ranks. The slaves generally do not seem to have vied with each other for white favor; nor did the house servants as a group betray the field hands to their masters.

The ways in which the slaves displayed solidarity often entailed considerable personal risk. Overseers expected the hands to help them subdue one of their number who resorted to physical resistance. Usually they did assist in subduing a rebel, either because they feared punishment or because they feared that the overseer would shoot the resistant slave, or because they thought the overseer justified in a particular case, or because they hated the slave in question, or because of any combination of these reasons. Yet, sometimes they refused to intervene or helped the victim to escape. Lucretia Alexander of Arkansas told of being held down by two slave girls while her master prepared to whip her. "They didn't much want to hold me anyhow," she said. "Some niggers would catch you and kill you for the white folks; and then there were some that wouldn't. I got loose from them."[8] Field hands often simply ignored a master's or overseer's call for help even when they knew they would be punished.[9]

The slaves reached out from their own farms and plantations to forge bonds of sympathy and cooperation, which served them well during the wartime desertions. Their religion in particular brought them together physically and spiritually. Success, however limited, resulted in part from an impressive system of communications, for their ability to transmit information—and misinformation—over long distances astounded their masters, who felt certain that every fiery statement by northern abolitionists reverberated through the plantations.[10] The slaveholders undoubtedly engaged in some exaggeration. William Wells Brown had never heard of Garrison or the abolitionists despite having worked as a hired boatman in St. Louis, of all places.[11] Yet, Peter Worsley's remarks about mid-twentieth-century Melanesia hold true for the Old South as well: "Europeans often underestimate the facility with which news and ideas and even material objects, can be passed on even in societies lacking modern techniques of communication."[12] James Stirling wrote during the 1850s: "There is no plantation so remote but what the echoes of this national warfare reach it, awakening to new thoughts and impulses all but the utterly degraded."[13]

The main methods of communication remain somewhat elusive. Folklore, black and white, attributes special significance to the African-style "talking drums," although some doubt of the extent of their use may be permitted.[14] R. Q. Mallard, less melodramatically but more plausibly, drew attention to the large number of slaves who had 'broad wives and who regularly moved about.[15] A large number of slaves hired out for limited periods and carried information from one place to another. Police jury minutes also reveal that many others had to work on roads and levees and undoubtedly brought political and other news back home. The simpler answer of Benjamin Russell, who had been a slave in South Carolina, may say enough:

> How did we get news? Many plantations were strict about this, but the greater the precaution the alerter became the slaves, the wider they opened their ears and the more eager they became for outside information. The sources were: Girls that waited on the tables and the drivers; they would pick up everything they heard and pass it on to the other slaves.[16]

The solidarity of the slaves grew within narrow limits. The slaves on one plantation often helped those on other plantations by protecting runaways or slipping food to those known to be underfed. When they knew each other, partied together, worshipped together, and married each other, their sense of extended family spread further than their own plantation. But without such specific ties their concern for each other remained slim, especially when masters worked to set them against each other by encouraging caste pretensions or inducing them to steal. The slaves, like many free and semifree rural folk the world over, simultaneously developed deep attachments to each other and a deep suspicion of outsiders. The definition of "outsiders" reflected a particular sense of community rather than a sense of class solidarity. The slaves defended themselves against much white aggression by their mutual assistance on the plantation or in the immediate neighborhood, but they could not easily go over to the offensive in league with slaves beyond their neighborhood, whom they greeted not so much with hostility as with suspicion or indifference. The web of paternalism in which they found themselves reinforced the provincial tendency to identify across class lines within a particular community. Hence, the slaves would refer to others from the same plantation as "same family to we," but would often more readily include their own white folks than they would blacks from other plantations.[17] The black preachers did much to expand the range of black brotherhood, but the struggle for unity could not easily be won in the absence of any means of organization.

Within each plantation divisive forces also existed, by no means solely or even primarily the much-discussed separation of house servants from field hands. Particularly in the Southwest but also in the older states, the domestic slave trade introduced a steady change of personnel that inhibited confidence. The slaves most frequently sold and resold qualified as tough and recalcitrant, but did not necessarily bring a positive influence with them. Many were criminal types by any definition, including the slaves' own. If some had found themselves sold for courageously defying cruel masters and overseers, many others had killed or dangerously quarreled with fellow slaves or had degenerated into antisocial beings who alternately tormented the whites and curried favor with them.

From slavery times to the present, black people have had to deal with "bad niggers" and "ba-ad niggers"—the greater the prolongation of the *a*, the greater the implicit approbation. In pure cases, which occurred among slaves about as frequently as pure cases of anything occur anywhere, the "ba-ad nigger" gave the white man hell, whereas the "bad nigger" terrorized other blacks. The real world being what it is, most ba-ad niggers were sometimes just bad, and vice versa. However much their lives as slaves and as oppressed black men among other oppressed black men gave a special quality to their behavior, these badmen basically represented a variation on a general theme. No one who has grown up in a lower-class urban neighborhood will fail to recognize the picture of some Tough Tony who would defend every kid on the block from outside aggression but who himself would probably inflict most of the beatings suffered by those under his protection. In some respects, bullies are the same everywhere, and however attractive and complex their personalities and actions, too many "bad niggers" (with or without the prolonged *a*) had a strong streak of the bully in them.

According to the myth, which does have a strong kernel of truth, every lower-class badman is a Robin Hood, avenging the poor and the downtrodden and harassing the Man. Eric Hobsbawm writes: "In any society as miserably poor and oppressed as that of the Sicilians there is a vast potential reserve of strong-arm men, as there is of prostitutes. The 'bad man' is, in the expressive phrase of French criminal slang, *affranchi*; and there are no other individual methods of escaping the bondage and virtual serfdom but bullying and outlawry."[18] Blacks, like oppressed peoples elsewhere, have glorified their badmen and preferred to see them as bad only by those unjust white standards which they have had the strength and courage to defy.

> I'se Wild Nigger Bill
>   Frum Redpepper Hill,
> I never did wo'k, an' I never will.
> I'se done kill de boss;
>   I'se knocked down de hoss;
> I eats up raw goose widout apple sauce![19]

The slaves viewed their badmen ambivalently, for they felt the effects of both sides of their behavior. In a deeper sense, the ambivalence reflected the contradictory social significance of that pattern for the quarters as a whole.

In many cases the balance tipped decisively toward the hero. Could slaves have had anything except admiration for their fellows on one of Isaac Franklin's plantations, whose defiance and physical resistance broke one overseer after another?[20] In a plantation world that did its futile best to emasculate black men, should we wonder at the expressions of pride in "incorrigible" fathers? Robert Falls, an ex-slave from Tennessee, proudly said of his father, "He was as mean as a bear. He was so bad to fight and so troublesome he was sold four times to my knowing and maybe a heap more times." In the recollections of ex-slaves and in slave songs, the intransigent father who was sold away often appeared in such a light. In the case of Robert Falls, his mother fell into the same category. She was so bad that, after she was sold, the slave traders sent her back.[21] Sarah Wilson remembered Uncle Nick, one terrible ba-ad nigger, who fought whites all the time and—too good to be true?—stole their food to feed hungry slaves.[22] These were the heroes. But in getting themselves killed or sold they also left their wives and children to face Ole Massa alone.

The slaves did not always appreciate their local badmen. "Dey was mean slaves," said James Lucas, an ex-slave from North Carolina, "de same as dey was mean marsters." David Blont, an ex-slave from North Carolina, had no better way to condemn his cruel overseer than to say that he was "meaner den a mean nigger." Rose Williams, who, as a slave in Texas, had been forced to marry and who hated her husband, described the perfect bully: "He am big and 'cause he so, he think everybody do what him say." A postwar black song made the point:

> In come a nigger named Billy Go-helf,
> Coon was so mean was skeered uf hisself;
> Loaded wid razors an' guns, so they say,
> 'Cause he killed a coon most every day.[23]

As a result, too often the slaves felt the need for protection against their heroes. When the driver had the character and physical strength to interpose himself, nothing much was lost. But when he did not, the slaves had to turn to their master and to slip further into dependency on whites. John S. Wise, from the vantage point of the Big House, told of his butler, Tom, who regularly raided the wine cellar. Measures finally had to be taken, not so much because of the thefts, which planters learned to take in stride, but because "his distemper developed an inclination to knock the heads of his fellow servants, male and female, on the slightest provocation."[24] Jake McLeod, an ex-slave from South Carolina, told of a man who elicited no sympathy from his fellow slaves when he was "unmercifully" whipped by his master, for his transgression had consisted in beating up another slave.[25] When Anderson, a slave in Missouri, faced trial for assault, the court learned that he drank excessively and, when drunk, "was in the habit of beating and wounding other slaves."[26] Probably few slaves offered sympathy to the man who got 150 lashes for teaching their children how to gamble.[27] Frank Adamson, who had also been a slave in South Carolina, vigorously defended his "good master, bestest in de land" for using a whip." 'Cause," he explained, "you'll find a whole passle of bad niggers when you gits a thousand of them in one flock."[28]

Many "model" slaves—"good Negroes," "good boys"—emerged suddenly as independent men and women, especially during and after the war, but many "bad niggers" at the same time emerged as model good boys. Mary Boykin Chesnut wrote with chagrin of a particularly trusted black who ran off to the Federals and wrote with joy of Clairborne, "that black rascal," whom everyone expected to be the first to defect but who saved the plantation home from being fired by enemy troops.[29] A planter near Augusta, Georgia, told John Richard Dennett in 1865 that some of the worst characters among the slaves had suddenly emerged as the white man's most valued and trusted allies.[30] These black gentlemen remind us of nothing so much as of the hoodlums who joined the forces of law and order in Mussolini's *squadristi* and Hitler's SA, or closer to home, of the "poor white trash," "ba-ad" characters among their own people because always ready to terrorize blacks.

One clue to the turnabout of some of the slaves with early reputations for bothering the whites may be found in the reports of those who fought white efforts to discipline them and yet proved good and reliable workers. These were the individualists who wanted to be left alone, but who gave no trouble when allowed to work in their own way. A master might, if he could without disrupting general discipline, look the other way. But if he could not or would not, then he would have a rough and rebellious man or woman on his hands.[31] These slaves provided a defiant individuality that strengthened the other slaves' ability to resist the master as an all-commanding pure will. But they were not likely to be of much help in building a spirit of community solidarity in the quarters, for their power derived precisely from their being loners.

Survival of the group and consolidation of its sense of community required an active accommodationism, which, if it were not to degenerate into passivity and self-negation, had to combine a spirit of defiance with all the tactics of getting along. Morton Rubin, writing of a plantation county during the twentieth century, points out that a "good Negro"—to the black community— is one who helps others even if he has to play up to the whites by being "good" in white terms. From the black point of view, there is a great difference between being a "good Negro" and being a "white man's nigger." The latter, in fact, is often brutal in his relations with blacks and dependent upon white protection to keep him from having to answer for crimes and outrages.[32] This type, which has had a long history in every class society, appeared frequently on the slave plantations.[33]

The prevalence of informers in the slave quarters would be incomprehensible without an understanding of the ambivalence called forth by the bullies. If the masters had had to rely only on traitors and spies, on classic Toms, they would not have had so easy a time. The slaves, once they learned the identity of informers, could ostracize them or worse. The negative significance of the "bad nigger" lay in his transforming many slaves, perhaps most at any given moment, into informers as a matter of self-preservation. An ex-slave admitted having told on a girl who had weighted her cotton bag with rocks. Why? Because the informer wanted her whipped as retribution for a beating she had inflicted.[34] A slave ran away and hid after killing his overseer. Normally, slaves helped each other in such situations. In this case, once he appeared, the other slaves handed him over. We have to guess at the reasons.[35] The slaves did not necessarily jump for joy over a fellow who shirked work, for they might have to take up the slack and had a right to expect everyone to share the misery up to his capacity.[36] Even when a slave was ba-ad rather than bad, he aroused considerable ambivalence. Frederick William Turner III writes of black—and white—folk heroes:

> In the eventual defeat and violent death of the outlaw we witness the triumph of the forces of law and order, those forces which guarantee our survival. We allow ourselves to participate vicariously in the successes of the outlaw, and we are one with him as his career rises to meteoric heights. But in his hour of defeat the outlaw is alone; we have left him to join the forces of law and order, and we take a certain pleasure in witnessing his violence turned against him.[37]

The best of the bad niggers—the really ba-ad ones—deserved some of the admiration they called forth in song and story, but their contribution, however essential, lay in its negativity. They were, for the most part, the nihilists of the quarters. Oppressed peoples cannot avoid admiring their own nihilists, who are the ones most dramatically saying "No!" and reminding others that there are worse things than death. No people wholly lacking such an attitude can expect to survive. But for the whole people the aim remains to live, not to die heroically. To live and forge themselves into a people the slaves had to resort to more restrained tactics. The ba-ad niggers' negativity, and even that of those many bad niggers who were not in the white man's pocket, provided an indispensable spur to the collective's positive work. But they remained basically outsiders, marginal men, who had to be sacrificed whenever the business of living needed to be pushed forward.

Frantz Fanon, commenting on the violence of life under certain colonial conditions, suggests that colonizers often strive to keep alive old feuds among the colonized:

> While the settler or the policeman has the right the live-long day to strike the native, to insult him and to make him crawl to them, you will see the native reaching for his knife at the slightest hostile or aggressive glance cast on him by another native; for the last resort of the native is to defend his personality vis-à-vis his brother. . . . Tribal feuds only serve to perpetuate old grudges deep buried in the memory. By throwing himself with all his force into the *vendetta*, the native tries to persuade himself that colonialism does not exist, that everything goes on as before, that history continues.[38]

As if prefiguring Fanon's indictment of the oppressor's regime, although actually aiming toward a different end, Judge Nash of the North Carolina Supreme Court remarked: "They [the slaves] sometimes kill each other in heat of blood, being sensible to the dishonor in their own caste of crouching in submission to one of themselves."[39]

The slaves quarreled a good deal, fought often enough to cause concern among their masters and overseers, and occasionally killed each other. "The niggers wasn't whipped much," recalled Richard Jackson, an ex-slave from Texas, " 'cept for fightin' 'monst themselves."[40] Much quarreling went on in the Big House, in which cooks and Mammies exercised despotic power, were quick with their hands, and from time to time took blows in return.[41] Quarrels in the quarters occurred over anything and everything, but hard blows were struck more selectively; although anything—an insult, a gesture—might lead to violence, usually much weightier provocation was required.

Curses and insulting language could provoke violence because the slaves did not use either lightly. They did use coarse language but did not, by the white standards of the time, do much swearing. Vulgarity of speech can only be defined by local convention and sensibility, but by their own standards the planters did badly, unless of course their ladies were present. In the rougher regions of the South the solemnity of the houses of justice proved no deterrent; judges and witnesses alike used language that left visitors gasping.[42] The yeomen, including their women, did even worse than the planters, and the poor whites were a scandal. The slaves often bore the brunt of white obscenity, especially from overseers. They resented it and saw in it a mark of contempt; sometimes they protested against it.[43]

The Reverend C. C. Jones charged that the slaves swore fright-fully, but the Union troops who occupied the South Carolina and Georgia lowlands found the opposite to be true. The Reverend Mr. Jones's son-in-law, the Reverend R. Q. Mallard, came closer to the truth when he wrote that the slaves' language was sometimes "coarse," "rarely vulgar," and "never profane."[44] Generally, the slaves' sometime reputation for vulgar language rested on the rough-speaking urban slaves and free Negroes, not on the country people.[45]

Hard cursing, by their own standards, could be heard every-where,[46] but the contradictory reports should be seen in a different light. The slaves personalized their religion, and Moses, Jesus, Mr. Linkum, and "de Big Massa" (God) often merged into a single living being. Hence, what whites took for profanity usually was one or another kind of respectful religious imagery. For the rest, the "coarseness" but not "vulgarity" to which the Reverend Mr. Mallard referred reflected a strong penchant for earthiness. How-ever much "swearing" and "vulgarity" the plantation slaves may have engaged in—hardly a matter of importance apart from its possible provocation to physical retaliation—they did riddle their speech with sexual, physical, and other allusions that contributed immeasurably to their cultivation of ambiguity. Thus, "Tittawisa" (or "Titty 'ouisa"), which was the normal way to refer to a slave named Louisa, meant "Sister Louisa" but also identified her by physical attribute in a way whites, for all their own foul language, considered coarse.[47] But if one slave really cursed another out, he could expect a harsh response.

Cases of murder and manslaughter, as documented in the rec-ords of the state supreme courts, offer a better idea of the sources of violence in the quarters. Conflicts over women (or men) pro-vided the most important immediate cause, with stealing and gam-bling disputes also prominent. "Jealousy," wrote David Gavin, that planter of the South Carolina low country who had his own problems with women, or rather not enough such, "seems to be common amongst women, white and black, some quarrels amongst my slave women I find originate in that."[48] Gavin expressed a one-sided view. Men more often than women resorted to violence out of jealousy. The innermost thoughts of the participants remain closed, but one speculation may be permitted. Black men could not, without risking their lives—which they often did—protect their women against the sexual violence of white men. All the more, then, however irrational it might seem to others, would they appoint themselves as protectors of the chastity of women who did not ask for protection and did not always want it. They defended their own manliness and their women's virtue, although the women did not necessarily see their actions that way.

From time to time the slaves killed each other.[49] The killing of a slave by a slave occurred often enough for southern periodicals such as the *Planter's Banner* of St. Mary's Parish, Louisiana, to take note of the crime and the sentence laconically: "Another Negro Sentenced."[50] In such cases the black defendant had a much better chance for a fair trial than in cases of violence against whites.[51] Instances of capital punishment and such severe sentences as twenty years at hard labor suggest some effort to protect black life and not merely slave property.[52]

In many other cases slaves who murdered slaves escaped with short prison terms, branding, whipping, transportation, and other lighter forms of punishment.[53] It would be easy to conclude that the masters and their courts worried more about the pecuniary loss involved in hanging a slave than they did about accounting for the life of the dead black. Whites showed such contempt for the loss of black lives in postbellum times that southern black communities had to demand punishment of blacks for assaulting or killing other blacks. Yet, southern whites seem to have taken a tougher attitude before emancipation. If they handed down sentences that fell short of the extreme penalty, they often did so because they doubted premeditation and assumed that such crimes reflected momentary passions. No doubt racism perverted white perceptions and created its own injustices. But white restraint cannot be seen through postbellum lenses and dismissed merely as a manifestation of racism. To some extent it reflected a genuine attempt to grapple with the quality of life in the quarters.

An account in the diary of the articulate John Berkley Grimball of South Carolina may serve as an illustration. His slave, Moses, got into a fight with a slave belonging to another planter. The other man pulled a knife. Moses struck him with a stick and killed him. Grimball secured the best lawyer he could, but feared that Moses would hang. After a trial before a magistrate and five free-holders, Moses was found guilty of "murder in the second degree or manslaughter" and sentenced to confinement for six months with fifty lashes per month, unless his master sold him out of the state after three months. Grimball's comments make it clear that the fear of pecuniary loss did not take precedence in his mind. "Such is the sentence," he wrote, "which (seeing, as I believe it was, a mere fight) I think a very severe one. . . . At the end of the three months I shall ship him—to save him the balance of the whipping—and also because he is now exceedingly obnoxious to the neighborhood."[54] When a slave killed a slave from another plantation, his master often responded in a manner that suggests a sense of duty, as well as sympathy for his own.

Slaveholders responded much more sternly when their slaves hurt others on the same plantation. In a way this distinction made sense. The slaveholders always tried to instill a corporate spirit in their slaves and to encourage them to identify with others on the plantation, black and white, against outsiders. Thus the Reverend C. C. Jones, who was not naive in these matters, could express shock when one slave drowned another. He could hardly believe that a slave would kill another from the same plantation—the same "family." His son, Charles Jr., who was if anything more hard-headed, was no less shocked when he heard that "a Negro [was] supposed to have been murdered by his fellow-servant."[55]

Many masters were determined to preserve order in the quar-ters, for the sense of "family" itself hung in the balance. But in addition, all quarrels threatened morale, decorum, discipline, and productivity. From the masters' point of view the defense of the family and the preservation of order and productivity comple-mented each other and merged into one image of what life should be. Thus they arrogated to themselves, when they could, the role of arbiter of their slaves' lives in this as in other respects.

The declarations of the slaveholders make clear their attitudes, pretensions, and interests. D. R. Hundley claimed that the slaves often poisoned each other and only rarely poisoned whites, and added:

And it is utterly confounding for what trivial causes they will take the life of a fellow-slave. Sometimes it is simply a dispute about a game at cards or marbles; sometimes the being supplanted by a rival in the confidence of the master or overseer is the exciting cause; but much more frequently jealousy leads to the fatal deeds, or a strong desire to get rid of a troublesome wife or husband in order to solace themselves with some new "affinity."[56]

A few years later, W. P. Bocock of Alabama instructed his overseer: "No Negro will be suffered under any pretense whatever to strike another—excepting always such moderate correction as it may be necessary for parents to use with their children."[57] With this attitude slaveholders generally intervened to settle matters in accordance with their own judgment. "On account of the changes, interruptions and interferences in families," wrote Reverend C. C. Jones, "there are quarrelings and fighting, and a considerable item in the management of plantations is the settlement of family troubles. Some owners become disgusted and wearied out, and finally leave their people to their own way."[58]

Shrewd masters, caught between a desire to assert their own authority and that weariness of which the Reverend Mr. Jones spoke, tried to compromise by setting up some kind of judicial system in which blacks and whites both participated. "Each and every one," wrote B. McBride in 1830, "should have a fair trial for a crime touching character, before punished, and when punished, avoid the whip as much as possible."[59] W. W. Hazard of Georgia wrote in support a year later:

> When any quarrel or disturbance occurs on my plantation, one or two not implicated are examined in the presence of the accused, who have the right to correct false statements, and establish their innocence, by reference to other testimony, which is immediately produced by the driver, or if absent, and the case is an important one, judgment is arrested until the necessary information can be procured.[60]

Some dozen years later, William Ethelbert Ervin of Mississippi sounded the same theme: "All quarreling and matters of differences between parties to be settled by arbitration, the arbiters being chosen one by each part & they choosing the third." If convicted by a majority, the slave would be liable to as many as twenty lashes at Ervin's discretion. Alexander Telfair of Savannah, Georgia, on the other hand, took a different line: "If there be any fighting on the plantation, whip all engaged in it—for no matter what the cause may have been, all are in the wrong."[61] These various reactions reveal that the slaves were asserting their wish to settle matters among themselves and that many masters were seeking some kind of compromise.

But, with due notice of the masters' claims, propaganda, and self-serving assertions, did the slaves actually inflict great violence upon one another? Did they in fact require the masters' heavy hand or velvet glove? Any answer must be tentative, for the question cannot be posed counterfactually. No estimate can be made of the results that would have followed if the masters' surveillance had not obtained. But the slaves do not seem to have treated each other nearly so harshly as Fanon's remarks on colonials or slaveholders' assertions or blithe assumptions might suggest.

On close inspection, the slaves' reputation for violence against one another rests on two specific circumstances, which often became one: drunken blacks, like drunken whites, resorted to violence more frequently than did sober blacks; and slaves in the loose social setting of the towns resorted to violence more frequently than did those in the more disciplined countryside. These circumstances merged because town slaves had easier access to liquor and were much more prone to drunkenness and disorder than were plantation slaves. Moreover, a certain number of victims of violence from sober plantation slaves were notorious informers and regarded as traitors to their fellow slaves.[62] Suspicions about the extent of violence in the quarters are raised by the comments of such observant travelers as Lyell and Olmsted. Lyell wrote from Georgia in the mid-1840s: "There were more serious quarrels, and more broken heads, among the Irish in a few years, when they came to dig the Brunswick Canal, than had been known among the negroes in all the surrounding plantations for half a century." A decade later Olmsted wrote from northern Alabama that all talk of hiring Irish workers instead of blacks had come to naught because they were too quarrelsome and violent toward each other.[63] These and similar comments undoubtedly reflect a widespread hostility toward the Irish, but they also reveal much about the planters' more sober estimate of black behavior.

Slaves in Virginia, wrote a slaveholder, "are more generally good-tempered than other people—they are kind towards each other."[64] Quickness of temper had always proceeded along with extraordinary courtesy. "The contrabands," wrote Lucy Chase, "are very mindful of the courtesies due each other. Good day and good health are their daily wishes. . . ." And Colonel Higginson reported with admiration the unfailing courtesy of his black troops toward one another. Frederick Douglass, who did not romanticize any aspect of slave life, saluted "the general temper and ardent friendship of my brother slaves," which produced the little happiness he had found in slavery. The Reverend C. C. Jones, who complained so stridently about slave violence, ended by admitting that, all things considered, they hurt and killed each other less often, proportionately, than any other people in the country.[65] The planters in the Sea Islands, according to one of their most careful historians, "found their laborers mild and forgiving, quick to start a quarrel, but as quick to forget it."[66]

With half the slaves in the South on units of four black families or less and another quarter on units of ten families or less, relationships among the slaves were often a family matter. "Lord, dere was a heap of Niggers on dat place," said Georgia Baker, "and all of us was kin to one another." Most of the slaves' quarrels consisted, as it were, of family affairs, and the occasional violence more often than not grew out of a flash of passion rather than a prolonged grudge. Life could be turbulent, even dangerous, but it rarely became vicious.[67]

The pattern of slave behavior had its white counterpart; together they derived from and contributed to a regional culture that long survived its plantation, frontier, and folk origins. Willie Morris, writing of his boyhood in Mississippi, reflects:

> That curious Mississippi apposition—of courtliness and extraordinary kindliness on the one hand, and sudden violence on the other —was a phenomenon which never occurred to me. We would laugh off the violence, engaging in it occasionally ourselves, while conducting ourselves according to the code as courteous and only slightly syrupy gentlemen, always ready with the proper word or the hospitable gesture. The apposition was merely a fact of our life, suggesting no irony. Among our elders, and even in the vaguest of "social" situations, the thing that mattered was *form*.[68]

The violence that slaves inflicted on each other fell far short of the appalling southern norm, whereas their kindness and courtesy equaled or exceeded it.

The masters reacted too quickly, in part because they feared the effect of any disorder on labor discipline and in part because their self-image required constant meddling in the lives of people whom they could not admit to be capable of taking care of themselves. For whatever reasons, they did work to calm disputes and minimize violent confrontation, but the positive results of their efforts would have fallen far short had they not intersected with a similar thrust from the quarters. The slaves, often led by their drivers and their preachers, made an effort to live together in peace. They had to: life was too close for anything else. And, as that Virginia slaveholder observed, despite their share of jealousy, suspicion, pettiness, and violence, they did try to be "kind towards each other."

"ALL NEGROES ARE FATALISTS"

The southern medical profession expressed deep concern over the slaves' "apathy" and "fatalism." Dr. William A. Booth, for example, fretted over the resignation shown by so many slaves during the great cholera epidemic of 1849: "The worse it rages the less they regard it."[1] R. R. Gibbes, writing from his plantation in South Carolina, picked up the theme:

> Negroes are generally fatalists, and believe that every one has his time appointed to die, and if it be "come" they expect to die; and, if not, they will get well without medicine. . . . Frequently have I found the patient's bed turned from its position of the day before, in order that he might die "with his face towards the rising sun," and often have I had it restored and informed them that their "time had not come *to go home*," as they call it.[2]

Attempts to grapple with black behavior encouraged the rise of a notable school of racist medicine, which won considerable support from within the medical profession but also drew heavy fire. Some leading medical men responded sensibly to the idea that whites and blacks might have different susceptibilities to disease and tried to pursue the question scientifically. Nevertheless, many slaveholders took the theories of such ideologically motivated physicians as Samuel A. Cartwright, Josiah Nott, and John Stainback Wilson seriously and indulged in various pseudoscientific speculations about black psychological traits.[3] In particular, many slaveholders tried to adapt their own behavior to presumed black psychology and its ostensible somatic effects, including an alleged African fatalism and apathy.[4]

Northerners who went south during the war found themselves confronted by the black behavior that had given rise to these grand theories. The attitude described by Gibbes and the physicians appears in the remark of the recently freed black man to whom Elizabeth Hyde Botume had expressed condolences on the loss of a child. "Oh we mustn't say that," he answered. "We mustn't fly in the face of Providence. The Massa call my leetle gal an' him mus' go. Ef him call him, him wanted him, an' us can't say nothing."[5] Miss Botume had company among other northern whites who had taken up work with the freedmen. Edward S. Philbrick, William Gannett, Thomas Wentworth Higginson, and others were faced with the same problem.[6]

The slaveholders complained bitterly about black apathy and indifference and especially about an alleged unconcern for the future, and the blacks themselves sometimes concurred. "A nigger," remarked James Johnson, an ex-slave from South Carolina, "wants what is in sight and not dat what he can't see; it can look out for itself."[7] In one sense the slaveholders got precisely what they asked for. Consider, for example, the pontificating of C. T. Botts, editor of the *Southern Planter:* "No laborer should have his attention distracted or his time occupied in thinking about what he should do next; the process of thought and arrangement should devolve wholly upon the superintendent, and the manual laborer, to be most effective, should by constant repetitions perform mechanically, and almost without the effort, his daily task."[8] To the limited extent to which Botts's formula found application on the plantations, apathy, indifference, and fatalism found the strongest encouragement from above.

Too many contemporaries, black and white, described this fatalism to permit its dismissal as a figment of white racist imagination. Yet black religion, in its fullest extension as total world-view, exuded love of life, and most slaves did not succumb to the spirit-breaking thrust of plantation discipline. Many undoubtedly did fall prey to demoralization in the wake of excessive beatings, hidden hungers from dietary deficiencies, and a variety of psychological aggressions. The evidence of widespread dirt eating alone suggests, although it does not prove, that many suffered from wretchedly unbalanced diets and worked themselves into a stupor.[9] But the low level of suicide, among other things, cautions against hasty generalizations.

The assertion that slaves frequently committed suicide, quaintly put forward by some historians as a form of "day-to-day resistance to slavery," rests on no discernible evidence. J. H. Hammond, South Carolina's outstanding planter and political leader, affirmed: "However frequent suicide may have been among those brought from Africa, I can say that in my time I cannot remember to have known or heard of a single instance of deliberate self-destruction, and but one of suicide at all."[10] Governor Hammond could hardly have denied the mass suicides on slave ships, since they had drawn much comment over the years. The Africans who chose it had a special purpose, for often they believed that their action would lead to reincarnation in Africa. They also had a special incentive: to avoid being eaten by the whites, whom they often thought to be cannibals.[11] The rest of Hammond's report on the slaves in the South betrays a certain disingenuousness. Harriet Martineau took the opposite tack and declared suicides frequent.[12] Neither version commends itself.

Without adequate statistics, rough impressions will have to serve. Enough slaves committed suicide to constitute an indictment of the regime, especially when the apparent reasons are reviewed, but not nearly enough to suggest that they saw suicide as an acceptable means of resistance in other than isolated cases.[13] Most seem to have resorted to suicide to escape capture after having run away or to avoid punishment or sale. For the most part, however, the slaves clung to life tenaciously and sought other responses to their imposed misery.

The low incidence of suicide among the slaves set a pattern that carried well into the twentieth century. As of 1940, according to Gunnar Myrdal, the black rate was 4.0 per 100,000, in contrast with 15.5 for whites.[14] There is no reason to believe that the suicide rate shifted sharply with emancipation, as it did with the Russian serfs, among whom suicides noticeably declined after 1861.[15] In recent decades the suicide rate has risen among young urban blacks, as has the homicide rate, to which it is apparently related. In the rural Deep South, no marked change has occurred. That is, where the community has retained its traditional cohesiveness or recapitulated it in a new setting, suicide has remained infrequent.[16]

Sociologists and psychologists have advanced many theses to

explain suicide: fear of the unknown and passive surrender to a feared death; escape from responsibility; final despair in existence; escape from the intended murder of others; symbolic murder of those with whom one identifies; an attempt at mental blackmail against those we want to feel eternal remorse; the killing of an introjected enemy; an effort at rescue and revival; and others.[17] Suicide normally being an individual act, any of these might obtain in any case. Yet Joost A. M. Meerlo provides an illuminating clue to the infrequency of suicide among slaves when he suggests that about 70 percent of all suicides suggest a passive inner justification: "As long as the person is aware that one person cares for him (I mean really cares and not as a mechanical formula), he does not lose hope of conquering his inner conflicts."[18] The strong sense of stewardship in the quarters—of collective responsibility for each other—probably accounts for the low suicide rate more than does any other factor. The "fatalism" with which blacks accepted their blackness, with all its temporal limitations in the social order, and their life-affirming religion may be understood as analytically inseparable from the tradition of stewardship.

The slaves' fatalism, if so it may be called, had deceptively positive qualities, which developed in tandem with the religiously grounded joy in life manifest in their everyday behavior. The slaves, like their African forebears and many other premodern peoples, closely identified stoic courage in the face of endless trial with cruelty itself. Colonel Higginson linked the fatalism of his black troops to their familiarity with intense and frequent physical pain. He thought that they had become insensitive to inflicting pain on others through learning how to stand it themselves. In this respect the slaves unwittingly carried on the African pattern of rejecting self-pity as an invitation to further misery.[19] This quality helps account for the slaves' well-known brutality toward animals and their extraordinary ability to face every kind of disappointment and adversity with so little whining.

The slaves faced death with apparent equanimity, not because they cared little for life but because they considered death an extension of life. Their religion, as manifested in their daily lives —or, if you will, their daily lives as crystallized in their religion —vigorously affirmed life. But this affirmation prepared them to die. The attitude toward death inherent in their religion received enormous reinforcement from the conditions of their oppression. As Fanon wrote of the Algerians and other colonized peoples:

The disinherited in all parts of the world perceive life not as a flowering or a development of an essential productiveness, but as a permanent struggle against an omnipresent death. This ever-menacing death is experienced as endemic famine, unemployment, a high death rate, an inferiority complex and the absence of any hope for the future.

All this gnawing at the existence of the colonized tends to make of life something resembling an incomplete death. Acts of refusal or rejection of medical treatment are not a refusal of life, but a greater passivity before that close and contagious death.[20]

The slaves showed evidence of this tendency, but they transformed it into a positive force through the infusion of a powerful spiritual thrust of their own.

In other respects, too, the slaves' fatalism and apathy became weapons of resistance embodying the opposite of that loss of will which so many have read into them. Significantly, the slaves neither often drank to excess nor acted on their knowledge of the narcotic effects of hemp. Upper-class white ladies, including Mary Boykin Chesnut, dabbled in opium and other narcotics. The slaves did not.[21]

With the price of liquor about forty cents a gallon, even slaves had no trouble getting it. A bustling trade developed between slaves and déclassé poor whites, as well as more substantial peddlers and shopkeepers; the outcry against it created the impression that drunkenness ran rampant in the quarters. Actually, the outcry revealed the extent of the trade and its social implications rather than the extent of drinking among the slaves. Olmsted's report from South Carolina provides a fair statement of the slaveholders' concerns:

> I have been once or twice told that the poor white people, meaning those, I suppose, who bring nothing to market to exchange for money but their labor, although they may own a cabin and a little furniture, and cultivate land enough to supply themselves with (maize) bread, are worse off in almost all respects than the slaves. They are said to be extremely ignorant and immoral, as well as indolent and unambitious. . . . They are said to "corrupt" the negroes, and to encourage them to steal, or to work for them at night and on Sundays, and to pay them with liquor, and also to constantly associate licentiously with them. They seem, nevertheless, more than any other portion of the community, to hate and despise the negroes.[22]

With such unscrupulous white men to sell him liquor at a few cents a pint, almost any slave who was willing to stint himself on food and clothing could have his fill even without stealing or working in his spare time.

The big planters and their spokesmen led an unsuccessful fight for suppression of the trade and prosecution of white offenders.[23] In much of North Carolina and other regions in which lower-class whites dominated the juries and resentment of planter pretensions ran high, the courts cynically acquitted the offenders. Where the offenders were local toughs, respectable planters risked violence to their person or property if they complained.[24] In the heart of the plantation districts, however, the planters had greater resources and sometimes reversed the pattern of violence while also falling back on the law.[25] The police and the courts did their best. Offenders received fines of fifty to three hundred dollars and more and even short prison terms throughout the Lower South.[26] But once again, the slaveholders found themselves at a disadvantage because of their own unwillingness to permit black testimony against white men, for it excluded the principal witnesses.

Concern over the illicit trade in liquor did not focus on plantation drunkenness. Planters complained occasionally about the quarreling and bullying attendant upon heavy drinking in the quarters, but the problem never rose to major proportions. Complaints about drunkenness among slaves and free Negroes centered in the towns and cities, in which attention fell on the encouragement to theft, the breaking down of racial barriers, and the camaraderie between blacks and poor whites.[27] In the countryside, the great fear concerned the protection of runaways by poor whites who courted favor among slave thieves and who might even become sympathetic enough to encourage insubordination and rebellion. Grogshops and contact between blacks and poor whites at drinking and gambling parties had long been suspected of playing a role in the Prosser, Vesey, and similar plots.[28] A South Carolina planter expressed these fears in 1860 over a situation he admitted to have been innocent enough:

> Yesterday went to Cyprus camp meeting. There was an alarm there on Friday night of an insurrection of the negroes and patrols were put out, but it proved to be false, nothing more destructive was found amongst the negroes than spirits, some good and some very bad, which they had no doubt bought of mean democratic white men who are no better than abolitionists.[29]

The slaves everywhere did a thriving business in stolen goods with these "mean democratic white men." More than anything else, the laws against trading with slaves aimed to suppress the stealing.[30] The slaves' easy access to liquor did not often create large-scale plantation drunkenness.

The slaveholders had another complaint that reveals something about their attitude toward their slaves. In many cases, wrote Charles Woodson of Prince Edward County, Virginia, the whites who dealt with the slaves had "unexceptionable general character." Still hé expressed apprehension, for even when the slaves paid with their own money or with goods they had procured honestly by hunting, working their gardens, or making useful items in their spare time, "It renders the slave independent in a great measure of his master." The slave, he added, worked more conscientiously for himself than for his master and would shepherd his strength at his master's expense. Fanny Kemble, on the other hand, pointed out that the slaves in precisely these cases could easily be cheated by unscrupulous whites with whom they had to do business.[31]

Knowledge of heavy drinking among the laboring classes of England led many abolitionists, as well as some temperance-minded southerners, to assume its existence among the slaves, especially since the grogshops of the towns and more heavily concentrated plantation districts seemed to be recapitulating the English scene.[32] Yet whites and blacks, southerners and travelers, reported no great problem among the slaves. The Union troops who occupied the Sea Islands, expecting to find demoralization and dissipation, were pleasantly surprised by their absence. Colonel Higginson, for example, reported little drunkenness among his black recruits despite easy access to liquor.[33] Lyell and Mrs. Schoolcraft had long before insisted on the same point, and in postbellum South Carolina gambling but not drunkenness plagued the black community.[34]

Only occasionally did planters or former slaves report chronic drunkards or even periodically heavy drinkers among the slaves.[35] Even less often did such complaints fall on the women, who seem to have restricted their consumption of alcohol to light drinks. Most masters let their slaves drink freely during the Christmas holiday and at special holiday barbecues, when in fact many did get drunk. Masters had no objection to heavy drinking at these times so long as no violence resulted. A few masters provided liquor to their slaves at all times and relied on their self-control to

avoid excess. Rarely, apart from holiday frolics, at which getting
drunk became almost a test of manhood for the young men, did
widespread drunkenness occur among the slaves, although it did
among masters, overseers, and neighboring poor whites.[36]

For the most part, the slaves confined their serious drinking to
the allotted times and limited their everyday intake to a shot of
whiskey in cold weather. Even at their balls they used persimmon
or locust beer or cider, which they made themselves, usually with
no objection from masters. William B. Smith of Virginia recalled:
"An old servant in my family was remarkable for making good
persimmon beer, and whenever I would pass the door of his house,
he never failed to invite me in to taste his beer." Smith quoted the
slave as saying, "Come, master, drink some beer; simmon beer and
ash-cake is equal to *cash*; but it don't make *glad* come like whiskey."[37] And West Turner, who had been a slave in Louisiana, told
how it was done:

> We made persimmon beer, too. Jest stuck our persimmons in a keg
> with two or three gallons of water and sweet potato peelings and
> some hunks of corn bread and left it there until it began to work. It
> sure is good to drink 'long with cracklin' bread and potatoes.[38]

The slaves preferred a safer vice than heavy drinking—chewing,
sniffing, and smoking tobacco. Both men and women freely used
tobacco while working as well as when at leisure, and they spent
a considerable portion of their money and exchangeable goods for
it. When they could, they raised their own and soaked it in sugar
and honey for chewing purposes. Keeping the slaves reasonably
quiet meant keeping them in tobacco, and the same rule applied
to blacks with both the Union and the Confederate armies. "Tain't
no fun, chile," an old black woman explained to her inquisitive
thirteen-year-old daughter. "But it's a pow'ful lot o' easement.
Smoke away trouble, darter. Blow ole trouble an' worry 'way in
smoke."[39]

In view of the easy access to hard liquor, the general sobriety of
the slaves speaks well for their community strength and resistance
to demoralization. The contrast between the behavior of the slaves
and that of the Indians compels attention, especially since drunkenness among the Indians of the Southeast mushroomed precisely
among the "half-breeds" who had sacrificed their traditional culture and adopted white ways without, however, winning acceptance as white men.[40] Black sobriety may also testify to the depth

of the religious commitment and the moral influence of the preachers. These matters must remain objects of speculation, along with another that may speak well for the plantation diet. If Keith Thomas is right in suggesting that much of the heavy drinking among the seventeenth-century English poor resulted from dietary cravings caused by excessive reliance on cereals, then the diet of the slaves, with its adequate quantity of meat, must appear good by comparison.[41]

Southern whites had a genius for attributing their own faults to the slaves, and the dither over the alleged abuse of alcohol provides one more illustration. Still, the slaveholders behaved with greater restraint than did the Atlantic slave traders, who deliberately fostered heavy drinking on the African coast and then tried to justify their gangsterism on the grounds of having to save the Africans from licentiousness.[42] The sobriety of the slaves becomes the more impressive when considered in relation not only to the drinking of the laboring poor of England and other industrial countries, but also to that of the whites among whom they had to live.

The First Assembly of the new colony of Virginia in 1619 had to take measures to combat white drunkenness, and the planters, as well as the middle-class and lower-class whites, maintained their reputation down to the end of the old regime.[43] A distressing number of the South's greatest men had—as Alonza Fantroy Toombs said mournfully of his beloved old master, Robert Toombs of Georgia—this one great fault.[44] If the habits of the southern whites are explained by the pressures of frontier life in both North and South, as well they might be,[45] the slave regime itself preserved those frontier conditions as part of its process of development.

The use of whiskey in white homes of all classes caused visitors to gasp. A mint julep before breakfast had become the custom early in the colonial period among the well-to-do, and whiskey at table in place of wine or beer was normal among the middle and lower classes.[46] Looking back from the vantage point of 1908, Eliza Frances Andrews recalled having always placed a bottle of wine or brandy or both in the room of a visiting gentleman, not only for a nightcap but for an eye-opener in the morning.[47]

The slaves were not amused. Drunken masters too often got ugly and took out their aggressions on their slaves. More important, drunken masters more often than not became improvident and lost their fortunes, with the result that the old place had to be sold and families and friends separated. The slaves did have a drinking problem, about which they often commented, but it concerned their masters' drinking.[48]

Slaveholders usually interpreted every kind of behavior among their slaves in such a way as to justify the status quo. Since the slaveholders sought to transform their slaves into extensions of their own will, they could not easily explain the apparent apathy or acknowledge the widespread evidence of submerged hostility. They had to sacrifice both logic and ideological purity to self-interest and to try to instill a fear that might accomplish what other measures could not.

Many slaves grew up in mortal fear of their masters and indeed of all white men. The number and proportion may have been much smaller than normally supposed, although most no doubt recognized that any white could hurt them at any given moment. That recognition also constituted fear, but it simultaneously engendered anger and spiritual resistance. White southerners too often took a narrow view of this fear. "The negro," wrote Ingraham, "has a habitual fear of the white man, which has become a second nature."[49] The language in John McDonough's will especially deserves attention, for this big planter and businessman of Louisiana had earned his reputation as a man genuinely concerned with the welfare of black people:

> Having been the friend of the black and colored man through . . . my long life, I will now give to them (the free black and colored man, wherever he may be throughout our . . . country) a parting counsel. . . . That they may separate themselves from the white man . . . and depart to the land of their fathers . . . where they and their posterity . . . may be safe—may be happy . . . having none to make them afraid.[50]

During the eighteenth and nineteenth centuries advertisements for runaways often referred to slaves who stuttered and had a downcast look or, specifically, to those who spoke haltingly to white men. Historians have interpreted these data as evidence of anxiety and fear.[51] Yet, these slaves' being runaways suggests something more, as does the occasional evidence of stuttering among "impertinent" house slaves, independent-minded and spirited mechanics, and others who clearly did not qualify as weaklings or Toms.[52] And significantly, modern black blues singers often use a calculated stutter to convey emotions they regard as too intense for words.[53]

The stuttering, stammering, and downcast looks before white men betrayed not only fear but smoldering anger and resentment. Their recurrence among runaways also lends some support to recent theories that associate stuttering with a sense of isolation, with fathers vague or distant, with domineering mothers, and with an inability to cope with authority.[54] Recent psychological researches cannot be projected back in an attempt to construct a depth psychology of strangers long since dead. But these researches do conform in a general way to a perception of many slaves as seething with hostility toward those who commanded the paternalistic relationship in which they found themselves embedded, especially when authority manifested itself in ways that must have seemed arbitrary, capricious, insensitive, and brutal. William B. Hamilton of Red River Landing, Louisiana, wrote his wife a troubled and puzzled letter:

> Wednesday night last Old Fanny dropped off very suddenly. She became very unruly, and the Major was punishing her a little, when she fainted right off. We had a coroner's inquest and postmortem examination made. The punishment was very light; there were no extensive external injuries upon the body, and from the doctor's examination he found the heart congested. This was caused by violent passion; or some sudden and violent mental emotion.[55]

The slaves' kind of fatalism proceeded in harmony with their submerged anger and merged with its apparent opposite—a doctrine of chance. As such, it illustrates a politically pregnant remark of Georg Simmel:

> Fate is generally defined as the agency which determines the development of that which man does not represent himself—although his own actions and his own being may be involved in these deciding powers. Because of this meeting of the inner being with something alien to it, the concept of fate contains existentially a motive of chance; which evidences a fundamental tension in the soul with regard to the meaning of life; at even those times fate acts as the very performer of man's will.[56]

Florestan Fernandes's reading of the attitude of Brazilian slaves holds true for American slaves as well in a sense akin to Simmel's remarks:

> Apathy may be seen as a potentially dynamic condition, as a choice that involved the predisposition to use the limp-body technique to

the end . . . deliberately using the only form of resistance and voluntary adaptive behavior that the Negro and mulatto had at their disposal. . . . The extreme apathy of the Negro and mulatto revealed itself to be a method of personal self-assertion while it hid its significance as a means of collective resistance.[57]

A people at bay or in a prolonged period of defeat in which the initiative belongs to the enemy can transform fatalism into a tremendous moral power. During those times fatalism becomes a way of holding on to the idea of final deliverance—of final victory. It negates the idea of submission at the precise moment and in the precise ways that it seems to surrender to it.

THE RUNAWAYS

The boldest slaves struck the hardest blow an individual could against the regime: they escaped to freedom. During the 1850s about a thousand slaves a year ran away to the North, Canada, and Mexico. Increased vigilance by the slaveholders and their police apparatus may have reduced the number from 1,011 in 1850 to 803 in 1860 as the census reports insist, but even so, the economic drain and political irritation remained serious. The slaves in the border states, especially the extreme northern tier, had a much better chance to escape than did those in Mississippi or Alabama. But even in Texas, Arkansas, and Louisiana slaveholders had to exercise vigilance, for many slaves went over the Mexican border or escaped to friendly Indians.[1]

Who ran away? Any slave might slip into the woods for a few days, but those whose departure rated an advertisement and organized chase—those who headed for freedom in the North, the southern cities, or the swamps—fell into a pattern. At least 80 percent were men between the ages of sixteen and thirty-five.[2] The age profile contains no surprise, but the sex profile does. At least one-third of the runaways belonged to the ranks of the skilled and privileged slaves—those with some education and with some knowledge of the outside world—and women occupied these ranks only as house servants. In view of the physical strength and general assertiveness of the women, their stronger ties to children and family probably account for much of their unwillingness to defect.[3] Many of the young women had children before they had husbands; the young men could more readily fly, for they often had not yet assumed responsibilities toward a woman or children even if they were already fathers.

For every slave who struck out for freedom, many—perhaps many hundreds—ran away a short distance and for a short period of time with a more limited objective. The circumstances that provoked slaves to run away varied enormously, but a few recurred often and, taken together, account for the overwhelming majority. Those who left for Mexico or the North obviously had made a decision to repudiate slavery in its every aspect, but the decision to go, even on the part of the most self-conscious slaves, often came in response to a specific provocation of the kind that sent thousands of others into the woods for short periods.

The whip provided the single biggest provocation to running away. Many slaves ran in anticipation of a whipping or other severe punishment, and others in anger after having suffered it. In some cases—too many—slaves ran not simply from a particular whipping but from the torments regularly inflicted by cruel or sadistic masters or overseers.[4] A planter who signed himself "Clod Thumper" laid down some "Maxims for Young Farmers and Overseers" that referred to these circumstances with a lighter touch than the slaves might have appreciated:

> Africans are nothing but brutes, and they will love you the better for whipping, whether they deserve it or not. Besides, by this manly course you will show your spunk. To be sure, a half dozen of them may take to the woods, but that is no loss to you.[5]

An ex-slave added another and more somber perspective. "They didn't do something and run," he insisted. "They run before they did it, 'cause they knew that if they struck a white man there wasn't going to be a nigger. In them days they run to keep from doing something."[6] Other provocations included insults, which some slaves reacted against even more readily than they did to the whip,[7] and the pressure of excessive driving, especially during the cotton-picking season. In addition, every large plantation likely had a habitual runaway. This type appeared everywhere and made a practice of leaving for periodic vacations in the woods and then returning to take his punishment, apparently regarding the one as well worth the price of the other. Samuel A. Cartwright, the celebrated physician-ideologue, reviewing the number of runaways in general and of habituals in particular, gravely announced that the problem lay with the blacks' unique susceptibility to a strange disease, "drapetomania," or the compulsion to run away from home.

A large if undetermined number of slaves ran away to rejoin loved ones from whom they had been forcibly parted. Newspaper advertisements frequently contained such words as "He is no doubt trying to reach his wife." Slaveholders had great trouble with newly purchased slaves who immediately left to try to find parents or children as well as wives.[8] In some instances the slaves had unexpected success when their masters, touched by the evidence of devotion and courage, reunited the family by resale.[9] In many more cases family ties prevented slaves from running away or kept them close to home when they did run. Olmsted reported from the lower Mississippi Valley that planters kept a sharp eye on mothers, for few slaves would leave permanently if they had to leave their mothers behind to face the master's wrath.[10] Mary Bell of Kentucky noted desertions during the war and commented: "A great many come back, mostly in a dreadful condition and strange to say their masters and mistresses nurse them through long spells of illness, a great many die. It is hard to turn them away on account of their mothers and fathers who are faithful and attached."[11]

Among the deterrents to making the long run to the free states none loomed larger than the fear of the unknown. The slaves needed more than the courage to leave family, friends, and familiar surroundings. The youth of the typical runaway suggests that many would have taken the necessary risks, but few slaves knew where to go. Most knew only the immediate area and often only a narrow strip of that. Even many skilled and relatively sophisticated slaves lacked an elementary knowledge of geography and had no means of transportation at their command.[12] Only rarely, if we except those aided by abolitionists, did slaves have the knowledge, resources, and presence of mind to forge papers and calmly board a stagecoach or railroad train.[13]

If most slaves feared to think about flight to the North, many feared even to think of short-term flight to the nearby woods or swamps. The slaves faced particularly difficult conditions in the swampy areas alongside the great plantation districts of Louisiana and the eastern low country. An old woman on the Georgia coast told Fanny Kemble that the slaves thought it useless to run away. " 'Tain't no use," she explained, "what use nigger run away?—de swamp all around; dey git in dar, an' dey starve to def, and de snakes eat 'em up—massa's nigger, dey don't neber run away."[14] During the war Colonel Higginson observed that the blacks of the South Carolina low country feared the great unknown beyond their immediate area. "The few negroes who did not believe in alligators," he wrote, "believed in sharks; the sceptics as to sharks were orthodox in respect to alligators; while those who rejected both had private prejudices as to snapping turtles."[15]

The slaves had good reason to fear their surroundings, for the dangers presented by their own ignorance and by nature accompanied those presented by a hostile and vigilant white community. Solomon Northup wrote:

> No man who has never been placed in such a situation can comprehend the thousand obstacles thrown in the way of the flying slave. Every white man's hand is raised against him—the patrollers are watching for him—the hounds are ready to follow on his track, and the nature of the country is such as renders it impossible to pass through it with any safety.[16]

The hounds to which Northup referred played a big role in restraining some who might have run away and in tracking those who did. The howling of dogs worried Colonel Higginson's black troops, for, as a corporal explained, they worked as the "detective officers of slavery's police."[17] Some slaveholders kept their own "nigger dogs"—especially fierce hounds trained to track down runaways—but many more enlisted those belonging to poor whites who earned a living as professional slave catchers. John Berkley Grimball, for example, paid a Mr. McCawdry a flat fee of thirty-five dollars a year to hunt any of his slaves who might run off.[18] These professionals operated throughout the slave states but primarily in the Lower South. Although some observers claimed that a fortune could be made at slave catching, poor and dissolute white men probably did most of this work.

The dogs more than the men struck terror into the slaves. They bit, tore, mutilated, and if not pulled off in time, killed their prey. A black woman who had had several children by her master and who was nursing at the time had a breast chewed off, and other horror stories were reported by the slaveholders themselves. One planter in Louisiana recorded a slave's being badly bitten and remarked, "Think he will stay home a while."[19] Slaveholders took a particularly callous attitude toward the fate of those runaways who resisted capture and had dogs set on them. Such slaves would never be much good to their owners anyway and might just as well serve as an example to the others.[20]

Some slaveholders condemned the use of dogs as barbarous and disgraceful, but most accepted it as a fact of life. They did not even bother to claim as excuse, as they might have, that the dogs' howling on the scent alerted the neighborhood and facilitated capture.[21] The dogs' cruel work on the attack was too apparent to be disguised. The slaveholder who publicly announced that he had told his overseer, "Dogs kept for the purpose of catching negroes will not be allowed under any consideration," said quite enough without further explanation.[22] Judge Lumpkin of the State Supreme Court of Georgia, never a man to mince words or allow sentiment to interfere with the protection of slave property, said in 1855 that the South had already lost 60,000 slaves to the North, that rough measures were in order, and that the courts would uphold the use of dogs in full cognizance of its effects.[23]

Slaves intent on running away used their wits against the dogs. They went to their conjurers for grave-dirt potions to rub on their feet to throw the dogs off the scent.[24] When they employed more formidable devices to misdirect the dogs, as the boldest and shrewdest slaves did, the conjurer's potions no doubt strengthened their self-confidence; when they relied on grave-dirt alone, the results were likely to be less happy. On the whole, the dogs did excellent work for the slaveholders. They tracked down and caught large numbers of runaways and discouraged many others from running off at all.

When safely in the woods, the runaway faced a new set of troubles. If a cold snap set in, he found himself reluctant to build a fire, for it might attract white attention. If he had to slip deep enough into the woods to avoid dogs, informers, slave catchers, and hostile white farmers and poor whites, he probably had gone too far to get food and supplies from fellow slaves. Many consequently fell seriously ill from hunger and exposure and either had to drag themselves back to the plantation or welcome capture.[25] Reviewing the obstacles to running away even temporarily and locally, Joe Gray Taylor comments:

The quarter had no mansions, but the swamp offered no comfortable beds. The plantation diet was not sumptuous, but rabbits were hard to catch. The whip of the overseer sang on the plantation air, but many never felt its bite. Those who did feel it often preferred that lash to moccasins, mosquitoes, and alligators. Indeed, alligators were said to prefer black meat.[26]

Slaveholders, especially in the Lower South, apparently saw the matter as Taylor suggests, for they usually took a calm view of their runaways and expected an early return. After all, their slaves had a long way to go to get to the free states, hardly knew the way, faced trying conditions in the woods, and sooner or later—usually sooner—would come home.[27]

And yet, large numbers of slaves did brave the elements, the dogs, and the patrols; did swallow their fears; and did take to the woods. No plantation of any size totally avoided the runaway problem. Everywhere, the slaveholders had to build a certain loss of labor-time and a certain amount of irritation into their yearly calculations. The kindest, most humane, most self-consciously paternalistic masters suffered almost as much as the others, the main difference being that they fretted more and more readily felt personally affronted and betrayed.[28] Harriet Martineau caustically remarked in the 1830s: "Slaves do run away in much greater numbers than is supposed by any but those who lose them, and those who help them." During the same decade Judge O'Neall of South Carolina observed: "Occasional flights of a slave from his master's service for special causes would not constitute any material or moral defect."[29] The shrewd Judge O'Neall knew that any other ruling would have made a substantial minority of the South's slaves ineligible for sale at normal market prices.

From the earliest days the slaveholders confronted a serious runaway problem. During the seventeenth and eighteenth centuries white indentured servants and newly imported Africans ran off in large numbers.[30] Skilled mechanics, house servants, and other privileged slaves constituted an estimated one-third to one-half of those running away; ordinary field hands, therefore, were making a substantial contribution of their own.[31] During the early decades of the nineteenth century southern public opinion responded calmly to the problem, although the numbers had not necessarily decreased, but with the rise of the abolition agitation in the 1830s concern grew over the threat of flight to the free states.[32]

White concern during the late antebellum period focused on runaways who sought to escape from the South, not merely to hole up in the woods awhile; and it especially focused on the much exaggerated efforts of northern abolitionists to encourage and aid escapes. Larry Gara has shown that white efforts never reached the peaks southerners assumed and that well-planned and successfully executed escapes owed much more to assistance from other slaves, free Negroes, and black abolitionists.[33] It is not certain that a sharp rise in successful escapes occurred after 1830, but increasingly, the slaveholders feared that they had a serious problem. The tempers of southern whites passed the boiling point during the 1850s.

The number of slaves who took to the woods for days, weeks, or months could not have risen nearly so high if runaways had not counted on substantial help from fellow slaves. In many cases, runaways stayed close to home and relied on slaves from their own plantations, including members of their immediate families, to slip them food and keep them informed of their master's temper so that they could return at the most propitious moment. Sometimes, a fellow slave negotiated with a master to effect return in exchange for a promise of leniency.[34] These efforts by fellow slaves carried considerable risk, for the slaveholders might punish the whole slave force and would certainly whip an individual collaborator with especial severity.[35]

Slaves from one plantation assisted runaways from other plantations under certain circumstances. The slaves from neighboring plantations often knew each other well. They met for prayer meetings, corn shuckings, Christmas, and other holiday barbecues; often formed close attachments; and sometimes extended their idea of a plantation family to at least some of these friends and acquaintances. Within this wider circle, the slaves would readily help each other even if they shunned those they regarded as strangers. But even strangers might find succor if they were fleeing the plantations of slaveholders known to be cruel. In those cases they often found food and supplies and sometimes found shelter on plantations filled with slaves they hardly knew.[36] Slaves who lived near towns and cities had an easier time, for urban slaves and free Negroes had enough freedom of movement to protect them.[37] The danger of betrayal remained high in both town and country, however, for a single informer could undo the work of many loyal brothers and sisters. The disloyalty and divisiveness so excoriated by David Walker, among other black militants, often involved a small percentage of the slave population—small, but large enough to sow distrust, suspicion, and fear.[38]

Some of the slaves who ran away ran to other white people. In scattered cases they ran to whites who would help them escape. A few white men protected runaway slaves at great personal risk, and less altruistic whites took in runaways to ease their own labor shortage.[39] Primarily, however, runaways who turned to whites turned to other slaveholders. Slaves knew which slaveholders in their vicinity would listen to sad stories and use their influence to save runaways from a bad beating. A slave who had taken to the woods for a while sometimes went to a reputedly kind slaveholder and asked him to intercede with the master for leniency. Others ran straight to a neighboring slaveholder in anticipation of stern punishment by their master for some misdeed, real or alleged.[40] At the very least this stratagem resulted in a cooling-off period, so that a master who insisted on a whipping would be less likely to inflict it in the heat of passion and therefore to make it excessive. At the most, the white neighbor, whether flattered by the slave's confidence or normally softhearted, would prevail on the master to settle for a light whipping or none at all. Many masters acceded to such requests as a courtesy to their neighbors, and others because their slave's willingness to surrender induced them to give him the benefit of some doubt. Slaves sometimes ran to a local slaveholder to ask him to inform their master about the overseer's cruelty or to ask protection from a brutal master. Ex-slaves attested to the readiness of slaveholders to intercede with each other in any or all of these circumstances.[41]

One or two reports from slaveholders may illustrate the emotions and attitudes to which the slaves appealed. Joseph Bieller of Louisiana wrote to his father, Jacob, in 1830:

> Bug came to my house on the second as a runaway. . . . He has done bad enough by runing away but his comeing here is not so bad as to have got in joal and run you to exspence. I shou like verry much to swap you one of my boys for him and give you the difference. I will give you one hundred dollars more than any other person will give I am truly sorry to see him as a runaway I hope you will not be so hard on him as you was the last time he came here no one knows but myself what feeling I have for him Black as he is we were raised together I shou be glad we could live together. . . .[42]

In South Carolina a decade earlier, a slave of Captain John Single-ton ran away when someone stole fodder from a barn he had been charged to lock. William R. Davie, to whom the slave ran for protection, wrote Captain Singleton:

> Frightened by what the servants told him of your displeasure and intention to make the overseer punish him severely, he without further reflection "ran away," then however his sense of duty and attachment to you got the better of his fears and he had determined to return home, but expecting he would be taken up, thought it was best to come to me and get a pass. I shall give him one to enable him to return without delay, and should his account be found correct I hope you will forgive him.[43]

The frequency with which these incidents occurred suggests that the slaves had found an effective but dangerous method for reducing, if not eliminating, punishment. By understanding the bond of courtesy between slaveholding neighbors and by giving a master time to control his temper and consider the probable ill effects of severity on the morale of the quarters, the slaves devised a useful if limited psychological weapon of defense. At the same time, in turning to another slaveholder, another master, they strengthened the doctrine of paternalism among the whites as well as among themselves.

Groups of slaves, as well as individuals, left the plantations for the swamps or woods, and they confronted the regime with a different and more formidable challenge. Slaves usually fled in groups in order to re-establish labor norms. Olmsted reported that the slaveholders of the Georgia and South Carolina low country did not dare to increase their slaves' tasks for fear of provoking mass desertions designed to force reconstitution of norms. Throughout the South the arrival of a new overseer with a reputation as a tough taskmaster would be met by the desertion of the bolder spirits, who were quick to test his resolve and let him know that they too had rights and power. In other cases, small groups took to the woods in order to pressure an unpopular master into selling them.[44] These actions paralleled strikes by free workers, for they aimed at winning concessions within the system rather than at challenging the system itself. But, like strikes by free workers, they contained a germ of class consciousness and demonstrated the power of collective action. In both respects they combatted the sense of impotence that the slaveholders worked so hard to instill in their slaves.

The contribution of local runaways to a spirit of autonomy in the quarters cannot easily be measured against that of the slaves who struck out for freedom in the free states. Each group had its important role. If the success of these local runaways in winning concessions for the quarters may be criticized for its corporatist limits within the status quo, so too the success of those who broke decisively with slavery to reach freedom may be criticized for its limited impact on the quarters. Abolitionists pointed out in antebellum times, as W. E. B. Du Bois and others did subsequently without in any way attempting to denigrate runaways they respected as heroic figures, that the Underground Railroad served as a safety valve for slavery by drawing off those who might have led insurrections.[45] This criticism retains force but requires qualification: it is not certain that the great majority of those who so courageously risked their lives to reach the free states would have participated in, much less led, insurrections. The psychology of the insurgent, especially in those inhibiting circumstances of the Old South, may have been far removed from that of the individual runaway, however much the two had in common as fearless spirits.

Those who fled to freedom made an inestimable contribution to the people they left behind, which must be weighed against their participation in a safety-valve effect. These were the slaves who, short of taking the path of insurrection, most clearly repudiated the regime; who dramatically chose freedom at the highest risk; who never let the others forget that there was an alternative to their condition. If more favorable conditions for insurrection had existed and if the slaves had risen more often than they in fact did, these runaways might easily be honored as those whose individual action emboldened the collective spirit. The danger in focusing on the drain of insurrectionary leadership, even on the assumption that runaways could have provided such a leadership, lies in a questionable assumption of cause and effect. If the possibilities for successful insurrection had not so closely approximated zero, especially during the nineteenth century, those runaways with insurrectionary inclinations might have stayed put. That they chose to leave as individuals may say no more than that they saw the futility of insurrection and the probable destruction of their people. They may, that is, have made the greatest contribution to the spirit of collective resistance that objective conditions made possible.

THE BRIGHT AND MORNING STAR

Accommodation and resistance developed as two forms of a single process by which the slaves accepted what could not be avoided and simultaneously fought individually and as a people for moral as well as physical survival. The hegemony of the slaveholders— their domination of society through command of the culture rather than solely through command of the gun—has no meaning except on the assumption of deep class antagonisms and on the further assumption that command of the culture could not readily have been established without command of the gun. The slave-holders' hegemony, as reflected in their relationship to non-slaveholding whites, for example, did not eliminate the chasm between the classes of white society. Antebellum political struggles often became sharp and reflected class antagonisms, which appear to have been sharpening during the 1850s. To speak of the slaveholders' hegemony is to speak of their ability to confine the attendant struggles to terrain acceptable to the ruling class—to prevent the emergence of an effective challenge to the basis of society in slave property.

The slaveholders established their hegemony over the slaves primarily through the development of an elaborate web of pater-nalistic relationships, but the slaves' place in that hegemonic sys-tem reflected deep contradictions, manifested in the dialectic of accommodation and resistance. The slaves' insistence on defining paternalism in their own way represented a rejection of the moral pretensions of the slaveholders, for it refused that psychological surrender of will which constituted the ideological foundation of such pretensions. By developing a sense of moral worth and by asserting rights, the slaves transformed their acquiescence in pa-ternalism into a rejection of slavery itself, although their masters assumed acquiescence in the one to demonstrate acquiescence in the other.

The slaves' world-view emerged primarily in their actions. But at each point at which this implicit world-view conflicted with that of the masters and provoked a crisis within the web of paternalistic relations, the slaves moved, as peoples generally do at such moments, toward articulating their position. Some slaves always reflected on the theoretical implications of their position. But even the preachers, drivers, and mechanics could not decisively organize their people politically and, therefore, could not move them toward explicit class consciousness. They did, however, contribute toward the formulation of a protonational consciousness, expressed primarily through a religious sensibility, that enabled a mass of oppressed individuals to cohere as a people.

The rise of a religious community among the slaves, with that looseness of organization inevitable in a slaveholding society and with its specific theological tendencies, ordered the life of the collective. Ralph Ellison's comment on the problems of black people in the twentieth-century South applies with added force to the slave period:

> The pre-individualistic black community discourages individuality out of self-defense. Having learned through experience that the whole group is punished for the actions of a single member, it has worked out efficient techniques of behavior control. For in many Southern communities everyone knows everyone else and is vulnerable to his opinions.[1]

No people can respond in this way unless it has achieved considerable moral coherence. For the slaves such moral coherence was the more important since they could not provide the institutional coherence achieved by the postbellum black churches.

The slaves' religion developed into the organizing center of their resistance within accommodation; it reflected the hegemony of the master class but also set firm limits to that hegemony. Not often or generally did it challenge the regime frontally. It rendered unto Caesar that which was Caesar's, but it also narrowed down considerably that which in fact was Caesar's. Black religion, understood as a critical world-view in the process of becoming—as something unfinished, often inconsistent, and in some respects even incoherent—emerged as the slaves' most formidable weapon for resisting slavery's moral and psychological aggression. Without it or its moral equivalent, "day-to-day resistance to slavery" might have been condemned to the level of a pathetic nihilism, incapable of bridging the gap between individual action against an oppressor and the needs of the collective for self-discipline, community élan, and a sense of worth as a people rather than merely as a collection of individuals. With it, the slaves were able to assert manhood and womanhood in their everyday lives and were able to struggle, by no means always successfully, for collective forms of resistance in place of individual outbursts.

However much the slaves, as Christians, felt the weight of sin, they resisted those perversions of doctrine which would have made them feel unworthy as a people before God. Their Christianity strengthened their ties to their "white folks" but also strengthened their love for each other and their pride in being black people. And it gave them a firm yardstick with which to measure the behavior of their masters, to judge them, and to find them wanting. The slaves transformed the promise of personal redemption, prefigured in the sign of Jonas, into a promise of deliverance as a people in this world as well as the next. Through tests of flood and fire they laid the moral and spiritual foundations for the struggle of subsequent generations of black Americans to fulfill that prophecy they have made their own:

> *But that which ye have already hold*
> *fast till I come.*
> *And he that overcometh, and keepeth*
> *my works unto the end, to him will I*
> *give power over the nations. . . .*
> *I am the root and the offspring of*
> *David, and the bright and morning star.*
>
> —Revelation, 2:25–26; 22:16

THE FATE OF PATERNALISM IN MODERN BOURGEOIS SOCIETY: THE CASE OF JAPAN

In arguing that southern paternalism grew out of slavery and that all paternalism rests on a master-servant relationship—that it is incompatible with bourgeois social relations—I have been speaking of the social system as a whole and its attendant hegemonic ideology. Something approximating paternalism enters into every form of human relations, including the most thoroughly bourgeois. But the existence of such an element does not in itself mean more than, say, the presence of ideas and sentiments reflecting wage-labor relationships in a generally slave or seigneurial society. The destruction of slavery meant the end of paternalism as the reigning southern ideal of social relations; it did not mean the total disappearance of paternalism as an ingredient in social relations. Thus, there can be no question that a significant number of white landlords in the Mississippi Delta region, for example, developed relationships with black (and white) tenant farmers during the twentieth century that echoed the patterns of the Old South. Neither can there be any question that as bourgeois social relations have intruded themselves into the remnants of the plantation system, paternalism has steadily declined. In the Old South, slavery encouraged and supported the spread of paternalism. In the New South, some planters and tenants have fought a rear-guard action against its erosion.

The subordination of one race to another or of the people of any country to a welfare state does not constitute a paternalistic order in any historically meaningful sense. A common declaration that the strong must protect and lead the weak in return for obedience and labor gives all nonliberal systems of class rule a certain similarity. But some such tendency, however feeble, characterized even the classically bourgeois regimes of nineteenth-century England and France and has come to play a greater role in all capitalist countries during the twentieth century. What demands explanation and excites wonder is not its presence in most societies but the appearance of its classical antithesis during the industrial revolution. Accordingly, I have defined paternalism in a narrow way in order to avoid the trap of trying to encompass almost all of world history under a single formula and in order to construct a discrete analysis of the particularities of different if overlapping ideologies and systems of social control. Some consideration of the subordination of one collectivity to another is nonetheless necessary for an understanding of the peculiar conjuncture of the Old South's two systems of social control: that of class, which paradoxically meant not the subordination of one class *en bloc* to another but of the individuals within one class to individuals within another; and that of race, which created a different set of social tendencies and problems.

The paternalism of the master-slave relationship had, in fact, little of importance in common with the systems of group subordination of the industrializing societies of the nineteenth century, and therein lay the source of the uniquely nonbourgeois character of the antebellum regime despite its many capitalist features and its commitment to production for a world market. Bourgeoisies have sometimes gone far toward encouraging paternalism, and some bourgeois regimes have gone much further in trying themselves to play the collective *padrone*. Some of the early industrialists of England and New England—one thinks of Wedgewood and the early cotton manufacturers of Lowell—made valiant (or infamous) attempts to regulate the lives of their laborers in accordance with their own understanding of patriarchal duty. But the exigencies of marketplace competition, not to mention the subsequent rise of trade-union opposition, reduced these efforts to impediments to the central tendency toward depersonalization.[1] Nor have welfare-state programs, which have swept the field during the twentieth century, turned back the clock; rather, they have eliminated only the most grossly inhumane and politically dangerous manifestations of the free market in labor. The paternalistic industrialists meanwhile went the way of those aristocratic bourgeois and bourgeois aristocrats of early modern Europe—the *noblesse de robe* of

France, for example—who tried to combine the roles of capitalist entrepreneur and traditional seigneur.[2] When the time came, Girondists and Jacobins alike settled scores with what was left of them. The more modern tendency, exemplified by such firms as IBM, represents both a response to the threat or actuality of unionization and a way of avoiding the worst features of depersonalization without altering its essence. It would be the purest folly to see in these developments a continuation of the essentially personal paternalistic relationship of master to servant.

Those modern states which have most directly attempted to play the role of collective *padrone* fall roughly into the category Marx referred to as having taken the "second" or "Prussian" road to capitalism. That is, they have been those states which imposed bourgeois revolution from above through the metamorphosis, usually at gunpoint, of a traditional ruling class into a bourgeois one: Germany, for example, or even more impressively Japan. The ruling class transformed itself under external compulsion and internal ferment: defeat at the hands of Napoleon in Prussia; the threat of foreign invasion after Perry's expedition in Japan. In these circumstances the new regimes could make extreme nationalist appeals for discipline and for a rededication to the supposed solidarity of the traditional order. The rhetoric of restoration and tradition cloaked a revolutionary transformation of the social structure and, at most, slowed the dissolution of personal bonds ideologically as well as socially.

Japan, the greatest success story of continuity in traditionalism, may serve as an example, for it reveals much about the relationship of individual paternalism to a collective system of control.[3] Despite considerable flux within each of such rigidly defined social classes as nobles, samurai, peasants, and merchants, the lines separating one class from another hardened during the seventeenth century. In a manner suggestive of Western European feudalism, the Japanese constructed a system of vertical loyalties and reciprocal obligations. Within the elaborate village organization of a seigneurial economy, the family played a central role for peasants and merchants as well as for samurai. Yet, the pressures of a land-crowded environment and the exigencies of rice culture encouraged a powerful egalitarianism on all levels of society, although not between them. Not only did political inhibitions to excessive private accumulation remain, but within each family the power of the father was hedged in. If he had great prestige and authority, to which his wife and children would normally defer, he nonetheless had to consult the family as a whole on major matters of common interest and represent their collective judgment, not his own private judgment, in the village. Thus, an egalitarian bias qualified Japanese paternalism at its source.

The relationship of the peasants to their lords was also qualified, but in a different way. The exchange of labor services, economic surplus, and social deference for protection and leadership theoretically defined the peasant-samurai relationship. But with the rise of a centralized national state, most notably with the institutional changes introduced by the great shogun, Ieyasu, in the early seventeenth century, the direct power of the samurai over the peasants met serious checks from above and gave way in time to the power of the state itself. In this ingenious system of politically centralized seigneurialism the trappings and some of the substance of a personal lord-peasant relationship survived alongside a rising system of state protection, which simultaneously reinforced the ideology of the lord-peasant relationship and set definite limits to its political and economic content. The egalitarian tendencies inherent in the family structure and projected onto the village community developed in a steady tension with the hierarchical structure of society and its components.

Those specialists who see the Meiji Restoration as a bourgeois revolution from above and those who see it as roughly equivalent to the establishment of a centralized and modernized prebourgeois absolute monarchy agree on the continuity of certain centralized patterns under the new regime. Even today, relations between capital and labor display many traits of patron and client. The egalitarian elements that qualified the paternalism of Tokugawa Japan undoubtedly helped to ease the transition to a new industrializing regime by providing an alternative to Western bourgeois individualism without directly challenging traditional patterns of deference. The equivalent of the Protestant work ethic which Robert N. Bellah has discovered in Tokugawa religion and samurai ideology no doubt reinforced the shift, which was, however, a shift in the relative strength of long-present egalitarian and subordinative tendencies.

From this point of view, the success of the Restoration in maintaining social order during a period of rapid economic and political transition may in part be accounted for by the appearance of ideological continuity—the appeal for a restoration of "traditional" loyalty to the emperor and a reaffirmation of old values. The relevant question centers on whether the older paternalism—the actual personal relationship of patron and client—can be sustained within a new economic system that is essentially bourgeois in its social relations, no matter how thoroughly integrated into a political system of state protection. Thorstein Veblen suggested many decades ago that the advance of capitalism in Japan would eventually erode the old ideology and move it toward a variant of Western Europe's bourgeois culture. More recently and deeply, Harry Harootunian has demonstrated the extent to which the intellectual and social currents that culminated in the Restoration prepared the way for the revolutionizing of the culture as well as the economy.

The Meiji regime reinforced the ideology of reciprocal personal obligations, but of obligations to the state as personified in the emperor rather than to specific lords; it completed the process begun by the early Tokugawa shoguns, who steadily detached the peasants from the samurai and in fact virtually reduced the samurai to the equivalent of a stipended bureaucratic officialdom. The ease with which the new regime led the masses through the transition—an ease that ought not to be exaggerated in view of the peasant unrest of the early Meiji period—may be accounted for not only by this essential ideological continuity but by the skill with which it fitted loyalty to the emperor as symbolic *padrone* into the obvious necessity for national cohesion to resist foreign domination. Thus paternalism, strictly defined, carried over into the relationship of labor to capital and received massive support from its identification with overriding demands for a national unity that all classes could perceive as vital to their interests. But it served as only one of many tools in the management of drastic social change—the opposite of its traditional function as a guiding ethos. With the shattering defeat of World War II and the subsequent social and economic reforms, it is now doubtful that that identification can be maintained much longer. In any case, from the beginning it had papered over a fundamental rupture in personal relations and thereby had replaced traditional seigneurial paternalism with a quite different if superficially similar method of social control.

ABBREVIATIONS USED
IN NOTES

The testimony of former slaves interviewed during the 1930s by the WPA (see A Note on Sources) is cited by abbreviated reference to George P. Rawick's edition, *The American Slave: A Composite Autobiography* (19 vol.; Westport, 1972–). Thus,

Rawick, ed., *S.C. Narr.*, II (2), 60.

refers to the testimony of an ex-slave living in South Carolina at the time of the interview. The volume number, II, refers to the second volume in the set as a whole—in this case it is the first volume of the South Carolina narratives. The number in parentheses (2) refers to Part 2 of the narratives for South Carolina; the last figure, 60, refers to the appropriate page. In some cases the testimony was not arranged in parts within a given state, so that no number appears in parentheses between the volume number and page number.

AA	*American Agriculturalist*
ACP	*American Cotton Planter*
ACPSS	*American Cotton Planter and Soil of the South* (new series)
AF	*American Farmer*
AH	*Agricultural History*
AHQ	*Alabama Historical Quarterly*
AHR	*American Historical Review*
BHM	*Bulletin of the History of Medicine*
CP	*Carolina Planter*

CSSH	*Comparative Studies in Society and History*
CWH	*Civil War History*
DBR	*De Bow's Review*
FHQ	*Florida Historical Quarterly*
FR	*Farmer's Register*
GHQ	*Georgia Historical Quarterly*
HAHR	*Hispanic American Historical Review*
JAH	*Journal of American History*
JMH	*Journal of Mississippi History*
JNH	*Journal of Negro History*
JSH	*Journal of Southern History*
J.Soc.H.	*Journal of Social History*
KHSR	*Kentucky Historical Society Register*
LH	*Louisiana History*
LHQ	*Louisiana Historical Quarterly*
MHSB	*Missouri Historical Society Bulletin*
Mo.H.R.	*Missouri Historical Review*
MVHR	*Mississippi Valley Historical Review*
NCHR	*North Carolina Historical Review*
NOMSJ	*New Orleans Medical and Surgical Journal*
PB	*Planters' Banner*
SA	*Southern Agriculturalist*
SAQ	*South Atlantic Quarterly*
SC	*Southern Cultivator*
SCHM	*South Carolina Historical Magazine*
SHQ	*Southwestern Historical Quarterly*
SLM	*Southern Literary Messenger*
So.Cab.	*Southern Cabinet*
SP	*Southern Planter*
SS	*Soil of the South*
THQ	*Tennessee Historical Quarterly*
VMHB	*Virginia Magazine of History and Biography*
WMQ	*William & Mary Quarterly*

MANUSCRIPT COLLECTIONS CITED IN NOTES

NC refers to collections at the Southern Historical Collection, University of North Carolina; LSU refers to collections in the State Department of Archives and History, Louisiana State University. An asterisk indicates that typescripts of the original manuscripts are available and have been used.

Acklen Papers, NC

Samuel A. Agnew Diary, NC*

Colonel David Wyatt Aiken Autobiography, NC

Archibald D. Alston Papers, LSU

Harrod C. Anderson Papers, LSU*

Anonymous Diary, 1835–1837, LSU

Archibald Hunter Arrington Papers, NC

Ashland Plantation Book, 1852, LSU

John D. Ashmore Plantation Book, NC*

Aventine Plantation Diary, State Department of Archives and History, Jackson, Mississippi

Mrs. Eleanor J. W. Baker Papers, Duke University

Everard Green Baker Diaries and Plantation Notes, NC*

Simmons Jones Baker Account Book, NC

Barbour Papers, University of Virginia

George S. Barnsley Papers, NC

R. R. Barrow Residence Journal, NC

Mary Bateman Diary, LSU

Thomas L. Bayne Autobiographical Sketch, NC*

Bayside Plantation Records, NC*

Taylor Beatty Diary, NC*

Mary Jeffries Bethell Diary, NC*

John Houston Bills Diary, NC*

Priscilla "Mittie" Munnikhuysen Bond Papers, LSU

Emily Morrison Bondurant Reminiscences, NC*

James P. Bowman Papers, LSU

Boykin Papers, 1836–1859, NC

Esther G. Wright Boyd Notes and Recollections, Tennessee State Library and Archives, Nashville*

Branch Family Papers, NC

Brashear Family Papers, NC

Gustave A. Breaux Diaries, Tulane University

Audley Clark Britton and Family Papers, LSU

Charles Wetmore Broadfoot Papers, 1831, NC

Annie Laurie Broidrick, "A Recollection of Thirty Years Ago," LSU*

Catherine Barbara Broun Diary, NC*

Charles Bruce and Family Papers, Library of Congress

Bumpus Journals, NC

John C. Burruss Papers, in the George M. Lester Collection, LSU

William Henry Burwell Papers, NC

Tod R. Caldwell Papers, NC

Cameron Papers, NC

Eliza Eve Carmichael Diary, NC*

Charles Clark and Family Papers, State Department of Archives and History, Jackson, Mississippi

Mrs. Eliza Clitherall Autobiography and Diary, NC*

Coleman Family Records, University of Virginia

Concordia Parish (La.) Inquest File, LSU

Confederate Collection: Letters, Tennessee State Library and Archives, Nashville

Cooper Papers, Tennessee State Library and Archives, Nashville

John Hamilton Cornish Papers, NC*

Susan Cornwall Diary, NC*

Correspondence: Slavery, Tennessee State Library and Archives, Nashville

Henry Craft Diary, NC*

John Matthews Winslow Davidson Diary, NC*

William R. Davie Papers, NC

Louis M. DeSaussure Journals, NC

Stephen D. Doar Account Book, Library of Congress

Emily Caroline Douglas Papers, LSU

Edward Dromgoole and Richard B. Robinson Papers, Duke University

Stephen Duncan Account Book, LSU

Edgefield County (S.C.) Military Record: Col. John Hill Plantation Diary, NC*

Belle Edmondson Diary, NC*

Elliott-Gonzales Papers, NC

William Ethelbert Ervin Journal, NC*

Alexander K. Farrar Papers, LSU

Susan Fisher Papers, NC

Henry Fitzhugh Letterbook, Duke University

Andrew Flinn Plantation Diary, NC (microfilm)

Joel B. Fort Papers, Tennessee State Library and Archives, Nashville

John Edwin Fripp Papers, NC*

Alson Fuller Account Book, NC

General Edmond T. Gaines Papers, Library of Congress

Katherine Polk Gale, "Recollections of Life in the Confederacy," NC*

David Gavin Diary, NC*

Edward J. Gay and Family Papers, LSU

William Proctor Gould Diary, NC (microfilm)

William P. Graham Papers, NC

Iverson L. Graves Papers, NC

James Hervey Greenlee Diary, NC*

John Berkley Grimball Diaries, NC*

Meta Morris Grimball Diary, NC*

Peter W. Hairston Diary, NC

James H. Hammond Papers, Library of Congress

Francis Hanson Diary, NC*

Thomas W. Harriss Papers, Duke University

Ernest Haywood Papers, NC

Hephzibah Church Books—Merritt M. Shilig Memorial Collection, LSU*

William P. Hill Diary, NC

Mrs. Isaac Hilliard Diary, Tulane University*

William Henry Holcombe Diary and Autobiography, NC*

George F. Holmes Letterbook, Duke University

Caroline Mallett Hooper Papers, NC (microfilm)

Franklin A. Hudson Diaries, NC*

Meredith Flournoy Ingersoll, compiler, "Excerpts from 'History of the Flournoy Family,'" LSU*

Jackson-Prince Papers, NC

Joseph Jaynes Plantation Account Books, Duke University

John C. Jenkins and Family Papers, LSU*

William L. Johnston Account Book, Duke University

B. B. Jones Book, NC

John Jones Papers, Duke University

Kelvin Grove Plantation Book, NC (microfilm)

Killona Plantation Journal, State Department of Archives and History, Jackson, Mississippi

John Kimberly Papers, NC

Thomas Butler King Papers, NC

Laurence Family Papers, Tennessee State Library and Archives, Nashville

Alexander Robert Lawton Papers, NC

Francis Terry Leak Diary, NC*

LeBlanc Family Papers, LSU

A. Ledoux & Company Record Book, LSU

William S. Hamilton Papers in the George M. Lester Collection, LSU

Levert Papers, NC

Liddell Papers, LSU

Francis Lieber Papers, Library of Congress

Louisiana, Historical Records Survey: Church Archives, LSU

Louisiana, Police Jury Minutes, LSU

Andrew Macrery Papers, LSU

Eliza L. Magruder Diary, LSU*

Manigault Papers, NC

Eliza Ann Marsh Diary, NC*

S. W. Marshall Account Book, Virginia Historical Society, Richmond

Nicholas B. Massenburg Farm Journal, NC*

Mary Ann Colvin Mayfield Papers, LSU*

Duncan G. McCall Plantation Journal and Diary, Duke University

E. E. McCollam Diary and Plantation Record, NC*

William McKean Letterbook, Virginia Historical Society, Richmond

William McKinley Book, NC (microfilm)

William N. Mercer Papers, LSU

Minis Collection, NC

William J. Minor and Family Papers, LSU

Dr. Luico Mitchell Account Book, North Carolina State Department of Archives and History, Raleigh

James Monette Day Book and Diary, LSU*

Columbus Morrison Journal and Accounts, NC

Mullins Papers, NC

Frank Nash Papers, NC

Negro Collection: Letters and Papers, Duke University

John Nevitt Plantation Papers, NC*

Newstead Plantation Diary, NC (microfilm)

North Carolina Manumission Society Minutes, NC*

Haller Nutt Papers, Duke University

Orange Grove Plantation Papers, Tulane University

Palfrey Papers, LSU

Ebenezer Pettigrew Plantation Papers, North Carolina State Department of Archives and History, Raleigh

Pettigrew Papers, NC

Louise Taylor Pharr Book, NC

Ulrich Bonnell Phillips Papers, Yale University

Physician's Account Book, 1824–1839, Library of Congress

Physician's Fee Book, 1847–1850, NC

Physician's Record Book, 1855–1862, NC

Pickens-Bonham Papers, Library of Congress

Plantation Record Book, 1850–1861 (in French), Tulane University

Pocket Plantation Record, University of Virginia

Pre Aux Cleres Plantation Record Books, LSU

William B. Price Papers, Duke University

Prudhomme Papers, NC

Alexander F. Pugh and Family Papers, LSU*

John H. Randolph Papers, LSU

David Rees Papers, Tulane University

Rufus Reid Papers, NC

William W. Renwick Papers, Duke University

Francis DuBose Richardson Memoirs, NC* (microfilm)

Alfred Landon Rives Papers, Duke University

Benjamin and B. W. Robinson Account Books, NC

Joseph Toole Robinson Papers, 1853–1866, LSU

John Rogers, "Life and Times of John Rogers of Carlisle, Kentucky," NC*

Martha Schofield Diary, NC*

Marsh Scuddeo Letters, LSU

H. M. Seale Diary, LSU

Abraham and James H. Sheppard Papers, Duke University

Henry E. Simmons Letters, NC

Singleton Family Papers, NC

Slave Papers, Library of Congress

Slavery Collection, LSU

Small Collections: Carson Family Papers, Tennessee State Library and Archives, Nashville

Charles Smallwood Diary, NC (microfilm)

Josiah Smith, Jr., Lettercopy Book, NC

Mrs. Smith Journal, Duke University

Whiteford Smith Papers, Duke University

Alonzo Snyder Papers, LSU

Leonidas Pendleton Spyker Diary, LSU*

Frank F. Steel Letters, NC

Robert H. Stewart Account Books, LSU

Stirling Papers, LSU

Joseph B. Stratton Papers, LSU

Tayloe Papers, University of Virginia

Edward Telfair Papers, Duke University

Ella Gertrude Clanton Thomas Journals, Duke University

Lewis Thompson Papers, NC

Ruffin Thomson Papers, NC

John C. Tibbetts Correspondence, LSU

Tillman and Norwood Medical Ledgers, NC

Walker Timberlake Papers, Duke University

Clarissa E. (Leavitt) Town Diary, LSU*

Nicholas P. Trist Papers, NC

H. M. Turner Physician's Record Book, NC

United Kingdom, Public Records Office: Colonial Office Papers, London

William D. Valentine Diaries, NC

Wade Family Papers: Slave Papers, Library of Congress

Dr. Walter Wade Plantation Diary, Mississippi State Department of Archives and History, Jackson

Samuel Walker Diary, Tulane University*

Henry Clay Warmoth Magnolia Plantation Journals, NC

Henry Watson, Jr., Papers, Duke University

Joseph Watson Correspondence, LSU

Weeks Papers, LSU

Weeks Papers (Letter from Trent), NC

James Wilson White Papers, NC

Maunsel White Papers, NC (microfilm)

William Rollinson Whittingham Papers, Duke University

Calvin Henderson Wiley Papers, NC

Sarah Hicks Williams Papers, NC

W. H. Wills Papers, NC

Robert W. Withers Books, NC

Witherspoon-McDowall Papers, NC

Carter G. Woodson Papers, Library of Congress

Robert and Newton D. Woody Papers, Duke University

Wooster Papers, NC

Wyche-Otey Papers, NC

Benjamin C. Yancey Papers, NC

A NOTE ON SOURCES

The slaveholders' papers and publications can hardly be accepted as "objective," especially when they purport to describe slave attitudes. The accounts of travelers, who varied considerably in talent, length of stay, and social attitudes, carry no more independent authority. But, taken together and with other contemporary white sources, they have much to offer, and no comprehensive treatment can afford to ignore them. The problem is to weigh them against black testimony as well as against each other.

Black testimony, however, is usually indirect. John Blassingame, in *The Slave Community*, demonstrates that the published accounts of runaway slaves can be illuminating. But they too require enormous care, for even when not distorted by northern abolitionist editing, they remained the accounts of highly exceptional men and women and can be as misleading in their honesty and accuracy of detail as in their fabrications. George P. Rawick has chosen to rely primarily on the interviews with ex-slaves conducted during the 1930s. In *Sundown to Sunup* he analyzes that testimony as brilliantly as one might hope for. But here too there are problems: the informants were very old; most had been children when emancipation came and had lived most of their subsequent lives as free persons. Moreover, many had been interviewed by whites under circumstances that may have imposed inhibitions. Other scholars, most impressively Sterling Stuckey and Lawrence Levine, are analyzing the spirituals and folklore materials in an effort to uncover the essentials of slave life.

I have tried to weigh different kinds of testimony against

each other and have felt safest when various kinds of sources—slaveholders' diaries and letters, southern periodicals, travelers' accounts, runaway-slave accounts, the WPA narratives, and folklore materials—seem to agree on what, how, and where, even if they disagree on interpretation and value judgment. In most cases a judgment had to be based on wide reading in different sources. My frequent use of "many," "most," "probably," "on balance," and "typically" reflects the difficulties of precise quantification. When materials invited or permitted measurement, I have tried to measure and have gratefully drawn on the quantitative work of Robert W. Fogel and Stanley Engerman and others. But the subject of this book is the quality of life, which largely defies measurement. For example, it would be wrong, not merely pointless, to seek in the slave narratives a precise measurement of the character of masters—to try to balance the testimony of those slaves who said they had good masters against those who said the opposite. Some testimony will command the respect of those who have studied the slave period and other testimony simply will not; a qualitative judgment, however subjective, is unavoidable. And how does one quantify a put-on?

I have readily and heavily used some plantation diaries and ex-slave accounts while slighting others. Two decades of work in the history of southern slave society have helped form my own estimates of what is and is not typical—what does and does not ring true. Another historian, having read as much (or as little), might well interpret the record differently; indeed, many have. I offer my reading as one historian's considered judgment and can only warn nonspecialists that all the sources are treacherous and that no "definitive" study has been or ever will be written. I hope, therefore, that even nonspecialists will make some effort to weigh my interpretations against those of such outstanding authorities as Du Bois, Woodward, Phillips, Stampp, Elkins, Aptheker, Rawick, and Blassingame and will recognize that the writing of history is a process of constant revision and debate.

The interviews with ex-slaves conducted during the 1930s by the Federal Writers Project of the Works Project Administration are finally being published by Greenwood Press in Westport, Connecticut, thanks to Professor Rawick's efforts. Greenwood has brought out nineteen volumes so far under the title *The American Slave: A Composite Autobiography*, the first volume of which is Rawick's stimulating interpretative essay, *Sundown to Sunup: The Making of the Black Community* (1972). The next sixteen volumes (II–XVII) contain the interviews conducted by the WPA; see my list of abbreviations, pages 667–668 above, for the method of citation used in this book. Volumes XVIII and XIX consist of interviews conducted by scholars at Fisk University. I have used the earlier publications rather than those in Professor Rawick's series and have cited them as follows:

Fisk University, *Unwritten History of Slavery*
> Fisk University, *The Unwritten History of Slavery: Autobiographical Accounts of Negro Ex-slaves* (comp. and ed. Ophelia Settle Egypt, J. Masuoka, and Charles S. Johnson; Washington, D.C., 1968 [1945]). This is the microcard edition; the pagination is the same as in Volume XVIII of the Rawick series.

Fisk University, *God Struck Me Dead*
> Fisk University, *God Struck Me Dead: Religious Conversion Experiences and Autobiographies of Negro Ex-slaves* (comp. and ed. A. P. Watson, Paul Radin, and Charles S. Johnson; Nashville, Tenn., 1945). The pagination differs from that of Volume XIX of the Rawick series.

Several volumes of excerpts from the slave narratives appeared before the Rawick edition, and I have cited two of them in place of the fuller work since they are easily available in paperback editions: Benjamin A. Botkin, ed., *Lay My Burden Down: A Folk History of Slavery* (Chicago, 1945), and Norman R. Yetman, ed., *Life Under the "Peculiar Institution": Selections from the Slave Narrative Collection* (New York, 1970), which contains excellent discussions and analyses of the interview projects.

Others have written valuable books based on the narratives and black folk sources. These are cited here in abbreviated form:

Lester, *To Be a Slave*
> Julius Lester, *To Be a Slave*. Illustrated by Tom Feelings (New York, 1968).

Saxon *et al.*, *Gumbo Ya-Ya*
> Lyle Saxon, Edward Dreyer, and Robert Tallant, *Gumbo Ya-Ya: A Collection of Louisiana Folk Tales* (New York, 1945).

WPA, *Negro in Virginia*
Work Projects Administration. Workers of the Writers Program, State of Virginia, *The Negro in Virginia* (New York, 1940).

WPA, *Drums and Shadows*
Work Projects Administration. Savannah Unit, Georgia Writers Project, *Drums and Shadows: Survival Studies Among the Georgia Coastal Negroes* (Athens, Ga., 1940).

NOTES

BOOK ONE, PART 1

ON PATERNALISM

1. LeRoi Jones (Amiri Baraka), *Blues People: Negro Music in White America* (New York, 1963), pp. 54, 39.
2. I have explored these developments in *The World the Slaveholders Made: Two Essays in Interpretation* (New York, 1969), Pt. 1.
3. See David Brion Davis, *The Problem of Slavery in Western Culture* (Ithaca, N.Y., 1966).
4. See esp. Philip D. Curtin, *The Atlantic Slave Trade: A Census* (Madison, Wis., 1969).
5. Despite pretenses, paternalism exists only as an echo of a displaced era when it passes into modern bourgeois society. Those interested in the argument on this point may consult the Appendix, "On the Fate of Paternalism in Modern Bourgeois Society: The Case of Japan."

FARMERS, PLANTERS, AND OVERSEERS

1. Farms and small plantations existed throughout the South but were especially common in the northern tier of slave states, in which tobacco and hemp cultivation predominated. For the technical and economic inhibitions to largeness of scale in these regions, see Ulrich Bonnell Phillips, *Life and Labor in the Old South* (Boston, 1948), pp. 80, 126; James Hopkins, *A History of the Hemp Industry in Kentucky* (Lexington, Ky., 1951), pp. 4, 17; and Richard L. Troutman, "The Physical Setting of the Bluegrass Planter," *KHSR*, LXVI (Oct., 1968), 367–377.
2. For a discussion and evaluation of their views see Robert McColley, *Slavery and Jeffersonian Virginia* (Urbana, Ill., 1964), p. 58.
3. E. S. Abdy, *Journal of a Residence and Tour in the United States of North America* (3 vols.; London, 1835), II, 291; Frederick Law Olmsted, *A Journey in the Back Country, 1853–1854* (New York, 1970 [1860]), pp. 64–65; James Stirling, *Letters from the Slave States* (London, 1857), p. 46.
4. Fredrika Bremer, *The Homes of the New World: Impressions of America* (2 vols.; New York, 1853), II, 249, 527.
5. Meredith Flournoy Ingersoll, comp., "Excerpts from 'History of the Flour-

noy Family.' " For a contrasting view see the remarks of Gov. John A. Winston of Alabama, Alabama House of Representatives, *Journal, 1857–1858,* p. 28. For the view of a "Small Farmer" see J. D. B. De Bow, ed., *Industrial Resources of the Southern and Western States* (3 vols.; New Orleans, 1852–1853), II, 337.

6. Rawick, ed., *Okla. Narr.,* VII (1), 131; also p. 177; *Texas Narr.,* IV (1), 264; Yetman, ed., *Life Under the "Peculiar Institution,"* p. 322.

7. See, e.g., Rawick, ed., *Texas Narr.,* V (4), 233; Fisk University, *Unwritten History of Slavery,* pp. 59–60.

8. Rawick, ed., *Texas Narr.,* V (4), 6. Also IV (2), 6, 56, 105, 145, 159; Yetman, ed., *Life Under the "Peculiar Institution,"* pp. 111, 113, 160, 255; Josiah Henson, *Father Henson's Story of His Own Life* (New York, 1962 [1849]), p. 153; Samuel Spencer, Jr., *Booker T. Washington and the Negro's Place in American Life* (Boston, 1955), p. 14.

9. D. R. Hundley, *SP,* XII (Aug., 1852), 243; D. R. Hundley, *Social Relations in Our Southern States* (New York, 1860), pp. 352–353. Also Frederick Law Olmsted, *A Journey in the Seaboard Slave States* (New York, 1856), p. 447; Joseph Holt Ingraham, *The South-West* (2 vols.; New York, 1968 [1835]), II, 26; Frances Anne Kemble, *Journal of Residence on a Georgian Plantation* (New York, 1863), p. 28; Fisk University, *Unwritten History of Slavery,* p. 145; Philip Graham, ed., "Texas Memoirs of Amelia E. Barr," *SHQ,* LXIX (April, 1966), 487.

10. For an intensive study of these conditions see Lyle Wesley Dorsett, "Slaveholding in Jackson County, Missouri," *MHSB,* XX (Oct., 1963), 25–37.

11. Kenneth M. Stampp, *The Peculiar Institution: Slavery in the Ante-bellum South* (New York, 1956), p. 331.

12. Olmsted, *Seaboard,* p. 350; *Back Country,* p. 158; Sir Charles Lyell, *A Second Visit to the United States of North America* (2 vols.; New York, 1849), I, 268; Ulrich Bonnell Phillips, "Plantations with Slave Labor and Free," *AHR,* XXX (July, 1925), 743.

13. Olmsted, *Back Country,* p. 239.

14. G. J. O. Ojo, *Yoruba Culture: A Geographical Analysis* (London, 1966), p. 159.

15. For a typical comment by an observant traveler see William Howard Russell on the South Carolina and Georgia coast: *My Diary North and South* (New York, 1965 [1862]), p. 71. Reports such as this one are largely responsible for having misled historians.

16. Yetman, ed., *Life Under the "Peculiar Institution,"* pp. 98, 264; Elizabeth Ware Pearson, ed., *Letters from Port Royal, 1862–1868* (New York, 1969 [1906]), p. 272. Also William Y. Thompson, *Robert Toombs of Georgia* (Baton Rouge, La., 1966), p. 88.

17. Charles W. Stetson, *Washington and His Neighbors* (Richmond, Va., 1956), p. 106; Gerald W. Mullin, *Flight and Rebellion: Slave Resistance in Eighteenth-Century Virginia* (New York, 1972), pp. 22–32.

18. For a sampling of various sources from different parts of the South see Harriet Martineau, *Society in America* (3 vols.; New York, 1966 [1837]), III, 330; C. Carson to W. S. Waller, June 4, 1849 in the Small Collections: Carson Family Papers; Valentine Diary, Feb. 8, 1850; H. E. Lawrence to Cornelius Lawrence, April 9, 1852, in the Brashear Family Papers; John H. North to Mrs. E. B. Lyons, Feb. 4, 1850, and J. W. Woodruff to J. P. Bowman, April 15, 1857, in the Bowman Papers; F. L. Riley, ed., "Diary of a Mississippi Planter," July 10, 1853, *Publications of the Mississippi Historical Society,* X (1909), 444; James C. Bonner, ed., "Plantation Experiences of a New York Woman," *NCHR,* XXXIII (July, 1956), 392; Davidson Diary, April 19, 1853; Charles C. Jones, Jr., to C. C. Jones, Feb. 4, 1863, in Robert Manson Myers, ed., *The*

Children of Pride: A True Story of Georgia and the Civil War (New Haven, Conn., 1972), p. 1025; Joel B. Fort Recollections; Katherine M. Jones, ed., *When Sherman Came: Southern Women and the "Great March"* (Indianapolis, 1964), pp. 25, 262; Helen Tunnicliff Catterall, ed., *Judicial Cases Concerning American Slavery and the Negro* (5 vols.; Washington, D.C., 1929–1937), II, 138–139; Susan Dabney Smedes, *Memorials of a Southern Planter* (ed. Fletcher M. Green; New York, 1965 [1860]), pp. 40, 196; Olmsted, *Seaboard*, p. 433; Edwin Adams Davis, ed., *Plantation Life in the Florida Parishes of Louisiana, 1836–1846, as Reflected in the Diary of Bennet H. Barrow* (New York, 1963), p. 100.

19. Rawick, ed., *S.C. Narr.*, II (2), 80–81; III (3), 97–99; *Texas Narr.*, IV (2), 16.

20. Absenteeism was the curse of the Caribbean. See Joseph Lowell Ragatz, *The Fall of the Planter Class in the British Caribbean* (New York, 1928); Vincent Harlow, *A History of Barbados, 1625–1685* (Oxford, 1926); Noel Deerr, *The History of Sugar* (2 vols.; London, 1949), I, 205; and Orlando Patterson's devastating indictment, *The Sociology of Slavery* (London, 1967). For Cuba, see Ramiro Guerra y Sánchez, *Sugar and Society in the Caribbean* (trans. Marjory M. Urquidi; New Haven, Conn., 1963); Fernando Ortiz, *Cuban Counterpoint: Tobacco and Sugar* (trans. Harriet de Onís; New York, 1947), p. 64. For Saint-Domingue, see Gabriel Debien, *Plantations et esclaves à Saint-Domingue* (Dakar, 1962), pp. 9–15, 40, 43, 49–55. Even Brazil, which closely approximates the United States in this respect, suffered more absenteeism than is generally commented on. For one thing, too many planters preferred to live in the coastal cities. See Caio Prado Júnior, *The Colonial Background of Modern Brazil* (trans. Suzette Macedo; Berkeley, Calif., 1967), p. 342; C. R. Boxer, *Salvador de Sá and the Struggle for Brazil and Angola* (London, 1952), pp. 14–15. And in general, D. B. Davis, *Problem of Slavery*, pp. 157–158.

21. J. H. Hammond, "Letters on Slavery," in E. N. Elliott, ed., *Cotton Is King and Pro-slavery Arguments* (New York, 1969 [1860]), p. 128.

22. Theodore Weld, *American Slavery as It Is: Testimony of a Thousand Witnesses* (New York, 1839), *passim*; also J. H. Easterby, ed., *South Carolina Rice Plantation as Revealed in the Papers of Robert F. W. Allston* (Chicago, 1945), p. 9.

23. John Spencer Bassett, *Slavery in the State of North Carolina* (Baltimore, 1899), p. 83; Bennett H. Wall, "The Founding of Pettigrew Plantations," *NCHR*, XXVII (Oct., 1950), 417; Phillips, *Life and Labor*, p. 235. Among the great planters of 1850 we find men like Thomas C. Warren, who held 353 slaves in one county; James C. Johnson, who held 272 in another; and Thomas P. Devereaux, who held 580 in two.

24. Albert Virgil House, ed., *Planter Management and Capitalism in Ante-bellum Georgia* (New York, 1954), p. 50; R. Q. Mallard, *Plantation Life Before Emancipation* (Richmond, Va., 1892); Guion Griffis Johnson, *A Social History of the Sea Islands* (Chapel Hill, N. C., 1930), pp. 74–75; James C. Bonner, *A History of Georgia Agriculture, 1732–1860* (Athens, Ga., 1964), p. 48; Olmsted, *Seaboard*, p. 419.

25. Weymouth T. Jordan, *Ante-bellum Alabama: Town and Country* (Tallahassee, Fla., 1957), p. 44; Ruth Ketring Nuermberger, *The Clays of Alabama: A Planter-Lawyer-Politician Family* (Lexington, Ky., 1958), *passim*; James Benson Sellers, *Slavery in Alabama* (2nd ed.; University, Ala., 1950), pp. 180–182.

26. Charles S. Sydnor, *Slavery in Mississippi* (Gloucester, Mass., 1965), p. 69; Olmsted, *Back Country*, pp. 15, 28, 46, 73, 119, 160; Joseph Holt Ingraham, *The Sunny South* (Philadelphia, 1860), pp. 259–260; Leak Diary, Dec. 4, 1858 (V, 491 ff.).

27. V. Alton Moody, *Slavery on the Louisiana Sugar Plantations*, (reprinted from *LHQ*, April, 1924), p. 19; J. Carlyle Sitterson, *Sugar Country: The Sugar Industry*

in the South, 1753–1950 (Lexington, Ky., 1953) pp. 45, 52, 57, 70, 73, 76–77, 81, 96; Joseph Karl Menn, *Large Slaveholders of Louisiana—1860* (New Orleans, 1964), pp. 96–97; Mercer Papers, 1839; Orange Grove Plantation Diary, Dec. 25, 1849; Frank Lawrence Owsley, *Plain Folk of the Old South* (Chicago, 1965 [1949]), p. 88; Robert Douthat Meade, *Judah P. Benjamin: Confederate Statesman* (New York, 1943), pp. 61–62.

28. For some examples from different areas see Margaret Armstrong, *Fanny Kemble: A Passionate Victorian* (New York, 1938), pp. 330–331; Duncan Clinch Heyward, *Seed from Madagascar* (Chapel Hill, N.C., 1937), p. ix; Holman Hamilton, *Zachary Taylor: Soldier in the White House* (Indianapolis, 1951), pp. 18–19.

29. Gideon Bridgers, *AF*, XIII (1831), 48, 152. See also the speech of J. L. Bridgers to the North Carolina Agricultural Society, *Transactions, 1857*, p. 17; *CP*, I (1844–1845), 25; Charles S. Sydnor, *A Gentleman of the Old Natchez Region: Benjamin L. C. Wailes* (Durham, N.C., 1938), pp. 112–113.

30. Maunsel White to Maunsel White II, Aug. 24, 1860.

31. A. H. Arrington to Kate Arrington, Feb. 17, 1857.

32. The following discussion has benefitted from two excellent studies: William Kauffman Scarborough, *The Overseer: Plantation Management in the Old South* (Baton Rouge, La., 1966), and John Spencer Bassett's introduction to the important collection, *The Southern Plantation Overseer as Revealed in His Letters* (Northampton, Mass., 1925). My main criticism of these studies is that they slight the activity and influence of the slaves in the overseer-planter conflicts.

33. *DBR*, XXI (Sept., 1856), 279. This was an old theme. See, e.g., the instructions of Richard Corbin, Esq., of Virginia in 1759, in Ulrich Bonnell Phillips, ed., *Plantation and Frontier Documents: 1649–1863*, (2 vols.; Cleveland, Ohio, 1909) I, 109.

34. Stampp, *Peculiar Institution*, p. 38. For a downward revision see Robert W. Fogel and Stanley Engerman, *Time on the Cross: The Economics of Slavery in the Antebellum South* (2 vols.; Boston, 1974).

35. Scarborough, *Overseer*, pp. 9–10. The relevant figures are 18,859 for 1850 and 37,883 for 1860.

36. Solon Robinson, "Negro Slavery in the South," *DBR*, VII (Nov., 1849), 380.

37. Phillips, *Life and Labor*, p. 326. A case in point occurs in the diary of J. B. Grimball, Oct. 6, 1840. Grimball expresses satisfaction that his overseer is quitting, although he is "humane to the negroes." He just could not get out a good enough crop.

38. Gavin Diary, May 3–6, 1859; John C. Burruss to John W. Burruss, March 29, 1850; Haller Nutt Journal of Araby Plantation, Nov. 1–4, 1843, March 31, 1844; Henry Palfrey to William Palfrey, Nov. 30, 1833; Rawick, ed., *Texas Narr.*, IV (1), 122; Catterall, ed., *Judicial Cases*, III, 202, 344, 652.

39. A. H. Arrington to Kate Arrington, Feb. 13, 1860.

40. See, e.g., Bills Diary, July 15, 1853, Oct. 24, 1857; R. R. Barrow Residence Journal, July 31, 1857.

41. Manigault Plantation Book, Jan., 1858; also Moses Liddell to St. John R. Liddell, Nov. 7, 1845.

42. Leak Diary, Oct. 17, 1854.

43. Scarborough, *Overseer*, pp. 45–46, 102; Easterby, ed., *South Carolina Rice Plantation, passim*; Bassett, *Southern Plantation Overseer*, p. 3.

44. See, e.g., J. B. Grimball Diary, Nov. 22, 1853, Nov. 28, 1855; E. G. Baker Diary, July 1, 1852; Coleman Diary, Sept. 21, 1831.

45. George Teamoh Journal, Pts. 1–2, pp. 8–9, in the Woodson Papers.

46. H.C., "On the Management of Negroes," *SA*, VII (July, 1834), 369.
47. William M. Otey to Mrs. Octavia Aurelia Otey, Nov. 13, 1851, in the Wyche-Otey Papers.
48. *Ibid.*, Nov. 14, 1858.
49. Thomas Alexander to Lt. [J. H.] White, Sept. 9, 1864, in the James Wilson White Papers. Hatred of an overseer by the slaves more often than not eventually got him fired; see, e.g., Chase C. Mooney, *Slavery in Tennessee* (Bloomington, Ind., 1957), p. 161.
50. See Scarborough, *Overseer*, p. 126.
51. Quoted in Weymouth T. Jordan, *Hugh Davis and His Alabama Plantation* (University, Ala., 1948), pp. 49, 54.
52. Louis Morton, *Robert Carter of Nomini Hall* (Charlottesville, Va., 1964 [1941]), p. 112; McColley, *Slavery and Jeffersonian Virginia*, pp. 59–60.
53. Phillips, ed., *Plantation and Frontier*, I, 113; also Sitterson, *Sugar Country*, p. 56.
54. *The Life and Times of Frederick Douglass* (New York, 1962), p. 47; also p. 66. See also Yetman, ed., *Life Under the "Peculiar Institution,"* p. 170 (William Hutson of Georgia), and p. 325 (Clara C. Young of Mississippi); Benjamin Drew, *The Refugee; Or, A North-Side View of Slavery* (New York, 1968 [1856]), pp. 141–142.
55. J. B. Grimball Diary, Sept. 12, 1832, Oct. 17, 20, 1832. For the postscript on Richard's machinations see Nov. 2, 3, 15, 1832.
56. Hundley, *Social Relations*, pp. 184–185.
57. Charles M. Manigault to Louis Manigault, Nov. 22, 1856.
58. A. T. Goodloe, "Management of Negroes," *SC*, XVIII (April, 1860), 130–131.
59. T. E. Blont, "Rules for the Government of Overseers," *SC*, V (April, 1847), 62.
60. A Subscriber, "Plantation Economy," *ACP*, II (May, 1854), 149–150.
61. J. L. Eubanks to A. H. Arrington, Oct. 14, 1860, in the Arrington Papers.
62. For some samples of masters' interventions and slaves' attitudes see R. R. Barrow Residence Journal, May 3, 9, 1858; George Teamoh Journal, p. 22, in the Woodson Papers; Rawick, ed., *Miss. Narr.*, VII (2), 58, 144; *Ga. Narr.*, XII (2), 347.
63. Interloper, "Overseers," *ACPSS*, II (June, 1858), 197.
64. Bobby Frank Jones, "A Cultural Middle Passage," unpubl. Ph.D. dissertation, University of North Carolina, 1965, p. 55.
65. Frances Butler Leigh, *Ten Years on a Georgia Plantation Since the War* (London, 1883), p. 226.
66. Isaac DuBose Seabrook, *Before and After: Or, The Relations of the Races at the South* (ed. J. H. Moore; Baton Rouge, La., 1967 [written but not published in 1895]), p. 59.
67. Rawick, ed., *Ala. Narr.*, VI (1), 432.
68. *Life and Times of Frederick Douglass*, p. 27.
69. *Ibid.*, Ch. 15 and pp. 92, 179–185.
70. Henry Clay Bruce, *The New Man: Twenty-nine Years a Slave, Twenty-nine Years a Free Man* (York, Pa., 1895), pp. iv, 28, 30, 31.
71. For some ex-slave reflections see Rawick, ed., *S.C. Narr.*, III (4), 171; *Okla. Narr.*, VII (1), 77, 112, 136.
72. See, e.g., Stirling, *Letters from the Slave States*, p. 265. On the origins of the term "trash," see the interesting exchange between W. P. Trent and Stephen B. Weeks as reflected in Trent to Weeks, March 12, 1892, in the Weeks Papers.
73. The primary sources—travelers' accounts and slaveholders' papers and reminiscences—may be consulted at random. But see the general discussion by Stampp, *Peculiar Institution*, pp. 149–150.
74. Rawick, ed., *Ark. Narr.*, X (5), 20; *Mo. Narr.*, XI, 302.

75. G. A. Ingraham to Susan Fisher, Dec. 27. 1840, in the Fisher Papers. For a discussion of the general criticism of whites as implied by contempt for poor whites, see Stampp, *Peculiar Institution*, pp. 380–381.

76. Herbert Aptheker, *American Negro Slave Revolts* (New York, 1963), pp. 233–234 and *passim;* James Hugo Johnston, *Race Relations in Virginia and Miscegenation in the South, 1776–1860* (Amherst, Mass., 1970), pp. 101–104, 138.

77. Lewis G. Clarke, *Narrative of the Sufferings of Lewis Clarke* (London, 1846), p. 25; Olmsted, *Seaboard*, p. 682. Also Thomas Wentworth Higginson, *Army Life in a Black Regiment* (Boston, 1962 [1869]), p. 110.

78. Fisk University, *God Struck Me Dead*, p. 121; Rawick, ed., *S.C. Narr.*, II (2), 279–281; III (3), 51; III (4), 165; *Texas Narr.*, V (4), 101; *Ala. Narr.*, VI (1), 106, 279; *Okla. Narr.*, VII (1), 354; *N.C. Narr.*, XV (2), 345.

79. Kemble, *Journal*, pp. 89–90.

THE HEGEMONIC FUNCTION OF THE LAW

1. Max Weber, "Politics as a Vocation," *From Max Weber: Essays in Sociology* (trans. and ed. H. H. Gerth and C. Wright Mills; New York, 1946), p. 121.

2. Marxist legal theory is, to say the least, undeveloped. But Rudolf Schlesinger makes a good contribution in *Soviet Legal Theory: Its Social Background and Development* (2nd ed.; London, 1951), Chs. 1 and 2; and the brief remarks of Gramsci are indispensable. See *Selections from the Prison Notebooks of Antonio Gramsci* (trans. and ed. Quintin Hoare and Geoffrey N. Smith; New York, 1971), pp. 195–196, 246–247.

3. Charles S. Sydnor, "The Southerner and the Laws," *JSH*, VI (Feb., 1940), 3–24, made a fine beginning, which still awaits criticism and development.

4. Gramsci, *Prison Notebooks*, p. 247.

5. The best discussion of these questions remains that of G. W. F. Hegel, *Philosophy of Right* (trans. and ed. T. M. Knox; London, 1967). Herbert Marcuse has skillfully criticized Hegel's argument, which undoubtedly breaks down at a critical point, but I do not think Marcuse or anyone else has yet resolved the problems therein posed; see *Reason and Revolution: Hegel and the Rise of Social Theory* (Boston, 1954).

6. On southern slave law in general see Catterall, ed., *Judicial Cases*, Vols. I–V; John Codman Hurd, *The Law of Freedom and Bondage in the United States* (New York, 1858–1862); Thomas R. R. Cobb, *An Inquiry into the Law of Negro Slavery* (New York, 1968 [1858]); William Goodell, *The American Slave Code in Theory and Practice* (New York, 1853). Good discussions from different points of view may be found in Ulrich Bonnell Phillips, *American Negro Slavery* (New York, 1952 [1918]), in Stampp, *Peculiar Institution*, and in all the separate studies of slavery in the states. The development of the law as a repressive mechanism against blacks is treated in Mary Frances Berry, *Black Resistance/White Law: A History of Constitutional Racism in America* (New York, 1971), esp. Chs. 1–5. Among the many more specialized studies, mention should be made of Lloyd Imes, "The Legal Status of Free Negroes and Slaves in Tennessee," *JNH*, IV (July, 1919), 255–261; Katherine Ann McGeachy, "The North Carolina Slave Code," unpubl. M.A. thesis, University of North Carolina, 1948; and esp. A. E. Keir Nash, "Fairness and Formalism in the Trials of Blacks in the State Supreme Courts of the Old South," *Virginia Law Review*, LVI (Feb., 1970), 64–100, and "The Texas Supreme Court and the Trial Rights of Blacks, 1845–1860," *JAH*, LVIII (Dec., 1971), 622–642.

7. William Styron, *The Confessions of Nat Turner* (New York, 1967), pp. 21–22.

8. *Ford v. Ford*, 1846, in Catterall, ed., *Judicial Cases*, II, 530.

9. Catterall, ed., *Judicial Cases*, II, 517.

10. *Ibid.*, III, 35.

11. *Ibid.*, II, 41.

12. *Ibid.*, V, 179.

13. *Ibid.*, II, 277, 289, 365.

14. *Ibid.*, I, 311, 312, 334. See also I, 154 (Judge Cabell of Virginia).

15. For the long historical record, splendidly analyzed, see D. B. Davis, *Problem of Slavery*.

16. By the late eighteenth century many Russian serfs had virtually become slaves. Yet, as Jerome Blum says, they refused to see themselves as such. With marvelous illogic by modern standards of property but with marvelous logic by traditional, they told their masters, "We are yours, but the land is ours." See *Lord and Peasant in Russia from the Ninth to the Nineteenth Century*, (Princeton, N. J., 1961), p. 469.

17. W. W. Hazard, "On the General Management of a Plantation," *SA*, IV (July, 1831), 350–351.

18. Thad W. Tate, Jr., *The Negro in Eighteenth-Century Williamsburg* (Charlottesville, Va., 1965), pp. 4–5, suggests a gradual decline in the status of the blacks during 1640–1660, with their legal confirmation as chattels effected after 1675. By 1705 the matter was definitively settled at law with the promulgation of a consolidated slave code. The literature is vast, but in addition to Tate see esp. Winthrop D. Jordan, *White over Black: American Attitudes Toward the Negro, 1550–1812* (Chapel Hill, N.C., 1968), pp. 82 ff. For an introduction to South Carolina as well as the Upper South see Wesley Frank Craven, *The Southern Colonies in the Seventeenth Century, 1607–1689* (Baton Rouge, La., 1949). More specifically, see H. M. Henry, *Police Control of the Slave in South Carolina* (New York, 1968 [1914]).

19. Stampp, *Peculiar Institution*, p. 23.

20. Ulrich Bonnell Phillips, "Slave Crime in Virginia," *AHR*, XX (Jan., 1915), 336–340. Phillips notes that in Nottoway County in 1789 a slave was executed for entering a kitchen and stealing one silver spoon.

21. Clement Eaton, *The Freedom-of-Thought Struggle in the Old South* (rev. ed.; New York, 1950), pp. 129–130; W. J. Cash, *The Mind of the South* (New York, 1941), p. 45.

22. Lt. Charles C. Jones, Jr., to C. C. Jones, July 25, 1862, in Myers, ed., *Children of Pride*, p. 939.

23. See, e.g., *George (a Slave) v. State of Mississippi*, 1859, in Catterall, ed., *Judicial Cases*, III, 363.

24. *Commonwealth of Virginia v. Jerry Mann*, 1820, in Catterall, ed., *Judicial Cases*, I, 133.

25. Phillips, *American Negro Slavery*, pp. 458 ff., or his article on slave crime cited in note 20 above.

26. See, e.g., Catterall, ed., *Judicial Cases*, II, 551, 556; III, 30–31, 35, 74, 92–93, 109, 325, 327, 328, 342, 381–382, 556; V, 162, 190; and the cases cited in notes 28 and 29 below.

27. Breaux Diary, July 25, 26, 1859.

28. Catterall, ed., *Judicial Cases*, III, 237. See also II, 77, 81, 191, 211, 413, 551, 554, 556; III, 133, 176, 214–215, 237, 556, 581, 673; V, 230, 237, 244; Orville W. Taylor, *Negro Slavery in Arkansas* (Durham, N.C., 1958), pp. 233–234; Sydnor, *Slavery in Mississippi*, pp. 84–85. And esp. Nash, "Fairness and Formalism," pp. 64–100.

29. See, e.g., *Nathan v. State of Missouri*, 1844, in Catterall, ed., *Judicial Cases*, V, 162.

30. Catterall, ed., *Judicial Cases*, III, 133, 152, 153, 162–163, 173, 185, 200–201, 210–211, 221,

225–226, 239–241, 246–247, 258–259, 285–286, 301–302, 322–324, 327, 332, 342, 344, 362, 364, 372–376, 556–557, 592, 657, 659, 676; also V, 154, 312.

31. Letitia Woods Brown, *Free Negroes in the District of Columbia* (New York, 1972), pp. 51 ff.

32. See, e.g., *State of Alabama v. Abram (a Slave)*, 1847, in Catterall, ed., *Judicial Cases*, III, 162.

33. Judge Ruffin's decision was read widely in Europe as well as America; we can only speculate that it may have helped sober those who took a rosy view of southern slavery. See Julius Yanuck, "Thomas Ruffin and the North Carolina Slave Law," *NCHR*, XXI (Nov., 1955), 456–475.

34. J. G. deRoulhac Hamilton, ed., *The Papers of Thomas Ruffin* (4 vols.; Raleigh, N.C., 1918–1920), IV, 255–257; Earnest James Clark, Jr., "Slave Cases Argued Before the North Carolina Supreme Court, 1818–1858," unpubl. M.A. thesis, University of North Carolina, 1959, pp. 34–35.

35. Catterall, ed., *Judicial Cases*, II, 70, 71.

36. E. J. Clark, Jr., "Slave Cases Argued Before the North Carolina Supreme Court," p. 38.

37. Rawick, ed., *Texas Narr.*, IV (1), 48; also Fisk University, *Unwritten History of Slavery*, p. 56; Yetman, ed., *Life under the "Peculiar Institution,"* p. 253; Rawick, ed., *Texas Narr.*, V (4), 152; *Ala. Narr.*, VI (1), 283; *Ark. Narr.*, IX (3), 342, 354; *Obio Narr.*, XVI, 46.

38. Henry, *Police Control of the Slave*, p. 75.

39. Mallard, *Plantation Life Before Emancipation*, pp. 43–44.

40. Rawick, ed., *Texas Narr.*, IV (1), 25–26.

41. Philip Alexander Bruce, *Economic History of Virginia in the Seventeenth Century* (2 vols.; New York, 1935 [1895]), II, 117.

42. Catterall, ed., *Judicial Cases*, I, 224–225.

43. In E. N. Elliott, ed., *Cotton Is King and Pro-slavery Arguments*, p. 29.

44. Catterall, ed., *Judicial Cases*, II, 273, 274, 333, 355–356 (Judge O'Neall quoted), 377. Also Gavin Diary, Nov. 20, 1856.

45. Catterall, ed., *Judicial Cases*, II, 605.

46. *Ibid.* V, 275.

47. See, e.g., Catterall, ed., *Judicial Cases*, II, 50, 549; III, 148, 151, 151–152, 154, 214, 233, 263, 283–284, 338, 371–372; also Bassett, *Slavery in the State of North Carolina*, p. 20; Clement Eaton, *The Growth of Southern Civilization, 1790–1860* (New York, 1961), p. 78; Nehemiah Adams, *A South-Side View of Slavery* (4th ed.; Boston, 1860), pp. 38–40.

48. See, e.g., Joe Gray Taylor, *Negro Slavery in Louisiana* (Westport, Conn., 1963), p. 226; Haller Nutt to Alonzo Snyder, April 30, 1844, in the Snyder Papers.

49. See, e.g., Gilberto Freyre, "Social Life in Brazil in the Middle of the Nineteenth Century," *HAHR*, V (Nov., 1922), 597–628; Gilberto Freyre, *The Masters and the Slaves: A Study in the Development of Brazilian Civilization* (trans. Samuel Putnam; New York, 1956), p. xxxix; C. R. Boxer, "Negro Slavery in Brazil: A Portuguese Pamphlet (1764)," *Race*, V (1964), p. 43; Stanley J. Stein, *Vassouras: A Brazilian Coffee County, 1850–1900* (Cambridge, Mass., 1957), p. 136; C. L. R. James, *The Black Jacobins: Toussaint L'Ouverture and the San Domingo Revolution* (New York, 1938), pp. 22–24; T. Lothrop Stoddard, *The French Revolution in Santo-Domingo* (2nd ed; New York, 1963), pp. 59–60; Deerr, *History of Sugar*, II, 351; Elsa V. Goveia, "The West Indian Slave Laws of the Eighteenth Century," *Revista de ciencias sociales*, IV (March, 1960), 75–108; J. Harry Bennett, *Bondsmen and Bishops: Slavery and Apprenticeship on The Codrington Plantations of Barbados, 1710–1838* (Berkeley, Calif., 1958), p. 24; Jaime Jaramillo Uribe, "Esclavos y señores en la sociedad colombiana del siglo XVIII," *Anuario colombiano de historia social y de la cultura*, I (1963), 3–55; Hubert

H. S. Aimes, *A History of Slavery in Cuba, 1511–1868* (New York, 1907), pp. 149–51, 177.

50. Olmsted, *Seaboard*, p. 487.

51. John Belton O'Neall, *The Negro Law of South Carolina* (Columbia, S.C., 1848), p. 20.

52. Sydnor, "Southerner and the Laws," p. 11.

53. George Fitzhugh, *Cannibals All! Or, Slaves Without Masters* (Cambridge, Mass., 1960 [1857], p. 79.

54. Louisiana, Ascension Parish, Police Jury Minutes, 1837–1856.

55. H.C., "On the Management of Negroes," *SA*, VII (July, 1834), 367–370.

56. A Minister of the Gospel, " 'Tatler' on the Management of Negroes," *SC*, IX (June, 1851), 84–85.

57. Bills Diary, Sept. 24, 1852; see also "Management of Slaves—Report of a Committee of the Barbour County Agricultural Society," *SC*, IV (Aug., 1846), 113–114; J. G. Taylor, *Negro Slavery in Louisiana*, p. 226; Chalmers S. Murray, *This Our Land: The Story of the Agricultural Society of South Carolina* (Charleston, S.C., 1949), p. 92.

58. Bremer, *Homes of the New World*, II, 511, 612.

59. Rawick, ed., *Texas Narr.*, V (3), 6, 119; George Teamoh Journal, Pts. 1–2, p. 32, in the Woodson Papers; Rawick, ed., *Okla. Narr.*, VII (1), 302; also *Ga. Narr.*, XIII (4), 218; Lester, *To Be a Slave*, p. 52; Fisk University, *Unwritten History of Slavery*, p. 5; Yetman, ed., *Life Under the "Peculiar Institution,"* p. 124.

60. See Catterall, ed., *Judicial Cases*, III, 597 (*State of Louisiana v. Morris, 1852*); also III, 154; V, 300; Gavin Diary, Nov. 9, 1855; Bremer, *Homes of the New World*, I, 278; Eaton, *Growth of Southern Civilization*, p. 79.

61. Richardson Memoirs, p. 43; Mary Woodrow to Mayor of Alexandria, Va., June 21, 1813, in Slave Papers, Library of Congress; Catterall, ed., *Judicial Cases*, III, 491–492.

62. See, e.g., A Young Planter, "Communication," *CP*, I (July 15, 1840), 209–210; R. F. W. Allston to Adele Petigru Allston, Nov. 27, 1853, in Easterby, ed., *South Carolina Rice Plantation*, p. 117; Bennet H. Barrow Diary, May 21, 1839, in E. A. Davis, ed., *Plantation Life in the Florida Parishes of Louisiana*, p. 148.

63. W. E. B. Du Bois, *Black Reconstruction in America* (New York, 1962 [1935]), p. 10; see also Dwight Lowell Dumond, *Antislavery Origins of the Civil War in the United States* (Ann Arbor, Mich., 1959), pp. 43–44.

64. See esp. John Hope Franklin, *The Militant South* (Cambridge, Mass., 1956), pp. 35, 39, and *passim*, where the role of slavery in encouraging violence is thoughtfully explored along several lines.

65. Quoted in Sydnor, "Southerner and the Laws," p. 12. This article is the most important contribution we have to this problem. I have drawn on it freely but also departed from it in some essentials.

66. Johan Huizinga, *The Waning of the Middle Ages: A Study of The Forms of Life, Thought and Art in France and the Netherlands in the Fourteenth and Fifteenth Centuries* (London, 1924), Ch. 1, "The Violent Tenor of Life," may profitably be read as suggestive for the Old South without making an equation of the two societies.

67. This tradition has lingered on in the twentieth century. Some southern states continue to accept physical force as a legitimate reply to personal insult. See, e.g., Wex S. Malone, "Insult in Retaliation—The Huckabee Case," *Mississippi Law Journal*, XI (April, 1939), 333–339.

68. The categories are Max Weber's. See esp. Max Rheinstein, ed., *Max Weber on Law in Economy and Society* (Cambridge, Mass., 1966), pp. 302 ff.; and Weber, *The Theory of Social and Economic Organization* (London, 1947), *passim*.

69. See, e.g., Max Weber, *General Economic History* (Glencoe, Ill., 1950).

70. Max Weber, "The Social Causes of the Decay of Ancient Civilization," *Journal of General Education*, V (Oct., 1950), 75–88.

71. Marxists therefore reject the idea of a special historical stage of "commercial capitalism" and insist on centering their analysis in the productive sector and its social relations. The best introduction to the question, apart from Marx's *Capital*, remains Maurice Dobb, *Studies in the Development of Capitalism* (New York, 1947). I have tried to develop some of the implications of this line of attack with reference to the relationship of the rise of slavery in the New World to the commercial revolution and the rise of capitalism in Europe in Pt. 1 of *World the Slaveholders Made*.

72. Special mention should be made of C. B. McPherson, *The Political Theory of Possessive Individualism: Hobbes to Locke* (Oxford, 1962), and Richard Schlatter, *The Idea of Property: The History of an Idea* (London, 1951)—two pioneer efforts in Marxian analysis. The struggle for a bourgeois concept of property and for the overthrow of traditional concepts, with France and the French Revolution as case studies, will be explored in two forthcoming works by Elizabeth Fox-Genovese: *Social Origins of the Girondist Bourgeoisie: A Contribution to the Marxian Interpretation of the French Revolution*, and *The Forging of a Bourgeois Ideology: A Study of the Development of French Physiocracy*.

73. The relationship of southern slave law and its implicit theory of property to those of ancient Rome is explored in Arnold A. Sio, "Interpretations of Slavery: The Slave Status in the Americas," *CSSH*, VII (April, 1965), 289–308, esp. p. 296.

74. Hence Hegel could denounce slavery as an outrage and a manifest contradiction to the essence of an emergent theory of right, which he saw as resting on a bourgeois theory of property. See *Philosophy of Right*.

75. Sydnor, "Southerner and the Laws," pp. 8–9; Fogel and Engerman, *Time on the Cross*, pp. 128–129.

76. See esp. Rheinstein, ed., *Max Weber on Law in Economy and Society*, p. 9.

77. See D. B. Davis, *Problem of Slavery*, esp. pp. 33, 40, 57–58, 256, 269–270. My own view of the role of the Catholic ethos in the shaping of New World slave societies may be found in "Materialism and Idealism in the History of Negro Slavery in the Americas," Ch. 2 of *In Red and Black: Marxian Explorations in Southern and Afro-American History* (New York, 1971), and in Pt. 1 of *World the Slaveholders Made*.

78. See, e.g., Barnsley Notebook, 1904. See the studies of Prado, *Colonial Background of Modern Brazil*, pp. 323, 330–332, 335, 392; Gilberto Freyre, *The Mansions and the Shanties: The Making of Modern Brazil* (New York, 1963), pp. 17, 23, 266; Boxer, *Salvador de Sá*, pp. 34–36; J. H. Parry, *The Spanish Seaborne Empire* (New York, 1966), Ch. 10; Arthur S. Aiton, "The Asiento Treaty as Reflected in the Papers of Lord Shelburne," *HAHR*, VIII (May, 1928), 167–177; Salvador de Madariaga, *The Rise of the Spanish Empire in America* (London, 1947), p. 271; and the references cited above in note 49.

79. Fisk University, *Unwritten History of Slavery*, p. 75.

IN THE NAME OF HUMANITY AND THE CAUSE OF REFORM

1. G. G. Coulton, *Medieval Panorama: The English Scene from Conquest to Reformation* (Cambridge, 1944), p. 705.

2. On the role of the churches as a proslavery force for humanization of plantation practice, see esp. Caleb Perry Patterson, *The Negro in Tennessee, 1790–1865*

(New York, 1968), p. 117; William S. Jenkins, *Pro-slavery Thought in the Old South* (Chapel Hill, N.C., 1935), pp. 210–211; Willie Greier, "North Carolina Baptists and the Negro, 1727–1877," unpubl. M.A. thesis, University of North Carolina, 1944; Ralph Thomas Parkinson, "The Religious Instruction of Slaves, 1820–1860," unpubl. M.A. thesis, University of North Carolina, 1948, esp. pp. 20–22. For the recollections of the Rev. A. M. Moore, ex-slave from Harrison County, Texas, on the increase of black preachers and the relaxation of opposition to black religious meetings, see Rawick, ed., *Texas Narr.*, V (3), 119.

3. For accounts of the steady suppression of dissent and the effective if limited use of violence, see Charles S. Sydnor, *The Development of Southern Sectionalism* (Baton Rouge, La., 1948), and Eaton, *Freedom-of-Thought Struggle.*

4. Ulrich Bonnell Phillips, "Conservatism and Progress in the Cotton Belt," *The Slave Economy of the Old South: Selected Essays in Economic and Social History* (ed. Eugene D. Genovese; Baton Rouge, La., 1968). Phillips here presents the argument that slavery would have been reformed out of existence if the abolitionists had left the South alone.

5. In general see Stampp, *Peculiar Institution*, pp. 232–234; also Tate, *Negro in Eighteenth-Century Williamsburg*, p. 175; McColley, *Slavery and Jeffersonian Virginia*, p. 72; John H. Russell, *The Free Negro in Virginia, 1619–1865* (Baltimore, 1913), p. 52; Henry, *Police Control of the Slave*, pp. 168–174; C. P. Patterson, *Negro in Tennessee*, p. 17

6. Quoted in J. H. Johnston, *Race Relations and Miscegenation*, p. 148.

7. Quoted in Du Bois, *Black Reconstruction*, p. 5. For an interesting illustration of the humanitarian impulse within a wider acceptance of slavery see Norman Dain, *Disordered Minds: The First Century of Eastern State Hospital in Williamsburg, Virginia, 1776–1866* (Charlottesville, Va., 1971), p. 112, an account of John Minson Galt, head of the Eastern State [Mental] Hospital in Williamsburg, Va., who worked for consideration of the plight of mentally disturbed blacks but emphatically defended slavery and the idea of black inferiority.

8. See Donald J. Senese, "The Free Negro and the South Carolina Courts, 1790–1860," *SCHM*, LXVIII (July, 1967), 140–153, esp. p. 148; Simms in E. N. Elliott, ed., *Cotton Is King and Pro-slavery Arguments*, pp. 238–239; Lester B. Baltimore, "Southern Nationalists and Southern Nationalism, 1850–1870," unpubl. Ph.D. dissertation, University of Missouri, 1968. The Catholic slaveholding countries undoubtedly had a more favorable attitude toward manumission, although the extent of the actual practice remains in dispute. But for the most part, slavery in those countries existed within or side by side with a seigneurial social system, so that release from slavery did not necessarily alter the more fundamental social relationships, and the less virulent racism allowed for a more open policy.

9. See McColley, *Slavery and Jeffersonian Virginia*, esp. pp. 90, 115–116; Joseph Clarke Robert, *The Road from Monticello* (Durham, N.C., 1941); W. D. Jordan, *White over Black*, p. 368.

10. Quoted by Ulrich Bonnell Phillips, *The Life of Robert Toombs* (New York, 1913), p. 161; also p. 166.

11. Walker Diary, July 25, 1857 (p. 33); *DBR*, XIX (Aug., 1855), 130; "Exemption of Slaves from Sale Under Execution," *SC*, XI (Oct., 1853), 309; Bremer, *Homes of the New World*, I, 277; II, 488; Allan Nevins, *The Emergence of Lincoln* (2 vols.; New York, 1950), II, 161–162; J. B. Sellers, *Slavery in Alabama*, pp. 169, 191; Sydnor, *Slavery in Mississippi*, p. 64; Wallace B. Turner, "Kentucky Slavery in the Last Ante Bellum Decade," *KHSR*, LVIII (Oct., 1960), 298.

12. See Joseph Sturge, *A Visit to the United States of America in 1841* (London, 1842), p. 61, and Stirling, *Letters from the Slave States*, p. 285, both of whom report conversations with slaves. Also Bremer, *Homes of the New World*, II, 434; Lyell, *Second Visit*, I, 209, 216–217; Olmsted, *Seaboard*, p. 97, and *Back Country*, p. 81; A Farmer of Lower Virginia, "Slavery in Virginia," *FR*, IV (July, 1836), 180; H.C., "On the Management of Negroes," *SA*, VII (July, 1834), 367–370; "Religious Instruction of Negroes," *Quarterly Review of the Methodist Episcopal Church, South*, I (July, 1847), 319–338; Bonner, *Georgia Agriculture*, p. 203.

13. Rawick, ed., *Texas Narr.*, IV (1), 26; Martineau, *Society in America*, II, 172; G. W. Featherstonhaugh, *Excursion Through the Slave States* (New York, 1968 [1844]), p. 125.

14. J. G. Taylor, *Negro Slavery in Louisiana*, p. 46; Sitterson, *Sugar Country*, pp. 90, 436; Lyell, *Second Visit*, II, 125; "Sugar and Slavery in Louisiana," *SC*, V (April, 1847), 55; Earl W. Fornell, "The Abduction of Free Negroes and Slaves in Texas," *SHQ*, LX (Jan., 1957), 379.

15. Forrest McDonald, *E Pluribus Unum: The Formation of the American Republic, 1776–1790* (Boston, 1965), p. 65. Also McColley, *Slavery and Jeffersonian Virginia*, p. 6; "Travelers' Impressions of Slavery in America from 1750 to 1800," *JNH*, I (Oct., 1916), 404–433; "James Madison's Attitude Toward the Negro," *JNH*, VI (Jan., 1921), 77–78; W. E. B. Du Bois, *The Suppression of the African Slave-Trade to the United States of America, 1638–1820* (New York, 1969 [1898]), pp. 12, 152.

16. See the forthcoming study by Peter H. Wood, *Black Majority*; also M. Eugene Sirmans, *Colonial South Carolina: A Political History, 1663–1763* (Chapel Hill, N.C., 1966), pp. 108, 209.

17. David Duncan Wallace, *The Life of Henry Laurens* (New York, 1915), pp. 66–67; G. G. Johnson, *Social History of the Sea Islands*, p. 34; Josiah Smith, Jr., to George Austin, Jan. 31, 1774, in the Smith Papers; Heyward, *Seed from Madagascar*, p. 75; Jeffrey R. Brackett, *The Negro in Maryland* (Baltimore, 1889), p. 124.

18. In general see Eaton, *Growth of Southern Civilization*, p. 81. Also Ingraham, *South-West*, II, 183; Major Amos Stoddard, *Sketches, Historical and Descriptive, of Louisiana* (New York, 1832), p. 332; J. W. DuBose, "Recollections of the Plantation," *AHQ*, I (Spring, 1930), 71; Frank F. Steel to Anna Steel, Dec. 15, 1859.

19. See Hammond's "Letter to Thomas Clarkson," in E. N. Elliott, ed., *Cotton Is King and Pro-slavery Arguments*.

20. Martineau, *Society in America*, II, 151; W. Freeman Galpin, ed., "Letters of an East Tennessee Abolitionist," *East Tennessee Historical Society Publications*, No. 3 (Jan., 1931), pp. 135–149; E. Merton Coulter, *John Jacobus Flournoy: Champion of the Common Man in the Ante-bellum South* (Savannah, Ga., 1942), p. 47.

21. A. T. Goodloe, "Management of Negroes," *SC*, XVIII (April, 1860), 130–131; and N. D. Guerry's reply in XVIII (June, 1860), 176–177.

22. Chancellor Harper in E. N. Elliott, ed., *Cotton Is King and Pro-slavery Arguments*, pp. 64–65.

23. A Reader, "Agricultural Laborers," *SA*, VIII (Jan., 1835), 8; cf. *ACP*, II (Aug., 1854), 253.

24. Garnett Andrews, in Southern Central Agricultural Society, *Transactions, 1846–1851*, pp. 98–99.

25. John Stainback Wilson, "The Peculiarities and Diseases of Negroes," *ACPSS*, IV (July, 1860), 319.

26. *Ibid.*, p. 20; see also *DBR*, III (May, 1847), 421, for a similar theme.
27. See the anonymous review of Ariel Abbot's *Letters Written in the Interior of Cuba* in *Southern Review*, IV (Aug.–Nov., 1829), 123–136; R. E. Caffrey's report on his trip to Cuba in *PB*, XV (March 7, 1850), n.p.; Noah B. Cloud, "The Cotton Power, an American Power," *ACPSS*, II (Nov., 1858), 331; William K. Scarborough, ed., *The Diary of Edmund Ruffin* (2 vols.; Baton Rouge, La., 1972), March 4, 1859 (I, 290). The best introduction to the Cuban situation is Franklin W. Knight, *Slave Society in Cuba During the Nineteenth Century* (Madison, Wis., 1970). For the eighteenth century see Herbert Klein, *Slavery in the Americas: A Comparative Study of Cuba and Virginia* (Chicago, 1967). Also Deerr, *History of Sugar*, II, 359; Aimes, *History of Slavery in Cuba*, pp. 47, 61, 77, 86, 159, 178, 143–144, 254–255, 266; Allan Nevins, *Ordeal of the Union* (2 vols.; New York, 1947), II, 63–64.
28. See, e.g., Bremer, *Homes of the New World*, II, 309, 437; Stirling, *Letters from the Slave States*, p. 109.
29. Stanley M. Elkins, *Slavery: A Problem in American Institutional and Intellectual Life* (Chicago, 1959), esp. Ch. 2.
30. For a fuller discussion of the different meanings of "treatment" and their significance, see my "Treatment of Slaves in Different Countries: Problems in the Application of the Comparative Method," *In Red and Black*, Ch. 7.
31. Curtin, *Atlantic Slave Trade*.
32. See the papers of K. G. Davies and Johannes Posthma in Stanley Engerman and Eugene D. Genovese, eds., *Race and Slavery in the Western Hemisphere: Quantitative Studies* (Princeton, forthcoming).
33. Richard Dunn, *Sugar and Slaves: The Rise of the Planter Class in the English West Indies, 1624–1713* (Chapel Hill, N.C., 1972); H. O. Patterson, *Sociology of Slavery*, pp. 46–47, 74; J. H. Johnston, *Race Relations and Miscegenation*, p. 184; Frances Trollope, *Domestic Manners of the Americans* (London, 1927), p. 246.
34. Hundley, *Social Relations*, pp. 289–290.
35. See, e.g., Lyell, *Second Visit*, I, 262; II, 78–79; Bremer, *Homes of the New World*, I, 296; W. H. Russell, *My Diary North and South*, p. 143. But for another opinion, at least so far as clothing is concerned, see Stirling, *Letters from the Slave States*, p. 263.
36. Quoted in G. D. H. Cole and Raymond Postgate, *The British Common People, 1746–1939* (London, 1946), p. 276.
37. It is enough to cite one last will and testament to this effect, for it came from a master who provided for the emancipation of his slaves. See *Heirs of Henderson v. Rost and Montgomery Executors*, 1850, in Catterall, ed., *Judicial Cases*, III, 605.
38. Kemble, *Journal*, pp. 7–8.
39. *Die Schnellpost* (Ulm), Jan. 10, 1838, typed translation at Louisiana State University. I wish to thank Mrs. Meyer, then at the Department of Archives and History, LSU, for bringing to my attention this item, which had originally been in her own family's papers.
40. Raimondo Luraghi, *Storia della guerra civile americana* (Turin, 1966), pp. 57, 69.
41. Jürgen Kuczynski, *The Rise of the Working Class* (New York, 1967), p. 181.
42. Eric J. Hobsbawm, *The Age of Revolution, 1789–1848* (Cleveland, Ohio, 1962), pp. 167, 198, 205–208, and *Industry and Empire* (New York, 1968), pp. 69–70; Hobsbawm and George Rudé, *Captain Swing* (New York, 1968), pp. 51–52; E. P. Thompson, *The Making of the English Working Class* (New York, 1962), p. 209; Shepherd Clough, *France: A History of National Economics, 1789–1939* (New York, 1964), pp. 34–35, 52, 162; George Duby and Robert Mandrou, *A History of French Civilization* (New York, 1964), pp. 213, 219, 450–451; Theodore S.

Hamerow, *Restoration, Revolution, Reaction: Economics and Politics in Germany, 1815–1871* (New York, 1966), pp. 76–77, 227; Geroid Tanquary Robinson, *Rural Russia Under the Old Regime* (New York, 1967), pp. 37, 41–42, 116.

43. Ulrich Bonnell Phillips, *Georgia and State Rights* (Washington, D.C., 1902), p. 153.

44. "The Negro: Personal Experience of a Southern Slaveholder," *DBR*, III (May, 1847), 419. Also *SA*, I (Dec., 1828), 523–528; III (May, 1830), 237–240.

45. Olmsted, *Back Country*, p. 182; Anonymous Diary, 1835, at Louisiana State University, p. 3; C. P. Patterson, *Negro in Tennessee*, pp. 66–67. The slave narratives (see, e.g., Rawick, ed., *American Slave*, Vols. IV, VI, VII) suggest 4 A.M. as the norm in the cotton and sugar regions of the Southwest, where conditions were supposed to be harshest.

46. For some indications of the range see Olmsted, *Back Country*, p. 50, and *Seaboard*, p. 109; and Weld, *Slavery as It Is*, p. 36. My estimates roughly concur with the ten-hour to twelve-hour day assigned in the factories. See the data in Charles B. Dew, *Ironmaker to the Confederacy: Joseph R. Anderson and the Tredegar Iron Works* (New Haven, Conn., 1966), and Robert S. Starobin, *Industrial Slavery in the Old South* (New York, 1970).

47. Mrs. E. C. Hamilton to William Hamilton, May 31, 1860, in the Lester Collection.

48. Bonner, *Georgia Agriculture*, p. 201. On a two-hour-or-more break as a summer norm see Charles S. Davis, *Cotton Kingdom in Alabama* (Montgomery, Ala., 1939), p. 79; Minnie C. Boyd, *Alabama in the Fifties: A Social Study* (New York, 1931), p. 43; Olmsted, *Seaboard*, p. 109; Agricola, "Management of Negroes," *DBR*, XIX (Sept., 1859), 361; Robert Collins, "Management of Slaves," *DBR*, XVII (Oct., 1854), 424; M. W. Philips, "Plantation Economy," *SC*, IV (Aug., 1846), 127; Rawick, ed., *S.C. Narr.*, II (1), 10; *Texas Narr.*, IV (1), 147.

49. Herbert Anthony Kellar, ed., *Solon Robinson: Pioneer and Agriculturalist* (2 vols.; Indianapolis, 1936), II, 381; Lester B. Shippee, ed., *Bishop Whipple's Southern Diary, 1843–1844* (Minneapolis, 1937), p. 29; Pearson, ed., *Letters from Port Royal*, p. 45, n. 1; House, ed., *Planter Management and Capitalism in Georgia*, p. 53; Phillips, ed., *Plantation and Frontier*, II, 117; Easterby, ed., *South Carolina Rice Plantation*, p. 346; "Management of a Southern Plantation," *DBR*, XXII (Jan., 1857), 40.

50. Sidney Andrews, *The South Since the War* (Boston, 1971 [1865–1866]), p. 181.

51. Deerr, *History of Sugar*, II, 354–359; Bremer, *Homes of the New World*, I, 312, 333; II, 328; Knight, *Slave Society in Cuba*, pp. 67 ff.; Raúl Bonilla Cepero, *Obras históricas* (Havana, 1963), p. 46; Waldemar Westergaard, *The Danish West Indies Under Company Rule* (New York, 1917), pp. 158–159; Stewart L. Mims, *Colbert's West India Policy* (New Haven, Conn., 1912), p. 322; H. O. Patterson, *Sociology of Slavery*, pp. 68–90; Elsa V. Goveia, *Slave Society in the British Leeward Islands at the End of the Eighteenth Century* (New Haven, Conn., 1965), p. 130; Michael Craton and Michael Walvin, *A Jamaican Plantation: The History of Worthy Park, 1670–1970* (Toronto, 1970), p. 105.

52. See, e.g., Kuczynski, *Rise of the Working Class*, pp. 92, 96, 112, 113; Hamerow, *Restoration, Revolution, Reaction*, p. 79; Clough, *France: National Economics*, pp. 159, 258; Charles Morazé, *La France bourgeoise, XVIIIᵉ–XXᵉ siècle* (Paris, 1946), pp. 48–54; Norman Ware, *The Industrial Worker, 1840–1860* (Chicago, 1964), pp. xii–xiii, 6–7, 73, 84, 128–130.

53. This was the Sardinia in which Antonio Gramsci grew up. See Giuseppe Fiori, *Antonio Gramsci: Life of a Revolutionary* (New York, 1972), Ch. 6.

54. For contrasting assessments of health standards see William Dosite Postell, *The Health of Slaves on the Southern Plantations* (Baton Rouge, La., 1951); and Richard H. Shryock, "Medical Practice in the Old South," *SAQ*, XXIX

(April, 1930), 172–182. For instances of unusually high expenditure to treat slaves see Mitchell Account Book, p. 148; Smallwood Diary, Vol. III; Price Papers, Vol. I (Oct. 18–Nov. 23, 1843, Jan. 13–23, 1844), Vol. II (July 6–7, 1846); Burwell Papers, Vol. III; Tillman-Norwood Medical Ledgers, I, 4–19; Johnston Account Book, Oct. 1–7, 1855; Stirling Papers, Aug. 24, 1842; Catterall, ed., *Judicial Cases*, III, 490, 520–521. The more general estimate of expenditure and the remarks on physicians' services are based primarily on: Physician's Record Book, 1855–1862; Physician's Fee Book, 1847–1850, p. 43; Physician's Book in the Minis Collection, VI, 84; H. M. Turner, Physician's Record Book, Vol. IV (March 15, 1851, Feb. 6, 1857); Physician's Account Book, 1824–1839; B. B. Jones Books, III, 1, 28; Price Account Book, Vol. I (July, 1843), Vol. II (Aug. 14–22, 1846); Jaynes Plantation Book, p. 111; Robinson Account Books, Vols. XIX–XX; Wade Diary, I, 33 ff.; Dr. Luico Mitchell Account Book, p. 167; Tillman-Norwood Medical Ledgers, I, 57, XX, 133; Graham Papers, VIII, 33, 204; Stock Farm Records in Jenkins Plantation Book; Aventine Plantation Diary; Sheppard Papers; Nutt Papers; Randolph Papers; Clark and Family Papers, Vol. XII (Oct. 19, 1853); Henry Watson Book, 1832–1848; Morrison Journal and Accounts, 1845–1862; Fuller Account Book, 1856–1860. Also *DBR*, VII (Nov., 1849), 436; VIII (Jan., 1850), 18. For a fuller discussion of the relevant problems see my "Medical and Insurance Costs of Slaveholding in the Cotton Belt," *JNH*, XLV (July, 1960), 141–155.

55. P. A. Bruce, *Economic History of Virginia in the Seventeenth Century*, II, 105–106; Hunter Dickinson Farish, ed., *Journal and Letters of Philip Vickers Fithian, 1773–1774: A Plantation Tutor of the Old Dominion* (Williamsburg, Va., 1943), p. 169; Morton, *Robert Carter of Nomini Hall*, p. 108; Austin Steward, *Twenty-two Years a Slave and Forty Years as a Freeman* (Canandaigua, N.Y., 1867), p. 11; McColley, *Slavery and Jeffersonian Virginia*, pp. 60–61; Mullin, *Flight and Rebellion*, p. 50; Fisk University, *Unwritten History of Slavery*, pp. 3, 5; Larry Gara, ed., "A New Englander's View of Plantation Life: Letters of Edwin Hall to Cyrus Woodman, 1837," *JSH*, XVIII (Aug., 1952), 350.

56. Avery O. Craven, "Poor Whites and Negroes of the Ante-bellum South," *JNH*, XV (Jan., 1930), 17; Bassett, *Southern Plantation Overseer*, p. 124; Olmsted, *Seaboard*, p. 506; S. Andrews, *South Since the War*, p. 182; Sam Hilliard, "Hog Meat and Cornpone: Food Habits in the Ante-bellum South," *Proceedings of the American Philosophical Society*, CXIII (Feb., 1969), 1–13.

57. Weld, *Slavery as It Is*, p. 33; cf. J. J. Tobias, *Crime and Industrial Society in the Nineteenth Century* (New York, 1968), pp. 240–243.

58. C. R. Boxer, *The Dutch Seaborne Empire, 1600–1800* (New York, 1965), pp. 61, 75; Henri Sée, *Economic and Social Conditions in France During the Eighteenth Century* (New York, 1912), pp. 21, 37.

59. G. T. Robinson, *Rural Russia*, pp. 94–95; G. E. Fussell, *The English Rural Laborer* (London, 1962), Ch. 10; Clough, *France: National Economics*, pp. 158–159; M. M. Green, *Ibo Village Affairs* (New York, 1947), pp. 42–43; Conrad Arensberg, *The Irish Countryman* (New York, 1949), p. 52; Pember Reeves, *Round About a Pound a Week* (London, 1914), *passim*.

60. See, e.g., K. Onwuke Dike, *Trade and Politics in the Niger Delta, 1830–1885* (Oxford, 1956), p. 156.

61. D. E. Huger Smith, "Plantation Boyhood," in A. R. Huger Smith, *Carolina Rice Plantation of the Fifties: Thirty Paintings in Water-Colour. Narrative by Herbert Ravenel Sass* (New York, 1936); Roger W. Shugg, *Origins of Class Struggle in Louisiana* (Baton Rouge, La., 1968), p. 72; Catterall, ed., *Judicial Cases*, III, 60; W. E. B. Du Bois, *John Brown* (New York, 1962), p. 35; WPA, *Negro in Virginia*, pp. 150–151.

62. *PB*, XIV (March 15, 1849), reprinted from the *Tribune*. Also Olmsted, *Back*

Country, p. 83; V. S. Naipaul, *The Loss of El Dorado: A History* (New York, 1970), p. 156; Earl E. Thorpe, *Eros and Freedom in Southern Life and Thought* (Durham, N.C., 1967), p. 23.

63. Fitzgerald Ross, *Cities and Camps of the Confederate States* (Urbana, Ill., 1958 [1865]), p. 32; Smedes, *Southern Planter*, p. 149. Also Bassett, *Slavery in the State of North Carolina*, p. 61.

64. Such references may be found throughout the volumes of Rawick, ed., *American Slave.*

65. E. A. Davis, ed., *Plantation Life in the Florida Parishes of Louisiana*, pp. 431 ff.; Eaton, *Growth of Southern Civilization*, p. 61.

66. *Southern Patriot*, Feb. 10, 1826, as quoted in William W. Freehling, *Prelude to Civil War: The Nullification Controversy in South Carolina, 1816–1836* (New York, 1966), p. 66.

67. Andrew Flinn Plantation Rules, 1840; Lyell, *Second Visit*, I, 265; S. Andrews, *South Since the War*, p. 25.

68. See "Duties of an Overseer," in *Affleck's Cotton Plantation Record and Account Book*, copies of which may be found in many sets of plantation papers, or the reprint in *ACP*, II (Dec., 1854), 353–356; W. D. Jordan, *White over Black*, p. 433, n. 9; Rusticus, "Plantation Management and Practice," *ACPSS*, I (Dec., 1857), 372–375; Moses Liddell to St. John R. Liddell, Jan. 6, 1845.

69. Quoted in Sitterson, *Sugar Country*, p. 235.

70. Rawick, ed., *Texas Narr.*, IV (1), 56. See also the remarks of Rawick, *Sundown to Sunup*, pp. 57 ff.

71. Steward, *Twenty-two Years a Slave*, p. 13; Saxon *et al.*, *Gumbo Ya-Ya*, p. 234; P. C. Weston, "Management of a Southern Plantation," *DBR*, XXII (Jan., 1857), 40; Eaton, *Growth of Southern Civilization*, p. 61.

72. Willie Lee Rose, *Rehearsal for Reconstruction: The Port Royal Experiment* (New York, 1967), p. 110; Rawick, ed., *American Slave*, passim, any volume.

73. Phillips, *American Negro Slavery*, p. 271, which relies on the Hammond Papers; also Plantation Rules, 1840, in the Flinn Plantation Diary.

74. Frederick Bancroft, *Slave Trading in the Old South* (Baltimore, 1931), p. 102; Ingraham, *South-West*, II, 287–288.

75. Solomon Northup, *Twelve Years a Slave* (New York, 1970 [1853]), p. 45.

76. Rawick, ed., *Texas Narr.*, IV (1), 15.

77. Nathan Bass, "Essay on the Treatment and Management of Slaves," Southern Central Agricultural Society [of Georgia], *Transactions, 1846–1851*, p. 198.

78. Cornwall Diary, Jan. 31, 1861.

79. Higginson, *Army Life*, pp. 43, 53.

80. Hegel, *Philosophy of Right*, pp. 70–71.

81. Mary Boykin Chesnut, *A Diary from Dixie* (ed., B. A. Williams; Boston, 1949), March 14, 1861 (p. 21).

82. See Debien, *Plantations et esclaves à Saint-Domingue*, pp. 66–67; C. L. R. James, *Black Jacobins*, p. 12 and Ch. 1 generally.

83. Rolando Mellafe, *La Esclavitud en Hispano-América* (Buenos Aires, 1964), p. 83.

84. W. D. Jordan, *White over Black*, pp. 154–155, 473; Sirmans, *Colonial South Carolina*, p. 66; E. R. Turner, *The Negro in Pennsylvania* (New York, 1969), p. 29.

85. Olmsted, *Seaboard*, p. 619; J. G. Taylor, *Negro Slavery in Louisiana*, pp. 184, 226–227; Benjamin Robinson Account Book, Nov. 21 and Dec. 2, 1850 (XX, 123, 126).

86. *Worsley v. State*, 1850, in Catterall, ed., *Judicial Cases*, II, 545.

87. Du Bois, *Black Reconstruction*, pp. 8–9.

88. Bell Irvin Wiley, "The Movement to Humanize the Institution of Slavery

During the Confederacy," *Emory University Quarterly*, V (Dec., 1949), 207–220; also Bell Irvin Wiley, *Southern Negroes, 1861–1865* (New Haven, Conn., 1938), pp. 168–172.

89. In addition to the public utterances of the reformers see *The Private Journal of Henry William Ravenel, 1859–1887* (ed. A. R. Childs; Columbia, S. C., 1947), p. 219; Eliza Frances Andrews, *War-Time Journal of a Georgia Girl, 1864–1865* (New York, 1908), p. 127; Mary Jones Journal, Jan. 11, 1865, in Myers, ed., *Children of Pride.* Also B. F. Riley, *History of the Baptists in Alabama from the Time of Their First Occupation of Alabama in 1808 Until 1894* (Birmingham, Ala., 1895), p. 291. J. S. Buckingham, among others, saw earlier amelioration as a response to abolitionist criticism; see *Slave States of America* (2 vols.; New York, 1968 [1842]), II, 431–432.

OUR BLACK FAMILY

1. Robert Lowell, *The Old Glory: Benito Cereno* (New York, 1965), p. 177.
2. David Gavin of South Carolina, recovering from a serious illness, offered a prayer: "Grant the blessings O Lord, grant them to my brothers, friends, relatives, to our negroes ennable them to be good and faithful servants and us kind and just masters and mistresses. . . ." Diary, Nov. 21, 1857.
3. Charles Colcock Jones, *Suggestions on the Religious Instruction of the Negroes in the Southern States* (Philadelphia, 1847), p. 13.
4. *Plantation and Farm Instruction, Regulation, Record, Inventory and Account Book for the Use of Managers on the Estate of Philip St. George Cocke* (Richmond, Va., 1852), copy in the Barbour Papers.
5. Rawick, ed., *Okla. Narr.*, VII (1), 105.
6. Thomas P. Jones, "The Progress of Manufactures . . .", *Textile History Review*, III (July, 1962 [1827]), p. 159; Eleanor J. W. Baker Journal (1848), p. 16.
7. Insanity in masters manifested itself sometimes in extreme indulgence but usually in cruelty. For evidence of its being an occasional problem see Catterall, ed., *Judicial Cases*, II, 463–464; III, 209, 337; John Lane to John C. Burruss, Feb. 15, 1833, in the Burruss Papers; Rawick, ed., *Ark. Narr.*, IX (4), 53.
8. Nott in De Bow. ed., *Industrial Resources*, II, 298; Kate Stone, *Brokenburn* (ed. J. Q. Anderson; Baton Rouge, La., 1955), July 17, 1861 (p. 41); Holcombe Diary, June 2, 1855.
9. Bond Diary, Aug. 26–27, 1861 (pp. 60–61).
10. *State v. Hoover*, 1839, Catterall, ed., *Judicial Cases*, II, 85–86.
11. Charles W. Ramsdell, ed., *Laws and Joint Resolutions of the Last Session of the Confederate Congress (November 7, 1864–March 18, 1865), Together with the Secret Acts of Previous Congresses* (Durham, N.C., 1941), p. 104.
12. McCall Diary, Dec. 29, 1853; E. F. Andrews, *War-Time Journal of a Georgia Girl*, p. 62; also Autobiographical Sketch (ms.).
13. Olmsted, *Back Country*, pp. 381–382.
14. Iris Origo, "The Domestic Enemy: The Eastern Slaves in Tuscany in Fourteenth and Fifteenth Centuries," *Speculum*, XXX (July, 1955), 340.
15. Ramón Menéndez Pidal, *The Spaniards in Their History* (New York, 1950), p. 70; Freyre, *Masters and Slaves, passim.*
16. Jack P. Greene, ed., *The Diary of Colonel Landon Carter of Sabine Hall* (2 vols.; Charlottesville, Va., 1965), I, 27.
17. Isaac L. Baker to W. S. Hamilton, 1823, in the Lester Collection.

18. Chesnut, *Diary from Dixie*, Dec. 8, 1861 (p. 172).
19. Yetman, ed., *Life Under the "Peculiar Institution,"* pp. 142, 252, 259, 282; see also Charles Ball, *Slavery in the United States: A Narrative of the Life and Adventures of Charles Ball* (Lewiston, Pa., 1836), p. 14; H. C. Bruce, *New Man*, p. 65; Rawick, ed., *Ark. Narr.*, IX (4), 55; X (5), 56; *Fla. Narr.*, XVII, 146.
20. See the trenchant remarks of Harmannus Hoetink, *The Two Variants of Caribbean Race Relations* (London, 1967), p. 16.
21. Quoted in Sydnor, *Slavery in Mississippi*, p. 242.
22. Thorpe, *Eros and Freedom*, p. 27.
23. Anne Firor Scott, *The Southern Lady: From Pedestal to Politics, 1830–1930* (Chicago, 1970), p. 17. Contemporary expressions of the inseparability of slavery from the rest of the social fabric abound in the writings of Fitzhugh, Hughes, Holmes, *et al.*, as well as in those with less propagandistic intention; see, e.g., J. B. O'Neall's speech in the *Proceedings of the State Agricultural Society of South Carolina*, Sept. 11, 1844, p. 219, or the article in *SLM*, XXV (Aug., 1857), 81. Georg Simmel argues: "The more narrowly unified the group, the more can the hostility among its members have quite opposite consequences." Intimacy, he continues, will allow the group to withstand great strain, but, "A group whose very principle is a considerable unity and feeling of belongingness is to this extent particularly threatened by every inner conflict." See Simmel, *Conflict and the Web of Group Affiliations* (Glencoe, Ill., 1955), p. 65.

A DUTY AND A BURDEN

1. John S. Wise, *The End of an Era* (Boston, 1900), p. 36.
2. Byrd, as quoted in Mullin, *Flight and Rebellion*, p. vii; Greene, ed., *Diary of Col. Landon Carter*, I, 27, 140–141.
3. Quoted in Charles Charleton Coffin, *The Boys of '61* (Boston, 1882), p. 447.
4. E. N. Elliott, Introduction to *Cotton Is King and Pro-slavery Arguments*, p. vii.
5. William Gilmore Simms, "The Morals of Slavery," in *ibid.*, pp. 274–275.
6. Edward A. Pollard, *Black Diamonds Gathered in the Darkey Homes of the South* (New York, 1968 [1859]), pp. 41–42, 44–45.
7. Quoted in C. P. Patterson, *Negro in Tennessee*, p. 79.
8. Martineau, *Society in America*, II, 313–315, 343.
9. Olmsted, *Seaboard*, p. 44.
10. W. H. Russell, *My Diary North and South*, p. 75; also Scott, *Southern Lady*, pp. 46–49.
11. Olmsted, *Back Country*, p. 265.
12. Quoted in Scarborough, *Overseer*, p. 103.
13. Rachel Weeks O'Connor to David Weeks, Oct. 14, 1824, in the Weeks Papers.
14. Quoted in W. B. Turner, "Kentucky Slavery in the Last Ante Bellum Decade," *KHSR*, LVIII (Oct., 1960), 297.
15. Mary Burruss McGehee to John W. Burruss, May 29, 1836.
16. Quoted from family correspondence by Ulrich Bonnell Phillips, "Racial Problems, Adjustments and Distrubances," in J. A. C. Chandler *et al.*, *The South in the Building of the Nation* (13 vols.; (Richmond, Va., 1909–1913), IV, 206.
17. Moses Liddell to St. John R. Liddell, April 7, 1841. See also the similar expression of R. F. W. Allston to his son, Charles Petigru Allston, Nov. 8, 1860, in Easterby, ed., *South Carolina Rice Plantation*, p. 169; and J. H. Sheppard to Abraham Sheppard, Jr., July 31, 1822.

18. B. Ballard to Lewis Thompson, Feb. 9, 1845, in the Thompson Papers.
19. "Duties of Christian Masters," pp. 67, 70, in the Wiley Papers.
20. Newstead Plantation Diary, Dec. 25, 1858.
21. Walker Diary, Dec. 10, 1859.
22. Mary C. Jones to C. C. Jones, Dec. 3, 1861, in Myers, ed., *Children of Pride*, p. 809.
23. Chesnut, *Diary from Dixie*, Dec. 8, 1861, Jan. 16, 1862, June 10, 1862 (pp. 172, 184, 244).
24. Here and elsewhere in this book where southern women are discussed, I have benefitted greatly from reading Anne Firor Scott's *Southern Lady*—a seminal book that suffers only from its brevity.
25. Joel B. Fort Recollections; also Craft Diary, July 17, 1863 (p. 134).
26. Magruder Diary, May 21, 1846.
27. Yetman, ed., *Life Under the "Peculiar Institution,"* p. 45.
28. *Ibid.*, p. 218; George Teamoh Journal, Pts. 1–2, pp. 27–28, in the Woodson Papers.
29. Catherine Carson to W. S. Walker, Jan. 26, 1836, in the Small Collections: Carson Family Papers.
30. Martineau, *Society in America*, II, 310.
31. See, e.g., Yetman, ed., *Life Under the "Peculiar Institution,"* pp. 225, 226.
32. Higginson, *Army Life*, pp. 109, 151; Bremer, *Homes of the New World*, II, 243; Rose, *Rehearsal for Reconstruction*, p. 85; J. B. Sellers, *Slavery in Alabama*, p. 112.
33. Rawick, ed., *S.C. Narr.*, II (2), 136; Yetman, ed., *Life Under the "Peculiar Institution,"* p. 225.
34. E. F. Andrews, *War-Time Journal of a Georgia Girl*, June 7, 1865 (p. 292).
35. Hiram B. Tibbetts to John C. Tibbetts, Dec. 28, 1848; see also Walker Diary, June 20, 1856. Walker was a staunch proslavery planter.
36. E. G. Baker Diary, April 24, 1861 (II, 95).
37. "Chancellor Harper on Slavery" in E. N. Elliott, ed., *Cotton Is King and Pro-slavery Arguments*, p. 94.
38. Kate Stone, *Brokenburn*, p. 8.
39. Catterall, ed., *Judicial Cases*, III, 43. See the discussion of these attitudes in *The Narrative of William Wells Brown, a Fugitive Slave* (Reading, Mass., 1969 [1848]), pp. 75–77.
40. Eugene H. Berwanger, *The Frontier Against Slavery: Western Anti-Negro Prejudice and the Slavery Extension Controversy* (Urbana, Ill., 1967), pp. 138–139, n. 4. More generally see Eric Foner, *Free Soil, Free Labor, Free Men: The Ideology of the Republican Party Before the Civil War* (New York, 1971). The argument, although wholly excessive, had some point. As Roi Ottey and William T. Weatherby wrote of the emancipation of the blacks in New York: "Their plight in many instances became worse, for they were thrown into the world of competition with little training or skill to shift for themselves"; *The Negro in New York: An Informal Social History* (New York, 1967), p. 75.
41. Edmund Ruffin, *Address to the Virginia State Agricultural Society on the Effects of Domestic Slavery* (Richmond, Va., 1853), p. 5; A., "The Influence of Slavery on the Progress of Civilization," *ACPSS*, III (June, 1859), 171; Andrew Garnett, in Southern Central Agricultural Society, *Transactions, 1851*, p. 100; Mary H. Schoolcraft, *Plantation Life: The Narratives of Mrs. Henry Rowe Schoolcraft, 1852–1860* (New York, 1969), pp. iii–iv, and p. 20 of the "Letters"; also William C. Daniell, "An Address Delivered at the Opening of a Convention to Organize an Agricultural Association of the Slaveholding States," *ACP*, II (Feb., 1854), 34. I have discussed Fitzhugh and tried to assess the significance of the defense of slavery in the abstract in *World the Slaveholders Made*, Pt. 2.

OF CONCUBINES AND HORSES

1. See Edward L. Keenan, *The Kurbskii-Groznyi Apocrypha: The Seventeenth-Century Genesis of the Correspondence Attributed to Prince A. M. Kurbskii and Tsar Ivan IV* (Cambridge, Mass., 1971), for an account of the evidence and for the probable authorship.

2. Quoted in Wall, "Founding of Pettigrew Plantations," *NCHR*, XXVII (Oct., 1950), 409–410.

3. Quoted in Rose, *Rehearsal for Reconstruction*, p. 108.

4. W. E. Abraham, *The Mind of Africa* (London, 1967), p. 74.

5. In *Toulmin v. Chadwick*; see J. B. Sellers, *Slavery in Alabama*, p. 226.

6. Catterall, ed., *Judicial Cases*, III, 605–606.

7. Arda Walker, "Andrew Jackson: Planter," *East Tennessee Historical Society, Publications*, No. 15 (1943), p. 32.

8. Northup, *Twelve Years a Slave*, p. 150.

9. Schoolcraft, *Plantation Life*, p. 482 n.; p. 18 of the "Letters."

10. E. G. Baker Diary, Feb. 13, 1849, July 8, 1849, Dec. 25, 1852, Dec. 28, 1852 (I, 3, 39–40, 111).

11. *Jim (a Slave) v. State*, 1854, in Catterall, ed., *Judicial Cases*, III, 36; see also Charles Colcock Jones, *The Religious Instruction of the Negroes in the United States* (New York, 1969 [1842]), p. 166.

12. Rawick, ed., *Indiana Narr.*, VI (2), 132; WPA, *Negro in Virginia*, p. 88.

13. On the more general aspects of this dialectic see esp. Georges Balandier, *Political Anthropology* (New York, 1970), pp. 103, 109–110; and Simmel, *Conflict*.

14. I hope to explore this question more fully in a subsequent publication.

15. For some reflections of ex-slaves on the paternalism of the planters toward the lower-class whites, see Rawick, ed., *S.C. Narr.*, II (1), 14, 87, 105, 161; III (3), 2, 119; III (4), 39, 254.

16. Hannah Arendt, "Reflections on Violence," *New York Review of Books*, XII (Feb. 27, 1969), 23. I have closely paraphrased her in this sentence. See Buckingham, *Slave States of America*, II, 25, for a discussion of the difficulties with authority encountered by slaveholders' sons in college.

17. Willie Morris, *North Toward Home* (Boston, 1967), p. 9.

18. Holcombe Diary, dated Aug. 5, 1855, but probably written in 1861. For remarkably similar statements see J.W.D., "Southern Literature," *Southern Eclectic*, II (Sept., 1853), 63–65; B., "The New Social Propositions," *SLM*, XX (May, 1854), 295; [William M. Samford?], *Southern Dial*, I (Nov., 1857), 9; speech of the Rt. Rev. Stephen Elliott, Jr., Southern Central Agricultural Society, *Transactions, 1851.* Also E. Merton Coulter, *Thomas Spaulding of Sapelo* (Baton Rouge, La., 1940), pp. 31–32; Alexis de Tocqueville, *Democracy in America* (trans. Phillips Bradley; 2 vols.; New York, 1945), I, 364, 395; Achille Murat, *America and the Americans* (Buffalo, N.Y., 1851), p. 17; A. du Puy Van Buren, *Jottings of a Year's Sojourn in the South* (Battle Creek, Mich., 1859), p. 143.

19. Featherstonhaugh, *Excursion Through the Slave States*, p. 158.

20. Lyell, *Second Visit*, I, 262.

21. *Ibid.*, I, 261.

22. Quoted in W. T. Jordan, *Hugh Davis*, p. 18.

23. Francis Lieber, *Remarks on the Final Adjournment of the Loyal Publication Society* (n.p., n.d.), p. 1. A copy of this pamphlet may be found in the Lieber Papers. See also the remarks of Col. Stanton Elmore in William Garrott Brown, ed.,

A Gentleman of the South: A Memory of the Black Belt from the Memoirs of the Late Col. Stanton Elmore (New York, 1903), p. 128; Mrs. A. M. King to Thomas Butler King, Dec. 27, 1844; Martineau, *Society in America*, III, 11.

24. Seabrook, *Before and After*, p. 46.
25. Du Bois, *Black Reconstruction*, pp. 52–53. See also Francis Pendleton Gaines, *The Southern Plantation: A Study in the Development and Accuracy of a Tradition* (New York, 1925), p. 159.
26. Kemble, *Journal*, pp. 286, 295, 301, 303, 305.

THE MOMENT OF TRUTH

1. While I was sampling opinion across the South, Willie Lee Rose was studying Virginia and the South Carolina low country intensively. Our conclusions coincided. She presented her evidence and ideas in a splendid paper, which unfortunately she has not published. Having had the privilege of hearing it and having learned from it, I regret its remaining unpublished all the more. Leon Litwack, also working simultaneously, arrived at similar conclusions; see his "Free at Last," in Tamara K. Hareven, ed., *Anonymous Americans: Explorations in Nineteenth Century Social History* (Englewood Cliffs, N.J., 1971), pp. 130–171, and his forthcoming book on the transition from slavery to freedom. C. Vann Woodward, in different terms, has traced some of the more important political consequences of these developments in *The Strange Career of Jim Crow* (New York, 1955), and in "The Political Legacy of Reconstruction" *The Burden of Southern History* (Baton Rouge, La., 1960). For an account of the Russian experience with serfs, which suggests some of this pattern, see P. Kropotkin, *Memoirs of a Revolutionist* (Boston, 1899), p. 49.
2. See the essays of Harper (pp. 79–83) and Hammond (p. 112) in E. N. Elliott, ed., *Cotton Is King and Pro-slavery Arguments*.
3. Bremer, *Homes of the New World*, I, 389; Craft Diary, Feb. 8, 1864 (p. 180).
4. Rose, *Rehearsal for Reconstruction*, p. 109.
5. Charles S. Johnson, *Shadow of the Plantation* (Chicago, 1966), p. 131. Leon Litwack has suggested—in private discussion—that many former slaves who recalled their masters as dying of broken hearts seem to have telescoped time and read the death of an old master, which occurred much later, back into 1865. Rereading the narratives, I must agree. But the ex-slaves' reaction then becomes all the more significant. See also the accounts in Fisk University, *Unwritten History of Slavery*, p. 28; Botkin, ed., *Lay My Burden Down*, p. 204 and Pt. 5, *passim*; Rawick, ed., *S.C. Narr.*, II (1), 248; III (3), 234; *Okla. Narr.*, VII (1), 283.
6. Broun Diary, May 1, 1863; Katharine M. Jones, ed., *Ladies of Richmond* (Indianapolis, 1962), p. 107; John H. Phillips to B. O. Tayloe, Oct. 10, 1862, Oct. 31, 1862, in the Tayloe Papers; Henry L. Swint, ed., *Dear Ones at Home: Letters from the Contraband Camps* (Nashville, Tenn., 1966), pp. 68–69; Lester, *To Be a Slave*, p. 147.
7. Clarence Poe, ed., *True Tales of the South at War: How Soldiers Fought and Families Lived, 1861–1865* (Chapel Hill, N.C., 1961), p. 139; also Ann Wooster to [?], Jan. 10, 1865, in the Wooster Papers.
8. Heyward, *Seed from Madagascar*, pp. 154–155; see also Easterby, ed., *South Carolina Rice Plantation*, pp. 200, 216; *The Journal of Charlotte Forten: A Free Negro in the Slave Era* (ed. R. A. Billington; New York, 1967), p. 183; Elizabeth Hyde Botume, *First Days Amongst the Contrabands* (New York, 1968), p. 59.

9. Chesnut, *Diary from Dixie*, pp. 486, 92–93, 293, 354.

10. Manigault Diary, May, 1862, June 12, 1862, March 22, 1867, and *passim* for 1862–1867.

11. Rawick, ed., *S.C. Narr.*, II (2), 82.

12. Mary A. H. Gay, *Life in Dixie During the War, 1861–1865* (Atlanta, Ga., 1901), p. 286.

13. Thomas Journal, 1865.

14. E. F. Andrews, *War-Time Journal of a Georgia Girl*, pp. 70, 179, 272, 318, 321–322 (entries for Jan.–June, 1865).

15. Cited in Robert Ascher and Charles H. Fairbanks, "Excavation of a Slave Cabin: Georgia, USA," *Historical Archeology* (1971), p. 5.

16. *Hargroves v. Redd*, 1871, in Catterall, ed., *Judicial Cases*, III, 103.

17. These and other relevant letters may be found in Myers, ed., *Children of Pride*, Bk. 2, pp. 885–1342. See esp. C. C. Jones to Charles C. Jones, Jr., April 28, 1862 (p. 886); C. C. Jones to Charles C. Jones, Jr., July 10, 1862 (pp. 929–930); Charles C. Jones, Jr., to C. C. Jones, July 19, 1862 (p. 934); C. C. Jones to Charles C. Jones, Jr., July 21, 1862 (p. 935); John Jones to Mary Jones, Dec. 7, 1863 (pp. 1121–1122); Mary Jones to Mary S. Mallard, Feb. 5, 1864 (pp. 1140–1141); Eva B. Jones to Mary Jones, June 13, 1865 (pp. 1273–1274); Eva B. Jones to Mary Jones, July 14, 1865 (pp. 1280–1281); Mary Jones to Eva B. Jones, Aug. 5, 1865 (pp. 1286–1287); John Jones to Mary Jones, Aug. 21, 1865 (pp. 1291–1293); Mary Jones to Mary S. Mallard, Nov. 7, 1865 (pp. 1303–1305); Mary Jones to Mary S. Mallard, Nov. 17, 1865 (pp. 1307–1309); Mary Jones to Mary S. Mallard, Dec. 9, 1865 (pp. 1311–1313); Mary Jones to Mary Ruth Jones, May 18, 1866 (pp. 1336–1337); Charles C. Jones, Jr., to Mary Jones, May 28, 1866 (pp. 1337–1339); Mary Jones to Charles C. Jones, Jr., May 28, 1866 (pp. 1339–1342). The quotations from Mary Jones's journal may be found on pp. 1241, 1247, and 1248.

18. Kate Stone, *Brokenburn*, April 15, 1863, Oct. 10, 1865, Nov. 17, 1865 (pp. 193, 363, 365–366.). Also George H. Hepworth, *The Whip, Hoe, and Sword*, (Freeport, N.Y., 1972 [1863]), p. 144.

19. Douglas Autobiography, p. 168. Also Breaux Diaries, Oct. 13, 1863, Nov. 23, 1863; J. Thomas May, "The Medical Care of Blacks in Louisiana During Occupation and Reconstruction, 1862–1868: Its Social and Political Background," unpubl. Ph.D. dissertation, Tulane University, 1970, pp. 14–15; J. Carlyle Sitterson, "The McCollams: A Planter Family of the Old and New South," *JSH*, VI (Aug., 1940), 359–360.

20. Frank Wysor Klingberg, "The Case of the Minors: A Unionist Family Within the Confederacy," *JSH*, XIII (Feb., 1947), 39, 44.

21. Elise Young to W. N. Mercer, Dec. 28, 1853, and Wilmer Shields to W. N. Mercer, Dec. 19, 1865, in the Mercer Papers.

22. Agnew Diary, Oct. 29, 1862, Oct. 31, 1862, Nov. 1, 1862 (II, 191–194).

23. Quoted in Wiley, *Southern Negroes*, p. 52, n. 43; for Alabama, see W. T. Jordan, *Hugh Davis*, pp. 155–166.

24. Rawick, ed., *Texas Narr.*, IV (2), 8; V (3), 53, 83–84.

25. Yetman, ed., *Life Under the "Peculiar Institution,"* pp. 280, 321, 118.

26. Quoted in Armstead L. Robinson, "In the Aftermath of Slavery: Blacks and Reconstruction in Memphis, 1865–1870," unpubl. undergraduate thesis, Yale University, 1969, p. 96.

27. Rawick, ed., *Texas Narr.*, IV (4), 23, 54.

28. Charles H. Bohner, *John Pendleton Kennedy: Gentleman from Baltimore* (Baltimore, 1941), p. 169; Smedes, *Southern Planter*, pp. 219–220; Rawick, ed., *S.C. Narr.*, II (2), 90, 113, 222, 261; III (3), 132, 205; *Texas Narr.*, IV (1), 110, 120, 122, 132, 142, 254, 295; the narratives from other states may be consulted at random.

29. J. B. Grimball Diary, March 3, 1862, July 17, 1863; M.M. Grimball Diary, March 22, 1863.
30. For a sensitive treatment of the situation in South Carolina see Carol Rothrock Bleser, *The Promised Land. The South Carolina Land Commission: A Study of a Reconstruction Institution* (Columbia, S. C., 1969).
31. The best general introduction to the postwar disintegration of paternalism remains Woodward's *Strange Career of Jim Crow*, but a full and comprehensive study is long overdue.
32. Quoted in May, "Medical Care of Blacks in Louisiana," p. 56.
33. Wise, *End of an Era*, p. 74.
34. As copied by Manigault, Plantation Book, 1865.

BOOK ONE, PART 2

TO THE MANOR BORN

1. Smedes, *Southern Planter*, pp. 125, 219.
2. On the attitudes of colonials toward their oppressors see the suggestive remarks of Albert Memmi, *Dominated Man* (New York, 1968), p. 5; on the aristocratic attitudes of the slaves see Ralph Ellison, *Shadow and Act* (New York, 1964), p. xv, and the writings of Faulkner, to which he refers.
3. Yetman, ed., *Life Under the "Peculiar Institution,"* p. 72; Sitterson, *Sugar Country*, p. 90.
4. Northup, *Twelve Years a Slave*, p. 322.
5. Higginson, *Army Life*, p. 260.
6. Sydnor, "Southerner and the Laws," *JSH*, VI (Feb., 1940), 14.
7. Pearson, ed., *Letters from Port Royal*, p. 230.
8. Quoted in Robert S. Starobin, "Privileged Bondsmen and the Process of Accommodation: The Role of Houseservants and Drivers as Seen in Their Own Letters," *J.Soc.H.*, V (Fall, 1971), 57.
9. It is in this context, I believe, that Frantz Fanon's dictum takes on meaning: "It is always easier to proclaim rejection than actually to reject." *The Wretched of the Earth* (New York, 1965), p. 177.
10. Rawick, ed., *Miss. Narr.*, VII (2), 149.
11. See the interesting remarks of Bremer, *Homes of the New World*, I, 385–386.
12. Kemble, *Journal*, p. 139; Leigh, *Ten Years*, p. 95; also Botume, *First Days Amongst the Contrabands*, p. 65. Edward Brathwaite writes about Jamaica: "In their everyday lives, also, the slaves observed carefully the courtesies of language"; *Creole Society in Jamaica, 1770–1820* (Oxford, 1971), p. 238.
13. Melville J. Herskovits, *The Myth of the Negro Past* (Boston, 1962), pp. 141–142.
14. Bertram Wilbur Doyle, *The Etiquette of Race Relations in the South: A Study in Social Control* (New York, 1971).
15. Lyell, *Second Visit*, I, 224.
16. Du Bois, "Politeness," in Meyer Weinberg, ed., *W. E. B. Du Bois: A Reader* (New York, 1970), 427. Originally published in *Crisis*, March, 1911.
17. Bremer, *Homes of the New World*, I, 511.
18. C. S. Johnson, *Shadow of the Plantation*, p. 27.
19. Scarborough, ed., *Diary of Edmund Ruffin*, I, 6.

20. "Management of Slaves," *SC*, IV (March, 1846), 44.
21. Yetman, ed., *Life Under the "Peculiar Institution*," p. 274.
22. Chesnut, *Diary from Dixie*, p. 42.
23. Rawick, ed., *S.C. Narr.*, III (3), 61; *Ala. Narr.*, VI (1), 325; VI (1), 435.
24. Howard W. Odum and Guy B. Johnson, *The Negro and His Songs: A Study of Typical Negro Songs in the South* (New York, 1968), pp. 253–254.
25. Ambrosio Donini, *Lineamenti di storia delle religioni* (Rome, 1959), pp. 207–210; also Eric J. Hobsbawm, *Primitive Rebels* (Manchestor, 1959), pp. 118–119.
26. Ruth Benedict, The *Chrysanthemum and the Sword: Patterns of Japanese Culture* (New York, 1967 [1946]), pp. 222, 223.
27. Helen Merrell Lynd, *On Shame and the Search for Identity* (New York, 1958), p. 43.
28. E. A. Davis, ed., *Plantation Life in The Florida Parishes of Louisiana*, p. 175; similarly, Rawick, ed., *Ark. Narr.*, IX (4), 166; X (6), 44.
29. Phillips, *Life and Labor*, p. 244.
30. John Richard Dennett, *The South as It Is, 1865–1866* (ed. Henry M. Christman; New York, 1965), p. 122.
31. Mooney, *Slavery in Tennessee*, p. 157.
32. E. F. Andrews, *War-Time Journal of a Georgia Girl*, p. 183.
33. Martineau, *Society in America*, II, 321.
34. Higginson, *Army Life*, p. 109.
35. Mary Jones to Mary S. Mallard, Nov. 7, 1865, and Jan. 17, 1866, in Myers, ed., *Children of Pride*, pp. 1303, 1319.
36. *Father Henson's Story of His Own Life*, p. 19.

DE GOOD MASSA

1. The volumes edited by Rawick, *The American Slave: A Composite Autobiography*, may be consulted at random. For a sample see Fisk University, *Unwritten History of Slavery*, pp. 7–8, 15, 17, 27, 33–34, 42, 61, 63, 77, 101–102, 103–106, 109, 111, 115, 121, 129, 148.
2. Fisk University, *Unwritten History of Slavery*, p. 42; also Rawick, ed., *S.C. Narr.*, II (2), 70.
3. Yetman, ed., *Life Under the "Peculiar Institution*," pp. 173–174.
4. WPA, *Negro in Virginia*, p. 156; for a case of a slave who lived under masters of the most diverse types, see Northup, *Twelve Years a Slave*. Also James W. C. Pennington, *The Fugitive Blacksmith*, in Arna Bontemps, ed., *Great Slave Narratives* (Boston, 1969), p. 197; *Life and Times of Frederick Douglass*, pp. 45, 96, 106; Steward, *Twenty-two Years a Slave*, pp. 16, 19.
5. Fisk University, *Unwritten History of Slavery*, p. 81.
6. WPA, *Drums and Shadows*, p. 100; also Fisk University, *Unwritten History of Slavery*, p. 149.
7. Saxon *et al.*, *Gumbo Ya-Ya*, pp. 16–17.
8. Yetman, ed., *Life Under the "Peculiar Institution*," pp. 140, 142.
9. *Ibid.*, p. 162.
10. Fisk University, *Unwritten History of Slavery*, p. 65.
11. Yetman, ed., *Life Under the "Peculiar Institution*," pp. 237, 238.
12. See "Some Undistinguished Negroes," *JNH*, III (April, 1918), 196–197; C. P. Patterson, *Negro in Tennessee*, p. 133.
13. See, e.g., Penelope Campbell, *Maryland in Africa: The Maryland State Colonization Society, 1831–1857* (Urbana, Ill., 1971), esp. pp. 144–145; Hollis R. Lynch,

"Pan-Negro Nationalism in the New World," in August Meier and Elliott M. Rudwick, eds., *The Making of Black America: Essays in Negro Life and History* (2 vols.; New York, 1969), p. 51. For the similar and yet in some essential respects different experience of Brazilian slaves who returned to West Africa, see Richard Ralston, "The Return of Brazilian Freedmen to West Africa in the Eighteenth and Nineteenth Centuries," *Canadian Journal of African Studies*, III, (Fall, 1969), 577–593.

14. See, e.g., the correspondence in the Slave Papers of the Library of Congress; also York Walker to Isaac Wade, July 30, 1858, and Granville Woodson to Mrs. C. E. Wade, Feb. 16, 1853, in the Wade Family Papers; Susan Capart to John Kimberly, March 1, 1859, in the Kimberly Papers; Randall Kilby to John R. Kilby, June 26, 1856; Richard Blount [Richard McMarine, Esq.] to Julius Johnston, June ?, 1858, in the Pettigrew Papers; Moses Legans to McDowell Reid, Oct. 20, 1843, in the Reid Papers; Sydnor, *Slavery in Mississippi*, pp. 235, 238.

15. Phillips, ed., *Plantation and Frontier,* II, 161–164; Berwanger, *Frontier Against Slavery*, pp. 74–75; Featherstonhaugh, *Excursion Through the Slave States*, p. 38.

16. Rawick, ed., *Ala. Narr.*, VI (1), 387.

17. Rawick, ed., *S.C. Narr.*, II (1), 12; similarly, *Ark. Narr.*, X (6), 36.

18. Rawick, ed., *Texas Narr.*, IV (1), 262.

19. Henry Palfrey to William Palfrey, March 12, 1844.

20. Bremer, *Homes of the New World*, I, 509–510.

21. Botume, *First Days Amongst the Contrabands*, p. 86.

22. Rawick, ed., *Texas Narr.*, V (3), 153.

23. Stirling, *Letters from the Slave States*, p. 201.

24. James M. McPherson, *The Negro's Civil War: How Negroes Felt and Acted During the War for the Union* (New York, 1965), pp. 242–243. See also Bill G. Reid, "Confederate Opponents of Arming the Slaves, 1861–1865," *JMH*, XXII (Oct., 1960), 249–270. See also the recent study, with documents, Robert F. Durden, *The Gray and the Black: The Confederate Debate on Emancipation* (Baton Rouge, La., 1972).

25. As quoted in Charles H. Wesley, "The Employment of Negroes as Soldiers in the Confederate Army," *JNH*, IV (July, 1919), 247. Also Alvy L. King, *Louis T. Wigfall: Southern Fire-Eater* (Baton Rouge, La., 1970), pp. 206–208.

26. Quoted in Albert D. Kirwan, ed., *The Confederacy* (New York, 1961), p. 215.

27. Poe, ed., *True Tales*, pp. 133, 134; also Laura A. White, *Robert Barnwell Rhett: Father of Secession* (New York, 1931), pp. 238–239.

28. Chesnut, *Diary from Dixie*, pp. 203, 292, 456.

29. Rawick, ed., *S.C. Narr.*, III (4), 39.

30. Smedes, *Southern Planter*, p. 156; or see Emma LeConte, *When the World Ended: The Diary of Emma LeConte* (ed. E. S. Meiers; New York, 1957), pp. 46–47.

31. Spencer, *Booker T. Washington*, pp. 16–18.

32. Yetman, ed., *Life Under the "Peculiar Institution,"* p. 243.

33. Elizabeth Keckley, *Behind the Scenes. Or, Thirty Years a Slave and Four Years in The White House* (New York, 1868), p. 74 (the physical abuse to which she refers had come under previous masters, not the Davises); Botume, *First Days Amongst the Contrabands*, p. 192.

34. Chesnut, *Diary from Dixie*, Feb. 13, 1862 (p. 189).

35. Botkin, ed., *Lay My Burden Down*, pp. 115, 205.

36. WPA, *Negro in Virginia*, p. 46.

37. Rawick, ed., *Okla. Narr.*, VII (1), 284.

38. Rawick, ed., *Miss. Narr.*, VII (2), 117.

39. E. F. Andrews, *War-Time Journal of a Georgia Girl*, pp. 286, 322.

40. Rawick, ed., *Ala. Narr.*, VI (1), 80.
41. Yetman, ed., *Life Under the "Peculiar Institution,"* p. 75; Rawick, ed., *Texas Narr.*, IV (2), 244.
42. Rose, *Rehearsal for Reconstruction*, p. 348; also M. T. Judge, "On The Devotion of Slaves to Masters," March 30, 1913, in Correspondence: Slavery, Tennessee State Library and Archives; Dennett, *South as It Is*, pp. 199–200; Botume, *First Days Amongst The Contrabands*, p. 142; George Brown Tindall, *South Carolina Negroes, 1877–1900* (Baton Rouge, La., 1964), pp. 55–56; Ottey and Weatherby, *Negro in New York*, p. 21.
43. K. M. Jones, ed., *Ladies of Richmond*, p. 289.
44. Chesnut, *Diary from Dixie*, p. 532.
45. Du Bois, *Black Reconstruction*, p. 59.

OUR WHITE FOLKS

1. Keckley, *Behind the Scenes*, pp. 41, 241–242.
2. Rawick, ed., *Texas Narr.*, IV (2), 162; V (3), 33, 140.
3. Yetman, ed., *Life Under the "Peculiar Institution,"* p. 276.
4. Philip Durham and Everett L. Jones, *The Negro Cowboys* (New York, 1965), pp. 3, 24.
5. Fisk University, *Unwritten History of Slavery*, p. 2. For some other examples of masters protecting their slaves from patrollers, see Mrs. Lucy to Uncle John, Sept. 4, 1849, in the Nash Papers; Ulrich Bonnell Phillips, "Historical Notes of Milledgeville," *Gulf States Historical Magazine*, II (July, 1903), 165–166. Ross thought the slaves' attitude reminiscent of that of Scottish clansmen; see *Cities and Camps*, p. 84. Also William I. Thomas and Florian Znaniecki, *The Polish Peasant in Europe and America* (2 vols.; New York, 1958), I, 172.
6. Phyllis Jennings to Mary Pettigrew, June 10, 1803, in the Pettigrew Papers.
7. Northup, *Twelve Years a Slave*, p. 20.
8. Holcombe Autobiography, I, 19; Frank F. Steel to Anna Steel, Dec. 15, 1859. Also Sarah Hicks Williams to Mr. and Mrs. Samuel Hicks, Oct. 10, 1853, in the Williams Papers.
9. Gay, *Life in Dixie*, p. 63.
10. See, e.g., Harriet Martineau, *Retrospect of Western Travel* (2 vols.; New York, 1838), I, 161; Farish, ed., *Journal and Letters of Philip Vickers Fithian*, pp. 184, 199; Rawick, *S.C. Narr.*, II (2), 324; J.B. Sellers, *Slavery in Alabama*, p. 128; Rose, *Rehearsal for Reconstruction*, pp. 85, 114. For the symbolic meaning of the egg among the Ashanti, see Laurens van der Post, *African Cooking* (New York, 1970), p. 62.
11. See Sir Charles Lyell, *Travels in North America* (2 vols.; London, 1845), I, 169; J. B. Sellers, *Slavery in Alabama*, p. 80; Rose, *Rehearsal for Reconstruction*, p. 160.
12. See, e.g., Chesnut, *Diary from Dixie*, pp. 538–540; Leigh, *Ten Years*, pp. 14, 21, 77, 177, 236.
13. Mary Cable, "We and They in Rhodesia," *New Yorker*, Feb. 19, 1966, p. 37.
14. Harvey Wish, "Slave Disloyalty Under the Confederacy," *JNH*, XXIII (Oct., 1938), 435–450, esp. p. 449.
15. Vernon Lane Wharton, *The Negro in Mississippi, 1865–1900* (Chapel Hill, N.C., 1947), p. 17; John Knox Bettersworth, *Confederate Mississippi: The People and Politics of a Cotton State in Wartime* (Jackson, Miss., 1961), pp. 163–164; Aptheker, *Slave Revolts*, pp. 94–95; Mooney, *Slavery in Tennessee*, p. 178; Rawick, ed., *S.C. Narr.*, III (4), 213–215; Magnolia Plantation Journal, Oct. 21, 1862, in

the Warmoth Papers; Pugh Plantation Diary, Nov. 4–6, 1862; Albert Virgil House, ed., "Deterioration of a Georgia Rice Plantation During Four Years of Civil War," *JSH*, IX (Feb., 1943), 113; Scarborough, *Overseer*, pp. 149, 153, 155; Wiley, *Southern Negroes*, p. 76.

16. Rose, *Rehearsal for Reconstruction*, pp. 16, 106–107, 145; also Litwack, "Free at Last," in Hareven, ed., *Anonymous Americans*, esp. pp. 154–156; Mary E. Massey, *Refugee Life in the Confederacy* (Baton Rouge, La., 1964), p. 237.

17. For squeals of outrage from masters and mistresses who usually failed to notice that their lives were being spared, see M.M. Grimball Diary, Aug. 4, 1863; Minor Plantation Diary, Jan. 3, 1863; Cornish Diary, Feb. 22, 1865, June 18–21, 1865; LeConte, *When the World Ended*, p. 40; K. M. Jones, ed., *When Sherman Came*, pp. 220, 268; Agnew Diary, March 4, 1864 (IV, 191–192); Bayside Plantation Records, May 1, 3, 4, 11, 1863; H. E. Lawrence to Frances E. Lawrence, Dec. 10, 1862 (?), in the Brashear Family Papers.

18. Kate Stone, *Brokenburn*, April 25, 1863 (pp. 197–198).

19. *Journal of Charlotte Forten*, pp. 57, 74, 178.

20. Kelly Miller, *Out of the House of Bondage* (New York, 1969 [1914]), p. 23.

21. Northup, *Twelve Years a Slave*, pp. 62–63.

22. Yetman, ed., *Life Under the "Peculiar Institution,"* p. 38.

23. Kate Stone, *Brokenburn*, Sept. 5, 1864 (p. 298); Easterby, ed., *South Carolina Rice Plantation*, p. 211; T. R. Gray, "Confessions of Nat Turner," reprinted in Herbert Aptheker, *Nat Turner's Slave Revolt* (New York, 1966).

24. Yet in some areas the potential for great violence in a "race war" caused widespread fright. See, e.g., S. Andrews, *South Since the War*, p. 207.

25. Rawick, ed., *Texas Narr.*, IV (2), 134.

26. Rawick, ed., *S.C. Narr.*, III (4), 54.

27. *Ibid.*, III (4), 119.

28. Kemble, *Journal*, p. 34; Swint, ed., *Dear Ones at Home*, pp. 36–37. Also De Leon, *Four Years in Rebel Capitals*, p. 315.

29. Pearson, ed., *Letters from Port Royal*, p. 14.

30. Botkin, ed., *Lay My Burden Down*, pp. 14, 15, 94, 110, 142, 148, 234.

31. Yetman, ed., *Life Under the "Peculiar Institution,"* p. 30.

32. Lyell, *Second Visit*, I, 255.

33. Rawick, ed., *S.C. Narr.*, II (1), 67; III (2), 141; II (1), 167, 250, 299.

34. *Ibid.*, II (1), 5–6.

35. Rawick, ed., *Okla. Narr.*, VII (1), 296.

36. *Ibid.*, VII (1), 209.

37. Rawick, ed., *S.C. Narr.*, II (1), 106.

38. Lyell, *Second Visit*, I, 208.

39. Greene, ed., *Diary of Col. Landon Carter*, June 28, 1770 (I, 429).

40. Martineau, *Society in America*, I, 309–310; II, 317. Also Bremer, *Homes of the New World*, II, 332; Chesnut, *Diary from Dixie*, p. 152. See also the remarks of Hugh Washington of Virginia, quoted in Mullin, *Flight and Rebellion*, p. 31, or of William Dunbar of Alabama, quoted in J. B. Sellars, *Slavery in Alabama*, pp. 13–14.

41. Ross, *Cities and Camps*, p. 137.

42. Bonner, ed., "Plantation Experiences of a New York Woman," *NCHR*, XXXIII (July, 1956), 402; (Oct., 1956), 546.

43. Rose, *Rehearsal for Reconstruction*, p. 366.

44. S. Andrews, *South Since the War*, pp. 26, 181–182, 234.

45. Dennett, *South as It Is*, p. 78.

46. Matthew Gregory Lewis, *Journal of a West India Proprietor, Kept During a Residence on the Island of Jamaica* (New York, 1969 [1834]), pp. 231, 408, 140.

47. Mary Jones to C. C. Jones, Jr., July 7, 1858, in Myers, ed., *Children of Pride*, p. 427.
48. I have profited here from Simmel's essay, "Faithfulness and Gratitude," without, however, accepting some of its main interpretations. See K. H. Wolff, ed., *The Sociology of Georg Simmel* (New York, 1950), p. 388, and generally, pp. 387–390.
49. Octave Mannoni, *Prospero and Caliban: A Study of the Psychology of Colonization* (trans. P. Powesland; London, 1956), p. 44.
50. Antonio Gramsci, *The Modern Prince and Other Writings* (New York, 1967), pp. 66–67.
51. Quoted in John M. Cammett, *Antonio Gramsci and the Origins of Italian Communism* (Stanford, Calif., 1967), p. 9.
52. Higginson, *Army Life*, pp. 16, 34, 42–43, 52.

SOME VALIANT SOLDIER HERE

1. S. Andrews, *South Since the War*, pp. 179–180, 324.
2. B. H. Nelson, "Some Aspects of Negro Life in North Carolina During the Civil War," *NCHR*, XXV (April, 1948), 166; see also Paul W. Gates, *Agriculture and the Civil War* (New York, 1965), pp. 23, 60–62, 78, 119.
3. James H. Brewer, *The Confederate Negro: Virginia's Craftsmen and Military Laborers, 1861–1865* (Durham, N.C., 1969); Dew, *Ironmaker to the Confederacy*.
4. For an excellent summary of the problems facing slaves who wanted to desert, see Litwack, "Free at Last," in Hareven, ed., *Anonymous Americans*, pp. 135–136; for Mississippi, see D. Clayton James, "Mississippi Agriculture, 1861–1865," *JMH*, XXIV (April, 1962), 129–141.
5. When the Yankees had cut roads and white southerners were locked in, their slaves sometimes loyally went through the lines and returned with needed supplies. See, e.g., Broun Diary, Jan. 25, 1863; Edmondson Diary, Jan. 2, 3, 4, 1864.
6. For examples see WPA, *Negro in Virginia*, p. 123; Yetman, ed., *Life Under the "Peculiar Institution,"* p. 74.
7. S. Andrews, *South Since the War*, p. 128.
8. Quoted in J. M. McPherson, *Negro's Civil War*, p. 39.
9. Among the various brief surveys see esp. Benjamin Quarles, *The Negro in the Making of America* (New York, 1968), p. 117, and more fully, his *Negro in The Civil War* (Boston, 1953).
10. On this much-told story see esp. Benjamin Quarles, "The Abduction of 'The Planter,' " *CWH*, IV (March, 1958), 5–10.
11. J. M. McPherson, *Negro's Civil War*, p. 147; also Massey, *Refugee Life*, pp. 237–238.
12. Woodward, "Equality: The Deferred Commitment," Ch. 4 of *Burden of Southern History*; the words quoted are on p. 82.
13. Botkin, *Lay My Burden Down*, p. 206.
14. Rawick, ed., *S.C. Narr.*, III (3), 26; *Ark. Narr.*, X (5), 193, 202; see also, Agnew Diary, Aug. 15, 1862, May 7, 1863, Dec. 7, 1863 (II, 121, 379; IV, 92–93); James W. Melvin to A. C. Britton, Feb. 17, 1863, in the Britton Papers; Mary S. Mallard Journal, Dec. 21, 1864, and Mary Jones Journal, Dec. 22, 1864, Jan. 10, 1865, Jan. 11, 1865, in Myers, ed., *Children of Pride*; K. M. Jones, ed., *When Sherman Came*, pp. 173 ff.; Pearson, ed., *Letters from Port Royal*, p. 155; Swint, ed., *Dear Ones at Home*, p. 160; and generally, Wiley, *Southern Negroes*, p. 14; Rose, *Rehearsal for Reconstruction, passim*.
15. Bond Diary, May 12, 1862, Nov. 15, 1862.

16. See, e.g., Pt. 4 of Botkin, ed., *Lay My Burden Down*. For the harsh conduct of Sherman's troops toward the blacks, see Joel Williamson, *After Slavery: The Negro in South Carolina Reconstruction* (Chapel Hill, N.C., 1965), p. 23.
17. Rawick, ed., *S.C. Narr.*, II (1), 97.
18. Peter Burchard, *One Gallant Rush: Robert Gould Shaw and His Brave Black Regiment* (New York, 1965), pp. 110–111.
19. The land question is discussed in Du Bois, *Black Reconstruction;* Robert S. Allen, *Reconstruction: The Battle for Democracy* (New York, 1946); Bleser, *Promised Land;* and Christie Farnham Pope, "Southern Homesteads for Negroes," *AH*, XLIV (April, 1970), 201–212.
20. Wiley, *Southern Negroes*, pp. 83–84.
21. Lester, *To Be a Slave*, p. 130.
22. See, e.g., Roland C. McConnell, *Negro Troops of Antebellum Louisiana: A History of the Battalion of Free Men of Color* (Baton Rouge, La., 1968); Benjamin Quarles, *The Negro in the American Revolution* (Chapel Hill, N.C., 1961); Willard B. Gatewood, Jr., ed., *"Smoked Yankees" and the Struggle for Empire* (Urbana, Ill., 1971), which contains a revealing collection of letters from black participants in the Spanish-American War.
23. See, in general, Quarles, *Negro in the Civil War;* Dudley Taylor Cornish, *The Sable Arm: Negro Troops in the Union Army, 1861–1865* (New York, 1956); and among the older works by participants see esp. George Washington Williams, *A History of Negro Troops in the War of the Rebellion* (New York, 1888).
24. For the important story of black recruitment in the border states see two articles by John Blassingame: "The Recruitment of Negro Troops in Missouri During the Civil War," *Mo.H.R.*, LVIII (April, 1964), 326–338; and "The Recruitment of Colored Troops in Kentucky, Maryland, and Missouri, 1863–1865," *Historian*, XXIX (Aug., 1967), 533–545.
25. Mrs. Laura E. Buttolph to Mrs. Mary Jones, June 30, 1865, in Myers, ed., *Children of Pride*, p. 1279.
26. Quoted in Burchard, *One Gallant Rush*, p. 115, n. 1.
27. These songs appear in a number of places in the slave narratives. See, e.g., Rawick, ed., *Ga. Narr.*, XIII (4), 215, 349.
28. Dennett, *South as It Is*, p. 291.
29. Quoted in Du Bois, *Black Reconstruction*, p. 99.

BOOK TWO, PART 1

THE CHRISTIAN TRADITION

1. Quoted by R. H. Tawney, *Religion and the Rise of Capitalism* (Gloucester, Mass., 1962), title page.
2. For a trenchant discussion often quoted out of context by hostile critics, see Karl Marx and Frederick Engels, *On Religion* (Moscow, 1957), pp. 41–42.
3. See Balandier, *Political Anthropology*, pp. 100–101.
4. I have taken the liberty of following, even of paraphrasing, George Santayana's masterful *Reason in Religion*, Vol. III of *The Life of Reason* (New York, 1962), esp. pp. 12–15; see also E. E. Evans-Pritchard, *Theories of Primitive Religion* (Oxford, 1965).
5. Friedrich Nietzsche, "Beyond Good and Evil," *The Philosophy of Nietzsche* (New York, 1927), p. 432. For a good although not fully convincing critique,

see Max Scheler, *Ressentiment* (trans. W. W. Holdheim and ed. Lewis Coser; New York, 1961), esp. Ch. 3.

6. Yet even Nietzsche found something to admire in Christianity—its ability to tame the masses. More interestingly, he regarded Christianity as a kind of plebeian revenge, born of envy, against the aristocracy. In his view it promoted dissembling and deception. The Christianity of the slaves in a way bears him out, but in a way very much removed from anything he could imagine.

7. Ernst Troeltsch, *The Social Teaching of the Christian Churches* (trans. Olive Wyon; 2 vols.; London, 1950), I, 295–296.

8. Karl Kautsky, *Foundations of Christianity* (trans. H. F. Mins; New York, 1953), pp. 355–356. Thus, Kautsky finds Christianity's primary role in the subjugation of the free urban masses of the empire rather than in any strengthening of lordship over the slaves themselves.

9. The most interesting attempt at such an interpretation by a Marxist is that of Archibald Robertson, *The Origins of Christianity* (2nd ed.; New York, 1962). But see also Clifford Geertz, "Religion as a Cultural System," in Michael Banton, ed., *Anthropological Approaches to the Study of Religion* (New York, 1966), pp. 1–46.

10. Donini, *Lineamenti di storia delle religioni*, pp. 196–199; Julien Freund, *The Sociology of Max Weber* (trans. Mary Ilford; New York, 1968), p. 202.

11. Troeltsch, *Social Teaching of the Christian Churches*, I, 39.

12. Robertson, *Origins of Christianity*, p. 182; also pp. 80 ff., 119, 183. Within the black liberation movement the boldest voice urging the revolutionary interpretation of the historical Jesus has been that of Rev. Albert Cleage, for whom Jesus was the leader of a black (that is, nonwhite) Israel in a national-liberation struggle against an allegedly white nation of Rome. The Rev. Mr. Cleage's emphases are suggestive: he hates Paul; lauds the Book of Mark; attacks the Book of John; and takes as major texts Matthew 10:34–36 ("I came not to send peace, but a sword") and Luke 11:23 ("He that is not with me is against me"). His national-racial interpretation aside—although it is absolutely essential from his own point of view—his reading of Christian history recapitulates that of a long line of Christian revolutionaries, including Thomas Münzer and one or two other lily-whites. See *The Black Messiah* (New York, 1969).

13. See., e.g., Rawick, ed., *S.C. Narr.*, III (4), 192; *Okla. Narr.*, VII (1), 78; WPA, *Drums and Shadows*, p. 180. For a remarkable Russian parallel see the speech of a landowner to his serfs as quoted in Hobsbawm, *Age of Revolution*, p. 149.

14. Troeltsch, *Social Teaching of the Christian Churches*, I, 82; and the cogent analysis of Antonio Gramsci, *Il Materialismo storico e la filosofia di Benedetto Croce* (6th ed.; Turin, 1955), pp. 91–98.

15. See the discussion of Georg Simmel, *Sociology of Religion* (trans. C. Rosenthal; New York, 1959), p. 44.

16. Troeltsch, *Social Teaching of the Christian Churches*, I, 57.

17. Donini, *Lineamenti di storia delle religioni*, p. 207.

18. For a discussion of these cults in depth see Peter Worsley, *The Trumpet Shall Sound: A Study of the "Cargo Cults" in Melanesia* (London, 1957); for their place in the history of such movements in general, see Vittorio Lanternari, *Religions of the Oppressed* (New York, 1963). On "de Big Massa," see esp. Botume, *First Days Amongst The Contrabands*, pp. 104, 141, 154, 242.

19. On the general history of slavery as a problem for the Christian churches, see D. B. Davis, *Problem of Slavery*. But see also the qualifications introduced

into these generalizations by Mircea Eliade, "Paradise and Utopia: Mythical Geography and Eschatology," in Frank E. Manuel, ed., *Utopias and Utopian Thought* (Boston, 1966), pp. 260–280.

20. Troeltsch, *Social Teaching of the Christian Churches*, I, 43.

SLAVE RELIGION IN HEMISPHERIC PERSPECTIVE

1. The following discussion of the British Caribbean owes much to the pioneer history of Bryan Edwards, *The History, Civil and Commercial, of the British West Indies* (5th ed.; 5 vols.; London, 1819); and Edward Long, *The History of Jamaica* (3 vols.; London, 1774). Among recent studies the most generally useful for Jamaica have been H. O. Patterson, *Sociology of Slavery*, pp. 40, 86–87, 182, 207–209; Philip D. Curtin, *Two Jamaicas: The Role of Ideas in a Tropical Colony* (Cambridge, Mass., 1955); pp. 49, 70; F. W. Pitman, "Slavery on the British West India Plantations in the Eighteenth Century," *JNH*, XI (Oct., 1926), pp. 659–661. For the Leewards see Goveia, *Slave Society in the British Leeward Islands*, pp. 196, 265–268, 284. For Barbados see Bennett, *Bondsmen and Bishops*, *passim*. Also of value is C. E. Pierre, "The Work of the Society for the Propagation of the Gospel in Foreign Parts Among the Negroes of the Colonies", *JNH*, I (Oct., 1916), 349–357.

For the Baptists and Methodists in the British Caribbean, I have relied most heavily on Goveia, *Slave Society*, esp. pp. 270–294; H. O. Patterson, *Sociology of Slavery*, esp. pp. 209–215; and Curtin, *Two Jamaicas, passim*. See also John W. Davis, "George Liele and Andrew Bryan, Pioneer Negro Baptist Preachers," *JNH*, III (April, 1918), esp. pp. 121–123; and "Letters Showing the Rise and Progress of the Early Negro Churches of Georgia and the West Indies (Documents)," *JNH*, III (April, 1918), 119–127; A. P. Newton, *A Hundred Years of the British Empire* (New York, 1940), pp. 47–48; and Bernard Semmel, *Jamaican Blood and Victorian Conscience: The Governor Eyre Controversy* (Boston, 1963), p. 34.

On the Afro-Caribbean religious movements see esp. H. O. Patterson, *Sociology of Slavery*, pp. 182–205; Curtin, *Two Jamaicas*, esp. pp. 28–32, 170; Goveia, *Slave Society*, pp. 245–248. I have also profited from an unpubl. undergraduate honors thesis: Howard Stroger, "Coromantine Obeah and Myalism," Rutgers University, 1966. Also Pitman, "Slavery in the British West India Plantations," pp. 651–652; Bennett, *Bondsmen and Bishops*, pp. 80–81; Eric Williams, *Negro in the Caribbean* (Manchester, 1942), p. 43; M. G. Lewis, *Journal of a West India Proprietor, passim*; and *DBR*, XXVIII (Feb., 1860), p. 209.

2. For the Dutch Caribbean see esp. Boxer, *Dutch Seaborne Empire*, pp. 149–153; also Edgar J. McManus, *A History of Negro Slavery in New York* (Syracuse, N. Y., 1966), pp. 19–20. In the Danish Caribbean the Moravian missionaries, who arrived in 1733, had considerable success in reducing African religious beliefs and practices to socially manageable proportions; see Westergaard, *Danish West Indies* p. 159.

3. For the French islands I have relied most heavily on C. L. R. James, *Black Jacobins*; James G. Leyburn, *The Haitian People*, including S. W. Mintz's splendid introduction (New Haven, Conn., 1966); and Alfred Métraux, *Voodoo in Haiti* (trans. H. Charteris; New York, 1972), also with an introduction by Mintz. Also Maya Deren, *Divine Horsemen: The Living Gods of Haiti* (London, 1953); Melville J. Herskovits, *Life in a Haitian Valley* (New York, 1937); Harold Courlander, "The Gods of the Haitian Mountains," *JNH*,

XXIX (July, 1944), pp. 339–372; and of special importance for the role of Vodûn during the revolution, Odette Mennesson-Rigaud, "Le role de Vaudou dans d'indépendence d'Haiti," *Présence Africaine*, Nos. 17–18 (Feb.–May, 1958), pp. 43–67. For the remarks of Raynal and de Wimpffen see T. L. Stoddard, *French Revolution in Santo-Domingo*, pp. 22, 24.

4. The Church's role in the slave trade and in both Africa and Brazil is discussed with a critical eye by C. R. Boxer in a number of impressive books: *Salvador de Sá*, pp. 79, 127–128; *Portuguese Society in the Tropics: The Municipal Councils of Goa, Macao, Bahia, and Luanda, 1510–1800* (Madison, Wis., 1965), pp. 131–132; and *Race Relations in the Portuguese Colonial Empire* (Oxford, 1963), pp. 7–21. The roles of the papacy and the British government are noted in Alan K. Manchester, *British Pre-eminence in Brazil: Its Rise and Decline. A Study in European Expansion* (Chapel Hill, N.C., 1933), p. 217; and René Maunier, *The Sociology of Colonies: An Introduction to the Study of Race Contact* (trans. E. O. Lorimer; 2 vols.; London, 1949), I, 293–294.

Gilberto Freyre's books present a radically different picture from that presented by Boxer and should be consulted: *Masters and Slaves*, pp. 173, 191–192; *Mansions and Shanties*, Ch. 24, pp. 314–315, 321–322, and 327 (for the quotation on the street rioters); *New World in the Tropics: The Culture of Modern Brazil* (New York, 1963), pp. 70, 88.

For useful summary accounts of the Jesuits see Manoel de Oliveira Lima, *The Evolution of Brazil Compared with That of Spanish and Anglo-Saxon America* (ed. P.A. Martin; Stanford, Calif., 1914), p. 28; C. Vianna Moog, *Bandeirantes and Pioneers* (trans. L. L. Barrett; New York, 1959), p. 156; João Dornas Filho, *A Escravidão no Brasil* (Rio de Janeiro, 1939), esp. pp. 21, 105; Orestes Popescu, *El Sistema económico en las misiones Jesuíticas* (Bahía Blanca, Argentina, 1952). On the planters and abolitionists and the religious question see Robert Brent Toplin, *The Abolition of Slavery in Brazil, 1880–1888* (New York, 1972), Ch. 3; Roy Nash, *The Conquest of Brazil* (New York, 1926), pp. 127–128; Stein, *Vassouras*, pp. 199–203.

Of special importance is Roger Bastide's impressive study, *Les Religions africaines au Brasil* (Paris, 1960). Bastide is especially critical (see p. 150)—properly, in my opinion—of the early Marxist analysis of the role of religion in slave insurrection, presented by Aderbal Jurema in *Insurrecões negras no Brasil* (Recife, 1935). Bastide has also made useful analyses of the relationship between specific Afro-Brazilian cults and such factors as historical moment and stratification within the black community; see "The Negro in Latin America," *International Social Science Bulletin*, IV, No. 3 (1952), 483; and Bastide's chapter on "Efeitos do preconceito de côr," in Bastide and Florestan Fernandes, *Brancos e negros em São Paulo* (2nd ed.; São Paulo, 1959). For a perceptive discussion of certain problems of method, see Thales de Azevedo, *Cultura e situação racial no Brasil* (Rio de Janeiro, 1966), Ch. 9.

Afro-Brazilian religions are perceptively discussed in Charles Wagley, *An Introduction to Brazil* (New York, 1963), esp. pp. 38–39; Donald Warren, Jr., "The Negro and Religion in Brazil," *Race*, VI (Jan., 1965), 199–216; Arthur Ramos, *The Negro in Brazil* (Washington, D. C., 1951), pp. 81–93; and Russell G. Hamilton, "The Present State of African Cults in Bahia," *J.Soc.H.*, III (Summer, 1970), 357–373.

For the slight participation of the blacks in the prophetic movements that have seared Brazil from time to time, see Lanternari, *Religions of the Oppressed*, Ch. 4. For an unforgettable account of one of those movements see Euclides da Cunha's masterpiece, *Rebellion in the Backlands* (trans. Samuel Putnam; Chicago, 1944).

I have discussed the relationship of secular to clerical power in Brazil and the evolution of the class structure itself in *World the Slaveholders Made*, and have presented a view of the theoretical relationship of ideology and material structure in "Materialism and Idealism in the History of Negro Slavery in the Americas," Ch. 2 of *In Red and Black*. Of special value for a consideration of these questions is Prado, *Colonial Background of Modern Brazil*, pp. 386, 395–397, 411.

5. The discussion of Cuba relies heavily on Knight, *Slave Society in Cuba*; Klein, *Slavery in the Americas*, is especially useful for the eighteenth century. See also, Fernando Ortiz, *Los Negros esclavos* (Havana, 1916); Manuel Moreno Fraginals, *El Ingenio* (Havana, 1964); and Esteban Montejo, *The Autobiography of a Runaway Slave* (New York, 1968), pp. 34–36. Rolando Mellafe's *La Esclavitud en Hispano-América*, p. 86, contains a useful statement of the general conditions in the Spanish colonies. See also the essay by Colin Palmer, "Religion and Magic in Seventeenth Century Mexican Slave Society," in Engerman and Genovese, eds., *Race and Slavery*.

BLACK CONVERSION AND WHITE SENSIBILITY

1. Scarborough, ed., *Diary of Edmund Ruffin*, Dec. 10, 1857 (I, 136–137).
2. I have quoted from Eric R. Wolf, *Sons of the Shaking Earth* (Chicago, 1964), who discusses the conversion of the Mexican Indians to the Catholicism of their Spanish conquerors. (see p. 175). In later years white southerners switched from accusing the slaves of insincerity for reasons of protection to insincerity for reasons of frivolous social intercourse—a standard by which white church attendance might also be questioned. See Ingraham, *South-West*, II, 55–56; J. B. Sellers, *Slavery in Alabama*, p. 122.
3. Marcus W. Jernegan, "Slavery and Conversion in the American Colonies," *AHR*, XXI (April, 1916), 504–527. See also John Mitchell Justice, "The Work of the Society for the Propagation of the Gospel in Foreign Parts in North Carolina," unpubl. M.A. thesis, University of North Carolina, 1939.
4. These circumstances, as they obtained in Virginia, have been discussed in numerous works on the colonial period of American history. But for an interesting special case, discussed in hemispheric perspective, see William Renwick Riddell, "The Baptism of Slaves on Prince Edward Island," *JNH*, VI (July, 1921), 307–309. Some attention to the religious instruction of slaves was manifested in Virginia at least as early as the 1720s; see Tate, *Negro in Eighteenth-Century Williamsburg*, pp. 92–99, 117.
5. Luther P. Jackson, "Religious Development of the Negro in Virginia from 1760 to 1860," *JNH*, XVI (April, 1931), 168–239; also Parkinson, "Religious Instruction of Slaves," unpubl. M.A. thesis, University of North Carolina, 1948.
6. For evidence of demands for more humane treatment of slaves in the wake of the revivals, see Morton, *Robert Carter of Nomini Hall*, p. 241; George William Pilcher, "Samuel Davies and the Instruction of Negroes in Virginia," *VMBH*, LXXIV (July, 1966), 293–300; Guion Griffis Johnson, "The Camp Meeting in Ante-bellum North Carolina," *NCHR*, X (April, 1933), 106; and for a particular set of records showing the diverse administrative actions that might be taken, see the Hephzibah Church Books, 1819–1820, in the Merritt M. Shilig Memorial Collection, typescript at Louisiana State University.

7. Sirmans, *Colonial South Carolina*, pp. 77, 99–100, 231.
8. See, e.g., McColley, *Slavery and Jeffersonian Virginia*, p. 63.
9. In some parts of the South the suspicion was solidly grounded. See, e.g., Asa Earl Martin, *The Anti-slavery Movement on Kentucky Prior to 1831* (Louisville, Ky., 1918), pp. 84–87.
10. Freehling, *Prelude to Civil War*, pp. 336–337; also pp. 72–76. Cf. George Dangerfield, *The Era of Good Feelings* (New York, 1963), p. 224; Luther P. Jackson, "Religious Instruction of Negroes, 1830–1860, with Special Reference to South Carolina," *JNH*, XV (Jan., 1930), 72–114; Frank J. Klingberg, *An Appraisal of the Negro in Colonial South Carolina* (Washington, D. C., 1941).
11. See Claude R. Rickman, "Wesleyan Methodism in North Carolina," unpubl. M.A. thesis, University of North Carolina, 1952.
12. Rev. Edward Thomas to Rt. Rev. R. W. Whittingham, March 10, 1836, in the Whittingham papers.
13. Quoted in James H. Boykin, *North Carolina in 1861* (New York, 1961), p. 98.
14. J. B. Sellers, *Slavery in Alabama*, p. 294; Sydnor, *Slavery in Mississippi*, p. 55; Anson West, *History of Methodism in Alabama* (Nashville, Tenn., 1893), p. 710; J. G. Taylor, *Negro Slavery in Louisiana*, p. 149; Sitterson, *Sugar Country*, p. 101; Mooney, *Slavery in Tennessee*, pp. 96–97; Bremer, *Homes of the New World*, II, 434.
15. Jackson, "Religious Instruction of Negroes, 1830–1860," pp. 72–114.
16. J. H. Davie to Robert Davie.
17. Freehling, *Prelude to Civil War*, p. 335.
18. For J. H. Hammond's view of the frequency of religious services for slaves, see *The Pro-slavery Argument, as Maintained by the Most Distinguished Writers of the Southern States*, (Charleston, S.C., 1852), p. 133, and *DBR*, VIII (Feb., 1850), 123; also C. C. Jones, *Religious Instruction*, p. 95; *ACPSS*, III (July, 1859), 201–204; Kemble, *Journal*, pp. 56–57; Wendell Holmes Stephenson, *Isaac Franklin: Slave Trader and Planter of the Old South, with Plantation Records* (University, La., 1938), p. 112. For a sampling of plantation manuscripts from different parts of the South see J. W. Witherspoon to Susan K. McDowall, Jan. 2, 1847, in the Witherspoon-McDowall Papers; Massenburg Farm Journal, March 8 and March 15, 1840; Cornish Diary, 1843–1844; Hanson Diary, Dec. 16, 1860; Magruder Diary, April 11, 1846, March 3, 1856; Ervin Journal, 1848; Hilliard Diary, 1850; Hudson Diary, April 22, 1853; E. G. Baker Diary, Aug. 8, 1856; Magnolia Plantation Journal, Oct. 18, 1856, in the Warmoth Papers; Bayside Plantation Records, March 17, 1861; Minor Plantation Diary, Feb. 10, 1863.
     For a sample of the various activities of plantation mistresses in bringing religious instruction to the slaves see Magruder Diary, 1846 and 1856; Hanson Diary, Sept. 15, 1858, March 30, 1860; Broun Diary, Nov. 29, 1863; Clarissa E. (Leavitt) Town Diary, Feb. 1, 1853; Bethell Diary, Jan., 1845, Dec. 9, 1857, June 6, 1860; Eliza Clitherall Autobiography, ms. II, 2; and Wise, *End of an Era*, p. 37.
19. F. L. Riley, ed., "Diary of a Mississippi Planter," *Publications of the Mississippi Historical Society*, X (1909), 453; Chalmers Gaston Davidson, *The Last Foray. The South Carolina Planters of 1860: A Sociological Study* (Columbia, S.C., 1971), p. 83; C. P. Patterson, *Negro in Tennessee*, p. 146; *ACP*, II (Aug., 1854), 253–254.
20. *Narrative of William Wells Brown*, p. 12; cf. Col. John Hill Plantation Diary in the Edgefield (S.C.) Military Record, 1830.
21. W. E. B. Du Bois, "Reconstruction and Its Benefits," *AHR*, XV (July, 1910), 781–799; J. G. Taylor, *Negro Slavery in Louisiana*, p. 149; Heyward, *Seed from Madagascar*, p. 185; Davidson, *Last Foray*, pp. 85, 96; Rawick, ed., *Texas Narr.*, IV (2), 60; Bondurant Reminiscences, typescript pp. 8–13.

22. Quoted in Phillips, "Radical Problems, Adjustments and Distrubances," in Chandler *et al.*, eds., *South in the Building of the Nation*, IV, 210.
23. Quoted in C. S. Davis, *Cotton Kingdom in Alabama*, p. 89.
24. Copies of Affleck's book may be found in many collections of plantation manuscripts. These particular instruction were reprinted in *ACP*, II (Dec., 1854), 353–356.
25. See Jenkins, *Pro-slavery Thought*, pp. 13, 17. For a good general discussion of the ways in which religion was used for social control see Eaton, *Growth of Southern Civilization*, p. 87.
26. George De Berniere Hooper to Caroline M. Hooper, May 13, 1853; John Rogers to "My Dear Children . . .," April 5, 1842, in the Renwick Papers; E. G. Baker Diary, Sept. 4, 1859, (II, 48) also Dec. 30, 1855 (I, 37); Mooney, *Slavery in Tennessee*, p. 92.
27. Yetman, ed., *Life Under the "Peculiar Institution,"* pp. (45–46.)
28. *Ibid.*, p. 91.
29. Greenlee Diary, Dec. 31, 1848; also Rogers Journal, pp. 150–151.
30. Plantation Diary, 1861–1865, in the Minor Papers.
31. E. F. Andrews, *War-Time Journal of a Georgia Girl*, p. 72.
32. Walter Brownlow Posey, *The Baptist Church in the Lower Mississippi Valley, 1776–1845* (Lexington, Ky., 1957), p. 91.
33. Martineau, *Society in America*, II, 319.
34. As quoted in a letter from Mary Jones to Charles C. Jones, Jr., Dec. 22, 1856, in Myers, ed., *Children of Pride*, p. 277.
35. William McKean to James Dunlop, Dec. 2, 1811, in the McKean Letterbook.

LET THE DEAD BURY THE DEAD

1. Aptheker, *Slave Revolts*, p. 166.
2. Edwin Vernon Morgan, *Slavery in New York with Special Reference to New York City* (London, 1898), pp. 21–22.
3. Mullin, *Flight and Rebellion*, p. 148.
4. *FR*, IV (July, 1836), 181.
5. For positive ex-slave recollections, which, however, vary widely in their reports of the degree of latitude permitted by slaveholders, see Fisk University, *Unwritten History of Slavery*, pp. 5, 131; Yetman, ed., *Life Under the "Peculiar Institution,"* pp. 65, 70, 189; Rawick, ed., *S.C. Narr.*, II (2), 15, 51, 89, 198; II (1), 229; *Texas Narr.*, IV (2), 58; V(3), 56, 117; *Ala. Narr.*, VI (1), 22, 155, 279–280, 307, 332, 398; *Okla. Narr.*, VII (1), 95, 99, 208, 264; *Ga. Narr.*, XII (1), 5, 77, 98, 127, 154, 208; XII (2), 5; XIII (3), 17, 159; XIII (4), 118; *Kansas Narr.*, XVI (1), 65.
    For negative reports see Fisk University, *Unwritten History of Slavery*, pp. 54, 151; Yetman, ed., *Life Under the "Peculiar Institution,"* pp. 70, 127; Rawick, ed., *Texas Narr.*, IV (2), 85; *Okla. Narr.*, VII (1), 113; *Ga. Narr.*, XII (1), 98. For the case of a master whom the slaves considered kind and who nonetheless took no pains with black funerals, see Rawick, ed., *Texas Narr.*, IV (1), 52.
6. Yetman, ed., *Life Under the "Peculiar Instituion,"* p. 92.
7. Stewart Account Books, 1841–1860; Yetman, ed., *Life Under the "Peculiar Institution,"* pp. 70, 92, 257.
8. Smedes, *Southern Planter*, pp. 22–23.
9. Judith Page (Walker) Rives to Alfred L. Rives, Dec. 5, 1856. See also Rev. C. C. Jones to Charles C. Jones, Jr., July 30, 1858, and Mary E. Roberts to Mary Jones, May 31, 1861, in Myers, ed., *Children of Pride*, pp. 433, 690–691.

10. Foby, "Management of Servants," *SC*, XI (Aug. 1853), 226–228.

11. *Jones v. Fort*, 1860, in Catterall, ed., *Judicial Cases*, III, 243. For an illustration of the trouble masters sometimes had to go to in order to make necessary funeral arrangements for their slaves, see Bond Diary, Jan. 27, 1863.

12. Rawick, ed., *Texas Narr.*, IV (2), 85.

13. See Yetman, ed., *Life Under the "Peculiar Institution,"* p. 65; Rawick, ed., *S.C. Narr.*, II (1), 333–335; *Texas Narr.*, IV (2), 58; V (3), 56, 117; *Ala. Narr.*, VI (1), 307, 332, 398; Fisk University, *God Struck Me Dead*, p. 159.

14. Schoolcraft, *Plantation Life*, p. 162. Also WPA, *Drums and Shadows*, p. 192; Rawick, ed., *S.C. Narr.*, II (1); II (2), 15, 89, 198. Cf. Lewis, *Journal of a West India Proprietor*, p. 327.

15. Rawick, ed., *S.C. Narr.*, II (2), 89, 198.

16. Julia E. Harn, "Old Canoochee—Ogeechee Chronicles: Life Among the Negroes," *GHQ*, XVI (June, 1932), 148–149.

17. See, e.g., Higginson, *Army Life*, p. 44; Seabrook, *Before and After*, p. 93. But note that whites believed that the blacks had a special dread of cemeteries after dark; W. G. Brown, ed., *Gentleman of the South*, p. 205.

18. E. Franklin Frazier, "The Negro Slave Family," *JNH*, XV (April, 1930), 215–216.

19. Geoffrey Parrinder, *African Traditional Religion* (London, 1962), p. 99; Herskovits, *Myth of the Negro Past*, p. 201; Newbell Niles Puckett, *Folk Beliefs of the Southern Negroes* (New York, 1968 [1926]), pp. 87, 103. For an excellent account of Afro-Jamaican funeral practices see Brathwaite, *Creole Society*, pp. 216–17.

20. Philip Alexander Bruce, *Social Life in Virginia in the Seventeenth Century. An Inquiry into the Origin of the Higher Planting Class, Together with an Account of the Habits, Customs, and Diversions of the People* (Williamstown, Mass., 1968 [1907]), pp. 218–219.

21. Higginson, *Army Life*, p. 44.

22. Puckett, *Folk Beliefs*, pp. 93–94; John S. Mbiti, *African Religions and Philosophy* (New York, 1969), p. 150.

23. WPA, *Drums and Shadows*, p. 59; WPA, *Negro in Virginia*, p. 76; Ojo, *Yoruba Culture*, p. 168.

24. For parallel white practices in Virginia in the 1830s see Abdy, *Journal of Residence and Tour*, II, 227. For black practices in Africa and the South see Parrinder, *African Traditional Religion*, p. 99; WPA, *Drums and Shadows*, p. 227; WPA, *Negro in Virginia*, p. 77; Frazier, "Negro Slave Family," pp. 216–217; Leigh, *Ten Years*, p. 165; Clyde Vernon Kiser, *Sea Island to City: A Study of St. Helena Islanders in Harlem and Other Urban Centers* (New York, 1969), p. 84; Fisk University, *Unwritten History of Slavery*, p. 5.

25. These affairs caused much concern among the whites, especially in the cities; see Wiley, *Southern Negroes*, p. 105, n. 28; Botume, *First Days Amongst the Contrabands*, p. 103. On the slaves' insistence on staying up with the body as a sign of respect, see Pearson, ed., *Letters from Port Royal*, pp. 253–254.

26. Posey, *Baptist Church in the Lower Mississippi Valley*, pp. 16–17.

27. See, e.g., Farish, ed., *Journal and Letters of Philip Vickers Fithian*, p. 241; Cornish Diary, March 17, 1843, April 14, 1843, Jan. 29, 1846; Hanson Diary, Nov. 23, 1859; Ingraham, *South-West*, II, 125. The white Regular Baptists had a special problem, for many of them opposed all graveside preaching on theological grounds; see Posey, *Baptist Church in the Lower Mississippi Valley*, p. 16.

28. See William E. Hatcher, *John Jasper, The Unmatched Negro Philosopher and Preacher* (New York, 1908), p. 37; Harry Toulmin, *The Western Country in 1793: Reports on Kentucky and Virginia* (San Marino, Calif., 1948), pp. 21, 29; Kemble,

Journal, pp. 112–114; Olmsted, *Seaboard,* pp. 25, 405; Schoolcraft, *Plantation Life,* pp. 161–162; Pennington, *Fugitive Blacksmith* in Bontemps, ed., *Great Slave Narratives,* p. 254; Yetman, ed., *Life Under the "Peculiar Institution,"* p. 146; Rawick, ed., *S.C. Narr.,* II (1), 73; *Texas Narr.,* V (3), 117.

29. For extended descriptions see the references to Kemble and Schoolcraft in note 28 above; also Olmsted, *Seaboard,* p. 449. Fragments of descriptions from ex-slaves—see Rawick's edition of the narratives—add up to a similar picture. Also Harold Courlander, *Negro Folk Music, USA* (New York, 1963), p. 200. On the hymns see Rawick, ed., *Ala. Narr.,* VI (1), 22, 155; *Okla. Narr.,* VII (1), 208, 264; *N.C. Narr.,* XV (2), 133; Amelia Thompson Watts, "A Summer on a Louisiana Cotton Plantation in 1832," in the Pharr Book.

30. Yetman, ed., *Life Under the "Peculiar Institution,"* p. 332.

31. Olmsted, *Seaboard,* p. 26; Puckett, *Folk Beliefs,* p. 95.

32. Pollard, *Black Diamonds,* p. 89.

33. Puckett, *Folk Beliefs,* pp. 246, 248.

34. Robert Farris Thompson, "African Influences on the Art of the United States," in Armstead L. Robinson *et al.,* eds., *Black Studies in the University* (New Haven, Conn., 1969), p. 149 and generally pp. 122–170.

35. Peter H. Wood, *Black Majority* (forthcoming).

36. Puckett, *Folk Beliefs,* p. 105.

37. Hortense Powdermaker, *After Freedom: A Cultural Study of the Deep South* (New York, 1968), pp. 122, 249; cf. Gunnar Myrdal, *An American Dilemma: The Negro Problem and Modern Democracy* (New York, 1944), p. 310.

38. See, e.g., Saxon *et al., Gumbo Ya-Ya,* pp. 244–245 and Chs. 15 and 16.

39. For an interesting discussion of white middle-class attitudes among twentieth-century southerners, which are not so far removed from the particular black attitudes under consideration here, see Christopher Crocker, "The Southern Way of Death," in J. Kenneth Morland, ed., *The Not So Solid South: Anthropological Studies in a Regional Subculture* (Athens, Ga., 1971), pp. 114–129.

40. Hobsbawm, *Industry and Empre* p. 69.

41. Reeves, *Round About a Pound a Week* pp. 67 ff.

42. Joost A. M. Meerlo, *Suicide and Mass Suicide* (New York, 1968), p. 133. Significantly, the Slave Act of the British Virgin Islands of 1783 and the earlier Act of 1780 in Antigua forbade any except the plainest slave funerals on the grounds that they represented a tendency on the part of the slaves to equalize themselves with the whites; see Goveia, *Slave Society in the British Leeward Islands,* p. 167.

43. The indignation of the slaves at having their graves raided by white medical students should be seen in this fuller context. See the letter by Susan M. Cummings to C. C. Jones, March 12, 1856, in Myers, ed., *Children of Pride,* p. 194.

THE WHITE PREACHERS

1. Joe Madison King, *A History of South Carolina Baptists* (Columbia, S.C., 1964), p. 141; also H. Shelton Smith, *In His Image, But . . . : Racism in Southern Religion, 1780–1910* (Durham, N.C., 1972), Ch. 1.

2. For reports by ex-slaves on minister-masters who were kind and humane, see Yetman, ed., *Life Under the "Peculiar Institution,"* p. 86 (Andy Marion); Rawick, ed., *S.C. Narr.,* II (1), 157; *Texas Narr.,* IV (1), 157–158; IV (2), 23, 64; *Ala. Narr.,* VI (1), 63, 332; *Indiana Narr.,* VI (2), 21.

   For sample reports of minister-masters who were cruel, see Rawick, ed., *Indiana Narr.,* VI (2), 201; *Ga. Narr.,* XII (2), 12; *N.C. Narr.,* XIV (1), 217;

Keckley, *Behind the Scenes*, Chs. 1 and 2; Fisk University, *God Struck Me Dead*, p. 185. H. C. Bruce, *New Man*, p. 85, provides accounts of both types. For an account of the Rev. Richard Fuller, proslavery ideologue and slaveholder, see Rose, *Rehearsal for Reconstruction*, esp. pp. 111–112, 115–119, 349. The Rev. Mr. Fuller was popular with his slaves, yet they walked out on him after the war when his trusted driver refused his appeals.

3. Wesley M. Gehwehr, *The Great Awakening in Virginia, 1740–1790* (Gloucester, Mass., 1965), pp. 235–236; Eaton, *Freedom-of-Thought Struggle*, pp. 131–143; B. F. Riley, *Baptists of Alabama*, pp. 276–277.

4. Holcombe Autobiography (ms.), Pt. 2, Ch. 1, pp. 1–2. See also Josiah Henson's telling recollection of the baker-preacher, John McKenney, in *Father Henson's Story of His Own Life*, pp. 27–28.

5. John Witherspoon to Susan D. Witherspoon, May 23, 1837, in the Witherspoon-McDowall Papers.

6. Stratton Diary, March 1, 1851; Hill Diary, Nov. 24, 1846; J. H. Witherspoon to Mrs. Susan McDowall, July 9, 1846, in the Witherspoon-McDowall Papers; Hanson Diary, Oct. 14, 1858; N. L. Garfield to Levert, April 27, 1857, in the Levert Papers; Cornish Diary, April 19, 1865; Spyker Diary, June 21, 1852.

7. Freehling, *Prelude to Civil War*, pp. 301–302.

8. Letter to *Farmville Journal*, Oct. 16, 1856, as quoted in Ira Berlin, "Slaves Who Were Free: The Free Negro in the Upper South, 1776–1861," unpubl. Ph.D. dissertation, University of Wisconsin, 1970. Also C. C. Jones, *Religious Instruction*, p. 176.

9. E. F. Andrews, *War-Time Journal of a Georgia Girl*, p. 69.

10. Doyle, *Etiquette of Race Relations*, p. 46.

11. Rawick, ed., *Okla. Narr.*, VII (1), 201.

12. Agnew Diary, Dec. 31, 1865 (VI, 303).

13. *Ibid.*, Sept. 1854 (I, 146).

14. Cornish Diary, Jan. 3, 1845.

15. Bremer, *Homes of the New World*, I, 289.

16. Valentine Diary, Nov. 4, 1851.

17. C. C. Jones, *Suggestions*, pp. 14–15; Fripp Papers, Dec. 19, 1857. For an account of white ministers who took a view opposite to that of the Rev. Mr. Jones, see William M. Wrightman, *The Life of William Capers, D.D.* (Nashville, Tenn., 1859), p. 345.

18. *PB*, March 21, 1850.

19. Cornish Diary, Oct. 10, 1847.

20. Bumpus Journal, May 19, 1842.

21. C. C. Jones, *Suggestions*, p. 28.

22. Myers, ed., *Children of Pride*, Bks. 1 and 2, *passim*.

23. Rawick, ed., *Texas Narr.*, IV (2), 103; Yetman, ed., *Life Under the "Peculiar Institution,"* p. 222.

24. Rawick, ed., *Texas Narr.*, IV (2), 117; Northup, *Twelve Years a Slave*, p. 97; also H. C. Bruce, *New Man*, pp. 71–72; Fisk University, *God Struck Me Dead*, p. 149. For a sympathetic account of the efforts of white preachers see Blassingame, *Slave Community*, Ch. 2. White preachers varied their texts a good deal and often did deliver messages of spiritual equality before God. But they could not avoid the theme of submission to slavery, and they thereby often ruined good efforts. For the variety of texts see Parkinson, "Religious Instruction of Slaves," unpubl. M.A. thesis, University of North Carolina, 1948, pp. 79–80; Myers, *Children of Pride*, p. 102; Stratton Diary, 1843–1851.

25. Rawick, ed., *Texas Narr.*, V (4), 7; IV (2), 167; V (3), 213; Chesnut, *Diary from Dixie*, p. 171; WPA, *Negro in Virginia*, p. 108; also Yetman, ed., *Life Under the "Peculiar Institution,"* p. 13.

26. C. C. Jones, *Religious Instruction*, p. 199.
27. As quoted in Aptheker, *Slave Revolts*, p. 57.
28. Robert Michelet, *Satanism and Witchcraft* (New York, 1970), pp. xii–xiii.
29. See Ch. 5 of Jeffrey Kaplow, *The Names of Kings: The Parisian Laboring Classes in the Eighteenth Century* (New York, 1972).
30. Keith Thomas, *Religion and the Decline of Magic*, (New York, 1971) p. 152. Consider too the remark of the duchess of Buckingham on Methodism: "It is monstrous to be told that you have a heart as sinful as the common wretches of the earth." As Christopher Hill comments, her response "tells us less about Methodism than about the ruling class"; *Reformation to Industrial Revolution* (New York, 1967), p. 228.

ORIGINS OF THE FOLK RELIGION

1. Herskovits, *Myth of the Negro Past;* E. Franklin Frazier, *The Negro Church: The Negro in America* (New York, 1966), and *The Negro Family in the United States* (Chicago, 1966).
2. Ojo, *Yoruba Culture,* p. 158 and *passim.* See also the statement of Mary H. Kingsley, as excerpted in Thomas Hodgkin, ed., *Nigerian Perspectives* (London, 1960), pp. 17–18. Of the numerous studies of West African religion the most relevant to the points made in this section are Mbiti, *African Religions and Philosophy,* esp. pp. 97 ff.; Parrinder, *African Traditional Religion;* Kenneth Little, "The Mende in Sierra Leone," in C. Daryll Forde, ed., *African Worlds: Studies in the Cosmological Ideas and Social Values of African Peoples* (London, 1954), p. 112; Abraham *Mind of Africa;* Balandier, *Political Anthropology;* M. M. Green, *Ibo Village Affairs,* pp. 55–56, 94–95; the several works by Rattray on the Ashanti; and Max Weber, *Sociology of Religion,* pp. 17–18.
3. For a striking illustration see the report of the conversion experience in Fisk University, *God Struck Me Dead,* pp. 26–27. For Africa see Abraham, *Mind of Africa,* p. 47; J. B. Danquah, *The Akan Idea of God* (London, 1944), p. 82; E. Bolaji Idowu, *Olódùmarè: God in Yoruba Belief* (London, 1962), pp. 148–149; Mbiti, *African Religions and Philosophy,* pp. 97 ff., and his *New Testament Eschatology in an African Background* (New York, 1971), p. 138.
4. Santayana, *Reason in Religion,* p. 16.
5. For an Asian parallel see Benedict, *Chrysanthemum and Sword,* p. 98.
6. Higginson, *Army Life,* pp. 17, 27, 253, 255.
7. WPA, *Negro in Virginia,* p. 110.
8. Fisk University, *Unwritten History of Slavery,* pp. 10, 106.
9. WPA, *Negro in Virginia,* p. 199.
10. *Religious Herald* (Richmond, Va.), Feb. 17, 1832, quoted in Berlin, "Slaves Who Were Free," unpubl. Ph.D. dissertation, University of Wisconsin, 1970; also Joseph B. Earnest, *The Religious Development of the Negro in Virginia* (Charlottesville, Va., 1914), p. 97, n. 96.
11. Rawick, ed., *S.C. Narr.,* III(3), 5.
12. James Redpath, *The Roving Editor, Or, Talks with Slaves in the Southern States* (New York, 1859), p. 260.
13. Rev. R. Q. Mallard to Mary Mallard, May 18, 1859, in Myers, ed., *Children of Pride,* p. 483.
14. For sympathetic reports of growing black interest in conversion and of belief in its sincerity, see Mrs. Smith Journal, 1793; Cornish Diary, Jan. 12, 1843, Dec. 21, 1848, and *passim;* Clarissa E. (Leavitt) Town Diary, March 27, 1853; Parson Brownlow, "Religion of the Negroes," *SC,* XVI (Dec., 1858), 378; *DBR,* XVIII (May, 1855), 575, 612; Chancellor Harper in E. N. Elliott, ed.,

Cotton Is King and Pro-slavery Arguments, p. 37; Pollard, *Black Diamonds*, p. 35.

15. Catterall, ed., *Judicial Cases*, III, 313.

16. For the views of a large planter, an English visitor, and a prominent journalist see J. B. Grimball Diary, March 20, 1855; Kemble, *Journal*, p. 84; and Pollard, *Black Diamonds*, p. 58.

17. C. C. Jones, *Religious Instruction*, pp. 127–128. Also Earnest, *Religious Development of the Negro in Virginia*, pp. 27–29.

18. A Minister of the Gospel, " 'Tatler' on the Management of Negroes," *SC*, IX (June, 1851), 84–85; also Orlando Kay Armstrong, *Old Massa's People: The Old Slaves Tell Their Story* (Indianapolis, 1931), p. 246.

19. Olmsted, *Back Country*, p. 109.

20. Hundley, *Social Relations*, pp. 328–329.

21. See Calvin Henderson Wiley, "Duties of Christian Masters," p. 94, in the Wiley Papers; "Autobiography of Emily Donelson Walton," pp. 9–10, in the Laurence Family Papers; Sydnor, *Slavery in Mississippi*, p. 61; Sitterson, *Sugar Country*, p. 102.

22. De Bow, *Industrial Resources*, II, 321.

23. Wilson, "Peculiarities and Diseases of Negroes," *ACPSS*, IV (Jan., 1860), 46–47.

24. Carpenter, "Observations on the Cachexia Africana," *NOMSJ*, I (Oct., 1844), pp. 146–165.

25. WPA, *Drums and Shadows*; Puckett, *Folk Beliefs, passim*; Rawick, ed., *Ga. Narr.*, XIII (4), *passim*.

26. K. Thomas, *Religion and the Decline of Magic* p. 50.

27. See WPA, *Drums and Shadows*; Morton Rubin, *Plantation County* (New Haven, Conn., 1951); Robert Tallant, *Voodoo in New Orleans* (New York, 1946); Puckett, *Folk Beliefs;* Powdermaker, *After Freedom*, pp. 286 ff.; Saxon *et al.*, *Gumbo Ya-Ya*, pp. 248 ff., 545; Herskovits, *Myth of the Negro Past*, pp. 250 ff.; Earnest, *Religious Development of the Negro in Virginia*, p. 136.

28. The size of the white clientele for black voodoo might reach one-third or one-half of the total, even during the twentieth century. See Powdermaker, *After Freedom*, pp. 295–296.

29. Harn, "Old Canoochee—Ogeechee Chronicles," *GHQ*, XVI (June, 1932), 147.

30. See, e.g., Guion Griffis Johnson, "Social Characteristics of Ante-bellum North Carolina," *NCHR*, VI (April, 1929), 155; Mann Butler, "Details of Frontier Life," *KHSR*, LXII (July, 1964), 224.

31. Rawick, ed., *Texas Narr.*, V (4), 184.

32. *Narrative of William Wells Brown*, p. 40; Catterall, ed., *Judicial Cases*, III, 367–368; II, 43; II, 414.

33. *Life and Times of Frederick Douglass*, pp. 136–138. See also H. C. Bruce, *New Man*, Ch. 5, for an account of the conjurer's power over the slaves by an ex-slave who regarded conjurers as self-serving frauds.

34. WPA, *Drums and Shadows*, p. 28.

35. Yetman, ed., *Life Under the "Peculiar Institution,"* p. 63.

36. Botkin, ed., *Lay My Burden Down*, p. 39; also Rawick, ed., *S.C. Narr.*, II (1), 69, 143; *Mo. Narr.*, XI, 55.

37. W. F. Allen *et al.*, *Slave Songs of the United States* (New York, 1871), p. 108; John G. Clinkscales, *On the Old Plantation: Reminiscences of His Childhood* (Westport, Conn., 1916), p. 12; Puckett, *Folk Beliefs*, p. 553; Odum and Johnson, *Negro and His Songs*, p. 39; Rawick, ed., *Ark. Narr.*, IX (4), 262; O. K. Armstrong, *Old Massa's People*, pp. 140–141. For a discussion of the trickster among African and non-African peoples see Edward Norbeck, *Religion in Primitive Society*, (New York, 1961) pp. 78 ff.; Paul Radin, *The Trickster: A Study in American Indian Mythology* (New York, 1972).

38. Rawick, ed., *Texas Narr.*, IV (2), 9, 238.
39. Ingraham, *South-West*, II, 258; Pollard, *Black Diamonds*, pp. xi–xii; Heyward, *Seed from Madagascar*, p. 165.
40. Herskovits, *Myth of the Negro Past*, pp. 242–243, 252–253; Geoffrey Parrinder, *Witchcraft: European and African* (London, 1958), p. 133; Shippee, ed., *Bishop Whipple's Southern Diary*, p. 36; Rawick, ed., *Ga. Narr.*, XIII (3), 345. The place of the devil in the lives of European peasants in the process of conversion to Christianity requires further study but does seem to pose some interesting parallels to the slave experience; see, e.g., Thomas and Znaniecki, *Polish Peasant*, I, 283–284.
41. William E. Barton, "Old Plantation Hymns," in Bernard Katz, ed., *Social Implications of Early Negro Music in the United States* (New York, 1969), p. 84.
42. Rawick, ed., *Ala. Narr.*, VI (1), 186; *S.C. Narr.*, II (1), 160.
43. Puckett, *Folk Beliefs*, p. 166. Whites in New Orleans and elsewhere have joined the cult, but its leadership has always been black.
44. Tallant, *Voodoo in New Orleans, passim.*
45. For the significance of the snake in African mythology see Geoffrey Parrinder, *African Mythology* (London, 1967), pp. 38–50; also see the interesting political implications in Karl Polanyi, *Dahomey and the Slave Trade* (Seattle, Wash., 1966), pp. 131–132; for its wider place in the non-Western world see Worsley, *Trumpet Shall Sound*, p. 252.
46. Puckett, *Folk Beliefs*, p. 146. For an example of the practice see Sydnor, *Slavery in Mississippi*, p. 61.
47. Yetman, ed., *Life Under the "Peculiar Institution,"* pp. 189–190. For white attitudes see Moody, *Slavery on the Louisiana Sugar Plantations*, p. 89; J. G. Taylor, *Negro Slavery in Louisiana*, p. 134; Stampp, *Peculiar Institution*, p. 374; Posey, *Baptist Church in the Lower Mississippi Valley*, p. 46.
48. Botkin, ed., *Lay My Burden Down*, p. 29.
49. Yetman, ed., *Life Under the "Peculiar Institution,"* p. 201.
50. Rawick, ed., *Indiana Narr.*, VI (2), 59. For similar "successes" see *Ark. Narr.*, XI (7), 20–21; *Ga. Narr.*, XIII (3), 345.
51. Rawick, ed., *S.C. Narr.*, III (3), 158; *Mo. Narr.*, XI, 101.
52. Botkin, ed., *Lay My Burden Down*, p. 46; Rawick, ed., *Texas Narr.*, V (3), 161.
53. Rawick, ed., *Okla. Narr.*, VII (1), 40; Fisk University, *Unwritten History of Slavery*, p. 46.
54. See, e.g., Rawick, ed., *S.C. Narr.*, II (1), 2; *Texas Narr.*, IV (1), 5; *Ark. Narr.*, X (6), 7; *Ga. Narr.*, XII (1), 89.
55. See the remarks of V. S. Naipaul on the widespread white fear of them as terrorists, *Loss of El Dorado*, pp. 156, 171.
56. Yetman, ed., *Life Under the "Peculiar Institution,"* pp. 115–116.
57. *Ibid.*, p. 53.
58. Rawick, ed., *Texas Narr.*, IV (2), 3, 64; Botkin, ed., *Lay My Burden Down*, p. 83.
59. "Autobiography of Emily Donelson Walker," in the Laurence Family Papers.
60. See the account of Patsy Moses of Tennessee in Rawick, ed., *Texas Narr.*, V (3), 142–144.
61. See WPA, *Drums and Shadows*, pp. 7, 92; Puckett, *Folk Beliefs*, p. 209; Stampp, *Peculiar Institution*, p. 394.
62. See Parrinder, *African Traditional Religion*, pp. 16–17, 27, and *Witchcraft*, p. 111; C. Daryll Forde, *The Yoruba-Speaking Peoples of South-Western Nigeria* (New York, 1950), p. 31; Mbiti, *African Religions and Philosophy*, p. 170. One politically relevant function of charms deserves comment. Rev. C. C. Jones, *Religious Instruction*, p. 128, delicately hints that some blacks believed that charms

could dissolve bullets and that this belief could become a deadly matter during an insurrection. It never did become a problem in the South, but the Rev. Mr. Jones knew what he was about. African peoples have often put this belief to revolutionary use. During the left-wing rising in Zaire (the former Belgian Congo) after the murder of Patrice Lumumba, the rebels used "Mulele's Water," named after their leader, to counter their troops' fear of death by guaranteeing invulnerability.

63. Wyndham B. Blanton, *Medicine in Virginia in the Eighteenth Century* (Richmond, Va., 1931), pp. 45, 173, 212–213; Phillips, *Life and Labor*, pp. 165, 283; WPA, *Negro in Virginia*, p. 75; Morton, *Robert Carter of Nomini Hall*, pp. 115–116. Black doctors commonly attended whites on the plantations in Surinam, according to Capt. J. G. Stedman.

64. See Tate, *Negro in Eighteenth-Century Williamsburg*, p. 131; Joseph Ivor Waring, *A History of Medicine in South Carolina, 1670–1825* (Columbia, S.C., 1964), p. 51.

65. See, e.g., C. P. Patterson, *Negro in Tennessee*, p. 36.

66. See, e.g., Yetman, ed., *Life Under the "Peculiar Institution,"* p. 286.

67. On white medical practice in general see John Duffy, "Medical Practice in the Ante-bellum South," *JSH*, XXV (Feb., 1959), 53–72. Also Virginia Jayne Lacy and David Edwin Harrell, Jr., "Plantation Home Remedies: Medicinal Recipes from the Diary of John Pope," *THQ*, XXII (Sept., 1963), 259–265; C. S. Davis, *Cotton Kingdom in Alabama*, p. 89.

68. W. T. Jordan, *Ante-bellum Alabama*, p. 77.

69. Rawick, ed., *S.C. Narr.*, III (4), 19; *Texas Narr.*, IV (1), 244.

70. John Hamilton to William Hamilton, Feb. 4, 1860, in the Lester Collection.

71. Kemble, *Journal*, p. 63.

72. Walter Fisher, "Physicians and Slavery in the Antebellum Southern Medical Journal," in Meier and Rudwick, eds., *Making of Black America*, I, 163; see also Craton and Walvin, *Jamaican Plantation*, p. 133. For evidence from the planters themselves of dissatisfaction with white medical performance by both doctors and planters who served as amateur doctors, see Catterall, ed., *Judicial Cases*, III, 188; James W. Melvin to A. C. Britton, Sept. 29, 1862, in the Britton Papers; and Smedes, *Southern Planter*, p. 29. For a more positive black view of white doctors see Pearson, ed., *Letters from Port Royal*, pp. 15, 31.

73. Schoolcraft, *Plantation Life*, pp. 235–236, 240; Ingraham, *South-West*, II, 123. Also Lyell, *Second Visit*, I, 264.

74. Kate Stone, *Brokenburn*, p. 372.

75. *Life and Times of Frederick Douglass*, p. 42.

76. See St. John R. Liddell to Moses Liddell, Feb. 14, 1852; Charles C. Jones, Jr., to Rev. C. C. Jones, June 20, 1854, in Myers, ed., *Children of Pride*, p. 46.

77. Sydnor, *Slavery in Mississippi*, pp. 48–49; Rawick, ed., *Miss. Narr.*, VII (2), 69, 166; Fisk University, *Unwritten History of Slavery*, pp. 46, 91. For a general discussion of rational, empirical, and magical elements in folk medicine see Erwin H. Ackernecht, "Natural Diseases and Rational Treatment in Primitive Medicine," *BHM*, XIX (May, 1946), 467–497.

78. Rawick, ed., *Texas Narr.*, IV (2), 91–92; *Okla. Narr.*, VII (1), 299. Cf. Goveia, *Slave Society in The British Leeward Islands*, p. 248; H. O. Patterson, *Sociology of Slavery*, p. 191.

79. Rawick, ed., *Texas Narr.*, V (4), 13; V (3), 169; *S.C. Narr.*, II (1), 24; *Kansas Narr.*, XVI, 47; *Ohio Narr.*, XVI, 59.

80. WPA, *Drums and Shadows*, pp. xx, 57; Puckett, *Folk Beliefs*, pp. 167–168, 192, 259, n. 2; Rawick, ed., *Ga. Narr.*, XII (1), 84.

81. These measures were by no means limited to rural slaves. See Richard C. Wade, *Slavery in the Cities* (New York, 1964), p. 138.

82. W. E. B. Du Bois, *The Souls of Black Folk* (New York, 1964 [1903]), p. 144.
83. Abraham, *Mind of Africa*, p. 49; Parrinder, *African Traditional Religion*, pp. 104–106; Puckett, *Folk Beliefs*, pp. 300, 358, 360, 366 ff.; George Way Harley, *Native African Medicine: With Special Reference to Its Practice in the Maró Tribe of Liberia* (Cambridge, Mass., 1941), esp. pp. 5, 142–152, 227–228. For a good account of Afro-Caribbean ideas and practice, see Gwendolyn M. Hall, *Social Control in Slave Plantation Societies: A Comparison of Saint-Domingue and Cuba* (Baltimore, 1971), pp. 73–74.
84. See Norbeck, *Religion in Primitive Society*, pp. 213, 215, 226; K. Thomas, *Religion and the Decline of Magic*, pp. 12, 91; Ivar Paulson, *The Old Estonian Folk Religion* (trans. Kitching and Kovamees; Bloomington, Ind., 1971), p. 174; Ralph C. Croizier, "Medicine, Modernization, and Cultural Crisis in China and India," *CSSH*, XII (July, 1970), 275–291; and May, "Medical Care of Blacks in Louisiana," unpubl. Ph.D. dissertation, Tulane University, 1970, pp. 167–168, 176–177.
85. Coulton, *Medieval Panorama*, p. 111.
86. See Eileen Power, *Medieval People* (9th ed.; London, 1960), p. 30; Coulton, *Medieval Panorama*, p. 9; Robert Kreiser, "Miracles and Convulsions in Paris, 1727–1737," unpubl. Ph.D. dissertation, University of Chicago, 1971.
87. K. Thomas, *Religion and the Decline of Magic*, pp. 587 ff.; George Caspar Homans, *English Villagers of the Thirteenth Century* (New York, 1960), esp. pp. 375–379.
88. Paulson, *Old Estonian Folk Religion*, p. 151; Rawick, ed., *Ga. Narr.*, XII (1), 151.
89. Fanon, *Wretched of the Earth*, p. 44.

THE GOSPEL IN THE QUARTERS

1. Scarborough, ed., *Diary of Edmund Ruffin*, Feb. 20, 1859, (I, 284).
2. Herskovits, *Myth of the Negro Past*, pp. 232–234.
3. The ultimate complexity of the problem is suggested by the parallel success of fundamentalist sects among colonial peoples. See Worsley, *Trumpet Shall Sound*, p. 235.
4. Arthur Huff Fauset, *Black Gods of the Metropolis: Negro Religious Cults of the Urban North* (Philadelphia, 1971), pp. 101–102.
5. Henry George Spaulding, "Negro 'Shouts' and Shout Songs," in Bernard Katz, ed., *The Social Implications of Early Negro Music in the United States* (New York, 1969), pp. 4–5. Also G. G. Johnson, *Social History of the Sea Islands*, pp. 150–151; James Weldon Johnson, *The Book of American Negro Spirituals* (New York, 1925), pp. 33–34; Courlander, *Negro Folk Music*, pp. 194–195; Kiser, *Sea Island to City*, p. 79.
6. Thomas Merton, *Seasons of Celebration: Meditations on the Cycle of Liturgical Feasts* (New York, 1965), p. 248. The place of the dance in the Afro-American cult known as Voodoo is discussed by John Q. Anderson, "The New Orleans Voodoo Ritual Dance and Its Twentieth Century Survivals," *Southern Folklore Quarterly* (Dec., 1960), 135–143.
7. Richard Allen, quoted in Eileen Southern, *The Music of Black Americans: A History* (New York, 1971), p. 87.
8. In North Carolina the Methodists worked harder than the Baptists among the slaves and recruited more widely. See Bassett, *Slavery in the State of North Carolina*, Ch. 3. Also J. M. King, *South Carolina Baptists*, pp. 127–129; Parkinson, "Religious Instruction of Slaves," unpubl. M.A. thesis, University of

North Carolina, 1948, p. 52; Everett Dick, *The Dixie Frontier: A Social History of the Southern Frontier from the First Transmontane Beginnings to the Civil War* (New York, 1964), p. 188; Posey, *Baptist Church in the Lower Mississippi Valley*, pp. 89–93; Quarles, *Negro in the Making of America*, p. 58; and in general, Carter G. Woodson, *The History of the Negro Church* (Washington, D.C., 1921).

9. R. B. Semple, *History of the Rise and Progress of the Baptists in Virginia* (Richmond, Va., 1810), p. 101; Robert, *Road from Monticello*, p. 7; C. P. Patterson, *Negro in Tennessee*, p. 20; J. G. Taylor, *Negro Slavery in Louisiana*, p. 138; William L. Richter, "Slavery in Ante-bellum Baton Rouge, 1820–1860," *LH*, X (Spring, 1969), 125–146; Swint, ed., *Dear Ones at Home*, p. 125; Gaston Hugh Wamble, "Negroes and Missouri Protestant Churches Before and After the Civil War," *Mo.H.R.*, LXI (April, 1967), 321–347. The experience in Canada is instructive, for there too blacks established their own churches; see Robin W. Winks, *The Blacks in Canada: A History* (New Haven, Conn., 1971), pp. 53, 71. For some interesting reflections by white ministers on the question of racial separation, see Whitefoord Smith, Memorandum, July 18, 1849; also July 23, 1849; Hanson Diary, March 30, 1860.

10. Wade, *Slavery in the Cities*, pp. 83, 161–162, 167–168; also Benjamin Elizah Mays and Joseph William Nicholson, *The Negro's Church* (New York, 1969), p. 3; Benjamin Elizah Mays, *The Negro's God as Reflected in His Literature* (New York, 1969), pp. 30–65; Walter H. Brooks, "Evolution of the Negro Baptist Church," *JNH*, VII (Jan., 1922), 11–22; Christopher Rush, *A Short History of the Rise and Progress of the African Episcopal Church in America* (New York, 1843), esp. pp. 18, 60–61, 91, for efforts in the North and relations with white churches.

11. Phillips, *American Negro Slavery*, p. 321; cf. C. C. Jones, *Religious Instruction*, pp. 90–91.

12. See E. U. Essien-Udom, *Black Nationalism: A Search for an Identity in America* (New York, 1964), pp. 31, 37–38.

13. Olmsted, *Back Country*, p. 93.

14. South Carolina had as good a police system as any and also a no-nonsense tradition in matters of social control, yet the laws were enforced only during times of stress. See Henry, *Police Control of the Slave*, pp. 133–141.

15. Rawick, ed., *Texas Narr.*, V (4), 198.

16. Fisk University, *Unwritten History of Slavery*, p. 87.

17. Rawick, *Sundown to Sunup* pp. 41 ff.; John F. Szwed in personal correspondence. Also, Rawick, ed., *Indiana Narr.*, VI (2), 98.

18. E. F. Andrews, *War-Time Journal of a Georgia Girl*, Feb. 12, 1865 (p. 89).

19. Botkin, ed., *Lay My Burden Down*, p. 146.

20. Yetman, ed., *Life Under the "Peculiar Institution,"* p. 13 (testimony of Lucretia Alexander of Arkansas).

21. *Ibid.*, p. 53.

22. Rawick, ed., *Texas Narr.*, IV (1), 11; *Ark. Narr.*, IX (4), 254; *Mo. Narr.*, XI, 305.

23. Rawick, ed., *S.C. Narr.*, II (2), 135.

24. Saxon *et al.*, *Gumbo Ya-Ya*, p. 242; Rawick, ed., *S.C. Narr.* II (2), 87.

25. Some elite house slaves, free Negroes, and urban slaves—by no means all and probably not the majority—were quite uncomfortable in these circumstances and preferred to pray in the "white" manner. See, e.g., Mary Sharpe to C. C. Jones, June 2, 1856, in Myers, ed., *Children of Pride*; Mrs. Smith Journal, 1793, p. 22; Olmsted, *Seaboard*, p. 405.

26. Max Weber, *The Sociology of Religion* (trans. Ephraim Fischoffs; Boston, 1964), p. 157. On spirit possession in Brazil see Warren, "The Negro and Religion in Brazil," *Race*, VI (Jan., 1965), esp. p. 201; in Haiti, Métraux, *Voodoo in Haiti*,

pp. 120–122; also Roger Bastide, *Sociologie et psychoanalyse* (Paris, 1950), p. 252; H. U. Beier, "The Egungen Cult Among the Yorubas," *Présence Africaine*, Nos. 17–18 (Feb.–May, 1958), pp. 33–36; Georges Balandier, *Ambiguous Africa: Cultures in Collision* (trans. Helen Weaver; New York, 1965), pp. 46–47; Worsley, *Trumpet Shall Sound*, p. 61; Norbeck, *Religion in Primitive Society*, pp. 99, 100.

27. Du Bois, *Souls of Black Folk*, p. 142.

28. See the illuminating discussion by Evans-Pritchard, *Theories of Primitive Religion*, p. 46, and his analysis of Radin's views on p. 247.

29. For a good summary discussion see Southern, *Music of Black Americans*, p. 96.

30. Olmsted, *Seaboard*, p. 460.

31. On the African origins of the call-and-response pattern in the spirituals see esp. Alan Lomax, "The Homogeneity of African–Afro-American Musical Style," in Norman E. Whitten and John F. Szwed, eds., *Afro-American Anthropology: Contemporary Perspectives on Theory and Research* (New York, 1970), Ch. 9, and his other stimulating writings. Also John W. Work, *American Negro Songs and Spirituals* (New York, 1940), p. 9; John J. Szwed, "Afro-American Musical Adaptation," *Journal of American Folklore* (Mar., 1969), 219–228; Charles W. Joyner, *Folk Song in South Carolina* (Columbia, S.C., 1971), pp. 6, 71; and the general discussion of slave songs, stories, and folklore in Blassingame, *Slave Community*, Ch. 1 and pp. 57 ff. The Rev. Henry H. Mitchell has pointed out that shouting and the like among lower-class southern whites and Pentecostals provide an important link between the white and black variants of Christianity and ought to be valued as such; see *Black Preaching* (Philadelphia, 1970), p. 101.

32. Mitchell, *Black Preaching*, p. 50.

33. Rawick, ed., *Texas Narr.*, V (3), 266.

34. Cash, *Mind of the South*, p. 58.

35. Olmsted, *Seaboard*, pp. 455–457.

36. Mitchell, *Black Preaching*, pp. 49–50, 101, 112–113, 133.

37. See, e.g., Puckett, *Folk Beliefs*, p. 535; Powdermaker, *After Freedom*, pp. 246, 260–261.

38. Olmsted, *Seaboard*, p. 123.

39. E. F. Andrews, *War-Time Journal of a Georgia Girl*, June 28, 1865 (p. 321).

40. Posey, *Baptist Church in the Lower Mississippi Valley*, pp. 70–71.

41. Toulmin, *Western Country in 1793*, p. 30.

42. See, e.g., Keckley, *Behind the Scenes*, p. xii, for a combination of these tendencies. The graveyard incident is from Sydnor, *Slavery in Mississippi*, pp. 251–252.

43. K. Thomas, *Religion and the Decline of Magic*, p. 111.

44. Rawick, ed., *S.C. Narr.*, II (1), 93.

45. See the perceptive analysis of Lawrence Levine, "Slave Songs and Slave Consciousness," in Hareven, ed., *Anonymous Americans*, pp. 118–121. For the continued strength of this doctrine see St. Clair Drake and Horace R. Cayton, *Black Metropolis: A Study of Negro Life in a Northern City* (2 vols.; New York, 1962), II, 615–616; Raymond Julius Jones, *A Comparative Study of Religious Cult Behavior Among Negroes, with Special Reference to Emotional Group Conditioning Factors* (Washington, D.C., n.d.).

46. Olmsted, *Seaboard*, pp. 123–124.

47. For an account of the polemic over the meaning of the curse in relation to the condition of Africa, see Eugene D. Genovese, "A Georgia Slaveholder Looks at Africa," *GHQ*, LI (June, 1967), 189.

48. Rawick, ed., *Texas Narr.*, IV (1), 239; also *Ala. Narr.*, VI (1), 5, 336.

49. Rawick, ed., *S.C. Narr.*, III (3), 205–207.

50. *Ibid.*, II (1), 7. For the good-from-evil preaching see J. G. Williams, *"De Ole Plantation"* (Charleston, S.C., 1895), p. 12; Rawick, ed., *Ga. Narr.*, XII (1), 296.

51. Puckett, *Folk Beliefs,* p. 110; cf. K. A. Busia, "The Ashanti," in Forde, ed., *African Worlds,* p. 197; Eva L. R. Meyerowitz, "Concepts of the Soul Among the Akan of the Gold Coast," *Africa,* XXI (Jan., 1951), 24–31.

52. See Clifford Geertz, *The Religion of Java* (New York, 1960), p. 232; Paulson, *Old Estonian Folk Religion,* pp. 22, 166; Mbiti, *African Religions and Philosophy,* Chs. 5–6.

53. Abdy, *Journal of Residence and Tour,* II, 292.

54. Miles Mark Fisher, *Negro Slave Songs in the United States* (Ithaca, N.Y., 1953), pp. 71–72; also pp. 137, 146, 156. The conversion account in Fisk University, *God Struck Me Dead,* p. 84, would appear to support Dr. Fisher's interpretation. We may recall that many recent black movements deny or minimize an afterlife; see Essien-Udom, *Black Nationalism,* pp. 153 ff., 251; and Cleage, *Black Messiah.*

55. Howard Thurman, *The Negro Spiritual Speaks of Life and Death* (New York, 1947), pp. 17, 27–28, 38, 51; Levine, "Slave Songs and Slave Consciousness," p. 114. Also Mbiti, *African Religions and Philosophy,* p. 4 and Ch. 14.

56. Wharton, *Negro in Mississippi,* p. 20.

57. Du Bois, *Souls of Black Folk,* p. 189; also *The Gift of Black Folk: The Negroes in the Making of America* (New York, 1970), Ch. 7; Mays, *Negro's God,* p. 21. Geroid Tanquary Robinson has cited the Russian peasants' songs of resistance and compared them to the spirituals; see *Rural Russia Under the Old Regime,* p. 48.

58. Harriet Beecher Stowe, quoted in Charles H. Nichols, *Many Thousand Gone: The Ex-slaves' Account of Their Bondage and Their Freedom* (Leiden, 1963), pp. 99.

59. E. F. Andrews, *War-Time Journal of a Georgia Girl,* Feb. 12, 1865 (p. 91). See also the reaction in *Journal of Charlotte Forten,* p. 203.

60. James Miller McKim, "Negro Songs," in Katz, ed., *Social Implications of Early Negro Music,* p. 2. See also Alvan Sanborn, ed., *Reminiscences of Richard Lathers* (New York, 1907), p. 5; Trollope, *Domestic Manners of the Americans,* p. 299.

61. J. Kennard, quoted in Southern, *Music of Black Americans,* p. 103.

62. T. S. Eliot, "The Metaphysical Poets," *Selected Essays* (London, 1936), pp. 286–287.

63. Alexander K. Farrar to W. B. Foules, Dec. 6, 1857, in the Farrar Papers.

64. See the stimulating discussion by Weber, *Sociology of Religion,* pp. 106–108.

65. E. P. Thompson, *Making of the English Working Class,* p. 34.

66. Yetman, ed., *Life Under the "Peculiar Institution,"* p. 232.

67. Broidrick, "A Recollection of Thirty Years Ago" (ms.); cf. Hatcher, *John Jasper,* p. 177.

68. Rawick, ed., *S.C. Narr.,* II (1), 53–54.

69. Kemble, *Journal,* p. 22.

70. Higginson, *Army Life,* p. 27; Rawick, ed., *S.C. Narr.,* III (4), 159; Botkin, ed., *Lay My Burden Down,* pp. 16 ff.; Fisk University, *Unwritten History of Slavery,* p. 112; E. F. Andrews, *War-Time Journal of a Georgia Girl,* (July 21, 1865), p. 339; C. C. Jones, *Religious Instruction,* p. 26. For an alternative interpretation of Jesus, as well as of the other theological questions discussed in this section, see James H. Cone, *The Spirituals and the Blues* (New York, 1972).

71. Rawick, ed., *S.C. Narr.,* II (1), 151.

72. *Ibid.,* II (1), 91, also p. 151.

73. See the analysis of Levine, "Slave Songs and Slave Consciousness," p. 121; see also Fisher, *Negro Slave Songs,* for a different interpretation that is nonetheless compatible with Levine's.

74. Lester, *To Be a Slave,* p. 79. As Powdermaker says, the slaves, deprived of

their African history, seized the biblical history of the Jews and made it their own; *After Freedom*, pp. 231–232.

75. Weber, *Sociology of Religion*, p. 185.
76. G. G. Coulton, *Ten Medieval Studies* (Cambridge, 1930), pp. 190–191.
77. See Paul Radin's introduction to Fisk University, *God Struck Me Dead*, p. viii.
78. Fisk University, *God Struck Me Dead*, p. 61.

THE BLACK PREACHERS

1. The most useful sources for this sketch have been: For ex-slave and related black accounts: Rawick's edition of the slave narratives—all volumes; Yetman, ed., *Life Under the "Peculiar Institution,"* pp. 36, 141, 147, 157; Saxon *et al.*, *Gumbo Ya-Ya*, p. 245; *Narrative of William Wells Brown*, p. 36; H. C. Bruce, *New Man*, p. 72; WPA, *Drums and Shadows*, p. 60. Also Howard Thurman, *Deep River: Reflections on the Religious Insight of Certain of the Negro Spirituals* (New York, 1955); T. C. Schilling, "Sketch of Thomas Landell," Dec. 16, 1941, unpubl., in Louisiana, Historical Records Survey: Church Archives (West Feliciana Parish, Conveyance Records of St. Paul #2 Baptist Church, Black); James Weldon Johnson, *God's Trombones: Seven Negro Sermons in Verse* (New York, 1927), Preface; Grace Sims Holt, "Stylin' Outta the Black Pulpit," in Thomas Kochman, ed., *Rappin' and' Stylin' Out* (Urbana, Ill., 1972), pp. 189–195; Elkin T. Sithole, "Black Folk Music," in *ibid.*, pp. 65–82; and W. E. B. Du Bois's indispensable *Souls of Black Folk*.

Among the more informative travelers' accounts: Lyell, *Second Visit*, II, 14, 213–214; Bremer, *Homes of the New World*, I, 352, 354, 376; II, 157–158; Olmsted, *Back Country*, p. 110, and *Seaboard*, pp. 408, 451. Also Wrightman, *Life of William Capers*, pp. 124 ff. (Capers's account of Henry Evans); Parkinson, "Religious Instruction of Slaves," unpubl. M.A. thesis, University of North Carolina, 1948; O. W. Taylor, *Negro Slavery in Arkansas*, pp. 180–181; J. S. Bassett, *Slavery in the State of North Carolina*, Ch. 3; J. G. Taylor, *Negro Slavery in Louisiana*, pp. 136, 146; Rawick, *Sundown to Sunup*, pp. 38, 84–85; Hatcher, *John Jasper*; Southern, *Music of Black Americans*, pp. 134, 145; C. S. Davis, *Cotton Kingdom in Alabama*, p. 89; Berlin, "Slaves Who Were Free," unpubl. Ph.D. dissertation, University of Wisconsin, 1970, p. 131; Frazier, "Negro Slave Family," *JNH*, XV (April, 1930), 249; Margaret Burr DesChamps, "John Chavis as a Preacher to Whites," *NCHR*, XXXII (April, 1955), 165–172; and Robert Cruden, *The Negro in Reconstruction*. (New York, 1969). See also two of the essays in Katz, ed., *Social Implications of Early Negro Music:* John Mason Brown's "Songs of the Slave" and Henry Cleveland Wood's "Negro Camp Meeting Melodies." Also "Letters Showing the Rise and Progress of the Early Negro Churches of Georgia and the West Indies," *JNH*, I (Jan. 1916), 69–92.

2. Aptheker, *Slave Revolts, passim*; J. H. Johnston, *Race Relations and Miscegenation*, pp. 40, 134–139; also John W. Cromwell, "Aftermath of Nat Turner's Insurrection," *JNH*, V (April, 1920), 208–234.

3. J. B. Sellers, *Slavery in Alabama*, p. 232.

4. Quoted by Christoper Hill, *The Century of Revolution, 1603–1714* (New York, 1966), p. 83. Colonel Leath, superintendent of the Memphis school system in 1870, apparently agreed. He forbade the use of prayers and of the Bible in black schools. See A. L. Robinson, "In the Aftermath of Slavery," unpubl. undergraduate thesis, Yale University, 1969, p. 227.

5. See, e.g., "Eighteenth Century Slaves as Advertised by Their Masters," *JNH*, I (April, 1916), 202–205.

6. Olmsted, *Seaboard*, p. 568.

7. Olmsted, *Back Country*, pp. 92 ff., 186–187.

8. Hairston Diary, Dec. 8, 1845.

9. Bondurant Reminiscences, p. 57.

10. C. C. Jones, *Religious Instruction*, esp. pp. 58, 158, 175–177; also, C. C. Jones, *Suggestions*, esp. p. 18; similarly, the remarks of Fredrika Bremer, *Homes of the New World*, II, 156.

11. See D. E. Huger Smith, "A Plantation Boyhood," in A. R. Huger Smith, *Carolina Rice Plantation of the Fifties*, p. 75; Hill Diary, Aug. 8, 1846; Eleanor J. W. Baker Journal, p. 14; William G. Proctor, "Slavery in Southwest Georgia," *GHQ*, XLI (March, 1965), 10; Martha Boman, "A City of the Old South: Jackson, Mississippi," *JMH*, XV (April, 1953), 1–32.

12. Ross, *Cities and Camps*, p. 83.

13. Rawick, ed., *Ala. Narr.*, VI (1), 383, 299–305; *Okla. Narr.*, VII (1), 303–304; *Texas Narr.*, IV (1), 2; V (3), 119, 219; V (4), 16; Fisk University, *God Struck Me Dead*, p. 6; B. F. Riley, *Baptists in Alabama*, pp. 80, 186–187.

14. Yetman, ed., *Life Under the "Peculiar Institution,"* p. 95.

15. WPA, *Negro in Virginia*, p. 77.

16. Rawick, ed., *S.C. Narr.*, III (3), 180–181; *Miss. Narr.*, VII (2), 58; *Ala. Narr.*, VI (1), 52.

17. Rawick, ed., *S.C. Narr.*, II (2), 128; *Texas Narr.*, V (3), 184; also *S.C. Narr.*, II (1), 246, 345.

18. Courlander, *Negro Folk Music*, p. 156; Saxon *et al.*, *Gumbo Ya-Ya*, p. 67.

19. Posey, *Baptist Church in the Lower Mississippi Valley*, pp. 20–21. The morals of the white clergy came into question early and in the sedate churches as well; see, e.g., Catterall, ed., *Judicial Cases*, I, 91, for an entertaining scandal in Virginia in 1771.

20. Simmel, *Sociology of Religion*, pp. 31–32.

21. Botkin, ed., *Lay My Burden Down*, p. 118; also Fisk University, *Unwritten History of Slavery*, p. 94.

22. See, e.g., Wiley, *Southern Negroes*, p. 107.

23. Fisk University, *Unwritten History of Slavery*, p. 2.

24. Hiram R. Revels Autobiography, p. 5, in the Woodson Papers. See also Wharton, *Negro in Mississippi*, p. 160.

25. Mitchell, *Black Preaching*, p. 134; also Rawick, ed., *Texas Narr.*, V (4), 186.

26. Rawick, ed., *Texas Narr.*, IV (2), 9; also *Ohio Narr.*, XVI, 89; *Va. Narr.*, XVI, 12; *Fla. Narr.*, XVII, 214.

27. Rawick, ed., *Indiana Narr.*, VI (2), 56.

28. Yetman, ed., *Life Under the "Peculiar Institution,"* p. 337; also Fisk University, *Unwritten History of Slavery*, p. 106.

29. Lyell, *Second Visit*, II, 213–214.

30. *Ibid.* p. 14.

31. Toulmin, *Western Country in 1793*, p. 30; Rawick, ed., *Texas Narr.*, IV (2), 44; Earnest, *Religious Development of the Negro in Virginia*, p. 104, n. 2.

32. WPA, *Negro in Virginia*, p. 247.

33. R. Ingraham to Susan Fisher, Jan. 5, 1840, in the Fisher Papers.

34. Bremer, *Homes of the New World*, I, 290.

35. Quoted in King, *South Carolina Baptists*, p. 126.

36. J. G. Williams, *"De Ole Plantation,"* pp. 2, 11. See also Swint, ed., *Dear Ones at Home*, p. 126, for a black minister's attack on "lily-white corruption" when ostensibly retelling familiar Bible stories.

37. Powdermaker, *After Freedom*, p. 245.

38. Bremer, *Homes of the New World*, II, 159.

39. On the language of the preachers in general see Bruce A. Rosenberg, *The Art of the American Folk Preacher* (New York, 1970), esp. pp. 7, 47, and 51; LeRoi Jones, *Blues People*, pp. 45–46; and Mike Thelwell, "William Styron and the Rev. Mr. Turner," in John Henrik Clarke, ed., *William Styron's Nat Turner: Ten Black Writers Respond* (Boston, 1968), pp. 75–76; and esp. Mitchell, *Black Preaching*. See also the references to the section, "The Language of Class and Nation," pages 754–755 below

40. Bassett, ed., *Southern Plantation Overseer*, p. 13, expressed this view after a detailed study of overseers' correspondence, the reading of which will bear him out..

41. Chesnut, *Diary from Dixie*, pp. 148–149. See also Marsh Scuddeo to Chat W. Scuddeo, Dec. 20, 1846; Anne S. Fishburne, *Belvidere: A Plantation Memory* (Columbia, S.C., 1949), pp. 25–26.

42. Rosenberg, *Art of the American Folk Preacher*, esp. pp. 10, 14, 17, 40, 47, 115–116; Mitchell, *Black Preaching, passim*; also Levine, "Slave Songs and Slave Consciousness," in Hareven, ed., *Anonymous Americans*, p. 106; LeRoi Jones, *Blues People*, pp. 45–46. On the African origins of the call-and-response style see J. W. Johnson, *Book of American Negro Spirituals*, pp. 23–25; Henry Edward Krehbiel, *Afro-American Folksongs: A Study in Racial and National Music* (4th ed.; New York, 1914), pp. 13, 22, 56 ff., 100.

   The repeated reference in the antebellum sources to grunts, groans, and the like raises an interesting question. George Shepperson, on hearing an early version of this chapter, asked if there was any evidence of speaking in tongues. I had to answer that I did not know. It is not at all impossible that observers like Olmsted heard precisely that. Consider his description of a black preacher's funeral sermon: "His manner was earnest, and the tone of his voice solemn and impressive, except that, occasionally, it would break into a shout or kind of howl at the close of a long sentence" (*Seaboard*, p. 25). In the urban cults of the northern ghettos, speaking in tongues has often been required or encouraged, and the link between certain features of the slave experience and twentieth-century black religion, especially Pentecostal, remains to be studied; see Fauset, *Black Gods of the Metropolis*, pp. 20, 69.

43. Henry E. Simmons to Anna Simmons, June 6, 1863.

44. For an account of some of the antics of the white Baptist preachers see Posey, *Baptist Church in the Lower Mississippi Valley*, p. 27.

45. WPA, *Negro in Virginia*, pp. 250–251; also Hatcher, *John Jasper*, pp. 453, 463. See the handsome tribute to Jasper in Francis Pendleton Gaines, *Southern Oratory: A Study in Idealism* (University, Ala., 1946), pp. 9–10.

46. Bremer, *Homes of the New World*, I, 490–491.

47. Olmsted, *Back Country*, pp. 188–190; J. G. Williams, *"De Ole Plantation,"* p. 1; Lyell, *Second Visit*, I, 245.

48. Charles Keil, *Urban Blues* (Chicago, 1966), p. 166. See the parallel drawn by the Rev. Henry H. Mitchell between the work of the preacher and that of the jazz musician; *Black Preaching*, pp. 198–199.

49. My understanding of the prophetic tradition, as developed below, owes most to the great work of Max Weber. In particular, see his *Sociology of Religion*, esp. Ch. 4, and *Ancient Judaism* (trans. H. H. Gerth and D. Martindale; Glencoe, Ill., 1952); esp. Ch. 11. A number of Weber's ideas have been developed and clarified by his followers and critics. Especially useful are Talcott Parson's introduction to *The Sociology of Religion*; Freund, *Sociology of Max Weber*, esp. pp. 195–196; and Arthur Mitzman, *The Iron Cage: An Historical*

Interpretation of Max Weber (New York, 1969), esp. pp. 189–221. Also of special value are the discussions in Worsley, *Trumpet Shall Sound*; Lanternari, *Religions of the Oppressed*; and Norbeck, *Religion in Primitive Society*. While respectfully dissenting, I have learned much from Eric Voegelin's great work, *Order and History*, (3 vols., more coming; Baton Rouge, La., 1956–), esp. Vol. I, *Israel and Revelation*.

50. Even in Haiti's great revolution millennialist and messianic prophecy played only a fleeting role. See Métraux, *Voodoo in Haiti*, p. 46.

51. Botume, *First Days Amongst the Contrabands*, pp. 109, 174.

52. The following discussion has been much influenced—up to a point—by Norman Cohn's "Medieval Millenarism: Its Bearing on the Contemporary Study of Millenarian Movements," in Sylvia Thrupp, ed., *Millennial Dreams in Action: Studies in Revolutionary Religious Movements* (New York, 1970), pp. 31–43; also Norman R. Cohn, *Pursuit of the Millennium* (London, 1957).

53. Cohn, "Medieval Millenarism," p. 31.

54. Eric Wolf, *Peasant Wars of the Twentieth Century* (New York, 1969), p. 177; Worsley, *Trumpet Shall Sound*, pp. 227–228.

55. See esp. Worsley, *Trumpet Shall Sound*, p. 225.

56. See Joseph Needham, *Time and Eastern Man* (Glasgow, 1965), pp. 47–49. The categories that Needham invokes are drawn from the work of Paul Tillich. Mbiti writes: "In the strict biblical sense of *prophets* and the prophetic movement, there are no prophets in African traditional societies, as far as I know" (*African Religions and Philosophy*, p. 190). On reincarnation see Idowu, *Olódùmarè*, pp. 190 ff..

57. Some ramifications of this conjuncture are suggestively explored in David F. Aberle, "A Note on Relative Deprivation Theory as Applied to Millenarian and Other Cult Movements," in Thrupp, ed., *Millennial Dreams in Action*, pp. 209–214. Also N. A. Mashkin, "Eschatology and Messianism in the Final Period of the Roman Republic," *Philosophy and Phenomenological Research*, X (Dec., 1949), 206–228.

58. Friedrich Engels, *The Peasant War in Germany* (New York, 1932), pp. 74–75.

59. Worsley, *Trumpet Shall Sound*, esp. pp. 73, 92. For an excellent discussion of postmillennial accommodationism see George Shepperson, "The Comparative Study of Millennial Movements," in Thrupp, ed., *Millennial Dreams in Action*, pp. 44–52, esp. 44–45. Shepperson points out that, strictly speaking, the millennium is not the perfect state but the thousand-year transition to it. I do not think that this qualification affects the argument I am making here.

60. Few "prophetesses" appeared among the slaves, although they abounded among other peoples in millennialist movements and have also appeared in the cults of the northern black ghettos.

61. Mitchell, *Black Preaching*, p. 30; Cleage, *Black Messiah*, p. 5.

RELIGIOUS FOUNDATIONS OF THE BLACK NATION

1 C. Eric Lincoln, *The Black Muslims in America* (Boston, 1961), p. 54.

2. Du Bois, *Gift of Black Folk*, esp. pp. 178, 188.

3. Rawick, ed., *S.C. Narr.*, III (4), 172.

4. Washington Wills to Richard Wills.

5. Leigh, *Ten Years*, p. 78.

6. H. H. Mitchell, *Black Preaching*, p. 203.

BOOK TWO, PART 2

TIME AND WORK RHYTHMS

1. Rawick, ed., *Texas Narr.*, V (4), 54.
2. Johann David Schoepf, *Travels in the Confederation, 1783–1784* (2 vols.; trans. A. J. Morrison; Philadelphia, 1911), II, 118. The Bagby quotation is from Bancroft, *Slave Trading*, p. 88.
3. Troeltsch, *Social Teaching of the Christian Churches*, I, 321.
4. *Ibid.*, II, 611, 808–809; also II, 554, 609. James L. Peacock suggests that Calvinism in the South has substituted fundamentalist attacks on certain social taboos for a worldy asceticism translatable into a bourgeois work ethic. This line of criticism deserves further investigation. See "The Southern Protestant Ethic Disease," in Morland, ed., *The Not So Solid South*, p. 109.
5. This discussion has drawn on the perceptive analyses of Christopher Hill, *Century of Revolution*, pp. 84–58; Rawick, *Sundown to Sunup*, pp. 128–129; and Michel Foucault, *Madness and Civilization: A History of Insanity in the Age of Reason* (trans. R. Howard; New York, 1965).
6. See esp. Weber, *Sociology of Religion*, pp. 169, 177. Alternatives to this Western tradition do exist; see, e.g., Robert N. Bellah, *Tokugawa Religion: The Values of Pre-industrial Japan* (Glencoe, Ill., 1957), for the Japanese case.
7. Fisk University, *God Struck Me Dead*, p. 7.
8. H. H. Mitchell, *Black Preaching*, pp. 107, 113; also p. 130.
9. Mbiti, *African Religions and Philosophy*, pp. 5, 17, 19; *New Testament Eschatology in an African Background*, Ch. 2.
10. Ojo, *Yoruba Culture*, p. 201.
11. See esp. Henri Mendras, *The Vanishing Peasant: Innovation and Change in French Agriculture* (trans. J. Lerner; Cambridge, Mass., 1970), pp. 55–56.
12. *Ibid.*, p. 62. The interesting discussion in Mullin, *Flight and Rebellion*, pp. 42–45, suffers from a failure to relate African time-reckoning to preindustrial European. As Eileen Power notes, Charlemagne named the months of the year precisely according to seasonal work rhythms; in her rendering from the Frankish: Winter, Mud, Spring, Easter, Joy, Plow, Hay, Harvest, Wind, Vintage, Autumn, and Holy Month (*Medieval People*, p. 27). See also Homans, *English Villagers*, esp. Ch. 23. The months as named by Charlemagne strikingly parallel the months designated by Africans; see Eva L. R. Meyerowitz, *The Sacred State of the Akan* (London, 1951), pp. 142–143; Mbiti, *African Religions and Philosophy*, p. 21. Even today, clock sensitivity varies enormously according to class and ethnicity in the United States; see Gay Gaer Luce, *Body Time: Physiological Rhythms and Social Stress* (New York, 1972), p. 13.
13. E. P. Thompson, "Time, Work Discipline and Industrial Capitalism," *Past and Present*, No. 38 (Dec., 1967), p. 60.
14. Hobsbawm, *Industry and Empire*, p. 67.
15. E. P. Thompson, "Time, Work Discipline and Industrial Capitalism," pp. 90–91.
16. *Ibid.*, p. 86; Elwin H. Powell, *Design of Discord, Studies of Anomie: Suicide, Urban*

Society, *War* (New York, 1970), p. 8; Karl Marx, *The Grundrisse* (ed. and trans. David McLellan; New York, 1971), p. 148.

17. "We didn't own no clocks in dem days. We just told de time by de sun in de day and de stars at night. If it was clouded we didn't know what time it was" (Jane Simpson, ex-slave, in Yetman, ed., *Life Under the "Peculiar Institution,"* p. 279); also Fisk University, *Unwritten History of Slavery*, p. 146.

18. John Horton, "Time and Cool People," in Lee Rainwater, ed., *Soul* (Chicago, 1970), pp. 31–50; Rawick, ed., *Texas Narr.*, IV (4), 57. See also the exasperated remarks of Harrod C. Anderson, a planter, Diary, Nov. 16, 1855.

19. *Life and Times of Frederick Douglass*, p. 27. For other black complaints see WPA, *Negro in Virginia*, pp. 29 ff., and Lester, *To Be a Slave*, p. 30.

20. See, e.g., the careful account kept by the overseer on a sugar estate in Louisiana: Seale Diary, 1857.

21. Printed slave list for 1856 in the Haywood Papers; Bruce Papers, box II, folder 1855; Macrery Papers, 1847; Negro Collection of Duke University (certificates of freedom for New York, from 1799).

22. Barnsley Diary, Jan. 9, 1860.

23. Luce, *Body Time*, p. 114.

24. Quoted in H. H. Mitchell, *Black Preaching*, p. 131.

A "LAZY" PEOPLE

1. Greene, ed., *Diary of Col. Landon Carter*; see Greene's introduction, I, 21–22, and the diary itself, I, 483 and *passim*.

2. *Ibid.*, II, 625.

3. Olmsted, *Back Country*, pp. 228–229.

4. Lewis H. Blair wrote in 1889: "Like a malignant cancer which poisons the whole system, this degradation [of the Negro] seems to intensify all the other drawbacks under which we labor." In *A Southern Prophecy: The Prosperity of the South Dependent upon the Elevation of the Negro* (ed. C. Vann Woodward; Boston, 1964), p. 26.

5. See, e.g., T. R. Dew, in E. N. Elliott, ed., *Cotton Is King and Pro-slavery Arguments*, p. 364; Hundley, *Social Relations in Our Southern States*, p. 262; S. Andrews, *South Since the War*, pp. 177, 183. See also Starobin, *Industrial Slavery in the Old South*, and Genovese, *Political Economy of Slavery*, Chs. 8–9.

6. Macrae quoted in WPA, *Negro in Virginia*, p. 224; LeConte, *When the World Ended*, p. 24.

7. Rawick, ed., *S.C. Narr.*, II (1), 22. The aristocratic Mrs. Chesnut apparently agreed: see *Diary from Dixie*, p. 505. Also C. Vann Woodward, *American Counterpoint: Slavery and Racism in the North-South Dialogue* (Boston, 1971), p. 35.

8. See esp. E. P. Thompson, *Making of the English Working Class*, p. 277.

9. Ingraham, *South-West*, II, 124. Also Hepworth, *Whip, Hoe, and Sword*, pp. 49–50.

10. Kemble, *Journal*, p. 94. See also E. F. Andrews, *War-Time Journal of a Georgia Girl*, p. 340.

11. See Cruden, *Negro in Reconstruction*.

12. Martineau, *Society in America*, II, 45.

13. Smedes, *A Southern Planter*, p. 44. For a parallel northern view see the remarks of a New England tutor on a Virginia plantation in 1837: Gara, ed., "New Englander's View of Plantation Life," *JSH*, XVIII (Aug., 1952), 342–354.

14. Greene, ed., *Diary of Col. Landon Carter*, II, 733, 755; also II, 834.

15. Quoted in C. C. Jones, *Religious Instruction*, p. 144.
16. Daniel Dennett, *PB*, XIV (Jan. 11, 1849), editorial.
17. Quoted by Eaton, *Growth of Southern Civilization*, p. 14.
18. See Sarah W. Graves to Iverson L. Graves, Jan. 30, 1849; E. G. Baker Diary, March 31, 1850; A. H. Arrington to Kate Arrington, Jan. 30, 1857; R. R. Barrow Residence Journal, Aug. 28, 1857; Lyell, *Second Visit*, II, 84; J. J. Ampère, *Promenade en Amérique: L'États-Unis, Cuba, Mexique* (2 vols.; Paris, 1860), II, 114; Abdy, *Journal of Residence and Tour*, II, 214.
19. *Southern Watchman*, May 31, 1865, as quoted in E. Merton Coulter, "Slavery and Freedom: Athens, Georgia, 1860–1866," *GHQ*, XLIX (Sept., 1965), 287.
20. Leigh, *Ten Years*, p. 25.
21. *Ibid.*, pp. 26, 54.
22. *Ibid.*, pp. 79, 156, 192, 202.
24. Higginson, *Army Life*, p. 14.
25. D. E. Huger Smith, "A Plantation Boyhood," in A. R. Huger Smith, *Carolina Rice Plantation of the Fifties*, p. 69.
26. Durham and Jones, *Negro Cowboys*, p. 30.
27. Chesnut, *Diary from Dixie*, pp. 199–200.
28. Schoolcraft, *Plantation Life*, p. 49.
29. For a useful introduction to this subject see W. T. Jordan, *Ante-bellum Alabama*, pp. 84–96.
30. *ACP*, II (March 1854), 76; original emphasis.
31. Martineau, *Society in America*, II, 297.
32. Eaton, *Growth of Southern Civilization*, p. 83; also Du Bois, *Black Reconstruction*, pp. 38–39.
33. See the discussion by Paul W. Gates, *Agriculture and the Civil War*, p. 60.
34. Charles Pettigrew, *Last Advice of the Rev. Charles Pettigrew to His Sons*, copy of pamphlet in the Pettigrew Papers.
35. Rawick, ed., *Okla. Narr.*, VII (1), 80.
36. W. D. Jordan, *White over Black*; Rawick, *Sundown to Sunup*, esp. p. 132.
37. Rawick, ed., *S.C. Narr.*, II (2), 266; also the testimony of Charles Watson in III (4), 188.
38. Harper in E. N. Elliott, ed., *Cotton Is King and Pro-slavery Arguments*, p. 95. On the view of Africa see Genovese, *Political Economy of Slavery*, Ch. 3, and "A Georgia Slaveholder Looks at Africa," *GHQ*, LI (June, 1967), 186–193.
39. Rawick, ed., *S.C. Narr.*, II (1), 251 (Charlie Davis); III (4), 8 (Sam Rawls); III (3), 43 (James Johnson); III (3), 50 (Jane Johnson); III (3), 57 (Mary Johnson); III (3), 276 (Sam Polite); *Miss. Narr.*, VII (2), 69 (Fanny Smith Hodges).
40. W. Arthur Lewis, *The Theory of Economic Growth* (Homewood, Ill., 1955), p. 107.
41. Kemble, *Journal*, p. 120.
42. Odum and Johnson, *Negro and His Songs*, p. 255.
43. Quoted by Doyle, *Etiquette of Race Relations*, p. 72.
44. Yetman, ed., *Life Under the "Peculiar Institution,"* p. 74.
45. Martineau, *Society in America*, I, 274.
46. Quoted by Litwack, "Free at Last," in Hareven, ed., *Anonymous Americans*, p. 153.
47. Rose, *Rehearsal for Reconstruction*, pp. 110, 123.
48. Northup, *Twelve Years a Slave*, p. 98. See also Rawick, ed., *S.C. Narr.*, II (1), 10–11, 15; III (3), 5; H. C. Bruce, *New Man*, p. 41.
49. Rawick, ed., *S.C. Narr.*, III (3), 38 (Adeline Johnson); pp. 274–275 (Sam Polite).
50. Rawick, ed., *Texas Narr.*, Vols. IV and V, *passim*; also Fernando Henrique Cardoso, *Capitalismo e escravidão no Brasil meridional* (São Paulo, 1962), pp. 119–132.

51. Rawick, ed., *Texas Narr.*, IV (1), 16.
52. *Ibid.*, IV (2), 84 (Austin Grant); also IV (1), 35 (Sarah Ashley); IV (1), 237 (Eli Coleman).
53. Smedes, *Southern Planter*, p. 31; Anderson Papers Diary, July 19, 1858. Southern periodicals often discussed the need for good treatment specifically as an inducement to good work; see, e.g., *SP*, III (Sept., 1843), 205–206.
54. As quoted in *Plantation and Farm Instruction, Regulation, Record, Inventory, and Account Book*, printed by J. W. Randolph of Richmond, Va., during the 1850s and circulated widely. These books may be found in various collection of plantation papers; see, e.g., Marshall Account Book.
55. Samuel A. Cartwright, *Ethnology of the Negro or Prognathous Race* (New Orleans, 1857), p. 11.

THE BLACK WORK ETHIC

1. Du Bois, *Gift of Black Folk*, pp. 14, 29.
2. *Ibid.*, p. 30.
3. Santayana, *Life of Reason*, Vol. II, *Reason in Religion*, p. 132.
4. For a brief discussion and references to the literature see my *Political Economy of Slavery*, Ch. 3. Also Mendras, *Vanishing Peasant*, p. 69. The Africans might well have agreed with the French peasants that a brave man *(courageux)* is by definition a hard worker. See also the interesting comparison of the Irish and Africans in Abraham, *Mind of Africa*, pp. 98–99.
5. See Menéndez Pidal, *Spaniards in Their History*, p. 21.
6. Olmsted, *Back Country*, p. 81.
7. *Ibid.*, p. 106; Frederick Law Olmsted, *Journey Through Texas: Or, A Saddle Trip on the Southwestern Frontier* (New York, 1969 [1859]), p. 33; Dennett, *South as It Is*, p. 114. See André Hodeir, *Jazz: Its Evolution and Essence* (trans. D. Noakes; New York, 1961), p. 240, for a description of the structure of jazz that parallels these facets of the work ethic.
8. See, e.g., Allan H. Spear, *Black Chicago: The Making of the Negro Ghetto, 1890–1920* (Chicago, 1967), p. 156.
9. Yetman, ed., *Life Under the "Peculiar Institution,"* p. 10.
10. Rawick, ed., *Ala. Narr.*, VI (1), 347.
11. Colin Clark and Margaret Haswell, *The Economics of Subsistence Agriculture* (4th ed.; London, 1970), pp. 139–141.
12. See esp. Rose, *Rehearsal for Reconstruction*, and Bleser, *Promised Land;* also S. Andrews, *South Since the War*, pp. 97–98, 206, 221–222, 339; *Journal of Charlotte Forten*, p. 178.
13. See the account of Clara Brim of Louisiana in Rawick, ed., *Texas Narr.*, IV (1), 148.
14. Northup, *Twelve Years a Slave*, p. 99.
15. For the historical growth of this practice in industry, as well as for a vigorous insistence that it strengthened rather than weakened the system of social control, see Starobin, *Industrial Slavery;* also S. Sydney Bradford, "The Negro Ironworker in Ante-bellum Virginia," in Meier and Rudwick, eds., *Making of Black America*, p. 142; Fletcher M. Green, "Gold Mining in Ante Bellum Virginia," *VMHR*, XLV (July, Oct., 1937), 227–235; 357–366.
16. E. A. Davis, ed., *Plantation Life in the Florida Parishes of Louisiana;* also on Barrow see Eaton, *Growth of Southern Civilization*, p. 61; Smedes, *Southern Planter*, p. 31; W. T. Jordan, *Hugh Davis*, pp. 105–107; Wall, "Founding of

Pettigrew Plantations," *NCHR*, XXVII (Oct., 1950), 409.

17. Frederick Marryat, *A Diary in America* (Paris, 1839), p. 186; Bonner, ed., "Plantation Experiences of a New York Woman," *NCHR*, XXXIII (July, 1956), 395; Phillips, *Life and Labor*, p. 283. In a typical performance for planters as a group, William Ethelbert Ervin of Lowndes County, Miss., paid thirty-five slaves $63.10 for work done during the Christmas holiday of 1846; Ervin Journal, Dec. 31, 1846, and entries for the subsequent years. See also Fisk University, *God Struck Me Dead*, p. 121.

18. The special conditions of the sugar harvest often required Sunday work and the postponement of the Christmas holiday until sometime in January. In such cases, slaves were generally compensated in time and presents.

19. *Rice v. Cade, et al.*, 1836, in Catterall, ed., *Judicial Cases*, III, 512.

20. Ellison, *Shadow and Act*, p. 27.

21. For a good discussion see Keil, *Urban Blues*, pp. 170–171.

22. The account of corn shucking draws most heavily on the following: Bremer, *Homes of the New World*, I, 370–371—note esp. her remarks on the songs as "histories" and her account of courtship patterns; Yetman, ed., *Life Under the "Peculiar Institution,"* pp. 62, 70, 267, 314; Fisk University, *Unwritten History of Slavery*, pp. 46, 50, 69, 148, 150. Relevant material in Rawick, ed., *American Slave*, may be found as follows: *S.C. Narr.*, II (1), 23; III (1), 283–284; III (4), 89–90; *Texas Narr.*, IV (1), 112, 118, 206, 260, 261; IV (2), 175; V (3), 119, 214, 266; V (4), 53, 104–105, 197–198; *Ala. Narr.*, VI (1), 49, 89, 193, 216, 280, 360, 412; *Okla. Narr.*, VII (1), 136, 230; *Ark. Narr.*, IX (3), 68, 291; *Ga. Narr.*, XII (1), 71, 99; XIII (4), 19. See also George Teamoh Journal, Pts. 1–2, pp. 14–15, in the Woodson Papers.

23. Rawick, ed., *Ala. Narr.*, VI (1), 89.

24. Rawick, ed., *Texas Narr.*, V (3), 214.

25. Yetman, ed., *Life Under the "Peculiar Institution,"* p. 267.

26. Fisk University, *Unwritten History of Slavery*, p. 50.

27. Bremer, *Homes of the New World*, I, 370. These huskings were rooted in English tradition and became major events among the white servants and black slaves of New England. See William Dawson Johnston, *Slavery in Rhode Island, 1775–1776* (Providence, R.I., 1894), p. 138.

28. For "Massa in the Great House" see Southern, *Music of Black Americans*, p. 181; for "Massa's Niggers Am Slick and Fat" see Doyle, *Etiquette of Race Relations*, pp. 22–23.

29. Wise, *End of an Era*, pp. 44–45; Rawick, ed., *Ala. Narr.*, VI (1), 193; also VI (1), 183; Smedes, *Southern Planter*, pp. 47, 126. See also C. S. Davis, *Cotton Kingdom in Alabama*, p. 67.

30. Rawick, ed., *Ala. Narr.*, VI (1), pp. 150–151. See also *Texas Narr.*, IV (1), 158; Fisk University, *Unwritten History of Slavery*, p. 4.

31. J. G. Taylor, *Negro Slavery in Louisiana*, p. 77. The Rice Coast of Georgia and South Carolina had a similar experience; see Heyward, *Seed from Madagascar*, p. 25. For Jamaica, see H. O. Patterson, *Sociology of Slavery*, p. 68.

32. See esp. Moody, *Slavery on Louisiana Sugar Plantations*, pp. 77–78; J. G. Taylor, *Negro Slavery in Louisiana*, pp. 77–78; Sitterson, *Sugar Country*, pp. 132–136; Ingraham, *South-West*, I, 240–241. For particularly useful sets of plantation papers see those of R. R. Barrow, Residence Journal, esp. Dec. 13, 1857; and Bond Diary, Dec., 1861, and Jan., 1862. For a striking English parallel see E. P. Thompson, "Time, Work Discipline and Industrial Capitalism," *Past and Present*, No. 38 (Dec., 1967), pp. 56–97. For similar conditions in the hemp region see Hopkins, *Hemp Industry in Kentucky*, pp. 61–63.

33. Rawick, ed., *Texas Narr.*, IV (1), 79; V (4), 65.

34. Rawick, ed., *Ala. Narr.*, VI (1), 151. For comments by South Carolina ex-slaves that suggest a holiday view of cotton picking see *S.C. Narr.*, III (3), 62; III (3), 115; III (4), 89–90; *Ga. Narr.*, XII (2), 6, 228, 348; XIII (3), 63, 100; Yetman, ed., *Life Under the "Peculiar Institution,"* pp. 62–63. For corroboration see the reviews of plantation records in J. G. Taylor, *Negro Slavery in Louisiana*, p. 66; C. S. Davis, *Cotton Kingdom in Alabama*, p. 64. But also see the opposite accounts in Sydnor, *Slavery in Mississippi*, pp. 103–104; J. B. Sellers, *Slavery in Alabama*, p. 267.

35. Virginia Clay-Clopton, *A Belle of the Fifties* (New York, 1905), p. 220; Kate Stone, *Brokenburn*, p. 4; *Private Journal of H. W. Ravenel*, p. 252; J. G. Taylor, *Negro Slavery in Louisiana*, p. 66; Rawick, ed., *Texas Narr.*, IV (2), 16; *Ala. Narr.*, VI (1), 151, 365.

36. William R. Bascom, "Acculturation Among the Gullah Negroes," *American Anthropologist*, LXIII (1941), 43–50. For a good general discussion see Rawick, *Sundown to Sunup*, pp. 17, 27–28.

37. Scarborough, ed., *Diary of Edmund Ruffin*, April 5, 1857 (I, 52); also Botume, *First Days Amongst the Contrabands*, p. 80; Higginson, *Army Life*, p. 250. See also the remarks of Mamadou Dia on African traditions of collective work: *Réflexions sur l'économie de l'Afrique noire* (Paris, 1961), p. 27.

38. Rawick. ed., *S.C. Narr.*, III (3), 152–153; II (1), 345; *Ark. Narr.*, X (5), 143; Martineau, *Society in America*, II, 157.

39. LeRoi Jones, *Blues People*, pp. 17–18, 41, 61, 67.

BOOK THREE, PART 1

LIFE IN THE BIG HOUSE

1. Broidrick, "Recollection of Thirty Years Ago," ms. pp. 3, 5; [John Stainback] Wilson, "The Negro—His Peculiarities as to Disease," *ACPSS*, III (July, 1859), 228–229; J. A. McKinstry to H. C. Nixon, Feb. 11, 1913, in Correspondence: Slavery, Tennessee State Library and Archives.

2. Winthrop D. Jordan, "American Chiaroscuro: The Status and Definition of Mulattoes in the British Colonies," *WMQ*, 3rd Ser., XIX (April, 1962), 186; also Jordan, *White over Black*, pp. 169, 178.

3. For evidence of a wide range of color in the selection of house servants see Olmsted, *Seaboard*, pp. 36, 421; Bremer, *Homes of the New World*, I, 280; Lyell, *Second Visit*, I, 208; Kate Stone, *Brokenburn*, pp. 8–9, 171; DuBose, "Recollections of the Plantation," *AHQ*, I (Spring, 1930), 71; Fisk University, *Unwritten History of Slavery*, p. 45.

4. Wade, *Slavery in the Cities*, esp. pp. 30 ff.; also Phillips, "Historical Notes of Milledgeville, Ga.," *Slave Economy of the Old South*, pp. 176–187.

5. For accounts of large house staffs on the plantations see J. B. Grimball Diary, May 7, 1857, Jan. 17, 1862; D. E. Huger Smith, "Plantation Boyhood," in A. R. Huger Smith, *Carolina Rice Plantation of the Fifties*, pp. 82, 91–92; E. F. Andrews, *War-Time Journal of a Georgia Girl*, p. 180; Rose, *Rehearsal for Reconstruction*, p. 126; Ingraham, *South-West*, I, 116; Eunice Dillon to Sarah Graves, March 26, 1835, in the Graves Papers. For a stark Russian contrast to the generally small American households see Kropotkin, *Memoirs of a Revolutionist*, p. 29.

6. See, e.g., Gowne Plantation Book in the Manigault Plantation Records;

Catherine Carson to W. S. Waller, Jan. 26, 1836, in the Small Collections: Carson Family Papers; Olmsted, *Back Country*, p. 47; G. M. Brown, "Biography of Mary Ann Colvin Mayfield," p. 47, in the Mayfield Papers.

7. *DBR*, XVIII (May, 1855), 573; also N. Adams, *South-Side View*, p. 29.

8. Olmsted, *Seaboard*, p. 28.

9. The origins of these caste distinctions are discussed in P. A. Bruce, *Social Life in Virginia in the Seventeenth Century*, pp. 170–171; W. D. Jordan, *White over Black*, p. 405; Phillips, *Life and Labor*, pp. 47 ff.

10. Charles C. Jones, Jr., to C. C. Jones, June 30, 1858, in Myers, ed., *Children of Pride*, p. 427.

11. Sydnor, *Slavery in Mississippi*, p. 3; Sitterson, *Sugar Country*, p. 91; Kemble, *Journal*, p. 153.

12. Yetman, ed., *Life Under the "Peculiar Institution,"* p. 60; Heyward, *Seed from Madagascar*, p. 74; Lyell, *Second Visit*, II, 20; Fisk University, *Unwritten History of Slavery*, p. 112.

13. Ingraham, *South-West*, II, 30; also Olmsted, *Seaboard*, p. 559; J. G. Williams, "*De Ole Plantation*," p. 12.

14. Rawick, ed., *S.C. Narr.*, II (1), 225.

15. In the Sea Islands, the field slaves did defer. See Botume, *First Days Amongst the Contrabands*, p. 132; Rose, *Rehearsal for Reconstruction*, p. 7; elsewhere, we find little evidence.

16. Pollard, *Black Diamonds*, p. 61.

17. Lynd, *On Shame and the Search for Identity*, p. 40.

18. Fisk University, *Unwritten History of Slavery*, p. 103; also Botkin, ed., *Lay My Burden Down*, p. 138; Rawick, ed., *Ala. Narr.*, VI (1), 329; *Miss. Narr.* VII (2), 158; *Fla. Narr.*, XVII, 356; Olmsted, *Seaboard*, p. 421; Smedes, *Southern Planter*, pp. 150–151. For Jamaican parallels see H. O. Patterson, *Sociology of Slavery*, pp. 58–63.

19. Bremer, *Homes of the New World*, I, 277, II, 435.

20. See, e.g., Saxon et al., *Gumbo Ya-Ya*, p. 429; E. A. Davis, ed., *Plantation Life in the Florida Parishes of Louisiana*, p. 106; Magruder Diary, July 6, 1855; Bethell Diary, June 22, 1862.

21. Bancroft, *Slave Trading*, pp. 228–229; also pp. 145, 154–155, 202, 323.

22. Stephenson, *Isaac Franklin*, p. 153; Bancroft, *Slave Trading*, p. 202.

23. Carmichael Diary, Oct. 14, 1837; Magruder Diary, Nov. 19, 1854; also Pettigrew Papers, item for Dec. 18, 1847; Elizabeth Allston Pringle, *Chronicles of Chicora Wood* (New York, 1922), p. 159.

24. Kemble, *Journal*, pp. 66–67; also Trollope, *Domestic Manners of the Americans*, p. 246.

25. WPA, *Negro in Virginia*, pp. 43, 156–157; Drew, *Refugee*, pp. 51, 259; Rawick, ed., *Texas Narr.*, IV (1), 37; Sitterson, "The McCollams," *JSH*, VI (Aug., 1940), 349–350.

26. For some samples of different situations see Louis B. Wright and Marion Tinling, eds., *The Great American Gentleman: William Byrd of Westover in Virginia. His Secret Diary for the Years 1709–1712* (New York, 1963), pp. 203, 210, 229. 244; Redpath, *Roving Editor*, p. 319; E. F. Andrews, *War-Time Journal of a Georgia Girl*, p. 292; Pringle, *Chicora Wood*, p. 83.

27. Steward, *Twenty-two Years a Slave*, p. 17; see also *Life and Times of Frederick Douglass*, p. 62; Weld, *Slavery as It Is*, p. 53; Olmsted, *Back Country*, p. 274. For some parallels see Marc Raeff, *Imperial Russia, 1682–1825: The Coming of Age of Modern Russia* (New York, 1971), p. 110; Blum, *Lord and Peasant in Russia*, p. 457 ff.

28. For a typical complaint see WPA, *Negro in Virginia*, p. 43.

29. Olmsted, *Seaboard*, pp. 195–196.

30. Cecilia, "Management of Servants," *SP*, III (Aug., 1843), 175.
31. Bonner, ed., "Plantation Experiences of a New York Woman," *NCHR*, XXXIII (July, 1956), 391; *PB*, XIV (Jan. 11, 1849), editorial; Charles Manigault, "Souvenirs of Our Ancestors and My Immediate Family," ms. p. 12; Chesnut, *Diary from Dixie*, Nov. 12, 1861 (p. 159), Feb. 26, 1865 (p. 488); also Lyell, *Second Visit*, II, 72. For an insight into the role of servants in shaping the prestige and status of their masters, see Thorstein Veblen, "Menial Servants During the Period of War," *Essays in Our Changing Order* (New York, 1934), p. 270.
32. Yetman, ed., *Life Under the "Peculiar Institution,"* pp. 312, 40. Kate Stone, *Brokenburn*, p. 9, comments on the hard work of the washerwomen.
33. Kemble, *Journal*, p. 223; Botkin, ed., *Lay My Burden Down*, p. 223; Yetman, ed., *Life Under the "Peculiar Institution,"* pp. 69, 268; Fisk University, *Unwritten History of Slavery*, pp. 93, 95, 101, 115; Fisk University, *God Struck Me Dead*, p. 185; Rawick, ed., *S.C. Narr.*, II (2), 91; III (4), 9; Steward, *Twenty-two Years a Slave*, pp. 18–19.
34. Sarah Hicks Williams to Mr. and Mrs. Samuel Hicks, Oct. 10, 1853, in the Williams Papers; also Martineau, *Society in America*, II, 309.
35. Sydnor, *Slavery in Mississippi*, p. 44.
36. See, e.g., Katherine Chatham, "Plantation Slavery in Middle Florida," unpubl. M.A. thesis, University of North Carolina, 1938, p. 76; for the complaint of an ex-slave see Rawick, ed., *Texas Narr.*, IV (1), 37.
37. See, e.g., Rawick, ed., *S.C. Narr.*, III (3), 73. For similar complaints from house slaves in the Caribbean and Brazil see Goveia, *Slave Society in the British Leeward Islands*, p. 141; Stein, *Vassouras*, p. 167.
38. Mrs. Hilliard Diary, June 9, 1850; Smedes, *Southern Planter*, p. 65; also Wright and Tinling, eds., *William Byrd: His Secret Diary*, pp. 90, 94.
39. Scarborough, ed., *Diary of Edmund Ruffin*, Feb. 19, 1860.
40. Yetman, ed., *Life Under the "Peculiar Institution,"* p. 167.
41. Kate Stone, *Brokenburn*, p. 9.
42. Rawick, ed., *S.C. Narr.*, III (4), 148.
43. WPA, *Negro in Virginia*, p. 82.
44. See, e.g., Drew, *Refugee*, p. 223; Magruder Diary, *passim*.
45. See, e.g., E. F. Andrews, *War-Time Journal of a Georgia Girl*, p. 346; see also Rawick, ed., *Texas Narr.*, IV (1), 115, 164, 223; V (4), 110; *Ark. Narr.*, IX (3), 318; X (6), 60, 174; *Ga. Narr.*, XII (1), 162, 320; XIII (4), 38; XIV (1), 279.
46. Rawick, ed., *Ala. Narr.*, VI (1), 169.
47. Rawick, ed., *Texas Narr.*, IV (2), 119; V (4), 219; *S.C. Narr.*, II (2), 195, 292; Fisk University, *God Struck Me Dead*, p. 198; Stirling Papers, Cotton Book for 1828; C. C. Jones to Charles C. Jones, Jr., Oct. 2, 1856, in Myers, ed., *Children of Pride*, p. 243.
48. Quoted in W. T. Jordan, *Hugh Davis*, p. 95; also Clay-Clopton, *Belle of the Fifties*, p. 4; Rawick, ed., *Ala. Narr.*, VI (1), 104; Fisk University, *Unwritten History of Slavery*, p. 135.
49. Steward, *Twenty-two Years a Slave*, p. 21.
50. For illustrations from white and black sources of frequent and intense field work by house slaves see Catterall, *Judicial Cases*, II, 561; Greene, ed., *Diary of Col. Landon Carter*, II, 683; Myers, ed., *Children of Pride*, p. 244; Olmsted, *Back Country*, p. 236; Magruder Diary, Aug. 26, 1847; LeBlanc Family Papers, 1862; Magnolia Plantation Journal, March 28, 1860, in the Warmoth Papers; Ashmore Plantation Book, Aug. 31, 1853; Lawton Plantation Diary, Jan. 10, 1817; Ralph B. Flanders, "Two Plantations and a County in Ante-bellum Georgia," *GHQ*, XII (March, 1928), 10; Swint, ed., *Dear Ones at Home*, p. 42;

Drew, *Refugee*, p. 130; Yetman, ed., *Life Under the "Peculiar Institution,"* p. 199; WPA, *Negro in Virginia*, p. 250; Fisk University, *Unwritten History of Slavery*, pp. 143, 170; *Narrative of William Wells Brown*, p. 12; Rawick, ed., *S.C. Narr.*, III (3), 185; IV (1), 267; *Texas Narr.*, IV (1), 267; *Indiana Narr.*, VI (2), 98, 111, 169; *Miss. Narr.*, VII (2), 26, 130; *Ark. Narr.*, IX (3), 127, 364; X (5), 209; X (6), 17.

51. Quoted by Scott, *Southern Lady*, p. 47. See also C. S. Davis, *Cotton Kingdom in Alabama*, p. 59; Yetman, ed., *Life Under the "Peculiar Institution,"* pp. 8, 140.

52. W. T. Jordan, *Hugh Davis*, p. 102. See also Kate Stone, *Brokenburn*, p. 33; Sitterson, "The McCollams," pp. 349–350.

53. Yetman, ed., *Life Under the "Peculiar Institution,"* pp. 133–134, 334; Drew, *Refugee*, p. 225.

54. Yetman, ed., *Life Under the "Peculiar Institution,"* p. 94; Rawick, ed., *S.C. Narr.*, III (4), 25.

55. Drew, *Refugee*, p. 177; Northup, *Twelve Years a Slave*, p. 120 and *passim*; Alexander K. Farrar to H. W. Dukes, Sept. 4–5, 1857, in the Farrar Papers.

56. Fisk University, *Unwritten History of Slavery*, p. 112; also Rawick, ed., *Ark. Narr.*, X (5), 35–36.

57. Rawick, ed., *Ala. Narr.*, VI (1), 220; WPA, *Negro in Virginia*, p. 157; Sydnor, *Slavery in Mississippi*, pp. 88–89; George Teamoh Journal, Pts. 1–2, pp. 11–12, in the Woodson Papers.

58. Constance McLaughlin Green, *The Secret City: A History of Race Relations in the Nation's Capital* (Princeton, N.J., 1967), p. 65.

59. For a suggestive discussion of some analogous structures in the colonial world, see Memmi, *Dominated Man*, p. 48.

60. Trollope, *Domestic Manners of the Americans*, p. 249.

61. Olmsted, *Seaboard*, p. 46.

62. Quoted in W. D. Jordan, *White over Black*, p. 388.

63. Quoted in Blum, *Lord and Peasant in Russia*, p. 459.

64. Wiley, *Southern Negroes*, p. 16; Du Bois, *Black Reconstruction*, p. 94. The northern espionage apparatus took full advantage of the situation and even placed house servants in the home of Jefferson Davis; see, e.g., K. M. Jones, ed., *Ladies of Richmond*, p. 118.

65. Chesnut, *Diary from Dixie*, p. 28. More generally see J. Williamson, *After Slavery*, p. 34.

66. There is a good brief discussion of this activity in Lester, *To Be a Slave*, pp. 91 ff.; also WPA, *Negro in Virginia*, pp. 145, 148, 173; Drew, *Refugee*, p. 167.

67. Yetman, ed., *Life Under the "Peculiar Institution,"* p. 222.

68. C. S. Johnson, *Shadow of the Plantation*, p. 21. Eventually, Red Ann forged a pass and fled to freedom.

69. Olmsted, *Seaboard*, p. 410.

70. Eleanor J. W. Baker Journal, 1848, p. 16.

71. Olmsted, *Seaboard*, p. 18.

72. For some specific illustrations see Rawick, ed., *Indiana Narr.*, VI (2), 138; Cornish Diary, Dec. 8, 1846; K. M. Jones, ed., *Ladies of Richmond*, pp. 95–96; Chesnut, *Diary from Dixie*, July 9, 1861 (p. 79).

73. *Father Henson's Story of His Own Life*, pp. 31–33; more generally, see J. G. Taylor, *Slavery in Louisiana*, p. 127.

74. Broidrick, "Recollection of Thirty Years Ago," ms. p. 5.

75. See Bateman Diary, 1856, esp. p. 25; Bayne Autobiographical Sketch, ms. p. 4; Rawick, ed., *Mo. Narr.*, XI, 244–245; Thomas Diary, Sept. 16, 1866; Chesnut, *Diary from Dixie*, pp. 295, 321.

76. Machado de Assis, *Dom Casmurro* (trans. Helen Caldwell; Berkeley, Calif., 1966), p. 112;

77. Federico García Lorca, *The House of Bernarda Alba* (New York, 1947).

78. Smedes, *Southern Planter*, p. 151.

79. Chesnut, *Diary from Dixie*, p. 482.

80. K. M. Jones, ed., *Ladies of Richmond*, p. 89.

81. As described and quoted by Linda Wolfe, *The Cooking of the Caribbean Islands* (New York, 1970), p. 92.

82. Mrs. Hilliard Diary, Jan. 20, 1850.

83. Heyward, *Seed from Madagascar*, p. 191.

84. Edward McGehee Burruss to Kate Burruss, Jan. 1, 1864, in the Lester Collection.

85. Fisk University, *Unwritten History of Slavery*, p. 7.

86. Mooney, *Slavery In Tennessee*, pp. 90–91; Walker Diary, April 8, 1856 (p. 23).

87. Quoted in Nuermberger, *Clays of Alabama*, p. 15.

88. E. G. Baker Diary, July 1, 1854 (I, 7–9); also, July 2, 1860 (II, 70–71).

89. Ruffin Thomson to his father, Nov. 6, 1862, Dec. 4, 1862. See also the will of A. H. Arrington, Aug. 24, 1859; *PB*, XIV (July 19, 1859), n.p.; J. B. Grimball Diary, April 21, 1858; for similar expressions for other house slaves see Bethell Diary, May 15, 1863, or the scattered remarks of Anna Matilda King in the Journal of the Thomas Butler King Papers.

90. Yetman, ed., *Life Under the "Peculiar Institution,"* pp. 134–135; Rawick, ed., *Okla. Narr.*, VII (1), 132; *Narrative of William Wells Brown*, p. 33; also Fisk University, *Unwritten History of Slavery*, pp. 67–68.

91. Yetman, ed., *Life Under the "Peculiar Institution,"* p. 162; see also p. 269, and Botkin, ed., *Lay My Burden Down*, p. 118, for similar expressions.

92. Rawick, ed., *S.C. Narr.*, II (1), 6; *Texas Narr.*, IV (1), 83; also IV (2), 61; Bremer, *Homes of The New World*, I, 374.

93. Steward, *Twenty-two Years a Slave*, p. 54; Kemble, *Journal*, p. 310; also Rawick, ed., *Ark. Narr.*, IX (4), 55; Bassett, *Southern Plantation Overseer*, p. 178.

94. Fisk University, *Unwritten History of Slavery*, p. 3.

95. See, e.g., Beatty Diary, May 30, 1864. For an interesting letter to a body servant from his master see W. H. Wills to Washington Wills, March 12, 1865.

96. Ross, *Cities and Camps*, p. 83; also K. M. Jones, ed., *Ladies of Richmond*, pp. 129–130; Featherstonhaugh, *Excursion Through the Slave States*, p. 46.

97. Mary Jones to Charles C. Jones, Oct. 9, 1856, in Myers, ed., *Children of Pride*, p. 248.

98. Quoted in Clement Eaton, *Henry Clay and the Art of American Politics* (Boston, 1957), pp. 64–65.

99. Amelia Thompson Watts, "A Summer on a Louisiana Cotton Plantation in 1832," in the Pharr Book, p. 96; see also WPA, *Negro in Virginia*, pp. 36, 39, 41.

100. Berlin, "Slaves Who Were Free," unpubl. Ph.D. dissertation, University of Wisconsin, 1970, p. 83; Greene, ed., *Diary of Col. Landon Carter*, Vol. II, for years 1776–1777; Mullin, *Flight and Rebellion*, p. 75.

101. Easterby, ed., *South Carolina Rice Plantation*, pp. 274, 281–294; also Yetman, ed., *Life Under the "Peculiar Institution,"* p. 69; Wiley, *Southern Negroes*, p. 143, n. 35.

102. Wiley, *Southern Negroes*, pp. 17, 136–137.

103. Higginson, *Army Life*, p. 57; Henderson is quoted to this effect in Doyle, *Etiquette of Race Relations*, pp. 131–132, as is Bruce in Melvin I. Urofsky, "Blanche K. Bruce: United States Senator, 1875–1881," *JMH*, XXIX (May, 1967), 129.

104. Blair, *Southern Prophecy*, p. 144.

105. Broidrick, "Recollection of Thirty Years Ago," ms. pp. 6–7.

106. Pollard, *Black Diamonds*, pp. 22-25, 92-94.
107. Yetman, ed., *Life Under the "Peculiar Institution,"* pp. 119-120, 262; Botkin, ed., *Lay My Burden Down*, p. 125; Rawick, ed., *Mo. Narr.*, XI, 303.
108. Rawick, ed., *S.C. Narr.*, III (3), 38-39.
109. For a useful review of Mammy's position and role see Jessie W. Parkhurst, "The Role of the Black Mammy in the Plantation Household," *JNH*, XXIII (July, 1938), 349-369. Parkhurst, however, draws different conclusions than the ones presented here.
110. Du Bois, *Gift of Black Folk*, pp. 188-189.
111. Olmstead, *Seaboard*, p. 556.
112. Dennett, *South as It Is*, p. 14; Rawick, ed., *S.C. Narr.*, III (4), 218.
113. Laura S. Tibbetts to Sophia Tibbetts, Jan. 23, 1853; similarly, M. O. Tayloe to B. O. Tayloe, Dec. 14, 1843.
114. M. Cain to Minerva R. Cain, April 14, 1833, in the Caldwell Papers.
115. Botkin, ed., *Lay My Burden Down*, p. 173.
116. Quoted in Parkhurst, "Role of the Black Mammy in the Plantation Household," p. 355.
117. Drew, *Refugee*, p. 156; Botkin, ed., *Lay My Burden Down*, p. 174.
118. *DBR*, V (Jan., 1858), 321; Kemble, *Journal*, pp. 28-29; Walker Diary, Feb. 17, 1856; Mrs. E. C. Hamilton to William Hamilton, May 31, 1860, in the Lester Collection. For critical views see C. C. Jones, *Religious Instruction*, p. 137; Pringle, *Chicora Wood*, p. 82.
119. Chesnut, *Diary from Dixie*, Feb. 16, 1865 (p. 478).
120. Pringle, *Chicora Wood*, p. 251.
121. E. F. Andrews, *War-Time Journal of a Georgia Girl*, pp. 293-294 n.; also p. 355.
122. Smedes, *Southern Planter*, pp. 16, 23, 38-39, 50, 271, 297. See also M. D. Cooper to William Cooper, Nov. 22, 1842.
123. Hotel and tavern servants will be left aside here, but they had a particularly bad reputation for insolence and aggressive behavior. See Sydnor, *Slavery in Mississippi*, p. 8; Ingraham, *South-West*, I, 183; L. W. Brown, *Free Negroes in the District of Columbia*, p. 130.
124. Olmsted, *Seaboard*, p. 195.
125. *Ibid.*, p. 194 n. See also Brackett, *Negro in Maryland*, p. 133; Rachel Weeks O'Connor to A. C. Conrad, May 26, 1836, in the Weeks Papers.
126. See, e.g., Manigault Plantation Record Book, March 22, 1867; Chesnut, *Diary from Dixie*, March 15, 1864 (p. 394); David L. Smiley, *Lion of Whitehall: The Life of Cassius M. Clay* (Madison, Wis., 1962), p. 71; Pugh Plantation Diary, Aug. 26, 1861.
127. Magruder Diary, July 26, 1857, and *passim* for 1854-1857.
128. Chesnut, *Diary from Dixie*, pp. 139-140, 145-152.
129. T. S. Eliot, "The Love Song of J. Alfred Prufrock," *The Complete Poems and Plays, 1909-1950* (New York, 1958), p. 6.

THE MEN BETWEEN

1. See, e.g., Magnolia Plantation Journal for 1856, in the Warmoth Papers; Orange Grove Plantation Diaries for 1849; Olmsted, *Back Country*, p. 47.
2. See Catterall, ed., *Judicial Cases*, II, 359; R. R. Barrow Residence Journal, Jan. 1. 1857; Nevitt Papers for 1827; William Edwards Clement, *Plantation Life on the Mississippi* (New Orleans, 1952), p. 179; Olmsted, *Seaboard*, p. 206; Wiley, *Southern Negroes*, pp. 50-51.

3. For evidence of black overseers and of drivers who virtually had the power of overseers in seventeenth-century Virginia, see P. A. Bruce, *Economic History of Virginia in the Seventeenth Century*, II, 18, n. 2; Catterall, ed., *Judicial Cases*, I, 78. For the Upper South during the nineteenth century, see Scarborough, *Overseer*, pp. 17–18; Scarborough, ed., *Diary of Edmund Ruffin*, I, 86–87; Rosser H. Taylor, *Slaveholding in North Carolina: An Economic View* (Chapel Hill, N.C., 1926), p. 83; WPA, *Negro in Virginia*, p. 64; Olmsted, *Seaboard*, p. 437. For the Lower South see [F. G. Ruffin], "Overseers," *SP*, XVI (May, 1856), 148; J. G. Taylor, *Negro Slavery in Louisiana*, pp. 80–81; Eron Rowland, *Varina Howell: Wife of Jefferson Davis* (New York, 1931), p. 275; N. Adams, *South-Side View* p. 97; Pon Pon Plantation Book, April 12, 1840, in the Elliott-Gonzales Papers; Gould Diary, Jan. 2, 1855; Martineau, *Society in America* I, 303; Coulter, *Thomas Spaulding of Sapelo*, pp. 85–86; Ralph B. Flanders, *Plantation Slavery in Georgia* (Chapel Hill, N.C., 1933), p. 143; W. T. Jordan, *Hugh Davis*, pp. 63–65; Rawick, ed., *S.C. Narr.*, II (1), 122–123; II (2), 88, 212; III (3), 274; III (4), 66, 117; *Texas Narr.*, V (3), 76, 184; V (4), 129; *Okla. Narr.*, VII (1), 77, 98, 124, 227; *Ark. Narr.*, IX (3), 139; *N.C. Narr.*, XIV (1), 3, 301.

4. See the white and black testimony in Drew, *Refugee*, pp. 139, 252–254; Yetman, ed., *Life Under the "Peculiar Institution,"* p. 196; Greene, ed., *Diary of Col. Landon Carter*, June 12, 1771 (I, 574); W. T. Jordan, *Hugh Davis*, p. 96; Leak Diary, Dec. 16, 1845; Ashmore Plantation Journal, p. 72; J. G. Taylor, *Negro Slavery in Louisiana*, p. 67; Katherine Polk Gale, "Recollections of Life in the Confederacy," ms. p. 7.

5. G. G. Johnson, *Social History of the Sea Islands*, p. 79; Rose, *Rehearsal for Reconstruction*, pp. 81, 133; Easterby, ed., *South Carolina Rice Plantation*, p. 151; Pearson, ed., *Letters from Port Royal*, pp. 37–38, n. 1. See also Rawick, ed., *S.C. Narr.*, II (1), 118–119; III (4), 46; *Texas Narr.*, IV (2), 151.

6. Lyell, *Second Visit*, II, 19.

7. Heyward, *Seed from Madagascar*, p. 113.

8. R. R. Barrow Residence Journal, April 21, 1855. See also the tribute to a dead driver from Rachel O'Connor, quoted in J. G. Taylor, *Negro Slavery in Louisiana*, p. 81.

9. Minor and Family Papers, item dated "Southdown, Sept. 21, 1862."

10. For cases of inheritance of jobs and of special selection at youthful ages see Olmsted, *Seaboard*, p. 436; Rawick, ed., *Texas Narr.*, V (3), 197, 204; *S.C. Narr.*, III (4), 61, 66.

11. For ages see Ulrich Bonnell Phillips and James Daniel Glunt, eds., *Florida Plantation Records from the Papers of George Noble Jones* (St. Louis, Mo., 1927), pp. 511, 566; Heyward, *Seed from Madagascar*, p. 113; Kelvin Grove Plantation Book, 1857; Coffin, *Boys of '61*, p. 449; Manigault Plantation Books, 1833–1861; D. E. Huger Smith, "Plantation Boyhood," in A. R. Huger Smith, *Carolina Rice Plantation of the Fifties*, pp. 64–65.

12. William S. Pettigrew to his sister, ca. 1860.

13. See C. S. Davis, *Cotton Kingdom in Alabama*, pp. 71–72; Rose, *Rehearsal for Reconstruction*, pp. 81, 87; Drew, *Refugee*, p. 45; Yetman, ed., *Life Under the "Peculiar Institution,"* p. 24; Rawick, ed., *S.C. Narr.*, III (3), 119, 218–219; *Texas Narr.*, V (3), 204. See also the letter from a literate driver to his master, Ben Sturn to William Elliott, Nov. 11, 1848, in the Elliott-Gonzales Papers.

14. See, e.g., *S.C. Narr.*, II (1), 198; Pearson, ed., *Letters from Port Royal*, p. 37.

15. Sydnor, *Slavery in Mississippi*, p. 75; Scarborough, *Overseer*, p. 83; Heyward, *Seed from Madagascar*, pp. 92, 102, 104; Phillips and Glunt, eds., *Florida Plantation Records*, p. 435; Botkin, ed., *Lay My Burden Down*, p. 178; WPA, *Negro in Virginia*, p. 64; Cotton Book for 1828 in the Stirling Papers; William S.

Pettigrew to Moses and Henry, July 28, 1858; Joan Caldwell, "Christmas in Old Natchez," *JMH*, XXI (Oct., 1959), 261.

16. D. E. Huger Smith, "Plantation Boyhood," pp. 72–73.

17. Rawick, ed., *S.C. Narr.*, II (2), 36; E. F. Andrews, *War-Time Journal of a Georgia Girl*, p. 283.

18. Rawick, ed., *Ala. Narr.*, VI (1), 117.

19. Kemble, *Journal*, p. 228, also pp. 239, 255; Rawick, ed., *S.C. Narr.*, II (2), 304; *Miss. Narr.*, VII (2), 13; Thomas Journal, 1865; Sydnor, *Slavery in Mississippi*, pp. 75, 209–210.

20. Rawick, ed., *S.C. Narr.*, III (3), 49; II (2), 49; Yetman, ed., *Life Under the "Peculiar Institution,"* p. 55; Heyward, *Seed from Madagascar*, pp. 157, 204.

21. Botkin, ed., *Lay My Burden Down*, pp. 85, 91, 94, 121; Yetman, ed., *Life Under the "Peculiar Institution,"* pp. 224–225; Drew, *Refugee*, p. 73; Kiser, *Sea Island to City*, p. 61; Rawick, ed., *Ala. Narr.*, VI (1), 2, 52, 66; *Texas Narr.*, V (3), 212, 238; V (4), 7, 180; *Okla. Narr.*, VII (1), 21.

22. See, e.g., the remarks in Featherstonhaugh, *Excursion Through the Slave States*, p. 37.

23. A. M. Lobdell to Lewis Stirling, Oct. 5, 1838, in the Stirling Papers; also Sydnor, *Slavery in Mississippi*, p. 75; Ledoux & Company Record Book, Jan. 2, 1857.

24. See, e.g., Rawick, ed., *S.C. Narr.*, II (2), 237; *Texas Narr.*, IV (1), 191; Henry, *Police Control of the Slave*, pp. 27–28; Mallard, *Plantation Life Before Emancipation*, pp. 45–46; Phillips, ed., *Plantation and Frontier*, II, 94.

25. R. King, Jr., "On the Management of the Butler Estate," *SA*, I (Dec., 1828), 523–529.

26. Rawick, ed., *Okla. Narr.*, VII (1), 216; *Texas Narr.*, IV (2), 46; IV (1), 285–286; Drew, *Refugee*, p. 139; Phillips and Glunt, eds., *Florida Plantation Records*, p. 391; Weld, *Slavery as It Is*, p. 72; E. A. Davis, ed., *Plantation Life in the Florida Parishes of Louisiana*, p. 181; and more generally, Nichols, *Many Thousand Gone*, pp. 62–63, and J. B. Sellers, *Slavery in Alabama*, pp. 66, 248–249.

27. H. O. Patterson, *Sociology of Slavery*, p. 62.

28. Hazard, "On the General Management of a Plantation," *SA*, IV (July, 1831), 350–354.

29. These and many other letters may be found in the Pettigrew Papers. Some have been excerpted by Robert Starobin in a stimulating article, which comes to different conclusions from my own; see "Privileged Bondsmen and the Process of Accommodation," *J.Soc.H.*, V (Fall, 1971).

30. See, e.g., Drew, *Refugee*, pp. 19, 252–253; "Letters of George Washington . . ." *JNH*, II (Oct., 1917), 411; Bills Diary, Dec. 10, 1853; Nevitt Diary, July 20, Aug. 10, Aug. 27, Sept. 14, Dec. 14, 1827, and Jan. 18, 1828; R. R. Randolph to Benjamin C. Yancey, Dec. 21, 1850, in the Yancey Papers; Edward T. Tayloe to B. O. Tayloe, Aug. 20, 1833; Wall, "Founding of Pettigrew Plantations," *NCHR*, XXVII (Oct., 1950), 410, 412; Mooney, *Slavery in Tennessee*, p. 153; Chatham, "Plantation Slavery in Middle Florida," unpubl. M.A. thesis, University of North Carolina, 1938, pp. 66–67.

31. Redpath, *Roving Editor*, pp. 269–283; Aptheker, *Slave Revolts*, pp. 211, 214; Catterall, ed., *Judicial Cases*, III, 200–201.

32. Drew, *Refugee*, pp. 45–46.

33. See, e.g., George Teamoh Journal, Pt. 3, p. 60, in the Woodson Papers; Rawick, ed., *S.C. Narr.*, II (2), 309; Catterall, ed., *Judicial Cases*, III, 454–455.

34. Catterall, ed., *Judicial Cases*, III, 669; Olmsted, *Seaboard*, p. 438; Yetman, ed., *Life Under the "Peculiar Institution,"* pp. 30, 193, 222, 294–295; Rawick, ed., *S.C.*

Narr., II (2), 88; *Texas Narr.,* IV (2), 202; V (4), 129; *Ala. Narr.,* VI (1), 2; *Okla. Narr.,* VII (2), 50, 129.

35. Northup, *Twelve Years a Slave,* pp. 226–227.
36. WPA, *Negro in Virginia,* p. 156.
37. Saxon *et al., Gumbo Ya-Ya,* p. 234; also Rawick, ed., *Ga. Narr.,* XII (1), 189.
38. Kemble, *Journal,* pp. 89, 239.
39. Quoted in J. G. Taylor, *Negro Slavery in Louisiana,* p. 81.
40. See, e.g., D. E. Huger Smith, "Plantation Boyhood," p. 65; Foby, "Management of Servants," *SC,* XI (Aug., 1853), 228; WPA, *Drums and Shadows,* pp. 159 ff.; Olmsted, *Back Country,* pp. 48, 81, 82; Rawick, ed., *Ga. Narr.,* XII (1), 43, 74; XII (2), 184; *N.C. Narr.,* XIV (1), 47.
41. Rawick, ed., *S.C. Narr.,* III (3), 65; *Texas Narr.,* IV (2), 72; *Ala. Narr.,* VI (1), 193, 431; Drew, *Refugee,* pp. 168–171; J. B. Grimball Diary, July 11, 1835; C. S. Davis, *Cotton Kingdom in Alabama,* p. 59; Scarborough, "Southern Plantation Overseer: A Re-evaluation," *AH,* XXXVIII (Jan., 1964), 15.
42. Isaac Stephens to William Elliott, Oct. 22, 1849, in the Elliott-Gonzales Papers.
43. See the discussion in Phillips, *American Negro Slavery,* p. 281.
44. *Father Henson's Story of His Own Life,* p. 23; Fisk University, *Unwritten History of Slavery,* p. 72; WPA, *Negro in Virginia,* p. 136.
45. Plantation Manual, in the Hammond Papers.
46. Chesnut, *Diary from Dixie,* June 11, 1862 (pp. 244–245). Drivers did not require the help of overseers to plunder a master; they did quite well on their own, when they so chose; see, e.g., Charles Pettigrew to Ebenezer Pettigrew, Oct. 25, 1804.
47. Schoolcraft, *Plantation Life,* p. 111; Drew, *Refugee,* p. 71; Haller Nutt to Alonzo Snyder, Dec. 15, 1844, in the Snyder Papers.
48. See, e.g., Wilson, "Peculiarities and Diseases of Negroes," *ACPSS,* IV (Sept., 1860), 416; Bass, "Essay on the Treatment and Management of Slaves," Southern Central Agricultural Society, *Transactions, 1846–1851,* p. 200.
49. Olmsted, *Seaboard,* pp. 436–437; Bremer, *Homes of the New World,* II, 488; Rawick, ed., *Texas Narr.,* IV (2), 195; Seabrook, *Before and After,* p. 60; Sitterson, *Sugar Country,* pp. 90–91.
50. See, e.g., the remarks of Heyward, *Seed from Madagascar,* pp. 184–185.
51. Rawick, ed., *S.C. Narr.,* II (2), 166.
52. Kemble, *Journal,* p. 168; C. C. Jones to Charles C. Jones, Jr., Sept. 11, 1854, in Myers, ed., *Children of Pride;* Leigh, *Ten Years,* p. 184; Catterall, ed., *Judicial Cases,* p. 320; Easterby, ed., *South Carolina Rice Plantation,* p. 63.
53. For an example see Drew, *Refugee,* p. 131.
54. See, e.g., Olmsted, *Seaboard,* p. 451; *Back Country,* p. 125; C. C. Jones, *Religious Instruction,* p. 57; Yetman, ed., *Life Under the "Peculiar Institution,"* p. 95; Rawick, ed., *Texas Narr.,* IV (1), 274.
55. The narratives may be consulted at random; see also M. M. Fisher, *Negro Slave Songs,* pp. 120–125; David Walker, *One Continual Cry: David Walker's Appeal to the Colored Citizens of the World (1829–1830)* (ed. Herbert Aptheker; New York, 1965), p. 86.
56. Scarborough, ed., *Diary of Edmund Ruffin,* Jan. 12, 1860 (I, 391). See also Harn, "Old Canoochee—Ogeechee Chronicles," *GHQ,* XVI (Jan., 1932), 146.
57. *Father Henson's Story of His Own Life,* p. 48.
58. Phillips, *Life and Labor,* p. 200; Lyell, *Second Visit,* I, 266; Leigh, *Ten Years,* pp. 181 ff.; J. T. Trowbridge, *The South: A Tour of Its Battlefields and Ruined Cities* (Hartford, Conn., 1866), p. 386; E. Merton Coulter, *James Monroe Smith: Georgia Planter* (Athens, Ga., 1961), *passim;* Rubin, *Plantation County,* p. 29.
59. Rawick, ed., *Okla. Narr.,* VII (1), 253–255.

60. Quoted in Sitterson, *Sugar Country*, p. 211. See also Thomas Journal, 1865, p. 4; Rawick, ed., *S.C. Narr.*, II (2), 304; *Ark. Narr.*, X (5), 339; Pearson, ed., *Letters from Port Royal*, p. 315.

61. See, e.g., Yetman, ed., *Life Under the "Peculiar Institution,"* pp. 24–25; Pearson, ed., *Letters from Port Royal*, pp. 12, n. 3, 234.

62. For a striking parallel see the discussion of the relationship of lords, village headmen, and peasants in Thomas C. Smith, *The Agrarian Origins of Modern Japan* (Stanford, Calif., 1969), pp. 59–60.

63. For some illustrations of the special relationships that could develop see Spyker Diary, Dec. 29, 1858; Bond Diary, Dec. 22, 1861, and Jan. 19, 1862; Leigh, *Ten Years*, pp. 34–35.

64. Heyward, *Seed from Madagascar*, p. 98.

65. For some examples see Olmsted, *Seaboard*, pp. 102–103; Higginson, *Army Life*, pp. 28, 219, 260; Andrew Forest Muir, "The Free Negro in Jefferson and Orange Counties, Texas," *JNH*, XXXV (April, 1950), 195.

66. "Souvenirs of Our Ancestors and My Immediate Family," Manigault Plantation Records.

67. See, e.g., Curtin, *Two Jamaicas*, p. 84; S. Vaughan to William Bullock, esp., Feb. 5, 1824, in U.K. Public Records Office, C.O. 137/157; M. G. Lewis, *Journal of a West India Proprietor*, pp. 181–182; Stoddard, *French Revolution in Santo-Domingo*, p. 246; C. L. R. James, *Black Jacobins*, pp. 19, 89.

68. Northup, *Twelve Years a Slave*, pp. 248–249.

69. Rawick, ed., *Texas Narr.*, IV (1), 3. For the remarkable career of Benjamin Montgomery see Wharton, *Negro in Mississippi*, p. 42.

70. The ambiguities and revolutionary potential of such mediatory groups are suggestively explored in Eric Stokes, "Traditional Resistance Movements and Afro-Asian Nationalism: The Context of the 1857 Mutiny Rebellion in India," *Past and Present*, No. 48 (Aug., 1970), pp. 100–118.

MEN OF SKILL

1. Marcus W. Jernegan, "Slavery and the Beginnings of Industrialism in America," *AHR*, XXV (Jan., 1920), 239. See also Richard B. Morris, *Government and Labor in Early America* (New York, 1946), pp. 31 ff.; Tate, *Negro in Eighteenth-Century Williamsburg*, p. 26; Morton, *Robert Carter of Nomini Hall*, p. 96; Arthur Pierce Middleton, *Tobacco Coast: A Maritime History of Chesapeake Bay in the Colonial Era* (Newport News, Va., 1953), p. 161; Annie Lash Jester, *Domestic Life in Virginia in the Seventeenth Century* (Williamsburg, Va., 1957), pp. 50–51; McDonald, *E Pluribus Unum*, p. 70; WPA, Georgia Writers Project, Savannah Unit, "Drakies Plantation," *GHQ*, XXIV (Sept., 1940), 207–235.

2. See, e.g., Walter Cline, *Mining and Metallurgy in Negro Africa* (Menasha, Wis., 1937), pp. 11–17; S. F. Nadel, *A Black Byzantium* (New York, 1942), pp. 85–86.

3. R. B. Morris, *Government and Labor*, pp. 182–188; Charles H. Wesley, *Negro Labor in the United States, 1825–1925: A Study in American Economic History* (New York, 1927); Phillips, "Slave Labor Problem in the Charleston District," *Slave Economy of the Old South*; Phillips, ed., *Plantation and Frontier*, II, 360–368; Leonard Price Stavisky, "Industrialism in Ante-bellum Charleston," *JNH*, XXXVI (July, 1951), 319.

4. Killona Plantation Journals, March–November, 1839 (I, 60 ff.); Henry Watson Papers, 1847, 1853; Withers Plantation Book, 1827; McKinley Plantation Book, 1852; E. G. Baker Plantation Journal, 1853; De Bow, ed., *Industrial*

Resources, I, 161; Rawick, ed., *Ga. Narr.,* XIII (3), 2; Graves Papers, Vol. XV; Cameron Papers, Vol. CXIII.

5. See, e.g., Hammond Account Book, 1850; Doar Account Book, 1853, 1857; McKinley Book, p. 17; Bruce Plantation Accounts, 1852-1859 (boxes 1-2); McCall Journal, 1851; Sheppard Journal, 1849, 1857; S. J. Baker Account Book, 1846; Spyker Diary, Jan. 15, 1857; Haller Nutt Journal, 1849; Phillips, ed., *Plantation and Frontier,* II, 38; J. B. Grimball Papers, 1843.

6. Catterall, ed., *Judicial Cases,* II, 279; V, 147; Kemble, *Journal,* p. 25; H. R. Sass, "Narrative," in A. R. Huger Smith, *Carolina Rice Plantation of the Fifties,* pp. 24-26; Coulter, *Thomas Spaulding of Sapelo,* p. 61; Ulrich Bonnell Phillips, *A History of Transportation in the Eastern Cotton Belt to 1860* (New York, 1908), p. 26.

7. Gerald M. Capers, Jr., *Biography of a River Town. Memphis: Its Historic Age* (Chapel Hill, N.C., 1939), p. 79; W. T. Jordan, *Hugh Davis,* p. 153; Olmsted, *Seaboard,* p. 426; N. Adams, *South-Side View,* p. 35; Rawick, ed., *N.C. Narr.,* XV (2), 2; O. W. Taylor, *Negro Slavery in Arkansas,* p. 79.

8. Bonner, *Georgia Agriculture,* p. 96.

9. Brewer, *Confederate Negro,* p. 17 and *passim.*

10. Morton, *Robert Carter of Nomini Hall,* pp. 106-107; McManus, *Negro Slavery in New York,* pp. 49-51; Marguerite B. Hamer, "A Century of Manumission: Sidelights on Slavery in Mid-Eighteenth Century South Carolina," *NCHR,* XVII (July, 1940), 232-260.

11. J. B. Sellers, *Slavery in Alabama,* pp. 198-202, 212-214; W. T. Jordan, *Hugh Davis,* pp. 79-81; Mooney, *Slavery in Tennessee,* pp. 31-34; Julia Hering, "Plantation Economy in Leon County, 1830-1840," *FHQ,* XXIII (July, 1954), 45; Cornelius O. Cathey, *Agricultural Developments in North Carolina* (Chapel Hill, N.C., 1956), pp. 54-55; O. W. Taylor, *Negro Slavery in Arkansas,* pp. 34, 73; *SC,* XII (Jan., 1854), 31.

12. For the extent of hiring out slaves by small farmers and overseers, see Owsley, *Plain Folk,* p. 16; Bancroft, *Slave Trading,* p. 146; Sydnor, *Slavery in Mississippi,* p. 173; Joseph Davis Applewhite, "Some Aspects of Society in Rural South Carolina in 1850," *NCHR,* XXIX (Jan., 1952), 43; Abigail Curlee, "The History of a Texas Slave Plantation 1831-1863," *SHQ,* XXVI (Oct., 1922), 106-107; Ingraham, *South-West,* II, 251; Lewis Atherton, ed., "Life, Labor, and Society in Boone County, Missouri, 1834-1852," *Mo.H.R.,* XXXVIII (April, 1944), 281, 284; William Bell to William Otey, Jan. 25, 1860, in the Wyche-Otey Papers.

13. Wade, *Slavery in the Cities,* pp. 38-42; Robert C. Black III, *The Railroads of the Confederacy* (Chapel Hill, N.C., 1952), pp. 29-30; Joseph Clarke Robert, *The Tobacco Kingdom* (Durham, N.C., 1938), pp. 197, 203 ff.; Eaton, *Growth of Southern Civilization,* p. 65.

14. For illustrations of hiring out slaves as punishment see Catterall, ed., *Judicial Cases,* II, 91, 583. For standard complaints see the comments of George S. Barnsley of Georgia in his diary, following the entry of Dec. 27, 1860; William McKean to James Dunlop, Feb. 23, 1816, in the McKean Letterbook; J. B. Hawkins to Charles Alston, Nov. 28, 1847, in the Alston Papers.

15. See, e.g., Slave Paper No. 11, Library of Congress; William A. Bibb to Nicholas Trist, Jan. 6, 1832, in the Trist Papers; Rawick, ed., *Texas Narr.,* V (3), 111.

16. Morton, *Robert Carter of Nomini Hall,* p. 107, n. 61; Catterall, ed., *Judicial Cases,* II, 374; III, 16; Thomas Martin to F. T. Martin and F. I. Levert, Oct. 5, 1857, in the Levert Papers; Edgar Alston to his mother, Aug. 25, 1847, in the Alston Papers; WPA, *Negro in Virginia;* Rawick, ed., *Mo. Narr.,* XI, 24; Stampp, *Peculiar Institution,* p. 185.

17. For the early legislation see W. D. Jordan, *White over Black,* p. 404; cf. Goveia,

Slave Society in the British Leeward Islands, pp. 140–141, 159, 163. For some typical outbursts of criticism see Frank G. Ruffin, "Hiring Negroes," *SP,* XII (Dec., 1852), 376–379; Charles C. Jones, Jr., to C. C. Jones, Oct. 1, 1856, in Myers, ed., *Children of Pride;* Report of the Read Committee in *DBR,* XXVI (May, 1859); Martin Richards, "Reopening the African Slave Trade," *ACPSS,* III (June, 1859), 172–173.

18. O. W. Taylor, *Negro Slavery in Arkansas,* p. 90; Ralph B. Flanders, "The Free Negro in Ante-bellum Georgia," *NCHR,* IX (July, 1932), 257; Coulter, "Slavery and Freedom: Athens, Georgia," *GHQ,* XLIX (Sept., 1965), 265–266; Henry, *Police Control of the Slave,* p. 100; Richter, "Slavery in Ante-bellum Baton Rouge," *LH,* X (Spring, 1969), 129–130; Wade, *Slavery in the Cities,* pp. 48, 51.

19. See, e.g., Pollard, *Black Diamonds,* p. 37; WPA, *Negro in Virginia,* p. 33; J. G. Taylor, *Negro Slavery in Louisiana,* pp. 160–161.

20. Clement Eaton, "Slave Hiring: A Step Toward Freedom in the Upper South," *MVHR,* XLVI (1960), 663–678.

21. Richard B. Morris, "The Measure of Bondage in the Slave States," *MVHR,* XLI (Sept., 1954), 219–240.

22. Greene, ed., *Diary of Col. Landon Carter,* II, 568.

23. Kemble, *Journal,* p. 114; *Life and Times of Frederick Douglass,* p. 42; Heyward, *Seed from Madagascar,* p. 112; Kellar, ed., *Solon Robinson,* I, 455; Lyell, *Second Visit,* I, 267; Pringle, *Chicora Wood,* pp. 13–14.

24. Kemble, *Journal,* p. 152; Yetman, ed., *Life Under the "Peculiar Institution,"* p. 228; Rawick, ed., *S.C. Narr.,* III (3), 201.

25. J. H. Hammond, *DBR,* VIII (June, 1850), 518.

26. Olmsted, *Seaboard,* p. 252; F. L. Riley, "Diary of a Mississippi Planter," *Publications of the Mississippi Historical Society,* X (1909), 454, ed. n.

27. See esp. the probing essay of Gwyn A. Williams, *Artisans and Sans-Culottes: Popular Movements in France and Britain During the French Revolution* (New York, 1964), esp. p. 20. The parallel between William's evaluation of the English and French artisans and the skilled slaves commands immediate attention.

28. Klingberg, *Appraisal of the Negro in Colonial South Carolina,* pp. 45–46; R. B. Morris, *Government and Labor,* p. 31.

29. James A. Porter, "Four Problems in the History of Negro Art," *JNH,* XXVII (Jan., 1942), 11–12; Clarence John Laughlin, *Ghosts Along the Mississippi: An Essay on the Poetic Interpretation of Louisiana's Plantation Architecture* (New York, 1961), Prologue; and generally, the good, brief discussion of the transition from Africa to America in Quarles, *Negro in the Making of America,* pp. 18, 32.

30. Klingberg, *Appraisal of the Negro in Colonial South Carolina,* p. 45; WPA, *Drums and Shadows,* esp. the illustrations following p. 194.

31. R. F. Thompson, "African Influences on the Art of the United States," in A. L. Robinson *et al., Black Studies in the University,* p. 156.

32. *Ibid.,* p. 142.

33. *Ibid.,* pp. 141–142.

FREE NEGROES

1. Phillips, "Racial Problems, Adjustments and Disturbances," *Slave Economy of the Old South,* pp. 60–61.

2. *Ibid.,* p. 61.

3. C. P. Patterson, *Negro in Tennessee,* p. 174.

4. See Nelson, "Some Aspects of Negro Life in North Carolina During the Civil War," *NCHR*, XXV (April, 1948), 143–166.
5. Missouri was an exception. There, manumission laws were liberalized. See Harrison Anthony Trexler, *Slavery in Missouri, 1804–1865* (Baltimore, 1914), pp. 210–223.
6. Robert C. Reinders, "The Decline of the New Orleans Free Negro in the Decade Before the Civil War," *JMH*, XXIV (April, 1962), 88–98.
7. Senese, "Free Negro and the South Carolina Courts," *SCHM*, LXVIII (July, 1967), 140–153.
8. Fornell, "Abduction of Free Negroes and Slaves in Texas," *SHQ*, LX (Jan., 1957), 369–386.
9. Berlin, "Slaves Who Were Free," unpubl. Ph.D. dissertation, University of Wisconsin, 1970, *passim*, but esp. pp. 270–300.
10. For a useful summary of the main statistics and a good introduction to the subject see E. Franklin Frazier, *The Negro in the United States* (rev. ed.; New York, 1963), esp. pp. 63–65.
11. Eugene D. Genovese, *The Political Economy of Slavery: Studies in the Economy and Society of the Slave South* (New York, 1965), Ch. 6, esp. pp. 136–141; J. Carlyle Sitterson, "Hired Labor on Sugar Plantations of the Ante-bellum South," *JSH*, XIV (May, 1948), 192–205.
12. See Marvin Harris, *Patterns of Race in the Americas* (New York, 1964), pp. 79–94.
13. For a general introduction see Stampp, *Peculiar Institution*, pp. 194–195, 216.
14. Charles S. Sydnor, "The Free Negro in Mississippi Before the Civil War," *AHR*, XXXII (July, 1927), 781; Marina Wikramanayake, "The Free Negro in Ante-bellum South Carolina," unpubl. Ph.D. dissertation, University of Wisconsin, 1966; Sellers, *Slavery in Alabama*, p. 379.
15. Cobb, *Inquiry into the Law of Negro Slavery*, pp. 314–315; Phillips, *Georgia and State Rights*, p. 156.
16. Roger Wallace Shugg, "Negro Voting in the Ante-bellum South," *JNH*, XXI (Oct., 1936), 357–364.
17. See the analysis by C. P. Patterson, *Negro in Tennessee*, pp. 166 ff.
18. W. D. Jordan, *White over Black*, p. 126.
19. See Hurd, *Law of Freedom and Bondage*, I, 242; but for some qualifications see J. H. Russell, *Free Negro in Virginia*, p. 117.
20. Brackett, *Negro in Maryland*, pp. 190–191.
21. Donald Edward Everett, "Free Persons of Color in New Orleans, 1803–1865," unpubl. Ph.D. dissertation, Tulane University, 1952, p. 171.
22. Hurd, *Law of Freedom and Bondage*, I, 241; II, 88, 286.
23. Muir, "Free Negro in Jefferson and Orange Counties, Texas," *JNH*, XXXV (April, 1950), 193.
24. Harold Schoen, "The Free Negro in the Republic of Texas," *SHQ*, Pt. 1, XXXIX (April, 1936), 292–308; XL (Oct., 1936), 85–113.
25. Carter G. Woodson, *The Education of the Negro Prior to 1861* (New York, 1968), pp. 128–129; Frazier, *Negro in the United States*, p. 74. In an undeveloped slave state like Florida about 30 percent of the free Negro males and 40 percent of the females were literate, although it is difficult to know just what "literate" really meant; Russell Garvin, "The Free Negro in Florida Before the Civil War," *FHQ*, XLVI (July, 1967), 7.
26. Sellers, *Slavery in Alabama*, p. 363; J. Merton England, "The Free Negro in Ante-bellum Tennessee," *JSH*, XXI (Feb., 1955), 54–56.
27. Brackett, *Negro in Maryland*, p. 197.
28. Bassett, *Slavery in the State of North Carolina*, p. 34.
29. W. D. Jordan, *White over Black*, p. 130. For areas of friction see Flanders, "Free

Negro in Ante-bellum Georgia," *NCHR*, IX (July, 1932), 281.

30. W. D. Jordan, *White over Black*, p. 129.

31. A full study of the immigrant population of the antebellum cities is long overdue, but a number of studies are now under way. At the moment all generalizations must be especially tentative.

32. Wikramanayake, "Free Negro in South Carolina," pp. 148–149. For a general assessment see Berlin, "Slaves Who Were Free," p. 335 and *passim;* also Fisk University, *Unwritten History of Slavery*, pp. 17, 33, 38; Saxon *et al.*, *Gumbo Ya-Ya*, p. 217; Nevitt Diary, April 6, 1829; F. L. Riley, ed., "Diary of a Mississippi Planter," *Publications of the Mississippi Historical Society*, X (1909), 481, n. 45.

33. O. W. Taylor, *Negro Slavery in Arkansas*, pp. 252–253; John H. Franklin, "The Free Negro in the Economic Life of Ante-bellum North Carolina," in Meier and Rudwick, eds., *Making of Black America*, pp. 218–219. Also John H. Franklin, *The Free Negro in North Carolina, 1790–1860* (New York, 1969 [1943]); W. A. Evans, "Free Negroes in Monroe County During Slavery," *JMH*, III (Jan., 1941), 42. For an account of a free Negro artisan who owned a slave boy and used him to insure debts, who worked for leading white families but could not always find work, who married a slave and had a child by her, and who was protected by a white patron—in short, whose life exhibits the vicissitudes of existence even for a fairly secure free Negro—see John H. Franklin, "James Boon, Free Negro Artisan," *JNH*, XXX (April, 1945), 150–180.

34. Franklin, "Free Negro in Ante-bellum North Carolina," p. 217, n. 6; England, "Free Negro in Ante-bellum Tennessee," p. 54. On tenancy in general see R. B. Morris, "Measure of Bondage in the Slave States," *MVHR*, XLI (Sept., 1954), 219–240.

35. Brackett, *Negro in Maryland*, pp. 180–181, 190, 224.

36. McColley, *Slavery and Jeffersonian Virginia*, p. 74.

37. Luther P. Jackson, "The Virginia Free Negro Farmer and Property Owner, 1830–1860," *JNH*, XXIV (Oct., 1939), 390–421.

38. England, "Free Negro in Ante-bellum Tennessee," pp. 37–58. Also Fletcher M. Green, ed., *Ferry Hill Plantation Journal* (Chapel Hill, N.C., 1961), pp. 16, 29.

39. I am indebted to Herbert G. Gutman for having compiled these data and made them available to me. We know little about the life of the free Negroes anywhere, but Gutman's unpublished researches and the work of Theodore Hershberg destroy at least one myth. Statistical analyses show that, overwhelmingly, free Negroes lived in two-parent households and presumably in family units. Their economic position was generally better in the South than in the North, but their family structure proved to be the reverse. Although much stronger than the stereotype would have it, the free Negro family in southern cities was weaker than its northern counterpart. Thus Frazier's thesis falls, for he derives his critique of the Negro family from the presumed consequences of economic determinants. It would seem, then, that the greater access of northern Negroes to religious and social institutions of their own choosing had more effect than occupational status. Unfortunately, apart from some knowledge of southern Negro efforts to build their own churches and social clubs, we know very little about their community life; see Hershberg's essay on the blacks in Philadelphia in Engerman and Genovese, eds., *Race and Slavery*.

40. Russell B. Nolan, "The Labor Movement in St. Louis Prior to the Civil War," *Mo.H.R.*, XXXIV (Oct., 1939), 18–37.

41. J. G. Taylor, *Negro Slavery in Louisiana*, p. 158.

42. Franklin, "Free Negro in Ante-bellum North Carolina," p. 222.

43. Herbert Aptheker, "Buying Freedom," *To Be Free* (New York, 1968), pp. 31–40, esp. pp. 35–36.
44. "Some Undistinguished Negroes" (documents), *JNH*, III (Jan., 1918), 91; Rawick, ed., *Indiana Narr.*, VI (2), 58.
45. Quoted in Wikramanayake, "Free Negro in South Carolina," p. 97.
46. See Slave Paper No. 9, Library of Congress.
47. Carter G. Woodson, *Free Negro Owners of Slaves in the United States in 1830* (Washington, D.C., 1924), p. vi. Woodson cites another case of interest:

> The editor [he writes of himself] personally knew a man in Cumberland County, Virginia, whose mother was purchased by his father who had first bought himself. Being enamored of a man slave, she gave him her husband's manumission papers that they might escape together to free soil. Upon detecting the plot, the officers of the law received the impression that her husband had turned over the papers to the slave and arrested the freedman for the supposed offense. He had such difficulty in extricating himself from this complication that his attorney's fees amounted to $500. To pay these he disposed of his faithless wife to that amount.

See also Mercer Papers, contract dated Feb. 9, 1834; Catterall, ed., *Judicial Cases*, I, 210; Rawick, ed., *Ala. Narr.*, VI (1), 135–136.
48. John H. Russell, "Colored Freemen and Slave Owners in Virginia" (with documents), *JNH*, I (July, 1916), 234–235, 241–242.
49. Franklin, "Free Negro in Ante-bellum North Carolina," pp. 224–225, 230.
50. Stampp, *Peculiar Institution*, pp. 194–195.
51. Laura Foner, "The Free People of Color in Louisiana and St. Domingue: A Comparative Portrait of Two Three-Caste Societies," *J.Soc.H.*, III (Summer, 1970), 406–430.

In Louisiana, ten free Negroes owned 50 or more slaves in 1830—in other words, enough to qualify not merely as planters but as big planters. By 1860 the number of such holdings had fallen to six, but they contained 493 slaves, or a mean average of 82 per holding. Every one of these big planters was a mulatto. The wealthiest of these Negro slaveholders was August Dubuclet of Iberville Parish, whose real property alone was valued at $200,000; his plantation totaled more than 1,200 acres, half of which were under cultivation, and housed 94 slaves. Antoine Decuir of Point Coupee owned more than 1,000 acres and 112 slaves in Iberville Parish. In general, the genuine slaveholders among the free colored of Louisiana had French names and were mulattoes who had inherited substantial wealth from white fathers. In much of Louisiana also, Negro slaveholding appears to have been a subterfuge, especially in the towns, but the existence of big planters among the Negroes, even in small numbers, drew much comment.

In South Carolina, too, one finds a core of large slaveholders among the free Negroes. At the end of the eighteenth century, for example, one free Negro owned about 200 slaves. William Ellison of the Sumter District, who was himself freed at the age of 29, rose to become a major planter, patented his own cotton gin, bought a plantation house from the governor of South Carolina, acquired about 100 slaves, was accepted into the exclusive white Episcopal church of Sumter, and upon his death was buried in the white cemetery. Both his daughters married white men of substantial means. Eventually, his children found it advisable to emigrate, but not before the highly charged 1850s. Until then they had found easy acceptance in white society.

Negro planters—that is, big slaveholders—existed elsewhere, but only in Louisiana (and secondarily in South Carolina) do they seem to have been of more than symbolic importance. Even in Alabama, where special historical and legal circumstances existed around Mobile to protect free Negroes, the influence of the treaty of annexation of 1819 and prior Spanish influence are clear in this respect. See Menn, *Large Slaveholders of Louisiana*, p. 92, n. 2, and pp. 93–94; Everett, "Free Persons of Color in New Orleans," pp. 210–230; Richter, "Slavery in Ante-bellum Baton Rouge" *LH*, X (Spring, 1969), 147–165; Wikramanayake, "Free Negro in South Carolina," pp. 100, 127–128, 240; J. B. Sellers, *Slavery in Alabama*, pp. 386–387, 392.

52. Many of the free Negroes of Mobile had Spanish or French names; see J. B. Sellers, *Slavery in Alabama*, p. 385.

53. See Foner, "Free People of Color in Louisiana and St. Domingue," and Everett, "Free Persons of Color in New Orleans," *passim*.

The caste pretensions of these free Negroes, and especially of the mulattoes, quadroons, and octoroons, would be of purely local interest, if not a mere curiosity, had they not misled several generations of historians. Even so outstanding a scholar as E. Franklin Frazier improperly extrapolated from conditions in Charleston and New Orleans and, given his enormous prestige, taught two generations of white and black historians and sociologists to view the southern free Negro from the vantage point of the South's two small brown elites. According to Frazier: "In the cities of the South, especially in Charleston, South Carolina, and in New Orleans, the communities of free mulattoes became almost an intermediate caste between the whites and slaves. They acquired considerable wealth, including slaves; they maintained conventional standards of sex and family life; they were cultivated people who often sent their children to Europe for education and in order to escape racial prejudice." Frazier's judgment received strong support from scholars who became entranced with the Brown Fellowship Society, which arose as a highly restricted, well-to-do mulatto organization in Charleston in 1790 and lasted a hundred years. The society emphasized white blood, free ancestry, economic success, and, in the words of its historian, E. Horace Fitchett, "a devotion to the tenets of the slave system." It is only one short step from being fascinated by this organization of fifty people or with the colored elite of New Orleans to such sweeping and false generalizations as that these groups provided postbellum leadership to the black masses; that they carried the only viable tradition of family stability among southern Negroes; or that free Negroes in general either were of this kind, at least in aspiration, or were impoverished and déclassé. In fact, these elites were exceptional, not only in the formal sense that all elites are by definition exceptional, but in the substantive sense that a prominent, large, and influential group of free Negro elites emerged in only one or two or three cities in the South. See Frazier, *Negro Church*, p. 62, and *Negro Family*, pp. 153 ff., 198; E. Horace Fitchett, "The Traditions of the Free Negro in Charleston, South Carolina," *JNH*, XXV (April, 1940) 139–152. See also C. M. Green, *Secret City*, p. 23, for an account of the openhanded spirit of a mulatto elite toward blacks.

54. R. B. Morris, "Measure of Bondage in the Slave States," pp. 219–240; England, "Free Negro in Ante-bellum Tennessee," pp. 37–58.

55. Franklin, "Free Negro in Ante-bellum North Carolina," p. 218. J. H. Russell (*Free Negro in Virginia*, p. 131) says that free Negro-slave marriages were common. See also Evans, "Free Negroes in Monroe County," p. 42; Bassett, *Slavery in the State of North Carolina*, p. 35; Wade, *Slavery in the Cities*, pp. 251–252; J. H. Franklin, "James Boon, Free Negro Artisan," pp. 150–180; Rawick, ed., *Texas Narr.*, V (4), 19; *Ark. Narr.*, IX (3), 191; X (5), 93.

56. Yetman, ed., *Life Under the "Peculiar Institution,"* p. 335; Drew, *Refugee*, p. 205;

Catterall, ed., *Judicial Cases*, III, 448; Rawick, ed., *Texas Narr.*, IV (2), 45; *N.C. Narr.*, XIV (1), 119.

57. Rawick, ed., *Texas Narr.*, IV (2), 19; V (3), 122; *Indiana Narr.*, VI (2), 16, 130; *Ga. Narr.*, XII (1), 186; H. C. Bruce, *New Man*, p. 76; George C. Osborne, "Plantation Life in Central Mississippi as Revealed in the Clay Sharkey Papers," *JMH*, III (Oct., 1941), 280.

58. Wade, *Slavery in the Cities*, pp. 249–252.

59. Berlin, "Slaves Who Were Free," p. 394.

60. Drew, *Refugee*, p. 205.

61. Redpath, *Roving Editor*, p. 128.

62. Walker, *One Continual Cry*, p. 111.

63. Berlin, "Slaves Who Were Free," p. 595.

64. *Life and Times of Frederick Douglass*, p. 50.

65. *Ibid.*, p. 198; *Patriot* (N.C.), Oct. 12, 1844; *Aurora* (Wilmington, N.C.), Oct. 30, 1850; Charles C. Jones, Jr., to Mary Jones, Oct. 27, 1860, in Myers, ed., *Children of Pride*, p. 624; Reinders, "Decline of the Free Negro," p. 218; Dorsett, "Slaveholding in Jackson County, Missouri," *MHSB*, XX (Oct., 1963), 34. Similarly, where free Negroes secretly operated schools for slaves, they took enormous risks; see, e.g., Reinders, "Decline of the Free Negro," p. 220. For a case study see Edmund Berkeley, Jr., "Prophet Without Honor: Christopher, Free Person of Color," *VMHB*, LXXVII (April, 1969), 180–190.

66. Aptheker, *Slave Revolts*, esp. p. 249; but see also McColley, *Slavery and Jeffersonian Virginia*, p. 111; W. D. Jordan, *White over Black*, p. 401, n. 47; Gerald Mullin, "Slavery in Eighteenth-Century Virginia," unpubl. Ph.D. dissertation, University of California, 1968), pp. 356, 390; and Alice Dunbar-Nelson, "The People of Color of Louisiana," *JNH*, II (Jan., 1917), 63.

67. Aptheker, *Slave Revolts*, p. 92.

68. Everett, "Free Persons of Color in New Orleans," p. 77.

69. Kenneth Wiggins Porter, "Florida Slaves and Free Negroes in the Seminole War, 1835–1842," *JNH*, XXVIII (Oct., 1943), 390–421.

70. Wiley, *Southern Negroes*, pp. 111, 112, 125, 147, 160, 216. See the petition of the free Negroes of Columbia, S.C., in the Pickens-Bonham Papers, Jan. 10, 1861.

71. The volumes of *DBR* may be consulted almost at random for those complaints. See also Phillips, "The Slave Labor Problem in the Charleston District," *Slave Economy of the Old South*, pp. 191–214; Mooney, *Slavery in Tennessee*, pp. 81, 179–180.

72. See, e.g., William McKean to James Dunlop. Aug. 17, 1811, in the McKean Letterbook; Walker Diary, 1856; Thomas Martin to F. T. Martin and F. I. Levert, Oct. 5, 1857, in the Levert Papers; C. C. Jones, Jr., to C. C. Jones, Oct. 6, 1859; in Myers, ed., *Children of Pride*, p. 524; C. C. Jones, *Religious Instruction*, p. 140; "On The Management of Negroes," *ACPSS*, II (Jan., 1858), 21; reprint from *Montgomery Mail* in *SC*, XIV (June, 1856), 192; Catterall, ed., *Judicial Cases*, II, 577.

73. Joseph G. Tregle, Jr., "Early New Orleans Society: A Reappraisal," *JSH*, XVIII (Feb., 1952), 34.

MISCEGENATION

1. Du Bois, *Gift of Black Folk*, pp. 144, 146.

2. Quoted in John Oliver Killens, *Black Man's Burden* (New York, 1965) p. 127.

3. The range of 13–25% may be found in Du Bois, *Black Reconstruction*, pp. 3–4. He was of course guessing, but so has everyone else been, usually without

his care. The 25% figure would seem the upper limit in any case and is probably too high.

4. See the discussion by O. W. Taylor, *Negro Slavery in Arkansas*, pp. 198–199.

5. See Frazier, *Negro in the United States*, pp. 67–70; also J. G. Taylor, *Negro Slavery in Louisiana*, pp. 162–163.

6. *Patriot*, (N.C.) July, 19, 1845. The "white" element in the lighter-skinned Africans remains in dispute; see, e.g., Creighton Gabel, "Prehistoric Populations of Africa," in Jeffrey Butler *et al.*, eds., *Boston University Papers on Africa* (2 vols.; Boston, 1965–1966), I, 3–37.

7. Wade, *Slavery in the Cities*, pp. 23–25, 122; Kelly Miller, *Out of the House of Bondage*, pp. 51–52; Woodward, *Strange Career of Jim Crow*, p. 16; Edward Byron Reuter, *The Mulatto in the United States* (Boston, 1918), p. 114; Terry Seip, "Slaves and Free Negroes in Alexandria," *LH*, X (Spring, 1969), 151; C. M. Green, *Secret City*, p. 33; Myrdal, *American Dilemma*, p. 126.

8. *Patton v. Patton*, 1831, in Catterall, ed., *Judicial Cases*, I, 318.

9. *Ibid.*, I, 302, 334; II, 281; III, 72, 95; IV, 181, 212–213, 228, 271, 491, 507, 613, 646, 683, 687, 696; V, 224–225, 247–248.

10. See, e.g., Powdermaker, *After Freedom*, p. 97; Allison Davis *et al.*, *Deep South: A Social Anthropological Study of Caste and Class* (Chicago, 1941), pp. 40, 237; Rawick, ed., *Texas Narr.*, VII (1), 18, 124. Also Drake and Cayton, *Black Metropolis*, I, 131, for some illuminating remarks on the attitude of black prostitutes in Chicago toward northern and southern white clients. In general, see Frazier, *Negro Family*, pp. 53–57, 65, 151.

11. J. H. Johnston, *Race Relations and Miscegenation*, *passim*; Eaton, *Growth of Southern Civilization*, p. 92; Berlin, "Slaves Who Were Free," unpubl. Ph.D. dissertation, University of Wisconsin, 1970, pp. 264–265; J. G. Taylor, *Negro Slavery in Louisiana*, pp. 162–163. For an obvious attempt to manumit a child without admitting paternity see the petition of Robert Stanley, 1841, in Louisiana, West Feliciana Parish, Police Jury Minutes.

12. William Gilmore Simms, *The Pro-slavery Argument* (Charleston, S.C., 1852), p. 221.

13. Olmsted, *Seaboard*, pp. 127, 601–602.

14. Origo, "Domestic Enemy," *Speculum*, XXX (July, 1955), 337; also Blum, *Lord and Peasant in Russia*, pp. 426–427. On the southern fancy-girl markets see Bancroft, *Slave Trading*, pp. 112, 131, 217–218, 328–334, 356; J. Winston Coleman, *Slavery Times in Kentucky* (Chapel Hill, N.C., 1940), p. 159; Bremer, *Homes of the New World*, I, 373; Saxon *et al.*, *Gumbo Ya-Ya*, pp. 225–226.

15. Northup, *Twelve Years a Slave*, p. 65.

16. On the free quadroons of New Orleans see the brief, judicious discussion by Eaton, *Growth of Southern Civilization*, p. 146.

17. Bonner, *Georgia Agriculture*, pp. 113, 189.

18. E. A. Davis, ed., *Plantation Life in the Florida Parishes of Louisiana*, p. 206.

19. D. Clayton James, *Ante-bellum Natchez* (Austin, Tex., 1964); Capers, *Memphis: Its Historic Age*, pp. 62, 68; James P. Shenton, *Robert John Walker: A Politician from Jackson to Lincoln* (New York, 1961); Alexander K. Farrar to H. W. Drake, Sept. 4, 5, 1857, in the Farrar Papers; Proctor, "Slavery in Southwest Georgia," *GHQ*, XLI (March, 1965), 9; Bertram W. Korn, *Jews and Negro Slavery*, (Philadelphia, 1950), pp. 51, 54; E. F. Andrews, *War-Time Journal of a Georgia Girl*, pp. 293–294; Martineau, *Society in America*, II, 335.

20. Wikramanayake, "Free Negro in Ante-bellum South Carolina," unpubl. Ph.D. dissertation, University of Wisconsin, 1966, pp. 127–128, 240; Monroe N. Work, ed., "Some Negro Members of Reconstruction Conventions and

Legislatures and of Congress," *JNH*, V (Jan., 1920), 118; Woodson, *Free Negro Owners of Slaves*, pp. vi, vii.

21. Joe M. Richardson, "A Negro Success Story: James Dallas Burruss," *JNH*, L (Oct., 1965), 274; Rawick, ed., *Ark. Narr.*, X (6), 97; also *N.C. Narr.*, XV (2), 230.

22. Rawick, ed., *Texas Narr.*, V (3), 46; *Ark. Narr.*, IX (3), 25–26; *N.C. Narr.*, XV (2), 219; *Ohio Narr.*, XVI, 77; *Fla. Narr.*, XVII, 62; Yetman, ed., *Life Under the "Peculiar Institution,"* pp. 232, 259; Fisk University, *Unwritten History of Slavery*, p. 87; *Narrative of William Wells Brown*, p. 7; *Life and Times of Frederick Douglass*, pp. 48–49.

23. See, e.g., Henry E. Simmons to Anna Simmons, Nov. 23, 1862; Records of Births in the Stirling Papers, 1806–1865; Olmsted, *Seaboard*, p. 622; Weld, *Slavery as It Is*, p. 11.

24. Henry Hughes, *Treatise on Sociology* (Philadelphia, 1860), p. 31.

25. For suggestive discussions of this question see J. H. Johnston, *Race Relations and Miscegenation*, pp. 230 ff.; Thorpe, *Eros and Freedom*, p. 8.

26. Thorpe, *Eros and Freedom*, p. 26.

27. Rawick, ed., *S.C. Narr.*, II (2), 305; III (3), 194–195, 210, 261; III (4), 32, 161; *Texas Narr.*, IV (1), 106, 153, 202, 224, 240, 252, 307; IV (2), 42, 69, 205; *Indiana Narr.*, VI (2), 50, 57; *Okla. Narr.*, VII (1), 233; *Ark. Narr.*, IX (3), 113, 342; IX (4), 122; X (5), 39, 74; X (6), 55–56; *N.C. Narr.*, XIV (1), 341; XV (2), 266, 396; *Fla. Narr.*, XVII, 186. Also Fisk University, *God Struck Me Dead*, p. 174, and *Unwritten History of Slavery*, pp. 37–39, 109, 127, 132; Pennington, *Fugitive Blacksmith*, in Bontemps, ed., *Great Slave Narratives*, pp. 197–198; Northup, *Twelve Years a Slave*, pp. 188 ff.

28. See, e.g., Catterall, ed., *Judicial Cases*, III, 181–182, 188, 238–239, 243, 354, 371, 387.

29. Phillips, *American Negro Slavery*, p. 205; Stampp, *Peculiar Institution*, p. 355; O. W. Taylor, *Negro Slavery in Arkansas*, pp. 201–202; J. G. Taylor, *Negro Slavery in Louisiana*, p. 232; Sydnor, "Free Negro in Mississippi," *AHR*, XXXII (July, 1927), 786–787. See also Olmsted, *Seaboard*, pp. 601–602, and *Back Country*, p. 116 n.

30. Bancroft, *Slave Trading*, p. 325.

31. A Reader, "Agricultural Laborers," *SA*, VIII (Jan., 1835), 8.

32. Harper in E. N. Elliott, ed., *Cotton Is King and Pro-slavery Arguments*, pp. 44–45; also p. 61.

33. J. H. Johnston, *Race Relations and Miscegenation*, pp. 193–194, 205. This problem persisted for race-conscious whites into the postbellum period; see Tindall, *South Carolina Negroes*, p. 299.

34. Quoted in Everett, "Free Persons of Color in New Orleans," unpubl. Ph.D. dissertation, Tulane University, 1952, p. 149.

35. M. T. Judge, "Devotion of Slaves to Masters," ms. p. 95, in Correspondence: Slavery, in the Tennessee State Library and Archives.

36. Journal of Araby Plantation, in the Nutt Papers; also Phillips, *American Negro Slavery*, pp. 273–274; Rachel Weeks O'Connor to David Weeks, July 8, 1832; and Nov. 16, 20, 1833, and to A. T. Conrad, April 12, 1835, in the Weeks Papers.

37. Wallace, *Henry Laurens* p. 67; Catterall, ed., *Judicial Cases*, III, 620; Rawick, ed., *S.C. Narr.*, II (2), Feaster; *Ala. Narr.*, VI (1), 46; J. G. Taylor, *Negro Slavery in Louisiana*, p. 219; J. B. Sellers, *Slavery in Alabama*, p. 62; Wiley, *Southern Negroes*, p. 52, n. 43.

38. Phillips and Glunt, eds., *Florida Plantation Records*, p. 25; Kemble, *Journal*, pp. 162, 194, 199; Mooney, *Slavery in Tennessee*, p. 160; Sitterson, *Sugar Country*, p. 107; J. G. Taylor, *Negro Slavery in Louisiana*, p. 233; WPA, *Negro in Virginia*, pp. 84–85; Rawick, ed., *S.C. Narr.*, II (1), 128; *Texas Narr.*, V (3), 191; *Miss. Narr.*,

VII (2), 4; *Ark. Narr.*, IX (3), 27; X (6), 103; *Ga. Narr.*, XIII (4), 310; *N.C. Narr.*, XV (2), 132; W. H. Russell, *My Diary North and South*, p. 149.

39. Scarborough, *Overseer*, p. 54. Some key South Carolina districts, with their percentage of married overseers: Beaufort, 72%; Charleston, 61%; Colleton, 74%; Georgetown, 58%. In Mississippi, some key counties: Hinds, 32%; Lowndes, 58%; Yazoo, 33%; Natchitoches, 60%. In Louisiana: Ascension Parish, 58%; Plaquemines, 50%; St. Mary, 46%; Terrebonne, 73%. In Virginia: Prince George, 57%; Richmond, 58%. In North Carolina: Northampton, 60%; Stokes, 92%.

40. Catterall, ed., *Judicial Cases*, V, 153; O'Neall, *Negro Law of South Carolina*, p. 13.

41. See J. H. Johnston, *Race Relations and Miscegenation*, Ch. 10, for a comprehensive introduction to the evidence. Also Catterall, ed., *Judicial Cases*, II, 11–12, 53, 109, 132, 143, 183, 196, 289, 339; III, 51, 193, 261, 336; Stampp, *Peculiar Institution*, p. 352. In the seventeenth century the practice was common; see Philip A. Bruce, *Institutional History of Virginia in the Seventeenth Century* (2 vols.; Gloucester, Mass., 1964), I, 83, and *Economic History of Virginia*, II, 111.

42. Rawick, ed., *Ark. Narr.*, IX (3), 191; IX (4), 56; *Ga. Narr.*, XII (1), 45; *N.C. Narr.*, XV (2), 106–107, 197, 213, 260; Robert C. Reinders, "Slavery in New Orleans in the Decade Before the Civil War," *Mid-America*, XLIV (Oct., 1962), 219; Tallant, *Voodoo in New Orleans*, p. 52 and *passim*; Wharton, *Negro in Mississippi*, pp. 227–229; L. W. Brown, *Free Negroes in the District of Columbia*, p. 29 and Ch. 4; England, "Free Negro in Ante-bellum Tennessee," *JSH*, XXI (Feb., 1955), 37–58; Schoen, "Free Negro in the Republic of Texas," *SHQ* Pt. 1, XXXIX (June, 1936), 294 ff.; Pt. 6, XL (July, 1937), 92; Redpath, *Roving Editor*, p. 316; J. B. Sellers, *Slavery in Alabama*, p. 246; Catterall, ed., *Judicial Cases*, I, 357; *Louisiana Gazette*, Nov. 12, 1819.

43. Flournoy to Allston, Dec., 1858, in Easterby, ed., *South Carolina Rice Plantation*, p. 146. Also Abdy, *Journal of Residence and Tour*, III, 29; Wikramanayake, "Free Negro in Ante-bellum South Carolina," p. 11.

44. Lyell, *Second Visit*, I, 271; *Journal of Charlotte Forten*, pp. 150, 181; Higginson, *Army Life*, pp. 1, 10; Heyward, *Seed from Madagascar*, p. 79.

45. Yetman, ed., *Life Under the "Peculiar Institution,"* pp. 61, 262, 295, 307; Fisk University, *Unwritten History of Slavery*, p. 14; Rawick, ed., *S.C. Narr.*, III (4), 178; *Texas Narr.*, IV (1), 76–77; *Ala. Narr.*, VI (1), 158; *Miss. Narr.*, VII (2), 109; *Ark. Narr.*, IX (4), 39; *N.C. Narr.*, XIV (2), 57, 302; H. C. Bruce, *New Man*, p. 74. See also B. F. Jones, "A Cultural Middle Passage," unpubl. Ph.D. dissertation, University of North Carolina, 1965, p. 188, for an analysis of the narratives' evidence.

46. For some specific illustrations of the resistance of the women see Yetman, ed., *Life Under the "Peculiar Institution,"* p. 124; Catterall, ed., *Judicial Cases*, III, 405.

47. Freyre is the frankest on this question; see *Masters and Slaves*, pp. 70, 75–76, 262, 268, 278–279, 324, 350–353, and *Mansions and Shanties*, pp. 374, 381–383, 414. But see also Prado, *Colonial Background of Modern Brazil*, pp. 106–108, 118–120, 401; Boxer, *Race Relations in the Portuguese Colonial Empire*, pp. 13–16, 27–39; Vianna Moog, *Bandeirantes and Pioneers*, pp. 69, 110, 132, 158.

48. See esp. Edward W. Phifer, "Slavery in Microcosm: Burke County, North Carolina," *JSH*, XXVIII (May, 1962), 148.

49. Gavin Diary, Sept. 29, 1855, Aug. 1, 1856, July 22, 1859.

50. "Morality versus Psychology," *NOMSJ*, I (May, 1844), 111.

51. Catterall, ed., *Judicial Cases*, I, 346.

52. Myers, ed., *Children of Pride*, pp. 1067–1069, 1083–1086, 1154–1155, 1194–1195.

53. Wright and Tinling, eds., *William Byrd: His Secret Diary*, pp. 183–184 and

passim; Maude Woodfin and Marion Tinling, eds., *Another Secret Diary of William Byrd* (Richmond, Va., 1942), pp. 93, 157, 168, 174; Louis B. Wright, ed., *The Prose Works of William Byrd* (Cambridge, Mass., 1966), pp. 60–61, 79, 96, 144. It is not clear, however, that Byrd had sexual relations with black women.

54. Woodward, *American Counterpoint*, p. 75. Also Olmsted, *Seaboard*, p. 601. For ex-slaves' recollections of the responses of plantation wives to their husbands' philandering with the slaves, see Rawick, ed., *S.C. Narr.*, II (1), 150; II (2), 14, 36–37; *Okla. Narr.*, VII (1), 362.

55. For an excellent summary and analysis of the evidence see Scott, *Southern Lady;* also Woodward's essay, "Protestant Slavery in a Catholic World," in *American Counterpoint*.

56. Chesnut, *Diary from Dixie*, pp. 21–22, 44, 122.

57. W. D. Jordan, *White over Black*, p. 149; also pp. 474–475.

58. W. Morris, *North Toward Home*, p. 79.

59. Bastide and Fernandes, *Brancos e negros em São Paulo*, p. 208.

60. On this and related matters see Calvin C. Hernton, *Sex and Racism in America* (Garden City, N.Y., 1965), which manages to combine astute observation, shrewd analysis, and tasteful wit.

61. "Certainly there must have been sadists among slaveholders and property in human beings gave their passions full sway. Whip scars on young girls indicate more than normal 'correction,' and there were numbers of such instances." J. G. Taylor, *Negro Slavery in Louisiana*, p. 184.

62. Rawick, ed., *S.C. Narr.*, II (2), 232; II (1), 34; also III (4), 34, 41, 45.

THE LANGUAGE OF CLASS AND NATION

1. Kelly Miller, *Out of the House of Bondage*, (New York, 1971), p. 20.

2. Origo, "Domestic Enemy," *Speculum*, XXX (July, 1955), 338.

3. Thomas Kochman, "Rapping in the Ghetto," in Lee Rainwater, ed., *Soul* (Chicago, 1970), p. 74.

4. I have drawn especially on J. L. Dillard, *Black English: Its History and Usage in the United States* (New York, 1972), and the work of William A. Stewart, which greatly influenced that of Dillard. See esp. Stewart, "Sociolinguistic Factors in the History of American Negro Dialect," *Florida Foreign Languages Reporter*, V (Spring, 1967), and "Continuity and Change in American Negro Dialects," *Florida Foreign Languages Reporter*, VI (Spring, 1968); the papers of Roger D. Abrahams, esp. " 'Can You Dig It?': Black Uses of Black English," as well as his *Deep Down in the Jungle* (rev. ed.; Chicago, 1970) and *Positively Black* (Englewood Cliffs, N.J., 1969); and an unpublished paper by Mervyn C. Alleyne, "The Linguistic Continuity of Africa in the Caribbean." The earlier work of Herskovits enormously influenced the more recent work.

5. Herskovits argues this matter strongly in *Myth of the Negro Past*, p. 50, and *Life in a Haitian Valley*, pp. 22–23. Of special importance is the work of Joseph H. Greenberg; see "Niger-Congo," in R. O. Collins, ed., *Problems of African History* (Englewood Cliffs, N.J., 1968), pp. 70–71. See also Gladwyn Murray Childs, *Umbundu Kinship and Character* (London, 1949), p. 190.

6. Mullin, *Flight and Rebellion*, p. 46.

7. See, e.g., C. C. Jones, *Religious Instruction*, p. 17; Dillard, *Black English*, *passim;* and P. H. Wood, *Black Majority*.

8. Thus, in Dutch Surinam the lingua franca was a pidgin English, which

widened the cultural distance between the Dutch-speaking planters and the African slaves. See Boxer, *Dutch Seaborne Empire*, p. 241.

9. Clement Eaton, *A History of the Old South* (New York, 1949), pp. 6, 7–8. For recent expositions of the traditional point of view, with criticisms of the work of Stewart, Dillard, *et al.*, see Juanita V. Williamson and Virginia M. Burke, eds., *A Various Language: Perspectives on American Dialects* (New York, 1971), esp. the articles by Kurath, Brooks, Farrison, Davis, and Williamson.

10. See Lyell, *Second Visit*, II, 20, 23; Kemble, *Journal*, p. 211; Andrews, *South Since the War*, pp. 131, 227–230, 351; Dennett, *South as It Is*, p. 121; P. H. Wood, *Black Majority*.

11. J. L. Dillard has pointed out the similarities between southern black English and that of the Jamaican maroons; see "The History of Black English in Nova Scotia—A First Step," unpubl. See also Rubin, *Plantation Country*, p. 89. Stewart has pointed out that although blacks and whites both use "ain't" in place of "is not," blacks also use it in a way that whites rarely if ever do —to negate verbs in the past tense. Whites need not do it for the obvious reason that; unlike blacks, they use the usual English past tense. But a black might say, "Dey not like dat" to mean "They did not like that," rather than (as a white would) "They are not like that."

12. George W. Cable, "Creole Slave Songs," in Katz, ed., *Social Implications of Early Negro Music*, p. 47; Nichols, *Many Thousand Gone*, p. 70.

13. White Virginians actually took pride in their use of African words during the eighteenth century. See Schoepf, *Travels in the Confederation*, II, 62.

14. Rawick, ed., *S.C. Narr.*, III (3), 27–28 (Marie Jenkins). The volumes of narratives contain innumerable such items. See also Higginson, *Army Life*, p. 206; Botume, *First Days Amongst the Contrabands*, pp. 67, 222.

15. The following remarks by William J. Entwistle in his essay, "The Portuguese and Brazilian Language," Ch. 3 in H. V. Livermore, ed., *Portugal and Brazil: An Introduction* (Oxford, 1953), p. 35, may be considered: "They [certain words of Brazilian Portuguese] are from a Bantu dialect (Kimbundo) or from Yoruba (Nago), but they are not really numerous outside of Negro verse. The Portuguese settler gave orders to his Negro slaves in Portuguese, but to make them intelligible it was necessary to strip them of grammatical superfluities. The result is a dialect with a quite un-Portuguese grammatical structure, without the *s* of the plural nouns or distinction of person in the verbs, other than the first person and the rest."

16. In the account of ex-slave James Hayes of Texas we find an illustration. His mistress was grieving for her dead husband. One day, however, she finally laughed, as a result of the following exchange. A slave said, "I got no 'lasses." The mistress rebuked him: "Say *mo*lasses." The slave replied, "Why say molasses [= mo' 'lasses, that is, more molasses] when I'se got no 'lasses?" Rawick, ed., *Texas Narr.*, IV (2), 127.

17. William A. Stewart, "On the Uses of Negro Dialect in the Teaching of Reading," unpubl.

18. See David Dwyer, *An Introduction to West African Pidgin English* (East Lansing, Mich., 1967), p. 98.

19. Redpath, *Roving Editor*, p. 32. Generally, see Grace Sims Holt, " 'Inversion' in Black Communication," in Kochman, ed., *Rappin' and Stylin' Out*, pp. 152–159.

20. Lester, *To Be a Slave*, p. 84.

21. Higginson, *Army Life*, p. 28; Botume, *First Days Amongst the Contrabands*, p. 74.

22. Olmsted, *Seaboard*, p. 29.

23. Rawick, ed., *S.C. Narr.*, II (1), 210; also Powdermaker, *After Freedom*, p. 47; Botume, *First Days Amongst the Contrabands*, p. 177; Swint, ed., *Dear Ones at Home*, p. 189.
24. Quoted in J. M. McPherson, *The Negro's Civil War*, p. 43.
25. See the suggestive discussion in Memmi, *Dominated Man*, p. 75, in which he describes what he calls "colonial bilingualism"; also see H. M. Lynd, *On Shame and the Search for Identity*, p. 171.
26. *Life and Times of Frederick Douglass*, p. 44.
27. Yetman, ed., *Life Under the "Peculiar Institution,"* pp. 16–17.
28. Rawick, ed., *Ala. Narr.*, VI (1), 377.
29. Heyward, *Seed from Madagascar*, pp. 188–189; Pearson, ed., *Letters from Port Royal*, p. 25; for the Southwest, see Smedes, *Southern Planter*, p. 19 n., and J. B. Sellers, *Slavery in Alabama*, p. 74.
30. Stirling, *Letters from the Slave States*, pp. 51, 56, 245. Stirling praised the "good English" of the slaves in Kentucky and Tennessee as being superior to that of the whites; see p. 56. See also *Journal of Charlotte Forten*, p. 160.
31. "The Negroes interviewed frequently speak fairly correctly at first but when they begin to talk of old times lapse into dialect." Interviewer's note in Rawick, ed., *N.C. Narr.*, XV (2), 340.
32. Gramsci, *Modern Prince*, pp. 58–60.
33. Mbiti, *African Religions and Philosophy*, p. 101.

BOOK THREE, PART 2

THE NAMING OF CATS

1. T. S. Eliot, "The Naming of Cats," in *Old Possum's Book of Practical Cats* (New York, 1939), pp. 9–10.
2. Catterall, ed., *Judicial Cases*, III, 482.
3. P. A. Bruce, *Social Life in Virginia in the Seventeenth Century*, p. 154.
4. T. C. Smith, *Agrarian Origins of Modern Japan*, p. 59.
5. Fisk University, *Unwritten History of Slavery*, p. 9; *Narrative of William Wells Brown*, p. 43. Some slaves and freedmen did remain indifferent; see, e.g., Yetman, ed., *Life Under the "Peculiar Institution,"* p. 319.
6. See Seale Diary, Oct. 16, 1857, in which the slaves are listed with such surnames as Clark, Taylor, and Davis; A. Heise to James Bowman, July 11, 1862, in the Bowman Papers, in which runaways are listed with surnames; also R. R. Barrow Residence Journal, July 25, 1857; and W. H. Stephenson, *Isaac Franklin*, pp. 104, 139 ff. For a French equivalent see the LeBlanc Papers for the 1850s [in French].
7. Heyward, *Seed from Madagascar*, p. 98; also D. E. Huger Smith, "A Plantation Boyhood," in A. R. Huger Smith, *Carolina Rice Plantation of the Fifties*, p. 71.
8. Many freedmen did take their master's name for a variety of reasons. See, e.g., Yetman, ed., *Life Under the "Peculiar Institution,"* pp. 21, 33, 35, 45, 59, 112, 182; G. M. Brown, "Biography of Mary Ann Colvin Mayfield," p. 7, in the Mayfield Papers.
9. See E. F. Andrews, *War-Time Journal of a Georgia Girl*, p. 347; Rawick, ed., *S.C. Narr.*, II (2), 33, 107, 233 (Susan Hamilton); *Texas Narr.*, IV (1), 51, 54; *Ark. Narr.*, IX (3), 105, 120; Yetman, ed., *Life Under the "Peculiar Institution,"* p. 116.
10. For some illustrations of concern to have the father's name, even if he had

been sold away early and was a dim memory, see Yetman, ed., *Life Under the "Peculiar Institution,"* p. 10; Rawick, ed., *S.C. Narr.,* II (1), 66.

11. Yetman, ed., *Life Under the "Peculiar Institution"* p. 39.
12. Rawick, ed., *S.C. Narr.,* III (3), 24.
13. See, e.g., Fisk University, *Unwritten History of Slavery,* p. 44.
14. Lester, *To Be a Slave,* p. 148.
15. Aleck Woodward in Rawick, ed., *S.C. Narr.,* III (4), 256.
16. *Ibid.,* III (4), 44; also *Ark. Narr.,* IX (3), 120. Often some branch of the master's family would provide a suitable name; see the selections of the 56 blacks on the Gay estate in Iberville Parish, La., in the Gay Papers, 1864.
17. Rubin, *Plantation County,* p. 159; also Pearson, ed., *Letters from Port Royal,* p. 271.
18. For a variety of white and black sources that indicate selection by slaves, not masters, see Lyell, *Second Visit,* I, 263; Bassett, *Southern Plantation Overseer,* pp. 190, 193, 201; John Bieller to Jacob Bieller, Aug. 27, 1827, in the Snyder Papers; Harn, "Old Canoochee—Ogeechee Chronicles," *GHQ,* XVI (June, 1932), 114–135; W. C. Harrison to William H. Taylor, Feb. 2, 1856, in the Dromgoole-Robinson Papers; WPA, *Negro in Virginia,* p. 82; Rawick, ed., *S.C. Narr.,* II (1), 112.
19. Yetman, ed., *Life Under the "Peculiar Institution,"* pp. 325–326.
20. Heyward, *Seed from Madagascar,* p. 67.
21. Greene, ed., *Diary of Col. Landon Carter,* I, 131, 430.
22. See the typical names in Ivan E. McDougle, *Slavery in Kentucky, 1792–1865* (Westport, Conn., 1970), pp. 24–25. See also Curlee, "History of a Texas Slave Plantation," *SHQ,* XXVI (Oct., 1922), 98; Botume, *First Days Amongst the Contrabands,* p. 49; Tooke Papers, 1860; Pre Aux Cleres Plantation Record Book, 1852–1853.
23. See, in general, L. D. Turner, *Africanisms in the Gullah Dialect* (New York, 1969); Newbell Niles Puckett, "American Negro Names," *JNH,* XXIII (Jan., 1938), 35–48; Dillard, *Black English;* Peter H. Wood, "The Roots of Black English," in *Black Majority* (forthcoming). For the prevalence of Africanisms on the coast see also Lyell, *Second Visit,* I, 263; D. E. Huger Smith, "A Plantation Boyhood," p. 71; Easterby, ed., *South Carolina Rice Plantation,* pp. 331 ff.; Rose, *Rebearsal for Reconstruction,* p. 97; Heyward, *Seed from Madagascar,* p. 97; Botume, *First Days Amongst the Contrabands,* pp. 47 ff., 55; Coulter, *Thomas Spaulding of Sapelo,* p. 86; and Kemble, *Journal,* and Leigh, *Ten Years,* for the Butler estate. Also Schoen, "Free Negro in the Republic of Texas," Pt. 1, *SHQ,* XXXIX (April, 1936), 297.
24. Yetman, ed., *Life Under the "Peculiar Institution,"* p. 175.
25. Ojo, *Yoruba Culture,* p. 234; Puckett, *Folk Beliefs,* p. 334; Swados, "Negro Health on the Ante-bellum Plantations," *BHM,* X (Oct., 1941), 464.
26. Thurman, *Negro Spiritual Speaks of Life and Death,* pp. 45–46; W. F. Allen *et al., Slave Songs of the United States,* p. 37.
27. R. Q. Mallard to Mrs. Mary S. Mallard, March 24, 1858, in Myers, ed., *Children of Pride,* p. 403.

THE MYTH OF THE ABSENT FAMILY

1. Lee Rainwater and William L. Yancey, *The Moynihan Report and the Politics of Controversy* (Cambridge, Mass., 1967), which includes the text of the report; Frazier, *Negro in the United States* and *Negro Family;* Elkins, *Slavery.*
2. For a brief general critique of prevailing notions of family disorganization see Charles V. Willie, "The Black Family in America," *Dissent,* Feb., 1971, pp.

80–83. The specialized literature is growing rapidly. For one of the most careful and responsible of the older studies see Drake and Cayton, *Black Metropolis*, II, 582–583.

3. See, e.g., Myrdal, *American Dilemma*, p. 935; Jessie Bernard, *Marriage and Family Among Negroes* (Englewood Cliffs, N.J., 1966), p. 21; Powdermaker, *After Freedom*, p. 143.

4. See esp. Peter Kolchin, *First Freedom: The Responses of Alabama's Blacks to Emancipation and Reconstruction* (Westport, Conn., 1972), Ch. 3; Herbert G. Gutman, "Le Phénomène invisible: La Composition de la famille et du foyer noirs après la Guerre de Sécession," *Annales: Économies, Sociétés, Civilisations*, XXVII (July–Oct., 1972), 1197–1218. Of special interest in these studies are the data from marriage certificates in the Union archives, which show an impressive number of cases in which slaves had lived together for ten years and longer, sometimes much longer.

5. Mullin, *Flight and Rebellion*, p. 109; Sydnor, *Slavery in Mississippi*, p. 103; Bancroft, *Slave Trading*, p. 206.

6. Quoted in M. Le Page Du Pratz, *History of Louisiana or of the Western Parts of Virginia and Carolina* (London, 1924), p. 365.

7. WPA, *Negro in Virginia*, p. 74; Fisk University, *Unwritten History of Slavery*, p. 136.

8. See, e.g., Agnew Diary, Aug. 19, 1862 (II, 124a–124b); Sitterson, *Sugar Country*, pp. 103–104; the correspondence of Charles C. Jones, Jr., and C. C. Jones, Oct., 1856, in Myers, ed., *Children of Pride*.

9. James W. Melvin to A. C. Britton, Feb. 11, 1863, in the Britton Papers.

10. Catterall, ed., *Judicial Cases*, I, *passim*; III, 89–90, 160; V, 182; also C. P. Patterson, *Negro in Tennessee*, pp. 57, 154.

11. Kenneth Stampp, having studied the wills of a large number of slaveholders, concludes that the financial return to the heirs constitute the overriding consideration; see *Peculiar Institution*, p. 204. But see also J. B. Sellers, *Slavery in Alabama*, p. 168, for a somewhat different reading.

12. Quoted in Phillips, *Life and Labor*, p. 243.

13. For some evidence of masters who went to great lengths to keep the families of even recalcitrant slaves together, or who took financial losses to avoid separations, see the Witherspoon-McDowall Correspondence for 1852; Richard Whitaker to A. H. Boykin, Nov. 17, 1843, in the Boykin Papers; J. B. Hawkins to Charles Alston, Nov. 28, 1847, in the Alston Papers; William Otey to Octavia A. Otey, Nov. 20, 1855, in the Wyche-Otey Papers; Ernest Haywood Correspondence, 1856–1857; Lewis Stirling to his son, Jan. 10, 1843; Henry A. Tayloe to B. O. Tayloe, Jan. 5, 1835; Correspondence of Joseph Bryan of Savannah, Ga., a slave trader, in the Slave Papers, Library of Congress; Gavin Diary, July 2, 1857; George W. Clement to Capt. John P. Wright, Oct. 28, 1849, in the Pocket Plantation Record. For evidence and analyses in secondary works see esp. R. H. Taylor, *Slaveholding in North Carolina*, p. 85; Phillips, *Life and Labor*, pp. 274–275; McColley, *Slavery and Jeffersonian Virginia*, pp. 66–68.

14. See, e.g., Morton, *Robert Carter of Nomini Hall*, p. 111; Joseph Clay to Edward Telfair, Dec. 6, 1785, in the Telfair Papers; Heyward, *Seed from Madagascar*, p. 88; W. T. Jordan, *Hugh Davis, passim*; Myers, ed., *Children of Pride, passim*; John Lynch to Ralph Smith, Oct. 13, 1826, in Pocket Plantation Record; J. B. Grimball Diary, June 20, 1835, Jan. 11, 1860, July 17, 1863; C. C. Mercer to John and William Mercer, July 28, 1860; wills dated Dec. 12, 1849, July 9, 1857, Feb. 2, 1862, in the Lawton Papers; A.G.G. to Thomas W. Harriss, Oct. 28, 1848, in the Harriss Papers; Gavin Diary, Sept. 9, 1856; William McKean to James Dunlop, April 4, 1812, in the McKean Letterbook; Eaton, *Henry Clay*, pp.

120-121; John Kirkland to his son, Sept. 15, 1858, in the Wyche-Otey Papers.

15. See, e.g., Lyell, *Second Visit*, I, 209-210; Stirling, *Letters from the Slave States*, p. 260.

16. Fisk University, *Unwritten History of Slavery*, pp. 1, 33: Rawick, ed., *S.C. Narr.*, II (1), 206; III (3), 2; *Texas Narr.*, IV (2), 110; *Indiana Narr.*, VI (2), 10; George Teamoh Journal, Pts. 1-2, p. 31, in the Woodson Papers.

17. Schoepf, *Travels in the Confederation*, II, 148; Metcalfe to Liddell, June 24, 1848, in the Liddell Papers. Also Charles M. Manigault to Louis Manigault, Jan. 8, 1857; John W. Pittman invoice and note, in the Slave Papers, Library of Congress.

18. In general see Rawick, *Sundown to Sunup*, p. 90.

19. For illustrations of each of these cases see Fisk University, *Unwritten History of Slavery*, pp. 140, 143; Phillips, *Life and Labor*, p. 270; Henry [the Driver] to William S. Pettigrew, July 1, 1857, in the Pettigrew Papers; Eliza G. Roberts to Mrs. C. C. Jones, May 20, 1861, and Mary Jones to Mary S. Mallard, Nov. 7, 1865, in Myers, ed., *Children of Pride*.

20. Rawick, ed., *Kansas Narr.*, XVI, 71; *Ohio Narr.*, XVI, 12.

21. Charles West to John Jones, July 23, 1855, in the John Jones Papers; Chatham, "Plantation Slavery in Middle Florida," unpubl. M.A. thesis, University of North Carolina, 1938, p. 80. See also *Father Henson's Story of His Own Life*, pp. 147-148, 157; Fisk University, *Unwritten History of Slavery*, p. 78.

22. WPA, *Negro in Virginia*, p. 34.

23. *DBR*, VIII (Feb., 1850), 122. For a discussion of the state laws designed to protect families from separation see Bancroft, *Slave Trading*, pp. 197-199.

24. Quitman as quoted in Bancroft, *Slave Trading*, p. 308; Chesnut, *Diary from Dixie*, p. 18.

25. Wise, *End of an Era*, p. 84; also pp. 85-86.

26. As quoted by R. E. Park in his introduction to Doyle, *Etiquette of Race Relations*, p. xxvii.

27. Kate Stone, *Brokenburn*, p. 84. Or see the remarks of the court in *Nowell v. O'Hara* (S.C.), 1833, in Catterall, ed., *Judicial Cases*, II, 352.

28. See Applegarth's statement in the Slave Papers, Library of Congress.

29. See, e.g., Judge DeSaussure of South Carolina in *Gayle v. Cunningham*, 1846, in Catterall, ed., *Judicial Cases*, II, 314; or Judge Slidell of Louisiana in *Bertrand v. Arcueil, ibid.*, III, 599-600.

30. Fogel and Engerman, *Time on the Cross*, pp. 126-144. See also the suggestive article by William Calderhead, "How Extensive Was the Border State Slave Trade: A New Look," *CWH*, XVIII (March, 1972), 42-55.

31. J. A. McKinstry to H. C. Nixon, Feb. 11, 1913, in Correspondence: Slavery, Tennessee State Library and Archives. In general see Bancroft, *Slave Trading*, esp. Chs. 2 and 10.

32. *Life and Times of Frederick Douglass*, p. 96.

33. Bremer, *Homes of the New World*, II, 93.

34. Quoted in Du Bois, *Gift of Black Folk*, p. 143.

35. Swint, ed., *Dear Ones at Home*, p. 124.

ROMANCES OF THE FIELD

1. See esp. D. B. Davis, *Problem of Slavery*, pp. 452, 462, 468-470; and W. D. Jordan, *White over Black*, pp. 32ff.

2. See esp. Denis Pierre de Pédrals, *La Vie sexuelle en Afrique noir* (Paris, 1950); Mbiti, *African Religions and Philosophy*, pp. 146 ff.; Parrinder, *African Traditional Religion*, p. 95; Abraham, *Mind of Africa*, p. 82; Marcel Griaule and

Germaine Dieterlen, "The Dogon," in Forde, ed., *African Worlds*, p. 92; Kenneth Little, "The Mende of Sierra Leone," in *ibid.*, pp. 131–132; M. M. Green, *Ibo Village Affairs*, pp. 200 ff.; Balandier, *Ambiguous Africa*, pp. 25, 28. There are some striking parallels between African and Japanese attitudes toward the sexual education of children; see Benedict, *Chrysanthemum and Sword*, pp. 270, 280. Furthermore, the gap between traditional African and seventeenth-century aristocratic attitudes was much narrower than that between traditional African and later European bourgeois attitudes; see esp. Philippe Ariès, *Centuries of Childhood: A Social History of Family Life*, (New York, 1962), pp. 100 ff.

3. Freyre, *Masters and Slaves*, pp. 326–327, 404, 470–471, and *Mansions and Shanties*, p. 117; Boxer, *Portuguese Society in the Tropics*, p. 102; C. S. Johnson, *Shadow of the Plantation*, pp. 188–189; Kiser, *Sea Island to City*, pp. 72–73.
4. Blanton, *Medicine in Virginia in the Eighteenth Century*, p. 156; also Ulrich Bonnell Phillips, "A Jamaican Slave Plantation," *AHR*, XIX (April, 1914), 545.
5. See Walter Fisher, "Physicians and Slavery in the Antebellum Southern Medical Journal" in Meier and Rudwick, eds., *Making of Black America*, I, 157; Mary Louise Marshall, "Samuel Cartwright and States' Rights Medicine," *NOMSJ*, XCIII (Aug., 1940), 74–78; Swados, "Negro Health on the Antebellum Plantations," *BHM*, X (Oct., 1941), 471–472; Scott, *Southern Lady*, p. 53.
6. Olmsted, *Back Country*, p. 117, n.
7. The record books of physicians who lived in or near cities and serviced nearby plantations suggest as much, but we do not have enough material to make a firm judgment. Such evidence may well exist, however, and may await a diligent special investigator. See Physician's Account Book, ca. 1830, Washington, D.C.; Physician's Fee Book, 1847–1850; Physician's Record Book, 1855–1862, Wilmington, N.C.
8. Morton, *Robert Carter of Nomini Hall*, p. 115; O. W. Taylor, *Negro Slavery in Arkansas*, p. 155; Plantation Record Book, 1850–1861 [in French], undated account near the back of the book.
9. Leak Diary, May 4, 1857, reported four such cases. Others reported one or two occasionally. See, e.g., House, ed., *Planter Management and Capitalism in Georgia*, pp. 13, 49; St. John R. Liddell to Moses Liddell, May 10, 1853; Chatham, "Plantation Slavery in Middle Florida," unpubl. M.A. thesis, University of North Carolina, 1938, p. 62; J. B. Sellers, *Slavery in Alabama*, p. 116; Flanders, "Two Plantations and a County of Ante-bellum Georgia," *GHQ*, XII (March, 1928), 10. Reports of venereal disease appeared occasionally in court cases; see Catterall, ed., *Judicial Cases*, II, 170, 321; III, 164, 214.
10. Rose, *Rehearsal for Reconstruction*, pp. 61, 64, 172.
11. Redpath, *Roving Editor*, p. 45.
12. Laurence M. Keitt, *Slavery and the Resources of the South* (reprinted from the *Congressional Globe*; Washington, D. C., 1857), p. 4.
13. Phillips, "Historical Notes of Milledgeville," *Slave Economy of the Old South*; David Kaser, "Nashville's Women of Pleasure in 1860," *THQ*, XXIII (Dec., 1964), 379–382; Reinders, "Slavery in New Orleans in the Decade Before the Civil War," *Mid-America*, XLIV (Oct., 1952), 211–221; Olmsted, *Seaboard*, pp. 507–509; Catterall, ed., *Judicial Cases*, I, 362; Bremer, *Homes of the New World*, II, 477; Valentine Diary, July 23, 1853; Fogel and Engerman, *Time on the Cross*.
14. Thorpe, *Eros and Freedom*, esp. pp. 156–163; also Hernton, *Sex and Racism in America*.

15. Morgan, *Slavery in New York*, p. 21; WPA, *Negro in Virginia*, p. 85; Yetman, ed., *Life Under the "Peculiar Institution,"* pp. 34, 92; Rawick, ed., *Texas Narr.*, V (3), 69, 223; C. C. Jones, *Religious Instruction*, pp. 134, 143; E. F. Andrews, *War-Time Journal of a Georgia Girl*, p. 320; DuBose, "Recollections of the Plantation," *AHQ*, I (Spring, 1930), 63–75; O. W. Taylor, *Negro Slavery in Arkansas*, p. 190.

16. Rawick, ed., *Texas Narr.*, IV (2), 223; *S.C. Narr.*, II (1), 61, 104; II (2), 23, 201; III (3), 167; *Indiana Narr.*, VI (2), 193–195; Swint, ed., *Dear Ones at Home*, p. 36.

17. Botkin, ed., *Lay My Burden Down*, p. 161.

18. Fisk University, *Unwritten History of Slavery*, p. 4.

19. *Ibid.*, pp. 68, 78, 147, 148, 151; Yetman, ed., *Life Under the "Peculiar Institution,"* p. 221; Rawick, ed., *Texas Narr.*, IV (1), 80; *Indiana Narr.*, VI (2), 139; *Fla. Narr.*, XVII, 268; Puckett, *Folk Beliefs*, p. 128; WPA, *Negro in Virginia*, p. 85.

20. Yetman, ed., *Life Under the "Peculiar Institution,"* p. 270; Fisk University, *Unwritten History of Slavery*, passim; WPA, *Negro in Virginia*, p. 69; Rawick, ed., *Texas Narr.*, IV (1), 188.

21. Fisk University, *Unwritten History of Slavery*, p. 57; Rawick, ed., *S.C. Narr.*, II (1), 224–225.

22. For black testimony on this point see Rawick, ed., *Texas Narr.*, IV (2), 246; V (3), 18; *Ark. Narr.*, X (6), 163; *Ga. Narr.*, XIII (4) 85, 189.

23. Kate Stone, *Brokenburn*, p. 345; and generally, Scott, *Southern Lady*, pp. 25, 37, 42.

24. See, e.g., Rawick, ed., *Texas Narr.*, V (3), 192; V (4), 4, 75, 103; Bernard, *Marriage and Family Among Negroes*, p. 82.

25. WPA, *Negro in Virginia*, pp. 82, 140; also Rawick, ed., *Ga. Narr.*, XII (2), 296; XIII (4), 38–39. But for indications of interference by masters for breeding purposes see Martineau, *Society in America*, II, 328; Rawick, ed., *Okla. Narr.*, VII (1), 73; *Ark. Narr.*, IX (3), 128.

26. Phillips, *Life and Labor*, pp. 203–204; Yetman, ed., *Life Under the "Peculiar Institution,"* pp. 199, 322; Botkin, ed., *Lay My Burden Down*, p. 161; Rawick, ed., *S.C. Narr.*, II (2), 23; WPA, *Negro in Virginia*, pp. 83–84.

27. Yetman, ed., *Life Under the "Peculiar Institution,"* p. 70.

28. *Ibid.*, p. 335.

29. *Narrative of William Wells Brown*, p. 38; Yetman, ed., *Life Under the "Peculiar Institution,"* p. 39; DuBose, "Recollections of the Plantation," p. 72; C. S. Davis, *Cotton Kingdom in Alabama*, p. 91.

30. Buckingham, *Slave States of America*, II, 196; J. G. Williams, *"De Ole Plantation,"* pp. 21–22. The slaves' attitude is the more remarkable when we consider that marriage for love in Europe did not arise as a general practice until the growth of the industrial city; see Gideon Sjoberg, *The Preindustrial City: Past and Present* (New York, 1965), pp. 151–152.

31. Hegel, *Philosophy of Right*, pp. 111–112; Herskovits, *Myth of the Negro Past*, p. 64; Parrinder, *African Traditional Religion*, p. 97; Arensberg, *Irish Countryman*, pp. 77 ff.; Geertz, *Religion of Java*, p. 53.

32. Olmsted, *Seaboard*, p. 132; *Back Country*, p. 89; Bassett, *Slavery in the State of North Carolina*, p. 91; Cornwall Diary, Jan. 31, 1861 (p. 56); C. S. Johnson, *Shadow of the Plantation*, p. 50.

33. Yetman, ed., *Life Under the "Peculiar Institution,"* p. 307.

34. Fisk University, *Unwritten History of Slavery*, p. 17. The slaves' tolerance of sexual practices that shocked white sensibilities (in theory, at least) did not extend to incest. A slaveholder in Georgia, for example, had to sell a slave who had fathered a child by his own daughter because the other slaves threatened to kill him; see Yetman, ed., *Life Under the "Peculiar Institution,"* p. 46.

35. J. W. DuBose, *The Life and Times of William Lowndes Yancey* (2 vols.; New York, 1942 [1892]), II, 435; Du Bois, *Souls of Black Folk*, p. 108.

36. Bills Diary, Oct. 30, 1854.

37. *DBR*, XXIX (June, 1851), 623.

38. S. Andrews, *South Since the War*, p. 178.

39. C. C. Jones, *Religious Instruction*, p. 142.

40. Scott, *Southern Lady*, pp. 54–55; Guion Griffis Johnson, "Courtship and Marriage Customs in Ante-bellum North Carolina," *NCHR*, VIII (Oct., 1931), 392; Botkin, ed., *Lay My Burden Down*, pp. 167, 195.

41. See, e.g., Posey, *Baptist Church in Lower Mississippi Valley*, pp. 45–46; Joseph A. Thacker, Jr., "The Concept of Sin in Kentucky During the Period 1830–1860," *KHSR*, LXVI (Oct., 1968), 125; Olmsted, *Back Country*, p. 276; Dennett, *South as It Is*, p. 146.

42. See, e.g., Powdermaker, *After Freedom*, pp. 68, 157.

43. Farish, ed., *Journal and Letters of Philip Vickers Fithian*, Sept. 5, 1774 (p. 241); Wright and Tinling, eds., *William Byrd: His Secret Diary*, June 17, 1710 (p. 82); Magruder Diary, April 19, 1857; W. T. Jordan, *Hugh Davis*, p. 98; Fisk University, *Unwritten History of Slavery*, p. 115; Rawick, ed., *S.C. Narr.*, II (1), 72; *Indiana Narr.*, VI (2), 139.

44. Yetman, ed., *Life Under the "Peculiar Institution,"* p. 291.

45. Botume, *First Days Amongst the Contrabands*, pp. 152, 155, 160.

46. Chesnut, *Diary from Dixie*, p. 122; also the speech of Gov. Collier of Alabama, excerpted in J. B. Sellers, *Slavery in Alabama*, p. 167; Hammond in *DBR*, VIII (Feb., 1850), 123; Higginson, *Army Life*, p. 258; Katherine Polk Gale, "Recollections," ms. pp. 14, 34; Robert Collins, "Essay on the Management of Slaves," *SC*, XII (July, 1854), 206; Easterby, ed., *South Carolina Rice Plantation*, p. 30; *Howard v. Howard*, 1858, in Catterall, ed., *Judicial Cases*, II, 221; Olmsted, *Back Country*, p. 112; Mallard, *Plantation Life Before Emancipation*, p. 49; D. E. Huger Smith, "A Plantation Boyhood," in A. R. Huger Smith, *Carolina Rice Plantation of the Fifties*, p. 77.

47. Leigh, *Ten Years*, p. 164.

48. Rawick, ed., *S.C. Narr.*, III (3), 49–50.

49. Yetman, ed., *Life Under the "Peculiar Institution,"* pp. 221–222.

50. Marrs, *Life and History*, p. 10.

51. Rawick, ed., *S.C. Narr.*, II (1), 16.

52. Frazier, "Negro Slave Family," *JNH*, XV (April, 1930), 249; Higginson, *Army Life*, p. 258.

53. Yetman, ed., *Life Under the "Peculiar Institution,"* p. 102.

54. Fisk University, *Unwritten History of Slavery*, pp. 64, 68, 104, 127, 131, 137. Also Rawick, ed., *Ark. Narr.*, IX (3), 159, 176.

55. Joel B. Fort Recollections

56. Martineau, *Society in America*, III, 100.

57. Olmsted, *Seaboard*, p. 448. See also Mooney, *Slavery in Tennessee*, p. 93, Pearson, ed., *Letters from Port Royal*, p. 41.

58. John Anthony Caruso, *The Southern Frontier* (Indianapolis, 1963), p. 347. Also Rawick, ed., *Ala. Narr.*, VI (1), 256, 387; Hundley, *Social Relations*, p. 348; Bremer, *Homes of the New World*, I, 394; Courlander, *Negro Folk Music*, p. 154; Odum and Johnson, *Negro and His Songs*, p. 169.

59. Botkin, ed., *Lay My Burden Down*, pp. 121–122; H. C. Bruce, *New Man*, p. 97; Rawick, ed., *S.C. Narr.*, II (2), 39; III (4), 249; *Indiana Narr.*, VI (2), 140.

60. Paul C. Palmer, "Servant into Slave: The Evolution of the Legal Status of the Negro Laborer in Colonial Virginia," *SAQ*, LXV (Summer, 1966), 365.

61. Rawick, ed., *Ga. Narr.*, XII (1), 88–89; H. C. Bruce, *New Man*, p. 73; Frazier, *Negro Church*, p. 34.

62. Stephen Pearl Andrews to George Frederick Holmes, Jan. 21, 1855, in the Holmes Letterbook.

63. James Weldon Johnson, in *Negro Americans, What Now?* (New York, 1934), pp. 29–30, told his people that sex had gone to the white man's head and had become corrupt. He expressed hope that black people would retain their "lusty" and "wholesome" attitudes as long as possible.

64. J. G. Taylor, *Negro Slavery in Louisiana*, p. 124; Sydnor, *Slavery in Mississippi*, p. 62; Smedes, *Southern Planter*, pp. 9–10; Henry, *Police Control of the Slave*, p. 29. For an illustration of the special directions given to overseers by planters concerning regulation of these marriages, see Marshall Account Book, 1855–1857.

65. Phifer, "Slavery in Microcosm," *JSH*, XXVIII (May, 1962), 148; Pennington, *Fugitive Blacksmith*, in Bontemps, ed., *Great Slave Narratives*, pp. 209–210; Rawick, ed., *Indiana Narr.*, VI, 139.

66. Catterall, ed., *Judicial Cases*, II, 208–209.

67. "Management of Slaves," *SC*, IV (March, 1846), 43–45. See also E. A. Davis, ed., *Plantation Slavery in the Florida Parishes of Louisiana*, pp. 406 ff.; Frank F. Steel to Anna Steel, Dec. 15, 1859; A. S. Brown to T. W. Harriss, Dec. 23, 1846 in the Harriss Papers. Slaves from off the plantation sometimes had an easier time appealing to a master or mistress about a cruel overseer; see Hairston Diary, Dec. 31, 1845.

68. See Yetman, ed., *Life Under the "Peculiar Institution,"* pp. 47, 306, for some representative instances.

69. Thomas Journal, Sept. 16, 1866; WPA, *Negro in Virginia*, p. 84.

70. For an overseer's report on some of these adventures see Charles B. Duke to John H. Bills, Oct. 14, 1860, in the Bills Papers.

71. Rawick, ed., *S.C. Narr.*, II (1), 231.

72. Yetman, ed., *Life Under the "Peculiar Institution,"* p. 24 (Mary A. Bell); Rawick, ed., *Indiana Narr.*, VI, 128; generally, G. G. Johnson, *Social History of the Sea Islands*, p. 132.

73. For a typical illustration of a planter's concern to unite a slave family see Edward A. Tayloe to B. O. Tayloe, Feb. 5, 1834. For slave reactions during the war see Fisk University, *Unwritten History of Slavery*, p. 2.

BROOMSTICKS AND ORANGE BLOSSOMS

1. B. McBride, "Directions for Cultivating Various Crops at Hickory Hill," *SA*, III (May, 1830), 237–240; Robert Collins, "Management of Slaves," *DBR*, XVII (Oct., 1854), 425; Wilson, "Peculiarities and Diseases of Negroes," *ACPSS*, IV (Sept., 1860), 415. The message never did quite reach the overseers, who remained almost wholly indifferent; see Bassett, *Southern Plantation Overseer*, pp. 260–261. And for a planter who was violently opposed to slave weddings on principle, see Sarah Hicks Williams to Mr. and Mrs. Samuel Williams, May 22, 1855.

2. Rawick, ed., *Ala. Narr.*, VI (1), 372; *S.C. Narr.*, II (2), 234, 329; III (2), 18, 136; *Texas Narr.*, IV (1), 63, 79; IV (2), 18; *Ark. Narr.*, X (5), 59; Cornish Diary, Dec. 16, 1860; Smedes, *Southern Planter*, p. 42; Mrs. Lacy to Uncle John, Sept. 4, 1849, in the Nash Papers; deposition of Fanny Grundy, Sept. 4, 1884, in Dickinson ms., "Race Problems—Slave Marriages," Tennessee State Library and Archives.

3. See, e.g., McCall Plantation Journal and Diary, April 30, 1853: Spyker Diary,

Sept. 19, 1857, Dec. 25, 1858; William B. Hamilton, Jan. 1, 1858, in the Lester Collection; Magruder Diary, Dec. 26, 1846; Laura S. Tibbetts to Sophia Tibbetts, Jan. 23, 1853.

4. C. C. Jones, *Religious Instruction*, p. 233. For ministers who did perform slave weddings see Cornish Diary, Dec. 16, 1860; Stratton Diary, 1840–1860; Henson Diary, Dec. 29, 1859; also Alex Reeves to Walker Timberlake, June 5, 1847, in the Timberlake Papers; N. L. Garfield to Levert, April 27, 1857, in the Levert Papers; Fisk University, *Unwritten History of Slavery*, pp. 14, 46, 60, 74, 107, 131; Rawick, ed., *S.C. Narr.*, III (3), 202.

5. Redpath, *Roving Editor*, pp. 40, 66; C. P. Patterson, *Negro in Tennessee*, p. 18.

6. Pennington, *Fugitive Blacksmith*, in Bontemps, ed., *Great Slave Narratives*, p. 255; Olmsted, *Back Country*, p. 154.

7. J. A. McKinstry to H. C. Nixon, Feb. 11, 1913, in Correspondence: Slavery, Tennessee State Library and Archives; Agnew Diary, May 28, 1864 (IV, 287); J. G. Taylor, *Negro Slavery in Louisiana*, p. 128; Rawick, ed., *Texas Narr.*, IV (2), 57, 136; *Ga. Narr.*, XII (1), 323; XIII (4), 201, 237; *Narrative of Lewis Clarke*, p. 277.

8. For some accounts of white ladies' activities in arranging invitations see Ross, *Cities and Camps*, p. 235; Redpath, *Roving Editor*, p. 313; Phillips, *American Negro Slavery*, p. 314. For fuller descriptions of slave weddings and the stir they caused in the Big House see Sarah Rootes Jackson Daily Journal, May 26, 1836, in the Jackson-Prince Papers; Mooney, *Slavery in Tennessee*, p. 93; Tyrone Power, *Impressions of America During the Years 1833, 1834, and 1835* (2 vols.; Philadelphia, 1836), II, 50; Mary Jones to Charles C. Jones, Jr., Jan. 31, 1856, in Myers, ed., *Children of Pride*, p. 289, plus the Jones family correspondence for Jan., 1861, pp. 641–648; Bond Diary, Jan. 4, 1862; Clarissa E. (Leavitt) Town Diary, Feb. 2, 5, 1853; Bremer, *Homes of the New World*, I, 376; Rawick, ed., *Texas Narr.*, IV (1), 78.

9. Ingraham, *South-West*, II, 128–129.

10. Leak Diary, Oct., 1856; see also Jan. 24, 1857.

11. Yetman, ed., *Life Under the "Peculiar Institution,"* p. 164.

12. Stampp, *Peculiar Institution*, p. 329.

13. Cornish Diary, Dec. 23, 1843.

14. Judith Page (Walker) Rives to Alfred L. Rives, Jan. 17, 1858.

15. See, e.g., WPA, *Negro in Virginia* pp. 80 ff.; *Narrative of William Wells Brown*, p. 39. For a kind master who was a practicing minister but had broomstick weddings for his slaves, see Rawick, ed., *Texas Narr.*, IV (2), 23.

16. Parrinder, *African Traditional Religion*, pp. 96–98; G. G. Johnson, "Courtship and Marriage Customs in Ante-bellum North Carolina," *NCHR*, VIII (Oct., 1931), 400.

17. Quoted by Dick, *Dixie Frontier*, p. 92.

18. WPA, *Negro in Virginia*, p. 80.

19. Quoted by J. B. Sellers, *Slavery in Alabama*, p. 125.

20. J. G. Williams, *"De Ole Plantation,"* p. 23.

HUSBAND AND FATHERS

1. Robert Collins, "Essay on the Management of Slaves," *SC*, XII (July, 1854), 206.

2. Foby, "Management of Servants," *SC*, XI (Aug., 1853), 226–228; Sitterson, *Sugar Country*, p. 57.

3. Hazard, "On the General Management of a Plantation," *SA*, IV (July, 1831), 351; cf. Catterall, ed., *Judicial Cases*, II, 123.

4. Chancellor Harper in E.N. Elliott, ed., *Cotton Is King and Pro-slavery Arguments*, p. 31. For a more convoluted expression of similar ideas, which reaches lyrical proportions, see Hughes, *Treatise on Sociology*, pp. 154–155.

5. Rawick. ed., *Texas Narr.*, IV (1), 76; Redpath, *Roving Editor*, p. 66. See also Kemble, *Journal*, p. 167.

6. Rawick, ed., *S.C. Narr.*, II (2), 36; *Okla. Narr.*, VII (1), 28; *Ark. Narr.*, IX (3), 231; *N.C. Narr.*, XIV (1), 101; *Ga. Narr.*, XII (2), 13; Greene, ed., *Diary of Col. Landon Carter*, II, 777; J. H. Johnston, *Race Relations and Miscegenation*, pp. 306–307.

7. See, e.g., Scarborough, *Overseer*, pp. 99–100; Weld, *Slavery as It Is*, p. 47; Rawick, ed., *Mo. Narr.*, XI, 171.

8. See Martineau, *Society in America*, II, 142; Catterall, ed., *Judicial Cases*, III, 362–363; Fisk University, *Unwritten History of Slavery*, pp. 1–2; and in general, James Hugo Johnston, "A New Interpretation of the Domestic Slave System," *JNH*, XVIII (Jan., 1933), 42.

9. E. F. Andrews, *War-Time Journal of a Georgia Girl*, p. 349; Kate Stone, *Brokenburn*, p. 219.

10. This problem long outlived slavery and cast a shadow over black male-female relations, discussion of which would best be reserved for blacks. See esp. Joyce Ladner, *Tomorrow's Tomorrow: The Black Woman* (New York, 1971).

11. *Father Henson's Story of His Own Life*, pp. 6–7.

12. Keckley, *Behind the Scenes*, pp. 22, 25–28; Mrs. Smith Journal, 1793, pp. 17–18; Phillips and Glunt, eds., *Florida Plantation Records*, p. 63; Trollope, *Domestic Manners*, pp. 246–247; Rawick, ed., *S.C. Narr.*, III (3), 17; J. M. McPherson, *Negro's Civil War*, pp. 62–63; Minor Plantation Diary, Sept. 28, 1863; Blassingame, "Recruitment of Colored Troops in Kentucky, Maryland, and Missouri," *Historian*, XXIX (Aug., 1967), 539–540.

13. Rawick, ed., *N.C. Narr.*, XIV (1), 3; also *S.C. Narr.*, III (3), 193. I have found only one reference to hunting by women; see *Ark. Narr.*, IX (4), 6.

14. Puckett, *Folk Beliefs*, p. 75.

15. Rawick, ed., *Texas Narr.*, IV (1), 67; *S.C. Narr.*, II (2), 138.

16. Dick, *Dixie Frontier*, p. 35; Hundley, *Social Relations*, p. 343; Rawick, ed., *S.C. Narr.*, II (2), 215.

17. Schoolcraft, *Plantation Life*, pp. 42–43; House, ed., "Deterioration of a Georgia Rice Plantation During Four Years of Civil War," *JSH*, IX (Feb., 1943), 108; G. G. Johnson, *Social History of the Sea Islands*, pp. 85–86; Sydnor, *Slavery in Mississippi*, p. 34, n. 58; Wall, "Founding of Pettigrew Plantations," *NCHR*, XXVII (Oct., 1950), 409; Fisk University, *Unwritten History of Slavery*, p. 136; Hundley, *Social Relations*, pp. 343–344.

18. Ascher and Fairbanks, "Excavation of a Slave Cabin," *Historical Archeology* (1971), pp. 3–17. See also Dick, *Dixie Frontier*, p. 96; Lyell, *Second Visit*, II, 17; Northup, *Twelve Years a Slave*, p. 200; Saxon *et al.*, *Gumbo Ya-Ya*, p. 238; Yetman, ed., *Life Under the "Peculiar Institution,"* pp. 61, 268, 331; Fisk University, *Unwritten History of Slavery*, p. 44; Rawick, ed., *S.C. Narr.*, III (3), 56; *N.C. Narr.*, XIV (1), 105.

19. See, e.g., the correspondence between Joseph Bieller of Louisiana and his father, Jacob, in the Snyder Papers.

20. J. G. Williams, *"De Ole Plantation,"* pp. 62–63.

21. Greene, ed., *Diary of Col. Landon Carter*, I, 72–73, 75, 335; C. S. Davis, *Cotton Kingdom in Alabama*, p. 93; Botume, *First Days Amongst the Contrabands*, p. 95.

22. Heyward, *Seed from Madagascar*, pp. 124, 127; D. E. Huger Smith, "Plantation

Boyhood," in A. R. Huger Smith, *Carolina Rice Plantation of the Fifties*, p. 67; F. L. Riley, ed., "Diary of a Mississippi Planter," *Publications of the Mississippi Historical Society*, X (1909), 434; Olmsted, *Seaboard*, p. 447; Catterall, ed., *Judicial Cases*, II, 219; V, 305; Yetman, ed., *Life Under the "Peculiar Institution,"* p. 73; Rawick, ed., *N.C. Narr.*, XV (2), 418; J. G. Taylor, *Negro Slavery in Louisiana*, pp. 126, 180.

23. Mooney, *Slavery in Tennessee*, p. 13; J. B. Sellers, *Slavery in Alabama*, p. 235; Louisiana, Ascension Parish, Police Jury Minutes, I, 36 (1837–1856); Leak Diary, March 21, 1853.

24. Rawick, ed., *Texas Narr.*, IV (2), 234; also G. W. Cable, "Creole Slave Songs," in Katz, ed., *Social Implications of Early Negro Music*, pp. 62–63. For descriptions of these festive hunts see B. F. Jones, "A Cultural Middle Passage," unpubl. Ph.D. dissertation, University of North Carolina, 1965, pp. 125 ff.; Phillips, *American Negro Slavery*, p. 314; J. G. Williams, *"De Ole Plantation,"* p. 61; D. Maitland Armstrong, *Day Before Yesterday: Reminiscences of a Varied Life* (New York, 1920), pp. 76–77.

25. Ervin Journal, p. 46.

26. W. T. Jordan, *Hugh Davis*, p. 95.

27. F. L. Riley, ed., "Diary of a Mississippi Planter," pp. 343–344; Seale Diary, March 7, 1857; Monette Day Book and Diary, *passim;* LeBlanc Record Book, 1859–1866.

28. WPA, *Negro in Virginia*, pp. 88–89; Rawick, ed., *S.C. Narr.*, III (3), 104; Scott, *Southern Lady*, p. 30.

29. Botume, *First Days Amongst the Contrabands*, pp. 221, 226.

30. Fisk University, *God Struck Me Dead*, p. 161.

31. Yetman, ed., *Life Under the "Peculiar Institution,"* p. 71.

32. Rawick, ed., *Texas Narr.*, IV (1), 2.

33. Odum and Johnson, *Negro and His Songs*, pp. 54, 55; Higginson, *Army Life*, p. 211.

34. Yetman, ed., *Life Under the "Peculiar Institution,"* pp. 310–311.

35. See, e.g., the account in Fisk University, *Unwritten History of Slavery*, p. 105.

36. Ulf Hannerz, "Another Look at Lower-Class Black Culture," in Rainwater, ed., *Soul*, p. 173.

37. Keil, *Urban Blues*, p. 26.

38. John Womack, *Zapata and the Mexican Revolution* (New York, 1969), p. 6. See also Pennington, *Fugitive Blacksmith*, in Bontemps, ed., *Great Slave Narratives*, p. 211; Rawick, ed., *S.C. Narr.*, III (3), 260; *Ark. Narr.*, X (5), 27; *N.C. Narr.*, XIV (1), 5.

39. Thomas Wentworth Higginson, *Black Rebellion* (New York, 1969), pp. 148, 144.

WIVES AND MOTHERS

1. Botume, *First Days Amongst the Contrabands*, p. 53. Also Rawick, ed., *Ga. Narr.*, XIII (3), 53.

2. Kemble, *Journal*, p. 263.

3. Rawick, ed., *Texas Narr.*, IV (1), 54. Also *S.C. Narr.*, II (2), 66, 114; *Texas Narr.*, V (3), 190; *Ga. Narr.*, XII (2), 41, 187; WPA, *Negro in Virginia*, p. 65; Kiser, *Sea Island to City*, p. 60.

4. For general surveys see Bonner, *Georgia Agriculture*, p. 87; J. B. Sellers, *Slavery in Alabama*, p. 66; J. G. Taylor, *Negro Slavery in Louisiana*, p. 62; Phillips and

Glunt, eds., *Florida Plantation Records*, p. 515; and Myers, ed., *Children of Pride*, *passim*. For the recollections of ex-slaves see Jeremiah W. Loguen, *Reverend J. W. Loguen as a Slave and as a Freeman* (New York, 1970 [1859]), p. 18; Rawick, ed., *S.C. Narr.*, II (2), 80; III (4), 36; *Texas Narr.*, IV (1), 223; *Miss. Narr.*, VII (2), 158, 165; *Mo. Narr.*, XI, 130, 261; *Ga. Narr.*, XII (1), 113; XII (2), 250, 269, 322; XIII (4), 217; *N.C. Narr.*, XIV (1), 93, 180, 215, 312, 313; XV (2), 57, 130, 149, 159. Fogel and Engerman doubt that many women plowed, but I fear that they have been misled by the records of the larger plantations, which exhibited a greater sexual division of labor; see *Time on the Cross*, p. 141.

5. Sydnor, *Slavery In Mississippi*, p. 96; Bonner, ed., "Plantation Experiences of a New York Woman," *NCHR*, XXXIII (July, 1956), 400; *Life and Times of Frederick Douglass*, p. 142; Rawick, ed., *Ala. Narr.*, VI (1), 46, 338; Fisk University, *Unwritten History of Slavery*, p. 13; Northup, *Twelve Years a Slave*, pp. 155–156; Yetman, ed., *Life Under the "Peculiar Institution,"* p. 252.

6. Rawick, ed., *Texas Narr.*, IV (2), 109.

7. See, e.g., Kate Stone, *Brokenburn*, p. 87; John Palfrey to William Palfrey, May 30, 1832.

8. Drew, *Refugee*, p. 259.

9. K. Thomas, *Religion and the Decline of Magic*, p. 17.

10. Ariès, *Centuries of Childhood*, p. 39. Ariès may well push his argument too far. See Natalie Zemon Davis, "The Reasons of Misrule: Youth Groups and Charivaris in Sixteenth-Century France," *Past and Present*, No. 50 (Feb., 1971), pp. 55–56.

11. Kemble, *Journal*, p. 95. For some illustrations of white concern about the high death rate of the slave children see Elizabeth Manigault, Gowrie, and Silk Hope Plantations, Slave Records, Sept.–Oct., 1834; K. W. Skinner to C. M. Manigault, July 12, 1851, in the Manigault Papers; J. H. Randolph to Moses Liddell, Nov. 13, 1851, in the Liddell Papers.

12. This argument has been pressed as far as it can go—much too far in fact—by Raymond and Alice Bauer, "Day to Day Resistance to Slavery," *JNH*, XXVII (Oct., 1942), 415–417.

13. J. H. Johnston, *Race Relations and Miscegenation*, p. 308; Rawick, ed., *Okla. Narr.*, VII (1), 302. Also Catterall, ed., *Judicial Cases*, V, 139; C. C. Jones to Charles C. Jones, Jr., Dec. 10, 1859, in Myers, ed., *Children of Pride*, pp. 544–545.

14. For a discussion of the economic pressures for infanticide in Japan see Johannes Hirschmeier, *Origins of Entrepreneurship in Meiji Japan* (Cambridge, Mass., 1964), pp. 73, 121; G. B. Sansom, *Japan: A Short Cultural History* (New York, 1931), pp. 516–517.

15. Ingraham, *South-West*, II, 125; Lyell, *Second Visit*, I, 264; Weld, *Slavery as It Is*, p. 12; R. R. Gibbes, "Southern Slave Life," *DBR*, XXIV (Jan., 1858), 324; G. G. Johnson, *Social History of the Sea Islands*, p. 96; Sydnor, *Slavery in Mississippi*, p. 64.

16. See William B. Price Books, I (1836–1843) and II (Aug. 14–22, 1846); B. B. Jones Book, III (1838); Turner Physician's Record Book, 1857.

17. See, e.g., E. P. Thompson, *Making of the English Working Class*, p. 328.

18. M. C. Mitchell, "Health and the Medical Profession in the Lower South, 1845–1860," *JSH*, X (Nov., 1944), 434.

19. Stampp, *Peculiar Institution*, p. 316.

20. Greene, ed., *Diary of Col. Landon Carter*, I, 494; Olmsted, *Seaboard*, pp. 658, 698, and *Back Country*, p. 47; J. B. Sellers, *Slavery in Alabama*, p. 128; Sydnor, *Slavery in Mississippi*, pp. 64–65.

21. Willie Lee Rose has suggested, in an unpublished paper, that the consequences of this practice were far-reaching and require expert medical and

psychological review. At the moment we can only note the possibilities. Some planters worried about it; see, e.g., J. Channing to Edward Telfair, Oct. 3, 1787, in the Telfair Papers.

22. Rawick, ed., *Texas Narr.*, V (3), 237; for an extreme case see V (2), 220. Also Bascom, "Acculturation Among the Gullah Negroes," *American Anthropologist*, XLIII, no. 1 (1941), 39; Kemble, *Journal*, p. 254; Olmsted, *Back Country*, p. 199; Frazier, *Negro Family*, p. 112.

23. Yetman, ed., *Life Under the "Peculiar Institution,"* p. 227.

24. See, e.g., Rawick, ed., *Texas Narr.*, IV (1), 37; *Ark. Narr.*, XI (7), 193.

25. Schofield Diary, Feb. 5, 1866.

26. *Narrative of William Wells Brown*, p. 35; also pp. 2, 10.

27. *Father Henson's Story of His Own Life*, pp. 10, 14.

28. George Teamoh Journal, Pts. 1–2, pp. 27, 29, in the Woodson Papers.

29. For an able defense of this view, with which I cannot agree, see Bernard, *Marriage and Family Among Negroes*, pp. 68 and esp. 73.

THE CHILDREN

1. *Jordan v. State*, 1857, in Catterall, ed., *Judicial Cases*, III, 56.

2. Catterall, ed., *Judicial Cases*, II, 358; Dennett, *South as It Is*, pp. 131–132.

3. Mullin, *Flight and Rebellion*, p.

4. Bancroft, *Slave Trading*, pp. 202, 208; but see also p. 197.

5. Morton, *Robert Carter of Nomini Hall*, pp. 102–103; W. T. Jordan, *Hugh Davis*, p. 76; R. H. Taylor, *Slaveholding in North Carolina*, p. 18, n. 46; Phillips, *Life and Labor*, p. 174; Stampp, *Peculiar Institution*, pp. 57–58.

6. J. H. Hammond, in E. N. Elliott, ed., *Cotton Is King and Pro-slavery Arguments*, p. 138.

7. See, e.g., Heyward, *Seed from Madagascar*, pp. 178–179; Yetman, ed., *Life Under the "Peculiar Institution,"* pp. 79, 202; Rawick, ed., *S.C. Narr.*, II (1), 205, 230, 263; II (2), 88, 105, 145; III (3), 126, 202, 232, 271. The plantation records and slave narratives for other states reveal the same pattern.

8. Lyell, *Second Visit*, I, 262; C. S. Davis, *Cotton Kingdom in Alabama*, p. 58; Fisk University, *Unwritten History of Slavery*, pp. 117, 146, 154; Yetman, ed., *Life Under the "Peculiar Institution,"* pp. 40, 144; WPA, *Negro in Virginia*, pp. 60–61; Rawick, ed., *S.C. Narr.*, II (2), 124–125, 129; III (4), 273; *Texas Narr.*, V (3), 258; V (4), 89; *Ala. Narr.*, VI (1), 17, 51.

9. R. R. King, "On the Management of the Butler Estate," *SA*, I (Dec., 1828), 523–529; Schoolcraft, *Plantation Life*, p. 39 and p. 12 of the "Letters"; F. L. Riley, ed., "Diary of a Mississippi Planter," *Publications of the Mississippi Historical Society*, X (1909), 465; Yetman, ed., *Life Under the "Peculiar Institution,"* pp. 264, 288; Rawick, ed., *S.C. Narr.*, II (2), 12; III (4), 158; *Texas Narr.*, IV (2), 19, 56; V (3), 2; V (4), 48, 95; *Ala. Narr.*, VI (1), 44, 149; *Ga. Narr.*, XII (2), 259; *N.C. Narr.*, XIV (1), 321; XV (2), 57; H. C. Bruce, *New Man*, pp. 14, 24.

10. Macrery Papers, 1855; Cotton Book, Aug. 30, 1828, in the Stirling Papers; Moody, *Slavery on the Louisiana Sugar Plantations*, p. 46; C. S. Davis, *Cotton Kingdom in Alabama*, p. 63. For some ex-slave recollections of the odd jobs see Saxon *et al.*, *Gumbo Ya-Ya*, p. 232; Yetman, ed., *Life Under the "Peculiar Institution,"* pp. 71–72.

11. Schoolcraft, *Plantation Life*, p. 42.

12. Olmsted, *Seaboard*, pp. 443 ff.; Rawick, ed., *S.C. Narr.*, III (4), 128.

13. W.H. Russell, *My Diary North and South*, p. 149.

14. Kuczynski, *Rise of the Working Class*, pp. 105–106 and Tab. 1; Hamerow, *Restoration, Revolution, Reaction*, pp. 235–236; Hobsbawm, *Age of Revolution*, pp. 50–51.

15. Quoted by E. P. Thompson, *Making of the English Working Class*, p. 329. I shall follow Thompson's account, esp. pp. 328–349, although, as everyone knows, he is terribly unscientific and permits himself to become enraged over the destruction of the lives of children—something no scientific historian is supposed to do. R. M. Hartwell, *The Industrial Revolution and Economic Growth* (London, 1971), Ch. 17, challenges Thompson's generalizations but admits, "There is evidence enough of the exploitation and ill-treatment of children in factories to justify contemporary and subsequent indignation" (p. 395).

16. E. P. Thompson, *Making of the English Working Class*, p. 349. For the extent of criminality and degeneracy among these children see Tobias, *Crime and Industrial Society*, pp. 88, 101.

17. See the grim accounts in Pitman, "Slavery on the British West India Plantations," *JNH*, XI (Oct., 1926), 601–604; H. O. Patterson, *Sociology of Slavery*, pp. 156–157; Craton and Walvin, *Jamaican Plantation*, p. 127.

18. See the remarks of Bremer, *Homes of the New World*, I, 337, on the children of the Big House; for the children of the nonslaveholders see esp. Robert E. Corlew, "Some Aspects of Slavery in Dickson County [Tennessee]," *THQ*, X (Sept., 1951), 239.

19. Rawick, ed., *Miss. Narr.*, VII (2), 27; also Ingraham, *South-West*, II, 126.

20. W. D. Jordan, *White over Black*, pp. 161–162; Moody, *Slavery on the Louisiana Sugar Plantations*, p. 80; Schoepf, *Travels in the Confederation*, II, 47; G. G. Johnson, *Social History of the Sea Islands*, p. 139; Ingraham, *South-West*, I, 236; Power, *Impressions of America*, II, 63; Botkin, ed., *Lay My Burden Down*, p. 90.

21. For accounts and descriptions see J. A. McKinstry to H. C. Nixon, Feb. 11, 1913, in Correspondence: Slavery, Tennessee State Library and Archives; Chesnut, *Diary from Dixie*, p. 167; Fisk University, *Unwritten History of Slavery*, pp. 6, 130; Rawick, ed., *S.C. Narr.*, II (1), 28, 167; II (2), 146; III (3), 15, 56–57, 62, 124, 186; *Texas Narr.*, IV (1), 45, 63; V (4), 49; *Miss. Narr.*, VI (1), 361; VII (2), 72, 101; *Ark. Narr.*, IX (3), 167.

22. Rawick, ed., *Texas Narr.*, IV (1), 97. See also the remarks of Esteban Montejo, *Autobiography of a Runaway Slave*, pp. 30–31.

23. Catherine Devereaux Edmonston, March 19, 1861, in Poe, ed., *True Tales*, p. 108; also Olmsted, *Seaboard*, p. 32.

24. Saxon *et al.*, *Gumbo Ya-Ya*, p. 447.

25. An Owner of an Estate in Mississippi, "Management of Negroes upon Southern Estates," *DBR*, XIX (June, 1851), 624.

26. Yetman, ed., *Life Under the "Peculiar Institution*," p. 265.

27. C. C. Jones, *Religious Instruction*, pp. 113–114; Drew, *Refugee*, p. 141.

28. Rawick, ed., *S.C. Narr.*, III (3), 27.

29. Olmsted, *Seaboard*, p. 424. See also Gibbes, "Southern Slave Life," *DBR*, XXIV (Jan., 1858), 324; Mary Ames, *From a New England Woman's Diary in Dixie in 1865* (Springfield, Ill., 1906), p. 64. D. E. Huger Smith, "A Plantation Boyhood," in A. R. Huger Smith, *Carolina Rice Plantation of the Fifties*, p. 62; Schoolcraft, *Plantation Life*, pp. 38–39; O. K. Armstrong, *Ole Massa's People*, p. 127.

30. Rawick, ed., *S.C. Narr.*, II (1), 119; III (3), 10; *Texas Narr.*, IV (1), 66; V (3), 189; *Ala. Narr.*, VI (1), 43; *Ark. Narr.*, IX (3), 209; X (6), 42, 154. But any volume may be consulted at random.

31. F. L. Riley, ed., "Diary of a Mississippi Planter," Jan. 23, 1849, p. 427.

32. Marengo Planter, "This Season's Work," *ACP*, II (Sept., 1854), 280.

33. Kemble, *Journal*, p. 121; also pp. 31–32, 52, 66 269, 312.
34. See, e.g., Rawick, ed., *Okla. Narr.*, VII (1), 300.
35. See, e.g., Keckley, *Behind the Scenes*, p. 19; H. C. Bruce, *New Man*, p. 106.
36. For some white complaints see C. C. Jones, *Religious Instruction*, p. 113; Mallard, *Plantation Life Before Emancipation*, p. 52.
37. Rose, *Rehearsal for Reconstruction*, p. 135; Swint, ed., *Dear Ones at Home*, p. 123.
38. See Rawick, ed., *S.C. Narr.*, II (1), 102, 286, 347; III (3), 158; *Texas Narr.*, V (4), 122; Fisk University, *God Struck Me Dead*, p. 185. Also M. Ames, *Diary in Dixie in 1865*, p. 34.
39. Fisk University, *Unwritten History of Slavery*, p. 100.
40. Ellison, *Shadow and Act*, pp. 96, 101; also James Baldwin, *The Fire Next Time* (New York, 1963), pp. 40–41.
41. *Life and History of the Rev. Elijah P. Marrs*, p. 11.
42. Rawick, ed., *S. C. Narr.*, II (1), 293.
43. See Rawick, ed., *S.C. Narr.*, II (1), 227; *Ala. Narr.*, VI (1), 33, 227; *Ga. Narr.*, XIII (4), 34; Fisk University, *Unwritten History of Slavery*, pp. 5, 110, and *passim*.
44. Rawick, ed., *Ga. Narr.*, XII (1), 312; XII (2), 111, 189; *Fla. Narr.*, XVII, 63.
45. Rawick, ed., *S.C. Narr.*, III (4), 9.
46. Rawick, ed., *Ga. Narr.*, XII (1), 65–66; Fisk University, *God Struck Me Dead*, p. 161; and generally, G. G. Johnson, *Social History of the Sea Islands*, pp. 138–139.
47. Rawick, ed., *Texas Narr.*, IV (1), 130.
48. Rawick, ed., *S.C. Narr.*, II (1), 101.
49. F. L. Riley, ed., "Diary of a Mississippi Planter," Aug. 8, 1860 (p. 469) and Sept. 23, 1865 (p. 450).
50. Rachel Weeks O'Connor to Mary Weeks, Jan. 23, 1826, in the Weeks Papers; W. C. Harrison to William H. Taylor, Jan. 18, 1853, in the Dromgoole-Robinson Papers. See also Charles C. Jones, Jr., to Mary Jones, Nov. 22, 1856, in Myers, ed., *Children of Pride*, p. 266; Walker Diary, Feb. 17, 1856; J. B. Sellers, *Slavery in Alabama*, pp. 128–129; *Father Henson's Story of His Own Life*, p. 8.
51. Rawick, ed., *N.C. Narr.*, XIV (1), 21; also C. S. Johnson, *Shadow of the Plantation*, p. 38; Olmsted, *Seaboard*, p. 92.
52. Rawick, ed., *N.C. Narr.*, XIV (1), 22.
53. Gibbes, "Southern Slave Life," p. 323.
54. "Autobiography of Emily Donelson Walton," typescript p. 10, in the Laurence Family Papers; *DBR*, XIX (Sept., 1859), 363; Joel B. Fort Recollections; Rawick, ed., *S.C. Narr.*, II (1), 225; *Texas Narr.*, V (4), 73.
55. Mallard, *Plantation Life Before Emancipation*, p. 10; D. E. Huger Smith, "A Plantation Boyhood," p. 81; Wise, *End of an Era*, pp. 52–53; Pollard, *Black Diamonds*, p. 49; Lyell, *Second Visit*, II, 24–25; Olmsted, *Seaboard*, p. 113; WPA, *Negro in Virginia*, pp. 73–74; Yetman, ed., *Life Under the "Peculiar Institution,"* p. 140; Phillips, *American Negro Slavery*, p. 313.
56. Pharr Book, pp. 105–106.
57. See, e.g., Fisk University, *Unwritten History of Slavery*, p. 140; *Life and History of the Rev. Elijah P. Marrs*, pp. 9–10; Rawick, ed., *Indiana Narr.*, VI (2), 17; *Life and Times of Frederick Douglass*, pp. 81, 83, 101.
58. Rawick, ed., *Texas Narr.*, IV (2), 33. For some illustrations of such attachments see Louisiana, West Feliciana Parish, Police Jury Minutes, 1850; John Palfrey to Edward Palfrey, Sept. 8, 1816; Clement, *Plantation Life on the Mississippi*, p. 2.
59. Stampp, *Peculiar Institution*, p. 378.
60. See, e.g., Rawick, ed., *S.C. Narr.*, II (1), 149; II (2), 178; *Okla. Narr.*, VIII (1), 77.
61. See, e.g., Sydnor, *Slavery in Mississippi*, p. 65.
62. Rawick, ed., *Texas Narr.*, IV (1), 88.

63. Rawick, ed., *Indiana Narr.*, VI (2), 27–28.
64. Flanders, "Two Plantations and a County of Ante-bellum Georgia," *GHQ*, XII (March, 1928), 11–12; Seabrook, *Before and After*, p. 69.
65. Yetman, ed., *Life Under the "Peculiar Institution,"* p. 182.
66. See the indignant remarks of Martineau, *Society in America*, II, 342; Trollope, *Domestic Manners of the Americans*, p. 245, n. 2; Seabrook, *Before and After*, p. 67.
67. Northup, *Twelve Years a Slave*, p. 261; also Pennington, *Fugitive Blacksmith*, in Bontemps, ed., *Great Slave Narratives*, p. 208.
68. See, e.g., Lester, *To Be a Slave*, pp. 127–128.
69. Rawick, ed., *S.C. Narr.*, II (2), 50.
70. A Reader, "Agricultural Laborers," *SA*, VIII (Jan., 1835), p. 8.
71. Stuart Noblin, *Leonidas La Fayette Polk: Agrarian Crusader* (Chapel Hill, N.C., 1949) p. 22; also Col. David Wyatt Aiken Autobiography; Mary Burruss McGehee to John H. Burruss, May 29, 1836; Gatewood, ed., *"Smoked Yankees,"* p. 75; Pollard, *Black Diamonds*, pp. 79–80.
72. Lyell, *Second Visit*, II, 168; Stirling, *Letters from the Slave States*, p. 26.
73. Bremer, *Homes of the New World*, II, 233–234.
74. Kemble, *Journal*, pp. 57–58.
75. Quoted in Eaton, *Henry Clay*, p. 66.

THE OLD FOLKS

1. E. F. Andrews, *War-Time Journal of a Georgia Girl*, pp. 101–102; Schoolcraft, *Plantation Life*, pp. 79–80.
2. Quoted in Phillips, *Life and Labor*, p. 175.
3. William S. Pettigrew to Moses, July 12, 1856.
4. Solon Robinson, "Negro Slavery in the South," *DBR*, VII (Nov., 1849), 381.
5. See, e.g., J. B. Sellers, *Slavery in Alabama*, p. 69; Catterall, ed., *Judicial Cases*, III, 190; Holcombe Diary, April 13, 1855; Yetman, ed., *Life Under the "Peculiar Institution,"* p. 275; Rawick, ed., *Texas Narr.*, V (4), 48; *Miss. Narr.*, VII (2), 19.
6. See esp. Brackett, *Negro in Maryland*, p. 149.
7. Josiah Nott, "Statistics of Southern Slave Population," *DBR*, IV (Nov., 1847), 286.
8. See, e.g., O. W. Taylor, *Negro Slavery in Arkansas*, p. 81.
9. Saxon *et al.*, *Gumbo Ya-Ya*, p. 30.
10. Easterby, ed., *South Carolina Rice Plantation*, p. 348; Bremer, *Homes of the New World*, I, 293–294.
11. S. Andrews, *South Since the War*, p. 321; May, "Medical Care of Blacks in Louisiana," unpubl. Ph.D. dissertation, Tulane University, 1970, p. 52; and generally, Wiley, *Southern Negroes*, pp. 4–5.
12. Stampp, *Peculiar Institution*, p. 318.
13. Lester, *To Be a Slave*, pp. 126–127.
14. House, ed., *Planter Management and Capitalism*, p. 35.
15. Leigh, *Ten Years*, p. 58; Wiley, *Southern Negroes*, p. 250; Rose, *Rehearsal for Reconstruction*, p. 303; J. M. McPherson, *Negro's Civil War*, pp. 121–122.
16. Lyell, *Second Visit*, I, 262.
17. D. E. Huger Smith, "A Plantation Boyhood," in A. R. Huger Smith, *Carolina Rice Plantation of the Fifties*, p. 89. Also Pollard, *Black Diamonds*, pp. 30–31;
18. *Journal of Charlotte Forten*, p. 157.
19. Botume, *First Days Amongst the Contrabands*, p. 210. Also Ingraham, *South-West*,

II, 241–242; *Life and History of Rev. Elijah P. Marrs*, p. 77; Rawick, ed., *Texas Narr.*, IV (1), 272.

20. Abraham, *Mind of Africa*, p. 71; Parrinder, *African Traditional Religion*, p. 24; Herskovits, *Myth of the Negro Past*, p. 15; also Benedict, *Chrysanthemum and Sword*, p. 98. In Jamaica, where masters often let old slaves shift for themselves, the strength of this African attitude saved many from misery; see H. O. Patterson, *Sociology of Slavery*, p. 158.

21. Gavin Diary, Sept. 13, 1856; *Life and Times of Frederick Douglass*, p. 43; Yetman, ed., *Life Under the "Peculiar Institution*," p. 167; Fisk University, *Unwritten History of Slavery*, p. 131.

22. Northup, *Twelve Years a Slave*, pp. 186–187.

23. Ingraham, *South-West*, II, 242.

24. Fisk University, *Unwritten History of Slavery*, p. 46 and *passim*; Rawick, ed., *S.C. Narr.*, II (2), 58, 89; III (3), 128; *Texas Narr.*, IV (2), 91–92, 111, 285; IV (4), 13.

25. Meerlo, *Suicide and Mass Suicide*, p. 64; Powell, *Design of Discord*, pp. 16–17.

HEARTH AND HOME

1. Tatler, "The Management of Negroes," *SC*, VIII (Nov., 1850), 163.

2. See esp. "Management of Slaves," *FR*, V (May, 1837), 32–33; The Editor, "Agricultural Survey of the Parish of St. Matthews, S.C.," *So.Cab.*, I (April, 1840), 196–203; Tatler, "Management of Negroes," pp. 162–164; Foby, "Management of Servants," *SC*, XI (Aug., 1853), 226–228; R.W.N.N., "Negro Cabins," *SP*, XVI (April, 1856), 121–122; Southron, "The Policy of the Southern Planter," *ACPSS*, I (Oct., 1857), 292–296. Also the following from *DBR:* "The Negro: Personal Experience of a Southern Slaveholder," III (May, 1847), 419; Solon Robinson, "Negro Slavery in the South," VII (Nov., 1849), 380; "Management of Negroes upon Southern Estates," XI (June, 1851), 623; Robert Collins, "Management of Slaves," XVII (Oct., 1854), 423; Agricola, "Management of Negroes," XIX (Sept., 1859), 359.

3. Eaton, *Growth of Southern Civilization*, pp. 60, 101–102; O. W. Taylor, *Negro Slavery in Arkansas*, pp. 147–148. Plantations that kept good records confirm this estimate; see, e.g., Orange Grove Plantation Diaries, 1849. The published census for 1850 and 1860 suggest a norm of about 5.75.

4. Schoolcraft, *Plantation Life*, p. 34.

5. C. C. Jones, *Religious Instruction*, p. 116; also C. S. Davis, *Cotton Kingdom in Alabama*, p. 81; C. P. Patterson, *Negro in Tennessee*, p. 66; Olmsted, *Back Country*, p. 74; Lyell, *Second Visit*, I, 249.

6. A Southron, "Hints in Relation to the Dwellings and Clothing of Slaves," *FR*, II (April, 1835), 703. Little change took place in this respect during the subsequent decades.

7. Bonner, *Georgia Agriculture*, p. 199; Rawick, ed., *S.C. Narr.*, III (3), 210.

8. Rawick, ed., *Texas Narr.*, V (3), 152.

9. Rawick, ed., *S.C. Narr.*, II (1), 150.

10. For indications of the spread of raised houses see Flanders, "Two Plantations and a County of Ante-bellum Georgia," *GHQ*, XII (March, 1928), 6; Sydnor, *Slavery in Mississippi*, p. 39; W. T. Jordan, *Hugh Davis*, p. 168; C. S. Davis, *Cotton Kingdom in Alabama*, p. 80; Rawick, ed., *Texas Narr.*, IV (1), 55. But even by 1860 most cabins were still on the ground; see, e.g., Boyd, *Alabama in the Fifties*, p. 46.

11. Planters generally saw the advantage of brick chimneys even if they were not prepared to spend the money to build them. There was, however, strong opposition to brick cabins for the slaves; they were considered too damp and dangerous to health. For discussions and descriptions of brick cabins and the campaign for more brick chimneys, see "Report of the Cambridge Agricultural Society on the Situation of Whitfield Brooks' Plantation," Nov. 21, 1844, in State Agricultural Society of South Carolina, *Proceedings of the Agricultural Convention, 1839–1845*, p. 287; Col. R. H. Powell "An Essay Presented to the Alabama State Agricultural Society at Its Annual Meeting in November, 1856," *ACPSS*, I (March, 1857), 71; Manigault Plantation Books, 1833; Schoolcraft, *Plantation Life*, p. 36; Stephenson, *Isaac Franklin*, pp. 97, 107; Moody, *Slavery on the Louisiana Sugar Plantations*, p. 73; Olmsted, *Seaboard*, pp. 44, 422; Rawick, ed., *Texas Narr.*, V (3), 73.

12. Olmsted, *Seaboard*, p. 111; Fisk University, *Unwritten History of Slavery*, p. 54; Rawick, ed., *S.C. Narr.*, II (1), 150, 205; *Texas Narr.*, V (4), 123; *Ga. Narr.*, XII (1), 63; Massenburg Farm Journal, III, 510.

13. Ascher and Fairbanks, "Excavation of a Slave Cabin," *Historical Archeology* (1971), p. 6.

14. Schoepf, *Travels in the Confederation*, II, 153; "Travelers' Impressions of Slavery in America from 1750 to 1800," *JNH*, I (Oct., 1916), 408; McColley, *Slavery and Jeffersonian Virginia*, p. 61; Higginson, *Army Life*, p. 31; Olmsted, *Seaboard*, p. 432.

15. Yetman, ed., *Life Under the "Peculiar Institution,"* p. 52.

16. Botkin, ed., *Lay My Burden Down*, p. 62; Rawick, ed., *S.C. Narr.*, II (1), 190; III (3), 211.

17. Rawick, ed., *S.C. Narr.*, II (1), 272; *Texas Narr.*, IV (2), 55–57; *Ala. Narr.*, VI (1), 283. 353. For a Big House recipe for candles which calls for a mixture of lard, saltpeter, and alum, see Mary S. Mallard to Mary Jones, Dec. 14, 1861, in Myers, ed., *Children of Pride*, p. 818.

18. McColley, *Slavery and Jeffersonian Virginia*, p. 62; Mullin, *Flight and Rebellion*, p. 51; Stampp, *Peculiar Institution*, p. 311.

19. WPA, *Negro in Virginia*, p. 67. See Niemcewicz's obvious exaggerations as reported on p. 68.

20. Martineau, *Society in America*, II, 357–358; Stirling, *Letters from the Slave States*, p. 264; G. G. Johnson, *Social History of the Sea Islands*, pp. 90–91; Olmsted, *Seaboard*, pp. 659–660; Hugh C. Bailey, *Hinton Rowan Helper: Abolitionist-Racist* (University, Ala., 1965), p. 7; Kemble, *Journal*, p. 24.

21. See, e.g., Reeves, *Round About a Pound a Week*, pp. 18–22, 48–49. On twentieth-century Ireland see Arensberg, *Irish Countryman*, p. 64.

22. See, e.g., Morazé, *La France bourgeoise*, pp. 48–54; Kuczynski, *Rise of the Working Class*, pp. 92, 94; Frederick Engels, *The Condition of the Working Class in England in 1844* (London, 1968), pp. 27–37, 53; Fussell, *English Rural Laborer* p. 53; E. P. Thompson, *Making of the English Working Class*, pp. 318, 321, 429; Boxer, *Dutch Seaborne Empire*, pp. 55, 59; Ware, *Industrial Worker*, pp. 12–13 and Ch. 2; Traian Stoianovitch, "Material Foundations of Preindustrial Civilization in the Balkans," *J.Soc.H.*, IV (Spring, 1971), 228–229, 242.

23. Quoted in C. P. Patterson, *Negro in Tennessee*, p. 65.

24. See, e.g., Henry A. Tayloe to B. O. Tayloe, May 20, 1841; *DBR*, IX (1850), 325; Martineau, *Society in America*, II, 161; W. H. Russell, *My Diary North and South*, pp. 140–141.

25. Yetman, ed., *Life Under the "Peculiar Institution,"* p. 192; C. C. Jones, *Religious Instruction*, p. 116; W. T. Jordan, *Hugh Davis*, p. 82; Easterby, ed., *South Carolina Rice Plantation*, p. 347; Magruder Diary, Feb. 6–7, 1846; J. T. Robin-

son Papers, 1850s; Spyker Diary, 1850s; E. G. Baker Diary, Aug. 10, 1848; and generally, Phillips, *American Negro Slavery*, p. 267.

26. C. S. Davis, *Cotton Kingdom in Alabama*, p. 79.

27. K. W. Skinner to Charles Manigault, June 29, 1851, and Louis to Charles Manigault, Dec., 24, 1854, in the Manigault Papers; Lyell, *Second Visit*, I, 249; Olmsted, *Seaboard*, p. 422; W. T. Jordan, *Hugh Davis*, p. 82; Fisk University, *Unwritten History of Slavery*, p. 5; Sydnor, *Slavery in Mississippi*, p. 39; Pierce Butler, *The Unhurried Years* (Baton Rouge, La., 1948), p. 60; Moody, *Slavery on the Louisiana Sugar Plantations*, p. 74.

28. Monette Daybook and Diary, July 18–21, 1855, describes the week-long organization of these efforts.

29. Rawick, ed., *S.C. Narr.*, III (3), 153–154; *Okla. Narr.*, VII (1), 18, 303; Bremer, *Homes of the New World*, I, 296–297; Kemble, *Journal*, p. 255.

30. Solon Robinson, "Negro Slavery in the South," *DBR*, VII (Nov., 1849), 381–382.

31. For Mack, the proud hunter, see Jane Harris Rogers, "The Model Farm of Missouri and Its Owner," *Mo.H.R.*, XVIII (Jan., 1924), 153–154. The words quoted are John Hunter's; see Rawick, ed., *Ark. Narr.*, IX (3), 360.

32. Schoolcraft, *Plantation Life*, pp. 234–235.

33. Ingraham, *South-West*, II, 109–110.

34. See Maurice Halbwachs, *The Psychology of Social Class* (trans. Claire DeLavenay; Glencoe, Ill., 1958), pp. 33, 40 (on the French peasants); and Stoianovitch, "Material Foundations of Preindustrial Civilization in the Balkans," p. 241.

35. See, e.g., Manigault Plantation Book, 1837; Northup, *Twelve Years a Slave*, p. 154; Weld, *Slavery as It Is*, p. 95; Rawick, ed., *Texas Narr.*, IV (1), 266; V (3), 189.

36. R. F. Thompson, "African Influences on the Art of the United States," in A. L. Robinson *et al.*, *Black Studies in the University*, pp. 144–145. African preferences cropped up occasionally. In Alabama, Susan Snow's mother refused to have a plank floor in her cabin and insisted on the dirt floor she had known in Africa; see Yetman, ed., *Life Under the "Peculiar Institution,"* p. 291.

37. Sitterson, "The McCollams," *JSH*, VI (Aug., 1940), 359; Sitterson, "Hired Labor on the Sugar Plantations of the Ante-bellum South," *JSH*, XIV (May, 1948), 202; Rawick, ed., *Ala. Narr.*, VI (1), 22.

38. R. H. Taylor, *Slaveholding in North Carolina*, p. 81, says that most slaves in North Carolina built lofts or lean-to sections for their children. See also Rawick, ed., *N.C. Narr.*, XV (2), 13; J. A. McKinstry to H. C. Nixon, Feb. 11, 1913, in Correspondence: Slavery, Tennessee State Library and Archives; Olmsted, *Back Country*, p. 74; Mallard, *Plantation Life Before Emancipation*, p. 30; Lyell, *Second Visit*, I, 249. Fanny Kemble (*Journal*, p. 30) and the Rev. C. C. Jones (*Religious Instruction*, p. 116) also describe these measures while condemning their inadequacy and the general lack of privacy.

39. See Debien, *Plantations et esclaves*, p. 37; Pitman, "Slavery on the British West India Plantations," *JNH*, XI (Oct., 1926), 606; H. O. Patterson, *Sociology of Slavery*, p. 55; J. H. Bennett, *Bondsmen and Bishops*, p. 33.

40. *Father Henson's Story of His Own Life*, p. 18.

41. Northup, *Twelve Years a Slave*, p. 170.

42. Wilson, "Peculiarities and Diseases of Negroes," *ACPS's*, IV (July, 1860), 319–320; *PB*, XIV (Aug. 2, 1849), n.p.

43. For earlier samples of the procedures in assignment of bedding, see Lawton Diary, Jan. 22, 1819, and Nov., 1825; DeSaussure Journals, p. 4 (1835). The plantations records for the 1850s show no general change; see, e.g., Reid Papers, I, 106, 113 (1854); De Bow, ed. *Industrial Resources*, II, 334; Boyd, *Alabama in the Fifties*, pp. 45–46.

44. See, e.g., Rawick, ed., *S.C. Narr.*, III (3), 119.
45. Spyker Diary, Jan. 6, 1857; Rawick, ed., *S.C. Narr.*, II (1), 52, 205; II (2), 172; *Texas Narr.*, IV (1), 85, 203.
46. J. A. McKinstry to H. C. Nixon, Feb. 11, 1913, in Correspondence: Slavery, Tennessee State Library and Archives; Rawick, ed., *Ga. Narr.*, XII (1), 24; *Ohio Narr.*, XVI, 50; Leigh, *Ten Years*, p. 232; Fisk University, *Unwritten History of Slavery*, p. 9.
47. R.W.N.N., "Negro Cabins," *SP*, XVI (April, 1856), 122; Puckett, *Folk Beliefs*, p. 416.
48. P. A. Bruce, *Economic History of Virginia in the Seventeenth Century*, II, 106.
49. W. H. Russell, *My Diary North and South*, p. 140.
50. Olmsted, *Seaboard*, p. 698.
51. Duncan Account Book for Feb., 1864; Dennett, *South as It Is*, p. 210.
52. Northup, *Twelve Years a Slave*, pp. 194–195; Steward, *Twenty-two Years a Slave*, p. 11; Rawick, ed., *S.C. Narr.*, II (1), 52; II (2), 83, 272, 328; III (3), 64, 200; *Texas Narr.*, V (3), 239.
53. Fisk University, *Unwritten History of Slavery*, p. 108.
54. Rawick, ed., *S.C. Narr.*, III (4), 51, 253; *Texas Narr.*, IV (1), 76, 225; V (3), 139.
55. Rawick, ed., *Texas Narr.*, IV (4), 83, 148; *Ala. Narr.*, VI (1), 364; *Okla. Narr.*, VII (*), 306–307; Fisk University, *Unwritten History of Slavery*, p. 104; Weld, *Slavery as It Is*, p. 46.
56. Rawick, ed., *Texas Narr.*, IV (1), 267; *Ala. Narr.*, VI (1), 359; *Ga. Narr.*, XIII (4), 7; D. E. Huger Smith, "A Plantation Boyhood," in A. R. Huger Smith, *Carolina Rice Plantation of the Fifties*, p. 71; Northup, *Twelve Years a Slave*, p. 169.
57. See esp. W. Darrell Overdyke, *Louisiana Plantation Homes* (New York, 1965), pp. 168–170; John Desmond, *Louisiana's Antebellum Architecture* (Baton Rouge, La., 1970), pp. 70–71; Laughlin, *Ghosts Along the Mississippi*, Pls. 46–48.
58. *Life and Times of Frederick Douglass*, p. 40.
59. See esp. James C. Bonner, "Plantation Architecture of the Lower South on the Eve of the Civil War," *JSH*, XI (Aug., 1945), 370–388.
60. Rawick, ed., *Texas Narr.*, IV (1), 271; *Okla. Narr.*, VII (1), 112.
61. Rawick, ed., *Texas Narr.*, V (3), 51–52.
62. Rawick, ed., *Okla. Narr.*, VII (1), 307. Also D. E. Huger Smith, "A Plantation Boyhood," p. 60, who pointedly remarks that the slaves always called the master's house the "Big House" or "Great House" even when it was small and modest.
63. Yetman, ed., *Life Under the "Peculiar Institution,"* p. 224.
64. *Ibid.*, p. 100.
65. Bassett, *Southern Plantation Overseer*, p. 261.
66. A. O. Craven, "Poor Whites and Negroes of the Ante-bellum South," *JNH*, XV (Jan., 1930), 16. Also Olmsted, *Seaboard*, pp. 111–112; Cash, *Mind of the South*, pp. 24–25; Dick, *Dixie Frontier*, pp. 80, 84; Phillips, *Georgia and State Rights*, p. 154; Hundley, *Social Relations*, p. 260; Seymour V. Connor, "Log Cabins in Texas," *SHQ*, LIII (Oct., 1949), 105–116.
67. E. F. Andrews, *War-Time Journal of a Georgia Girl*, p. 93.
68. See, e.g., Wright, ed., *Prose Works of William Byrd*, p. 143; Lyell, *Second Visit*, II, 63; and the hair-raising account of Gov. Gilmer's overnight visit with a yeoman family in northwest Georgia in James C. Bonner, *Georgia's Last Frontier: The Development of Carroll County* (Athens, Ga., 1971), pp. 36–37.
69. S. Andrews, *South Since the War*, p. 180; also Dennett, *South as It Is*, p. 103.
70. Olmsted, *Seaboard*, pp. 384–386, and *Back Country*, pp. 198, 205, 231–232.
71. Yetman, ed., *Life Under the "Peculiar Institution,"* p. 335.
72. J. M. Brown, "Songs of the Slave," in Katz, ed., *Social Implications of Early*

Negro Music, p. 28. See also Fisk University, *Unwritten History of Slavery*, p. 6.

73. Olmsted, *Back Country*, p. 142; also Fisk University, *God Struck Me Dead*, pp. 171–174.

74. Harn, "Old Canoochee—Ogeechee Chronicles," *GHQ*, XVI (June, 1932), 149.

75. Lyell, *Second Visit*, I, 264.

76. Alexander Humboldt, *The Island of Cuba* (New York, 1856), pp. 225–226.

77. Rawick, ed., *S.C. Narr.*, II (1), 250.

GARDENS

1. Kate Stone, *Brokenburn*, p. 6. For accounts of the extent of the practice see Evangeline Walker Andrews, ed., *Journal of a Lady of Quality; Being the Narrative of a Journey from Scotland to the West Indies, North Carolina, and Portugal in the Years 1774 to 1776* (New Haven, Conn., 1922), 176–177; Sam Bowers Hilliard, *Hog Meat and Hoecake: Food Supply in The Old South, 1840–1860* (Carbondale, Ill., 1972), pp. 182–185; Flanders, *Plantation Slavery in Georgia*, p. 146; Phillips and Glunt, eds., *Florida Plantation Records*, p. 30; Brackett, *Negro in Maryland*, p. 104; WPA, *Negro in Virginia*, pp. 70–71; W. T. Jordan, *Hugh Davis*, p. 104; Moody, *Slavery on the Louisiana Sugar Plantations*, pp. 65–66; Bonner, *Georgia Agriculture*, p. 200; McDougle, *Slavery in Kentucky*, p. 73; Owner of an Estate in Mississippi, "Management of Negroes upon Southern Estates," *DBR*, XXIX (June, 1851), 624; Bass, "Essay on the Treatment and Management of Slaves," Southern Central Agricultural Society, *Transactions, 1846–1851*, pp. 195–201; Curlee, "History of a Texas Slave Plantation," *SHQ*, XXVI (Oct., 1922), 79–127.

2. Rawick, ed., *S.C. Narr.*, II (2), 111; III (2), 172, 219; *Texas Narr.*, IV (2), *passim*.

3. See, e.g., G. G. Johnson, *Social History of the Sea Islands*, p. 137; also Rawick, ed., *S.C. Narr.*, III (3), 113; *Texas Narr.*, V (4), 22.

4. See, e.g., Olmsted, *Seaboard*, pp. 443 ff., and *Back Country*, p. 182; Pennington, *Fugitive Blacksmith*, in Bontemps, ed., *Great Slave Narratives*, pp. 253–254; Rawick, ed., *S.C. Narr.*, III (4), 53; *Texas Narr.*, IV (1), 215; *Ala. Narr.*, VI (1), 10; *Okla. Narr.*, VII (1), 251; Fisk University, *Unwritten History of Slavery*, p. 144.

5. Henry, *Police Control of the Slave*, p. 147.

6. Sydnor, *Slavery in Mississippi*, p. 97; Phillips, *Life and Labor*, p. 283; Kirwan, ed., *Confederacy*, pp. 59–60; Sitterson, *Sugar Country*, p. 98; Litwack, "Free at Last," in Hareven, ed., *Anonymous Americans*, pp. 153–154; N. Adams, "A Northerner's Experience in re Southern Slavery," *DBR*, XVIII (May, 1855), 575; "On the Management of Negroes," *ACPSS*, II (Jan., 1858), 20–21; Gibbes, "Southern Slave Life," *DBR*, XXIV (Jan., 1858), 324; Harrod C. Anderson Journal, Feb. 4, 1860; Rawick, ed., *S.C. Narr.*, III (3), 66; *Texas Narr.*, IV (1), 85; V (3), 58.

7. Olmsted, *Seaboard*, pp. 439, 442–443, and *Back Country*, p. 75; Wall, "Founding of Pettigrew Plantations," *NCHR*, XXVII (Oct., 1850), 414; Moses Liddell to St. John R. Liddell, Jan. 9, 1839; Schoolcraft, *Plantation Life*, p. 48; Myers, ed., *Children of Pride*, pp. 978, 987, 1017, 1126.

8. Ingraham, *South-West*, II, 54; Rawick, ed., *S.C. Narr.*, III (3), 66; III (4), 219; *Okla. Narr.*, VII (1), 251.

9. My discussion of the British Caribbean and especially Jamaica relies heavily on a number of splendid articles by Sidney W. Mintz, which happily are

being collected in book form: see Mintz, *Afro-Caribbeana* (forthcoming). The most important of these for our immediate purposes are "The House and the Yard Among Three Caribbean Peasantries"; "Currency Problems in Eighteenth-Century Jamaica and Gresham's Law"; "Historical Sociology of the Jamaican Church-Founded Free Village System"; "The Contemporary Jamaican Internal Market Pattern"; "The Sociology of Jamaican Freedman Villages"; and "Origins of the Jamaican Market System." For the Sunday markets in Barbados see J. H. Bennett, *Bondsmen and Bishops*, pp. 23–24. For the Leewards see Goveia, *Slave Society in the British Leeward Islands*, pp. 238–239. For additional modern treatments of Jamaica see esp. Curtin, *Two Jamaicas*, pp. 11, 19; H. O. Patterson, *Sociology of Slavery*, pp. 216–229; Douglas Hall, *Free Jamaica: 1838–1865* (New Haven, Conn., 1959), p. 19; Pitman, "Slavery on the British West India Plantations," *JNH*, XI (Oct., 1926), 595, 608. All slave societies, even the most brutal, made some provision for slave gardens, but the British Caribbean stands out as a particularly important case. For Cuba see Montejo, *Autobiography of a Runaway Slave*, p. 24. For Brazil see Freyre, *Masters and Slaves* and *Mansions and Shanties*, *passim*, and Stein, *Vassouras*, p. 170. For Saint-Domingue see Stoddard, *French Revolution in Santo-Domingo*, p. 58.

10. U.K. Parliamentary Speeches, April 2, 1792.
11. For the example of Natchez see the contemporary account of Ingraham, *South-West*, I, 54–55, and the modern discussion by Sydnor, *Slavery in Mississippi*, pp. 77 ff., 99.
12. Rose, *Rehearsal for Reconstruction*, p. 367; W. H. Russell, *My Diary North and South*, p. 77; Olmsted, *Seaboard*, p. 422.
13. J. M. McPherson, *Negro's Civil War*, p. 127.
14. Du Bois, *Black Reconstruction*, p. 123.
15. C. S. Davis, *Cotton Kingdom in Alabama*, p. 61.
16. Schoolcraft, *Plantation Life*, p. 161.
17. Catterall, ed., *Judicial Cases*, II, 113–114.
18. Rusticus, "Plantation Management and Practice," *ACPSS*, I (Dec., 1857), 375.
19. R. R. King, Jr., "On the Management of the Butler Estate," *SA*, I (Dec., 1828), 525.
20. See, e.g., Agricola, "Management of Negroes," *DBR*, XIX (Sept., 1859), 362; Robert Collins, "Essay on the Management of Slaves," *SC*, XII (July, 1854), 206; Olmsted, *Seaboard*, p. 689.
21. E. A. Davis, ed., *Plantation Life in the Florida Parishes of Louisiana*, p. 407.

KITCHENS, HIGH AND LOW

1. As quoted in Berwanger, *Frontier Against Slavery*, p. 127.
2. W. Morris, *North Toward Home*, p. 387.
3. Wise, *End of an Era*, p. 66.
4. Not everyone thought highly of southern cooking; see the acid comments of Featherstonhaugh, *Excursion Through the Slave States*, p. 27, or S. Andrews, *South Since the War*, p. 20. Here, we shall bracket the question of how good southern cooking really is—an impossible question in any case, and too dangerous for someone brought up on pasta and veal cutlets to fool with. Suffice it to say that it has enjoyed a reputation as our one distinguished regional American cuisine, and that that reputation must be accounted for.
5. Mallard, *Plantation Life Before Emancipation*, p. 18.

6. C. M. Green, *Secret City*, p. 43; Northup, *Twelve Years a Slave*, p. 67; Durham and Jones, *Negro Cowboys*, pp. 45, 49–51.

7. Saxon *et al.*, *Gumbo Ya-Ya*, p. 145; Lyell, *Second Visit*, II, 126; Bremer, *Homes of the New World*, I, 292; Rawick, ed., *Texas Narr.*, V (3), 17; WPA, *Negro in Virginia*, p. 38; Northup, *Twelve Years a Slave*, p. 95.

8. Amelia Thompson Watts, "A Summer on a Louisiana Plantation in 1832," p. 100, in the Pharr Book; Bremer, *Homes of the New World*, II, 280; W. T. Jordan, *Hugh Davis*, p. 77; Bancroft, *Slave Trading*, p. 313.

9. W. H. Russell, *My Diary North and South*, p. 150.

10. Hilliard, "Hog Meat and Cornpone," *Proceedings of the American Philosophical Society*, CXIII (Feb., 1969), 12.

11. Bob Jeffries, *Soul Food Cookbook* (Indianapolis, 1970), p. vii.

12. Frances D. and Peter J. Ribotti, *French Cooking in the New World* (Garden City, N.Y., 1967), p. 5.

13. Bonner, ed., "Plantation Experiences of a New York Woman," *NCHR*, XXXIII (July, 1956), 397.

14. Daniel P. Mannix and Malcolm Cowley, *Black Cargoes: A History of the Atlantic Slave Trade, 1518–1865* (New York, 1962), pp. 15–16. On the exchange of foods among Africa, Europe, and the Americas see Alfred W. Crosby, *The Columbian Exchange: Biological and Cultural Consequences of 1492* (Westport, Conn., 1972), Ch. 5.

15. Wolfe, *Cooking of the Caribbean Islands*, pp. 20, 38; Goveia, *Slave Society in the British Leeward Islands*, p. 245.

16. *American Heritage Cookbook* (2 vols.; New York, 1964), II, 611.

17. Hilliard, "Hog Meat and Cornpone," pp. 1–13. On the attitude of the Nation of Islam see Essien-Udom, *Black Nationalism*, p. 28; Lincoln, *Black Muslims in America*, p. 81.

18. R. Nina Rodrigues, *Os Africanos no Brasil* (3rd ed.; São Paulo, 1945), pp. 200–202; Wolfe, *Cooking of the Caribbean Islands*, pp. 16–17, 50; Lewis, *Journal of a West India Proprietor*, p. 151. In turn the Americas contributed enormously to Africa's store of foods; see Robert L. Reynolds, *Europe Emerges: Transition Toward an Industrial World-wide Society* (Madison, Wis., 1961), p. 317; Pedro Calmon, *Historia social do Brasil: Espirito do sociedade colonial* (3rd ed.; São Paulo, 1941), p. 176; Pope-Hennessy, *Sins of the Fathers*, pp. 36–37; Basil Davidson, *Black Mother: The Years of the African Slave Trade* (Boston, 1961), pp. 277–278.

19. Schoolcraft, *Plantation Life*, p. 234.

20. Contrast, e.g., the reports of weekday distribution in Rawick, ed., *S.C. Narr.*, II (1), 27, 119, 158, and *Ala. Narr.*, VI (1), 426, with the more frequent reports of weekend distribution: *S.C. Narr.*, II (2), 56, 275; *Texas Narr.*, IV (1), 215, 257; IV (2), 166, 205, 208; V (3), 68, 188, 190; *Okla. Narr.*, VII (1) 234, 282; Glunt and Phillips, *Florida Plantation Records*, pp. 461 ff.; W. T. Jordan, *Hugh Davis*, p. 83; D. E. Huger Smith, "A Plantation Boyhood," in A. R. Huger Smith, *Carolina Rice Plantation of the Fifties*, p. 88.

21. See Flanders, "Two Plantations and a County of Ante-bellum Georgia," *GHQ,* XII (March, 1928), 7; *DBR*, XIX (Sept., 1859), 359. Unmarried slaves were usually fed in a communal kitchen, but they might choose to eat alone.

22. Southron, "The Policy of the Southern Planter," *ACPSS*, I (Oct., 1857), 295.

23. Rusticus, "Plantation Management and Practice," *ACPSS*, I (Dec., 1857), 375. Also Ralph Butterfield, *ACPSS*, II (Sept., 1858), 293–294; J. B. Sellers, *Slavery in Alabama*, pp. 95–98; C. S. Davis, *Cotton Kingdom in Alabama*, pp. 83–84.

24. Rawick, ed., *S.C. Narr.*, II (2), 56; also D. E. Huger Smith, "A Plantation Boyhood," p. 88; G. M. Brown, "Biography of Mary Ann Colvin Mayfield," in the Mayfield Papers.

25. Rawick, ed., *S.C. Narr.*, II (2), 339.
26. Rawick, ed., *Ga. Narr.*, XII (1), 289; also XIII (3), 81.
27. Rose, *Rehearsal for Reconstruction*, p. 89.
28. Rawick, ed., *Ala. Narr.*, VI (1), 384; *Texas Narr.*, IV (2), 1; *S.C. Narr.*, II (1), 291.
29. Rawick, ed., *S.C. Narr.*, III (3), 18; Northup, *Twelve Years a Slave*, p. 187.
30. Northup, *Twelve Years a Slave*, p. 201. Most ex-slaves spoke of opossum with particular fondness; see, e.g., Rawick, ed., *Texas Narr.*, IV (2), 160.
31. Yetman, ed., *Life Under the "Peculiar Institution,"* p. 96; also Rawick, ed., *Texas Narr.*, IV (1), 203; *Ohio Narr.*, XVI, 44.
32. Rawick, ed., *S.C. Narr.*, II (1), 301. Louisa Davis gives the recipe as fully as any; for an example of similar preparation well to the west, see *Texas Narr.*, IV (1), 218.
33. Saxon *et al.*, *Gumbo Ya-Ya*, p. 239; Hilliard, "Hog Meat and Cornpone," pp. 6–7.
34. Odum and Johnson, *Negro and His Songs*, p. 240; for some other 'possum songs see J. G. Williams, *"De Ole Plantation,"* p. 61.
35. Rawick, ed., *Ga. Narr.*, XIII (4), 120.
36. Hilliard, "Hog Meat and Cornpone," pp. 6–7; Hilliard, *Hog Meat and Hoecake*, p. 47; Swint, ed., *Dear Ones at Home*, p. 90.
37. Buckingham, *Slave States of America*, II, 294.
38. Rawick, ed., *Indiana Narr.*, VI (2), 54.
39. Rawick, ed., *Texas Narr.*, IV (1), 253; IV (2), 61; V (3), 274; *N.C. Narr.*, XIV (1), 215; XV (2), 22, 145, 423.
40. See, e.g., the instructions in the Minor Plantation Diary, 1861–1868.
41. Margaret Cussler and Mary L. De Give, *'Twixt the Cup and the Lip: Psychological and Socio-cultural Factors Affecting Food Habits* (New York, 1952), pp. 133, 156.
42. Rawick, ed., *Okla. Narr.*, VII (1), 98; M. C. Boyd, *Alabama in the Fifties*, p. 44.
43. Rawick, ed., *S.C. Narr.*, II (2), 55.
44. Fisk University, *Unwritten History of Slavery*, p. 46; WPA, *Negro in Virginia*, p. 70; Rawick, ed., *Ark. Narr.*, IX (3), 96–97, 181.
45. Rawick, ed., *S.C. Narr.*, II (2), 40.
46. Rawick, ed., *Texas Narr.*, IV (2), 233.
47. Olmsted, *Back Country*, p. 162.
48. *Private Journal of H. W. Ravenel*, p. 117; Yetman, ed., *Life Under the "Peculiar Institution,"* pp. 53, 214; Northup, *Twelve Years*, p. 67; Rawick, ed., *Texas Narr.*, IV (1), 157, 228; IV (2), 183; *Ark. Narr.*, IX (3), 136; Higginson, *Army Life*, p. 18. The slaves throve on sorghum, which became a standard addition to their diet, as well as to that of many whites; see Boyd, *Alabama in the Fifties*, pp. 33, 44; Bonner, *Georgia Agriculture*, p. 86.
49. K. W. Skinner to Charles Manigault, May 17, 1851, in the Manigault Papers; Pearson, ed., *Letters from Port Royal*, p. 53; also WPA, *Negro in Virginia*, p. 71.

CLOTHES MAKE THE MAN AND THE WOMAN

1. Henry Fitzhugh to Buchanan, Feb. 2, 1756, in the Fitzhugh Letterbook; J. Channing to Edward Telfair, Aug. 10, 1786, in the Telfair Papers; Mrs. Smith Journal, 1793, p. 11; Toulmin, *Western Country in 1793*, p. 18; Tate, *Negro in Eighteenth-Century Williamsburg*, p. 73; W. D. Jordan, *White over Black*, p. 85; McColley, *Slavery and Jeffersonian Virginia*, p. 62.
2. Quoted in Wilson, "Peculiarities and Diseases of Negroes," *ACPSS*, V (March, 1860), 176.

3. *PB*, XIV (Aug. 2, 1849), n.p.; *DBR*, XIX (Sept., 1849), 359; XXIV (Jan., 1858), 323.

4. WPA, *Negro in Virginia*, p. 71; C. S. Davis, *Cotton Kingdom in Alabama*, p. 84.

5. I have had to arrive at this estimate impressionistically by reading agricultural journals and plantation records; the difficulty arises from the customary lumping of expenditures for clothing with expenditures for other supplies. See, e.g., *DBR*, VIII (Jan., 1850), 18; *CP*, I (1844–1845), 111–112; Phillips, ed., *Plantation and Frontier*, I, 135; Watson Papers for 1847–1861; Leak Diary, V, 491 ff.

6. Robert Collins, "Management of Slaves," *SC*, XVII (Oct., 1854), 424.

7. Sydnor, *Slavery in Mississippi*, pp. 27–28; Bonner, *Georgia Agriculture*, pp. 198–199; C. P. Patterson, *Negro in Tennessee*, p. 66; Sitterson, *Sugar Country*, p. 92; *DBR*, XXIX (June, 1851), 624; Leak Diary, II, 17 ff., 110 ff.; Spyker Diary, Nov. 28, 1858.

8. Kate Stone, *Brokenburn*, p. 7; Bonner, ed., "Plantation Experiences of a New York Woman," *NCHR*, XXXIII (July, 1956), 395–396; John Palfrey to Henry Palfrey, March 22, 1815.

9. Phillips and Glunt, eds., *Florida Plantation Records*, pp. 244 ff.; Fisk University, *Unwritten History of Slavery*, pp. 104, 136, 153; Rawick, ed., *S.C. Narr.*, II (1), 27.

10. WPA, *Negro in Virginia*, p. 72.

11. Spencer, *Booker T. Washington*, p. 15.

12. See, e.g., the attempt at careful measurement in the Cotton Book for 1828, in the Stirling Papers; also Heyward, *Seed from Madagascar*, pp. 181–182.

13. Botkin, ed., *Lay My Burden Down*, p. 121; also p. 60.

14. Rawick, ed., *Texas Narr.*, V (4), 123; also *Okla. Narr.*, VII (1), 49; Kate Stone, *Brokenburn*, p. 7; WPA, *Negro in Virginia*, p. 73.

15. The range of $1.00–1.25 appears regularly in plantation manuscripts, although occasionally a planter went as high as $1.75. See, e.g., E. G. Baker Diary, Sept. 25, 1857, Sept. 16, 1859.

16. See *Plantation*, I (March, 1860), 44–45, for a typical blast at northern shoe manufacturers; also De Bow, ed., *Industrial Resources*, II, 130.

17. Rawick, ed., *S.C. Narr.*, III (3), 128; also *Texas Narr.*, IV (2), 220.

18. E. A. Davis, ed., *Plantation Life in the Florida Parishes of Louisiana*, p. 188; Ledoux & Company Record Book, Jan. 18, 1857; I. W. Dunlop Diary, April 22, 1860, in the J. T. Robinson Papers; Olmsted, *Back Country*, pp. 80, 182; Robert Collins, "Management of Slaves," *SC*, XII (July, 1854), 206; Wilson, "The Negro—His Peculiarities as to Disease," *ACPSS*, III (July, 1859), 228–229; Phillips, *American Negro Slavery*, p. 267; Rawick, ed., *Texas Narr.*, IV (1), 78; *Ala. Narr.*, VI (1), 212; Fisk University, *God Struck Me Dead*, p. 160.

19. J. G. Williams, *"De Ole Plantation,"* p. 4.

20. Rawick, ed., *Ala. Narr.*, VI (1), 391; Fisk University, *Unwritten History of Slavery*, p. 50; WPA, *Negro in Virginia*, p. 91.

21. E. F. Andrews, *War-Time Journal of a Georgia Girl*, p. 101; Rawick, ed., *Ga. Narr.*, XII (2), 227; Fish University *Unwritten History of Slavery*, pp. 19, 56, 154; Paul Buck, "Poor Whites of the Old South," *AHR*, XXXI (1925–1926), 52–54.

22. Rawick, ed., *Texas Narr.*, V (3), 18; *Ark. Narr.*, IX (3), 181; *Ga. Narr.*, XII (2), 227; Ingraham, *South-West*, II, 127.

23. Rawick, ed., *S.C. Narr.*, II (2), 113, 206; *Okla. Narr.*, VII (1), 102; Lyell, *Second Visit*, II, 26.

24. D. B. Davis, *Problem of Slavery*, p. 450; Henry Larson and May Pellaton, *Behind the Lianas: Exploration in French Guiana* (Edinburgh, 1959), p. 96; Boxer, *Golden Age of Brazil*, p. 19.

25. Dike, *Trade and Politics in the Niger Delta*, pp. 49–50.
26. Featherstonhaugh, *Excursion Through the Slave States*, p. 95.
27. Kemble, *Journal*, p. 24; Buckingham, *Slave States of America*, II, 305; S. Andrews, *South Since the War*, pp. 182, 222.
28. W. T. Jordan, *Ante-bellum Alabama*, pp. 100–104.
29. Buckingham, *Slave States of America*, II, 6–7; Olmsted, *Seaboard*, p. 19; Pearson, ed., *Letters from Port Royal*, pp. 15, 18.
30. Redpath, *Roving Editor*, p. 97.
31. Yetman, ed., *Life Under the "Peculiar Institution,"* p. 58.
32. Swint, ed., *Dear Ones at Home*, p. 65; Rose, *Rehearsal for Reconstruction*, pp. 55, 236.
33. J. B. Grimball Diary, Nov. 20, 1848, and *passim*; "Souvenirs of Our Ancestors of My Immediate Family," in Manigault Plantation Records; Moses Liddell to St. John R. Liddell, March 6, 1851.
34. See, e.g., W. T. Jordan, *Hugh Davis*, pp. 84–85; Margruder Diary, 1840s and 1850s; Myers, ed., *Children of Pride*, p. 265.
35. Martineau, *Society in America*, I, 296–297.
36. Kemble, *Journal*, p. 58; also pp. 179–180.
37. Rawick, ed., *Miss. Narr.*, VII (2), 44; also p. 152. For historians' reviews of evidence from plantation and small-farm areas see Bonner, *Georgia Agriculture*, p. 199; and Corlew, "Some Aspects of Slavery in Dickson County," *THQ*, X (Sept., 1951), 241.
38. C. C. Jones, *Religious Instruction*, pp. 145–146. See also Lyell, *Second Visit*, I, 265; Olmsted, *Seaboard*, pp. 27–28, 112, 391.
39. Rawick, ed., *S.C. Narr.*, II (2), 47, also p. 62; also Smedes, *Southern Planter*, pp. 34–35.
40. Rawick, ed., *Texas Narr.*, IV (1), 40; *Ga. Narr.*, XIII (4), 187; *Fla. Narr.*, XVIII, 134; Yetman, ed., *Life Under the "Peculiar Institution,"* p. 180; Schoolcraft, *Plantation Life*, pp. 63–64; Olmsted, *Back Country*, p. 271.
41. Heyward, *Seed from Madagascar*, p. 182.
42. Martineau, *Society in America*, I, 301–302.
43. Rawick, ed., *Texas Narr.*, IV (1), 95; *Ark. Narr.*, X (6), 44.
44. Fisk University, *Unwritten History of Slavery*, p. 105; Rawick, ed., *S.C. Narr.*, II (2), 127; also Wise, *End of an Era*, p. 37; Botume, *First Days Amongst the Contrabands*, pp. 50, 228–229; Steward, *Twenty-two Years a Slave*, p. 23.
45. J. G. Williams, *"De Ole Plantation,"* p. 23.
46. WPA, *Negro in Virginia*, pp. 72–73; Smedes, *Southern Planter*, p. 34.
47. Phillips, "Racial Problems, Adjustments and Disturbances," in Chandler et al., eds., *South in the Building of the Nation*, IV, 204; Belle Becker Sideman and Lillian Friedman, eds., *Europe Looks at the Civil War*, (New York, 1955), p. 64; Lester, *To Be a Slave*, p. 45.
48. Rawick, ed., *Ala. Narr.*, VI (1), 47; also Smedes, *Southern Planter*, pp. 38.
49. Ingraham, *South-West*, II, 243.
50. For incidence of improvised pig-bone buttons, as well as metal ones, see Ascher and Fairbanks, "Excavation of a Slave Cabin," *Historical Archeology* (1971), p. 12; for Nancy Williams see WPA, *Negro in Virginia*, pp. 88–89.
51. Phillips, *Life and Labor*, p. 283.
52. Odum and Johnson, *Negro and His Songs*, p. 140.
53. Rawick, ed., *S.C. Narr.*, III (3), 195; also Bremer, *Homes of the New World*, I, 296; Kemble, *Journal*, p. 27; Northup, *Twelve Years a Slave*, p. 214.
54. WPA, *Drums and Shadows*, pp. 121, 145, 164; Montejo, *Autobiography of a Runaway Slave*, p. 16.
55. Puckett, *Folk Beliefs*, pp. 220–221; Claude Lévi-Strauss, *The Savage Mind* (Lon-

don, 1966), pp. 64–65; Victor W. Turner, "Colour Classification in Ndembu Ritual: A Problem in Primitive Classification," in Banton, ed., *Anthropological Approaches to the Study of Religion*, pp. 47–84.

56. Kate Stone, *Brokenburn*, p. 7; Rawick, ed., *S.C. Narr.*, IV (2), 1, 151; *Ala. Narr.*, VI (1), 149.

57. Chesnut, *Diary from Dixie*, p. 31; Bremer, *Homes of the New World*, I, 264; Amelia Thompson Watts, "A Summer on a Louisiana Cotton Plantation (1832)," in the Pharr Book; Cornwall Diary, Jan. 31, 1861; Doyle, *Etiquette of Race Relations*, p. 76; West, *Methodism in Alabama*, p. 564.

58. See Melville and Frances Herskovits, *Suriname Folk-lore* (New York, 1936), pp. 4–5.

59. For parallels and suggestive discussions of this question see Hill, *Reformation to Industrial Revolution*, p. 34; Frantz Fanon, *Dying Colonialism* (trans. Haakon Chevalier; New York, 1967), p. 35; and esp. Stoianovitch, "Material Foundations of Pre-industrial Civilization in the Balkans," *J.Soc.H.*, IV (Spring, 1971), 243 ff.

60. O'Neall, *Negro Law of South Carolina*, pp. 24–25.

61. The Memorial is printed in full in Phillips, ed., *Plantation and Frontier*; see esp. II, 112–113.

62. White women during the antebellum period had marched on to their own proper place, which cynics might think marked a kind of servility in itself. They increasingly provided a market for perfumes, colognes, powderpuffs, hair tonics, oils, etc. See Boyd, *Alabama in the Fifties*, p. 112.

63. McManus, *Negro Slavery in New York*, p. 64.

64. Ingraham, *South-West*, II, 193.

65. S. Andrews, *South Since the War*, pp. 186, 187.

66. Rawick, ed., *Ark. Narr.*, IX (4), 294.

READING, WRITING, AND PROSPECTS

1. Quoted by Worsley, *Trumpet Shall Sound*, p. 246.

2. Hill, *Century of Revolution*, 94, 174.

3. Quoted by Kuczynski, *Rise of the Working Class*, p. 109.

4. E. N. Elliott, ed., *Cotton Is King and Pro-slavery Arguments*, pp. 35, 36, 124; Catterall, ed., *Judicial Cases*, III, 33. See also *Life and Times of Frederick Douglass*, p. 93; *DBR*, XXIX (June, 1851), 625; Bass, "Essay on the Treatment and Management of Slaves," Southern Central Agricultural Society, *Transactions, 1846–1851*, p. 196.

5. Quoted in Eric J. Hobsbawm, *Bandits* (New York, 1969), p. 50.

6. See W. D. Jordan, *White over Black*, p. 107; Henry, *Police Control of the Slave*, pp. 164–165; Coulter, "Slavery and Freedom: Athens, Georgia" *GHQ*, XLIX (Sept., 1965), 264; James B. Lawrence, "Religious Education of the Negro in the Colony of Georgia," *GHQ*, XIV (March, 1930), 41, 57.

7. C. S. Davis, *Cotton Kingdom in Alabama*, p. 94, J. B. Sellers, *Slavery in Alabama*, pp. 117–118; O. W. Taylor, *Negro Slavery in Arkansas*, p. 187; R. I. Brigham, "Negro Education in Ante Bellum Missouri," *JNH*, XXX (Oct., 1945), 405–420.

8. *Father Henson's Story of His Own Life*, p. 137.

9. Du Bois, *Black Reconstruction*, p. 638; also Myrdal, *American Dilemma*, p. 887.

10. Wade, *Slavery in the Cities*, pp. 173, 176; Reinders, "Slavery in New Orleans

in the Decade Before the Civil War," *Mid-America*, XLIV (Oct., 1962), 220; C. C. Jones, *Religious Instruction*, p. 115; Stirling, *Letters from the Slave States*, pp. 295–296; Richter, "Slavery in Ante-bellum Baton Rouge," *LH*, X (Spring, 1969); Mooney, *Slavery in Tennessee*, pp. 95–96; G. A. Ingraham to Susan Fisher, Dec. 27, 1840, in the Fisher Papers; Eva B. Jones to Mary Jones, June 13, 1865, in Myers, ed., *Children of Pride*; Swint, ed., *Dear Ones at Home*, p. 190.

11. Mooney, *Slavery in Tennessee*, p. 78; G. G. Johnson, *Social History of the Sea Islands*, p. 153; North Carolina Manumission Society, "Minutes, 1816–1834," mss., letter from J. O. Gales, Sept. 6, 1816; Chatham, "Plantation Slavery in Middle Florida," unpubl. M.A. thesis, University of North Carolina, 1938; Simms in E. N. Elliott, ed., *Cotton Is King and Pro-slavery Arguments*, p. 200; C. C. Jones, *Suggestions*, p. 7; Bremer, *Homes of the New World*, I, 276; Olmsted, *Back Country*, pp. 12–13, 143, 181; Lyell, *Second Visit*, I, 267; Higginson, *Army Life*, p. 1; Rawick, ed., *S.C. Narr.*, II (1), 225; III (4), 52; *Texas Narr.*, IV (1), 73; V (3), 89, 116; *Indiana Narr.*, VI (2), 56, 78, 109, 113, 211. Also Eaton, *Freedom-of-Thought Struggle*, Ch. 3.

12. Sydnor, *Slavery in Mississippi*, p. 54; Mooney, *Slavery in Tennessee*, p. 95; Brigham, "Negro Education in Ante Bellum Missouri," p. 418; Bonner, ed., "Plantation Experiences of a New York Woman," *NCHR*, XXXIII (July, 1956), 395; Charles H. Moffat, "Charles Tait, Planter, Politician, and Scientist of the Old South," *JSH*, XIV (May, 1948), 229.

13. For white encouragement and support, see the testimony of ex-slaves in Rawick, ed., *S.C. Narr.*, II (1), 192, 327; II (2), 39–40; III (3), 119; III (4), 52, 165, 167, 178; *Texas Narr.*, IV (2), 23, 141–142, 161, 186, 244; V (3), 115, 121, 163; V (4), 71, 78; *Ala. Narr.*, VI (1), 59, 160, 212, 257, 332, 410; *Okla. Narr.*, VII (1), 25, 31, 41, 95, 145, 213; *Miss. Narr.*, VII (2), 45; *Ark. Narr.*, X (5), 363; *Ga. Narr.*, XII (1), 83, 257; XII (2), 42; XII (4), 78, 92; *N.C. Narr.*, XIV (1), 95, 332; *Fla. Narr.*, XVII, 146; *Life and History of Rev. Elijah P. Marrs*, pp. 12–16; H. C. Bruce, *New Man*, p. 25.

14. Catherine Devereaux Edmondston in Poe, ed., *True Tales*, pp. 103–104; also O'Neall, *Negro Law of South Carolina*, p. 19; Autobiography of Hiram R. Revels, pp. 1–2, in the Woodson Papers.

15. *Life and History of Rev. Elijah P. Marrs*, p. 12; George Teamoh Journal, Pts. 1–2, p. 43, in the Woodson Papers; Dennett, *South as It Is*, p. 175; Rawick, ed., *S.C. Narr.*, II (2), 50 (Edmund Carlisle); *Texas Narr.*, V (4), 53; *Ga. Narr.*, XIII (4), 214; Yetman, ed., *Life Under the "Peculiar Institution,"* pp. 257, 313; Buckingham, *Slave States of America*, I, 168.

16. Du Bois, "Reconstruction and Its Benefits," *AHR*, XV (July, 1910), 797.

17. S. Andrews, *South Since the War*, Ch. 14, esp. pp. 127–130, 181 f., 227, 336 (quoted), 389; cf. Buckingham, *Slave States of America*, II, 429.

18. In addition to such general works as Rose, *Rehearsal for Reconstruction*, A. A. Taylor, *The Negro in South Carolina During Reconstruction* (Washington, D.C., 1924), J. Williamson, *After Slavery*, Powdermaker, *After Freedom*, and Du Bois, *Black Reconstruction*, see such specialized accounts as that of Claude Elliott, "The Freedman's Bureau in Texas," *SHQ*, LVI (July, 1952), 1–24; Joe M. Richardson, "The Evolution of the Freedman's Bureau in Florida," *FHQ*, XLI (Jan., 1963), 223–238.

19. Gehwehr, *Great Awakening in Virginia*, p. 236.

20. Bremer, *Homes of the New World*, II, 194.

21. Fisk University, *Unwritten History of Slavery*, p. 33.

22. Lyell, *Second Visit*, II, 16.

23. Tindall, *South Carolina Negroes*, p. 6.

24. Smedes, *Southern Planter*, p. 43.
25. Kemble, *Journal*, p. 8.
26. Botume, *First Days Amongst the Contrabands*, p. 4.
27. Kemble, *Journal*, p. 271.

DE BIG TIMES

1. See, e.g., Olmsted, *Back Country*, p. 49; Lyell, *Second Visit*, II, 13; H. C. Bruce, *New Man*, pp. 62–63; Rawick, ed., *S.C. Narr.*, II (1), 152, 166, 171, 301, 304, 327, 333; II (2), 1, 51, 105, 196, 213, 238, 241; III (3), 49, 56, 115, 118, 174, 221; III (4), 10, 31, 56, 58, 71, 168, 248, 255. Reports from other states are in the same vein.
2. Farish, ed., *Journal and Letters of Philip Vickers Fithian*, pp. 128, 265; J. G. Taylor, *Negro Slavery in Louisiana*, p. 33; Sitterson, *Sugar Country*, p. 97.
3. Yetman, ed., *Life Under the "Peculiar Institution,"* pp. 16, 144, 155; Fisk University, *Unwritten History of Slavery*, pp. 55, 109.
4. Minor Plantation Diary, Jan. 20, 1850.
5. Phillips, *Life and Labor*, p. 5; C. S. Davis, *Cotton Kingdom in Alabama*, p. 4; Magnolia Plantation Diary in the Warmoth Papers; James W. Malvin to A. C. Britton, Dec. 26, 1862, in the Britton Papers; Pugh Plantation Diary, Dec. 7, 1859; Liddell Plantation Book, Nov. 31, 1843; Mallard, *Plantation Life Before Emancipation*, p. 34.
6. Ingraham, *South-West*, II, 276; also Hilliard, *Hog Meat and Hoecake*, p. 29.
7. Sydnor, *Slavery in Mississippi*, p. 12; J. B. Sellers, *Slavery in Alabama*, p. 72; Dick, *Dixie Frontier*, p. 92; Magnolia Plantation Journal in the Warmoth Papers; Smedes, *Southern Planter*, p. 38; E. G. Baker Diary, Aug. 10, 1848; Monette Diary, July 20, 1849; Ashland Plantation Record Book, 1852; Macrery Diary, 1855.
8. See, e.g., Easterby, ed., *South Carolina Rice Plantation*, p. 346; Rees Plantation Diary, July 19, 1822; McCall Journal and Diary, Dec. 16, 1852; McCollam Diary, Jan. 28, 1847; J. B. Grimball Diary, Jan. 6, 1834.
9. Olmsted, *Back Country*, p. 14; Rawick, ed., *Texas Narr.*, V (4), 135.
10. W. T. Jordan, *Hugh Davis*, p. 103; *PB*, XIV (Aug. 9, 1849), n.p.
11. "Plantation Rules," 1840, in the Flinn Diary.
12. Quoted in W. T. Jordan, *Ante-bellum Alabama*, p. 92.
13. Quoted in C. P. Patterson, *Negro in Tennessee*, p. 72.
14. Botkin, ed., *Lay My Burden Down*, p. 118.
15. Yetman, ed., *Life Under the "Peculiar Institution,"* p. 141.
16. Fisk University, *Unwritten History of Slavery*, p. 136; WPA, *Negro in Virginia*, p. 63; Rawick, ed., *S.C. Narr.*, II (1), 27, 100; III (4), 251; *Texas Narr.*, IV (2), 93; V (3), 220; *Ga. Narr.*, XII (3), 319.
17. Sitterson, *Sugar Country*, p. 97.
18. For periodic dances sponsored by the masters see W. H. Russell, *My Diary North and South*, p. 140; McCall Diary, June 4, 1853; Leak Diary, Jan. 5, 1860; Spyker Diary, Aug. 1, 1857; Monette Diary, June 5, 1852. For regular Saturday night dances see Rawick, ed., *S.C. Narr.*, II (1), 327; II (2), 169; III (3), 115.
19. See, e.g., Boyd Notes and Recollections, p. 8; William B. Smith, "The Persimmon Tree and the Beer Dance," *FR*, VI (April, 1838), 58–61.
20. There are scattered references to these fights in the slave narratives, and they are part of southern folklore. There is little evidence, however, that they were widespread.
21. Rawick, ed., *S.C. Narr.*, II (1), 16 (Frank Adamson); *Texas Narr.*, IV (1), 135; *Ga. Narr.*, XIII (4), 224; *Kansas Narr.*, XVI, 23; O. W. Taylor, *Negro Slavery in Arkansas*, pp. 207–208.

22. Boyd Notes and Recollections, p. 8; Smedes, *Southern Planter*, p. 123; Olmsted, *Seaboard*, p. 128; E. F. Andrews, *War-Time Journal of a Georgia Girl*, p. 382.

23. E. A. Davis, ed., *Plantation Life in the Florida Parishes of Louisiana*, Jan. 1, 1859.

24. *Father Henson's Story of His Own Life*, p. 20.

25. W. W. Gilmer, "Management of Servants," *SP*, XII (April, 1852), 107.

26. Olmsted, *Seaboard*, p. 91; Bonner, ed., "Plantation Experiences of a New York Woman," *NCHR*, XXXIII (Oct., 1956), 531; Caldwell, "Christmas in Old Natchez," *JMH*, XXI (Oct., 1859), 264; also J. M. McPherson, *Negro's Civil War*, p. 171.

27. WPA, *Negro in Virginia*, p. 95; also pp. 91–92; Fisk University, *Unwritten History of Slavery*, p. 130; Steward, *Twenty-two Years a Slave*, p. 20; Rawick, ed., *S.C. Narr.*, II (1), 1–2; *Texas Narr.*, IV (1), 10.

28. Gavin Diary, June 6, 1856; McBride, "Directions for Cultivating Various Crops at Hickory Hill," *SA*, III (May, 1830), 239; Pocket Plantation Records, Agreement between Ralph Smith and Overseer, 1813; [Anon.], "Management of Slaves," *SC*, IV (March, 1846), 44; Tatler, "Management of Negroes," *SC*, VIII (Nov., 1850), 162–164; Foby, "Management of Servants," *SC*, XI (Aug., 1853), 227; Judge Bay in Catterall, ed., *Judicial Cases*, II, 276. Also Olmsted, *Seaboard*, p. 442; Yetman, ed., *Life Under the "Peculiar Institution,"* p. 128.

29. Wright and Tinling, eds., *William Byrd: His Secret Diary*, Feb. 25, 1711; Greene, ed., *Diary of Col. Landon Carter*, I, 442, II, 558; Bassett, *Southern Plantation Overseer*, p. 12.

30. In general see Courlander, *Negro Folk Music*, pp. 219–220; Southern, *Music of Black Americans*, pp. 45–47, 66–67, 157.

31. Lester, *To Be a Slave*, p. 111; also Rawick, ed., *S.C. Narr.*, II (2), 127, 215, 329.

32. This version is from Rawick, ed., *Texas Narr.*, IV (2), 167. There are many others.

33. Lester, *To Be a Slave*, pp. 105–106; also WPA, *Drums and Shadows*, pp. 189, 208–209.

34. Clarissa E. (Leavitt) Town Diary, Feb. 26, 1853.

35. WPA, *Negro in Virginia*, pp. 92–93.

36. For illustrations of holidays extending well beyond the usual three days see *Narrative of Lewis Clarke*, p. 79, in which a six-day holiday is described as common in Kentucky; Rawick, ed., *Miss. Narr.*, VII (2), 167; *Ohio Narr.*, XIV, 64; Newstead Plantation Diary, 1859; Liddell Plantation Book, 1841–1844; McCall Plantation Diary, Dec. 30, 1852; J. T. Robinson Papers, 1860; J. F. Corsbee to N. D. Woody, Dec. 31, 1857, in the Woody Papers; Haller Nutt Journal, 1847; Orange Grove Plantation Diary, Jan. 5, 1846; J. G. Taylor, *Negro Slavery in Louisiana*, p. 128.

37. W. C. Hickmon, "Weather and Crops in Arkansas, 1819–1879," *Monthly Weather Review*, XLVIII (Aug., 1920), pp. 447–450; Newstead Plantation Diary, Dec. 25, 1858; Pugh Plantation Diary, Dec. 23, 1859; McCall Plantation Journal and Diary, Dec. 25, 1852.

38. E. A. Davis, ed., *Plantation Life in the Florida Parishes of Louisiana*, pp. 85, 139; Easterby, ed., *South Carolina Rice Plantation*, p. 347; Pearson, ed., *Letters from Port Royal*, p. 32.

39. Rawick, ed., *S.C. Narr.*, III (3), 285, *Texas Narr.*, IV (2), 99; V (3), 234.

40. For a basically accurate if somewhat romantic account of the Christmas holiday in the patriarchal Natchez region, see Caldwell, "Christmas in Old Natchez," pp. 257–270. Also R. Ingraham to Susan Fisher, Jan. 5, 1840, in the Fisher Papers; Judith Page Rives to Alfred L. Rives, Jan. 12, 1858; McCall Plantation Journal and Diary, Dec. 29, 1852.

41. Olmsted, *Seaboard*, pp. 101–102; Sydnor, *Slavery in Mississippi*, p. 80.

42. Mrs. Hilliard Diary, Dec. 25, 1849; Kate Stone, *Brokenburn*, p. 76; Saxon *et al.*,

Gumbo Ya-Ya, p. 232; Yetman, ed., *Life Under the "Peculiar Institution,"* p. 332; Rawick, ed., *Texas Narr.*, IV (1), 131.

43. Liddell Plantation Book, Dec., 1842; Randolph Plantation Expense Book, 1850; Bills Diary, Dec. 26, 1856; Leak Diary, 1859-1860; Stirling Papers for 1854, 1857; W. C. Harrison to William H. Taylor, Jan. 26, 1857, in the Dromgoole-Robinson Papers; H. Hamilton, *Zachary Taylor: Soldier in the White House*, pp. 35-36; De Bow, ed., *Industrial Resources*, II, 331; Olmsted, *Back Country*, pp. 51-52; Redpath, *Roving Editor*, p. 138; J. G. Taylor, *Negro Slavery in Louisiana*, p. 200.

44. See, e.g., Olmsted, *Seaboard*, p. 75; Bruce Journal, Dec. 25, 1850; Bills Diary, Dec. 25, 1856; Jackson-Prince Plantation Account, Dec. 25, 1833; Ervin Journal, Dec. 25, 1846; J. F. Corsbee to Newton D. Woody, Dec. 31, 1857, in the Woody Papers.

45. Clemson quoted in Rosser H. Taylor, "The Gentry of Ante-bellum South Carolina," *NCHR*, XVII (April, 1940), 127; also St. John R. Liddell to Moses Liddell, Dec. 28, 1851; Lewis, *Journal of a West India Proprietor*, p. 333; and the remarkable "Petition for Compensation for the Loss of Slaves by Emancipation in the Danish West Indies," *JNH*, II (Oct., 1917), 423-428.

46. Wilson, "Peculiarities and Diseases of Negroes," *ACPSS*, IV (Aug., 1860), 367.

47. Yetman, ed., *Life Under the "Peculiar Institution,"* p. 190 (Prince Johnson); Rawick, ed., *S.C. Narr.*, III (3), 286 (Junius Quattelbaum). Also *Ark. Narr.*, IX (3), 138; *Ga. Narr.*, XII (1), 76, 87.

48. Rawick, ed., *Texas Narr.*, IV (2), 100.

49. Breaux Diary, Jan. 1, 1859.

50. E. A. Davis, ed., *Plantation Life in the Florida Parishes of Louisiana*, passim; Shippee, ed., *Bishop Whipple's Southern Diary*, Dec. 27, 1843 (p. 51); Rawick, ed., *S.C. Narr.*, III (4), 54; Botume, *First Days Amongst the Contrabands*, p. 90.

51. See, e.g., Magnolia Plantation Journal, Oct. 4, 1858, in the Warmoth Papers; Stephenson, *Isaac Franklin*, p. 112; Sitterson, *Sugar Country*, p. 100; Rawick, ed., *Texas Narr.*, IV (1), 190; *Indiana Narr.*, VI (2), 53; H. C. Bruce, *New Man*, p. 13.

52. See, e.g., McCollam Diary and Plantation Record, June, 1845; Amelia Watts Thompson, "A Summer on a Louisiana Cotton Plantation in 1832," p. 96 in the Pharr Book; Nevitt Diary, Aug. 25, 1827; W. S. Pettigrew to Moses, July 12, 1856; Hundley, *Social Relations*, p. 355; Phillips and Glunt, eds., *Florida Plantation Records*, pp. 307, 508.

53. Rawick, ed., *Ala. Narr.*, VI (1), 391.

54. Rawick, ed., *Okla. Narr.*, VII (1), 304; F. L. Riley, ed., "Diary of a Mississippi Planter," *Publications of the Mississippi Historical Society*, X (1909), 425.

55. Schoepf, *Travels in the Confederation*, II, 118.

56. Kemble, *Journal*, pp. 96-97; W. T. Jordan, *Hugh Davis*, p. 84; Clitherall Autobiography, II, 2.

57. See, e.g., Nevitt Diary, July 4, 1827; F. L. Riley, ed., "Diary of a Mississippi Planter," p. 356; Bateman Diary, July 4, 1856; Britton Diary, July 8, 1863; Kate Stone, *Brokenburn*, p. 38; Monette Daybook and Diary, July 4, 1857.

58. Rawick, ed., *Texas Narr.*, IV (1), 286; also IV (1), 190; *S.C. Narr.*, II (2), 58-59, 262; *Miss. Narr.*, VII (2), 145; Fisk University, *Unwritten History of Slavery*, pp. 37, 135.

59. *Life and Times of Frederick Douglass*, pp. 146-147.

60. Quoted in Abe C. Ravitz, "John Pierpont and the Slaves' Christmas," *Phylon*, XXI (Winter, 1960), 384-385.

61. Quoted in Phillips, "Plantations with Slave Labor and Free," *AHR*, XXX (July, 1925), 742. See also the statement of John Brown, a planter in Arkansas,

quoted in O. W. Taylor, *Negro Slavery in Arkansas*, pp. 206–207.

62. Quoted in Hering, "Plantation Economy in Leon County," *FHQ*, XXXIII (July, 1954), 33.

63. Nevitt Diary, Dec. 27, 1828.

64. See, e.g., Marsh Diary, Jan. 8, 1850; Prudhomme Diary, Dec. 24–26, 1860; Magruder Diary, Dec. 19, 1846, Dec. 23, 1854; Louis Manigault Diary, Dec. 25, 1854; Catherine Carson to W. S. Walker, Jan. 26, 1836, in the Small Collections: Carson Family Papers; Edward McGehee Burruss to his sisters, Dec. 29, 1862, in the Lester Collection.

65. Hiram B. Tibbetts to John C. Tibbetts, Dec. 28, 1848.

66. Foby, "Management of Servants," *SC*, XI (Aug., 1853), 227–228. Also Rusticus, "Plantation Management and Practice," *ACPSS*, I (Dec., 1857), 374.

67. John N. Evans to John W. Burruss, Jan. 1, 1836, in the Lester Collection.

68. This contradictory significance was nothing new in the history of class rule. The evidence presented by Natalie Zemon Davis for sixteenth-century France, for example, adds up to a similar story. See "Reasons of Misrule: Youth Groups and Charivaris in Sixteenth-Century France," *Past and Present*, No. 50 (Feb., 1971), p. 41.

69. Northrup, *Twelve Years a Slave*, p. 221; also pp. 213–215, 220.

70. Rawick, ed., *Texas Narr.*, IV (2), 173.

71. WPA, *Negro in Virginia*, p. 87.

72. *Life and Times of Frederick Douglass*, pp. 146–147.

73. Rawick, ed., *Texas Narr.*, V (4), 172.

74. *Ibid.*, V (3), 126.

75. See the discussions in Rawick, *Sundown to Sunup*, pp. 97–100; Blassingame, *Plantation Community*, Ch. 1; Puckett, *Folk Beliefs*, pp. 31–32, 36–37; and Abraham, *Mind of Africa*, p. 95.

76. See Pollard, *Black Diamonds*, p. 101; "Folk-lore Scrapbook," *Journal of American Folk-Lore*, XII (July–Sept., 1899), 226–228. The slaves could also satirize themselves; see, e.g., Shippee, ed., *Bishop Whipple's Southern Diary*, p. 50.

77. See esp. Ellison, *Shadow and Act*, pp. 66–68.

78. *Ibid.*, p. 70.

79. Nietzsche, "Beyond Good and Evil," *Philosophy of Nietzsche*, p. 444.

80. C. C. Jones, *Religious Instruction*, p. 110; see also Schoolcraft, *Plantation Life*, p. 180 n.

81. Quoted in Olmsted, *Seaboard*, p. 518.

82. "Management of Slaves," *FR*, V (May, 1837), 32.

BOOK FOUR

THE SLAVE REVOLTS

1. This section is merely an excerpt of a long manuscript on the slave revolts of the New World and the place of the southern slave revolts in the hemispheric story. At first I thought I would include that material in this book, but it became clear that it would merely prove a long digression. Therefore, I include these excerpts in the hope that their generalizations will be de-

fended and documented shortly in a separate work. At that time I shall explore the significance of the revolution in Saint-Domingue and the place of the slave revolts, including those of the United States, in the general history of the revolutionary movements of the modern world. At that time also, I shall provide the bibliographical essay omitted here.

2. Phillips, "Racial Problems, Adjustments and Disturbances," in Chandler *et al.*, eds., *South in the Building of the Nation*, IV, 236; also Phillips, *Georgia and State Rights*, p. 153.

3. Chesnut, *Diary from Dixie*, pp. 264–265.

4. Gould Diary, Dec. 25, 1856. Also Rosannah P. Rogers to David L. Rogers, Oct. 29, 1831, in the Renwick Papers; Elizabeth Watters to John Huske, Nov. 1, 1831, in the Broadfoot Papers; Gaines Papers, 1831.

5. Eaton, *Growth of Southern Civilization*, p. 97; also Eaton, *Freedom-of-Thought Struggle*, Ch. 4, "The Fear of Servile Insurrection".

6. See, e.g., Moses Liddell to St. John R. Liddell, July 21, 1845, and M. Gillis to St. John Liddell, ?, 1856, in the Liddell Papers.

7. See, e.g., Thomas L. Clingman, *Selections from the Speeches and Writings of Thomas L. Clingman* (Raleigh, N.C., 1877), p. 239; George Fitzhugh, "Disunion Within the Union," *DBR*, XXVIII (Jan., 1860), 1; Scarborough, ed., *Diary of Edmund Ruffin*, I, 456–458.

8. See E. N. Elliott, ed., *Cotton Is King and Pro-slavery Arguments, passim;* Coffin, ed., *Boys of '61*, p. 453; Garnett Andrews, address to Southern Central Agricultural Society, *Transactions, 1846–1851*, p. 96.

"ROAST PIG IS A WONDERFUL DELICACY, ESPECIALLY WHEN STOLEN"

1. Morton, *Robert Carter of Nomini Hall*, p. 106; Tate, *Negro in Eighteenth-Century Williamsburg*, p. 127; Mullin, *Flight and Rebellion*, p. 60; Josiah Smith, Jr., to George Austin, April 11, 1774, in the Smith Lettercopy Book.

2. Pinckney as quoted in Freehling, *Prelude to Civil War*, p. 63; Posey, *Baptist Church in the Lower Mississippi Valley*, p. 50.

3. See Flinn Plantation Diary, 1840; Bills Diary, May 31, 1853; Leak Diary, March 19, 1859; Bayside Plantation Records, Nov. 22, 1861; D. E. Huger Smith, "A Plantation Boyhood," in A. R. Huger Smith, *Carolina Rice Plantation of the Fifties*, p. 68; and more generally, Sitterson, *Sugar Country*, pp. 102–103; J. G. Taylor, *Negro Slavery in Louisiana*, pp. 107–108.

4. William McKean to James Dunlop, Dec. 11, 1816, in the McKean Letterbook; W. T. Jordan, *Hugh Davis*, pp. 101–104.

5. J. G. Taylor, *Negro Slavery in Louisiana*, pp. 208–209.

6. C. C. Jones, *Religious Instruction*, p. 135; Kemble, *Journal*, p. 278.

7. Olmsted, *Back Country*, p. 74.

8. Mary Branch to William Branch, Jan. 18, 1862.

9. "Management of Negroes," *SA*, n.s., II (July, 1842), 387.

10. Thomas Affleck, communication to U.S. commissioner of patents, *Report on Agriculture, 1849*, p.. 162.

11. Catterall, ed., *Judicial Cases*, II, 373.

12. "Plantation Accounts, 1833–1834," entry on next to last page, in the Jackson-Prince Papers; also Magruder Diary, Feb. 10, 1846.

13. Valentine Diary, Jan. 1, 1851.

14. Charles Pettigrew to Ebenezer Pettigrew, Oct. 25, 1804.

15. McBride, "Directions for Cultivating Various Crops Grown at Hickory Hill," *AA*, III (May, 1830), 238.

16. Easterby, ed., *South Carolina Rice Plantation*, p. 213.

17. J. B. Sellers, *Slavery in Alabama*, p. 257.
18. Olmsted, *Seaboard*, p. 117.
19. Freyre, *Mansions and Shanties*, p. 330; D. Hall, *Free Jamaica*, p. 195; H. O. Patterson, *Sociology of Slavery*, p. 222; Origo, "Domestic Enemy," *Speculum*, XXX (July, 1955), 342–343.
20. Tobias, *Crime and Industrial Society*, p. 98.
21. J. H. Johnston, *Race Relations and Miscegenation*, p. 79.
22. Yetman, ed., *Life Under the "Peculiar Institution,"* p. 53; also Rawick, ed., *Indiana Narr.*, VI (2), 82.
23. H.C., "On the Management of Negroes," *SA*, VII (July, 1834), 370; School-craft, *Plantation Life*, p. 71.
24. Mooney, *Slavery in Tennessee*, p. 72.
25. Rawick, ed., *Texas Narr.*, V (3), 190–191.
26. Rawick, ed., *Texas Narr.*, V (3), 247; *Ala. Narr.*, VI (1), 87; *S.C. Narr.*, II (1), 2.
27. Rawick, ed., *Texas Narr.*, IV (2), 181; *Narrative of Lewis Clarke*, p. 23.
28. S. Andrews, *South Since the War*, p. 177.
29. Botume, *First Days Amongst the Contrabands*, p. 279.
30. Saxon *et al.*, *Gumbo Ya-Ya*, p. 430.
31. Rawick, ed., *Texas Narr.*, IV (2), 163; *Ga. Narr.*, XII (2), 119; also *Life and Times of Frederick Douglass*, p. 50; *Narrative of William Wells Brown*, pp. 20–21.
32. J. G. Williams, *"De Ole Plantation,"* p. 11.
33. Yetman, ed., *Life Under the "Peculiar Institution,"* p. 182 (Henry Johnson); E. A. Davis, ed., *Plantation Life in the Florida Parishes of Louisiana*, Sept. 15, 1840 (p. 211); also Rawick, ed., *Ark. Narr.*, IX (3), 128; *Mo. Narr.*, XI, 94, 208; *Ga. Narr.*, XIII (4), 185; *Fla. Narr.*, XVII, 291; Fisk University, *God Struck Me Dead*, p. 46; Catterall, ed., *Judicial Cases*, III, 235.
34. Fisk University, *Unwritten History of Slavery*, p. 130.
35. *Ibid.*, pp. 4–5.
36. Yetman, ed., *Life Under the "Peculiar Institution,"* p. 178.
37. Rawick, ed., *Texas Narr.*, IV (1), 35; *Ark. Narr.*, IX (4), 12; *Mo. Narr.*, XI, 267, 325.
38. *Narrative of Lewis Clarke*, pp. 23–24.
39. Rawick, ed., *S.C. Narr.*, III (4), 105.
40. Lyell, *Second Visit*, I, 264; Olmsted, *Seaboard*, pp. 111–112, 422; W. H. Russell, *My Diary North and South*, pp. 77–78; also Sydnor, *Slavery in Mississippi*, p. 41; Yetman, ed., *Life Under the "Peculiar Institution,"* p. 13.
41. Smedes, *Southern Planter*, p. 61; Catterall, ed., *Judicial Cases*, III, 86; Boyd, *Alabama in the Fifties*, p. 45; Hazard, "On the General Management of a Plantation," *SA*, IV (July, 1831), 350–354; C. C. Jones, *Religious Instruction*, p. 135.
42. See, e.g., J. G. Williams, *"De Ole Plantation,"* pp. 3, 39.
43. Leigh, *Ten Years*, pp. 235–236, 238, 296; Pearson, ed., *Letters from Port Royal*, pp. 320–323; Powdermaker, *After Freedom*, p. 120.
44. See, e.g., Campbell, *Maryland in Africa*, p. 84; Richard Blount [Richard McMarine] to James Johnston, June, 1858, in the Pettigrew Papers.
45. Leyburn, *Haitian People*, p. 47.
46. Aptheker, *Slave Revolts*, pp. 141–142; Stampp, *Peculiar Institution*, pp. 126–127.
47. Powdermaker, *After Freedom*, p. 120. See also the remarks of Baldwin, *Fire Next Time*, pp. 35–36; Johnie Scott, "The Coming of the Hoodlum," in Budd Schulberg, ed., *From the Ashes: Voices of Watts* (New York, 1967), p. 115.
48. From *The Brothers Karamazov*, as quoted in Michael Cherniavsky, *Tsar and People: Studies in Russian Myths* (New York, 1969), p. 201.
49. For a suggestive discussion of some of the theoretical implications of these distinctions, see Lynd, *Shame and the Search for Identity*, p. 37.

50. C. C. Jones, *Religious Instruction*, pp. 135–136; cf. Greene, ed., *Diary of Col. Landon Carter*, Sept. 12, 1771 (II, 628).

51. See, e.g., R. H. Barrow, *Slavery in the Roman Empire* (London, 1928), pp. 31–32; Naipaul, *Loss of El Dorado*, p. 109.

52. Bremer, *Homes of the New World*, I, 291–292.

53. *Narrative of William Wells Brown*, p. 23.

54. See, e.g., J. M. McPherson, *Negro's Civil War*, pp. 149–150. The literature on African attitudes is large, but see esp. Mannoni, *Prospero and Caliban*, p. 72.

55. For a stimulating discussion of relevant historical patterns see Georg Simmel, "The Lie," in Wolff, ed., *Sociology of Georg Simmel*, pp. 312–316.

56. Herskovits, *Myth of the Negro Past*, p. 156.

57. Pope-Hennessy, *Sins of the Fathers*, pp. 134–135.

58. Higginson, *Army Life*, p. 12.

59. Yetman, ed., *Life Under the "Peculiar Institution,"* p. 150.

60. See, e.g., Rawick, ed., *S.C. Narr.*, II (1), 103; II (2), 45; Pennington, *Fugitive Blacksmith*, in Bontemps, ed., *Great Slave Narratives*, pp. 227–228.

61. *DBR*, XXXI (Sept., 1861), 301.

62. H. C. Bruce, *New Man*, pp. 114–115.

STANDING UP TO THE MAN

1. K. Thomas, *Religion and the Decline of Magic*, p. 531.

2. Hobsbawm and Rudé, *Captain Swing*, pp. 79 ff.

3. Stampp, *Peculiar Institution*, p. 127.

4. A. L. King, *Louis T. Wigfall*, p. 99. For Dallas and the evidence of some politically inspired arson see William W. White, "The Texas Slave Insurrection of 1860," *SHQ, LII* (Jan., 1949), 259–285.

5. See Aptheker, *Slave Revolts*, pp. 144–148, 178; Starobin, *Industrial Slavery*, pp. 88–91; McManus, *Slavery in New York*, p. 85; Hopkins, *Hemp Industry in Kentucky*, p. 138; Freehling, *Prelude to Civil War*, p. 61; Catterall, ed., *Judicial Cases*, III, 622.

6. See, e.g., Nevitt Diary, Jan. 13, 1827; A. M. Lobdell to Lewis Stirling, Oct. 5, 1838, in the Stirling Papers; E. A. Davis, ed., *Plantation Slavery in the Florida Parishes of Louisiana*, Sept. 6, 1839, July 21, 1840, Dec. 2, 1843; Gould Diary, Jan. 18–19, 1840; Phillips, ed., *Plantation and Frontier*, II, 121; Phillips, *Life and Labor*, p. 247.

7. Hilliard Diary, June 19, 1850.

8. Magruder Diary, Jan. 31, 1855.

9. Scarborough, ed., *Diary of Edmund Ruffin*, I, xxv.

10. *Ibid.*, II, (forthcoming).

11. Hobsbawm and Rudé, *Captain Swing*, pp. 79–80, 205 (words quoted), 284–285.

12. Tate, *Negro in Eighteenth-Century Williamsburg*, p. 140.

13. Debien, *Plantations et esclaves à Saint-Domingue*, pp. 60, 63, 68; C. L. R. James, *Black Jacobins*, pp. 16–17; Naipaul, *Loss of El Dorado*, pp. 112, 171, 326–327.

14. Pope-Hennessy, *Sins of the Fathers*, pp. 65, 227; Brackett, *Negro in Maryland*, pp. 132–133; Phillips, "Slave Crime in Virginia," *AHR*, XX (Jan., 1915), 337–338; Aptheker, *Slave Revolts*, pp. 192, 197–198, 241–242.

15. McDougle, *Slavery in Kentucky*, p. 38; Martineau, *Society in America*, II, 330; Scarborough, *Overseer*, p. 172; Biographical Sketch of H. C. Anderson, p. 2, in the Anderson Papers; Magruder Diary, July 29, 1856; Leak Diary, July 31, 1852; Rawick, ed., *S.C. Narr.*, III (3), 158.

16. *S.C*, VII (Sept., 1849), 140; Olmsted, *Back Country*, p. 56. Phillips thought that masters were killed more frequently than overseers. J. B. Sellers disagrees; see *Slavery in Alabama*, p. 45. The subject needs careful study; my reading of the fragmentary evidence leads me to agree with Sellers.

17. Quoted by Stampp, *Peculiar Institution*, p. 131.

18. See, e.g., any volume of Catterall, ed., *Judicial Cases;* Phillips, ed., *Plantation and Frontier*, II, 117–121; newspapers such as the *New Orleans Bee*, Jan. 13, 1842, March 21, 1845; plantation journals—Bills Diary, March 14, 1854, or E. G. Baker Diary, June 2, 1854; family letters—J. W. Metcalfe to St. John R. Liddell, Oct. 31, 1856, in the Liddell Papers, or Malichi J. White to William S. Pettigrew, Feb. 20, 1858, in the Pettigrew Papers; ex-slave accounts— Rawick, ed., *S.C. Narr.*, II (1), 27; *Ala. Narr.*, VI (1), 7, 47, 60; *Okla. Narr.*, VII (1), 135, 161; Botkin, ed., *Lay My Burden Down*, pp. 174–175. Generally, see J. H. Johnston, *Race Relations and Miscegenation*, pp. 21–29.

19. See Farish, ed., *Journal and Letters of Philip Vickers Fithian*, pp. 242, 245; Mary E. Bothwell to William W. Renwick, Jan. 12, 1842, in the Renwick Papers; notes in Christoper Edelen estate records for 1860, Slavery Collection, Louisiana State University; and more generally, J. B. Sellers, *Slavery in Alabama*, pp. 245–260.

20. See, e.g., Catterall, ed., *Judicial Cases*, III, 239–241; II, 364, 372–373, 375–376.

21. Hurricane, "The Negro and His Management," *SC*, XVIII (Sept., 1860), 276–277; also Alexander Clayton, "Southern Slave Laws," *DBR*, VIII (Jan., 1850), 23; Ingraham, *South-West*, II, 258; Pugh Plantation Diary, Feb. 24, 1861; Louisiana, Ascension Parish, Police Jury Minutes, 1837–1856. More generally, see Eaton, *Growth of Southern Civilization*, p. 80; Stampp, *Peculiar Institution*, pp. 214–215; W. T. Jordan, *Ante-bellum Alabama*, p. 54; Franklin, *Militant South*, pp. 72 ff., 172; J. G. Taylor, *Negro Slavery in Louisiana*, p. 204.

22. Yetman, ed., *Life Under the "Peculiar Institution,"* p. 93.

23. For some examples see WPA, *Negro in Virginia*, p. 144; George Teamoh Journal, Pt. 3, pp. 58–59, in the Woodson Papers.

24. Rawick, ed., *Ark. Narr.*, IX (3), 95; *Indiana Narr.*, VI (2), 14.

25. Rawick, ed., *Ark. Narr.*, IX (3), 35; *N.C. Narr.*, XV (2), 321; *Va. Narr.*, XVI, 12; Fisk University, *God Struck Me Dead*, p. 177, and *Unwritten History of Slavery*, p. 146; Aptheker, *Slave Revolts*, pp. 147–148; Yetman, ed., *Life Under the "Peculiar Institution,"* pp. 229, 313; H. C. Bruce, *New Man*, p. 98.

26. *Life and Times of Frederick Douglass*, p. 52.

27. See, e.g., Botkin, ed., *Lay My Burden Down*, p. 7.

28. Catterall, ed., *Judicial Cases*, V, 247; J. H. Johnston, *Race Relations and Miscegenation*, pp. 21–26; J. B. Sellers, *Slavery in Alabama*, pp. 248–249; Redpath, *Roving Editor*, pp. 315–316; R. R. Barrow Residence Journal, July 25–27, 1857; D. J. Weeks to James Sheppard, Sept. 20, 1854, in the Sheppard Papers; J. G. Taylor, *Negro Slavery in Louisiana*, p. 203; Rose, *Rehearsal for Reconstruction*, p. 131; *Narrative of William Wells Brown*, pp. 2–4; Northup, *Twelve Years a Slave*, *passim*; Fisk University, *Unwritten History of Slavery*, pp. 14–15, 19, 34, 56, 69, 116, 125, 131, 136, 139, 143; Rawick, ed., *S.C. Narr.*, II (2), 145, 167, 234; *Texas Narr.*, IV (1), 125, 139, 205, 303; IV (2), 213–214; *Indiana Narr.*, VI (2), 162; *Okla. Narr.*, VII (2), 17; *Mo. Narr.*, XI, 2; *Ga. Narr.*, XII (1), 15, 25; XIII (3), 5; XIII (4), 170; *Ohio Narr.*, XVI, 52; *Tenn. Narr.*, XVI, 9.

29. Olmsted, *Back Country*, p. 82.

30. Botkin, ed., *Lay My Burden Down*, p. 175. See also Schofield Diary, Jan. 12, 1866; Rawick, ed., *Okla. Narr.*, VII (1), 7, 359.

31. G. M. Wharton to Cooper, April 13, 1850, in the Cooper Papers.

32. Gavin Diary, Nov. 13, 1862.

33. Bauer and Bauer, "Day to Day Resistance to Slavery," *JNH*, XXVII (Oct., 1942), 406–412; Louis Manigault to Charles Manigault, April 19, 1853, and Charles to Louis, April 20, 1853; Spyker Diary, May 9, 1857; Buckingham, *Slave States of America*, I, 402.

34. Ingraham, *South-West*, II, 124, 131.

35. Phillips, *Life and Labor*, p. 325; Flanders, *Plantation Slavery in Georgia*, p. 149.

36. See, e.g., Spyker Diary, May 24, 1857; J. P. Bingham to St. John R. Liddell, March 5, 1841, in the Liddell Papers; Joseph Bieller to Jacob Bieller, April 7, 1829, in the Snyder Papers.

37. Ingraham, *South-West*, II, 286; House, ed., *Planter Management and Capitalism in Georgia*, pp. 60–61; Fisk University, *Unwritten History of Slavery*, p. 69; Olmsted, *Back Country*, p. 348; Sydnor, *Slavery in Mississippi*, p. 16.

BROTHERS, SISTERS, AND NO-'COUNTS

1. Rawick, ed., *Mo. Narr.*, XI, 284.

2. Catterall, ed., *Judicial Cases*, II, 523.

3. C. C. Jones, *Religious Instruction*, p. 130.

4. *Ibid.*, pp. 144, 143 (quoting Gooch and Seabrook). Also H., "Remarks on Overseers and the Proper Treatment of Slaves," *FR*, V (Sept., 1837), 302.

5. Pearson, ed., *Letters from Port Royal*, p. 287.

6. H. C. Bruce, *New Man*, p. 99. See also Fisk University, *Unwritten History of Slavery*, pp. 14, 30.

7. Fisk University, *Unwritten History of Slavery*, pp. 4, 56; Yetman, ed., *Life Under the "Peculiar Institution*," p. 331.

8. Yetman, ed., *Life Under the "Peculiar Institution*," p. 13.

9. See, *e.g.*, the statement of A. Foster at the inquest into the death of a slave, in Concordia Parish Inquest File, Louisiana, 1857; Acklen Papers, 1861; Marshall Account Book, printed instructions, 1850s; Bassett, *Southern Plantation Overseer*, p. 146; J. B. Sellers, *Slavery in Alabama, passim*; J. G. Taylor, *Negro Slavery in Louisiana*, p. 203.

10. See, e.g., Martineau, *Society in America*, II, 152.

11. *Narrative of William Wells Brown*, p. 49.

12. Worsley, *Trumpet Shall Sound*, p. 50.

13. Stirling, *Letters from the Slave States*, p. 298. Also Redpath, *Roving Editor*, pp. 284–286; Du Bois, *Gift of Black Folk*, p. 90.

14. See, e.g., WPA, *Drums and Shadows*, pp. 91, 140.

15. Mallard, *Plantation Life Before Emancipation*, p. 51.

16. Rawick, ed., *S.C. Narr.*, III (4), 52–53.

17. Botume, *First Days Amongst the Contrabands*, p. 103, also pp. 120–121; Fisk University, *Unwritten History of Slavery*, p. 54; Wise, *End of an Era*, p. 149; Steward, *Twenty-two Years a Slave*, p. 31; Power, *Impressions of America*, II, 80. Contrast Rawick, ed., *Ark. Narr.*, IX (4), 87, in which slaves slipped food to others on a plantation with a master who did not issue adequate rations, with Catterall, ed., *Judicial Cases*, III, 588, in which slaves shot and killed a slave from another plantation for stealing. For general hostility toward outside slaves see *Father Henson's Story of His Own Life*, pp. 13–14. On the readiness of slaves to combine against thieves from other plantations see West, *Methodism in Alabama*, p. 601; Buckingham, *Slave States of America*, I, 86–87; Rawick, ed., *Texas Narr.*, V (3), 2.

18. Hobsbawm, *Primitive Rebels*, p. 38.

19. The song, in this version at least, is probably postbellum. See H. C. Brearley, "Ba-ad Nigger," *SAQ*, XXXVIII (Jan., 1939), 75, and generally his discussion, pp. 75–81.

20. Stephenson, *Isaac Franklin*, pp. 99 ff., 111.

21. Yetman, ed., *Life Under the "Peculiar Institution,"* pp. 116–117.

22. *Ibid.*, p. 327. For another such Robin Hood see Fisk University, *God Struck Me Dead*, p. 178.

23. Rawick, ed., *S.C. Narr.*, III (4), 52; *Texas Narr.*, V (4), 176; *Miss. Narr.*, VII, 91–99; *N.C. Narr.*, XIV (1), 111, also p. 80; Willie Sheppard to James Sheppard, July 16, 1859; Botkin, ed., *Lay My Burden Down*, p. 161; Howard W. Odum and Guy B. Johnson, *Negro Workaday Songs* (Westport, Conn., 1926), p. 9.

24. Wise, *End of an Era*, p. 150.

25. Rawick, ed., *S.C. Narr.*, III (3), 157.

26. *Ewing v. Thompson*, 1850, in Catterall, ed., *Judicial Cases*, V, 178. See also Phillips, ed., *Plantation and Frontier*, II, 39.

27. Rawick, ed., *S.C. Narr.*, II (2), 289.

28. *Ibid.*, II (1), 15.

29. Chesnut, *Diary from Dixie*, p. 503. See also Smedes, *Southern Planter*, pp. 167, 171–172.

30. Dennett, *South as It Is*, p. 261.

31. See, e.g., Yetman, ed., *Life Under the "Peculiar Institution,"* pp. 213, 292–293; H. C. Bruce, *New Man*, pp. 36–37.

32. Rubin, *Plantation County*, pp. 90–91; also Allison Davis *et al.*, *Deep South*, p. 24.

33. See, e.g., the lengthy account of the blacksmith, Jacob, in Moses Liddell to St. John R. Liddell, July 1, 1840.

34. Fisk University, *Unwritten History of Slavery*, p. 69.

35. O. W. Taylor, *Negro Slavery in Arkansas*, p. 108; Greene, ed., *Diary of Col. Landon Carter*, April 25, 1766 (I, 291).

36. See the interesting account in Lewis, *Journal of a West India Proprietor*, p. 205.

37. Frederick William Turner III, "Badmen, Black and White: The Continuity of American Folk Traditions," unpubl. Ph.D. dissertation (folklore), University of Pennsylvania, 1965; cf. Ulf Hannerz, "The Significance of Soul," in Rainwater, ed., *Soul*, pp. 20–21.

38. Fanon, *Wretched of the Earth*, p. 43.

39. *State v. Caesar*, 1849, in Catterall, ed., *Judicial Cases*, II, 134.

40. Rawick, ed., *Texas Narr.*, IV (2), 195.

41. These altercations could become vicious, as when one cook split the head of another with a chair. See Kate Stone, *Brokenburn*, pp. 170–171; Edward T. Tayloe to B. O. Tayloe, July 16, 1855.

42. Shippee, ed., *Bishop Whipple's Southern Diary*, p. 27 (Florida, 1847).

43. See the caustic attack on overseers for using profane language to the slaves in Clod Thumper, "Maxims for Young Farmers and Overseers," *ACPSS*, I (March, 1857), 77–87. Also Olmsted, *Back Country*, p. 263; Doyle, *Etiquette of Race Relations*, p. 29; Rose, *Rehearsal for Reconstruction*, pp. 116–117.

44. C. C. Jones, *Religious Instruction*, p. 137; Rose, *Rehearsal for Reconstruction*, p. 101; Higginson, *Army Life*, pp. 18, 254; Mallard, *Plantation Life Before Emancipation*, p. 10; also Olmsted, *Back Country*, p. 144; DuBose, "Recollections of the Plantations," *AHQ*, I (Summer, 1930), 115.

45. See, e.g., Coulter, "Slavery and Freedom: Athens, Georgia," *GHQ*, XLIX (Sept., 1965), 264–293.

46. See, e.g., Yetman, ed., *Life Under the "Peculiar Institution,"* p. 323; Olmsted, *Seaboard*, p. 403; Fisk University, *God Struck Me Dead*, p. 1.

47. M. M. Fisher, *Slave Songs*, *passim*, argues that the slave songs were full of such

earthy references, which prudish collectors after the war carefully dropped from the printed texts.

48. Gavin Diary, July 9, 1856. See also C. C. Jones, *Religious Instruction*, p. 136; Pearson, ed., *Letters from Port Royal*, p. 211; Catterall, ed., *Judicial Cases*, III, 594; J. B. Sellers, *Slavery in Alabama*, pp. 251, 261.

49. See E. J. Clark, Jr., "Slave Cases Argued Before the North Carolina Supreme Court," unpubl. M.A. thesis, University of North Carolina, 1959, pp. 53 ff.; there are a number of cases, drawn from local newspapers, in the Ulrich Bonnell Phillips Papers at Yale University. See also Catterall, ed., *Judicial Cases*, III (Alabama, Mississippi, Louisiana), pp. 134, 174, 205, 245–246, 253, 260–261, 308, 312, 329, 356, 485, 590, 594–595, 597, 598, 634–635, 672.

50. *PB*, XIV (April 12, 1842).

51. Stampp, *Peculiar Institution*, p. 227. Using the same evidence, I have concluded that Stampp takes too critical a view; but without a detailed study the question must remain in doubt.

52. For the cases referred to above see the sentences in Catterall, ed., *Judicial Cases*, III, 174, 356, 554, 590, 594–595, 672; also Bills Diary, June 30, 1854; Leak Diary, Aug. 21, 1852.

53. See, e.g., Sydnor, *American Revolutionaries in the Making*, p. 81; Magruder Diary, April 12, 15, 1855; Henry, *Police Control of the Slave*, p. 54.

54. J. B. Grimball Diary, May 5, 6, 9 (words quoted), 1840.

55. C. C. Jones to Charles C. Jones, Jr., June 7, 1854,and Charles C. Jones, Jr., to C. C. Jones, June 20, 1854, in Myers, ed., *Children of Pride*, p. 47.

56. Hundley, *Social Relations*, 332; also printed in *DBR*, XVII (Oct., 1854), 425.

57. Quoted in C. S. Davis, *Cotton Kingdom in Alabama*, pp. 47–48; also p. 60.

58. C. C. Jones, *Religious Instruction*, p. 134. See also Phillips, *American Negro Slavery*, p. 237; Schoolcraft, *Plantation Life*, p. 12 of the "Letters"; Rawick, ed., *S.C. Narr.*, II (2), 129–130; *Ala. Narr.*, VI (1), 216.

59. McBride, "Directions for Cultivating Various Crops Grown at Hickory Hill," *SA*, III (May 1830), 239.

60. Hazard, "On the General Management of a Plantation," *SA*, IV (July, 1831), 351.

61. William Ethelbert Ervin, "Rules to be observed on my place from and after the First of January, 1847," in the Ervin Journal; Telfair quoted in Phillips, ed., *Plantation and Frontier*, II, 128. Telfair's remarks were in a great feudal tradition. A Japanese lord in 1445, for example, ordered the execution of all quarreling peasants; see Sansom, *Japan: A Short Cultural History*, p. 419.

62. See, e.g., Anne Newport Royall, *Letters from Alabama, 1817–1822* (ed. Lucille Griffith; University Ala., 1969), pp. 248–249; Richter, "Slavery in Ante-bellum Baton Rouge," *LH*, X (Spring, 1969), 147–165. For some instances of killing informers see Catterall, ed., *Judicial Cases*, II, 452; Buckingham, *Slave States of America*, II, 87.

63. Lyell, *Second Visit*, I, 266; Olmsted, *Back Country*, I, 211.

64. H.C., "On the Management of Negroes," *SA*, VII (July, 1834). 369.

65. Swint, ed., *Dear Ones at Home*, p. 36; Higginson, *Army Life*, p. 29; Fisk University, *Unwritten History of Slavery*, p. 105; *Life and Times of Frederick Douglass*, p. 153; C. C. Jones, *Religious Instruction*, p. 136.

66. G. G. Johnson, *Social History of the Sea Islands*, p. 153.

67. Rawick, ed., *Ga. Narr.*, XII (1), 44; also XII (1), 66, 71; XII (2), 120. The heat of passion, however, could produce grievous physical damage; see, e.g., E. A. Davis, ed., *Plantation Life in the Florida Parishes of Louisiana*, May 27, 1845 (p. 357), which describes how a woman smashed her husband's hip with a hatchet.

68. W. Morris, *North Toward Home*, pp. 126–127.

"ALL NEGROES ARE FATALISTS"

1. E. D. Fenner, ed., *Southern Medical Reports* (2 vols.; New Orleans, 1849–1850), I, 215.
2. Gibbes, "Southern Slave Life," *DBR*, XXIV (Jan., 1858), 322.
3. See esp. the following articles by Samuel A. Cartwright: "The Diseases and Physical Peculiarities of the Negro Race," in Fenner, ed., *Southern Medical Reports*, II, 421–429; "Philosophy of the Negro Constitution," *NOMSJ*, IX (Sept., 1852), 195–208; "Ethnology of the Negro or Prognathous Race," *NOMSJ*, XIV (March, 1858) 149–163. See the attacks on Cartwright by James T. Smith, *NOMSJ*, VIII (Sept., 1851), 228–237; H. V. Wooten, *NOMSJ*, XI (Jan., 1855), 448–456; editorial, *Charleston Medical Journal and Review*, VII (Oct., 1852), 719–720. For an attempt to account for racial differences scientifically see *Proceedings of the Second Annual Meeting of the Medical Society of North Carolina*, May, 1851. For an example of the support Dr. Cartwright received from the gullible see *Plantation*, I (Dec., 1860), 654–655.
4. See, e.g., Wilson, "The Negro—His Peculiarities as to Disease," *ACPSS*, III (July, 1859), 228–229; for a critical appraisal see Swados, "Negro Health on Ante-bellum Plantations," *BHM*, X (Oct., 1941), 460–472, esp. p. 462.
5. Botume, *First Days Amongst the Contrabands*, pp. 104–105.
6. J. M. McPherson, *Negro's Civil War*, pp. 57–58; Rose, *Rehearsal for Reconstruction*, p. 96; Higginson, *Army Life*, p. 54.
7. Rawick, ed., *S.C. Narr.*, III (3), 43.
8. Editor's Note, *SP*, III (Aug., 1843), 176.
9. Shryock, "Medical Practice in the Old South," *SAQ*, XXIX (April, 1930), 160–161; Swados, "Negro Health on Ante-bellum Plantations," p. 471: Boyd, *Alabama in the Fifties*, p. 44; Moody, *Slavery on the Louisiana Sugar Plantations*, p. 272; Jewel Lynn De Grummond, "Social History of St. Mary's Parish, 1845–1860," *LHQ*, XXXII (Jan., 1949), 82–83; Carpenter, "Observations on the Cachexia Africana," *NOMSJ*, I (Oct., 1844), 146–165; Magruder Diary, Sept. 23, 1847; Catterall, ed., *Judicial Cases*, III, 607, 621, 622, 673–674.
10. Hammond, quoted in in E. N. Elliott, ed., *Cotton Is King and Pro-slavery Arguments*, pp. 230–231.
11. Pope-Hennessy, *Sins of the Fathers*, pp. 105–206; B. Davidson, *Black Mother*, p. 57; Boxer, *Salvador de Sá*, p. 231; G. M. Hall, *Social Control in Slave Plantation Societies*, pp. 21–23.
12. Martineau, *Retrospect of Western Travel*, I, 178.
13. See the good summary discussion by Quarles, *Negro in the Making of America*, p. 75. For scattered evidence of suicides see Phillips, *American Negro Slavery*, pp. 271–272, and *Life and Labor*, p. 258; Sydnor, *Slavery in Mississippi*, p. 94; C. S. Davis, *Cotton Kingdom in Alabama*, p. 87; O. W. Taylor, *Negro Slavery in Arkansas*, p. 231; Mullin, *Flight and Rebellion*, p. 60; Phillips, ed., *Plantation and Frontier*, II, 94; Catterall, ed., *Judicial Cases*, II, 425; III, 128, 347, 638; Botkin, ed., *Lay My Burden Down*, pp. 183–184; Rawick, ed., *Texas Narr.*, V (3), 46, 248; *Indiana Narr.*, VI (2), 46, 170; *N.C. Narr.*, XV (2), 333; Fisk University, *God Struck Me Dead*, p. 182; *Narrative of William Wells Brown*, p. 14.
14. Myrdal, *American Dilemma*, p. 982.
15. Thomas Masaryk, *The Spirit of Russia* (2 vols.; London, 1919), II, 571–573.
16. Herbert Hendin, *Black Suicide* (New York, 1969), p. 47; Powell, *Design of Discord*, pp. 38–39.
17. See the summary discussion in Meerlo, *Suicide and Mass Suicide*, pp. 24–25 and

passim; Powell, *Design of Discord*, esp. pp. 7–47; Emile Durkheim, *Suicide* (Glencoe, Ill., 1962).

18. Meerlo, *Suicide and Mass Suicide*, p. 60.
19. Higginson, *Army Life*, p. 54. Also Herskovits, *Dahomey*, I, 99–103; II, 16–19, 53–54.
20. Fanon, *Dying Colonialism*, p. 128.
21. See, e.g., Hopkins, *Hemp Industry in Kentucky*, p. 214. Evidence of at least moderate use of opium appears in the journals of the white ladies. I find no evidence of use by slaves.
22. Olmsted, *Seaboard*, pp. 84–85.
23. For public and private expressions of concern see J. H. Hammond in De Bow, ed., *Industrial Resources*, III, 35; *PB*, XIV (May 24, 1849), editorial; *DBR*, XV (Sept., 1853), 277; C. C. Jones, *Religious Instruction*, p. 138, and *Suggestions*, p. 13; Gavin Diary, Feb. 11, 1859; Moore Rawls to Lewis Thompson, Oct. 28, 1860, in the Thompson Papers; D. E. Huger Smith, "Plantation Boyhood," in A. R. Huger Smith, *Carolina Rice Plantation of the Fifties*, p. 95.
24. Olmsted, *Seaboard*, pp. 440–441; Gavin Diary, Nov. 9, 1855; Catterall, ed., *Judicial Cases*, II, 21.
25. See, e.g., *Rhodes v. Bunch*, 1825, in Catterall, ed., *Judicial Cases*, II, 2. Slaveholders in South Carolina tore down an offender's home, and he sued. The judge awarded damages of one cent and bluntly expressed sympathy for the vigilante action.
26. See, e.g., Catterall, ed., *Judicial Cases*, III, 234, 258, 599, 631, 688; V, 260 (Alabama, Louisiana, Arkansas). In Missouri, by contrast, $20 fines were normal; see *ibid.*, V, 170, 184–185, 206.
27. Wade, *Slavery in the Cities*, pp. 84–85, 149; Olmsted, *Texas*, p. 33.
28. Mullin, *Flight and Rebellion*, Ch. 5; Freehling, *Prelude to Civil War*, p. 334; Hundley, *Social Relations*, pp. 229–230; Bassett, *Plantation Overseer*, p. 52; Featherstonhaugh, *Excursion Through the Slave States*, pp. 158–159.
29. Gavin Diary, Oct. 29, 1860.
30. For a case study see E. J. Clark, Jr., "Slave Cases Argued Before the North Carolina Supreme Court," unpubl. M.A. thesis, University of North Carolina, 1959, pp. 91–92. Also Mullin, *Flight and Rebellion*, p. 61; Greene, ed., *Diary of Col. Landon Carter*, II, 648–649; C. P. Patterson, *Negro in Tennessee*, p. 19; Sitterson, *Sugar Country*, p. 103.
31. Charles Woodson, "On the Management of Slaves," *FR*, II, (Sept., 1834), 248; Kemble, *Journal*, pp. 83, 234–235.
32. For an account of the drinking problem among the English poor and some of its social consequences see Tobias, *Crime and Industrial Society*, pp. 32, 210 ff.; cf. Blum, *Lord and Peasant in Russia*, pp. 432–433.
33. Higginson, *Army Life*, pp. 18, 38; Pearson, ed., *Letters from Port Royal*, p. 15; Rose, *Rehearsal for Reconstruction*, p. 101.
34. Lyell, *Second Visit*, I, 263, 266, 269; Schoolcraft, *Plantation Life*, p. 15 of the "Letters"; A. A. Taylor, *Negro in South Carolina*, p. 122; Booker T. Washington, *The Negro in the South* (ed. Herbert Aptheker; New York, 1970).
35. See, e.g., Greene, ed., *Diary of Col. Landon Carter*, I, 396–397, 411–412; Alread Moore Haywood to George W. Haywood, March 17, 1857; F. M. Green, ed., *Ferry Hill Plantation Journal*, Jan. 4, 1838, and Jan. 15, 1839; Fisk University, *Unwritten History of Slavery*, p. 73.
36. Floyd, "Management of Servants," *SC*, XI (Oct., 1853), 301; Rawick, ed., *S.C. Narr.*, II (1), 284; III (3), 94, 222, 283; III (4), 13; *Texas Narr.*, V (4), 90; *N.C. Narr.*,

XIV (1), 106–107; Yetman, ed., *Life Under the "Peculiar Institution,"* pp. 71, 200.
37. W. B. Smith, "The Persimmon Tree and the Beer Dance," *FR*, VI (April, 1838), 58.
38. Saxon *et al.*, *Gumbo Ya-Ya*, p. 239.
39. WPA, *Negro in Virginia*, p. 73. See also Hundley, *Social Relations*, p. 339; W. T. Jordan, *Hugh Davis*, p. 104; M. F. Ingersoll, comp., "Excerpts from 'History of the Flournoy Family' " (ms.); Mary Jones to Charles C. Jones, Jr., Dec. 22, 1856, in Myers, ed., *Children of Pride*, p. 277; Rawick, ed., *Texas Narr.*, IV (1), 164; Ross, *Cities and Camps*, p. 235; Higginson, *Army Life*, pp. 31, 38. Tobacco was of course also highly popular among the whites. Sidney Andrews was staggered by the extent of its use in North Carolina; see *South Since the War*, p. 182.
40. Mary E. Young, *Redskins, Ruffleshirts, and Rednecks: Indian Allotments in Alabama and Mississippi 1830–1860* (Norman, Okla., 1961), pp. 10–11.
41. K. Thomas, *Religion and the Decline of Magic*, pp. 18–19.
42. Pope-Hennessy, *Sins of the Fathers*, p. 62.
43. Jester, *Domestic Life in Virginia*, pp. 72–74; P. A. Bruce, *Social Life in Virginia*, p. 178; Buckingham, *Slave States*, I, 170; Holcombe Autobiography, I, 25–27 : J. B. Grimball Diary, March 10, 1847; Haller Nutt Journal of Araby Plantation, Feb. 19, 1848; Lt. Charles C. Jones, Jr., to C. C. Jones, March 7, 1862, in Myers, ed., *Children of Pride*, p. 857; S. Andrews, *South Since the War*, pp. 376–377. Gaines, *Southern Plantation*, pp. 160–161, compares the white South's reputation for excessive drinking with the reality and finds the reputation well deserved.
44. Rawick, ed., *Ala. Narr.*, VI (1), 384.
45. Allan M. Winkler, "Drinking on the American Frontier," *Quarterly Journal of Studies on Alcohol*, XXIX (June, 1968), 413–445.
46. Hilliard, "Hog Meat and Cornpone," *Proceedings of the American Philosophical Society*, CXIII (Feb., 1969), 10–11.
47. E. F. Andrews, *War-Time Journal of a Georgia Girl*, pp. 7–8. See also B. F. Riley, *Baptists of Alabama*, pp. 127 ff., 176 ff., 239.
48. See, e.g., *Narrative of Lewis Clarke*, p. 22.
49. Ingraham, *South-West*, II, 260. See also the apparently corroborating remarks scattered through Walker, *One Continual Cry*, and Northup, *Twelve Years a Slave*.
50. Catterall, ed., *Judicial Cases*, III, 628–630.
51. Mullin, *Flight and Rebellion*, pp. 98–103; but see also Stampp's more careful judgment, *Peculiar Institution*, p. 381; Lorenzo Greene, "The New England Negro as Seen in Advertisements for Runaway Slaves," *JNH*, XXIX (April, 1944), 137.
52. See, e.g., Thomas Journal, p. 9; Joseph Bieller to Jacob Bieller, Aug. 27, 1827 in the Snyder Pagers; Higginson, *Army Life*, p. 172.
53. Kiel, *Urban Blues*, p. 125; also Kochman, "Rapping in the Ghetto," in Rainwater, ed., *Soul*, p. 57.
54. See esp. Murray A. Snyder, "Evaluating the Personality of the Stutterer," in Dominick A. Barbara, ed., *The Psychotherapy of Stuttering* (Springfield, Ill., 1962), Ch. 2.
55. William B. Hamilton to Mrs. William B. Hamilton, June 2, 1858; in the Lester Collection.
56. Simmel, *Sociology of Religion*, pp. 9–10.
57. Florestan Fernandes, *The Negro in Brazilian Society*, (trans. D. Skiles *et al.*; New York, 1971) p. 127.

THE RUNAWAYS

1. De Bow, ed., *Industrial Resources*, III, 426; Arthur C. Cole, *The Irrepressible Conflict, 1850–1865* (New York, 1934), p. 271; *DBR*, XXV (1858), 458; Mooney, *Slavery in Tennessee*, p. 58; Olmsted, *Texas*, pp. 324 ff.; Paul Adams, "Amelia Barr in Texas, 1856–1868," *SHQ*, XLIX (Jan., 1946), 367.
2. In North Carolina during 1850–1860, 208 advertisements yielded 82% between the ages of 16 and 35 and 81% male. (I am indebted to Professor Paul Gaston for placing his notes at my disposal.) In Alabama, J. B. Sellers intensively studied advertisements at Huntsville and found 85% male for 1820–1860; see *Slavery in Alabama*, p. 293. See also J. G. Taylor, *Negro Slavery in Louisiana*, p. 179; McManus, *Negro Slavery in New York*, pp. 106, 112.
3. Josiah Henson, with his own wife as an illustration, insisted that the problem lay "with a woman's instinct [to cling] to hearth and home." *Father Henson's Story of His Own Life*, p. 107.
4. See, e.g., Carl Bernhard, Duke of Saxe Weimar Eisenach, *Travels Through North America During the Years, 1825–1826* (Philadelphia, 1828), II, 5; J. G. Taylor, *Negro Slavery in Louisiana*, p. 183.
5. Clod Thumper, "Maxims for Young Farmers and Overseers," *ACPSS*, I (March, 1857), 77.
6. Quoted by Lester, *To Be a Slave*, p. 29.
7. See, e.g., Bassett, *Southern Plantation Overseer*, p. 63; Scarborough, *Overseer*, p. 172.
8. See note 5 (p. 758 above) to the section "The Myth of the Absent Family" in Book Three, Part 2.
9. See, e.g., Rawick, ed., *Texas Narr.*, V (4), 41; *Ark. Narr.*, X (6), 35.
10. Olmsted, *Back Country*, p. 48; Rawick, ed., *Texas Narr.*, IV (2), 44–45; also p. 177.
11. Mary Walker Meriwether Bell, fragment, Confederate Collection: Letters, Tennessee State Library and Archives.
12. *Narrative of Lewis Clarke*, p. 30; *Life and Times of Frederick Douglass*, pp. 161–163; Redpath, *Roving Editor*, pp. 92, 115, 125; W. H. Russell, *My Diary North and South*, p. 76.
13. For reference to such daring see Catterall, ed., *Judicial Cases*, I, 356. Also, for two runaways who negotiated large distances to engage in horse stealing, see Bole to Lizzie Mullins, Feb. 26, 1859, in the Mullins Papers.
14. Kemble, *Journal*, p. 140.
15. Higginson, *Army Life*, p. 156.
16. Northup, *Twelve Years a Slave*, p. 240; also p. 95.
17. Higginson, *Army Life*, p. 71.
18. J. B. Grimball Diary, Feb. 6, 1861; Applewhite, "Some Aspects of Society in Rural South Carolina in 1850," *NCHR*, XXIX (Jan., 1952), 55; Scarborough, *Overseer*, pp. 91–92.
19. Botkin, ed., *Lay My Burden Down*, p. 123; Eaton, *Growth of Southern Civilization*, p. 73; Weld, *Slavery as It Is*, pp. 108, 155; Northup, *Twelve Years a Slave*, p. 136.
20. Olmsted, *Back Country*, pp. 214–215.
21. WPA, *Negro in Virginia*, p. 139.
22. Daniel Lee [?], "Rules of the Plantation," *SC*, VII (July, 1849), 103.
23. Catterall, ed., *Judicial Cases*, III, 45 (*Moran v. Davis*, 1855).
24. Puckett, *Folk Beliefs*, p. 248.

25. Weld, *Slavery as It Is*, p. 108; Greene, ed., *Diary of Col. Landon Carter*, I, 305; Rees Plantation Journal, Jan. 22, 1834; John Palfrey to W. T. Palfrey, July 16, 1833.

26. J. G. Taylor, *Negro Slavery in Louisiana*, p. 175.

27. J. B. Sellers, *Slavery in Alabama*, pp. 292–293, W. T. Jordan, *Hugh Davis*, pp. 99–100; Henry A. Tayloe to B. O. Tayloe, Feb. 16, 1835.

28. See, e.g., Nevitt Papers, 1826–1830; James Usher to Richard Singleton, June 27, 1827, in the Singleton Family Papers; advertisement for runaway dated Nov. 13, 1857, in the Pettigrew Papers.

29. Martineau, *Society in America*, II, 121; Judge O'Neall in *Johnson v. Wideman*, 1839, Catterall, ed., *Judicial Cases*, II, 373.

30. W. F. Craven, *Southern Colonies in the Seventeenth Century*, pp. 215–216; W. D. Jordan, *White over Black*, p. 184, n. 15; Mullin, *Flight and Rebellion*, pp. 39–47; R. H. Taylor, *Slaveholding in North Carolina*, p. 10; John Palfrey to James Johnston, July 1, 1810, in the Palfrey Papers.

31. Tate, *Negro in Eighteenth-Century Williamsburg*, pp. 148, 152; Mullin, *Flight and Rebellion*, pp. 36–37, 94–96, and *passim*.

32. For the shift in opinion in a key border state see McDougle, *Slavery in Kentucky*, p. 52.

33. Larry Gara, *The Liberty Line: The Legend of the Underground Railroad* (Lexington, Ky., 1961).

34. Scarborough, *Overseer*, p. 90; Redpath, *Roving Editor*, p. 127; Weld, *Slavery as It Is*, pp. 11, 21, 24; Yetman, ed., *Life Under the "Peculiar Institution,"* pp. 239–241; Fisk University, *Unwritten History of Slavery*, pp. 23, 45, 99, 124, 130; Rawick, ed., *Mo. Narr.*, XI, 273; *Ga. Narr.*, XIII (3), 96; XIII (4), 301.

35. Scarborough, *Overseer*, p. 92; Olmsted, *Back Country*, pp. 87–88; *Life and Times of Frederick Douglass*, p. 165; McCollam Diary, April 20, 1847. Collective punishment of villages from which peasants fled was resorted to often in feudal times; see, e.g., Peter Duus, *Feudalism in Japan* (New York, 1969), p. 79.

36. O. W. Taylor, *Negro Slavery in Arkansas*, p. 215; *Narrative of William Wells Brown*, p. 5; Yetman, ed., *Life Under the "Peculiar Institution,"* p. 142; Rawick, ed., *Texas Narr.*, IV (2), 206; V (3) 248–249, 263.

37. Wade, *Slavery in the Cities*, p. 215; Richter, "Slavery in Ante-bellum Baton Rouge," *LH*, X (Spring, 1969), 139.

38. See Walker's blast at free Negroes in *One Continual Cry*, pp. 85–86. Yet a large majority of urban free Negroes probably helped runaway slaves when they could.

39. See, e.g., Sydnor, *Slavery in Mississippi*, pp. 8, 112. The five volumes of Catterall, ed., *Judicial Cases*, contain scattered references to whites who protected slaves as a matter of principle and at great risk.

40. Bassett, *Southern Plantation Overseer*, pp. 129, 153–154; R. R. Barrow Residence Journal, Jan. 2, 1858; J. G. Taylor, *Negro Slavery in Louisiana*, p. 182. For Caribbean parallels see Bremer, *Homes of the New World*, II, 401–402; Lewis, *Journal of a West India Proprietor*, p. 115.

41. Northup, *Twelve Years a Slave*, p. 146; Yetman, ed., *Life Under the "Peculiar Institution,"* p. 161; Rawick, ed., *Okla. Narr.*, VII (1), 17.

42. Joseph Bieller to Jacob Bieller, Sept. 14, 1830, in the Snyder Papers.

43. William R. Davie to Capt. John Singleton, April 16, 1819, in the Davie Papers; also Seale Diary, Jan. 10, 1857; S. Rawlings to James Barbour, March 29, 1850, in the Barbour Papers.

44. Olmsted, *Seaboard*, pp. 435–436; J. B. Sellers, *Slavery in Alabama*, p. 269; Scar-

borough, *Overseer*, p. 90; Bassett, *Southern Plantation Overseer*, pp. 55–57.

45. See, e.g:, Du Bois, *John Brown*, p. 94. Also the remarks of Hobsbawm on the possible relationship of peasant unrest and emigration in Sicily, *Primitive Rebels*, p. 97.

THE BRIGHT AND MORNING STAR

1. Ellison, *Shadow and Act*, pp. 100–101.

APPENDIX. ON THE FATE OF PATERNALISM IN MODERN BOURGEOIS SOCIETY: THE CASE OF JAPAN

1. The struggle between paternalistic values and the new industrial society in England is best explored in Karl Polanyi, *The Great Transformation: The Political and Economic Origins of Our Time* (New York, 1944); and in E. P. Thompson, *Making of the English Working Class*, esp. pp. 203–204, 341–343, 543–544, and "The Moral Economy of the English Crowd in the Eighteenth Century," *Past and Present*, No. 50 (Spring, 1971), pp. 76–136, esp. pp. 83, 95. See also the critical evaluations of Thompson's views: A. W. Coats, "Contrary Moralities: Plebs, Paternalists and Political Economists," *Past and Present*, No. 54 (Feb., 1972), pp. 130–133; and Elizabeth Fox-Genovese, "The Many Faces of Moral Economy: A Contribution to a Debate," *Past and Present*, No. 58 (Feb., 1973), pp. 161–168.

2. See esp. Franklin Ford, *Robe and Sword: The Regrouping of the French Aristocracy After Louis XIV* (Cambridge, Mass., 1953), pp. 167–168. The old regime in Russia, to which that of the South has sometimes usefully been compared, presents its own complexities, for although the relationship of noble to serf abstractly suggests that of master to slave or at least of lord to dependent, the reality was something else. On the one hand, the nobles developed a well-earned reputation for absenteeism, indifference, and unmitigated brutality to those whose labor supported them. On the other hand, the peasants, when their condition as serfs had not deteriorated to *de facto* slavery, had their own means of collective self-defense. The nobles did not generally emerge as protectors of the serfs or even as meddlers in their daily lives. As a result, the tendency of the peasants to look to a *padrone* was transferred to the tsar, with well-known political consequences, until the revolutionary crises of 1905–1917. On the face of it, therefore, paternalism in Russia exhibited some similarities to that of the Old South and some to that of Japan, but basically it was unique. See esp. Michael Cherniavsky's brilliant *Tsar and People*; also Blum, *Lord and Peasant in Russia*, esp. pp. 362–367, 409–410; Raeff, *Imperial Russia, 1682–1825*, pp. 109 ff.; G. T. Robinson, *Rural Russia Under the Old Regime*.

3. I have relied especially on Bellah, *Tokugawa Religion*; Benedict, *Chrysanthemum and Sword*; Duus, *Feudalism in Japan*; John Whitney Hall, "Feudalism in Japan—A Reassessment," *CSSH*, V (Oct., 1962), 15–51; H. D. Harootunian, *Toward Restoration: The Growth of Political Consciousness in Tokugawa Japan* (Berkeley, Calif., 1970); Barrington Moore, Jr., "Modern Bourgeois Society," *Social Origins of Dictatorship and Democracy: Lord and Peasant in the Making of the Modern World* (Boston, 1966), Ch. 5; E. Herbert Norman, *Japan's Emergence as a Modern State: Political and Economic Problems of the Meiji Period* (New York,

1940); Sansom, *Japan: A Short Cultural History*; T. C. Smith, *Agrarian Origins of Modern Japan*; Thorstein Veblen, "The Opportunity of Japan," *Essays in Our Changing Order*, pp. 248–266.

I am especially indebted to Professor John Whitney Hall for giving the material on Japan a specialist's critical reading.

SUBJECT INDEX

An index of personal names appears on pages 814–823.

NAME INDEX

A subject index appears on pages 803–813.

ABOUT THE AUTHOR

Eugene D. Genovese began *Roll, Jordan, Roll* in 1962, after having worked for more than a decade in other aspects of slavery, using as his main sources plantation records, family papers, slave narratives, and travelers' accounts. He says of his work: "I started studying the masters and decided I could not understand much about them unless I studied the slaves closely. Once I started, they became an obsession."

Born in 1930 in Brooklyn, Professor Genovese graduated with a B.A. from Brooklyn College in 1953 and received his Ph.D. from Columbia University in 1959. He taught at the Polytechnic Institute of Brooklyn (1958–63), Rutgers University (1963–67), and Sir George Williams University in Montreal (1967–69), and has been a visiting professor at Columbia (1967) and Yale (1969). He has been chairman of the history department at the University of Rochester since 1969. In 1973, he was elected a Fellow of the American Academy of Arts and Sciences and a Fellow of the Center of the Behavioral Sciences (1973–74).

Professor Genovese is author of *The Political Economy of Slavery: Studies in the Economy and Society of the Slave South; The World the Slaveholders Made: Two Essays in Interpretation;* and *In Red and Black: Marxian Explorations in Southern and Afro-American History.* He is editor of *The Slave Economy of the Old South: The Selected Essays of Ulrich B. Phillips; Slavery in the New World: A Reader in Comparative History* (with Laura Foner); *The Slave Economies* (2 vols.); and *Plantation, Town, and County: Essays on the Local History of American Slave Society* (with Elinor Miller). He has contributed articles to *The Nation, The New York Review of Books, Atlantic Monthly, The American Historical Review, Journal of Southern History, Journal of Negro History,* and many other journals. He is a member of the editorial board for the *Journal of Social History.*

VINTAGE POLITICAL SCIENCE AND SOCIAL CRITICISM

VINTAGE FICTION, POETRY, AND PLAYS

VINTAGE HISTORY—AMERICAN

VINTAGE CRITICISM: LITERATURE, MUSIC, AND ART